Fredericksburg!
Fredericksburg!

CIVIL WAR AMERICA

Gary W. Gallagher, editor

Frederic

Frederic

George C. Rable

ksburg!
ksburg!

THE UNIVERSITY OF NORTH CAROLINA PRESS

Chapel Hill & London

© 2002

The University of North Carolina Press

All rights reserved

Manufactured in the United States of America

Designed by Richard Hendel

Set in Charter and Champion types

by Tseng Information Systems, Inc.

Library of Congress Cataloging-in-Publication Data

Rable, George C.

Fredericksburg! Fredericksburg! / by George C. Rable.

p. cm. — (Civil War America)

Includes bibliographical references and index.

ISBN 0-8078-2673-1 (cloth : alk. paper)

1. Fredericksburg (Va.), Battle of, 1862.   I. Title.   II. Series.

E474.85 .R24   2002

973.7'33—dc21   2001027915

06   05   04   03   02   5   4   3   2   1

For, as always,
Kay, Anne, and Katie,
and with deep gratitude
for colleagues at
Anderson University (1979–1998)
and the
University of Alabama (1998–)

Contents

Acknowledgments xi

Prologue 1

Chapter 1. Armies 7

Chapter 2. Politics 28

Chapter 3. Strategy 42

Chapter 4. Marching 63

Chapter 5. Delay 80

Chapter 6. Camp 100

Chapter 7. History 116

Chapter 8. Discontent 132

Chapter 9. Preparations 143

Chapter 10. Crossing 156

Chapter 11. Orders 174

Chapter 12. Artillery 190

Chapter 13. Breakthrough 204

Chapter 14. Attack 218

Chapter 15. Perseverance 237

Chapter 16. Futility 255

Chapter 17. Retreat 271

Chapter 18. Carnage 288

Chapter 19. Wounds 307

Chapter 20. News 323

Chapter 21. Recrimination 338

Chapter 22. Winter 354

Chapter 23. Freedom 371

Chapter 24. Morale 389

Chapter 25. Mud 408

Epilogue 427

Order of Battle 437

Notes 451

Bibliography 589

Index 659

Maps & Illustrations

MAPS

Fredericksburg battlefield, dawn, December 13
   xvi

Theater of operations 10

March to Fredericksburg 67

The armies on December 10 149

Meade's attack and breakthrough,
   December 13, noon–1:00 P.M. 206

The Confederates stop Meade's and Gibbon's
   attacks, December 13, 1:00–2:00 P.M. 211

French's and Hancock's assaults against the
   Confederate left, December 13, noon–1:00 P.M.
   223

Howard, Sturgis, and Griffin support the attacks
   on the Confederate left, December 13,
   2:00–3:00 P.M. 240

Confederate counterattack against the Federal
   left begins, December 13, 2:00–3:00 P.M. 245

ILLUSTRATIONS

President Abraham Lincoln and Maj. Gen.
   George B. McClellan meet after Antietam 8

Gen. Robert E. Lee 21

Lt. Gen. James Longstreet 22

Lt. Gen. Thomas J. Jackson 23

Maj. Gen. Ambrose E. Burnside 51

Burnside profile, *American Phrenological Journal,*
   March 1862 54

Maj. Gen. Henry W. Halleck 58

Maj. Gen. Edwin V. Sumner 59

Maj. Gen. William B. Franklin 60

Maj. Gen. Joseph Hooker 61

Aquia Creek and Fredericksburg Railroad, construction crew at work 65

Aquia Creek Landing, Virginia, wharf, boat, and supplies 66

Confederate president Jefferson Davis 76

Fredericksburg, Virginia, from the east bank of the
  Rappahannock River 85

Thanksgiving in Camp 120

Fredericksburg, Virginia, showing destroyed railroad bridge
  and Confederate troops 148

Alfred Waud, *96th [N.Y.] Engineers Building Pontoon Bridge at
  Fredericksburg* 159

Destruction in Fredericksburg 163

David English Henderson, *Departure from Fredericksburg
  before the Bombardment* 167

Stone wall at the base of Marye's Heights 220

Secretary of State William H. Seward 331

Christmas Eve 369

Alfred Waud, *The Mud March* 416

David English Henderson, *The Return to Fredericksburg after the Battle* 428

Acknowledgments

Any project that began so many years ago—in
1992, to be precise—is bound to accumulate a
host of debts. It is not surprising that my first
research stop was the Fredericksburg and Spotsylvania National Military Park, where Robert K.
Krick has assembled a superb collection and
equally valuable staff. The red and blue bound
volumes in one corner of Bob's office contain
copies of innumerable documents related to the
important battles fought in the area and much
more. Bob is unfailingly generous in making
these treasures available to researchers, and as
an extra bonus, visitors standing at the copy machine receive a steady stream of acerbic Krickian
observations on all manner of things. Donald
Pfanz also shared his encyclopedic knowledge of
the collections, encouraged me to look at unpro-
cessed documents in his office, and conducted
an invaluable tour of the Marye's Heights area,
including a successful search for the railroad cut
where so many Federals faced, as they would
have said, "galling" Confederate fire. Once my
writing was under way, Donald kindly agreed to
read the battle-related chapters and made many
useful suggestions. Noel Harrison enthusiastically shared his wonderfully detailed knowledge
of the local area and sites. Frank O'Reilly conducted an excellent tour of the area occupied
by the Federal left and Confederate right that
he so expertly treated in the best tactical study
available on any phase of the campaign.

At the United States Army Military History
Institute, Richard Sommers kept hauling out
manuscript boxes and patiently worked with this
neophyte military historian. A Mellon Fellowship
from the Virginia Historical Society allowed for a

very productive week of research in Richmond, where Nelson Lankford, Frances Pollard, and Graham Dozier made working with their collections easy and pleasant. As usual, the staffs in Special Collections at Duke University and the Southern Historical Collection at the University of North Carolina provided outstanding service. I also received excellent assistance at the William L. Clements and Bentley Historical Libraries at the University of Michigan. At the Library of Congress the staff efficiently answered questions and kept the manuscripts coming, despite being flooded with historians in town for a professional meeting. All across the country, archivists and librarians proved almost unfailingly helpful in responding to requests for information and photocopies.

Eric Walther proved to be a boon companion on a research trip to North Carolina, where he almost always chose good restaurants. At Anderson University two student secretaries, Kim Baker and Lori Miller, helped compile information on regimental casualties. As always, my great friend and former department chair at Anderson, J. Douglas Nelson, took a great interest in this project and in me. Doug knows very little about Civil War history, but this did not prevent him from commenting on this book or sending a few gentle barbs in my direction. I suppose the infamous "Lunch Bunch" at Anderson University deserve some acknowledgment for their fellowship and good cheer, but they are—both present and former members—a strange group of human beings. Nancy Leonard, Robert Kenzer, and Guy Hubbs kindly supplied some helpful research materials. A good friend, Phil Lambooy, provided much encouragement over the years as well as some valuable citations on religious materials. Three old LSU buddies, Marius Carriere, Chip Dawson, and Frank Wetta, asked some stimulating and often irreverent questions as we gathered each year for the Southern Historical Association annual meeting. Daniel Sutherland generously shared notes and photocopies from his own research on the Fredericksburg campaign. As is his wont, T. Michael Parrish kept my mailbox filled with fugitive sources and citations that I would never have found without his sharp eye and warm interest. Gretchen Schneider and her staff at the East Central Indiana Library Services Administration cheerfully and efficiently handled numerous interlibrary loan requests. William Marvel—a fine historian and generous friend—shared much Burnside material and answered many questions about the campaign. Bill will not entirely agree with my interpretation of Burnside, but his efforts have shaped my thinking on the entire project.

Financial support from the Falls Faculty Development Fund at Anderson University and the Summersell Fund in Southern History at the University of Alabama helped defray travel and photocopying expenses.

Several talented people provided useful readings. Carol Reardon carefully critiqued the prologue. Three friends and colleagues at the University of Alabama lent their expertise to the project. Forrest McDonald offered some shrewd and invaluable advice on the "Freedom" chapter and introduced me to the Bowers Park tennis crowd. Howard Jones read the diplomatic history sections and always took a great interest in the project. Lawrence F. Kohl set me straight on the Irish Brigade and shared many insights on the Civil War in general. Lectures at Ohio State University and Pennsylvania State University provided early opportunities to test ideas about developing a new kind of campaign study. A shortened version of the chapter on the sack of Fredericksburg appeared in *North and South* magazine, edited by Keith Poulter. An invitation from James Marten to deliver the Frank L. Klement Lecture at Marquette University—parts of which appear in Chapters 20 and 21—forced me to rethink the question of how battle news was communicated and interpreted.

A number of years ago Gary W. Gallagher asked me to do an essay on the battle's carnage for the Fredericksburg volume in his renowned Military Campaigns of the Civil War series. Since then his steady encouragement, valued friendship, and most recently, careful reading of the entire manuscript has helped bring this project to fruition. An anonymous reader for the University of North Carolina Press provided positive and helpful suggestions for one last round of cuts. At the University of North Carolina Press David Perry offered much support and encouragement from the beginning and did not wince too much over the manuscript's length. As the book moved through editing and production, Ron Maner managed all the nagging details with friendly patience and remarkable efficiency. Stephanie Wenzel expertly copyedited the manuscript. Two old friends performed yeoman service. A. Wilson Greene read every page and offered sound advice on matters large and small. His recommendations forced me to tighten many chapters and to explain better the purpose of the entire manuscript, though his unfailing friendship and entertaining letters have been even more appreciated. In addition, Will and Maggie Greene warmly welcomed me to their home during several research trips. Thomas E. Schott dragged me into the age of electronic editing, but more importantly, his incredible editorial skills and willingness to plow through hefty manuscripts continue to amaze me and far exceed the obligations of even a long friendship.

My wife, Kay, patiently listened to many tales of Fredericksburg without getting too bored. Many of the more obscure titles cited in the notes and bibliography are there because of her superb skills as an interlibrary loan librarian. Daughters Anne and Katie briefly visited the Fredericksburg battlefield once, without much enthusiasm. They along with Kay have often reminded me over the years about what is truly important. The dedication expresses only a small part of my debt to them as well as to many colleagues over the years who have enriched the lives of students while offering their friendship and example to an appreciative historian who has often needed their guidance and encouragement.

Fredericksburg!
Fredericksburg!

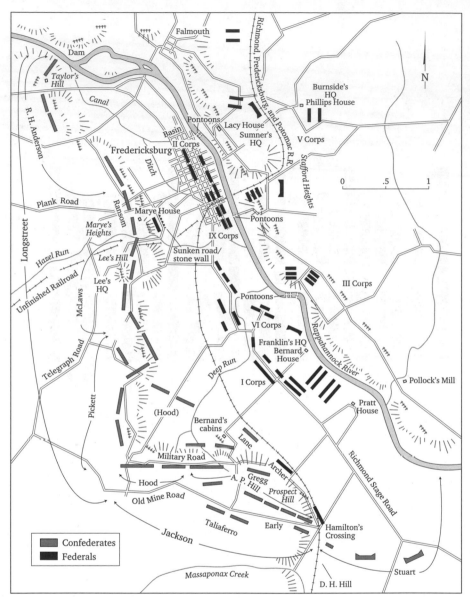

Fredericksburg battlefield, dawn, December 13

Prologue

About three in the afternoon on that hot July day, the men in gray and butternut emerged from the woods and hollows near Seminary Ridge. With skirmishers in advance, they moved out smartly, confident they could once again whip the Yankees. They marched toward the Emmitsburg road and would converge on a clump of trees and a sharp angle in a stone wall on Cemetery Ridge. Only 13,000 they were, and yet they would have to cross three-quarters of a mile of gently rolling land to assault a formidable and well-prepared enemy.

Those soldiers, the men of Winfield Scott Hancock's Second Corps—rest ing a bit after an earlier Confederate artillery barrage—beheld a stunning and magnificent and unforgettable sight: lines of troops moving across the undulating fields and climbing over fences, stopping to realign where the ground offered protection. Federal batteries began ripping the oncoming Rebs with shell and shrapnel. As the Confederates neared the Emmitsburg road, canister tore holes in the lines. Under this intense fire, the troops of James J. Pettigrew's and George E. Pickett's Divisions along with Isaac Trimble's two brigades began losing their formations. Yet they continued to advance, their objective now in sight and seemingly in reach.

Most of the veterans on Cemetery Ridge knew how to prepare for what they termed hot work. As Pettigrew's men crossed the Emmitsburg road and headed straight toward the stone wall north of the angle, soldiers from the 14th Connecticut poured a withering fire into them. "Give them Hell," Sgt. Benjamin Hirst hollered. "Now We've got you. Sock it to the Blasted Rebels. Fredericksburg on the other Leg."[1] To the south, Pickett's men also closed in on their objective. Except for a few sporadic shots, Alexander Hays's and John Gibbon's divisions held their fire until the Rebels got to within 300 or 400 feet of their line. With some skillful maneuvering and improvisation, they then poured their rounds into the front and both flanks of the still-advancing Confederates. As New Yorkers and Ohioans curled around Pettigrew's left and some Vermont troops swept down on the Confederate right, brigades from Pickett's Division became badly intermingled. The swirling mass nevertheless pushed toward some rocky ground just south and west of the clump of trees, a section of the Union line held by two brigades of Gibbon's division. With the Confederates no more than 100 feet away, men from the 20th Massachusetts rose and fired. "We were feeling all the enthusiasm of victory," Capt. Henry L. Abbott reported, "the men shouting out,

'Fredericksburg,' imagining the victory as complete" all along the line. "The moment I saw them [the Confederates] I knew we should give them Fredericksburg," Abbott later told his father.[2]

It seems curious that in the midst of this desperate struggle, with the issue still in doubt, soldiers would suddenly invoke memories of a battle fought more than six months earlier. But both Federal regiments had good reason for recalling Fredericksburg. On December 11, 1862, Abbott's 20th Massachusetts had crossed the Rappahannock River under fire to secure a bridgehead for the army's long-delayed pontoons. The regiment had taken more casualties in street fighting with some tenacious Mississippians than it would suffer at Gettysburg. On December 13 Hirst's 14th Connecticut, among the first regiments to charge the Confederate defenses on the outskirts of Fredericksburg, got cut to pieces. For these New England boys, Fredericksburg had been far bloodier work than Gettysburg.[3] On the afternoon of July 3, 1863, both regiments could exact revenge on the Rebels, visiting upon them the same horrors the bluecoats had experienced at Fredericksburg.

Too often historians operating largely from hindsight have treated Fredericksburg as a large, costly, but not especially significant battle. Contemporaries viewed this engagement much differently, in ways ranging from the mundane to the metaphysical. For the Army of the Potomac and for the whole northern war effort, Fredericksburg was a nadir. The shouts of "Fredericksburg, Fredericksburg" did not merely reopen old wounds or relieve old frustrations; these cries summoned a host of memories for both sides. Fredericksburg had come to signify both courage and carnage, a costly and, some might say, meaningless valor. Recriminations, exultation, and most of all death dominated recollections of what had happened back in December.

The influence of the departed George B. McClellan remained with the Army of the Potomac; his most ardent friends, including a number of high-ranking officers, were still convinced that only Little Mac could effectively lead them. On the Confederate side, Robert E. Lee and his army seemed nearly invincible after their "easy" victory at Fredericksburg. There was also the hapless Ambrose E. Burnside, modest and likable, to be sure, and perhaps a victim of military and political intrigue. Doubts about his ability to command an army grew and festered, leaving deep demoralization and political trouble in their wake. Heavy questions of responsibility weighed down the army and the entire North.

For the soldiers, thinking about Fredericksburg and its aftermath stirred up painful memories of a winter campaign: hard marches in cold rain, wet clothes and blankets and shelter tents, smoky shanties, short rations, and cheerless holidays. There had been temporary logistical problems in the northern army, and more intractable and ominous shortages among the Confederates. Snow, sudden freezes, rapid thaws, and mud had only aggravated the loneliness of camp life and worries about home. For the Federals, massive bloodshed wedged between Thanksgiving and Christmas raised troubling doubts about God's will and, for the Confederates, prompted cocksure assertions of divine favor.

The agony, suffering, uncertainty, regrets, and assessments of defeat and victory extended far beyond the battlefield. Dead officers were sent home for burial. The wounded crowded the Washington hospitals, while Richmond received its own share of sufferers along with many refugees from Fredericksburg itself. It would be a tough winter in the Confederacy. Signs of civilian disaffection and political unrest became more evident, while manpower and supply problems refused to go away. Across the northern states, news of yet another disastrous defeat spread like a great smothering blanket. Republicans had fared poorly in the recent state and congressional elections; Abraham Lincoln had grown depressed, his leadership uncertain and tentative. Even his seemingly deft handling of a cabinet crisis only a few days after the battle and the final Emancipation Proclamation could not quiet nagging doubts about the administration. The rising price of gold in New York, talk of a negotiated settlement, the growing confidence of Peace Democrats, and nervous reactions in London, Paris, and even Vienna and St. Petersburg made the repercussions of Fredericksburg hard to exaggerate but also tricky to gauge. Were the Army of the Potomac and the northern public really so demoralized as they appeared? Was Burnside finished? Would McClellan return? Would Lincoln's government collapse?

Battles are never isolated events, and the rippling effects of Fredericksburg respected few boundaries.[4] Herman Melville wrote a poem, Louisa May Alcott tended the wounded, Walt Whitman visited the Union camps near Falmouth, and in London Karl Marx fumed over Burnside's failure. Generals and common soldiers alike worried about the future as they shivered in winter quarters. Rumors, speculation, orders issued and canceled, and late or no pay all sapped morale. The Confederates fared no better in their equally squalid camps, but they exuded optimism to the point of overconfidence.

Whatever the despair over the carnage or the celebration of victory, the ways of God remained inscrutable. Who could look back on recent events without sadly noting the frightening costs of what at one time had seemed to both sides a glorious crusade sure to end in a quick, nearly bloodless victory? Perhaps patriotism was, in the common parlance of the camp, "played out," though soldiers and civilians alike could be remarkably resilient. One thing was certain: despite some Confederate hopes for peace, the suffering and dying seemed destined to continue as if the war had escaped all bounds of human control.

It was not surprising, then, that Union soldiers in July 1863 still felt the reverberations of Fredericksburg. So many hard thoughts, so much effort to find meaning in random events . . . so hard a struggle merely to survive in a world given over to destruction and bloodshed where most of the ordinary joys, pleasures, challenges, and even sorrows of life became overshadowed by that ever present and insatiable demon, civil war.

★ ★ ★

The story of Fredericksburg is, of course, much more complex than it appears at first glance. Battle studies, with only a nod toward the political context, all too often concentrate so much on strategy and tactics that they neglect many elements of vital importance to common soldiers and civilians.[5] Such works often give short shrift to the aftermath of an engagement, especially the carnage and political reverberations. As a general observation—surely a few exceptions could be found—historians interested in political and especially military affairs naturally focus on particular, unique events and changes over time. In contrast, social, cultural, and to some extent economic historians examine patterns and constants.

Yet all people, and especially soldiers, are creatures of habit who are buffeted by unpredictable events. Campaigns and battles clearly intrude on the commonplace rhythms of military (and civilian) life, but at the same time all the ordinary and expected events shape reactions to the extraordinary and unexpected. In the pages that follow I have tried to illuminate and fuse both aspects of historical experience. Soldiers were never just cogs in the proverbial military machine; before they donned uniforms, they were husbands and sons and brothers, and so they remained. The state of their stomachs was not unrelated to how they assessed the course of the war. Their loneliness, spiritual longings, boredom, and frustration deeply influenced their reaction to military and political developments. Morale thus became a complex intermix of certain universals of camp life along with marching, fighting, carnage, and fear.

The "old" military history dealt largely with leaders, dissecting strategy and tactics carefully, sometimes brilliantly. The "new" military history has focused on soldier life and its connections to larger social themes. But gaining a fuller understanding of a battle requires looking at both sides of the equation and mixing the elements. It requires a blending of the everyday and the spectacular, the mundane and the sublime. It involves examining what the privates expected to happen as well as what the generals planned. It means treating the people involved as full human beings.

*I can't offer you either honours or wages;
I offer you hunger, thirst, forced marches,
battles and death. Anyone who loves his
country, follow me.*
—*Garibaldi*

1 Armies

Few people could be neutral about Maj. Gen. George B. McClellan. Both loved and reviled, the "Young Napoleon"—as admirers dubbed him—curiously combined strengths and weaknesses. A superb organizer but cautious fighter, McClellan earned the respect, admiration, and especially affection of countless officers and enlisted men. Yet he was nothing if not deliberate, and he readily produced reams of excuses for inaction. His obsessive secretiveness raised questions about his willingness to fight and even about his loyalty. At once arrogant and insecure, he treated his military and civilian superiors with condescension and occasionally contempt.

McClellan regularly and all too indiscreetly questioned the military and political judgment of President Abraham Lincoln, Secretary of War Edwin M. Stanton, and Gen. in Chief Henry W. Halleck. McClellan favored a war of maneuver with limited objectives, fought by conventional rules, and even tried to protect civilian property. Whatever his private views on slavery, he opposed forcible emancipation. Nor did he discourage national Democratic leaders from using him as a cat's-paw against the Lincoln administration. A man of deeply conservative instincts, McClellan sometimes saw himself as God's appointed agent in the war, and with a conviction bordering on megalomania, he fully believed that the fate of the Union rested in his hands.

President Abraham Lincoln and Maj. Gen. George B. McClellan meet after Antietam (Library of Congress)

This egotistic confidence, however, failed to mask deep fears about supposed enemies, whether real, potential, or imaginary.

Had he not saved the Army of the Potomac after the retreat from the Virginia Peninsula and John Pope's debacle at Second Bull Run? And had not his victory at Antietam been a great masterpiece and a vindication of his generalship? Unfortunately Robert E. Lee's army had escaped destruction; Lincoln and his advisers failed to recognize McClellan's genius. Halleck and Stanton had refused to provide the needed men and supplies. Worse, they had plotted to poison the president's mind against him.

As the warm days of early fall 1862 passed quickly with the Army of the Potomac still immobile, Lincoln abandoned his gingerly approach to the touchy McClellan. "You remember my speaking to you of what I called your over-cautiousness," the president wrote on October 13. "Are you not over-cautious when you assume that you can not do what the enemy is constantly doing? Should you not claim to be at least his equal in prowess, and act upon the claim?" Attack the Rebels' communications, the president urged. Strike at Lee's army. Obviously irritated, Lincoln closed his letter with a flippant remark that surely enraged McClellan: "It is all easy if our troops march as well as the enemy; and it is unmanly to say they can not do it."[1]

At last prodded to action, on October 26, 1862, McClellan got the Army of the Potomac moving. He required eight days to bring his troops across the Potomac on pontoon bridges and march twenty miles into Virginia. With supply routes established along the Orange and Alexandria and Manassas

Gap railroads, McClellan meandered toward Warrenton. Heartened, Lincoln nevertheless fretted over the slow pace. For his part the general was sulking. A sarcastic inquiry from the president about the state of his cavalry horses had made him "mad as a 'march hare.'" McClellan told his wife, Ellen, "It was one of those dirty little flings that I can't get used to when they are not merited." Although more men were still needed to fill depleted regiments, he informed Lincoln that he would "push forward as rapidly as possible to endeavor to meet the enemy." But even as McClellan advanced, he kept one eye fixed on his enemies in Washington. "If you could know the mean & dirty character of the dispatches I receive you would boil over with anger," he informed Ellen. His customary martyr's pose degenerated into outright scorn for his superiors: "But the good of the country requires me to submit to all this from men whom I know to be greatly my inferiors socially, intellectually & morally! There never was a truer epithet applied to a certain individual than that of the 'Gorilla.'" McClellan railed against Halleck, vowed to "crush" Stanton, sparred with Quartermaster Gen. Montgomery Meigs, and argued with Herman Haupt over rail transportation. Yet at least for a few days at the beginning of November he sounded confident to both his wife and the president.[2]

Many of the troops shared his confidence. The sight of such a magnificent force on the move especially impressed the exuberant new recruits, not yet ground down by the hardships of marches, the dullness of camp, or the horrors of combat. "God is on our side," averred a pious Hoosier, "and now I believe that the movement is taking place which . . . will terminate this unholy rebellion."[3] The men's letters reported great progress and predicted imminent triumph. The Rebel capital appeared to be within reach, and a New York private offered to "give many a good day's rations to be present at the taking of Richmond."[4]

Delays and defeats had not seriously dampened the army's spirits, nor had the naïveté of the early war been entirely knocked out of the soldiers. But after more than a year's hard fighting, it had become clear, at least to most veterans, that victory would not come easily or cheaply. Even men who believed the current campaign would be decisive did not sound that sanguine. "I expect a hard fight," Lt. Col. Joshua Lawrence Chamberlain of the 20th Maine admitted, because the Confederates "are admirably handled & fight with desperation." A New York surgeon agreed that "Blood must flow" before the rebellion was finally defeated.[5] Fearful of carnage yet cautiously hopeful, the Army of the Potomac nonetheless got caught up in the excitement of a campaign that apparently offered such promise of success.

So did the northern public. As the march began, newspapers carried

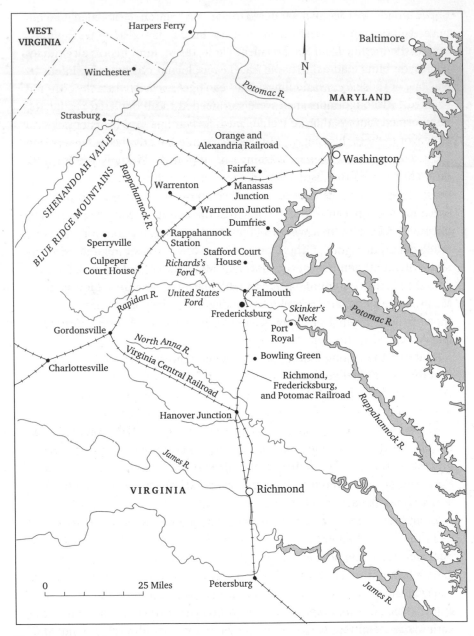

Theater of operations

glowing reports of McClellan's advance into Virginia. Sensational dispatches had erroneously predicted certain victory before, but once again the press whipped up enthusiasm for the latest "On to Richmond." Echoing confident soldiers, editors claimed that the Rebel capital would be in Union hands by the new year. This campaign, declared the conservative *Boston Post*, should silence McClellan's radical Republican critics once and for all. Ironically, the much abused commander of the Army of the Potomac had broader political support than even his Democratic friends recognized. Moderate Republican editors also issued cheerful bulletins and praised McClellan's generalship. Perhaps this time the results would match the buildup.[6]

Such wishful thinking, however, hardly prepared anyone for a winter campaign, and because McClellan had squandered so many beautiful fall days after Antietam, this new drive against the Rebels began ominously late in the year. The rigors of life in the field during early November clouded the Pollyannas with a bracing shower of reality. The weather grew colder each day. When orders got confused and footsore regiments took wrong turns, the prolonged exposure only elicited louder complaints. After a day trudging through mud and finding a key bridge had been burned by the Confederates, the men of the 11th New Hampshire finally settled into camp around midnight. "Cold enough to freeze an Icelander," groaned Willard Templeton as the men huddled around fires with the wind blowing rain into their faces. During this "toughening," as surgeon Daniel Holt termed it, many men fell ill, and some died.[7]

On November 7, in the Federal camps stretching from Snicker's Gap toward Warrenton, a winter storm left four inches of sleet and snow on the ground. The next morning at White Plains, Elisha Hunt Rhodes of the 2nd Rhode Island shook the snow off his blanket and almost decided not to write in his diary. He did, however, express one half-frozen, sardonic wish: "How I would like to have one of those 'On to Richmond' fellows out here with us in the snow."[8] Keeping warm, especially at night, proved nearly impossible. After sleeping on the cold ground, a young New Hampshire private declared himself "completely used up and so tired and stiff that I could scarcely walk." Even with roaring fires the most ingenious soldiers could keep only half their bodies from freezing at any given time. Nor could they avoid the acrid smoke from wet wood. Stoics burrowed into their overcoats and kept their feet near the fires.[9]

Fortunate regiments bedded down in two-man shelter tents. Propped up with sticks or muskets with a pole across the top, they measured a little more than five feet long and a little less than five feet wide. One Rhode Islander thought a shelter tent afforded hardly more room than a "good sized doghouse"; a Pennsylvanian dismissed it as a mere "pocket handkerchief." More reflective soldiers, however, felt thankful for not being among the many who slept with an unimpeded view of the heavens. Besides, a good fire could make those drafty tents feel luxurious on a chilly night.[10]

Soldiers humorously recounted their sufferings in letters and especially in memoirs; many prided themselves on surviving the ordeal. In words echoed by scores of other men, New Yorker James Post concluded, "It's really astonishing how much the human system can endure," but he still asked his wife to send some "thick" underwear immediately. Although much better supplied than their opponents, the soldiers in the Army of the Potomac occasionally suffered from clothing shortages, especially when Rebel cavalry raided supply trains. Some Federals also went barefoot. As the 131st Pennsylvania approached Middleburg, Virginia, the soles fell off Howard Helman's shoes, exposing his feet to sharp stones. The new boots he received that evening badly pinched during the next day's march. Even fellows with decent shoes developed painful blisters.[11]

Infrequent washing helped wear out clothes. Underwear, pants, shirts, and jackets appeared dingy and quickly became ragged. Lice thrived amidst the filth, and fighting them was a constant, largely unsuccessful battle. For soldiers accustomed to the standards of middle-class cleanliness, filthy, vermin-infested clothing symbolized how much the war had changed daily life and undermined civilized values.[12]

Complaints about lice and ragged clothing, however, paled beside the grumbling over short rations. Soldiers could endure almost anything so long as they had enough to eat, but even the well-provisioned Army of the Potomac could not keep the men adequately fed during marches. Supply wagons fell behind, became mired in mud, or got lost on country roads. Veterans knew enough to eat heartily before a march began; along the way, men wolfed down rations and then went hungry later. Newly enlisted regiments learned these lessons through hard experience. Men in the 24th Michigan began shouting "Bread! Bread!" whenever they saw high-ranking officers.[13]

Food was not just important; it was an obsession. Meals were described to the last detail, including the exact number of hardtack consumed. Roughly three inches square, these "crackers" were a staple of the military diet and certainly well named because they could break teeth unless soaked in pork grease or crumbled into coffee. Camp wags held that they were best consumed in the dark so the worms or weevils crawling out would escape notice. After grinding down his back teeth on hardtack, young Robert Carter declared that it "wasn't fit for hogs."[14] A few crackers and some raw salt pork could hardly satisfy a soldier in a cold camp at the end of a long day's march.

Regiments, however, occasionally lacked even the hardtack and the pork. Sometimes only roasted corn and a cup of coffee stood for breakfast, while corn kernels scrounged from the mules made a poor dinner. The cooking utensils alone might turn the stomach of the hungriest soldiers. "A dirty, smoke-and-grease begrimed tin plate and tin dipper have to serve as the entire culinary department," John Haley of the 17th Maine noted.[15] But the soldiers and their clothes were no cleaner than the plates or cups, and if the food would not bear close inspection, no wonder some worried that the war might turn a generation of young men into barbarians unfit for home life.

Such musings assumed, however, that the beloved soldier boys would survive the war, and even though McClellan committed his precious troops to combat slowly, sparingly, and reluctantly, this hardly ensured their well-being. The greatest threat to the Army of the Potomac—or any other Civil War army—came not from the hard marches or even enemy bullets. The physical demands of the campaign—the cold, the cheerless bivouacs, the worn-out shoes, and the poor food—made them vulnerable to an insidious, deadly foe: disease. For many soldiers the greatest shock of army life was watching comrades fall, not on blood-soaked battlefields but in camps and hospitals to unexpected enemies such as typhoid or dysentery or even childhood maladies.[16] As the weather grew colder in early November, a few soldiers bravely claimed that outdoor living was toughening them up, but in reality the exposure took a heavy toll. Each morning, stiff with rheumatism, men arose for the day's march after a night punctuated by nagging coughs. Hungry soldiers allowed their stomachs to overrule their brains and devoured sutlers' pies, overpriced, indigestible, and almost sure to cause diarrhea.[17]

Unfortunately the common camp diseases, many of which were aggravated by poor sanitation and badly cooked food, followed men on the march. The rates of typhoid fever remained nearly as high as they had been during the pestilent summer months on the Virginia Peninsula. The incidence of dysentery and diarrhea (the latter undoubtedly a much underreported malady) had fallen considerably, though the mortality rate was rising. Diarrhea struck without warning and often defied treatment. A New York private dosed himself with laudanum and stayed in his tent, but a week later he sampled some cider and "loosened up my bowels again." As McClellan's march began, the 11th New Hampshire left camp without Sewall Tilton. The poor man had suffered from diarrhea for five weeks. His weight had fallen and his hands trembled so much that he could barely write. More than a month later, weaker yet, he was seeking a discharge from the army.[18]

If you could be here, a Connecticut soldier advised his mother, "and see the poor fellows dying around you, worn out by marches and disease and see the misery brought upon us by this awful war, then you would be still more anxious to have the war ended." Each day men saw friends from home, boys in their own company, and complete strangers buried along the roads or in camp. Hospitals in Maryland and northern Virginia and around Washington were full. Disease thinned the ranks of the most robust regiments and reduced others to skeletons. On October 29 Sgt. George S. Gove recalled in his diary how the 5th New Hampshire had left Concord a year earlier more than 1,000 men strong but now could muster only about 200 fit for duty.[19] Ever present death and the fear of whom it would strike next depressed even the strongest soldiers.

Somehow being tossed into a hastily dug hole, what passed for burial with "military honors," seemed almost obscene. After watching such a ceremony for one of his comrades, Capt. Andrew Boyd of the 108th New York penned a stark, Victorian epitaph: "He died for his country, with no dear mother nor dear sister to receive his last dying words." Was this any way to treat a soldier who had died far from home? How would the rituals of mourning proceed with the family absent and perhaps not even aware that the poor fellow was gone? News of death traveled slowly, sometimes haltingly to the home front: a list of the dead from the Washington hospitals, a brief eulogy in a comrade's letter published in the local newspaper, or maybe a hastily scrawled chaplain's note.[20] Even without engaging the enemy, for many soldiers death had become a familiar companion, a daily remainder of their peril.

Men naturally sought temporary escapes from these tensions and fears. They especially looked to alcohol for solace. Loud singing and drunken revelry rent the night even when the army was on the march. Tales of widespread dissipation exaggerated the problem but also alarmed the folks at home. Health warnings and religious injunctions against young men falling into bad habits proliferated. An address issued to the army by a temperance lecturer asserted that medical and scientific evidence proved that alcohol was a poison. Soldiers should think how much money could be saved and how many victories might be won if they would take a pledge of total abstinence. Some men avoided these temptations, a *New York Tribune* editorialist hoped, but he conceded that many would not. For troops in northern Virginia and nearby Maryland, Washington offered other diversions. Henry Thompson, a young drummer in the 15th Connecticut, informed his wife that the nation's capital teemed with prostitutes. He had gone to a saloon where he met six or seven "bad women." The meals ran from 37 cents to $1.00, but should an unwary lad venture upstairs, there were "extra" costs.[21] What Thompson's wife thought of her husband's apparently firsthand knowledge unfortunately has been lost to history.

Alcoholism and venereal disease could weaken an army at the beginning of a campaign, but the most serious challenges to discipline came when food ran low. A shortage of hardtack in the 9th New York prompted a night raid on the quartermaster's wagon. Hungry men broke open four boxes with axes and, with reasoning similar to that applied by southern slaves who raided masters' smokehouses, saw nothing wrong with stealing government property to feed government troops. Soldiers also justified forays against the wagons of sutlers who had charged exorbitant prices. With soft bread going for 15 cents a loaf, hardtack-weary soldiers from the 108th New York and other regiments stationed near Warrenton seized some 1,800 loaves.[22]

Hungry Yankees also cast covetous eyes toward Confederate larders. Many soldiers were profoundly shocked to see how much the Virginia countryside had already been ravaged. "It is almost a desert," remarked a sergeant of the famous Iron Brigade. Once-fine homes stood empty, and even the fashionable resort at White Sulphur Springs lay in ruins. A New Yorker considered the barren landscape fit only for wolves. With no coffee, wheat, or other supplies, poor civilians would hardly survive the coming winter.[23]

A few tenderhearted men felt compassion for the southerners' plight, but most spared little sympathy for Rebels regardless of age, gender, or condition. To Union soldiers, white southerners appeared to be primitive, backward people, at once ignorant and arrogant. Men and women alike spat tobacco, smoked pipes, and wallowed in vice. Laziness, poverty, and slavery had blighted both the land and the people; planter nabobs oppressed slaves and poor whites alike. What the region really needed, many New England soldiers believed, was an infusion of Yankee energy and morality.[24]

Such perceptions were hardly new, but by the fall of 1862, the nature of the war was changing. Despite McClellan's conservative views, many enlisted men and a growing number of officers no longer put much store in protecting civilian property. Northern soldiers and their friends back home talked of carrying the war into southern farmhouses and fields. Although tough talk did not always translate into harsh actions and conservative attitudes persisted during the fall of 1862, some soldiers kept expanding the boundaries of acceptable behavior.[25]

Foraging—whether officially condoned or not—became both commonplace and difficult to control. To Pvt. Edwin O. Wentworth of the 37th Massachusetts the rationale was simple: "The people here are all rebels. We have had a grand time killing and eating their sheep, cattle and poultry." Officers often ignored such pillaging so long as they received a share, and in any case hungry soldiers cared little about property rights. A Maine recruit joked about seizing hogs from a woman supposedly related to Robert E. Lee: "We didn't feel enough interest in their genealogy to ask whether their pig-ships' names were Lee or Fitzhugh." A few men still paid for any goods taken, though others handed their Rebel hosts counterfeit Confederate bills printed in Philadelphia.[26] Actions that would have seemed extraordinarily callous a year or even a few months earlier no longer caused much unease as the war steadily eroded conventional moral standards.

The seizure, consumption, and even destruction of property began when-ever the troops stopped at the end of a day's march. Soldiers grabbed nearby fence rails to kindle roaring fires, an action that posed no great ethical di-lemma for either enlisted men or officers.[27] With the fires going, foraging parties fanned out into barns, chicken houses, and hog pens. Few soldiers asked any longer whether the owners were loyal to the United States; they had decided to fend for themselves, and if supply wagons failed to appear, they would live off the land. Even men who pitied suffering families and might still be inclined to pay for food grabbed what they wanted if they encountered any resistance.[28]

Confederate livestock faced mortal danger from soldiers tired of the usual salt pork. A lieutenant herding some sheep into camp, according to a young soldier in the 131st Pennsylvania, looked "more like a butcher than a com-mander." Raw recruits might be satisfied with chasing rabbits until they saw veterans feasting on lamb. Near White Plains, members of the 10th Massa-chusetts slaughtered so many sheep that the place was dubbed "Camp Mut-ton."[29] Other soldiers used dogs to drive squealing hogs toward their hungry comrades. "A nice pig generously introduces himself to the guard & is ac-cepted as a martyr to the cause of the Union," a Minnesotan wryly remarked. The fresh pork reminded lonely farm boys of home, but the cooking seldom evoked memories of a mother's kitchen. When a fat old hog turned belliger-ent, a sergeant in the 17th Maine pinned it to the ground with his bayonet. After the beast was heaved into a large frying pan, it "continued to puff and froth." Such a sight, John Haley observed with disgust (and no little exag-geration), "reduced our gustatory pleasure in pork to the minimum and we had no stomach for it after all." But many ravenous soldiers could not afford to be finicky. Men from the 24th Michigan cut off some meat from a cow that had been dead several days. During any halt in the march the countryside became what Jacob Heffelfinger termed "one vast slaughter shop."[30]

The men also struck at enemy chicken coops. An Indiana soldier watched bemusedly as twenty other Hoosiers chased squawking chickens and gobbling turkeys around a barn lot. At night pickets drifted away from their posts to snare unwary ducks or geese from sleeping farmers. Fresh poultry sizzling in a skillet whetted the appetites of weary men at the end of a day's trek across the Virginia countryside. After a sumptuous meal of fried chicken, flaky biscuits, and fine butter, Capt. Charles Haydon of the 2nd Michigan reflected that the "jollity & good feeling [would be] little understood by those who have never tried it."[31] The longing for simple pleasures made men more than willing to defy orders, beard angry civilians, readjust their scruples, and risk capture by Confederate cavalry.

Inclination and desire, however, clashed with military discipline because officially the soldiers were still supposed to protect civilian property. Yet the logic of this policy escaped many men. Explaining to a hungry recruit why he should guard some traitor's house or barn no longer carried much weight. Who could justify having a provost guard fire on a shivering private caught stealing straw on a cold night? To Captain Haydon, the explanation was clear: "Contractors must be enriched & political pimps rewarded" so they could overcharge the government for hay, grain, or fresh meat. Such illicit profits would vanish if the army was permitted to live off the land. "I have seen a sick soldier refused a drink of water by a Union guard lest . . . he . . . might possibly do some injury to rebel property," Haydon railed. Regiments and brigades that defied orders and "swept the country pretty clean" had his approval.[32]

Yet even some enlisted men still hesitated to abuse civilians and feared that widespread plundering would demoralize the army. These sensitive souls bemoaned the disgraceful conduct of others and generally blamed worthless stragglers, though the question of responsibility remained devilishly tricky. Pvt. Edward King Wightman, an educated and opinionated New Yorker, had enjoyed a fine supper while guarding a large house near Warrenton. After he and his comrades departed, however, other Federals ransacked the place. The straitlaced Wightman haughtily remarked that "most of our common soldiers are scarcely above brutes by nature." A Pennsylvania chaplain believed that "rebel property is too carefully guarded" but also acknowledged that "we certainly can not permit our army to be a band of marauders."[33] The most difficult decision was where to strike the balance.

Orders to safeguard civilian property remained in force even though they were often honored more in the breach than in the observance. Seeing how much destruction had already taken place, a Pennsylvania corporal predicted that a recently issued edict against looting would be universally ignored. A clever group of New Jersey soldiers even pretended to be provost guards in order to seize an already pilfered calf from some unsuspecting Vermonters.[34] Many officers routinely disregarded orders against foraging, and some directly benefited from raids on civilian food supplies. A wink-and-nod policy generally prevailed. The colonel of the 6th Wisconsin made up in clarity what he lacked in subtlety, telling his troops, "Don't you let me see or hear of your foraging on this march. I think I see a smokehouse near that white residence. Go back to your quarters." When later awakened from a convenient nap and presented with hams, fresh eggs, and flour, he solemnly inquired whether the men had violated his instructions. One clever forager, presumably with a straight face, claimed that a friendly farmer had insisted the men take this load of provisions. "That's all right," the colonel sighed with relief, "I was afraid you had stolen them." He then put another egg on his tin plate.[35]

Some conscientious officers tried to stop the plundering, but their best efforts often failed ludicrously. Maj. Gen. George Gordon Meade came upon Lt. Ernest Wright of the 13th Pennsylvania Reserves chasing a pig and chided him about disobeying orders. Wright snapped back that "he had little respect" for such edicts and, not surprisingly, got arrested for his cheekiness. But after learning of Wright's excellent service record, Meade ordered his release. Futility quickly degenerated into farce. Despite an edict against sheep stealing, Brig. Gen. Winfield Scott Hancock caught members of the Irish Brigade in the act of slaughtering several of the woolly creatures. Threatening the miscreants with his sword, Hancock prepared to bring down the full force of his wrath on them, when a frightened sheep jumped up, bleated loudly, and ran off. On another occasion he spied some soldiers apparently fleeing from enemy pickets. As he rode up closer, however, the reality of the situation came into focus. "Enemy! the rebs be damned!" he exploded, "It is a damned flock of sheep they are after."[36]

The most stringent measures failed to stop the plundering. Courts-martial handed out stiff sentences but to little avail. Imposing fines, forcing offenders to wear barrels shirts inscribed with the word "thief," and even stringing up men to cross bars did little to reduce foraging. Moreover, such punishments were extremely unpopular in the ranks, and woe betide the officer who crossed the line of what enlisted men considered to be acceptable treatment. Enraged soldiers assaulted one martinet with burning fence rails and bayoneted another to death in his tent.[37] With little regard for the conservatism of the upper command, McClellan's troops learned to carry on a far more destructive war than had been conceivable only a few months earlier.

Sharp-tongued Virginians who berated Yankees at every opportunity reinforced the growing belief in the Army of the Potomac that ending the war required crushing such rebellious spirits. The defiance of Confederate women had already become legendary, and confrontations between soldiers and "secesh females" acquired a set-piece quality. The Federals' descriptions of hostile women were colorful but largely interchangeable: "Three saucier vixens could not be found in all rebeldom"; "the women at the doors look sour and cross"; "more inveterate secessionists I have never encountered." Even children acted out their parts as rabid Confederates. One little girl told a group of Massachusetts soldiers that she hated the Yankees because they had brought cold weather.[38]

With incredible gall, some women begged soldiers to guard their property while still spouting secessionist gasconade. Even women who appeared meek sometimes spat fire. When men from the 20th Maine politely asked for milk, one "amiable lady" wished them all dead. Hot-blooded Confederates avoided contact with the Federals and angrily tore up northern newspapers. An eighteen-year-old declared that she had no desire to enter heaven if Yankees were there but that she would gladly kiss the most unkempt soldier in the Confederate army.[39]

Nor would Confederate women succor their enemies. Near Middleburg, Virginia, a lady in mourning attire hid the pump handle to prevent a foraging party from getting a drink of water. A few fanatics, whose devotion to the southern nation well exceeded their good sense, tried to assault Federal soldiers. In a battle over chickens one woman hurled a stone at a member of the 10th Massachusetts and broke his jaw.[40]

Violent confrontations made for exciting stories in postwar memoirs and regimental histories, but for the southern civilians involved, these incidents signaled the final stages of resistance preceding a painful adjustment to military reality. However noteworthy their confrontations with fiery belles, the Federals also met women who shattered stereotypes, as harsher treatment forced even ardent Confederates to act more circumspectly. Relations between invader and invaded naturally remained tense but also grew more complex in ways that confounded expectations on both sides. Some women —whether Unionists or not—hoped that the Federals might restore order and bring some relief from irregular foraging. Others disdained politics and even entertained soldiers around the supper table, a rare treat for men used to the rough fare and rougher conditions of march and camp.[41]

However pleasant such encounters might be, by the beginning of November much of the bluecoats' exuberance had worn thin. Once again combing his body and clothes for lice, a disheartened member of the 10th Massachusetts grumbled, "If I could only get home the Union might go to H–ll."[42] The march left in its wake many stragglers as well as rumors of officers running off for the pleasures of Washington and other cities. "The boys are pretty well played out," a Pennsylvanian conceded.[43]

Such laments prompted speculation about the Army of the Potomac settling into winter quarters before a battle could be fought. Even if a bloody engagement took place and the army retreated once again, some men preferred being taken prisoner to staying in the ranks. Rumors of European intervention, financial uncertainty, and peace negotiations all circulated between home front and camp, reinforcing a deepening gloom about the course of the war.[44] More ominous were signs of despair in the army. Seeing no prospect for ending the war soon, General Meade poured out his frustration: "The South accepts ruin, and is willing to have all its material interests destroyed if it can only secure its independence. The North, owing to the villainous system of paper money, the postponement of taxation and of the draft, has not yet realized the true condition of the country." But even if the northern people and the rosewater politicians would accept sterner measures, whether northern armies could win in the eastern theater remained doubtful. "The South has able generals," a Maine chaplain conceded sadly. "We have not been bold and daring enough; we have at times been too cautious for our own good."[45] This was a remarkable understatement, for surely caution had been McClellan's watchword, and only the most sanguine believed that he could match wits with Robert E. Lee, whose reputation for invincibility grew almost as rapidly in the North as it did in the South.

Standing nearly six feet tall, weighing around 190 pounds, and sporting a thick gray beard the Virginian looked every inch the classic gentleman. Yet his deep piety and sense of duty appeared at odds with an intense and sometimes costly aggressiveness. The unassuming humility he displayed with generals, staff, and family was partly misleading because by the fall of 1862, it belied a man who had become a very confident commander. So, too, his robust appearance belied a weakening heart and a curious fatalism. He dressed in a simple uniform and ate plain food, but there was about Lee a strength and even a fierceness that inspired respect, admiration, and awe in the Army of Northern Virginia.[46] After Joseph E. Johnston was badly wounded at the battle of Seven Pines on June 1, 1862, Lee had assumed command and won a series of strategic victories and established a psychological ascendancy over his Federal opponents. Although Lee tried to avoid the sin of pride and worried that people expected too much of him, even this model of humility and introspection could not help but sense his own mastery of command.

Gen. Robert E. Lee (Francis
Trevelyan Miller, Photographic
History of the Civil War, 2:235)

The recent campaign into Maryland and the bloody draw at Sharpsburg
had been costly, but this had not tarnished Lee's reputation or checked his
aggressiveness. Luckily, McClellan had been inactive for several weeks after
the battle, thus allowing Confederates precious time to rebuild and reorga-
nize their forces. Despite persistent supply problems, Lee managed to re-
organize the cavalry and consolidate artillery batteries with patient diplomacy.[47]

The most visible change in the Army of Northern Virginia was the creation of two corps to replace a less formal command structure.[48] Lt. Gen.
James Longstreet would command the First Corps. At age forty-one "Old
Pete," as he was known in the army, was one of Lee's most reliable subordinates. A large man with a florid complexion and a normally cheery disposition, he had become much more reserved since three of his children had died
of scarlet fever at the beginning of the year. A native South Carolinian in an
army dominated by Virginians, this cautious disciple of defensive warfare
offered a striking contrast to Lee and other more aggressive generals.[49]

Lee chose Lt. Gen. Thomas J. "Stonewall" Jackson to command the Sec-

ond Corps. After a disappointing performance during the Seven Days campaign, Jackson had returned to form by the fall of 1862 and had become indispensable to Lee. Yet Jackson could be a troublesome subordinate, and he had engaged in some nasty disputes, notably with his capable division commander Maj. Gen. Ambrose P. Hill. Two years younger than Longstreet, "Old Jack," nevertheless acted older. Officers and enlisted men admired Jackson but also found him unbending and occasionally harsh. Although Confederate president Jefferson Davis apparently harbored some reservations about Jackson, no one could doubt he was a fearsome fighter who had become the Confederacy's most popular hero.

Jackson tended to be reserved and humorless (except around playful cavalry commander Maj. Gen. J. E. B. Stuart). Fearless and self-confident, he had trouble understanding human weaknesses in others and drove his men with a relentlessness that bordered on the maniacal. Jackson reminded people of an Old Testament prophet pronouncing judgment on hapless mortals. As devout as Lee and nearly as fatalistic, Jackson wrote to his wife shortly after the birth of their daughter, "Do not set your affections upon her, except as a gift from God. If she absorbs too much of our hearts, God may remove her from us."[50] Though the ways of providence remained both mysterious and terrible, he vowed to serve God by wreaking bloody vengeance on the Yankees with a remorseless fury that struck fear in the North and evoked awe in the South.

Lee had chosen two capable (albeit sharply contrasting) corps commanders, and despite persistent problems in various divisions and brigades, the

start of McClellan's advance did not trouble him much. Lee knew his opponent and had taken his measure. He ordered Jackson to Winchester, while Longstreet, screened by Stuart's cavalry, marched toward Culpeper. The Confederate high command exuded confidence. Lee's appearance in Richmond on November 1 for a conference with Davis sparked new rumors of European intervention, an impending armistice, and even an end to the war. By November 6, as McClellan's forces massed near Warrenton and Federal cavalry probed toward the Rappahannock River, Lee returned to Culpeper. He instructed Jackson to march up the Shenandoah Valley and prepare to join Longstreet. Stuart, mourning the recent death of his young daughter, poured himself into the work of shielding Longstreet's movements and providing intelligence on enemy activity. The Confederates also suffered from the cold, and they faced much more serious supply problems than the Federals; but Lee was not that concerned. He expected McClellan's strength to "decrease the farther he removes from his base" and looked for a chance to "strike a successful blow."[51]

Lee also hoped that improved discipline and vigorous enforcement of the conscription laws might swell the ranks of his army. Straggling had become rampant during the Maryland campaign, but in Lee's view, better officers and sterner measure might reduce the problem. Courts-martial imposed harsh sentences—including hard labor, bucking and gagging, and the ball and chain—for soldiers convicted of being absent without leave. Furloughs became a rarity.[52] Although discipline improved and many absentees returned to the ranks, Lee's men never became textbook soldiers. The typical Confederate remained an independent cuss who enjoyed his fun without worrying too much about regulations.

As Indian summer faded and the air grew sharper and clouds looked more ominous in late October and early November, footsore and hungry Confederates had a convenient excuse for swigging "apple jack" or some other alcoholic concoction. Soldiers had to wade through icy streams—"ten thousand needles sticking through your flesh would not have hurt any worse," a Georgian claimed—and early snowfalls along with cold winds only added to their misery.[53] The men huddled together under blankets or shivered in thin "fly" tents. Lucky ones found shelter in an abandoned farmhouse. Large fires, constantly attended, supplemented hastily constructed brush huts. Longstreet advised his troops to heat the soil with daytime fires and sleep on the warmer, drier ground at night. Fiddles and banjos had generally fallen silent. The chill air quieted the most exuberant spirits.[54]

Newspaper reports of their boys suffering from exposure disturbed Confederate civilians. "Our poor soldiers" was a lament heard around domestic firesides as winter approached. Newspapers carried appeals for blankets and clothing, and women pledged their time to sew for local regiments; but soldier and civilian perceptions of the war were diverging. "Those of our people who are living at home in comfort have no conception of the hardships which our soldiers are enduring," Brig. Gen. Elisha Franklin Paxton complained. While speculators prospered by overcharging the government for everything the army needed, civilians rationalized their own indifference by arguing that the War Department should provide for the soldiers.[55] Such logic chopping offered no relief to the men in the field.

Despite official schedules of clothing allowances and descriptions of a "standard" Confederate uniform, from the beginning of the war the average soldier had been shabbily attired. Whole regiments took on a ragtag appearance in ill-fitting clothing of various styles and colors. These "uniforms"—if such they can be called—soon became worn. Officers scoured the countryside for pants or shirts, while many men relied on wives, mothers, and sisters to supply their needs. After receiving a package from his mother and sister, Harvey Hightower of the 18th Georgia exulted, "I tell you [I] feel like a white man." Few enlisted men or officers were so fortunate. Claiming it was too cold to take off his shirt for a much needed washing, a Mississippi officer informed a female cousin that he had no socks or drawers at all.[56]

A man without underwear was certainly an extreme case, but barefoot soldiers on the march had become a common sight. In late October the 48th Virginia in Jackson's corps had 130 men without shoes; a sergeant in the 9th Virginia in Longstreet's corps reported 17 of the 57 men in his company marching toward Culpeper barefoot. Near Strasburg, Virginia, a North Carolina chaplain watched men clear away snow to bury a comrade; several of the mourners were shoeless. Small, sharp stones along the roads cut into the feet of men who also had to traverse steep, rocky ground.[57] The plight of soldiers with frozen and often bleeding feet deeply affected most officers. A colonel in the 6th South Carolina marveled at his men's uncomplaining patriotism, but perhaps he had not often lingered around the campfire or listened to their comments on the march.[58]

Ill-clothed and shoeless soldiers increasingly went hungry. A poor wheat crop in Virginia and a shortage of transportation portended "failure and ruin," Commissary Gen. Lucius B. Northrop warned. At the rate Lee's men were consuming beef and pork, another Richmond official predicted, either the army must go on half-rations or supplies would be exhausted by the first of the year.[59] By early November soldiers felt the pinch. Breakfasts (if any) were spartan, little flour or pork was available, prices for sugar and salt were exorbitant, and food that at home would have seemed fit only for slaves was now devoured with relish. To a Maryland artillerist a simple ration of fresh pork and cornmeal was such a "rarity" that it deserved mention in his diary.[60] Civilians occasionally offered the men delicacies such as jars of pickles, but many farmers charged extortionate prices: apples were 50 cents apiece; honey, $1.50 a pound; molasses, $4.00 per gallon; coffee, $3.00 a pound; and lowly crab apples, 75 cents a dozen. Even with tighter discipline in the ranks, there was bound to be irregular foraging.[61]

The cold, shortages, and hunger, along with Antietam's lingering horrors, had not demoralized Lee's men but perhaps had made them more reflective and surely more receptive to religious appeals. Spiritual matters had often been neglected in both armies during the first year of the war. Despite complaints of widespread indifference, however, there were signs of religious awakening in the Army of Northern Virginia. By late October and early November some chaplains were holding evening services with strong support from Jackson and even from the often impious Brig. Gen. Jubal Early. Lee himself sometimes joined the men for prayers. The Evangelical Tract Society flooded the camps with devotional literature, and soon the first evidence of revivalism—a wave of evangelical fervor that would ebb and flow through Confederate ranks for the rest of the war—manifested itself in extended meetings and dramatic reports of conversions. In Washington recently elected Ohio congressman James A. Garfield feared that Lee, Jackson, and Stuart had "inspired their men with a kind of Cromwell spirit which make their battalions almost invincible."[62]

Confederates did believe that the Lord of Hosts would soon deliver them from their enemies. The repeated devastation of the Virginia countryside by Federal armies, including McClellan's advancing forces, only intensified their faith. The "vandal hordes"—a recurring phrase in many accounts— seemed capable of almost any crime, from grabbing the last morsel of bread from defenseless women and children to despoiling churches. The Yankees' insulting and vulgar language along with their cant and hypocrisy especially infuriated lower-ranking Confederate officers, who feared for the safety of their own homes and families.[63]

The inevitable cruelties and hardships of war perhaps stirred Lee's soldiers to fight, but they also cast a pall over both army and home front. Even that old firebrand Edmund Ruffin worried about supply and manpower problems in the Army of Northern Virginia. A cavalry officer attending a church service near Snicker's Gap observed a lady sitting ahead of him "shiver in agony of prayers and tears" as her colonel husband was suddenly called away by an aide. "Many of us are destined yet to share the fate of our dead and wounded comrades," General Paxton noted gloomily on his eighth wedding anniversary, "but . . . I feel that my place must be filled and my duty done, if it cost me life and bring sorrow to the dear wife and little ones." Like General Lee, Paxton saw himself as both an instrument and in some ways a puppet of God's will. With Hancock's men approaching Fauquier County, Amanda Edmonds concluded that the gathering Yankees had "every advantage over us." In such desperate straits only the "goodness of God . . . and our generals can save us," yet her comments bespoke more anxiety than assurance.[64]

Throughout the fall Confederates would remain optimistic, but their optimism was increasingly tempered by an acknowledgment of their own problems and the mounting costs of war. Although with considerably more sophistication than the average soldier, Lt. Ujanirtus Allen of the 21st Georgia well summed up the general mood in a letter to his wife: "You may think I speak of battles quite indifferently. No one dreads them more than myself. But if we must fight let us go at it hoping and praying and with a determination to do our best. We can not controll circumstances, neither does our own fate rest in our own hands."[65]

Soldiers in both armies had to weigh the hazards of a winter campaign. At the end of the first week in November, McClellan's forces were near Warrenton, scattered from Manassas Junction to the east with cavalry as far west as Sperryville. Lee's army remained divided in the face of this formidable foe, with Longstreet at Culpeper and Jackson in the Shenandoah Valley near Winchester. But as so often happens, the clash of arms that appeared certain to occur within days never took place. The politics of war would suddenly change the course of the campaign.

War is simply a continuation of political intercourse, with the addition of other means.
—Karl von Clausewitz

2 Politics

On November 1, 1862, in Albany, New York, a Democrat perusing his local party newspaper, the *Atlas and Argus* might well have paused over an ominous official announcement: county commissioners would administer a recently authorized militia draft. A description of exemptions was there, too, along with notice of a commissioners' meeting on November 6 to hear appeals of men seeking relief from conscription. Six days later in Rochester, New York, the Republican sheet, oddly titled the *Daily Democrat and American,* reported that the city's draft office was being flooded with phony medical affidavits after false reports about an impending call-up had caused a panic.[1]

By the fall of 1862 the combined effects of disease, battles, expiring enlistments, and desertions had created a manpower crisis in the North. Spring and summer recruitment had lagged, and in July Congress had authorized a militia draft of over 300,000 men for nine months' service. Governors, griping all the while about War Department procedures, had scrambled to fill their states' quotas with volunteers, hoping to avoid a draft at least until after the autumn elections.[2] Lincoln's recently issued preliminary Emancipation Proclamation would mean little if there were not enough troops available to win a major battlefield victory in the eastern theater.

Besides stirring controversy, the conscription and bounty system offered opportunities for a few enterprising citizens. Some agents promised to collect bounties, advise families in the subtleties of military law, and secure exemptions. For $2.00 a young man might purchase George W. Raff's comprehensive *Manual of Pensions, Bounty, and Pay*. Did this mean that patriotism had been replaced by a more selfish calculus? Bounty men and conscripts made notoriously unreliable soldiers and sometimes deserted their regiments while still in training camp. Volunteers expressed cool contempt for men who had to be bribed or dragooned into service.[3]

Recruitment had inevitably become entangled in state politics. McClellan had hoped to replenish skeleton regiments with new recruits, but delicate negotiations between federal and state officials caused irksome delays. Governor Andrew Curtin, for instance, asserted the right of Pennsylvanians to join new regiments and elect their officers. Faced with uncooperative state officials and enlistees reluctant to serve with veteran regiments, Stanton finally decided to abandon, at least temporarily, any effort to force the issue.[4]

Public officials treaded carefully for fear of provoking armed resistance. From Massachusetts, where Governor John A. Andrew kept troops on alert to suppress rioting; to Pennsylvania, where the Molly Maguires vigorously opposed conscription; to Indiana, where two enrollment officers were murdered, the threat of violence lurked beneath the surface of public debate. Many citizens had begun to feel the force of government in general and centralized power in particular for the first time in their lives, and the adjustment was painful. A mob of nearly a thousand Belgian Catholics and German Protestants gathered under a banner proclaiming "No Draft" and ransacked the Osaukee County, Wisconsin, courthouse, destroying documents and pummeling a local draft commissioner. Only a strong show of military force by the governor prevented a similar outbreak in Milwaukee. Jittery Washington officials tried to prevent news of these disturbances from passing over the telegraph lines.[5]

Given the public outcry, obstructionist tactics by state governors, and the War Department's caution, it is not surprising that the militia draft raised only around a quarter of the men authorized by Congress. As a Republican editor in Wisconsin noted with alarm (and some accuracy), the greatest resistance to the draft occurred in the most heavily Democratic counties.[6] Indeed, the political unity of the war's first year was crumbling. Even as armies in the western theater were advancing and defeating Rebel armies, little progress had been made in the eastern theater, and the war threatened to settle into a bloody standoff. Alarm about conscription and opposition to the recently adopted emancipation policy helped revive the Democratic Party. The approaching congressional and state elections placed Lincoln on the defensive and emboldened the opposition.

A key battleground was New York, a heavily populated, closely competitive state with labyrinthian politics. Secretary of State William H. Seward was never far removed from his home turf's political battles, and his chief henchman, Thurlow Weed, still pulled wires in the state Republican Party. Both Seward and Weed favored creating a "Union" coalition to unite moderate Republicans with War Democrats, but their old nemesis and fervent radical Horace Greeley insisted the Republican Party stand foursquare for emancipation.

Rejecting Maj. Gen. John A. Dix, the Seward-Weed faction's gubernatorial candidate, the state Republican convention nominated Brig. Gen. James S. Wadsworth, an ex-Democrat and Free-Soiler. While serving as military governor of the District of Columbia, Wadsworth, as befitting an old Van Buren Democrat, denounced the southern "aristocracy" and vowed to "save the lives of white men who are perishing by the thousands in this country." This statement, along with earlier remarks about blacks being a "docile people" and "industrious peasantry," were clearly intended to blunt the Democrats' racist attacks on emancipation; but Wadsworth was no doughface on slavery, and his acceptance letter unequivocally endorsed emancipation. Only a few days before the election the general proudly declared himself an abolitionist and denounced Democrats as secret disunionists.[7]

★ ★ ★

Attempting to build a coalition with backers of the old Constitutional Union Party, Democrats nominated conservative Horatio Seymour for governor. A veteran of many bruising factional quarrels, Seymour, an old-fashioned states' rights Democrat, condemned government centralization without renouncing the war itself. Posing as a moderate alternative to the radical Republicanism of Wadsworth and Greeley, Seymour vigorously campaigned not so much as an enemy of the Lincoln administration but as a constitutional strict constructionist and Unionist. Without succumbing to the defeatism of the peace faction, he could make racist appeals against emancipation and criticize the arbitrary arrests of citizens. To Seymour, McClellan represented the military ideal, a general who would conduct the war along safely conservative lines.[8] Ironically like Lincoln, Seymour tried to appeal to a broad political center.

By late fall Democrats were campaigning with energy and confidence.

One enterprising firm was even marketing Seymour lithographs at $1.00 each. A Democratic ratification meeting in Albany on October 31, complete with a 100-gun salute and marching clubs, attracted a crowd of more than 7,000. Indignantly denying Republican charges that a vote for Seymour was a vote for Jefferson Davis, speakers explicitly linked their party to McClellan and tried to isolate the radicals by suggesting that even Lincoln would not be entirely displeased if Seymour won the election.[9]

This absurd notion notwithstanding, the prospect of losing New York frightened Republicans. A Seymour victory would mark the Union's death knell, several editors warned. England and France would likely recognize the Confederacy and intervene in the war. Reactionaries in London would rejoice, and the Rebels in Richmond would exult as the American republic tottered toward its downfall. The Democratic standard-bearer might pretend to sustain the war effort, but he was a traitor at heart. Greeley wildly predicted that Seymour would recall New York regiments from the field and "inaugurate an insurrection against the General Government."[10] All across the country anxious Republicans followed the New York canvass with great interest, and many foresaw disaster.[11]

On election day large crowds gathered near the offices of New York City's major newspapers to scan the latest bulletins. Prominent New York lawyer George Templeton Strong's initial hopes for a light turnout were dashed when he learned that Seymour had carried the city by around 31,000 votes. "God help us," he scribbled in his diary.[12] Seymour won the state by a slender majority of less than 11,000 of more than 600,000 votes cast (Republicans held on to their legislative majority), but this relatively narrow margin hardly made his triumph any less significant. As Democrats reveled in a victory over "radicalism," Seymour lauded the people for having risen up against the forces of patronage and corruption to protect constitutional rights.

The state's leading Democratic newspaper, the *New York World,* echoed these sentiments. All New Yorkers desired was the preservation of their liberties, vigorous prosecution of the war, and an end to political interference with generals in the field.[13] This oblique reference to McClellan only hinted at the larger military significance of the election.[14] In Oswego, New York, fervent abolitionist Ruth Whittemore wrote her eighteen-year-old brother, then serving in the 50th New York Engineers, that with Seymour as governor, "you might as well throw down your arms and hurrah for Jeff Davis." Her neighbors, "stinking 'Secesh' Democrats," even now "hoped every man would be shot that went to fight against the South." In the Army of the Potomac news of Seymour's win heartened Democrats who welcomed the possibility of an early end to the war but depressed other soldiers who worried that the Union had been lost.[15]

Bitter recrimination further weakened New York Republicans. Moderates, convinced that a more conservative candidate would have beaten Seymour, blamed the radicals. Even Republican editors in neighboring Connecticut feuded over which faction had been responsible for the New York debacle. Weed moved quickly, advising the newly elected governor to avoid extreme measures, and the more cynical Republicans speculated that Seymour would pay more attention to distributing patronage than to assailing the Lincoln administration. Others hoped Seymour would not betray the public trust, despite his associations with unsavory peace advocates in New York City.[16]

New York radicals refused to accept responsibility for the defeat. Instead they blamed the Weed-Seward faction for undermining Wadsworth's candidacy. Concessions to moderates, abolitionist editors argued, had weakened the party's moral and political appeal, and the nation's leading religious weekly credited an unholy trinity of liquor dealers, proslavery men, and secret traitors with electing Seymour. Brig. Gen. John Cochrane, who was angling for Wadsworth's former command in Washington, informed Lincoln and Secretary of the Treasury Salmon P. Chase that the people were so disappointed with the slow progress of the war that "they have been aching for a head to smash." The hapless Wadsworth was their first victim.[17]

But he was not the only candidate to get his head smashed. All across the country Republicans had gone down to defeat or eked out narrow victories. Outside New England, voters turned out many incumbent congressmen, and the Democrats captured the critically important states of New Jersey, Pennsylvania, Ohio, Indiana, and Illinois. In some areas Democratic margins were thin, but the Republican majorities had fallen off in districts once considered safe.[18] A flood of depressing telegrams and letters arrived in Washington for Lincoln and his advisers; the president pored over the details of both congressional and state contests.[19]

Attempts to rally public opinion and form a broad-based Union coalition were floundering by the fall of 1862. The Democrats, seemingly moribund for the first year and a half of the war but now resurgent and combative, sought the right issue to use against the administration and the Republicans. As longtime defenders of laissez-faire and small government, they instinctively turned to a classic defense of liberty. The nature of the crisis was unmistakable: government tyranny threatened sacred rights. During the summer of 1862 federal marshals had detained persons accused of supporting the Confederacy but had paid most attention to draft evaders. Lincoln had tacitly approved "arbitrary arrests" and on September 24 had officially suspended the writ of habeas corpus to enforce the militia draft. With some hesitancy Republicans supported these measures and deplored opposition attempts to erect legal barriers to conscription. But in denouncing "military despotism" the Democrats had struck a responsive chord as even their opponents reluctantly conceded.[20]

After the last vote was tallied in early November, Democrats concluded that the civil liberties question had helped carry the day.[21] However that might be, they continued to press the issue throughout November and into December. Stung by the attacks, many Republicans, including some radicals, admitted that government officials had been overzealous and thus had provided a political opening for unscrupulous "demagogues."[22]

On November 22 the War Department ordered the discharge of "political" prisoners who had been arrested for discouraging enlistments or opposing the draft. Even the imperious Stanton later acknowledged that mistakes had been made. Republicans hoped this gesture would end the clamor against the government and defuse the civil liberties issue.[23] Cynics naturally traced this newfound sense of justice to the election returns. The *New York Herald* extravagantly described the prisoners' release as "opening the doors of our Bastilles" and denounced Stanton as a barbarian. Democrats kept repeating what soon became their political mantra: "The Constitution as it is; the Union as it was; the Negroes where they are."[24]

The last clause in this catchphrase was no afterthought. Fear of emancipation had become a staple of party rhetoric. Throughout the campaign Democrats had roundly condemned abolitionists and explicitly defended a "white man's" government. They had sketched out for their supporters a series of horrors that would certainly appear in the wake of emancipation. Thousands of black immigrants flocking to the North taking jobs away from white husbands and fathers would be just the beginning. Political equality and miscegenation would follow, bringing to American streets bloody scenes reminiscent of the French Revolution.[25]

Victorious Democrats cheered the rout of abolitionism. Conservative friends (or pretended friends) of the Lincoln administration claimed that the election returns proved how wrong the president had been to abandon his once moderate course and yield to the radicals on the slavery question. The Union would now be safe from extremists in both sections, triumphant Democrats predicted. Congressman Samuel S. Cox of New York lampooned the Republican opposition with a racist version of the Ten Commandments: "Thou shalt not take unto thee any graven image of ebony. . . . Thou shalt not take the name of Liberty in vain. . . . Thou shalt not degrade the white race by such intermixtures as emancipation will bring. . . . Thou shalt not bear false witness against their neighbors, charging them falsely with disloyalty. Thou shall not covet their neighbor's servants . . . nor tax the people for their deliverance." Such debates on the home front spilled over into the army camps. For politically savvy soldiers the fate of slavery remained a matter for intense discussion. Some agreed that voters back home had repudiated the abolitionists, and one New Yorker hoped that the election had scotched the careers of "political preachers" who were "really wolves in sheep's clothing."[26] Perhaps the war against the southern disunionists would not become an uncontrollable revolution after all.

For their part emancipationist Republicans and their abolitionist allies worried that Democrats might just be right, that a conservative tide would sweep away their hard-won gains. Senator Charles Sumner of Massachusetts considered the election in New York "worse for our country than the bloodiest disaster on any field of battle." But he and other radicals stood fast and spurned any compromise on the slavery question. A few more sound Republican newspapers might stay the course of political reaction, Horace Greeley irritably suggested, because "the newspaper is the chief bulwark of the Republican cause, as the Grogshop is the natural citadel of our adversaries." Other wishful thinkers hoped the recent defeats might force Lincoln to join forces in a permanent alliance with the antislavery radicals. Yet even the most sanguine could hardly ignore rumors that the president considered the preliminary Emancipation Proclamation the greatest mistake of his political life. And who could be sure what direction the administration might take when such marplots as Seward and Weed still wielded so much influence?[27]

Sumner and his friends were right in one respect: the greatest danger stemmed not so much from the Democrats, at least in the short term, but from divisions in Republican ranks. Conservative and moderate party leaders had often sidestepped emancipation during the recent campaign to accommodate their constituents' racial prejudices. After the elections, some of these same Republicans complained that the administration's antislavery stance had cost the party precious votes in tightly contested districts.[28] Little wonder, then, that reports circulated of the party waffling on the slavery question. Senator John Sherman of Ohio, an influential moderate, now considered the preliminary Emancipation Proclamation "ill timed," and conservatives pressed Lincoln to delay issuing a final Emancipation Proclamation.[29]

Although the claim that many loyal voters were in the army was obviously a convenient excuse, Republicans firmly believed that this had cut into their political base. By the same token, stay-at-home Democrats had led their party to victory.[30] But whether soldiers in the Army of the Potomac were strong Republicans was debatable. Democrats bragged how McClellan's many friends in the ranks had warmly supported Seymour. According to a New York artilleryman, "Republicanism is played out in the army." Democrats had reportedly been steadily gaining strength with the soldiers.[31]

"Messrs. Lincoln, Seward, Stanton & Co., you have done your work badly, so far. You are humbugs. My business is stopped, I have got taxes to pay, my wife's third cousin was killed on the Chickahominy, and the war is no nearer an end than it was a year ago. I am disgusted with you and your party and shall vote for the governor or the congressman you disapprove, just to spite you." Thus George Templeton Strong described the typical Democratic voter. Most people remained loyal, he believed, but they had lost faith in the national administration. The increasingly beleaguered Lincoln came under enfilading fire from both ends of the political spectrum. "You are surrounded by an atmosphere of treachery, disloyalty and slavery," a New York radical warned the president. "Do you ever realize that the desolation, sorrow, and grief that pervades this country is owing to you? That the young men who have been maimed, crippled, murdered, and made invalids for life owe it to your weakness, irresolution, and want of moral courage?"[32]

The president endured the barrage of criticism stoically for the most part. When his old Illinois friend Orville Hickman Browning held forth at length about how the preliminary Emancipation Proclamation had badly hurt the party, Lincoln sat in stony silence. Visitors upbraided the president in his own office. An enraged Pennsylvania Republican used an awkward double negative but still got his point across: "I am sorry to say it was not your fault that we are not all beaten." Some disgruntled partisans had even been heard to say that Lincoln should be strung up to the nearest lamppost. Such harsh invective proved how precipitously Lincoln's political stock was falling. Typically, he summoned up a bit of dark humor to deal with the criticism: "I feel like the boy in Kentucky who stubbed his toe while running to see his sweetheart, and who said he was much too big to cry, but far too badly hurt to be able to laugh."[33]

The fact remained that many citizens who might otherwise have voted Republican had indeed grown disgusted and impatient with the war's halting progress. Even administration loyalists grumbled about the military stalemate. As the first disappointing election returns trickled in from the October states, Chase privately noted the people's dissatisfaction with a "mismanaged war." Strategic blunders and incompetent generals had left "loyal soldiers to rot in camp or be slaughtered on the field," one of the secretary's Ohio supporters groused. "We abhor this milk & water course at Washington," a Michigan Republican sputtered.[34] The whining of the party's congressional leaders and even first-term members must have been especially painful to Lincoln. "Hundreds of Republicans," Senator Lyman Trumbull of Illinois fulminated, "who believed that their sons and relatives were being sacrificed to the incompetency, indisposition, or treason by proslavery Democratic generals, were unwilling to sustain [the] administration."[35]

According to many newspapers the elections had been a referendum on the conduct of the war. Radicals accused conservative generals of exhausting the voters' patience, while moderates emphasized a broader frustration with indecisive campaigns and bloody battles. Public disappointment over "another winter of delay will be something terrible to contemplate," a Philadelphia newspaper warned.[36] Despite adopting an understandably defensive tone, Republicans tried to sound confident. The Lincoln administration now had no choice but to carry on the war more aggressively. The people demanded victories; unsuccessful generals would have to go. Some editors denounced McClellan by name; others vaguely predicted a reorganization of both the army and the cabinet.[37]

Civilians and soldiers alike execrated the war's sluggish progress. Aside from politics and partisanship, the central question remained how and when the Confederates would be defeated. Impatient civilians demanded results. Disillusioned soldiers wondered whether their hardships, sacrifices, and bloodshed would ever lead to victory, the only thing that could silence public criticism. As one sophisticated Bostonian observed, "Military success is everything—it is the verdict which cures all ills."[38] Easily enough said, but battlefield victories against Confederate forces in the East remained frustratingly elusive, and the demoralization at home and in camp sparked rumors of peace.

★ ★ ★

Only days after the elections Lincoln began receiving urgent letters describing the supposed eagerness of Confederate leaders to begin negotiations. Shortly after he won a House seat by running on a peace platform, prominent New York Democrat Fernando Wood informed the president of the Rebels' readiness to send representatives to the next Congress in exchange for a general amnesty. Lincoln dismissed such reports as "groundless" and refused to countenance private diplomacy.[39]

Republicans tried to squelch talk of a negotiated settlement with powerful, seemingly self-evident arguments. First, the Confederates would accept nothing short of southern independence. Given Rebel distrust of Peace Democrats, even if some form of reunion was acceptable, the *Chicago Tri-*

bune predicted that Confederates would insist on coming back with their own president and vice-president, likely demanding amnesty and guarantees for "slave breeders."[40] Only the disloyal clamored for peace under such conditions. "Northern Democrats will fall into the embrace of the Southern Confederacy as gently as a courtesan sinks into the arms of her paramour," one Republican editor sniffed. Not only would Democrats welcome back traitors, but they risked inciting civil strife in the North to do it. Prominent divine Henry Ward Beecher did not doubt "that there are men in New York who would inaugurate blood, murder, and revolution, if they dared." Unfortunately, disaffection on the home front was spreading to the troops. A Pennsylvania colonel worried that traitorous talk was doing more damage to the Army of the Potomac than 50,000 Rebel reinforcements.[41]

Indeed, the northern elections had also heartened the Rebels. Confederate newspapers filled their columns with reports of peace sentiment in the northern states. Virginia's Governor John Letcher, it was rumored, had been in contact with the slippery Fernando Wood.[42] Such stories revived hopes for a diplomatic breakthrough.

Talk of an armistice or settlement naturally spread to Lee's army, where optimists foresaw peace by spring, if not sooner. Soldiers of course longed for a cessation of hostilities and grasped at the meagerest straws in the political wind. Maj. Gen. Lafayette McLaws, one of Longstreet's steadiest division commanders, rejoiced that "more Christian spirits" would soon displace defeated Republicans. Other officers agreed that dissension in the North might eventually bring down Lincoln's government and speculated that Seymour and his New York friends would help stop the fighting.[43]

Confederates hoped for continued political convulsions that would confound their enemies. Three of President Jefferson Davis's most strident newspaper critics decided that the elections had deeply divided the Federals, would cripple their armies, and might even lead to a general uprising in the northern states. Ardent fire-eater Edmund Ruffin rejoiced over the growing political discord across the North and believed that an armistice followed by a convention of the states would likely occur during the next several months.[44]

Few leading Confederates, however, held such sanguine views. Most newspapers discouraged their readers from placing any faith in treacherous northern politicians. "These Yankee Democrats," the *Richmond Daily Whig* warned, sought power for their own purposes. Surely so-called conservatives would prove just as faithless as Lincoln and the Republicans. So long as northern capitalists were making money from the war, calls for peace meant little, and in any event it was too late to restore the old Union after all the sacrifices the South had made. Nor was there evidence, despite the honey-tongued oratory of Horatio Seymour or Fernando Wood, that the northern Democracy had become a peace party.[45]

Even if northern conservatives could be trusted, the newly elected Congress would not assemble for over a year, and in the meantime the war would continue. The elections held out "no hope of speedy results," a Georgia editor cautioned. Senator William Lowndes Yancey of Alabama had no more faith in the northern Democrats than in the northern abolitionists. "Let us build our own unity upon their fierce party strife and jealousies. Upon their clashings of party interests, let us bind together our patriotic energies."[46]

The possible impact of the northern elections on international diplomacy could not be so easily dismissed. For months newspapers North and South had speculated about possible European intervention in the war, and during the late summer of 1862 the British had begun edging in that direction. Thinking that October might be the right time for a mediation offer, Foreign Secretary Lord John Russell had begun sounding out the French government. But the cabinet was divided, and despite his own belief that the Federals were losing the war, Prime Minister Henry John Temple, Lord Palmerston, remained cautious and delayed making a final decision.[47]

In France the talented foreign minister Edouard Drouyn de Lhuys had clung to an attitude of strict neutrality even as Emperor Napoleon III had pushed for a more aggressive policy. The discussions in Paris and London were approaching a climax before news of the American elections reached the continent. Growing unemployment in the French textile industry, sharply higher food prices, and perhaps some public sympathy for the Confederate cause along with hopes for assistance in his Mexican venture finally spurred Napoleon III into action. On November 7 he called for the Russian, French, and British governments to propose mediation of the American conflict with an immediate six-month armistice and suspension of the Union blockade.[48]

After a long discussion on November 10 and 11 the British cabinet rejected the French overture. The Russians did likewise.[49] This did not entirely kill mediation because much would still depend on the military situation and whether Lincoln proceeded with emancipation. Domestic politics, however, threatened to force Palmerston's hand. By December 1862 the loss of southern cotton had thrown several hundred thousand textile workers out of work, and still more were on relief. Newspapers on both sides of the Atlantic publicized the distress in England's northern industrial districts. Manufacturers clearly favored mediation, as did labor leaders, though the latter were reluctant because of the slavery question.[50]

Any talk of mediation made official Washington edgy. Foreign interference in American affairs would only unite the North, Seward asserted with more hope than conviction. He tried to reassure the American minister in London, Charles Francis Adams, about recent Republican losses at the polls, but even the dour New Englander must have smiled over the secretary of state's tortured analysis of the American elections: "People have become so confident of the stability of the Union that partisan combinations are resuming their sway here, as they do in such cases in all free countries." So Seymour's victory in New York could actually be interpreted as a sign of political health! Seward instructed the American minister in Paris to make no comment on Napoleon III's mediation offer. He kept his own remarks on recent diplomatic developments inserted into the president's annual message to Congress—remarkably bland.[51] Lincoln and his advisers nonetheless feared that a continued military stalemate might provide an excuse for foreign intervention. Consequently, their impatience with McClellan and other commanders grew. Only success on the battlefield could end this threat to American sovereignty.[52]

Even after the British had spurned mediation for the time being, rumors persisted that the French might act on their own. British opinion remained volatile. As news of the elections reached London, a new flurry of speculation began about a change in the ministry's policy toward the United States. Even sympathetic antislavery politicians such as John Bright worried about the American administration's apparent weakness. Irish nationalist William Smith O'Brien pointedly defended the Confederacy's right of self-determination.[53] Frederick Engels and Karl Marx discussed the American war from a more radical perspective. A sarcastic Engels had little sympathy for a people that "allowed itself to be continually beaten by a fourth of its own population and which after eighteen months of war has achieved nothing more than the discovery that all its generals are idiots and all its officials rascals and traitors." Engels and Marx had trouble fitting the "bourgeois republic" into their theory of class warfare, and their private letters reveal much perplexity about the course of the American conflict. Believing that his comrade was too pessimistic, Marx concluded that despite the vicissitudes of northern politics, the Confederates were losing the war.[54]

Diplomatic indecision on the mediation question and European misunderstanding of the significance of the American elections caused great consternation in the United States. Many northerners condemned foreign meddling in U.S. affairs, especially by the British, and vilified the English upper class for sympathizing with the southern aristocracy. The British nobility appeared hell-bent, one Boston editor grumbled, on conciliating the "Richmond oligarchy." Old resentments against European corruption and dynastic intrigue fanned hostilities. A New Jersey sergeant in the Army of the Potomac contemptuously dismissed England as that "little island across the sea."[55]

Leading Democrats spurned foreign mediation and declared their unswerving commitment to preserving the Union. Conservative victories in the recent elections, the *New York Herald* noted optimistically, made British intervention less likely and might even spark a counterrevolution in the Confederacy.[56] Some Republicans also played down the importance of the French mediation proposal and even suggested that British hostility to the American republic was abating. In their view the northern people controlled their own destiny so long as they defeated the Rebels on the battlefield.[57]

Most Confederates would have agreed on the decisive importance of battles, but southern diplomats closely followed each twist and turn of international politics. Naturally the northern election returns and the French mediation effort pleased them. Convinced that the cotton famine in England might yet prove decisive, James M. Mason in London boasted that "the ability of our generals and prowess of our arms is everywhere acknowledged in Europe." England's rejection of mediation only temporarily dampened such exuberant spirits. Even Secretary of State Judah Benjamin half expected the French to intervene in the war without waiting for British cooperation.[58]

"King cotton" might make European intervention inevitable, optimists such as Mason still believed. Yet rumors of imminent diplomatic recognition had circulated since the beginning of the war, and now even hopeful Confederates hedged their bets.[59] Skeptics appeared to be in the ascendancy. After many previous disappointments, who could still expect help from France or Great Britain? The European powers were in reality enemies of the South, and any prospect of foreign recognition was, according to an Augusta, Georgia, editor, a mere "bubble." The chimera of British or French navies breaking the blockade had too long weakened the people's will to make sacrifices. Confederates stood alone, Governor John Letcher of Virginia warned, and would have to "rely upon ourselves and fight it out."[60]

A growing sense of self-reliance and dependence on divine favor shaped general opinion. "We have to conquer a Peace with our good swords & by God's help we will do so!" plantation mistress Catherine Edmondston stoutly maintained.[61] Ironically, both sides now agreed that more blood would have to be shed before the war would end. Northern newspapers pressed for a winter campaign, and a strategic military victory had become a political necessity for Republicans. The abolition wing of the party in particular feared that Lincoln might draw back from emancipation. Seymour and other Democratic leaders urged the president to conduct the war in a more "constitutional" way, and the recent retreat on "arbitrary" arrests only made them more aggressive. The unpopularity of the draft and the military deadlock all boded well for the political opposition.

For Confederates the future appeared surprisingly bright. The northern elections and talk of foreign intervention temporarily heartened the war-weary. Public confidence in Confederate arms ran high, though Jefferson Davis's unrelenting opponents made national unity ever more elusive. The costs of the war continued to mount even when Confederate armies won important victories. Realists understood that the Yankees might appear demoralized but were sending ever larger armies into the field. Confederates, however, might hope that November would bring a lull in the fighting, a respite from the relentless pressure on dwindling resources, and a chance to replenish anemic regiments. Unfortunately General McClellan had at last bestirred himself. Yet the Army of the Potomac was moving slowly, and General Lee fully expected his soldiers to defeat a familiar and predictable opponent once again.

3 Strategy

Abraham Lincoln was worried that the northern people had still not made up their minds that the war was in earnest. "They have got the idea into their heads that we are going to get out of this fix, somehow by strategy!" he told a group of Sanitary Commission volunteers in early November. "General McClellan thinks he is going to whip the rebels by strategy; and the army has got the same notion. They have no idea that the war is to be carried on and put through by hard, tough fighting . . . and no headway is going to be made while this delusion lasts."[1] The recent elections convinced the president that too many people did not grasp the war's awful calculus. As news of the Republican defeats sank in and rumors of foreign intervention spread, the president increasingly vented his frustration on White House visitors.

"He has got the slows," Lincoln testily remarked after McClellan allowed Lee to slip between the Army of the Potomac and the Richmond defenses. Slow: that one word described the Army of the Potomac's commander perfectly. As the president's secretary John G. Nicolay explained, Lincoln admired McClellan's abilities, and his "high personal regard" had led him to "indulge" the general's "whims and complaints and shortcomings as a mother would indulge a baby." Despite the Democratic campaign to elevate the "Young Napoleon" to a national hero by a "most vigorous and persistent system of puffing in the newspapers," McClellan had never lived up to his reputation. He was "constitutionally too slow, and has fitly been dubbed the great American tortoise."[2]

Lincoln had solid military reasons to get rid of McClellan, but political imperatives had momentarily stayed his hand. Timing, Lincoln well knew, in both political and military affairs was everything. So just as he had waited to replace Maj. Gen. Don Carlos Buell in the western theater until after the October states had voted, he hesitated now to move against the popular McClellan before the New York elections.[3] On November 5, with Seymour's victory certain, the president at last ordered Gen. in Chief Henry W. Halleck to remove McClellan and appoint Maj. Gen. Ambrose E. Burnside of the Ninth Corps to command the Army of the Potomac. Fearing that McClellan harbored Caesarean ambitions and might defy the administration, Stanton took the precaution of sending Brig. Gen. Catharinus P. Buckingham, an older staff officer who had graduated from West Point with Robert E. Lee, to deliver the president's order.[4]

Around ten on the evening of the fifth, Stanton summoned Buckingham to the War Department. Entering the secretary's third-floor office, Buckingham ran into Halleck and, ironically enough, General Wadsworth, who had just lost the New York governorship to Seymour. Stanton led Buckingham into a small room and handed him two envelopes, one addressed to McClellan, the other to Burnside. The general was to make sure that Burnside accepted the command first, and then he was to deliver the order to McClellan in person. Should Burnside absolutely refuse the command, Buckingham was to return to Washington without seeing McClellan.[5]

Buckingham arrived at Ninth Corps headquarters south of Salem, Virginia, on November 7 toward evening. Finding Burnside asleep in an upstairs room of a small frame house, Buckingham awoke the general and handed him the momentous envelope. Burnside "did not feel competent to command and [stated] that he was under very great personal obligations to McClellan," Buckingham later reported. Prepared for just such a reply, Buckingham played his trump card: if Burnside refused the appointment, it would be offered to Maj. Gen. Joseph Hooker. Even the genial Burnside considered Hooker a dangerous and unprincipled intriguer, and so he reluctantly acceded to Lincoln's wishes.[6]

Buckingham, Burnside, and two aides traveled through a snowstorm back to army headquarters at Rectortown. The night had grown bitterly cold as they reached McClellan's tent around 11:30 P.M. Having just finished a cup of tea with Brig. Gen. Herman Haupt, the superintendent of military railroads, McClellan had begun writing a letter to his wife, Ellen. Buckingham and Burnside knocked on the tent pole.

As McClellan remembered it, the two men looked "very solemn" but tried to make polite conversation. Buckingham, however, recalled nervously blurting out the purpose of the visit and thrusting the envelope into McClellan's hands. McClellan read the orders and then calmly remarked, "Well, Burnside, I turn the command over to you." Little more than a month later Burnside vividly recalled the shock: "I then assumed the command in the midst of a violent snow-storm with the army in a position that I knew but little of."

After Burnside and Buckingham left, McClellan resumed the letter to Ellen. "I am sure that not a muscle quivered nor was the slightest expression of feeling visible on my face, which he [Buckingham] watched closely. They shall not have that triumph," McClellan wrote proudly. Toward his successor, he was condescending: "Poor Burn feels dreadfully—I am sorry for him." Typically, McClellan had only arrogant disdain for his superiors: "They have made a great mistake—alas for my poor country—I know in my innermost heart she never had a truer servant."[7]

McClellan's disappointment and anger quickly surfaced. On November 9 he told a staff officer that death seemed preferable to leaving his army in another's hands. He voiced similar sentiments at an officers' reception that evening: "I feel as if the Army of the Potomac belonged to me. It is mine. I feel that its officers are my brothers, its soldiers my children. This separation is like a forcible divorce of husband and wife."[8]

It was not a wholly inapt analogy. Many officers and enlisted men reacted to news of McClellan's removal with the despair of a jilted lover. "The army is in tears," declared a Pennsylvania captain. Those who had served with the general through several campaigns were especially distraught; even in the newer regiments, men expressed regret.[9] Demoralization seemed inevitable. A foreboding of impending disaster hung over the camps; the most disgruntled no longer appeared to care about the Union's fate. A Pennsylvania recruit expected the Army of the Potomac to be driven out of Virginia and Confederate independence established. Some soldiers were temporarily overwhelmed by an utter hopelessness.[10]

The initial shock soon gave way to spirited indignation. "There is one opinion upon this subject among the troops," Brig. Gen. John Gibbon, the able commander of the Iron Brigade, asserted, "and that is the Government has gone mad." The president had treated a skillful and selfless patriot contemptibly. Unable to comprehend the decision, the men engaged in what a

Minnesotan described as "tall swearing." Regimental letters to local newspapers dramatically conveyed the uproar to the home folks.[11]

Soldiers always complain, of course, but the anger ran much deeper than the usual grousing at the end of a hard day. The more outspoken officers threatened to resign their commissions. Empty blustering or not, at the time it appeared serious.[12] "Lead us to Washington," one general supposedly begged McClellan, and "we will follow you there." Reckless talk came easy, and there is no evidence that any of this vexation ever got beyond the talking stage; but disaffection clearly infected the army's upper echelons. Brig. Gen. Andrew Atkinson Humphreys, a longtime McClellan supporter with a legendary penchant for profanity, reportedly spouted that he "wished the Confederates would get into Washington and drive the whole d—d abolition posse into the Potomac." The Maine soldier who recorded this incident noted how many high-ranking officers adamantly insisted on McClellan's restoration to command. "No stone is left unturned to keep alive this feeling of distress among the privates and lower-grade officers."[13]

With no encouragement from their hero, however, most soldiers could do little but gripe, though some veteran officers did try to leave the service. A Rhode Island sergeant who deemed McClellan's departure "the hardist blow this Armey ever had" regretted that enlisted men could not resign.[14] As it turned out, however, neither could their officers. A general order from the War Department forbade any officer from resigning in the face of the enemy. Strongly appealing to patriotism and ethnic pride, Brig. Gen. Thomas Francis Meagher of the famous Irish Brigade reminded his disgruntled men that they fought for a cause, not for an individual. Adj. James B. Thomas of the 107th Pennsylvania would stay in the army only "because I have taken an oath to do so. . . . Before I think I had a higher motive."[15]

For many others the "higher motive" was exactly the point. The soldiers in the Army of the Potomac would remain steadfast even if they strongly disagreed with the government's military policies. However grudgingly, the men would respect Lincoln's authority as commander in chief. "The American soldier is true to his country, true to his oath, and resolved to fight the rebellion to the bitter end no difference who commands," a member of the 6th Wisconsin maintained. "[I] am not a McClellan man, a Burnside man, a Hooker man, i am for the man that leads us to fight the Rebs on any terms he can get."[16] Soldiers repeatedly noted the simple imperative to obey orders. Denying stories that the Army of the Potomac had become demoralized, Republican newspapers reported the men eager to meet the enemy in battle.[17]

Some soldiers in fact welcomed the change in command because, like Lincoln, they had gradually lost confidence in McClellan as a fighting general.

They readily recalled the spring fiasco on the Virginia Peninsula and could easily tick off the mistakes made during the recent Antietam campaign. Unable to understand why they could not whip the ragged Rebels, they blamed McClellan's lack of aggressiveness. A sarcastic Indiana veteran wondered why the Young Napoleon, despite abundant opportunities, had not yet "given some evidence of military genius." Campfire arguments erupted between McClellan's staunch defenders and his now emboldened detractors.[18]

Many bluecoats, of course, occupied the broadly confused middle. Refusing to embrace the blind devotion of McClellan's friends or the equally fanatical hatred of his enemies, they often sounded painfully ambivalent. Contradictory reactions appeared within a single paragraph of a single letter; soldiers kept changing their minds about McClellan's departure for days or even weeks. As a Pennsylvania captain later put it, he and his comrades felt like a young man who loses his lady love, suffers exquisite agony, but then decides there are other women in the world.[19] Such sentiments were easily enough expressed, but many officers and enlisted men worshiped McClellan. For better or for worse, those affections would not fade so quickly.

While some generals command fear or respect, McClellan inspired lasting devotion. Soldiers explicitly described their "love" for Little Mac, an attachment comparable to the admiration of the French for Napoleon. Not even George Washington had been so beloved by his men. One disheartened engineer referred to McClellan simply as "our Georgy." Sounding like a young man writing to his father, a New York colonel told the general how he had "grown up under your care." For weeks after Burnside took command, soldiers sitting around the campfires at night would sing, "McClellan is the man."[20]

True believers clung to an unswerving faith in McClellan's military genius. No other general would ever command such devotion from so many soldiers in the Army of the Potomac.[21] "Confidence" was the word that most often appeared in diaries and letters, and to men with such confidence it quickly became an article of faith that McClellan would have led them to victory had he not been shamefully removed. To sack a successful general in the midst of a march into enemy territory appeared the height of folly. The "idol of the Army," as a New York private dubbed McClellan, would surely have captured Richmond.[22] Whether the Army of the Potomac would ever have such faith in another commander remained an open question. Hotheads swore they would never fight for anyone but their beloved Little Mac.[23] Such sentiments may have made Burnside nervous, though it was difficult to gauge their significance. Most soldiers would do their duty; but the effects in the army would be lasting, and the political consequences for the Lincoln administration were potentially devastating.

Rather than criticizing the president, however, many men simply cursed what a Massachusetts recruit termed "wire pulling politicians" trying to manage the war from Washington. If only such schemers would leave their comfortable offices and take the places of the long-suffering soldiers. The boys had grown tired of being "dupes and tools of mad politicians," a Wisconsin sergeant groused, and were counting the days until their terms of enlistment expired.[24] "Patriotism no longer rules but fanaticism," a Michigan private protested. Abolitionists, the culprits who had supposedly pressured Lincoln into dismissing McClellan, became convenient scapegoats. "It was nothing but the nigar lovers of the North who took him from us," a Pennsylvania private concluded.[25]

Yet even McClellan's most fervent supporters realized that their hero had been steadily losing popular favor, especially among civilians who considered many generals too cautious and blithely spoke of conducting a winter campaign. These critics were "men who have no spunk enough to leave their mammy long enough, let alone to face the enemy," Pennsylvania private Alexander Adams railed, "men who are setting on their asses by their warm fires and enjoying all the comforts of home, running down men who are enduring hardships all the time and risking their lives to restore their country."[26]

McClellan had polarized both the country and the officer corps, turning the Army of the Potomac into a hothouse of intrigue. To Republicans McClellan's popularity in the ranks had been greatly exaggerated. Only the general's closest associates and what a Wisconsin soldier (himself just elected to Congress) called "political Generals of the Fernandy Wood school" would regret the Young Napoleon's departure. McClellan himself may have been a loyal man, a Regular army officer commented; but the "election of the New York traitors; the gallows-birds who have damned McClellan by befriending and admiring him" had led to talk of dictatorship, and this had spelled the general's doom.[27] So he would leave, mourned by many but scorned by others.

Little Mac seemed oblivious to the latter. In a typically egotistical address he recalled how the Army of the Potomac had "grown up under my care." After praising the men's loyalty and sacrifices, he added a final sentence that must have pleased his Democratic friends: "We shall ever be comrades in supporting the Constitution of our country and the nationality of its people." Privately he was less discreet. During one farewell visit with some officers he proposed a presumptuous toast: "The Army of the Potomac, God bless the hour I shall be with you again." He had to hold back tears as he bade goodbye to old friends.[28]

Burnside had graciously arranged for McClellan to review the troops one last time. The men, often several ranks deep, lined the roads for more than three miles near the army's newly established Warrenton headquarters. By eight in the morning on November 10 the men of the First, Second, and Fifth Corps, with bayonets gleaming and artillery scattered along the route, waited to catch a final glimpse of their hero. McClellan rode a fine stallion with his staff trailing behind, but occasionally the soldiers broke ranks to gather around him.[29] Even amid the boom of cannon, the cheers from these bareheaded veterans seemed deafening. Men wildly tossed caps into the air, officers saluted with swords, and color-bearers waved tattered regimental flags.[30] Some old soldiers wept. Even men who acknowledged McClellan's faults broke down under the strain of intense emotion. "The Army of the Potomac has just returned from its funeral," a private in the Fifth Corps somberly remarked. Some men cheered and sobbed and fumed at the same time, their oaths and threats rent the air, and their denunciations of political stay-at-homes occasionally exhausted profane vocabularies.[31]

In some units, especially the newer ones, nobody cheered, and McClellan did not even review Burnside's old Ninth Corps. One New York veteran sourly refused to shout for McClellan and instead wished he were back home.[32] Some soldiers stuck to their accustomed pose of scornful indifference. A Pennsylvania corporal wondered why anyone considered McClellan, Burnside, or any other general better than ordinary mortals. An orderly in Hancock's division took much more interest in breakfast than in the "rise and fall of generals."[33]

Yet few officers and enlisted men could be so cavalier about such a dramatic change. McClellan himself struggled with deep emotions. He rode along sadly surveying the troops and could not keep from weeping. "I never before had to exercise so much self control," he commented in a hastily scribbled note to Ellen. "The scenes of today repay me for all that I have endured."[34] The next morning a red-eyed McClellan and several of his staff prepared to leave for Trenton, New Jersey. His uneventful departure from the army relieved nervous Republicans, perhaps prematurely. Democratic kingpins soon bought the general a fine house on West 31st Street in New York and began touting him as a presidential candidate. Calling for an armistice and a negotiated settlement of the war, peace advocates loudly praised Seymour and McClellan.[35]

No sooner had McClellan left the army than the political fireworks began. Democrats seized every opportunity to use McClellan against the administration. Comparing Little Mac to George Washington, the *New York Herald* praised him as a "great general and perfect patriot" who had been "mostly falsely and basely maligned and abused." McClellan's military genius was as obvious as Lincoln's ineptitude. Why had the abolitionists pressured the president into recklessly removing the general on the eve of a great victory? McClellan was just the latest "sacrifice" to "appease" what New York congressman Samuel S. Cox termed the "ebony fetish."[36]

For their part abolitionists rejoiced that the great obstacle in their war against slavery had at last been removed. Through Charles Sumner's rose-colored glasses, McClellan's dilatoriness now appeared providential. It had ensured that the rebellion would not be defeated before slaves were declared free. Buell had departed and now McClellan. Apparently the administration's infatuation with conservative generals was over; surely there would now be no retreat from emancipation.[37]

Although both Democrats and abolitionists exploited Lincoln's decision for their own purposes, political considerations cut in several other directions. McClellan's removal heartened Republicans regardless of their factional loyalties and thus boosted Lincoln's standing in the party. "The country will breathe freer," a Racine, Wisconsin, editor predicted, "when it learns that this prince of laggards, not to say traitors, has at last been removed from the command of the Army of the Potomac." If anything, the president had been far too patient with someone who had let the Confederates escape repeatedly from his grasp. In rural Republican strongholds the press heartily agreed that Lincoln had acted none too soon.[38]

Denying Democratic charges that McClellan had been shelved because of his political views, Republicans insisted that the president had made a strictly military decision. Even Seward's conservative friends welcomed Little Mac's departure. Privately Republicans speculated that the recent elections may at last have given Lincoln some backbone. Had the president moved sooner, the party might not have suffered such heavy losses, but few Republicans cared to dwell on past mistakes. Instead they looked to the future, hopeful about the prospects of a more aggressive military strategy.[39]

A few editors and politicians sounded as ambivalent as some of the soldiers about the change in command. Quietly sustaining Lincoln's course seemed wisest, but conservative and moderate Republicans remained uneasy about where the war might be heading, and for good reason.[40] Lincoln had made a risky decision. Whether Burnside or anybody else could lead the Army of the Potomac any more successfully than McClellan was by no means clear. Certainly no one matched McClellan's organizational talents and ability to inspire devotion. Neither Lincoln nor Halleck had been able to impose their strategic ideas on the army's recalcitrant generals, many of whom were Little Mac's allies. McClellan had shown signs of learning how to deploy his magnificent army in battle, but his slowness, excessive caution, constant complaints, loose talk, and near-insubordination had tried even Lincoln's legendary patience.[41]

That McClellan had been about to win a dramatic victory over an increasingly confident Robert E. Lee, as the general's admirers would always believe, was a doubtful proposition. Yet installing a new commander in early November meant several weeks' delay, pushing any campaign late into the fall, when inclement weather could stymie the best-laid plans. For Lincoln the choice of McClellan's successor had posed no end of difficulties.

Many Republicans would have welcomed the appointment of "Fighting Joe" Hooker. While in Washington convalescing from a painful foot wound suffered at Antietam, Hooker had courted several influential politicians, including Salmon P. Chase and his politically ambitious daughter, Kate. Criticism of McClellan's sluggishness and possible disloyalty quickly became their chief topic of conversation. Hooker's endorsement of the preliminary Emancipation Proclamation greatly pleased the radicals, and by late October many people in Washington expected him to supplant McClellan. Yet Lincoln knew about Hooker's reputation as an intriguer and McClellan hater. His loose, indiscreet chatter had done nothing to endear him to either the president or Halleck.[42]

Hooker's liabilities then made the appointment of Ambrose E. Burnside seem prudent. Born in Liberty, Indiana, on May 23, 1824, Burnside had worked for a time as a tailor's apprentice. He received an appointment to the U.S. Military Academy at West Point, where unlike his future opponent Lee, he accumulated scores of demerits. The convivial proprietor of a local saloon regularly drank toasts to the three men he admired most: St. Paul, Andrew Jackson, and his favorite customer, Ambrose Burnside.[43] Although he narrowly escaped disciplinary dismissal, Burnside compiled a respectable academic record and in 1847 managed to graduate eighteenth in a class of thirty-eight cadets. He covered himself in gambling debts rather than glory during subsequent service as an artillery officer in the Mexican War. Assigned to an isolated post in New Mexico, he fought boredom by designing a breech-loading carbine for the cavalry. Burnside married Mary Richmond Bishop from Providence, Rhode Island, in 1851 and two years later resigned his commission to begin manufacturing his carbine. For various reasons this business failed, and by the eve of the Civil War he was working as a cashier for a railroad owned by none other than George B. McClellan.

Shortly after the bombardment of Fort Sumter, Burnside accepted com-

Maj. Gen. Ambrose E. Burnside
(Library of Congress)

mand of the 1st Rhode Island infantry regiment. His leadership of a brigade at the First Battle of Bull Run earned him a quick promotion to brigadier general. Burnside's first opportunity for independent command came in January 1862 when he directed an amphibious expedition that captured Roanoke Island off the North Carolina coast. Success against greatly outnumbered Confederates had come when Union victories were scarce and by March had earned Burnside another star. Clearly he seemed destined for higher command, but his flaws as a general had already emerged. He delegated authority to his brigade commanders, yet his close attention to organizational and logistical minutiae sometimes drove Burnside to the point of exhaustion. Besides, he had a trusting nature, a quality that would hardly serve him well in the backbiting Army of the Potomac.

Frustrated by McClellan's failure on the Virginia Peninsula, in July 1862 Lincoln had offered Burnside command of the Army of the Potomac. With much self-effacement Burnside had declined. After Lee had begun his invasion of Maryland in September, Lincoln repeated the offer, and the general had again refused. At Antietam Burnside had commanded the Ninth Corps, and its performance, especially the supposedly tardy crossing of the famous bridge on the southern part of the battlefield, had stirred controversy and damaged his reputation. The once cordial relationship with McClellan had cooled during September and October; Little Mac evidently had come to consider Burnside a potential rival.[44]

Burnside's appointment to command the Army of the Potomac seemed logical enough. After all, in North Carolina he had shown promise directing a successful campaign. Though hardly a close student of strategy, Burnside was intelligent and hardworking. Even Chase, who clearly preferred Hooker, admitted that Burnside had "some excellent qualities" and believed that the administration would strongly support him. Stanton also favored Burnside, though Lincoln apparently did not consult the cabinet on the matter.[45]

Like McClellan, Burnside had been a Democrat before the war, but unlike his erstwhile friend, he had come to favor emancipation. Burnside had few political enemies; more significantly, he had few political friends. His selection aroused no partisan bickering, a plus for Lincoln, but Burnside himself had no political base of support should he run into trouble. As Prussian military theorist Carl von Clausewitz has pointed out, a successful commander must understand politics and be able to deal with politicians, yet Burnside remained a political innocent. Where McClellan tended to espy numerous enemies near and far, Burnside could discern none, regardless of proximity.[46]

Contemporaries considered Burnside an impressive physical specimen. A six-footer with a large face and balding head, his bushy, brown sideburns curved around his lips into a full mustache. This luxuriant facial hair and his dark, deep-set eyes rendered his appearance distinctive and memorable. Burnside's dress mirrored a frank, hearty simplicity. Careless about his uniform, he often rode about in a plain jacket and fatigue cap. Soldiers appreciated his informality, cheerfulness, and good humor.[47] Burnside's honest humility stood in striking contrast to the devious arrogance of McClellan or Hooker. Even the general's detractors found him amiable and appealing.

In many ways Burnside was his own toughest critic, and genuine modesty was his worst failing. "I do not feel equal to it," he confessed to Brig. Gen. Orlando Willcox the morning after taking command. In his first order to the army he expressed "diffidence" about his own ability. The enormity of this new assignment soon became a crushing burden. Through the prism of his own limitations, Burnside saw fearsome, almost insurmountable difficulties. He had trouble sleeping and kept telling anyone who would listen that he was not the man for the job.[48]

Lincoln, who well understood the need for self-confidence in politics, should have been wary of appointing a man who had repeatedly expressed sincere doubts about his own capabilities. Even Burnside realized that the entire country, from the president to the corn shucker, expected an immediate advance against the Confederates. In such a campaign, the general's mistrust of his own abilities and a penchant for second-guessing himself could become fatal handicaps.

"Burnside, it is said, wept like a child, and is the most distressed man in the army, openly says he is not fit for the position," Maj. Gen. George Gordon Meade reported the day after McClellan's removal. Even generals who were not charter members of the diehard McClellan faction wondered why they should have confidence in a commander who had so little confidence in himself.[49] The rank and file shared the top leadership's concern. Some soldiers insisted they would never have the same faith in Burnside they had in McClellan. Newspaper reports that Burnside would speedily crush the rebellion elicited howls of ridicule around campfires.[50]

At this point, however, such opinions hardly predominated, as the general's easy manner and simple patriotism made him naturally popular. Whether the change was for the best or not, and despite suspicions that Burnside had conspired with Washington politicians to replace their hero, even ardent McClellan men grudgingly admired their new commander. Yet Burnside would have little time to prove himself, and rumors persisted that Hooker would soon take his place.[51]

More hopeful bluecoats forecast that Burnside's victories would soon erase all memory of McClellan. The sturdy devotion of Burnside's old Ninth Corps was reportedly inspiring the rest of the army.[52] Many soldiers expressed confidence in his military skill. "He has been my man for the last eight months," a New York officer informed his brother. Although they surely should have known better by this time, some sanguine veterans (and many new recruits) predicted the speedy defeat of the Rebels.[53]

The northern public naturally took great interest in Burnside, and speculation about his abilities had already gone far afield. Throughout the war the *American Phrenological Journal* had regularly published profiles of leading northern generals. In the spring of 1862 during the North Carolina campaign an anonymous writer had offered a detailed phrenological analysis of the latest Union hero, Ambrose E. Burnside. His skull shape indicated a "large brain" and "very active nervous system." The general displayed "clearness of perception," "quickness of thought," an "excellent power to plan," and a "will which no opposition can subdue." His "Cautiousness" seemed to be "comparatively weak" while his "Combativeness and Destructiveness appear to be large." As if to confirm its ludicrousness, this phrenological reading had concluded that Burnside possessed "rather large Self-Esteem" and a firmness akin to that of Stonewall Jackson.[54]

Such pseudoscientific musings had undoubtedly convinced some readers and bemused others, but they clearly illustrate how deeply the war had

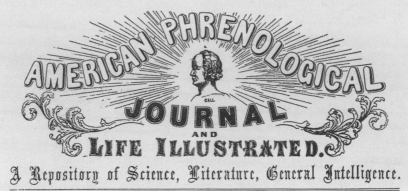

AMERICAN PHRENOLOGICAL JOURNAL AND LIFE ILLUSTRATED.

A Repository of Science, Literature, General Intelligence.

VOL. XXXV. NO. 3.]   NEW YORK, MARCH, 1862.   [WHOLE NUMBER, 279.

Published by
FOWLER AND WELLS,
No. 308 Broadway, New York.
AT ONE DOLLAR A YEAR, IN ADVANCE.

Contents.

	PAGE		PAGE
Ambrose E. Burnside, Phrenological Character and Biography	49	Dr. Luther V. Bell	66
Who are Happiest?	66	A Sunbeam and a Shadow	62
Words and Ideas	61	Problem: to Analyze the Intellect and Knowledge	63
A Shelf in our Cabinet—No. 2	62	The Master of the North	64
The Five Gateways of Knowledge—No. 2—The Nose	63	The American Star	67
People of whom more might have been Made	61	Talk with Readers	67
Prisoners and Prison Keepers	65	Lord Campbell's Brain	67
Electric	59	Education and Training Phrenologically Considered—No.2	64
Samuel H. Felton, Phrenological Character and Biography	65	Opinions of the People	49
		To Correspondents	69
		Advertisements	70

AMBROSE E. BURNSIDE.

PHRENOLOGICAL CHARACTER AND BIOGRAPHY.

PHRENOLOGICAL CHARACTER.

This gentleman has two qualities which mark his constitution and character; these are, intensity and endurance. He has a compact, firm, substantial body; he has, at the same time, a large brain, a very active, nervous system, and great susceptibility. We judge from his organization that one branch of his family is remarkable for intensity of feeling, clearness of perception, quickness of thought, and general sensitiveness; while the other branch is noted for endurance, hardihood, power, toughness, courage, and will-power; and our subject appears to have in himself these qualities combined in nearly equal degree.

His brain is large in the thinking department; he has an excellent power to plan, is capable of taking in large views of truth, and of comprehending the philosophy of subjects

BRIG.-GENERAL AMBROSE E. BURNSIDE.

clearly. His perceptive organs are well developed, hence his mind is ready, prompt, and positive.

His head is remarkably high, indicating Firmness to a very great degree. He has a will which no opposition can subdue, and an earnestness of purpose which is increased

rather than diminished by difficulties. He appears to have large Conscientiousness, Veneration, and Benevolence. He ought, therefore, to be known for the love of justice, respect for superiors, and kindness toward all. His Cautiousness, so far as we can judge by the likeness, is comparatively weak; hence, we judge that he is a stranger to fear, and liable to expose himself too much. His Combativeness and Destructiveness appear to be large, and we infer that he is bold, earnest, and executive.

He has talent for mathematics, for mechanics, is fertile in resources, able to adapt himself to ends on the spur of the moment, or to carry out a systematic course of engineering. His Language is fairly indicated. He is a good, but not a great talker. He expresses himself in strong and unqualified terms, and impresses the hearer with an idea that he is in earnest. He has rather large Self-Esteem, believes in his own power, trusts to his own skill and ability, and relies on himself; and in an emergency, if questions of importance were left to his discretion, he would weigh all the circumstances and the responsibilities, and decide and act with more

Burnside profile, American Phrenological Journal, *March 1862*

reached into the recesses of American life. If phrenologists had indeed been paying attention to Burnside, then the war had become all consuming. It is significant that, like most other assessments of Burnside before Fredericksburg, even this one had been favorable.

Burnside's appointment generated surprising enthusiasm among politicians. In November 1862 hardly anyone had anything bad to say about the general, at least publicly. For Democrats it was enough that he had long been

McClellan's friend (apparently reporters had not yet caught wind of their recent contretemps). Building on his predecessor's masterful strategy, Burnside would soon march triumphantly toward the Rebel capital.[55] In some ways Republican editors agreed, but they plainly expected a greater aggressiveness. "GOD SPEED GENERAL BURNSIDE!" *Harper's Weekly* proclaimed. "March and fight" will replace "wait and dig," a Philadelphia newspaper correspondent predicted. Most Republicans applauded the appointment, and Rhode Island governor William Sprague arranged a 100-gun salute to honor the state's adopted son, who now commanded the largest field army in the world.[56]

Some radical Republicans, although they appreciated Burnside's belated support for emancipation, worried that Lincoln's choice reflected a lingering caution and debilitating conservatism. A *New York Tribune* reporter who had met Burnside considered him a man of distinctly limited ability; a *Chicago Tribune* editorial deplored efforts by some newspapers to turn the general into a second Napoleon. Working as his father's secretary in London, young Henry Adams, the already world-weary skeptic, coldly commented, "I do not believe in Burnside's genius."[57] At this point all opinions, however informed or groundless they might be, amounted to little more than speculation. Given the stakes involved and the consuming interest, rash predictions, unfounded expectations, and far-fetched rumors were inevitable.

Confederates also assessed the significance of McClellan's departure and with equally mixed results. Southern generals had always been able to rely on McClellan's lethargy, a Georgia editor noted with sly contempt and rare candor. Privately at least, the Confederate high command agreed. "We always understood each other so well," General Lee remarked about McClellan. "I fear they may continue to make these changes till they find some one whom I don't understand." Such a statement suggested overconfidence, while southern newspapers tried to goad the deposed general into marching on Washington.[58]

The removal of McClellan, often described as the Yankees' ablest general, boded well for southern fortunes, or so many Confederates believed.[59] The southern press waxed enthusiastic. A desperate northern administration had not been able to abide having a Democratic general leading a heavily Democratic army; Lincoln and Seward would pay the political price.[60] Reports from deserters and prisoners about demoralization in the Army of the Potomac made for cheerful reading. A Richmond newspaper claimed that Halleck had been forced to visit the Federal camps to quell the protests. "All Yankeedom is in an uproar," a young Charleston woman gloated.[61]

As for the new Federal commander, he seemed beneath contempt. At the beginning of the war Burnside had been "little better than a loafer about Washington, having failed in everything he had undertaken," the *Richmond Daily Whig* sniffed. Should the bluecoats be foolish enough to try an advance on Richmond so late in the year—and many Confederates wondered if they could—the weather would stop them dead in their muddy tracks. "Freezing nights and bogy roads are incompatible with the safe retreat of a beaten foe," explained the *Charleston Mercury*. The Yankee government itself seemed to be tottering toward collapse.[62]

Despite the wildly exaggerated tone of many editorials, Confederates had good reason to rejoice as the end of the year approached. The northern elections, McClellan's removal, reports of Yankee demoralization, and the appointment of an incompetent commander all had engendered a buoyant faith in southern prospects.

General Burnside, of course, was preparing to quash that faith. After officially assuming command on November 9, he established headquarters at the nearly deserted town of Warrenton, Virginia. Once a thriving village of more than 600 inhabitants, Warrenton, which boasted a respectable hotel, a few businesses, several churches, and some impressive private homes, had grown shabby under the press of war. Many stores were closed, and the sick and wounded of both armies crowded the streets. Coffins filled the Presbyterian church, while local women tended an already sizable Rebel cemetery on the edge of town. "Neglect and decay" could be seen "everywhere," one Union staff officer remarked, and most of the locals stayed indoors.[63]

A little over a week after Burnside took command, some soldiers from the 133rd Pennsylvania tramped into Warrenton to buy soft bread, a long-sought-after luxury. They discovered a true seller's market: high prices and an extremely doubtful product. Soon, however, livestock and poultry began to disappear from pens and coops. "We steal every thing we come across," a hungry Michigan recruit bragged to his father.[64]

Yet the pickings were slim because John Pope's army during the summer and retreating Confederates more recently had already stripped the area of provisions. Ninth Corps bivouacs near Warrenton with names such as "Hungry Hollow" and "Camp Starvation" accentuated the problem. Salt pork and sugarless coffee became staples as even the accursed hardtack grew scarce. Available food was often inedible. "The pork was so mean that we consigned it to the flames," a Maine private observed ruefully.[65] The army's scattered divisions fared little better elsewhere in northern Virginia. Hardtack was low, supply wagons were late, and men were hungry. The story was the same at Waterloo, New Baltimore, White Sulphur Springs, and other places.[66]

Most of these supply problems were temporary, and the commissary wagons quickly caught up with the soldiers. But even as the men broke open the "cracker" boxes and Burnside tinkered with his campaign plans, the weather worsened. Snow fell at Warrenton on the day McClellan was removed, again on the day Burnside took command, and three days later on November 12. Already the bluecoats realized that a winter campaign with no shelter except fly tents would be deadly. With tongue only partly in cheek, a Michigan man in the First Corps teasingly informed his wife that he might not be able to undress and climb into bed immediately when he returned home but would have to sleep outdoors for the first couple of nights.[67]

In the wake of this exposure came sick lists, fatal fevers, and camp burials. Of the approximately 700 men in the 13th New Hampshire, some 200 had been hospitalized by mid-November. Medical treatment in the Army of the Potomac had improved since the summer, but there were still negligent or drunken surgeons absent from their posts. Helpless patients lying on foul beds "crawling with vermin" went unwashed for days. The wretched conditions spurred Dr. Mary Walker to supervise the transfer of the most seriously ill to Washington hospitals. Amid general neglect and growing indifference to death, one nurse asked, "Does war makes us worse than the heathen?"[68]

With a lull in the fighting and the air turning cold, the army might have gone into winter quarters. Understanding why McClellan had been removed, however, Burnside did not dare to consider that alternative.[69] On the very day he took command, the general responded to Halleck's insistent request for a campaign plan. After feints in the direction of Culpeper or Gordonsville, the Army of the Potomac would "rapidly move" toward Fredericksburg and from there advance on Richmond. The line of march would effectively shield Washington from Lee's army—always a sensitive point with Lincoln and Stanton. Burnside laid out the advantages of this more direct route, with its short, defensible line of communications, but needlessly added that even if some Confederate forces headed north while Richmond was being captured, "the loss of a half a dozen of our towns and cities in the interior of Pennsylvania could well be afforded." There is no evidence that anyone in the corridors of the War Department fussed over this curious passage, an indication perhaps of the administration's willingness to accept almost any plan that promised to end the costly stalemate in the East. Burnside carefully listed his subsistence needs and requested that pontoons be sent for use in bridging the Rappahannock. He proposed dividing the Army of the Potomac into three wings but did not go into detail about organizational changes.[70]

Burnside had sounded a decisive note in his first important dispatch to the War Department. Whether he had spent enough time considering alter-

natives is doubtful. But the political pressures were inescapable, and a successful offensive demanded not only decisiveness but speed. Given the strategic objectives and need for an immediate advance, Burnside's plan had considerable merit and some potential for success.[71]

After receiving Burnside's proposal, Halleck requested a meeting and on November 12 traveled to Warrenton with Herman Haupt and Quartermaster Gen. Montgomery Meigs. In some ways Halleck's trip marked a departure from his usual passivity and avoidance of responsibility. Despite his reputation as a military scholar, "Old Brains" did not impress his contemporaries. He looked less like a general and more like an overly prosperous banker, with his bald forehead, double chin, and slight paunch. His blunt, almost clipped manner of speaking could not disguise a wariness of others and frequent hesitation to express his own views. As general in chief he hated making decisions and seldom provided the kind of clear, detailed advice Lincoln or the army commanders needed.[72]

Following a pleasant meal at a local hotel, Halleck, Meigs, Haupt, and Burnside settled down to business. The meeting, however, began on a sour, albeit familiar, note. Burnside still insisted that someone else should have been appointed to command the army. "I am not fit for it," he repeated. Tired of such talk, Halleck impatiently asked for details of a plan that he already distrusted. Burnside obligingly explained the advantages of the Fredericks-

Maj. Gen. Edwin V. Sumner
(National Archives)

burg route, but Halleck urged sticking with the line of advance toward Culpeper and Gordonsville. Haupt, the railroad man, naturally preferred the
shorter Fredericksburg route. After more discussion Halleck refused to issue
any orders but agreed to present Burnside's ideas to Lincoln. If the president
approved, Burnside would march the army to Falmouth and cross the Rappahannock River on pontoon bridges. Halleck would arrange to have the
pontoon trains moved to Falmouth.[73]

Burnside's proposal to abandon the line of advance that the administration had pressed on McClellan did not please Lincoln, and he likely shared
Halleck's reservations about the Fredericksburg route. Yet the president
hesitated to show any lack of confidence in his new commander, and so on
the morning of November 14 Halleck wired Burnside the administration's
response: "The President has just assented to your plan. He thinks that it
will succeed, if you move rapidly; otherwise not."[74] Burnside recognized the
necessity for concentrating his forces and marching, but this curt and unenthusiastic response from Washington hinted at trouble ahead.

His plans approved, Burnside ordered the reorganization of the Army
of the Potomac into three grand divisions, with the Eleventh Corps, commanded by Maj. Gen. Franz Sigel, as a reserve force.[75] The Right Grand Division (Second and Ninth Corps) would be commanded by Maj. Gen. Edwin V.
Sumner. At age sixty-five Sumner was the oldest corps commander in the
army. Dubbed "Bull" because of his booming voice, bravery under fire, and
an old army story about a musket ball that had once bounced off his thick

Maj. Gen. William B. Franklin
(National Archives)

head, Sumner had three notable characteristics: unwavering loyalty, limited ability, and precarious health.

Maj. Gen. William B. Franklin would command the Left Grand Division (First and Sixth Corps). Franklin had graduated at the top of the same West Point class (1843) in which Ulysses S. Grant had ranked twenty-first. The cautious Franklin was a McClellan loyalist of the first order, albeit a capable engineer and solid administrator. Throughout the coming campaign his lack of enthusiasm and initiative would border on insubordination.

Hooker would lead the Center Grand Division (Third and Fifth Corps). Distasteful as it was to him, Burnside had to make the appointment. Hooker could not be ignored; he had the appropriate rank, powerful political connections, and undoubted abilities as a soldier. But in an army that he thought he should command (and with Republican editors continuing to puff him in fawning editorials), Joe Hooker would hardly be a model subordinate.[76]

Creating the grand divisions added another layer to the command structure, and either the corps or grand division commanders could easily become superfluous. Under this scheme Burnside would have less contact with the corps commanders and even less with the vitally important division commanders. The cavalry and artillery remained scattered among the grand divisions. Although Burnside greatly reduced the swollen adjutant general's staff, the reorganization had ensured that communications and staff work would only become more complex and difficult. All these important changes also delayed the advance toward Fredericksburg.[77]

As the reorganization proceeded, the soldiers waited, complaining as usual and speculating about the future. "We are making history," Col. Robert McAllister of the 11th New Jersey told his family. "The eyes of the world are

Maj. Gen. Joseph Hooker
(National Archives)

upon us." Even ardent McClellan men sounded a note of enthusiastic patriotism. "Love of country, especially such a country as ours where the blessings of a free government and the best of institutions are enjoyed alike by all, should be paramount to every other," a New York staff officer believed. Soldiers broadly embraced the values of a middle-class democracy, and many tried to conform to its model of virtuous citizenship.[78] Duty remained their polestar as they sat in their tents or around the campfires pondering what might happen over the next week or so.

Yet nervousness about Burnside, a lingering preference for Little Mac, and uncertainty about where the army might be headed also made soldiers uneasy. Men in the newer regiments and even some veterans might dream of reaching Richmond, but many still expected (or, rather, hoped) the army would soon go into winter quarters.[79] Such thoughts partly reflected a crisis in confidence. Perhaps Confederate generals were superior, and maybe even their soldiers were braver. A Michigan recruit bitterly remarked that none of his comrades would ever see the Rebel capital except as prisoners of war. The new Congress would press for peace negotiations, a Massachusetts officer predicted, and if the enemy held out until spring, "the Confederacy is a fixed fact."[80]

Whether stemming from a prickly personality, momentary pique, or genuine despair, such pessimistic statements probably no more reflected the army's general opinion than did the wildly optimistic declarations. Yet some disillusionment with the whole enterprise was unmistakable. Pvt. Roland E. Bowen of the 15th Massachusetts badly wanted to come home but doubted his chances. "If I ever do," he exploded to his wife, "I will see this Union in the bottom of Hell before I have any thing to do with another war." A greatly frustrated Michigan captain wrote in his diary, "We are fooled, beaten, bamboozled, outflanked, hoodwinked & disgraced by half our numbers. . . . All the devils in Hell could not stand before this army if it were led & handled [by a capable commander]." A beautiful fall had already gone to waste: "Hell & furies it is enough to drive a man mad if he has one particle of regard for his country." A chastened sadness and a Lincolnesque fatalism crept into soldiers' letters and diaries. "If a ball takes off a limb, they must at least discharge me," an orderly in Hancock's division remarked. "If the ball touches my heart the Almighty will give my discharge nor stop to make it out in duplicate."[81]

Worries about Confederate intentions compounded these fears. That sly old fox Lee might not even contest the crossing of the Rappahannock and instead adopt a Fabian policy of luring the Army of the Potomac away from its supply base. Of course, any rumors involving a movement by Jackson, who was seen by many northerners as nearly invincible, made folks edgy.[82]

"The war languishes. We are slowly invading Virginia, but there is nothing decisive or vigorous done there or elsewhere," George Templeton Strong noted glumly. But he had a "foreboding," a sense that this lull in the war was about to end and there was about to begin a "terrible, crushing, personal calamity to every one of us; when there shall be no more long trains of carriages all along Fifth Avenue bound for Central Park, when the wives and daughters of contractors shall cease to crowd Stewart's and Tiffany's, and when I shall put no burgundy on my supper table. . . . 'Without the shedding of blood there is no remission of sins.' It is impossible this great struggle can pass without our feeling it more than we have yet felt it." Few civilians engaged in such morose ruminations. Screaming headlines began appearing in the newspapers again as editors seated behind great desks in comfortable chairs composed editorials clamoring for a rapid advance toward the Rebel capital. Burnside would be the man; the end of the war was now in sight; steadfast veterans would push on to victory.[83] Brave young men in blue had only to march toward the Rappahannock.

I have destroyed the enemy merely by marches.
—Napoleon I

4 Marching

Herman Haupt, single-minded in pouring his considerable talent and energy into moving military supplies quickly over the railroads, always seemed to encounter snags. Washington red tape and generals who made impossible demands were bad enough, but what really irritated the impatient Pennsylvanian were delays. He wanted his trains to move—constantly. "Trains must not stand still, except when loading and unloading," he told Burnside, "and the time for this should be measured by minutes, not by hours." Manassas Junction was the main bottleneck, and the irascible Haupt upbraided Brig. Gen. Daniel E. Sickles when he discovered that the general's "agent" there had reportedly diverted engines to make unloading cars more convenient for his troops.

Haupt's men, too, were often tactless and sometimes profane; but shipping supplies along a single-track railroad was no easy task, and Haupt refused to let a mere general or even the secretary of war stand in his way. When Stanton ordered officers to cooperate in unloading the trains and then tried to require railroad workers to provide receipts for all supplies, Haupt refused. This prompted one of Stanton's famous rages, but he nevertheless gave up on having the order enforced.[1]

Haupt still had his hands full. Anticipating a change in the Army of the

Potomac's supply base, Haupt had argued for rebuilding the stretch of the Richmond, Fredericksburg, and Potomac Railroad between Aquia Creek and Falmouth. This would allow supplies to be moved down the Potomac to Aquia Creek and on by rail to camps north of Fredericksburg.

As early as mid-October Haupt had brought the necessary lumber and other materiel to Washington. A month later, transports and troops were already on their way to Aquia Creek, and Haupt, along with a retinue of other officers, was busy inspecting wharves and partially destroyed track at Aquia Creek. After four days of work, by November 22 Haupt's industrious engineers had rebuilt 800 feet of wharf and landed one engine. After two more days a bridge over Potomac Creek was in operation; two days after that the first engine was chugging toward Falmouth.

Haupt's achievement had been impressive. The span over Potomac Creek stood nearly four stories high and had required more than 40,000 cubic yards of timber. Railroad cars loaded with supplies were placed on huge Schuylkill barges (two parallel barges bolted together) and floated down to Aquia Creek. From there they could be hooked onto engines and taken to Falmouth. Soon twenty trains a day ran over the repaired tracks. Shipments from Alexandria reached Falmouth within seventeen hours, including time for unloading and loading at Aquia. Of course, problems persisted. Unnecessary items got shipped, enterprising boys snuck onto trains hoping to sell their newspapers in the camps, and "contraband goods" being sent by "Jews, sutlers and others" sometimes evaded Haupt's sharp lookout. Worse, shivering soldiers routinely stole wood intended for stoking the engines or would wash clothes upstream from water stations, so that "soap and other impurities" clogged the trains' boilers.[2]

Haupt already knew what Burnside and other generals were learning: the railroad was transforming military strategy. To one engineer the newly rebuilt wharves at Aquia seemed as "busy as I ever saw the docks of new york in her palmiest dayes."[3] Watching the trains leave for Falmouth, an observer could easily see how dependent the army had become on this marvel of the age. Railroads determined lines of march and sometimes dictated campaign strategy.

Troops moved great distances by rail, but wagons, horses, and mules remained the backbone of military transportation. Soldiers marched to battlefields accompanied by cavalry, artillery, and supply trains. A four-horse team could haul 2,800 pounds of supplies along good roads but considerably less on a rough country lane, especially after a rain. An army used up horseflesh. The Federals generally had enough horses, though even before Burnside took command, disease had hobbled many animals. A Wisconsin chap-

Aquia Creek and Fredericksburg Railroad, construction crew at work
(National Archives)

lain succinctly described the problem: "The heel becomes very sore and the hoof separates from the skin so that when they [the horses] step, it opens, splits, and cracks." No one seemed to know what caused the malady, though a Pennsylvanian speculated that perhaps the animals had been eating too much corn and not enough hay. Some cattle and horses also suffered from a usually fatal "black tongue" disease.[4]

These problems threatened to slow Burnside's movement before it had even begun. In various artillery batteries, anywhere from one-third to one-half of the horses were useless, and raids on local farmers alleviated only part of the deficit.[5] Cavalry officers blamed wet weather, poor forage, and hard riding for worsening the problem, but some regiments just took better care of their animals. Whatever the causes, the horses suffered, stumbling on hooves that seemed ready to fall off, "blood and matter squirting out all around the foot," according to one trooper. Quartermaster General Meigs informed Burnside that it might not be possible to provide enough healthy horses for both the supply trains and the cavalry.[6]

Federal cavalry was already advancing toward the Rappahannock before the army itself began moving. Especially nervous about Jackson's where-

Aquia Creek Landing, Virginia, wharf, boat, and supplies (Library of Congress)

abouts, Union troopers tried to keep tabs on Lee's army. Sharp skirmishing with Confederate cavalry occasioned some loss of baggage and supplies but few casualties. Burnside feinted with cavalry and detached infantry toward White Sulphur Springs in hopes of making Lee think he still intended to advance on Culpeper along the Orange and Alexandria Railroad. Later, as the army began its march to Fredericksburg, Federal cavalry continued to monitor Rebel movements, especially along the Rappahannock fords.[7]

With the railroad to Falmouth still under repair and without making sure the greatly needed pontoons had left Washington, Burnside ordered his army forward. At 5:00 A.M. on November 15, Sumner's Right Grand Division began leaving Warrenton; by late morning most of his men were on the road heading southeast.[8] Marching four abreast and carrying between forty and fifty pounds of equipment per man, the soldiers could go about two and a half miles an hour, but delays were common, especially in early morning when the men ate hurried breakfasts and tried to repack the tents. Soldiers would often have to leave the road to let artillery or supply wagons pass; some regiments trudged through nearby fields on parallel routes. Clausewitz noted that a modern army "was accustomed to consider a fifteen-mile

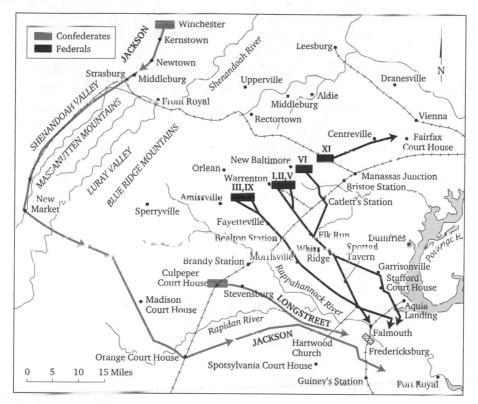

March to Fredericksburg

march a day's work," and Sumner's troops matched this standard.[9] The advance regiments covered the forty miles to Falmouth in around two and half days, arriving on November 17. Compared with McClellan's more leisurely pace or to any reasonable expectation, for that matter, Burnside had moved quickly.[10]

Yet even as the first of Sumner's men neared Falmouth, rain began to slow the march, and all along the route soldiers in the trailing regiments noticed shoes stuck in the mud. Men were soon using rails to pry artillery pieces out of the muck. "Wet and disagreeable," a mud-spattered Massachusetts corporal in the Irish Brigade tersely noted.[11] The new regiments quickly lost their illusions about the glories of field service and inevitably straggled, littering the roadside with surplus baggage.

Inexperienced officers working with poor maps added to these woes by making wrong turns, getting lost, and then doubling back. After a roundabout and arduous journey through the countryside, a veteran in Brig. Gen. Oliver Otis Howard's division noted how his comrades exercised the soldiers' sovereign right to complain: "Oh what deep and heartfelt curses did I repeatedly hear heaped upon the generals, the war, the country, the rebels, and everything else."[12]

Pvt. Joseph E. Hodgkins of the 19th Massachusetts thought he had as much to gripe about as anyone. His regiment had marched about forty miles in three days, sometimes in the rain (or perhaps snow, as the regimental history later claimed). During the night of November 18 Hodgkins "laid across two or three corn hills" and slept fitfully. On guard duty two days later he had gotten "pretty well soaked" and finally flopped down in a sopping blanket, "wet to the skin." His experience was typical. Campaigning in such weather struck many as ludicrous; it seemed cold enough for snow. Men awoke to find an inch or two of water running through their shelter tents. And sometimes they had to light damp wood with flint and steel because they had no matches.[13]

Besides being cold and wet, soldiers were usually hungry. The supply trains were mired in mud or for some other reason had not caught up with the infantry. A New York regiment had ten "crackers," coffee, and a little fresh meat for the daily marching ration, but a New Hampshire outfit had to endure an entire day without water. The fortunate might snare a rabbit along the way, while the more enterprising (or ravenous) might stumble through the dark, ford creeks, and fall into muddy ditches searching for the commissary wagons. Officers with more compassion than discretion doled out a few tablespoons of whiskey to their sullen men, but the tipplers would soon quaff their portion and then beg, buy, or steal the precious elixir from the teetotalers. The ensuing fights, black eyes, bloody noses, and hangovers hardly improved morale.[14]

Short rations, long days, general exposure, and a few unexpected annoyances soon took their toll. Some Buckeye soldiers making their way to Falmouth through a pine forest faced an onslaught of wood ticks. These pesky creatures clung to legs, necks, and heads, and their bites caused unbearable itching for several days. More generally, men already weakened by maladies such as diarrhea and typhoid fever merely grew sicker from the added exertion. Older recruits fell victim to neuralgia and rheumatism from sleeping on cold, damp ground. But the youngest soldiers also suffered. A nineteen-year-old in the 21st Connecticut, after keeping up with his regiment for several days, collapsed from exhaustion at the end of the march and awoke with his legs in water. Feverish and delirious, he was taken to a field hospital. In and out of consciousness and even hallucinating that his mother had arrived to see him, he soon died. After several other men suffered a similar fate, soldiers christened the place "Camp Death."[15]

But for all the misery, the appearance of the advancing Federals remained impressive. There was something grand about so many soldiers tramping along the roads, through woods, and across fields. The men would naturally complain of the cold, the mud, and the food, but the marching itself made them exuberant. A New Yorker captured the scene: "It is a splendid sight. There is something majestic and grand in the march of so large an army." With their long lines of troops and hundreds of campfires glowing in the night, the vast legions appeared irresistible. Standing at her cabin door eyeing the passing spectacle, an awestruck woman agreed: "Dear suz! I didn't s'pose there wuz so many folkses in the world."[16]

The coming campaign would surely test whatever enthusiasm the Federal soldiers could muster. "Almost anyone can be a soldier in summer," Capt. Charles Haydon commented both soberly and self-assuredly, "but to have served faithfully one's country in the winter of the year & of its hopes will be a lasting source of pride & gratification." Hard fighting now seemed likely, but a Vermont corporal predicted that the Federals would cut off Lee from Richmond and starve his army.[17]

Such optimism, however, had little tangible basis. What did most of the enlisted men, or their officers for that matter, really know of Burnside's plans? With the weather turning colder, they could only pray that their new commander would proceed quickly and decisively. Some soldiers, still smarting from the removal of their idol McClellan, claimed to prefer the old James River route to Richmond or simply wished the army would settle into winter quarters. Others, again under the lingering McClellan influence perhaps, fretted about going into battle against supposedly much larger Confederate forces. Marching could, after all, produce as much despair as exhilaration. The patrician Oliver Wendell Holmes Jr. had seen the worst fighting of the war so far at Antietam, and as he traveled over the "muddy & cut up roads" of northern Virginia, he concluded that "we never shall lick 'em." With the cynicism of a combat veteran and the cocksureness of a Brahmin intellectual, he declared the subjugation of the Rebel states an impossible task.[18]

Behind Sumner's forces the rest of the army was also advancing toward Falmouth. Despite some grumbling about laboring on the Sabbath, on November 16 the First and Sixth Corps left their camps around Warrenton and New Baltimore. As a McClellan protégé, Franklin naturally hoped to move "without fatiguing the men too much." Regardless of bad roads, some wrong turns, and a few broken-down wagons, by November 18 the first regiments of the Left Grand Division had reached Stafford Court House.[19]

It had rained most of the way. The diaries, letters, and regimental histories often mentioned rain only in passing, and it is tempting for historians to do the same. Yet the foul weather did more than bog down artillery, soak uniforms, or saturate blankets. The rain dampened spirits and marked an ominous beginning to an important campaign. As the soldiers noted their slow progress, morale sank almost as quickly as a caisson in the mud. Slippery climbs up treacherous hills wore the men out physically but also drained their psychological reserves. After a day in a cold, driving rain a Wisconsin officer wrote home from his "BIVOUAC IN THE BRUSH TEN MILES FROM ANYWHERE, IN STAFFORD CO., VA." One meticulous member of the 13th Massachusetts measured the mud on November 20; it was two inches deep. The next day it was three inches, and after a two-day halt five inches of ooze all the way to the commissary wagon.[20]

Soldiers naturally dwelled on their immediate miseries. Mule drivers exhausted their profane vocabularies as did infantrymen who had lost their shoes and slogged along in their stocking feet. With forgivable exaggeration a Massachusetts soldier claimed that the "amount of muscular energy required to lift your feet with ten pounds or more of mud clinging to each foot, can hardly be appreciated except by persons who have a knowledge of the sacred soil of Virginia."[21]

As Sumner and Franklin advanced toward the Rappahannock, Hooker's Center Grand Division became the rear guard. On the morning of November 17 the Fifth Corps set out for Warrenton Junction while the Third Corps headed toward Bealeton. Both corps eventually converged on the area around Hartwood Church and then turned east to cross the road between Stafford Court House and Falmouth near Potomac Creek. Perhaps hoping to win over a troublesome subordinate, Burnside commended Hooker "for carrying out so successfully the most difficult part of the late movement— bringing up the rear."[22]

This reference to "bringing up the rear" could just as easily have rankled the egotistical Hooker, but his assignment had hardly been easy. Given the complexity of the routes and the condition of the roads, many regiments alternately marched or waited in rain-soaked camps for nearly a week. The men in Brig. Gen. George Sykes's division dubbed their soggy bivouac near Hartwood Church "Camp Misery."[23]

Pvt. Howard Helman, a seventeen-year-old printer who had enlisted in the 131st Pennsylvania only three months earlier, left a careful record of the trek from a foot soldier's perspective. On November 17 Helman's feet were quite sore from marching at what he considered a rapid pace in a steady drizzle. The second day was even worse because his regiment was supposed to keep up with the supply train and rescue stuck wagons. It rained the next day, and the exhausted Helman had to sit up most of the night because of "rheumatism" and a "severe pain across the lungs." On November 20 and 21 the men stayed in camp but were nearly out of food. The following day they headed out again. The "roads kept getting worse" and they had nothing to eat, but somehow they made it to a "nice piece of ground" near Potomac Creek.[24]

Because their march began later and lasted longer, Hooker's troops bore the brunt of the inclement weather. Stories about pouring water out of boots and scores of dead horses and mules left lying along the army's track may have been embroidered, but rain and wind made setting up camp at the end of a long day nearly impossible. Any logical stopping place had typically become a sea of mud. Tent pegs would not hold, and the canvas blew all over. Tents that did stay up had rivulets of water running underneath, soaking blankets and other gear. Fires started with damp wood sputtered out in the drizzle. A disgusted member of 133rd Pennsylvania, sounding rather like the biblical prodigal son, announced he would now gladly pay five dollars for the privilege of sleeping in "his father's hog pen."[25]

At the end of a dreary day the Virginia countryside appeared all that more desolate. Words such as "miserable," "tumble down," and "forlorn" described the land and its people. Dilapidated farms, many now deserted, with overgrown fields dotted the landscape. "Old cleared ground and a cow is the wealth of the farmers," Col. Robert McAllister of the 11th New Jersey noted sadly. "Children don't wash at all."[26]

Empathy for Rebels, however, no matter how forlorn their appearance, was in short supply. The New England troops in particular expressed condescension, at best, and contempt, at worst, toward the poor Virginians, a downtrodden people who had failed to absorb the Yankee virtues of thrift and learning. The change in attitude—already noticeable during McClellan's final days—became even more pronounced during and after the march toward Fredericksburg. Speaking for many of his comrades, a Rhode Island artilleryman declared, "We dont think it any sin to take what we want to eat from secesh." What a New York surgeon called "stolen luxuries" satisfied hunger but, more importantly, afforded "revenge[, a] sweet morsel [that] . . . rolled with pleasure under the tongue." The reduction of Virginia to a vast wasteland might simply be an inevitable consequence of civil war. After a beautiful young woman begged some New Hampshire soldiers not to steal the hay from her family's barn, they found it "rather tough to withstand her tears" but went about their plundering. Hardened to such pleas, these same men had just the day before burned down a "secesh" barn.[27]

Foraging became a great game, born of necessity, the soldiers would have stoutly maintained, but also affording spiteful amusement. Nor did cleaning out Confederate larders mean distinguishing between wealthy disunionists and more humble yeomen. Hungry Federals bolted down pork and beef that tasted all the sweeter for having been stolen from their enemies, rich or poor.[28]

The moral dilemma of feasting on other folks' misery now received humorous treatment. Stomachs full at last, the men relaxed around campfires recounting hairbreadth escapes from irate, shotgun-wielding farmers. "There is one thing certain the people will not be troubled feeding chickens this winter," a newly enlisted chaplain chortled. Capt. Frank Sterling of the 121st Pennsylvania eagerly shared with his sister what he undoubtedly considered a clever analysis of the moral problem: "Quite a number of times fine pieces of pork, mutton etc. have come into my possession whose previous history I do not think it would have been safe to have followed up too closely. Under such circumstances I always follow [the apostle] Paul's advice namely eat what is set before me without asking questions."[29]

Much to the dismay of conservative officers, this new toleration, indeed relish, for plundering civilians was spreading. A member of the 79th New York sadly informed his mother that soldiers from Ohio, Michigan, and Indiana bragged about their depredations. Already frustrated over trying to maintain discipline in his division, General Hancock exploded when he discovered that even the chaplain in the Irish Brigade had been filching turnips.[30] Some commanders still posted guards to prevent men from sneaking off to raid chicken coops or pigpens, and occasionally punishment was meted out for unauthorized foraging. In one of the Pennsylvania reserve regiments an hourly roll call prevented the men from scouring the countryside for fresh delicacies.[31] Such strict measures, however, were rare. More often than not even high-ranking officers simply looked the other way. Be it honey or fresh mutton, the officers enjoyed their share of the spoils.[32]

Growing impatience in Washington and elsewhere for an offensive campaign left little time or energy for safeguarding Rebel property. The Army of the Potomac's rapid march in the cold and rain reflected this new sense of urgency, yet the men themselves remained confused about what it meant. Soldiers had been sharply critical of the logistical failures, though many still declared themselves well pleased with Burnside and his aggressive strategy. "The knapsacks weighed like lead & the mud pulled like wax, & the rain came down in torrents," a Pennsylvania sergeant in Hooker's grand division observed melodramatically, "but we are going towards Richmond so we don't care for all they are able to put on us." To such determined souls the Confederate capital suddenly appeared within reach, and though that chimera had bedazzled volunteers before, the most hopeful new recruits even saw the end of the war in sight.[33]

All the same, many soldiers greatly resented pressure from the newspapers and politicians. With his usual acerbity General Meade complained that "it is most trying to read the balderdash in the public journals about being in Richmond in ten days." Still convinced that the James River was the only practical route to the Confederate capital, Meade wondered why officials in Washington, especially Halleck, did not understand this. Men who had struggled through the rain and mud could only wish that those editors who so loudly demanded a winter campaign could have accompanied the army on its recent march.[34]

The first sketchy newspaper comments on the army's advance toward Fredericksburg appeared on November 18, the day after Sumner's men reached Falmouth. The familiar "On to Richmond" headlines and optimistic editorials blanketed the Republican press. McClellan partisans complained that the Army of the Potomac would at last receive all the troops and support necessary for conducting an offensive campaign — as if they had not before — and they even insisted that Burnside was resisting pressure from Halleck to move forward too quickly. Few newspapers had anything but praise for the new commander or his campaign plans, and the more confident editors foresaw the Confederates falling back to defend their capital. "Hard fighting" lay ahead, the always sanguine *Philadelphia Inquirer* admitted, but "Richmond will soon be ours." Having thrown off the incubus of "McClellanism," the Army of the Potomac was showing unaccustomed energy and spunk.[35]

To skeptics, all of this sounded ominously familiar, but wishful thinking, nagging impatience, and political desperation clouded judgment. The logic of events seemed simple enough: McClellan had been removed for being too slow, and Burnside had moved forward quickly. The newspapers were already building up unreasonable expectations for the approaching campaign, and ironically enough every editorial praising Burnside only put more pressure on him, his generals, and his troops. Even enthusiastic support could hardly build confidence in a man prone to doubting his ability and second-guessing his own decisions. Nor could the insistent demands of a restless public revitalize an army still plagued by factionalism and whose apparently growing devotion to its new commander had yet to be seriously tested.

★ ★ ★

If the northern people oscillated between utter despondency and naive faith, public opinion in the Confederacy seemed more sanguine, equally contradictory, for sure, but much less mercurial. "The history of mankind cannot afford a parallel with the wonderful energies displayed and brilliant triumphs achieved by these Confederate States," Governor John Gill Shorter informed the Alabama legislature. Even Zebulon Vance, the recently elected governor of North Carolina and no ardent Confederate nationalist, believed that as the "ephemeral patriotism" and "the tinsel enthusiasm of novelty" were disappearing, the people would soon have to display a "stern and determined devotion to our cause which alone can sustain a revolution." According to Maj. Gen. Lafayette McLaws, the Yankees "acknowledge our superiority of courage and spirit." Fighting for self-government just as their revolutionary forebears had done and proudly assuming the mantle of "rebels," many Confederate soldiers now looked toward victory.[36]

To complement an often unjustified confidence, Confederates tended not only to denigrate but underestimate the enemy. If the southern cause stood for the spirit of 1776 and political purification, the northern government embodied all the evils of political consolidation and military despotism. Confederates expressed as much contempt as hatred for the Federals by repeatedly emphasizing supposedly fatal flaws in the Yankee character. A series of editorials in the *Richmond Daily Whig*—hardly a fire-eater sheet—expressed widely held beliefs. Not only did the Federals fight for an unjust cause ("the advantage of moral force is all on our side"), but they had evolved into "the vilest race on the face of the earth." Their wickedness was nearly unfathomable: "besotted and intolerant, rapacious and stingy, fraudulent and roguish, boastful and cowardly, contentious and vulgar, envious and spiteful."[37]

Faith in the purity of the cause and the wickedness of the enemy easily turned into self-righteousness. Pious Confederates saw themselves as crusaders against Yankee infidels; battlefield victories became signs of divine favor. As one Richmond editor fervently asserted, the "just God . . . who had baffled the devices of our enemies, will continue to aid us in our struggle for independence of the most corrupt and wicked despotism of modern times."[38] Of course many ministers and other Bible-believing folk doubted that God would simply punish the heathen Yankees without using the scourge of war to chastise the Confederacy's perhaps chosen but often backsliding people.

Many citizens had apparently grown weary of self-sacrifice and were taking advantage of others' suffering. "Speculators" and "extortioners" were widely condemned for driving up prices and impoverishing the people. These harpies, one soldier warned, "are stabbing the very vitals of the republic." Petitions to governors and letters to newspapers complained of merchants hording scarce supplies until they rotted rather than selling them to poor families at reasonable prices.[39]

In such a cruel and selfish world, perhaps it was up to the female population to hold the people to a higher standard of morality. Given the "patriotic and intense feeling" of so many women, Governor Francis Pickens of South Carolina maintained, "no men who have such mothers, such wives, and such sisters, were ever born to be enslaved." On November 14, the day Lincoln had given his grudging approval to Burnside's change of base, a letter from a "lady" appeared in the *Richmond Daily Enquirer* urging the women of the Confederacy (with their "female domestics") to join together at noon on December 1 to pray for peace and the success of southern arms, a call that echoed across the South.[40]

The fires of southern patriotism still burned brightly. And lest the Yankees (or fainthearted southerners) decide that the Confederacy could be starved into surrender, the *Richmond Daily Examiner* set them straight: "The sufferings of our people, poverty at our firesides, and the rags of our armies, instead of being hailed as signs of submission, should strike the North pale with despair. They are proofs of heroic resolution; they are endured without complaint; they are sacrifices to liberty in which we glory."[41]

Yet the hardships faced by southern families could hardly be relieved by patriotic editorials. The government's fiscal difficulties remained serious, and people showed little stomach for tough medicine. Even editors who railed against wartime opportunism drew back from price controls or other measures that interfered with free markets. "Prices must always be regulated by . . . supply and demand," Jefferson Davis intoned, and for the government to meddle with ordinary commerce would only undermine public confidence.[42]

Davis had never been a bold politician or an original thinker, but in November 1862 his caution seemed justified. He had already expended much political capital pushing for conscription and the suspension of habeas corpus, and even with the war going fairly well, critics multiplied. Richmond buzzed with rumors that the president acted as his own secretary of war, interfered with his generals, and insulated himself from ordinary citizens. The cabinet, according to the *Richmond Daily Examiner,* presented a "living satire on the statesmanship of the South and the intelligence of the country."[43] Ironically, growing confidence in southern arms made carping seem less dangerous while simultaneously discouraging the adoption of policies that would have demanded greater sacrifices from ordinary citizens.

The recently appointed secretary of war, James A. Seddon, faced a familiar problem: the army's ever growing demand for soldiers. Near the end of November the War Department summoned absent officers back to their commands on pain of losing their commissions and threatened absent en-

Confederate president Jefferson Davis (Library of Congress)

listed men with being treated as deserters. The necessity for vigorous en-forcement of the conscription laws became obvious as Federal armies pre-pared for offensive operations late in the year.[44]

Unfortunately for the Davis administration, some governors and editors still considered the draft a violation of both individual liberties and states' rights. Yet the early flood of enthusiastic volunteers had long since slowed to a trickle. On the day that Burnside reorganized the Army of the Potomac into grand divisions, thirteen advertisements for Confederate substitutes ap-peared in the *Richmond Daily Dispatch*. A member of the 21st Virginia asked his father for help in procuring a substitute because even if it cost $1,000, he could earn more than that in a year working at home.[45]

Political backbiting and efforts to avoid conscription, however, did not signify general demoralization. Public confidence in Lee remained high even among the government's harshest critics. Lee would look for an offensive opening and knew that giving up more territory would only add to the suf-fering of his beloved and already war-ravaged Virginia.[46] With Jackson still in the Shenandoah Valley, the Army of Northern Virginia remained divided, but Lee showed little concern and would not reunite his forces until Burnside tipped his hand.

Much would depend on the Federals' line of march and on accurate intel-ligence about their movements. Lee's seemingly invincible cavalry chief, the dashing Stuart, had become the toast of Richmond and a magnet for attractive women (despite his deeply religious, abstentious, and somewhat prud-ish character).[47] Stuart would serve as the army's eyes and ears; but his men badly needed more carbines, and some three-fourths of their horses suffered from the same tongue and hoof ailments that were hobbling the Federal cavalry. The War Department promised to buy a thousand horses in Texas, but when they might arrive was anybody's guess.[48]

As Stuart's cavalry prowled the countryside, Lee advised Jackson to be ready to march should Burnside head toward Fredericksburg or cross the Rappahannock at some other point. Lee had not worried that Burnside might steal a march on him and trusted Jackson's judgment on the timing of any move to rejoin the main body of the army in Culpeper. To impede the enemy advance, Lee had ordered the railroad between Aquia Creek and Fredericksburg destroyed along with the bridges and culverts, but both he and Davis were reluctant to have the tracks south of the Rappahannock torn up until it was absolutely necessary.[49]

On November 15 the *Richmond Daily Enquirer* reported the enemy advancing toward Fredericksburg. That same day Lee, unsure about either the direction or the timing of Union movements, sent an infantry regiment and an artillery battery to strengthen a small force stationed there. If Burnside's troops had already crossed the Rappahannock and occupied the town, Lee would withdraw his forces to the North Anna River. Anticipating that Fredericksburg could not be held, the War Department and the president reluctantly authorized the destruction of the railroad between Fredericksburg and Hanover Junction. Lee remained uncertain about Burnside's intentions because he had not yet received intelligence that the bluecoats were rebuilding the wharves at Aquia Creek. As Sumner's troops approached Falmouth on November 17, Lee still thought it likely that Burnside would transfer his army south of the James River.[50]

Timing remained critical. So far Burnside had moved rapidly without Lee discovering his intentions. Learning that Sumner's men were approaching Falmouth, on November 17 Lee ordered two of Longstreet's divisions commanded by McLaws and Brig. Gen. Robert Ransom Jr. to head immediately toward Fredericksburg. As these units left their camps the next morning, some of Stuart's cavalry splashed across the Rappahannock to scout out enemy movements and arrived at Warrenton just as the last Federals were leaving. At this point Lee could not be certain that the rest of Burnside's army was following Sumner and still preferred to assume a strong defensive position along the North Anna River. There he could take advantage of the Federals' elongated line of communications and launch a counterattack. Two days later Lee better understood the Federal movements and telegraphed Davis: "I think burnside is concentrating his whole army opposite Fredericksburg." Given Lee's apparent calm, Richmond officials simply assumed that the Army of Northern Virginia could stop Burnside.[51]

On November 18, in the midst of all-day rain, McLaws's men left Culpeper Courthouse and headed toward the Rapidan River on treacherous roads. Preparing to cross the river at Raccoon Ford, some soldiers took off their shoes and socks before wading into the icy, knee-deep waters. "Men yelled, cursed, and laughed," the brigade historian recalled. Others kept their shoes on rather than risk having their feet cut by rocks in the riverbed. One embarrassed recruit who had removed most of his clothes had to promenade without pants past a house full of curious ladies. The soldiers trudged through rain again the next day and reached Fredericksburg around noon on the twentieth.[52]

Ransom's Division marched more slowly, completing the trek two days later. Wet, hungry, and miserable, these soldiers (many of whom were barefoot) were every bit as disconsolate as their Yankee counterparts.[53] The artillery had an even harder time because the men had to strain as much as the horses to pry up gun wheels out of the mud. "A more drenched and disgusted set was never seen," a member of the famous Washington Artillery recalled. To compound the misery, a hard-hearted surgeon refused to dole out a whiskey ration to the shivering men.[54]

By November 23 Longstreet's other three divisions (commanded by major generals Richard H. Anderson, George E. Pickett, and John B. Hood) had reached the Fredericksburg vicinity. Lee had intended to send these divisions back toward the North Anna River, but when Burnside made no move to cross the Rappahannock, he ordered them to join McLaws and Ransom. Their more circuitous route afforded the men an even more protracted dose of discomfort. Shoe top–deep mud in some places caused considerable straggling. After marching several days in the rain, the men lay stiff and sore in their makeshift camps. Nearly 40,000 Confederate soldiers bivouacked in and around Fredericksburg, but Lee had still not decided whether to fight there or retreat to the North Anna.[55]

"If the enemy attempt to cross the [Rappahannock] river, I shall resist it, though the ground is favorable for him," Lee informed the War Department as the last of Longstreet's troops were arriving. Lee's tone perhaps betrayed his annoyance with the government's insistence that he not pull back. But the men in the ranks were not troubled. All along they kept telling their home folks of the "big fight" brewing.[56] The mere appearance of Marse Robert in the camps near Fredericksburg inspired confidence. "Feel better satisfied in going into a fight under him than anyone else," a South

Carolinian chirped, giving voice to a near-universal sentiment in the Army of Northern Virginia. Burnside's momentary advantage of surprise was gone. Once again Lee's soldiers blocked the road to Richmond. Surveying some excellent defensive positions in the hills behind Fredericksburg, Brig. Gen. Thomas R. R. Cobb bragged that his brigade alone could "whip ten thousand of them attacking us in front." Hearing enemy drums and bands playing across the river, the pious Georgian was itching for a fight, trusting in protection from a "Righteous God."[57]

Civilians echoed this optimism. Should Burnside's army be decisively beaten at Fredericksburg, Edmund Ruffin predicted, a northern peace party would end the war in two months, and without European intervention. Some observers still doubted that a major offensive would be launched so late in the year, but should the Federals attack Fredericksburg, the *Richmond Daily Examiner* assured its readers, the result could only be a disaster for Union arms. And Burnside? He "will enter the Hades of lost reputations," the *Richmond Daily Dispatch* predicted.[58]

The next weeks or even days might change the entire course of the war. With armies in motion, even the Federals sounded more cheerful. For the troops, marching itself, despite all its hardships, often had a salubrious effect on morale. For sure, the temporary discomfort and supply problems produced plenty of grumbling and also sowed seeds of skepticism about the campaign, but the dissipation of the torpor and lethargy caused by the lull in the fighting since Antietam had been almost palpable. Burnside believed that he must strike quickly, and Lee, caught a bit off guard at first, stood ready to counter any thrust toward Richmond. The Federals hoped for a dramatic victory, though the lingering effects of McClellanism and nagging doubts about Burnside's ability dampened enthusiasm. The Confederates faced growing logistical problems and no little internal dissension, but from General Lee to the humblest private, they exuded confidence.

All delays are dangerous in war.
—*John Dryden*

5 Delay

The shooting had begun before Sumner's grand division even reached Falmouth. On November 15 some of J. E. B. Stuart's "horse artillery" had shelled Federal supply trains and infantry moving toward the Rappahannock River.[1] This early skirmishing seemed to presage a much bigger fight—but not just yet. Although Burnside had advanced rapidly, the vitally important pontoons had not arrived. Frustrating delays plagued the Federals and gave Lee time to reunite his army, resupply, and prepare his defenses around Fredericksburg.

On November 17 harassing fire from a Confederate light artillery battery across the Rappahannock greeted Sumner's men as they reached Falmouth. A New York battery with longer-range and more accurate Parrott rifles scattered the Rebels in less than ten minutes. From her second-floor vantage point, Jane Howison Beale watched people running through the streets. Young women from a local paper mill "stampeded" when a shot hit their building. Lee reported, somewhat misleadingly, that Confederate forces in Fredericksburg had prevented the Yankees from crossing the river.[2]

Burnside arrived at Falmouth on November 19, and Lee reached Fredericksburg the following day. That morning Federal artillery mistakenly opened fire on a fifteen-car train carrying civilians out of town. This incident reconfirmed Confederate notions about their enemies' character. "Was [there] ever greater cowardice, more unmanly or baser conduct?" a North Carolina plantation mistress raged. "Did you ever hear of such hellish malignity?" General Cobb fumed. According to the *Richmond Daily Enquirer* the dastardly Yankees had fired eighteen rounds at cars filled with women and children, causing one young mother to almost die of fright. Given their conduct the bluecoats must soon receive a "terrible retribution."[3]

Yet Lee still could not prevent the advance units of the Federal army from crossing the Rappahannock and assumed he would have to fall back. The opportunity to occupy Fredericksburg tantalized the Federals, especially General Sumner, who gazed longingly across the river. The silver-haired old soldier understood military and political realities: he knew delay at this point could prove disastrous. Tall and slender with a neatly trimmed beard, Bull Sumner was nearing the end of his military career but had lost none of his own reputation of bravery. He could cross the Rappahannock and seize the Rebel guns. Nor did the task appear difficult. One of his division commanders noticed that a cow had easily waded through water hardly more than three feet deep. Sumner asked Burnside for permission to cross into Fredericksburg if he could find a good place to ford the river. The commanding general demurred. Fearing that rising waters would cut off Sumner's men, and perhaps recalling all the trouble that having troops astride the Chickahominy River had caused McClellan during the Peninsula campaign, Burnside decided to wait for the pontoons.

Burnside also may have overestimated immediate Confederate strength, and in any case by the time the army reached Falmouth, rain was falling and the river was rising. Burnside presumed the pontoons would arrive shortly, and he had already ordered quartermasters to gather a twelve-day supply of "grain and small commissary stores."[4] Had the new commander made his first mistake? If Fredericksburg could be immediately occupied, the most impatient soldiers believed, Richmond could be in Federal hands by Christmas. "Remarkable counsels prevail," a New Hampshire captain wrote in disgust. "We must wait—wait for pontoons to cross on, which will be simply waiting for the rebel army to arrive and entrench itself."[5] Too many fine fall days had already gone to waste.

Bad weather raised new doubts back home. Newspapers reported the Rebels strengthening their defenses in Fredericksburg and speculated that the army might spend the winter at Falmouth. If Burnside did not advance quickly, the Confederates would build more extensive fortifications around Richmond, and for students of the recent Crimean War, it seemed the Federals might face another siege of Sevastopol. Ever since the removal of McClellan, editor Manton Marble of the *New York World* sniffed, all the Democrats' worst forebodings had come true. The "Halleck-Stanton" campaign in Virginia was obviously grinding to a halt.[6]

Republican newspapers, despite sometimes contrary reports in their own columns, naturally tried to scotch talk of the campaign fizzling. On November 22 the *Philadelphia Inquirer* carried a large map of the Fredericksburg area on the front page. "Nothing that can be seen or foreseen seems able to interfere with a continued advance," an editor commented. With a swipe at McClellan, Horace Greeley proclaimed Burnside's line of march "the one which a great General would have adopted at the outset." *New York Times* correspondent William Swinton reported Burnside pressing forward without waiting for supplies, as a more cautious general (again read McClellan) would have done. Yet Swinton's dispatch included this jarring prediction: "Christmas will either see us in Richmond or shattered in overwhelming defeat."[7]

Burnside had good reason for not crossing the Rappahannock before the pontoons arrived, but allowing Sumner to occupy Fredericksburg would not have been that risky. Federal artillery on Stafford Heights would have deterred Longstreet's men from attempting to drive them out of the town. To defeat Lee, Burnside would have to strike quickly and boldly. Unfortunately his campaign plan hinged on the timely arrival of the pontoons, and he could not adjust to meet new contingencies.

Sumner obeyed the orders against crossing the Rappahannock and even claimed later that Burnside had been right. But Hooker was neither so dutiful nor so honest. Taller than average and blessed with large, bluish-gray eyes, as well as a drinker's florid complexion, to many of his contemporaries Hooker looked like a great general. The foot injury suffered at Antietam still troubled the commander of the Center Grand Division. Only recently had he been able to wear a shoe, and he still had to use a cane. Despite a reputation as a drunkard, rake, and conniver, Hooker had many friends in the army and of course in Washington. Newspapers kept suggesting that Fighting Joe would soon replace Burnside, and Hooker did nothing to quell such speculation.[8]

After establishing his headquarters near Hartwood Church, Hooker asked permission to cross the Rappahannock above Fredericksburg and strike at Lee. Burnside declined, worried, as with Sumner's proposed crossing, that the unpredictable river might entrap his men. Yet before Burnside had responded, Hooker—utterly disregarding the chain of command—sent a long private dispatch to Stanton outlining his own ideas for the campaign. Hooker wanted to use his 40,000 or so men to surprise Lee before Jackson could link up with Longstreet. "The enemy . . . have counted on the McClellan delays for a long while, and have never failed in their calculations," he said, knowing full well what Stanton thought of McClellan. It would be several days before the pontoons could be laid across the Rappahannock, the general predicted. The criticism of Burnside had been implicit but obvious. Hooker (with support from his political allies) was angling for the command.[9]

With the campaign temporarily halted, Burnside and the various generals in Sumner's grand division established their headquarters near Falmouth. Poor farms and a few scattered church buildings of no great value were the only signs of civilization in economically depressed Stafford County. As "barren as the wastes of Africa," claimed a New York cavalry trooper who had surely never seen that continent. Most white men and slaves had left, but the usual complement of what Federals called (sometimes with irritation, often with bemusement) "negrah families" remained.[10]

Nestled in the narrow floodplain between the river and Stafford Heights, the village of Falmouth in 1860 had some 150 buildings and around 500 people. "It is an old shabby town," a Federal staff officer remarked contemptuously. "The streets are irregular and dirty, the men take kindly to whiskey and tobacco. The women are not tidy. The niggers have mostly skedaddled. In short, the whole concern looks as though they were rapidly going to the Devil." Run-down mills and other sorry-looking buildings stood idle. Many inhabitants who had not already departed were leaving as Sumner's troops arrived; those who remained struck one Minnesotan as densely ignorant. As in the surrounding countryside, the women and children appeared destitute.[11]

Even without prodding by politicians the Federals would hardly wish to tarry in such a place. Around nine in the morning on November 21 Burnside, Sumner, and Provost Marshal General Marsena Rudolph Patrick conferred about arranging for the capitulation of Fredericksburg. In a brief letter addressed to Mayor Montgomery Slaughter and the Common Council, Sumner complained that several buildings harbored Confederate sharpshooters. Moreover the mills, factories, and railroad were sustaining "armed bodies in rebellion against the Government of the United States." The general demanded the surrender of Fredericksburg by five that afternoon. If the local officials did not capitulate, he would grant them sixteen hours to evacuate sick and wounded soldiers along with women and children before he proceeded "to shell the town."[12]

Mayor Slaughter, who did not receive Sumner's letter until 4:40 in the afternoon, could only buy time. He denied responsibility for firing on the Federals and assured the general that the Confederates would not use Fredericksburg to manufacture or transport supplies. But "while their troops will not occupy the town, they will not permit you to do so," he added, and in the next breath requested more time to remove the "sick and wounded, the women and children, the aged and infirm."[13]

Wagons and ambulances soon began evacuating civilians. Suspecting that Burnside and Sumner sought a pretext to shell the town, General McLaws explained that the Confederate high command knew "too well the treacherous, fiendish Yankees character to give them any such excuse for the exercise of their natural brutality." Yet once Longstreet's corps arrived, it hardly mattered if the Federals crossed the river. They would still be no closer to the Confederate capital than McClellan had been, a Richmond editor observed. That Burnside was now reduced to terrorizing women and children meant that Richmond was "safe for the winter."[14] Without the pontoons, however, the river remained a near-impassible barrier, and by November 22 Sumner's men had pulled back from the Rappahannock. Uncertainty and doubt, not the cheerfulness and confidence of the recent march, held sway on the Union side of the river.[15]

The object of all this maneuvering, the town of Fredericksburg, was originally built around the tobacco trade, but its fortunes had steadily declined after the War of 1812. Near the end of the 1850s, though, a burst of mill construction accompanied by a wave of boosterism offered hope for future growth. On the eve of the war the town had 5,023 inhabitants, nearly one-third of whom were either slaves or free persons of color. The other two-thirds, the white citizens, although lukewarm secessionists, generally adhered to the Confederate cause. Alternately occupied by both sides in recent months, Fredericksburg braced itself as the contending armies showed up once again on its doorstep.[16]

Naturally the arrival of Sumner's men in Falmouth, coupled with the pitifully small Confederate force in town, caused great alarm. "Our hearts sank within us," wrote Jane Beale, while on a nearby plantation Kate Corbin feared being "given again unto Satan." Appreciative citizens shouted, "God bless you, boys!" when Longstreet's men began gathering on the surrounding hills.[17]

As Burnside reached Falmouth, many of Fredericksburg's white families and their slaves were already preparing to leave. With Federal artillery plainly visible on Stafford Heights, women and children, old people, and even the sick crowded the roads leading out of town. Their fortitude and patriotism impressed Lee, other Confederate officers, and even the Federals. After hearing how several women had supposedly fallen to their knees pleading with Lee not to surrender the town even at the price of fire and

*Fredericksburg, Virginia, from the east bank of the Rappahannock River
(Library of Congress)*

destruction, one of Sumner's staff officers remarked, "Were the ladies of the North to imitate the South they would make heroes of us all." Such women, however, had little time to strike virtuous poses. Regardless of their economic means, they faced tough choices. Should they leave? If so, when? And where should they go?[18]

Many decided that now was the time, and soon the streets and country roads became stages for heartrending scenes: here a panic-stricken widow somehow became separated from her three young girls; there frightened mothers with toddlers and feeble elderly trudged through the mud in the frosty air. Household goods overflowed carts and wagons, and discarded furniture lay scattered in the refugees' wake. Confederate soldiers watched the procession with dismay, wondering where the people would go and if they would ever return.[19]

Some folks took shelter in churches or barns, but many had to sleep in "brush and blanket" makeshifts or huddle around fence corners. Near Salem Church, three miles west of town, women and children pieced together tents from old quilts and counterpanes. The sight of "delicate women, beautiful girls, and tender young children" driven from "comfortable homes" saddened a Confederate artillery officer. White southerners reared to value honor, respectability, and social distinctions now faced an anomalous situation because even in Virginia the war had already had a leveling effect. One of Pickett's men noticed an especially pathetic group standing watch over their bedding and scanty provisions while waiting for tents to be set up. During the cold nights the cries of shivering children echoed through the woods.[20]

Refugees overflowed nearby country houses and outbuildings. Hospitable home owners covered their sofas with sheets and spread pallets on the floors, while hotel lobbies and billiard rooms in nearby villages served as temporary quarters. Once-proud white families could not disdain sleeping in slave cabins.[21]

In this topsy-turvy world more fortunate refugees, some with body servants in tow, fled by rail to Richmond. Many arrived on November 23 and 24, but the exodus continued for the rest of the week. Some eventually scattered to Petersburg or Charlottesville, but most jammed the Confederate capital, already overflowing from earlier waves of refugees. Families without prior arrangements spent their first night in town sleeping on cars in the station. The trains eventually disgorged a mass of confused, distraught, and desperate women and children.[22]

A formerly comfortable Fredericksburg merchant lived with his wife and three young daughters in a damp Richmond basement. A mother and her four children crowded in a single room, supported only by the small earnings of one daughter who signed Confederate notes in the Treasury Department. Less fortunate refugees without political connections had trouble finding any work. Benevolent local women raised only modest sums for displaced families; the influx of hungry mouths drove up food prices; the high costs of muslin and calico brought homespun dresses back into fashion.[23]

When most of the Federals pulled back from the riverbank and settled in camps, a few brave souls returned to their Fredericksburg homes. Maria Hamilton hoped the Rappahannock would prove both "a barrier and safeguard to us." For the rest of November and into December, while some families still left, others decided to take their chances back in town. Yet life was anything but normal. The churches were closed, and rumors could still send folks packing at a moment's notice. To Confederate soldiers Fredericksburg seemed eerily deserted.[24]

That a town associated with young George Washington and national heroes such as Hugh Mercer, John Paul Jones, and James Monroe—what had once been, according to a Richmond editor, a place of "intelligence, refinement, and moral elevation"—should become a scene of "exile, desolation, and ruin" sparked great indignation. Some soldiers recoiled in horror imagining their own families being forced out into the cold; others vowed bloody vengeance. Even devout Christians, ignoring scriptural admonitions about loving enemies, called for retribution against the "vandal hordes."[25]

For the time being, however, the few people still in town were safe enough because Burnside had decided against crossing the Rappahannock until the pontoons arrived. But nearly everything related to the pontoons had gone wrong. During the November 12 meeting with Halleck, Meigs, and Haupt, there had apparently been desultory discussion about the need for bridging material. Burnside had erroneously assumed that pontoons were already en route from Berlin, Maryland, to Washington and that Halleck would expedite their movement to Falmouth. Brig. Gen. Daniel P. Woodbury, a West Point graduate and veteran engineer, working with Haupt on reconstructing the wharves at Aquia Creek, also had responsibility for transporting the pontoons. Halleck later claimed that Burnside was supposed to issue any necessary orders to Woodbury.[26]

In fact, an order to transport pontoons to Washington had been sent on November 6—not by telegraph but through the mails—and so did not reach Berlin until November 12. Capt. Ira Spaulding of the 50th New York Engineers had managed to get thirty-six pontoon boats to Washington by November 14. Halleck apparently believed, however, that at least some of them had arrived earlier, because on the twelfth he had ordered Woodbury to move all bridging material to Aquia Creek.[27]

A hopeless mess ensued: Woodbury, Spaulding, and Halleck either misunderstood each other or simply failed to communicate. On November 14 Burnside's chief engineer, Lt. Cyrus B. Comstock, had wired twice asking about the progress of the pontoons. Burnside had assumed the pontoons would arrive as Sumner's men reached Falmouth, but the best that Woodbury could promise was that one pontoon train—the heavy boats and equipment came by wagon—might be sent overland from Washington on November 16 and that a second train might be sent by water. Horse and harness problems had delayed the overland train's departure until the afternoon of November 19, the day Burnside arrived at Falmouth. All this time Spaulding had assumed there was no great hurry.[28]

Woodbury had supposedly advised Halleck to delay the army's movement for five days to allow more time for transporting the pontoons, but the general in chief had brushed aside the suggestion. Neither Halleck nor anyone else apparently discussed this matter with Haupt or Meigs. In fact, nobody in Washington appeared to grasp the importance of the pontoons to the success of the campaign. If thirty-six pontoon boats could leave Washington on November 16 or 17 as Woodbury had originally promised, Burnside decided to proceed with the march to Falmouth as scheduled. Yet with delays already occurring, he should hardly have counted on smooth sailing. As Clausewitz and other commentators have pointed out, the unexpected disrupts military plans and tests a commander's judgment. Given the political pressure for an advance, Burnside could not afford to remain at Warrenton long, but if the army's advance depended on such precise timing and coordination, it was doomed to fail.[29]

On November 22 Burnside sent an angry but diplomatically worded letter to Halleck. He complained about the delays and the failure of commissary wagons to reach Falmouth while his army was on the march.

> I cannot make the promise of probable success with the faith that I did when I supposed that all parts of the plan would be carried out. . . . I do not recall these facts in any captious spirit, but simply to impress upon the General-in-Chief that he cannot expect me to do as much as if all the parts of the plan had been carried out. . . . I am not prepared to say that every effort has not been made to carry out the other parts of this plan; but I must, in honesty and candor, say that I cannot feel that the move indicated in my plan of operations will be successful after two very important parts of the plan have not been carried out, no matter for what reason. The President said that the movement, in order to be successful, must be made quickly, and I thought the same.

Predictably, Halleck denied responsibility for any delays and suggested that Burnside call General Woodbury "to an account." The general in chief later attributed the entire fiasco to "accident and the elements." Because of further delays in loading the pontoons on wagons and hauling them from Belle Plain, not until November 24 did any pontoons reach Falmouth.[30] By November 27 the rest of the pontoons had finally straggled in, ten days late by Burnside's reckoning. Sumner still wanted to cross the Rappahannock, but unsure about Jackson's location and intentions, Burnside decided not to attack Longstreet.[31]

Burnside's inaction did not stop rumors of bridges being laid, and even wary veterans could still work up some enthusiasm for another crack at Lee. A soldier in the 22nd Massachusetts distilled his thoughts into several powerful sentences: "I am for pushing this matter ahead, and never faltering, until . . . every rebel hearthstone is desolate, to secure our former prosperity and bring about peace; and my bones may moulder in Virginia if thereby one 'jot or tittle' is added to the good of the Federal army." However much he dreaded the sound of whizzing bullets, his devotion to the Union kept him going. He hated military life but could not abandon the sacred cause: "I have taken my life in my hands to meet the foe, and for Freedom and the Old Constitution I will battle on."[32]

Although new recruits were most likely to express confidence in Burnside and despite delays and hardships many soldiers still praised their new commander, steady determination mingled with somber reflections on the bloody work ahead or the potential death toll in winter camps. A chaplain in the 133rd Pennsylvania declared, "Many who are now buoyant with life will lie mangled and torn on the field." A colonel in the 37th Massachusetts asked, "Will the country blame Burnside, if in carrying out a plan of necessity and one adopted by the Administration, he shall leave upon the cold, unwelcome soil of Virginia many a cherished son and brother, fallen not by bullet or saber, but stricken down by continued and severe exposure?" An officer in the 79th New York stated, "The field of battle with all its horrors is redeemed somewhat by the thought that the dead on both sides have fallen in a cause sacred in their own eyes at least." Such grim comments surely depressed the home folks and contrasted sharply with newspaper headlines trumpeting a glorious campaign in progress.[33]

Emotions swung back and forth wildly. Inactivity frustrated everyone, and soldiers began cursing Meigs and other bureaucrats for causing the delay. Whatever the reason, "the army will not brook disappointment," a Pennsylvania lieutenant maintained. Surely the bridges would be thrown across the Rappahannock in a day or so. Indeed, from November 21 on, the engineering officers seemed to be working feverishly.[34]

But still nothing much happened. Suspecting that roads to Richmond were becoming quagmires after the recent rains, a Hoosier volunteer drew the obvious conclusion: "No general—no army can conquer the elements." The failure to cross the Rappahannock was allowing the Confederates to concentrate their forces, and one of Burnside's most loyal supporters feared the Army of the Potomac now faced between 60,000 and 100,000 Rebel troops.[35] Even if demoralization had not exactly set in, Federal prospects appeared to grow darker with each passing day.

For his part Lee did not know what to make of the Federals' rapid advance and sudden halt. As late as November 23 he was still moving artillery to the North Anna River, and with Jackson at Winchester, the Army of Northern Virginia stood in some danger. Although Lee recognized the political pressure on the enemy, he hesitated to bring the rest of his army to Fredericksburg immediately because he hoped that Jackson might be able to fall on Burnside's flank.[36]

On November 18 Lee suggested that Jackson begin transferring divisions out of the Shenandoah Valley and across the Blue Ridge Mountains, though he gave Stonewall considerable leeway on the timing of his march. As was his wont, Jackson did not dally. By November 21 he had left Winchester and had begun moving up the Valley Pike. His troops welcomed the change. "This army is in the best condition I have ever known it," an artillery sergeant told his mother. "The men are cheerful almost to recklessness." The Federals were likely to cross the Rappahannock, Lee advised Jackson, and it was "desirable that the whole army should be united." Whatever inner turmoil Lee may have experienced, his correspondence during this period betrayed no sense of urgency or even a hint that the Federals posed any great threat to his army.[37]

Jackson maintained his usual reticence; his staff learned little about their marching schedule or destination. An English newspaper correspondent thought Jackson "genial" and "courteous" but careless about dress and spartan in habits. So it was much to everyone's surprise when, on the morning of November 24, the general donned a new uniform coat, a gift from Jeb Stuart, and even a new hat. The sight of a suddenly dapper Stonewall Jackson greatly amused his aides, who like the rest of the officers, seemed confident, eager for battle.[38]

Reveille sounded at 4:30 A.M., and two hours later Jackson's "foot cavalry" was on the road, making 13 to 17 miles a day through the valleys and mountains. The last of Jackson's men neared Fredericksburg on December 3; they had tramped roughly 175 miles in twelve days, and they looked it. An English observer noted their "dingy homespun dress, nondescript caps, . . . unshaven, unwashed, uncombed heads and faces."[39]

To many soldiers this journey was unforgettable. On November 24, as Jackson's men left New Market heading southeast across the mountains, they entered spectacular country. As they crested the Blue Ridge, the awesome and beautiful scene before them made a powerful impression. The turnpike road wound "about like a serpent," a Georgia private marveled, and for these men the image of the roads slithering like a long snake to the top of the mountain and then down stuck in their minds for years. "Thousands of bivouac fires, flashing and glowing on the mountain side," a South Carolinian recalled, punctuated the night.[40] But with the breathtaking landscape came a sudden chill. Men would awaken with frost in their hair, food frozen in their haversacks, and sometimes their blankets dusted with snow.[41]

Hundreds of men began the trek barefoot; still more would be without shoes or socks by the end. One sympathetic woman in Winchester noted how "cold and red and dirty" the soldiers' feet looked. Worse were large bleeding cracks in toes and feet that left red traces along the line of march. Such scenes called to mind harrowing tales from the American Revolution. An Alabama colonel insisted that barefoot men in his regiment ride in ambulances. But most simply endured. "It is useless for a man to say what he can stand and what he cannot stand unless he tries," a sore-footed Georgia sergeant mused. "I find as much depends upon the energy and spirits of a man, as his strength."[42]

The same could be said of the generals and the whole army. Union forces, in Lee's view, would likely cross the Rappahannock downstream near Port Royal under protection of their gunboats rather than attack Fredericksburg directly. By November 28, though, Lee confessed to being mystified: "What the designs of the enemy are I do not know." The army's activities reflected the confusion. Even as some men from Pickett's Division began tearing up railroad tracks between Fredericksburg and Hamilton's Crossing—a sure sign of impending withdrawal—Brig. Gen. William Nelson Pendleton worked at improving artillery positions along the Rappahannock.[43]

Few Confederates seemed to expect a fight at Fredericksburg. Even if the Yanks crossed the Rappahannock, a North Carolina lieutenant promised that "we will give them a merry time." Others bragged how they were "going to walk right through Burnside and gobble him up."[44] Confidence reigned in Richmond and throughout the eastern Confederacy for a host of reasons: Burnside's entire campaign rested on a grand delusion about his army's irresistible strength; attacking Fredericksburg would play into Lee's hands; the bluecoats were obviously stalled on the Rappahannock; the Army of the Potomac would soon have a new commander; after another defeat the northern people would finally realize that the Confederates could not be easily crushed. Only the strongly anti-Davis *Charleston Mercury* offered a demurrer: "There is no path to security for the Confederate States, but one of bloody victory over a bloodthirsty foe. The task before us is one where doubt cannot interpose, timidity cannot shrink, humanity cannot soften. Failure is destruction."[45]

All easily enough said, but like the Federals, Confederate troops at Fredericksburg, with Jackson's men still on the march, had begun to feel the bite of winter. Soldiers huddled around fires, though frost lay on their blankets in the morning. Even officers had trouble keeping warm.[46] Shortages of tents and blankets epitomized pervasive supply problems. Bureaucratic disputes had slowed rail transportation, and Unionist underground activity also may have disrupted shipments from Richmond to Fredericksburg. The Richmond, Fredericksburg, and Potomac Railroad supplied Lee; but the bridge over the South Anna River was not rebuilt until November 24, and in any case the trains were unloaded at Hamilton's Crossing to keep any stores out of Federal artillery range.[47]

Enlisted men suffered most from the shoe shortage. In mid-November more than 6,000 men in Longstreet's corps were barefoot. Even after a large shipment from Richmond, some 2,000 men still had no shoes, and perhaps as many as 3,000 others wore shoes that would never withstand another march. A Virginia cavalryman described the most common cause for straggling: "many of our soldiers barefooted walking over frozen ground, and muddy roads, their feet torn and lacerated by stones, and unable to keep up, obliged to fall in the rear." Quartermaster Gen. Abraham C. Myers tried to pressure draft-exempt tanners to increase their output, but much to Lee's dismay, he also had some 2,000 soldiers detailed to make shoes in Richmond, Atlanta, and Columbus, Georgia. Even then one shipment of government shoes, Lee complained, was "of a very inferior character, and unfit for service."[48]

The shoe crisis called forth imaginative but sadly ineffective measures. Longstreet issued a general order in early November directing the men to fashion moccasins from the hides of recently slaughtered cattle. With the hair sides turned in to keep feet warm, these substitutes proved to be only marginal stopgaps. The cowhide moccasins not only stank but also became slippery in snow and mud, and they quickly wore out. Some men preferred remaining barefoot or wrapping their feet in rags and straw.[49] Jackson's men also cobbled together moccasins, and with equally little enthusiasm. On the march the leather stretched during the day but at night dried and shrank so that men hobbled. Sometimes they had to cut the torturous things off their feet, though a few soldiers were still wearing theirs in early December.[50]

The pain of frostbitten feet could be felt by the politicians. When Confederate troops—many without shoes—had marched through Richmond in early November, the president's political enemies blasted the quartermaster general. Suggesting that Myers, Davis, and the cabinet should go barefoot instead of these noble heroes, the *Richmond Daily Whig* had excoriated the administration: "The Government cannot be trusted. It has no forethought, or is entirely indifferent to the conditions of the men." After a letter appeared in several papers urging people to donate shoes, this same editor scathingly lampooned high officials "sitting by a rousing fire, toasting their well-shod feet, and thinking of anything but the soldiers." Such timeservers did little but draw their bloated salaries and dispense patronage to their friends.[51]

The pro-Davis *Richmond Daily Enquirer* claimed that the number of barefoot soldiers had been greatly exaggerated but still encouraged a local committee to collect shoes. Yet even charitable appeals often contained none too subtle swipes at the administration. The acerbic *Charleston Mercury* disingenuously reminded its readers that there was "something more important and pressing for the people now than to sit in judgment on delinquent officials" and that it was up to them to "supply the neglect of their public agents." Indeed the needs were overwhelming and the situation dangerous.

Families of barefoot soldiers petitioned for their discharge, and behind such pleas lurked threats of desertion.[52] "I wouldn't care much [if] the Confederacy was broke into a thousand fragments no how for they treat the army like so many dogs," wrote a tattered Georgian. Some men had no socks or mittens; others lacked shirts or drawers. Regimental letters in newspapers described men wearing shoes and clothing unfit even for slaves, a telling reference in a slaveholders' republic.[53]

Although faith in Lee and confidence in their own fighting ability took the edge off many complaints, food shortages were another matter. Temporary privations might be understood and endured, but scanty rations day after day eventually sapped men's physical and emotional reserves. In November 1862 the War Department outlined the dimensions of the crisis for General Lee: there were 100,000 fewer hogs than last year, poor corn crops in Tennessee and northwestern Georgia, and less than half the usual wheat production in Virginia. Reduced rations of flour and fresh beef could hardly sustain an army during arduous campaigning. Lee's quartermasters bought some food from farmers, but local supplies were soon exhausted. The Army of Northern Virginia consumed a thousand head of cattle each week, and at that rate beef would disappear in two months.[54]

Exposure, tattered clothes, and meager rations naturally spawned illness. Some fevers had persisted into the fall months, as did an outbreak of smallpox after Antietam. With the approach of winter, men simply could not shake off colds. Intestinal diseases still proved deadly; a North Carolinian told of one diarrhea sufferer who had died on his way to the sinks.[55] Settling into winter quarters would only add poor sanitation to the problem of persistent shortages.

Illness and discomfort aside, there remained the dull routine of drill and picket duties, which spurred a search for diversion. Stuart's staff held dinner parties (albeit with spartan menus) and even visited a nearby estate for a fox hunt. Literate men devoured books, including dictionaries and almanacs; several of Jackson's officers read or recited from Shakespeare, William Makepeace Thackeray, and Charles Dickens. The Washington Artillery's Literary and Dramatic Association performed a "roaring farce" titled "The Lady of Lyon," with the soldiers playing both male and female parts. Any appearance of real women in the camps, especially if they were well dressed and attractive, created a stir, and more enterprising fellows sought out female company in the surrounding countryside. One romantic South Carolinian crossed over to a small island in the Rappahannock to catch a glimpse of a beautiful young lady who supposedly lived there.[56] Such a fairy tale fit nicely the sentimentalism of the age.

There are also accounts of less savory diversions, however. Confederate soldiers, far from models of decorum, naturally hankered to leave camp, even if only briefly. The height of adventure was to sneak past guards, go into Fredericksburg, and devour greasy pies or dried-up apple turnovers. One hapless sutler charging outlandish prices for gingerbread lost not only his horses and the wheels off his wagon, but his goods as well.[57] Confederate enlisted men and officers committed more serious breaches of discipline as well. Instances of theft and vandalism filled court-martial records, and evidence of what soldiers euphemistically called "horizontal refreshment" appeared in medical reports of venereal disease.[58]

Alcohol accompanied and stimulated other vices. A bottle of brandy sent from home occasioned a celebration that easily got out of hand. Noisy tipplers serenaded their sleeping comrades past midnight, engaged in raillery against officers, or gave impromptu speeches satirizing Confederate supply problems. A dram of whiskey punch or some other concoction hit the spot on a cold night. After one of his men absconded to Richmond on a drunk and ended up missing the battle of Fredericksburg, Brig. Gen. James J. Archer, whose brigade needed every man in line that day, adopted a teetotal position: "I wish all the liquor in the universe was poured out & sunk."[59]

The men were no more likely to give up liquor than they were to swear off cards or dice. Gambling appeared to be a besetting sin for Confederate soldiers. A Louisiana chaplain in Jackson's corps had tried to stamp out this vice, but whenever he was away, the boys broke out the cards. The resourceful chaplain once slipped back into camp, grabbed more than $60 from a large pot, and donated the money to Richmond orphans. In mid-November General Lee issued a general order expressing dismay that "a habit so pernicious and demoralizing would be found among men engaged in a cause . . . demanding the highest virtue and purest morality in its supporters." Attempts to suppress gambling, however, failed. On rare Confederate paydays, poker, keno, and other popular games cleaned out many a poor private. Inveterate gamblers played from morning until night, and despite efforts to stop such activities, soldiers set up chuck-a-luck boards in an area called the "Devil's Half-Acre" and lay in wait for unwary country boys. The folks back home, of course, were spared news of such wickedness. Indeed, one army correspondent assured his readers that the "soldier with his sister's testament in his pocket and his mother's precepts in his heart cannot stoop to a vice so low and so degrading."[60]

Letters home, especially those addressed to sweethearts, wives, mothers, and sisters, often presented a sanitized version of camp life. But however circumspect, correspondence maintained essential ties between soldiers and their communities. Approximately four of five Confederates were literate, although some were only marginally so, judging by their often exotic spelling and tortured syntax. From the camps around Fredericksburg many Confederates sent news of their recent movements to their home folks—everything from hastily scribbled notes to carefully drafted letters running seven or eight pages. Captured Yankee stationery alleviated a chronic shortage of paper, and families did not object to letters written with stubby pencils.[61]

Yet when a soldier wrote home, he had little assurance that his letters would arrive safely or that he would receive a response. Because the railroad stopped five miles from Fredericksburg, Lee asked Postmaster Gen. John H. Reagan to either leave army mail in Richmond or turn it over to his chief quartermaster. The post office could hardly be expected to deliver often illegibly and inaccurately addressed mail to regiments on the move. But such entreaties, no matter how reasonable, failed to satisfy civilian or military critics.[62]

Even if the post office had been unusually efficient, soldiers still would never have thought they heard from home often enough. Many began their letters with complaints that sometimes filled a page or more about their loved ones neglecting to write. The soldiers themselves had reasonable excuses for their spotty correspondence. "Don't measure the length of your letters by mine," a Virginia cavalry officer admonished his wife. "I have to write sitting on the bare ground, with the flag of my saddle for a desk, and with fingers so cold the pen will scarcely stay in them, to say nothing of the ever varying smoke which keeps me in constant tears." Soldiers and civilians alike devised schedules for writing or numbered their letters to track delivery, but their ingenuity could not counteract the delays and inefficiencies of the postal system.[63]

Mail was essential for both soldiers and civilians. Letters could boost morale, and their absence could stifle it. A quartermaster in Pickett's Division thought his wife's missives never seemed long enough, and he did not even mind deciphering the cross-written sentences. "Tell me everything you do, say, think, and dream," he urged. "The slightest circumstance of home is full of interest to me and affords me untold pleasure." An Alabama lieutenant pointedly commented about how soldiers needed to know that their sacrifices were appreciated. "Give the boys letters written in a cheerful, hopeful spirit and they are more conducive to health than medicine and more potent to prevent desertion than the articles of war." Yet letters, both sent and received, brought their share of pain as well. "These hours devoted to communication with dear ones at home bring their bitter fruits of memory," a South Carolina captain remarked.[64]

The sheer distance from families brought past wrongs, minor arguments, and unspoken apologies more clearly to mind. Letters carried undercurrents of regret. The dullness of camp combined with the fear of combat intensified feelings of isolation and despair. Had he known how long he would be away from home, John French White of the 32nd Virginia confessed to his wife, he never would have enlisted.[65] It would be a mistake, however, to equate such comments with demoralization. Patriotism and a sense of honor and comradeship kept soldiers at their posts. In Americus, Georgia, Penelope Pryor hoped that her husband, Capt. Shepherd Green Pryor of the 12th Georgia, could come home soon. She strove for "fortitude and patriotism" but, having recently buried two brothers, could not imagine coping with the loss of a husband. He carefully explained to her the impossibility of furloughs and the army's need for every available man. Their correspondence proceeded in delicate counterpoint. "I am content to bow submissively to my affliction," she wrote. "You must bear my absence as well as you can do," he replied.[66]

Separation sometimes strengthened relationships, but love could easily wilt under wartime pressures. Many men were better able to express their feelings through the mail than in person. A lovesick Georgia major promised his sweetheart he would continue writing even if he did not hear from her for six months. "You and I, Hester, should know each other and love each other sufficiently well to have no doubts as to one another's feelings and wishes. . . . We may never be one, but our destinies are blended. Neither can ever efface the impression made by the other."[67] Idle weeks in camp could set a man thinking about trust and loyalty. Affection might fade, but it could just as easily grow stronger, especially under the powerful influence of imagined hopes for the future.

Married men who went to war wanted their families to remain unchanged, as if time could somehow stop for civilians. They enjoyed receiving letters offering glimpses of life at home and liked to imagine their loved ones enjoying simple domestic pleasures. The correspondence, however, turned bittersweet because many men badly missed their children. Word of a son who had contracted whooping cough, reports of school troubles, and even stories of minor mischief caused worry. The death of a child stirred their deepest emotions, especially in the absence of a spouse with which to share the trauma. That great romantic J. E. B. Stuart warbled about sending his wife "a small box with little mementos of this humbug husband that you make so much fuss over" before he lapsed into a mournful lament for their daughter, who "loved her Pa like idolatry and is now lifeless clay."[68]

Children died, but children were also born. Newly enlisted recruits or

men who had recently returned from furloughs worried about their pregnant wives and fretted over the absence of home news. Their concerns were
not allayed by the sometimes coy language with which women discussed
their condition. One exasperated Virginia volunteer finally suggested that
his beloved stop resorting to euphemisms and write in plain language. For
their part soon-to-be mothers dreaded giving birth alone. Difficult deliver-
ies and postpartum complications only made the separation of husband and
wife more agonizing. In Fluvanna County, Virginia, Arabella Speairs Pettit,
severely ill for weeks after the birth of a son, praised her "noble husband,"
artillery sergeant William B. Pettit, for bearing their "severe trials" with a
"mind far superior to his poor weak wife's." All the "painful trouble" she was
enduring "on account of your love for me" saddened Pettit. With a dollop of
guilt and a larger dose of self-satisfaction, he rejoiced that the "hollowness
of heart, faithlessness, indifference or downright hate" that characterized
so many marriages had not stained his own.[69]

Financial worries added to the difficulties of marriage at a distance.
Wives, struggling to keep their children clothed and fed, asked for instructions from absent husbands about land sales, debts, and taxes. Advice was
considerably more plentiful than dollars, though. "If God spares my life," a
Georgian wrote his wife, "I will send you some [money] before Christmas
Day." Even when Confederate soldiers were paid—and most regiments were
badly in arrears—enlisted men seldom had much cash to send home.[70]

Men were supposed to care for their families but could not play their accustomed parts as patriarchal protectors of hearth and home. It is tempting
to exaggerate temporary changes in marital roles and overanalyze shifting
power relationships, but the most important questions at the time were more
mundane and practical. Letters and newspapers from home overflowed with
reports of shortages and high prices. Would wives have enough wood for the
winter? What about warm clothes for the children? Would there be enough
to eat? "I fear desertion will be frequent . . . if there is not something done
for the support of the soldiers' families," a western North Carolina woman
predicted after corn hit $2.00 a bushel.[71]

All these woes, especially the death of loved ones back home, demanded
more than human strength, and many soldiers came to rely on their religious
faith. Robert E. Lee himself set the tone. Weeks after his daughter Annie had
died of typhoid, he searched for consolation in pious formulas: "But the Lord
gave, and the Lord has taken away; blessed be the name of the Lord. . . . I
had always counted, if God should spare me a few days of peace after this
cruel war was ended, that I should have her with me. But year after year my

hopes go out, and I must be resigned." In the midst of bloody combat and personal trials, soldiers thanked God for his many mercies and hoped that their lives might be preserved for some great future work.[72]

Yet Christians also realized that in wartime, sin was an especially insidious foe. "Vice of all kinds [is] sadly prevalent in the army," a Virginian commented. "May God in His mercy check this." Swearing, drinking, gambling, and—if one dared say it—whoring became commonplace. So did irreverent and ribald talk. Men grew accustomed to working on Sundays, though Stonewall Jackson still refused to read letters on the Sabbath and warned that if the Confederate Congress did not ban Sunday mails, the southern nation could hardly "escape [God's] wrath."[73]

Even as prayer, Bible reading, and religious services helped some men cope with daily troubles and fear of death, in many regiments the spirit of the Lord seemed far away. Chaplains offered communion, baptized converts, visited the sick, and buried the dead, though these good shepherds were always in short supply and their flocks often indifferent. Congress had authorized the employment of chaplains but soon slashed their pay from $85 to $50 a month. These men of God occupied an anomalous position. They shared the soldiers' poor clothing, short rations, and uncertain pay but were not supposed to take up arms. Earning the respect of the enlisted men proved difficult, especially for those who lacked the energy and eloquence to touch the hearts of hardened veterans. Some chaplains served only briefly before retreating to pulpits back home; others grew discouraged over spiritual listlessness in the ranks.[74]

With Lee's men settling into camps around Fredericksburg, revival services that had begun earlier in the fall continued, as many as five or six a day among the scattered brigades. Nightly meetings drew large crowds, and scores of men responded to the altar calls. To many officers, Christian soldiers were simply better soldiers, and those who witnessed the great bloodletting of Antietam and other recent battles were ripe for conversion. Jackson welcomed signs of religious zeal, though some of it was probably manufactured to impress pious officers, and he predicted that God would surely bless the army.[75]

In the midst of lively revivals, soldiers brooded over the state of their souls. The Sabbath nurtured homesickness and, for some, thoughts about what it meant for Christians to kill other Christians. Even the most confident volunteers could not suppress gloomy introspection about the evils of war, but faith helped them deal with uncertainty and danger. If the worst happened, dutiful Christian soldiers could count on reuniting with their loved ones in heaven. A sergeant in the 18th Mississippi who contemplated joining a church scanned various psalms for assurance of divine protection. Although "resigned to my dreary fate on earth," he could find comfort in God's promise to deliver the righteous from their enemies.[76]

Deliverance would come in the Lord's good time, of course, and how long that would be was anyone's guess. The rapid Union advance to Fredericksburg had been followed by an unexpected lull. Frustrated by the delay in the arrival of the pontoons, Burnside appeared immobilized by uncertainty, his army stalled along the Rappahannock. The threat of Yankee shelling had frightened many civilians out of town, but then nothing happened. At first baffled about Federal intentions, Lee was gathering his two corps to counter the enemy advance. As frustration and doubt grew among the Federals, the Confederates struggled with supply problems while awaiting their opponents' next move. The consolations of evangelical Christianity could not entirely assuage loneliness and family worries. For both armies the certainties of a winter campaign, the trials of camp life, and preparations for battle heightened anxieties. For the Federals especially, the scattered bivouacs along the Rappahannock seemed all too temporary, and the prospects of a fight still loomed very much in their minds.

But all that I could think of, in the darkness
and the cold,
Was that I was leaving home and my folks were
growing old.
—*Robert Louis Stevenson*

6 Camp

"We put our little 'dog-tents' upon the sticky red mud of Virginia; made smoky fires outside, of wet wood . . . warmed and dried as we could, standing by the wretched fires in the rain; then we spread our blankets on the soft mud, and slept. We slept; for we were tired out; but we awoke stiff, rheumatic, and cross. . . . It has rained about five days of the week."[1] Thus a Connecticut officer summed up camp life near Falmouth. Storm fronts had followed Burnside's advance toward the Rappahannock, the damn pontoons had not arrived, and the weather was turning cold.

Sleet and snow now occasionally mixed with the rain. "Ice forms half an inch thick at night," a surgeon in the Sixth Corps claimed. During the most bitter nights corporals of the guard strolled about making sure pickets did not freeze to death, a real danger as winter approached. During daytime thaws the rain, sleet, and snow turned the earth into a quagmire. A member of the 13th New Hampshire wryly remarked, "Virginia weather and mud is responsible for nine tenths of the profanity in the army."[2]

Soldiers could adjust to cold weather, but no one got used to wet feet or damp clothes. Not only did it seem to rain most days, but when it snowed, it was that heavy late fall kind of snow that soon soaked through everything. On a typical night sodden blankets covered men who had fallen asleep in wet clothes and then might wake to an inch of water in their tents. One Pennsylvanian informed newspaper readers back home that the soldiers could stand such adversity and even conquer it, but few of his comrades sounded as hopeful. "Muttering" was the most polite word used to describe their response.[3]

Newer regiments often lacked tents. Men slept near fires or stood up all night with blankets over their heads to avoid waking up in a mud puddle.[4] Soldiers with flimsy shelter tents fared little better. High winds or driving rain easily penetrated these poor defenses against the elements. "I never thought . . . I should see the day when I would regard a Negro cabin as a luxury," remarked a Mississippi-born Federal artillery officer. Not only did the tents easily flood, but as one strapping six-foot, one-inch recruit lamented, you had to lie down "with both ends stick[ing] out."[5] The men remained in camp limbo, expecting to move (and perhaps fight) at any time but also weighing the wisdom of setting up more permanent living arrangements.

The more industrious soldiers built chimneys, a tricky and hazardous undertaking. Those fortunate enough to have tents pitched on a hillside might simply dig out a convenient fireplace, but makeshifts of sticks daubed with mud and covered with barrels were more common. Officers enjoyed watching such improvement going up, in part because the labor itself seemed to do the men good. More practically, privates relished a snug tent warmed by a small fire on a cold night, but the blessing was hardly unmixed. "We try to imagine . . . an old-fashioned fireplace at home," a Massachusetts lieutenant observed, "but the smoke and ashes in our eyes and the cold wind at our backs very quickly dispels the illusion." Of course the chimneys (and tents) sometimes caught fire.[6]

Building a chimney was a tedious, time-consuming job. Camp wisdom held that marching orders usually came right after such a project had been completed. By the end of November and the beginning of December, however, many men assumed they would soon be in winter quarters and began to erect sturdier structures. Sounds of saw and axe reverberated through the camps all day.[7]

Soldiers typically erected huts and covered them with tents; some notched their logs and built pitched roofs, while others dug down a couple of feet and set the timber vertically. Whatever the design, the plentiful Virginia mud filled the chinks. Typically these shelters accommodated between four and eight men. Tenderfoot regiments watched veterans raising "shanties" and quickly followed suit. Quality of construction naturally varied from what a Pennsylvania chaplain termed "neat and tasteful" to "sorry, shabby concerns."[8]

Whether they slept out in the open, in tents, or in huts, the men had to work hard simply to get warm. Some companies kept large fires going day and night. Although a few soldiers used coal, most relied on whatever wood they could scrounge nearby, and the supply rapidly thinned out. Chopping wood took time and could be dangerous with poor quality axes. It could also be frustrating. After hauling wood for a half-mile, a Massachusetts infantry-man bitingly noted that "some of the boys [who] were never known to bring a stick . . . always wanted the best seat at the fire."[9]

In later years men fondly recalled pleasant evenings spent around roaring fires, but at the time their watering, burning eyes received more notice. Green wood produced acrid smoke, and the wind always blew it into their faces. A Maine recruit claimed he could see no more then ten feet in any direction, perhaps a blessing because many of his comrades had taken on a decidedly sooty appearance. Sparks ignited blankets, even boots. Little wonder soldiers ruefully named their bivouacs "Camp Misery" or "Smoky Hollow."[10]

The sight of Maine troops in torn pants and underwear drilling on a cold day underscored the fact that some men had completed their recent march in a decidedly threadbare state. Though the Federals looked like parade-ground soldiers compared to the ragged Confederates, a few regiments had gone for two months without a change of clothes.[11]

The army's halt along the Rappahannock allowed the baggage trains finally to catch up with the brigades, and quartermasters began issuing over-coats, wool shirts, and underwear. These items brought "comfort and joy" to a Massachusetts recruit but provoked a cynical response from a New Hamp-shire private. Drawing new clothes likely meant a battle in the offing because the government "want[s] the dead well dressed that are left on the field."[12]

By the fall of 1862, however, the word "shoddy" had entered the American lexicon to describe clothing supplied by unscrupulous contractors. With Jacksonian outrage Democratic editors blasted "monopolists" who gouged the taxpayers but cared little for the soldiers' well-being. Footwear was a case in point. Boots too heavy for marching blistered the feet. They often fit badly, the soles quickly gave out, and bare toes poked into the cold air. Even new shoes usually leaked. Men would write whole paragraphs in letters listing the specifications for shoes or boots they wanted sent from home.[13]

The war in some respects remained a public-private endeavor with soldiers still relying on packages from home to round out their often spare wardrobes. Soldiers might clumsily sew up or patch old clothes, and the men generally carried what they called a "housewife"—needles, thread, and thimble. Few soldiers mentioned washing clothes. Laundry days were probably rare—a good thing in late November because drying wet clothes would have been nearly impossible.[14]

Nor were dirty-looking fellows in warm uniforms eating all that well. "Why did I leave three square meals a day to be a soldier?" was stock camp humor. Thinking about good food only made matters worse. "If you write any more about Turky i shall go cracy," a Massachusetts volunteer admonished a relative. Soldiers sat around the fires cursing all manner of folks, including their officers, for the skimpy rations. Perhaps the officers were negligent, but sometimes the commissaries shorted the men and lined their own pockets by selling government food to sutlers or other extortioners.[15]

More likely, however, the transportation had gone awry. Burnside's supply lines stretched from the Aquia Creek and Belle Plain landings on the Potomac River to camps scattered north and east of the Rappahannock. Before the engineers repaired the rail connection to Falmouth, 800 tons of supplies had to be hauled daily over atrocious roads where wagons easily became stuck or tumbled down embankments. For some soldiers this meant either a long journey along the kidney-jarring roads or backbreaking labor extricating wagons and mules from the mud.[16]

Consequently, during the first week or so after the march many of Burnside's men went hungry. Even hardtack sold at a premium, and when boxes finally arrived at the camp of a Pennsylvania regiment, the "boys walked into them like mince pies." Sometimes the crackers and the salt pork were wormy. One box of such fare, months old, prompted wags to explain that the letters "B.C." on the side (which actually stood for "Brigade Commissary") meant "Before Christ." Yet the famished hardly cared. A broken bottle of cornmeal in the 133rd Pennsylvania presented no problem. The men baked it up into "dodgers . . . chew[ed] it fine and pick[ed] the pieces of glass out between our teeth." An apocryphal tale more than likely, but several regiments dubbed their bivouacs "Camp Starvation."[17]

The standard Federal ration of a pound of meat and a pound of hard bread, though sufficient in quantity, fell short in variety and nutrition. Commonly enough, ravenous men would wolf down a three-day supply of food in one day and then go hungry.[18] Thinking they had fared better with McClellan, soldiers nicknamed broken hardtack soaked in pork fat "Burnside stew." The amenities of dining were ignored. "When we get home again," a New Hampshire recruit mused, "we will not any more sit at the table to eat, but will seize our grub in our fists, and eat it on the wood pile, or in the back yard like soldiers."[19]

After days of hardtack and salt pork, nearly anything else seemed like sumptuous fare. A Minnesotan pronounced rice and boiled potatoes a "rich dish." Soft bread, vegetables, pickles, molasses, and plain bean soup elicited appreciative comments.[20] Every regiment had specialists in scrounging extra food, foragers who cleaned out local farmers or bolder spirits who pilfered provisions from their own officers. General Sumner lost a fine turkey to some audacious thieves; men who had stolen a skinned rabbit from their company commander brazenly serenaded the camp with a chorus of "Who Stole Captain Trout's Rabbit?"[21]

More scrupulous soldiers wangled passes to buy overpriced food in Falmouth, where flour sold for 12½ cents a pound; bread, 25 cents a loaf; a quarter of a beef liver, 25 cents; and a pound of fresh pork, 25 cents. Although dickering likely occurred, enlisted men could scarcely afford anything between visits of the paymaster. "I'll eat hard bread and salt pork before I'll pay such enormous prices," declared a Connecticut officer, "and to 'secesh' at that."[22]

Such thrift and loyalty were admirable, but growling stomachs hardly cared. Whenever a sutler arrived in camp, hungry soldiers flocked around his wagon and soon parted with their hard-earned cash. Everyone knew the price of goods back home and therefore most viewed sutlers as at best a necessary evil. A sutler charging 50 cents for a pound of butter and $2.00 for a plug of Navy tobacco, a Pennsylvania recruit grumbled, "had fairly embedded himself in greenbacks." According to the *New York Herald,* sutlers had paid only 25 cents for that plug of tobacco.[23] A discernible strain of anti-Semitism ran through such talk. These traders were nothing but "Jews that have come here to swindle the soldiers," a New Hampshire volunteer groused. The *New York Times* reported that Jews had swarmed out of New York and Philadelphia and Baltimore to make outlandish profits selling cheap merchandise.[24]

Frustrated officers threatened to expel sutlers, but enlisted men took matters into their own hands. Bored, drunk, or simply fed up, soldiers staged midnight "raids," tearing down tents or tipping over wagons and taking what they wanted. With cries of "let's go for him, he has got enough of our money," a large group of soldiers "cleaned out" one sutler and wrapped the miscreant up in his own tent fly.[25] These men were playing a risky game. A few such incidents might drive down prices; but if they happened too often or the men got out of control, the provost guards would step in, and the sutlers might disappear altogether.

Soldiers would have been wealthier and probably healthier if sutlers had been banished from the camps. Words such as "unpalatable," "unspeakable," or "indigestible" accurately described their pies and other baked goods.[26] Besides being cheated, the men might have to live with the effects of their indulgence for months. A naive lad tempted by expensive pastry would end up making frequent trips to the camp sinks.

Illness in the Federal armies had held steady since the sickly summer months. The Army of the Potomac was only marginally healthier now than it had been in July, though one surgeon claimed at least a third of the men receiving medical treatment should never have been enrolled.[27] A regimental sick list of 150 or more was not uncommon. Although suffering no significant casualties since the Peninsula campaign, the 2nd Michigan now mustered only around 600 men of an original 1,080. On November 28 an Augusta newspaper devoted its entire front page to listing men from Maine currently in hospitals.[28]

Widely varying cleanliness and sanitation standards helped explain disparities in disease rates. A Connecticut volunteer reported a well-ordered camp with plenty of spring water, while a Pennsylvania corporal told his sister that no one should be afraid of a little dirt in coffee or meat. In some camps rats ran freely, even scurrying over sleeping men at night. Surgeons' detailed instructions on constructing and maintaining sinks escaped the attention of ignorant, careless, or indifferent volunteers. A New York doctor suggested that any man who defecated or urinated in camp should have to wear a barrel over his head with the "offensive matter . . . shoveled upon the barrel-head directly under the offender's nostrils." It is unlikely that such a punishment was ever carried out. Besides, Virginia's clay soil made effective sanitation difficult in the most scrupulously policed camps.[29]

By the end of 1862 mortality rates from disease were reaching wartime highs. Childhood maladies had hit hard during the first wave of recruitment, and now a second outbreak of measles occurred. Like the Rebels, Yankees also contracted smallpox, and several regiments began vaccinations. Medical reports included the usual run of headaches and colds; damp weather and sleeping on the ground naturally led to rheumatism, bronchitis, and pneumonia. Anyone awake at night could hear continual coughing.[30]

Fevers and intestinal diseases remained the real killers. By the fall the number of typhoid deaths was rising again. The Army of the Potomac would lose 116 men to the disease in November and 287 the following month. Pvt. Peter W. Homer of the 1st New Jersey Cavalry contracted typhoid in early December. Quite "emaciated," he was finally admitted to a Washington hospital on January 2, 1863. Suffering from an "exhausting diarrhea, from ten to twelve thin watery evacuations daily," he also complained of "abdominal tenderness." By mid-month his condition had improved. But two more serious bouts of diarrhea at the beginning and end of February seriously weakened him, and on March 2, at age twenty-six, he died.[31]

Diarrhea and dysentery, the most deadly of all camp diseases, persisted even after the weather had turned cool. Doctors usually prescribed bland diets, but some adopted more radical measures such as rectal injections with tincture of opium. Soldiers had their own favorite remedies, such as strong tea, but the army diet, poor sanitation, and lethal sutler pies often kept them trotting to the sinks. By the time chronic sufferers reached a regimental hospital, much less one in Washington or Philadelphia, they often had only a few days to live. Autopsies revealed badly inflamed, discolored intestines and colons, sometimes with spots and black deposits.[32]

On November 30, 1862, Pvt. James R. Woodworth of the 44th New York began caring for his tent mate, Albert A. Smith, who had "no control of his bowels and nasties his clothes and blankets." One night after Smith had done this three times, Woodworth spent the next day boiling his clothing. Delirious much of the time, poor Smith imagined himself in combat and, during one violent fit, sliced another soldier's hand with a hatchet. Finally taken to the new camp hospital, Smith died shortly after midnight on December 7. The next day Woodworth, who loved his twenty-two-year-old friend "almost as a brother," helped bury him and carved his name and regiment into a pine pole.[33]

By the time of Smith's death, surgeons were establishing hospitals in vacant houses, though a Massachusetts colonel complained that the generals had taken the best buildings for themselves, leaving feverish men to shiver in drafty barns or freeze in fly tents. Anticipating large numbers of sick and wounded, Medical Director Jonathan Letterman stocked 500 hospital tents.[34] Quiet, intense struggles with disease took place in these tents where generals seldom ventured and whose horrors home folks either refused to contemplate or could not fathom.

It was little wonder some men avoided seeking medical help until it was too late. Soldiers actually feared the hospitals more than typhoid or dysentery. The gruel was bad enough, and bullets sometimes seemed kinder than the human attendants in these places. Surrounded by dying men every day, surgeons grew callous and stewards sometimes stole from their helpless charges. One poor fellow was even murdered for his money. Doctors were bound to be criticized either for being rough with truly ill men or for coddling malingerers. Officers complained that soldiers were too easily sent to convalescent camps, and what a crusty Regular termed a "vast number of shirks, semi-sick, pretended sick, and bald-faced liars" somehow received furloughs.[35]

Increasing numbers of men, however, breathed their last in the hospitals or in their tents. A Michigan soldier wrote to his wife that two comrades had died on December 4 and another was near death.[36] Funerals, though commonplace, still made a deep impression. An escort marching slowly with arms reversed carried the deceased in a rude coffin made from cracker boxes or barrel pieces, sometimes accompanied by a dirge from the regimental band or perhaps a fife and muffled drum. A chaplain would read some scripture, offer a prayer, and repeat the man's dying words about faith in Christ. Then soldiers fired three volleys over the grave, usually at sunset, and everyone marched back to camp, perhaps to the tune of "Yankee Doodle." Men who witnessed these simple ceremonies often recalled the details years later.[37]

Soldiers long remembered the first death in their regiment, an event that brought many a young man face-to-face with his own mortality. As John M. Brackett of the 21st Connecticut was lowered into the grave, Dwight Vick thought about the wife and three children his comrade had left back home and perhaps about his own family as well.[38] Some of the men were less sentimental. One soldier decided that the $5.00 owed him by a recently deceased friend should be used to ship the man's body home. The pervasiveness of death hardened soldiers to pain and honed an edge of cynicism. "But it's all right," a Pennsylvania lieutenant remarked after several men died in camp, "They're paid 13 dolls. a month to come out here and be buried, the government bearing the funeral expenses." If Halleck and the War Department had sent enough supplies, perhaps not so many boys would have died.[39]

But as always the humdrum days passed. In the midst of the campaign, life in camp began to fall once again into familiar patterns. If a fellow could get enough to eat and had a warm fire, he might spend an agreeable evening telling stories or gabbing about everything from women to politics. A relaxed smoke at the end of the day could almost make up for other hardships. Such ordinary pleasures cemented friendships and fostered the kind of unit cohesion that turned highly individualistic, democratic citizens into soldiers who would obey orders and fight well. As they developed pride in themselves, their companies, and their regiments, men soon came to believe that soldiers from their state were the best in the army. Shared suffering in camp, not to mention on the battlefields, forged them into a true band of brothers—brothers who had their squabbles but who would also pull together in a crisis.[40]

Because the army had not yet moved into winter quarters, recreation remained simple and serendipitous. The men played a little baseball or rode horses. A few glee clubs sang old songs around the fires at night, but familiar tunes and sentimental lyrics only added to the ennui of camp life.[41]

Approximately 90 percent of Federal soldiers were literate, so there was a steady demand for reading matter, everything from newspapers to Shakespeare. Some regiments had their own libraries hauled about in boxes by a surgeon or chaplain. Pious soldiers pored over the testaments and tracts while others devoured illustrated newspapers such as *Frank Leslie's* and *Harper's Weekly* or perused trashy novels. The men especially enjoyed newspapers; even for those with little education a "company reader" helped them keep up with affairs back home. Soldiers passed around books and papers until they fell apart. They begged their families for almost any kind of printed material to while away the idle hours. Cut off from newspapers and magazines during the recent march, a Pennsylvanian now understood how "war and barbarism" went hand in hand.[42]

Boredom, bad food, and cold were a surefire recipe for trouble. Tempers grew short and enlisted men became insubordinate, failing to show up for roll calls or falling asleep on picket duty. Topping the list of offenses were drinking, gambling, fighting, and stealing, not to mention simply taking off for a lark somewhere. Even with the army on the march, far too many of its officers lingered in Washington and other northern cities. What a Baltimore editor termed the government's "rose-water policy" encouraged laxity and even desertion. Despite strict orders to the contrary, officers still left camp too often, and some naive privates did not realize they needed a pass to visit Falmouth.[43]

One New Yorker tried to reassure folks back in Rochester that the demoralizing effects of camp life had been greatly exaggerated, but families had reason to worry. Alcohol posed the largest temptation. Despite the provost marshals' diligence, contraband whiskey entered the camps in hollowed-out books and other clever devices. Officers, including several generals, were notorious drinkers, and enlisted men followed suit. In the 21st Massachusetts an accommodating chaplain brought hard liquor from Washington, presumably for medicinal use, but a spree with the 51st New York earned him a severe reprimand for "degrading his cloth and disgracing his calling." Nighttime tippling occasioned noisy brawls, sometimes punctuated with bayonet wounds and cannon firing. Many a surgeon or quartermaster fell victim to the bottle. According to official military statistics, alcoholism rates had leveled off since the beginning of the war, which only meant the problem remained serious.[44]

The soldiers cultivated other vices to varying degrees. In contrast to Lee and his pious officers, Federal generals did little to discourage gambling. And there were always women. Venereal disease rates naturally declined the farther the army traveled from the Washington brothels. Even visiting matrons from the Sanitary Commission attracted attention, and the mere appearance of a woman in camp usually merited a detailed description in a diary or letter. Some men cared little about a female's loyalty. One hapless cavalry lieutenant on picket duty near Stafford Court House was captured by Confederates and lost his commission after supping pleasantly with a Virginia woman.[45]

Various incidents highlighted a larger dilemma made more troublesome by the unexpected and unwelcome halt in the Federal advance. Few soldiers could argue with the need for discipline in the ranks, but agreement on how to define discipline and how to maintain it remained elusive. Officers who were sticklers for regulations risked alienating enlisted men who resented anyone lording it over them and who bristled over the slightest mistreatment. "I can't say that I feel very free today," a Massachusetts recruit mused on his twenty-first birthday. "I am a high private in the front rank, and subject to the orders of a man." Nothing pleased the average soldier more than to see a martinet's pretensions deflated. The members of one New York regiment cheered heartily when several officers in Howard's division were court-martialed for consuming rations rightfully belonging to enlisted men.

Like their Confederate counterparts, the Federals considered themselves independent citizens of a republic and resisted becoming cogs in a military machine. Maintaining discipline with soldiers who shunned hierarchy and questioned orders tried the patience and ability of inexperienced officers. Many of the "men" were hardly more than young boys, and their enlistment began a transformation into adulthood just as the more common vices —notably swearing, drinking, gambling, whoring, and brawling—marked their coming of age. Once when a fun-loving but not terribly bright private in a Rhode Island battery refused to stop horsing around while loading hay, a saber-waving sergeant accidentally stabbed him to death. Higher-ranking officers refused to bring charges against the sergeant, and a captain threatened to punish severely anyone who even hinted at vengeance. To accommodate the widely varying degrees of maturity among the men, officers tried to establish a balance between regulations and respect for individuals. The boys insisted on being treated like men, but the looser and more democratic ways of the war's first two years slowly gave way to a harsher discipline—a discipline designed to foster both self-control and courage.[46]

Punishments were thus a delicate matter because they tended to be both severe and public. Insubordination merited stern correction. When a private in the 13th New York told a corporal to go to the devil, or words to that effect, he had to carry a thirty-pound log strapped to his back for ten hours and forfeit a month's pay. Other infractions received equally stiff penalties. Anyone caught stealing had to either stand on a barrel or march around camp wearing a board emblazoned with the word "thief." According to a Pennsylvania volunteer, such treatment seemed excessive for a "little fellow who stole a few crackers . . . when he was nearly starved." Men guilty of various misdemeanors might be sentenced to policing the camp for several days; in some regiments offenses such as unauthorized foraging and drunkenness drew fines.[47]

Dirty hands, faces, or muskets discovered during inspections could also earn offenders a trip to the guardhouse. Occasionally carelessness about appearances signified deep-seated problems. Men became so homesick they no longer cared about themselves or anything else. When recruits fell into this kind of funk, it took severe measures by their comrades to shock or scare them out of it.[48]

The best medicine for homesickness was encouraging words from family and friends. In 1862 the U.S. Post Office issued some 251,307 stamps, but that number soared to 338,340 the following year as the volume of wartime correspondence soared. Home news boosted morale almost as much as victories or good rations. Writing and reading letters did far more than ease camp monotony. It allowed soldiers to convey some sense of their momentous (and mundane) experiences to civilians.[49]

The soldiers' desire for letters easily surpassed the abilities of even conscientious home folks to supply them. Although the Federals delivered the mail more efficiently than the Confederates, Burnside's troops would never have believed it. And of course when one regiment received no mail, a neighboring outfit always seemed to be tearing through a large sack of letters. With armies so often on the move, prompt delivery could hardly be guaranteed even for properly addressed letters, by no means a certainty itself. Most soldiers endured lengthy periods with nary a missive. "It does not suit a man with a family to be in the army," Col. Robert McAllister sadly remarked after more than six weeks with no word from home.[50]

Irregular mail threatened relationships already strained by separation: "i do not know if i have Relatives or Friends yet on the Earth," a Michigan volunteer wrote sadly. Regular correspondence became a test of love and devotion; no word from home drove some men to the verge of a mental breakdown. A sudden halt in mail immediately betokened trouble at home, perhaps illness or death. The soldiers themselves seldom found much time for writing letters on the march, and they assumed their friends and families had more opportunities to keep up a correspondence. Descriptions of awkwardly scratching out a note on a cracker-box desk in flickering light on a cold night with smoke blowing in the eyes were undoubtedly meant to make the home folks feel guilty and prod them into writing more often themselves.[51]

The men treasured letters and read them until they nearly fell apart. "You do not know how consoling and comforting your letters are," a New York surgeon informed his wife. "As you say, 'it is almost like seeing you,' and they are the only things which reconcile me to my situation." Some soldiers carefully preserved their correspondence, but others burned it rather than risk its capture by Confederates who would likely read it for amusement or mockery.[52]

The soldiers' letters ultimately revealed men torn between patriotic and family obligations. They might speak of duty and honor, and women might even embrace those values, but that hardly lessened the trauma of separation. "The soldier when he enters the field, is presumed to sever all ties of home," mused a Wisconsin surgeon. But this was impossible, just as "a man cannot have a home without a country, but what is country without a home, that center of all his hopes and his affections!" The soldier enlisted to fight for his family but soon realized how much he was expected to sacrifice for so little reward. "Strike from his affections that of home and family, and how much of country will be left? When I get back I'll ask some old bachelor to tell me." Company and regiment became partial substitutes for family and community, but the men's hopes and dreams remained at home. "Bless the dear children," Lt. Col. Joshua Lawrence Chamberlain of the 20th Maine wrote with deep feeling. "I don't dare to think of them too much. It makes me rather sad, & then I do not forget that I am here in the face of death every day."[53]

Thoughts of home often rushed in without warning and could not be controlled. Sitting in his tent with a fire burning, an Indiana major imagined his wife and children attending church. Seeing Confederate civilians driven from their houses prompted even the more hard-hearted Federals to think about how their own families would fare under similar circumstances. The unforgiving Virginia mud and rain and snow only made the more familiar surroundings of home seem more attractive. "I have seen no state I like so well as I do Michigan," commented one lonesome Wolverine.[54]

Being away from home turned many soldiers into hopeless romantics who stared at family pictures or penned ardent love letters. George W. Ballock, a member of General Hancock's staff, told his wife how he longed for the day when "I can leave war . . . and bask once more in the sunshine of your love." At age thirty-seven he admitted that the "stern realities of life may have somewhat tempered the vivacity of youth." Yet he loved her with all his heart, and his "only regret is, Jennie, that I have not been able to love you better." Tonight, he assured her in one letter, "you will be with me in dreams. I shall feel your loving arms around me. Your soft cheek will be pressed to mine." These conventional sentiments, which might run for a page or more in letter after letter in which these men never seemed to run out of adjectives to describe their wives' perfection, did not disguise the erotic undertones. Although sexual desire was seldom expressed openly, a plain-speaking New Hampshire sergeant commented on the "hearty" appearance of a comrade recently returned to the regiment: "I reckon it didn't hurt him any to sleep with a woman a spel."[55]

Memories of playing with children, the simple pleasures of a walk or a game, were bittersweet. Short notes and school compositions from their children helped men retain home ties. Although fathers could offer a few words of advice or admonitions about the importance of good character, the war often intruded into efforts to maintain customary relationships. Dreaming about a frolic with his son and daughter, a New York engineer awoke in "desolate woods with my wearied and fatigued comrades sleeping around." In the "dead of night" he could only pray for a safe return home while realizing how quickly his children would be grown. More ominously, a New York infantryman had a nightmare about Frankie, Charlie, and little Alta climbing a steep mountain. He at first saw a "vast army of soldiers in battle array," but this turned out to be an "army of angels making heavenly music and our children were hurrying to join them."[56]

Yet for most families keeping love alive involved much less frightening and more mundane matters. From Lancaster, Wisconsin, Catherine Eaton begged her husband, Samuel, a chaplain in the famous Iron Brigade, to wangle a furlough. Struggling as a minister's wife in his absence but gaining confidence in "find[ing] my sphere," she prized his letters yet grew sad as the holidays approached. Fearing that Samuel might shrink his new flannel shirt, she sent detailed washing instructions. Their son, James, reported doing well in Latin and Greek but doubted he could handle both during the next school term. Soldiers savored such homey details. Pvt. James R. Woodworth of the 44th New York nearly cried when he received letters from his wife, Phoebe. He laughed at reports of their little sons' pranks and wrote fervently of his undying love. A pious man, Woodworth liked to imagine them both reading scripture at the same time and hoped their separation would bring them closer to God.[57] There were no dramas here, merely the struggles of ordinary families in an extraordinary time.

Despite the obvious strains of separation, the usual joys and sorrows of family life persisted, but now the women dealt with them alone. However much couples tried to preserve traditional relationships, wives had to do much more on their own because their husbands could offer nothing but advice-filled letters. Women might worry about their menfolk being corrupted by camp life and might even try to assert traditional moral authority at a distance, but more practical matters took precedence. Money problems worsened with pay so often in arrears; soldiers could do little for their struggling families but urge economy. Working out disagreements by mail proved even more difficult. Pained by news of his father's remarriage, a Maine volunteer hesitated to send the expected best wishes. Pvt. Edwin O. Wentworth of the 37th Massachusetts complained about his wife making coats when she had her hands full taking care of their daughter, Anna. Carrie Wentworth had larger concerns, and as rumors of an impending battle circulated, she spoke for countless women. "I do hope the war may speedily close. . . . Still, before that time, there must be some hard fighting. I hope you may not see it. I suppose I am selfish, but we all are."[58]

As always, death permanently severed relationships, at least in this world. The soldiers could not help thinking about countless families desolated by the deaths of loved ones in hospitals and on battlefields. Yet many of these same men had to cope with the loss of friends and family at home. A Pennsylvanian advised his fiancée not to mourn her deceased grandmother excessively or become "old maidish." Soldiers steeled themselves with that religious fatalism so pervasive among the Civil War generation. Noting the irony of his beloved wife dying quietly at home while he survived the hardships of war, a Massachusetts man reduced his grief to a familiar formula: "Such are the inscrutable decrees of providence." Given the frequency of death at home and in the field, it should not be surprising that between 1862 and 1863 sales of life insurance policies more than doubled.[59]

Loneliness remained a constant as soldiers went about their normal routines. By the end of November and early December, the Army of the Potomac had largely settled into the camps along the Rappahannock. The soldiers spent their days drilling—typically a company drill in the morning, battalion drill in the early afternoon, and a dress parade toward evening. A Pennsylvania captain estimated that this amounted to around four hours for older regiments and five hours for newer ones. All this precise maneuvering was designed to avoid accidental shootings in tightly packed formations. It also helped generals prepare their troops for combat, though the lessons might be quickly forgotten once the bullets started flying. Many outfits clearly needed the training, and even as soldiers groused about the numbing repetition and the tedium of reviews by high-ranking generals, the men came to take pride in their regiments' proficiency on the parade ground.[60]

As much as they disliked drill, soldiers usually loathed picket duty. One late November morning privates William McCarter and Samuel Foltz of the 116th Pennsylvania retired from their post along the Rappahannock to a vacant brick building in Falmouth. By three in the afternoon, however, they were back on picket again, this time in the open. They had little food, though a man from another regiment shared a large turnip with McCarter. Soon the wind picked up, and their eyes began to water, ears began to hurt, and blood began slowly congealing in their veins—or so it seemed. McCarter and Foltz huddled against a bridge abutment, cursing the orders that forbade fires. Unable to stand the numbing cold any longer, Foltz slipped back into town, but McCarter stayed and tried to fight off sleep with his coat pulled over his head. About 11:00 P.M. the sergeant of the guard found him, still standing but hunched over and presumed dead. Once back in the brick building, however, McCarter responded to warm blankets and strong coffee. That same night three men from other regiments did freeze to death.[61]

Because both sides considered firing on a picket little better than murder, such duty was largely uneventful though certainly monotonous and uncomfortable. The men would rotate between various posts front and rear.[62] Suffering like McCarter from the cold and dampness, some volunteers defied orders and started fires. After standing guard in the rain, pickets often had to sleep in wet clothes. Typically they complained and threatened mutiny but did their duty.[63]

Improving roads to speed the arrival of badly needed supplies made a lot more sense to the average volunteer than standing picket, but it also meant much harder work. Detachments of soldiers cut timber for "corduroying" roads and reconstructing bridges between Belle Plain and Falmouth. Two regiments of the Third Corps used 300 teams of horses to build a 1,100-foot expanse through a swamp. With some exaggeration a Pennsylvania private boasted of working ten hours on the roads with the mud up to the mules' bellies.[64] Other men unloaded or guarded supplies at Aquia Landing, built earthworks to protect artillery, or dug sinks. Whether this activity meant the army was about to fight again or go into winter quarters became the most hotly debated topic around the campfires.[65]

During this quiet period men calculated ways to improve their own positions in the army. For some soldiers enlistment had temporarily relieved the frustration of searching for a civilian career, and however much they might talk of fighting for ideals such as the Union, many could not hide their intense desire for promotion. An enlisted man in the 44th New York who badly wanted to become an officer pressed his father to lobby the governor for a commission. Lieutenants looked to be captains, and captains to become majors; the higher the rank, the more burning the ambition. Colonels and brigadier generals who otherwise complained of officers trying to wield political influence wrote directly to Lincoln and members of Congress pleading their cases. Maj. Gen. George Gordon Meade, a division commander longing for corps command, bitterly complained to his wife about "intrigues and bickering" in the army slowing his ascent. With some justification Maj. Elijah H. C. Cavins of the 14th Indiana decided that too many generals cared more about promotions than about winning the war.[66]

Yet could the two goals be so neatly separated? As the army languished in camps along the Rappahannock, the Federals suffered from the usual but sometimes deadly aspects of camp life: the cold, the food, the disease, the boredom, and the loneliness. There was nothing extraordinary about their lives during the last part of November 1862, but the commonplace formed the backdrop for what lay ahead. Everyday experiences shaped the attitudes of men as they also pondered their immediate future. Ambitious officers need not have worried; there would soon be plenty of opportunities for promotion.

We cannot escape history.
—*Abraham Lincoln*

7 History

Abraham Lincoln was losing his customary patience. The Army of the Potomac had quickly advanced toward the Rappahannock but now seemed stalled. "I do not clearly see the prospect of any more rapid movements," the president complained, perhaps worrying that Burnside had turned out no better than McClellan. Not realizing how the pontoons had delayed the enterprise, Lincoln requested an immediate parley with Burnside.[1] On the evening of November 26 the two met aboard the steamer *Baltimore* in Aquia Creek and spent the next morning discussing campaign plans. Burnside reported that most of Lee's army was "at and near" Fredericksburg but still proposed crossing the Rappahannock and attacking the Rebels. Because such an operation would be admittedly risky, Lincoln suggested gathering 25,000 men south of the Rappahannock at Port Royal and an additional force on the north bank of the Pamunkey River. The main army could then cross the Rappahannock while the two smaller forces prevented Lee from retreating into the Richmond defenses. Both Halleck and Burnside objected that this would take too much time, and so the idea was dropped. The country could wait until Burnside was ready, Lincoln supposedly said, and Halleck would not force the general into a battle prematurely. Yet there is little question Burnside felt political pressure to launch an attack. Perhaps his sense of inadequacy or fear of never measuring up to McClellan along with his frustration over the pontoons now made him suddenly cautious.[2]

Lincoln had attempted to keep this meeting secret, but on November 28 the *New York Times* reported the trip to Aquia Creek and two days later revealed that the president had conferred with Burnside. Shortly after his return to Washington, Lincoln appeared depressed. Talking with some women visitors, he sadly conceded, "I have no word of encouragement to give."[3]

The army's mood was decidedly mixed. Lingering rumors that McClellan would assume command of an army operating south of the James River and complaints about "trickster politicians" could still be heard in the camps. "McClellan is removed because he failed to move where Halleck desires," Michigan private Edward Taylor opined. "And have we the assurance that Burnside will be supported by the Administration and that his appointment is not a cover to something further?" This "temporary appointment" would likely pave the way for the ascension of a radical such as John C. Frémont. "I have no faith now," Taylor concluded glumly.[4]

Although some soldiers feared that the administration expected too much from Burnside, many still expressed faith in their new commander. In striking contrast to McClellan, the general's informality and lack of pretense continued to win friends. Expecting a forward movement soon, a veteran of the general's faithful Ninth Corps affectionately praised "Old Burny" for "managing things right."[5]

Soldiers' expectations ran the gamut, and the range of opinion suggested both continued frustration and apprehension. Hearing that Burnside was conferring with Lincoln, a New Yorker simply wanted matters settled before the weather got worse. Others were already feeling the effects of the late season. "The day is cold and raw, and I have the blues," an Ohio colonel confessed. "I almost wish I had resigned. Surely, I have no relish for this winter campaign."[6] Delays were inevitable in military life, as veterans well knew. Even talk of winter quarters or a thirty-day armistice almost seemed more depressing. "I am sick of the war and so is the entire army," groused a Massachusetts private.[7]

Sheer uncertainty buffeted emotions. "We are liable at any moment to be called upon either to advance or skedaddle," a Rhode Islander advised his sister. "We have been here a week now looking at the rebles like two bulldogs neither one daring to bark." That some men described the roads as dry and fit for campaigning while others did little but complain about mud suggests wide variations in mood and morale. A great battle seemed likely to begin any day—but then again maybe not.[8]

On the other side of the river Confederate confidence soared as the last brigades from Jackson's corps arrived. Soldiers exulted over press reports of political pressure on Burnside.[9] Official Richmond remained convinced that the Army of Northern Virginia could easily defend the capital. Lee had foiled the Yankees thus far, and should he soundly whip them again, the always sanguine *Richmond Daily Enquirer* predicted, the Army of Northern Virginia might even capture Washington. An armistice and early peace would quickly follow.[10]

In the meantime Lee's soldiers were throwing up a few earthworks and preparing artillery positions in the hills surrounding Fredericksburg. Though much of the work took place at night, the Federals could see the results each morning. A "warm reception"—in the soldiers' euphemistic language—would obviously await any bluecoats crossing the river.[11]

Republican editors back home paid little heed to such obstacles, and their coverage of the army's advance remained upbeat if not wildly optimistic. A large map labeled "Burnside before Fredericksburg" appeared on the front page of the *Chicago Tribune.* One small-town Pennsylvania newspaper even offered the ominously familiar headline "On to Richmond." *Harper's Weekly,* however, sounded a cautious note: "If we do not take Richmond before Christmas, the Army of the Potomac will lose more men from disease in their winter-quarters than have perished in the bloodiest battle of the war."[12] Should Burnside fail to achieve a complete victory, he appeared fated for disaster.

The Army of the Potomac's apparent halt along the Rappahannock, however, failed to dampen popular enthusiasm for this latest offensive. "The Confederate chiefs are obviously bewildered," a Connecticut editor wrote hopefully. By the end of November, news of the pontoon problems appeared in the press, and for the time being Quartermaster Gen. Montgomery Meigs became the favorite whipping boy.[13] Republicans tried to quell their own impatience and defended Burnside by claiming that once the campaign succeeded, no one would remember these momentary delays. Yet as one radical editor warned, destroying Rebel armies—not merely capturing Rebel cities—remained the key to victory.[14] For civilians and soldiers alike, the demands for what a Massachusetts recruit termed "no more dilly-dallying with rebels" could not be ignored. Democrats sounded their own discordant notes, charging that Burnside operated under direct orders from Chase, Stanton, and Halleck. A New York editor even discerned a return to the poky McClellan strategy.[15]

With the army apparently stalled, some correspondents remained in Washington and missed reporting the campaign when the War Department stopped issuing passes for civilians, but reporters already at Burnside's head-quarters sent dispatches describing the Confederates' defensive prepara-tions. Exactly what Rebel forces had already arrived remained unclear. As usual Jackson's exact location was of prime interest, and the Confederate positions appeared impressive. Taking Fredericksburg would be "the most stupendous undertaking which has been presented to any military com-mander during the war," a *New York Times* reporter warned. Even among Republicans, doubts multiplied. Newspaper dispatches lost their breathless quality, and editorial comments carried an edge of despondency.[16]

Under pressure to advance but in danger of being mauled, Burnside appeared to have no good options. The tardy pontoons had thwarted his original plans, but even his friends were becoming nervous and impatient. Caught in the political and military crossfire, he might have to consider a different strategy.

★ ★ ★

On Thanksgiving Day Burnside returned from the meeting with Lincoln for a pleasant reunion with his wife. Yet for other soldiers, the holiday seemed much like any other day in camp.[17] There was guard duty, picket patrol, and brigade inspections—the usual routine. Officers might cancel drill, but aside from some extra mail and packages, there was not much to celebrate. On such a "cheerless day," a Maine corporal recalled, only the pranksters managed to escape the gloom and loneliness.[18]

In many camps, of course, there were religious services and other cere-monies. For New Englanders especially, observing at least some Thanks-giving traditions became an obsession. Chaplains offered prayers for peace and brief sermons on the meaning of the holiday. A regimental band played patriotic airs. In some camps men fell into formation for a reading of their governor's Thanksgiving proclamation. To cynical veterans such activities seemed poor substitutes for a regular Thanksgiving dinner.[19]

But this was the middle of the nineteenth century, and such affairs could not be complete without some speech-making. Officers waxed eloquent about the sacred Union cause or warned the men against various tempta-tions. Chaplains urged the boys to stay sober and tried to focus their minds on gratitude and other elevated sentiments. Yet on this blustery day the men most appreciated any speaker who kept his remarks brief. Having listened to two sermons dealing with matters such as self-sacrifice, the nobility of mili-tary service, and the evils of swearing, a Massachusetts officer charitably decided that "both . . . preachers labored as hard to find cause for thankful-ness" as the men did.[20]

Thanksgiving in Camp (Harper's Weekly, *November 29, 1862*)

Gratitude did not come easily for soldiers with growling stomachs. That there was nothing to eat but hardtack and salt pork became a common Thanksgiving Day refrain in diaries and letters. Because supply problems still plagued the army, some regiments lacked even these staples and so "gave themselves unreservedly to the exhilarating and pleasant recreation of d—ing the quartermaster." A few paragons tried to be thankful for army rations; others found humor in the situation. Officers in the 13th New York held a "special" dinner, with each man bringing hardtack prepared in a different way. A Massachusetts regiment offered a choice of entrées: "salt pork stuffed with hard crackers . . . or a slice of pork between two crackers."[21]

Sarcasm assuaged hunger pangs only briefly. "Thanksgiving day—full of memories, but turkeyless to us," a Rhode Islander remarked. A Maine recruit noted how men from his regiment had raided a butchering yard, where they scraped fat from entrails and even ate lungs. "While our friends at home suffer through roast turkey, mince pie, and plum pudding," he wrote, "we cram ourselves on air pudding." But in the end there was nothing amusing about a Thanksgiving Day spent in a dreary camp eating barely digestible food. "The boys were mighty blue," a Massachusetts lieutenant confided to his sister. "I was homesick as a dog."[22]

Many enlisted men tried to round up a respectable Thanksgiving meal, but their efforts usually fell far short. A few ginger cookies, shortcakes with molasses, or a small apple pie seemed like special treats.[23] Soldiers often settled for a lot less: "rather ancient" chickens; "flat, sour, heavy biscuits," two dozen for 50 cents in Falmouth; soup made from desiccated vegetables; a cow's heart; and the "rarity" of boiled tripe. A tablecloth thrown over a makeshift table recaptured in some small way the atmosphere of Thanksgiving at home. Although a raw Michigan recruit considered his dinner of pork and beans the finest he had eaten in camp, "it was the first time in many years that I had been without a piece of turkey." What rankled even more was to watch generals and other officers, as one Massachusetts volunteer put it, "faring like princes." To see and worse yet smell the succulent geese, turkey, and other fixings while breaking your teeth on hard bread sent spirits drooping.[24]

Yet for some soldiers more than for many other Americans, the historical meaning of Thanksgiving also weighed on their minds. With a tinge of chauvinistic literalism, these men appreciated the preservation of their own lives and the continued health of their families. "We are to day an *unbroken* Circle upon probationary ground," a New Hampshire sergeant cautioned his wife.[25] How easy to envision the family gathering around the table for the traditional holiday feast or attending a Thanksgiving church service. Whatever the tensions and problems his folks had faced, a soldier in camp remembered a room filled to overflowing with love and affection. The men regaled comrades with old stories, recalled holiday traditions, and described what they would be eating back home. A New York private jokingly commissioned an older brother to devour his share of the family dinner. The pleasant sketch appearing in some illustrated newspapers of an extended family crowded around a Thanksgiving table groaning with rich food contrasted starkly with the spartan realities of army life. Yet the troops also tried to imagine the war at an end, the family circle restored, and everyone grateful for the blessings of peace.[26]

On November 27, 1862, such blessings seemed far away. The desolation of the Virginia countryside was depressing enough, but so was the condition of many regiments. To "see the poor fellows around you dying, worn out by marches and disease" only added to the ennui. "I ought to be happy," a New York lieutenant told a friend back home. "I use to be the gayest, happiest, jolliest dog of all." Broken in health and spirits, he now felt "as unhappy and miserable" as anyone in the regiment. He could not help but think that the northern people had somehow wronged him, McClellan, and the entire army. But he vowed to stick it out and like many others discovered unexpected reservoirs of patriotism within himself.[27]

For the northern public this Thanksgiving became a great celebration of religious nationalism. "Christianity and civilization are engaged in deadly conflict with the paganism and barbarity of feudal ages," declared one small-town editor. Others agreed that the fate of liberty hung in the balance. Yet the usual catchphrases could not conceal the disputed nature of these ideas. Republicans emphasized the wickedness of the rebellion and the need to end partisan strife, while Democrats prayed for what an Indianapolis editor termed the "complete restoration of constitutional liberty" and thanked the Almighty for the triumph of conservatism in the recent elections.[28]

The more general hope was that the war would serve some larger purpose by stimulating public virtue. As Governor Edwin Morgan of New York observed in his Thanksgiving proclamation, even war "does not shut out all sunshine from our homes." People continued to work and love while the "storm without makes them gather closer together about the family hearth. With less of egotism and of worldly pride than before, chastened by adversity, they are happier than ever." The war would weed out arrogance and luxury, but both the theology and the politics remained confused.[29] After all, in the view of many orthodox Christians such a cataclysm had to originate in sin. Some clergy lamented the prevalence of individual vices such as swearing, Sabbath-breaking, and intemperance, while others railed against national iniquities such as moneygrubbing, political corruption, and especially slavery. Even conservatives came to believe that God would use the war to end human bondage. The people should rejoice on this Thanksgiving Day, Henry Ward Beecher declared, because the nation would soon be freed from this grievous offense.[30]

Families with loved ones in the army clung all that more fervently to holiday traditions. They attended church, gathered around the table, and munched on the usual apples, candy, and nuts after dinner; but how hard it was to enter the spirit of the occasion. Catherine Eaton told her husband how they had likely "thought of each other at the same moment many times" on Thanksgiving Day. Other women carried food to army hospitals or served meals to the poor in some of the nation's worst neighborhoods. If people would contrast the prosperity of New York with the desolation of Virginia, a Dutch Reformed clergyman suggested, they would count their many blessings. This surely belabored the obvious and offered cold comfort to families who had lost loved ones, feared they soon would, or struggled along without a breadwinner. Two Philadelphia ministers feebly advised their parishioners to be thankful that things were no worse.[31] Yet Thanksgiving had originated as a celebration of deliverance from hunger and despair, and many Americans must have wondered as the year 1862 neared its end when their deliverance from the horrors of civil war would come.

God sometimes seemed so far away. The war sorely tested civilians, but it threatened to consume the soldiers' faith. Notably pious people were naturally much concerned about the state of religion throughout the country but especially worried about the army. Would the men hold fast to their spiritual moorings, or would camp life and battle destroy their moral character? The war slowed the onslaught of secular influences; soldiers and civilians increasingly relied on religious language to describe their daily struggles with separation, danger, and death. Clergy and laity alike invoked God's power to restore order to increasingly chaotic lives.[32]

On a mid-November day two members of the 19th Indiana strolled through a pine grove and discussed the Lord's tender mercies. Such simple piety that emphasized the essentials of faith suited many soldiers because the war raised some battling theological questions. It must be part of God's plan to be in this "miserable forsaken country," a New York private concluded while standing picket along the Rappahannock. Men read the Bible and various religious tracts for guidance about their role in the country's unfolding destiny. The sacred history, especially in the Old Testament, gave individual sacrifice not only a larger but also a transcendent meaning. But this relationship became easily muddled in the men's minds. Despite all the carnage of the past year, a belief that the Lord protected individuals from harm persisted and made prayer even more essential. Yet the men prayed not only for their own safety but also for the spiritual welfare of their families and for the Almighty's blessing on their commanders. That God answered such prayers remained a cornerstone of wartime faith.[33]

But in a righteous cause, where were the Christian soldiers? Sunday seemed like any other day in the army. For some men, simply to enjoy a quiet Sabbath at home became a humble but profound wish. The devout missed hearing church bells, dressing up for services, and even listening to exhortatory sermons. The trouble was that camp life hardly inspired spiritual discipline. "My experience goes to convince me that religion stands a poor show for increase in the Army," a Maine private lamented.[34]

Because "man and beast" needed the "prescribed weekly rest," Lincoln ordered that "Sunday labor in the Army and Navy be reduced to the measure of strict necessity." His language suggests more practical than spiritual considerations, but the president duly acknowledged the "Divine will" and called for the "orderly observance of the Sabbath by the officers and men." Although some regiments began holding Sunday services, and the New York Times applauded the president's effort to safeguard soldiers' health and morals, chaplains noted that indifference to the Sabbath had already taken root and were doubtful about the Lord ever blessing an army that so often marched on Sunday.[35]

This is not to say that religious obligations were completely ignored. To the contrary, Sunday services took place despite the cold weather and over the sound of drums and axes echoing through the camps. And they were held regardless of rude interruptions. After rowdies disrupted a prayer meeting, a New Jersey chaplain had to chastise one overzealous worshiper for swearing and then thrashing the ringleader. Such an episode illustrates not only the anomalous status of religion in the army but also the difficulties of spiritual leadership. At first colonels selected regimental chaplains. Eventually Congress required that only ordained clergy be appointed but also cut their pay from $1,700 to $1,200 a year.[36]

Many soldiers enjoyed the Sunday services in part because the chaplains often preached from texts with direct military applications and labored to fortify their listeners for the trials of army life. As with the Confederates, the most respected Federal chaplains held prayer meetings, visited the hospitals, and shared in the common hardships.[37] The press often portrayed chaplains as shiftless cowards who hid in their tents when it was cold—"religious shirks," according to a Hoosier correspondent. Instead of admiration, chaplains faced ridicule and became the butt of practical jokes even from pious soldiers. According to one thoughtful Pennsylvania volunteer, these supposed men of God frequently abandoned their posts and seldom exhibited a character consistent with their "high calling." But then the officers with their incessant profanity hardly set a good example, and this same Pennsylvanian could only bemoan the "low ebb to which religion and morality have descended in the army."[38]

According to Pennsylvania chaplain Alexander M. Stewart, it was an "uphill business to accomplish anything for Jesus in the camp." The seeming indifference of the men and their commanders was a constant trial. "What are the abominations of savages and heathens compared with the wickedness of our army?" Stewart asked, a question many of his colleagues would echo.[39]

Whether the benefits justified the costs of supporting chaplains was debatable, claimed one coolly practical staff officer, especially when the successes tended to be both small and short lived. Chaplain Andrew Jackson Hartsock of the 133rd Pennsylvania persuaded his men to burn two decks of cards but recognized that soldiers without much reading matter easily got bored, quickly tired of the same old conversations around the campfires, and gambled to "while the time away." He formed the "Regimental Christian Union" by compiling a list of men who strove to live a purer life and "escape the wrath to come."[40] If organization were a key to military success, perhaps it could yield spiritual fruits as well.

★ ★ ★

Chaplain Hartsock and his colleagues usually focused on personal piety, and certainly Lincoln's order had recognized the importance of Sabbath observance; but the president increasingly used religious language to address public questions, most notably slavery. Although the preliminary Emancipation Proclamation had been couched in starkly military terms, Lincoln had earlier assured a group of visiting clergy, "Whatever shall appear to be God's will, I will do."[41] Moral and pragmatic considerations could not be easily separated anyway, and the political calendar would force the president to confront the question again soon in his annual message to Congress. Given the delay in the Army of the Potomac's advance on Richmond and the recent elections, the president himself needed consolation.

Not so the victorious Democrats, who now pressed the administration to withdraw the Emancipation Proclamation. The northern people were fighting for the Union, not for abolition, they argued, and Lincoln should heed the voters' message. The Confederates seemed ready to negotiate if only the administration adopted a more reasonable stance on slavery. Of course when argument failed, there was always racial fear, and conservative editors continued to warn—in often lurid fashion—that the northern states would soon be inundated with former slaves.[42]

Republicans were vulnerable on this last point and beat a hasty retreat. Even as the *Chicago Tribune* ridiculed reports about an impending "nigger invasion" of the North, editor Joseph Medill maintained that the Emancipation Proclamation was primarily a means to suppress the rebellion and secure free institutions for white people. Defending Lincoln's policy as a purely military measure defined the Republican mainstream. Both publicly and privately, bellwether moderate Henry J. Raymond, editor of the *New York Times,* made it clear that loyal people would support the destruction of slavery strictly on the grounds of necessity. In short, no one could say abolitionists controlled the Republican Party.[43]

Antislavery zealots feared losing ground after the elections and worried that Lincoln would disappoint them once again. In their view this hardly seemed the time for caution or retreat. Emancipation was what Confederates most feared, and the time was ripe to destroy the South's landed aristocracy. Any further delay, Frederick Douglass warned, would only play into the hands of Jefferson Davis. But would the president have enough backbone to forge ahead?[44]

All sides tried to gauge the army's reaction to this debate, but that was no easy task given the range of opinion. A minority of soldiers agreed with the abolitionists that emancipation would strike a deathblow against a rebellion concocted by wealthy slaveholders. Maj. Elijah Cavins of the 14th Indiana denied favoring social equality or intermarriage but considered slavery a "relic of barbarism" deeply offensive to God. He had come to believe that all people have the right to pursue happiness and that even the mostly kindly treated slaves "dream of liberty."[45]

More typically, however, soldiers appeared largely indifferent to the moral dimensions of the issue and described themselves as single-minded patriots fighting to preserve the Union. Perhaps concerned about the effect of slavery on white labor, they cared little about the condition of the slaves. A fair number of men expressed a vitriolic hostility to both emancipation and black people, blaming abolitionist agitation for prolonging the war. Let those who "howler about the evils of slavery or the injustices of the slave holder, come and serve as a private soldier for one month and I will bet One thousand dollars they will be as willing to settle this war as they are to abuse the Army for not making forward movements," a Pennsylvania private informed a judge back home. Accusing Greeley, Sumner, and other radicals of manufacturing "political capital," a disgusted Massachusetts recruit claimed that not one in fifty of his comrades would reenlist after seeing so many lives needlessly sacrificed. The war, he insisted, would likely create a new political party hostile to wire-pullers, speculators, and abolitionists—a party that would receive overwhelming support from men in uniform.[46]

Most soldiers, however, were neither ardent abolitionists nor diehard reactionaries. They clearly were not fighting for black equality or primarily to rid the country of slavery, though many eventually came to accept Lincoln's pragmatic arguments for emancipation. Direct exposure to slavery in Virginia sometimes had a profound effect on political attitudes.[47] Slavery had obviously blighted the state. The run-down farms and sallow-faced children all bespoke a society dominated by haughty aristocrats who degraded white labor. The mental and moral inferiority of southerners, an article of faith for many Yankees, was there for all to see. If nothing else the war should humble what a Pennsylvania chaplain called the "towering pride of old Virginia." Idle planters and their pampered children would soon learn to live and work in a society freed from the incubus of slavery.[48]

As for the slaves, many soldiers hardly knew what to make of these strange people. Pity, condescension, bewilderment, and a certain fascination shaped their reactions. The Federals either emphasized appalling conditions in the slave quarters or claimed that physical mistreatment had been greatly exaggerated. Evidence of racial mixing struck soldiers as both exotic and frightening. Slaves, they discovered, were a varied lot. Many seemed appallingly ignorant; some appeared deathly afraid of the Federals; others expressed strong religious convictions and showed remarkable knowledge about the war.[49]

Refugee slaves often worked in the Federal camps. "I have got me a little nig & am going to try and civilize him," Burnside's aide Daniel Reed Larned bragged to his sister. Other officers considered blacks improvident and comical but nevertheless welcomed their labor. Rather like the slaveholders, they did not see black people as fully human and sometimes used them for sadistic amusement. The most popular prank involved grabbing slaves of various ages, throwing them onto a blanket, and having a dozen or more strong men toss them as high as twenty feet in the air. "It was confoundedly mean," a New York private admitted, "but I laughed myself double at it." In the 35th Massachusetts a captain made a man named Adam stand on his head. The captain then whacked him with a sword to bring him "back upon his feet again in double quick time." Such antics, one lieutenant casually recorded in his diary, made the men "nearly split our sides with laughter."[50] Yankees sometimes proved to be cruel emancipators, and former bondsmen must have found "freedom" to be a mixed blessing.

The Army of Northern Virginia also had "servants," but there was nothing ambivalent about their status. Human bondage was a given, a part of daily life, and remained what Vice-President Alexander H. Stephens had called it more than a year earlier: the "cornerstone" of the Confederacy. In a letter to his father a North Carolina captain added a request for a slave to a list that included towels and handkerchiefs. In late November the Engineer Bureau asked for approximately 4,500 slaves from fourteen counties to build more fortifications around Richmond. At the same time the Tredegar Iron Works advertised for 500 black men to work in coal mines and at the furnaces. Notices of runaway slaves and black crime, including a counterfeiting ring involving one of the president's house servants, filled the newspapers.[51] Thus slaves remained an indispensable, omnipresent, and troublesome property.

Classical defenses of slavery continued to appear during the war and remained at the heart of Confederate intellectual life. According to the *Charleston Mercury* slavery had produced the highly developed sense of honor that defined the southern character, a habit of command that brought success in politics and, more importantly, victory on the battlefield. Tales of faithful slaves protecting their masters and mistresses from Yankee marauders became staples of wartime propaganda. Even those bold souls who called for reform—such as a convention of Episcopal bishops who urged slaveholders to encourage marriage, to avoid breaking up families, and to offer religious instruction—were buttressing rather than subverting the institution. Some Confederate soldiers, without exploring the paradox, claimed to be fighting for both liberty and slavery.[52]

Refusing to concede the moral high ground, slaveholders generally dismissed the Emancipation Proclamation as another example of cant and hypocrisy. Given the treatment of free blacks in the North, who could believe that the money-grubbing Yankees cared a whit about the poor slaves? One Richmond newspaper derisively reported, "A negro proposes that President Davis should retaliate upon Lincoln's proclamation by declaring all the Northern negroes slaves after the first of January next."[53] Yet beneath such swagger fear had always lurked. Attempts to ridicule the Emancipation Proclamation clashed with the commonly held view that the Federals were really attempting to incite slave insurrections. No less an authority than President Davis himself raised the alarm about the "horrors of a servile war"; state legislatures moved to strengthen internal security. A frightened Virginia woman worried that white people might soon be massacred, but her husband, an artillery sergeant in Lee's army, tried to reassure her that the slaves would not dare strike in the middle of a war.[54] Whether this tortured logic relieved her mind is doubtful. Nevertheless the threat of emancipation inspired Confederates to fight all that much harder for southern independence.

For Yankee and Rebel alike, however, talk about the future of slavery was little more than poorly informed speculation. Much still depended on Lincoln's course. Even the president's critics gave him credit for honesty and purity of heart, but by the fall of 1862 many people were questioning his steadiness of purpose. After long refusing to move against slavery, Lincoln had suddenly issued the preliminary Emancipation Proclamation. Yet now, given the more conservative political climate, would he revert to a more cautious policy? Lincoln appeared more depressed than ever. Even his customary humor carried with it an air of ineffable sadness. "His hair is grizzled, his gait more stooping, his countenance sallow, and there is a sunken deathly look about the large cavernous eyes," a frequent visitor to the White House noted.[55] Despite unsolicited advice from many quarters, Lincoln kept his own council.

On December 1, the opening day of the third session of the 37th Congress, the Reverend Byron Sunderland, chaplain of the Senate, prayed that the Emancipation Proclamation would "inspire some salutary fear in the rebels of the South [and in] . . . the false and lying prophets of the North." Both houses then awaited the reading of the president's annual message. Lincoln began with the fatalistic observation that the "Almighty" had not yet chosen to "bless us with a return of peace" and would do so "in His own good time," then followed with brief comments on the war, the usual summary of foreign relations, and synopses of department reports.[56]

The most significant section of his address dealt with the future of slavery. Lincoln still favored compensated emancipation and had not abandoned the chimerical notion of colonizing former slaves in Latin America. He proposed a constitutional amendment to put slavery on the road to extinction by the end of the century. These measures, he argued, would prove much less costly in lives and treasure than continuing a bloody civil war. Lincoln did not believe that free blacks should be forced to leave the country and, seeking to assuage northern racial fears, argued that most would remain in the southern states. Yet he did not present the various proposals as a substitute for the Emancipation Proclamation, and that became a source of confusion. He closed this cautious state paper, which seemed to take several different tacks, with a rhetorical flourish: "Fellow-citizens, *we* cannot escape history. . . . The fiery trial, through which we pass, will light us down, in honor or dishonor, to the latest generation. . . . In *giving* freedom to the *slave,* we *assure* freedom to the *free*—honorable alike in what we give, and what we preserve. We shall nobly save, or meanly lose, the last best, hope of earth."[57] As if replying to Confederate propagandists, the president linked national honor to emancipation. But how to square gradual and compensated emancipation (essentially a peacetime proposal) with the Emancipation Proclamation (a measure born of military necessity) was by no means clear. Often quoted in the future, the message as a whole struck some discordant notes for the present.

The political reaction, even among those with strong opinions about slavery, was mixed and contradictory. A certain amount of abolitionist outrage was to be expected. William Lloyd Garrison excoriated Lincoln as a man "manifestly without moral vision" whose public papers "all bear the same marks of crudeness, incongruity, feebleness, and lack of method." Henry Ward Beecher, the famed antislavery preacher, warned the administration to stand by the Emancipation Proclamation or be destroyed. Frederick Douglass and other black leaders deplored talk of colonization. Some abolitionists, however, muted their criticism and expressed their reservations about compensated emancipation in remarkably mild language. Lincoln would still do the right thing on January 1, 1863, they hoped.[58]

There were no essential contradictions between the message and the Emancipation Proclamation, staunch Republicans maintained. Horace Greeley dusted off that old bogey the "slave power," an idea that had long papered over strategic and tactical differences within the Republican Party. Editors praised Lincoln generally without mentioning any particular parts of the message or lauded his honesty in contrast to the Democrats' disloyalty.[59]

For sure, doubts about gradual and compensated emancipation—decried as a "weak and absurd scheme" by newly elected Ohio congressman James A. Garfield—could not be easily suppressed. Even if the Rebel leaders would accept this plan, Congress would never appropriate the necessary funds. The message might contradict the preliminary Emancipation Proclamation, but few Republicans seemed ready to repudiate the president's policies, however unclear or wavering they might appear.[60]

Some conservative newspapers applauded Lincoln's renewed call for gradual and compensated emancipation. Several editors praised his "statesmanship," duly noting the radical Republicans' dismay. The president's moderate proposals might win over disaffected voters and even become the basis for a negotiated peace.[61] Perhaps fearing just such an eventuality and riding high from their recent victories, leading Democrats would have none of it. Blasting Lincoln's obsession with "the inevitable nigger," a Rochester, New York, editor deplored the administration's indifference to the suffering of the soldiers and their families. Racial phobias continued to carry their political weight, especially in the cities and the rural Midwest.[62]

Confederates saw Lincoln's message as a sign of Yankee desperation and welcomed divisions among their enemies. "He [Lincoln] is quaking in his knees, evidently, and peace must come soon," an artillery sergeant confidently predicted. Many white southerners scoffed at compensated emancipation. "What do you say to selling our negro property to old Abe and quitting the war?" Brig. Gen. William Dorsey Pender lightheartedly asked his wife.[63]

Like many northerners, Confederates hardly knew what to make of Lincoln's latest proposals. If some thought the president was moderating his course, others believed he remained committed to the Emancipation Proclamation. The message was "full of abolition," a Richmond editor maintained; it "breathes the same heartless, cold-blooded, and murderous fanaticism" that had caused the war, a Georgia minister sadly noted. Lincoln remained what he always had been: an abolitionist at heart. Moreover, the message overflowed with lies and evasions. Between George Washington and Abraham Lincoln, the *Richmond Daily Whig* commented, one could see "the zenith and nadir of the glory of the Great Republic."[64] But no matter whether Rebels saw the Yankees as more desperate or merely fanatical, they remained united in the fervent conviction that they could win their independence.

Of course military events could easily make interpretations of Lincoln's message irrelevant. As critics pointed out, the president had said little about the war, but soldiers in the Army of the Potomac read the message carefully. Lincoln's seemingly temperate course had considerable appeal in the ranks, where partisan politics meant little. "It meets my views exactly," a Pennsylvania private remarked. "It is broad and deep, but yet so simple a child can understand it." Lincoln's moderation on slavery drew more support than his lofty rhetoric. As a New Yorker who had objected to the Emancipation Proclamation declared, "I believe in getting rid of slavery at any cost, but think Father Abraham has proposed the wisest plan I have heard yet."[65] More conservative soldiers thought Lincoln had devoted entirely too much attention to slavery. A disgruntled New Yorker complained that white soldiers had to eat hard, moldy bread while fugitive slaves dined on soft bread. Given Lincoln's apparent commitment to abolition, he seemed "bound to die with the [Republican] party," a Third Corps volunteer told his parents.[66] But it would be many of these same soldiers who would do the dying. And it would be the soldiers who would have the most to say about the immediate course of history, even more than the president.

Now is the winter of our discontent. . . .
—William Shakespeare

8 Discontent

Like Abraham Lincoln, Ambrose E. Burnside was feeling the full weight of responsibility. "He is working night & day and has been sick ever since he took command," trusted aide Daniel Reed Larned reported. "He has slept but little and is most arduous in his labors and does not spare himself even for the common necessities of health." Shortly before the meeting with Lincoln, Burnside appeared to be driving himself almost beyond endurance.

But to what end was Burnside pushing himself? Most of the pontoons had finally arrived, yet so had most of Lee's army. Federal signal officers at Falmouth had cracked the Confederates' flag alphabet but intercepted no messages of importance. The famous aeronaut Thaddeus Sobieski Constantine Lowe could send up reconnaissance balloons 1,000 feet, though he had not yet arrived in Falmouth. In New York McClellan claimed to "pity" poor "Burn" because the public expected so much of him, though as Larned noted, should the current campaign fail, Little Mac's newspaper friends would let him have it "right and left."[1]

If only the general could strike a blow before winter weather halted all campaigning. But where? The Union high command was divided. Brig. Gen. John Gibbon, a former West Point classmate of Burnside's now commanding a division in the First Corps, decided that the delays and bad roads made any crossing into Fredericksburg impossible. Instead he advised—and here the McClellan influence was still evident—that Burnside transfer the army to the James River and seize the Confederate rail center at Petersburg. General Sumner favored crossing the Rappahannock downstream to turn the Rebels' right flank, while other officers preferred moving upstream to fall on Lee's left. Burnside apparently considered this latter option because he ordered batteries placed to protect Banks and United States fords. But with more pontoons arriving, a head-on attack against Lee remained a live option.[2]

Burnside had earlier requested gunboats be sent up the Rappahannock to open the river for quartermaster vessels and to cover troop movements. He had revised his initial plans because of the pontoon delay and now hoped to cross the river at Skinker's Neck, twelve miles or so downstream from Fredericksburg where the terrain seemed favorable. Franklin, however, objected, and Hooker still pressed for a crossing well above the town. In fact, the Skinker's Neck crossing was fraught with peril. Even if Burnside could steal a march on Lee, such a massive movement of men and supplies in early December would require perfect weather and better luck.[3]

Burnside might also have crossed farther downstream at Port Royal under the protection of Federal gunboats, but Maj. Gen. D. H. Hill's Division stood athwart that route. Late in the afternoon of December 4, Rebel artillery shelled four Yankee gunboats near Port Conway and succeeded in driving them off after an hour-long exchange of fire. With typical invective and much bravado, Hill reported that the "ruffians" had shelled Port Royal, a town "full of women and children," but that God had mercifully protected the "inoffensive inhabitants." According to Hill the "pirates" suffered six killed and twenty wounded, but the Federals reported no casualties. The gunboats, however, quickly left the area and anchored downstream awaiting orders from Burnside.[4]

The prolonged encampment of the army caused ominous rumblings in Union ranks. The president received a letter from Anson Stager, superintendent of the military telegraph, damning General Franklin. The commander of the Sixth Corps, Maj. Gen. William F. "Baldy" Smith, supposedly warned Burnside against assaulting Lee's strong defensive position, though Smith's loyalty to his chief was as questionable as his memory. Hooker's headquarters, of course, buzzed with intrigue and backbiting. Meade reported overhearing Fighting Joe "talking very freely about our delay." The ambitious Hooker expected to lead any advance on Richmond and was currying favor with the irascible Stanton. Rumors of Hooker's ascension to command of the Army of the Potomac, some of which emanated from the general's staff, cropped up every other day or so.[5]

Politically sophisticated soldiers concluded that Burnside's stalled advance had hurt his standing with the army and the country. The clamor at home was rising to a crescendo despite some sympathy for Burnside, even from the McClellan crowd. "If Burnside does not move soon," a Hoosier sergeant predicted, "his head will be demanded and drop in the basket."[6] With the pontoons available at last, many soldiers could not understand why they had not crossed the river. The delay only gave Stonewall Jackson more time to bring up his troops. No answer to these musings, veterans realized, would be forthcoming. Soldiers had little choice but to wait and complain, especially about the lack of reliable news.[7]

Idle speculation fostered wishful thinking: perhaps Burnside was waiting for another Federal army to threaten Richmond from the east, or maybe the Rebels were preparing to withdraw from Fredericksburg. Normally sanguine soldiers became edgy. Expecting a bloody fight soon, a Massachusetts recruit wondered why he should risk his life "just to please the croakers at home."[8] Patriotism of this variety might not survive many more hardships or setbacks. Morale was mercurial, and whether the army crossed the river to fight or went into winter quarters, the men's spirits might falter.

Many bluecoats, however, did not expect a battle. The idea of a winter campaign seemed, in soldier parlance, "played out." The Virginia weather, a Pennsylvania private declared, would prove "just as fatal to a campaign as frost is to cucumbers, or arsenic to rats." Apt or not, the analogies reflected the expectations and frustrations of troops who had tasted defeat before.[9] Men who had only a few weeks earlier welcomed reports of an advance against the Rebels were apparently "played out" themselves.

The Confederate defenses also sobered once-enthusiastic bluecoats. In his unpretentious headquarters tent, Lee pored over reconnaissance reports and scanned northern newspapers. Lee knew he could not prevent Burnside's army from occupying Fredericksburg, given the commanding Federal artillery positions on Stafford Heights. But with the excellent ground his own forces occupied, he had decided against a retreat to the North Anna River. Still expecting another Federal army to advance along the James toward Richmond, Lee suggested bringing reinforcements from the West but did not press Jefferson Davis on the matter. Like Burnside, Lee increasingly felt weighed down by responsibility and public expectation: "I tremble for my country when I hear of confidence expressed in me. I know too well my weakness, and that our only hope is in God." But for many Rebels, Lee's character partook of the divine. This "quiet, urbane Christian gentleman," noted a Richmond editor, inspired "reverence" among Confederates, who were beginning to believe he could work miracles.[10]

In the meantime Confederate preparations proceeded. Anticipating that the Federals would avoid attacking the high ground and instead attempt to turn the Confederate left, Longstreet's artillery chief, Lt. Col. Edward Porter Alexander, had pits dug on the reverse slopes of these hills. He placed some guns on the crest where they could sweep the plain behind the town. Parapets and traverses were built and improved as engineers and artillerists argued about the appropriate height for earthworks; the men manning the guns naturally favored piling the dirt high. Longstreet ordered all approaches to Marye's Heights along the Plank and Telegraph roads examined and measured, and Lee inspected the artillery positions.[11]

Despite efficient and energetic activity, the distribution of artillery pieces between the two corps of Lee's army still bothered Jackson. Moreover the Federals had more experienced artillery officers and better ammunition, not to mention superior guns. Confederates most needed more mediumbore Napoleons, but Lee also requested additional 10-pounder Parrotts and 3-inch rifles. Some larger Parrotts could be useful as well, he thought.[12]

Lee remained quietly confident, however, and still was not worried about Jackson's scattered troops strung out from Hamilton's Crossing to Guiney Station and along the Rappahannock from Skinker's Neck to Port Royal. Although Lee held a formidable defensive position, uncertainty about when and where Burnside might cross the river had for the moment rendered his forces dangerously divided. The men, however, exuded optimism, and some even spoiled for a fight. "He is Burnsides now," a Georgia lieutenant crowed, "but if he will come out in good weather he will be Burnt-all-over." As one North Carolinian told his wife, the next battle might be the last.[13]

Given the obvious strength of the Rebel positions, it seemed likely that Burnside would try a flanking maneuver, perhaps even another "change of base." In any event, until the army actually neared the Rebel capital, a big fight remained improbable.[14] Yet rumors of an impending battle refused to die. After all, why had there been no official orders to build winter quarters? And why were some officers so enthusiastic? Colonels were itching for a fight, claimed one Michigan recruit, eager to have a "star on their shoulder" and willing to "sacrifice half their regiment."[15]

Colonels might have been itching to fight, but not here. "The time for crossing has gone by," a New Jersey officer lamented the day after Thanksgiving. Enlisted men sensed it too; an attack against those positions would produce staggering casualties.[16] Every delay deepened the pessimism infecting the ranks, and with veterans expressing a fatalistic defeatism, the newer regiments quickly caught the disease. Even the most stalwart soldier admitted succumbing to a seemingly pervasive despair. The idea of whipping the Rebels in battle seemed ludicrous. What is more, it all seemed without purpose, a "worthless war doing no one any good," a Michigan volunteer sourly commented. There was too much phony glory and moneymaking, a New Hampshire soldier agreed. "There is no soul in this war to an ignorant man," a Pennsylvania private reported to a friend back home, "not half as much as in the southern side."[17]

Clamor from the home folks and political pressure from Washington added to the uncertainty, and the rumor mill was grinding overtime. "Why we remain here idle, while we are having such beautiful weather, is a mystery to us all," an artillery officer complained to his sweetheart back in Ohio. The word "mystery" frequently cropped up in soldiers' letters as November faded into December. Rumors did not simply pass from person to person but instead were discussed, argued, evaluated, and modified. Veterans and neophytes alike exchanged the latest tales, and their reactions ranged from gullibility to skepticism. The men loved to debate the wild reports, idle gossip, and more solid speculation that floated about in camp nearly all the time.[18] Burnside and Lincoln would likely have understood and sympathized with the perplexity in the ranks. More than either fading determination or growing discouragement, a sad bewilderment encircled politicians and soldiers alike.

★ ★ ★

Confederates, too, wondered why the Federals remained idle. But then suddenly winter arrived with a vengeance. December 5 brought rain, then sleet, and finally several inches of snow (some soldiers claimed there was hail as well).[19] December 6 saw snow on the ground and bitter cold; water froze five feet away from a campfire.[20] On December 7 the temperature dipped into the low twenties. December 8 was still colder in the early morning at 16 degrees; a captain washing his face found the water had begun to freeze before he could dry off.[21]

The Army of Northern Virginia, as many Confederates freely admitted, was hardly prepared for the cold. Great roaring fires kept the men warm at night. Cutting and gathering wood began taking up much of their time, and areas near the camps were soon stripped of trees. Fires brought additional irritants besides uneven warmth: acrid smoke as well as sparks that set coats and blankets ablaze on windy nights. Sleeping on the ground in these conditions was a special kind of discomfort. An Alabamian with only one blanket happily became a hospital steward to enjoy snugger quarters, while a South Carolinian with three blankets thought he had "no right to complain." Many Confederate regiments did not receive tents until the first week of December.[22]

Although a South Carolina volunteer added a "resolution" about needing a coat as a wry postscript to a letter home, the persistent clothing shortage was no joking matter. One grateful Georgian deemed a recently received overcoat was worth $50 to him. Other men begged for underwear or socks; in the threadbare Army of Northern Virginia, the list of needed items steadily lengthened.[23]

On December 8, General Orders No. 100 established new clothing allowances for the Confederate armies. The orders mandated an adequate issue of clothing twice a year, but the troops could hardly believe it would happen. Wealthy men who had raised regiments right after Fort Sumter had already reneged on promises to keep soldiers decently clothed. Families and charitable groups struggled to make up the shortfall. Several members of Gen. William E. Barksdale's Mississippi brigade tried to talk Lee into allowing a man from each company to bring back winter clothing from home. Articles about officers in fancy uniforms and enlistees in rags dotted the newspapers.[24]

Yet reports indicate that the condition of Lee's army began to improve after this first cold snap. More government-issue clothing and boxes from home reached the camps. Some men even claimed to have nearly everything they needed.[25] Unfortunately, however, these fresh supplies did not include footwear. Men who donned new underwear or even fine overcoats too often went barefoot, or nearly so. Chronic shoe shortages, especially among Jackson's men, as well as complaints about ill-fitting government footwear persisted. In Richmond debate still raged over who was responsible and what could be done.[26]

In some regiments the absence of palatable food rivaled the rarity of good shoes. The supply problems so evident in early November had abated only slightly. "I don't think old Jeff Davis can feed us much longer and we will all have to starve or come home," a North Carolinian predicted. Around the campfires the men talked of little besides what they did *not* have to eat, and they muttered the usual idle threats about raiding the commissary wagons.[27] What they did have to eat was beef—variously described as "tough," "blue," and "dry"—along with flour, bread, or crackers. Besides being indigestible, these provisions were inadequate because the army remained on half-rations.[28]

Typically, soldiers tried to make the best of even wretched conditions, perhaps spurred by the growing conviction that no more real fighting would occur that year. Spirited snowball fights erupted among Stuart's cavalry. The famous Washington Artillery, attached to Longstreet's corps, built a makeshift theater from blankets and tents for their Literary and Dramatic Association. With winds howling against the pine brush and the audience seated on logs before great fires, the troupe produced a rendition of the light comedy "Lady of Lyons" with a strapping, petticoat-clad sergeant in the role of Pauline.[29] The audience could only hope that Burnside would not spoil the entertainment.

★ ★ ★

Not that Burnside's better-supplied troops always fared that much better. Soldiers bivouacked north and east of the Rappahannock were fortunate compared with those moving into new camps or ordered forward shortly after Thanksgiving. On December 1 Brig. Gen. George W. Getty's division of the Ninth Corps broke camp near Washington. During an excruciatingly slow march the men trudged through snow and suffered greatly even with shelter tents and five days' cooked rations. Some Rhode Islanders hooted at the "[13th] New Hampshire babies" for falling out along the way, though a member of this outfit claimed that army shoes—"very poor things excepting upon dry ground"—had slowed them down. Most regiments were on the road for eight days; they arrived hungry, soaked to the skin, covered with mud, and dead for sleep.[30]

Baldy Smith's Sixth Corps received marching orders just as the cold weather hit. Brig. Gen. William T. H. Brooks's division left camps near Stafford Court House on December 4 heading for Belle Plain. Caught in drenching rain that turned to snow, the men marched into a fierce wind. Uniforms soon became stiff with ice and snow. Nearly worthless shelter tents and a single blanket per man offered little protection against this kind of cold.[31] Brig. Gen. Francis L. Vinton's brigade, passing through Stafford Court House on December 4, also felt the full bite of the storm. The catalog of woes was long: wet feet, wood that would not burn, the impossibility of sleep, and ambulances stuck in freezing mud (six men in one brigade died en route). Later describing the experience, a Wisconsin surgeon used the word "miserable" five times in one sentence.[32]

Delays, exposure, and hunger also ravaged Brig. Gen. John Newton's division. From one dreary, "colder than Greenland" bivouac, Lt. Charles Harvey Brewster of the 10th Massachusetts admitted to his mother that patriotism was waning. "McClellan was right and I believe this campaign . . . will be only second in horrors to Napoleon's Russian Campaign." Water froze in tin cups, the wind chilled men to the bone, and only the "miserable hard crackers" kept them from starving. This was usual soldier hyperbole, perhaps, but Brewster rightly wondered how an army could possibly fight under such conditions.[33]

Men already settled into camps were not necessarily more comfortable.

Several days before the bad weather hit, a Hoosier private noted, "We are not well fixed for winter." When the cold rain of December 5 turned to sleet and snow, Rebel pickets on the other side of the river held up painted signs announcing "winter quarters." The next morning a blanket of snow covered the ground (some three to five inches, according to soldier estimates), and temperatures plummeted. "We might as well be on Lake Superior," a Michigan volunteer claimed. One Pennsylvanian enjoyed watching his comrades slip and slide down a steep hill onto the parade ground, but the usual camp humor wore as thin as a government blanket.[34]

December 7 brought worse conditions. The sky cleared; but the wind blew snow around, and the air shimmered raw. A Michigan lieutenant awoke with his hair frozen stiff "sticking in all directions like porcupine quills." Joints ached and wet feet became sore. "Winter is upon us savagely," gasped a Pennsylvania chaplain whose thoughts naturally turned to Washington's men at Valley Forge.[35] The air still did not feel as cold as back home, a New Yorker decided, but a New Hampshire volunteer considered the temperature frigid even by New England standards.[36]

Men on picket duty during and after the storm had the roughest time. Sentinels covered with snow looked like "plaster statues," one colonel thought. Soldiers stationed at reserve posts with the luxury of fires kept reasonably warm, as did those lucky enough to have gloves or mittens, but everyone began to lose feeling in their feet.[37]

Back in the camps the cold simply compounded the usual miseries of army life. Water froze in buckets; chunks of ice rattled in canteens. Men unable to sleep would walk through the camps to keep from freezing. After one restless night, a New York volunteer voiced a popular sentiment: "Wish they would bring out some of them 'On to Richmond' chaps and give them a chance." Sheer exhaustion might finally induce fitful slumber.[38] Men began sleeping in groups of two to five, often in "spoon" fashion, sharing blankets. Those on the outside of the spoon got cold, but shifting positions required unusual coordination and often simply frayed tempers.[39]

Shelter tents inadequate in early November were worthless now. "More like a dog kennel than a habitation for men," a Michigan captain groused. About all a fellow could do was roll up in a blanket and stay inside or sit bundled up in an overcoat playing cards. At least by this time soldiers knew where all the leaks were, a New Yorker remarked sarcastically. Still, tents were better than nothing. While a New Hampshire recruit wearing overcoat and gloves sat on a knapsack in a small tent hunched over trying to compose a letter, horses and mules, some half-starved, froze to death outside.[40]

The snow and cold had forced regimental officers to order or at least allow their men to begin building sturdier quarters. Soldiers erected log huts, taking special pride in chimneys, and some laid out streets. One newly enlisted New York captain even crafted a primitive furnace from old camp kettles. A Fifth Corps lieutenant dropped live coals from a nearby fire in a hole dug in the tent floor: "I don't know which it will do first asphyxiate me or warm up the tent." To be sure, many a shanty was little better than a "hog house," as one Connecticut soldier described them, but any jury-rigged structure seemed preferable to the flimsy shelter tents.[41]

Keeping warm had become a simple matter of survival. Sick lists were lengthening; 283 men were ill in one Ninth Corps brigade alone. Each morning more ailing soldiers would show up for the surgeon's call. Hospital tents filled quickly. Cases of frostbite appeared, and deaths from exposure occurred in several regiments. Fevers and pneumonia took the highest toll, but despite the cold, unsanitary conditions proved no less unhealthy as dysentery and other intestinal complaints continued to debilitate regiments. Camp burials became final, sobering reminders of a winter campaign's ultimate price.[42]

Although few Yanks looked as threadbare as the Rebels, some were nearly as poorly shod. Shoe shortages plagued all three grand divisions, and letters home often carried specifications for much-needed boots. Brig. Gen. Daniel E. Sickles claimed that 2,000 soldiers in his division did not have shoes good enough for marching. Officers had little choice but to excuse such men from duty.[43]

The soldiers' wrath sometimes fell on what a New York surgeon called "drunken and dishonest Quarter Masters." But it fell most often on shady contractors who supplied the army with shoes that quickly wore out and poorly made socks that immediately raised blisters.[44] Especially galling was the common assumption that none of these supply problems were *real.* The typical Federal soldier had less patience with shortages than his Confederate counterpart because he *knew* that his suffering stemmed mostly from venality or incompetence.

This was particularly true of food. If all the speculators in Washington had to eat army rations, a Michigan soldier fumed, the war would be over in a week. One Pennsylvanian in Meade's division declared, only half-humorously, that the army fed the officers' horses first, then the officers, then the mules, and finally the enlisted men. But at least the quantities were sufficient, and some soldiers actually grew to relish the spartan fare. "Am getting to be a great admirer of hardtack," an orderly in Hancock's division wryly observed. "Begin to regard them as the Arab does his dates. Salt pork too is a very good institution." A Pennsylvania private even claimed that crackers and pickled pork (the "fatter the better") had cured his bowel complaints.[45]

Adequate supplies along with the occasional special treat undoubtedly helped Federals endure the cold and perhaps buttressed morale, especially among regimental officers who occasionally enjoyed corn cake, fried Indian pudding, chicken stew, or some soft bread. Ingenuity brought its own satisfaction. A Michigan sergeant sent his girlfriend a detailed description of a tasty soup made from ordinary rations.[46] By early December food was plentiful; some men claimed to be growing fat. Shortly after the snowstorm Capt. James Remington of the 7th Rhode Island reported having all the fixings for a regular homemade supper: baked beans and pork, potatoes, onions, vinegar, pepper, tea, coffee, and sugar.[47]

Paymasters also arrived to settle accounts with some regiments. The men received anywhere from two to six months' pay, but this covered only the period through October, and so the Treasury remained in arrears.[48] Suddenly these soldiers had money to buy the extras that made camp life more bearable. Anticipating quick profits, several entrepreneurs purchased everything from apples to whiskey (the latter item smuggled in cases marked "Bibles") for sale to their suddenly flush comrades. Sutlers and gamblers gathered to clean out the unwary.[49]

Many camps, however, saw no fresh greenbacks. No pay for two, four, or six months became common laments. Men were so strapped that they could not afford small items such as paper or stamps. One rumor had it that the Treasury was short some $160 million of the amount needed to pay all the soldiers.[50]

The unpaid men quite understandably tended to lose heart. Crammed into cold tents and eating the same old hardtack and salt pork, soldiers readily vented their frustrations and disgust with the whole enterprise. The Lincoln administration, a disgruntled New York lieutenant asserted, seemed to think that all was going well even though his regiment had not been paid in five months. A Pennsylvania sergeant advised his brother not to join the army. Making matters worse, folks back home seemed indifferent to both the men and their families. Printing a letter from a soldier who had not been paid for six months, an Indiana newspaper editor drew what he considered two obvious conclusions: peace could not be won on the battlefield, and the Democrats deserved to take over the reins of government.[51]

At the end of the first week in December, both armies still nervously waited. Plagued by rumors, uncertainty, supply problems, and now the bitter cold, the long-suffering soldiers hardly knew what to expect. Two men, a Pennsylvanian and a New Yorker, wrote similar letters home describing how they wished the paymaster would arrive soon so they would not have to carry money across the Rappahannock River and into battle.[52] Within a day or two, however, the safety of their cash would be the least of their worries.

Despite the Confederacy's painfully obvious logistical shortages, Lee and his army were buoyantly optimistic. The future appeared bright if they could just throw back the invaders one more time. The less confident Federals, though, had far greater resources to withstand the rigors of the season—a good thing, too, because the Union high command was still hamstrung by delay and indecision.

From camp to camp, through the foul womb of night,
The hum of either army stilly sounds;
That the fix'd sentinels almost receive
The secret whispers of each other's watch.
Fire answers fire, and through their paly flames
Each battle sees the other's umber'd face;
Steed threatens steed, in high and boastful neighs
Piercing the night's dull ear; and from the tents
The armourers, accomplishing the knights,
With busy hammers closing rivets up,
Give dread note of preparation.
—William Shakespeare

9 Preparations

A military campaign at the beginning of winter, the season of death, made a certain macabre sense. Yet at the end of the first week in December it was hard to imagine the soldiers in chilly camps near Falmouth, Stafford Court House, or White Oak Church suddenly marching into battle. The cold weather had already used up many Union regiments, or so some soldiers thought. The potential death toll (as much from the elements as from enemy bullets) appeared staggering.[1]

Burnside's troops noticed the political effects of the military stalemate. There were few Republicans in the army anymore, a New Jersey corporal claimed; "political demagogues have taken the patriotism out of the common soldiers," a New Hampshire sergeant agreed. Talk of an armistice or even a peace settlement blew in with the cold weather and the lingering effects of recent Democratic election victories. "I will bet you a silk dress against six doughnuts and a mince pie that our regiment will be disbanded before next April," Massachusetts private Edwin Wentworth sportingly predicted to his wife.[2]

Camps began to resemble construction sites on the way to becoming winter quarters. With tents being logged up and generally improved, Walt Whitman's brother George assumed there would be no fighting any time soon.[3]

But contrary evidence appeared, too, such as large siege guns in Falmouth. The fire of patriotism still burned brightly in some soldiers, certain that the Almighty would bless the fortunes of Union arms. Talk of taking Richmond before the new year persisted, though it would not happen without "some hard fighting," a First Corps adjutant admitted.[4]

There would certainly be a hard fight if Burnside had his way. He had assembled a formidable host. The Army of the Potomac now numbered approximately 120,000 men in the three grand divisions, with the Eleventh and Twelfth Corps in reserve within reasonable marching distance.[5] Having decided against crossing the Rappahannock at the fords above Fredericksburg or at Skinker's Neck, Burnside chose to attack where Lee would least expect it: Fredericksburg itself. Many of his generals lacked confidence in their commander, and perhaps he in them. In both the War Department and among the Army of the Potomac's high command, the seeds of misunderstanding and confusion were still being sown, and just as with the pontoon fiasco, they would eventually ripen into backbiting and recrimination.

★ ★ ★

Public confidence in Burnside, however, remained remarkably high. Although nearly a month had passed since McClellan's departure, editors still lauded the new commander as an unassuming but energetic soldier. His lack of political ambition—in sharp contrast to McClellan, whose name was already being bruited about for the 1864 Democratic presidential nomination—also won favor. Pontoons had caused the delay, Republican senator Zachariah Chandler of Michigan, a leading radical, believed, and he still expected a fight near Fredericksburg soon. Burnside appeared "cheerful, if not confident" to Senator Charles Sumner of Massachusetts. Meigs, Halleck, or the cabinet received much of the blame for the stalled offensive.[6] Rather than criticizing Burnside, Democrats noted how the general now faced the same political pressure that had undone their hero McClellan. On one hand, unscrupulous abolitionists would welcome another military defeat to prevent the war from ending before their schemes for emancipation reached fruition. On the other hand, if the army went into winter quarters, an incompetent and corrupt administration would bear the responsibility.[7]

More ominous to the public were reports of Confederate strength that cropped up in newspapers of all political stripes. Conservative papers worried about reinforcements being sent to Lee from the West and the apparently impregnable defenses at Fredericksburg. Even the staunchly Republican *Philadelphia Inquirer* bemoaned the 130,000 men the enemy was supposedly assembling.[8] "On to Richmond" editors suddenly sounded hesitant. They began wondering about the lateness of the season, and some Republicans admitted that winter weather precluded active campaigning. The northern public seemed largely apathetic, the *New York Times* conceded sadly, perhaps because people had already read too many sensational dispatches announcing impending battles that were never fought.[9]

Out of Washington came fresh reports that Burnside would attack Lee at Fredericksburg. Even as the cold snap began, Republican editors predicted that the army was about to cross the Rappahannock. The shivering, starving Rebels could not possibly stand against the northern hosts, and false reports of a Confederate retreat back into the Richmond defenses also circulated. According to Horace Greeley, the decisive moment of the war was at hand, and the end was perhaps only a few months or weeks ahead.[10]

Newspapers kept screaming for military action. However important the fighting in the West, they maintained, the rebellion must be crushed in Virginia. Even the usually cautious *New York Herald* talked of Richmond's imminent fall, while the similarly moderate *Albany Evening Journal* declared "the fate of the Republic hangs upon the campaign." Soundly whipping Lee's army would seal the Confederacy's doom.[11] But this veneer of confidence barely concealed an anxious impatience. Despite the thousands of men added to the ranks since summer, a heavy blow against the Rebels had yet to be struck. The boys had grown tired of moving toward Richmond by "jerks and twitches," wrote one soldier. Senator Chandler may have been patient with Burnside, but he worried that Seward, "the evil genius of this inaction," still sought a "disgraceful compromise" with traitors. "Something must be done or we are lost," he insisted.[12]

Ironically, Susan Emeline Jeffords of Warrenton, Virginia, would have agreed. She most dreaded the two armies going into winter quarters. The Yankees would then continue to pillage, and spring would find local families in desperate straits. In Richmond, Lucy Meade considered "a fight with all its horrors . . . preferable to this awful suspense." Noting the depletion of the woods and how many large Yankee guns perched ominously on Stafford Heights, Fredericksburg refugees and several editors expected a battle any day.[13]

Confederates eagerly anticipated the fight because they expected to win. The press also ridiculed the demoralized Army of the Potomac, filled with raw recruits and commanded by a mediocre general who feared meeting Lee in battle. Editors even quoted military scholars on the difficulties of crossing a river with a large army. Though Lee might still withdraw to a stronger defensive position, Richmond appeared safe. Superior federal numbers could not overcome financial problems, internal strife, and what some optimists considered almost certain European intervention. Should the Yankees foolishly launch a winter campaign, disaster would surely follow. "We await the results with tranquil and trustful hearts," a Charleston editor declared.[14]

The longer the Federals hesitated, the sooner Burnside would be removed from command. The Yankees would then surely have to acknowledge their failure to conquer the Confederacy. Near the end of November, Virginia governor John Letcher wrote privately that Lee's army "cannot be whipped, and the people they represent can never be subjugated." On the very day that Burnside would begin crossing the Rappahannock, Senator Benjamin H. Hill of Georgia asserted that the "darkest day of the crisis is behind us" and that southern independence would soon be won. Leading Confederates used words such as "crushing," "overwhelming," and "complete" to describe all-but-certain victory. Hard as it might be to imagine Burnside in the role of Napoleon, Lee would become another Wellington at a second Waterloo.[15]

The inactivity and ineffectiveness of the Union cavalry—especially when contrasted with the daring skill of Jeb Stuart's horsemen—only added to Yankee malaise and bolstered Rebel spirits. On Thanksgiving troopers from Brig. Gen. Wade Hampton's brigade had splashed across the Rappahannock and the following day had overrun Federal pickets near Hartwood Church, capturing more than ninety prisoners, a hundred horses, and as many carbines. Subsequent raids had netted fancy provisions intended for Burnside and his officers. Confederate horsemen unused to rich food feasted on pickled oysters, lobsters, smoked beef tongues, plums, and nuts.[16] On December 2 a detachment from the 9th Virginia Cavalry had crossed the Rappahannock at Leeds' Ferry, well downriver from Fredericksburg. Surprising some sleepy pickets, they bagged around fifty Federals before making good their escape back across the river.[17] That same day another small body of Confederate cavalry had attacked pickets from the 1st New Jersey Cavalry near Dumfries and snared fourteen prisoners without firing a shot. According to an unusually candid and colorful report by enraged lieutenant colonel Joseph Kargé, the Union officer in charge, a second lieutenant, had left his command to "provide for his belly," dining with "an attractive female" whose husband was a captain in the Confederate army. Little wonder that a staunch administration newspaper dismissed Union cavalry operations as disgraceful.[18]

Yet how could efficiency and discipline be maintained with soldiers languishing in camps half expecting to go into winter quarters? With the two armies so close together, standard orders against fraternization were often ignored. By this stage of the war, firing at enemy pickets seemed little better than murder, and the men stationed along the Rappahannock observed an informal truce. In plain sight of one another, pickets on both sides of the river tried to match George Washington's legendary feat by hurling stones toward the opposite bank. The most adventurous crossed the river at night for quick visits with their erstwhile foes.[19]

There was method in this madness. Yankees longing for a good smoke eagerly traded coffee for tobacco with Rebels who had tired of ersatz brews. Newspapers were also popular items of exchange. The men often rigged up little sailboats to float across and warned each other at the approach of officers. Attempts by generals to stop this illicit traffic and prevent men from shouting back and forth across the river were largely futile.[20] While the brass might worry about security breaches, chilled soldiers at watch on the riverbank rarely did.

Contacts between pickets seldom involved military secrets anyway. They mostly centered on what was commonly called "blackguarding." According to the Yankees, the Rebels specialized in profane jokes and sectional slurs. On the other hand, General McLaws described the Federals as mostly "depraved wretches" spouting "vulgarities." A more dispassionate Pennsylvania chaplain considered the exchanges of "insulting slang and profanity" about even.[21]

The Confederates often got the best of these verbal jousts, largely because they acted as if they were winning the war. The southerners could be playful: "Yanks, before you can take Fredericksburg, you will get up Early, go through a Longstreet, cross a Lee, jump over a Stonewall, and climb two Hills." Or ironic: "When are you coming over, blue coat?" "When we get ready, butternut." "What do you want?" "Want Fredericksburg." "Don't you wish you may get it." Or dismissive and bloodcurdling at the same time: to a Yankee inquiry "Why don't you fellows wear good clothes?" a ragged Reb quickly responded, "These are good enough to kill hogs in."[22]

Confederates hardly believed the bluecoats would dare cross the river. A cavalry captain doubted Burnside would be "such a fool," but if he did cross, "it is a mere question of how many dead he will leave for us to bury." Most Rebels expected no fighting before next spring—if then.[23] Others disagreed, but whether the Confederates really thought a battle would take place or not, soldiers of all ranks remained supremely confident. Jeb Stuart was typical. With Lee's veterans in "fighting trim," he foresaw a "glorious victory."[24]

"One cannot imagine the degree of confidence and high spirits displayed by the men," General Pender told his wife. The soldiers placed their faith in Lee, who in turn came to believe that his great army was nearly invincible. The Confederate commander regularly inspected his defensive posi-

Fredericksburg, Virginia, showing destroyed railroad bridge and Confederate troops (National Archives)

tions, anxious to engage the enemy. Unaware of where Burnside might cross and wary of Union reinforcements, Lee accordingly left his own divisions scattered along the Rappahannock.[25]

A pessimistic War Department clerk in Richmond, however, guessed that Lee had no more than 30,000 to 40,000 "effectives." Federal estimates of Lee's strength generally exceeded 100,000 and ran as high as 200,000. He actually had about 80,000 troops strung out up and down the river. The strength of Lee's position, however, more than compensated for any numerical disparity. Almost from the day of his arrival, Lee had put his soldiers to work improving on the inherent advantages offered by the broken range of heavily wooded hills behind the town. A new military road and field telegraph lines linked the defenders and allowed for rapid movement of forces to any point of attack. Lee deployed his men in depth where necessary and spread them thinner where the terrain offered greater protection. All in all, the Confederate positions had far more strong points than weak ones.[26]

Put simply, Lee held the high ground west of Fredericksburg, and the Federals would have to cross a river to get at him. Even if Burnside managed to do this, Confederate guns could make it difficult for the Federals to

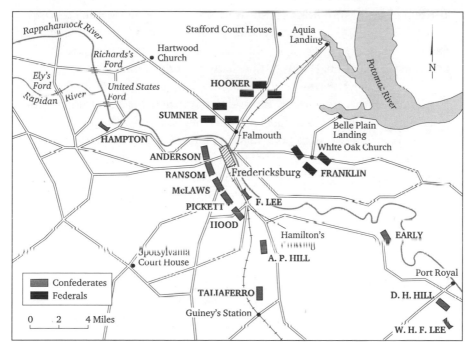

The armies on December 10

hold the town. Lee had more than 60 batteries manned by at least 4,500 troops. Entrenchments sheltered the long-range guns, while lighter pieces, deadly against infantry, were concealed in the woods, more or less protected from superior Federal firepower. Enough guns stood in reserve to counter the flank attacks Porter Alexander and others considered likely. Most importantly, artillery could be brought to bear on any threatened point. By the same token Federal artillery on Stafford Heights would prevent Lee from counterattacking, and Jackson recognized this problem immediately. "I am opposed to fighting here," he told one of his division commanders. "We will whip the enemy but gain no fruits of victory."[27]

Burnside's preparations had not proceeded so smoothly. His plan of attack apparently remained sketchy, but he was determined to make the crossing at Fredericksburg. He hoped to seize the military road that the Confederates had built and thereby slice Lee's army in two. Unfortunately he had few trusted confidants aside from staff officers. Even Clara Barton noticed the confusion in camp; she overheard two generals discussing the army's future plans with Burnside standing nearby silent as a sphinx. One thing is certain: he did not inspire universal confidence. One colonel told reporter Murat Halstead the army still longed for Little Mac, a fact punctuated by a group of drunken officers Halstead overheard singing "McClellan's Our Leader, So March Along." At a meeting of Sumner's corps, division, and brigade commanders on the night of December 9, "words were not minced," according to Maj. Gen. Darius N. Couch. Apparently Sumner alone stood by Burnside while everyone else criticized the "rashness" of his strategy.[28]

Alerted to this dissension, Burnside summoned his subordinates for a meeting at Sumner's headquarters the following day. They assembled around noon in a two-story brick mansion known as Chatham, built in 1771 but more recently owned by a rabid secessionist named J. Horace Lacy. Had their business not been so urgent, the generals might have strolled in the terraced garden or listened to tales about General Washington's visits to the stately house. Instead they gathered inside for a stern lecture. Burnside laid out his battle plans and then sharply noted the critical tone of some generals. Hancock quickly denied any personal animosity but pointedly noted the high ground behind Fredericksburg held by the enemy. Burnside, however, was brooking no objections. He had assumed command reluctantly, he said, but now he had made up his mind about where and when to cross the river. "Your duty is not to throw cold water," Brig. Gen. Oliver Otis Howard remembered Burnside saying, "but to aid me loyally with your advice and hearty service." Sumner, Couch, and the other generals either pledged their support or kept quiet.[29]

Typical of a person lacking self-confidence, Burnside had chosen the wrong time to be decisive or—more accurately—stubborn. Not only had he failed to make his plans clear, much less justify them, but he had dragooned his generals into silent or sullen acquiescence when he most needed their counsel and assistance. Nor did his repeated expressions of inadequacy and reluctance to accept the command inspire confidence. To be fair, though, whom could Burnside trust? Commanding an army filled with disgruntled, impossible-to-satisfy McClellan loyalists, Burnside was about to launch a difficult and complex offensive with at best uncertain support from vitally important subordinates.

★　★　★

With the decision to engage Lee made at last, the camps sprang to life. As couriers scurried about and artillery trains rumbled, teamsters began hauling pontoons toward the river. Orders went out on December 9 for men to place the usual sixty rounds of ammunition in their cartridge boxes and three days' cooked rations in their haversacks. Held in readiness to march at a moment's notice, the troops were instructed to move forward steadily when the order came and not even pause to assist the wounded. Things were looking serious; even the musicians were carrying muskets.[30]

The weather continued cool, and many soldiers looked back longingly on their abandoned shanties, though large campfires still inspired camaraderie. While some men brewed coffee, filled canteens, or patched clothes, young Pennsylvanians in the Irish Brigade talked, laughed, and joked while devouring "salt horse" and fresh beef. Pvt. William McCarter remembered how boys who had not yet seen a big fight stayed up that night talking in small groups about what would happen the next day.[31]

McCarter and his comrades perhaps overdramatized their plight, but even veterans on the eve of battle often sounded like sentimentalists. The worst of war did not turn many soldiers into true cynics. As William James observed, most people are inherently conservative and make only the smallest adjustments in their beliefs even under horrendous circumstances. Thus the Civil War generation, locked into the formulas of their culture, clung to familiar verities. Many soldiers recalled being serenaded by bands on both sides during those early December days. The Federals would play "The Star-Spangled Banner" or "John Brown's Body," and the Confederates would respond with "The Bonnie Blue Flag" or "Dixie." Occasionally Union musicians might then strike up a Rebel tune, and vice versa. Near sundown one evening, however, bands on both sides played "Home Sweet Home," which drew cheers—and some tears for the homes and loved ones many would never see again.[32]

As always right before a battle, men thought about "home," a word that evoked a thousand meanings. Thoroughly Victorian Clara Barton imagined soldiers dreaming of a wife, a mother, or a sister. She noticed a light in one general's tent and wondered if he was composing a "last farewell" to his family. As a few men drafted wills and more wrote letters home, many became acutely aware of their physical surroundings. General Howard sat near a fireplace, his papers spread on a large portfolio, with "Tom, a little colored boy" holding an inkstand and candlestick. An officer in the 16th Maine remembered years later the military forms scattered about in his tent—morning reports, memorandums, orders to be copied, and various documents awaiting endorsements—and his sword and sash hung ready for a dress parade that would never be held.[33]

Soldiers expressed a bluff, manly confidence in their letters home, surely in many cases to cover their fright. "The boys are all well and hearty and thinks soldiering is a fine thing," one Federal informed his wife. "I don't anticipate any trouble at all," a Vermonter reassured his mother. On the eve of battle, men grasped at any bit of plausible good news. Rumors circulated in all three grand divisions that the Rebels were evacuating Fredericksburg.[34] At a moment of maximum tension, men naturally tended to believe what they wanted to believe, trying to transform their hopes into reality. Some veterans still expected the campaign to open the road to Richmond, and a Rhode Island officer urged his mother to so inform any skeptics at home. That the war could be decided by one great battle remained an article of faith. As a sanguine New Yorker put it, "an Austerlitz for the enemy—we hope a Waterloo for us."[35]

Pessimists of course would have their say. Delays had already dashed their hopes for capturing Richmond during the current campaign or for gaining success at Fredericksburg, for that matter. Any sensible person gazing across at the formidable Rebel defenses could predict the outcome. "The country is clamoring for General Burnside to drive his army to butchery," a Wisconsin officer lamented. A brigade commander in Hancock's division agreed, fearing the Confederates would "slaughter us by the thousands."[36]

In a sense the casualties were mounting before a single shot was fired. Men continued to succumb to disease. Hospital tents sometimes sheltered "beats" or "shirkers," though with the prospect of a battle where every able-bodied man would be needed, hard-boiled doctors tried to weed out the cowards. Some convalescents determined to join the fray despite their infirmities. Lt. Charles Harvey Brewster of the 10th Massachusetts, suffering horribly from diarrhea and dosed with a noxious combination of quinine, opium, castor oil, and turpentine, tried to catch up with his regiment. But after he managed to find the division's wagons, the "griping pains" in his bowels prevented him from joining his comrades in crossing the river.[37]

Being labeled cowards seemed a far worse fate to such men than the dangers of combat. In an era when men (and women) could utter phrases such as "death before dishonor" with utter seriousness and express cold contempt for those who feigned illness or avoided danger, battle became a test of character. A patriotic man preferred risking his life with his comrades. "I want to show 'em the stuff I've got in me," a cook in a Massachusetts regiment avowed, pleading with a lieutenant to let him advance with his company. Soldiers anticipating their first big battle fought the immemorial demons of war: the fear of death and the fear they would not face it bravely. A New Jersey corporal admitted that not everyone in his regiment seemed ready for the ordeal but thought most seemed cheerful. "I hope that come what will it will never be said I was a coward."[38]

Many civilians and soldiers believed courage sprang from a conviction that God would wrap deserving individuals in his loving arms. Faith had become central to combat motivation: a basic trust that the Lord would not only guide men through the ordeal but would also carry the army to victory. So soldiers prayed not only for their own safety but also for the triumph of their cause. "What a blessed consolation that the Lord is a prayer hearing and prayer answering God," a Maine volunteer exclaimed.[39] Chaplains helped the men by collecting mail, securing personal effects, and holding meetings. The "pious and the profane have some heart throbs which are similar," a Wisconsin chaplain observed.[40]

For many volunteers the Christian soldier remained a powerful ideal, and however pat the evangelical formulas, they bespoke a simple, sincere conviction. "Oh, Mother the consolation of feeling that Jesus is mine & I am his is more than all the vain pleasures of this world," a New Yorker professed. By the same token the humble prayers of folks back home could carry the men through their fiery trial. Although divine protection did not mean safeguarding the Christian soldier from all harm that naive expectation had long since vanished—a devout man dying in combat could rest secure in his salvation and anticipate the joys of a heavenly reunion with loved ones. In letters written on the eve of battle, soldiers tried to steel both themselves and their families for whatever fate might befall them. Henry Brantingham of the 28th New Jersey urged his wife not to "give way to doubts and fears." The Lord had always cared for them and would continue to do so. All he dreaded was "the sorrow it would cost my dear wife and friends" if he should be killed. "But if it is the will of God that I should thus pass into Eternity I trust that all will be well." He did not think this would happen, but he wanted to assure her that "my trust is in God, and I feel perfectly composed." A few days later a Rebel bullet ushered him into Eternity.[41]

Premonitions of death haunted some men's thoughts, and all struggled with powerful emotions, from a fatalistic despair to an almost manic cheerfulness. Some laughed nervously, others talked openly of their fears, while a few feigned indifference to danger. The sight of long ambulance trains and stretcher-bearers certainly made emotional control difficult. An ominously large pile of coffins stacked near a freight station in Falmouth forcibly reminded soldiers that this night could be their last on earth and led them to ponder how many poor boys would not survive the battle. Camp songs and whiskey punch scarcely chased away these dark thoughts.[42] A Pennsylvania chaplain sounded an apocalyptic note: "Sad, strange night. The pent-up fires will soon leap forth to destroy the precious work of God."[43] The bloody war would have free reign, and death would have the victory.

On the other side of the Rappahannock the Confederates shared some of these forebodings. Although Rebels still hoped that Burnside would abandon any offensive plans until spring, a brave woman shouted from across the river that the Yankees were busy cooking rations—a sure sign of an impending move. Longstreet sent out last-minute details to complete work on artillery redoubts and instructed battery commanders to have their horses in harness an hour before sunrise the following day, December 11.[44]

Along the Confederate lines men slept fitfully, grappling with demons of their own: visions of Yankees already crossing on the pontoons, or of their dead children summoning them to a heavenly home. General Pender, often an imperious and selfish husband, was in a confessional mood. He assured his wife that he always sought her happiness. "If I have failed it has not been for lack of love or the desire." A Georgia infantryman worried about the wickedness of so many comrades prone to gambling, profanity, and other vices, largely indifferent to religion. "What then must be their feelings as the Messenger of Death strikes them," he wondered. "But it is then too late to pray after the devil comes."[45]

★ ★ ★

If not the devil himself, fervent Rebels easily saw Burnside as his vice-regent. Having decided to cross the Rappahannock where the Confederates least expected, Burnside still hoped to smash Lee's army before Jackson's scattered divisions could arrive. A great victory still seemed possible. Sumner was to send his grand division directly into Fredericksburg while Franklin crossed downstream and Hooker remained in reserve, prepared to join either wing. All three commanders were to be ready to move at daybreak on December 11. Two days earlier, clearly hoping for Halleck's endorsement, Burnside had briefly described his plan to "turn" the Confederate position. He offered to send more details by cipher. Citing security problems, the general in chief scotched this idea. As for the plan, he offered neither approval nor advice. This was Burnside's show.[46]

Was the attack doomed from the start? Had Burnside been politically pressured into making this ill-considered movement? The earliest writers on the battle excoriated Burnside for simply throwing his army against impregnable Confederate defenses. A commander should never do what his enemies desire, they said. By crossing the river where and when he did, Burnside had severely limited his tactical options and had risked the destruction of his army. Over the years historians have stressed a similar theme, questioning not only the strategy employed but also the tactics of the river crossing itself.[47] Yet as an early British student of the battle recognized, Lee's army was a good half-day from being united, and had Burnside moved rapidly, he might have been able to reach the Confederate military road. Indeed as Clausewitz has observed, shallow rivers such as the Rappahannock are relatively easy to cross and pose no great strategic obstacle to offensive action. Furthermore, a river crossing offered an opportunity for a flanking movement against the Confederates, but success would depend on coordinating the operations of the three grand divisions.[48]

For all of these operations the pontoons would be of critical importance. On December 8 a memorandum from Lt. Cyrus B. Comstock, the chief of engineers, described how five pontoon bridges were to be laid: two near Chatham leading into the upper part of Fredericksburg, one near the steamboat landing into the southern part of town, and two (later changed to three) more than a mile downstream just below Deep Run. The work would begin at 3:00 in the morning on December 11.[49] Coordination of infantry and artillery, however, rested on sketchy and ill-defined orders. Inevitably the pontoon trains would get entangled with the infantry, and even the carefully engineered approaches down the relatively steep banks to the crossing points would turn treacherously slick in the early morning hours.[50]

The Army of the Potomac finally stood poised to move. The road from Antietam to Fredericksburg had been long and torturous. On the night of December 10 it was hard to believe that more than a month had gone by since McClellan's removal. The rapid march and the sudden halt along the Rappahannock were soon to be forgotten as the long-anticipated battle unfolded. Unlike the Confederates—Lee was still not convinced that Burnside would assault these strong positions—the Federals had begun to have doubts, and even though a certain optimism prevailed in some quarters, the night of December 10 seemed freighted with somber thoughts. In just a few hours, as the soldiers would say, "the ball would open."

Months of partisan bickering, military politics, and public pressure would culminate in the long-awaited battle. Burnside would test his plan, his generals, his soldiers, and himself. Lee waited confidently, unsure of exactly where the Federals would strike, but seemingly ready to counter any move. Back home, worried civilians North and South waited impatiently—sometimes selfish, sometimes doubtful, sometimes oblivious to the difficulties of conducting a campaign so late in the year. The weather had turned cooler; both armies had marched through mud, rain, and snow. Disease had dogged the soldiers' paths, supplies had run short, and speculation about the immediate future had gone long. The men had almost settled into winter quarters. But at last, perhaps, all the suffering and preparation and doubt would have served some purpose. The reign of king rumor was about to end.

And crimson-dyed was the river's flood,
For the foe had crossed from the other side,
That day, in the face of a murderous fire
That swept them down in its terrible ire;
And their life-blood went to color the tide.
—Nathaniel Graham

10 Crossing

The bridge building began early in the morning of December 11, with the temperature in the mid-twenties, skim ice clinging to the riverbanks, and everything cloaked in a dense, stubbornly persistent fog. The job at hand required both skill and time. Wagons drawn by six mules bore the pontoons to the river. One group of engineers placed a heavy timber abutment on the ground and secured it with stakes; then a six-man team maneuvered a boat into place, turning it parallel to the shore and anchoring it in position. At this point several balks (floor timbers measuring twenty-five feet long and a little more than four inches wide) were laid over the first boat, "lashed" into place, and then topped with chesses (boards approximately fourteen feet long and twelve inches wide) laid across them. Side rails laid along the chesses over the outside balks completed the job. Another pontoon would be floated out approximately thirteen feet from the first, and the process continued until the bridge was secured to an abutment on the opposite shore.[1]

Beginning at 5:00 A.M., the 15th New York Engineers took a little over three hours to complete their bridge below Deep Run, two miles southeast of Fredericksburg. But just as the final balks were going into place, Rebel pickets opened fire, wounding six Federals. A battalion of Regulars from the U.S. Corps of Engineers was supposed to lay another bridge just south of this first span, but manhandling thirty boats down embankments to the water's edge delayed them until about 7:00 A.M. Two hours later the work party drew fire—and audible curses—from about a hundred of Hood's Texans. A Confederate major reportedly shouted, "You damned Yankees, go to hell." One bluecoat was wounded, and two others were taken prisoner before Federal artillery fire scattered the Rebs. By 11:00 A.M. the completed bridges awaited Franklin's infantry and artillery.[2]

Sumner's orders were to cross his grand division, march through Fredericksburg, and seize the high ground behind the town. Franklin was instructed to move down the "old Richmond Road, in the direction of the railroad" and attack the Confederates without waiting for Sumner to begin his assault. The Richmond Stage Road ran to Bowling Green and eventually to the Confederate capital, but not toward the railroad. Army maps, however, mislabeled a country lane branching off toward Hamilton's Crossing as "Road to Bowling Green."[3] So the long-awaited assault began with vague orders and cartographic confusion; indeed by this time Burnside himself was having second thoughts.

Franklin began crossing his infantry at 4:00 P.M., but Burnside now told him to send over only one brigade to guard the bridgeheads. With the 2nd Rhode Island acting as skirmishers, Brig. Gen. Charles Devens Jr.'s brigade from the Sixth Corps advanced toward the pontoons about sundown with fixed bayonets and grim determination. The men fell into step as a band began to play, but this set the bridges swaying dangerously. Until the music was ordered stopped, it seemed likely that men would be dumped into the icy water. Meanwhile Confederate skirmishers lurking behind a large haystack and swarming around the Bend—a two-story wooden house owned by prosperous slaveholder Alfred Bernard—began sniping at the Federals. A member of the 37th Massachusetts noticed how the men's faces turned "pale" as they first came under fire, but Union artillery and musket fire quickly scattered the Rebels. The bluecoats fanned out as they reached the western riverbank. Massachusetts troops who entered the Bernard house suddenly found themselves in unaccustomed luxury: artwork on the walls, fine carpets, a seven-foot mirror, a heavy rosewood bed, and a mahogany wardrobe. With the common soldiers' typical contempt for a wealthy Rebel's property, they grabbed flour and whiskey, tore down a barn, milked cows, and enjoyed fresh beef.[4]

Most of Franklin's men (and some of Hooker's as well) spent the day marching toward the pontoon crossings and waiting several hours in the mud before finally settling into cold bivouacs. Some officers used the time to deliver spread-eagle speeches, while soldiers hastily scribbled notes home.

A Michigan regiment fortunate enough to receive two months' pay arranged with the chaplain to send the money home before they crossed the river. With the cannonading upstream as backdrop (Federal artillery was pounding Confederate positions in town), they sat on their knapsacks "joking, laughing and eating crackers and pork," apparently little concerned about what lay ahead. It was the same elsewhere. "The men all seem cheerful and anxious to meet the rebels," a New Jersey recruit observed.[5]

Rolling up their blankets against the cold, soldiers drifted off to sleep. Men without fires stirred restlessly in the chill air or stomped about the camps trying to stay warm. Others huddled near the bluffs of the Rappahannock.[6] Of course the sometimes overpowering fear of death kept many men awake. During the "terrible suspense" of waiting, soldiers became helpless victims of their own vivid imaginations. "If a man's knees shake at all," a Maine recruit observed, "it is while marching the last mile toward the fight." Anticipation created an agonizing tension. Franklin's men could hardly expect an uneventful crossing on the morrow, what with the boom of heavy guns along Stafford Heights still in their ears and the certainty of something big happening only a mile or so upstream.[7]

While engineers working on the lower bridges had encountered only light resistance, all hell had broken loose in Fredericksburg itself. On the night of December 10, after surveying the crossing site near Chatham, Capt. Wesley Brainerd of the 50th New York Engineers had scribbled a note to his father. "To night the grand tragedy comes off. If I am killed and should this meet your eye, please accept it as my 'good bys,' remember me to all my friends and I beg of you to look after the interests of my Dear Wife and Little Daughter. And so, dear Father, Good bye."[8]

Brainerd stepped out of his tent at midnight, and by 3:00 A.M., undaunted by the bone-chilling fog and the thirty- to fifty-foot bluffs down which the captain's men had dragged the pontoons, both the 15th and 50th New York Engineers were at work on bridges—two at the upper end of town and one at the lower end (usually called the "middle bridge"). The men could make out the flickering campfires more than 400 yards away on the opposite bank but also noticed them being extinguished. Three hours later, with one of the upper bridges and the middle bridge about two-thirds complete and the other upper bridge about one-quarter finished, Confederate infantry suddenly began popping away at the engineers. The bullets struck lashers, chess carriers, and balk carriers, and a minié ball instantly killed Capt. Augustus Perkins of the 50th New York Engineers. Wounded soldiers flopped into the boats while others crawled back to safety. Four times crews ventured out to complete the bridges but came scurrying back, and by 10:00 A.M. the New

Alfred Waud, 50th [N.Y.] Engineers Building Pontoon Bridge at Fredericksburg
(Library of Congress)

Yorkers had suffered fifty casualties, including a seriously wounded Captain
Brainerd.[9]

Supporting infantry who berated the fainthearted engineers for retreating too quickly soon had to eat their words. General Woodbury led forty
volunteers from the 8th Connecticut onto one of the bridges, but after Confederate fire felled twenty or so, the rest beat a hasty retreat. Two supporting regiments in Hancock's division also suffered casualties near the upper
bridges.[10]

As some Federals had feared, Lee had been ready for them. Around
5:00 A.M. McLaws ordered two signal guns fired to alert Confederate troops
that the long-awaited battle was about to begin.[11] Lee of course had for some
time recognized that the commanding enemy artillery positions on Stafford
Heights meant that his army could not hold Fredericksburg if the Federals
chose to cross the Rappahannock there. Nor did he wish to shell the Yankee

divisions once they occupied the town. His strategy was to buy time: harass the bridge builders, delay the crossing, and allow Jackson's scattered brigades to reassemble while Longstreet's men re-deployed. Should Burnside choose to attack his strong defensive positions, so much the better.[12]

Longstreet's corps was stretched thinly along a secure defensive line. Maj. Gen. Richard H. Anderson's Division held the extreme left extending from Taylor's Hill to the Orange Plank Road. To his right, perched on Marye's Heights, stood Brig. Gen. Robert Ransom Jr.'s division. McLaws occupied Telegraph Hill (the site of Lee's headquarters and thereafter dubbed "Lee's Hill") on Ransom's right. Maj. Gen. George E. Pickett's and Maj. Gen. John B. Hood's Divisions were placed along the long ridge from McLaws's right to Hamilton's Crossing. Although the commanders were a curious mixture of personalities and abilities—from the stolid Anderson to the untested Ransom, from the steady McLaws to the flamboyant Pickett—there was no gainsaying the strength of their positions.[13]

Confederate batteries had been placed in rifle pits and behind log breastworks. Ammunition chests had been removed from the limbers and hidden behind the traverses. Because much of the digging had taken place in freezing temperatures and with tools in short supply, there was little protection in these relatively shallow works for either the ammunition or supporting infantry.[14] Even as the Federals were laying the bridges, Lee—up early as usual—was fiddling with gun placements and drafting last-minute instructions. He had no intention of engaging the enemy batteries on Stafford Heights, so Longstreet directed Rebel gunners to fire only at the pontoons and infantry attempting to cross, while his artillery chief Porter Alexander kept batteries well concealed behind houses and ridges.[15]

Given the layout of the town, Confederate artillery was virtually useless against the Federal engineers, so the job of harassing the Yanks fell to Brig. Gen. William E. Barksdale's Mississippi brigade of McLaws's Division. A onetime fire-breathing newspaper editor, Mexican War officer, Mississippi congressman, and ardent secessionist, Barksdale proved a brave and resourceful soldier whose stubborn aggressiveness perfectly suited Lee's needs. Establishing his headquarters on Princess Anne Street at the three-storied Market House, the town's commercial center, Barksdale stationed the 17th and 18th Mississippi along the riverbank from the upper part of town to a quarter-mile below Deep Run, holding the 13th and 21st Mississippi in reserve behind Marye's Heights. Once the shooting started, these regiments took supporting positions along Caroline Street, allowing for the movement of troops to any threatened point along the riverbank.

From the warehouses, shops, and houses along Water Street the Mississippians could fire at their enemies on the opposite shore or any body of troops trying to cross the river. Once across, however, Union forces could find shelter under the steep banks on the Fredericksburg side. Although an eventual Federal bridgehead could not be prevented, McLaws intended to make it as costly as possible. Barksdale's men were dug in along the riverbank behind dirt-filled barricades, and the rifle pits were connected to town cellars by protective "zigzags."[16]

Lt. Col. John Fiser, commanding the 17th Mississippi, warned off civilians living near the river when word came that the bridges were being constructed and deployed seven companies along the riverbank. Alert Mississippians had heard bridging material being hauled down from Stafford Heights but were under orders to keep quiet until the Yankees got closer. The fire they opened around 5:00 A.M. had a "stunning effect," according to Fiser. It drove the bridge builders back repeatedly, and the Federal guns hauled down to the riverbank accomplished little in the fog. Several companies from the 8th Florida had been detached from Anderson's Division to support Fiser on the left by firing from "point-blank range of the enemy above the [upper] bridge."

On the southern end of town the right wing of the 17th Mississippi along with several companies from Col. William H. Luse's 18th Mississippi lined the riverbank with sharpshooters and waited. The bridge builders "were working with the precision of clockwork," a sergeant later described the scene. "It was a beautiful but solemn and mournful sight; the dark forms of the pontoniers were dimly reflected through the fog in the rippling waters." Around 7:00 A.M. Rebel musketry drove the engineers from the bridge; according to Luse, Federal infantry support "broke ranks and were with difficulty rallied." A Richmond newspaper reported with some exaggeration that the Mississippians' fusillade had "filled the air with the legs, arms, and disjointed members of dead Yankees."[17]

Ironically, the Federal engineers might have considered this an accurate description of what had transpired. Despite the completion of the lower bridges, the operation as a whole had been disastrous. The burden of failure was pressing down on Burnside's shoulders. Up by 4:00 A.M., the Federal commander spent most of the day at his headquarters in the Phillips House, a recently abandoned, two-story brick Gothic Revival structure complete with elaborate furnishings (even indoor plumbing) located a mile east of the river on the higher shelf of Stafford Heights and offering a panoramic view of Fredericksburg. Burnside, however, hardly enjoyed the scene spread before him. Increasingly impatient and then furious as the Rebels thwarted the engineers, Burnside finally ordered his artillery chief, Brig. Gen. Henry J. Hunt, to "bring all your guns to bear upon the city and batter it down."[18]

A longtime McClellan supporter, the opinionated Hunt had undeniable tactical skills. Appalled by gunners who squandered ammunition, Hunt preached appropriate rates of fire at various distances. On the evening of December 10 he had placed his guns along a nearly five-mile line from above Falmouth to Pollock's Mill opposite the Confederate right flank. The daunting mission of these batteries was to "control the enemy's movements on the plain," to "reply to and silence" Confederate batteries along the high ground behind Fredericksburg, to "command the town," to protect the bridge builders and their supporting regiments, to cover troops crossing the pontoons, and to secure the army's somewhat vulnerable left flank. Hunt divided some 147 guns into four sections, each with several specific tasks. The early morning fog, however, thwarted Hunt's gunners. Even after the mist began to lift, heavy cannonading silenced Barksdale's sharpshooters only momentarily, and the Rebels quickly resumed their murderous fire on the pontoniers. Eyewitnesses testified to the deafening noise of the artillery fire (a Massachusetts recruit described it as louder than at Antietam—impressive if true) and its earth-shaking force. This early barrage, however, largely wasted ammunition, and the bridge building remained at a standstill. Hunt later claimed that he opposed Burnside's order to shell the town and considered such an action "barbarous," but no contemporary evidence supports his story. Given Hunt's own description of the artillery's mission, it is more likely that at the time he shared Burnside's angry impatience over an entire army being delayed by a few infantry regiments.[19]

The heavy fog was lifting at 12:30 P.M. as Hunt's men prepared, in the words of a section commander, to "open a rapid fire along the whole line, with the object of burning the town." The Yankee guns on Stafford Heights were soon hurling solid shot and shells into Fredericksburg. A second lieutenant in Battery A, 5th U.S. Artillery, reported that his four 20-pounder Parrotts got off nearly 500 rounds that day. Other outfits reported an average closer to 50 rounds per piece. The larger guns husbanded precious ammunition. With the town shrouded in haze and smoke, the 4.5-inch rifles of the 1st Connecticut Heavy Artillery in the left center section fired off a round every ten to fifteen minutes with what its commander guessed was "considerable effect."[20]

It was the most intense bombardment they had ever heard, several eyewitnesses reported. The great guns seemed to fire ever more rapidly, and men ran out of words to describe what they saw and heard.[21] They strained

Destruction in Fredericksburg (National Archives)

to recapture the frightening cacophony of so many cannon. "Talk of Jove's thunder," a Buckeye scribbled in his diary. "Had the ancients heard so frightful and so incessant a noise they would have sunk into the ground with terror." Others wrote of a "sharp" report or "deep thunder," of a "hissing, whizzing, whirring, screeching sound" as shots and shells of various sizes flew across the Rappahannock. A New York private noted the "loud purring" of the solid shot and "musical singing" of shells that together "made the grandest discord of sound I have ever heard." Some slaves in the area decided that "judgment day had come."[22]

It seemed so indeed for the town of Fredericksburg. Watching buildings collapse under the bombardment, a New Hampshire soldier thought the place was becoming "a hell." After two hours of intense artillery fire, entire blocks lay in ruins with only walls standing as stark reminders of what had once been homes or businesses; the elm trees in front of one fine mansion had been "pierced, torn, twisted or split asunder."[23] Solid shot turned many homes into what a Connecticut recruit aptly called "complete pepperboxes." Ninety-eight cannonballs had reportedly hit a single residence on Caroline Street. In one house a solid shot smashed a fine piano; in another a shell struck a child's playhouse, scattering toy dogs and dolls around the room. Hardly a building remained unscathed. The town had been knocked to pieces.[24]

The bombardment of Fredericksburg seemed to raise the war's barbarity to an ominously higher level. There was no sanctuary; nothing seemed sacred. Sighting their guns with precision, young artillerists even targeted houses of worship. Taking aim at the town clock in St. George's Episcopal Church, a two-story brick Romanesque structure on the east side of Princess Anne Street, Union gunners nicked the spire and sent one shell through a wall. A nearby Baptist church was hit a score or more times.[25]

For observers with an apocalyptic turn of mind, the sight of the church steeples poking above the fog and smoke was unnerving, and the outbreak of fires heightened the sense of judgment and doom. Watching the batteries flash in the gloaming, a member of the Irish Brigade saw a "sheet of flame" appear to engulf the town. Between twenty-five and forty buildings were badly burned, and later visitors noted blocks of charred ruins.[26] Oblivious to the noise and destruction, some veterans sat, ate, repeated stale camp jokes, or listened to a band playing "The Girl I Left Behind Me" over the racket. But most soldiers could not take their eyes off the artillery spectacle, the most engrossing sight they had seen for weeks.[27]

The destruction of what many Federals conceded had once been a charming town strained the power of language. The roaring cannon and sharp crack of small arms fire seemed almost beyond description. A New Jersey man wrote of a "tremendous rain of shot and shell," but this likely would have struck many soldiers as far too tepid. Words such as "magnificent" and "sublime" often appeared in diaries and letters. But many soldiers penned paragraphs and pages whose evocative powers still somehow fell short.[28] Part of the problem arose from a painful moral ambivalence. Many Union soldiers could not watch the bombardment of Fredericksburg with either awe or equanimity. The devastation of Rebel property might be easily justified or even welcomed, but the historical associations of the town with Washington and the founding of the republic also made its destruction profoundly sad. Some of the gunners and even spectators felt twinges of conscience. "There are many things connected with this war that seem hard for an enlightened and Christianized nation such as we claim to be," a New York volunteer confessed to his mother.[29]

Watching the cannonade, the Confederate high command seemed both fascinated and appalled. "These people delight to destroy the weak and those who can make no defense; it just suits them," Lee fumed. Yet even these words—harsh by the Virginian's usually genteel standards—exhibited a steely self-control. While the Federal artillery on Stafford Heights commanded the town, Lee still hoped "to damage them [the Union forces] yet." Such staunch determination filtered down in the ranks, though some men also expressed a fervent desire for bloody vengeance. Brig. Gen. Winfield

Scott Featherston instructed his brigade on the Confederate left to shoot the Federals just as they would a bear or squirrel and reckoned his boys could "whip the whole Yankee army."[30]

Barksdale's tenacious defense doubtless bolstered such confidence. Although the men of the 17th Mississippi thought the bombardment "the most terrific they were ever under," they held their positions—but not without a price. One private "had his brains splattered by a shot"; another was severely wounded by a bounding cannonball. Walls and chimneys came tumbling down, and falling bricks killed or severely injured several men. As Barksdale and his staff munched on hardtack dipped in honey—a rare treat—a Parrott shell fell in their midst. Although it did not explode, a piece of slate fell off a building and badly bruised the general.[31]

Even during the shelling Barksdale skillfully shifted various companies to shore up defenses along the riverbank. Most of the 8th Florida anchored the left wing of the 17th Mississippi until around 11:00 A.M., when a wall collapsed on its commander, Capt. David Lang. The regiment's performance suffered accordingly. Three companies (along with several others from the 21st Mississippi) were detached to support the right wing of the 17th Mississippi in its defense of the middle pontoon crossing along the wharves. The Floridians proved utterly worthless. Their new commander, Capt. William Baya, repeatedly disobeyed orders and refused to fire at the pontoniers for fear of attracting attention from Federal artillery. But who could blame these men for wanting to escape the firestorm? A courier in the 18th Mississippi had earnestly prayed that he not disgrace the family name by any cowardly act as he dodged shot and shell. He soon needed all the help the Lord could provide as he saw one fellow's head torn off by a shell and three other men fall wounded.[32]

Despite the intense cannonade, Barksdale's brigade stood firm. As the guns fell silent around 2:30 P.M., Yankee engineers scrambled out to complete their work, but again the Mississippians drove them back. Nine times Fiser's men had stopped the bridge builders, and even the usually impassive Lee beamed over each report of another repulse. Barksdale offered to help douse the fires ignited by Federal shells, but Longstreet told him, "You have enough to do to watch the Yankees." The Mississippians were of course doing much more: Barksdale bragged that he would present Marse Robert with "a bridge full of dead Yankees."[33]

Along Marye's Heights, Confederates cheered the stout resistance but watched the bombardment with horror, fascination, and awe. Porter Alexander claimed then and later that this was the greatest artillery barrage he ever witnessed. Lt. Edward Patterson of the 9th Alabama was at once aghast and enthralled by the sights and sounds: "Never before have I ever witnessed a scene of such terrible beauty. Or heard music so grand, at the same time so mournfully beautiful." After rambling on about "shrieking" shells, booming guns, and the flashes of fire from Stafford Heights, he finally despaired of recapturing the scene: "But why attempt a description of that which is indescribable? Words are too barren, they are powerless to convey to the mind a picture that can in any way compare with the reality."[34]

For the inhabitants of Fredericksburg, terror overwhelmed any sense of sublimity. For several weeks civilians had nervously watched for signs of Federal movements. "I have breathed under this roof," one woman had told a British reporter at the end of November, "living I cannot call it." But when the attack had not come immediately, refugees had drifted back to their homes. As the guns began booming on the morning of December 11, hapless civilians scrambled for their basements, and a few even crawled into wells or cisterns. Damp cellars, however, were not always safe havens. The local postmaster's house caught fire, forcing the family into the garden; they spent the day cowering behind a plank fence. In Jane Beale's house on Lewis Street, a Presbyterian minister led a frightened group in reciting the Twenty-seventh Psalm. Just as a 12-pound shot struck the building, they reached the verse "Though an host should encamp against me, my heart shall not fear."[35]

Maybe such piety had some effect, because the civilian death toll was amazingly small—probably no more than four people, two of each race and gender—but details on these casualties are sketchy. Rumors bespoke other deaths. On December 12 a New Jersey chaplain visited a man struck by a shell fragment and not expected to live. A Mississippi soldier heard that a fleeing mother had been killed by a shell, leaving her screaming baby covered in blood. Whether true or not such stories reaffirmed deeply held convictions about Yankee barbarism.[36]

The sight of more refugees fleeing from Fredericksburg—some from burning houses during the height of the bombardment—intensified Confederate outrage. As terrified civilians dodged falling shells, members of the Washington Artillery wagered whether one poor fellow would safely reach Marye's Heights. Men, women, and children escaped in whatever was available—ambulances, carriages, wagons, or carts—or they hurried along on foot toward the Confederate lines and safety. Some had no coats; others made do with what was handy. One woman wrapped herself in an ironing board cover for her flight along the Plank Road.[37]

Elderly people, many of them frail and ill, were finally driven from their homes and staggered along, sometimes carrying heavy bundles. But women and young children with little more than the proverbial clothes on their

David English Henderson, Departure from Fredericksburg before the
Bombardment *(Gettysburg National Military Park)*

backs presented the most heartrending sight and sure grist for Rebel propaganda. Many Confederate soldiers could vividly recall their wails and
piercing screams years later. Despite some embroidering, the *Richmond Daily
Examiner* described real suffering: small children, "their little blue feet tread-
ing painfully the frozen ground, blindly following their poor mothers who
knew as little as themselves where to seek food and shelter." The "distressing
sight" of women and children running from burning buildings even touched
the hearts of some Federal artillerists.[38]

Not many Confederates would have believed that a damned Yankee could
harbor any tender feelings. It was just like those black-hearted fiends to shell
a town filled with women and children. Recounting the horrible scenes,
many soldiers vowed vengeance. Some men gave the piercing Rebel yell as
women and children passed through their ranks. Others offered the poor
refugees their own meager rations. The news of the bombardment and exodus spread quickly. In a nearby county one young woman, eager for retribution, longed to hear that Philadelphia or New York or Boston was in flames.
Northern savages now warred against women and children, trumpeted the
Richmond press. "The most unprovoked and wanton exhibition of brutality

that has yet disgraced the Yankee army," declared the *Richmond Daily Dispatch.* "Modern Goths and Vandals," fumed the *Lynchburg Daily Virginian.* The women's nobility and stoicism (forgotten for the moment were their screams and cries) won universal praise. Watching refugees flee from the "vile fiends of Lincoln," a Georgia infantryman felt "proud" of "being able to render assistance to these unfortunate females."[39]

At least Barksdale's men had repulsed the Yankee engineers. Burnside was nearly beside himself when the bridge builders—even after the artillery barrage—still could not finish their work. He remained adamant that the pontoons had to be completed that day. Hunt and Woodbury finally suggested that volunteers cross the river in boats, establish a bridgehead, and drive the vexing Rebels out of town.[40]

The task of leading what was immediately dubbed a "forlorn hope" fell to the 7th Michigan (Col. Norman J. Hall's brigade, Howard's division), a veteran regiment already bloodied at Fair Oaks and Antietam. Led by Lt. Col. Henry Baxter (soon to be wounded during the crossing), around seventy men sprang from the riverbank willows and bushes, pushed three pontoon boats from shore, and jumped in. From Chatham, Clara Barton heard their voices echoing, "Row! Row!" as Barksdale's troops began plugging away once more. While a few reluctant members of the 50th New York Engineers rowed the boats, the Wolverines lay flat in the bottoms. Once they were out about 100 yards, the high bank on the Fredericksburg side afforded them some protection. Even before the boats had landed, men jumped out, splashed ashore, and began clambering up to Water Street to the left of the pontoon crossing.[41]

The Yankees quickly bagged some thirty prisoners. Barksdale's troops fell back to Caroline Street, where they stoutly resisted any further Federal advance. No longer able to hold his position, the general realigned his forces to contain the bridgeheads and control as many of the streets running toward the river as possible.[42]

Closely behind the 7th Michigan came the 19th Massachusetts, another veteran outfit in Hall's brigade. After landing, they deployed in houses along Water Street to the right of the pontoon crossing. Advancing toward Caroline Street, they came under a "shower of bullets" from Barksdale's men, who had squirreled themselves away in houses and cellars and behind barrels, boxes, and fences. Stout Confederate resistance exacted a high price for the advance. Company B lost ten of its thirty men in five minutes, and the regiment finally had to withdraw with heavy losses. The street fighting had proved especially nasty. One wounded Massachusetts private had reportedly been bayoneted seven times by Rebels, and a story later circulated that four of Barksdale's men had been "killed in cold blood by the Yankees." The Federals, now under orders to bayonet any Confederates found firing from a house, took few prisoners.[43] Although most soldiers still hesitated to carry out such edicts, the growing savagery of the war had immediate consequences for Fredericksburg. This brief but brutal fight seemed to unleash a new blood lust on both sides.

After the engineers resumed their work and with one upper bridge finally completed around 4:30 P.M., the remaining regiments in Hall's brigade started across. As the troops squeezed into a four-block area, Hall finally ordered the 20th Massachusetts, which because of confused orders had crossed the river in boats, to "clear the street leading from the bridge [Fauquier Street]" of Barksdale's men. These members of the famous Harvard Regiment, commanded by Capt. George N. Macy, proved equal to the task. The men scrambled up the riverbank and, as they moved toward Caroline Street in column by companies, suddenly came under intense fire. A Fredericksburg citizen dragooned into guiding the regiment through the streets fell dead at the first volley. Marching four abreast, the Massachusetts troops provided easy targets for Barksdale's concealed marksmen. Bluecoats "began dropping at every point," Pvt. Josiah Murphey recalled. He soon became one of the casualties. Turning to his left to fire down Caroline Street, nineteen-year-old Murphey was suddenly hit in the face, fell to the ground, and "cursed the whole southern confederacy from Virginia to the gulf of Mexico." But despite heavy losses, the Bay Staters forced their way into houses and drove Barksdale's weary soldiers out. When the regiment appeared temporarily stalled, Macy prodded his men with sulfurous oaths, which he did not hesitate to shower on the 7th Michigan when it refused to advance. Macy and the intrepid Capt. Henry L. Abbott, despite the growing darkness, mounting casualties, and milling confusion, kept re-forming their men and pushing them toward Princess Anne Street, where Barksdale had rallied most of his troops.[44]

But the regiment's losses were staggering. An advance of no more than fifty yards had cost more than 100 men, and altogether over a third of the 335 soldiers who had crossed the Rappahannock were now casualties. The streets, according to Lt. Henry Ropes, were "heaped with bodies." But cold numbers hardly convey the human price of battle. Company I, composed largely of sailors and fishermen from Nantucket Island, had suffered injuries ranging from superficial to mortal. Hit in the right big toe by a spent ball, lanky nineteen-year-old Pvt. James Barrett was in great pain. A minié ball had fractured the left knee of Pvt. Jacob G. Swain. Two days later the eighteen-year-old had his leg taken off at the lower third of the thigh; he would not survive a second amputation the following fall. Pvt. Albert C. Parker, a blue-eyed, sixteen-year-old shoemaker, took a bullet through his penis and suffered permanent disability. The good luck of others stood in striking contrast. Another shoemaker, twenty-one-year-old Pvt. George C. Pratt, reported sixteen bullet holes in his uniform but not a scratch on him. The officers noted what Macy termed "fearful" losses but also basked in praise for their conspicuous gallantry. Capt. Oliver Wendell Holmes Jr. doubted there was a better regiment in the entire Army of the Potomac.[45]

Barksdale's troops shared in both the encomiums and the blood: nearly 30 killed, some 150 wounded, and more than 60 taken prisoner or missing. The official tabulation of the numbers and names required over three tightly packed pages. But again such lists tell very little of the human story. "The Rebs lay thick along the fence just as they had fallen," a lieutenant in the 19th Massachusetts noted in his diary. "Killed by our round shot and shell. Some with heads off, others arms and legs off, and some mutilated in a horrible manner." Several Mississippians joined their Federal counterparts on the amputation tables. Cpl. J. W. Alexander of the 13th Mississippi lost both legs; Sgt. A. D. Sadley of the 21st Mississippi lost his right leg and his left foot. A member of the 17th Mississippi survived to mourn his brother, whose body soon lay in a "cold grave upon the banks of the Rappahannock." He recalled their childhood frolics and most of all their love. It was so hard to imagine losing a brother even with the assurance they would soon meet in a "better world."[46] For each of the dead, someone undoubtedly felt a similar grief because valor exacted such a high price.

But to Lee and his generals the price seemed worth paying. Barksdale's men had delayed the Federal crossing longer than anyone might have expected or even hoped. At the middle pontoon crossing the 18th Mississippi, despite some belated support from two other regiments in McLaws's Division, had to retire for fear of being flanked. Shortly after 3:15 P.M. 100 men from the 89th New York crossed the Rappahannock in four pontoon boats. Storming buildings in groups of twenty-five, by 4:00 P.M. they had cleared the lower part of Fredericksburg. In thirty minutes the middle bridge was complete. The New Yorkers gobbled up more than sixty prisoners, most of whom were from the ineffectual Florida companies deployed along the river.[47]

About 7:00 P.M. McLaws ordered the remnants of the Mississippi brigade withdrawn from Fredericksburg. According to Longstreet, Barksdale remained so "confident of his position that a second order was sent him before he would yield the field." Yet the collapse of his line in the lower part of town and the danger to his forces along Princess Anne Street posed by the repeated attacks of the bloodied but unbowed 20th Massachusetts made a retreat wise if not imperative. To bring his men back through the streets before dark, however, would have risked coming under deadly Federal artillery fire, so Barksdale's reluctance was understandable. The 21st Mississippi was assigned to cover the withdrawal, but when Lt. Lane Brandon learned from prisoners that one of his old Harvard classmates, Captain Abbott of the 20th Massachusetts, was leading a Yankee platoon, he kept counterattacking until he was finally placed under arrest for disobeying orders. All in all, Barksdale handled the retreat deftly, and soon his command was resting behind a stone wall at the base of Marye's Heights.[48]

At last Burnside had his bridges. At the Phillips House the prevailing assumption remained that the Army of the Potomac had finally stolen a march on Robert E. Lee. Burnside was pleased, reporting "very slight losses," the river spanned, and troops crossing. There were even plans for Haupt to rebuild the railroad bridge across the Rappahannock.[49]

The Federals appeared ready to strike a decisive blow. Realizing the necessity for prompt action, Halleck pressed for sending reinforcements into Fredericksburg during the night. Even as the 20th Massachusetts slugged it out with Barksdale's men in the streets of Fredericksburg, the rest of Hall's brigade was crossing the upper bridges. As these troops quickly moved to support their comrades engaged in the bloody street fighting, they came under Rebel artillery fire. Although the shelling produced lethal results, General Howard admonished some of the enlisted men that attempting to dodge projectiles was futile. But when a shell whizzed over the general's head, he instinctively ducked. This amused men in the 127th Pennsylvania who had just seen one of their officers struck down by a shell fragment and now mockingly repeated the general's advice. "Dodging appears to be natural," Howard good-naturedly conceded.[50]

The rest of Howard's men endured scattered Rebel artillery fire and helped drive the last of Barksdale's sharpshooters from several houses. At one street corner a Massachusetts volunteer counted at least fifteen dead bluecoats; other men noticed Rebel bodies lying in the streets.[51] Around 8:00 P.M. Col. Rush C. Hawkins's brigade from Burnside's old Ninth Corps tramped across the middle pontoon bridge. The boys cheered as they entered the lower part of Fredericksburg, and pickets fanned out onto the now eerily deserted streets. Ordered not to sleep, some soldiers began building fires.[52]

The Federals had secured the town, but Lee was satisfied, in fact more than satisfied. He had managed to delay the Federal crossing long enough for Jackson to bring in his dispersed divisions the next day. Moreover, Burnside seemed hell-bent on attacking the strongest defensive positions Lee's army had ever held. Each new report of more bluecoats coming over the bridges appeared to light his face with anticipation. Like the Federals, however, many of Lee's men had spent an uncomfortable day waiting. Some read old letters from families and sweethearts one last time, and most nervously anticipated what the next day might bring.[53]

They could hear the Federal troops crossing the bridges. Those men closest to the enemy in town dared not have fires on a night when temperatures again plummeted into the twenties. One picket in Brig. Gen. Joseph B. Kershaw's brigade froze to death, and many men stayed up all night just to keep warm. Other Rebels set several haystacks and fence rails afire. Wrapped in blankets and bedded down for the night on frozen ground, most could have echoed the words of a soldier on the extreme left of Lee's line: "We sleep on our arms tonight and expect bloody work tomorrow."[54]

As did the Federals on both sides of the Rappahannock. Like Franklin's men to the south, most of Sumner's troops had spent the day marching toward the river and then back, waiting in the mud, trying to sleep, writing letters, and talking. But thousands had also watched the engineers trying to bridge the Rappahannock, and the opening of Hunt's massive artillery barrage had sent hearts pounding. Inactivity and suspense were almost worse than advancing into line of battle, many said. Even as onlookers, they sometimes fell victim to a stray Rebel shot. After marching down to the Rappahannock in the midst of the bombardment, a Connecticut soldier recalled, his regiment doubled back to camp "in rather a sullen humor."[55]

The bluecoats also noticed ominous signs of what lay ahead. The sight of a wounded soldier lying on a sheet soaked with blood and being pulled along on an artillery caisson, his left side opened up and part of his arm torn off by a shot, suddenly brought a seventeen-year-old boy in the 12th Rhode Island face-to-face with mortal danger. He imagined himself being carried off the field while his loved ones at home fretted over his fate. Though loath to believe that their generals would order them to attack such stout defenses, many Union soldiers prepared to meet their maker. "If I could only feel that I was a Christian, I would go cheerfully," declared one Connecticut volunteer. He had tried to serve his country and his God but was painfully aware of his shortcomings. Most of his comrades, he suspected, were even less prepared to finish their life on earth.[56]

Sunset brought the day to a merciful close. The gathering darkness highlighted the flash of cannon, burning fuses arched across the dark sky, and bursting shells briefly illuminated the town. Some of the Yankees lost their bearings in the crowded streets. A sergeant and his squad of eleven men from the 127th Pennsylvania stumbled onto a Confederate patrol and were soon on their way to Libby Prison in Richmond. Meanwhile some of their comrades discovered more Rebel casualties in the second story of an old stone house; one poor fellow, severely wounded in the legs and slowly bleeding to death, begged the Pennsylvanians to finish him off. Many soldiers tried to escape these horrors by sleeping, but on both sides of the river the cold air and frozen ground made any rest fitful at best. Like the Confederates, some Federals simply paced about to keep their blood circulating.[57]

Church bells sounded during the night. Whether they were ominous portents or sources of familiar comfort depended on one's perspective. Badly weakened by loss of blood, Captain Brainerd sat on a chair in a large room of the Lacy House. All around him men cried, groaned, sank into sleep, or died. In Fredericksburg itself, Federals gathered in the streets, eating, drinking, smoking, and talking quietly about the battle to come. Although some would later claim that on this night they could see nothing but disaster ahead, at the time their opinions were mixed. A certain buoyant optimism had not entirely vanished from the Army of the Potomac. The men of the Irish Brigade, according to one witness, appeared to be in "excellent spirits" and welcomed rumors that other Federal armies were converging on Richmond and Petersburg from the east.[58] After all, Burnside had at last gotten troops across the river, and the campaign could proceed in earnest. The drive on the Confederate capital would now be launched. Lee, of course, had other ideas.

Order, counter-order, disorder
—Helmuth von Moltke

11 Orders

Military orders can range from general orders for an entire army to special orders for a particular unit or an individual soldier. There are written orders and verbal orders, orders followed and orders ignored, orders drafted, orders contemplated, and orders never considered. December 12 would be a day remembered for orders issued and orders not issued and much second-guessing about both.

With the pontoon bridges finally completed in the gathering darkness on December 11, Burnside decided not to risk pushing too many soldiers into the already crowded streets or onto the plain below the town. On the following day, then, he would still be positioning troops and not issuing orders for an attack.[1] Burnside had worked on his plans well into the night of December 11, but he was nevertheless up at 4:00 A.M. the next morning. He spent most of the day at the Phillips House conferring with generals and drafting instructions. Sumner was directed to move his men across the river according to his own best judgment. Despite advancing years, Sumner remained aggressive and watched the crossing closely, apparently longing to join the troops.[2]

At the foggy sunrise on December 12, Brig. Gen. William H. French's division (Second Corps) began crossing the uppermost bridge. An ominous hint of what lay ahead came in the taunt of a Confederate prisoner headed in the opposite direction on the bridge· "Never mind, Yanks, you chaps will ketch hell over there." Paying it little mind, French's men hurried through the streets to join Howard's regiments near the outskirts of town and suffered a few casualties from desultory Rebel artillery fire during the day.[3]

In three columns Hancock's division began crossing the second of the upper bridges around 8:00 A.M. Marching four abreast, they too took some casualties from Confederate shells. The appearance of a professional embalmer handing out business cards to members of the Irish Brigade as they stepped off the abutment hardly improved anyone's mood. The men's curses rang in the ears of this ghoulish entrepreneur as the division swung into line along Water Street to move up in support of Howard and French. Noticing a few dead Confederates, some of Hancock's troops marveled at how the bodies still looked so eerily fresh and natural. It would be a sad Christmas in Mississippi, a Pennsylvania officer commented. Even worse was the much clearer sight of the formidable Rebel defensive positions. A New Hampshire recruit predicted that when the order came to advance, they would move forward "knowing full well that death is there with open arms bidding them welcome." Not everybody was so glum. A captain in the Irish Brigade still believed that "certain victory waited this army" and said later he would have treated anyone who doubted this proposition with "scorn and contempt."[4]

Three divisions of the Ninth Corps crossed the middle bridge a bit later and fanned out into the lower sections of Fredericksburg. The endless ribbons of bluecoats moving toward the riverbank impressed those still waiting on the Falmouth side. This great host appeared as an irresistible juggernaut that would sweep the Rebels away. Yet neither this daunting spectacle nor the martial music nor the officers' speeches inspired some soldiers as much as more tangible stimulants. Troops of Brig. Gen. Samuel D. Sturgis's division were issued whiskey rations just before they reached the bridges. Because some of them would not touch liquor, the more avid tipplers quaffed more than their share and soon were, a Massachusetts lieutenant reported, "pretty well corned." One unsteady fellow nearly staggered into the Rappahannock as his regiment neared the pontoons.[5]

Given the difficulties of the preceding day and the crossing, the Federals had neither the inclination nor the opportunity to celebrate the successful occupation of Fredericksburg. Confederate artillery fire again erupted as the Ninth Corps crossed the middle bridge and occupied the lower part of town. A Michigan volunteer in Brig. Gen. William W. Burns's division had his head blown off, and one regiment apparently panicked when an exploding shell sent three men sprawling in the mud. Huddled along the riverbank to escape the fire, many new recruits got their first taste of real war. Their loud, laughing bravado hardly concealed their nervousness, one officer perceptively noted.[6]

To the south, as a brigade band jauntily played "Dixie," Franklin's infantry and some artillery moved across the bridges. By early afternoon two divisions were posted on either side of Deep Run, with one held in reserve. Oddly, Confederate artillery did not immediately open on these troops as they reached open ground toward the Richmond Stage Road. Nonetheless, intermittent fire during the afternoon and early evening kept many soldiers hugging the muddy ground. Col. Alfred T. A. Torbert reported that his brigade stationed near Deep Run was shelled "without effect," but that opinion depended on one's perspective. A solid shot came close to taking one colonel's head off, and even though many shells fell short, a dozen or so dead and seriously wounded men littered the ground.[7]

Once the Sixth Corps was across the river, Maj. Gen. John F. Reynolds's First Corps tramped over the bridges and into position by late afternoon. Officers again remarked on the general absence of Confederate artillery fire, but Lee would hardly unmask his guns, especially with Jackson's men still on the march. By the standards of Civil War battlefields, this was ideal ground for maneuvering, but positioning nearly 60,000 troops between the river and the Richmond Stage Road became increasingly difficult. According to soldiers in Meade's division, the movement of the bluecoats over the bridges had been slow, "something like molasses out of a jug."[8]

Gibbon's division fell into line behind the Richmond Stage Road to the Sixth Corps' immediate left; Meade held the ground between Gibbon's left and the river; behind him, Brig. Gen. Abner Doubleday's division stood in reserve. Although Gibbon and Meade had faced some Confederate fire, Doubleday's men attracted more attention perhaps because the fog had lifted by the time they came off the bridges. Few of the shells had much effect other than to goad inexperienced troops into some long-range picket shooting, a waste of ammunition unlikely to harm any Rebels, a member of the 2nd U.S. Sharpshooters condescendingly sniffed.[9]

But fate remained as fickle as ever. During the crossing several soldiers had tossed their playing cards onto the bridges or into the water. After all, the Lord would hardly bless an army bent on gambling, and provoking divine wrath on the eve of a great battle seemed foolhardy. As if to punctuate this thought, a solid shot from a Whitworth gun struck a knapsack and threw a deck of cards into the air. "Deal me a hand!" yelled some nearby soldiers.[10] From the common soldier's viewpoint, such portents loomed large and outweighed troop positions, officers' orders, or even the enemy's formidable defenses. By this time new uncertainties and fears had crowded out more hopeful thoughts.

★ ★ ★

An army plagued with doubts showed signs of cracking under the strain of impending combat. A general breakdown occurred almost as soon as the soldiers entered Fredericksburg. The aggressive foraging in northern Virginia had set the stage for a loosening of restraints in protecting enemy property. Frustrated veterans, hungry soldiers, and terrified boys on the eve of their first fight took out their frustrations on a now defenseless town. The businesses and homes of the city provided easy prey for enlisted men and likely a fair number of officers, too.

Beginning on the night of December 11 and intensifying into the following day, soldiers looted with an awesome, frightening alacrity and thoroughness. Second Corps troops broke into the Bank of Virginia and reportedly hauled away haversacks filled with banknotes. No business escaped the looters. Entering drugstores, they smashed bottles on the floors. In jewelry stores men stole as many watches as they could carry away (likely for later resale to the fellows back in camp) or donned cheap pins and brooches. Silver and jewels dating from Washington's day disappeared from the local Masonic lodge. The idea of holy ground or sacred objects had become for the time being irrelevant. The Episcopal church lost a four-piece communion set (it was returned after the war); a Connecticut volunteer caught one man carrying off a pulpit Bible.[11]

During this saturnalia of destruction, soldiers drew little distinction between public buildings and private dwellings. Compared to this reckless, unrestrained thievery, traditional foraging seemed like harmless fun. However much some Federals may have longed to have McClellan back, his punctilious attitude about protecting Rebel property was long gone. Officers commandeered private homes for their headquarters.[12]

Virtually any vacant dwelling became fair game for marauding troops. "The soldiers have free license for today and are happy in ransacking the houses of the wealthy for articles of value," a member of the provost guard told his parents. The men might pause over unusual books, paintings, or other artifacts, but they almost always hauled off more practical items such as food, clothing, musical instruments, and toys.[13]

Simple foraging ran a distinct second to wanton destruction, however, a task that some regiments performed with manic efficiency. Observers and participants alike vividly described the carnival of destruction. The more elaborate the furnishings, the more thorough the vandalism. Keys of an ornate piano were fingered briefly and then suddenly smashed with axes.

A small piece was slashed from a large Brussels carpet for use as a saddle blanket. Vases and statues were hurled into expensive mirrors, and cut-glass goblets were thrown through plate-glass windows. Vintage wine was spilled onto the ground. Soldiers even dumped out plain flour in their utter contempt for Confederates and their property, though relatively well-provisioned Yankees hardly had to worry about preserving what had become scarce commodities in the beleaguered Southland. Soldiers also invaded the deepest recesses of their enemies' private lives by slashing family portraits or ripping open beds with bayonets or rifling diaries and letters. To leave an unmistakable message, some men scrawled "damned Rebels" or what one termed "ribald verses on the walls."[14]

The looting turned many houses into veritable shambles. Once-gracious parlors were "strewn with . . . dirt and filth," noted an observant Hoosier, "and even ladies' clothing thrown in confusion or torn to pieces." Rare books lay tattered and torn on the floors of despoiled libraries. Piles of miscellaneous trash littered the corners of various rooms. Some members of the 19th Massachusetts, who had done such hard fighting the day before, filled their canteens with molasses and poured the goo all over one house.[15]

The Federals had turned Fredericksburg into a chaotic world where the functions of various private and public spaces seemed oddly if not obscenely confused. While the interiors of many homes became great trash heaps, expensive furniture was strewn in the streets. Looters lounged about on stuffed sofas or chairs, ate off fine china, drank from gold and silver cups, or even pounded on pianos al fresco. Men hauled out featherbeds to sleep under the heavens. The destruction spilled onto the streets. Furniture was smashed—one mahogany bureau was used for kindling—and old books became stepping-stones for muddy boots. All manner of household goods lay on sidewalks or in the streets. To the men of one New Hampshire regiment it seemed a "mighty whirlwind" had swept through Fredericksburg.[16]

The town became a bizarre mixture of the anomalous and the unexpected. Amidst the Rebel bodies still lying about and all the debris, soldiers also noticed dead cats and dogs that had been killed during the bombardment. Sometimes the indoor sights were downright macabre. In a house in the lower part of town a New Yorker enjoyed his evening meal of roasted chicken and jelly, his tin cup of scalding coffee resting on a dead Confederate. In the streets men reclined on expensive furniture while cooking up messes of slapjacks. For a while it must have seemed that the Army of the Potomac was holding a giant pancake supper. Men eagerly filled their haversacks with flour and soon had the frying pans sizzling. In their hungry haste to relieve the monotony of hardtack and salt pork, members of the 48th

Pennsylvania cooked up what turned out to be rather hard "Johnny Cakes" and then discovered that their "flour" was actually plaster of Paris. Amassa Kimball of the 15th Massachusetts, enjoying some honey with his meal, suddenly jumped up and shouted, "Jerusalem! I'm bit." He had left several beehives too close to the fire. In an instant his comrades were shedding their socks, pants, and even drawers.[17]

For many soldiers grabbing food seemed much more practical than hauling off valuable household goods that might easily be lost or have to be abandoned. A full belly was its own reward. "We are obliged to the secesh for potatoes & fresh meat for dinner," a young Minnesotan lightly remarked in his diary. Even in the poorer sections of town the soldiers scrounged poultry, pork, and corn. Unusual treats molasses, fish, sugar, tomatoes, cream, peaches, candy, preserves, ham, and pickles—merited appreciative comments in letters and diaries. Many years later a sergeant in Hancock's division recalled the delicious taste of pilfered lard spread over crackers.[18]

After stuffing themselves the men longed for a smoke or chaw, but like coffee in the Army of Northern Virginia, tobacco in the Army of the Potomac had often been a scarce item. Near the middle pontoon bridge, however, soldiers found scuttled tobacco and began hauling precious boxes up with ropes and iron hooks. A few impatiently dove into the icy water determined to retrieve their share.[19]

The discovery of alcohol in various homes and businesses brought even more smiles to campaign-weary faces. A Pennsylvanian in the Second Corps remembered the "congenial" warmth produced by his first-ever taste of whiskey. Emptying barrels of drugstore liquor into canteens and dumping or smashing bottles, the soldiers both struck a blow against the Rebels and looked to their own comfort. Adding to whiskey rations already issued to several regiments shortly before they crossed the bridges, some soldiers got roaring drunk. "Ah, General, let us sing and dance to-night; we will fight the better for it tomorrow," several carousers shouted at the pious and temperate O. O. Howard. The unconscious forms of unrestrained tipplers soon mingled with other debris on the streets. One scene was especially rich: a group of intoxicated Massachusetts soldiers, carrying a hapless goose and a black bottle (contents unidentified), chased a frightened pig and sang "I Dreamt I Dwelt in Marble Halls" as they staggered along Caroline Street and nearly ran into Confederate pickets.[20]

Drunkenness and the release from strict discipline it produced combined to spawn a kind of street theater. Twirling parasols and strolling through the streets in hoop skirts, wearing calico or silk dresses, bonnets stuck awkwardly on their heads, Burnside's brawny Yankees burlesqued the ideal of the "southern lady." Members of the street-fighting 19th Massachusetts must have especially enjoyed sauntering about aping the conventions of polite society: "Good evening, Mrs. Smith" and "How do you do this evening, Miss Jones?" After expropriating the extensive wardrobe of one Fredericksburg matron, a freshly recruited New York regiment held their own fashion show until their colonel dispersed them with a few blistering oaths, several no doubt ridiculing their supposed lack of manhood.[21]

Dress-wearing revelers played music on stolen fiddles and pianos to accompany the frolicking of "quadrilles and contra dances." Some of the dirtiest fellows in one regiment wore the "choicest silks," while their "partners" were attired with "long tail coats and plug hats." Exaggerated manners mocked the social affectations of southern aristocrats. "Between sets the ladies would sit on the curb-stones and the gentlemen would do the honors." Consumed by laughter, the cotillion's chronicler admitted he could not "do justice to the scene." In other parts of the city, men cavorted atop pianos. The merrymaking and drunken high jinks reached a culmination when members of the 20th Massachusetts hauled out an eighteenth-century family coach and hitched it to a mule. One man wearing the "mask of a negro" drove along Caroline Street while two of his comrades dressed as Confederate belles sat in the back seat "scattering smiles and kisses to an applauding crowd."[22] Great fun here, and no little emotional release, but inventive mockery also lay at the heart of such bizarre performances. What better way to puncture the pretensions of southern honor and humiliate those notorious "secesh females" than by having common soldiers cavort in women's clothes stolen from the wardrobes of Fredericksburg's leading families?

Amidst the vandalism and carnival, some men began picking up souvenirs. Appropriately enough, an officer in the Harvard Regiment grabbed editions of Plutarch and Byron along with a few children's books. Others preferred fancy silver goods. Many soldiers settled for small, insignificant items such as a glass ball, a crocheted baby's sock, and even a small piece of cloth scooped from the river. Almost anything might serve as a memento worth shipping home.[23]

Preserving and mailing what a Connecticut volunteer dubbed a "keepsake from rebeldom" could be difficult, though a surgeon in Hancock's division managed to send an entire box of "trophies" received from a patient. Soldiers who crossed the river later or were stationed in poorer parts of town often found slim pickings. Others refused to be encumbered with impedimenta right before going into battle, and of course many desirable items simply could not be carried off. A report of one man shipping a sewing machine home to his wife seemed implausible.[24]

Whether looting or destroying, the Yankees went about their work with frightful thoroughness, as if exacting Old Testament vengeance against their foes. "Our soldiery completely sacked . . . near every house," a Pennsylvanian proudly and matter-of-factly informed his hometown newspaper. A New Yorker admitted spending most of December 12 carrying off "every thing of value." Yet long lists of items smashed or pilfered hardly recaptured the atmosphere of a military horde unleashed on a nearly deserted town. "Ludicrous" and "disgraceful," one artillery lieutenant called scenes he had witnessed: "Everything that they could not eat or wear they destroyed in pure wantonness." A Massachusetts recruit noted, with considerable surprise, that some houses contained furnishings rivaling those of his native Boston. Much of Fredericksburg appeared gutted, mute witness to how relentlessly marauding troops had tried to destroy everything in their path.[25] Even if the soldiers' accounts exaggerated the damage, they also spoke volumes about changing attitudes on the nature of the war.

Many bluecoats relished the devastation. Their justifications fell into three broad categories: enjoyment, retaliation, and the nature of war. "We lived high," appeared often in diaries and letters. Even after the carnage on December 13, a New Hampshire volunteer confessed, "we kinded of hated to leave the city for I tell you we had a good time there." After the battle a few soldiers emphasized the pleasures rather than the horrors of their recent experience. They could still almost taste (or at least describe) the pilfered food, and perhaps for some these memories helped blot out darker recollections.[26]

The stout resistance of Barksdale's men and the scattered Confederate artillery fire also offered a convenient excuse for sacking the town. As a member of Burnside's headquarters guard put it, "The cursed Rebels brought it all on themselves by their own maddened folly." For those soldiers from godly homes whose families worried about the effects of army life on their moral character, a spirit of righteous vengeance might cover the proverbial multitude of sins. "Men who at home were modest and unassuming now seemed to be possessed with an insatiate desire to destroy everything in sight," one artillery officer noticed. An undeniable callousness held sway among men who continued to loot even while under fire and then joked about it.[27]

For folks back home who might question whether the bombardment and sack could be justified, Pvt. Roland E. Bowen had a terse response: "Mother you know but very little about War." Yet some civilians as well as many soldiers were by this time adjusting their beliefs about the character of war. The romantic ideals of the antebellum decades had not disappeared, but they were eroding, especially in the armies. Inured to violence and death, men developed a hardy toughness simply to survive. Bowen had watched hogs chewing on a Confederate corpse but was "too busy stealing to drive them away." "Such is War," he shrugged. This attitude could justify nearly anything, though even the extensive damage did not satisfy the more blood-thirsty. "I wish that we had burnt the whole of it [Fredericksburg] over their heads," a Connecticut volunteer informed his father.[28]

Such strong statements—not to mention the wrecked town—graphically illustrated how quickly discipline could break down and how easily "civilized" men turned into a mob. But not everyone admitted it. Despite overwhelming evidence, some Federals maintained at the time and years later that no wanton destruction occurred in Fredericksburg. General Couch made the preposterous claim that Federals had not damaged much property. Other officers writing to their families also minimized the pillaging, as did some northern newspapers. For years afterward soldiers either tried to draw fine distinctions between occasional looting and willful vandalism or claimed that stragglers and shirkers had been largely responsible.[29]

This is not to say that all (or even most) enlisted men looted or that all (or even most) officers looked the other way. In one house owned by a staunch Rebel who happened to be the brother-in-law of their commander, Brig. Gen. Alfred Sully, some Minnesotans safeguarded valuable portraits painted by the general's father, famous artist Thomas Sully. Homes used as officers' quarters suffered little damage; a few houses even received guards. During the heavy fighting on December 13 scattered cavalry and provost guards prevented looting. Provost General Patrick fumed over the breakdown in discipline and lashed out with his riding crop at one fellow caught carrying off a great load of carpeting and bedding. He sent one hapless group of officers with "Mantle Ornaments hanging at their saddles" back to Hooker's headquarters, though it is doubtful that Fighting Joe cared.[30]

A fair numbers of soldiers, who could hardly believe that the fortunes of war respected neither gender nor age, were appalled at what they had witnessed. For men who had grown up husbanding their resources and property, watching the wanton destruction of valuables and ordinary household items was almost more than they could stand. Children's toys scattered about in the wreckage especially unnerved family men. Others were distressed when looters cleaned their guns with ladies' silken gowns. Surgeons and even chaplains had reportedly joined the vandals. One volunteer believed the sack of Fredericksburg had been "done in a manner worthy of the Gothic of the Goths or the hungrish of the Huns."[31]

One Regular was especially disgusted that the pillaging had been carried out by the Army of the Potomac: "I am ashamed to be considered an officer belonging to it." Men shuddered to think that such wholesale devastation might be repeated elsewhere. Some soldiers naturally claimed that neither they nor their regiment had joined in the vandalism.[32] Perhaps guilty consciences masked the truth, but especially in the more sober aftermath of a great battle, men had a chance to ponder their behavior. Some did not like what they had discovered about their comrades or themselves.

Victims of the bombardment and sack neither philosophized nor analyzed the Federals' conduct; instead they inventoried their property. Estimates for household goods damaged or stolen ranged from a few to several thousand dollars per household. Citizens itemized missing furniture, crockery, silverware, clothing, sheets, books, and food. Nearly anything had been fair game. Emilie Caldwell had lost paintings, carpeting, wineglasses, sauce tureens, and a dressing gown; her list went on for two full pages. By contrast Lucy Southard counted up ordinary household items, including "every piece of clothing my [five] children had except what they had on." Several people claimed to have lost nearly everything. "I can tell you much better what they left, than what they destroyed," one man observed ruefully. Reports of the destruction plunged those civilians who had fled before the bombardment into even greater despair.[33]

Profound sadness often alternated with intense anger. In one widely circulated anecdote a Federal general solicitously offered a woman safe passage across the Rappahannock. Indignantly spurning the suggestion, she claimed to have "no more business beyond that river than a Yankee has in heaven." An equally feisty matron cheered on a group of Confederate artillerymen, "Give it to the d—d rascals, boys." Even respectable ladies might be excused for using strong language, but bravado could hardly conceal the growing realization that life would not get back to normal any time soon. Another sad fact, as a few civilians conceded, was that earlier Confederate occupations of Fredericksburg had also taken a toll, and now the Yankees had cleaned almost everyone out.[34]

Confederate soldiers, already sympathetic to the refugees, grew livid over the sack of Fredericksburg. "A monument to the barbarity of the abolitionists," fumed a young staff officer. Only "savages" would have destroyed the local YMCA library, one of Barksdale's men raged. Bitterness overflowed in words such as "Goths," "Vandals," and "scoundrels."[35]

These latest outrages reconfirmed stock Confederate images of Federal malevolence. Gruesome tales of civilian suffering immediately became staples of unofficial propaganda. Reporters and soldiers writing to the newspapers offered stock yarns of brave young women breathing patriotic fire against the cruel Yankees. Besides printing long lists of items destroyed, the press harped on the sightings of bluecoats accoutered in women's pilfered clothing. The Federals now seemed capable of the most heinous crimes, even stealing Bibles. Letter writers only hinted at even darker offenses, letting their readers' imaginations fill in the details. The Yankees had even desecrated the churches, claimed a member of the 7th South Carolina under the pseudonym "Stuart." They had "covered the walls with ribaldry and vulgarisms too obscene to be repeated." In a Georgia newspaper "Tivoli" reported that "all sorts of insulting and filthy deeds were performed in conspicuous places where they could not help but meet the eye and disgust the senses."[36]

Spirited editorials drew inflammatory conclusions. The pillage of Fredericksburg was the "most infamous crime ever perpetrated upon this continent," declared the usually temperate *Richmond Daily Dispatch.* The Federal army, showing its true character, had become little better than a "barbarous horde of Bedouin Arabs." The typical Yankee, the editor continued, was "a compound of cant, cunning, treachery, avarice, cruelty, and cowardice, mingled in such nice proportions that it is hard to tell which predominate." The semiofficial voice of the Davis administration, the *Richmond Daily Enquirer,* claimed that the "councils of Hell" summoning up "the worst spirits of the damned" could hardly have done more damage to helpless Fredericksburg than the "Union restoring Yankees." Even reasonably sophisticated readers came to believe the Federals capable of nearly any imaginable outrage.[37]

At the time it was easy to believe that the devastation of Fredericksburg had pushed the war to a new level of destructiveness and cruelty. Even some of the Federals conceded that a fearful precedent had been set. The meaning of noncombatant appeared to be in flux. However much they might condemn their enemies' wanton disregard for civilian lives and property, Confederates must also have wondered if this war would any longer be fought solely between the contending armies.

★ ★ ★

Those armies, however, now stood on the brink of combat. In the late afternoon of December 12, Burnside, still working to complete his battle plans, rode out with Franklin, Reynolds, and Smith to examine his lines south of Fredericksburg and get some sense of Confederate troop positions.[38] Franklin and the other generals proposed having the First and Sixth Corps launch a massive assault against Lee's right flank; they also pressed Burnside to bring two Third Corps divisions across to protect the bridges. This plan would have required considerable shifting of forces during the evening and into the night, and for the moment Burnside would not endorse it. He left

Franklin and the others with a promise to issue orders later and, after visiting other generals, returned to his own headquarters around midnight.[39]

Burnside's own thinking is difficult to reconstruct, but he must have realized that any element of surprise had been lost. More importantly, Lee had received precious time to summon Jackson's Division. He would be able to muster some 80,000 men against the Federals' 120,000. Despite the delays, however, Burnside still evidently hoped to seize part of the recently constructed military road at some point near Hamilton's Crossing, thus forcing the Confederates to abandon their defensive line. Unfortunately most of his top commanders were beginning to have serious doubts. Perhaps Burnside lacked the tenacity and strength of character necessary to push forward a battle plan in the face of obstacles and diversions.

Whether Lee had yet taken Burnside's measure is uncertain, but he seemed quietly confident as he reconnoitered the Confederation lines. To one anonymous observer the neatly dressed, sturdily erect Confederate chieftain appeared quite "calm and composed." His December 12 dispatches to the War Department matter-of-factly reported the crossing of enemy troops and then went on to other things, including suggestions on the transfer of forces along the Carolina coast.[40] His sangfroid was contagious. Longstreet shuffled brigades around, and McLaws, thoroughly familiar with the ground to his front, extended his lines below Marye's Heights. "We waited for the enemy with perfect calmness and with confidence in our ability to repel them," he later wrote. On the left of the Confederate line a lieutenant in Anderson's Division deemed the Rebel position unassailable: "It would be like murder to kill them [advancing Federals] in such a place."[41]

In several ways, however, the strength of the Confederate left could be a decidedly mixed blessing. After all, these formidable positions could just as easily deter as incite an attack. The real weakness of the Rebel defenses, as Lee and his generals recognized, was on the right toward Hamilton's Crossing. As the Federals tramped across the pontoons on the morning of December 12, Lee ordered up A. P. Hill from near the Yerby House to occupy the area being vacated by Hood between Deep Run and Hamilton's Crossing. Brig. Gen. William B. Taliaferro, commanding Stonewall's old division, would advance from Guiney Station in support of Hill.

Having arisen at 4:00 A.M., Jackson later joined Lee and Stuart in checking out the ground. About noon, at Lee's request, Jackson ordered Early, still at Skinker's Neck, and D. H. Hill, then guarding the river near Port Royal, to rejoin the rest of the corps. Jackson told D. H. Hill that he expected the real attack to fall on the right, and the prospect excited him. Watching the troops moving into line, Old Jack began to whistle—a rarity for that straitlaced commander and likely a sign of eagerness for combat. He seemed impatient and repeatedly dispatched couriers to check on the progress of Early and D. H. Hill. Guards placed along the approaches to Fredericksburg enforced Draconian orders against straggling. Surgeons would examine men claiming illness, and shirkers would be given a cavalry escort to the "first major-general whose command was going into the fight, to place them in [the] front and most exposed portion of his command." Although a few soldiers deserted and more than 500 men would be sent in under guard over the next two days, one of Jackson's staff officers attested that many soldiers were spoiling for a fight, convinced they could "trounce Mr. Lincoln's people well."[42]

Jackson's troops advancing toward Hamilton's Crossing were not necessarily looking forward to doing battle, however. A. P. Hill's men noticed surgeons scouting locations for field hospitals. To one of Hood's soldiers these arriving troops resembled a funeral procession. A lieutenant in Early's division tramping along in the cold and dark was saddened about heading into a slaughter pen with so many men unprepared to meet their maker. Thoughts of blood and death naturally oppressed many Rebels, but just as on the other side, putting up a brave front remained important. Pointing to women and children still leaving Fredericksburg, a member of Brig. Gen. James H. Lane's brigade shouted, "Look at that fellows. If that will not make a Southern man fight, what will?"[43]

Uncertainty about whether the rest of Stonewall's brigades would arrive in time caused some anxious moments. Early's division had to travel some fifteen miles, and because the orders were not received until late afternoon, the men would still be marching after midnight.[44] The orders for D. H. Hill arrived near sundown; his troops would have to travel roughly twenty miles over poor roads. "The march that night was one of the hardest I ever saw," a Tar Heel captain informed his father. The roads were "jammed with wagon trains & artillery some mired down, broken & capsized." Men trudged along cursing, stumbling into stragglers, losing their regiments, and then double-quicking to catch up. Many outfits did not reach their camps (a few miles from Hamilton's Crossing) until 3:00 A.M. on December 13. At best, soldiers caught an hour or two of sleep in the woods. A member of the Richmond Howitzers found the experience surreal: "Here an army ill-fed, ill-clothed, and worse paid, is rushing with a sort of frenzied delight towards . . . a terrible battle-field." But his amazement reflected the remarkable fact that morale in the Army of Northern Virginia remained high regardless of shortages and exposure. These men would fight, and eagerly at that.[45] Yet Lee and Jackson were still operating with an extremely thin margin of error.

As Franklin and other Federal generals clearly recognized, the Confederate right presented a tempting target, but Burnside had not struck quickly enough.

★ ★ ★

On the night of December 12, Rebels and Yankees speculated about these matters, worried about tomorrow, or tried not to think about it. After an unusually warm day the temperature fell into the thirties after sundown. One Confederate considered it a typical Virginia evening for that time of year: "enough frost in the atmosphere to make a glowing fire agreeable; enough to freeze the top crust of mud in the roads," though Kershaw later reported that with no fires permitted, one picket froze to death. Soldiers told stale camp jokes and laughed uproariously to cover their nervousness. Each man, however, had to find his own way to calm prebattle jitters. Alcohol might help, but even for officers whiskey was hard to come by. Stonewall Jackson wrapped himself in an overcoat and sat quietly reading his Bible.[46]

As for the Yankees, many of them had spent the day sacking the town, and the vandalism continued well into the evening. Consequently the Union forces experienced a much wider range of comfort and discomfort on the eve of battle. At one extreme Franklin and the staff officers from the First and Sixth Corps luxuriated at Mannsfield, a two-story Georgian house owned by wealthy slaveholder Arthur Bernard, whom General Reynolds had ordered arrested and shipped off to Aquia Landing. The house had fine paintings, a spacious library, and a well-furnished drawing room with a warm coal fire and nicely lit candelabras. "I for once thanked my stars that I was a staff officer," admitted Col. Charles Wainwright, chief of artillery for the First Corps.[47]

On the crowded streets of Fredericksburg few soldiers enjoyed such sumptuous accommodations. With fires generally forbidden, many men had only cold rations for supper. Amateur musicians continued to pound out tunes on pianos that had been dragged outdoors. Regimental bands occasionally chimed in with "Hail Columbia" or "The Star-Spangled Banner."[48]

The chilly night air penetrated to the bone as fog again lay heavily on the town. A Rhode Island corporal, praying the new day would come soon, recalled kicking the ground to keep the blood circulating in his toes. The unfortunates on picket duty crawled back to their bivouacs stiff from the dampness. Morning would find blankets frozen to the ground. A few horrified fellows discovered in dawn's light that they had slept among dead Rebels.[49] But whether in featherbeds or a hayloft; stretched out on a mattress, cornstalks, a brush heap, or fence boards; or lying in a gutter, many of the bone-tired men finally fell asleep. Some were even comfortable. Despite the mud and frost, a member of the Irish Brigade "slept as sound i think as ever i slept in my life." One hopeful Pennsylvanian was determined to dream of "onward to Richmond."[50]

Thinking kept many others awake. For soldiers going into their first fight, vague notions of combat derived from textbook accounts, romantic tales, and perhaps boyhood dreams of heroism had been at least partially dispelled by disillusioned veterans. Yet a striking contrast remained between soldiers eager for the fray and those who would go forward compelled only by absolute necessity.[51] Even inexperienced troops glancing toward the Confederate positions knew the next day's battle would be bloody. What would it cost to storm the Rebel batteries so menacingly visible on the high ground or the more concealed positions near Hamilton's Crossing? One Hoosier dreaded "rushing" toward a "slaughter pen"; a nameless private sardonically remarked to a Cincinnati reporter that the Johnnies had not minded the Federals getting into Fredericksburg but getting out would be an entirely different matter. If the Confederates still seemed unsure about their enemies' intentions, the Union forces remained equally uncertain and considerably more fearful about what lay ahead. Perhaps Lee had lured Burnside's troops across the Rappahannock and now planned to destroy them.[52]

Such general forebodings, however, gave way to a focused concern for the particular individual's fate. Getting "hit" was something most soldiers thought of on the eve of battle. Some would even dream about suffering a horrible wound. As a Connecticut volunteer mused, many men would die the next day, but the nagging question remained, "Will it be me?" Perhaps God would spare his life, and he could hope and trust that he might be permitted to return home someday. Yet he concluded his diary entry, "It may be the last time I shall write and if so will he who finds it please send this last token to my uncle." Some soldiers claimed to have premonitions about not surviving the morrow and instructed comrades about sending their effects to the home folks. After one doctor in the 55th New York repeatedly declared, "I am a dead man," an exasperated colonel ordered him to a hospital in the rear.[53]

As always, there were thoughts of home—thoughts that might not only calm nerves but also give the troops something to fight for. A fastidious New Jersey colonel told his wife what to do should he be wounded or killed, including details on the recovery and burial of his body. With such matters arranged, he could steel himself for the big fight. Other soldiers simply put up a brave front for their families. "You must not worry about me, Libbie," one of Howard's men advised his wife. "For you know I have been, as you say, lucky, thus far and I feel I shall continue to be." Whether this sounded cheerful or fatalistic was uncertain, but other soldiers sought more solid re-assurance. One devout volunteer whose parents were reportedly notorious swearers and drinkers gathered much of his company together for prayer. He was prepared to die and hoped that each comrade was ready to meet his maker.[54]

While his soldiers settled down for the night, General Burnside continued to prepare orders for the next day. At last he would carry out his attack, and maybe then he could escape the relentless political pressure or even prove to the McClellan faction his fitness for command. That those orders would consign many men to their deaths—a thought that had certainly crossed the minds of the soldiers in their chilly bivouacs—simply meant that those godly souls praying for the Almighty's protection had better do so even more fervently.

Am I not shot
With the self-same artillery?
—Richard Lovelace

12 Artillery

The fog lay thick across the valley of the Rappahannock once again on the morning of December 13; visibility was no better than fifty or sixty yards. Yanks and Rebs caught a few final minutes of sleep in the chilly thirty-degree weather. Burnside was up early, having slept no more than four hours and nearing the limits of physical endurance. At this critical juncture he was faltering and hardly exhibited the proper balance of flexibility and firmness necessary for directing a battle against a skillful foe on unfavorable ground.[1]

Still determined to seize the military road running along the Confederate lines and split Lee's army in two, Burnside hurriedly put finishing touches on a battle plan and drafted orders for the day before 6:00 A.M. He dispatched Brig. Gen. James A. Hardie with a rough pencil copy of the orders to Franklin's headquarters. Hardie, friendly with both McClellan and Hooker, had known Franklin at West Point, and perhaps that was why Burnside picked him for this assignment. How he may have interpreted Burnside's intentions as he wound his way toward the Rappahannock through mud and over frozen ground is unknown. Franklin had been impatiently expecting to receive word from headquarters ever since the preceding evening's conference with Burnside. Around midnight he had even dispatched an aide to the

Phillips House to hurry matters along. He sat up most of the night waiting for orders, but Hardie did not arrive at Mannsfield until around 7:30 A.M.[2]

The document Hardie delivered to Franklin was a model of imprecision: "Keep your whole command in position for a rapid movement down the old Richmond Road and . . . send out at once a division at least to pass below Smithfield, to seize if possible, the height near Captain Hamilton's on this side of the Massaponax, taking care to keep it well supported and its line of retreat open."[3] What exactly had Burnside ordered Franklin to do? Make an attack against Lee's right flank, or a mere diversion against Prospect Hill? Unfortunately, later self-serving testimony by Franklin, Burnside, and other generals, along with the vaguely worded orders themselves, hardly cleared up this question. Confusion about the local road system on various maps makes sorting out the truth even more difficult.[4]

In the meantime Sumner would attempt to capture Marye's Heights, and if both movements succeeded, the Confederates would likely "evacuate the whole ridge between these points." Two of Hooker's divisions would remain in the rear at the bridges to support Franklin, who was further instructed to "keep your whole command in readiness to move at once, as soon as the fog lifts." These last two points suggested that Burnside expected Franklin to be using most of his troops for the assault on Prospect Hill and in the movement down the Richmond Stage Road to flank the Rebel right.[5]

Unfortunately for Burnside, the force of the attack depended on Franklin's understanding and judgment, and that general had never shown much imagination or aggressiveness. Camp scuttlebutt claimed that Franklin, an old McClellan loyalist supposedly jealous of Burnside, might attempt to sabotage the battle plans. Such loose talk was hardly unusual in the Army of the Potomac, and how seriously it should be taken is far from clear. Yet one fact is indisputable: Franklin narrowly construed Burnside's instructions to mean that he was to conduct essentially a reconnaissance in force with at least one well-supported division. Other misinterpretations added to the confusion. Baldy Smith later claimed that his Sixth Corps could not have moved down the Richmond Stage Road without uncovering the bridges, but Burnside's order had clearly provided for the defense of these crossings. The word "seize" seemed to imply that the high ground near Hamilton's Crossing was undefended; "carry" would have been more consistent with normal military usage. Such ambiguities gave Franklin all the excuses he needed to proceed cautiously, indeed timidly. Although Franklin would later claim that the orders contradicted an understanding reached with Burnside the previous evening, by 7:40 he had already chosen a division to spearhead the attack. It is also likely that Franklin had lost faith in Burnside and that any assault against the Confederate right would be neither powerful nor well supported.[6]

With Jackson's final two divisions still moving into place on the morning of December 13, Lee's right flank was temporarily vulnerable, and Confederate writers have conceded that Burnside had an opportunity to strike a blow.[7] The thick fog prevented the Rebels from observing their opponents' opening moves, but they could hear "the indescribable buzz, like the distant and uncertain noise of bees, that so plainly tells the trained soldier that an army is going into line of battle."[8]

The wooded hills and the open plain broken up by small streams and poor roads chewed up by wartime traffic certainly favored the defenders. Burnside's only significant geographical advantage was Stafford Heights, the platform for his artillery. The Confederate lines along the range of hills behind the town ran from Taylor's Hill on the north near the dam above Falmouth to Marye's Heights behind Fredericksburg, then slightly southwest to Telegraph Hill (later called Lee's Hill), and finally to Prospect Hill near Hamilton's Crossing on the south. Although not especially imposing, these gentle slopes formed naturally strong defensive positions. South of Fredericksburg, Hazel Run and Deep Run broke up the riverside plain between Burnside's two grand divisions. This made mutual reinforcement between Franklin and Sumner difficult and essentially dictated separate (though it was hoped coordinated) assaults against the Confederates.[9]

At Fredericksburg, as in many battles, the ground itself would exert what Clausewitz termed a "decisive influence on the engagement." The terrain would shape the tactics of each side as well as the outcome of the battle. The plain and heights south of Fredericksburg had what Clausewitz considered the three characteristics that most affect the course of military operations: first, obstacles (some seemed slight but would nevertheless prove important) to the Federals approaching Jackson's lines; second, uneven ground along with the thick fog that impaired visibility (much more for Franklin than for Jackson); and finally, the excellent cover for both infantry and artillery offered by the Confederate positions.[10]

Franklin's troops would have to advance across open ground while exposed to battery fire. Even though the plain provided room for maneuvering, its features could impede any offensive thrust. The Richmond Stage Road ran roughly parallel to the river about three-quarters of a mile away. Mounded earth and ditches on both sides along with fences and scattered cedars made this thoroughfare, according to Franklin, "an exceedingly strong feature in the defense of the ground," but the hedgerows could slow any attacking force as well. To Franklin's front lay muddy fields of wheat and corn stubble traversed by drainage ditches. Beyond them, some 1,000 yards past the Richmond Stage Road, ran the tracks of the Richmond, Fredericksburg, and Potomac Railroad. The ground sloped gently down toward the roadbed, and at one point woods lapped across the tracks. On the other side of the railroad the ground rose gradually toward the wooded crest held by Jackson's troops.[11]

Around 35,000 Confederate infantry supported by fifty-four artillery pieces awaited Franklin's attack. Although mud on top of frozen ground, a shortage of tools, and the last-minute shifting of troops had prevented construction of gun pits or other defensive works, Jackson had approximately eleven men per yard—in military parlance a "deep formation." A. P. Hill's famous Light Division occupied the front line running from Deep Run nearly to Hamilton's Crossing. Two divisions formed a backup line: Brig. Gen. William B. Taliaferro's four brigades on the left, and Early's sleepy-eyed men on the right. Two brigades of Stuart's cavalry hovered on Jackson's right flank between Hamilton's Crossing and Massaponax Creek.[12]

The placement of artillery batteries presented several difficulties. Because Hill's line arced back and the high ground was wooded, it would be impossible to sweep the field of fire. On Prospect Hill Lt. Col. Reuben Lindsay Walker, a superb artillerist, commanded five batteries (fourteen guns). On Hill's left near Arthur Bernard's slave cabins, Capt. Greenlee Davidson had three more batteries (nine guns). About 200 yards to the right of Davidson and across the railroad tracks, Capt. John B. Brockenbrough placed an additional three batteries (twelve guns). This last group was in front of Hill's lines, close to the skirmishers. Eighteen guns from Stuart's horse artillery further protected the right flank.

Despite being thus favorably placed, the guns did not cover between 800 and 1,000 yards of Hill's front, according to the estimate of Jackson's artillery chief, Col. Stapleton Crutchfield. The guns could not oblique far enough right or left to defend the weak point in the center of Jackson's line. Although trees masked much of Jackson's artillery, they also limited maneuverability. In short, the nature of the terrain meant that Jackson could not effectively deploy more than a third of his artillery.[13]

One glaring weak point diminished the strength of Jackson's position. Hill had left a 600-yard gap between Lane's North Carolina brigade on the left and Brig. Gen. James J. Archer's mixed brigade of Alabamians, Georgians, and Tennesseans to the right. This ground, where the woods extended beyond the railroad, was swampy and covered with thick undergrowth. A brigade commanded by Brig. Gen. Maxcy Gregg stood more than a quarter-mile behind the gap.[14] Concerned about what he considered faulty deployment, Lane informed Hill, who apparently declined to station troops in such a marshy place, evidently relying instead on the uninviting ground to deter a Federal attack there.[15]

Hill, doubtless distracted by news of his oldest daughter's death from diphtheria and never known for meticulous defensive preparations, had been careless in positioning his troops. His official report made no comment on the gap between Lane and Archer. Even more mysterious is the lack of evidence about Hill's activities or even his whereabouts during the battle. Jackson's report tersely suggested that Hill had been responsible for the brigade alignment. By the time of the battle, however, the two generals had been embroiled in a nasty feud for over two months. Hill had recently referred to Jackson as "a crazy old Presbyterian fool." Candidly describing himself as a "porcupine—all bristles and all sticking out too," Hill had predicted that "the Almighty will get tired, helping Jackson after awhile, and then he'll get the damndest thrashing."[16] No evidence suggests that Hill was undermining Jackson at Fredericksburg, but he was clearly not up to par.

Sorting out Jackson's responsibility is equally difficult. Given the testy relationship, he probably had not conferred with Hill about the terrain. He had pressed for an attack on the Federals before the fog lifted, but Lee had demurred. Jackson's habitual aggressiveness was far less striking this morning than his appearance. The chronically rumpled Old Jack was once again wearing his new uniform—the recent gift from Stuart—and looked uncharacteristically dapper. His old fatigue cap had been replaced by a fine grayish-blue lieutenant general's hat resplendent with gold braid. Wherever Jackson went during the day, the bright new uniform elicited considerable amazement and not a few humorous jibes. So another tale became part of the Stonewall legend; in retrospect the sparkling new uniform dramatized the day's signal importance for the Confederacy. The eccentricities of great battle captains add to their mystique, and Jackson's oddities certainly burnished his reputation as a pious and fearsome fighter. Confederates in general had enormous faith in him, but on this morning the usually careful Jackson—reported to be praying as he rode along—may have overlooked the ominous gap in Hill's lines.[17]

★ ★ ★

The Federals would discover the breach soon enough. After mulling over Burnside's orders, Franklin gave Reynolds the go-ahead to launch the assault. Meade's division would lead the attack supported by Gibbon on the right with Doubleday protecting the left. Reynolds, a hard-bitten Regular army officer, commanded enormous respect from the volunteers as well as from his fellow officers. Even the ambitious Meade, who acknowledged a natural rivalry with his corps commander, considered him a fine soldier and good friend. Yet as with A. P. Hill's performance, Reynolds's role, too, remains murky. Apparently he spent much of the day on artillery details.[18]

Meade's division included the Pennsylvania Reserves along with a couple of newly recruited Keystone State regiments. The famous Pennsylvania Reserves—so designated because they had initially been militia regiments raised in excess of the state's quota of volunteers—were rugged, battle-toughened veterans, bloodied and depleted by hard fighting in the Seven Days, Second Bull Run, and Antietam campaigns. Meade, their commander and the senior division commander in the First Corps, had been angling for a corps command and blamed the McClellan clique for delaying it; in fact, he had even consulted with Hooker on the matter.[19] But for all his ambition and notorious temper, Meade shunned political intrigue and was a solid general, in many respects an excellent choice to lead the assault.

Unfortunately Meade was at best doubtful of success. He complained to Franklin that attacking with a single division would simply repeat the mistakes of Antietam, where piecemeal assaults had yielded little but heavy casualties. His division could take the heights, Meade believed, but could not hold them. Typically laconic, Franklin replied that these were Burnside's orders and they would have to be obeyed. As one staff officer later described it, "Meade went in by God and he went in like a gentleman." Franklin directed the division to advance from near Smithfield down a local farm lane directly toward the Confederate lines on Prospect Hill.[20]

With the fog beginning to lift, around 9:00 A.M. Meade's three brigades accompanied by artillery approached the Richmond Stage Road. Men unslung their knapsacks and began tearing away the hedgerows on both sides of the thoroughfare. Once across, they grabbed cedar branches to form makeshift bridges for artillery to pass over a drainage ditch. Col. William Sinclair's brigade led the way onto a slight crest facing the railroad, followed by Col. Albert Magilton's brigade 300 yards to the rear. Brig. Gen. Conrad Feger Jackson's brigade aligned perpendicular to Sinclair and Magilton protecting the left flank. It took nearly an hour to get these troops into position.[21]

Through the mist Lee, Jackson, Longstreet, and Stuart could now glimpse the Federal host. The advancing blue lines deeply impressed Confederate observers, who long afterward penned descriptions of fluttering flags, gleaming bayonets, and bright uniforms. Contemporary accounts used words such as "grand" and "magnificent"; one Tennessean described it as "one of the most imposing sights ever beheld on the American Continent." For Yankee and Rebel alike, the geography of Fredericksburg offered a remarkable panorama for viewing the battlefield, and many on both sides would comment about how unusual it was to watch so much of the fighting unfold.[22]

Observing the enemy's advance, Confederates on Telegraph Hill seemed entirely nonplussed. As usual, the stiff and earnest Jackson became an easy target for playful teasing. Longstreet asked him if all those lines of Yankees frightened him, but of course he received a deadly serious response: "Wait till they come a little nearer, and they shall either scare me or I'll scare them." Just to make sure that no one misunderstood, Jackson responded to a later jab from Longstreet, "Sir, we'll give them the bayonet." Old Jack then rode back along the lines, instructing artillery officers to reserve their fire until the enemy came within range. His fighting blood obviously up, Jackson remarked, "I am glad the Yankees are coming." He spoke with the assurance of a general not only holding a strong defensive position but also sure that God would safeguard the right. A firm belief in providence produced a calm resignation in many of Jackson's men also. "What my fate may be I know not," mapmaker Jedediah Hotchkiss mused in a hastily written letter to his wife. "I can only trust in a merciful God, whose favor has never forsaken me, and hope for his protection. May he grant us victory, and may it be the means of bringing peace to our distracted land."[23] So, too, the piety of some young artillery officers, rapidly becoming legends in the Army of Northern Virginia, would soon be tested.

The equally devout (albeit always playful) Stuart also enjoyed a grand view of the unfolding drama. One of his officers had seen Federal ambulance drivers and litter carriers marking with red and yellow flags old barns and various outbuildings for field hospitals. Stuart had placed Maj. John Pelham in charge of the eighteen guns on Jackson's right. Twenty-four years old, Pelham had not quite completed his West Point education when the war broke out. Slender, fair-haired, and blue-eyed, a veritable boy in appearance, Pelham had been nicknamed "Sallie" by fellow cadets. But he was a spirited and intrepid officer nonetheless. On this morning he had tied a red and blue striped necktie (a gift from a British observer) around his cap.[24]

Pelham's attitude was as audacious as his attire. He proposed hauling a gun or two well ahead of the advancing Federals and then pouring an enfilading fire into their flank. Stuart, no stranger to audacity, readily assented. Pelham promptly placed a 12-pounder Napoleon at the intersection of the Richmond Stage Road and a country road that ran northeast from Hamilton's Crossing. Pelham unlimbered in a shallow depression screened by cedar hedges. Meade's troops, though, were plainly visible to the Rebel artillerists less than 400 yards away. At 10:00 A.M. Pelham opened on the Federals with a solid shot.[25]

Nothing so terrorizes infantry as artillery fire from the flank and rear, and some bluecoats immediately hit the ground, their faces pressed against the muddy earth. Pvt. Joseph Pratt of the 1st Pennsylvania Reserves had been one of those fellows who always claimed to be having premonitions of death. Indeed, just that morning an officer had told him to stay back and guard the knapsacks. Right before Pelham opened fire, Pratt had decided to stick with his company. He took only a few steps before he was hit by a Rebel round. Pratt joked about the wound being "good for a month's furlough" but died a few days later. Meade's artillery, joined by the heavier guns across the river, quickly responded to the deadly enfilading fire, but without much effect because the Federals had trouble finding Pelham's lone gun. Some cannon on Stafford Heights could not be depressed far enough, while defective shells posed more danger to Yankee infantry than to the Rebels. On the other hand, a well-aimed Confederate round mowed down seven members of the 121st Pennsylvania, and one poor wretch was cut in half by a solid shot.[26]

Fully five Union batteries tried to zero in on the elusive Pelham. Stuart deployed skirmishers as well as Capt. John Esten Cooke with a Blakely rifle to support his intrepid artillerist. Pelham continued calmly directing the fire of his beleaguered Napoleon, instructing his men to hit the ground after each round. They began taking casualties, however, and Pelham soon had to help man the gun himself. Advancing Federal infantry and accurate artillery fire that broke the Blakely's axle and killed two gunners underscored the precariousness of his position. Stuart—on no less than three occasions—sent orders to withdraw, but only when the limbers were nearly empty did Pelham finally do so.[27]

Pelham's skillful maneuvering and rapid fire had not only delayed Meade but had also thoroughly shaken the Pennsylvanians. Later Federal reports claimed that the Union left had been enfiladed by an entire battery.[28] Pelham's daring against long odds made for a dramatic tale that Confederates never tired of retelling. Thus was born a legend shorn of the qualifications and complexities of the events themselves. Pelham had delayed the Federal assault for nearly an hour, which allowed D. H. Hill's weary troops more time to move into a supporting position in Jackson's rear. Yet Pelham may in fact (as even Lee perhaps believed) have opened prematurely on the advancing bluecoats. Given the natural strength of Jackson's lines, Franklin's caution, and the accumulation of Federal delays, his contribution to Confederate success that day has perhaps been exaggerated.

Any postmortem discussion over tactical fine points, however, is largely irrelevant. Pelham became the perfect Confederate hero, the dashing young officer who had stalled an entire division and several batteries with a single gun. (Confederates guessed that between a dozen and twenty Federal cannon had fired toward Pelham's position). Watching from his hilltop headquarters, Lee uttered the famous words that assured the Alabamian's place in the Confederate pantheon: "It is glorious to see such courage in one so young." In a dispatch to the War Department the next day, Lee dubbed his young artillerist "the gallant Pelham," a sobriquet that became permanently attached to him. That Stuart's cavalrymen, other artillerists, and some of Jackson's infantry had such a good view of this engagement helped spread Pelham's renown as an exemplary officer.[29] However inspiring to soldiers, civilians, and young people, the lessons drawn from Pelham's exploits were far from simple. The single-gun heroics overshadowed Federal tactical errors and obscured Union opportunities lost. More importantly, although Pelham's performance helped build esprit de corps, it also fostered an overconfidence apparent during and long after the battle of Fredericksburg. Ironically, Pelham's bravery and tactical skill could mislead the unwary. Federal advantages in every resource could not forever be overcome by gallant young officers whose ranks would grow ever thinner. Pelham himself, the prototype, would de dead in less than four months.

But for now his gallantry had disrupted the Federal plans. Not only had he held up Meade's advance, but his spirited attack would also keep Doubleday's division guarding the Federal left the entire day rather than supporting Meade and Gibbon—a signal accomplishment in itself. Reynolds ordered Doubleday to drive off the pesky Confederate cavalry; two batteries (assisted by the Regulars across the river) began shelling Stuart's troopers on the left flank. Doubleday then ordered the Iron Brigade to advance toward woods where Rebel cavalry had taken shelter.[30]

Led by the newly enlisted 24th Michigan on the left and the veteran 7th Wisconsin on the right, the troops moved forward. After one Michigan man had his head blown off by a Confederate shell and another lost an arm, the regiment wavered until Col. Henry A. Morrow steadied them by putting companies through the manual of arms. Both regiments stumbled into ravines and thick undergrowth in the woods but also managed to capture several disoriented Confederates and grab horses that the Rebels could ill afford to lose. A Maryland battery plunged ahead with the Federal infantry, making it still hotter for Pelham.[31]

With the threat to his left quelled for the moment, Meade swung Feger Jackson's brigade into line on Sinclair's left and trained several batteries toward Prospect Hill. Wainwright hurried more First Corps artillery forward to support Gibbon's advance on Meade's right. Reynolds ordered four batteries (eighteen guns in all) to shell the woods held by A. P. Hill's troops. Around 11:00 A.M. Yankee gunners, joined by others across the river, opened a nearly hour-long bombardment. It drew little response from the largely hidden Rebel guns more than 1,000 yards away. Meanwhile Meade's men still lay on the cold ground, which was now turning oozy. Smoke from the guns blew back over the troops and obscured the area leading down toward the railroad. The cruel chaos of battle had begun in earnest: a recruit from one of the new Pennsylvania regiments saw a horse shot in the head while still hitched to a caisson and another poor beast running to the rear dragging its entrails along the ground. Trails shattered and axles broke as recoiling guns slid around in the mud and hit frozen ground.[32]

Throughout the morning Federal artillery exacted a steady toll, dealing death bolts randomly, arbitrarily, and anonymously. Even what Lindsay Walker on Prospect Hill termed the earlier "desultory fire" had been bothersome. Battery commanders were forced to relocate their guns to avoid the enemy rounds. Two of Brockenbrough's pieces were brought back across the railroad tracks. One of the first shots had landed in the midst of Walker's group and killed Lt. James Ellett of the Crenshaw Artillery just as he was positioning his guns.[33]

Capt. David McIntosh, one of Walker's commanders, recalled the unpleasant experience of enduring this barrage: "The worst ordeal the soldier has to encounter is to lie still, and do nothing under heavy fire." But the orders that morning allowed no other course. Confederate guns were not to engage in a long-range artillery duel but instead wait until the infantry was in range (roughly 800 yards) before opening fire. Old Jack sat quietly on horseback, setting an example of courage for the troops while shells flew. As a sharpshooter's bullet passed between Jackson and his aide Lt. James Power Smith, Jackson coolly remarked, "Mr. Smith, had you not better go to the rear? They may shoot you!" A North Carolina major who saw Jackson riding along while the troops cheered wildly noticed how "his eyes seemed to be on fire, so eager was he for the fray." Not everybody, of course, shared Old Jack's enthusiasm. Soldiers who had bragged about how brave they would be in a fight suddenly turned pale; some lay flat on the ground; others crouched behind large trees. The latter tactic proved unwise. Several men were injured and at least one was killed by falling tree limbs snapped off by artillery shells.[34]

★ ★ ★

Yet as frightful as it was, the cannonade inflicted mostly accidental and incidental damage because the Federal gunners had not been able to sight their targets. Confederate batteries had hardly been disabled as Union infantry prepared to go forward once again. Reynolds instructed Meade to advance toward the woods (where troops crossed the railroad) and Gibbon to move forward on the right. Feger Jackson's and Sinclair's brigades comprised two-thirds of this assault line, and Gibbon's division supplied the other third. Brig. Gen. Nelson Taylor's brigade was in the lead, and the division's other two brigades were stacked up behind it. Under cover of slow artillery fire, the long blue line, 8,000 strong, crossed over a slight rise and began descending toward the railroad.[35]

With guns charged and lanyards drawn taught, Rebel artillerists tensed. "Minutes seemed like hours," one officer recalled. "One holds his breath and then breathes hard." As the first bluecoats approached a tree around 800 yards in front of Walker's batteries, the Confederates opened up with shells, spherical case (a projectile filled with shrapnel), and double-shotted canister. Pelham's fifteen guns, practically at right angles to the Federal line of advance, raked Meade's troops in a murderous crossfire. Stuart, moving about quickly directing fire, had several close calls but seemed oblivious to danger. Brockenbrough and Davidson also opened on Gibbon. All told, Jackson brought between forty and fifty guns to bear on the Federal infantry.[36]

Walker's guns, Jackson later reported, were "pouring such a storm of shot and shell into his [the enemy's] ranks as to cause him first to halt, then to waver, and at last to seek shelter by flight." The lines, savagely rent by the fire, staggered. Officers tried to close them up, but some bluecoats broke for the rear. Gibbon ordered his men to hit the ground, and Meade's brigade commanders followed suit. "Now the dogs of war are being let loose," one of the Pennsylvania Reserves melodramatically noted in his diary. "The rebs are throwing their rotten shells all around us, much to our discomfort." Other soldiers complained of enemy batteries hurling "railroad iron." Far in Gibbon's rear a Maine volunteer "hugged the ground for dear life" even as one of his comrades was killed by a spent cannonball.[37]

Not only in Reynolds's corps but in the Union army generally on this day the number of injuries and deaths caused by artillery fire would be unusually high. A Maine sergeant in Gibbon's division suffered a severe skull fracture from a shell fragment. Pieces of bone pressed down on his brain, causing partial paralysis, and he died a little more than a month after being hit. Rebel shells killed horses as well as men. Lt. John Simpson, commanding the 1st Pennsylvania Light Artillery, Battery A, lost so many animals that he had to conduct a "change of front" by hand.[38]

Confederate artillerists cheered as their projectiles plowed through the Union ranks. "Oh! It did me good to see the rascals run," exclaimed a South

Carolina gunner. The Yankees skedaddled like "frightened deer," a member of the Richmond Howitzers later told his mother. But the exaltation was tinged with sadness as well. Veterans had been on the receiving end of such a hailstorm before and knew they might well face the screaming shells themselves within minutes. Under such circumstances anger and awe did not always overwhelm ordinary human sympathies. Observing the carnage, one of Walker's men declared, "Lord be marsiful to their poor souls."[39] He might well have invoked a similar mercy for himself and his comrades who would need it soon enough.

In technical military terms the Federals responded with "counter-battery fire," but those who witnessed and survived this barrage would not have used such sterile language. Wainwright, with support from several Sixth Corps batteries, had between forty and fifty cannon working to silence the now unmasked Confederate guns. Capt. Frank Amsdun's Pennsylvanians, who would expend 348 case shot and 236 shells throughout the day, lobbed many of these rounds in Walker's direction. Several of the pieces fouled rapidly, while continuous recoil snapped two axles. Federal artillerists scored several direct hits on Confederate caissons, causing breathtaking explosions.

But the contest was hardly one-sided. The 2nd Maine battery still faced a "very galling" crossfire from Brockenbrough and Pelham. Reynolds, for a time, put a halt to counterfire toward the Hamilton's Crossing area because the rounds were passing so closely over Gibbon's infantry. Shells whooshed only a foot above their heads, a Massachusetts volunteer claimed, and one man was badly wounded in the hip by friendly fire. As Capt. James Hall was redirecting his guns, a Confederate solid shot passed between him and several officers, smashing and exploding a limber chest. Enraged, Hall dismounted, sighted one of the guns, and sent a shell whizzing toward Prospect Hill. In a startling display of marksmanship and luck, the return shot struck a Rebel caisson, evening the score.[40]

Hall then directed his fire toward Brockenbrough on the right with dramatic effect. Davidson had reportedly been slow to support Brockenbrough's beleaguered gunners, several of whom had been downed by artillery fire and Federal sharpshooters. Brockenbrough, one of his battery commanders, and several other officers were wounded. Broken axles, defective fuses, high casualties (among men and horses), and weak infantry support finally forced these batteries to pull back across the railroad.[41]

Near the Bernard slave cabins, Davidson's men were also pressed hard. The Rebels with their light pieces were no match for the Federals, who hammered them with shot and shell. Likewise plagued by poor ammunition and a broken axle, Davidson soon had four disabled cannon. Behind these guns the shells fell thick and fast among Pender's brigade. A Tar Heel captain raised his head just long enough to see a sergeant hit in the breast by an exploding shell that tore off the top of his head. The man dropped onto his hands and knees, and for at least a minute his brains "quivered" until he finally flopped on his face. Several others suffered mortal wounds.[42]

Dividing their attention between Federal artillery and the advancing infantry, Walker's gunners fought an uneven battle as the Union batteries pounded their position. So many horses were killed that Prospect Hill was quickly dubbed "Dead Horse Hill," but the human casualties were more appalling. The Pee Dee Artillery lost nearly twenty men. One gunner had some shrapnel go through his coat. A minié ball struck his ramrod, and a splinter grazed his head. A piece of shell struck the gun he was serving and knocked him to the ground. Another shell fragment barely missed a leg. Under this intense fire some men from Capt. Willie Pegram's section abandoned their guns. The diminutive but combative Pegram, however, wrapped himself in the battery flag and strode among the cannon rallying his men. An equally daring but fatalistic member of the Crenshaw Battery refused to take cover while under fire. "I'll be killed just as quick laying down as standing up," he told his comrades and proved something of a prophet when a bullet fatally pierced his heart.[43]

On the right of Jackson's lines, with the help of two more batteries sent by Crutchfield, Pelham kept up an enfilading fire against the Federals. The young major seemed to be everywhere, dashing among the cannon, according to one artillerist, like a "boy playing ball." Pelham jauntily promised to keep one of his men in the thick of the fight until he was killed. Well-aimed shells continued to scatter Yankee infantry to the "boisterous cheers and repeated huzzahs of [the] men."[44]

Determined to silence the pesky artillery on his left, Wainwright dispatched several batteries (mostly from Doubleday's division) to do the job. For a half-hour about fourteen Yankee guns concentrated on the Rebel batteries, a "fearful" exchange of fire, Wainwright claimed.[45] "You men stand killing better than any I ever saw," Pelham remarked to a lieutenant in the Rockbridge Artillery whose command was being hit hard. An exploding limber chest mortally wounded a few officers and disabled guns. Even Pelham reportedly took to his heels during the more deadly fireworks.[46]

By now the Confederates had lost eleven guns, three limbers, and a caisson. Those cannon still in working order hardly had enough horses. Losses included several capable battery commanders. But Rebel artillery had performed well, delaying Meade's assault and inflicting considerable damage and casualties on the Yankee batteries. Doubleday would be tied down protecting the Federal left for the rest of the day. General Franklin now brought up Brig. Gen. David B. Birney's Third Corps division to form a strong supporting line along the Richmond Stage Road.[47] With the attack on the left stymied, the timing of Burnside's battle plan had gone out of kilter.

The intermittent and sometimes intense artillery duel had left a lasting impression. "Such a scene at once terrific and sublime," wrote one Confederate, could only be compared to the "bombardment of Sebastopol." Had the fiends of hell been let loose in these furious barrages? As Federal shells landed among Early's men, a Georgia volunteer suddenly realized that an exploding shell could snuff out his life at any time, though "Providence ordered it otherwise."[48] Yet he and many other infantrymen on both sides would not have to wait long to find out whether they would survive through God's grace or just dumb luck.

*Go into emptiness, strike voids, bypass
what he defends, hit him where he does
not expect you.*
—Ts'ao Ts'ao

13 Breakthrough

With Confederate artillery apparently neutralized, the next steps seemed obvious: an advance through the fields and across the railroad tracks, then a charge up a hill and into the Rebel lines. But what reads like one great effort in a battle narrative was in reality much more halting and confused. Even well-drilled regiments—not to mention brigades—do not move as units. Soldiers themselves, mouths dry, breathing difficult, and a generally heavy feeling, were hardly the proverbial well-oiled cogs in a military machine. Men already nervous amidst smoke, noise, earth-shaking reverberations of the artillery duel, and the thud of sharpshooters' bullets against human flesh now prepared for the test of courage. Some yelled or cursed to relieve the tension. Meade jokingly suggested to Col. William McCandless of the 2nd Reserves that he might soon earn a brigadier's star. "More likely a wood overcoat," the colonel sardonically replied.[1]

At 1:00 P.M. Sinclair's brigade with Feger Jackson to the left and Magilton following began moving past the artillery and down toward the railroad. As the exhausted artillerists shouted at the infantry to do their duty, Meade came across one terrified soldier who remained immobile until whacked hard with the flat of the general's sword.[2] The man could easily catch up with his outfit because, from the first, this advance illustrated the differences between battles fought in textbooks, plans laid out on maps, and attacks by flesh-and-blood soldiers.

In the confusion Sinclair, only twenty-four years old and new to brigade command, apparently forgot about the 13th Reserves and left them behind with the artillery. The rest of his mud-spattered soldiers, along with Feger Jackson's and Magilton's troops, trudged through the marshy stubble fields, scrambling into or simply vaulting three ditches. Confederate infantry fire from the other side of the railroad and Rebel artillery rounds attended them the whole way. One member of Magilton's brigade considered this spot worse than the famous cornfield at Antietam.[3] Sinclair's men, heading directly into the gap between Lane and Archer, crossed the tracks and entered the woods with little trouble. But thick woods, mucky ground, and sheer terror were breaking up the formations; dense vegetation obscured the view on both sides; and regimental command was breaking down as men stumbled rather than surged forward.[4]

Slogging uphill through the undergrowth and expecting at any time to run into Rebels, Sinclair's men nevertheless had found the weak point in Jackson's line. But how could they exploit their good fortune? The difficult terrain played havoc with organization. "Regiments separated from brigades, and companies from regiments" amidst "all the confusion and disorder," Meade wrote later. This antiseptic description hardly recaptured the frightening disorder of this halting advance. Sinclair himself had been wounded crossing the railroad, and McCandless now "commanded" a brigade no longer functioning as a brigade.[5]

The 1st and 6th Reserves had already brushed aside one or two small groups of Confederates when they neared a line of stacked rifles. These belonged to Maxcy Gregg's brigade of South Carolinians. A bookish, fervent disunionist and capable general nearly fifty years old and rather deaf, Gregg had evidently overlooked the tactical importance of the gap between Lane and Archer or his brigade's potentially precarious position. Concern that his men might accidentally fire into retreating Confederates outweighed the possibility of charging Federals appearing in his front. To avoid casualties from friendly fire, Gregg had ordered his men to stack arms, and many huddled under trees to escape Federal artillery rounds. What one officer later described as a "dense forest mostly of small saplings" prevented both sides from seeing more than fifty yards in front of them. The Pennsylvanians first hit Orr's Rifles on the right of Gregg's line with a powerful volley. The South Carolinians returned fire, and soon the bullets were flying among the trees. Finally hearing the ruckus, Gregg rode over and loudly ordered the firing stopped. Officers barked out their commands: "Let the guns alone! Lie

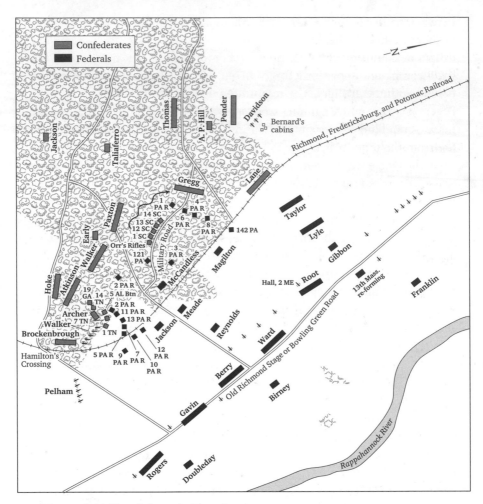

Meade's attack and breakthrough, December 13, noon–1:00 P.M.

down! Those are our men in front!" Arguments broke out among Gregg's troops about whether they were shooting at Yankees or Archer's pickets in retreat. Suddenly the Pennsylvanians overran the position, and the fighting became hand-to-hand. Gregg fell from his horse mortally wounded by a bullet in his spine. Now thrust into command, Col. Daniel H. Hamilton of the 1st South Carolina tried to save the brigade by throwing back his right wing to hold off the charging Federals.[6]

Meade's men were now astride the military road, and Burnside's objective of cleaving Lee's army in two appeared to be within their grasp. The South Carolinians could do little but hang on and wait for reinforcements. Together Orr's Rifles and the 1st South Carolina suffered nearly 250 casualties, with a heavy toll among the line officers. Although the situation appeared desperate, Stonewall Jackson's deep formation remained largely intact. The Pennsylvanians had been extremely lucky to overrun a brigade with only two regiments. The laggard 13th Reserves had eventually advanced up Prospect Hill, and after some meandering through the woods, the 2nd Reserves had reached the crest, where they now turned toward Archer's temptingly unsecured left flank. The rookie 121st Pennsylvania had not gotten far beyond the railroad.[7]

Without support Sinclair's men could neither maintain their position nor exploit the breakthrough. For a time, however, it appeared that the Federals would widen the gap and that more regiments would attain the crest of Prospect Hill. Not only had the Pennsylvanians swept past Archer's brigade; they now threatened to destroy it. Although "Little Gamecock" Archer had barely arrived from sick leave in Richmond to take command, he was a courageous, inspiring fighter. At the start of the Union assault Archer had instructed his troops to hold their fire until the enemy reached the railroad. He fretted about the gap in the Confederate line and about being outflanked, but his men peppered Feger Jackson's brigade with great effect. The "pop, pop, pop" of musketry fire had been "fearful," recalled a member of the 19th Georgia. Ironically this fusillade had forced some Federals to oblique into the lip of woods and thus right into the gap between the two Rebel brigades.[8]

But just as Archer's men were reveling in their apparent repulse of Meade's troops, all hell broke loose in the woods to their left. The 2nd Reserves and probably the 11th Reserves (one of Feger Jackson's outfits that had managed to cross the railroad) stumbled onto the Rebels' flank and began blasting away at the 19th Georgia from the left and rear. "They were slaughtered like sheep," claimed Adj. Evan M. Woodward of the 2nd Reserves, and for once such a cliché seemed both apt and accurate. The Pennsylvanians poured their fire directly into a shallow rifle pit, leaving the poor Georgians unable either to defend themselves or flee to safety.[9] After holding for about fifteen minutes, the Confederates "gave way," and men scurried off with their heads covered to avoid the flying lead. But soon the 7th Reserves were also shooting into the Rebels from the front. Caught in the deadly crossfire that also struck the 2nd Pennsylvania Reserves, the Georgians desperately tried to surrender. Only when Woodward waved his hat between the two sides, jumped down into the depression, and asked the Rebels to give up the fight did one of the Georgians shout back, "We will surrender if you will let us."[10] The surviving Georgians would be a skeleton force at best.

Thus the 14th Tennessee was left to defend the exposed left flank. After a bullet whizzed past one man's knee, he assumed it had come from a Confederate rifle and shouted for the "damned fools" to stop shooting; but he soon discovered that it was bluecoats hitting them from behind. Seeing Federals advancing through some small pines, Lt. Col. James W. Lockert ordered a retreat, later conceding that his troops "fell back in disorder."[11]

Officers and men in regiments on the brigade's right cursed these seeming cowards and reportedly fired into their fleeing comrades, but soon enough several companies in the 7th Tennessee also abandoned their position. Part of this regiment, however, along with the 1st Tennessee, stood its ground and fought until its ammunition was exhausted. Despite the severe wounding of several officers, these troops had stemmed the rout, but they would not be able to hold long without help. According to Archer's sobering arithmetic—and his bitterness was apparent even in his official report—the gap in A. P. Hill's line had cost the brigade nearly 250 killed or wounded and more than 150 missing (many captured).[12]

Having earlier absorbed the full fury of Archer's rifles, the men of Feger Jackson's brigade would have taken grim satisfaction in these numbers. Their commander was a bundle of contradictions. Born during the War of 1812, a Quaker who nevertheless had served in the militia, he volunteered in the Mexican War and enlisted again in July 1861. His Civil War record to date was spotty and slightly mysterious. Taken ill during the Second Bull Run campaign, his participation in the battles of South Mountain and Antietam is difficult to document. According to a Union nurse, Jackson was a "hard drinker and very profane"—not exactly a rarity in the Army of the Potomac. Yet there is no evidence that his reputed fondness for the bottle interfered with the performance of his duties.[13]

Certainly the task he faced early in the afternoon of December 13 might well have called for a stiff shot of commissary whiskey. Advancing to the left of Sinclair toward the Confederate position (with the 13th Reserves filling in the gap between the two brigades), Feger Jackson's men approached the railroad and laid down a heavy fire against Rebel skirmishers on the other side of the roadbed. Just as the Federals began crossing the tracks less than 200 yards away, Archer's men (right before the devastating assault on their own left flank) had unloosed several effective volleys. Fascinated and horrified, the Rebels watched scores of Pennsylvanians fall dead or wounded; those not hit appeared both confused and terrified. The 13th Reserves—the famous "Bucktails," known for their excellent marksmanship and deer tails on their caps—managed to reach the other side of the railroad, push into the woods, and even later support the attack on Archer's flank. But in the process they suffered horrendous casualties. Many of these Pennsylvanians scrambled for immediate shelter in the railroad cut and seemed "to melt away as did the mist of the morning before the sun," one member of the 14th Tennessee recalled.[14]

Unlike Sinclair men's, who had swept into the gap, Feger Jackson's troops made little headway. Coming under heavy fire, the 9th Reserves crowded behind a stone fence well short of the railroad. Separated from the rest of the brigade, they nevertheless managed to snipe away at Confederate artillerists. To their right the 10th and 12th Reserves hugged the railroad embankment while shooting at Archer's men. Some of the Pennsylvanians reportedly fired sixty or more rounds while taking a fair amount of punishment themselves. Watching from near the railroad, a frustrated Meade decided that Feger Jackson should move to the right and into the woods, but the young lieutenant delivering the orders took a fatal bullet in the chest. Another Confederate shot struck Feger Jackson's horse, throwing the general to the ground. As he attempted to lead his men on foot toward the woods, a bullet entered his skull above his right eye, killing him instantly. With their brigade commander dead, only the 5th and 11th Reserves managed to cross the railroad. Of all Meade's brigades, Feger Jackson's would accomplish the least, but it still paid a heavy price: 56 killed, 410 wounded, and 215 captured or missing.[15]

Despite breaching the Confederate line, Meade's assault was breaking up and losing its momentum. Sinclair's men had crossed the railroad, with the Second Brigade only 100 yards behind. Col. Albert Magilton, a classmate of Stonewall Jackson's at West Point and a veteran of the Seminole and Mexican wars, was also new to brigade command. As with Sinclair's and Feger Jackson's, his troops would not function as a brigade for long. Moving forward in tight formations, some of his troops got turned around as they came first under artillery fire and then withering musketry from Archer's brigade. After a brief rest on the railroad embankment and in the ditches, a sergeant in the 7th Reserves stirred them into action again. "Wide awake, fellows, let's give them hell," he hollered. The regiments attempted to charge, but they lost all organization in a mad dash for the woods and scurried for cover in the undergrowth. Companies stumbled forward almost blindly, either lacking or misunderstanding their orders. The 7th Reserves drifted to the left, came under fire, and gained some ground before joining the attack on Archer's left.[16]

After crossing the railroad, two of Magilton's regiments, the 3rd and 4th Reserves, followed Sinclair up Prospect Hill. Both headed toward the military road. The 3rd Reserves got within sight of the Rebel ambulance train and hospital tents but found themselves isolated and without support, vulnerable to a Confederate counterattack.[17]

Magilton's remaining regiments—the 8th Reserves and the 142nd Pennsylvania—advanced only a short distance before they were hit hard by Lane's North Carolinians. Three companies of the 142nd crossed the railroad and charged into the woods with a yell when "a terrific and most galling fire from the enemy's rifle-pits" staggered them. The Pennsylvanians returned fire, but Magilton ordered them to stop because he believed—wrongly as it turned out—that one of Sinclair's regiments lay ahead of them. This mistake contributed to the 250 casualties the regiment suffered in less than an hour of fighting. The 8th Reserves also lost nearly half their strength, and neither regiment had achieved very much. In his diary Sgt. Franklin Boyts of the 142nd recorded the theme of the day for Meade's division: "As we had no supports upon our flanks, we were forced to retire."[18]

Ironically, Lane's brigade itself, dishing out all this punishment on Magilton's two regiments, was in a precarious position. It could not stop other Federals—now clearly visible—sweeping beyond its right into the gap. Lane told Col. William Barbour of the 37th North Carolina to "hold his position as long as possible," and so three companies were pulled back at a right angle to protect the flank. Worrying about being turned, the Tar Heels kept up an intense fire against several of the Pennsylvania regiments. Little did they realize that the isolated and unsupported Yankees would soon be in even worse trouble.[19]

But Lane's regiments were surely in a tough spot. Unfortunately for the Tar Heels, the ground rose about fifty yards in front of the railroad, offering some protection for the 7th, 18th, and 33rd North Carolina but also preventing them from seeing any Federals advancing toward the lines. In the open and flat ground on Lane's right flank, the 28th and 37th North Carolina were vulnerable to artillery and small arms fire from several directions. These regiments would nearly exhaust their ammunition dealing with the threat to their flank.[20]

Yet more Federals were heading their way as Gibbon's brigades at last moved forward to support the Pennsylvania Reserves. Gibbon's baptismal experience leading a division was going to be rough. He had graduated from West Point in Burnside's class and later served in the Mexican and Seminole wars. A captain of artillery at the beginning of the war, he had quickly risen to the rank of brigadier general. Gibbon had ignored seniority in selecting brigade commanders and thereby ruffled several colonels' feathers. His oft-expressed contempt for volunteer officers and his exacting inspections

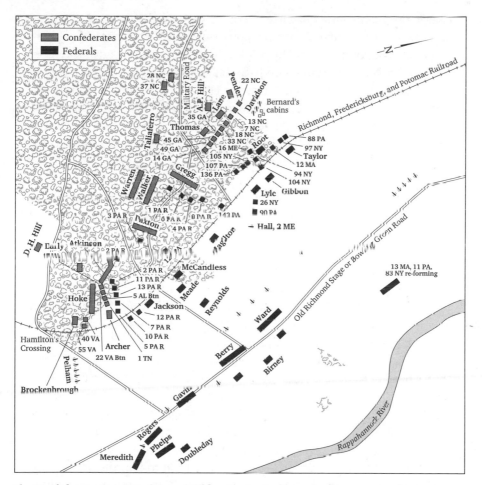

The Confederates stop Meade's and Gibbon's attacks, December 13, 1:00–2:00 P.M.

hardly made him a favorite. Yet Gibbon was a fine soldier of unquestioned courage and seemed well suited to work in tandem with Meade.[21]

Gibbon's troops had been up before dawn. In the early morning fog the men had stretched their stiff limbs and begun cursing even before breakfast. They had strolled about camp trying to get warm, gulping down hot coffee. After crossing the Richmond Stage Road, they had come under fire along the gently rising ground. They had lain in the mud, anxious to go forward as the cannon fire slackened around 1:00 P.M. Just as Meade's men were moving out, Brig. Gen. Nelson Taylor proposed a bayonet charge toward Lane's position. Gibbon said this would violate orders, and so the advance stalled for another half-hour. Meade later testified that Gibbon's officers failed to charge the enemy lines quickly enough, so perhaps the recent shake-up in brigade commands had yielded its poisonous fruit.[22]

In any case, by 1:30 P.M. Taylor's brigade had begun its advance under cover of rapid shellfire from two batteries Gibbon had ordered forward to within 200 yards of the woods. A recent Harvard law school graduate and Democratic politician, with his full beard Taylor nevertheless looked like the beau ideal of a Civil War general. Unfortunately his troops were already shaky. During the artillery barrage, when the 88th Pennsylvania on the brigade's right flank had moved forward to elevated ground, scores of men had abandoned the ranks and run suddenly to the rear in complete disarray. Only after one of Taylor's staff officers and a few of the regiment's own officers had stopped this "disgraceful and causeless retrograde movement" did these soldiers rejoin the brigade line.[23]

Ironically, however, during the attack itself these same Pennsylvanians, who along with the 97th New York enjoyed the advantage at least of being protected by the same small rise that shielded three of Lane's regiments, proved more stalwart than the outfits on Taylor's left wing. This was hardly surprising. The 11th Pennsylvania and 83rd New York had to advance over open ground under blistering fire from the 28th and 37th North Carolina. Three times the 11th Pennsylvania's colors drooped toward the ground. More than a third of its men, including its colonel, were hit in no more than thirty minutes of fighting. Casualties among the New Yorkers, including several officers felled by sharpshooters in the trees, matched those of the Pennsylvanians.[24] Here was a typical Union tale of Fredericksburg: two regiments blown off the field and two more pinned down and taking casualties.

When Gibbon ordered Col. Peter Lyle's brigade to join the attack, Taylor shifted the 88th Pennsylvania and 97th New York farther to the right to make room. Despite some uncertainty about Gibbon's exact orders, the line of six regiments crept toward the railroad. This time some of the bluecoats managed to ascend the slight hill and pour a destructive fire into the 33rd North Carolina, but as the Yanks came over the rise, the Tar Heels returned the favor. Both sides ran short of ammunition, growing frantic as they exhausted the standard sixty rounds. Displaying more valor than judgment, one intrepid private sat on the railroad tracks coolly firing at Lyle's men while an equally daring captain stood waving a cap to inspire his company. Lyle's troops held their position for nearly half an hour, but after they expended nearly every bullet, the 90th Pennsylvania and 26th New York were forced to lie down.[25]

The attack sputtered to a halt. Even though his men had thus far failed even to cross the railroad and he risked committing the classic blunder of reinforcing failure, Gibbon decided to commit the rest of his troops to the assault. Around 1:45 P M he ordered Col. Adrian R. Root to bring up the First Brigade. With three regiments (107th Pennsylvania, 105th New York, and 16th Maine) leading and two regiments (94th and 104th New York) stacked behind the New Englanders, the troops moved smartly across a plowed field and through the shattered remnants of Taylor's and Lyle's brigades. Once they were under heavy artillery and rifle fire, their pace slowed to a crawl. Contrary to orders, many men halted to return fire. Root cobbled together a line from regiments that had held their ground during earlier assaults.[26]

Spearheading the attack, the 16th Maine advanced the farthest and suffered the most casualties in the division. Already reduced by exposure and hard marching to a mere 427 men, this rookie regiment acquitted itself well in its first big fight. After exchanging fire with Lane's troops along the railroad, the men plunged ahead, driving a wedge between the 28th and 37th North Carolina. They encountered desperate resistance, vicious hand-to-hand combat with musket butts and bayonets. Out of ammunition, some of the Tar Heels hurled empty rifles—bayonets fixed—like harpoons. Not a few of the Maine soldiers seemed driven by a strange blood lust as they waded into the North Carolinians. One of them skewered a Rebel whom he accused of killing his brother. In the midst of this chaos Root's brigade steadily gained ground. However, a deadly volley from the 33rd North Carolina, before it withdrew back into the woods, slowed the advance. On the left of Lane's brigade the 7th and 18th North Carolina also pulled back at least fifty yards, and there the re-formed line held.[27]

To the left of the 16th Maine, the 105th New York and on their right the 12th Massachusetts advanced far enough to enter the woods and capture some prisoners. But like so many other outfits, they ran out of cartridges and received little support.[28] On the heels of the 16th Maine, the 94th New York (with the 104th New York close behind) joined the bayonet charge against Lane's position. Near the railroad, however, the New Yorkers became tangled up, and though they managed to enter the woods, they were soon stymied by confused orders. One company in the 104th lost more than a third of its men during this brief advance. "A battlefield is an awful scene," one private told his home folks. "No tongue nor pen can fully describe the horrors."[29] On both flanks the regiments in Root's makeshift line quickly became isolated. To the left the men of the 107th Pennsylvania had advanced enthusiastically but could not hold their position. Seven soldiers "showed the white feather," the adjutant later admitted; this regiment, too, lost nearly a third of its strength in casualties. Still further to the left, the 136th Pennsylvania found itself alone in the woods running out of ammunition. On the brigade's far right the 88th Pennsylvania charged against Lane's flank but was left behind as other regiments withdrew across the railroad.[30]

Coordinating Gibbon's advance with Meade's attack had failed. Gibbon's division had forced Lane's men back in fierce but uneven and disorganized attacks. The movement into the woods had soon degenerated into bloody and chaotic small-unit actions that accomplished little aside from amassing casualties. To be sure, some of Meade's men had poured through the gap in the Confederate line, and Gibbon's troops had made some progress against the North Carolinians, but unsupported, these positions could not be held or initial success exploited.[31]

★　★　★

Ironically, several Confederate regiments faced similar problems defending their weakened lines and launching counterattacks. Col. John M. Brockenbrough moved his brigade to the left in response to Archer's desperate pleas. The 47th Virginia and 22nd Virginia Battalion bolstered the embattled 1st Tennessee and 5th Alabama Battalion still desperately holding out against the Federal onslaught that had shattered Archer's left. Closing to within sixty yards of the Federals, the Virginians drove the Yankees back toward the railroad ("an enfilading fire that swept us down with murderous accuracy and compelled us to retire," wrote a Pennsylvania colonel), but Brockenbrough's other two regiments—the 40th and 55th Virginia—fell behind in the woods.[32]

Fortunately for Archer's forces, however, more help was on the way. Posted behind Walker's guns and Brockenbrough's infantry in thick woods, Early's division had seen little of the fighting. A messenger from Archer pleaded for reinforcements just as an order came from Jackson to hold the division in readiness to move toward the railroad near Hamilton's Crossing. Despite his gray hair and rheumatic body, the irascible and profane Early was an aggressive and able general. He hesitated but slightly. Word arriving from an artillery officer that large numbers of Yankees had swept into the "awful gulf" between Lane and Archer dispelled any indecision. It took a bold (or foolhardy) man to ignore a direct order from Stonewall Jackson, but about 1:30 P.M. Early sent Col. Edward N. Atkinson's Georgians off to rescue Archer.[33]

Five of the brigade's six regiments—for some reason the 13th Georgia failed to move—advanced about 250 yards, rending the air with Rebel yells. Crashing into the Pennsylvanians who had been making things so hot for Archer, they pushed the Yankees back toward the railroad. Some Confederates charged with less élan than others. A strapping conscript in the 60th

Georgia cowered behind a tree until Col. W. H. Stiles ordered him up. The man then fell backward shouting, "Lord receive my spirit." "The Lord wouldn't receive the spirit of such an infernal coward," Stiles sputtered. At that the soldier leaped up yelling, "Ain't I killed? The Lord be praised," and dashed forward, musket in hand. His cheering comrades had by this time wound their way through the trees toward the railroad and the copse of woods on the other side. Their biggest problem now was exposure to a possible Federal counterattack. Although Atkinson's men were hit by Union artillery as they emerged from the woods and neared the railroad, the Georgians did not stop.[34]

Early sent Col. James A. Walker's brigade around Atkinson's left to drive the Federals out of the gap and relieve the pressure on Lane's North Carolinians. Passing through another Confederate brigade, Walker's troops ran into remnants of Meade's attacking force and pushed them back toward the railroad. "The Rebels and our men were all mixed up together," wrote a member of the 1st Reserves. "I did not know whether I could even get out alive or not." Untouched by enemy bullets, a private in the 142nd Pennsylvania got torn up by blackberry bushes in his haste to escape. Although Walker had routed the Yankees to his front, he also realized the danger to his left from a couple of Gibbon's stray regiments that had remained on the other side of the tracks, so he halted his men and drew back the 13th Virginia to protect the flank.[35]

In fact, Hill's lines remained vulnerable. Early therefore dispatched Col. Robert F. Hoke's brigade to shore up Archer's right. As some of Hoke's troops passed through the remnants of Gregg's South Carolinians, the mortally wounded Gregg, braced against a tree, waved them toward the enemy with his cap. The Federals continued to cheer, with more bravado than confidence, even as Hoke's brigade drove them toward the railroad. "The yanks showed their backs," one Georgian exulted.[36]

Meade was furious. His initially successful attack was faltering for lack of support. A ball passing through his slouch hat did not lessen his anger, most of which was directed toward Brig. Gen. David Birney, whose Third Corps division was supposed to be supporting the attack. A Philadelphia lawyer of sturdy abolitionist stock, Birney thus far sported a lackluster war record. At 11:20 on the morning of the attack, Brig. Gen. George Stoneman, commanding the Third Corps in Hooker's Grand Division, ordered Birney to cross the Rappahannock. Subsequently Reynolds sent the division forward to help Meade. Several advance regiments, coming under heavy Confederate artillery fire, fell back to the Richmond Stage Road.[37]

Meade dispatched, by his reckoning, three separate pleas to Birney for assistance. It never came. The tangled command structure, especially the extra layer of bureaucracy created by the grand divisions, along with poor communications and timid generalship all contributed to the mess. Stoneman was Birney's immediate superior, but Birney had been instructed to follow Reynolds's orders, not Meade's. He later claimed that he had thought Meade's attack was "a mere feint, a diversion," but his punctilio would cost precious lives.[38]

After two unanswered requests for assistance, Meade galloped to the rear, hell-bent on finding Birney. Meade tore into the hapless brigadier with a ferocity that nearly defied description. According to one lieutenant, Meade's profanity "almost makes the stones creep." Birney lamely claimed to be awaiting new orders from Franklin, but this explanation did nothing to ease the situation. "General, I assume the authority of ordering you up to the relief of my men," Meade thundered. But even as the division advanced belatedly to assist the retreating Pennsylvanians, Meade continued to storm. Cornering Reynolds later in the afternoon, he exploded, "My God, General Reynolds, did they think my division could whip Lee's whole army?"[39]

Meade harped on the matter for weeks after the battle. Franklin had not understood the importance of the attack, he thought, but obviously neither had Reynolds. "The slightest straw would have kept the tide in our favor," Meade told his wife. Personal loss exacerbated Meade's distress. His beloved aide Arthur Dehon had been shot through the heart as he delivered instructions to Feger Jackson shortly before Jackson himself fell mortally wounded.[40]

The usually sterile official reports barely concealed the anger of Meade's men. "I cannot close," Col. Robert Anderson of the 9th Reserves wrote, "without expressing the conviction that had we been promptly supported, that portion of the field gained by the valor of our troops could and would have been held against any force that the enemy would have been able to throw against us." This assertion ignored both the difficulty of winning any decisive advantage in wooded terrain and the inherent strength of Stonewall Jackson's lines, but it quickly became an article of faith among many Federals and even some Confederates. Similar might-have-beens also appeared in letters to small-town newspapers, and later conversations with Rebel officers reinforced the Federals' conviction that a well-coordinated attack could have carried the position and won the day.[41]

Persistent recriminations and Meade's fulminations aside, the real issue and the genuine tragedy was, of course, the casualties. "You can hardly call it a battel it was more like a Butcher Shop then any thing els," a badly shaken color-bearer from the 7th Reserves told his father. By the time Meade's men had recrossed the railroad and reached comparative safety, the killed, wounded, or missing numbered at least a third of the division. Ten of the fifteen regiments suffered more than 100 casualties. Hardest hit was the 13th Reserves: it lost 161 soldiers in two hours of fighting. The gross statistics did not concern most soldiers. Their world revolved around their company, the boys with whom they had marched, laughed, griped, suffered, and fought. A private in Company G of the devastated 11th Reserves discovered that 24 of 30 men in his outfit had been wounded; a sergeant in Company C of the 142nd Pennsylvania noted that there were only 36 men left of the 60 who had entered the fray.[42]

"The sights are too horrible to describe with pen and ink," this same sergeant informed his parents. "We were mowed down like grass upon the field." The men in his company could only hope that Fredericksburg "may have been the first and last fight." A busy surgeon confirmed that many of the dead and wounded had been left in the woods. For days missing men wandered back to their regiments. The grumbling, cursing survivors saved their choicest words for the inept generals who had sent them into such a fight without proper support.[43] Yet for all Burnside knew, his left wing was driving the Confederates. The battle plan appeared to be working, and now it was time to hit the Rebels' other flank.

*I approve of all methods of attacking
provided they are directed at the point
where the enemy's army is weakest
and where the terrain favors them
the least.*
—Frederick the Great

14 Attack

The telegrams from James Hardie were terse but encouraging.

9:00 A.M.: "General Meade just moved out. . . . Skirmishers, however, heavily engaged at once with enemy skirmishers."

11:00 A.M.: "Meade advanced half a mile and holds on. . . . No loss so far of great importance."

Noon: "Birney's division is now getting into position. . . . Reynolds will order Meade to advance."

At his Phillips House headquarters Burnside read these dispatches intently. Though ensconced on the second floor with a powerful spyglass, he could not see much of Fredericksburg through the morning fog and much less to the south, where Franklin's troops were fighting. Burnside in fact remained befogged in several other senses. He placed too much faith in cryptic information from Franklin, grasping at any sign of progress on the left so as to set the rest of his battle plan in motion. Unable to see most of the battlefield, he would have to rely on judgment and instinct to decide if and when to order an assault against the Confederate center on Marye's Heights. Ideally his mind needed to be clear and well rested, but the loss of sleep was catching up with him. An aide later claimed he found Burnside napping at midday in the attic of the Phillips House. Whatever the truth of that story (and the source is not entirely reliable), on this morning Burnside was not in the best condition to launch a risky attack against the strongest part of the Confederate line.[1]

Geography exerted an even more decisive influence on the Union right than it had on the left. Buildings offered some protection while concealing Federal strength from Lee, but once ordered to attack, the troops would have to leave this relatively safe haven and advance over mostly open ground. Two main roads ran west toward Marye's Heights. To the south, the Telegraph Road extended out from Hanover Street; at the edge of town it veered slightly southward before curling around the base of Marye's Heights. In an elongated triangle formed as the Telegraph Road diverged from the extension of Hanover Street were houses and gardens that would slow an attacking force but would offer limited cover. The Orange Plank Road (an extension of William Street) also ran west from Fredericksburg; it skirted a brick tannery and crossed Marye's Heights before heading toward Chancellorsville.

Just past the outskirts of town, more than a quarter-mile from Marye's Heights, the Federals would encounter a millrace across their line of march. This offshoot of a canal running from the Rappahannock to a basin on the northern edge of Fredericksburg was about five feet deep and fifteen feet wide. Only three bridges spanned the ditch, however, and one of those had been stripped of timber, leaving only the stringers. On December 12 Federal engineers had partially drained the millrace, though no one seemed to have considered it much of an obstacle. The ditch's steep bank on the far side would offer troops protection and an opportunity to reform lines. But beyond it, between the sheltering bank and Marye's Heights, lay 500 yards of mostly open ground with only a few buildings, fences, and a slight swale providing any cover. Not only could Confederate artillery sweep this area, but unknown to Burnside and his generals, the Telegraph Road became a sunken road as it wound along the base of Marye's Heights. The stone fences along each side could readily conceal a brigade or more of infantry.[2]

The stone wall on the Fredericksburg side stood about four feet high, and the Confederates had banked up earth against its face and to the south had hastily thrown up a few log breastworks and abattis. "What a place for infantry," a young officer in the Washington Artillery exclaimed. But the real strength of the position was Marye's Heights and the hills behind, from which shot and shell could be hurled against an attacking force. Rising

Stone wall at the base of Marye's Heights (United States Army Military History Institute)

sharply some forty feet above the Sunken Road and stone wall, Marye's Heights commanded both the Plank and Telegraph roads as they emerged from town.[3]

Although neither army had yet learned the value of field entrenchments, Longstreet had improved a naturally strong position. To the left of the stone wall between the Telegraph and Plank roads, the 24th North Carolina of Ransom's Division held a recently dug shelter trench. Nine guns from the Washington Artillery were posted in newly constructed gun emplacements near the crest, with seven more pieces on either side of this position to concentrate additional fire on the approaches to Marye's Heights. Twenty-one guns on Telegraph Hill pointed toward both the Telegraph Road and an unfinished railroad cut to the south of the stone wall that guarded a potentially vulnerable flank.[4]

Besides the 24th North Carolina on the left, three regiments from Cobb's brigade crouched along the stone wall. Brig. Gen. John Roger Cooke's brigade (Ransom's Division) stood about 200 yards behind Marye's Heights, and Ransom's own brigade lay within easy supporting distance. To the right, the rest of McLaws's Division continued to hold the area south of Hazel Run, while Anderson anchored the left flank.[5]

Riding to Lee's headquarters in the early morning fog, Longstreet could hear Union officers barking out commands across the way. To an artillery sergeant, the general appeared lost in thought as he surveyed the ground, speaking little, and then only in low tones. Still expecting the main Union attack to be against the Confederate right, Longstreet ordered Hood, with

Pickett in support, to hit the flank of any Federal force that moved against Jackson. By 9:00 A.M. Alexander could glimpse the outlines of Stafford Heights through the fog, and an hour later he could see the open ground behind Fredericksburg. Soon his careful defensive preparations would begin to pay off. After conferring with Lee and ribbing Jackson, Longstreet had a few artillery rounds lobbed into Fredericksburg to test the range. Some time after 11:00 A.M. (likely closer to noon) his guns opened on the streets and bridges. The purpose was to create a "diversion" to relieve the pressure on Jackson. With uncanny timing these shots screamed toward Sumner's men just as they were preparing to attack.[6]

At 6:00 A.M. Burnside had sent new orders instructing Sumner to "push a column of a division or more along the Plank and Telegraph roads, with a view to seizing the heights in the rear of the town. The latter movement should be well covered by skirmishers so as to keep its line of retreat open." Like the orders to Franklin, these directions also could be interpreted (or misinterpreted) in several ways, but Burnside promised to visit Sumner later. Timing was critical. If Franklin's troops made progress, forcing Lee to weaken his left, an attack by Sumner might just work.[7]

Burnside's decision—as he later admitted—assumed that by 11:00 A.M. Franklin had already launched an assault on the Confederate left. But Meade would not actually cross the railroad for another two hours. Burnside did not yet realize that what were supposed to be coordinated attacks would be anything but. Another logical, though faulty, premise of the plan assumed that the ongoing attack on the Rebel right would compel Lee to send reinforcements from Longstreet to Jackson. In fact Lee had not weakened this sector one iota. Burnside's thinking was not, as Baldy Smith later claimed, an "insolvable mystery," but if the success of a military engagement depends, as Clausewitz observed, on the commander's ability to "fight at the right place and right time," the chances for success were slim.[8]

Sumner conveyed Burnside's orders to Second Corps commander Darius N. Couch, who remained cool to the entire battle plan but whose troops would do much of the fighting. Couch selected French's division to lead the attack, supported by Hancock's division, with Howard's division guarding the upper part of Fredericksburg against a possible Confederate incursion there. Receiving Couch's orders at 9:30 A.M., French marched his brigades through the streets partially under cover of the morning fog.[9]

A graduate of West Point (class of 1837, which included such luminaries as Hooker, Early, John Sedgwick, Braxton Bragg, and John C. Pemberton), William H. French was a veteran artillery officer who had fought in the Seminole and Mexican wars. He had recently been promoted to major general after serving as a brigade commander during the Peninsula campaign and leading a division at Antietam. Maybe Couch's skepticism about Burnside's plans had filtered down to his subordinate because French's official report precisely detailed the nature and timing of various orders, as if he were justifying his own actions while expressing no faith in the operation itself. Described as "imperious and impatient," French elicited both obedience and hard work from his staff. French later stated privately that he had not reconnoitered the ground and that on December 13 he had protested launching the attack. In any event, he was not enthusiastic about his present task.[10]

As noon approached, French's troops moved through the streets toward the Plank and Telegraph roads just as the Confederate artillery began firing into Fredericksburg. The early morning orders issued to the commander of the Washington Artillery on Marye's Heights had been precise: "As soon as the enemy's infantry comes in range of your long-range guns General Longstreet wishes you to open upon them with effect. Be particular in acquiring the bearing and range of the streets of the town. The enemy passing through them will give you an opportunity to rake him, which you will of course take." Confederate artillerists would long remember the "magnificent sight" of the blue lines snaking through the streets of Fredericksburg even as they prepared to unleash the fury of their guns.[11]

French's men, who had spent the early morning hours reading mail, could hardly have anticipated the firestorm. Indeed, General Couch had to order some brazen souls to discard their recent plunder before going into battle. Brig. Gen. Nathan Kimball's brigade emerged from town first with an unusually heavy line ("cloud") of 700 skirmishers from two Ohio regiments and one Delaware unit.[12] Their orders were to drive off Confederate skirmishers, keep at their heels, and follow them into the Rebel breastworks.[13] As the first troops approached the millrace, the scattered Confederate artillery fire exploded into a concentrated barrage. Guns on Stansbury's Hill, Marye's Heights, and Telegraph Hill rained fire onto the Federal skirmishers and the three brigades following them. The shells burst "beautifully" among the bluecoats, an English observer commented. The gunners could hardly miss such easy targets. "Set 'em up again," one gunner in the Washington Artillery jeered as the solid shots bowled over Federals like ninepins.[14]

Yet as Longstreet and Col. James B. Walton of the Washington Artillery both noted with amazement, French's men kept pressing forward, even as the intense fire shattered formations. Before deploying his 8th Ohio as skirmishers, Col. Franklin Sawyer had spied fences as well as scattered shops and buildings farther out Hanover Street. These, along with the millrace, could slow the advance but also offer protection, and they soon became wel-

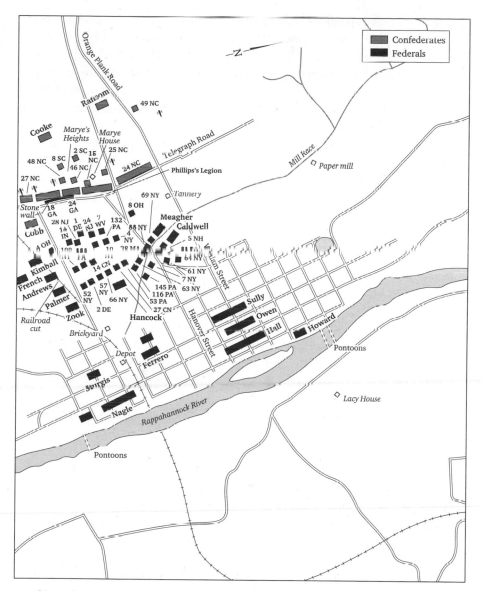

French's and Hancock's assaults against the Confederate left, December 13, noon–1:00 P.M.

come havens for men and officers alike. Artillery fire began raking the Buckeyes even as they moved out at the double-quick and neared the millrace. At the head of the column some twenty officers and men fell almost instantly. Confederates described "gaps" torn in the Federal lines or "lanes ploughed out of human bodies."

Still the bluecoats drove the few Rebels from the ditch, scrambled across the small bridge, and re-formed their line under the protection of the western bank. Unsure what had happened to the other two regiments of skirmishers, Sawyer led his troops forward, but progress was halting as men paused to tear down fences. Mounting casualties—enfilading fire from the right was especially deadly—forced soldiers to crouch behind fences near the few buildings standing between them and the last 100 yards of open ground leading to the stone wall. Several men broke down the door of a small grocery near where the Telegraph Road and Orange Turnpike diverged. Carrying wounded comrades inside, they found a woman—likely the owner's wife—hidden in the cellar. Under heavy fire they dragged her out to show them the well. By this time nearly a fifth of this small regiment had been killed or wounded.[15]

The other skirmishers fared no better. Both the 4th Ohio and 1st Delaware marched to the railroad depot; they turned there to cross the millrace, but a murderous fire dropped nearly a score of Buckeyes and several of the Delaware men. Remnants of both regiments somehow survived the artillery and advanced another 300 yards or so to reach the swale in front of the stone wall. Col. John S. Mason of the 4th Ohio issued the wildly unnecessary order for the skirmishers to lie down as Cobb's musketry drove them to the ground. This proved to be a very unlucky place, especially for Henry A. Darlington, a twenty-five-year-old printer and volunteer fireman from West Chester, Pennsylvania, who had joined the 1st Delaware as a sergeant. Recently promoted to second lieutenant, Darlington fell wounded, and as several comrades carried him from the field, a Confederate shell blew his body to pieces.[16]

The rest of Kimball's brigade was supposed to exploit the skirmishers' "success." With a jaunty, if jarring, "Cheer up, my hearties, cheer up! This is something we must get used to!" Kimball dispatched his four remaining regiments. They, too, crossed the millrace near the depot and then tried to move into line for the attack. More tightly packed, they suffered horribly from the artillery storm. Parts of the brigade reached the swale some 100 yards from the stone wall and even moved somewhat beyond but were stopped by what many bluecoats would later call a veritable sheet of flame, as Cobb's infantry rose and fired a withering volley into their ranks. In addition, the Washington Artillery was pouring in canister. The Yankees tried to advance across the mucky, uneven ground and through the fences, but once they got to the swale, their depleted ranks had no hope of reaching the stone wall. About this time Kimball received a serious thigh wound and was carried off the field; Mason assumed command. "The brigade was scattered all over the line no regiment entire," the Ohioan later wrote.[17]

The details of the engagement remain sketchy. "Shattered, torn and bleeding, our column still pushed—gained the open ground—drew up in line of battle and with bayonets fixed, rushed forward to the charge," an imaginative lieutenant in the 14th Indiana informed his hometown newspaper. This recital could apply to any number of Civil War engagements. The regiment's commander, Maj. Elijah H. C. Cavins, offered few details in either a letter to his wife or his official report. Other soldiers also stuck to general accounts of the fight.[18] These Hoosier veterans hesitated to recount their searing experience in any detail. Many of the Union regimental after-action reports for Fredericksburg were similarly terse. No one wanted to dwell on failure. Cavins's men did not shy away from reporting the casualties—after all, three brave color-bearers had fallen in a brief period—but they did not focus on how the casualties had occurred or say much about the fighting itself. In fact, it was an officer from another regiment, Colonel Sawyer of the 8th Ohio, who later penned the most graphic account of a young Hoosier who hid behind a stump trying to pick off Rebel gunners until both stump and man were blown to pieces by a Confederate shell.[19]

In the center of Kimball's line two rookie New Jersey regiments each suffered more than twice the casualties of the 14th Indiana. That morning the nine-month volunteers of the 24th New Jersey had tried to hide their nervousness with imitations of whizzing shells, jokes, and desultory reading; two sergeants had even fought a mock duel with swords. What the regiment encountered beyond the town was no laughing matter: "screeching" artillery rounds that quickly increased the number of dead and wounded. Some men fell to the ground too terrified to move; others desperately begged God to deliver them. Most finally reached the swale, pressing themselves against the ground and awkwardly trying to load their weapons.[20] No longer functioning as regiments or even as companies, the survivors simply fought to save their own lives. "This batel Was the grates Slaughter or the Most Masterley pease of Bootchery that has hapend during the Ware," one of them wrote with raw eloquence. "I have ben in one fight and I think it Will be the last for is the most horiabel place . . . amounted to Nothing except to slaughter the solgers for nothing."[21]

As Colonel Mason observed, the advance under intense artillery fire had so exhausted most of Kimball's men that they had to pause at the swale, out of both the energy and the support to go farther. Kimball later guessed that a fourth of the brigade fell during the attack. A member of the 28th

New Jersey marveled, "it is a greate wonder that it [the charge] dident kill us all."[22]

Behind the stone wall the Confederates had been more than ready. Admonished to withdraw if Anderson's Division on the left had to give way, Cobb had scoffed, "If they wait for me to fall back, they will wait a long time." This statement summed up the man. Cobb had been a hardworking, scholarly lawyer and ardent secessionist back in Georgia. Though bitterly disappointed that his brother Howell had not been elected Confederate president, the pious Tom Cobb scorned anyone who wavered in his commitment to the southern cause. Despite his lack of military experience, he had become a capable general and rapidly won the respect of Lee and others. On the morning of December 13 Cobb had solemnly warned his troops about the bloody work ahead but promised to remain with them until the end. He would keep his word.[23]

As Kimball's troops began advancing, General Ransom moved Cooke's brigade up to the crest of Marye's Heights and Willis's Hill. A few Georgians behind the stone wall had nervously begun firing. Cobb, stalking up and down the Sunken Road, reassured his anxious troops, ordering them to wait until "you [can] count the Yankee buttons." As Kimball's shot-up regiments finally reached the swale, the Georgians, under orders to aim low, loosed "a perfect sheet of flame . . . from behind the stone wall." These or similar words would be used countless times by the survivors on both sides. With double-shotted canister from Marye's Heights also ripping into the Federals, a Georgia hospital steward coined another soon-to-be-familiar phrase describing the area in front of the stone wall as a "complete slaughter pen."[24]

Through the smoke the Yankees could barely see their destroyers. Yet still more bluecoats approached the killing ground. French's other two brigades were supposed to follow Kimball at 150-yard intervals and overrun the Rebel line. But even before Col. John W. Andrews's brigade received the order to advance, one of the regimental commanders, Col. John E. Bendix of the 10th New York, was struck in the face by a shell fragment. Andrews had only three regiments; one had already been sent forward with the skirmishers. Around noon this small brigade "marched steadily up the slope and took a position in Kimball's rear." But with the Federal "line" already torn to pieces, Andrews could only send his troops forward to fill in the gaps. So many officers were hit, including Andrews, that regiments often became formless, leaderless masses hugging the earth for protection. The 10th New York, for example, lost nine of eleven officers and had three different commanders in less than an hour. Lt. Col. John W. Marshall called the situation "temporary confusion," a gross understatement. To survivors it seemed they had passed through a "storm" of metal, a death-dealing hail. Indeed, this analogy leaped often to mind and pen. One tall fellow in the 4th New York had pulled up his coat collar as if he were heading into a gale.[25]

Why did they keep going? This is the most difficult question posed about Fredericksburg and many other Civil War battles. Some men mechanically obeyed orders, others still burned with commitment to the Union cause, many fought for their comrades, and a few acted from motives that could not be easily or simply explained. Soldiers often had trouble articulating their combat reactions to their families or even to fellow soldiers or perhaps to themselves. If most were simply trapped between the demands of fear and duty, sheer inertia and the absence of acceptable alternatives kept them moving forward, often halfheartedly as the casualties mounted. This was not the kind of gallantry described in novels, but it was courage nonetheless.

Andrews's troops and each subsequent brigade had also endured the disheartening sight of the wounded and dead from the previous assaults scattered through the streets and fields. The men of the 132nd Pennsylvania, who had been badly bloodied at Antietam and were short of officers, apparently balked at the sight of the carnage. At one point the regimental adjutant had to retrieve the bulk of the regiment when only one company had followed him toward the front. Alongside an unfinished railroad cut, Confederate artillery shells—largely from Telegraph Hill—found their mark, dismembering or simply blowing men into indistinguishable pulp. Defying orders, shirkers carried the wounded to the rear. Several mud-covered men, spattered by blood and pieces of flesh, fired blindly toward the stone wall. A few pressed beyond the swale but could not stand against the withering fire. "[We were] blown off our feet," one private reported, "staggering as though against a mighty wind."[26]

Col. Oliver H. Palmer's brigade, the latest to pass the depot and head into Rebel artillery fire, encountered wounded men lying all about near the millrace; some already wore the pallor of death. One man with both legs shot off gamely tried to be encouraging: "Pass on boys. Don't stop to look at me." Delayed by enfilading fire for twenty minutes or longer, Palmer's troops were slow to reinforce Kimball and Andrews. The survivors then approached what amounted to infantry hell, "worse than Antietam," as many soldiers described it.

By this time some men had no heroic impulses left. A few officers in the 14th Connecticut reportedly feigned illness to avoid entering the fray, but enlisted men also looked to skedaddle with a wounded comrade. Yet most plodded forward; many wondered why the Federal artillery did not shell the Rebels. Scores of wounded and dying men entered their field of vision, and then a shell burst at the head of one company. Several men went down, one with his face shot away. A major in the 108th New York crawled over three board fences and was eventually hit by a ball that knocked off his cap and inflicted a painful though not especially dangerous scalp wound. A few minutes later a spent ball badly stung his leg. Remnants of companies dashed toward the stone wall, sometimes with cheers and shouts but always with the same fruitless results: just more killed and wounded to litter the field. Bullets caromed off cartridge boxes and canteens; shell fragments struck haversacks and blankets; both poked holes in hats and overcoats unless flesh stopped them. Deadly missiles seemed to swarm like wasps and struck men almost everywhere—most often in the thigh or arm but also in the parietal bone, the scrotum, or the knee. Three different soldiers stumbled over a Connecticut sergeant seriously wounded in the leg; finally the poor wretch managed to crawl into a hut with other casualties.[27]

"It seems as if our company and Regt were all gone," a Connecticut soldier summed up the result of French's assault. The words "shattered and broken" applied to every regiment. Officially the division casualties totaled a mind-numbing 1,160. The combination of artillery fire and concentrated rifle fire had mangled bodies almost beyond recognition. Several high-ranking officers had been wounded. Worse was the growing conviction that it had all been for nothing. "A perfect failure," a Pennsylvania private grumbled. A member of the 108th New York doubted there had ever been any chance for success: "We might as well have tried to take hell."[28]

A brief lull occurred as the last of French's troops stalled. The Georgians behind the stone wall decided they had repulsed a mighty legion with ease. Perhaps they had, but the reinforcements Ransom and McLaws fed into the Sunken Road during the assault had also helped. The 27th North Carolina in Cooke's brigade had scrambled down the crest—apparently without orders—to bolster Cobb's right and was soon joined by the 46th North Carolina. Kershaw also dispatched two South Carolina regiments to meet the next wave of Yankees. Even as the infantry fire subsided, the artillery on both sides continued to pound away. Near his headquarters at the Stephens House, Cobb was suddenly struck in the thigh by a piece of shrapnel. A handkerchief proved a poor tourniquet. The femoral artery had been torn, and by the time the wounded man was carried to a hospital behind Marye's Heights, he had already lost too much blood. In shock, Cobb fainted and soon died.[29]

The Georgians and Carolinians defending the Sunken Road had little time to mourn their fallen commander. More Yankees were pouring from the streets of Fredericksburg, led by the redoubtable Winfield Scott Hancock. Tall and stocky with brown-to-reddish hair, blue eyes, and a distinctive mustache and chin whiskers, Hancock exuded an air of steady confidence. Regardless of his dismay over the formidable Confederate defenses, he was expected to succeed where French had failed.[30]

"We had to march for a considerable distance by the flank through the streets of the town," Hancock wrote, "all the time under a heavy fire, before we were enabled to deploy; and then, owing to obstacles—among them a mill-race—it was impossible to deploy, except by marching the whole length of each brigade by the flank in a line parallel to the enemy's works, after we had crossed the mill race by the bridge." Hancock neglected to mention that the west bank of the millrace offered the troops considerable protection, but he hardly exaggerated the magnitude of the task before him. Whatever doubts he entertained, though, were private. He solemnly instructed his regimental commanders that the Confederate lines "must be carried at all hazards and at all costs."

Col. Samuel K. Zook commanded the lead brigade. A capable soldier, though like Hancock sometimes crusty and generally skeptical of the battle plan, Zook led his six regiments along the railroad cut through a brickyard and into line. As they turned toward Marye's Heights, a shell blew apart a poor fellow in the 57th New York, and a piece of skull temporarily knocked Cpl. Lawrence Floyd unconscious. Other men dodged bits of clothing and equipment. When another volunteer in the 57th was struck in the back, entrails flew in several directions. "Then I began to see the horrors of war," one young recruit informed his parents. It was not the only horror he saw. He also noticed a severed head lying on the ground and several men who had lost arms or legs. Amazingly, some of Zook's men, after tearing away or clambering over fences under relentless fire, reached the remnants of French's division, marked by flags planted 100 yards from the stone wall. Even though a third of the brigade had already been hit, some men drove beyond French's lines. Elements of the 53rd Pennsylvania got to within perhaps 50 yards of the stone wall before taking shelter in a few buildings earlier held by French's skirmishers. Once within range of Confederate infantry, one soldier noted, "the boys involuntarily pulled their hats down over their eyes as if breasting a storm."[31]

So many officers fell so quickly that the command of regiments sometimes passed to two or three men in a matter of minutes. The after-action reports often implausibly described a steady advance and failed to capture the chaos of the effort. The experience of a private in the 27th Connecticut was typical. About halfway up the hill "the brigade got rather confused and different regiments were mingled together." Fragments of companies gathered near the swale or behind fences or in buildings—wherever they could find some safety. The final casualty figures for Zook's brigade were staggering: over 500 men were killed, wounded, or missing, and there would be at least 26 leg and 15 arm amputations. The 57th New York had only 50 men left after the battle.[32]

From any vantage point Confederate officers could easily see the results of their well-prepared defense. As Longstreet later remarked, "Every gun that we had in range opened upon the advancing columns and ploughed their ranks by a fire that would test the nerves of the bravest soldiers." The Federals had moved out in "handsome style," he marveled, but also noted that they "did not meet the fire of our infantry with any heart." As before, Federal artillery rounds from Stafford Heights had little effect on the well-protected Confederate gunners who poured shot, shell, and canister into Hancock's soldiers.

With Tom Cobb dead, Col. Robert McMillan of the 24th Georgia assumed command of the troops in the Sunken Road. Calmly moving along the lines, he ordered his infantry to hold their fire. The men opened with devastating effect once the Yankees came in range. Cobb's regiments suffered only light casualties. Cooke and Ransom's brigades took heavier losses, especially in the regiments that remained on Marye's Heights under steady fire with little cover. The unfortunate 48th North Carolina, exposed to Federal artillery and stray infantry rounds most of the day, lost nearly 180 men.[33] Yet this outfit and the hard-hit 15th and 25th North Carolina were very much the exceptions as Ransom's and McLaws's troops confidently stood their ground with more bluecoats heading their way.

Closely following Zook came the Irish Brigade, one of the hardest-fighting outfits in the Army of the Potomac. The unit's battle flags had become so tattered that Brig. Gen. Thomas Francis Meagher had sent them back to New York. Because new ones did not arrive in time for the battle, Meagher ordered boxwood sprigs pinned to each man's cap as a reminder of their proud heritage.[34]

One of the war's great characters, Meagher had been born into a prosperous merchant family in Waterford, Ireland, where he early became a crusader for Irish independence. Arrested by British authorities and exiled to Tasmania, in 1852 he had turned up in California and eventually made his way to New York City. A self-promoter with the flair of P. T. Barnum and the charm of Aaron Burr, he had dabbled in law, but his real talent lay in oratory and politics. Raising troops for an Irish brigade of New Yorkers in the fall and winter of 1861, he had courted powerful leaders ranging from Governor E. D. Morgan to Archbishop John Hughes. In the fall of 1862 the 28th Massachusetts recruited in Boston and the 116th Pennsylvania from Philadelphia had joined Meagher's three New York regiments.[35]

Because of hard marching and bloody combat, the Irish Brigade appeared downright puny on the eve of Fredericksburg. Most of the regiments could muster no more than 250 soldiers. The 28th Massachusetts was relatively robust with 416 men, but the 63rd New York brought to the field only 162 rifles. Meagher characteristically claimed that his boys had never been in "finer spirits." This could well have been true of Meagher himself, a notorious drinker. On this day as on many others, controversy would dog Meagher, but he relished the limelight. His own troops were entranced by his natural charisma and respected his courage and leadership as well as his care for their creature comforts.[36]

Meagher, decked out in a dark green suit with black shoulder knots embroidered with silver stars and a yellow silk sash across his breast, had been up early on the morning of December 13 exhorting his men. A Rebel shell interrupted one of his speeches, and during its dramatic conclusion the "mangled remains—mere masses of bloody rags" from three members of the 69th New York were carried off. But nothing could stop the flow of Meagher's words, or his tears. The soldiers must fight hard for their adopted land, he urged the 88th New York, because they were the regiment dearest to his beloved wife. As officers issued final instructions, the men appeared solemn. A Jesuit priest strolled among them blessing Catholics and Protestants alike. For a few moments each man was left alone with his thoughts. Even through the smoke and haze and the overwhelming smell of gunpowder they could anticipate what lay ahead. Rebel shells bursting in the streets and the terrible suspense were added to the sight of the wounded. A German soldier whose foot had been shot off nevertheless rode along in a wheelbarrow coolly smoking a cigar; an ashen-faced captain was carried atop a window shutter after having one leg nearly shot clean off. As this grotesque parade passed, a young Pennsylvanian about to enter his first battle fainted.[37]

When the 116th Pennsylvania trudged out Hanover Street, the men heard a cat mewing amidst all the racket. Solid shots caromed through the streets, and a shell crumbled a brick chimney. The Irish Brigade started taking casualties before it even emerged from the supposed shelter of the town. A Pennsylvania sergeant with his head blown off fell to his knees still grasping his rifle; a single shell left eighteen members of the 88th New York hors de combat. Soldiers could now see the ground where French's and Zook's troops had been slaughtered.[38]

Between 12:30 and 1:00 P.M. Meagher's approximately 1,200 men crossed the dreaded millrace. Some used a rickety bridge; others scrambled over on the stringers; many, seizing the quickest way to the relative safety of the far bank, splashed through the shallow water. Sweating profusely, breathing heavily, their hearts pounding, soldiers threw themselves onto the ground and rested there for about ten minutes, waiting for orders. Having already been mauled by Rebel batteries (some men had fallen mortally wounded into the ditch), they now discarded blankets and haversacks. The "clink, clink, clink" of bayonets being fixed "made one's blood run cold," a private recalled. Officers' whispered orders heightened the terror as thoughts turned to the awful test that surely lay ahead. Dead men from French's division were strewn about them. One soldier had been hit by a solid shot, and his head, according to Pvt. William McCarter of the 116th Pennsylvania, now resembled a halved watermelon.[39]

"Irish Brigade, advance. Forward, double-quick, guide center." The men could see the smoke of infantry fire to their front. Once again the Rebel artillery enfiladed the lines. Gaping holes opened in the ranks, then closed; colors fell and rose again; too many men were being hit; walking wounded stumbled to the rear. An orderly sergeant in the 116th Pennsylvania jerked around, a hole in his forehead, blood splashing as he fell at a young lieutenant's feet. Forty percent of the men were hit before they had even fired a shot. So many officers and color-bearers went down that companies and regiments seemed to evaporate.

Somehow the survivors forced their way beyond French's lines. How far would be disputed for years, but a few men apparently got to within twenty-five yards of the stone wall. They now fired at will, but the Confederate volleys were steadier and deadlier. "Blaze away and stand it boys!" shouted Maj. James Cavanagh of the 69th New York, but he, too, was soon badly wounded. "Our men were mowed down like grass before the scythe," a member of the 88th New York wrote after the battle. The familiar description hardly did justice to this particular hell.

For the stranded Yankees near the wall, the whole affair had degenerated into small, bloody firefights. Some men took shelter near a brick house while others stacked pieces of wood fence into flimsy barricades. To Private McCarter it seemed that every second or third man along the line had been hit, and soon a bullet tore into his shoulder. He lay on the ground, still clasping his rifle, thinking the end had come. Praying quietly, he recalled feeling quite composed. But then a comrade fell by his side with a horrible stomach wound. "Oh, my mother," he gasped, twitched for a few seconds, and died. Meanwhile other soldiers still cursed and fired toward the Rebels;

running out of cartridges, they grabbed more from the dead and wounded. The bodies of the fallen provided some protection for the intrepid souls who advanced beyond the swale out into the open ground.

Remnants of a few companies scrambled over the third and last wooden fence, but this impotent assault sputtered with hardly enough officers left to lead a disorganized retreat. Not only had entire regiments been smashed up in little more than thirty minutes, but to the commander of the 28th Massachusetts it seemed that the brigade was simply gone. For the survivors who bemoaned the absence of artillery or infantry support, the terrible casualties represented a blood sacrifice to military incompetence.[40]

Confederates behind the stone wall might well have agreed with their enemies. Some men had fired so many rounds that their rifles had become fouled and their faces as sooty as blackface minstrels. Each time the blue columns inched forward, the "rattle" of Confederate rifles, according to one witness, sounded "like a thousand packs of Chinese crackers." Ironically many of the men so efficiently slaughtering the Irish Brigade were Irish too, including their commander, Colonel McMillan, who enjoined his troops, "Give it to them now, boys! Now's the time! Give it to them!" Yet under such circumstances compassion for enemies seemed natural. "Oh God, what a pity! Here comes Meagher's fellows," one Rebel cried as he spied the evergreen sprigs. Confederates observing this charge knew courage when they saw it, and now their brave foes lay bleeding and dying on ground that had once yielded corn for shipment to the starving in Ireland.[41]

Such ironies hardly mattered to Meagher's men as they lay on the ground expecting any minute to be blown up by a shell or picked off by a sharpshooter. And these scattered soldiers were the lucky ones. Three of five regimental commanders already had been hit; some line officers had been struck several times. It would be days before anyone would know how many were missing and likely dead. Were there even 250 men left in the brigade? It seemed so pitifully depleted that a corporal in the 28th Massachusetts assured his wife that the "rest of the fighting will have to be done without our aid."[42]

None of this carnage, however, prevented Hancock from sending in his last brigade. Brig. Gen. John C. Caldwell had been a teacher and farmer back in Vermont. Slow moving, stocky, easygoing, and occasionally lazy, he was a solid though unspectacular volunteer officer. Under galling artillery fire his sizable brigade of six regiments (nearly 2,000 men) moved through the streets dodging falling debris. To relieve the tension, Col. Robert Nugent, who commanded the 69th New York in the Irish Brigade, advised Col. Robert E. Cross of the 5th New Hampshire to make dinner reservations for them at the Spotswood House once he reached Richmond. Cross, already suffering from fever and chills, replied with a string of profanity.[43]

Caldwell pushed his men forward until they stumbled onto a cluster of troops firing ineffectually toward the Rebels. Some of Caldwell's soldiers on the left began popping away despite orders against firing before they had penetrated the Confederate lines. The general himself had to walk the brigade line to prod the men into motion again. On the right the 5th New Hampshire and 81st Pennsylvania advanced beyond the Stratton House, a two-story Greek Revival structure owned by a local wheelwright. The 5th New Hampshire, with two commanders already hit, now found its progress stymied by groups of men from the previous attacks firing wildly toward the Confederates. The surviving officers on that end of the line (the 81st Pennsylvania had four different commanders in a matter of minutes) simply could not form a battle line ("human valor had its limit," a young private decided). The few Granite Staters who managed to crawl over or slither through the last board fence likely came as close to the stone wall as any other Federals that day. But most men had been mowed down, and the regimental colors had fallen five or six times.[44]

The brigade line—earlier it had reminded a lieutenant in the 64th New York of martial scenes described in schoolbooks—fell apart. Toward the center the largely German 7th New York moved beyond two groups of men from earlier charges who had been pinned down. To its immediate left the fresh recruits of the 145th Pennsylvania had been hit by enfilading battery fire before crossing the millrace. The men advanced unsteadily over the muddy ground. With the left wing of the regiment cut off by a high board fence, the right began giving ground, slowly at first, then precipitously. Caldwell admitted that the regiment "broke and fell back." Even Hancock's report, which lavished praise on nearly every regiment and every officer, contained a hint of censure. Col. David B. McCreary, however, testily denied that his boys had skedaddled. Few soldiers commented on the hasty retreat, though one man blamed a German regiment in front of them—perhaps the 7th New York—for any confusion. Whatever the explanation, the Pennsylvanians stood under fire long enough to lose nearly half their number and for the regimental flag to receive fifteen holes.[45]

Even veterans had trouble advancing, a sergeant admitted. Col. Nelson Miles took a bullet in the throat as he tried to push the 61st and 64th New York beyond a wooden fence. Despite his departure from the field and the panicky withdrawal of the 145th Pennsylvania, the New Yorkers held their position and fired only when ordered but could not move beyond the sheltering fence.[46] Caldwell's men had been no more able than Zook's or Meagher's troops to keep going. This charge, like the previous ones, never seriously threatened the Confederate position.

A staff officer who claimed that half the brigade had been hit exaggerated only slightly. The stalwart 5th New Hampshire, 7th New York, and 81st Pennsylvania had lost nearly two-thirds of their strength, and even the shaky 145th Pennsylvania had suffered more than 200 casualties. Overall, Hancock estimated his losses at around 40 percent, including some 150 officers. Besides wounded commanding officers, the heavy toll among the staff officers and horses thwarted efforts to coordinate the attacks. Hancock himself almost became a casualty; a bullet pierced his coat and grazed his abdomen. "It was lucky I hadn't a full dinner," he remarked. A New York surgeon in Caldwell's brigade, contemplating the shuffling of command structure caused by the carnage, observed that "these changes admonish us that life is uncertain here and military rank or position subject to continued change." [47]

A common measure of Yankee valor on December 13 and for years thereafter was proximity to the stone wall. Despite the general assumption that Hancock's men came the closest, rival claims and sketchy reports have produced confusion and mild controversy. Perhaps some Federal lay dead only fifteen or twenty paces away, as several sources, including Confederate ones, suggested. Some contemporary evidence placed the 53rd Pennsylvania from Zook's brigade nearest the stone wall, but the 69th New York, the 88th New York, and the 116th Pennsylvania in the Irish Brigade have had their champions. What about the horribly bloodied 5th New Hampshire in Caldwell's brigade? Does it matter? Not much perhaps, but General Sumner recognized the uncommon valor of many regiments and later informed a group of congressmen who had never been close to a battle, "No troops could stand such a fire as that." [48]

Throughout the afternoon, men from French's and Hancock's divisions straggled back toward town. Many more simply pressed themselves against the ground, perhaps unable to move. "I wondered while I lay there," a young officer in the 57th New York later wrote, "how it all came about that these thousands of men in broad daylight were trying their best to kill each other." He could find no more "romance" or "glorious pomp" in war, only bitter thoughts about the fools who had ordered his regiment onto this killing ground. Now they simply had to stay put, still under fire from the front and occasionally from the rear. Whenever the shots were flying especially thick, Colonel Cross of the 5th New Hampshire "covered [his] face and counted rapidly to one hundred." If a man dared lift his head he could see fresh troops being shot down. [49]

Everyone, especially the wounded, was parched, but the Good Samaritan who tried to haul out a canteen to a thirsty soldier risked his life. Some men were hit repeatedly or watched as comrades were killed a few feet away. Soldiers wrapped themselves in blankets as if this might protect them against the leaden storm or even rolled dead bodies into macabre breastworks. Somehow they simply held on. "We might as well die here," declared the colonel of the 53rd Pennsylvania, and without ammunition there was little else they could do. Literally immersed in the carnage, men expected to die.[50]

Toward late afternoon the survivors of both French's and Hancock's divisions were withdrawn from the field. In ones and twos, men arose from among their dead and wounded comrades. But given the breakdown in command, only parts of companies and regiments made it back into Fredericksburg. In the Irish Brigade, it was literally every man for himself as soldiers recrossed the millrace. But reaching town did not guarantee safety. Just as one group of the brigade's soldiers neared the outskirts, a solid shot bounded down a street and mortally wounded a captain in the 63rd New York. He lived barely long enough for Chaplain William Corby to hear his confession. Thirsty troops drank water from gutters; with bowed heads they spoke gravely of fallen comrades. At dusk Fredericksburg seemed like a vast graveyard. "Sorrow hangs as a shroud over us all," commented one New York private.[51]

The price paid for using conventional assault tactics against well-protected infantry and massed artillery had been staggering. Yet both armies had not yet recognized the importance of field entrenchments or the necessity of flanking strong positions. Whether the rifled musket was revolutionizing warfare is still being debated by historians. Only weeks before Fredericksburg, Old Brains Halleck maintained that smoothbores were equally if not more effective in a "close engagement." As Pickett's Charge and Cold Harbor would later demonstrate, adjusting tactics to the size of Civil War armies and increased firepower was a slow process.[52] Given the thinking of the time, Burnside's limited information about the fighting on the Federal left, the poor staff work, the absence of effective reconnaissance, and ignorance of the terrain west of town, it is understandable that French's and Hancock's troops had been ordered to attack the strongest part of the Confederate line. It is truly appalling, however, that fresh divisions continued to cross the same ground for several more hours.

Perseverance, dear my lord, keeps honor bright.
— William Shakespeare

15 Perseverance

"Magnificent" seemed just the right word to describe the scene. The vast panorama on the Confederate left—brigade after brigade of Yankees vainly trying to reach the stone wall—inspired both awe and pity among Rebel witnesses, military and civilian. "It was the grandest sight I ever saw," wrote one artillerist. Like some "huge blue serpent" stretched out beautifully and temptingly, a Louisianan recalled, the Federal lines had been ripped and gouged repeatedly by the guns and by the merciless volleys from the Georgians and Carolinians behind the stone wall.[1]

From Howison's Hill, Confederate batteries delivered an oblique and sometimes enfilading fire against Federal troops in the streets on the south side of town. The guns on Telegraph Hill did likewise, two 30-pounder Parrott rifles proving especially effective. Strolling back and forth on what would soon be known as "Lee's Hill," the Confederate commander watched his men throw back the Yankees with seemingly greater ease each time. Plainly dressed in overcoat, light blue pants, and black felt hat, Lee said little, but as usual his calm demeanor inspired confidence.[2]

And why shouldn't he be unruffled? The entire Federal army, Longstreet assured Lee, could not overrun the Confederate left. Dramatically dashing forward on horseback, General Kershaw had not only taken command of the troops behind the stone wall but had also brought up reinforcements. Kershaw placed his South Carolinians behind the front-rank Georgians and North Carolinians, making the line four deep and roughly doubling the already overwhelming firepower. Most of the casualties suffered by Kershaw's men occurred as they descended Marye's Heights. Once the troops were in such a packed position, friendly fire presented a greater danger, but as the general proudly noted, despite the "rapid and continuous" fire (nearly sixty rounds per soldier), "not a man was injured by the fire of his comrades." The regiments still on Marye's Heights, however, remained under fire much of the day, as did Cooke's and Ransom's brigades. On an exposed knoll near the Marye House the 3rd South Carolina sustained 40 percent casualties from Federal batteries and scattered Union infantry fire. "The balls came as thick as hail," declared Tally Simpson, who credited God with preserving his life.[3]

The casualty figures marked the accumulation of anguish, anomalies, and close calls. One member of the 3rd South Carolina received such a disfiguring mouth wound that his company commander could not recognize him. The body of a lieutenant from this same badly cut-up outfit lay on the Telegraph Road. In one of those classic Confederate scenes lovingly retold and embellished for years, the officer's "faithful body servant" tenderly carried the corpse to the rear for shipment back to Newberry, South Carolina. And these were only 2 of almost 120 casualties in this regiment. Even though the 2nd South Carolina had lost only a third the number of men, there were plenty of horrors to recount. As the regiment reached Marye's Heights, a shell had scattered one private's head, brains, and body in three different directions. Jumping, rolling, and sliding down the hill, more men were hit. Once behind the stone wall, Pvt. J. R. Keese was shot through the lung. Grabbing a sergeant's leg, he begged for someone to finish him off. He died that evening.[4]

The placement of so many troops in such a vulnerable place had cost unnecessary casualties, but McLaws and Longstreet naturally assumed that they needed troops in position to help Kershaw quickly should the Yankees get too close to the stone wall. Fredericksburg had become a one-sided fight, but even in a one-sided fight the victorious army makes mistakes. Confident Confederates could cheer each repulse, though despite an overpoweringly strong defensive position, some regiments paid a high price.

★ ★ ★

The Yankees suffered far greater casualties. As the Federals advanced, General Couch watched brigades "melt like snow coming down on warm ground." The pretty analogy was far too gentle to describe the halting movements and terrible carnage, but after climbing the courthouse steeple, Couch had a much better view of the fighting. "Oh, great God! See how our men, our fellows are falling!" he exclaimed to General Howard. Orders for French and Hancock to "storm" the enemy works obviously could not be carried out, so Couch prepared to send in Howard's division—the last one in the Second Corps—to flank the Rebels out of the Sunken Road. The plan was to support the earlier assaults with fresh troops on either side. From the left Brig. Gen. Samuel D. Sturgis's division from the Ninth Corps was already attempting to assail the other end of the stone wall; from the right Howard's brigades would march out along both sides of Hanover Street.[5]

Brig. Gen. Oliver Otis Howard was an easy man to caricature. A devout Christian who held prayer meetings in his tent, Howard often lectured his troops on the evils of swearing and alcohol. Convinced that the Lord was using the "incompetency of our leaders" to humble the nation and further the antislavery cause, Howard and his equally pious brother Charles offered prayers of thanks for their deliverance after each battle. For all his piety, however, Howard was a brave soldier, though often an unlucky one.[6]

To support Hancock, Col. Joshua T. Owen's Second Brigade had to trek through the streets and across the millrace (largely through the water in two and threes). Moving into line to the left of Hanover Street, Owen advanced toward the Stratton House. But the "lines" he was to support had been "almost entirely annihilated," and so Owen ordered his men "to lie close to the ground." Fortunately the brigade had reached a point where the guns on Marye's Heights could not be depressed far enough to hit them, but Rebel infantry fire took a heavy toll. The soldiers held their position as if "glued to the ground," Owen proudly informed a Philadelphia newspaper, although scattered buildings, a small wood fence, and dead bodies provided the only cover. The unfortunates who raised their heads were often hit by Confederate sharpshooters. Prostrate and frightened men also had to endure triumphant enemy shouts, an "unearthly, fiendish yell" more "terrible" than an "Indian war whoop," a chaplain in the 127th Pennsylvania recalled.[7]

Howard sent Hall's brigade—regiments already bloodied in the street fighting of December 11—north of Hanover Street toward the shallow entrenchments to the right of the stone wall. Again the purpose was to flank the Confederates out of a seemingly impregnable position. But a movement born in confusion and desperation quickly ended in another bloody repulse. Running into a stream of wounded men from previous assaults, the brigade had trouble crossing the millrace. As the 19th Massachusetts moved up over the bank on the other side, several color-bearers were hit immediately, and other regiments did not move smoothly into line. Under lethal artillery fire

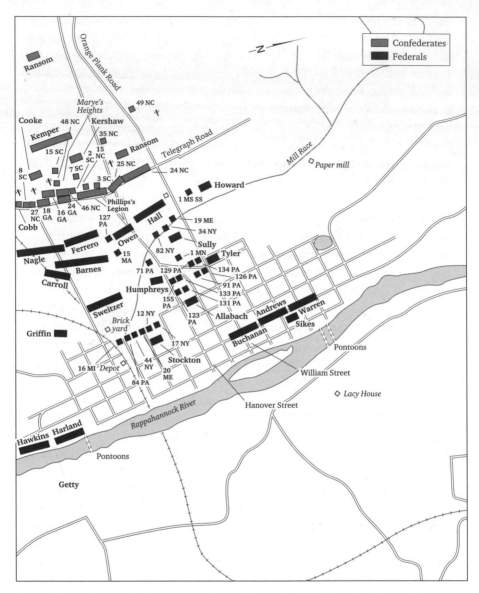

Howard, Sturgis, and Griffin support the attacks on the Confederate left, December 13, 2:00–3:00 P.M.

from the right and withering infantry fire to the front, the brigade fell apart. Parts of four regiments retreated. Even men of the stalwart 19th Massachusetts, after firing a couple volleys, fled back to the millrace bank. This left the 20th Massachusetts stranded and in trouble. Unable to advance and unwilling to retreat, the troops held their position, with no idea what to do.

One fellow had bullets go through his cap, strike his coat collar, and cut his blanket strap; miraculously, he was not wounded. Yet more than a third of his comrades were hit. Lt. Leander F. Alley died instantly when a bullet smashed through an eye and lodged in his brain. Owen's and Hall's brigades suffered some 500 casualties, to no discernible purpose.[8]

Brig. Gen. Alfred Sully dispatched three regiments from his brigade to Hall's beleaguered command and one to Owen; he held the 1st Minnesota in reserve. Later as another brigade passed by, the general reportedly commented, "There goes a lot of brave soldiers to hell." Although Sully kept as many men as possible out of harm's way, his troops could not escape the fury of the battle. The men of the 34th New York marching to support Hall soon heard the screams of the wounded and saw the ground being plowed by solid shot, but then they too were hit. One soldier lost both legs; a young boy—minus a leg and arm and being carried off the field—wanted his mother to know that he "died like a man." Sully undoubtedly protected some of his troops from becoming part of this fool's errand, but the costs of being "lightly engaged" were not cheap: in this case, 122 casualties, many of whom were killed or seriously wounded by artillery rounds. The survivors were covered with mud from exploding shells. "They hain't got me yet," Pvt. Roland E. Bowen of the 15th Massachusetts later reassured his mother.[9]

The same would not be true for many men sent in to shore up Hancock's left flank. Well before Howard's brigades had advanced along Hanover Street, Brig. Gen. Orlando Willcox, commanding the Ninth Corps in the lower part of Fredericksburg, had positioned Brig. Gen. Samuel D. Sturgis's division to enter the fray. Around noon he had ordered Sturgis to support Hancock. A half-hour later Brig. Gen. Edward Ferrero's brigade advanced along the railroad. The 51st New York was detached to support Lt. George Dickinson's battery, which had unlimbered on a bluff near a brick kiln, but Confederate artillerists quickly found them. Shells fell among the cannon, killing three (including Dickinson, who was struck in the head by spherical case shot) and wounding ten while twice driving all the gunners from their pieces.[10]

Ferrero was supposed to bring up his other four regiments under protection of this battery and then head toward Kershaw's supposedly vulnerable right flank. But neither the tactics, the geography, nor the commander seemed right. Rumor had it that Ferrero, the "New York dancing master," as he was derisively called because of his prewar profession, had been drinking, but even had he been cold sober, the odds against a successful attack that day were daunting.[11]

The men of the 11th New Hampshire entered their first battle leading the brigade across the railroad toward the outskirts of town. Dubbed the "$300 bounty boys," and despite faces turning pale and hearts seeming to rise into their mouths, they quickly gave the lie to any slanders about their courage. Advancing under the deadly artillery fire, they formed a line of battle to the right of the railroad, lay down, and finally slogged uphill toward Marye's Heights. Hysterical with fright, one volunteer shouted, "They'll kill every one of us: not a d—d one of us will be left to tell the story!" Nervous smirks could not hide the fact that many of his less demonstrative comrades agreed. "The day is lost!" yelled retreating Pennsylvanians from Hancock's division. Yet Ferrero's men pressed on, and once the brigade's survivors reached higher ground, they laid down the most intense fire that Confederates behind the stone wall would endure that day. Cries of "Give it 'em boys; give it 'em!" spread along the line. Men swore, chewed tobacco, and kept shooting for much of the afternoon, but more and more of them fell while little damage was being done to the Rebels.[12]

Here and there men performed with matchless valor. The 21st Massachusetts came under fire immediately after it emerged from Fredericksburg. A color sergeant from Company A suddenly went down, but Sgt. Thomas Plunkett from Company E grabbed the falling colors and kept marching toward the front. Bullets ripped holes in the flag, and a shell mangled Plunkett's arms. Yet even then he stood grasping the shattered staff with his bleeding stumps, saying, "Don't let it fall, boys."[13] Descriptions of Plunkett's bravery dominated later accounts of the regiment's ordeal.

The whole uphill advance had quickly produced enormous losses (a third of the 51st New York fell in five minutes). Seemingly minor obstacles proved deadly to the 35th Massachusetts. A wire fence surrounding a whitewashed cottage slowed the advance, as did a board fence, which was soon spattered with chunks of flesh and smeared with blood. Even where boards had been torn away from fences, the dead, dying, and wounded often blocked the way. Like the 11th New Hampshire, about all these men could do was lie down and hold on. "The air seemed to be so full of balls," said one Pennsylvania soldier, "that a finger could not be pointed toward the rebel batteries without being hit on the end with a bullet."

Men now fell at every step with limbs shattered or bowels or skulls ripped; a few soldiers feigned being wounded to avoid going any farther. The galling fire spared nothing. A fine black dog, the beloved mascot of the 51st New York, was mortally wounded. With no orders being issued, soldiers kept piling onto the slight rise for the rest of the afternoon; survivors soon ran out of ammunition. And there they stayed, still 200 yards from the stone wall.[14]

"We had no chance at them," declared Walt Whitman's brother George, "while they could take as deliberate aim as a fellow would at a chicken." Rebel cannon virtually blanketed the field. The Washington Artillery continued its lethal work, while from Telegraph Hill Confederate guns pounded any of Sturgis's men who ventured near the railroad cut. Bursting shells sometimes bowled over three or four soldiers at once. After one particularly spectacular hit, Lee commented, "Well done, give them another." Other observers gasped at seeing the awful gaps blown in the Yankee lines.[15]

The gunners had plenty of easy targets because Sturgis now swung his last brigade around Ferrero's left in a desperate effort to flank the Rebels out of the Sunken Road. Ravines near Hazel Run, however, thwarted this maneuver. Brig. Gen. James Nagle's troops therefore advanced along both sides of the railroad until they came under a terrific artillery crossfire. Regiments were blown apart, though isolated companies rallied to the colors. The railroad cut proved a deathtrap for men seeking shelter there; those that scrambled out were mowed down by artillery and musket fire. Bending down to reduce the chances of being hit, scattered groups of soldiers inched forward in the wake of Ferrero's men, crossing a plain littered with bodies. After being struck in the cheek and having several teeth knocked out, a New Hampshire soldier wandered about in shock, blood seeping from his mouth. A few men found refuge in a cellar near a brick house, but one fellow tearfully turned away new arrivals because there was no more room. Joining the remnants of Ferrero's command, Nagle's regiments lay on the ground, pinned down in a one-sided firefight. A member of the 6th New Hampshire attempting to roll over was hit in the neck, and a lieutenant rising up a bit too much took a ball in the hand.[16]

On the right side of Nagle's brigade the 7th Rhode Island came under fire for the first time. Watching remnants of the Irish Brigade slowly retreat, the men calculated their own chances for survival. Thick smoke shrouded the field in front of them. Soon after the regiment cleared the outskirts of town, a Confederate shell sprayed bloody pieces of lung from a lieutenant colonel over the regiment's commander, Col. Zenas R. Bliss. After a brief pause near a small rise, the regiment was ordered to reinforce Ferrero's thinly held right flank. These Rhode Islanders, too, had trouble negotiating the board fences, and at one point Colonel Bliss grabbed a rifle and began firing to steady his shaky men. With their flag pierced by sixteen bullets, the regiment finally reached the rise held by some of Ferrero's troops. Bliss later noted how the boys had "covered themselves with mud and glory," but actually their situation was desperate. They were "badly whipped," as Capt. Lewis Leavens admitted to his hometown newspaper.[17]

In a classic understatement, Cpl. Henry C. Heisler of the 48th Pennsylvania offered a prediction: "I think it will cost an awful lot of men yet before we can get them [the Confederates] out of their entrenchments." Soldiers in any of the attacking divisions would have agreed. At 1:30 P.M. General Couch had signaled Burnside, "I am losing. Send two rifle batteries." He sorely needed them. The Second Corps alone had suffered nearly 4,000 casualties; 1,000 or so more had been sustained by Sturgis's division.[18] By 2:00 P.M. everything had fallen apart. Franklin had hopelessly bungled his assignment, and without support Meade had been unable to capitalize on his breakthrough. On the Union right ten brigades had attempted to drive the Confederates out of the Sunken Road. None had come close. Yet Burnside would not give up, and so the carnage continued.

★ ★ ★

On Franklin's front, Meade's troops poured out of the woods, soon to be followed by Gibbon's men. Lane's North Carolinians had withstood assaults from their right and front, had fallen back nearly out of ammunition, but did not break. To the left more North Carolinians (commanded by Brig. Gen. William Dorsey Pender) along with two batteries firing double-shotted canister helped stave off an advance by Gibbon's right wing. "The head of the column went down like wheat before the reaper," one officer later boasted. But the Confederates suffered, too. A Rebel limber chest exploded in flames, tearing one of the gunners in half and "burn[ing the body] to a crisp." Pender's wounded left arm hung limp, and blood dripped through his fingers as he moved regiments into position to help Lane; but he dismissed the injury as a "trifle."[19]

The threat to Lane's left had been thwarted. Likewise, the move to the railroad by Col. James A. Walker's Virginians with assistance from Brig. Gen. Edward L. Thomas's Georgia brigade relieved pressure on Lane's right. In the tangled undergrowth Thomas had to move the brigade slowly in column toward the firing. Once up, these fresh troops, attacked by three separate lines of Federals, lacking immediate support, and running low on ammunition, soon gave ground themselves. Though hampered by the dense woods, the 49th Georgia blistered some of Gibbon's men. The delayed arrival of two more Georgia regiments, the 35th and 45th, piled up more Federal casualties. The Georgians would later claim that Lane's exhausted troops had fled through their ranks, but at least two North Carolina regiments kept fighting. Thomas eventually formed a loose brigade line and pushed the Yankees back toward the railroad. His men—some still barefoot—had fought well under trying circumstances on difficult terrain.[20]

To their right Early's brigades had sent Meade's regiments packing. Al-

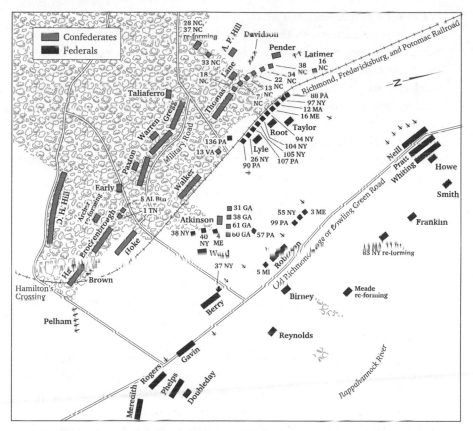

Confederate counterattack against the Federal left begins, December 13, 2:00–3:00 P.M.

though Franklin later claimed that the Pennsylvanians could be seen "leaving the wood at a walk," he admitted that the retreat had been far from orderly. "We had no line," Bates Alexander of the 7th Reserves confessed. With Rebel artillery and musket fire at their backs, scattered groups from Sinclair's and Magilton's brigades stumbled toward the Federal guns. Mystified by the lack of infantry support, remnants of Feger Jackson's brigade along the railroad soon joined the rout. Disjointed Confederate counterattacks drove the Pennsylvanians back through the fields toward the Richmond Stage Road.[21] All efforts to rally them failed. Meade raged and swore, threatening to have one officer shot. It did no good. "I've had enough of this sort of business," one hulking soldier declared as he headed toward the river. "Regardless of threat and force, and deaf to all entreaties," General Stoneman later reported, "they [Meade's men] sullenly and persistently moved to the rear."[22]

The retreat was no less chaotic than the Confederate counterattacks. Walker's troops, along with remnants of Archer's and Brockenbrough's commands, held their positions along the railroad, but Hoke's brigade crossed the tracks and soon came within range of Federal artillery. A piece of shell knocked Hoke's horse to its knees, and the general had to be untangled from a stirrup before the beast dragged him away. Darkness was falling, and Early, fearing the brigade might be flanked, ordered Hoke to pull half of his men back to the railroad and send the rest back up Prospect Hill. Since the Federal prisoners along the tracks outnumbered their captors, some tense moments passed before Confederate officers sorted everything out.[23]

Despite its cost, including the wounding of the brigade commander, the charge of Atkinson's Georgians became the stuff of legend. With wild cheers they began driving the Yankees back across the railroad, taking prisoners and bayoneting a few of their fleeing foes.[24] Yet even before they entered the copse of woods that lapped over the railroad, they ran into some of Meade's men as well as fresh troops coming suddenly through the trees to their left. At last Birney's reinforcements—in this case Brig. Gen. J. Hobart Ward's brigade—had arrived. They were too late to support Meade's attack and too late to stop the retreat but in time to surprise the jubilant Georgians.

As Ward's three regiments approached the copse of woods, fleeing Pennsylvanians momentarily disrupted the formations. "Go back! Go back!" they shouted. Undeterred, Ward's troops kept going, stumbling into two ditches and some fierce fighting on their way to the railroad. The 38th New York even crossed the tracks but soon came under devastating fire from some of Atkinson's Georgians. Ward's men then fell back; their commander estimated his losses at 300 of 800 men in five minutes. No doubt Ward's guess about the duration of the contest was off, but Atkinson's men certainly had fallen on the bluecoats with a fury.[25]

Watching this action from Telegraph Hill, Lee remarked to Longstreet, "It is well this is so terrible! we should grow too fond of it."[26] This much-quoted statement, revealing that even the regal and reserved Marse Robert occasionally succumbed to blood lust, summed up both the horror and excitement of the battle. It certainly must have been satisfying for Lee and other officers to watch Confederates on both ends of the field repulse their enemies with such apparent ease.

Satisfying it might have been from afar, but to Jackson's men counterattacking on the right, the glory was rapidly dissipating. Atkinson's Georgians swarmed around the retreating Federals but soon hit the ditches. To Colonel Evans it seemed that Reb and Yank alike tumbled in at the same time. Moving through the woods had broken up their formations, and so when the Georgians finally made their way out onto the plain, their charge for the Union batteries was spirited but disorganized.[27]

Hall's battery fired double-shotted canister toward the advancing Rebels at a range of 200 yards but quickly ran out of ammunition and had to be withdrawn. Birney dispatched two batteries to cover the retreat and two more regiments from Ward's brigade to support the Maine and New York men coming out of the woods.[28] The 57th Pennsylvania jumped into one of the drainage ditches to stop the oncoming Rebels, who were screaming "like savages." Holding their fire until the retreating regiments cleared the ditches, these men then poured it into Atkinson's troops. Yet they too, with their commander seriously wounded, finally had to fall back, leaving behind men who refused to abandon the comparative safety of the ditch.[29]

The position of the Federal guns remained precarious. Again the delay in bringing up support for the Pennsylvania Reserves nearly brought on disaster. While Ward's men were advancing and retreating, Birney moved Brig. Gen. Hiram G. Berry's brigade in from the left to partially cover Meade's retreat. Berry deployed his troops carefully. On his right he sent the 5th Michigan to protect several batteries. On the brigade left he exhorted members of the 17th Maine, declaring that the eyes of their fellow citizens would be upon them. In a sentimental age largely innocent of true cynicism, many men took such an appeal to state pride seriously. Although they hated to get their new uniforms dirty, these soldiers flattened themselves on the muddy corn stubble and opened what Berry termed a "withering fire" into the Confederates. To their right, Irishmen in the 37th New York let out a wild yell as they, too, blasted away at the Georgians.[30]

Just before these partially concealed troops began firing, some of Atkinson's men had moved to within seventy-five yards of Hall's abandoned guns and entered an area that would be rightly dubbed the "slaughter pen." Emerging unsupported from the copse of woods, they launched what amounted to a piecemeal assault against a larger force in a fairly strong defensive position. Not stopping to calculate the chances for success—a few Yankee cannon seemed to be there for the taking—the Georgians pushed forward, despite the increasing loss of mounted officers. Some Confederates actually reached the guns before being cut down.[31]

Their casualties would have been higher had the uneven ground not limited the killing power of the Federal artillery and infantry, and had confused orders not delayed the arrival of Birney's last brigade. To the right of Berry's men, Brig. Gen. John C. Robinson placed the 63rd and 114th Pennsylvania next to the heavily engaged 5th Michigan. The 114th Pennsylvania, a colorfully attired Zouave outfit, had never been in combat. Derided as "featherbed soldiers" and "bounty-slingers" by scornful veterans, these Philadelphians quickly proved their mettle. Led by Col. Charles H. T. Collis, an ambitious, Irish-born lawyer, they dragged the six endangered guns of Lt. Pardon S. Jastram's Rhode Island battery to safety. Then they joined the 5th Michigan and 63rd Pennsylvania in counterattacking Atkinson's troops. When a solid shot knocked General Robinson off his horse and an exploding shell killed a bugler and wounded a captain, the shaken men of the 114th paused. Collis grabbed the regimental colors and led his men forward. "The Rebs turned and broke like a pack of sheep," one soldier reported.[32]

The dead, wounded, and dying lay scattered throughout the woods and fields from the Richmond Stage Road to the railroad and beyond. Men from both sides remained trapped in the ditches, occasioning considerable debate, confusion, and a certain dark humor about just who was taking whom prisoner. Eventually Robinson's troops captured the wounded Colonel Atkinson and sixty other Georgians.[33] General Early gave the surviving enlisted men the proverbial heroes' welcome, but he berated their officers for driving beyond the railroad. Indeed their gallantry had come at a terrible price; there were more than 300 casualties in the four regiments that had joined the daring counterattack. Atkinson's troops, however, thought a great victory would have been won had they just been supported by Early's other brigades. The Yankees would have been driven into the river, one soldier still declared years later.[34] Perhaps so; but Franklin had more than a corps not yet engaged, and the farther the Rebels pushed, the more severe the artillery fire from the other side of the river. Ultimately the futile counterattacks of these Confederates had simply piled up casualties, much like the Federal assaults at the other end of the line.

For Reynolds's corps, disaster begat disaster because as Meade was being driven from the woods, Gibbon's disorganized assault sputtered also, and for a familiar reason: lack of support. Around 2:30 P.M. Gibbon received a painful wrist wound while directing fire by Hall's gunners and was replaced by General Taylor. Since there was little help to be had from the hard-pressed Federal batteries to the left, retreat became inevitable. Regiments such as the 90th Pennsylvania fought desperate rearguard actions to save Gibbon's collapsing left. Root's brigade withdrew reluctantly as parts of Thomas's, Lane's, and Pender's brigades drove Gibbon's entire division back across the railroad. A member of the 105th New York raced ahead of the charging Rebels to preserve the regimental colors. As enemy artillery poured canister into the Federals, a private in the 88th Pennsylvania cracked under the strain. He leaped to his feet screaming at the Confederates to stop firing. He was immediately hit in the head and fell dead without making another sound.[35]

Other outfits learned the price of gallantry. The 16th Maine had pushed as far into enemy lines as any regiment in the division. Finally forced to withdraw under Confederate musket fire, the men got hit by artillery once they emerged from the woods onto the open plain. Shells knocked soldiers senseless. "Yells of victory, cries of defeat, curses and groans, accompanied our hapless return," Lt. Abner Small recalled. All told, the regiment suffered horribly: 27 dead, 170 wounded, and 34 missing. Well under half the regiment answered roll call that evening; the highest-ranking officer in Company B was the fourth sergeant.[36]

Adding to the horror—and completely unexpected in the damp winter—artillery shells set the high broom sage on fire. Flames lapped around the wounded singeing hair, eyebrows, and whiskers. Through the smoke Col. Regis du Trobriand of the 55th New York could see desperate men struggling to escape, but even adrenaline could not force shattered limbs to move. This calamity appropriately ended the story of Gibbon's repulse. The ineffectual assault had produced more than 1,200 casualties. The wounded writhing on the ground with their faces burned away aptly symbolized the tragedy of this badly bungled operation.[37]

Despite the turn in the tide of battle, Franklin seemed absolutely passive and showed no inclination to send more troops into the fight. At 2:15 P.M. Hardie telegraphed Burnside: "Gibbon and Meade driven back from the wood. . . . Jackson's Corps attacks on the left. . . . Things do not look so well on Reynolds' front; still, we will have new troops in soon." The message did not indicate how cautiously Birney's troops had been funneled into the fight. Burnside was deeply disappointed. Still uncertain about how the attacks on Marye's Heights were going, he now realized that the Union effort on the left was stalled, an especially surprising turn of events in light of earlier dispatches.[38]

Still hoping Lee might be forced to weaken his left, Burnside ordered Franklin to "advance his right and front" against the Confederates. Without offering an explanation, Franklin said this was impossible. Upon receiving this response, Burnside muttered, "But he must advance," and dispatched another staff officer with a more explicit order instructing Franklin to attack with his entire force. Franklin again demurred. All the troops, except Brig. Gen. William W. Burns's division detached from the Ninth Corps to guard the bridges, were already engaged. Although technically correct, the statement was wildly misleading. Smith's Sixth Corps had come under artillery fire, and Doubleday's division in the First Corps had done little but guard the left flank against Confederate cavalry and artillery. At 2:40 P.M. Franklin reported that his left was in "danger of being turned" and asked for reinforcements. Whether this hint of panic was real or feigned is uncertain. His later claims were clearly contradictory: he had received no orders to attack; not enough daylight remained for an attack; and another attack would have brought disaster.[39]

On Franklin's left, Doubleday's troops had remained mostly idle since the Iron Brigade's morning clash with Rebel cavalry and artillery. The four brigades had taken positions behind the Richmond Stage Road, with the line curling back toward the river. Throughout the day the division artillery exchanged fire with enemy gunners on Prospect Hill. Intermittent though sometimes heavy Confederate artillery fire harassed brigades as they shifted to protect several Federal batteries. Members of the Iron Brigade, under fire but unable to shoot back, considered this a sore trial. A member of the newly recruited 24th Michigan thought the constant shelling "enough to make the stoutest heart shudder." Even veterans sweated, screamed in terror, and burrowed into the mud when shells flew over.[40] Rebel shells disintegrated knapsacks, sent playing cards flying, and sometimes caused painful though not always serious wounds. Blood spattered over the troops, and a ricocheting solid shot snuffed out one fellow's life. Why his regiment did not move against the Rebels baffled one Hoosier and doubtless many of his comrades.[41]

At least Doubleday's brigades were protecting the army's left flank, however. For most of the day the entire Sixth Corps did nothing productive. Several of Baldy Smith's batteries had engaged in the morning artillery duel, but Franklin kept the infantry in reserve guarding the bridgeheads. On the right near Deep Run, picket firing proved especially galling. Pender's 16th North Carolina had helped drive Gibbon's men back across the railroad. Advancing beyond the tracks, these Confederates engaged in a brief but sharp fight with the 15th New Jersey (part of Col. Alfred T. A. Torbert's New Jersey Brigade in Brig. Gen. William T. H. Brooks's division) stationed along Deep Run. Torbert sent two more regiments to strengthen the Federal skirmish line. Col. William B. Hatch of the 4th New Jersey led a vigorous charge toward the railroad embankment, gathering exhausted Rebels as prisoners.[42]

Through the smoke and noise Confederates detected a threat to Capt. Joseph W. Latimer's battery and the rest of Pender's men on A. P. Hill's left flank. Ordered by Hood to prepare for just such a contingency, Brig. Gen. Evander M. Law sent two green regiments, the 54th and 57th North Carolina, to save the guns. Spoiling for action, these Scotch-Irish and German troops brought courage as well as naïveté to the assignment. Like many raw recruits, they had fretted that the war might end before they saw any fighting. Now they were determined to silence the veterans' jibes and win Hood's respect. They not only routed the New Jersey regiments along the railroad but also pushed to within 300 yards of the Richmond Stage Road. In their enthusiasm, however, they advanced too far and came first under artillery fire before they were blistered by infantry rounds. "It was an awful sight to see their poor fellows going up in the air," a Union artillerist admitted as he counted eighteen Rebels knocked down by a single shot. Yet it took several messengers from Hood to end this heroic and foolhardy charge.[43]

The Federals were also in trouble. Colonel Torbert had sent the 23rd New Jersey toward the railroad to support the 4th New Jersey, but the former soon lost sight of the latter. Approaching the embankment in some confusion, the men of the 23rd hesitated, then fell back a short distance, although six companies finally managed to line up along the tracks. Smith and Torbert decided to withdraw both regiments rather than risk bringing on a general engagement. As the bluecoats retired in disarray, Confederate artillery pounded away, and Law's men pressed their advantage.

For both sides, however, the orders to retreat provoked dismay and anger. Malcontents in the Union ranks blamed division commander Brooks for throwing them into the fight and then bringing them out with nothing to show for their losses. An illiterate but articulate Tar Heel cursed "Durn ole Hood," who "jess didn't have no bus'ness 't all ter stop us when we'uns was uh whippin' them ar durn blue-bellies ter hell an' back." Yet for all the bravado, each side had bled more than enough. This sharp skirmish produced 224 casualties in the 57th North Carolina alone (somewhat amazingly, the 54th North Carolina got off rather easily with 46 casualties) and nearly 100 in the rest of Law's brigade (including some surprisingly heavy losses from artillery in supporting regiments that had not even crossed the railroad). For the entire Federal Sixth Corps more than a third of the casualties (162) were among Torbert's men. The fight had lasted only fifteen minutes.[44]

Gibbon's retreat and the sudden threat near Deep Run had left a gap to the right of Birney, but as the New Jersey and North Carolina troops slugged it out along the railroad around 3:00 P.M., Brig. Gen. Daniel E. Sickles's division arrived. Sickles, notorious for his political exploits and acquittal on charges of murdering his wife's lover, always had a flair for the dramatic entrance. Despite a hard-bitten New Jersey sergeant's opinion of Sickles—"don't know his head from his foot" (obviously cleaning up camp language)—the appearance of these troops on the field was certainly timely.

Sickles placed two brigades west of the Richmond Stage Road with a battery between them that joined Sixth Corps artillery in raking Law's North Carolinians. The 26th Pennsylvania and 1st Massachusetts (Brig. Gen. Joseph B. Carr's brigade) helped drive off the last of Law's butternuts.[45]

Federal casualty reports for Doubleday, Sickles, and most of the Sixth Corps offer dramatic evidence of Franklin's caution if not his dereliction. Indeed, it is easy to point to these relatively idle troops and wonder what might have been. Yet the soldiers' own perceptions were quite different. Even troops ensconced behind embankments and hedgerows reported being under fire much of the day. Complaints about "railroad iron," minié balls flying like "hail," and tons of shot and shell raining on their heads filled many accounts.[46]

Sixth Corps soldiers tried to convince the home folks and perhaps themselves that just like the men who had charged the Rebel lines, they too had fought bravely at Fredericksburg. Supporting a battery under fire was a greater test of courage than direct engagement in battle, they averred. Soldiers proudly related how well they had stood their ground, considering it a signal test of manhood. Only those who had been there could understand how hard it was simply to lie down with shells whizzing over head.[47] A Maine volunteer in Brooks's division believed his regiment could have been "raked from three points at any moment" by Rebel artillery. Some shells simply stuck in the ground or knocked over stacks of muskets. Men could see regiments heading for the railroad but not returning. As explosions threw dirt over them, privates (and if truth be told, their officers too) wormed themselves down into the cornfield furrows. One colonel in a New York regiment undoubtedly saved lives by whacking with a sword any man who raised his head.[48]

Luck deserted other soldiers. One man in the 6th Maine became the regiment's only casualty when a bullet tore into his calf muscles as he was defecating. How shocking it must have been to the home folks when news of deaths and serious wounds appeared in newspapers after initial reports that a particular unit had been held in reserve or only lightly engaged. Even ground-hugging soldiers took shell fragments or rifle balls in their heads or shoulders. One fine young man was killed while carrying water to wounded comrades. A New York captain simply told his sister how glad the boys were to see the sun set that day.[49]

Never satisfied with merely repulsing an enemy attack, however, Stonewall Jackson believed that failed Federal assaults invited counterattacks. The confusion of the Union withdrawal and the "success" of Atkinson's unsupported foray across the railroad suggested an opportunity for a decisive stroke. Jackson's countenance glowed with what one observer termed an "intense but suppressed excitement."[50]

Perhaps an artillery barrage might provoke another Yankee attack, and then the Confederates could destroy Franklin. Jackson ordered Capt. William T. Poague of the Rockbridge Artillery near Hamilton's Crossing to open on Doubleday's batteries. On the left Davidson's gunners also lobbed rounds toward the Union lines. But the Yankee guns responded, striking down horses and men. One Rebel gunner lying behind a stump near a "pile of filth" decided that under the circumstances "it smells sweet as a rose." Finally, the Confederates had little choice but to stop firing and scurry for cover.[51]

Cessation of this artillery duel left the Federals equally relieved because they had taken a beating. A solid shot had severed the arm of one Michigan soldier, and another shot had torn a man's head off. Throughout the "perfect shower of shot and shell," soldiers round lied on the ground or covered their heads with knapsacks. Wiser men sought greater safety. "When a man has to choose between laying in a ditch half full of water or getting his head blown off he will generally lay contented in the mud," a Wisconsin volunteer sagely observed.[52] He would have been well advised to stay put because the fight was not quite over.

Like many great commanders, Jackson always thought in terms of destroying the enemy's army. So the bloody standoff would hardly do. He now prepared to have D. H. Hill's Division "drive them into the river yonder." His plan was certainly unconventional: haul out artillery first to probe the Federal defenses and then follow with Hill's troops accompanied by as many men as the other divisions could muster. In addition, Stuart's artillery and cavalry would drive in the Federal left. Jackson's command, however, was in no condition to carry out this movement with daylight running out, and orders soon miscarried. Jackson wanted Early to lead the attack; but the Virginian was outranked by the prickly Hill, and in any case only two of his brigades were in position to join the assault. No word reached Taliaferro. A. P. Hill received his orders at dusk. How or if Hood was supposed to help is unclear.[53]

On the right the signal to launch the attack never came, so Stuart simply pushed his men forward. His artillerists attempted to "crowd" the Federals, but in advancing their guns ran into one of those pesky ditches. Even Stuart's aggressive troopers moved out reluctantly. They realized that few might survive this charge and expressed great relief when orders at last arrived from Jackson calling off the attack.[54]

The halt had not come soon enough for D. H. Hill's men. Yankee guns had silenced the artillery heading the Confederate charge. Hill's troops got tangled up in the woods; regiments separated from their brigades. Confusion reigned at twilight. Litter-bearers hauling back casualties from a North Carolina regiment followed a procession of mud-caked Yankee prisoners being marched to the rear. Men piled up against one another, halted, and simply lay down. Even Jackson later admitted that Union artillery "so completely swept the plain" that any infantry assault would have been hopeless.[55] This ill-conceived attack had been mercifully thwarted.

In striking contrast to the 2,338 combined casualties for A. P. Hill and Early, D. H. Hill and Taliaferro had each suffered 172 casualties.[56] At the end of the day Jackson had two relatively unscathed divisions. Across the field Franklin had Sickles's and Doubleday's divisions along with the entire Sixth Corps. Darkness ended the bloodletting but not speculations about what might have been.

Franklin's timidity had foiled Burnside's plans, but whether an all-out assault against Jackson's lines late in the day would have accomplished anything is doubtful. While trying to prod Franklin into attacking the Confederate right in force, Burnside himself turned persistence into sheer obstinacy as he threw his forces against the stone wall. The Second Corps and one Ninth Corps division had been crippled, but on the Federal right Burnside had an entire corps and one division (from Hooker's grand division) that had not seen action.

As the day wore on, Lee grew increasingly pleased with his well-executed defense, though Jackson typically favored a more aggressive strategy. Even with his two fresh divisions, however, and a couple more hours of daylight, it is doubtful that Old Jack could have done more than spread death and destruction more evenly through his corps. Yet neither Stonewall nor, apparently, his troops would entertain such gloomy thoughts. One of Taliaferro's men later told his wife, "A battle was fought that might have terminated the war could power have been given our Generals, like Joshua of old, to have stayed the sun an hour or two in its course."[57]

We fight, get beat, rise, and fight again.
—General Nathanael Greene

16 Futility

For the Army of the Potomac, December 13 could not end soon enough. In the early afternoon, with several hours of daylight left, Burnside had plenty more troops to funnel into the deathtrap on the outskirts of Fredericksburg. While many of his generals realized the impossibility of the situation, Burnside continued to function in both a physical and mental fog. As with many genuinely modest individuals, Burnside's apparent indecisiveness at times cloaked a stubborn doggedness. Unfortunately that stubbornness now overruled his good judgment. At Antietam McClellan had refused to press his attacks; Burnside would not make that mistake. Instead he would keep fruitlessly pounding away at the Confederate line. Unable to think calmly, he refused to modify his tactics and kept insisting that Marye's Heights must be taken. Reports from the field or the advice of subordinates now carried little weight, especially if such advice came from Joe Hooker.[1]

Hooker had been in a foul mood since midmorning after he learned that Birney's and Sickles's divisions had been detached from the Third Corps to support Franklin. He would have "nothing to act with" when the time came to support Sumner's attack, he complained to Burnside. Furthermore, he did not want Franklin to command his men. Rebuffed, the general became sullen and uncooperative. Burnside's secretary described him as "ungentle-manly and unpatriotic" throughout the day.[2]

Matters came to a head when Burnside ordered Hooker to reinforce Sumner. According to Hooker's later testimony, this was a fool's errand because a prisoner that morning had told several generals, including Burnside and Sumner, that the Confederates were just hoping the Federals would be reckless enough to attack along the Telegraph Road. Whether or not this was true, Hooker lacked faith in his mission and commander. After consulting with French, Hancock, Willcox, and Couch and personally reconnoitering the ground, Hooker sent an aide back to Burnside requesting the orders be canceled. Not only were many of the troops demoralized, he thought, but the Confederate positions were impregnable. The aide soon returned reporting Burnside's insistence that the attack proceed, but Hooker galloped back to the Phillips House to protest in person. Fretting about the waste of precious time, Burnside testily repeated the order. Hooker reportedly strode through the rooms roundly cursing, his words and tone bordering on insubordination.[3]

Under orders from Brig. Gen. Daniel Butterfield (commanding the Fifth Corps), Brig. Gen. Charles Griffin's division had begun crossing the river, with the first regiments deploying in the streets around 2:00 P.M. Others in the chain of command such as Griffin, a capable soldier and opinionated member of the McClellan clique, shared the doubts of Hooker and other ranking generals. While bringing artillery into position and noticing some infantry pass by, he reportedly snarled, "There goes one of my brigades to hell, and the other two will soon follow."[4]

That was exactly where they were headed. At 3:30 P.M. Butterfield ordered Griffin to support Sturgis. This fresh division, relief for Ferrero's battered men, soon fell victim to a fatal misapprehension. Somehow Butterfield got the idea that some of Couch's men had carried the heights and that Sturgis's troops were no longer receiving return fire. Butterfield passed the word along to Hooker. One dispatch reported Butterfield sending in Griffin—his "right bower"—but any euchre player would have recognized that even this powerful card could take but one trick, and at this point the hand (and likely the game) was lost.[5]

Moving toward Sturgis's men, who lay on the rising ground southeast of the stone wall, Col. Joseph A. Barnes's brigade marched along the railroad, crossed the railroad cut, and entered a storm of artillery shells and then the deadly rifle fire. In the noise and confusion, first one regiment and then another appeared to "lead" the brigade forward. The whirring of shells might temporarily clear the mind, one officer observed, and even spur a spir-ited charge. But the fresh troops fared no better than their predecessors. Running into a board fence, some soldiers tried to knock it to pieces with their clubbed muskets. Once past this obstacle, the men might get off three or four rounds before their lines "became completely riddled and disorga-nized." To make matters worse, the 18th Massachusetts drifted to the right and became separated from the rest of the brigade. Three times scattered groups of men inched forward but never very far. Some soldiers suppos-edly passed 50 yards beyond the farthest point reached by Sturgis's troops, though they soon fell back toward the fence or flopped to the ground. A lieutenant in the 18th Massachusetts claimed that only 47 men (of an origi-nal 300) reached the assault's high-water mark. Conscientious officers broke under the strain. "Colonel [Joseph] Hayes threw his arms about me and almost cried at this wicked murder," another young officer told his father. "It is no satisfaction to me that I led brave men to useless death."[6]

Conspicuous bravery, however, was not necessarily the rule in a brigade with apparently few textbook soldiers. Members of the 118th Pennsylvania, the famous "Corn Exchange" regiment, lingered over some tobacco found on the wharf. Even officers stopped to snatch up souvenirs from looted build-ings.[7] Several men laughed nervously as a "colored servant" was thrown into the air by an exploding shell. Remembering their recent bloody en-counter with some of Lee's retreating forces after Antietam, the troops form-ing on the streets showed "some hesitancy and unsteadiness," according to the regimental historian. Yet they finally joined the advance, uneasily eyed wounded soldiers huddled near the brick kiln, and stumbled through the fences. It seemed to one company officer that each man was on his own, and even the progress made to this point had at best been halting. "This is awful," one soldier cried as he saw the regiment's major hit in the arm. Dis-organized and demoralized, some men buried their faces in the mud, barely attempting to fire toward the stone wall. Others scurried back to the brick kiln as some officers either drifted toward town or tried to find their men.[8]

Barnes's troops, like many others, had seen badly wounded men stream-ing to the rear well before they had left the sheltering streets. Members of the 22nd Massachusetts stood aghast as they watched a soldier run-ning toward them, blood spurting from his throat, until he fell near one of the bridges. No one stopped to succor him. The Massachusetts regiment had already come across several dead men from Nagle's badly mauled 12th Rhode Island, but now they had to confront the horrors firsthand. As one dauntless fellow tried to lead them forward, a shell spattered his brains over his comrades. The poor sufferer "was gasping in that peculiar, almost inde-scribable way that a mortally wounded man has," wrote one soldier, "I shall never forget the pleading expression, speechless yet imploring."

Blinded by flying dirt and gravel, the Bay Staters reached the limits of en-durance. With sweat rolling down their faces, a few soldiers yelled, cursed, and fired, but most hit the ground. Aside from the pervading smell of death, Massachusetts men soon sniffed other pungent odors. In their haste to hit the ground, they had reached an area used as a sink by other troops. But few dared to move when the bullets buzzed about like bees, brushing clothes, hitting flesh, wounding, and killing. The unhurt and wounded alike lay in the mud trying to catch their breath, likely cursing the generals who had sent them into this little corner of hell.[9]

Yet it could have been much worse because Griffin's men were advancing just as some shifting of Confederate infantry and artillery reduced Rebel rates of fire. Pickett's troops had been idle all day; but around 2:00 P.M. Longstreet had ordered two of the Virginian's brigades to reinforce Ran-som and McLaws, and several regiments came into position about the time of Barnes's advance.[10] On Marye's Heights the Washington Artillery had been hotly engaged ever since the first late-morning assaults. An occasional Federal artillery round would tear into their redoubts, and stray rifle fire from Yankee infantry also proved pesky. One corporal dropped dead when a bullet entered his spine; several other wounded gunners were quickly re-placed. When they were nearly out of ammunition, Alexander brought up nine guns to relieve them, but the crews and horses attracted considerable fire. Even worse, the entire column briefly ground to a halt when the lead gun overturned on a narrow road. Seeing Confederate batteries being with-drawn, the Yankees began to cheer, contributing to the false impression that their attacks were succeeding. The respite, however, was limited because other Confederate batteries to the left and right continued to pour in enfi-lading fire.[11]

Sumner and Hooker swung some of their artillery into action and for a time made a fight of it with Alexander's fresh gunners. On the left Griffin placed the 5th Battery (E), Massachusetts Light Artillery, between the brick-yard and the poorhouse. The New Englanders drew Rebel fire but, even with their guns badly recoiling in the mud, sent more than 100 rounds toward the Confederate lines.[12] Just as Barnes's men began advancing, two of Sumner's batteries came into position to the left of Hanover Street beyond the mill-race. "I would rather lose my guns than my men," General Couch shouted when his artillery chief cautioned against this move. Capt. John G. Hazard's Rhode Islanders were only 150 yards from the stone wall and got off a few well-aimed shots, disabling at least one Rebel gun, but within no more than thirty minutes, fifteen horses and sixteen men (including Hazard and two other officers) were out of action. A New York battery unlimbered to the left and rear, relatively sheltered from enemy fire.[13] Regardless of a commander's skill, the Federal artillery in the Fredericksburg streets and on the plain beyond inflicted little damage on the well-protected Confederates.

Yet to many soldiers these tactical details hardly mattered. Like many battles, this one had assumed a life of its own. Pious men might perceive the divine hand at work, and even without teleological explanations, it seemed that the course of the fight had passed beyond human control. Still more Union troops were now crowding onto the field. Just as Griffin's first brigade advanced, Brig. Gen. Amiel Whipple (whose Third Corps division had crossed the river that morning to support Howard's division) sent Col. Samuel S. Carroll's small brigade to relieve Sturgis. The regiments swung around to Griffin's left, into and mercifully out of the deadly railroad cut. Pressing uphill, these troops managed to gain ground but at horrific cost. Even when the men, bayonets fixed, moved at the double-quick, Confederate artillery rounds tore holes in the formations, and once the bluecoats were within range of the stone wall, Rebel infantry stopped them cold. "As to firing my gun," a member of the 110th Pennsylvania told his sister, "I got wounded before we were allowed to fire." Even so, some men exhibited extraordinary bravery. One captain fell early in the charge, shot through the lungs, but still he urged his comrades forward. He even asked that his wife be told that he had died "defending the rights, liberties, and Flag" of his "bleeding country."[14]

Many others would soon have that privilege. By 4:30 P.M., with daylight fading on one of the year's shortest days, with Barnes's brigade already used up, and with Carroll's brigade blown apart, Griffin received orders to assault the Confederate line. Col. Jacob B. Sweitzer's brigade of Massachusetts, New York, Pennsylvania, and Michigan troops drew this hopeless assignment. The men advanced under enfilading artillery fire and apparently passed beyond most of Barnes's regiments, but they were forced to take shelter in the swale already packed with men from the previous assaults. Troops on the ground and stragglers stumbling toward the rear hardly encouraged the new arrivals. But some of Sweitzer's men fired away at the Confederate lines, only dimly seen in the gathering dusk. Amidst the smoke, noise, and general chaos, orders became confused (or were defied or simply could not be heard), and companies got turned around.

Like other Union attacks, this one extracted a high price. In the 32nd Massachusetts one of every ten men was either killed or wounded within ten minutes. A member of the 14th New York saw men fall on both sides and remained convinced years later that a fervent prayer the night before the battle had led God to spare his life. How else could he explain why some survived without a scratch when so many others were hit? Disorganization added to the bloody toll. Casualties climbed higher as panicky officers first ordered men to lie down, then to move forward, and then to come back. "Words cannot tell," a badly shaken Michigan volunteer scrawled in his diary that evening as he tried to sleep among the dead and dying.[15]

Attacking by brigades for much of the day had chewed up entire divisions. The dead were piled up in front of the stone wall, and hundreds of wounded men lay in the fields, ditches, or buildings. Survivors hung on hoping for relief or simply nightfall.[16] Unfortunately Griffin would send in his last brigade right after sunset. Could he have believed that throwing one more brigade into this swirling, bleeding mass would somehow break the Confederate line? This last effort would only round out the division's killed and wounded at the 1,000 mark.

A bugle call signaled Col. Thomas B. W. Stockton's men to join the fray, but two New York regiments failed to hear it. The troops were supposed to cross the millrace and move toward the swale, though this maneuver had no discernible purpose. One problem was that these men had already witnessed several futile assaults and had taken casualties of their own while waiting in the lower end of Fredericksburg near the railroad. Not surprisingly, an officer in the 20th Maine muttered, "God help us now," as the movement began and his men were struck by Rebel artillery rounds. Despite gardens, fences, ditches, and sardonic shouts from survivors of earlier assaults, some of Stockton's soldiers managed to reach the front and fired ineffectively toward the stone wall. Mercifully, the spreading darkness reduced the casualties, though with so many fragmented regiments scattered about, some of the losses must have come from friendly fire.[17]

Soldiers later confessed that they never expected to get off the field alive. A member of the 44th New York claimed, in proverbial fashion, that he would happily have given his right arm to escape with his life. In fact, two of his comrades lost their left arms, and others in the regiment sacrificed legs as well.[18] Even in accounts written years later, the sheer desperation and hopelessness of these final attacks appeared obvious. Neither officers nor enlisted men had much faith in what they were doing; it seemed as if they moved forward because the generals could not figure out anything else to do. Many boys entering combat for the first time aged rapidly in only a few minutes.

None suffered more than Brig. Gen. Andrew Atkinson Humphreys's division of recently recruited Pennsylvanians. These 4,500 troops had not yet "seen the elephant," and so many eagerly anticipated their first fight. Still crediting hazy reports that Couch's men were gaining ground (likely based on the sudden withdrawal of the Washington Artillery), Butterfield ordered Humphreys forward at about the same time Griffin moved to support Sturgis. The crest must be carried, Burnside kept insisting, and now much of Hooker's command was engaged or about to be.[19] Humphreys's men would take roughly the same route as French's and Hancock's. In the gloaming, artillery support meant little; Confederate gunners waited on hills that were now barely visible.

An often sickly topographical engineer, Humphreys was nevertheless a dashing commander. To his troops he epitomized coolness in the heat of battle. After riding with a column of men out Hanover Street, he sat calmly issuing orders with a cigar planted firmly in his mouth. In the twilight he inspected the millrace and even approached the swale that sheltered survivors. Apparently convinced that his brave boys could take the heights, Humphreys enthusiastically prepared to send them into the fight.[20]

Unfortunately Humphreys's flare for the dramatic overrode his judgment. Even worse, so did his romantic, outmoded notions of warfare. "I led the charge and bared my head," he bragged to his wife, "raising my right arm to heaven, the setting sun shining full upon my face gave me an aspect of an inspired being." He even admitted being "egotistical" but then continued in the same vein: "I felt gloriously, and as the storm of bullets whistled around me . . . the excitement grew more glorious still." To a friend he later wrote of feeling "more like a god than a man." His sentiments were gratifying, except that he led what a *Harper's Weekly* artist later dubbed the "forlorn hope." Even the weakest young men would not be left guarding knapsacks this time; instead they would advance into a nightmare.[21]

Just as these Pennsylvanians were forming in the streets for the third time that afternoon, Couch urgently requested their assistance. Humphreys rode out with Col. Peter H. Allabach's brigade. In the smoke and fading light the troops could not see far ahead, but after crossing the millrace, they gathered under the protection of the bluff. At this point hoping that one rapid thrust would cleave the Rebel lines, Humphreys ordered a bayonet charge—officers in front. With regiments aligned two abreast, Allabach inspected his lines trying to make sure the men's guns were not loaded. Meanwhile Humphreys announced in a mock heroic tone more suitable for the drawing room than the battlefield, "Gentlemen, I shall lead this charge. I presume, of course you will wish to ride with me?"[22]

After advancing 200 yards under artillery fire, Allabach's lead regiments halted in confusion when they stumbled onto remnants of Howard's division lying on the ground. Most of the Pennsylvanians quickly joined these troops, and some began firing contrary to orders. Survivors recalled the terrific noise, and a corporal admitted that "the thought of momentary death rushed upon us as the work of carnage began, and it required every exertion to hush the unbidden fears of my mind." Even official reports and regimental histories, which usually present an orderly view of battle, could not help but reflect the chaotic moments of sheer terror. Humphreys and other officers wanted the Second Corps troops withdrawn, but they could barely get their own soldiers to stop popping away into the falling darkness.[23]

"The men behaved very well under fire, and not until the brigade in front gave way and ran over our men was there any wavering in our line." This simple but not quite accurate statement from a private in the 131st Pennsylvania ignored the most unexpected problem Humphreys's men encountered: the survivors of earlier attacks sprawled on the ground in front of them. Such obstacles can impede, and these obstacles were not inert. Pockets of demoralized soldiers from Howard's, French's, and Hancock's divisions warned of certain death and by grabbing at trousers, shirts, canteens, or haversacks tried to stop the Pennsylvanians from charging toward that damned stone wall.[24]

Humphreys's men should have heeded these cries because Porter Alexander's guns had the range of any regiments that dared creep beyond the swale. From behind the stone wall the Georgians and Carolinians kept up a steady fire as men in the rear ranks loaded and passed guns to the front. Although Griffin's and Humphreys's nearly simultaneous assaults put Longstreet's troops under more pressure than at any other time that day, the lines held. A member of the 2nd South Carolina recaptured the scene: "At every advance we waited . . . until they got near us, when on knees or in stooping posture we would rise, and fire with terrible effect—stoop, reload, and fire again. . . . There could be but one result."[25]

Not yet realizing the hopelessness of the situation, Humphreys tried to force Allabach's frightened men to their feet for a grand bayonet charge. This required some prodigious swearing, especially when Confederate fire cut down his favorite horse (he would soon lose a second mount). To some observers Humphreys seemed perfectly calm as he shouted for the boys to give the Rebels "cold steel" because "that's what the rascals want."[26]

The attack itself—a weak charge and a feeble second effort that made little headway—belied such melodramatic descriptions. Regiments overlapped and divided, with companies scattering in different directions. "There was very little for any officer to do," a captain in the 131st Pennsylvania admitted. "The men did everything." Rebel artillery and infantry seemed to concentrate on Allabach's poor men, knocking staff officers from their horses, striking color guards, and mowing down hundreds of soldiers. Reverting to a cliché, albeit apt, Humphreys reported, "The stone wall was a sheet of flame." After being engaged fifteen minutes, a corporal in the 133rd Pennsylvania, lying in six inches of mud, felt perfectly calm and kept firing. Other men, however, "skedaddled," and regimental commanders reported several cases of "cowardice." Or was it simply good sense? Remnants of companies and regiments fell back in confusion, making it impossible for officers to hold positions beyond the swale.[27]

Even the failure of Allabach's charge did not end the attack. With Hooker praising the Pennsylvanians' gallantry, and with Butterfield and Burnside insisting the heights be carried, Humphreys brought up his remaining brigade. Col. Erastus B. Tyler, a onetime furniture dealer from Ohio who had risen quickly to brigade command, would lead his regiments two abreast over roughly the same ground covered by Allabach. Under command to advance with bayonets fixed and not to fire unless ordered, these soldiers also had to pass over Second Corps troops. With officers twelve paces to the front, a bugle sounded the charge. But Tyler's men, despite some display of enthusiasm, soon ran into a familiar obstacle: men lying on the ground crying out that the Pennsylvanians were heading toward certain death. A few officers even brandished swords to halt the advance. Tyler's first two regiments stepped over these troops but soon came under fire from the rear.[28]

Compared to fire from the front, this was a minor problem because Confederates behind the stone wall shot down scores of Pennsylvanians. What little impetus the attack had now disappeared. The formations came apart. The 126th Pennsylvania maneuvered past the Stratton House, a two-story brick Greek Revival structure that had already become a collection point for survivors from the previous assaults, but fences impeded further progress. Confused by the thick smoke and near-darkness, the Federals fired several volleys and fell back behind the swale.

For a time it seemed like nearly everyone had been hit. A second lieutenant in the 126th Pennsylvania saw men dropping on all sides with their "groans and shouts commingling with the roar and whistle of shell, the crack of musketry & whiz of bullets." Confessing he had no idea what to do, one young officer faced the ultimate terror: "I do honestly believe some of the bullets were not more than one inch from my face. I was expecting to fall every minute." A sergeant in the 134th Pennsylvania described a "withering fire" with bullets shaking a small tree "as if by a wind." At times Yankee rounds wreaked havoc in their own ranks. A group of men from Company K,

129th Pennsylvania, would jump up and fire every time they saw a Rebel cannon flash in the dusk. Officers' shouts of "cease firing" came too late, and some poor wounded Federal, likely stranded during an earlier assault, crawled back toward the lines.[29]

Humphreys's men had been engaged at least fifteen minutes, perhaps a half-hour, and maybe over an hour under artillery fire, long enough at any rate to pile up more than 1,000 casualties. Company officers had fallen at an appalling rate. Every regiment had noble young men killed or wounded, fine fellows remembered for their devotion to duty and good cheer, men with worried families back home, men who had predicted they would be among the first to be hit. For the survivors, the loss of beloved comrades gave human meaning to stark numbers. The division's official list of casualties filled more than fifteen closely written pages.[30]

It is hard to believe, but even this "forlorn hope" would not be the last assault on the Confederate lines that day. Around 5:00 P.M. Willcox had ordered Brig. Gen. George W. Getty's division to advance toward the left of the stone wall to relieve pressure on the Union right. Getty had been in the army since the 1840s, but more than half his troops had not yet engaged in battle. They had already witnessed considerable carnage, including several men ripped apart by shells, while spending the morning and early afternoon in the lower part of Fredericksburg along the railroad near the gas works. "I saw on either side death in its most horrid form," a member of the 9th New York mused. "And I asked myself, Where is Civilization? Where is Christianity? And was consoled by the belief that man was never made to be perfect in this blackguard world." Many other soldiers had observed the hopeless attacks and become demoralized, yet when the time came, many would go forward, however reluctantly. Shortly after he received orders to advance, Getty sent Col. Rush C. Hawkins's brigade forward into the darkness.[31]

Mercifully, Confederate gunners could no longer see the Yankees heading in their direction. After crossing the tracks, Hawkins's troops halted briefly at the railroad cut. "It looked like certain death," one Federal later scrawled in his diary. Misunderstanding his orders, Hawkins sent the 9th New York off to support a battery.[32] The remaining regiments proceeded up the slope toward the remnants of other brigades. Once close enough for the Confederates to target them in the twilight, they came under fire from their left and front. Stray shots from the rear forced men to the ground, where they fired halfheartedly toward the stone wall for about fifteen minutes. Suddenly a man in the 25th New Jersey screamed that they would all be taken prisoner, and the companies on the left broke for the rear; some apparently trampled members of the 89th New York in the process. Many enlisted men took this as the signal to crawl back to the millrace. Regimental officers naturally claimed that *other* regiments had shown the white feather, but in truth, maneuvering, much less attacking, was impossible. Darkness and slippery footing (in part caused by blood and gore that covered the field) foreclosed any success.[33]

The ordeal of the 13th New Hampshire, a newly recruited regiment that had arrived from Washington just days before, epitomized this final phase of the engagement. As the day had worn on, some men wondered about even getting into the fight, and one lieutenant had remarked about the setting sun: "I wish I could get up there and kick that thing down." But he eventually had to bring his men into column and march toward the noise. Hit by artillery fire before they reached the railroad embankment (some soldiers claimed there was more danger from errant Federal shells than from enemy rounds), the men marveled at the gun flashes from both sides eerily intruding on twilight's usual calm. Even as they were receiving some last patriotic admonitions at the railroad, a few soldiers were nervously firing over the heads of other Federals lying on the ground up ahead.

Slowed by mud after they had crossed the tracks and soon entangled with the 25th New Jersey, the Granite Staters slogged through marshy ground near Hazel Run and perhaps got to within twenty yards of the stone wall before they were hit by what Col. Aaron F. Stevens called the "startling crash" of Rebel shot, shell, and bullets. One lucky fellow knocked down by an exploding shell found himself pinned in the mud by two comrades; he wiggled out from underneath only to discover that both were dead and their blood had soaked his uniform. Men threw themselves down and fired a few shots, but they could not hold this dangerous position. Some later blamed the New Jersey troops for botching the assault, though officers could no longer drive anyone forward at this point. Some clearheaded soldiers openly asked what fool had ordered them into this hell. Later a proud captain reported that every man in his company had acquitted himself well before having to retreat. Another fellow came much closer to the truth: "If it had been in the day time so that they could see our position, they would have killed about every one of us."[34] He was right.

The casualties among Hawkins's men were about half those for the most heavily engaged brigades of Sturgis, Griffin, or Humphreys. Proportionally the division losses were even lower because Col. Edward Harland's brigade, positioned on a ridge near the railroad, was not sent forward. A Connecticut private welcomed the sunset that ended the mad assaults and kept his regiment out of the fight. Yet even though these soldiers had been spared the ordeal before the stone wall, they wanted folks back home to know how they had marched along dangerous streets, come under artillery fire, and suffered casualties.[35]

These green troops had lived to tell their tales because darkness had finally ended the slaughter—almost. Around 4:00 P.M. Butterfield had assigned Brig. Gen. George Sykes's division to form a defensive line along the millrace between Hanover Street and the Plank Road. After Humphreys's assault failed and in part because Hooker feared a Confederate counterattack, Sykes sent Lt. Col. Robert C. Buchanan's and Maj. George L. Andrews's brigades to cover the Pennsylvanians' withdrawal. Buchanan received orders to "take the enemy batteries in front at the point of the bayonet," but these were soon countermanded. With unintended irony, two regiments occupied the city cemetery. By 6:30 P.M. Sykes's brigades stood behind the millrace astride Hanover Street, where they came under Confederate artillery fire. Later in the evening they advanced to relieve Howard's men. Hooker claimed that this move came at Burnside's insistence and led to more casualties. The soldiers, however, could hardly tell where they were (some believed they had actually charged Rebel batteries), and they spent an uncomfortable night in the mud.[36]

"Our men only eighty paces from the crest and holding on like hell," Sturgis telegraphed back to Burnside's headquarters at nightfall. Indeed, hanging on was about all the Federals could do. Exhausted, scared, hungry, thirsty, and wounded, the troops had reached the limits of endurance. It mattered not where they were—near the stone wall, along the canal ditch, or back in town. All feared that in just a few hours the battle would start anew. Survivors could barely comprehend what had happened. With tears flowing down his cheeks, General French rode through Fredericksburg searching for his boys. "Adjutant, where is my division?" he implored. "Tell me where my men are. My God, I am without a command." While brazen thieves continued looting buildings, artillery and ammunition wagons jammed the streets. Reassembling regiments was nearly impossible. When roll was called in the 129th Pennsylvania, a wounded corporal declared himself present except "for a little of piece of me." At this point reports of who had been killed or wounded were sketchy and unreliable. Usually talkative soldiers fell silent, except for a few mumbled words about a fallen comrade. Others prayed quietly. Most buildings, of course, had been commandeered for hospitals or officers' quarters, so enlisted men remained outdoors. Men lay on the curbstones or pavement, trying to sleep, trying to forget.[37]

Desperate for rest after the day's horrors, the men could perhaps have handled the cold (temperatures dropped into the forties after sundown) had it not been for the unearthly cries of the wounded still lying on the field. For troops close to the front, the noise was unnerving. The incessant groaning and wailing, increasing steadily in volume, was more chilling than the night air. "Piercing and horrible," declared a lieutenant in Sykes's division. "More than humanity can bear," added one of Birney's men. Some fellows shouted out their regiments in hopes that a comrade would rescue them from this dreadful night. Still more pitiable were the variety of the sounds: screams, prayers, pleas for water, curses, moans, and sighs—an atonal hymn of horror sung in various regional and ethnic accents. The agony of soldiers who had been hit engulfed those who had survived the day unscathed. The cries of such desperate men offered no solace to the badly wounded. Some simply begged to die. "My God! My God!" one poor fellow called over and over until finally his voice grew weaker and at last faded out.[38]

The anguish smelted war's fierce hatred and touched chords of humanity. For the Confederates behind the stone wall or on Marye's Heights or in the woods behind the railroad, their erstwhile enemies now appeared as simply helpless sufferers. Even crusty veterans winced at the screams of pain, further proof (if such were needed) that the supposed glories of war hardly measure up to the fearful sacrifice. Defying orders, a few Rebel soldiers brought water to wounded Federals. "I can shoot them [the Yankees] as deliberately and eagerly as ever I did any game," a Georgia lieutenant explained, "but I can not pass a wounded man without doing what I can for him." Slaughtering enemies while acknowledging their humanity created a painful ambivalence. The psychological hardening—natural enough for soldiers surrounded by death—remained incomplete. This was especially true because Confederates had witnessed so much Yankee bravery that day, whether in the woods on the right or in front of the murderous stone wall on the left.[39]

Once the sun went down, bluecoats crept onto the field to aid their fallen comrades. Flickering lights bobbed and blinked across the killing ground as small groups, including surgeons, ventured out with lanterns. In the darkness they searched for regiments by feeling for numbers on caps or calling for men from particular outfits. But then some poor wretch would cry out, "Take me. Oh, take me." A New Jersey private in the Sixth Corps stumbled across men without heads or arms or legs. Unable to stand the sights or sounds, he gave up being a Good Samaritan and slunk back to camp.[40]

The wounded could hear ambulance wagons passing or the muffled conversations of rescue parties. One fellow with blood oozing from a shattered leg knew he could be saved. "Do for heaven's sake carry me in." In desperation and growing colder, he offered $50 and finally $100 to anyone who would help. Some Massachusetts troops, who found him dead the next morning, noted the look of "savage helplessness about the eyes" along with the clenched teeth in his "half-closed mouth." Other men gave up the struggle for life more readily. Some begged other soldiers not to touch them, to let them die, or even to finish them off with a bullet. A lieutenant with a mangled arm and leg lay on the field for several hours before finally blowing his brains out with a revolver. Yet ambulance teams and less organized groups brought many of the wounded—often carried on boards, doors, and shutters—into town and even across the river throughout the night.[41]

Despite a serious shoulder wound, Private McCarter of the Irish Brigade struggled back to safety on his own. Dizzy from loss of blood, he had hugged the ground for several hours but toward dusk tried to time his movements for the intervals between Confederate volleys. Though hit in the foot along the way, he crawled downhill and finally collapsed on a rubber blanket, his body wracked by fever and overwhelmed by thirst. A friend from his own company brought water and helped McCarter into an ambulance. When the ambulance got stuck in the mud, the driver furiously beat the horses until vehicle and passengers went careening over rocks and stumps. Two men died en route, but the party finally reached a house in town filled with other wounded men. Shaking with chills, McCarter entered the library and flopped down on the floor. But his pain and the groans of seven other wounded men in the room made sleep impossible.[42]

McCarter had arrived at a makeshift field hospital. Churches, public buildings, and private homes overflowed with wounded men, and more lay on porches or in yards. Throughout the night blood-covered surgeons with coats off and sleeves rolled up performed emergency amputations; more elaborate procedures would have to wait for daylight. The Baptist church had eight large operating tables; in several private homes surgeons did their cutting on dining room tables. Working by candlelight (with blankets covering windows to avoid drawing fire) was both tricky and dangerous. Because ether was too flammable, surgeons used chloroform, which in any case took effect more quickly—a necessity given the sheer numbers of wounded. During the early evening stray Confederate shots occasionally interrupted the surgeons' frantic labors.[43]

After working for six hours, a young Massachusetts soldier decided he never wanted to see a hospital again. One surgeon noted perceptively that those trying to save the wounded at least were too busy to ponder the day's horrors. Sometimes, however, a sense of futility overwhelmed the most dedicated doctors. Even as they worked, the ceaseless, haunting cries of other wounded men penetrated the walls. The sufferers with nowhere else to rest lay on floors slick with water, mud, and blood. Little could be done for many of them, one surgeon confessed, and he quit at midnight, exhausted.[44]

Bluecoats who had somehow escaped enemy shells and bullets tried to sleep; despite the screams of the wounded, men would doze. Bodies were shoved aside or piled up to make room on the ground. Some soldiers did not discover until morning that their blankets were blood-soaked or that men who had remained quiet through the night were, in fact, dead.[45]

While some soldiers slept well, even sprawled out on boards and despite cold and corpses and fears of another fight the next morning, others lay awake all night. A lieutenant in Sykes's division who had tossed his gum blanket on an "old manure heap" could not stop his mind from racing. Thoughts about the past "contrasted most disagreeably with the present." Death almost seemed preferable to facing another day of combat. Many men simply lay on the damp ground unable to sleep, unable to stop thinking about what tomorrow might bring.[46]

Their immediate future largely depended on Burnside and his generals. At 8:00 P.M. Butterfield gloomily reported to Hooker that everyone at Fifth Corps headquarters "seem[ed] to agree that it will be one of the most difficult of operations to carry this crest in front." He pointed out several natural obstacles and the Confederates' formidable defenses. Perhaps Franklin might yet force Lee to "evacuate" his defenses, but there was nothing very hopeful about this assessment. At 10:40, Butterfield sent Col. Rush Hawkins to brief Hooker and Burnside.

Earlier in the evening Burnside, along with Sumner, Hooker, and several staff officers, had dined on canned salmon, peas, and coffee at the Phillips House. At 9:00 P.M. Franklin joined the group, and a discussion of battle plans ensued. Burnside appeared oblivious to the day's losses and deaf to advice, dramatically declaring that he would lead his old Ninth Corps the next morning in a "column of attack by regiments" against the stone wall and Marye's Heights.

Deciding to investigate the situation himself, Burnside asked the grand division commanders to await his return. He crossed the river and met with Couch and perhaps Baldy Smith. The army commander acted energetic and cheerful but, according to Couch, also felt responsible for having led the army to a "great disaster." Whether or not this was true, like most of his soldiers, what Burnside probably most needed was sleep.

During the commander's absence Hawkins arrived at the Phillips House. He used a diagram to explain why the Confederate positions were impregnable. Sumner, Hooker, and Franklin grew drowsy, and one staff officer lay sprawled on a sofa; everyone fretted about Burnside's whereabouts because he did not return until 3:00 A.M. Whether he met with Hawkins or solicited further comment from his grand division commanders is uncertain, but he did not go to bed. At 4:00 A.M. he telegraphed the president: "We hope to carry the crest today."[47]

As Burnside mulled over his plans, Lee also held a council of war, fully expecting the Federals to renew their attacks the next day. Confident that any new assaults would be thrown back, Lee decided that Jackson should then counterattack against the Federal left. In light of the remarkably easy repulse of the enemy on December 13—and forgetting the temporary Federal breakthrough on the right—Lee and his generals naturally hoped to exploit their success. Chasing Burnside's army back across the Rappahannock or even destroying it seemed possible.[48]

For the moment, however, it would be enough to brace for the next day's fighting. Despite a shortage of tools, Longstreet's men began connecting artillery positions and digging additional rifle pits. On Jackson's front, soldiers from Gregg's South Carolina brigade chopped down trees for crude breastworks. Throughout the night Massachusetts troops in Griffin's division could hear the Rebels strengthening their lines. Ever the perfectionist, Porter Alexander shifted cannon about, planning to hurl incendiary shells into town should Burnside launch a night attack, and other artillerists prepared to rake ground already littered with the dead and wounded.[49]

Success or failure made all the difference in assessing the day's work. "It was the prettyest battle wee ever fought," a Georgia captain declared. If the Federals suffered through a night of gloom and fear, the Confederates noticed a beautiful moon and a restful calm. A few thoughts of home and family would be in order followed by the release of sleep. The Rebels could drift off more easily than their Yankee counterparts because they had grown even more confident of success. "Our men are in excellent spirits," one of Pickett's men wrote in his diary, "and expect to be victorious."[50]

Across the lines too many Federals had seen the upturned faces of the dead, and most regiments had witnessed more than enough fighting already. Who could forget all those futile charges on the stone wall? Walking among the corpses in the early morning darkness, Colonel Zook, whose brigade had endured so much during Hancock's advance, admitted that he "never felt so horribly since I was born." Unable to sleep and deeply depressed, he hoped never to go through such a night again.[51] Maybe it was better not to sleep; just wait for morning, wait for it to begin all over again.

To them that fleeth cometh neither power nor glory.
—*Homer*

17 Retreat

Early in the morning of December 14, with fog again shrouding Fredericksburg, war took a back seat to breakfast. For a captain in Sykes's division, fried pork on a stick, hardtack, and a pipe filled the bill. Others refused to settle for familiar camp fare. A Sixth Corps colonel joined several friends in slaughtering two hogs and filling haversacks with fresh pork. In town, soldiers wolfed down their pilfered preserves, fruit, and hotcakes off fine china while sipping wine.[1]

The plundering of Fredericksburg continued. Souvenir hunters hauled off glass and crockery; slaves joined the looters. One delighted Pennsylvanian found John Milton's *Complete Works*—including, presumably, "Paradise Lost"—lying in the street. Musket butts smashed mirrors, sabers hacked down candelabra, and molasses dripped down the tubes of a church organ.[2] Throughout the day soldiers pounded on pianos, and one fellow decked himself out in "socks and satins that would have done honor to the Queen of England." Alcohol lubricated the proceedings as soldiers sought escape from memories of yesterday and worries of tomorrow. "In Fredericksburg and having a bully time," a survivor of Hawkins's brigade breezily informed his sister.[3]

Yet waiting for orders took a heavy psychological toll. Lifting fog revealed Marye's Heights bristling with artillery and infantry. As the morning dragged on, tension mounted, especially in the Ninth Corps, which was slated to lead the assault. As they peered toward the Rebel lines, men could hear the cries of the wounded from nearby buildings. But minutes and hours passed, and still no orders came. A rumored dawn attack by Sykes's division had not occurred, nor had a midmorning assault. Some men received whiskey rations; others read mail; by noon soldiers were frying batter cakes.[4]

"I determined to stand my ground like a man and never flinch," Charles Granger of the 16th Connecticut wrote in his diary. "I commanded myself." Such self-control—a highly prized virtue in that era—was no mere stoic quality. It carried powerful religious overtones. Although the Sabbath passed largely unnoticed that day, pious soldiers sensed the Lord's presence. Faith in God and thoughts of heaven helped soothe apprehension. A chaplain in the 79th New York read a prayer, joined fervently by men preparing for the worst. Simple pleas for deliverance and a few last thoughts of loved ones praying at home brought some comfort, but one soldier simply "waited for the hour of death."[5]

In an odd and unexpected way, Burnside's generals answered the prayers. Over breakfast Sumner, Hunt, and Willcox had decided the proposed attack would surely fail. How to dissuade their commander became the problem. Burnside, assuming for some unknown reason that his losses so far had been no more than 5,000, had prepared orders for the attack. With brigades already moving into position, he visited Chatham at 10:15 for last-minute consultations. As usual Sumner cut to the heart of the matter and bluntly told his friend, "General, I hope you will desist from this attack; I do not know of any general officer who approves of it and I think it will prove disastrous to the army." Burnside was stunned. Ensuing discussions with several division and corps commanders revealed that all agreed with Sumner.[6]

After returning to the Phillips House and more discussion, by midafternoon Burnside had canceled the attack. The general was not well. His short naps during the day and early evening had not provided enough sleep. He felt nauseous after supper with Hooker, Butterfield, and several other generals—perhaps more from the company than from the food. For the time being the Army of the Potomac would hold Fredericksburg, but despite hours of debate, no other decisions had been reached.[7] Burnside had wisely called off the attack, yet he had no idea what to do next. Such dithering could prove a costly luxury because his badly mauled troops appeared vulnerable to a Rebel counterattack.

Lee might indeed have counterattacked had he realized the extent of Federal losses or had he known that Burnside would not renew the assaults.

Union artillery on Stafford Heights, however, still commanded the plain, and Franklin had more than a corps of fresh troops to parry any Confederate thrust. Moreover, Lee expected another Federal attack; information from a captured Yankee on Longstreet's front had indicated as much. A new assault would have pleased Lee. So when the enemy remained quiet, he chided Longstreet, "I am losing faith in your friend General Burnside."[8]

Ordinary soldiers sensed the enemy's hesitation, and a few stouthearted spirits longed for a counterattack to drive the Yankees into the Rappahannock. Officers knowingly quoted Lee as saying he could easily whip Burnside's army by noon. Throughout the day more fighting often seemed imminent because with the two armies still so close, it was hard to believe otherwise.[9]

Upon awakening, Longstreet's men had still been able to hear the moaning of the Federal wounded in front of the stone wall. Sgt. Richard Kirkland, Company E, 2nd South Carolina Infantry, could stand it no longer and asked permission to give them water. After some discussion General Kershaw reluctantly agreed. Filling as many canteens as he could carry, Kirkland climbed over the stone wall. Once Sykes's men realized what Kirkland was doing, they held their fire and even cheered his bravery.[10] Such acts bespoke a common humanity that hatred and relentless fighting had not entirely suppressed. They reaffirmed civilized values in the midst of a war that always threatened to destroy more tender impulses. All along Lee's lines a Confederate soldier here and there would scramble onto the field to relieve the thirst of a wounded foe.[11]

More common, however, was the Confederate behind the stone wall and along the heights who kept his opponents pinned down most of the day. Porter Alexander could not depress his guns far enough to hit the closest Federal regiments, but Rebel musketry covered the ground. To men in McLaws's and Anderson's Divisions, not much seemed to be happening aside from what one South Carolinian termed "spiteful sharpshooting." Losses were accordingly slight.[12] The greatest danger to the Confederates—and not really that serious a threat—occurred late in the morning when men from the 3rd and 4th U.S. Infantry entered John Hurkamp's tannery on the south side of the Plank Road. From the windows and a "loop-holed wall" they fired toward Rebel sharpshooters posted in several frame houses in front of the stone wall. This might have relieved pressure on other regiments in Sykes's division but had little effect on the tactical situation.[13]

For the rest of Sykes's men, December 14 brought unremitting misery punctuated with occasional danger. They were "unable to eat, drink, or attend to the calls of nature"—even a major's official report recaptured the basics of the experience. At daybreak Rebel sharpshooters stood poised to pick off any Federal who raised himself off the ground; lifting a hand drew fire. Stretcher-bearers were hit; near the cemetery seven men were wounded crawling over a wall. With skirmishers drawn back into the lines, men lay flat on their faces only eighty yards from the stone wall. Some soldiers cowered behind dead bodies or wounded horses; others prayed quietly as bullets whistled around them. After lying for hours in one position, some desperate lad could stand it no longer and would dash toward the rear or sneak away for tobacco. Officers compiled casualty lists by passing names along the lines. Muddy water and a few hardtack made up the day's sustenance; men reread letters or newspapers as the hours dragged on. By afternoon, soldiers simply had to stretch cramped legs and thus became more vulnerable to enemy bullets.[14]

To the left of Syke's regiments, members of the 20th Maine took "grim satisfaction" in watching the overbearing Regulars suffer. But many of Griffin's troops huddled together near the swale in even more desperate circumstances. This slight rise afforded only four to six inches of protection, so the soldiers had to flatten themselves tightly against the earth. Had the sun not come out, the grass would have remained wet all day. Bullets whizzed past regularly; occasionally a shell exploded. Not realizing that Alexander's gunners were low on ammunition, some Federals wondered why Rebel artillery did not blow them off the field. A Michigan recruit's diary reflected a common state of mind: "How would you like it . . . to lay there all day long—waiting—for what—thinking of what?" Memories of home, church, and friends kept passing through his mind.[15]

Some men could not withstand the strain, and despite orders not to return fire for risk of bringing on a general engagement, the more frustrated or foolhardy leaped to their feet and tried to nail some poor Reb whose head had popped up over the stone wall. They incongruously claimed to be keeping the Confederates pinned down. A Pennsylvania captain, likely inspired by the whiskey in his canteen, sprang up, grabbed the colors, planted them in the ground, and defiantly shook his fist toward the Rebels. A lieutenant followed suit. By some miracle neither man was hit.[16]

This sort of "bravery," if such it was, soon ran its course, and men took shelter wherever they could find it. Two Massachusetts brothers turned dead comrades into gruesome breastworks, tucking their heads under their bedrolls and pressing against the bodies. More fastidious fellows wrapped blankets around nearby corpses. Regiments thus remained on the field in these conditions for more than thirty hours. After a while men stopped counting the close calls; casualties slowly piled up.[17]

Danger stalked even the relatively fortunate troops who had moved to the rear or had been brought back into town. Rebel sharpshooters, for example, made crossing the street perilous. Worrying about stray bullets, a Minnesotan who had earlier felt ravenous could not eat a thing. "I lost a chunk of my Patriotism as large as my foot," he admitted.[18]

Along the Confederate right, nothing much happened. Jackson waited for any sign of a Yankee movement, impatient to launch a counterattack. He could see that Franklin still had formidable reserves. Early and Taliaferro now held the front line with D. H. Hill behind them and A. P. Hill's exhausted forces in reserve.[19] Throughout the day an occasional artillery round was fired (sometimes with deadly effect); sharpshooters on both sides picked off the unwary or the unlucky. Skirmishing—some of Hood's and Pickett's regiments supported Taliaferro—was about as close as anyone came to serious fighting. In Early's brigade some fools jumped up about trying to draw Yankee fire and then ducked behind trees.[20]

One Virginian recalled having "a beautiful view of the Yankee army," and indeed men on both sides spent much of the day staring across the lines.[21] But it was all a matter of perception. The view did not seem so beautiful to Federals who nervously held their ground and later exaggerated their danger. Descriptions of "heavy" Rebel cannonading appeared in some Union accounts.[22] Reports of "brisk" picket firing and "sharp" skirmishing, however, were confined to Gen. Joseph B. Carr's brigade (Sickles's division), where the Federals did suffer casualties.[23]

Like their counterparts on the right, Franklin's frontline troops lay in the mud exposed to sharpshooter fire. The occasional artillery round made the men hug the ground all that more tightly. Hardtack, pork, coffee, and even a bit of whiskey helped them endure the ordeal. Many soldiers expected a Rebel attack at any time, but as a Rhode Islander put it, they could only lie there "awaiting events." Pvt. Henry G. Milans of the 3rd Pennsylvania Reserves wrote home. He would carry a pocket watch into the battle almost certain to begin any minute, and should he fall, he wanted his son Joseph to have the watch, to hold it to his ear, and to consider its ticking final advice from his father. Joseph should love his mother always, be kind to his sisters, and make the Bible his "guide" throughout his life. As Milans heard cannon booming and the crack of musket fire, he explained that he was fighting so his family might "enjoy the blessing of a free Government and live under the blessing of a free Gospel and have the privaleges of education and a door open to eminance, welth, and happiness."[24]

The Federals tried to add up the butcher's bill and figure out what it all meant. Faces smeared with powder and sweat bearing sad and anxious expressions betokened once-naive young men who had matured quickly. Survivors in the hardest-hit regiments appeared disheartened, broken men barely able to comprehend how their ranks had been thinned so horribly. The Irish Brigade was a case in point. A Rhode Island corporal later claimed to have seen Meagher crying uncontrollably while Burnside tried to console him. In French's division a New Jersey company mustered its pathetic band in a billiard saloon. Clusters of stacked, orphaned muskets provided a crude estimate of the dead, dying, wounded, and missing.[25]

Unfortunately many of the casualties remained on the field. Even without a formal truce a few men would sneak out of the lines to recover the wounded. Groups of soldiers from each side occasionally ran into each other and clasped hands, much to the delight of their observant comrades. By afternoon Jackson guardedly permitted a cease-fire. Aside from a Rebel picket shooting off the toe of a Maine recruit (accidentally, perhaps, though the Yankee's friends had their doubts), the erstwhile enemies enjoyed the fraternizing.[26] Trading, eased along by convivial whiskey, proceeded smoothly; tobacco, for example, was bartered for a northern illustrated newspaper. A hapless hog caught running between the lines became a rare fatality as blue and gray divided the fresh pork.[27]

To see men who had tried to annihilate one another mixing freely was an odd and, to officers, disconcerting sight. Some issued strict orders against conversing with the enemy. One Confederate playfully asked Brig. Gen. Robert E. Rodes, "May we not tell them that we whipped them yesterday?" Some taunting naturally occurred.[28] Yet more was going on than idle banter. The shared experience of combat had fostered grudging respect. A Yankee surgeon admitted, according to one Georgia newspaper, that the Confederates "fight like the revolutionary fathers." No finer compliment could have been offered. More disconcerting was the Federals' discovery that their Rebel counterparts were "nice fellows" and could become "real friends." Recognizing a common humanity implicitly made resuming the slaughter more difficult, and indeed the reason for the officers' caution about such truces soon became apparent. Only the generals really wanted the war to continue, some enlisted men maintained. The privates could easily settle all outstanding differences among themselves.[29] Such easy talk perhaps did not mean much, but with so many dead and wounded still lying about, who could blame these soldiers for fantasizing about their own negotiated peace?

During the brief truce, some men buried a few dead comrades, though they could hardly stand on ceremony. Given the delays caused by Jackson's insistence on a written request and some untimely Federal artillery rounds, the wounded continued to suffer and die. During a more formal cease-fire the next day, the mood turned even more solemn. Soldiers showed much less interest in trading goods or exchanging pleasantries. Instead they went about the work with grim efficiency. After digging in the cold ground without proper tools, soldiers threw the bodies, some shrouded in thin blankets, into shallow trenches.[30]

Despite these efforts, death continued to assault all the senses from many directions. Empty buildings became charnel houses. Members of a Massachusetts battery bent on plunder burst into a room filled with dead Confederates. Corpses littered the railroad depot yard. But it was the appearance of the bodies, not their stench or even the staggering numbers, that left the most lasting impression. They lay on the ground contorted into every conceivable posture, limbs pointing in odd directions. Who could forget the armless, the legless, or the headless? Or the calm expressions on the faces of men shot through the heart who had died instantly? Or the sight of brains oozing from a head wound? Men on burial detail sometimes involuntarily shuddered as the gruesome sights overwhelmed their physical and psychological defenses. A New Jersey sergeant in the Sixth Corps especially noted the effects of shells: "the dead mashed into one complete jelly, their remains stringing over a distance of five yards." The begrimed faces on many corpses made these dead soldiers appear "common" to an aristocratic officer such as Oliver Wendell Holmes Jr. of the 20th Massachusetts.[31] Perhaps men took solace in social conventions, or maybe they could not face the fact that these globs of flesh and disfigured bodies had once lived and breathed like themselves. The chaotic landscape of the battlefield gave the lie to patriotic slogans, naive hopes, and even brave deeds.

For both sides the overwhelming presence of death at first produced horror and revulsion, but soon Yank and Reb alike psychologically closed themselves off from such sights. They could never entirely suppress strong emotions such as shame and guilt and fear, but even the men on burial details somehow learned to cope.[32]

To make matters worse, scavengers had often stripped the bodies—rather like cleaning a hog or skinning a squirrel, depending on the preferred metaphor. A fortunate Confederate might find a new rifle or a full haversack uncontaminated by the owner's blood. There was a raft of scarce items: a good overcoat, a warm blanket, or a sturdy pair of shoes that fit. An Alabama officer saw two barefoot soldiers standing over a Yankee who had received a mortal head wound, waiting for him to die so they could grab his shoes. One impatient fellow tried to pull a shoe off a supposedly dead Federal who suddenly stirred. "Beg Pardon Sir," the Rebel said, "I thought you had gone above."[33]

Such courtesy hardly characterized prevailing attitudes or practices. Some contemporary accounts describe a field of white-clad corpses, but others talk of bodies stripped naked. This ultimate humiliation for the Yankees—to be laid bare before their enemies—reflected the desperate shortages in Lee's army, as did bodies dug up for the clothing. Other indignities, such as cutting off a finger to steal a ring, reflected only barbarity. Just as Federals had lost their moral compass in sacking Fredericksburg, so Confederates now foraged among the dead with an alacrity they would have once found shocking.[34]

That barefoot men would steal shoes was self-justifying, and most Confederate accounts stressed sheer necessity. A Georgia captain admitted that he would "pass among the wounded and dead as carelessly as if they were stones." Although he and his comrades would readily share water with injured foes, they would also steal from the Yankee dead without a second thought. Yet such attitudes were still far from universal. As usual, Virginians blamed North Carolinians for any irregular behavior; a South Carolina volunteer claimed that only skulkers plundered the dead. At bottom lay the most familiar and frightening feature of war: dehumanizing the enemy. A cruel, barbarous foe deserved no mercy. The wretched bluecoats, according to one Confederate artillerist, had "burned houses and drove old men, women and mothers with infants at the breast, and little children into a December night to die of cold and hunger."[35]

During the burial truces, the Federals discovered how their dead had been stripped. Some shied away from mentioning in letters home that even men's underwear had been pilfered.[36] But more often than not the bluecoats described what they saw in tones of moral outrage. Stories spread that unscrupulous villains had pulled coats off the wounded. Although he admitted the poorly clad Rebels needed clothes, a member of the Irish Brigade denounced their "barbarity." Raging over such "diabolical" acts, a Maine recruit decided that slavery had "destroyed much of the finer sensibilities of the Southern people."[37]

Not for a minute, however, would Confederates concede the high moral ground. How could these Yankee hypocrites object to a ragged soldier grabbing an overcoat when they neglected and abused their own dead? "They would pitch them in like dogs," claimed one Georgian who had witnessed the Federal burial details. This was especially shocking because anonymous death terrified soldiers.[38] But for many Confederates the moral clincher for the argument about relative barbarity became the Federals' use of dead comrades as human breastworks. One Confederate soldier breathlessly wrote to his wife about how the Yankees had piled up the dead and thrown dirt over them to afford protection for the living. The press quickly picked up this theme. These heartless bluecoats, one Virginia editor declared, seemed more like "Mongol Tartars than Anglo-Saxons."[39] It was the height of irony: the treatment of the dead by both sides seemed to contemporaries a far greater outrage against civilized values than the slaughter that had produced so many corpses.

★ ★ ★

As the sun went down on December 14, the Federals settled in for another long night on the battleground. Mud stiffened in the cold air. On the streets of Fredericksburg, soldiers stoked their fires, fried their slapjacks, and listened to the fiddlers play. Inside the houses, men wrote letters or played cards by candlelight; others munched a quiet meal accompanied by a sip of whiskey. Outfits pinned down for a day and a half were at last relieved. Regiments from Howard's division, for example, replaced Sykes's exhausted Regulars. Both armies kept digging, strengthening their positions in anticipation of fighting the next day.[40]

Around 6:15 P.M. the sky suddenly began to light up. At first appearing below the horizon, the brightness intensified and spread across the northern heavens. Columns of light in varied hues shot up into the night sky, eerily revealing dead bodies still strewn over the landscape. Yankee and Rebel alike stood awestruck at the most magnificent aurora borealis most had ever seen.[41] Confederates saw nature exultant in their triumph. This rare and spectacular sight crowned their victory and augured well for the future. The streaks of red, a Richmond newspaper declared, signified "the blood of those martyrs who had offered their lives as a sacrifice to their native land."[42] Observers on the other side hoped the red, white, and blue light portended success for the Union cause, but many disheartened Federals doubted it. The spectacular light only threw the Union dead into starker relief. As if to confirm such thoughts, the sounds of familiar hymns swelled across the battlefield that night—a suitable requiem to accompany the celestial display.[43]

The tense anticipation on both sides came to nothing the following day. Confederate artillery chieftains busied themselves moving cannon about and improving their positions. But the recent ammunition shipment from Richmond barely got dented. Gunners lobbed a few rounds at the enemy to drive off pickets from the swale and send sharpshooters fleeing from the tannery. Scattered picket firing and the odd Federal artillery round barely disturbed Longstreet's troops, who dozed in their rifle pits.[44]

The Irish Brigade held a banquet in a small theater to celebrate the arrival of new regimental flags. A bevy of generals including Couch, Sturgis, Willcox, and of course Hancock headed a list of distinguished guests. Several toasts followed a fine dinner of turkey, chicken, and champagne shipped from Washington. Yet the brigade's staggering losses on December 13 left every third place vacant and cast a pall over the proceedings. General Meagher nevertheless launched into a typically florid oration, though Rebel artillery shells soon ended the speech-making.[45]

Jackson's front remained stationary. At some places along the lines, soldiers exchanged more or less friendly greetings. A few bursts of picket firing, an occasional artillery round, and stray bullets (some of which whizzed over Stonewall's head during an afternoon reconnaissance) constituted the only dangers the Confederates faced.[46] Around 3:00 P.M. a New Jersey battery fired on Rebels digging rifle pits, but that marked the extent of Federal aggressiveness for the day. Sporadic artillery fire, however, kept everybody edgy.[47]

Some men had the misfortune to catch a bullet on this "quiet" day. Luck ran out for a member of the 11th Pennsylvania Reserves who had survived Meade's assault on the woods two days before. Wounded in the thigh, he underwent an immediate amputation. Six weeks later, after enduring a second operation, he died. For a few soldiers the psychological stress became nearly as deadly. A member of the 19th Indiana suffered a wound in his left arm, likely self-inflicted.[48]

Covered with dirt and mud, lying in woods and ditches, Rebel infantrymen waited and tried to get warm. Confederates still hoped the Federals might foolishly advance because they believed that southern independence might be secured on this very field. Yet as the hours passed, the bluecoats stayed put. One Virginian on Jackson's front line got it right when he speculated that the badly mauled Yankees would not dare attack again.[49]

Many Federals spent the day anxiously waiting nonetheless. Incredibly, in outfits that had not yet seen much action, dreams of victory and confidence in Burnside persisted. Not yet realizing how badly the army had been bled on December 13, some still speculated that one great battle could end the war.[50] But even for the naively optimistic, December 15 proved a harrowing day. No one wanted to be the last casualty of Fredericksburg. The hours of terrible uncertainty provoked some desperate praying. Men who had already seen action probably joined in, even as they bitterly concluded that the appalling carnage had accomplished nothing. Not only did the Rebs hold their superior defensive positions, but a Confederate counterattack appeared likely. "We must whip them or they will drive us into the river," one Sixth Corps private sadly predicted. A battle-scarred chaplain in Humphreys's division had an even grimmer appraisal: "We are terribly cut up and in all probability badly defeated." The real mystery was why the Rebels did not destroy them, and so some soldiers easily credited rumors that the army was about to slip back across the Rappahannock.[51]

But Burnside had other ideas. During the night of December 14 and all through the next day, the Union high command debated about whether to renew the attacks, hold on to Fredericksburg, or retreat. Hooker, who commanded the Federal forces in town (approximately 12,000 men), had already pointed out his troops' vulnerability to artillery. Moreover, he feared soldiers were becoming demoralized from all the plundering. Worse yet, signal officers reported that the Confederate left had been "greatly strengthened."

Although depressed and apparently thinking about relinquishing command, Burnside consulted Hooker and other generals throughout the day. None of their advice was especially helpful. Butterfield favored flanking the Confederate right but still considered the James River the best route to Richmond. A few generals doggedly maintained that the Confederate works could be carried by storm. Sumner favored holding Fredericksburg, though for what purpose is unclear. Perhaps Burnside had come to realize that many of his generals were neither reliable nor loyal. "Political intrigue & jealousies in subordinates are greater enemies than an open foe," one staff officer noted.[52]

No advice from Washington was forthcoming. On December 13 Burnside had dispatched Maj. William Goddard to consult with Halleck. Goddard must have reported on problems in the army's high command because on December 15 Halleck wired Burnside: "You will be fully sustained in any measures you may adopt in regard to unreliable officers." But the general in chief was guarded about future campaign plans and suggested that Burnside "make some use of the spade"—presumably to hold the town against a Rebel counterattack.[53] A quick ride into Fredericksburg confirmed the uselessness of this suggestion. With a slouch hat protecting him from prying eyes but deep disappointment etched on his face, Burnside rode back across the river, where choking back tears, he finally issued the orders for the army to retreat.[54]

Throughout the day, ambulances had been crossing the middle pontoon bridge to pick up wounded and recrossing on one of the upper bridges. In addition to substantial foot traffic, there were also men being carried on beds, settees, boards, doors, and carts.[55]

Once the wounded had been safely removed, the generals worked feverishly to coordinate a complex and dangerous operation. On the Union left, divisions farthest from the bridges pulled back first. Bluecoats built great roaring fires to deceive the Rebels as they prepared to slip back toward the river. "Looks like a skedaddle," a Sixth Corps lieutenant scribbled sourly in his diary. Dirt and hay scattered over the pontoons muffled the sounds of marching feet. Orders about noise were strict: no speaking above a whisper; bayonets, canteens, and cups were to be secured or wrapped in blankets to avoid jingling. The weather cooperated, too. Heavy cloud cover concealed troop movements, and a stiff wind blowing directly into the Federal lines carried sounds away from the Confederates.[56]

When it came time to move, officers awoke their men with unwonted gentleness. A New Jersey corporal who had fallen asleep in a fine straw pile was furious but soon grasped the wisdom of a retreat. With Doubleday's division leading the way, Franklin's men began the silent tramp back across the bridges. By 4:00 A.M. the last of the pickets were safely on the other side of the Rappahannock.[57]

On the Federal right the Second Corps led the withdrawal. A two-company detachment carried boxes filled with dirt to spread over the bridges whenever artillery crossed. Along the forward lines men noisily dug more rifle pits while their comrades crept back toward town. To make this charade realistic, no one told the soldiers they were covering a retreat.[58] Dogs barked, and as the wind picked up, doors and shutters creaked. "It seemed as if all the hosts of hell were let loose in the city," a New Hampshire captain shuddered. A few larcenous fellows still grabbed mementos as they stooped low and headed toward the bridges. Even in the cool air the exhausted men worked up a nervous sweat worrying about being left behind and taken prisoner. Uncertainty about what the generals might be planning heightened anxiety. By 10:00 P.M. Couch's men had crossed the bridges.[59]

Elements of Butterfield's Fifth Corps either stayed in line longer or had more time to explore the nearly deserted town. Those closest to the Rebels maintained the ruse of an army determined to hold its ground and kept digging until after midnight. Other men marching back through the streets entered houses to awaken sleeping stragglers. A few soldiers still paused to enjoy some last fruits of captured Fredericksburg; others evacuated buildings, sometimes moving toward the front to relieve the advance pickets. Men still stumbled over dead bodies. The sights and sounds that night, according to a corporal in Humphreys's division, "made a feeling of dread creep over one." But for most of the men, including those from Sturgis's division who had been pinned down for nearly thirty hours, the ordeal appeared over at last.[60]

Some regiments, however, still had close calls—some last horrible moments—or even suffered a few casualties. Soldiers who at first had tromped toward the wrong bridges would arrive at the right ones just as the planks were being pulled up. Sykes's division formed the rearguard, with men from Warren's brigade sheltering themselves in rifle pits and barricading streets to foil any Rebel pursuit. Engineers had to reassemble bridges hastily as more bluecoats appeared on the opposite bank. (Some members of the 5th New York who arrived late were mistakenly charged with desertion.) The last of Sykes's troops crossed around 8:00 A.M. An hour later the bridges had been disassembled; boats ferried over stragglers for another hour or so. Men from several regiments later swore they were the last on around the Falmouth side.[61]

Only one regiment deserved that honor. Capt. John Lentz and a small detachment from the 91st Pennsylvania held a blockhouse where the railroad crossed Hazel Run. They never received orders to withdraw, and they remained there until 10:00 A.M. on December 16. A Confederate scouting party that had already captured some Federals approached the blockhouse, and one of the Rebels shouted, "Down with your guns, you sons of bitches." Lentz coolly allowed the butternuts to get closer and then ordered his men to fire. Surrounded on three sides, Lentz's boys had to dash back through streets now swarming with the enemy. Pvt. James Clark swam across the river for a boat, and the Pennsylvanians escaped—the last Federals to leave Fredericksburg.[62]

Despite some confusion over the number of troops in town and the timing of the withdrawal, the retreat came off better than anyone had a right to expect. The only hint of enemy interference was a few Rebel infantrymen sniping at the engineers tearing down the pontoons. After cutting bridges loose from the Fredericksburg side so they swung over to the eastern bank, the engineers spent the day packing up bridging material and sending boats upstream.[63]

Having escaped with their lives, Burnside's men again faced the more mundane discomforts of a late-season campaign. Driven by wind, one of those cold winter rains that can depress the hardiest soul had begun during the night. Men awoke wet and chilled, some in tents flooded with water on top of rubber blankets that afforded little protection. The sodden clothes, blankets, and other essentials elicited what an Ohio artillerist dubbed "tall grumbling." Soldiers who had crossed the bridges in the rain plodded up Stafford Heights and now struggled with the sloppy footing to reach their old camps.[64] It was the final indignity: tramping along in the rain and slogging through mud after a humiliating defeat, having left so many dead comrades in enemy hands.

In the 12th Rhode Island a third of the men had no shelter tents; that night, in the same brigade, a soldier reportedly died of exposure. Some men had left their gear on the other side of the river, while others had settled down before clouds had blown in without bothering to pitch tents. Forlorn fellows wrapped in soggy blankets contrasted sharply with those rare exuberant spirits who got fires going, managed to dry out clothes, or even enjoyed a drop of whiskey.[65]

The wretched conditions hardly mattered to some men. Huddled near a pathetic fire, lying in a haystack on a knapsack pillow, bone-weary soldiers at last got to rest and perhaps for a time blot out the horrors of the past few days. Wind and rain could not disturb their dreams. Settling down in camp, grateful to be alive, seemed like being "home" again.[66] That evocative word showed how the experience of battle could reshape a soldier's orientation toward the world. The recent bloodbath had transformed once roundly despised, muddy camps into cozy sanctuaries.

Yet these miserable bivouacs inevitably added to the campaign's toll. Some men had been sick going into battle, more were ill coming out of Fredericksburg, and now disease—rheumatism, diarrhea, and fevers—felled soldiers who had escaped Rebel shells and bullets. These deaths on the heels of the horrible carnage across the river seemed especially poignant and ironic. Even as regiments took stock of how many men had survived the battle, their sick lists grew.[67]

The fighting itself still sputtered, refusing to die out. Confederate artillerists hurled a few shells across the Rappahannock; the explosions disrupted breakfasts and knocked down tree limbs. Several regiments had to move out of range. In return, stray Yankee rounds picked off a couple of unlucky Rebels, though neither side inflicted much damage.[68]

Unfortunately the battle's ghastly detritus demanded immediate attention. During yet another burial truce on December 17 and 18, parties of wary Federals recrossed the river to perform one of war's most unpleasant tasks. General Wadsworth, who had just arrived from Washington, could only mutter, "My God, my God," when a Confederate staff officer estimated that there were at least 800 unburied Federal dead in front of Marye's Heights. From 600 to 1,000 corpses were thrown into two burial trenches, the vast majority unidentified. Like typical Americans intent on measuring even death, Federals and Confederates alike marveled at the numbers and the acreage over which the bodies were strewn.[69]

Hasty burials only compounded the battle's horrors. Intent on a quick finish to the loathsome task, Federals wrapped the stripped bodies in thin blankets and sometimes tossed them into a trench three or more layers deep. Rude boards with a name scrawled in pencil memorialized a few soldiers, or a chaplain might mumble some words; but most men received no such honors. A black body servant and newspaper correspondent serving in Sickles's division summarized the numbing effects of mass interments. So common had the grim work become "that the lifeless body of a man was looked upon as nothing more than that of a brute."[70]

For a few Federals, though, their ultimate fate still hung in the balance. On the morning of December 16, Confederates began snapping up prisoners, including an entire regimental band from the 114th Pennsylvania that had been left behind during the night. All told, Lee reported capturing some 900 Federals. At this stage of the war both sides remained eager to exchange prisoners. Provost Marshal Patrick paroled some Confederates to their Virginia homes, and on December 17 after a flurry of notes, many prisoners were sent back across the lines. More than 100 bluecoats, however, ended up in Richmond's Libby prison—including the Pennsylvania musicians and their brass instruments. Even soldiers lucky enough to have been paroled or exchanged right after the battle experienced anxious moments. Having heard all kinds of wild tales, Yankee prisoners feared being poisoned, but their reactions varied widely. While one captive tearfully begged his captors not to shoot him, another sneered, "Kiss my ass."[71]

Across the river the appearance of ragged, half-starved Confederate prisoners both comforted and frightened their captors. Clothed in various odds and ends, the Rebels hardly looked like fearsome warriors. Yet a Cincinnati reporter who examined a group of "lank, yellow, weather-beaten" North Carolinians thought otherwise. They most resembled "wild animals" who marched tirelessly and fought with abandon.[72] To gaze into the eyes of such men helped Federals understand why the battle had been so bloody.

While Rebs may have mystified Yanks, Confederates typically dismissed their enemies as coldhearted fiends who lacked human feeling. "The scoundrels ran off leaving the dead unburied," a Georgian commented shortly before the first Federal burial parties appeared. Southern soldiers recounted for the home folks how the Federals had dumped bodies into the trenches. "They care no more for the dead than they would for dogs and brush," one officer claimed. For the Rebels (and even a few bluecoats), tossing several hundred bodies into an old icehouse epitomized the war's heightened barbarity.[73]

Dark thoughts, however, could not entirely detract from the sheer sense of relief the Federals felt at being back across the river. Even the old McClellan crowd grudgingly gave Burnside high marks on handling the army's withdrawal. But men still had to grapple with what this sudden retreat meant because Fredericksburg's staggering price cast a pall over everything. "O, Dear Mother Why my life has been spared the Lord only knows," one New Yorker wrote home. "Our army has been badly whipped & thousands of firesides are made lonely and desolate." Despairing soldiers speculated how this latest defeat would damage the Union cause abroad and at home. Some thought they had been damned lucky to escape; many others credited divine providence. It seemed little short of miraculous that the Rebels had not driven the army into the river; so, too, that the wind and rain had covered the withdrawal.[74]

Few men were as God-fearing as Lee and Jackson. Surprised and chagrined by the sudden disappearance of their enemies, they hardly interpreted it as God's handiwork. For Confederates the second-guessing began immediately. Should Lee have attacked Burnside while the Federals still reeled from their losses? Geography and arithmetic weighed against that idea. The long Rebel defensive line would have been difficult to concentrate for an assault, and even then Federal batteries on Stafford Heights would have raked the town and plain. Lee could not estimate the Union casualties with any precision and had to assume that Burnside still had substantial reserves. Jackson's corps had suffered serious losses, and even the relatively easy triumph over the Yankees had proved temporarily disruptive. "No one knows how brittle an army is," Lee sagely remarked to Stuart. There were any number of reasons why the Confederates could not attack, but the truth is that Lee had been waiting for Burnside to renew the attacks and never expected the Federals to withdraw. A month later he jokingly remarked how eager Jackson had been to drive the Yankees into the river, but he remained sensitive about having miscalculated again.[75]

A few of Lee's soldiers raged against a lost opportunity to strike another blow at the infernal Yankees, but many more cheering Confederate troops moved into town and began ringing church bells to celebrate their victory.[76] With the Federals barely across the river, it was too early to assess the battle's consequences. Yet a swelling pride began appearing in official reports—perhaps understandably, for the Confederates had easily thrown back numerous assaults and held the field. Disappointment in their enemies' deft escape would quickly wear off.

On the other side of the Rappahannock, Burnside, his generals, officers, and enlisted men thought of little but the defeat and retreat.[77] The Army of the Potomac had lost another battle, and the campaign had failed. Burnside's army had not been destroyed, but it had been whipped, every assault repulsed. Whole brigades had been shattered, and in the end the places of heroic sacrifice had been abandoned to the enemy. It had been a demoralizing debacle. Death and suffering seemed the battle's chief legacies.

How are the mighty fallen in the midst of battle.
—2 Samuel 1:25

18 Carnage

The official numbers were sobering if not devastating: 1,284 dead, 9,600 wounded, 1,769 captured or missing, for a total of 12,653 Union casualties. The victors had also paid a high price: 595 killed, 4,061 wounded, 653 captured or missing, for a total of 5,309 Confederate casualties.[1] The figures required analysis, but even on their face, as crude measurements of the performance of each army and its commander, they revealed as much about the battle of Fredericksburg as any consideration of strategy and tactics. But to comprehend the losses beyond the cold statistics meant listening to soldiers discussing the casualties in the camps and hearing the news filter back to thousands of homes. It meant looking, without turning away, at all those bodies in front of the stone wall. It meant accompanying the dead back home and hearing the funeral sermons. It meant pondering the idea of Christian soldiers. It meant thinking anew about courage and maybe even cowardice.

Despite deceivingly precise figures, measuring the battle's final toll was in fact tricky. Even if an initially accurate count of the dead were possible—and it was not—the mortally wounded sometimes died weeks or even months later. Perceptions presented an even larger problem. As the army was re-crossing the Rappahannock, soldiers began calculating the losses for themselves. The most sanguine northern observers placed the total Federal casualties at around 12,000, but many thought them much higher.[2] Men who had seen little action guessed that the totals ran to 15,000 or more.[3] Other soldiers, however, overestimated the actual numbers by nearly 60 percent, claiming that losses had reached 20,000 or more. Because so many men had been able to see so much of the fighting, the carnage had been seared into their minds. Soldiers who cynically discounted newspaper casualty reports often assumed the "real" numbers had to be higher. Several bluecoats suggested Federals losses anywhere from three to ten times those of the Confederates.[4]

Rebels guessed the ratio had been around five to one. Typically, Lee's soldiers agreed with many of their foes across the river that Burnside had lost around 20,000 men. A few even pushed the Federal figure nearer 30,000. Whatever their estimates, to Lee's soldiers the numbers signified a smashing victory, and they eagerly shared the news in exultant letters home.[5]

Southern civilians therefore received wildly unreliable reports of Federal casualties. "The Yanks lay in perfect heaps in front us," one of Kershaw's men wrote home, and he placed Union losses at more than 20,000 men. Soon vivid descriptions (a soldier correspondent to a Georgia paper reported how "the Yankees were slaughtered like hogs") and inflated numbers circulated throughout the Confederacy. Only a few days after the Federal withdrawal from Fredericksburg, official Richmond considered the figure of 20,000 Union casualties authoritative.[6]

But the Yankees hardly knew the correct figure themselves. The *New York Tribune* reported a remarkably accurate 13,500 casualties on December 18, but some Republican editors, worried about sagging morale and the political consequences, published much lower figures. Ironically this fed skepticism among press-wary soldiers. It also played into the hands of Democrats who plausibly claimed the actual numbers were much higher and reflected the Lincoln administration's mismanagement of the war. Conservative editors could therefore use the widely bruited figure of 20,000 to badger Republicans while patriotically and safely praising the common soldiers' unparalleled valor.[7]

Yet sectional and political prejudice did less to skew the reported numbers than did the location of the bodies. Unlike battles where the dead lay scattered through thick woods, at Fredericksburg innumerable bodies lay in plain view along the railroad, in the streets, and especially in front of the stone wall. Tromping over the field, some Rebels even tried to count the bodies. A sergeant in Kershaw's brigade tallied 900 Federal corpses, but a lieutenant colonel in the same outfit heard that 1,300 bluecoats had been buried near the stone wall. Despite divergent estimates, Confederates agreed they had never seen so much carnage.[8]

The profusion of corpses made a lasting impression on Lee's men. Confederate descriptions emphasized three features of these killing fields. First, the dead covered many acres. English observers told Stuart they had never beheld anything comparable on European battlefields. Even the streets of Fredericksburg, one private commented, were "choked" with bodies.[9] Second, Confederates noticed heaps of bodies; one of Stuart's men counted 85 in a single pile. Such ghastly accumulations seemed to magnify the slaughter.[10] Third, Rebel accounts emphasized how "thick" the dead lay in particular areas: more than 100 bodies in a large garden; about 450 scattered across four acres. Many soldiers reverted to the old cliché about being able to walk on corpses for a quarter-mile or even the entire length of the stone wall without having to touch the ground.[11] Despite such vivid descriptions, however, folks at home must have struggled to grasp the extent of the butchery.

Soldiers could hardly forget the sights—hands, legs, arms and heads shot off and bodies mangled beyond recognition—reminding one Rebel of hog-butchering time back home. Yet these putrefying remains had once been human beings—whose final agonies appeared in glazed eyes, bent knees, or fingernails buried in cheeks.[12]

A few young men on their way to becoming seasoned veterans appeared (or at least pretended) to take these impressions in stride. Riding over the battlefield, one of Longstreet's staff officers noted how he "enjoyed the sight of hundreds of dead Yankees" and how it had done "my soul good." Anyone who had grown accustomed to a battlefield, one Georgia captain coolly informed his wife, considered such sights "grand." Christian soldiers reconciled hatred and revenge with their faith. Had not the vandal scum cruelly bombarded and sacked the town? Had not God Almighty (and General Lee) now visited them with just retribution? After seeing the ruined town, many Confederate soldiers concluded that the people of Fredericksburg had been rightly avenged. A Virginia infantryman from a most respectable family spoke for many others: "I hate them more than ever. . . . It seems to me that I don't do anything from morning to night but hate them more and more." The carnage no longer elicited much pity even from women. Standing near her gutted house, Mayor Slaughter's wife pointed to several dead Federals lying nearby and remarked, "I am repaid for all I have suffered by the sight of these."[13] It was a cruel and misleading statement. Hatred could for a time assuage the feelings of loss among both soldiers and civilians, but people could not entirely surrender to blind fury even as the war appeared to spiral out of human control.

A young Virginian contrasted the affectionate tone of a letter to his wife with a battlefield covered with dead bodies. Even wartime passions could not harden his heart against such horrors. Soldiers who rode over the bloody ground and noted the individual remains readily imagined loved ones at home awaiting the return of men being anonymously buried. Picking up a letter written by a northern woman to her now-dead husband, Milo Grow of the 51st Georgia mused that Fredericksburg would "cost a world of pangs and sorrows." The Yankee wife would never receive a response to her loving missive, and Grow could not help but empathize with the grief on the other side.[14]

Even a great victory carries many sorrows, one Richmond editor philosophized, and soon southern families suffered the anxiety of scanning newspaper casualty lists while praying to be spared the sight of that one sacred name among the dead or wounded or missing. In Milledgeville three newspaper columns recorded the losses from various Georgia regiments. Richmond and Charleston newspapers reported casualties almost immediately, but nothing appeared in many North Carolina or Georgia papers for another couple of weeks. The *Richmond Daily Enquirer* had the worst timing: three columns of casualties on Christmas Eve and two more on Christmas. In the Confederate capital, fragmentary reports dribbled out bad news to anxious family and friends, thus lengthening the agonizing suspense. Across the hinterlands, of course, word traveled still more slowly.[15]

In the North the news spread too quickly. An earlier attempt to have the Associated Press compile accurate casualty reports had foundered on the highly competitive nature of the newspaper trade. Reporters attempted to compile lists from regimental muster rolls, but clearly the emphasis was on speed rather than accuracy. On Monday, December 15, as the Army of the Potomac prepared to recross the Rappahannock, the *New York Tribune's* front page contained nothing but finely printed casualty lists and dispatches detailing a bloody battle at Fredericksburg, Virginia. Over the next several days all the New York papers filled their columns with the names of the dead, wounded, and missing. Some editors shielded their readers a bit by placing this information on a back page, but people gathered at newspaper offices for updated lists. Within a week the smaller papers were publishing casualty reports from their states and letters from particular regiments including more detailed information.[16]

Name after endless name in long printed columns drove home the costs of war. In Charleston, South Carolina, by December 20 the first meager battlefield reports appeared with telegrams tersely announcing the fates of particular soldiers. Young Emma Holmes found that her diary had become "nothing but a record of death." In New York City that same day, Elizabeth Freeman, though grateful for the safety of her son, commented about how word of heavy casualties at Fredericksburg had depressed everyone. From Lancaster, Wisconsin, Catherine Eaton advised her husband that only God's "restraining power" had saved his life. News of a great battle always cast families into pits of helpless anxiety. There was no way for anyone to be ready for the worst news if it came and their darkest fears were realized.[17]

After receiving the first accounts of a bloody battle in Virginia, a Michigan woman cried for three days before learning that her son had emerged unscathed. Many soldiers sent short notes to relieve the anxiety at home, but impatient families clamored for immediate news. Henry Wadsworth Longfellow fretted over his wounded nephew, a sergeant in the bloodied 20th Massachusetts. But he received no answer to a telegram sent to the Sanitary Commission and so wrote to a nurse in Washington and Senator Charles Sumner begging for information. All too often no word came—no name on a list and no account of a regiment's losses. Prayers and hopes became focused, selfish, and almost superstitious. A Maine volunteer perceptively remarked, "The peculiar feature of war is that each expects *someone else* to fall."[18]

Though soldiers often wrote home about the possibility of falling in battle and could identify with fallen comrades, they had trouble imagining their own deaths. They rarely avoided the normal denial and ambiguity that prevent people from dwelling on their mortality and allow them to go on with life in the midst of great dangers. Even Federals advancing against those solidly entrenched Georgians and Carolinians behind the stone wall often assumed that they would somehow survive.[19] Perhaps the "bravest" men simply avoided commenting on the subject, if for no other reason than to avoid frightening their nervous families.

As soldiers themselves recognized, rumors and false reports heightened fear at home. Men reported to have been badly wounded or killed might in fact have come through the battle without a scratch. On the other hand, a soldier would be listed as slightly wounded or rapidly improving on one day, and the next day he would be dead. In Madison Parish, Louisiana, Kate Stone learned that a Lieutenant Stone—not related to her family—had been killed at Fredericksburg. On Christmas morning an elderly neighbor informed the family that the dead man was, in fact, Kate's brother. A hastily procured newspaper soon confirmed the earlier account. Despite their relief, the Christmas celebration was ruined. The family later learned that their boy had been slightly wounded after all.[20]

Wounded soldiers still able to write reassured loved ones at home that they would survive. Their letters generally exuded a bluff optimism about their injuries and a pride in having done their duty. Yet sometimes the news was both indirect and less assuring. When Philip Hacker of the 5th Michigan was hit in the right groin by a minié ball, his brother quickly informed their parents. On the last day of the year Hacker was able to write but screamed in agony when anyone changed his bed. Stoically thankful that his wound was not worse but admitting that it was bad enough, he asked his mother to be brave. By the end of January, still in severe pain, he had submitted to God's will but bitterly complained that "this cursed war has blighted the hopes of being anybody." Less than a month later Hacker died of dysentery and complications from his wound.[21]

Hacker had slowly slipped away from his parents at a distance, but other families learned about their loved ones' fates firsthand. Only a few days after the battle, relatives began arriving in Falmouth. A Philadelphia woman who thought her son was dead wept profusely upon learning that he was recovering nicely. When his brother's name appeared on a list of wounded, Walt Whitman scoured field hospitals only to discover that George Washington Whitman had received a gash in his cheek from a shell fragment and was doing fine. But the saddest tidings awaited others. A New York woman bringing food to her wounded son found his name scratched on a wooden grave marker. Federal officers escorted ladies across the Rappahannock in fruitless searches for men already tossed into burial trenches. In an age when most people died in their beds, families deprived of a final farewell longed for the details of their boy's last moments. They needed to know where the body lay and sought reassurance that the sacrifice had not been in vain. Patriots still linked their relative's death to a sacred cause.[22]

Families cherished accounts from anyone who had been with their boys to the end. Friends and chaplains would assure loved ones that soldiers killed in battle or who had died right after an amputation had not suffered long. Their letters typically portrayed the men as calm, prayerful, and resigned to their fate. One comrade even included Capt. Washington Brown's dying words: "Oh Lord receive my spirit! Goodbye Eliza, dear mother and all the dear ones at home, I wish to meet you all in Heaven. I have prayed for you. Goodbye I am done." Piety, love of family, hopes for a reunion in the afterlife—Brown's words touched on many of the period's central images and values. Letters from superior officers usually described how such men had carried the colors, inspired the regiment, or succored the wounded.

Death transformed nearly everyone into a brave hero who had spoken lovingly of home and family. To dismiss this as sentimental Victorian mush overlooks an idealism and loyalty that soldiers on both sides would not have found unusual. Men who died in battle were the bravest of the brave, and so it became all that much harder to inform a man's loved ones that the body had been thrown into a shallow grave or remained in enemy territory.[23]

Families therefore made Herculean efforts to bring their loved ones home. A man detailed from the regiment sometimes accompanied an officer's corpse on a boat or train; more commonly a relative journeyed to retrieve a body. Generally, embalming or some other expedient took place beforehand. A surgeon in French's division used a case made of hardtack boxes and filled with charcoal to prevent an already badly mangled corpse from putrefying. What a religious periodical termed the "melancholy harvest" of war reached the grieving families soon enough. By custom, on Nantucket Island a steamer arriving with such ghastly cargo flew its flag at half-mast; eight men from that small place had been killed at Fredericksburg.[24]

As bodies returned, the funeral business North and South prospered. On Christmas the corpse of Lt. Leander Alley, a member of the 19th Massachusetts who had been killed in the street fighting on December 11, arrived on Nantucket Island. From the wharf a flag-draped hearse topped by a gilt eagle wound through the streets to the family home, where hundreds of people paid their respects. The next day schools and businesses closed, and after "impressive funeral services," scores of children followed a procession to the Unitarian cemetery. A few days later a three-mile-long cortege in Richmond accompanied the metallic caskets of Francis Dunbar Ruggles and two other men from the Washington Artillery. In the beleaguered Confederacy, however, even mourning cloth was in short supply, and often a brief prayer service at home (usually without the corpse) had to suffice. Even though nineteenth-century Americans had considerable experience with premature death, great battles laid a blanket of sorrow simultaneously on thousands of households.[25]

Too often the anguish was geographically concentrated; in New York City on January 16, 1863, a crowd packed St. Patrick's Cathedral to bid farewell to the dead of the Irish Brigade. The majestic simplicity of the building and its stained glass windows added to the somber atmosphere. Amidst strains of the "Dies Irae" from the Mozart Requiem sung by a choir led by Father Thomas Ouellet of the 69th New York, a large catafalque crowned with six tapers and a velvet pall embroidered with a white cross stood in memory of the brigade's more than 100 dead. Some of the wounded attended to honor their fallen comrades. A long and ornate sermon praised the soldiers for serving their "adopted country" and defending the Constitution. After the mass Meagher hosted a dinner at Delmonico's Restaurant. In a eulogistic address fueled by several toasts, the good general could not forgo political commentary and praised his men for bravely serving during a crisis for which Democrats bore no responsibility. Political recrimination would not take a day off for mourning.[26]

Protracted grieving followed any great battle, and horrific news or no news at all ruined the holiday season for thousands of families. On December 20 in Greensboro, Alabama, Fannie Borden wrote to her husband about her brother Ruffin "Bud" Gray, who was serving in Barksdale's brigade and about whom she had heard nothing. By Christmas, word had arrived that Bud had been mortally wounded by an artillery round. "How horrible to think of dying among strangers with no dear friend or relative near," she lamented. It was a common sentiment. Her inconsolable mother kept saying how much Bud must have suffered without warm clothing over the past several months. Fannie especially regretted that he had never made an "open profession of religion." At last the metal coffin reached Greensboro, and though the boy's mother wanted it opened for the funeral, that could not be done. A few pieces of gray hair clipped from his head showed how much he had aged during two years' service.[27]

★ ★ ★

In several senses "boys" had grown into men, but the youthfulness of the casualties seemed particularly appalling. Newspaper obituaries dwelled mournfully on the virtues of soldiers cut down in the prime of life, their future promise unfulfilled. Tender age and touching nobility became inextricably linked, especially in public statements about such losses. Whether they had been sturdy sons of New England following in their revolutionary ancestors' footsteps or scions of Virginia responding to honor's call, the dead soldiers left families struggling to cope with their obscenely premature deaths and repeatedly asking, "Why?"[28]

Why, especially, would the Lord allow so many Christian soldiers to suffer and die? The men's piety, lovingly sketched in many accounts, made the sacrifice of life all that more poignant. Some soldiers had professed their faith at a young age and even in the army had maintained close ties with pastors and local churches. Their eulogies featured long lists of virtues: how they had overcome the temptations of vice, had shunned swearing, and had dutifully observed the Sabbath. A Roxbury minister praised Lt. Edgar M. Newcomb of the 19th Massachusetts for avoiding the coarser features of camp life by exhibiting an almost "womanly purity and refinement." Although Confederate preachers emphasized similar qualities, they lifted up the ideal of the "Christian gentleman" in a more masculine fashion.[29]

Whatever the differences in emphasis, however, such model soldiers embodied a stern devotion to duty that could even conquer life's ultimate fear. Countless eulogies spoke of mortally wounded soldiers calmly facing death, submissive to God's will and with minds turned toward heaven. "All is well— my way is clear—not a cloud intervenes," a Georgia captain reportedly testified on his deathbed. Such men especially wished their families to know that they had died in full assurance of the resurrection. "It is all light ahead," Lieutenant Newcomb quietly said. Knowledge that loved ones retained their spiritual confidence to the very end proved a great comfort to God-fearing families. At Newcomb's funeral back in Boston a choir even sang, "I would not live alway."[30]

Religious and patriotic themes became inextricably entwined. Evangelical catchphrases and set-piece eulogies transformed wartime deaths into rituals of sacrifice. In dying for country, one also died for God. Saving (or creating) a nation exacted an awful price; by giving up their lives for their respective causes and comrades, soldiers reenacted the Easter drama—and with the same assurance of eternal life. Their suffering and deaths sealed the promise of salvation. From hospital beds some men claimed that they had required an amputation to bring them to repentance. Pain atoned for past sins. "I lost my arm, but I have found a savior," one soldier told a member of the Christian Commission. The effusion of blood signified the redemptive power of sacrifice. A few men experienced conversion literally in their last moments of life. The death of a sickly and badly wounded young volunteer in a Washington hospital on Christmas highlighted the spiritual significance of such vast carnage.[31]

The loss of so many devout young men (after a battle few bothered to note the thousands of soldiers who fell short of that standard) cast a pall on both sides, but particular deaths seemed to cast an even longer shadow. In official reports and soldier letters, many Confederates mourned for Tom Cobb, who had died commanding the Georgians behind the stone wall. They remembered him as a fine gentleman, a capable general, and above all a model Christian. At an elaborate funeral in Athens, Georgia, a mass of lawyers, judges, politicians, University of Georgia faculty, Masons, and firemen gathered to pay one last tribute. While a local editor lauded Cobb as a "Christian hero," a weeping crowd seemed overcome with grief. Lafayette McLaws remembered the Georgian as a "religious enthusiast," always seeking a "visible sign that Providence was with us." Such an exemplary life and its abrupt end led one soldier to muse that "the ways of God are past finding out."[32]

For Confederates, the Almighty's inscrutable nature manifested itself most dramatically in the deaths of young officers. Promises of divine protection made with such confidence early in the war now gave way, if not exactly to doubts, at least to a more complex theology. Even the triumphant Rebels had to acknowledge that many Christian soldiers had fallen. Randolph Fairfax, a private in the Rockbridge Artillery, had died instantly when struck in the corner of his left eye by a shell fragment. Confirmed in the Episcopalian faith at fourteen, he had shown a religious devotion and seriousness rare in one so young. In tortured fits of conscience he had worried about studying too hard and not preparing well enough for the last judgment. An excellent student at the University of Virginia, he had read scriptures at the local poorhouse and carefully observed the Sabbath. Eulogized by the Reverend Philip Slaughter as a fine soldier and a model Christian, Fairfax had led a blameless life that proved how military duty and religious devotion were both compatible and complementary. Such deaths, however, had a sobering effect. Fairfax had been variously described as a "beautiful youth" or "lovely boy" or "Christian hero" almost too fine for a corrupt world. Lee considered Fairfax the very embodiment of "self-denial and manliness" and tried to soften the loss by pointing out that he had been "translated to a better world."[33] Nonetheless, Fairfax's death also suggested that during a battle the Lord would not necessarily safeguard even his most faithful servants. Such examples of selfless devotion to duty would become part of the edifying history of the war for southern independence.

Sadly, eulogists on neither side remarked on the tragedy of devout young men killing one another in fratricidal war. Yankee preachers proved as one-sided in their recognition of sainthood as their southern counterparts. Cyrus Augustus Bartol, for example, extolled the virtues of Maj. Sidney Willard of the 35th Massachusetts, who had been wounded during Ferrero's advance on December 13 and had died the following day. In a memorial tribute delivered at West Church in Boston a week later, Bartol declared that Willard—"a good husband . . . a good soldier, a good Christian, a good man"—had fallen a martyr to the cause of civil and religious freedom. A superb student raised in the church who would leave a room to avoid foul language, he had nevertheless been patient with weaker comrades who yielded to the temptation of strong drink. He had bravely marched south to free the slaves, fully realizing the unfinished struggle for equal rights in the North. Like the Confederates, northern ministers and politicians hoped such lives would inspire young people to perform deeds of valor, but they also wondered why such an exemplary young man had been struck down in his first fight.[34]

Yet in contrast to Confederate civil religion, the northern variety seemed more equivocal, and eulogies sometimes carried divisive political messages. With emancipation still hanging fire, the deaths of soldiers with abolitionist convictions became opportunities to promote the antislavery cause. Although he had recently received a medical discharge, Chaplain Arthur B. Fuller, brother of famous transcendentalist Margaret Fuller, had insisted on crossing the pontoons on December 11 with some Massachusetts troops. He had died instantly when struck by several bullets, leaving a wife pregnant with their fourth child. Fuller's tragic story became a religious and political object lesson. As a brave Christian, a teetotaler, and an indefatigable supporter of Sunday schools, Fuller had lived a life that embodied what one minister called "practical Christianity." The Reverend James Freeman Clark likewise insisted that Fuller had died to rid the United States of slavery, an example that should lead others to buckle on the armor of righteousness in the fight for universal liberty.[35]

Given the volatile political atmosphere and recent Democratic gains at the polls, such conclusions could never go uncontested. On one level, the story of Gen. George D. Bayard's death simply evoked sympathy. Throughout the war he had struggled with various physical ailments, including an old arrow wound from his days fighting the Kiowa in Nebraska territory, but at Fredericksburg he commanded a cavalry brigade. Wondering if he should really be in a hospital, Bayard had written to his father less than a month before Fredericksburg that "honor and glory are before me—shame lurks in the rear." Moreover, he had already postponed his marriage to the West Point superintendent's daughter three times. On December 13, leaning against a tree in front of Franklin's headquarters and seemingly oblivious to danger, he suffered a severe hip wound from a ricocheting solid shot. He calmly asked how much longer he had to live, then wrote a farewell note to his parents. Bayard died the next morning. The funeral services took place on the day of his scheduled wedding. Yet this story offered more than poignant coincidence. Radical Republicans considered Bayard a martyr; Greeley claimed that he "died in full Anti-Slavery faith, converted on his many fields of battle." But a Cincinnati newspaper reported that Bayard said, "Tell McClellan that my last regret, as a military man, is that I did not die serving under him." In a battle for historical memory, Little Mac's friend Franklin and other conservatives claimed Bayard as one of their own.[36]

Confederate eulogists faced different problems in sorting out sometimes conflicting social and political values, especially in treating a well-known officer of uncertain spiritual conviction. Such was the case with Maxcy Gregg, a man who had never professed Christianity and had been mortally wounded as Meade's men poured into the gap on the Confederate right. In the early morning hours of December 14, Stonewall Jackson visited Gregg and urged him to "turn your thoughts to God and to the world to which you go." In great pain, Gregg nevertheless refused to cry out or show any emotion save resignation to his fate. His reputation as a man of inflexible will only grew among officers who gathered at the bedside during his final hours and heard him dictate a note to Governor Francis Pickens expressing his readiness to die for South Carolina.

Lee praised Gregg's "disinterested patriotism and unselfish devotion," but a man such as Gregg required a more grandiloquent eulogy. At the Presbyterian funeral service in Columbia on December 20, the Reverend Benjamin Morgan Palmer grappled with the significance of the general's life and death. He praised Gregg's perfectly balanced personality and his classical virtues that typified the state's leadership class. The general had been a "true man" whose "courage, honesty and strength were tempered with the softer graces of gentleness and love." Gregg resembled an honorable Roman hero "incapable of falsehood," with a finely tuned sense of justice; he was a "polished and courtly gentleman" whose quiet reticence concealed a steely inner core. Gregg had preferred the scholarly repose of the study to the base cunning and unseemly ambition of the world. Palmer had to skirt questions about the general's Christian convictions by assuring the audience that Gregg had expressed interest in religion and had no doubt privately made peace with his creator. Such a life should inspire all Confederates to redouble their efforts in the holy war against a "bold and infidel fanaticism [that] has undertaken to impeach the morality of God's administration, and with reckless blasphemy denounces as profligate the government of the universe."

Palmer had tried to conceal a real problem in a flood of rhetoric because the general's life clearly illustrated more stoic than Christian virtues. Gregg the fire-eating orator had exuded an almost primal sense of honor, but try as he might, Palmer could not really make him into a Christian martyr. The stern rectitude of a Carolina gentleman, the demands of relentless war, and the ideal of the Christian soldier just would not fit together.[37]

Regardless of such contradictions, the horrors of Fredericksburg could not undermine the era's prevailing evangelical dogmas. Survivors of the carnage on both sides remained convinced that God had protected them. Hence their only legitimate response was humble gratitude followed by trust that somehow the Lord would also keep them safe the next time. Soldiers who still held that God had specifically spared *them* could thus cope with the chaos of combat. These convictions, moreover, brought them closer to the home folks. Men took comfort in the thought of families in prayer; by the same token, images of Christian soldiers sustained civilian morale. A Virginia woman affirmed that God had miraculously spared her brother, and a Massachusetts lieutenant declared that nothing could have saved him but a mother's prayers.[38]

Faith-based certitude buttressed daily life in the midst of civil war, and even the sternest tests did not necessarily shake the foundations of spiritual assurance. But for some Federals after Fredericksburg, nagging doubts crept into letters home. A New Jersey volunteer still affirmed that God's "unflinching protection . . . never will fail while we put our whole trust in him," which was the only way he could explain how he had survived when "the bullets were flying so thickly." But whether this was spiritual or physical protection remained unclear because admittedly there had been "nothing to protect the union soldiers but the protection that Christ throwed around us when he said it is finished." The hope of resurrection could partially replace the old conviction that the Lord would spare the humble private's earthly life. A New Hampshire recruit decided that it was best not to think about such matters but instead to "obey orders and leave the rest to the God of battles." Yet the question remained: why did one man escape all injury when so many were falling around him? Obviously, Christian soldiers seemed to receive no special protection. Two notably pious friends in the 5th Pennsylvania Reserves, for instance, who had been struck down during Meade's advance eventually died as Rebel prisoners.[39] The war was testing religious conviction beyond what anyone could have imagined just a year earlier. Doubts did not necessarily signify a loss of faith, but they did reveal that the confidence of even the most devout Christians could hardly remain unfazed amid such vast destruction of life.

★   ★   ★

Because of the terrain at Fredericksburg, soldiers had observed wholesale dying firsthand. Normally men saw little beyond their own regiment or even their own company, but the wider vistas of this battlefield had intensified the horror.[40] Yet like all soldiers, they found combat nearly impossible to describe. "I was going to write about my feelings in going into battle," a Pennsylvania private told his mother, "but it cannot be done." Surrounded by smoke and noise, the men easily became disoriented. Once the first shot was fired, a Confederate remembered simply standing with his company and doing what he had to do.[41]

But even veterans believed they had never heard such artillery and musket fire, and the incessant volleys shredded nerves. One member of the

Pennsylvania Reserves had exerted himself so much during his regiment's advance and retreat that he vomited in a ditch. Clausewitz once described war as "primordial violence, hatred, and enmity . . . a blind natural force" nearly beyond human understanding or control. In the midst of a battle, an ordinary soldier reacted with savagery, a hatred of the enemy that could drive him to extraordinary feats of endurance and valor. During combat men entered a nameless world of unimaginable chaos. Planning, leadership, and religious faith counted for little; fate and luck ruled. Chance held everyone in its fickle hands—not only troops in the front lines but also men in the rear, who might be snuffed out by a random shot.[42]

Close calls became staples of campfire conversations and letters home. Stories about a diary, a folded letter, a hard biscuit, or even a stolen copy of *Pilgrim's Progress* stopping a potentially fatal bullet were legion. Such incidents fed prevalent superstitions though Fredericksburg did not produce the usual tales of pocket Bibles saving lives.[43] Belts, swords, musket butts, and even tin cups deflected minié balls; bullets sometimes sliced harmlessly through knapsacks or bedrolls. Any man emerging unscathed from such heavy fire and counting a half-dozen or more bullet holes in his clothing had been both lucky and courageous. Now he was blessed with irrefutable proof that he had held his ground when the lead flew.[44]

How men had dealt with the all-pervasive fear was another much-discussed subject. One Sixth Corps soldier told of watching boys cook their dinners while shells struck nearby; they would hit the dirt and "then rise as if nothing happened." Such composure impressed soldiers who acknowledged—at least to themselves—that everyone was scared. Men were not supposed to admit fear, but some simply could not move when the orders came to advance. Others nervously twitched or broke into a sweat. Getting through the ordeal—"no longer a slave to the fear that at first had nearly overpowered me," in the telling words of a Maine recruit—created a strange exhilaration, an intense appreciation for life. Officers typically and misleadingly described their bravest men as "fearless," but a whole gamut of emotions from terror to panic to bloodthirstiness to elation surged through soldiers under fire. Many men might have once defined courage as the absence of fear, but a battle such as Fredericksburg inevitably changed such ill-formed notions. Soldiers soon realized that they could not always coolly face the foe, but duty, loyalty, and devotion to the boys in the company could temporarily overcome basic instincts for self-preservation.[45]

In a sense, honor could likewise inspire bravery. A cook in the 19th Massachusetts had begged to join his comrades because he did not want anyone telling his wife back in Lynn that he had toted a kettle while his regiment was shouldering arms. Soldiers responded indignantly to the slightest imputation against their courage. The idea of an "honorable death" did not seem either ludicrous or pointless because noble examples fostered a more selfless patriotism. After all, soldiers in both armies claimed to be fighting for their homes. Families and friends would soon learn whether a man had done his duty or skulked in the rear. As a mortally wounded seventeen-year-old corporal was being carried off the field on a house shutter, he simply declared, "No man can call me a coward."[46]

Courage helped assuage the pain of failure, and even after a terrible whipping, honor remained. "We were defeated because bravery and human endurance were unequal to the undertaking," declared a soldier in Griffin's division. Everyone on the field at Fredericksburg had learned the sanguinary lessons about human limits; valor could not stop a bullet. Honor could not guarantee victory.[47] Fearless charges against strong positions increasingly seemed like madness.

Although soldiers on both sides spoke the language of honor, Confederates did so with a distinctly southern accent. Daring, gallantry, audacity, and a firm conviction that Rebels fought more fiercely than Yankees increasingly defined national identity. Col. Clement A. Evans of the 31st Georgia proudly reported that his men had "behaved with a courage characteristic of the Southern soldiers." According to other officers, their men had upheld the fighting reputation of particular states. Assuming a direct link between casualties and courage, a South Carolina colonel said of his regiment, "Ours is a bloody record, but we trust it is a highly honorable one."[48]

Thus ancient definitions of courage survived even in the face of horrific combat. Experience, disillusionment, and hardening might alter traditional notions of patriotism, but they did not destroy them. At the beginning of the war, many men had imagined battles as dramatic clashes between knightly heroes, and though such chivalric notions could not survive long, at the same time people wanted to believe that massive bloodshed could have some redeeming qualities. Sacrifice and even martyrdom still sounded like noble ideals, but romantic impulses clashed with harder reality. A Fourth of July militia drill back home was "boy's play" compared with the "work" of battle, thought Pvt. Edwin Wentworth. To read about combat "is well enough in a pleasant room," he mused, "but to *face the music* is quite another matter."[49]

Interestingly enough, Wentworth still chose a euphemism—"face the music"—to sum up his experience. With no intended irony or apparent reservations, many others talked simply of doing their duty and serving their country. Even the most melodramatic descriptions, such as General Sully's tribute to the 19th Maine, "who for the first time smelt gunpowder, and apparently did not dislike the smell of it," stirred pride. But officers had to do much more than recognize courage. Their own bravery solidified companies and regiments; leading by example worked much better than flowery exhortations. At the same time, however, a more democratic style had replaced aristocratic ideas of knightly valor. A captain in the Irish Brigade expressed the new ethos best: "Even the humblest private may be styled a hero."[50]

Whatever his rank, a courageous man was supposed to behave with humility and go about his duty without fanfare. Often the quiet soldiers found unexpected reservoirs of strength. As Yank and Reb alike noted, men who loudly boasted of their courage often quailed, cowered, or even ran off once the bullets started flying. In striking contrast, the best soldiers unostentatiously stayed at their posts even if they were dangerously wounded.[51]

Courage, according to Clausewitz, is an "emotion" essential for "moral survival." Indeed, both combat effectiveness and physical well-being rested on disciplined courage. Preserving character and preserving life became equally compelling goals, though not objectives that could be rationally reconciled or weighed. Battle inevitably created emotional turmoil. Seeing one's friends fall produced a rage that drove men to become "heroes" despite their better judgment. Once the first rushes of enthusiasm and adrenaline passed, the sight of the dead and wounded seemed far less impelling. Just as formations fragmented in hopeless charges, so, too, did combat spawn mental confusion as soldiers reacted unexpectedly. Some felt unusually collected in the midst of combat and seemed almost disappointed by their lack of excitement. A Massachusetts private marveled that though aroused to a fever pitch, he remained strangely calm at the same time. He would have run had he not been surrounded by comrades, he said, but like so many others, he feared appearing scared. Even this lowest common denominator of courage pushed soldiers to the limits of endurance. "Our men did all that flesh and blood could do," a Pennsylvania officer wrote to his sister.[52]

Not all flesh and blood withstood such trials, and despite many heroic examples, some men could not respond to duty's call. Anticipating combat was often the most difficult challenge. Court-martial records suggest that troops not directly engaged and under sporadic fire were the most likely to desert during a battle. Several Sixth Corps soldiers simply disappeared for a day or more. Likewise, some men in Howard's, Griffin's, and Sykes's divisions who had witnessed the early charges toward the stone wall broke for the rear. A few soldiers exaggerated the number of "cowards" in their ranks, perhaps to puff up their own valor, but it is likely that a third or more of the men in any regiment at Fredericksburg never fired a shot.[53]

Some men took to their heels whenever artillery rounds landed nearby, or they cowered behind trees or in ditches as their regiments moved to the attack. Every man knew of skulkers who somehow disappeared as soon as the shooting started, but many also acknowledged the thin line separating courage from cowardice. Some boys could literally not get off the ground. A Maine volunteer watched a comrade "gather himself together, gain his place in the ranks, and again drop behind." The man fell to his knees, tightly grasping his musket, yet he seemed to be paralyzed. He indignantly rejected the taunts of "coward" but literally could not move. Other men cried piteously for their families back home. Some refused to pretend. "I know I'm a coward, and a damned coward," wailed a Massachusetts soldier as he dodged the blows from the flat of an officer's sword and kept running. An equally candid fellow informed an astonished provost guard near one of the pontoon bridges that he was the "most demoralized man in the whole of the Army of the Potomac."[54]

Few soldiers could be so shameless and instead pretended to be wounded, refusing to be examined by a surgeon and stumbling toward the rear. As Gibbon's men withdrew from the woods, two stretcher-bearers carried off a large New Yorker, but he scampered away when they stopped for water. One cowardly lieutenant first claimed to be wounded and then ill before he was finally arrested. Other men hoped for some slight injury to justify an honorable withdrawal from combat. General Taliaferro cursed one fellow hiding behind a tree waving his arms who announced that he was "feelin' for a furlough." A few wounds were undoubtedly self-inflicted.[55]

The question of who would die in any given battle was not only fraught with theological difficulties but raised doubts about fate, luck, and justice. Many people believed that God decreed the hour of one's death, but many also placed much stock in superstitious portents. Soldiers would inevitably declare before every battle that they were goners for sure this time. A South Carolina infantryman bathed and changed his underwear because he did not want to be buried in dirty clothes. Like many others, a Pennsylvania adjutant scrawled final instructions for his family before becoming absolutely "prostrated" when a shell shattered a nearby tree. Some soldiers prayed quietly, convinced that the hour of their death rapidly approached. After Fredericksburg, stories circulated of men with such forebodings who had been killed instantly once their regiments were engaged.[56]

If enlisted men knew of comrades who had to be shamed or driven into battle, they also realized that their superiors occasionally blanched, broke into a sweat, pretended to be wounded, or even scurried to the rear. Such officers immediately lost the respect of their troops and often had to resign.

Concern about one's reputation at home drove many hesitant company commanders into battle. When a letter to a Rochester newspaper reported that a lieutenant in Griffin's division had hidden behind a fence during the battle, he heatedly denied the charge, but the damage had been done. Even helping a wounded comrade off the field (a common dodge by shirkers) often opened a soldier to vicious gossip that quickly reached local communities. After a Maine officer was cashiered for cowardice, army officials sent details of the case to newspapers closest to the man's home.[57]

Leaving the ranks during a fight was a serious offense, but given the gruesome realities of combat, generals were often lenient. Two lieutenants who had reportedly abandoned their posts on December 13 received only a reprimand; derelict privates often lost a month's pay or were fined some other small amount. Yet sentences varied significantly between divisions. Courts martial in Whipple's division, for instance, generally imposed $10-a-month fines for three months, but in Sykes's division the period was twice as long. Other commanding officers favored public humiliation. A man might be forced to wear a placard or barrel labeled "coward" or "skulker" for a month or more, or have his forehead inscribed with a "D" or a "C" in India ink. General orders announced the punishments during roll calls, and public humiliation of cowards brought derisive laughter from some of the troops. In the Sixth Corps several deserters had to carry around a twenty pound ball and chain or a heavy log for a month. Besides these punishments, sergeants and corporals were often busted to the ranks and fined. Stiffer sentences included hard labor for periods ranging from a month to the duration of a soldier's enlistment. Some enlisted men were drummed out of their regiments and imprisoned; a few officers were cashiered. Soldiers clearly had reservations about the more severe penalties, but a Massachusetts volunteer spoke for many others: "I rejoice to see the cowards humbled."[58]

At least the appearance of justice reestablished some sense of order in a chaotic world, but refined definitions of courage or cowardice did not necessarily help soldiers or their families sort out the meanings of so many deaths. The battle of Fredericksburg elicited fear, anxiety, and cruelty. Hundreds may have died, thousands more may have sustained grotesque injuries, but in the larger scheme of things, individual agony seemed irrelevant. As Clausewitz coldly noted, "We are not interested in generals who win victories without bloodshed." Some soldiers embraced this philosophy. A Confederate captain in Kershaw's brigade mournfully contemplated all the fine men killed since the beginning of the war. His affirmation that "they died [for] a *Just Cause*" seemed stock but also sincere. Yet even devout Christians had difficulty explaining the bloodshed. Men would not fully understand all the war's sacrifices, explained the Reverend J. O. Means at Lieutenant Newcomb's funeral, until the completion of God's master plan. But the plan was inscrutable, and its completion was submerged in an ocean of blood. For the time being, Means admitted, it seemed that the boys had simply been sacrificed and "nothing gained."[59] The dead at least no longer had either to suffer or to ponder. For the painfully wounded, however, both the agony and the hard questions had just begun.

He jests at scars, that never felt a wound
—*William Shakespeare*

19 Wounds

Burying the dead was hard, but treating the wounded could be overwhelming. First they had to be moved, and the wounded of Fredericksburg took various journeys. Some were brief: from the field on a litter (one Georgian claimed he "never did a harder day's work in my life") or in an ambulance jostling along dirt roads. Other journeys took longer. Prodded by the weather and a shortage of tents, Confederate military authorities began removing the wounded from farmhouses and temporary field hospitals on December 14 and loaded them onto railcars for transfer to Richmond hospitals.[1]

The following evening more than 800 wounded men arrived in Richmond; others went to Charlottesville, where one woman noted the "sickening sight" of trains carrying "bloody freight." The mayor of Richmond asked citizens to provide blankets, and women brought coffee, tea, soup, and milk to the depot. Ambulances, hacks, and omnibuses carrying the men to various hospitals crammed the streets.[2]

Transportation was a more critical problem for the Federals. Surgeons could make preliminary assessments, care for the superficially injured, and perform simple amputations in the field hospitals, but ultimately many of the wounded would have to be taken either to division hospitals nearer the camps or to much larger facilities in Washington and elsewhere. Here would follow more operations, more convalescence, and more dying. The key problem was efficiently moving the casualties, a task that until now had stymied both sides.

Considering the recent horrors of Antietam, the Federals might have faced another medical disaster. But by the end of 1862 a series of reforms—largely organizational—had vastly improved matters. Jonathan Letterman, appointed medical director of the Army of the Potomac by McClellan, had organized medical operations by division rather than by regiment, sacked several incompetent doctors, created surgical teams, stockpiled medical supplies at Aquia Landing, and supervised the setting up of field hospitals before the battle. For once the army had a surplus of blankets and an adequate number of hospital tents. "A new era has dawned for our wounded," a surgeon in the Ninth Corps enthused. Letterman still faced a shortage of wagons to carry supplies, but he had solved many logistical problems.[3]

Letterman had appointed a captain to command the ambulances in each corps, with lower ranking officers and sergeants placed in charge of divisions, brigades, and regiments. Regulations specified four-horse and two-horse ambulances for each regiment and outlined duties for each man. Only members of the ambulance corps—designated by a green band around the cap and half-chevrons on each arm—were to carry men from the field. Such rules were necessary because soldiers with little taste for fighting often pretended to succor the wounded. There were "always plenty of a certain class of skulkers" to accompany a wounded man to the rear, noted private Jacob Heffelfinger of the 7th Pennsylvania Reserves. But genuinely compassionate fellows said orders be damned as they hauled friends to safety. Several of these received medals of honor for extraordinary valor in rescuing fallen comrades.[4]

Rules and organization often became meaningless once a battle began. On the Union right, where ambulances were impractical, litter-bearers ventured onto the field to collect the wounded. But with only six such men per regiment allotted to this task, the system broke down under the mass of casualties. Some wounded had crawled back to safety, while others had remained on the field for a day or more. Even before the evacuation of the wounded on December 15, men were being carried on mattresses or floorboards. Litter-bearers came under fire and were sometimes hit themselves, but they managed to get the wounded to ambulances waiting near the bridges.[5]

Despite terrain difficulties, the ambulance corps operated efficiently at Fredericksburg, especially on the Union left, where the drivers could get much closer to the front. On December 13, despite considerable danger, ambulances had brought the wounded back toward Smithfield and other temporary field hospitals. Manned by a driver and two attendants, each ambulance carried canned meat, hard bread, condensed milk, and medical dressings. A regimental surgeon accompanied an ambulance, supervised the loading of passengers, and distributed tickets to those who had to wait for the next vehicle. The nearly 1,000 ambulances in the Army of the Potomac made transporting the wounded back across the river on December 15 relatively efficient.[6]

None of these accomplishments silenced critics. Admittedly, litter carriers were not the strongest, the most energetic, or the bravest soldiers, and the wounded never seemed to be carried from the field quickly enough. Typically, many of the men had to be moved several times, and some unfortunately got soaked in the cold rain on their way to division hospitals. A published letter from Griffin's division charged the ambulance corps with "criminal negligence" for failing to remove the wounded from the battlefield before midnight on December 13. One Irish Brigade soldier blasted the "lying government papers" for reporting that the casualties had been well cared for when many remained unattended for several days after the battle.[7] Perception naturally lagged behind performance, men in the ranks perhaps had unreasonable expectations, and the chronic grumblers also had political axes to grind. But given the extent of the carnage, a detached or objective view of the medical shortcomings was perhaps beyond human capability.

Miraculously, a few Federals who had lain for two or more days where they had fallen somehow survived. Immobilized by their wounds or weakened by loss of blood, they had simply waited, dreading that they would never get off that terrible field. For such men the will to live had helped them survive, but others clung agonizingly to life only to die later. On December 14 a soldier with a severe thigh wound hobbled through the streets of Fredericksburg using a rammer as a cane. At several field hospitals surgeons quickly diagnosed the case as hopeless and refused treatment. Faint from blood loss, the man finally lay down in a yard, where some Rhode Islanders from Getty's division later found him dead.[8]

Ironically, such seeming indifference reflected the improved organization that saved others. For a couple of days before the battle, assistant surgeons had set up hospital tents and cleared private homes. Medical directors from the three grand divisions had staked out buildings (some already hit by shellfire) almost as soon as the first Federals had crossed the Rappahannock. Fredericksburg had three field hospitals for the Second and Fifth Corps; four more facilities strung out from near the Bernard House to south of Smithfield served the First and Sixth Corps; on the Falmouth side of the river seven division hospitals clustered around the Phillips House, and there were one at the Lacy House and two more farther east. The locations were conveniently close to the bridges and may also have reflected an assumption that most Federal casualties would occur near the batteries and pontoon crossings on the Falmouth side.[9]

Letterman allotted two hospital tents (capacity around twenty men) for each regiment. The pine and cedar branches that covered the ground and the relatively mild weather afforded fairly comfortable accommodations. Stoves or open fires warmed the inside, while cooking for the patients was done outdoors. The uneven distribution of the wounded among the divisions caused overcrowding in some field hospitals while others stood nearly empty. For several days after the battle poor sufferers lay on bare floors with a haversack for a pillow and hardly any blankets. Confederates set up hospitals in barns and abandoned buildings, but initially many of the Rebel wounded lay on straw pallets in the woods.[10]

For both sides, hospital conditions ranged from comfortable to appalling. Some division hospitals had enough bedding, plenty of food, and warm drinks for the wounded, but others lacked stoves and offered patients little but hardtack. During the rain of December 16, water flowed into the tents and soaked the hay on which the wounded lay. Even though many of these problems were temporary, bitter complaints about the chilly tents and poor food quickly reached the home folks. Letterman had planned to accommodate most of the wounded in the division hospitals on the Falmouth side, and the Federal withdrawal from Fredericksburg greatly improved conditions for them.[11]

Three surgeons and three assistants worked in each field hospital. Assistant surgeons organized the kitchen mess and gathered straw, wood, water, and blankets. Beginning on December 13 and continuing for the next several days, the wounded flooded the hospitals and forced the War Department to dispatch more surgeons to Falmouth. During the night doctors made their rounds to make sure wounds had not started to bleed again or that the most painfully injured men had received enough opiates.[12]

Letterman had tried to weed out the worst surgeons and specified that the most skilled doctors, regardless of rank, treat the most seriously wounded. Army surgeons had often dismissed volunteer doctors as incompetents or quacks, but the contempt was mutual. Reports of drunkenness and even experimental surgery on the mortally wounded hardly inspired confidence among either soldiers or their families.[13]

The parade of wounded at first seemed endless. Men filthy from powder, smoke, and mud staggered toward the field hospitals. During the skirmishing on December 14, soldiers could still be seen hobbling along on makeshift crutches or being carried on stretchers. The next day on the Federal left, one fellow being brought off the field could barely contain both his surprise and his relief: "All right now! I shall not die like a dog in the ditch. . . . I shall see my mother again." A Connecticut volunteer whose brigade had remained safely behind the railroad during the twilight assaults toward the stone wall decided that many of the wounded were "lucky" because their fighting days were over and they "had nothing more to fear." The same would soon be true for the mortally wounded who lay largely unattended in woods, streets, or field hospitals. A Georgia prisoner who had expected abuse from his Yankee captors soon breathed his last softly calling for his wife, Martha.[14] As the torment ended for these soldiers, others fought for their lives. The hospitals witnessed tragedy and triumph, almost as if the battle of Fredericksburg was continuing on a different front.

Harried surgeons confronted a variety of difficult and ghastly injuries. Near Chatham a man who had suffered a shell wound that had torn off a piece of his skull and left part of his brain exposed somehow talked sensibly to anyone who could bear to look and listen; a New York chaplain observing a soldier with a similar wound noted how the exposed tissue "pulsated." The corps reports listed the types of wounds from head to toe. The small number of chest and abdominal wounds simply meant that such injuries usually killed men before they reached a division hospital. In the field hospitals, wounds to the legs, arms, shoulders, and the hip area (including the genitals) were much more common.[15]

Performing triage, especially when some fellows had been hit more than once, presented the greatest challenge for the surgeons. Solid shot, shells, and bullets all did far more damage than a dozen or so hard-pressed doctors in a division hospital could repair. Wounds were rarely clean because shrapnel and minié balls remained lodged in the body. One Pennsylvania major who had been hit by several shots had a bullet apparently lodged somewhere in his left thigh muscle. The wound appeared to heal, and the man could walk with a cane; but fifteen years later, discharges from the leg still required a daily change of dressing. Luck smiled on other men, however. Private McCarter of the Irish Brigade had suffered with his serious shoulder wound through the night of December 13 on the floor of a temporary field hospital in Fredericksburg. Still in "agony" the next morning, he begged a surgeon to remove the bullet. After cutting away McCarter's clothing and wiping through the clotted blood, the doctor finally found the bullet under the right arm. McCarter yelled "slash away," and soon the ball was extracted with surprisingly little pain.[16]

Many patients required more extensive operations. Minié balls flattened as they entered an arm or leg, dragging clothing, hair, and sweat; bullets and shell fragments shattered bones. In an era when postbattle amputations were routine, soldiers most dreaded coming under the surgeon's knife. In the First Corps alone, surgeons performed over 100 amputations before the Federal withdrawal; for the entire Army of the Potomac, the total exceeded 900. Surgeons quickly examined wounded men as they were carried in and then tagged them with a ticket describing what was to be cut off. Soon the surgeons and their assistants busily wielded their knives and other instruments in hour after hour of exhausting work. At a First Corps hospital near Smithfield a chaplain saw a badly wounded soldier "sighing and weeping with pain," but soon the man was lying on a bed of straw minus a leg *and* an arm.[17]

What everyone, even casual passersby, most noticed right after the battle were the piles of amputated limbs. Hands, arms, feet, and legs lay strewn about or in great heaps awaiting burial.[18] Whether all this cutting and hacking had done much good remained in doubt.

Leading British and French doctors still debated the efficacy of amputations, and the *American Journal of Medical Science* recommended the procedure only in doubtful cases where life was in danger; but the controversy mattered little to the sufferers whose fate hung in the balance. Some men lost a limb before they realized what was happening. That many needless amputations were performed became an article of faith among troops who accused surgeons of spurning more conservative options. A Rhode Island corporal was convinced that some medical officers used the wounded to practice their technique or instruct medical students. Thus fearful of the surgeons, other soldiers refused to let anyone saw on them, and a few even survived to brag about it. One captain philosophically remarked that a poor man had a hard enough time in the world with two legs, let alone just one.[19]

The wounded themselves or visitors who had witnessed amputations in the hospitals undoubtedly originated many rumors. In Fredericksburg morbidly curious men peered through windows observing the operations. Private McCarter vividly remembered the "ugly looking surgical tools" and one young surgeon covered with gore, sleeves rolled up, striding about smoking a cigar. Other soldiers recalled the "crunching" of a saw going through a bone, the "shrieks and groans" of the patients, or even the quiet struggles of men who still thrashed about before the chloroform took hold. All this suffering seemed futile for at least two reasons. First, in many instances doctors knew amputation did not guarantee survival of the patient. Second, given the outcome of the battle of Fredericksburg itself, heroic measures to save lives might be pointless. As one soldier who had lost a leg perceptively commented, it would not have been so bad "if we had been put in where we had the least chance," but as far as he could tell, his limb was "gone for nothing."[20]

Since there were only about thirty medical officers assigned to a division hospital, musicians, chaplains, and volunteers had to take up the slack. Although the War Department and newspapers discouraged civilians from visiting the wounded, a few women volunteers helped succor the hopeless, the despairing, and the convalescent. One man recalled hearing only one gentle voice, that of twenty-four-year-old Nellie Chase, who poured a bit of whiskey down his throat, washed the clotted blood from his face and hair, and insisted that a diffident surgeon examine his wounds. Some imperious doctors considered such kindness unwanted interference in hospital procedures; but the soldiers appreciated the gentle care, and in their delirium sometimes mistook female volunteers for their mothers.[21]

Despite hostile surgeons, transportation problems, and in some cases their own inexperience, the nurses made a difference for many patients. Clara Barton, a former teacher and civil servant who had been energetically assisting the soldiers ever since First Bull Run, arrived on December 7, began helping the first casualties on December 11, and managed to cross the river on December 13 to dress wounds. She remained at Chatham for the next couple of weeks tending patients and carefully recording deaths and burials. On returning to Washington, however, she could not get Fredericksburg out of her mind.[22]

Such physically and emotionally demanding work could be deeply satisfying but also enormously frustrating. The horrors, drudgery, and constant demands of suffering patients took their toll. Hardly able to describe Chatham's rooms and corridors overflowing with the wounded, Harriet Eaton mostly noticed the pathos: men clinging to life and so grateful for a smile or kind word; soldiers in excruciating pain begging for someone to write to their home folks. Completely drained, Eaton despaired over the future of the army. Yet such volunteers became godsends for the wounded. Isabella Fogg helped distribute food and linens to the hospitals in Hooker's grand division. She read the Bible to soldiers, wrote letters for them, bathed them, and offered a tearful goodbye to the dying.[23]

The sheer magnitude of the demand, however, overwhelmed the most dedicated volunteers and underscored the need for organized relief. By this point in the war the Sanitary Commission efficiently hauled supplies directly to the division hospitals. After bringing in stores by boat to Aquia Landing and then overland to a headquarters near the Phillips House, several ministers, doctors, and other agents handed out wool shirts, underwear, and socks. Relief kitchens dispensed crackers, dried fruit, condensed milk, and beef broth. Optimistic reports brimming with impressive statistics, however, told only part of the story. Relations between the Sanitary Commission and the Christian Commission competing for supplies and glory grew testy. Members of the Christian Commission, although uncertain about their own mission, criticized their "ungodly" rivals. Some of their volunteers distributed soft bread and butter to wounded men who had not enjoyed such delicacies for months, but more often ministers simply carried tracts and testaments. Truth be told, many of the wounded would have preferred more creature comforts to literature on the evils of gambling or swearing.[24] Effectively ministering to the wounded presented a similar challenge to both the Christian Commission and the Sanitary Commission, and despite the friction, both groups helped assuage much physical, emotional, and spiritual misery.

These devoted civilians entered places where generals were seldom seen and soldiers most feared to go. Here the almost inconceivable destructiveness of war was on display: men with eyes shot out, swollen tongues, or missing arms and legs. The piteous groans and nauseating smell of blood completed a massive assault on the senses. Barely recognizable human specimens covered by thin blankets lay dying on piles of straw. Their desperate, pleading expressions haunted visitors' memories.[25]

The flood of wounded during the first several days after the battle had swamped surgeons, their assistants, and other hospital workers. Not surprisingly, stories of various horrors soon reached the home folks, who knew nothing of how Letterman and his officers had actually improved medical organization. Many soldiers preferred to ignore the hospitals or exaggerate their deficiencies. Thus when a New Yorker in Getty's division claimed that the wounded were treated no better "than a pack of used up maimed dogs" and that hundreds more men would have survived the battle had they received better care, he sacrificed accuracy to colorful description.[26] Nonetheless, dramatic incidents and questionable anecdotes dominated popular perceptions.

But even the most graphic accounts often illustrated the nobility of the human spirit under great suffering. After the street fighting on December 11, Pvt. Josiah Murphey of the 19th Massachusetts had been carried to a room in the Lacy House. There he was laid between a Mississippi prisoner and another Nantucket man so racked with pain that he begged Murphey to kill him. Murphey noticed a bluecoat nearby whose brain was oozing through a hole in his head. He heard the screams of patients who could only be calmed by opiates and saw the dead being hauled out. Even amidst these scenes, many of the soldiers tried not to raise a fuss because they realized how much better off they were than others.[27]

Many of the wounded welcomed an extra blanket, soft bread, or a kind word, but their thankfulness also bespoke Victorian assumptions about what constituted manly character. In many ways soldiers and civilians alike expected the wounded to suffer stoically, though the hospitals required a new kind of courage. One New Yorker claimed he had seen legs and arms "carried out dors by the bushel." Though slightly wounded himself, he believed that the real test came in controlling one's emotions. "One gets used to such seens quicker than you would think it possible," he proudly reported to his wife. In the middle of so much misery many boys hesitated to cry out lest they appear weak. Their wounds proved their valor, but so did their endurance of pain. A New York lieutenant shot through the intestines quietly told a Philadelphia reporter that he would not live more than two days, and other men received and conveyed the worst news just as calmly.

Or did they? A soldier who had lost both hands joked that he could not steal chickens anymore but could still escort the ladies home. Did this forced cheerfulness help one get through the initial shock or merely delay the inevitable depression? Pain and despair clearly forced soldiers to call on deeper resources within and beyond themselves. A Pennsylvania chaplain praised a wounded colonel's "Christian resignation" and love for fellow sufferers; such spiritual fortitude, as another chaplain suggested, helped some men survive amputations against all odds.[28] The occasional miraculous recovery must have offered some hope to patients who had seen scores of bodies being carried from the field hospitals.

Death was so unpredictable. A New Hampshire captain who had confidently declared that he would recover without an amputation went under the surgeon's knife the next day and died two days later. Death was also pervasive as men died alone and often unnoticed for several hours. Mortality rates in Union field hospitals ranged from less than 2 to more than 6 percent, but the cold statistics hardly reflected what everybody "knew" to be true. Camp superstition held that soldiers entering a hospital seldom came back.[29] Memories of ghastly deaths undoubtedly inflated the numbers in many people's minds. In one hospital a corporal screamed and thrashed about calling for his wife most of the night. Once a nurse found a picture of his wife and little girl, he looked at them, smiled, and died.[30]

Regardless of actual numbers, the death toll struck observers as appalling. An assistant surgeon claimed with some exaggeration that it was not uncommon on a given morning to discover that half the patients in a hospital had died during the night. "The sight of the dead becomes a familiar one," Harriet Eaton noted matter-of-factly, and she was right. Corpses covered with a thin blanket, sometimes just a piece of cloth over the face, lay in rows near hospital tents. Names (usually of officers) carved on barrel staves stuck in the dirt identified the bodies; often lice still clung to their human hosts.[31]

One way or another the field hospitals quickly emptied. Some wounded died, others recovered, and the rest were moved to more permanent facilities. The medical story of Fredericksburg was in several ways heartening. The ambulance corps and surgeons had done a remarkable job, as the mortality statistics proved. Yet the suffering was hardly over. Many wounded ended up in Washington hospitals, where the second movement of the symphony of death, dying, and painful recovery began.

Letterman would have preferred treating the most seriously wounded in a special field hospital, but Burnside, whose mind was on launching another campaign, ordered their transfer to Washington, Philadelphia, and other points north. The first of the wounded reached Washington on December 17, and by December 26 the last casualties had arrived.[32]

The trip began with pitiable, painful movements. Wounded men found support on rude crutches or a good friend's strong arm; some were transported on a mattress or in an ambulance. Surgeons dressed the stumps of recent amputees hoping to prevent them from bleeding to death on the way. At Falmouth Station members of the Christian Commission handed out soda crackers and coffee with a dollop of spiritual consolation. Train delays prolonged the agony of wounded men crowding the platform or trackside tents. Even when the trains arrived, the sight of a freight car piled high with cracker-box caskets could hardly have been soothing. Nor was boarding the train. The loading of the most helpless cases was sometimes prevented by a crush of "cowardly stragglers, injured slightly if at all."[33]

The jolting ride to Aquia Creek might take three to four hours. Because special hospital cars outfitted by the Sanitary Commission were not yet in service, trains with double engines front and rear hauled nearly thirty cars of all sorts back and forth along the single-track line between Falmouth and the wharves. The most seriously wounded men had mattresses or fresh hay to lie upon, but for some there was neither straw nor blankets. Letterman had arranged for surgeons supplied with instruments, whiskey, and dressings to accompany the wounded. Even the best efforts of the Sanitary Commission and the doctors, however, could not prevent several deaths on the way to Aquia Creek or much ease the suffering of men riding on open cars in the winter. The hot toddies from Clara Barton perhaps provided as much comfort as anything.[34]

Aquia Creek, like Falmouth Station, was a bottleneck. Simply transferring the men to two waiting steamboats required several hours. At least a Sanitary Commission relief station served hot meals. As with the trains, the boat decks were often strewn with hay, and wounded men packed every crevice. Nurses from Washington hospitals and Sisters of Mercy attended the men during this final agonizing leg to Washington, but several more died en route.[35]

Beginning on an unseasonably mild December 17, the boats landed at the Sixth Street Wharf, where members of the Christian Commission greeted the hungry men with soft bread and applesauce. Nearly 3,000 wounded disembarked that day, 1,800 the next, and several hundred daily for the next week and a half. Journalist Noah Brooks witnessed the sad procession. "Faces grimed and blackened with smoke and powder, ragged, disheveled, and dropping with fatigue and weakness," men with mangled faces, some without fingers or arms, were "creeping, limping and hobbling along." Stretcher-bearers carried the most seriously wounded, and ambulances and omnibuses conveyed them to various hospitals. Brooks recalled the "vigor, hope, and ambition" of idealistic boys filled with visions of "glory" who had left the capital and now returned "broken, decrepit, useless, disfigured." Disgusted with delays in getting the wounded into the wards, a volunteer nurse wrote, "I think every man who comes a-soldiering is a fool."[36]

Nonetheless, her fellow volunteers and surgeons had been preparing for the Fredericksburg casualties for several days. Medical improvements had taken place in Washington also. Well-ventilated barracks hospitals elevated a couple feet off the ground had slowly replaced the churches, government buildings, and private homes that had been used since First Bull Run. To the untrained eye and especially to the nose, the improvements were less apparent. The stench from water closets and the sometimes filthy wards sickened visitors and even nurses. Although the hospitals readily accommodated the Fredericksburg casualties, reports of overcrowding persisted. Rancid mutton tallow used to dress wounds, careless attendants, and high rates of infection suggested that conditions sometimes remained deplorable. Yet as a Pennsylvania chaplain noted, the Washington hospitals provided much better care than had the field or division hospitals at Fredericksburg.[37]

Better conditions, of course, neither changed perceptions, ended complaints, nor made the wards less depressing. Everything from vile odors to ubiquitous lice revolted the senses. To Louisa May Alcott, the "disheartened look" of the men "proclaimed defeat, more plainly than any telegram of the Burnside blunder." Visitors and nurses alike grumbled about the sometimes rude and indifferent treatment accorded the weakest patients. In a long dispatch to the *New York Times,* Walt Whitman recounted the story of a twenty-year-old man from Plymouth County, Massachusetts, who, though prostrated by diarrhea, had fought in the battle. Afterward he developed a fever and grew steadily weaker from lying on the cold ground. On the open railcar to Aquia Creek, he could not sit up or cover himself with blankets. Similarly exposed on his journey up the Potomac, he lay helpless on the wharf until an ambulance finally carried him to a hospital. There a gruff "ward-master" insisted that he clean up and change his clothes before lying on the bed. The man nearly died of neglect before Whitman nursed him back to health with daily visits and extra food.[38]

Regardless of persistent problems (and Whitman often overdramatized particular cases), the wounded themselves testified to the surprisingly efficient and even kindly treatment they received in Washington hospitals. They appreciated careful attention, the occasional bath, special food, and especially sleeping in a bed, "a blessing I have not enjoyed for four months," commented one Massachusetts lieutenant.[39] Sometimes surgeons shipped convalescent patients back to hospitals in their native states, but these furloughs involved much red tape and often depended on political connections. Frustrated men tired of what one Pennsylvanian termed a "tyrannical arrangement" simply had a family member mail them civilian clothes so they could slip home.[40]

Whatever improvements had taken place, the usual reports of medical bungling kept tongues wagging in the army and at home. A Massachusetts infantryman praised the surgeons of the 50th New York Engineers at Fredericksburg who had resected four inches of bone from his right arm, but he claimed that poor treatment in a Washington hospital had allowed his hand to heal turned outward, thus greatly reducing strength in the arm. Yet even the sensitive Louisa May Alcott, who had seen egotistical surgeons arrogantly ignore patient questions or handle injured limbs with rough indifference, believed some doctors worried that their daily rounds of treating serious wounds might make them callous to human suffering. She especially admired one surgeon who enthusiastically took on the most difficult cases.[41]

Persistent criticism may have reflected unrealistic expectations. Soldiers, families, and civilians often blamed the doctors for inevitable deaths or long-term disabilities. Given the medical knowledge of the day, little could be done for many injuries. Serious head wounds were generally fatal. Picking out bone fragments from a skull, much less the more heroic resort to trephining—using a small circular saw to remove a "disk" from the cranium to relieve pressure on the brain—often proved futile. A surgeon might not realize when a bullet fragment had entered the brain, and the patient would die unexpectedly.[42] Spinal, chest, and abdominal wounds proved almost as deadly. Men suffering such injuries seldom lasted past the end of the year.[43]

Because the lead minié balls became misshapen when they entered the body and did not exit cleanly, surgeons often had trouble locating them. Probing and guesswork sometimes succeeded, though what at first appeared a simple wound might prove baffling. Failure to remove a bullet led to a painful, pus-filled infection. And even if the bullet was eventually found and extracted, the patient might die.[44] For men weakened by the difficult journey from Falmouth, resections and removal of bone fragments also carried great risk. Occasionally a patient simply died from the effects of anesthesia.[45]

Even with improved amputation techniques, patient prognoses remained doubtful for weeks or longer. A private in the 16th Maine sent to Lincoln Hospital in Washington after he lost both arms in a field hospital appeared to be doing well. The stumps were healing, his appetite was good, and he could sit up much of the day and seemed in good spirits. But after developing a "slight chill," he became restless and at times delirious. Stimulants, changes in diet, and drainage of abscesses brought no improvement. He lost control of his bowels and suffered from night sweats; signs of gangrene appeared. Befitting a hero of the American republic, this twenty-six-year-old whose regiment had advanced farther than any other during Gibbon's assault died on Washington's birthday. Even a patient strong enough to withstand an amputation in one of the general hospitals often succumbed to hemorrhages and infections.[46]

The symptoms of gangrene, which most frequently appeared in patients suffering from wounds to the extremities, included swelling of the limbs, "sloughing" of the wound, prickly sensations, sharp pains, a heavily coated tongue, occasional fever, and sleeplessness. Some of the most severe outbreaks had occurred after Antietam, but the problem persisted, especially in several Philadelphia hospitals. A young private who had served in the 8th Pennsylvania Reserves cried out so loudly and incessantly that he kept an entire ward awake. He eventually recovered, but for others, complications such as typhoid fever and even arthritis shadowed their convalescence.[47]

Unsure how to respond, relatives visiting the mortally wounded either acted like noisy busybodies or sat patiently awaiting the end. After Capt. Daniel Boisol of the 123rd Pennsylvania was brought to a Georgetown hospital with a serious bladder wound, his parents, wife, and young son gathered at the bedside, according to one observer, as "he died by inches" over the next ten days. Family members sometimes arrived just as their loved ones breathed their last. Hearing that her fiancé, a captain among the first skirmishers to advance toward the stone wall, had lost a leg, a young Ohio woman traveled to Washington in search of her beloved. They were married on January 4, 1863, even though he seemed dangerously weak. That very day a nurse noticed a drop of blood on his bandage and discovered that an artery had ruptured. In a few hours the bridegroom was gone.[48]

Volunteer nurses sometimes made room for families in their own quarters—an action that encapsulated the impetus behind their work. These women tried to make the large, impersonal hospitals homier. By changing linens, tending fires, fussing over food, and opening windows to release fetid air, the volunteers must have seemed quite domestic to their patients. Night nurses watched over the sleeping men—Louisa May Alcott studied facial expressions and snoring types—much like anxious mothers hovering over sick children. Delirious men cried out for their mothers, confusing them with the volunteers. Nurses washed their charges as if they were their young sons, though some soldiers shyly blushed at such intimate care. Conscientious volunteers read aloud or wrote letters for their "boys" but brought order to the wards. Clara Barton recorded the names of the wounded in books so families could learn of their whereabouts.[49]

Nurses, who generally focused their attention not on larger meanings but on individual cases, knew how much anguish the war had brought to so many families. So they did what they could to ease it. Though often "home sick, heart sick, and worn out," Alcott found "real pleasure in comforting, tending, and cheering these poor souls." Whether they voiced their appreciation or not, they seemed to love her. She considered most patients rather like scared schoolboys, "docile, respectful, and affectionate," and to her "truly loveable." Like other volunteers, Alcott described her nursing in the sentimental language so valued by close-knit middle-class families, and such accounts helped strengthen the bonds between soldiers and civilians. Thus when a Philadelphia newspaper reported a typically maudlin scene where a sixteen-year-old died with his head in the arms of a kind lady visitor, readers around campfires or at hearths could appreciate the poignancy. The mortally wounded soldier who told his nurse, "You are real motherly, ma'am," mirrored the mind of his generation.[50]

As medical battlegrounds and places where the lives of soldiers and civilians intersected, hospitals also embodied the religious tensions, fears, and hopes of the era. Alcott presented a stereotypical portrait of a hospital chaplain—"the wrong man in the wrong place," she thought—wandering about, "hands in his pockets, preaching resignation to cold, hungry, wounded men."

Yet Alcott's own religious prejudices included a condescending contempt for Irish Catholics. A Maine pastor recalled greeting the wounded with food, warm drinks, and stimulants, but also sympathetic words. Sometimes coldly practical nurses and doctors forgot that a wounded man needed spiritual solace as well as physical succor. "I spoke to the wounded about the Savior, who was wounded for them," a Massachusetts minister reported. The men seemed eager for the redemption message because it had been some time since they had even heard a prayer. Sundays in the hospital, as Alcott her self noted, brought a repose that induced some boys to speak quietly but movingly of home and family and faith.[51]

Volunteers who brought supplies and the nurses who tended the dying were struck by the men's simple courage. One lively fellow who had been shot through the cheek worried about what "Josephine Skinner" back home would think of his scar, but he decided it did not look that bad. Despite worrying about his family, a badly wounded soldier rested easier when re-assured that he had done his duty. "I must be marching on," one young man remarked to two nurses shortly before he died. To the wonder of occasional hospital visitors, pale, weakened soldiers could lie in bed and cheerfully inquire about comrades. Such noble fellows powerfully influenced others; they lived up to their era's most cherished ideals, notions of honor and brav-ery that were not mere copybook maxims but shaped the behavior of real people.[52]

Forced smiles from men in terrible pain hinted at certain models of char-acter but also showed how human agony continued long after the guns fell silent. A Vermonter who had lost a leg decided that it would have been much worse to lose a hand and believed that with a wooden leg, "I can so shape my life that it will be of but little inconvenience"; but these breezy comments in a letter written to a lady friend back home concealed more than they re-vealed. Some soldiers replayed the battle over and over in their minds. A New Jersey volunteer with a mild knee wound feverishly raved, grabbed a nurse's arm, and kept trying to dodge imaginary artillery shells. He could not lie still and so would let forth an "incessant stream of defiant shouts, whispered warnings, and broken laments," all the while calling out for a wounded friend who had shared a blanket with him on the way to a Wash-ington hospital but who had already died.[53]

Such small dramas were all that mattered to families, but hospital bu-reaucrats and even Sanitary Commission officials had to focus on supposedly larger issues. They sometimes offered only perfunctory assistance in track-ing down a wounded soldier, and the hospital lists remained notoriously in-complete. Families trying to find their way through the maze of army hospitals and government offices quickly grew discouraged. Packages of food and other items sometimes went astray even if properly addressed. But mostly the folks back home simply wanted some news of their boys. A nurse working at Georgetown Hospital wrote to a worried mother that she had not found the name "John Shure" on the official roster but after a lengthy search had at last tracked him down. He had fought bravely until a bullet passed through a lung. The nurse regretted not being able to sit with Shure during his final hours: "He thinks he is getting well but does not know his condition."[54]

Shure's agony deeply affected his family and friends; it seemed to mean little in the larger scheme of the war. But such small events and bits of news added up. The dreadful columns of killed and wounded that filled the newspapers cast a pall over the coming holiday season. In most people's minds, reports of dreadful suffering among the wounded at Falmouth and in the Washington hospitals far overshadowed real but often invisible improvements in medical treatment. What folks back home did know was that a great battle had been fought and that most of the casualties had been on the Federal side. They would spend the next several weeks and more sorting out this news.

Ill news hath wings, and with the wind doth go,
Comfort's a cripple, and comes ever slow.
—Michael Drayton

20 News

Early in the morning of December 12, the lank, sad-looking man trod across the grass between the Executive Mansion and the War Department, heading for one of his favorite haunts, the office of the U.S. Military Telegraph. There Abraham Lincoln often read aloud from Artemus Ward or some other humorist while waiting for the latest battlefield dispatches. Early news from Fredericksburg had been promising. On December 11 Sid Demming, chief Associated Press correspondent traveling with the Army of the Potomac, and J. G. Garland, a telegraph operator at Falmouth, had reported the shelling of the town, the successful crossing of the Rappahannock, and troops cheering Burnside. Their dispatches had gone directly to Anson Stager, superintendent of the military telegraph. Even a wire from General Sumner to his wife—"Fredericksburg is ours. All well."—ended up in the pile of telegrams. Lincoln eagerly read the thin slips of paper, but details remained sketchy. The Federal forces had secured a foothold, and there had been some skirmishing. So far so good.[1]

By the next morning, reports had arrived of fighting on the Federal left. An early afternoon dispatch noted intense artillery and musket fire. "Cannot tell from this point who has the best of the fight," Garland added. Then at 2:50 P.M. a telegram from Stager brought the best news yet: word from

Sumner's headquarters that "our forces have taken the first redoubt." An hour later a wounded New York colonel was quoted as saying, "We are getting the best of it." Yet the noise of the battle remained so intense that Stager could barely hear his instrument tapping out the messages, and he did report large numbers of wounded coming off the field. "The Rebellion is now virtually at an end," commented Lincoln, at least according to the *New York Times*.[2]

At 4:00 A.M. on December 14 Burnside wired the president that his troops held the "first ridge outside of the town" and "we hope to carry the crest today." But despite rumors that the Army of the Potomac had "done well," Secretary of the Navy Gideon Welles remained skeptical: "There is something unsatisfactory or not entirely satisfactory in this intelligence." What little information was available seemed ominously vague. "They [War Department officials] fear to admit disastrous truths. Adverse tidings are suppressed, with a deal of fuss and mystery, a shuffling over of papers and maps, and a far-reaching, vacant gaze at something undefined and indescribable." Then word started arriving of heavy casualties, and in official Washington hopes for a Union victory began to fade. Tension mounted especially because panicky friends of the administration jabbered about the fate of the Union hanging on this latest battle.[3]

On the evening of December 14 Lincoln met with Herman Haupt, who was just returning from Fredericksburg, and with Halleck. In something of a panic the president may have asked the general in chief to order Burnside's withdrawal from Fredericksburg, but predictably Halleck refused to assume responsibility. Haupt assured Lincoln that Burnside would likely bring the army back across the Rappahannock on his own. Later that evening reporter Henry Villard of the *New York Tribune,* who had slipped away from Falmouth hoping to scoop his rivals with news of the Fredericksburg disaster, called on Lincoln. The president impatiently pressed for details, and Villard finally blurted out the truth: this was the worst defeat ever suffered by the Army of the Potomac.[4]

For once the usually talkative president did not tell one of his droll stories, but for several days afterward he kept trying to come up with just the right anecdote to describe his plight. Subject to bouts of depression, Lincoln often used rustic humor to shake off his own dark thoughts, but after Fredericksburg, his yarns seemed more pathetic than funny. Maybe he was like the boy with a fierce dog by the tail, unable to hang on but afraid to let go, or like the old woman trying to sweep floodwaters from her cabin wondering whether her broom could outlast the storm. Many stuffy politicians, including cabinet members, could not appreciate such frontier tales and suspected that the president somehow misunderstood the gravity of the situation. Yet as Lincoln explained to Congressman Isaac Arnold of Illinois, "If I could not get momentary respite from the crushing burden I am constantly carrying, my heart would break."[5]

In this crisis, however, humor no longer helped much. Friends and visitors found Lincoln sadly subdued, not wallowing in self-pity perhaps, but expressing a sense of despair bordering on powerlessness. Interrupting one congressman's litany of gloom, Lincoln cried out that more bad news would drive him "crazy." He worried incessantly about the army and appeared terribly anxious. He mused about trading places with a soldier sleeping on the cold ground or even one killed in battle. In utter exasperation he told a friend, "If there is a worse place than Hell, I am in it."[6]

By December 15, with news of the battle arriving with the first of the wounded, a deepening gloom spread over the capital. The word "defeat" began cropping up in correspondence and no doubt on street corners, along with second-guessing over Burnside's tactics. News of the army's safe withdrawal across the Rappahannock hardly lifted anyone's spirits. This was worse than McClellan's retreat from the Peninsula, concluded the Chicago Tribune's Washington correspondent. A Mexican diplomat overheard people saying that southern independence now seemed assured.[7]

To forestall the spread of defeatism, the War Department clumsily attempted to prevent newspaper correspondents from telegraphing details of the battle, especially information about the staggering losses. Yet the war had revolutionized the use of the telegraph in reporting, and newspapers had roughly tripled the amount of space devoted to telegraphic dispatches. So maladroit attempts at official censorship were doomed to fail. The main result was delay and confusion in transmitting casualty lists. Even Republicans complained that these efforts only aroused public suspicion and made the defeat look worse.[8]

As usual the first accounts of the fighting had been breathlessly optimistic. "All Glorious on the Rappahannock," "Terrific Bombardment Yesterday," and "Fredericksburg in Ashes," blared the Chicago Tribune on December 12. Across the North, Republican newspapers reported in much the same vein; a Rhode Island editor crowed that those who had despaired over earlier delays did not really know Burnside.[9] News that the Army of the Potomac had captured Fredericksburg produced more favorable reports the next day.[10] On the morning of December 14 prospects remained bright. The New York Times lauded Burnside for concentrating his forces to defeat the Rebels, though the day's telegrams began hinting at a bloody defeat.[11]

By December 15 more details were slipping through the War Department censors. Republican newspapers, however, remained at least publicly cheerful. Expectations of still more fighting and predictions that the campaign could prove decisive persisted. Sanguine editors concluded that the Saturday engagement had tested enemy strength; now Burnside knew where to hit Lee's army. Yet ominously, a Boston editor sounded cautious perhaps without meaning to: "The news from our army at Fredericksburg contains nothing which should weaken hope or occasion despondency." A few papers began talking of a "repulse," but others found no reason for discouragement.[12]

The following day, front pages still carried dated accounts of Franklin's apparent success on the Federal left and the impending attack that would finish the job. Even word of Burnside's withdrawal from Fredericksburg hardly softened the bluff optimism. Rumors of an expedition under Maj. Gen. Nathaniel P. Banks sailing from New York to cooperate with the Army of the Potomac led to speculation that Burnside would soon renew the fight with reinforcements from another direction. He would yet triumph over Lee, a "slow man," according to the *Philadelphia Inquirer.* Only the timid would despair, declared a Connecticut editor, but bluster proved a thin disguise for desperation. "Don't treat the affair at Fredericksburg as a disaster," John W. Forney, a staunch Lincoln friend, frantically wired his managing editor in Philadelphia.[13]

Partisan demagogues, one Boston newspaper warned, could turn a temporary setback into an excuse for despair over the Union cause. But the demagogues hardly required assistance. Loud denials that the army was demoralized after withdrawing from Fredericksburg soon flooded the North. What had been lost aside from casualties? one prominent church publication asked, and then coldly added that the North had plenty more young men to send into the ranks. This cruel calculus—which was also offered by Lincoln around this time[14]—could still not paper over a defeat, and this same editor actually used the word "disaster" even as he maintained that the "heart of the nation does not waver." The logic grew even more strained. Advances and retreats occurred in any war, and indeed Burnside's withdrawal only proved his military prowess. Such a clever maneuver elicited comparisons to Napoleon and even the improbable assertion that Lee had been outfoxed. Renewed calls for an advance on Richmond and denial that the army would soon go into winter quarters signified more fear than hope.[15]

The brave front inevitably cracked. Given the high expectations for the campaign, recognition of the reality was a galling, often agonizing exercise. Another Union offensive had failed, a fact that haunted moderate Republicans. The editor of the bellwether *Springfield Daily Republican* sharply questioned any "senseless palaver about strategy" to conceal the truth but still drew a distinction between temporary "indignation and discouragement" and genuine "alarm" for the nation's future.[16]

Such mincing of words could hardly buttress public morale. In a dispatch composed on the evening of December 13, *New York Times* correspondent William Swinton reported that whatever anyone chose to call it, Fredericksburg had been a "defeat" and "a black day in the calendar of the Republic." One Democratic editor observed that even if Burnside advanced again with reinforcements, he would occupy a less favorable position than McClellan had held in June. Given the inflated estimates of Rebel numbers (some 200,000, according to the *New York Herald* and other papers), Burnside's tactics seemed even more foolhardy. Newspaper maps, which were often far from accurate, nevertheless showed the strength of the Confederate positions and bolstered such popular perceptions. Shocking descriptions of a battlefield strewn with dead and wounded only added to the gloom. Despondency spread rapidly, especially in cities where anxious crowds gathered around newspaper office bulletin boards.[17]

By December 17 even some Republican newspapers were calling the Fredericksburg affair a "disaster." The *Albany Evening Journal,* edited by Seward ally Thurlow Weed, bemoaned the "butcheries in which the flower of our youth is sacrificed." Newspapers muted criticism of Burnside, but Democrats pointedly ridiculed Republican efforts to minimize the catastrophe and began hinting that the real responsibility rested in Washington.[18]

Uncertain news had kept even political sophisticates on tenterhooks. In New York George Templeton Strong had eagerly scanned the first newspaper bulletins describing the crossing of Federal forces on December 11 but was not sure whether to interpret the sketchy information as evidence of a setback. Word that "one redoubt" had been taken by the Federals led Elizabeth Blair Lee in Silver Spring, Maryland, to speculate that perhaps this time a Union army had "outwitted" the Rebels, "a great comfort after frequent blunders." Despite delays in receiving information, civilian opinion in the North likely mirrored Lincoln's emotional roller coaster: early hopes, growing doubts, and then bitter disappointment. Although wary observers had steeled themselves for another disaster, for a while they, too, accepted the common newspaper fiction that Burnside had only been testing the enemy defenses.[19]

War-weary northern civilians had to reckon with another bloody repulse, though some readily declared—with how much assurance is unclear—that the results could have been much worse. Hopes persisted that Burnside might renew the attack, but word of another defeat spread rapidly across the northern states. Had the tide now turned in the Rebels' favor? A few conservative Democrats and McClellan supporters actually crowed over the debacle; some reportedly smiled at the Republicans' discomfiture. Yet many citizens simply appeared confused, unable to draw firm conclusions from fragmentary reports, and so went about their business. With the Christmas shopping season in full swing, people were spending money and enjoying amusements despite the tragedy along the Rappahannock. Newspapers allowed the home folks to participate vicariously in campaigns but also aroused deep anxieties and heightened the tensions of ordinary people waiting to hear about their friends and relatives. Thus word about Fredericksburg proved more disconcerting than informative.[20]

Newspapers helped people maintain ties between home and camp, but many civilians also sought escapes from the seemingly relentless news. Telegraphy and photography brought the war home to people who might have preferred to avert their eyes and ears. False hopes, recurring alarms, and cycles of exaltation and despair all frayed nerves. Depending on one's perspective, there was always either too much or never enough war news. For their part soldiers doubted that anyone at home really understood the realities of war, though some thought the Fredericksburg disaster might wake people up. Yet even as Burnside's men inevitably wondered about how their families were reacting to the latest news, they also resented public impatience. A member of the 10th Pennsylvania Reserves wrote a scathing letter to his hometown newspaper sarcastically inquiring what the "On to Richmond, stay at home guards" thought about all the casualties. Men unwilling to shoulder even their fair burden of taxes kept screaming for generals to advance as if soldiers were mere machines that could be thrown into battle without considering the limits of human endurance or the terrible costs.[21]

★ ★ ★

Although public pressure in the Confederate camp had a different tenor—especially after Fredericksburg—like Lincoln, Jefferson Davis was feeling the political heat, especially because of the deteriorating situation in the western theater. On December 10 the Confederate president had left Richmond for Chattanooga to visit the faction-riven Army of Tennessee. During his stay with Braxton Bragg's troops at Murfreesboro, Davis consulted with several generals about strategic and command problems. Back in Chattanooga on December 14, he received a War Department telegram about fighting at Fredericksburg. Anxious for news, he considered returning to Richmond immediately, but soon word of Lee's great victory arrived. Varina Davis later passed along rumors that Burnside had made a fire-breathing speech to his generals right before the battle and that these same officers had later refused to renew the attacks.[22]

Burnside's crossing of the Rappahannock on December 11 had actually heartened folks in Richmond, where Lee's own confidence shaped official attitudes and spilled into the streets. Even with the rumble of artillery in the distance, people seemed most worried that the Yankees would avoid a decisive contest. Soon reports of spirited fighting and brave counterattacks counterbalanced the sad news about the deaths of generals Cobb and Gregg. The sight of people strolling in their finery and "speculators" going about their brisk trade offered Kate Mason Rowland a "short oblivion" from worrying about the soldiers. On Sunday morning, December 14, despite fears of renewed fighting, people went to church as usual, and the capital appeared calm.[23]

With permission from the War Department, newspaper reporters had gone to Fredericksburg, and even with paper shortages and shrinking dailies placing war news at a premium, dispatches running a column and more began appearing a couple of days after the battle. Soon the Richmond papers were crowing about how the outnumbered Army of Northern Virginia had easily repulsed the enemy. Most accounts adopted a dashing, fearless tone and were short on detail and long on praise for Confederate valor. No one bothered to mention the anxious moments on the Confederate right, though most readers cared little for tactical fine points anyway. What folks longed for was good news, but because of telegraph problems, reports of Lee's victory traveled slowly beyond Virginia.[24]

For many civilians, anxiety and prayers for deliverance quickly gave way to thanks for another victory, for which Lee, Jackson, and God Almighty received lavish praise. North Carolina plantation mistress Catherine Edmondston believed that Lee had allowed the Federals to cross the Rappahannock so he could "cut them off in detail." Word of casualties (including false reports of J. E. B. Stuart killed and A. P. Hill taken prisoner) naturally tempered the rejoicing. "How I wish the war would end," a sixteen-year-old Florida girl wrote after reports of another battle in Virginia. "It throws a cloud over everything." Like many northern civilians, southerners had learned not to credit vague accounts of great victories and so eagerly sought detailed confirmation, though news of success brought its own improbable rumors. Had Burnside been killed? Was McClellan back in command? Was the Army of the Potomac in a state of mutiny? Civilians welcomed accounts of their enemies' despair, including word that the Yankees no longer found Lincoln's jokes very funny.[25]

★ ★ ★

Still reeling from the news of Burnside's defeat, Lincoln faced a political firestorm in Washington. A Peace Democrat's call for the president's impeachment was easily dismissed, but Republican confidence in the administration, already shaky after recent election losses, was eroding fast. Panic-stricken Ohio congressman William Parker Cutler decided that "God alone can take care of us." But even the Almighty recently seemed to favor Rebels and Democrats. Angry radicals began calling for a cabinet shake-up as soon as the first bad news from Fredericksburg reached the capital. Nervous moderates acknowledged the political fallout from the battle, and even Seward's friends pressed for changes. "The President and cabinet stink awfully in the nostrils of the American people," one conservative New Englander groused.[26]

Reports that Lincoln seldom consulted most of the cabinet had circulated for months. Both Seward and the president had approached the emancipation question gingerly, a particularly sore point with antislavery zealots. Salmon P. Chase's unbridled presidential ambitions and indiscreet conversation only enhanced the appearance of an administration divided and adrift. "Common sense, if not common honesty, has fled from the Cabinet," Senator William Pitt Fessenden of Maine had lamented shortly after Congress reconvened in early December.[27]

All the while Seward's political stock was plummeting. Charges that his influence was wrecking the Republican Party, rumors that he and Weed favored a compromise with the Rebels, and alarm at a resurgent Democracy energized administration critics. It seemed deliciously ironic that a man passed over in 1860 because of an undeserved reputation for radicalism had now become the radical Republicans' bête noire without having won the trust of party conservatives. No wonder the affable and kindly Seward was starting to look all of his sixty-one years. At the end of November a member of the sharp-eyed Adams clan had described him as "pale, old, and careworn." Fredericksburg would add a few more wrinkles to his face and give his enemies fresh political ammunition.[28]

On the afternoon of December 16 a caucus of Republican senators gathered in a Capitol reception room to discuss the latest military debacle. Senator Lyman Trumbull of Illinois considered Fredericksburg a political disaster. Minnesota senator Morton S. Wilkinson pointedly blamed Seward's malign influence for recent reverses, while Benjamin F. Wade of Ohio accused Lincoln of appointing commanders who did not support the government's policies. It was even suggested that somehow Seward had prevented the Banks expedition from cooperating with Burnside. A no-confidence motion directed against the secretary of state never came to a vote, but no one rose

Secretary of State William H. Seward (Library of Congress)

to his defense. Even though the caucus adjourned without taking action, its tone spelled trouble for the president.[29]

After learning of the caucus from Senator Preston King of New York, Seward penned a resignation letter, perhaps a bit hastily in light of the senators' hesitation to move forthrightly against him. They were similarly indecisive when they reconvened the next day to discuss various options, including a general resolution calling for a reconstruction of the cabinet. John Sherman of Ohio tartly suggested that the real difficulty lay with the president. Some senators may have argued for Lincoln stepping down, but Trumbull defended his honesty and patriotism. Finally, at Sumner's suggestion, a milder resolution vaguely calling for "changes" in the cabinet was adopted, and a committee of nine was appointed to call on the president.[30]

On the afternoon of December 18 Senator Orville Hickman Browning of Illinois, a conservative Republican and longtime confidant, stopped at the Executive Mansion. "They wish to get rid of me, and I am sometimes half disposed to gratify them," Lincoln snapped. In the grip of one of his fatalistic moods, he finally remarked, "We are now on the brink of destruction. It appears to me the Almighty is against us, and I can hardly see a ray of hope." For three hours that evening the senators harangued the president, mostly on Seward's shortcomings but also on the failings of Democratic generals, with a few bitter comments about the fall elections thrown in for good measure. Lincoln mostly listened, occasionally objected, but promised to consider the senators' resolutions.[31]

At 7:30 the next morning Lincoln and the cabinet (minus Seward) met with the senators (minus Wade). Lincoln led the delegation into his office and informed them that he had invited the cabinet for a "free and friendly conversation with the committee." Chase sheepishly conceded that the cabinet had been consulted on important questions, perhaps not as fully as might be desirable, but that there had been unity in administration councils. Fessenden suggested that the president seek the cabinet's advice but "might act on his own judgment." The atmosphere grew tense, and at Chase's urging, the cabinet members retired. Fessenden then pressed Lincoln to accept Seward's resignation, but the president refused even to ask for the senators' advice on the matter. The four-hour session finally broke up after midnight.[32] The senators' attempt to dictate to the president had clearly failed, and ironically, the Fredericksburg affair—the original spark for the crisis— had disappeared from the discussion.

Lincoln must have had a fitful night's sleep; right after breakfast the next morning he sent Secretary of the Navy Welles to talk Seward into withdrawing his resignation. Already Washington buzzed with rumors that the entire cabinet would quit. Still embarrassed, Chase dramatically announced that he had prepared a letter of resignation, but before he could capitalize on this theatrical gesture, Lincoln reached out a long arm to grab the document. "This cuts the Gordian knot," he exulted; "I see my way clear." An offer by Stanton to resign was brusquely refused, and an obviously discomfited Chase departed. With these resignations in hand, Lincoln felt free to keep both men in the cabinet and defy the Republican senators.[33] Yet this "resolution" of the crisis—with Lincoln appearing as a political mastermind— hardly ended cabinet divisions or silenced the chorus of criticism in the wake of the Fredericksburg disaster.

Lincoln likely took little comfort in his supposed triumph over the Republican senators. Even the haughty, condescending Sumner had come to "profoundly pity" the president during this agonizing period, but less self-important observers also commented on how bad Lincoln looked. The shock of Fredericksburg and the cabinet imbroglio left the administration reeling. Confusion and alarm if not demoralization spread beyond the capital. One New York editor pointed out the obvious: cabinet changes meant little at this juncture; what the country most needed were heavy blows struck at the rebellion.[34]

★ ★ ★

Unfortunately for the administration, no good news came from abroad either. The possibility of European intervention remained alive. Even though the British cabinet had recently rejected a French mediation proposal, U.S.

diplomats nervously awaited the latest war news. In London a report that Burnside had taken Fredericksburg momentarily raised hopes, but by Christmas Day, news of the Army of the Potomac's defeat had dashed them and dampened holiday spirits. Henry Adams feared "another Antietam, only worse" and began "screwing [his] courage up to face the list of killed and wounded." His father, Minister Charles Francis Adams Sr., wrote of a "profitless war," predicted that Burnside was finished, and suspected that both sides had perhaps worn themselves out fighting.[35]

Extensive reporting and editorial comment by the conservative *Times* of London presented an especially gloomy picture of U.S. affairs. "Another tremendous disaster has fallen on Federal arms," the *Times* commented on December 29. "So great has been the carnage, so complete and undeniable the defeat, that the North appears stunned by the blow." The Confederacy looked to be on the verge of winning independence. Even in England rumors swirled: McClellan would soon regain command; massive desertions might weaken Federal armies; Lincoln might well retreat on emancipation. Karl Marx raged over Union failures and even lent credence to the canard that Burnside had been forced by the press into attacking Lee. Word of the cabinet crisis confirmed that despair had engulfed the northern states. A New York correspondent for the *Times* described the soldiers' demoralization: "Slaughtered in vain at Fredericksburg with as much method as if they had been swine at Cincinnati, they ask one another why they should risk another such contest, without hope of achieving anything by it." Another reporter called December 13 a "memorable day to the historian of the Decline and Fall of the American Republic."[36]

Similarly gloomy reports and urgent requests for the latest information came from Brussels, Rome, and St. Petersburg. Northern diplomats acknowledged their fears but clung to their hopes.[37] The news from Fredericksburg dealt another blow to the Union cause, though it hardly created a groundswell for European intervention. Proposals for mediation, while not entirely dead, had reached their political apogee and were steadily losing support, especially in Great Britain.

Ironically, given how closely the British had recently come to intervention, Confederates now doubted that the Europeans would act. Bitter disappointments, including the failure of the so-called cotton famine to force the politicians' hand, had greatly frustrated southern diplomats. Even news of the "glorious victory at Fredericksburg," propagandist Henry Hotze admitted, hardly affected the fainthearted British cabinet. According to an agent of North Carolina governor Zebulon Vance, the English government "is too well pleased to see both North & South exhausted to stop the strife."

No loyal Confederate should expect anything from Europeans; only more Fredericksburgs would advance the southern cause. The Confederates appeared to be winning their independence on the battlefield, Minister James Mason believed, but neither Palmerston nor other cautious British politicians yet favored diplomatic recognition.[38]

Rebel diplomats and Hotze's propaganda sheet tried to exploit Yankee losses to prompt official recognition of the Confederacy as a sovereign and independent nation. But diplomacy had entered an odd phase. On one hand, leading Confederates doubted they would receive any help from England and France but, on the other hand, decided that their fledgling nation needed no such assistance. Only two days before the battle of Fredericksburg, in dispatches to Mason in London and John Slidell in Paris, Secretary of State Judah Benjamin had seemed most concerned about ending southern dependence on northern shipping and establishing direct trade with Europe. By mid-January Benjamin had decided that any large European loan to the Confederacy would have to await the end of the war. What with recent battlefield successes and the fading hopes for European mediation, planning for peace seemed more profitable to Benjamin. He even worried about stipulations against the African slave trade in future commercial agreements.[39]

Slidell, however, still held out hope for the French. The mercurial Napoleon III nursed imperial designs in Mexico and needed southern cotton. He certainly did not lack incentives for another diplomatic move, given the recent Democratic victories in the northern elections, the controversy over McClellan's removal, the Fredericksburg disaster, and especially the suffering in the French textile industry. On January 9 the French ministry sent a note to Washington suggesting direct negotiations between the two sides without the formality of an armistice. Seward rebuffed this watered-down mediation scheme, and the British expressed no interest in pushing the idea.[40]

Southerners reacted confidently to what might have been considered bad news. J. E. B. Stuart, who had earlier admitted having "strong hopes of France," still believed that southern independence must ultimately depend on divine aid and "our own strong armies." Other Confederates had considered the French more sincere than the British in their approach to the American conflict, and some believed that Napoleon III had virtually recognized southern independence. Edmund Ruffin had predicted that the French would intervene unilaterally to stop the war in America. Rumors of new French and British moves surfaced again in the wake of Fredericksburg.[41] Yet even as the French prepared their January mediation offer, Confederate soldiers and editors decided it did not much matter. "We would be better off to fight the battles out ourselves," a Virginia artillery officer decided. Only a victorious war could bring lasting peace. The latest diplomatic rumors met with understandable skepticism from southerners who had heard promising news before, only to have their hopes dashed. With little expectation of help from abroad, the keynote became self-reliance. The triumph at Fredericksburg confirmed faith in southern arms and proved the wisdom of abandoning the chimera of European intervention.[42] There was no need to cower before the potentates of Europe—unreliable friends at best—when General Lee and his men could defeat the Yankee hosts so handily.

The same news and speculation that had spread from the battlefield across the North and to European capitals also rebounded back to the camps. Soldiers eagerly read newspapers for the "latest intelligence" from Washington. Reports of political commotion back home, including the cabinet crisis and the latest diplomatic rumors, also affected army morale. Soldiers dreaded change, especially the unknown, and signs of political disturbances made them uneasy. "The troubles at Washington," a Twelfth Corps general feared, "are casting a greater gloom over the country than the affairs of the army." Rumors circulated that Lincoln himself might soon be out and a military dictator appointed in his place.[43]

Confederates paid equally close attention to affairs in Washington and welcomed reports of division in the North and Yankees devouring their own. Snippets from the northern press made for pleasant reading in winter camps. Accounts of the cabinet crisis became yet more evidence that the attempted subjugation of the southern people was bound to fail and that the war would soon be over. Speculations aside, one point was clear to most Confederates: Lee's victory at Fredericksburg had created a political crisis among their enemies.[44]

The New York gold market provided the most sensitive barometer of the impact of the battle and the effect of the political tremors in Washington. With news that Burnside had crossed the Rappahannock, gold prices had briefly fallen, but by December 16 they had crept up again as the first discouraging accounts from Fredericksburg reached New York. Greenbacks steadily lost value for the rest of December and the first two months of 1863, while gold prices rose from the low 130s to the high 150s. According to the newspapers the Fredericksburg debacle had forced up gold prices because people assumed that the Treasury would likely print more greenbacks. Foreign investors, having lost faith in the Union's chances for survival, were also reportedly buying gold. Experts disagreed about whether the combination of Fredericksburg and the cabinet crisis had spooked the markets, but increasing gold prices reflected sagging public confidence. A Baltimore editor forthrightly blamed the administration's timid military policies for speculation and gold hoarding. After Fredericksburg the value of government bonds dropped even more precipitously than the value of the greenbacks.[45]

Sophisticated Confederates followed the New York financial markets, and so rising gold prices buoyed southern hopes. One War Department official heard that Confederate bonds were selling briskly in New York. Regardless of wishful thinking about a northern economic collapse, the Confederacy suffered from much steeper inflation; consumer prices in the United States had increased only modestly. However, because workers' wages held steady throughout 1862, even small price hikes eroded incomes and pinched family budgets. As usual, perceptions mattered a great deal, and labor unrest in the cities grew. The macroeconomic picture, however dimly perceived, while not exactly stormy did evince some dark clouds on the horizon. Ballooning Federal expenditures and the burgeoning Union debt became rough indexes of Rebel resistance. Because revenues raised by taxes and bond sales were not keeping up with spending, by the end of 1862 Chase and his Treasury colleagues faced tough choices.[46]

Although clearly secondary to both the military crisis and the Seward affair in attracting public attention, Chase's financial policies had come under fire. The rapidly expanding money supply naturally touched raw nerves among Democrats, who were habitually given to fears about the conspiratorial manipulation of paper currency and stocks. Editors consistently criticized the administration for supposedly flooding the country with worthless greenbacks.[47] Yet Chase, with typical immodesty, believed that the New York money men had faith in his policies, and he felt a special obligation to bankers, especially Jay Cooke, and other investors who had promoted and purchased government bonds. In turn, the support of such powerful interests had undoubtedly helped him remain in the cabinet. The treasury secretary favored a uniform system of currency issued by national banks, and even in the midst of the post-Fredericksburg gloom and the cabinet crisis, he was lining up support in Congress and among Republican newspaper editors. But the creation of a national banking system in March 1863 would mean little if the recent string of military reverses continued.[48]

In the era of the telegraph, financial information was so readily transmitted that much of the North was being integrated into a national market, a development that seemed remarkable in hindsight. At the time, military news mattered most to people. The first dispatches from a battlefield could be completely misleading, though fairly reliable reports about Fredericksburg had reached northern newspaper readers within days. Farmers, housewives, grocers, bankers, congressmen, and the president—everybody—could read about the latest disaster for Union arms. The news traveled a bit slower in the Confederacy, but everyone there was just as eager for the latest word. Politicians and investors had precipitated the northern cabinet crisis and the surge in gold prices on the basis of fragmentary reports from the battlefield. Daily dispatches produced a glut of news that, whether trustworthy or not, fostered a sense of constant crisis and sped up the pace and intensity of life at home and in camp.

Modern war, as Clausewitz observed, mobilized the resources of a whole people, and these included thoughts and emotions.[49] Energy and enthusiasm replaced deliberation; vigor substituted for reflection. Even the literary world got caught up in this whirl. Stunned by word of the carnage along the Rappahannock, Herman Melville hastily scrawled a few lines of verse "for the slain at Fredericksburg," though the evocation of "patriot ghosts" ascending had such a clapdash quality that he did not bother to publish them in Battle-Pieces after the war. Lesser scribblers added stanzas of maudlin newspaper poetry that were quickly forgotten. Their images of artillery fire, light, and death expressed the immediate dismay and anger but offered nothing of lasting value. Ephemeral Victorian sentimentalism did not make much of an impression on an anxious northern public. It was a truly pressing, nonliterary question posed by poet and editor William Cullen Bryant that haunted Yankee minds: "How long is such intolerable and wicked blundering to continue?"[50]

A battle lost is a battle
one thinks one has lost.
—*Joseph de Maistre*

21 Recrimination

Who is to blame? is the universal and urgent question posed after a disastrous battle. Despite the panoramic qualities of Fredericksburg, Union soldiers still had trouble grasping the bigger picture and were as eager for news as the folks back home. Had the Banks expedition sailed? Was another Federal army approaching Richmond from the east? Had their hurriedly composed postbattle letters arrived safely? What did their families make of it all? [1]

Despite efforts to maintain ties between home and camp, the mental and emotional distance widened. Civilians, many soldiers believed, could never grasp the horrors of Fredericksburg or understand their courage and endurance because only men of doubtful character remained at home. A young Hoosier, among the first Federals to charge the stone wall, reckoned only "female men" were left back in Spencer, Indiana. Pride, however, could not make up for loneliness, homesickness, and—especially after Fredericksburg—discouragement. A private in the 44th New York wrote a long poem with a recurring couplet: "Backward, roll backward, oh time in thy flight / Make me a citizen just for a night." Tired of the food, the cold, and the bloodshed, he dreamed about the pleasures of home. The glory of soldiering had faded, and now he hoped for a medical discharge because his legs seemed shaky and he could better serve his country at home writing patriotic editorials.[2]

His comrades would have appreciated the sardonic tone but would have ridiculed his choice of occupation. Many Federals fully believed that spread-eagle journalism had spurred their generals into making the foolhardy assaults on the well-entrenched Confederates. Ever since the battle, the lying press had, as usual, covered up official incompetence. A worthless newspaper correspondent safely ensconced in a tree two miles from any fighting knew nothing of real war, a bitter lieutenant in French's division remarked, but instead kept "thirsting for blood."[3]

Whatever the latest editorials might proclaim, Richmond was not going to be taken any time soon. In letters written immediately after the battle, soldiers summed up the demoralizing effects. A New Jersey chaplain described the entire army as "sadly disheartened", a Pennsylvanian from Meade's battered division bluntly termed Fredericksburg the "worst disaster" since the beginning of the war. Others chose milder words, but their talk of "discouraged" or "discontented" regiments hardly brightened the picture.[4]

To the average enlisted man, explaining the defeat was simple: the Federals had attacked impregnable defenses. A Connecticut drummer writing from "Camp Trials, Tribulation, and Desolation" described Fredericksburg as a "regular Sebastopol," not an especially apt comparison but one that resonated with anyone who had a nodding acquaintance with the Crimean War. "Not a million men could have carried the position," one lieutenant declared with pardonable exaggeration. Many Federals had witnessed gaping holes being torn in the Union lines; to veterans it seemed like Malvern Hill reversed.[5]

"It was simply murder," raged one Pennsylvanian. Everyone from the private with simple common sense, to experienced officers who had checked out the ground, all the way up to General Hooker realized the futility of the assaults—or so several soldiers thought. And that made the average fellow's bravery all the sadder. "Our troops fought with the greatest determination and died with the utmost devotion," Hancock informed Senator Zachariah Chandler.[6]

But reports appeared that not all the men had acted so nobly. "Some of the volunteers fought well, others behaved shamelessly," one hard-bitten Regular informed his wife. Stories circulated about regiments that hesitated or broke for the rear. Such tales were standard after any battle, though in a broader sense they raised disturbing questions about the quality of Union troops. Some Federals now believed that they fought with less determination and élan than the Confederates. Half the army, according to one

Pennsylvania captain, thought mostly of their bounty money, and as for the Rebels, "They do fight well and worthy of a better cause."[7] Ever since McClellan had been repulsed on the Peninsula, the psychological momentum had shifted southward.

Fredericksburg helped engender, at least temporarily, a sense of defeatism because even the dullest soldiers realized that gallant charges had only piled up casualties. That melancholy conclusion cut deep into the marrow of courage and even the ability to carry on the usual camp routine. "Nothing gained"—the phrase cropped up often in letters home. Pointless sacrifices created the ultimate horror: carnage without meaning. All this "butchery"—another popular word—had occurred, and there seemed no end in sight.[8]

Years later an artilleryman remembered Fredericksburg as the Army of the Potomac's "Golgotha," but here the horrible "sacrifices" carried no promise of redemption. In the end the meaninglessness of the carnage struck the most mournful note. Echoing the book of Ecclesiastes, a soldier-poet asked about his dead comrades, "Was their effort vain?" The answer all too often weakened faith and spread despair. So long as memories of bloody fields haunted the soldiers' thoughts, so did doubt and depression.[9]

The boys were "blue" and ready to go home, but for the time being they settled for venting their frustrations in campfire discussions. Brooding over the defeat, men bitched about anything from politics to food. Even the best soldiers, Walt Whitman commented, needed to let off steam with typically profanity-laden complaints. Bitter words about worthless sacrifices and senseless bloodshed hit home. As one sergeant bluntly summed up the situation, "The Fifth New Hampshire regiment is played out."[10]

The camps around Falmouth reminded some soldiers of Valley Forge, and the combination of devastating defeat, cold weather, and physical discomfort made the comparison apt. "If any person wants to know what real hardship and misery are, let him join the Army of the Potomac," one Zouave volunteer suggested. A man in Sturgis's division claimed that his regiment was "not so well provided for as the hogs in Massachusetts." If only the "On to Richmond" crowd could visit the camps of the badly depleted regiments, take their turn on picket duty, and sleep on the damp ground, they would understand why the men had lost their appetite for war.[11]

A New Yorker visiting friends in a neighboring camp found them "sick of solgering like my self." Such a reaction was largely reflexive; many volunteers told anyone who would listen that they never wanted to witness such scenes of carnage again. New recruits, though, responded this way after any sizable battle. Many young men had seen enough and had no desire to repeat the experience. According to a Pennsylvania chaplain, soldiers now embraced a minimalist standard of courage: "Our battle-worn veterans go into danger when ordered, remain as a stern duty so long as directed, and leave as honor and duty allow." Drawings of officers leading charges that appeared in the illustrated newspapers elicited derisive howls of laughter in camp. Some soldiers swore they would never enter a battle again.[12] Such talk blunted anger, perhaps, and many of these men would still do their duty; but for several weeks after Fredericksburg such statements also reflected a deeper despondency about the Union cause.

For the most disheartened soldiers it seemed axiomatic that the conflict could never be ended by fighting, that battles would never save the Union.[13] The Rebels could not be whipped, period. Once-enthusiastic soldiers gave up on the idea of ever conquering the southern states.[14] Given these assumptions, the conclusion was obvious: the war would have to end soon. Only the prevaricating press would still claim that the Federals were itching for a fight or that any more lives should be sacrificed. The old fantasy about a peace settlement worked out by privates kept cropping up in camp discussions and letters home. Even the once odious word "compromise" crept into soldiers' correspondence, and speculation that Congress could settle everything during the coming winter sounded attractive to war-weary volunteers.[15]

Capt. David Jones in Taylor's brigade of Gibbon's division had seen enough fighting on December 13 to understand the widespread discouragement. The army was "daily becoming more demoralized." Some soldiers who had not been paid for a long time actually deserted, but Jones believed that problems extended far beyond the army camps. The American people had a "too impulsive shiftless temperament to endure a long war" and would give up on a "hopeless task." He wondered if there were officers capable of commanding such large armies and feared "the Rebs are too smart for us." Yet at the same time he clung to a vague belief that the government could do better and even suggested raising a million troops if necessary.[16]

Although his long, thoughtful, though disjointed letter listed many of the most common causes for post-Fredericksburg gloom, it also suggested the need to distinguish between grumbling and disaffection. Many soldiers who loudly complained about everything from poor generalship to lousy food would nevertheless stand to the colors when ordered. Dissatisfaction did not always mean demoralization. Even the despondent expressed some willingness to fight; with reinforcements they would try the Rebels again. Only a few days after the battle a hopeful Michigan captain claimed he "never felt more like fighting till the last man falls."[17]

Simple patriotism remained strong, and it was bolstered by staunch loyalty to comrades. To have any meaning an abstract love for the Union had to be translated into affection for one's family and fellow soldiers. Nothing could arouse a man's fighting spirit quicker than someone casting aspersions on the honor and courage of his company or regiment. Pride in how they had fought, even in defeat, remained strong. Idealistic young men spoke of "duty" without hint of irony or cynicism, and even officers who considered resigning their commissions could not in good conscience desert their comrades. They still had work to do, and the admonitions of parents, friends, and Sunday school teachers summoned them to persevere. "Rely upon me when duty calls," vowed Sgt. Walter Carter of the 22nd Massachusetts, whose canteen had been pierced by a Rebel shot during the battle. "My sense of right and love of country and its glorious cause would impel me forward to death, even if my poor nature hung back and human feelings gained control over me." Talk of the glorious Union by men bloodied in battle was not empty rhetoric but, rather, a reason for turning a deaf ear to grumblers and malcontents.[18]

One lieutenant admitted that some of the men might have been "cursing the stars and stripes" right after the battle, but "these same soldiers will fight like bull dogs when it comes to scratch." Indeed the grumbling veterans could be "relied upon more." The quickest way to end the war was to give the Rebs a good whipping and silence the "croakers" at home. If nothing else, the men had to prove that all the suffering had not been in vain. Fighting for those who had fallen involved not just a momentary passion for vengeance but a steady resolve that even incompetent leadership could not destroy.[19]

Such dedication often had deep religious roots. Although badly shaken, faith in divine protection for the individual persisted because men firmly believed not only in God's sovereignty but also in the inscrutability of his purposes. Despite the decline of Calvinism, many Christians still affirmed the Lord's mysterious and awesome control of human history. A soldier in Hancock's division who had lost many friends in the fight—"to all human appearances their lives are thrown away"—still believed that "God is wiser than we are and overrules all to accomplish ends for our good." Christians had to trust without always understanding because the Lord reigned over all, even in defeat.[20]

Students of the Old Testament could readily explain the entire conflict as punishment for sin, a scourge to abase the proud and reaffirm God's power. If only sinners humbled themselves, victory would follow. That the Almighty would yet come to the aid of free institutions, would yet vindicate the cause of liberty and progress, became the credo of this American civil religion. Loyalty to government meant loyalty to God even though human weakness spawned public dissension and divine displeasure. The defeat at Fredericksburg, one New York soldier affirmed, "had a purpose in thus humiliating our nation."[21]

The tangled relationship between individual iniquity, national sin, and divine purpose raised hard questions. That devout soldiers realized they might soon be killed, hoped for a heavenly reunion of loved ones, but still worried about their fate fit into the Lord's plan. Alarmed by reports of revival meetings in Lee's army, a Maine chaplain decided that perhaps God intended to humble the northern people through the bloody Fredericksburg debacle. Yet commonplace pieties seemed almost obscene. Alfred Castleman, a surgeon in the 5th Wisconsin, scorned the "pleasure [taken by] . . . our men of God, when, at their nightly prayers they in the same breath thank . . . God for the murders we have been permitted to perpetrate—the misery to inflict—and ask for peace on earth, and good will to man."[22] But then Castleman had struggled to repair the damage inflicted by bloodthirsty Christians on both sides.

Although affirmations of faith did not immediately dispel despair, they revealed new sources of strength. Memories of the recent slaughter certainly slaked a man's thirst for combat, but the army would survive. Despite loud complaints about all manner of things and the hardships of a winter encampment, patriotism, loyalty to comrades, and sheer determination were not quite "played out."

★　★　★

Victorious armies face different problems. The year 1862, which had brought a string of military disasters in the West and a serious threat to Richmond, was ending on a most positive note for Lee's bloodied but confident men. Their commander had fought a masterful defensive battle at Fredericksburg, yet the victory had not been decisive. The Yankees had "suffered heavily . . . but it did not go far enough to satisfy me," Lee admitted to his wife, Mary, a bit testily.

The Federals could still cross the Rappahannock at will, as Lee well knew, and Burnside would be reinforced. With the strategic situation largely unchanged, Lee remained poised to withdraw his forces to the North Anna River line. He had expected the Federals to renew the contest; Burnside, however, had refused to oblige. Despite a deep "disappointment," Lee tried to be philosophical: "We might have gained more but we would have lost more, & perhaps our relative condition would not have been improved." To daughter Mildred he quipped, "I am however happy in the knowledge that Genl Burnside & his army will not eat that promised Xmas dinner in Richmond to day." Months later Lee claimed that he had been "much depressed" by the outcome of Fredericksburg. "We had not gained a foot of ground and I knew the enemy could easily replace the men he had lost."[23]

Perhaps Fredericksburg had been a barren triumph, but jubilation generally overcame doubts. With the war entering its second winter, Burnside's defeat raised southern spirits at the end of a year of hard fighting.[24] Not only had the Confederates won a glorious victory, but some soldiers considered it "decisive." A member of the Richmond Howitzers speculated that Fredericksburg might be the last battle of the war; abandoning its usual skepticism, the *Richmond Daily Examiner* interpreted Burnside's retreat as a "confession of absolute defeat." The heavy casualties inflicted on the Federals—some Confederates believed that Burnside's army had been virtually destroyed—seemed suitable retribution for the wasting of the town. "Many of the vandal horde," a North Carolina infantryman exulted, "now lie on or beneath the soil that a few days ago they thought to desecrate."[25] The contrast between the sacred (soil) and the profane (enemy) limned common Confederate assumptions about the nature of the contest and about the vast gulf between the character and fighting ability of the two sides.

Despite admiration for all those charges toward the stone wall, many Confederates still contrasted brave southerners with cowardly northerners—a vital element of national identity for the fledgling southern republic. The craven foes had even stooped to manufacturing bullets specially designed to burst and infect wounds, the *Richmond Daily Enquirer* reported. Newspapers and some soldiers claimed that the Federals, driven by fixed bayonets and whiskey, had fought poorly and wavered against firm resistance. Their officers had failed to rally the faltering ranks, and only guards at the pontoon bridges had prevented the bluecoats from skedaddling back across the Rappahannock.[26]

"No one but an ass would have attempted to do what he [Burnside] did," one of Pickett's men snorted. Indeed, a Richmond editor described Burnside's order to renew the attacks on December 14 as an act of "incomparable stupidity." But like many Federals, some Confederates did not know whether to treat Burnside with contempt or pity. Like McDowell and McClellan, Burnside had failed miserably, but southern newspapers also reported that he had been under intense political pressure to attack Lee's army. Now he would be sacrificed, editors predicted, and be sent off to some backwater, a scapegoat for the failures of Lincoln and the cabinet.[27]

A Federal picket had reportedly shouted across the river asking if the Rebels had some "sorry corporal" to trade for Burnside—proof enough that the Army of the Potomac was "completely demoralized," a common phrase in Rebel letters and newspapers. According to a *Charleston Mercury* correspondent, 10,000 of Burnside's men were now refusing to fight. Confederates especially welcomed reports of partisan backbiting in Washington. Rumors circulated of Frémont replacing Burnside or of McClellan returning to command.[28]

Confederates who followed what one cavalryman called the "commotion . . . in Yankeedom" concluded that the Union war effort had been fatally damaged. Whatever the explanation, the long-awaited day of reckoning for the Yankees had arrived. "A proud and haughty people are humbled" as "reckless politicians" headed toward "speedy ruin," a Georgia volunteer rejoiced. The only thing northern speculators, those "traders in blood," cared about was making money from their nation's suffering, so another defeat would simply help fill their coffers. A Richmond editor venomously charged the Yankees ("the vilest of the human race") with enlisting the "low, brutal, obscene thieving wretches, gathered from the low quarters of the globe," to fight their battles. Refugees from "every prison house, penitentiary, and penal colony in the world" embodied the "immorality and ruffianism" so highly prized in the northern states. A Virginian in D. H. Hill's Division claimed that many of the Federal dead at Fredericksburg had been "tall and slender men" clearly of foreign extraction and that soon Confederates would be fighting the "real genuine blue bellied Yankees." Even William W. Holden's *North Carolina Standard,* a bastion of latent Unionism and a consistent critic of the Davis administration, thought Confederate prospects never seemed brighter.[29]

Weighing difficulties and discussing strategy had given way to crude bragging. The Confederates would capture Washington, and the Yankees would only visit Richmond as prisoners of war. Editorials, speeches, civilians' comments, and soldiers' letters brimmed with confidence. If the Federals cared to test Lee's army again, an eager young South Carolinian in Pickett's Division blustered, "let them come."[30]

Assertions of cultural superiority multiplied. The southern people, the *Richmond Daily Enquirer* trumpeted, displayed a superior "character, tone, and Christianity." Having defeated the mighty Federal host, barefoot men required no further proof of their virtue and invincibility. An unwavering faith in Lee negated sheer numbers as soldiers bragged that the Army of Northern Virginia had never been whipped. "No matter how large a force the nigger government may send against us," a Louisiana artilleryman avowed, Richmond would be safe. "The star of the rising empire of the South brightly ascends the horizon," a Georgia editor said, "and will soon culminate in unclouded majesty and splendor."[31]

The more sober-minded southerners disavowed this kind of bombast.

Despite the general rejoicing over the easy victory, some editors warned against overconfidence. The Yankees would undoubtedly try a different route to Richmond, much fighting remained, and people would have to endure some reverses before southern independence was won. A leading Presbyterian minister privately remarked, "We have not yet seen the worst of this war." Lee agreed and warned Secretary of War James A. Seddon that he must have more men. But Marse Robert had more faith than ever in his army and remained convinced that the "Almighty hand" would continue to bless southern arms.[32]

Christian convictions could foster emotions ranging from simple appreciation to dangerous hubris. Lee and Jackson, not to mention countless soldiers and civilians, expressed a humble thankfulness for the defeat of Burnside's army. Even in an official report, D. H. Hill acknowledged the "signal interposition of God in our favor . . . at Fredericksburg." That Lee's ragged, outnumbered army had triumphed only proved that the Lord protected the weak from the strong. Such convictions failed to immunize Confederates from spiritual arrogance. Assertions that the Almighty favored the Rebels confused the Lord's purposes with human endeavors. "God is on our side," declared a Richmond editor at the end of the year as he rejoiced over the Yankees' discomfiture. Though Pickett's Division quartermaster worried about the bitterness against the Federals in his own heart, he nevertheless called upon the Lord to "blot them out of existence."[33] To excoriate a godless foe while ignoring one's own transgressions had a long history, and many Confederates fell prey to sinful boastfulness.

In an evangelical culture, some Christians of course recognized the dangers of spiritual pride. Too many people indulged in self-righteous posturing and failed to realize that human weakness had brought on the war in the first place and that only sincere repentance could stay God's wrath. It was obvious that the southern states would still have to pass through severe trials before winning final victory. Stonewall Jackson understood how prophets such as Jeremiah had often called on the children of Israel to abandon their stiff-necked ways and believed that peace would only come when the people had turned away from wickedness. But the signs were hardly favorable. Soldiers still drank and swore, speculators pursued the almighty dollar, and citizens murmured against their leaders. Even the opening of a new theater in Richmond elicited a stern warning by a Baptist minister against indulging in vulgar amusements while the country remained in mortal danger.[34]

Cautionary voices, however, were drowned out by Confederates exulting over the victory. In Richmond and throughout the South, in official circles, around campfires, inside modest homes, and on street corners, confidence in the cause swelled. Problems that had seemed insurmountable a few months earlier appeared less formidable, and wild enthusiasm overwhelmed sober judgment.

★ ★ ★

For the Federals, anger spilled out in great torrents. In affixing responsibility for the Fredericksburg disaster, they lashed out at some favorite targets, venting their frustrations on bungling commanders, interfering politicians, partisan demagogues, and cheating contractors. If the troops had fought well, as most believed, then why had the Army of the Potomac suffered such a horrendous defeat? Given the incompetence of generals and the War Department, a frustrated New Yorker in Sickles's division frothed, the Federals might as well "let the south go to hell and disband the armies before it [the war] costs any more lives." A Hoosier in the Iron Brigade dismissed the Army of the Potomac as the "grandest humbug that has been imposed upon the public since the palmiest days of that prince of humbugs Barnum." Soldiers variously derided the "knaves" or "fools" or "ignoramuses" or "asses" managing the war.[35]

If only "the people in the North will rise up in their might & hurl the rotten politicians in Washington to Hades, and give us a Gen. to lead us or call us home before we die of exposure and or are killed in useless battles," a sergeant in Sykes's division ranted. Like many civilians, angry soldiers could not grasp how war on such an unprecedented scale had stretched conventional ideas about organization and strategy to their breaking point. Frontal assaults against a well-prepared enemy merited sharp rebukes, and with unusual perception the *Boston Daily Advertiser* observed that the "improvements in modern artillery and musketry make it practically impossible to carry entrenchments by assault in column." One point seemed obvious: the strategy of the entire campaign had been disastrous, and whether one blamed generals or politicians, there would be hell to pay. "We take that whipping like a parcel of schoolboys would taking a whipping," a Massachusetts volunteer informed his home folks. "One boy blames the other for getting them all whipped."[36]

The two favorite whipping boys were Halleck and Stanton. Soldiers and editors accused the general in chief of attempting to direct the campaign from his office.[37] Old Brains came under fire for two reasons. First, leading Democrats blamed him for the pontoon fiasco, and even Republican editors hesitated to defend him on that score.[38] Second, the general in chief's harshest critics charged him with ordering Burnside to cross the Rappahannock and launch the suicidal assaults. According to one camp tale, Halleck had sworn that the Army of the Potomac "must go to Richmond if every man had to go on crutches."[39] Some political insiders and a few soldiers blamed Stanton, who had won few friends in Washington, for issuing the fatal orders. Amidst rumored cabinet changes, the irascible secretary of war became a tempting political target.[40]

Other voices clamored for McClellan's return. Perhaps now people could appreciate Little Mac's caution compared with what a Maine chaplain termed Burnside's "rashness and dash."[41] McClellan never would have led his beloved boys into such a "slaughter house," many veterans declared.[42] As early as December 15 the cry "McClellan is the man" echoed in the camps near Falmouth, and calls for his reinstatement sparked heated discussion. "We *must* have McClellan back with unlimited and unfettered powers," Brig. Gen. Gouverneur K. Warren believed. "His name is a tower of strength to every one here."[43] Only McClellan could save the army. Soldiers fondly and inaccurately recalled the halcyon days with their old commander, who some believed had never been defeated, but then McClellan supporters had always been quick to defend a strategic retreat. Even a skeptical volunteer admitted that "McClellan stock is rising."[44]

A Confederate newspaper gleefully reported that a single word from McClellan would incite the Army of the Potomac to overthrow the Lincoln administration—a wild suggestion that did not appear entirely fanciful in Washington. Congressman James A. Garfield feared a "very insidious and determined scheme on the part of the Democracy . . . to make a kind of French coup d'etat in favor of McClellan." Talk of "military dictatorship" was needlessly alarmist, but an editorial drumfire recommending the general's restoration to command was real enough. The powerful Blairs and other conservative Republicans considered bringing back McClellan solely to boost morale in the army and the country at large. Shaken Republicans worried that the Army of the Potomac teemed with intrigue instigated by Little Mac's treasonous allies.[45]

Whatever people believed about Halleck, Stanton, or McClellan, the perpetrator of "Burnside's slaughter" had become the storm center of debate both inside and outside the army. One furious New Yorker suggested that "they aughto to Hang someone for this either Burnside or Halock."[46] Before Fredericksburg, soldiers had willingly given Burnside the benefit of the doubt, in part because his genial disposition offered a welcome change from that of the sometimes aloof McClellan. "Just the fellow for fine reviews in time of peace," an orderly in Hancock's division thought. But many men, especially those in the regiments that had been mauled, no longer believed that Burnside could command an army. Talk of the general being "played out" or of his "stock" having a "downward tendency" summed up camp senti-ments.[47]

Burnside's appearance no longer elicited huzzahs or even polite recognition from the troops; despite prodding by officers, a few halfhearted shouts and an embarrassed silence became the most common reaction. A little more than a week after the withdrawal, the devastated Irish Brigade pointedly refused to cheer for him. Indeed, barely more than stony silence could be expected from men who considered their commander the "butcher of the Army of the Potomac."[48]

But as with reports of demoralization, hostility to Burnside can be easily misinterpreted or exaggerated. Outrage among defeated soldiers is understandable, yet even the most angry often expressed some sympathy for their commander. A New Hampshire corporal who had been in the thick of the fight with Sturgis's division claimed that Burnside still had the soldiers' "whole confidence." One badly wounded fellow lying in a Washington hospital refused to hear any disparaging talk about his commander. The troops respected Burnside's nobility and generosity; rumors that he had been ordered to make the attacks turned him into a tragic figure in some quarters. Caught between Lincoln, Halleck, Stanton, and McClellan, Burnside naturally won sympathy from soldiers fed up with backbiting generals and meddling politicians.[49]

Burnside himself sadly took the criticism to heart. One commonly circulated tale described him riding through camp looking "pale as death," visibly shuddering when soldiers hurrahed for McClellan. A staff officer noted how Burnside had grown "careworn and miserable"—rather like Lincoln during this difficult period. The general spent more time alone brooding on the defeat, the unreliability of many officers, and Halleck's failure with the pontoons. "Jealousies and political intrigue are greater enemies than an open foe," the faithful Larned concluded.[50]

On December 18 Burnside met with members of the Joint Committee on the Conduct of the War in Falmouth. The committee's animus against conservative generals was well known, but the magnitude of the Fredericksburg losses had a sobering effect even on the most partisan members. With the cabinet crisis unfolding in Washington, Republicans hoped to limit the political damage of yet another defeat. Just before he left the capital, Zach Chandler confided to his wife, "The country is done unless something is done at once." Lamenting the "folly, folly, folly" and a president "too weak for the occasion," he railed against "these fools or traitor generals" who wasted "precious blood in indecisive battles."[51]

The committee members allowed Burnside to describe his plans and perspective on the battle at length, a process guaranteed to reinforce prevailing impressions of the general's straightforward honesty and political harmlessness. Burnside naturally dwelled on the pontoon question and hurried through the battle itself, but only one committee member bothered to ask questions. The general conceded the strength of the Confederate positions and that he might have chosen a better point of attack. Under interrogation he denied that Lincoln, Halleck, or Stanton had directed the army's movements and refused to blame anyone else for his shortcomings.[52]

As the testimony unfolded, the committee grew increasingly sympathetic to the beleaguered Burnside. Congressman George W. Julian of Indiana admired the general's humble honesty, willingness to take responsibility, and obvious lack of ambition for higher command. During his appearance General Sumner not only backed up Burnside but also maintained that within a few days "the army will be in excellent order again." Even Franklin refuted reports of widespread demoralization.[53]

Franklin later bragged to McClellan about "ventilat[ing] my opinions" before the committee "in a way that astounded them." He remained ignorant of how his feeble performance at Fredericksburg had disappointed Burnside and how ready McClellan's old enemies were to blame the disaster on his excessive caution. Ignoring the chain of command, Franklin, joined by Baldy Smith, even sent a letter to Lincoln proposing that 250,000 troops advance along the James River toward Richmond. The president must have smelled more than a whiff of McClellan's influence but wearily replied that this proposal left hanging the old question of how Washington would be properly defended.[54]

Hooker as usual played his own game. Appearing before the committee on December 20, he agreed that Halleck had promised that the pontoons would be ready in time but implied that Burnside should have expected delays. Hooker had favored crossing the army upstream from Fredericksburg, and he repeatedly pointed out how both his strategic and his tactical advice had been ignored. If he were to be credited, the only person with the intelligence, prescience, and will to command the Army of the Potomac was Joseph Hooker. He deplored the persistent influence of McClellan toadies such as Franklin and Smith, never hesitated to fault his superiors, and encouraged speculation that he might soon displace Burnside.[55]

The generals would in the end protect themselves, but in the meantime the country would have to decide how to weigh the defeat at Fredericksburg and whom to blame. Perhaps the northern people themselves had expected too much from the army, though criticizing impatient newspaper editors could not conceal the failure by thousands of men and millions of dollars to crush the rebellion.[56]

The political tremors continued. "The republican party is forever played out now the last Battle was its death knell," a disgusted New Yorker wrote to a brother serving in French's division. Editorials ridiculing Lincoln and lampooning official incompetence reflected growing confidence among administration opponents.[57] Democrats warned that the American people would not be patient forever. "The war is a failure!" one leading conservative newspaper shouted, and the country could no longer abide the administration's disastrous course. Even the temperate *Harper's Weekly* believed "matters are rapidly ripening for a military dictatorship."[58]

Orders from Washington had produced the Fredericksburg debacle, critics declared. The War Department had allegedly forced a reluctant Burnside to attack the Rebels' impregnable positions. Such stinging accusations again threw the administration onto the defensive. Even a few Republicans acknowledged that Lincoln and Stanton had faltered, but Democrats insisted that direct orders from Halleck and the president had sent hundreds of poor soldiers to their deaths.[59]

Acerbic editorials blasting Lincoln, Halleck, and Stanton angered Burnside. "I'll put a stop to that," he abruptly announced on December 19. Despite protests from several staff officers, he refused to dodge responsibility, drafted a public letter, and quickly arranged to meet with Lincoln. When he reached Washington about 10:00 P.M. the next evening, the president had already gone to bed but had not been able to sleep because of dyspepsia, and he hurriedly pulled on his trousers for a late night meeting. Lincoln expressed relief over the general's willingness to admit mistakes and thanked him warmly for being the first person ever to lift any responsibility from his shoulders. Back at Willard's Hotel some time after midnight, Burnside put the finishing touches on his letter. The next day he again conferred with Lincoln as well as with Halleck and Stanton. Lincoln reassured the nervous general in chief that Burnside was his "real friend," but the impatient secretary of war sharply rebuked the general for not having his letter ready for publication. Even the affable Burnside bristled at this remark, and Lincoln cajoled Stanton into making an apology.[60]

Burnside addressed his letter to Halleck and backdated it to December 17 to avoid the appearance that someone in the administration had forced him to write it. After describing the army's movements, the battle, and the reasons for withdrawing, Burnside explained how he had chosen the

Fredericksburg route against the advice of Lincoln, Halleck, and Stanton. He took complete responsibility for the defeat: the administration "left the whole management in my hands, without giving me orders."[61]

The soldiers credited Burnside for admitting his mistakes, a rare enough quality among general officers. Some men believed the letter helped restore confidence in their commander, though a colonel in Doubleday's division more perceptively noted that his comrades now thought of Burnside as a "high-toned, honorable man, but less of a general." And in fact Burnside's virtual confession of incompetence was hardly inspiring. He appeared weak, "an awful greenhorn," to an ardent McClellan supporter who deemed the letter the work of a "high-minded donkey." Hooting at the document's supposedly "manly statements," a lieutenant in Griffin's division considered Burnside's explanations "bosh, all bosh."[62]

Republican editors seemed to take the letter at face value and felt that Burnside's remarkable candor and plain honesty should restore public confidence. Yet the general had no real political allies. Unlike McClellan or even Frémont, no partisan faction felt any great loyalty toward him. Republicans praised his letter because it deflected criticism from the Lincoln administration. Presidential secretary John Hay published an anonymous editorial in a leading Missouri newspaper using Burnside's letter to counter complaints about the government. Hay, whether speaking for Lincoln or not, clearly acted in the administration's interest to contain political damage from the Fredericksburg disaster. Mistakes had been made, Republicans admitted, but they refused to allocate blame. At least Burnside's frankness and sincerity offered a welcome change from the usual evasions.[63]

Leading Democrats scoffed. The political chicanery was blatant in a document so helpful to an administration desperate to defend itself. "Very Remarkable, Very Curious, Very Generous and Very Naïve Letter from General Burnside," ran the headline in the *New York Herald.* Burnside, a Pennsylvania editor complained, "has stepped forward to shield the blundering Halleck, the ambitious Secretary of War, and the imbecile President." For many Democrats the disastrous decision to remove McClellan explained all that followed.[64]

Yet if Lincoln merited criticism for his course since Antietam, it was more for indecisiveness rather than interference. Although depressed and baffled, he had hardly lost his political touch, but now he seemed less surefooted. Take, for example, his bizarre letter of congratulations to Burnside's battered army. The obvious magnitude of the defeat notwithstanding, Lincoln claimed that "the attempt was not an error, nor the failure other than an accident." After commending the troops for their skill and bravery, he congratulated them because the number of casualties had been "comparatively so small." This time Lincoln's odd sense of fatalism was combined with an incredible misunderstanding of the battle's human costs.[65]

The president's letter boosted neither military nor public confidence. "Compared to what?" the First Corps artillery chief exploded after reading the comment on the casualties.[66] Lincoln's peculiar statements offered more political ammunition to administration opponents who already had more than enough. "As well attempt to hide the reeking graves of the soldiers under a coat of whitewash as varnish over the errors of the Generals and the blunders of the Cabinet," an Albany editor wrote. The *Boston Post* was even more pointed: "The bones may bleach, the wives and mothers weep, the soldiers murmur, the officers remonstrate, in vain; there is nobody to blame; a bloody sacrifice was not an error, but an accident."[67]

Public anger would not be so easily assuaged without someone to blame. After hearing from several more witnesses in Washington, two days before Christmas the joint committee released the testimony without comment to Congress. It soon appeared in newspapers. On learning of the committee's action, Lincoln himself snapped, "Why will people be such damned fools?" Although relieved not to be the scapegoat, Burnside reportedly "cringed" while reading some of the testimony. Republicans hoped to stanch the torrent of abuse against the government, but a "report" affixing no responsibility would hardly do that. "All of the officers clear themselves," a Wisconsin sergeant groused.[68]

Official Washington had run out of excuses. The big pile of rationalizations had done nothing but diminish the reputations of Burnside, Franklin, Halleck, Stanton, and Lincoln without moving the Army of the Potomac any closer to defeating Lee. Two days after the battle the *New York Tribune* had predicted that Burnside would soon force the enemy into the "decisive struggle of the war." Reinforcements would allow him to strike the Rebels again. Several days later the paper was claiming that Burnside had "outgeneraled" Lee in withdrawing his army from Fredericksburg; in fact, the Army of the Potomac would have easily won any battle fought on equal ground. An editorial on Christmas Day declared that aside from the casualties little had been lost at Fredericksburg. It remained for the *Tribune*'s bitter rival, the *New York Herald,* to state the obvious, although not without some relish: "At this Christmas time, when good fairies fill the air, we can hardly wonder at the sudden miracle which has shown us the Fredericksburg affair in its true light, and given us occasion for national joy instead of national sorrow."[69]

Only absolute necessity and prospect of great
advantages can excuse winter operations.
—Frederick the Great

22 Winter

Christmas was coming, but with the possibility of more fighting still hanging fire, few soldiers thought much about the holiday. Republican newspapers spurned any suggestion that the army go into winter quarters, and
from Rhode Island to Wisconsin editors kept beating the drums for a new
offensive. Europe required new evidence of northern determination, and in
any case Greeley reported the troops itching for another go at the Rebels.
Even conservative newspapers suggested alternate routes to Richmond and
agreed that Burnside should try to capture the Rebel capital before spring.[1]

Yet those shouting the loudest would not have to put up with the hardships of a winter campaign, and so the Union soldiers scoffed at their advice.
Lee's men, too, would suffer because their government had not remedied
serious supply problems. Somber reflection would thus taint Christmas in
both armies as the holidays only widened the psychological gulf between
soldiers and home folks. But for the time being, strategic questions also intruded.

As the weather turned colder, few soldiers showed much interest in campaigning. Rumors spread through the bivouacs that the army would, in fact,
be going into winter quarters, that a corps or even a grand division was going
to be withdrawn for garrison duty in Washington. But there had been no offi-

cial word, and the troops wondered impatiently how long they would have to lie on the ground without tents. With perhaps the example of Napoleon's Russian venture in mind, Col. Emory Upton of the 121st New York predicted that the army would lose 15,000 men to illness during a winter offensive.[2]

In some regiments the men had begun logging up tents and building huts only days after they had recrossed the Rappahannock. The sounds of axes, hatchets, and hammers cut through the crisp air, and within a week shanties dotted the landscape. That officers allowed men to log up their tents suggested the campaign was over, but uncertain of Burnside's intentions, savvy veterans hung back, waiting until they were sure. Getting a good start on a hut and then suddenly having to move would be the ultimate frustration.[3]

The construction was hardly uniform. Camps sprouted with an assortment of architectural styles, with liberal use of Virginia mud being the only common denominator. Some soldiers dug several feet into the ground, while others erected more conventional cabins, though the term "shebang" perhaps best captured the ramshackle appearance of these dwellings.[4] The dimensions were not even remotely standard.[5] Some huts were a snug 6 feet by 6 feet; more commonly the shanties were about 100 square feet. A central ridgepole covered by fly tents rose 6 feet or higher in the center. They had no windows and smoky barrel chimneys, and sunlight seldom penetrated the gloomy interiors unless the "door," usually an old piece of sack, was open. The most carefully constructed cabins were tight and warm, but more typically they were "dark, dirty, dismal, and cheerless."[6]

Many soldiers, however, reserved such comments for their diaries or their comrades. Letters to family emphasized the cozy warmth of newly built "homes." Word of a "snug little bed" doubtless eased one wife's worries about her Hoosier husband freezing to death. A Massachusetts artillery captain waxed almost lyrical: "When I come in evenings, hang up my cap, put on my slippers and sit down in my easy chair in front of a big, blazing fire, I am nearly as comfortable as in a parlor at home." He had not become a ruffian and instead maintained some semblance of civilized existence.[7]

The shanties at least provided shelter and a place to sleep. Soldiers fashioned beds from cracker boxes and barrel staves supported by sticks driven into the ground and covered with twigs or saplings. Hay, ticking filled with dry leaves, or pine boughs provided a modicum of comfort. Canteens and haversacks hung on pegs; a shelf over a fireplace held miscellaneous dinnerware; cracker boxes stored virtually everything else. Although cramped quarters bred both disease and despair, a New York lieutenant tried to accentuate the positive: "You could call the tent, fireplace, steps, floor, bed and all a clumsy heathenish affair—I call it the perfection of ingenuity, architecture, and engineering—and I find it more comfortable than a house."[8] Again the yearning for the familiar trappings of home helped men tolerate or even appreciate their crude surroundings.

Some fool knocking a chimney over or, worse, a fire quickly ended such reveries. Even without such mishaps, settling in for several months of stinging eyes and constant coughing intensified the misery. Clad in overcoat and gloves, Charles Haydon, a captain in the 2nd Michigan, squatted near a fire trying to avoid the smoke and wondering where all the heat had gone. He missed the conversations of friends and had grown tired of hearing bugles or drums or soldiers squabbling. Perhaps pining after old pleasures was a weakness, he conceded, but his misery also stoked "mingled hate, revenge, and a determination to uphold our cause to the last."[9]

He could have been referring to the "last" stick of kindling because both armies were rapidly denuding the countryside. Finding enough firewood had become a challenge, especially when nearby trees served as windbreaks. With farmers' fences and even outhouses falling under the axe, a division quartermaster predicted that "in another month we shall freeze as well as starve."[10] Chopping wood, tying it up in bundles, and dragging it back to camp became the most onerous of winter duties. According to one estimate, it took between 150 and 200 fires a day to keep a regiment warm and fed.[11]

The payoff for all the hard labor was a roaring fire to gather around at night. Soldiers huddled near the flames wrapped in whatever they could find. Many had shed their knapsacks and blankets before going into battle, and new blankets did not arrive immediately. The men had to line the notoriously thin army blankets with newspapers, but even then some soldiers slept in their clothes and used an overcoat for more cover.[12]

The Army of the Potomac was probably the best-equipped army in world history, but that fact was cold comfort—literally—to men convinced that they lacked decent clothes for the winter. "There is criminal negligence somewhere," a New Jersey colonel informed his sister. With no fear of demagoguery, Democrats charged that corrupt contractors and foot-dragging by bureaucrats were killing brave soldiers in Virginia while the government provided clothing for idle slaves and unemployed British workers.[13]

The reality was more prosaic. Despite spot shortages, War Department shipments of pants and overcoats soon reached the camps. No one had frozen to death, Cpl. Peter Welsh of the Irish Brigade scoffed, nor had he seen any man without pants, though some boys looked pretty ragged. Other Federals reported adequate clothing supplies.[14] The soldiers, of course, welcomed items from home, but shipping costs and delays gave pause to requests for boots or other bulky items. One New Hampshire recruit claimed his new gloves "fit like a duck's foot in a mud puddle" and his shiny boots would help "stamp out the rebellion." A member of the 24th Massachusetts reported that his regiment was "as fine a looking lot of soldiers as ever handled a musket or marched a mile." But his point was tinged with political bitterness: "Uncle Sam ought to be proud to think that we had such a fine lot of fellows volunteer to fight, bleed, and almost die for the sake of a cussed nigger."[15]

Everyone's outlook would have been brighter with better food. As regiments settled into camps, regular supply had resumed, yet the monotony of salt pork and hardtack grated on the soldiers. "This is the way us poor cusses halfto live" one New Yorker informed his sister. The usual grumbling over meals now carried political overtones. Few privates doubted that commissary officers skimmed off supplies, but even worse, crooked contractors sent the army rancid bacon crawling with maggots. Such charges in the wake of another military disaster added to the growing conviction that folks at home would never understand what soldiers had to endure in the field.[16]

Disease remained the deadliest enemy. The general health of many regiments was reportedly poor, and in fact mortality rates from sickness in the northern armies jumped dramatically between November and December. Nightly coughing, groaning, moaning, and labored breathing bespoke the costs of a winter campaign. Sometimes it seemed the army had become one vast hospital. Soldiers pictured folks at home reading about daring troop movements, unaware of how many men were fighting much less dramatic but equally deadly battles against illness.[17]

By the end of the year, some regiments appeared woefully depleted. The 13th New Hampshire reported no more than 400 effectives, with at least 250 men answering sick call in the morning or already in a hospital. The 24th New Jersey, one of the first regiments to charge the stone wall, was almost as reduced from disease after the battle and soon had fewer than 300 men fit for duty. Other outfits reported comparably depressing numbers.[18]

Despite the cooler weather, diarrhea—"this terrible complaint of the army"—still plagued the troops. One surgeon blamed adulterated coffee and the shortage of vegetables, but whatever the cause, the number of cases held steady and the death toll climbed. Typhoid fever proved even more devastating. Young men who appeared perfectly healthy suddenly fell ill and died within days. Contaminated water and a poor diet explained the outbreaks, though even men who understood how and why the disease spread adopted an attitude of helplessness inevitability. "Most of us have lost our courage and expectations of reaching home, or even dying on the battlefield—a fate less cruel than dying by inches," reported a Maine volunteer.[19]

These deaths were a familiar occurrence in division hospitals. Complaints of general disarray—drafty hospital tents, patients sleeping on straw or using knapsacks for pillows, and food shortages—persisted even after many of the wounded had recovered or been shipped to Washington. A musician in the 24th Michigan with a bad cold decided to visit a nearby hospital. "One look was enough for me," he gasped. "God forbid I should have to go there."[20]

The sheer numbers of the dying were numbing, and like any statistics, they failed to capture the poignancy of individual cases. Cpl. Samuel W. George of the 12th New Hampshire had left a wife and eight-month-old twins back in Concord. Nearly six feet tall with black hair and a dark complexion, this once vigorous thirty-six-year-old had become seriously ill in December. He languished in camp during the fighting on December 13. Several days afterward, in the final moments of his life, he managed to raise himself in bed for one last look at pictures of his wife and children. Such deaths, at once heartrending and commonplace, seemed especially pitiable to surviving comrades who also felt so far from family and friends. Relentless reminders of mortality compounded the post-Fredericksburg gloom.[21]

Funerals also added to the woe. There were three burials on three consecutive days in the 122nd Pennsylvania and three in one day in the 108th New York. The sound of fifes or a noisy Irish wake carried the same doleful message. With no chaplain available to offer final consolation, a plainspoken member of the 124th New York stretched his arms toward the heavens and implored, "Great God of battle—as we bury poor Tom's mangled body, let his soul enter Heaven—Amen!" Some men still wrote in the age's euphemistic style about a soldier's "last march" before "he is borne on Angel wings to join his God in glory," but Walt Whitman better recaptured the mood in one camp near Falmouth during a perfunctory burial: "Death is nothing here." Even a Maine nurse who fussed over patients sadly noted her own "indifference" as she closed the eyes, wrapped the face, and cut off a lock of hair from another dead soldier.[22]

The news of these deaths, usually conveyed in an officer's letter, often reached a man's home shortly after Christmas. Joseph Heisler had complained of rheumatism right before the battle, and by December 20 he had died of what was vaguely called "brain fever." His brother, Cpl. Henry C. Heisler of the 48th Pennsylvania, had him buried in a rough box and erected a crude headboard so at least the grave would be marked if their father ever came for the body. "It was very hard," Heisler wrote to a sister, "to see him die so sudden but here a man can be well and hearty one day and can die the next."[23]

In the midst of death and its reminders, camp life went on; regimental routine distracted fears of what lay ahead. Reveille, doctor's call, roll calls, meals, drill, dress parade, and taps continued day after day.[24] Junior officers inspected tents, sinks, and cooking facilities; they supervised endless drilling. Captains filled out forms in triplicate and, if they were ambitious, boned up on military science. At the top, a good colonel who kept his men occupied and earned their respect often made the difference between a miserable, unhealthy camp and a clean, orderly one. Even then only a road-building detail, provost duty in Falmouth, or unloading supplies at Aquia Landing broke up the tedium.[25]

Fortunately the picket truce generally held, and shouting across the Rappahannock sometimes led to an exchange of visits and meals. The Rebels were the "same kind of people we are," a New Yorker in Doubleday's division remarked as if much surprised by this discovery. A Michigan volunteer considered each side equally "sick of this unhuman wholesale slaughter" and believed the rank and file of both armies would vote for peace. Perhaps so, but both men missed an important distinction. Although some sharp repartee still continued, even sociable Confederates sounded more confident if not cocky. A fellow could hear them across the river whistling and singing, and when they talked of the war ending by spring, they meant with southern independence secured.[26]

Occasional fraternization with the Rebels merely enlivened dull times. Repairing tents, writing letters, or gathering wood hardly filled the idle hours. "Cut off from civilization" became a common lament. "One never thinks in the m[ornin]'g how to enjoy himself during the day, but how to get through it without positive suffering," wrote a Michigan officer. The hours passed sluggishly; a day sometimes seemed like an eternity. Peering from his tent across a "sea of red mud" or staring into the fire was driving a Massachusetts volunteer crazy. With nothing to do, he would "go to bed in sheer desperation then roll and toss all night."[27]

Seeing the same grimy-faced soldiers and listening to stale old jokes around campfires grew tiresome, so the boys welcomed any momentary relief. Civilian visitors, especially if they were female, were the best distractions. To hear the "rustle of silk would be the sweetest music" to a New York lieutenant who, like men in any age and clime, longed for the "sight of a pretty face" and the "silvery tones" of a woman's voice. Soldiers vividly recalled when they had last seen a woman and could describe in great detail any who ventured into camp, no matter how unpromising their appearance. Although laundresses seemed "amphibious creatures," deprivation bred uncommon boldness. One adventurous private in the 17th Maine tried to kiss the rather large "Dutch Mary" and got a hard whack with a wet shirt. Enterprising, well-dressed prostitutes ventured near the bivouacs and presumably made a living. Officers, however, worried more about their men taking up with Rebel belles who only inconsistently rebuffed Yankee lovemaking.[28]

Soldiers starved for culture could read, and many begged their families for printed matter. Although the soldiers would devour salacious literature, or any other kind for that matter, the Christian Commission flooded the army with testaments, tracts, and church papers, and if the agents can be believed, the men welcomed it all. Newsboys also appeared, hawking copies of the *New York Herald* for ten cents with cries of "another bloody battle." Other papers sold for less, but soldiers favored the twelve-page *Herald* because, despite its conservative politics, it was crammed with war news. Soldiers read aloud to their less literate comrades.[29] Just as camp gossip powerfully affected morale, so did news reports passed by word of mouth.

Games could, for a time at least, help divert young men from their worries and drain nervous energy. New York and New England troops enjoyed the relatively new sport of baseball. Raggedly played pickup games with scores such as 45-15, 33-1, or 19-17 amused players and spectators alike, especially when inexperienced boys awkwardly tried to master a difficult sport. In an era when a base runner could be put out by plunking him with the ball and regiments were not averse to wagering on the outcome, the rowdiness of the contests became part of the attraction.[30]

Other soldiers hungered for spiritual solace, and there were even stirrings of a religious revival in the army after Fredericksburg. On gray winter days a real worship service was something to treasure. A Pennsylvania captain described a particularly moving sermon delivered in a fierce wind as "quite a treat and . . . justly appreciated by all the men." Lively weekday prayer meetings were not as effective as Sunday services in securing bonds between families and soldiers who hankered for worship back home. "Thank God for the Sabbath the day of rest when you lift our souls from the low groveling earth to the heavens above," a Hoosier exulted. On Sunday afternoons conscientious chaplains visited the hospitals, and the men themselves sometimes passed the time singing hymns.[31]

These wholesome activities, however, cut against the grain of military life. "Never was there a place where the Gospel was more needed than in the army," claimed one Massachusetts minister who considered the "social atmosphere" quite "unfavorable" for leading a Christian life. Despite efforts of chaplains, officers, and even President Lincoln, Sabbath-breaking remained the rule rather than the exception. "There is no Sunday in the army" became a camp cliché. The customary day of worship and reflection was taken up with everything from pitching quoits to general inspections.[32]

Yet men's contemplation of the horrors of Fredericksburg seemed to have sparked small signs of religious awakening in the camps by late December. Chaplains and visiting evangelists held nightly meetings hoping to win lost souls to Christ. Though the number of converts grew steadily, this was far from a mass revival. The best news a Pennsylvania chaplain could report was that few ever refused a gift testament, but for individual soldiers who had perhaps seldom considered their mortality or relationship with God, the meetings could be real turning points. Many reflected on misspent youth and fretted over their shortcomings before receiving assurance of salvation. Soldiers struggling to lead a Christian life relished letters from home that encouraged their walk with Jesus. Devout men urged relatives to read the Bible and accept Christ as their savior. "Life is short. Death is certain," Virgil Mattoon of the 24th New York warned his brother, though he held out hope for an "unbroken family circle in Heaven."[33]

Religion remained a powerful tie between military and civilian life; but peaceful Sundays at home stood in stark contrast to the soldiers' current state, and many wondered if they would ever enjoy such simple pleasures again. The war itself remained the greatest test of faith, especially in the aftermath of Fredericksburg. When a Pennsylvania chaplain advised his listeners that everyone must be subject to the higher powers and that government was ordained by God, he broached a touchy subject. Soldiers not only had to connect northern war aims with divine purpose but had to obey their leaders, especially in light of the post-Fredericksburg political uproar. By the same token, a shivering soldier standing picket who could feel the Almighty's protection would somehow find the inner resources to survive the winter and fight again. Faith that God was watching over individuals at every moment had by no means disappeared despite daily evidence that raised serious doubts.[34]

Religious devotion, then, became another sign of soldier resilience. Cold weather, poor shelter, monotonous food, and widespread disease surely affected morale, yet the men could always grumble and relish simple diversions. Oaths sometimes drowned out the prayers, and the folks back home might never understand what their loved ones were enduring; but by late December it seemed clear that the Army of the Potomac would not fall apart. At least not yet.

★ ★ ★

Neither would the Army of Northern Virginia. Even after their smashing victory, Lee's men faced the same problems as their Federal counterparts.

The Confederates could not officially go into winter quarters so long as Burnside's intentions remained uncertain. "Very cold. No tents," a soldier in Jackson's old brigade reported. Makeshifts dotted the camps. Men burrowed into the ground and covered the hole with a blanket or used brush to block out the wind or fashioned wigwams from sticks, dirt, and straw.[35] Captured enemy tents sheltered some regiments, and more government tent flies arrived after the battle. Men with some thin canvas between themselves and the night air seemed fortunate. "I get along with it better than I could expect," a Georgia captain told his wife after recalling all the comforts at home.[36]

Veterans saw no reason to build more elaborate quarters when the army might move at any moment to counter another Yankee thrust across the Rappahannock. Better to stay in fly tents than waste time and energy constructing log huts that seemed to one Louisiana artillerist little better than slave quarters.[37] For the most part the confident Confederates did complain less than the Federals. Many claimed to be comfortable and even enjoying their crude homes. "Wee live know [sic] like folks and before we lived like hogs," asserted one North Carolinian who had managed to erect a "splendid house and chimney." Many more claimed to be "snug" and "warm."[38]

Self-assured Confederates could adjust to the discomforts. Great roaring fires with huge logs created a good deal of smoke, but Lt. Ujanirtus Allen of the 21st Georgia seemed to enjoy describing how sooty strands hung from his beard. Green wood and high winds compounded the discomfort. Yet knowing that "the Yankees could not drive us from our position" made Capt. Matthew Talbot Nunnally of the 11th Georgia feel almost cozy. Men could crouch near their tents, smoke a pipe, and perhaps even smile a bit.[39]

Soaring morale and proud determination, however, could not remedy the army's severe supply problems. Transportation bottlenecks left coats in Richmond and soldiers freezing in camp; government clothing often proved ill fitting; and complaints received vague, defensive replies from Richmond bureaucrats.[40] Worse yet, men were still barefoot or wearing shoes that had long outlived any usefulness. Relief would be elusive. The Confederate government had issued four patents for wooden shoe soles, and some of Longstreet's men were still making moccasins. One of four soldiers in Lee's only Louisiana brigade remained without shoes; others in the same outfit lacked blankets and even underwear. Soldiers sent home long lists of badly needed items, from boots to socks to overcoats.[41] The combined efforts of government, families, and charity never quite covered the needs (or bodies) of ragged Confederates.

Their stomachs were not filled either. Lee's commissary officers preferred buying food locally but remained dependent on shipments from Richmond. For their part War Department subsistence officers complained of poor support from the cavalry and blamed Lee. Commissary Gen. Lucius Northrop vetoed a scheme to trade government sugar for farmers' bacon. And so it went. Charges that badly needed supplies rotted in Richmond warehouses elicited familiar excuses about transportation shortages.[42]

But the sad truth was that Lee's men were hungry. Rations of flour, bacon, and beef had been steadily reduced. Three daily meals suddenly became two; involuntary fast days were common.[43] Fat pork and dry bread seldom satisfied a soldier's appetite. The bacon was often rancid and the beef tough. "I sometimes think they kill them [the cattle] to keep them from dying," a Virginia infantryman wryly commented.[44]

Short rations and cold weather weakened an army already suffering poor health. Letters home read like extended medical reports. Twenty percent of a regiment seriously ill was commonplace, and a daily "sick train" carried the worst sufferers to Richmond hospitals. The cold brought some men to the limits of endurance, so resignations, medical leaves, and severe disabilities thinned the ranks further.[45] Aside from the usual maladies, winter brought on fevers, chills, and aches. Fearing he had contracted fatal pneumonia, as had several of his comrades, one Alabamian rubbed his sore chest with turpentine and dosed himself with powdered morphine. Rheumatism also greatly afflicted the thinly clad Confederates.[46]

Miseries were always relative, of course. High morale mitigated various hardships, yet Lee's supply problems would continue and could not help but weaken his forces. Cold winds buffeted both armies crouched in tents or shanties. Military uncertainties and the thought of a winter campaign made everyone edgy. The approaching holidays would likely engender more depression and loneliness than cheer and celebration.

★ ★ ★

"My heart is filled with gratitude to Almighty God for his unspeakable mercies," Lee wrote to his wife on Christmas Day. "I have seen His hand in all the events of the war. Oh if our people would recognize it & cease from vain self boasting & adulation." Perhaps the sacred season would soften hatred and turn Yankees' hearts toward peace. And if Christmas failed to do this, Lee quickly added the hope that the "confusion that now exists in their [the Federals'] counsels will . . . result in good." The joys of former Christmases now sadly contrasted to "desecrated and pillaged" Virginia, he told his daughter.[47]

From his picket post Virginian Henry Krebs considered December 25,

1862, the most "unpleasant Christmas" in his life. Many forlorn soldiers lamented that it was just another dreary day in camp. "No egg nog, no turkey, no mince pie, nothing to eat or drink but our rations," one soldier lamented. It was a dull, cheerless time, and there were not even any young ladies around. Warm memories of home only added to the ennui. Spiritually minded men looked in vain for signs the army knew the meaning of the holiday. Even back home, secular traditions had already crowded out much of the religious significance; cards, shopping, and presents defined the holiday, especially in cities but elsewhere as well. And these were the things most often missed. A "festival that was formally devoted entirely to pleasure" nearly passed unnoticed in the camps, a Georgia lieutenant reflected.[48]

Many accounts of the day called it "ordinary." Even on Christmas most soldiers subsisted on the usual camp fare. A staff officer who had become adept at cooking dishes such as barbecued rabbit jauntily told his wife, "If the darkies all leave us, I shall be able to render you some assistance." More often, however, soldiers could not hide their sadness. Jesus himself, one Virginian remarked, would have been hard pressed to "furnish a holiday dinner out of a pound of fat pork, six crackers, and a quarter of a pound of dried apples." Filling his stomach became an imaginary exercise for a Mississippi private who listened intensely as another soldier lovingly described a $7.00 meal he had once eaten at a French Quarter restaurant in New Orleans.[49]

A fortunate few actually enjoyed real food. One pleasantly amazed Virginia infantryman devoured roast turkey, pig's head stew, baked shoat, turnips, and dried apple pudding. At a remarkably fine dinner with some high-ranking officers, artillery sergeant Ham Chamberlayne noted how they "were all as merry as if there were no war." Grateful farmers might offer a nice meal to soldiers guarding their property, but a respectable feed was prohibitively expensive. A $6.00 turkey, a $10.00 bottle of whiskey, or ginger cakes at three for $1.00 quickly deflated a fellow's enthusiasm, if not his wallet.[50]

Christmas highlighted the connections between physical needs, emotional pangs, and military morale. Witnesses of the recent carnage sensed what was missing during this normally joyous season: some liquid refreshment to anesthetize the memory. For men used to a cup of cheer at home, a "dull" Christmas readily translated into a "sober" Christmas when a gallon of whiskey cost $40 or more. Longing for his holiday brandy, one Virginian complained to his wife, "I have not smelled a drop this Christmas."[51]

Other soldiers got lucky. Some regiments managed a regular holiday spree with whiskey or eggnog, and camps grew boisterous with tipplers singing and carousing. Much of the drinking apparently took place in Pickett's Division, though even in Jackson's corps, Alabama and North Carolina troops created disturbances.[52] Older Christmas traditions survived even in an evangelical culture, and secularization of the holiday had proceeded even in the rural South. Most surprising, though, is the almost total silence about the day's spiritual significance for troops with at least a historical reputation for piety.[53]

Soldiers seldom mentioned Christmas religious services. Reading, foraging, setting off fireworks, yelling, and firing guns in camp helped pass the hours. In the 1st Georgia a private clad in a brown denim suit adorned with yellow paper stars conducted a mock battalion drill and a spirited ribbing of the regiment's colonel. Role reversal and carnival revelry had ancient roots and nicely matched many enlisted men's fun-loving and irreverent natures. A minstrel show in Hood's Division, described by one Texan as "supremely ridiculous," appears to have represented the high point of holiday entertainment in the Army of Northern Virginia.[54]

Such merrymaking provided some relief from routine but could never suppress thoughts of home. Memories of Christmases past—the children with their stockings, a cozy fire, a plump turkey, or traditional pound cake—churned up emotions. A miserable Mississippian hoped that at least he and his wife might be gazing at the same stars. For another soldier thoughts of hugging his wife and romping with their sons kept intruding on his attempt to write a letter home. Melancholy reflections, images of loved ones gathering for Christmas dinner, and cordial wishes for a good holiday at home only intensified the pangs of separation.[55]

On one level, Christmas on the home front followed familiar patterns: newspaper advertisements for books or perfume or brandy, the anticipation of wide-eyed children, and the bustle of holiday meals. In Richmond, young boys set off firecrackers. Yet now women also had to think about soldiers in the hospitals, and the demands on their charity ran up against shortages and inflation. If the Christmas spirit seemed far away to the soldiers, it did to many civilians also. One stricken Fredericksburg refugee had "Tommy's stocking" as her sole remaining "relic of Xmas." To make matters worse, Confederate soldiers had stolen the family's six turkeys on Christmas Eve. Everyone noticed how "different" the holiday seemed. A foreboding gloom overshadowed innocent joy. To a staff officer on leave in North Carolina the explanation seemed obvious: "All thoughts are absorbed in the war."[56]

Who could forget all the lives that had been lost during the year? A celebration of a long-ago birth painfully reminded people of ever present death but also became a marker for the course of the war. Even as people gamely tried to keep up seasonal traditions, peace seemed far away. Some Confederates, however, mixed holiday themes with an exuberant nationalism. "The Lord, who is the God of Battles, has looked with favor upon his children of the stubborn South," a North Carolina surgeon believed. "The bonfire this Christmas is the blaze of victory, and the glad tidings brought by the triumphant chorus of angels, proclaiming 'peace on earth, good will toward man,' mingle with these which declare the triumph of liberty, independence, and country." After a period of "universal defeat, disaster, and disgrace" the Yankees had little reason to celebrate, a Richmond editor observed, and then somewhat incongruously warned citizens about the dangers of complacency and overconfidence.[57]

Civil religion, however, could not allay the painful thoughts that inevitably accompanied a wartime holiday. With so many men away from home and prices so high, many people expected a "dull" Christmas, though one editor assured the children that Santa Claus would still come. War, however, predated Christ's birth, and humans had never been able to escape its cruelties. Admonitions to keep the faith in God and country—the heart of official Confederate propaganda—could not keep people from lamenting the wickedness of humanity and the elusiveness of peace. At the end of another year of bloody struggle, hatred, malice, and greed seemed ever more pervasive. Patriotism and determination ran deep in the Confederacy, yet recalling Christmas just one year ago, South Carolina private Tally Simpson found little to celebrate: "If all the dead . . . could be heaped in one pile and all the wounded be gathered together in one group, the pale faces of the dead and groans of the wounded would send such a thrill of horror through the hearts of the originators of this war that their very souls would rack with such pain that they would prefer being dead and in torment than to stand before God with such terrible crimes blackening their characters."[58]

★ ★ ★

Had Confederates visited the northern camps, they would have discovered that the Yankees, too, wondered what had become of the holiday. Fat pork and hardtack at two or even three meals made Christmas hard to swallow. "A gay old Christmas dinner," a Massachusetts volunteer ruefully wrote his mother, but at least he had not found bugs and worms in his crackers like one disgusted Michigan soldier. Leftover vegetable soup or a tough piece of beef made for sparse dining, even for men who had grown up poor. "I use to think times was hard at home but this is out of my head," a disconsolate Pennsylvanian told his sister. To make matters worse, enlisted men heard about generals and their staffs enjoying turkey, mutton, and other good things while they settled for the usual camp fare.[59]

Yet for all the complaining, the average Federal dined more sumptuously than his Confederate counterpart. Roast beef was a particular favorite, especially if accompanied by potatoes, onions, and biscuits, but pancakes for breakfast or an expensive turkey were likewise relished.[60] Some men delighted in simple fare such as beans, rice, and apples, but the sheer diversity of menus suggested that the Union government could supply a large army even under difficult winter conditions. Ingenuity and appetite made up for shortfalls. When one soldier chef concocted dumplings from crushed hardtack, pork grease, and dried apples, his comrades greedily devoured them.[61]

Whenever the train whistles blew, the men of the 116th Pennsylvania would yell, "boxes, boxes, boxes." It seemed just like home to a Maine volunteer. The boys would go to sleep on Christmas Eve "with feelings akin to those of children expecting Santa Claus." On Christmas Day, however, a long-expected box had still not appeared, and his "mental thermometer not only plummeted to below zero, it got right down off the nail and lay on the floor." Soldiers blamed such delays on the Adams Express or the War Department, and as always, many boxes arrived with the contents jumbled and provisions spoiled. Inevitably, too, boxes reached the camps addressed to men who had been killed or seriously wounded, and the contents would be quickly auctioned off.[62] Thus even feasting offered no respite from reminders of death.

Some regiments did draw a whiskey ration on Christmas Day. One Pennsylvania lieutenant even noted how men used to voting as "repeaters" back home got into line more than once. Soldiers understandably tried to assure their families that they had not spent the holiday in a drunken debauch. An Indiana major told his wife he did not drink nearly as much as he had at home, but he might have been lying or been deterred by the poor quality of the booze. Government-issue whiskey was often nasty, though that hardly stopped the hardcore drinkers.[63]

Statements about the entire army roaring drunk made for colorful exaggeration, but the whiskey punch flowed freely, especially among company officers. Provost guards remained on alert to quell disturbances. Men firing pistols or slashing the air with sabers presented some danger, though many tipplers passed out harmlessly before being carried back to their tents. Here and there a fistfight would break out or thirsty men would raid a sutler's stock, but that was the extent of the violence. One surgeon who deplored soldiers "making beasts of themselves" and acting like a "heard of swine," nevertheless understood that they probably considered "oblivion" better than "miserable recollection."[64]

Although the horrors of Fredericksburg still haunted men's minds, on

Christmas Day domestic concerns dominated their thoughts. Like the Confederates, Federals simply wished they were home. Imagining one were again with one's wife or children could relieve the oppressive dullness of camp. Men could envision the eager young folks hanging their stockings, the tree decorated, and families praying for their safety. As at Thanksgiving, the soldiers could see and almost taste the food or feel the warm family hearth and the familiar church pew.[65]

In lonely camps men prayed for their families and tried to rekindle the season's message of love and peace—no easy task in 1862. Thankfulness offered hope, but a hope tinged with sadness, especially when the usual exchange of gifts could not take place. One Michigan lieutenant noted Christmas Day briefly but then decided he had better tell his wife how much he loved her and appreciated her as a Christian mother. Perhaps he was expressing his true feelings, just in case. No wonder a New Hampshire private cherished a *Harper's Weekly* drawing titled *Christmas Eve* that showed a wife earnestly praying at home while in another panel her soldier husband sat near a small sentry fire. Walter Gordon McCabe's poem "Christmas Night of '62" recaptured not only the soldiers' often maudlin sentimentality but their dreams of family.

> There's not a comrade here to-night
> But knows that loved ones far away
> On bended knees this night will pray;
> "God bring our darling from the fight."[66]

Actually the home folks preparing for the holiday were as likely to be buying as praying. Advertising in northern newspapers was both more extensive and more elaborate than in the rapidly shrinking Confederate sheets. Column after column touted the latest fashions, makeup, books, and toys. New laborsaving sewing machines promised help for the harried housewife. The sale of superfluous objects such as napkin rings, card baskets, and berry dishes in Baltimore just as Burnside's army was poised to cross the Rappahannock seemed anomalous if not obscene. But even the worst battlefield news could not drown out the din of holiday commerce.[67]

December 1862 hardly seemed the appropriate time for a spending spree, however. To a Quaker woman living in Delaware, many people tried to balance "festivity" with charity. Folks seemed less "wrapped up in selfish enjoyment" and more willing to hold Christmas dinners for soldiers' children or visit the hospitals. In Washington, Elizabeth Walton Smith, wife of the soon-to-be-departing Secretary of the Interior Caleb Smith, organized spe-

Christmas Eve (Harper's Weekly, *January 3, 1863*)

cial meals for the sick and wounded in some twenty hospitals. Mary Lincoln, Stephen A. Douglas's widow, and several senators' wives waited tables.[68]

The joy and sadness of Christmas in 1862 made civilians and soldiers alike think more about their lives and times. Amidst wartime suffering, children would enjoy the holiday, and newspaper reports of gifts for the soldiers and visits to hospitals would impart to readers the usual warm, secure, and slightly smug feeling that Americans were decent people after all despite the war. To George Templeton Strong, Christmas still meant beautiful music and peace on earth even in a time of wrenching upheaval. For a Pennsylvania infantryman who had witnessed some of the worst carnage on December 13, the essential fact remained that he was still alive despite a surely perilous future.[69]

The feelings of the season could be summed up in the word "sacrifice." A member of the Irish Brigade, still reeling from the horrific bloodshed, kept thinking of all the widows and orphans. In New York, Pennsylvania, and Massachusetts it would be a "sad, sad Christmas" around "many an Irish hearthstone." Soldiers still lamented lives needlessly squandered for the sake of scheming politicians and perhaps for a cause now hopeless.[70]

Over all loomed the prospects for a winter campaign. Chilly winds, sparse rations, and camp routine had probably reduced optimistic Confederates' fighting edge despite apparently soaring morale. The better-supplied Federals could not yet shake the postbattle blues. Most of these men would still fight, and a remarkable number would eventually reenlist. The noble cause of liberty, a struggle for freedom and national unity, made Christmas worth celebrating, especially for Republicans with a strongly antislavery bent. Though many cynical soldiers would have ridiculed such sentiments after the slaughter at Fredericksburg, Pvt. Isaac Taylor of the 1st Minnesota, for one, remained steadfast: "May the peerless ray of Freedom's sun dispel the thickening gloom & bring us peace & unity."[71] Yet defining that word "freedom" remained a tricky and treacherous and anything but unifying exercise.

The cause of Freedom is the cause of God!
— *William Lisle Bowles*

23 Freedom

January 1, 1863, New Year's Day: a traditional occasion for letting off steam and taking stock. A Georgia regiment celebrated their individual and collective liberty by drinking rum and racing horses, two activities long associated with freedom-loving American males.[1] As with Christmas, of course, a boisterous celebration at New Year's might temporarily relieve melancholy, but soldiers and civilians alike still had to live with painful memories of the recent past.

Even optimistic Confederates recalled 1862 as a year of sadness and sorrow. Memories of former comrades lying in shallow graves on some soon-to-be-forgotten field cast a long shadow over efforts to foresee a brighter future. We "tax our ingenuity to devise means of killing each other," marveled an Alabama lieutenant. Fire-eater Edmund Ruffin worried that the Yankees had gained significant ground and could still muster superior numbers in any engagement. A nurse in Chattanooga, turning to an Old Testament image, wailed that "in every state of our beloved land there has been a temple erected to the insatiate Moloch."[2]

Yet the day's bright sunshine chased away dark thoughts. In brief remarks at Raleigh, North Carolina, Jefferson Davis declared, "The New Year comes in auspiciously for us. It finds us victorious at every point." The recent triumph of southern arms against overwhelming numbers portended well for the future and fanned hopes for peace. Even though the Yankees had driven her family from their home in Baton Rouge, Louisiana, young Sarah Morgan rejoiced that "every hour brings us nearer our freedom."[3]

Sarah Morgan's words were an odd choice for a Confederate, many northerners would have thought, because January 1 would likely bring the final Emancipation Proclamation. To a Pennsylvania sergeant, however, it was just another cold day spent on picket duty. Under such conditions some soldiers simply longed to eat halfway palatable food. "I set with my ars flat on the ground and thought of the past," Pvt. Philip Piper of the 110th Pennsylvania wrote to a cousin, but he was mostly thinking about his stomach, since his great wish for the New Year was to gorge on sausages and buckwheat cakes at home.[4]

Getting drunk might relieve the tedium, and whiskey had been associated with republican liberty at least since the American Revolution. In some officers' quarters, especially those of that old Democratic wheelhorse Dan Sickles, whiskey and champagne flowed freely, the latter hardly the drink of robust democracy. Liquor remained a disturbing symbol of male freedom. Drunken revelry not only set a poor tone for camp life but also stirred resentment among enlisted men, who generally endured a bone-dry holiday and disapproving officers. A New Jersey chaplain proudly reported sobriety in his regiment, where men for the first time in some years began the new year with "clear heads and furless tongues."[5] Perhaps the unaccustomed mental acuity prompted some serious meditation.

What had all the months of fighting accomplished? For Union soldiers staggered by the Fredericksburg slaughter, talk about needless sacrifices persisted. A Minnesotan's thoughts were typical: "The South is gaining & the North losing confidence in its cause." The previous spring the army had been within sight of Richmond's church spires, but now it languished more than sixty miles away. "We have traversed a country, leaving desolation & graves to mark our track, but we have gained absolutely nothing!" a provost guard lamented. Such sentiments resonated among northern Democrats who readily blamed an abolitionist clique in Washington for all military setbacks.[6] Nor was the connection between demoralization and partisanship coincidental. The new year would bring not only more fighting but also new arguments over liberty.

The American Civil War was a fight over freedom. But differing ideas—all advanced with determined vigor—about what freedom meant raised hard and troubling questions. Did freedom embrace all people, including those of African descent now owned by others as chattel slaves? Did freedom, North or South, include the privilege to attack government policies and encourage draft resistance? Did freedom encompass the right to break up the American union or permit mobilizing enough power to preserve it? Who was truly fighting for freedom, Yankees or Rebels? Did internal dissent in both sections help preserve or threaten freedom?

The ideal of freedom, so central to the American story, inevitably engendered conflicting definitions and interpretations. State papers, political speeches, newspaper editorials, published sermons, soldiers' letters, and informal conversations overflowed with talk of "freedom." A staple of American thought and language, freedom was a concept at once commonplace, sacred, and contentious. The glosses on its meaning were myriad, contradictory, and incendiary. An admixture of morality and Christianity, not to mention Lincoln's appeals to providence and his recognition of God's often inscrutable ways, further complicated sorting out definitions and determining which one(s) would at last prevail.[7] In addition, political power (and military might) remained central to the strident debate. As another costly year of war closed, shrill voices still stumped for particular notions of freedom to the exclusion of others. On New Year's Day the focus would be on the future of black people, but emancipation remained a bitterly divisive issue.[8]

★ ★ ★

As 1862 came to an end, the nation turned again toward the haggard-looking man in the Executive Mansion for an infusion of moral purpose and strategic direction. The Fredericksburg disaster kindled speculation that the president might delay or withhold the final Emancipation Proclamation. A doubtful Harriet Beecher Stowe, for one, had written to Charles Sumner asking if Lincoln would "stand firm" and begging the senator to keep up the political pressure for emancipation. Many abolitionists depressed over battlefield news also worried about the war dragging on and the European powers intervening. Recent events had "raised the hopes of McClellan copperheads," an irate Michigan citizen warned Senator Chandler. "For God's sake don't let the President go back on his proclamation."[9]

The principle was clear. As Henry Ward Beecher pointed out in one of his stirring addresses, all men regardless of color were entitled to liberty under the law of God. Yet bold declarations could not ease worries about the president's course. George Stephens, a black body servant and newspaper correspondent, wrote to the *New York Anglo-African* stressing the importance of issuing a final Emancipation Proclamation as promised. But Stephens had witnessed the carnage at Fredericksburg, and even though he emphatically believed that this defeat should not stay the president's hand, he understood why Lincoln might have to withhold the proclamation in light of conservative resurgence in the free states. Unlike some radicals, he would not ignore political realities. As Chase pointedly advised veteran abolitionist Wendell Phillips, it would greatly help matters if the abolitionists would sustain antislavery men in Washington and in the cabinet.[10]

The Fredericksburg defeat actually elicited some passionate calls for emancipation, but these appeals had distinctly military overtones. Tending the wounded in a Washington hospital, Hannah Ropes emphatically favored "immediate, unreserved emancipation," a policy obviously coupled with an aggressive war strategy. The opportune moment to destroy slavery had arrived, and the most ardent abolitionists shared Lincoln's basic belief that right must eventually prevail.[11] Whether they yet agreed on the timing of emancipation remained to be seen. In a typically fiery speech in New York, Gerrit Smith declared that all attempts to conciliate Rebels and northern Democrats had failed. Despite Fredericksburg, the rebellion would collapse once the administration dismissed doughface generals and spurned any compromise on the slavery question. Perhaps the Lord had allowed Burnside's defeat so the sin of slavery could be excised from the nation. Therefore "freedom" for the slaves became the key to victory. Such arguments combined moral fervor with pragmatic rationalization, because emancipation itself would bring several million slaves to the Union side and likely tip the balance in a war that might otherwise remain locked in bloody stalemate.[12]

Conservative Democrats, however, blamed the lack of military progress on Lincoln's embrace of abolition. Editor James Gordon Bennett charged that antislavery fanatics virtually controlled the War Department and had even been directing Burnside's moves. "Never did the very name of a radical so stink in the nostrils of the nation," he fumed. "Unworthy of the name of Americans or of men, these bloodthirsty and ferocious abolitionists should be . . . expelled from all civilized communities in this world and assigned to the company of Judas Iscariot and Benedict Arnold in the next."[13] It would be easy to dismiss such words as gasconade; but Bennett tied abolition to battlefield losses, and for many disgruntled citizens the connection made sense.

Amidst rising criticism the president largely kept his own counsel. Not until December 29 did he read a draft of the final Emancipation Proclamation to the cabinet. On December 31 Chase suggested changes. Lincoln made some modifications, but the final document remained very much his own. During the last week of 1862 the president appeared to have rebounded from both Fredericksburg and the cabinet crisis. Privately he made it clear that he would not retreat from emancipation, though some of his conservative friends still believed that the policy lacked popular support and could well prove ruinous. At one point Lincoln impatiently told a reluctant politician, "You must not expect me to give up the Government without playing my last card."[14]

At 11:00 A.M. on January 1, 1863, the traditional New Year's reception began at the Executive Mansion. The crush of visitors pushed forward to shake the president's hand, but one reporter thought Lincoln looked preoccupied. Perhaps he was thinking about Fredericksburg or what to do about Burnside, whom he had met with earlier in the morning. During the reception Seward's son Frederick carried the parchment copy of the Emancipation Proclamation upstairs. Spreading the document on the cabinet table, Lincoln inked the pen and then hesitated. "I never in my life felt more certain that I am doing right, than I do in signing this paper," he announced, perhaps to reassure both himself and others.[15]

In the proclamation Lincoln appealed to both justice and military necessity. Despite the subdued, legalistic tone of the document, the revolutionary implications were striking. Not only did the proclamation declare that slaves in areas currently controlled by the Rebels "henceforward shall be free," but it also asserted that black men could now fight for their freedom on land and sea.[16]

After months of desultory discussions about raising black regiments, Lincoln had now committed the government—at least on paper—to launching the experiment. Yet just as Fredericksburg cast a long shadow over the emancipation question, so, too, did the military stalemate hasten enrollment of Negro troops. After visiting hospitals near Falmouth with Clara Barton, Senator Henry Wilson of Massachusetts stood ready to "draft every last man who could carry a musket." Given the heavy losses, increasing desertions, and continuous laments over all the white lives sacrificed in vain, necessity powerfully challenged prejudice.[17]

Lincoln had announced two key decisions (emancipation and black troops) in one document, and they hit the country like a thunderclap. On New Year's Eve in several northern cities, interracial crowds had gathered in churches and public squares anticipating the glorious news. Larger groups assembled the next afternoon and evening awaiting final word. Lingering doubts still mingled with hopes, however. "Thus far the loyal north has trusted him [Lincoln], less for his ability than for his honesty," Frederick Douglass had commented in an editorial composed in late December but not published until January. The president should not "trifle with the wounds of his bleeding country . . . while the cold earth around Fredericksburg is wet with the warm blood of our patriot soldiers—every one of whom was slain by the slaveholding rebels." Should Lincoln delay, Douglass warned, he risked going down in history as an American Nero. On January 1 at a large meeting held at Tremont Temple in Boston, Douglass impatiently awaited news of the president's decision. When a messenger arrived late in the evening to announce that Lincoln had signed the final Emancipation Proclamation, the crowd erupted in shouts of praise and hymns of rejoicing.[18]

Antislavery stalwarts still reluctant to praise Lincoln described the Emancipation Proclamation as the culmination of a divine plan. Turning the fight into a crusade for freedom would surely strengthen the North's hand against the rebellion, the *Chicago Tribune* declared. The Emancipation Proclamation had saved a nation tottering on the brink of destruction, and Federal armies would now carry forward the great work of freeing the slaves and restoring the Union.[19] Even having the Army of the Potomac stalled along the Rappahannock seemed a minor problem, because supporters of emancipation clearly believed that a righteous crusade against slavery guaranteed victory on the battlefield.

To critics of emancipation, however, the proclamation seemed nothing more than a worthless, paper decree, more an act of desperation than of statesmanship. Faltering Union armies could not whip the Rebels, much less destroy slavery. Democrats declared themselves to be the true defenders of liberty and berated Lincoln as a dangerous tyrant and bumbling war leader. Having successfully played on racial fears during the recent election campaign, they again raised the specter of bloody slave revolts, black voting, and social equality. Emancipation marked the latest ploy by a desperate administration and could only portend the final destruction of the Union.[20]

Democratic opposition could be expected, but more worrisome to the administration was uncertain support on its own side. Lincoln had not been able to mollify conservative Republicans, and even some cabinet members harbored reservations. Secretary of the Navy Gideon Welles acknowledged the revolutionary nature of emancipation but predicted that "the immediate effect will not be all its friends anticipate or its opponents apprehend." Privately Seward and his cronies were decidedly lukewarm. That bellwether of moderation the *New York Times* remained skeptical about how well former slaves could handle freedom and sounded downright equivocal on the question of black troops.[21] Clearly some Republicans were hedging their bets, uncertain about the wisdom of emancipation, alarmed about Democratic calls for peace negotiations, worried over cries for McClellan's return to command, and waiting to gauge the soldiers' response.

A Connecticut artillerist who rejoiced that Lincoln had refused to back down on emancipation acknowledged that many of his comrades bitterly opposed the proclamation and that some Republicans had even switched parties. McClellan supporters of course railed against the president, but the initial outcry extended throughout the army. Turning the war into an anti-slavery crusade might only make the Rebels fight harder—a serious objection for soldiers who feared that the Confederates already enjoyed greater élan and higher morale. A divided North rent by party divisions and disaffection in the border states could hardly defeat a united South.[22]

The proclamation also provoked more visceral responses. Men who had enlisted to save the Union deeply resented becoming a tool for radical plotters who would risk destroying the republic to advance their schemes. If people at home wanted to fight for black freedom, let them enlist. A New Jersey volunteer enjoyed watching the regiment's only abolitionist trudge along with his knapsack.[23]

Even soldiers who denied that the army was demoralized cursed emancipation and the government. One phrase (in several variations) resounded: "The men will not fight for niggers." Young volunteers had been deceived by "brokers and officeholders" into believing they were "fighting for the Union," a Rhode Island private raged, when "it is a bull nigger they are fighting for." Conservative editors quoted soldiers who swore they would never risk their lives to free slaves. "'It's nothing but an abolition war, and I wish I was out of it,'" one Wisconsin soldier correspondent groused. "You can hear it everywhere, let those deny it who may. It is the truth, and why hide the truth. That is the sentiment, go where you will."[24]

Such fulminations, however, hardly plumbed the depth of racism in the ranks. "If I had my way about things I would shoot every nigger I come across," a private in the 14th Indiana frothed. With freed blacks heading north, he warned his sister, there would be an "awful bad smell amonxt you." A common complaint among soldiers—that blacks received preferential treatment from the government—carried its own irony because by this time using escaped slaves as officers' servants had already shown Federals to be less than ardent friends of freedom. Some regiments became notorious for their casual cruelty toward the fugitives. A Massachusetts volunteer spoke for many of his comrades: "We all hate the sight of a nigger worse than a snake."[25]

But even racism bore various shadings. A Pennsylvania captain expressed moral indifference to the slavery question: "I care not if the Niggers eat the Whites or Whites kill the Niggers." Others who at least recognized the evils of slavery clung to the shibboleth of colonization.[26] Indeed, racial attitudes like much else in Civil War America remained in flux, so fiercely expressed sentiments did not necessarily betoken attitudes carved in stone. Entrenched racial prejudice among the troops was often impervious to argument, but not to the course of the war itself. Military developments and to some degree the performance of black troops would vindicate the wisdom of emancipation and change white soldiers' attitudes as well.

For the present, however, opponents of the proclamation chafed at charges of disloyalty. "They [abolitionists] tell us because we are not willing to see the negro in our ranks . . . that we lack patriotism!" a Michigan private complained. McClellan supporters especially noted how they had bravely fought for the Union. From their perspective, Lincoln's emancipation policy had only further demoralized an already badly shaken army. Reports that the soldiers were ready to throw down their arms intensified in the wake of the Emancipation Proclamation. Such sentiments would soon wane, but in January 1863 the slavery question became one more source of division among already disheartened soldiers.[27]

Yet there was also quiet support for emancipation in the army. A Maine officer even suggested that any soldiers who cursed an abolition war ought to be sent south. Like the opponents of emancipation, its defenders offered a variety of arguments. For some men the simple immorality of slavery settled the question. To others a war against slavery became the key to military victory. "I would burn and destroy every city in the South, and emancipate every slave, if by doing so our cherished institutions could be preserved and handed to future generations," declared one Hoosier. A fair number of men remained ambivalent, hardly knowing what to expect from the emancipation policy.[28]

Confederates for the most part feigned indifference to Lincoln's supposedly empty gesture. "It is difficult to decide," the always acerbic *Richmond Daily Examiner* sniffed, "whether wickedness or folly predominate in this extraordinary document." Lincoln's refusal to free slaves in areas under Union military control revealed his craven hypocrisy. A paper decree would have no effect on the war, Confederate editors bravely maintained, and the general absence of comment among Lee's men suggested they agreed. Although many Confederates may not have been so nonplussed as they tried to appear, confidence in southern arms made the change in enemy policy seem much less frightening. The *Richmond Daily Dispatch* drew a striking contrast between northern words and southern deeds: "The South has given its answer to Lincoln's proclamation of emancipation at Fredericksburg and Murfreesboro."[29]

★   ★   ★

Discussions of the impact of emancipation on the nation's future did not take place in a political vacuum and were shaped by assessments of the military situation and renewed talk of a negotiated peace. All sorts of rumors alarmed already nervous Republicans. A frightened Ohioan advised Chase that Democrats planned to hold a national convention, depose Lincoln, and lead the northwestern states into a coalition with the Rebels. After Fredericksburg, predictions of an armistice or worse suddenly seemed believable. According to Sumner many senators had grown despondent, and Lincoln himself greatly feared "fire in the rear" from the northern Democracy. Not expecting a great battlefield victory any time soon, Republicans remained wary and downcast.[30]

Because their political opponents were raising anew the cry of "liberty," leading Democrats, who considered themselves true defenders of white democracy against abolitionist fanaticism, equated freedom with both racial purity and civil liberties. Even after release of some government prisoners, Democrats kept pounding away at the War Department's "arbitrary arrests." Acrimonious debate in Congress erupted over both the fate of particular prisoners and the larger question of political freedom. Democrats excoriated the hypocrisy of a government obsessed with emancipating black men but seemingly indifferent to the fate of white men tossed into prison because of their political beliefs.[31]

Many of these partisans believed they had found a champion in Governor Horatio Seymour of New York. Shortly after his election, Seymour had consulted with McClellan, and while New York Democrats courted the general's favor, the two men cautiously helped each other. In several respects Seymour, as befitting an old supporter of Stephen A. Douglas, remained a War Democrat, but he was increasingly wary of expanding federal power. He loyally supported troop enlistments, but on the civil liberties question he drew a principled political line. To leading conservatives in both parties Seymour had become a pivotal figure, apparently with an eye on the presidency. Editors eagerly anticipated his annual message to the legislature, and no less a wire-puller than Thurlow Weed sought to shape its contents.[32]

On Wednesday, January 7, Seymour's message dominated the political stage. More than two-thirds of the document addressed national affairs and struck a decided note of loyal opposition. Civil war was a reality, the troops deserved public support, and the Union remained indissoluble. Denying that the rebellion "can suspend a single right of the citizens," Seymour nevertheless stopped short of explicitly endorsing peace negotiations with the Rebels. Denunciation of martial law and support for civil liberties won warm support from leading Democratic editors. The governor had emphasized both patriotism and freedom, twin themes that received especially friendly coverage in the Irish American press. True loyalty that safeguarded the republic's traditions against dangerous abuses of power by the abolitionist-controlled Lincoln administration became a potent message for his party.[33]

Though Seymour's message was not especially memorable in content or language, its effectiveness could be measured by sharply worded Republican criticism. Greeley characterized the governor as a "demagogue" placed in office by "cowardice, drunkenness, and masked disloyalty." Other editors blasted him as a "hypocrite," his message "disgraceful," and his purpose "factious." Even the *New York Times,* at first mildly dismissive, intemperately attributed Seymour's election to the disfranchisement of loyal soldiers in the field and the machinations of liquor dealers.[34] The Republicans' harsh rhetoric betrayed their recognition of Seymour as a rising star and a serious threat to the administration.

A whiff of political danger in turn fed larger fears. Though reluctant to use the word "traitor," Republicans worried about the growing power of so-called Peace Democrats, whom they suspected of unduly influencing Seymour. Even conservatives such as Gideon Welles railed against the governor's "jesuitical insincerity," his "unhallowed partisan and personal aspirations." Longtime Democrat Maj. Gen. John Dix, who was commanding troops in New York City, warned that Seymour's views might even spark serious resistance to the forthcoming draft. According to Frederick Douglass, northern traitors now threatened the republic far more than Rebels. Though obviously heartened by the Emancipation Proclamation, he worried that the Army of the Potomac might "never win a great battle" and that a "divided North" would be no match for a "united South."[35] The aftershocks of Fredericksburg continued to shake northern confidence and weaken public will.

Republican alarms, however overwrought, reflected an apparent shift in the general mood, a defeatism that threatened to cross both party and ideological lines and perhaps force recognition of southern independence or at least a restoration of the Union based on humiliating concessions to the Rebels. Rumors of impending peace negotiations—made plausible by the appearance of quixotic and unauthorized "diplomats" in Richmond—revived talk of sectional compromise. Shortly before Fredericksburg, mercurial Horace Greeley had forecast a peace settlement within six months. After the battle he began corresponding with two leading Peace Democrats and in mid-January consulted with Henri Mercier, the French minister in Washington.[36] Spurred by newspaper editorials and public meetings, conservative Democrats trumpeted a potent message: if more fighting could not bring peace, a point that seemed obvious at the beginning of 1863, a convention of the states should negotiate an end to the war.[37]

Ohio congressman Clement L. Vallandigham, the most prominent and outspoken of the Peace Democrats, bluntly termed the war a failure and shortly after Fredericksburg called for a cease-fire. Thwarted by a Republican House majority that tabled his motions, Vallandigham spoke for an hour without interruption on the afternoon of January 14, 1863. After denouncing abolition and the suspension of habeas corpus, he drove home his most telling argument. "You have not conquered the South," he told his Republican colleagues. "You never will." Lincoln had transformed a war for the Union into a war for abolition: "With what success? Let the dead at Fredericksburg . . . answer." Federal troops should be withdrawn from the southern states and a peace established based on free trade and white supremacy.

This speech went too far even for many conservatives. Criticism of Vallandigham by Democrats in Ohio and elsewhere revealed deep divisions in the party between moderates such as Seymour and the peace faction. Yet in the aftermath of Fredericksburg the effects of war weariness, military blunders, and political disaffection made Republicans edgy. Pungent attacks on Vallandigham reflected frustration with a weakened and divided government that seemed to stumble from defeat to defeat.[38]

The political costs of the military stalemate kept mounting. In Indiana, Governor Oliver P. Morton and his supporters warned that "Copperheads" might provoke violence or even attempt to detach the old Northwest from New England. Peace meetings and rumors of secret societies sparked hysterical talk of conspiracies. Democrats in the Indiana House of Representatives thanked Seymour for his stout defense of civil liberties, introduced peace resolutions, and roundly condemned the Emancipation Proclamation.[39] If liberty meant the right to indulge in partisan attacks, then liberty seemed in no danger. Disputes between Republican governors and Democratic legislators in both Indiana and Illinois led to the effective dissolution of the state legislatures. Cries against "tyranny" or "treason" drowned out reasoned debate and lent weight to the more extreme voices in each party.[40]

The shock of Fredericksburg and disputes over emancipation sometimes pulled the Republicans in a more conservative direction, forcing several prominent radicals to fight for their political lives. Although Chase apparently toyed with the idea of seeking a senate seat from Ohio, recent Democratic gains led the Republican majority in the legislature to put aside factional bickering and reelect radical stalwart Benjamin F. Wade.[41] Elsewhere divided Republicans battled a resurgent Democracy. In Michigan another ardent antislavery man, Zachariah Chandler, faced a challenge from a moderate Republican who attacked the Joint Committee on the Conduct of the War for meddling in military affairs. Even though Chandler was easily re-elected by the legislature, he still fumed over the political effects of recent military failures. If he were ever president, Chandler told his wife, he would stop the Rebel sympathizers in their tracks by clapping Seymour into prison—a statement that nicely summed up the sort of reaction the governor's increasing prominence sparked among agitated Republicans. To bolster wavering Republicans, a radical New York editor suggested that the country badly needed more "earnest men" like Zach Chandler.[42] Attempting a political comeback in Pennsylvania, former secretary of war and minister to Russia Simon Cameron apparently tried to buy a senate seat with both patronage and cash. But in a legislature where the parties were evenly balanced, he fell two votes short amidst charges of corruption and threats of violence.[43] The tense atmosphere in several states created a surreal political climate. Democrats routinely denounced would-be Republican tyrants, but their own irregular procedures and calls for negotiations with the Rebels tested the limits of wartime dissent.

The exercise of political freedom only heightened the sense of danger among all groups, whether bitter racists who opposed emancipation, moderates who worried that the army was falling apart, or radicals who detected treason in every partisan attack. A cacophony of warring tongues precluded consensus on defining or protecting freedom. The fissures in both the parties and the nation along with insistent calls for peace presented Republicans with their most serious challenge since the secession crisis.

Radical dissatisfaction with the cabinet and the president persisted. A gloomy Pittsburgh editor blamed the administration's "irresolution and timidity" for strengthening the hands of northern traitors. Fainthearted Republicans feared being dragged down by military disasters.[44] Just as with the supposed demoralization in the Army of the Potomac, however, sound and fury did not bespeak genuine disaffection. Several Republican editors issued rousing calls for unity. Only if the party stood firm against the "Calhounites" of the South and their northern allies could political liberty and the heritage of the revolutionary fathers survive. Devotion to the Union cause and an energetic war policy could still bring victory; like the Israelites murmuring against Moses and Aaron in the wilderness—in the apt analogy offered by a Boston Unitarian minister—the northern people could still reject the counsels of despair and reach the political promised land.[45]

Political loyalty in this hothouse atmosphere meant resisting the siren calls for a negotiated peace on both practical and philosophical grounds. Parleying with the Rebels would be far worse than continuing the war, and in any case Confederate leaders had arrogantly spurned even the cowardly initiatives of the Peace Democrats.[46] Who could trust the motives of men ready to truckle with traitors? Selfish businessmen and politicians whose patriotism seldom extended beyond profits or patronage would happily bargain with the Rebels. Democratic partisans downplayed every victory and magnified every defeat, thereby giving aid and comfort to what one Boston editor still called the "slave power." Copperhead leaders, Republicans charged, secretly plotted the Union's destruction. Blasting Vallandigham's speech, Representative John A. Bingham of Ohio accused Democrats of openly siding with Rebels. Even a conservative editor warned Democrats that partisan attacks on the government and open sympathy for the nation's enemies would set them down in history as infamous traitors.[47]

The political fragmentation in the northern states—hastened by military losses, divisions over emancipation, and the revival of the Democratic Party—left the American Union in peril. Ideologues debated the meaning of freedom while partisans maneuvered for advantage. Political wrangling no doubt deepened public despair over the war's apparent lack of progress. In January 1863 it seemed entirely plausible that northern disunity might eventually destroy the republic. The war threatened to drag on indefinitely, and perhaps the prospect of more bloodshed with no end in sight proved to be the most depressing thought of all. Yet as a Pennsylvania captain declared on New Year's Day, the Army of the Potomac simply had to win a battle. Military success would revive the government's "timid supporters" and silence the "Peace shriekers of the Seymour ilk." Like so many others on both sides, he placed freedom at the heart of the war: "This is a contest, not between North and South; but a contest between human rights and human liberty upon the one side and eternal bondage on the other."[48]

★ ★ ★

Whose definition of freedom would prevail? Confederates maintained they were fighting for white liberty and the right of self-determination. Sumner, Douglass, Lincoln, Seward, Seymour, Vallandigham, Davis, and countless others had their own ideas about what was at stake in the war. Events converging in late December 1862 and early January 1863 had brought each view into remarkably sharp relief. Recrimination, racism, and a politics of both loyalty and liberty made the debates especially rancorous.

Which view would eventually triumph still largely depended on those bluecoats camped along the Rappahannock. After Fredericksburg, soldiers' calls for ending the war intensified; but how a settlement might be negotiated remained unclear, and the phrase "honorable peace" that cropped up in so many soldiers' letters lacked any precise meaning. For some only an unconditional restoration of the Union was acceptable; for others giving up emancipation or even recognizing Confederate independence would be "honorable" enough.[49]

Conservative soldiers felt the political winds blowing in the right direction. "We live in hopes of Democratic victories," a Connecticut volunteer informed his home folks. Highly literate and politically savvy men commented about everything from Indiana legislative battles to Seymour's message. Some had grown cynical and complained that Republican spoilsmen had descended to depths matched only during James Buchanan's notoriously corrupt presidency, and a Massachusetts private declared the party "about dead." More ominously, peace coupled with disunion no longer seemed unthinkable, and one Massachusetts private even applauded Vallandigham's resolutions.[50]

Most Federals, however, loathed Copperheads. One Hoosier railed against civilians who "find fault with everything connected with the war, and do all they can to discourage those who have friends in the army." Such malcontents hardly ever criticized the Rebels but instead harped about white men being forced to fight for black men. The circulation of conservative newspapers in the camps greatly angered some soldiers, especially midwesterners reading about disaffection back home. Such men applauded efforts by Republican governors to thwart "traitors" in the state legislatures and cared little about civil liberties. Political prisoners should have been hanged, one Indiana major declared; a Massachusetts private proposed executing a few disloyal New York peace men, including Governor Seymour.[51] Anger and disappointment fostered fear and uncertainty. Indeed, emotion more than ideology shaped attitudes during this tumultuous period. The frustrating military situation, the still-explosive question of emancipation, political disorder in several northern states, and signs of disarray in Washington all portended a bleak future for soldiers in their chilly camps.

★　★　★

Some Rebels, too, expressed dismay over the horrific costs of the war. Meditating on what he had seen at Fredericksburg, a Georgia soldier agonized over the suffering that even a victory brought: "Many a good and brave woman [who] could say 'husband' last Saturday morning when they rose . . . were widows when the sun set and many children that could say 'father' were orphans." These somber reflections, however, hardly expressed genuine despair. Conversations with Yankee stragglers and prisoners convinced many Confederates that their enemies were about to give up. The war would surely be over by spring, Jedediah Hotchkiss informed his wife. Civilians, including once-staunch Unionists, saw Confederate prospects brightening. "The papers are very encouraging," young Lucy Breckinridge noted in her diary. "We are beginning to hope for peace."[52]

Rumors of Federal officers resigning en masse, the Senate attempting to drive the Yankee president from office, and continuing cabinet divisions led some soldiers and civilians to conclude that the South could never be subjugated. Even a wildly implausible tale of a fistfight between Halleck and Stanton boosted confidence. A Virginian welcomed talk of foreign mediation and northern disaffection that "keep our spirits up and our hopes alive." Confederates eagerly devoured reports of a possible separation between the old Northwest and New England. To a sanguine Tar Heel editor, the victory at Fredericksburg had sealed the old Union's fate: "The people of the North are not blind nor deaf, nor will they always remain dumb. These failures have doomed the Lincoln Administration and . . . their hopes vanish."[53]

Word of powerful northern Democrats calling for negotiations gave Confederate optimism an even more tangible basis. Accounts of peace meetings in New York and other cities heartened Lee's men and even convinced a few skeptics that a settlement might be in the offing. Confederates greeted the statements of Seymour and Vallandigham with equal enthusiasm. Referring to a possible convention of the states, one North Carolina editor breezily decided that "the Yankees are getting sick of this war."[54]

But war-weary Rebels had heard it all before. Shortly after Fredericksburg a South Carolina plantation mistress had hoped the war might end soon, but by mid-January she found the "political horizon . . . again overcast." Peace seemed an elusive dream, a wish that overblown newspaper reports of troubles in Yankeeland could not fulfill. Col. Clement A. Evans wisely noted that despite all the press criticism of Lincoln, the Federals had shown no sign of abandoning the struggle.[55]

Soothing words from northern Democrats about restoring the old Union did not satisfy southerners determined to build their own nation. Several congressional resolutions made it clear that there could be no peace without recognition of the Confederacy as a sovereign power. Far too much blood had already been shed to accept a patched-together compromise. "Too late!" commented one War Department official about overtures for a convention of the states.[56]

Who could rely on the slippery promises of northern conservatives? To hold out hope for a peace settlement only invited disappointment, and soldiers especially warned their families against unrealistic expectations. Reports of peace meetings and diplomatic moves in the Yankee papers might

simply be ploys to lull unsuspecting southerners into a perilous complacency. After all, northern Democrats had betrayed their southern allies in
1861 and still cared more about spoils than justice. Seymour's states' rights
pronouncements meant nothing, the *Charleston Mercury* proclaimed. So
long as greedy Yankees—including conservative ones—could earn blood
money from the war, they would never recognize Confederate independence.[57] Therefore southerners would have to fight on, relying on unity and
determination in the face of a still-powerful enemy.

Just like northern Republicans, however, southern leaders faced internal
divisions. A strongly pro-Davis Charleston editor presented the official line:
"The voice of Government is the voice of God, and all its requirements and
commands are clothed with authority and power. It simply gives utterance
to obligations which have been binding by the Lord of all, and in making
known these duties, the Government we ourselves created simply acts as
the organ and instrument of the King of Kings and Lord of Lords." Thus
citizens obeyed both their rulers and their God. In contrast to this high-
blown theory, however, New Year's Eve editorials in rival North Carolina
newspapers mirrored actual political practice. While the *Raleigh Weekly Register* denounced factious opposition to the Confederate government in the
state legislature, the *Raleigh Weekly Standard* inveighed against southerners
who would ignore constitutional limitations to uphold military despotism.
Should he survive the war, a disgusted South Carolina soldier promised his
wife "never to dabble in the dirty pool of politics." So far at least, "our young
republic" had successfully defended the "great principles of liberty."[58]

Any consensus on those "great principles of liberty" kept threatening to
unravel. Jefferson Davis attempted to hold his nation together despite internal divisions, economic weaknesses, and the military losses of the past
year. Toward the end of his western tour, in a speech at Jackson, Mississippi,
he reminded Confederates of unbridgeable sectional differences. Pointing to
recent Yankee atrocities and long-standing conflicts between Puritans and
Cavaliers, he declared any further political connection between two such
different "peoples" impossible. Yet the president could not escape the history that had once united Americans. Back in Richmond he publicly praised
Virginians for fighting, just as in 1776, for the sake of freedom. Robert E.
Lee, "emulating the virtues of the heroic Light-horse Harry, his father," had
just won a great victory at Fredericksburg. With a rhetorical flourish Davis
maintained that the experience of war had knit together the states of the
Confederacy.[59]

In a message to the Confederate Congress a few days later, the president exuded confidence. The southerners' successful fight for their "rights and liberties" had taught the nations of the world once again "the impossibility of subjugating a people determined to be free." Buoyed by Fredericksburg, Davis expressed "profound contempt" for the "impotent rage" of the Emancipation Proclamation. But he also rejoiced that the document proved, finally and without doubt, the impossibility of reunion. Davis's defiant optimism struck just the right note, or so many Confederates believed, and for once even his most persistent critics held their fire.[60]

Yet the fledgling southern nation still faced a most uncertain future. Despite recent victories on the battlefield, price increases ravaged the economy, and the value of Confederate money kept falling. Secretary of the Treasury Christopher G. Memminger admitted that the large volume of treasury notes needed to finance the war had fueled a dangerous inflation. Complaints about "extortioners"—denounced by Davis as the "dregs and refuse of the land"—grew sharp and were sometimes tinged with anti-Semitism. Grain and potatoes needed to feed the people had reportedly been snapped up by distillers. Editorials against profiteering provoked decidedly defensive and somewhat frightened responses from businessmen. Petitions complaining about greedy merchants gouging widows and orphans poured in to the governors. Recognizing the connections between desertions and suffering on the home front, states devoted much of their budgets to aiding soldiers' families, and some congressmen even favored national relief measures.[61] These unprecedented laws provoked opposition to the expansion of government power. Impressments of supplies, especially with official compensation below market prices, seemed "gross oppression" even to the pro-Davis *Richmond Daily Enquirer.* Debates erupted in Congress pitting advocates of emergency powers against defenders of property rights.[62]

To many Confederates, conscription presented the most serious threat to fundamental liberties. The question of exemption, enlivened by charges of bribery and corruption, became a veritable tug-of-war between national, state, and local interests. Even a brief exchange in the Confederate House over the wisdom of allowing ministers to escape the draft turned into an impassioned discussion of centralized power.[63] The heat generated by these arcane questions is understandable. They touched matters that deeply affected the lives of ordinary people. While editors and politicians debated the theoretical wisdom of conscription, women across the Confederacy petitioned the War Department for the release of men whose health had failed or who were badly needed back home. Touching stories of families left with little to eat generally met with a curt bureaucratic dismissal. Yet the plain-tive question of a Mississippi woman to Governor John J. Pettus begged an answer: "What is to become of the women and children, if you call out *all* the men?"[64]

Indeed, larger issues of manpower loomed. Confederate armies simply needed more soldiers, regardless of state objections or pleas for exemptions. Even Davis's critics deplored political divisions and judicial challenges to conscription. Support for the draft remained strong in the military, where people were in the best position to realize that a victorious struggle for liberty required enrollment of enough men. Constitutional questions, one Richmond editor suggested, could be deferred until later.[65] But many Confederates could never lay aside such objections. So even with southern fortunes improving, debates over the meaning of freedom continued. But for all the theorizing and politicking, not to mention talk of peace, the main arbiters of the future course of freedom were for the moment dormant, shivering in army camps along the Rappahannock.

*The human heart is the starting point
in all matters pertaining to war.*
—Maurice de Saxe

24 Morale

On the day after Christmas, Halleck telegraphed Burnside about a possible enemy advance in the Shenandoah Valley; he considered it "probable" that the Confederates "will take advantage of the inactivity of the Army of the Potomac" to march toward Harpers Ferry. To Burnside the implied rebuke must have cut deeply even though he was already planning a new campaign. A cavalry expedition commanded by Brig. Gen. William Woods Averell would cross the Rapidan and Rappahannock, slide around Lee's left, and cut the rail line to Richmond. Averell would advance with a "thousand picked men," both Regular and volunteer cavalry, along with four artillery pieces and twenty engineers. Troopers would gallop toward the James River Canal east of Richmond and also strike at the Petersburg Railroad. With additional cavalry and infantry supporting these maneuvers, Burnside intended to cross the bulk of his army below Fredericksburg, though exactly where remained uncertain.[1] The plan was complicated and perhaps unworkable, as it required the coordinated movement of detached forces over a wide area. Given the skepticism of many officers and enlisted men in the aftermath of Fredericksburg and the factiousness, in some cases bordering on disloyalty, among Burnside's generals, the odds against success were long.

By December 27, detachments of cavalry, artillery, and infantry had left their camps. Some soldiers still anticipated going into winter quarters, expressed doubts about a new campaign, and expected the orders to be rescinded; others believed the unseasonably fine weather was perfect for such a movement. The first advance toward the upper fords of the Rappahannock and the Rapidan appeared to go well, but confusion about roads, the effects of wading through cold water, and shivering in chilly bivouacs with little food hardly made the men hopeful of success. The fear of being led into another slaughter like Fredericksburg dogged the march. A Massachusetts lieutenant in the Sixth Corps considered the entire movement a "desperate effort, in the dark, to retrieve his [Burnside's] fortunes by one who does not know what he is about, and I think the first idea of its feasibility . . . that Burnside will get will be when he sees his shattered army drowning in the Rappahannock."[2]

Unfortunately such attitudes extended much further up the chain of command. Around Hooker's headquarters, open criticism of Burnside poisoned the atmosphere. Fighting Joe, according to one artillery colonel, "talked as wildly as ever in condemnation of everybody." At a lavish Christmas dinner, staff officers toasted the general as the Army of the Potomac's next commander, and while feigning humility and embarrassment, Hooker promised in true mock heroic style to do everything in his power to crush the rebellion.[3]

Why Burnside had not been shelved baffled several generals, and the loss of faith among the high command grew palpable. A staff officer summarized what was rapidly hardening into conventional wisdom: "Burnside says he has no confidence in himself as commander of the army—can the Army then have confidence in him?"[4] Discontent pervaded the Left Grand Division, undoubtedly fanned by indiscreet remarks from Franklin and Baldy Smith. Again Burnside lacked powerful friends inside or outside the army, and so Hooker, the darling of radicals such as Chase and Chandler, openly maneuvered against him while diehard McClellanites freely sniped away.

In the Sixth Corps, Brig. Gen. John Newton had run out of patience. An illustrious West Point graduate, fine engineer, and capable general, Newton had complained even before the battle that the promotion policies in the Army of the Potomac gave more weight to seniority than to performance and had asked to join the Banks expedition. Only days after Fredericksburg one of Newton's division commanders, Brig. Gen. John Cochrane, wrote to Chase criticizing Halleck and Stanton. Cochrane had been a prominent New York Democrat for nearly thirty years, and even though he praised McClellan's old friends Franklin and Smith, he sounded more and more like a radical Republican as he warned the treasury secretary that the army had lost faith in Burnside.[5]

Both generals had informally discussed the army's low morale with Franklin and Smith, and none of the four approved Burnside's proposed flanking maneuver. Newton asked for leave to visit Washington — in itself an unusual request with the army preparing to move again — and vaguely told his superiors that he planned to meet with powerful members of Congress. Cochrane also expected to confer with congressmen and perhaps Lincoln. The two generals reached the capital on the afternoon of December 30, but because Congress was in holiday recess, Cochrane proceeded to the Executive Mansion hoping to see the president. He ran into Seward, who arranged for an interview.[6]

The conversation began awkwardly. Fearing to appear openly insubordinate, Newton hesitated to tell Lincoln that even privates had given up on Burnside, and so he proceeded cautiously and indirectly, all the while assuring the president that he had no intention of interfering with military operations. Here was more bad news to try Lincoln's patience, and he naturally suspected both generals of slandering Burnside and perhaps lobbying for a change in commanders. Newton described the army as dispirited, suggesting that the latest campaign plan could end in disaster, while letting the president draw his own conclusions about Burnside. A recent spate of resignations and desertions, Newton suggested, pointed to serious demoralization. With fervid protestations about unsullied patriotism and pure motives, the wily Cochrane added that he had overheard lower-ranking officers saying they would never cross the Rappahannock again. Lincoln quietly thanked the generals for the information but said little.[7]

This disquieting meeting had confirmed what the president had feared all along: the Army of the Potomac remained factious with the pernicious McClellan influence all too apparent. "I have good reason for saying you must not make a general movement of the army without letting me know," Lincoln tersely instructed Burnside. So just as Hooker reported his troops in motion, the entire plan was scrapped.[8]

For security reasons and likely to avoid responsibility himself, Halleck had earlier asked that details of any plans not be sent by telegraph, so it must have surely baffled Burnside to learn that the president had somehow gotten wind of the impending movement. Adding to the frustration, Averell enthusiastically reported his troops ready to splash through the fords should Burnside manage to change the president's mind. Many officers and soldiers must have been relieved to learn that the movement had been aborted. Burnside would have to sort all this out and determine just where he stood with the administration; on the last day of 1862 he boarded a steamer bound for Washington.[9]

At their meeting that afternoon, Lincoln told Burnside about the recent visitors without naming names. Shocked and infuriated to hear that two subordinates had scuttled his plans, Burnside would later barely recall the rest of the conversation. He described for the president the proposed thrust across the river, but Lincoln wished to consult with Halleck and Stanton before approving such a move. When Burnside pointedly asked which generals had gone behind his back, the president refused to say. Even the mild-mannered Burnside heatedly suggested that such men be dismissed from the service but acknowledged that if the country lacked confidence in his abilities, he would resign. In an obvious fit of pique, he added that neither the army nor the country had much faith in Stanton or Halleck.[10]

Burnside returned to Willard's Hotel and as was his wont worked into the early morning hours, this time drafting a letter essentially repeating what he had said earlier to the president. "I cannot conscientiously retain the command," he declared, "without making an unreserved statement of my views." Burnside readily admitted that not a single grand division commander had endorsed his latest campaign plan and again offered to resign. Early the next morning as the president was eating breakfast, Burnside, Halleck, and Stanton arrived for yet another meeting. Burnside handed his letter to Lincoln, who read and returned it without comment. With his usual candor Burnside repeated his statement about a general loss of confidence not only in himself but also in Halleck and Stanton. Whether he suggested that the secretary of war and the general in chief resign is unclear; in any case Lincoln ducked that question, and so the conversation drifted onto a discussion of strategy. Given the lack of support among his own generals, Burnside naturally wished for "some encouragement" from the administration if he were to cross the Rappahannock again and remarked that Halleck should "at least . . . sanction the move." But the meeting ended without a decision, and to the president it seemed that no one would take any responsibility.[11]

Over a three-day period Lincoln had faced two insubordinate generals, conferred with a faltering army commander, and heard nothing but evasive statements from his military advisers. Halleck's passivity had been especially annoying. In a sharply worded letter to the general in chief, Lincoln's usually well-controlled temper suddenly exploded. Noting that Burnside planned to cross the Rappahannock again but that the grand division commanders remained opposed, the president gave Halleck a brief lecture on responsibility: "If in such a difficulty as this you do not help, you fail me precisely in the point which I sought your assistance." Halleck should accompany Burnside "to the ground, examine it as far as practicable, confer with officers, getting all the elements for forming a judgment of your own." He must then tell Burnside whether he approved or disapproved of the campaign plan. Pulling no punches, Lincoln closed with a sentence that lacerated Halleck: "Your military skill is useless to me if you will not do this." At a New Year's reception held at Stanton's house, the secretary of war handed Lincoln's letter to Halleck. The hurt and outraged general in chief immediately submitted his resignation, but Lincoln, perhaps thinking better of a shake-up in the high command at this delicate time, withdrew his note.[12] Chronic cabinet divisions and now a blowup among his chief military advisers boded ill for the future of the Army of the Potomac.

The mood in the country had turned equally sour. "Many are very bitter against him [Burnside]," the wife of Michigan's Republican governor noted, "and even rejoice over the defeat." The weight of failure, high taxes, depreciating money, and so many deaths depressed many people, as even faithful Republicans sadly conceded. Fredericksburg had been a "wet blanket" on the home front, a recruiting officer reported. "Some [people] are discouraged, others angry at somebody they dont know who." So pervasive had the despair become that even the staid *Scientific American* published an editorial blaming the generals and politicians for the nation's woes.[13]

Burnside returned to Falmouth a sadder and angrier man. Back in camp he learned that the details of his plans had somehow leaked out there as well, and he swore to find out who had gone to Lincoln behind his back. The trip to Washington had done nothing to solve the dilemma. Burnside favored a campaign that his generals opposed and the government refused to endorse.[14]

These developments drove Hooker's stock higher, especially when he unexpectedly journeyed to Washington in early January. Loose talk with reporters about his distrust of Burnside and readiness to assume command only fueled speculation that the change would come soon. Hooker knew the value of newspaper puffery but also disclaimed military ambition, at least when he chatted with other generals. Even a colonel serving under Franklin who had never set eyes on Hooker remarked on his reputation as an unscrupulous intriguer.[15]

Dissension at the top inevitably trickled down into the ranks. An orderly in Hancock's division dismissed the entire Army of the Potomac as a "gigantic humbug" filled with partisan cliques. Complaints about self-promoters who would sacrifice lives to advance or destroy careers made for bitter campfire conversations. "The cabinet ought to be drawn up in line and shot by a file of Greeley's Negroes," a McClellan supporter raged. Too many officers, according to one widespread complaint, cared only for their pay and the bottle, and indeed a lull in campaigning always offered more chances to lobby for promotions.[16]

Unfortunately for Burnside, much of this desultory grumbling focused on the army's apparently rudderless state. "We need a leader" became the familiar cry. Where was the Napoleon for this crisis? In New York the McClellan crowd replied, and calls for Little Mac's return grew louder. Without the right commander, a Massachusetts colonel groaned, "the Star Spangled Banner sounds like a wail to me." Reading about William S. Rosecrans's success at Stones River, soldiers naturally wondered why the powers that be could not find a general to match Lee in the eastern theater.[17]

Good news from the West briefly lifted spirits in Washington and across the northern states. Perhaps the post-Fredericksburg clouds would soon disappear, and certainly some soldiers showed remarkable resilience. Lt. Col. William Franklin Draper of the 36th Massachusetts perceptively commented on how his own attitude had improved since he wrote a despairing letter right after the battle. Maybe Burnside could not lead the boys to victory, but he wondered whether any general could really manage such a large army.[18]

Scores of men, however, feared the South was winning. The old saw that fighting could never end the war still echoed through the camps. Not only did soldiers admit that they had lost their patriotism, but a few suffered from a corrosive nihilism. Contemplating the impossibility of defeating Lee, much less taking Richmond, a Connecticut volunteer described his comrades as thoroughly "disheartened and sick of the war."[19]

The effects of Fredericksburg hung over the camps like a heavy fog, deeply penetrating into the bone and sinew and heart of the army. A common fantasy centered on being taken prisoner in some bloodless skirmish and then being exchanged and paroled. Soldiers admitted they were unable to shake off depressing memories. After reading press reports that attempted to gloss over the slaughter, a member of the 11th Pennsylvania Reserves fired off an angry letter to his hometown paper questioning Burnside's abilities and noting how his outfit remained in "wretched and ragged condition."[20]

★ ★ ★

Disgruntled soldiers rightly linked despair over the strategic situation to physical hardships because military readiness and material comfort often went hand in glove. Despite steady improvement in the supply situation since the first days of confusion and chaos after the battle, nothing could stop the usual grousing about food. "The boys are most crasey for fear we shall have to giv thoes rebs another hack," a New Hampshire soldier wrote home, "but that is the least that troubles me as long as I can get enough to eat." Advising his brother to "steer clear" of the army, a member of the Iron Brigade added that "a good soldier cares more for a good meal than he does for all the glory he can put in a bushel basket."[21]

To soldiers subsisting on little but hardtack, pork, and coffee for a year or more, even desiccated vegetables had their charms. They made "queer tasting" soup that "smells very strong," a Michigan soldier commented. The good Lord only knew what was in the stuff; roots, dirty pieces of unidentifiable plant matter, and even sand hardly made for a savory meal. Gobbling up fried hardtack from less-than-sanitary utensils, a Maine chaplain thought it best to keep "eyes shut" and remember "it is all for our country."[22] But the spirit of patriotic sacrifice had worn thin.

Reports of widespread illness and unhealthy camps persisted despite improvements in shelter and food. Letterman estimated the rate of sickness for January 1863 at 8 percent, remarkably low by his lights, but many soldiers knew that there were many more men unfit for duty.[23] Regiments able to muster fewer than 300 men and companies reduced to a pathetic score all bespoke the staggering and unanticipated costs of the war. For once sheer numbers meant a great deal as soldiers sadly noted how many comrades in bright new uniforms had enlisted on some cheerful morning that now seemed so long ago and how few remained in the ranks.[24] The on-again, off-again campaign plans forced surgeons to prepare to move patients on short notice, and despite the construction of more hospitals near Aquia Creek, transporting the most serious cases raised the mortality rate.[25]

Whatever the actual numbers, January camp deaths loomed large to the soldiers. Days when several noble boys breathed their last became memorable, especially when bodies lay unburied. Between January 2 and 15 a sergeant in the 122nd Pennsylvania counted the deaths of seven comrades.[26] Lively, fun-loving fellows suddenly fell ill and were gone. A New York surgeon thought of men who had once occupied places of wealth and position at home now lying cold "with nothing but a blanket and mother earth over them." Other soldiers mused on how the Lord called his servants home without warning, like a "thief in the night," as the Bible said. "I have got So used to the dead March that [I] due not mind it any more," a Pennsylvanian told his wife.[27]

Volunteers built cracker-box coffins for what seemed like daily funerals; makeshift headboards or a sealed bottle with a scrap of paper listing the victim's name, regiment, and home address marked the graves. Services were brief: "the slow march, the arms reversed, the muffled drum, the piercing fife, the dirge . . . platoon fire over the grave, the quickstep march back to camp, two left to close the grave, and all is done." Soldiers witnessed so many funerals that in their minds Virginia became one vast graveyard, sacred ground that could never be surrendered to the Rebels.[28] Deaths of friends and comrades might redouble some soldiers' determination but more often dispirited companies and regiments.

In an age dependent on sketchy, inaccurate newspaper accounts and sometimes long-delayed letters, the desire to know that one's loved ones were safe could never be satisfied. Given the uncertain military situation, camp hardships, and all too frequent deaths, soldiers valued letters more than ever. The absence of mail sent morale plummeting, but nothing could brighten a day more than news from home. Tearing open a letter, especially from a wife or mother, brought tears to the eyes of hardened campaigners. Especially after Fredericksburg, soldiers needed to know that the home folks still cared about their sufferings. According to one officer, the distribution of mail became the "event of the day" to "us, poor devils, in the Virginia mud, in canvas houses."[29]

Of all the problems that plagued both armies, the pangs of loneliness hit some men the hardest. To recall a loving wife or playful child added to the sense of dull dissatisfaction if not outright despair that hung over an army in winter. Even sweet reveries suddenly became frightening. One night a New York sergeant dreamed of coming home only to find his wife indifferent to him and ready to take the hand of a well-dressed gentleman riding in a fancy carriage. Although he claimed that the smoke hurt his eyes as he wrote about this nightmare, he could not help but cry. Men whose minds drifted to domestic scenes also had to battle sometimes uncontrollable terror. Given all that he had seen, a New Hampshire sergeant confessed that he most feared being horribly wounded. Admonitions to bravery emanating from both home and camp could not ease such anxieties. Husbands and wives, though they seldom admitted it to each other, sometimes doubted their spouse's fidelity, and talk of purity and faithfulness could not conceal worries on that score.[30]

A vivid imagination could thus be a mixed blessing, but many men enjoyed picturing what their loved ones might be doing at home. Knowing that their families worried and prayed helped soldiers go about their daily tasks, no matter how mundane. Distance encouraged men and women to idealize one another. A Massachusetts officer warmly praised his wife for becoming the mainstay of the local soldiers' aid society. Less-than-perfect husbands naturally claimed to be changed men, and whatever the truth of such statements, many had grown to appreciate domestic life. "Home, how well we know how to estimate the value of that little word," a Pennsylvania lieutenant confessed to his wife. "It means all that men care for. Glory and honor sink into insignificance alongside . . . all its endearments."[31]

Yet home remained far away, and that irreducible fact added to the psychological strain of soldiers who found little diversion as they nervously waited for generals to decide on the army's next move. Soldiers naturally dreaded word of family illness, especially when misdirected letters held up news of recovery. The men recognized obvious signs of anxiety among their home folks, and separation itself created health problems. A corporal in the Irish Brigade suggested that his wife visit the doctor to get some medicine for her nervousness. Men rarely received furloughs to care for ailing family members or even attend a mother's funeral.[32]

The arrival of paymasters in late December and early January helped alleviate some worries for soldiers who had gone two, four, or even six months without receiving a single greenback. Suddenly flush with money, they dreamed of splurging on everything from apple fritters to soap, or for what an Irish Brigade corporal termed a "regular jollification." Sutlers and newsboys swarmed about the camps, and opportunistic soldiers gathered to collect high-interest loans from their less provident comrades or lure gullible lads into gambling away their pay. One New Jersey volunteer decided he would only send money to his wife if the paper money was holding its value back home, though few men seemed so calculating. Other soldiers, however, did not receive all their back pay, and a Rhode Island corporal recalled hearing derisive cheers for Jeff Davis.[33]

Many regiments received no pay at all. Rather than sending money home, soldiers had to beg their families for a few dollars to tide them over; some men had even run out of money for postage stamps. Living on official promises made for a spartan existence. Sardonically recapturing the feelings of many, a Pennsylvania surgeon whose pay was $600 in arrears remarked, "Uncle Sam treats his officers more like Dogs than Gentlemen."[34]

Bureaucratic foul-ups, including paymasters skipping soldiers who were on detached service, added to the dismay. In a kind of desperation reminiscent of Washington's army during the American Revolution, some soldiers sold state bounty warrants to speculators for ready cash. No one ever seemed to know when the paymaster was even *supposed* to arrive, let alone when he *would* arrive. The angry resignation of one Pennsylvania officer who not only suffered from chronic diarrhea but also claimed that his wife and children had been reduced to "absolute want of the common comforts of life" reached Lincoln's desk. If soldiers were not going to be paid, perhaps they should just go home. As would be the case with the Confederates later in the war, the connection between family hardships and demoralization in the army became clear. On January 18 twenty-three men in the 13th Pennsylvania Reserves quietly "stacked their arms" and "refused to serve until they are paid." The men were immediately arrested, and when some remained defiant, they ended up in irons.[35] This near mutiny showed just how dangerous the situation had grown, and Washington politicians took notice.

Chase admitted to the chairman of the Senate finance committee that the Treasury owed some $60 million to the soldiers and sailors but had only $12.5 million available for that purpose. This gloomy arithmetic indicated a genuine crisis. Congressional resolutions calling for the government to pay the men could not fill empty coffers, and printing more greenbacks now seemed inevitable even to those who normally worshiped hard money. In January and February the purchasing power of a soldier's monthly pay dipped to what was then a wartime low. Lincoln well understood the issue from his brief militia service in the Black Hawk War and, despite his own aversion to currency inflation, would approve nearly any congressional measure to remedy this rank injustice and political embarrassment.[36]

Even staunch Republican newspapers were outraged, and conservative editors eagerly seized on the issue. The president, the politicians, and government contractors all received their money while families suffered. Yet some bluecoats feared—and quite rightly—that there was simply not enough money in the Treasury. A New Yorker in Hancock's division sarcastically suggested that perhaps the men had not been paid because "they [the politicians] have not had Enough of us killed yet." A Minnesotan berated "villains at Washington" bent on "robbing the helpless Soldiers" to line their own pockets and even fantasized about the army marching to burn the capital.[37] Such reckless statements helped let off steam but also suggested that patience had worn thin.

Telltale signs of trouble appeared around the camps. Lazy fellows seemed all too numerous and remained impervious to discipline. Given the army's depressed state, customary complaints about drunken officers carried a sharper tone. A Hoosier private tied another common vice—gambling—to general demoralization: "The grand army of the Republic has one third playing cards, the other doing the duty, and the last third deserting as fast as they can."[38]

The last part of the statement was an obvious exaggeration but seemed believable at the time. The absentee rate in the Army of the Potomac had held steady since November at around 26 percent, but the aggregate numbers concealed a disturbing trend. Many of those who had been sick or wounded in the fall after a hard campaign season had either died, gone home, or recovered enough to return to the ranks, so in fact what appeared to be a serious yet stable problem actually signified a higher desertion rate. Desertion may have reached 200 men per day in January 1863, and several hundred officers remained absent without leave. The toll in particular regiments was even more striking. The 140th New York in Sykes's division lost 18 men during January 1863; nearly a score of new recruits for a Rhode Island battery absconded almost immediately; from a Sixth Corps camp near White Oak Church a surgeon noted how on a single night 19 enlisted men and non-commissioned officers had taken "leg bail."[39]

Each deserter had his own reason, from bounty jumping to health problems to family troubles, but a more general pattern also emerged. Although some soldiers had loudly talked of deserting over the Emancipation Proclamation, few ever did. Despair at home played a larger role. A Michigan woman informed her brother that the Fredericksburg defeat had sapped northern patriotism, and in early January he replied that the army's fighting spirit was largely "played out." A few weeks later he deserted. Many such men had just grown sick of the war, but the military stalemate and tardy pay further eroded morale and clearly pushed some soldiers over the edge. And for every man who actually deserted, several others considered it. "I hope the earth will sink between the two great armies so they cant get near each other," a disheartened Connecticut volunteer raved. "Let those that like to carry the flag at home come down here . . . and face the music." He would not yet abandon his post but did not rule out heading home.[40]

Clever stratagems foiled efforts to suppress desertion. Families shipped citizens' clothes to the camps, helping the soldiers to slip away undetected, or a man might suddenly disappear right after a helpful relative's visit. Eventually officers tried to intercept packages and banned civilian clothes in camp. General Patrick ordered the arrest of men caught without passes outside the picket lines and established procedures for cavalry to round up skulkers and stragglers during marches and battles.[41]

In theory, deserters could be shot, and soldiers dreaded being assigned to carry out these sentences; but in reality executions remained rare. Typically the poor miscreant would be marched around a square of men, have his head roughly shaved, and then be escorted from camp to the strains of the "Rogue's March." Often a "C" for coward or a "D" for deserter would be branded on the man's hip. Onlookers deplored this barbaric spectacle, though many also conceded the necessity for treating the offense with severity.[42]

When officers could resign and thus escape the punishment meted out to enlisted men who deserted, one could hardly blame a fellow for railing against the injustice. But it also seemed that deserters got off lightly, and the uncertainty of punishment clearly exacerbated the problem. The welcome such cowards sometimes received back home also raised hard questions about how popular will affected army morale. Democrats trumpeted reports of desertion and accused the government of suppressing the actual numbers. Even such a Republican stalwart as Senator William Pitt Fessenden of Maine refused to criticize unpaid soldiers for absconding and felt "heartsick" over the War Department's "miserable mismanagement."[43]

Yet despite the desertions and sagging morale, many soldiers slowly recovered from their post-Fredericksburg doldrums. Although Republican newspapers exaggerated what they reported as a rekindled fighting spirit, many rugged veterans understood they would soon have to face Lee again. Some regiments that had been horribly battered only a few weeks earlier now appeared fit to take the field. Love of country, a sense of duty, grim determination, and even personal honor survived regardless of complaints, pessimism, and despair. A Hoosier in French's division proudly served the "best government in the world" and hated to hear anyone in the army or at home lending comfort to the "enemies of Freedom." Indeed, memories of sacrifices already made and comrades lost sparked a patriotic revival—not the flag-waving and hurrahing variety but, rather, the quiet kind of resolve that carried armies to victory.[44]

Disillusionment and despair would not necessarily tear most men away from a still-firm commitment to finish their work. A Pennsylvania captain admitted being tempted to let others do the fighting but could never quite bring himself to act on this impulse. "I am a soldier and a good one," he noted with unaffected pride. He would "growl" after a fight, but when "an order came to storm a battery, nary a squeal would I make." This last statement made up for the bad food, the damp ground, and the harsh talk about Burnside or Lincoln. It overshadowed the swearing, the grumbling, and wild talk of mutiny. It perhaps counted for more than demoralization and even desertions. War demanded a great deal of soldiers and pushed them to the breaking point and beyond, but armies somehow managed to survive the worst. "This body of men is composed of material which is not easily broken," a Maine private decided. "All we want is competent leaders, men who are capable of the duties to be performed and we will show the country that we are a mighty army, a conquering host."[45]

As the soldiers endured the daily drills or stood on some cold picket post, they proved their mettle. Here the army revealed its strength of character, not merely a steady loyalty but the important ability to find comfort and even pleasure in the ordinary: a nice roaring fire, a piece of pork roasting on a stick, or even a simple night's sleep accompanied by pleasant dreams of home.[46] Such soldiers could be relied on not only for routine duties but for standing to the mark in the next fight.

Speculation about the army's future plans continued to dominate conversation in the capital and in the camps along the Rappahannock. Burnside returned from Washington depressed and likely disappointed that his resignation had not been accepted. Taking the unusual step on January 5 of writing directly to Lincoln, he informed the president that despite opposition from his own generals, orders had been issued for engineers and cavalry to prepare for crossing the Rappahannock again. Repeating the offer to relinquish command, he gave Lincoln the option to remove him at any time. Writing to Halleck, Burnside asked for strategic advice but acknowledged that the general in chief need not "assume any responsibility in reference to the mode and place of crossing." By this time Burnside knew his man, and Halleck's reply was defensive though not entirely discouraging. Claiming to have long favored a crossing of the Rappahannock above Fredericksburg and likely prodded by the recent blowup with Lincoln, Old Brains at least advised Burnside to make Lee's army and not Richmond his primary objective. After mentioning several contingencies and the possibility of feints at various points, Halleck's customary caution resurfaced: "As you yourself admit, it devolves on you to decide upon the time, place, and character of the crossing which you may attempt. I can only advise that an attempt be made, and as early as possible." Lincoln endorsed Halleck's reply but also responded directly to Burnside's letter. "Be cautious," he counseled, "and do not understand that the Government is driving you."[47] These words offered Burnside little comfort. He could still feel the political pressure without being entirely sure that his superiors would support his decisions.

News of Burnside's proffered resignation soon leaked out along with reports that Lincoln, having lost patience with both Halleck and the cabinet, would now direct war policy on his own. For his part Burnside forged ahead with his plans, no doubt relieved to be back in the field riding to reconnoiter the fords above Fredericksburg and conferring with generals and staff. Balloon ascensions aided in the reconnaissance, and Burnside himself reportedly rode in one of Lowe's contraptions. Unseasonably pleasant weather —not to mention cavalry movements and the ominous arrival of more pontoons—certainly suggested that the army would not long remain idle. Yet in camp and in Washington, contradictory rumors circulated. The troops would cross the river, the campaigning season was over, Hooker would soon replace Burnside, or even the American republic was entering its death throes: all seemed plausible. Frustrated by delays and false reports, one of

Burnside's faithful staff officers "wish[ed] all the newspapers were in the bottom of the sea."[48]

Opinion in the ranks had turned against Burnside. During a review of Sumner's grand division in early January, the reception was decidedly cool. "Old Burnside wanted to see how many more men he had [available] to kill off," one private sniffed. Even though men in the loyal Ninth Corps cheered their old leader, a chilling rain cut short the inspection and made Burnside's customary doffing of his hat and exposure of his bald pate seem slightly ridiculous.[49]

Formerly naive and hopeful volunteers had their eyes opened. A Massachusetts officer had once assumed that "our Generals devised plans almost superhuman in cunning—that . . . they had looked into the future and set the exact minute when the signal should be given for blows to be struck which were inevitably to crush the Rebellion." But he now considered the whole lot more like Dickens's Micawber, "waiting for something to turn up."[50] Unpaid, homesick, occasionally cold and even hungry, some ill unto death, soldiers had lost many illusions, but most remained at their posts. Men learned how to make themselves comfortable, at least comparatively so, and a winter camp sometimes presented a deceptively ordered and even placid appearance. But talk of a new offensive kept the boys on edge awaiting the next test—if not of their valor at least of their endurance—as the war stretched into the indefinite future.

★ ★ ★

Confederates were much more cheerful but no less uncertain, as everyone from newspaper editors to privates offered widely varying predictions on Burnside's next move. Surely the devastating defeat at Fredericksburg and the reported demoralization made it unlikely that the Federals would launch a winter campaign.[51] But thinking on the matter also ran the other way. Burnside still had a large army, and political pressure would likely force another thrust toward Richmond, perhaps with a crossing at Port Royal or even an advance along the old James River route.[52] So for the time, confusion reigned.

Lee kept his forces alert for any Federal move. Stuart's cavalry remained active and combative, conducting several forays that the Federals found nettlesome if not alarming. Only days before the battle of Fredericksburg, Brig. Gen. Wade Hampton had moved northeast in a raid on Dumfries that bagged fifty Yankees and twenty-four sutlers' wagons, a good haul for Rebel horsemen whom Stuart described as "thinly clad and scantily fed." On December 17 Hampton struck again in the same direction, this time reaching Occoquon, where he captured more prisoners and wagons before Federal cavalry drove him off. The general later boasted of quaffing Burnside's Christmas champagne, and reports of how he had ruined the bluecoats' holiday cheer appeared in the Confederate press, giving yet more reason for rejoicing to people eager to turn small successes into great triumphs.[53]

Under orders from Lee, Stuart led a larger expedition of 1,800 troopers that on December 27 reached Dumfries and Occoquon, snatching up more prisoners and wagons though not in the numbers anticipated and against stiffer Federal resistance. But despite hard marching, cold weather, and short rations, some Confederates described the raid as a lark; Yankee cavalry "ran like sheep," claimed one Virginian. Stuart even sent a cheeky note to Union Quartermaster General Meigs complaining about the poor quality of captured Union mules.[54]

The raid in fact had not accomplished much aside from reconfirming the already established superiority of Confederate cavalry. Flashy heroics did not alter the imbalance in men and resources. Lee saw "no sign" of the Army of the Potomac going into winter quarters and so as usual dragged his feet on sending reinforcements to other theaters. "General Burnside's army is increasing rather than diminishing," he informed Secretary of War Seddon. The fact remained, as Lee explained at length, that Confederate armies were not large enough to take advantage of enemy mistakes, and the southern people had not yet faced up to this stubborn and unpleasant reality. Even Lee recognized that esprit could not forever make up for such a disadvantage, and a Confederate surgeon concisely described the frustrating strategic situation: "The Yankee forces are so large that we cannot expect to gain more decided victories over them. All we can do is hold them in check until they are discouraged and worn out."[55] Like Lee, Jackson remained dissatisfied with the military stalemate. It galled him to hear Yankee bands playing on the other side of the Rappahannock, and pacing in his tent one day, he finally exploded: "Napoleon would not have permitted this. The enemy ought to be driven into the Potomac."[56]

It was better to be frustrated over an incomplete victory than disheartened by a crushing defeat, however, and optimistic Confederates bore the hardships of winter quarters reasonably well. Relative idleness, a North Carolinian noted, gave soldiers a feeling of cheerful "content[ment], irresponsible laughings, independent action, and practical spirit of jesting." Compared with marching and fighting, camp life became almost like "home." Each day the boys built their fires and ate their meals and went about their duties. "A dreamy sort of existence, a sort of trance," thought Jedediah Hotchkiss.[57]

Reading, visiting, and music ("Richmond Is a Hard Road to Travel") filled the hours between meals, drills, and picket duty. If one of the boys celebrated a birthday, his comrades might toss him into a Virginia mud puddle. Checkers and cards provided some amusement, as did an occasional baseball game; members of the 16th Mississippi bowled ninepins with cannonballs.[58] Whether held in woods or in logged-up tents complete with curtains and "artificial thunder," amateur theatricals attracted appreciative crowds. Yet men dressed as women with sheets tied around their waists or draped over barrel hoops reminded the soldiers of the greatest void in their social lives.[59]

As with the Federals, the rare appearance of any reasonably attractive woman in camp caused an immediate stir. The absence of "sweet creatures" saddened a romantic artillerist who resolved to cut quite the figure with young women after the war, but such sentimental effusions could not disguise disturbing changes. "The constant association with all the coarse elements of humanity," a South Carolina lieutenant feared, along with all the bloodshed and "abominable vices untempered by the sweet & angelic influence of women's society, is enough to upset what virtues a man may be possessed of at home."[60]

To preserve conventional moral standards became a perhaps hopeless battle. In Brig. Gen. George T. Anderson's brigade of Hood's Division a Christian association established a code of conduct based on the Ten Commandments, with added prohibitions against gambling and drunkenness.[61] Because camp life sorely tested a man's religious convictions, there was often a close connection between morals and morale. Enlisted men yearned for the prayer and fellowship of a Sunday at home. Observing the Sabbath strengthened commitment to the southern cause and reminded soldiers that they were fighting for their families and for their faith.[62]

With the war soon to enter its third year, many soldiers prayed for spiritual renewal. In makeshift log chapels, men held Bible classes and sang favorite hymns. Revival meetings soon overflowed even the 1,200-seat Presbyterian church in Fredericksburg, and beginning with Barksdale's brigade the number of converts grew rapidly. Preachers of various denominations conducted joint services, marking the first real signs of concerted evangelism in the army. The emphasis was on conversion rather than politics, on praying rather than fighting, but the message of salvation and reports of mass enthusiasm undoubtedly nourished military as well as spiritual hopes.[63]

For many soldiers the distance between the anxious bench and the picket line was not that great. But even with revival meetings and prayer services, the state of religion in Lee's army remained precarious, as Jackson and many chaplains readily acknowledged. Men who had not heard a sermon in months talked of returning home to worship God, as if worship seemed hardly possible in camp. "I have gone entirely wild," a Georgia sergeant confessed to his wife, "and if I ever get back I shall have my name taken off the church book for it is a shame and disgrace to the cause of Christ for it to be there." This statement no doubt exaggerated his shortcomings, but the mounting carnage of the war surely encouraged introspection and self-doubt. Even soldiers who anticipated a better world to come wrestled against the fear of death. For despite the obvious confidence produced by Fredericksburg, Gen. Frank Paxton knew that many men would never see the return of peace. "So darling," he wrote in closing a long letter to his wife, "I live upon the hope that this war may some day end, that I may survive it, and that you and I may spend many a happy day together."[64]

Worries about the army's (and the country's) spiritual state in part grew out of a loneliness that ate away at morale even in a victorious army. Élan developed from shared sacrifices and glorious victories but also depended on individual dispositions and emotional health. Sometimes word from home only added to the sadness that afflicted so many soldiers in camp. "I read over your letter a moment ago," a young South Carolinian wrote to a favorite aunt, "but its contents were so tinctured with a feeling of melancholy, that it added very little to cheer me up." When families described the pain of separation, soldiers had to steel themselves to persevere while hoping against hope for a happy reunion in the not too distant future. Even vivid images of a wife and child became bittersweet as soldiers felt both a powerful sense of duty and a gnawing fear of dying far from home.[65]

Swirling emotions buffeted these men, but love remained a powerful anchor. A soldier gently teased his wife about inviting a woman to warm up his tent. A couple suddenly realized that their deep affection for each other came without limits or conditions, unchangeable even in the face of war. A major who recalled the last night spent with his wife in the syrupy language of the era ("you never seemed lovelier to me than on that night") also noted with a barely suppressed eroticism how her "lips rival its [sic] purest carnation." An Alabama lieutenant imagining his wife sitting before a fire in her dressing gown claimed to be "homesick" but was obviously feeling horny.[66] Impulses both carnal and tender filled and overflowed letters, but the real world of war and inescapable burdens intruded on the most romantic reflections.

Home troubles could not be put on hold for the war's duration, and separation may have healed some old wounds but surely reopened others. Like the Federals, the poorly paid Confederates worried about their loved ones suffering from want of necessities. Some men coldly urged their wives to economize, while others relied on their spouses' judgment to allocate the family's shrinking resources. Distance complicated such problems and made misunderstandings more likely. The imperious General Pender often hurt his long-suffering wife, Fanny, with some ill-chosen words, and neither of them ever quite forgave or forgot. The travails of childbirth in the midst of war caused great anxiety at home and in camp, but even simple stories of a youngster's latest antics sometimes proved more sad than comforting. In Lexington, Virginia, Margaret Junkin Preston noticed how children's games had turned warlike, filled with shooting Yankees, taking prisoners, hobbling about on crutches, and punctuated with military jargon.[67]

Separation only intensified ordinary human miseries that in turn affected soldiers' attitudes and actions. Memories of children who had died before the war still devastated couples separated in their grief and no longer able to comfort each other. Christians might affirm that such trials strengthened the soul, but the deaths of relatives at home only added to the war's already overwhelming sorrows. Knowing he would likely never see many of his relatives and friends again, an Alabama surgeon reverted to an all-too-true cliché: "Man is a [sic] few days and full of trouble." Husbands and wives seemed worn down by care, and nightmares about the future were a constant reminder of life's transitory nature.[68]

Distraught soldiers, worried sick about their home folks or simply fed up with army life, took unauthorized furloughs, but compared with the steady exodus from the Federal camps, the desertions from Lee's army seemed less serious. Reports of Virginians slipping away right before Christmas could be expected, and many likely returned after the holidays. Although Jackson acknowledged that some men went home to help their hungry families, he favored shooting deserters. But during the winter of 1862–63 only a few executions took place.[69]

Most volunteers still answered duty's call. So long as they could scrounge up enough to eat, enlisted men enjoyed the comparative ease. Yet idleness eventually lost its charms. "Nothing doing," a Virginia artillerist noted in his diary. "Time hangs heavily on our hands. Camp life is decidedly dull and monotonous and even a lazy man gets tired of it." Military life held few attractions as days and weeks in winter camp stretched out in a fellow's imagination. Ambitious young men had plenty of time to think about their futures. "Though a humble private I have high aspirations," one of Barksdale's Mississippians confessed. "My heart often asks myself why cannot I be a great man."[70]

Watching the sluggish Rappahannock on picket duty left many a soldier alone with his thoughts. Even with a brush shelter and a fire, this was always an uneasy time, one of Jackson's veterans recalled. Despite the relatively mild days, the nights grew cold and damp. Exchanging news and insults with the Yanks across the way and rumors about impending movements made a man uneasy.[71] The army would not languish in camp forever.

On the other side of the river the thoughts of Burnside's men likely flowed in similar channels. For both armies, morale remained a critical question at the beginning of a new year. Federals pondered the army's future, their attitudes shaped by the horrors of Fredericksburg, a loss of trust in their leaders, monotonous hardships, the steady toll of disease, worries about home folks, and lack of pay. Desertions thinned the ranks and revealed the depths of demoralization, but the Army of the Potomac remained formidable, a badly shaken but still mighty host whose presence kept Lee and his commanders on alert. Suffering from many of the same problems of a winter encampment, the Confederates, too, made the best of listless days, taking their fun where they could find it, keeping up with the news from home, and marking time until the next campaign began. Their spirits remained high as faith in Lee and his generals overshadowed ominous shortages of men and supplies. Perhaps the fighting was over for the winter, as so many Rebs and Yanks hoped. Yet still feeling the pressure from Washington and painfully aware of the impatience and demoralization in the North, Burnside had little choice but to try his luck again.

An army can pass wherever a man can set foot.
—*Napoleon*

25 Mud

When would the government finally figure out what to do with the Army
of the Potomac? That was the question of the hour, according to the *New
York Times,* and it was repeated by editors, politicians, civilians, and soldiers. "The army can't lay here all winter," Col. Robert McAllister of the 11th
New Jersey decided. Little did the carping complainers living comfortably
at home "know of the suffering in our army—suffering by cold, wet, and
disease that are carrying down thousands of our brave men to an untimely
grave."[1] Veterans knew firsthand the difficulties of winter campaigning, but
practicalities never stopped armchair strategists.

Noted military thinker Horace Greeley claimed that this war somehow
differed from all previous wars: "Its boiling blood refuses to be tempered
by the fiercest blasts of Winter. Its immense armaments, its tremendous
stretches of exposed and raid-inviting frontier, alike forbid the thought of
months of hibernation." Burnside nursed no illusions about how long the
administration or the northern people would be patient. In a four-column,
front-page dispatch William Swinton of the *New York Times* described the
army as a "melancholy muddle." He quoted Halleck as saying, "The Army of
the Potomac has ceased to exist." Swinton thought Burnside a good-natured,
conscientious man who lacked both the confidence and the intelligence nec-

essary to command a large army. A run of good weather had already passed, and now it was too late to launch another offensive with demoralized troops. Swinton was no lone voice. Republican and Democratic editors insistently asked why the army remained idle.[2]

It was not totally idle, however. Cavalry and engineers scouted crossing points, while infantry detachments corduroyed roads. Dubious intelligence, including a report that part of Longstreet's corps had been ordered to Tennessee, caused further fits and starts.[3] General Patrick considered Burnside (perhaps again suffering from mental strain and overwork) "obtuse" and "very forgetful" about details. Yet his plan was in place: to cross the army upstream from Fredericksburg at Banks and United States fords with a diversionary maneuver below the town involving newly arrived infantry, navy tugs, mortars mounted on boats, and transport vessels. Other generals remained unconvinced. Besides having to contend with his army's internal bickering and sagging morale, Burnside was violating an important Clausewitzian principle: "When a battle is lost, the strength of the army is broken — its moral even more than its physical strength. A second battle without the help of new and favorable factors would mean outright defeat, perhaps even absolute destruction."[4]

Most soldiers would not have quibbled with the great Prussian theorist's statement. Despite evidence that the Federals had begun to recover from the effects of Fredericksburg, signs of demoralization had also returned. On Wednesday, January 14, after a cold rain, three discouraged soldiers noted the presence of something else that could sabotage any winter campaign: mud. Mules could hardly slog through the soft ooze, and the thought of pitching new camps much less moving an army appeared ludicrous. The prospect of more marching, sleeping without tents, and all without pay appalled one Maine volunteer. "Do you wonder . . . that the Soldier is disheartened, discouraged," he asked his sister. "If the government wants Soldiers that is ready to do Let them treat them as men not as Brutes."[5]

Fear, despondency, uncertainty, and a persistent loyalty whipsawed emotions. An Indiana cavalryman stripped the problem down to its most fundamental elements: the "great struggle of the war" had begun and "many thousands may perish." Yet to him the Army of the Potomac seemed tough enough to go up against Lee, and gritty determination survived even in demoralized regiments.[6] At the same time apprehension, doggedness, and hints of bravado made for an odd psychological mix. "I am getting to be a believer in pre-destination," a Massachusetts officer said, and indeed many soldiers sounded a note of Lincolnesque fatalism. Such an attitude expressed a sad indifference to the war, a demoralization that drained the patriotism and even the determination to fight for home and family right out of the troops.[7] What such diverse attitudes and emotions added up to, only the next campaign would tell.

Few portents held any promise for success. "Our army here is almost ruined and melting away rapidly," Senator Fessenden noted sadly. "Traitors are about as thick at the North as at the South, and how soon the government will find itself without support it is hard to say." Alarmists among Republican House members warned that McClellan Democrats dominated the officer corps, and conservative newspapers spread treason among the enlisted men. "Burnside is a slow coach and will do nothing effective," Senator Chandler observed.[8] The first reports of the Army of the Potomac leaving the camps aroused surprisingly little enthusiasm in the northern press, despite previous, unrelenting calls for action. Normally "On to Richmond" editors evidently anticipated another reverse, fully expecting Lee to counter any Federal thrust.[9]

Confederate cavalry kept a close watch on the Federals, and each day the infantry strengthened its positions. On January 16 Lee arrived in Richmond to confer with Jefferson Davis but hurried back to camp the next day amidst reports of Federals stirring across the river. He had no idea of Burnside's intentions and still would retire to the North Anna line should the Federals cross the Rappahannock again—a course of action that would displease Davis.[10] Rumors of enemy movements failed to shake the aplomb of Lee's soldiers. They did not need to know how Marse Robert planned to thwart the Yankees this time. Burnside might force them into battle again, but they harbored few doubts about the outcome.

★ ★ ★

Friday, January 16. Ready to march at last. "No one sorry to move," a New Hampshire volunteer claimed. "Almost anything is preferable to this vile camp." Burnside's headquarters ordered batteries to cover crossing points and teamsters to drag pontoons toward the river. "The morale of the army is not now right for such a move," a Michigan captain feared. Perhaps the orders would be countermanded.[11]

Saturday, January 17. In the early morning hours as word spread that the army would cross the river and flank the Rebels, quartermasters and ordnance officers scurried about. "I have yet to see the first man who approves of the movement," an officer in Doubleday's division grumbled. Not surprisingly, his comrades appeared "hopeless," "despondent," and "dispirited," to this McClellan loyalist. Yet reports of demoralization and threats of mutiny even circulated among Humphreys's stalwart Pennsylvanians and the Regulars in Sykes's division. Franklin suggested a delay until Monday so more roads could be corduroyed, but he may have simply been buying time, hoping for bad weather to foil Burnside's plans. By 10:00 A.M. the marching orders had been countermanded again. Cpl. George Mellish of the 6th Vermont spoke for many enlisted men: "All is uncertainty in the army."[12]

Sunday, January 18. "How long the present state of affairs and suspense will continue is known only to wise heads at Washington," a New Yorker in the Fifth Corps bitingly commented. Cooked rations placed in haversacks several days earlier had begun to spoil; men receiving boxes from home wolfed down food just in case they really did break camp this time. One thing was certain: the good weather would not last forever. Maybe God would bless this effort, but then again another slaughter might await. "I think the soldiers will go forward, very reluctantly," a New York artillery officer predicted. The boys understandably uttered more than a few prayers on this somber Sabbath. Still uncertain about timing, Burnside waited for a spy to return from the other side of the river and decided not to send troops across at United States Ford, where the Rebels appeared strong. Once again the anticipated movement never got started. A Massachusetts lieutenant colonel dubbed the army the "Snail of the Potomac."[13]

Monday, January 19. A conversation between Burnside, Franklin, and Smith grew heated. The latter two predicted the campaign would fail because the Rebels were too powerful and their own troops were too demoralized. Barely controlling his anger, Burnside dismissed their objections. After visiting Franklin's headquarters, First Corps artillery chief Wainwright was appalled: "Both his staff and Smith's are talking outrageously, only repeating though . . . the words of their generals. Burnside may be unfit to command this army; his present plan may be absurd, and failure certain; but his lieutenants have no right to say so to their subordinates. . . . Franklin has talked so much and so loudly . . . that he has completely demoralized his whole command, and so rendered failure doubly sure. . . . Smith and they say Hooker are almost as bad."[14]

Soldiers still assumed they would be leaving the camps soon, even though by early afternoon the movement was again postponed. For sure, a great number of troops would be "missing" once the army crossed the Rappahannock. A winter campaign with men already unhealthy held no charms for wary veterans. Some soldiers were reportedly "groaning Abe Lincoln & cheering Jeff Davis."[15]

Tuesday, January 20. The suspense ended. "The Army of the Potomac [is] about to meet the enemy once more," began General Orders No. 7. "The auspicious moment seems to have arrived to strike a great and mortal blow to the rebellion." Besides urging "gallant soldiers" to earn ever more lasting "fame," Burnside also enjoined "firm and united action of officers and men," a stark illustration of the problem. He was sending troops into a campaign against the advice of his senior generals, and their doubts had infected junior officers and enlisted men.[16]

Although some soldiers in green regiments and a few Ninth Corps stalwarts actually cheered the orders as they were read, most outfits responded tepidly or worse. In Howard's division members of the 15th Massachusetts and the 42nd New York "hooted" at both the orders and Burnside.[17] Too many men had given up on Burnside. "One more defeat would fix him," a New Yorker predicted. A veteran artilleryman claimed that "everyone has been praying for rain or a snow to stop it." Were the troops near mutiny, demoralized, or merely unenthusiastic? Their words expressed both momentary pique and deep disillusionment. Discerning the army's mood at this point required making fine distinctions, especially when a few soldiers were actually optimistic. A brave Ninth Corps volunteer could feel the country's gloom lifting and could almost hear people cheering the coming victory. Such eagerness was rare. A Michigan surgeon better expressed the skeptical fortitude that held the poor, battered Army of the Potomac together: "I hope the army will go to Richmond this time or to hell, and I don't care which."[18]

At 1:00 A.M. on January 20 Maj. Gen. John G. Parke, Burnside's chief of staff, had issued orders for Hooker's Center Grand Division to cross "just above Banks' Ford," with one division to assist General Woodbury in laying pontoons. Late in the morning Burnside filled in the details. Once over the river, Hooker would reestablish communication with Franklin (who would have crossed just below Banks Ford), "secure a position" on the Orange Plank Road west of Salem Church, and prepare to attack should the Confederates abandon their position at Fredericksburg and head south on the Telegraph Road. Hooker ordered his troops to be ready to march by 11:00 A.M.[19]

With temperatures inching above freezing and the roads in good shape, regiments began leaving their camps; a band struck up "The Girl I Left Behind Me." As the ground thawed during the afternoon, one New Yorker noticed "twelve foaming, panting, weary horses tugging at each slow-moving [artillery] piece." Assigned to assist with pontoons, Birney's division advanced to within less than two miles of Banks Ford. As usual, moving troops along country roads proved confusing and slow. Some of Hooker's men halted to let regiments from Franklin's grand division pass and consequently marched no more than a mile or two.[20]

In Sickles's division, soldiers cursed anyone who tried to prod them along and yelled for officers to climb off their horses and carry a knapsack like a real soldier. "I'm demoralized," one man shouted. From the beginning the march prompted sardonic humor, the veterans' perennial defense against official imbecility. Some men joked about "Burned Side." Others posed a riddle: Why was the Army of the Potomac like a frog? Answer: "It is always found in a mud puddle." One wit suggested the army had a "damned little head for so long a tail."[21]

Franklin's orders called for sending a division to assist with the pontoons, crossing the river below Banks Ford, advancing toward the Orange Plank Road, and finally turning east to confront the Confederates a little more than a mile away on Marye's Heights. Around noon from camps near White Oak Church, elements of the First and Sixth Corps headed west. Some regiments marched a dozen miles; others, only three or four on the jammed roads.[22]

"On the march today the disaffection produced by Franklin's and others' talk was very violent," Wainwright noted. "The whole army seems to know what they have said, and their speeches condemning the move were in the mouths of everyone"—an exaggeration no doubt, but suggestive of trouble ahead. Men naturally indulged their penchant for grumbling, and in some outfits straggling began immediately.[23]

By early evening, as tents were being pitched, rain had started, lightly at first, but by midnight the heavens had opened up. Water flowed into some tents; a gusty east wind blew others away. Lt. Samuel S. Partridge of the 13th New York, already feverish, spread his rubber blanket on the ground, wrapped himself up in soggy covers, and almost got comfortable after some friends tucked him in with a tarpaulin. Men futilely tried to dry out around smoky fires that mostly made their eyes water. In one of Birney's brigades a "generous" whiskey ration elicited much shouting and some fighting. At a loss for words, a Pennsylvanian wrote in his diary, "O! what a night."[24]

The cold, wind-driven rain seeped through uniforms and slashed the faces of soldiers without tents. Men stoically chewed hardtack and pork. During the night the cries from some sufferers kept almost everyone awake; boys threw blankets over their heads, sat on logs, and waited miserably for the gray dawn. Some men spent the night exchanging mordant jokes around sodden fires. One of the Pennsylvania Reserves who managed to fall asleep awoke the next morning in "about half a foot of water and . . . stiff as an old horse." With the endless night over, men staggered to their feet. Every stitch of clothing was wet, and waterlogged knapsacks weighed them down.[25]

Wednesday, January 21. At 4:00 A.M. reveille sounded for Hooker's men. The steady rain had produced a "complete sea of mud." Wagons sank up to their axles. But by lashing the teams and some "prodigious blasphemy," the "spiritless" troops crawled perhaps three miles. One of Sykes's Regulars summed up the situation: "Burnside cannot fight with troops out of heart." By early afternoon nearly everyone had fallen out of line exhausted.[26] Entire companies tugged at ropes to pull supply and ammunition wagons from the mire. Countless pairs of boots were filled with water and mud—the ultimate soldier misery. The rain had accomplished what many thought impossible: it had even ruined hardtack. With rations soggy and spoiled, mud-splatterd men grimly recalled how they had started at daybreak without so much as a dipper of morning coffee and now faced the prospect of no supper.[27] Such discomforts weighed far more heavily on their minds than grand strategy.

Franklin's troops slogged four or five miles, though few of the pontoons or artillery ever got close to where the bridges were to be laid. By noon many regiments had given up the struggle. As rear guard for the ammunition train, members of the 16th Maine had to unload wagons and heft boxes uphill, gaining no more than a half-mile. It was a "wade on to glory," a Wisconsin volunteer wryly commented. It had not taken long for every man and beast to become covered with what they ruefully called the "sacred soil" of Virginia. Soldiers and animals alike became nearly unidentifiable—a fact lovingly recounted and embellished for years afterward.[28]

Dropping out, panting, and sweating after several hours of great exertion, men sat on the same waterlogged blankets that had "seemed like so much lead" during the march. The air hung so heavy with moisture that smoke from fires hovered near the ground, adding to the wretchedness of yet another cheerless bivouac. After watching men toss away their gear while wrestling with mules and artillery, a Sixth Corps sergeant pointedly remarked that McClellan had been right about the futility of winter campaigning.[29]

"Mud is King!" a New York surgeon had written prophetically little more than a week earlier. "More of a sovereign, and a worse despot than cotton and ten thousand times more to be dreaded by such an army as ours when we want to move than all the inventions and machinations of our enemies." The reddish, weathered-clay soil held water and stuck to anything. The soldiers strained for words: "river of deep mire," "a vast mortar bed," "the mud is ass deep." It seemed almost alive as it sucked and grabbed men and equipment. "Your feet sink into it frequently ankle deep, and you lift them out with a sough," a Pennsylvania lieutenant recalled. An imaginative volunteer composed some appropriate doggerel:

> Now I lay me down to sleep
> In mud that's many fathoms deep;

> If I'm not here when you awake
> Just hunt me up with an oyster rake.[30]

As was obvious to all, rain had made the Virginia roads virtually impassable. By the morning of January 21 only three pontoon trains had neared Banks Ford, and Woodbury predicted it would be several more hours before they could be hauled the final mile over the sloppy roads. Across the river he noticed signs of Rebel preparations and suggested that the night's fires had alerted the enemy. Late and confused orders had once again foiled Burnside's plans, but the engineers and supporting infantry had shown little enthusiasm for the work. Some wagons had reportedly been sabotaged, and there were rumors that "bad whiskey" had slaked the fighting spirit. Worn-out teamsters abandoned their animals, wandered off searching for food, and in a few cases unhitched mules and rode away. A few of men with long ropes tried to drag pontoon trains up small rises, but by early afternoon they had given up from sheer exhaustion.[31]

"Profanity gulch" described a ravine where artillery pieces and wagons became hopelessly entangled. Unfortunately swearing could not extricate a battery from the mire. Attempts at prying guns loose with long levers and even double-teaming the horses proved futile. As wheels sank deeper, men waded in up to their ankles. Infantry detachments corduroyed more roads; but pieces of wood caught in wheel spokes, and one officer observed how even these thoroughfares quickly deteriorated into a "miry pine brush." Smashed-up and capsized pontoons, broken-down caissons, and pieces of guns and wagons marked the track of a failed campaign.[32]

The march was torture for the animals. Stouthearted army mules, creatures known for their endurance under rough treatment, could not handle the wretched footing. Once mired in mud, the hapless beasts stopped pulling and eventually died. A sketch artist noted how "clouds of vapor . . . rose from the overworked teams" straining under drivers' curses and whips. Horses lay along the roadsides dead or nearly so; some dropped in their harnesses; others broke their legs straining against heavy loads. A Pennsylvania lieutenant came across a heavy wagon stalled in a "slough." Four mules struggled to get out but could not, even after they had been cut loose from their traces. A chain fastened to one mule's neck and pulled by a wagon freed the animal but also broke its neck. A second mule shared the same fate. The other two mules stopped struggling as they sank deep into the muck, and their suffering was finally ended by merciful bullets.[33]

After breakfasting on tea and toast, Burnside and four staff officers rode off toward the river in the rain. Seeing the "careworn" general covered with

Alfred Waud, The Mud March *(Harper's Weekly, February 14, 1863)*

mud, one Vermonter decided that perhaps the infantry's burden was lighter than its beleaguered commander's. Around 5:00 P.M. Burnside and his party returned to camp. Discouraging dispatches awaited. Burnside himself had seen the sodden spectacle: twenty horses unable to budge a caisson, 100 soldiers struggling with a pontoon train, and animals and men used up. Yet he bristled at the pessimistic reports from Woodbury, Franklin, and Hooker, and complained that some generals had done everything possible to thwart his plans. Over dinner Burnside tried to appear cheerful. At 11:00 P.M., however, he telegraphed Halleck that a "severe storm" had delayed the march and allowed the Rebels to "discover our designs." He finally bowed to the inevitable: "It is most likely that we will have to change the plan."[34]

Thursday, January 22. At breakfast Burnside remarked that Hooker now placed the odds against success at nineteen to one; Franklin and Woodbury had offered similarly gloomy assessments. A *New York Times* correspondent overheard Fighting Joe dismissing the government as "played out" and talking about the need for a dictator. Facing generals as hopeless as the roads, Burnside finally ordered Hooker and Franklin to bring their troops back to the camps.[35]

Friday and Saturday, January 23–24. The return trip was pure hell. Infantry lugged fence rails, logs, and brush for corduroying roads. Even so, pulling artillery pieces killed more horses and mules. Guns and wagons sank to their axles, and it required the better part of two days to get the pontoons back to Falmouth. Foul tempers and finger-pointing between the infantry, artillery, and cavalry further slowed the retreat.[36]

Organization had simply broken down, and each man struggled along on his own. Straggling, already a serious problem during the early stages of the march, obliterated any sense of discipline. Plagued with diarrhea, Cpl. Joseph Bloomfield Osborn of the 26th New Jersey had naturally fallen behind. In the continuing rain the woods where he had taken shelter filled with cursing men, some vowing they would never "fight for the nigger." A few broke their muskets across trees, claiming that more than half of Franklin and Hooker's troops had done the same. A forlorn, mud-spattered group of twenty soldiers reaching their old bivouac identified themselves in response to challenge as "Stragglers of the Seventeenth Maine, Sir!"[37]

Sumner's troops shook their heads in amazement as they watched a stream of dirty and exhausted soldiers troop by their tents. Members of the faithful old Ninth Corps could hear Hooker's and Franklin's men offering "three groans" for Burnside or joining a lugubrious chorus of what was turning into a campfire favorite, "Burnside's Army Lies Floundering in the Mud."

A volunteer in Getty's division described one group of stragglers as "muddy, wet, ugly, sour, and insubordinate."[38]

★ ★ ★

More unpleasant surprises awaited the returning troops. Soldiers in Double-day's division discovered that some of Sigel's troops had taken over their old campsites. An Ohio regiment had torn down shanties for firewood, and other soldiers occupied huts that had been carefully constructed by First Corps outfits right after Christmas. After an exchange of curses, the interlopers usually departed.[39]

For several days after the Mud March a trickle of desertions turned into a steady stream. Many regiments reported that a man or two had run off during the preceding week. Pickets slipped away from their posts, and groups of deserters hid in the woods from cavalry patrols. The usual sentences of fines or hard labor would not likely stem this tide. Morale had apparently hit bottom.[40]

During and after the Mud March, officers and men in every corps, including troops in the Right Grand Division that had not even left their camps, received whiskey rations. "If no worse use is ever made of liquor than this," a New York surgeon remarked, "surely the cause of temperance has no reason to complain."[41] Such an opinion depended on one's perspective, of course. "Camp was like a pandemonium," said a New Jersey volunteer. Drunken men staggered around cursing Burnside, and one colonel speculated that the Rebels could have easily crossed the river and captured many prisoners. Exhausted and demoralized troops appeared determined to drown their troubles, and no beverage could serve better, a Pennsylvanian claimed, than commissary whiskey. As the precious liquor was being poured into canteens, a fight broke out in the 118th Pennsylvania. Men from the 22nd Massachusetts and the 2nd Maine joined the fray; when a major wielding two cocked six-shooters tried to restore order, they knocked him into the mud.[42]

The men had reason to drink. Not only had the latest campaign ground ignominiously to a halt, but without even bringing on a battle, it was killing people. Weakened soldiers had fallen ill and died along the way. Ambulances carried the sick back toward a newly constructed hospital at Aquia Creek, where some patients still lay on the ground in tents without fires. Meanwhile, burial details kept busy turning up the soggy earth.[43]

It seemed as if God again held the army's fate in his hands. On one hand, a "providential" rain had prevented another murderous battle. "Heaven muttered at the deed and sent an angel to stop it," a Connecticut sergeant declared. On the other hand, a thoughtful private who could hear church bells ringing in Fredericksburg reflected on how the Rebels were "praying earnestly for our discomfiture and utter annihilation." Still, "we have at least an equal number of good Christians at home," he told himself, "with just as good voices and just as determined spirits."[44]

Other soldiers, including Meade and Humphreys, believed the army might have won a great victory and played down reports of demoralization.[45] But despite a certain core of unyielding resolve, Burnside would not be spared scalding postmortems. Even men who felt sorry for their commander admitted that his best efforts had failed. Many others called for his head. Franklin's soggy troops openly vowed to "sit up nights cursing Burnside." An earthy Vermonter sarcastically remarked, "Burnside has shit his breeches this time." Doubts about the general's abilities had now hardened into convictions about his incompetence as cries for Little Mac's return reached a crescendo.[46]

Words such as "disheartened" or "desponding" and most of all "demoralized" appeared in letters describing the army's condition. The Mud March had been more discouraging than Fredericksburg, claimed one of Humphreys's Pennsylvanians.[47] Men talked of throwing down their arms. Presumably the Rebels would quickly follow suit, both armies would melt away, and peace would dawn. A Michigan private felt like a man in a sinking ship surrounded by sharks and "going swiftly . . . to the Devil." The very idea of a victory by this God-forsaken army seemed ludicrous to soldiers who again noted how many of their comrades were dying for no purpose.[48]

The army seemed "played out," in soldier parlance. "Its patriotism has oozed out through the pores opened up by the imbecility of its leaders, and the fatigues and disappointments of a fruitless winter campaign," a New Jersey corporal wrote sadly. Only "honor and self-respect and an adherence to their oath" prevented mass desertions. An equally disgruntled Massachusetts officer predicted the army would become a "source of great trouble to the government if things go on in this way much longer." Enlisted men swore they would never fight again; there appeared to be far "too many officers of the Governor Seymour stamp."[49]

Men who still cherished the Union cause or at least remained determined to complete their enlistment blamed "croakers"—in the ranks and at home —who spread their poison among the gullible. "Fault-finders and gloomy prophets," especially in the northern press, a Pennsylvania volunteer complained, were "doing more for the enemy than they can do for themselves." Spying a newspaper correspondent from some "On to Richmond" sheet, Pennsylvanians in the Sixth Corps peppered him with irreverent questions:

"Why don't the army move?" "When did you learn to be a general?" "Does your mother know you're out?" "What do you get apiece for lies?"[50]

The Confederates delighted in their enemies' plight. Reports rapidly spread from the camps to the newspapers and finally to the southern home front that the Army of the Potomac had become completely demoralized.[51] Southerners' response to Federal maneuvers had largely been contemptuous. Confederate soldiers had set up "hand boards" with "large letters" that read, "BURNSIDE STUCK IN THE MUD." Scornful pickets shouted to the Yanks with mockingly polite invitations to come over or offers to help with the pontoons. Rebel bands played "Dixie" and, for good measure, a few Union airs.[52]

As despondent bluecoats magnified the depressing effects of the Mud March, exuberant Confederates overstated their enemies' discomfiture. "If the Yankees had crossed the river, we would have whipped them easily" became their steady refrain. Next time, perhaps, General Lee would bag the entire lot. A Charleston correspondent reported the Army of Northern Virginia in high spirits and good health and full of boundless confidence. Less straggling, better clothing, comfortable quarters, and spirited drilling all bolstered an indomitable fighting spirit. An optimistic Georgian who expected the war to be over by July 4 began thinking about the hair-raising tales he would tell his wife after he returned home.[53] Lee refrained from such wishful thinking, but the mutual trust between a seemingly invincible commander and his brave troops sent Confederate hopes soaring to dangerous heights.

At the same time, northern spirits sank lower. Newspaper descriptions of artillery, wagons, men, and animals floundering in the mud soon appeared. Republican editors tried to play down signs of demoralization, but people did not find their assessments credible. "Northern dirt-eaters grow more insolent and shameless everyday," George Templeton Strong wrote wearily. "False, cowardly, despicable sympathizers with Rebellion" had gained far too much influence over a weak-kneed public. Reports of insubordination among Burnside's generals prompted the Joint Committee on the Conduct of the War to launch another investigation. *New York Times* editor Henry J. Raymond, who had spent several days at Burnside's headquarters during the Mud March, reported widespread discontent and suggested that either the troublemakers be removed or that a new commander be appointed.[54]

At last Burnside prepared to move against his enemies by drafting a set of orders that would have shaken the Army of the Potomac to its foundations. Numerous heads were going to roll. He proposed dismissing Hooker from the army for "unjust and unnecessary criticisms of the actions of his superior officers." Generals Newton and Cochrane and Brig. Gen. William T. H.

Brooks, a division commander in the Sixth Corps, would also be sacked. Generals Franklin, Smith, Sturgis, and Ferrero were "relieved from duty."[55] These blows to both Hooker and the McClellan faction would likely produce a political firestorm. But the commander's mind was made up, and when asked what he would do should Hooker attempt to incite a mutiny, Burnside replied that he "would swing him before sundown." In any case, he would travel to Washington seeking Lincoln's approval for the dismissals.[56]

The journey to the capital typified the man's bad luck. On January 23 at 8:30 P.M. Burnside, Raymond, Larned, and a servant started for Falmouth in an ambulance. In the foggy darkness the driver, who was both near-sighted and deaf, drove them over an embankment, and they became stuck near a pile of dead mules. The hapless party stumbled through the mud, taking three hours to cover the three miles to the station. But the engine had already left, so with Burnside carrying a lantern, the forlorn group trudged toward Stoneman's Switch and, after walking two miles, managed to flag down a locomotive. By the time they arrived at Aquia Landing, boarded a steamer, and reached Washington, it was after 6:00 in the morning.

Leaving his companions at Willard's Hotel, Burnside went off to see Lincoln. He handed the president General Orders No. 8 along with a note resigning his commission. Reiterating that he had never sought the command in the first place, Burnside somewhat petulantly remarked that he would gladly return to civilian life. "I think you are right," the president replied, "but I must consult with some of my advisers about this." Lincoln had received what amounted to an ultimatum. Burnside's sudden stubbornness left no room for diplomatic niceties, even for a president. In a response that likely surprised and irritated Lincoln, Burnside sharply commented, "If you consult with anybody, you will not do it [approve the order], in my opinion." Lincoln dismissed the objection: "I cannot help that; I must consult with them." The president could do as he pleased, Burnside observed icily.[57]

On Sunday morning, January 25, Lincoln informed Stanton and Halleck that he planned to replace Burnside with Hooker. He had not conferred with the cabinet, and he did not leave the matter open for discussion. Like much of the country, he had lost faith in Burnside. For all Fighting Joe's faults—his shameless plotting was no secret to Lincoln—there seemed little choice but to act now. When Burnside arrived around 10:00 A.M., Lincoln informed him of the decision. The general took the news with apparent equanimity, glad to be free of a terrible burden. He loyally hoped that Hooker would win a great victory. Lincoln would not hear of Burnside giving up his commission and instead granted him a much needed thirty-day furlough.[58]

Stanton issued orders relieving Burnside of command "at his own request." Sumner, largely because of his age, and McClellan's friend Franklin would also depart. At last Joe Hooker received the appointment for which he had schemed so long. After returning to Falmouth, Burnside visited Sumner's headquarters, where their conversation, undoubtedly reliving old triumphs and disappointments, ran well into the night.[59]

The next morning Col. Zenas Bliss of the 7th Rhode Island stopped by Burnside's headquarters and found the general in shirtsleeves, champagne bottle in hand. Over a convivial drink Burnside bitterly remarked, "They will find out before many days that it is not every man who can command an army of one hundred and fifty thousand men." At 10:30 A.M. several officers, including Hooker, arrived to bid their former commander farewell. Burnside addressed them with what General Patrick considered "some feeling"; he was overwhelmed to say, "There are no pleasant reminiscences for me connected with the Army of the Potomac." For a time the atmosphere grew tense. Yet he issued a gracious farewell order praising his successor as a "brave and skilled general" and wished the army "continual success until the rebellion is crushed." At noon Burnside, Sumner, and Larned departed for Washington.[60]

As word of the change spread, soldiers high and low had the final say. The sympathetic Meade concluded that Burnside had been unequal "to the command of so large an army" and "deficient in that large mental capacity which is essential in a commander." But Burnside "appeared much like Washington to the troops that knew him best," said a loyal Ninth Corps corporal, one of the few such ardent defenders left. Soldiers still admired Burnside's manly assumption of responsibility, and several men noted how uncontrollable factors—notably the weather—had ruined his plans. Perhaps fate or even God's will had been against him. No one could doubt Burnside's honesty or patriotism, but even admirers conceded his lack of self-confidence and the army's subsequent loss of faith in him.[61]

Some irreverent fellow had reportedly asked Burnside shortly before his removal, "When are you going to butcher again?" The story spoke volumes about the opinions of ordinary soldiers. Disheartened troops influenced by disaffected officers had recently howled and hooted at Burnside. A corporal in the First Corps thought news of the change in generals "too good to be true."[62]

The army's new commander condescendingly noted "the gloom and despondency which has settled over the mind of the army through the reverses and imbecility of my predecessor." But like Burnside, Hooker would have to deal with troops whose heart in many ways belonged to McClellan. Many veterans still believed that only the Young Napoleon could command the Army of the Potomac.[63]

★ ★ ★

Demoralization continued to dog the army. "Everybody appears indifferent to the appointment of Hooker," a Ninth Corps New Yorker wrote. "Heroes of many defeats we are not inclined to gratuitous confidence in anyone." This was not entirely accurate, because some soldiers welcomed the change and expressed great confidence in Hooker. Other men, however, feared they had become mere playthings to be marched about, thrown into battle, and slaughtered—all on the whim of some incompetent general, unscrupulous politician, or partisan editor. A New York private scorned the "chuckle heads at Washington" who kept replacing one failed commander with another.[64]

In the rough calculations of the common soldier, the war was simply no longer worth its staggering cost. The most disheartened men demanded peace on virtually any terms. Brave soldiers blamed skulkers, deserters, and all the disaffected folks at home for taking the fight out of many regiments. Why continue the slaughter, a Pennsylvania sergeant in Meade's division asked, when "pen and ink" could settle the entire matter?[65]

But the Army of the Potomac had already survived command changes, several disasters, and numerous prophecies of its imminent collapse. This is not to deny that the morale crisis was real or serious; it was. Yet even among fellows who cursed incompetent officers and railed against Copperheads, there remained a spark of hope, if not exactly optimism. These soldiers often despaired of their own government but not of their comrades, men who had stood the fire before and who would not shrink from it next time. Honor, now often defined as one's reputation in the company or regiment, would keep such men in the ranks. A fatalism about death coupled with the conviction that suppressing the rebellion required more fighting steeled them for the spring campaign. As a Massachusetts lieutenant rightly observed, the army had been somewhat demoralized ever since spring when it had been thrown back from the gates of Richmond but had fought well anyway.[66]

In a long letter explaining to his wife why he stayed in the ranks, Cpl. Peter Welsh of the Irish Brigade recaptured this spirit of hard-headed yet still idealistic patriotism: "This is my country as much as the man that was born on the soil and so it is with every man who comes to this country and becomes a citezen." Even a war filled with "erors and missmanagement" carried a "vital interest" for "people of all nations." Anticipating Lincoln's Gettysburg Address, Welsh defined the stakes:

This is the first test of a modern free government in the act of sustaining itself against internal enemys and matured rebellion[.] all men who love free government and equal laws are watching this crisis to see if a republic can sustain itself in such a case[.] if it fails then the hopes of millions fall and the designs and wishes of all tyrants will suceed[.] the old cry will be sent forth from the aristocrats of europe that such is the common end of all republics[.] the blatent croakers of the devine right of kings will shout forth their joy. . . . It becomes the duty of every one no matter what his position to do all in his power to sustain for the present and to perpetuate for the benefit [of] future generations a government and a national asylum which is superior to any the world has yet known.[67]

Perhaps better than any other statement from a common soldier, Welsh's tribute to American democracy explained how the Army of the Potomac would survive to fight another day.

That very question, however, still hung fire, especially with the northern public. The effects of the Fredericksburg campaign had shaken the Union's already wobbly foundations. The gloom in Washington was not lifting. Despair visited everyone from sober moderates, such as Senator John Sherman of Ohio, who believed that "military affairs look dark," to excitable radicals, such as Horace Greeley, who warned that the country stood on the "very brink of a financial collapse and a Copperhead revolution."[68]

Yet in the cities and elsewhere, despite scores of families in mourning for men recently killed, what one Philadelphia editor termed the "pleasure-seeking population" appeared "gayer than they ever were." It was a central irony of this war, indeed of many modern wars: "People are making money so fast they can afford to spend it freely." No wonder soldiers had grown discouraged, the wife of Michigan's Republican governor noted, "when people living in comfortable homes who have not paid a cost or given up a friend" were constantly "harping" about every real and imagined difficulty.[69]

There was nothing imaginary, however, about the general malaise. Loneliness, cold, bad food, disease, death, and the sheer boredom of winter quarters left both armies languid. In the face of chronic shortages of everything from horses to shoes, the Rebels exuded confidence, although thoughtful southerners recognized Confederate weaknesses. Democrat Horatio Seymour unnerved Republicans throughout the North even as the moody, mysterious Lincoln appeared more decisive. In both the United States and the fledgling Confederate nation, conscription threatened to pit neighbor against neighbor by raising the most basic and explosive questions about power and justice. Nervous Europeans read about the American bloodbath with both fascination and horror.

As some families struggled to make ends meet, their soldier boys also had to weigh the costs of war in the balance of their own commitment to cause and comrades. Reservoirs of patriotism remained substantial but not inexhaustible. For those with a metaphorical turn of mind, the men stuck in the muddy camps symbolized a nation mired in civil war. The cold and muck of winter—the season of death—provided a setting to match the gloom, particularly for the Federals. Yet also for reflective Confederates, including the poor people driven from their ruined homes in Fredericksburg, who understood that the Yankees were far from whipped, optimism could not always chase away darker thoughts. All across the fractured land, hard questions about the Lord's will and nagging fears about the future seemed as natural as the bare trees and fallow fields. Peace remained a distant, indistinct, and elusive dream.

Epilogue

On December 28, 1862, a Fredericksburg woman refuging in Richmond finally learned what fate had befallen her property. Her home had been commandeered as a temporary hospital, and the parlor table had been used for amputations. Blood and water still filled cups and vegetable dishes, and a Union soldier had been buried near the kitchen door. This was but one example of the desecration and destruction that returning Confederate soldiers sadly cataloged after the Yankees withdrew from the town. Besides fire damage on some blocks and innumerable shell holes in various buildings (at least twenty in the steeple of St. George's Episcopal Church), minié balls had peppered doors, and fences had been knocked down all over town. Furniture, clothing, trunks, and books, along with valuable business and family papers, still littered the streets. A Charleston newspaper correspondent angrily reported how the Yankees with their "muddy boots and jingling swords" had turned the once "elegant library" and the fine furnishings of the Bernard House into a bedlam.[1]

The physical destruction drove home the connection between the material concerns of daily life and the abstract world of ideology. The loss of food, clothing, shelter, and even privacy made the struggle against the Yankee invader much more tangible. Understanding the soldiers' suffering had become much easier for refugees still camped in the woods or sleeping in outbuildings.

The Federals' departure had not brought much relief to the people of Fredericksburg, nor had it even ended the looting. Although with less thoroughness and alacrity, Confederate soldiers, too, snatched up provisions and souvenirs. One local resident feared that the Rebels would likely take whatever the Yankees had left behind. "It is as you know," a bank employee lamented, "the fate of war and I must submit without a murmur." Deserted buildings offered too many temptations. "The conduct of our soldiers is most disgraceful," another citizen admitted, "and yet we must be silent for fear of giving encouragement to the enemy. To the dwellers on the frontier, civil war is no pastime." Much of the nearby countryside had already been devastated, and a sensitive Georgia captain observed, "These people have felt the pang of War in every sence form or Shape."[2]

Many civilians had heard the sounds of battle, assisted the wounded, and even donated nails for making coffins. Over the next several weeks refugees would drift back into Fredericksburg, some with toddlers or babies only days

David English Henderson, The Return to Fredericksburg after the Battle
(Gettysburg National Military Park)

old. A Mississippi infantryman worried that these "pitiful" children would not enjoy "much of a Christmas celebration," and neither would their parents. Some families had lost nearly everything; others went hungry. The social order showed signs of collapse. Not only had many slaves run off to the Yankees, but the ability to rely on friends and neighbors seemed to be crumbling as fast as the ruined buildings. Genteel families once known for their beneficence no longer had much to share with the destitute.[3]

Refugees daring or desperate enough to return while the Yankees lurked across the river entered a world of destruction. The town's elite had lost everything from fancy French beds to valuable artwork, but ordinary people, too, found their furniture broken up and their crockery smashed. Even people fortunate enough to recover household goods and find new lodgings often could not meet the exorbitant living expenses.[4]

General Lee's "acute grief" for women "flying from the enemy" had been somewhat assuaged by "the faces of old and young . . . wreathed in smiles and glow[ing] with happiness at their sacrifices for the good of their country." Lee, more familiar with upper-class women who entertained dashing officers at candy stews, expected "a kind Providence" to protect these noble people. Other soldiers met less-idealized specimens, poor mothers looking for lost children or begging for food.[5] Angry excoriations of the Yankees would not succor the destitute, whose ideas about patriotic sacrifice (or even divine protection) had been radically altered.

Their plight, however, also elicited a more practical response. After the battle Confederate regiments and brigades took up collections. Typically officers chipped in about $10 apiece, and privates, despite their low pay, gave an extremely generous dollar or two. Generals and even a few enlisted men gave $100 or more. Regiments generally raised around $500; some brigades, over $2,000. One of Jackson's staff officers claimed that $30,000 in donations had reached corps headquarters.[6] The soldiers appeared to be cheerful givers, and newspapers heralded their selfless devotion to suffering women and children.[7]

Helping the Fredericksburg refugees became a test of patriotic fervor for southern civilians as well. Beginning in Virginia, then spreading south and west as far as Mobile, local aid associations began raising money for what a Georgian described as "people rendered homeless by the Northern vandals." Anti-Yankee invective spiced pleas for generosity from people living in communities as yet untouched by the invaders. Women from ladies' relief groups fanned out from church meetings into the towns and countryside; some went door-to-door soliciting neighbors and friends.[8]

The combined donations from civilians, soldiers, and even city councils reached an impressive $170,000. Individuals and churches sent flour, bacon, and other provisions to hungry families near Hamilton's Crossing. Newspapers printed lists of contributions; 50 cents became the Confederate equivalent of the scriptural widow's mite. Slaves in the Army of Northern Virginia reportedly made generous, voluntary donations to the cause. "There's an item for the Northern freedom shriekers," a newspaper correspondent smugly remarked.[9]

But the imposing amounts raised hardly dented the overwhelming need. Throughout late January and February applications for assistance poured into Mayor Slaughter's office. One woman whose family had already received $100 in public money had not yet been able to replace all the groceries that had been stolen or spoiled. There were still mothers whose children had little clothing left and were nearly barefoot. Even refugees who had not yet returned to Fredericksburg begged the mayor for money to meet the skyrocketing costs of room and board. By March, Slaughter was again appealing for contributions. He praised the uncomplaining people of Fredericksburg, who had suffered heavy losses and remained steadfast in the southern cause.[10]

Slaughter exaggerated both the virtue and the unity of his community, yet the town's citizens had, in fact, paid a high price for loyalty—a price they would pay throughout the war years and beyond. Periodic threats from Yankee armies kept refugees from returning, and as late as October 1864 there were no more than 600 to 800 people in Fredericksburg. Signs of destruction remained after Appomattox. The Lacy House that had served as Sumner's headquarters stood deserted, its windows smashed, rooms filled with rubbish, and the names of Yankee soldiers scrawled on the walls. Visitors still noticed artillery damage in several town buildings. Eventually fields and orchards would cover up battle scars, but the stone wall still stood as a mute, austere reminder of almost unimaginable carnage. Local residents loved recounting how the Yankees had been beaten back time after time on that long-remembered December day, a signal victory in a disastrous war. By the 1870s, physical signs of the fighting had largely disappeared, but atop Marye's Heights stood a national cemetery, the ironic, final resting place for many Federal soldiers who had fruitlessly tried to reach that ground during the battle.[11]

★ ★ ★

Union soldiers understood how the destruction of Fredericksburg had made some Confederates fight all that much harder. For these men connections between the ordinary rhythms of daily existence and a willingness to risk one's life had always been at the heart of soldiering. Like all great battles, Fredericksburg had brought together the ordinary and the extraordinary. The common elements of material existence—food, clothing, and shelter—had shaped and, in turn, been shaped by the higher ideals of the flag, the Union, and freedom as well as more basic loyalties to a company or that friend standing next to you in the battle line. Human beings experience the ephemeral and the enduring simultaneously, which is why military campaigns involve much more than strategy, tactics, or horrific combat. Soldiers are more than fighters, and civilians are more than citizens. Bodies, minds, spirits: all become part of the story of war. This war in particular involved both revolutionary upheaval and the very human efforts of ordinary people somehow to hang on to the comforting and familiar even as the foundations of their lives appeared to be cracking and giving way. That cemetery on Marye's Heights, of course, literally marked the end of the story for so many young Americans.

In quite different ways the Confederate refugees and the rows of graves (mostly for unidentified soldiers) epitomized the suffering that had become synonymous with the word "Fredericksburg." But they could hardly encompass the lasting anguish the battle had spawned. Soldiers fortunate enough to survive serious wounds usually endured painfully slow and uncertain recoveries. After having his left leg amputated, in April 1863 Sgt. George Zuelch of the 7th New York still languished in a Washington hospital suffering pain, fever, and nausea. He would not be discharged for yet another thirteen months.[12]

But at least Zuelch's wound finally healed. Pvt. Andrew Cole of the 145th Pennsylvania had beaten the odds to survive removal of bone fragments from a skull wound (trephining). He was mustered out of service in December 1863; but in February 1864 the wound was still "open and discharging," and in all likelihood more bone would have to be removed. For other soldiers, too, old wounds remained swollen, saved limbs were useless, and pain was chronic.[13] After being shuffled from hospital to hospital and finally sent home, many veterans were left permanently, sometimes completely, disabled. A New Hampshire volunteer whose wound no longer troubled him eventually succumbed to the diarrhea contracted in camp. A Vermonter in the Sixth Corps who had been hit in the intestines and bladder managed to get along with a "urinary fistula" and "artificial anus," yet he died at age twenty-five only six years after he left the army.[14]

For such men the anguish of the battlefield had never gone away. The screams of the wounded echoed in their own cries of pain. The blood lust of combat, a raging, almost blind fury that often had little or nothing to do with causes or comrades, had produced horrific injuries. It might take years to repair the damage even partially. Some veterans endured several postwar surgeries, often because of hasty or botched amputations. A Pennsylvania private who lost a big toe to gangrene had to face another amputation in 1867 and still another the following year. He ended up losing two-thirds of his right leg. On three occasions between 1872 and 1874 a doctor examined an ex-private from the 7th Michigan who had undergone an amputation at the right ankle joint. Since the ends of the bones sometimes painfully extruded and discharges from the stump persisted, he recommended an amputation at the knee, though the records are silent on whether the hapless sufferer agreed to go under the knife again. But even saving a leg might also mean losing it, or worse. A New York corporal in Caldwell's brigade had been hit in the right femur during the skirmishing of December 14. A surgeon removed the ball, but the fractured limb was badly deformed. Bone fragments were extracted several times, and in June 1865 an amputation was performed at a New York hospital. After apparently improving, the man died in early October. Complications from amputations, abscesses, and pain dogged veterans' lives long after the war.[15]

Orators, poets, and writers of monument inscriptions eulogized the dead of Fredericksburg but ignored the badly wounded survivors for whom the battle remained a daily, tormenting memory for the rest of their lives.[16] Young people would later recall seeing the aging veterans marching in parades, living reminders of that glorious and terrible war; the private agonies of helpless fellows dependent on families or institutions seldom came into public view.

★   ★   ★

In many ways Fredericksburg had woven together the mundane, the horrific, and the transcendent. Everyday matters such as shelter, clothing, food, pay, and letters had loomed larger for the common soldiers than campaigns or strategies. Yet generals' plans along with privates' fears and junior officers' ambitions had influenced the pace and texture of military life. Bloody combat occurred in the context of family news, politics, ideology, religion, and rumor. It tore at emotions, often undermining or solidifying faith in leadership and the respective causes.[17] The approach of winter, dampness, smoke, rain, and mud had shown how a campaign encompassed much more than lines on a map, shifting batteries, or advancing brigades. Everything from shoe shortages to supply foul-ups to cavalry raids added to the miseries and anxieties of soldiers in the field.

The military significance of the battle loomed enormous at the time but has since been overshadowed by engagements such as Chancellorsville, Gettysburg, and the Wilderness. Yet because it was fought between the fall elections and the final Emancipation Proclamation, Fredericksburg exemplified Clausewitz's famous dictum about the connection between warfare and politics. The replacement of McClellan the political lightning rod with Burnside the political innocent had clearly reflected Lincoln's frustrations with generals who offered unsolicited policy advice without winning victories.

Burnside's initially rapid advance, however, had been foiled by poor planning in Washington, the pontoon delays, and his own unrealistic assumptions. As an army commander Burnside often lacked the flexibility to change either his strategy or his tactics in the face of new information or enemy movements. Both the location and the timing of the river crossing, after several delays, proved anew that coordination of movements and accurate intelligence had become crucial in maneuvering large armies—principles further illustrated by the reassembling of Lee's forces along with skillful defensive preparations on the Confederate left and the flawed alignments on the Confederate right. Given the natural strengths of the Rebel positions, however, Lee clearly had a lot more margin for error than Burnside.

Indeed, in hindsight it appears that the Federals could hardly have selected a worse place to fight, and any gains they might have achieved would have been short lived and costly. Yet the fighting had proved indecisive. As was typical of Civil War battles, the victors could not follow up their success. Staggering losses and a terrible defeat for the Federals yielded only modest gains for the Confederates. Longstreet may well have learned about the advantages of the tactical defensive, and Federal generals would certainly become more reluctant to order frontal assaults against well-entrenched troops; but whether such "lessons" would be effectively applied to the advantage of either side remained much in doubt. Few, if any, generals could effectively move and maneuver forces as large as the armies at Fredericksburg. A truly decisive victory would have required nearly flawless coordination and execution, but inadequate staff work, cumbersome command structures, and the chronic shortage of capable corps, division, and brigade commanders all meant that by the spring of 1863, it appeared that neither side could win the war on the battlefield—at least in the eastern theater. The battle of Fredericksburg marked the continuation of a military stalemate, an already well established pattern that greatly discouraged Lincoln and the northern public just as it satisfied but also frustrated the Confederate leadership.[18] In that sense the bloody battle whose results created powerful political reverberations was almost strategically insignificant.

The memories of Fredericksburg, however, would naturally focus on the extraordinary, the spectacular, and the terrible. The attempts to lay the pontoons in the heavy fog, the stout Confederate resistance, the deafening artillery bombardment, the hazardous crossing of the first Federal troops, the sharp street fighting, and the sack of the town had become striking features of the campaign before most of the troops on either side were even engaged. The tactical complexities of Franklin's attack and Jackson's counterattack were overshadowed by the repeated and senseless charges by Sumner's and Hooker's men toward the stone wall. The deadly Confederate artillery and withering infantry fire would not be soon forgotten by Yank or Reb.

Nor could anyone ignore the tenacity and futility of the attacks. Burnside's well-executed withdrawal from Fredericksburg could not for a moment atone for the bloodletting that came to define the battle in many people's minds. Staggering casualties, hasty burials, numerous amputations, and a painful struggle to find meaning in seemingly vain sacrifices all cast long shadows over the Federal camps, though even the victorious Confederates had to contemplate the high costs of war. From the hospital tents in Falmouth and the wards in Richmond and Washington rose the stench of blood, sweat, piss, and death. Depressing news reverberated throughout both "nations," back and forth between camp and home, and sent shock waves that echoed in Europe. The triumphant Rebels flirted with overconfidence even as the whipped Federals indulged in seemingly endless rounds of recrimination. On a more abstract level, both sides staked out a variety of positions on such burning issues as slavery and freedom, but for the soldiers, especially for the bluecoats, the realities of cold, disease, desertion, and mud often obscured these larger questions. Yet the most tangible and persistent kinds of suffering, including memories of slaughter and sacrifice, and even the agonies of the Mud March, could not overwhelm human resilience.

Some men still found strength in their religious faith, others in fighting for their families or even for a cause, though for many veterans in both armies Fredericksburg came to symbolize a raw courage that the home folks could never quite understand. Soldiers knew that bravery—displayed for all to see in the word "Fredericksburg" soon to be emblazoned on regimental flags—exacted a terrible price, and that despite all the grumbling, disillusionment, disaffection, and even desertion, many had, however reluctantly, paid the price. At the dedication of a monument to Humphreys's division in the National Cemetery at Fredericksburg on November 11, 1908, editor and political wheelhorse Alexander K. McClure compared the valor of his fellow Pennsylvanians to the courage of Pickett's men at Gettysburg. Sectional reconciliation had become a major theme on such occasions, and as a noncombatant McClure hardly carried the moral authority to describe much less assess what these men had endured. But by this time many old soldiers themselves had noted the obvious parallels between the two engagements. Humphreys's men had long been convinced that their gallantry had been unequaled during the war, but when they shook hands with some of Pickett's veterans, a former private in the 129th Pennsylvania decided that "although these two divisions failed in what they undertook they showed the stuff of which the American soldier is made."[19]

Several former bluecoats believed their bravery superior because they had made more assaults. They also liked to quote Lee, who after the war had supposedly praised the intrepid spirit of the Irish Brigade and other Union outfits at Fredericksburg.[20] Even on that hot July 3 in Pennsylvania, some Confederates recognized that they had experienced their own "Fredericksburg"—a word that evoked images of desperate and futile struggle. Over the years some ex-Rebels conceded that Federal attacks at Fredericksburg had set a standard for valor and persistence that even Pickett's charge had not matched.[21] Such claims rested on glittering and surprisingly blood-less generalities. In their recollections, the details of the physical anguish, political turmoil, factious backbiting, and spiritual doubts were obscured. But then the aging survivors likely had a perspective different from that of the young men in both armies who had stood their ground, faltered occa-sionally, cursed their fate, called on God to save them, and finally fallen on that harrowing thirteenth of December.

Order of Battle

ARMY OF THE POTOMAC
Maj. Gen. Ambrose E. Burnside

Right Grand Division
Maj. Gen. Edwin V. Sumner

SECOND ARMY CORPS
Maj. Gen. Darius N. Couch

FIRST DIVISION
Brig. Gen. Winfield S. Hancock

SECOND DIVISION
Brig. Gen. Oliver O. Howard

First Brigade
    Brig. Gen. John C. Caldwell
    Col. George W. Von Schack
    5th New Hampshire
    7th New York
    61st New York
    64th New York
    81st Pennsylvania
    145th Pennsylvania
Second Brigade
    Brig. Gen. Thomas F. Meagher
    28th Massachusetts
    63rd New York
    69th New York
    88th New York
    116th Pennsylvania
Third Brigade
    Col. Samuel K. Zook
    27th Connecticut
    2nd Delaware
    52nd New York
    57th New York
    66th New York
    53rd Pennsylvania
Artillery
    1st New York Light, Battery B
    4th U.S., Battery C

First Brigade
    Brig. Gen. Alfred Sully
    19th Maine
    15th Massachusetts
    Massachusetts Sharpshooters, 1st
        Company
    1st Minnesota
    Minnesota Sharpshooters, 2nd
        Company
    34th New York
    82nd New York (2nd Militia)
Second Brigade
    Col. Joshua T. Owen
    69th Pennsylvania
    71st Pennsylvania
    72nd Pennsylvania
    106th Pennsylvania
Third Brigade
    Col. Norman J. Hall
    Col. William R. Lee
    19th Massachusetts
    20th Massachusetts
    7th Michigan
    42nd New York
    59th New York
    127th Pennsylvania
Artillery
    1st Rhode Island Light, Batteries A
        and B

THIRD DIVISION
Brig. Gen. William H. French

First Brigade
  Brig. Gen. Nathan Kimball
  Col. John S. Mason
  14th Indiana
  24th New Jersey
  28th New Jersey
  4th Ohio
  8th Ohio
  7th West Virginia
Second Brigade
  Col. Oliver H. Palmer
  14th Connecticut
  108th New York
  130th Pennsylvania

Third Brigade
  Col. John W. Andrews
  Lt. Col. William Jameson
  Lt. Col. John W. Marshal
  1st Delaware
  4th New York
  10th New York
  132nd Pennsylvania
Artillery
  1st New York Light, Battery G
  1st Rhode Island Light, Battery G
Artillery Reserve
  Capt. Charles H. Morgan
  1st U.S., Battery I
  4th U.S., Battery A

NINTH ARMY CORPS
Brig. Gen. Orlando B. Willcox

FIRST DIVISION
Brig. Gen. William W. Burns

First Brigade
  Col. Orlando M. Poe
  2nd Michigan
  17th Michigan
  20th Michigan
  79th New York
Second Brigade
  Col. Benjamin C. Christ
  29th Massachusetts
  8th Michigan
  27th New Jersey
  46th New York
  50th Pennsylvania
Third Brigade
  Col. Daniel Leasure
  36th Massachusetts
  45th Pennsylvania
  100th Pennsylvania
Artillery
  1st New York Light, Battery D
  3rd U.S., Batteries L and M

SECOND DIVISION
Brig. Gen. Samuel D. Sturgis

First Brigade
  Brig. Gen. James Nagle
  2nd Maryland
  6th New Hampshire
  9th New Hampshire
  48th Pennsylvania
  7th Rhode Island
  12th Rhode Island
Second Brigade
  Brig. Gen. Edward Ferrero
  21st Massachusetts
  35th Massachusetts
  11th New Hampshire
  51st New York
  51st Pennsylvania
Artillery
  2nd New York Light, Battery L
  Pennsylvania Light, Battery D
  1st Rhode Island Light, Battery D
  4th U.S., Battery E

THIRD DIVISION
Brig. Gen. George W. Getty

First Brigade
Col. Rush C. Hawkins
10th New Hampshire
13th New Hampshire
25th New Jersey
9th New York
89th New York
103rd New York
Second Brigade
Col. Edward Harland
8th Connecticut
11th Connecticut
15th Connecticut
16th Connecticut
21st Connecticut
4th Rhode Island

Artillery
2nd U.S., Battery E
5th U.S., Battery A

CAVALRY DIVISION
Brig. Gen. Alfred Pleasonton

First Brigade
Brig. Gen. John F. Farnsworth
8th Illinois
3rd Indiana
8th New York
Second Brigade
Col. David McM. Gregg
Col. Thomas C. Devin
6th New York
8th Pennsylvania
6th U.S.
Artillery
2nd U.S., Battery M

Center Grand Division
Maj. Gen. Joseph Hooker

THIRD ARMY CORPS
Brig. Gen. George Stoneman

FIRST DIVISION
Brig. Gen. David B. Birney

First Brigade
Brig. Gen. John C. Robinson
20th Indiana
63rd Pennsylvania
68th Pennsylvania
105th Pennsylvania
114th Pennsylvania
141st Pennsylvania
Second Brigade
Brig. Gen. J. H. Hobart Ward
3rd Maine
4th Maine
38th New York
40th New York
55th New York

57th Pennsylvania
99th Pennsylvania
Third Brigade
Brig. Gen. Hiram G. Berry
17th Maine
3rd Michigan
5th Michigan
1st New York
37th New York
101st New York
Artillery
Capt. George E. Randolph
1st Rhode Island Light, Battery E
3rd U.S., Batteries F and K

SECOND DIVISION
Brig. Gen. Daniel E. Sickles

First Brigade
  Brig. Gen. Joseph B. Carr
  1st Massachusetts
  11th Massachusetts
  16th Massachusetts
  2nd New Hampshire
  11th New Jersey
  26th Pennsylvania
Second Brigade
  Col. George B. Hall
  70th New York
  71st New York
  72nd New York
  73rd New York
  74th New York
  120th New York
Third Brigade
  Brig. Gen. Joseph W. Revere
  5th New Jersey
  6th New Jersey
  7th New Jersey
  8th New Jersey
  2nd New York
  115th Pennsylvania
Artillery
  Capt. James E. Smith

New Jersey Light, 2nd Battery
New York Light, 4th Battery
1st U.S., Battery H
4th U.S., Battery K

THIRD DIVISION
Brig. Gen. Amiel W. Whipple

First Brigade
  Brig. Gen. A. Sanders Piatt
  Col. Emien Franklin
  86th New York
  124th New York
  122nd Pennsylvania
Second Brigade
  Col. Samuel S. Carroll
  12th New Hampshire
  163rd New York
  84th Pennsylvania
  110th Pennsylvania
Artillery
  New York Light, 10th and 11th
    Batteries
  1st Ohio Light, Battery H

FIFTH ARMY CORPS
Brig. Gen. Daniel Butterfield

FIRST DIVISION
Brig. Gen. Charles Griffin

First Brigade
  Col. James Barnes
  2nd Maine
  18th Massachusetts
  22nd Massachusetts
  Massachusetts Sharpshooters, 2nd
    Company
  1st Michigan
  13th New York
  25th New York
  118th Pennsylvania

Second Brigade
  Col. Jacob B. Sweitzer
  9th Massachusetts
  32nd Massachusetts
  4th Michigan
  14th New York
  62nd Pennsylvania
Third Brigade
  Col. T. B. W. Stockton
  20th Maine
  16th Michigan
  Michigan Sharpshooters, Brady's
    company
  12th New York

17th New York
44th New York
83rd Pennsylvania
Artillery
Massachusetts Light, 3rd and 5th
Batteries (C and E)
1st Rhode Island Light, Battery C
5th U.S., Battery D
Sharpshooters
1st U.S.

SECOND DIVISION
Brig. Gen. George Sykes

First Brigade
Lt. Col. Robert C. Buchanan
3rd U.S.
4th U.S.
12th U.S., 1st Battalion
12th U.S., 2nd Battalion
14th U.S., 1st Battalion
14th U.S., 2nd Battalion
Second Brigade
Maj. George L. Andrews
Maj. Charles S. Lovell
1st and 2nd U.S. (battalion)
6th U.S.
7th U.S. (battalion)
10th U.S.
11th U.S.
17th and 19th U.S. (battalion)
Third Brigade
Brig. Gen. Gouverneur K. Warren

5th New York
140th New York
146th New York
Artillery
1st Ohio Light, Battery L
5th U.S., Battery I

THIRD DIVISION
Brig. Gen. Andrew A. Humphreys

First Brigade
Brig. Gen. Erastus B. Tyler
91st Pennsylvania
126th Pennsylvania
129th Pennsylvania
134th Pennsylvania
Second Brigade
Col. Peter H. Allabach
123rd Pennsylvania
131st Pennsylvania
133rd Pennsylvania
155th Pennsylvania
Artillery
1st New York Light, Battery C
1st U.S., Batteries E and G
Cavalry Brigade
Brig. Gen. William W. Averell
1st Massachusetts
3rd Pennsylvania
4th Pennsylvania
5th U.S.
Artillery
2nd U.S., Batteries B and L

Left Grand Division
Maj. Gen. William B. Franklin

FIRST ARMY CORPS
Maj. Gen. John F. Reynolds

FIRST DIVISION
Brig. Gen. Abner Doubleday

First Brigade
Col. Walter Phelps Jr.

22nd New York
24th New York
30th New York
84th New York (14th Militia)
2nd U.S. Sharpshooters

Second Brigade
    Col. James Gavin
    7th Indiana
    76th New York
    95th New York
    56th Pennsylvania
Third Brigade
    Col. William F. Rogers
    21st New York
    23rd New York
    35th New York
    80th New York (20th Militia)
Fourth Brigade
    Brig. Gen. Solomon Meredith
    Col. Lysander Cutler
    19th Indiana
    24th Michigan
    2nd Wisconsin
    6th Wisconsin
    7th Wisconsin
Artillery
    New Hampshire Light, 1st Battery
    1st New York Light, Battery L
    4th U.S., Battery B

SECOND DIVISION
Brig. Gen. John Gibbon
Brig. Gen. Nelson Taylor

First Brigade
    Col. Adrian R. Root
    16th Maine
    94th New York
    104th New York
    105th New York
    107th Pennsylvania
Second Brigade
    Col. Peter Lyle
    12th Massachusetts
    26th New York
    90th Pennsylvania
    136th Pennsylvania
Third Brigade
    Brig. Gen. Nelson Taylor

    Col. Samuel H. Leonard
    13th Massachusetts
    83rd New York (9th Militia)
    97th New York
    11th Pennsylvania
    88th Pennsylvania
Artillery
    Maine Light, 2nd and 5th Batteries
    Pennsylvania Light, Battery C
    1st Pennsylvania Light, Battery F

THIRD DIVISION
Maj. Gen. George G. Meade

First Brigade
    Col. William Sinclair
    Col. William McCandless
    1st Pennsylvania Reserves
    2nd Pennsylvania Reserves
    6th Pennsylvania Reserves
    13th Pennsylvania Reserves (1st
      Rifles)
    121st Pennsylvania
Second Brigade
    Col. Albert L. Magilton
    3rd Pennsylvania Reserves
    4th Pennsylvania Reserves
    7th Pennsylvania Reserves
    8th Pennsylvania Reserves
    142nd Pennsylvania
Third Brigade
    Brig. Gen. C. Feger Jackson
    Col. Joseph W. Fisher
    Lt. Col. Robert Anderson
    5th Pennsylvania Reserves
    9th Pennsylvania Reserves
    10th Pennsylvania Reserves
    11th Pennsylvania Reserves
    12th Pennsylvania Reserves
Artillery
    1st Pennsylvania Light, Batteries A,
      B, and G
    5th U.S., Battery C

SIXTH ARMY CORPS
Maj. Gen. William F. Smith

FIRST DIVISION
Brig. Gen. William T. H. Brooks

First Brigade
    Col. Alfred T. A. Torbert
    1st New Jersey
    2nd New Jersey
    3rd New Jersey
    4th New Jersey
    15th New Jersey
    23rd New Jersey
Second Brigade
    Col. Henry T. Cake
    5th Maine
    16th New York
    27th New York
    121st New York
    96th Pennsylvania
Third Brigade
    Brig. Gen. David A. Russell
    18th New York
    31st New York
    32nd New York
    95th Pennsylvania
Artillery
    Maryland Light, Battery A
    Massachusetts Light, 1st
        Battery (A)
    New Jersey Light, 1st Battery
    2nd U.S., Battery D

SECOND DIVISION
Brig. Gen. Albion P. Howe

First Brigade
    Brig. Gen. Calvin E. Pratt
    6th Maine
    43rd New York
    49th Pennsylvania
    119th Pennsylvania
    5th Wisconsin

Second Brigade
    Col. Henry Whiting
    26th New Jersey
    2nd Vermont
    3rd Vermont
    4th Vermont
    5th Vermont
    6th Vermont
Third Brigade
    Brig. Gen. Francis L. Vinton
    Col. Robert F. Taylor
    Brig. Gen. Thomas H. Neill
    21st New Jersey
    20th New York
    33rd New York
    49th New York
    77th New York
Artillery
    Maryland Light, Battery B
    New York Light, 1st and 3rd
        Batteries
    5th U.S., Battery F

THIRD DIVISION
Brig. Gen. John Newton

First Brigade
    Brig. Gen. John Cochrane
    65th New York
    67th New York
    122nd New York
    23rd Pennsylvania
    61st Pennsylvania
    82nd Pennsylvania
Second Brigade
    Brig. Gen. Charles Devens Jr.
    7th Massachusetts
    10th Massachusetts
    37th Massachusetts
    36th New York
    2nd Rhode Island

Third Brigade
    Col. Thomas A. Rowley
    Brig. Gen. Frank Wheaton
    62nd New York
    93rd Pennsylvania
    98th Pennsylvania
    102nd Pennsylvania
    139th Pennsylvania
Artillery
    1st Pennsylvania Light, Batteries C
      and D
    2nd U.S., Battery G
Cavalry Brigade
    Brig. Gen. George D. Bayard
    Col. David McM. Gregg
    District of Columbia, Independent
      Company
    1st Maine
    1st New Jersey
    2nd New York
    10th New York
    1st Pennsylvania
Artillery
    3rd U.S., Battery C

Volunteer Engineer Brigade
    Brig. Gen. Daniel P. Woodbury
    15th New York
    50th New York
Battalion U.S. Engineers
    Lt. Charles E. Cross
Artillery
    Brig. Gen. Henry J. Hunt
Artillery Reserve
    Lt. Col. William Hays
    32nd Massachusetts Infantry,
      Company C
    New York Light, 5th Battery
    1st Battalion New York Light,
      Batteries A, B, C, and D
    1st U.S., Battery K
    2nd U.S., Battery A
    4th U.S., Battery G
    5th U.S., Battery K
Unattached Artillery
    Maj. Thomas S. Trumbull
    1st Connecticut Heavy, Batteries B
      and M

ARMY OF NORTHERN VIRGINIA
Gen. Robert E. Lee

FIRST CORPS
Lt. Gen. James Longstreet

MCLAWS'S DIVISION
Maj. Gen. Lafayette McLaws

Kershaw's Brigade
    Brig. Gen. Joseph B. Kershaw
    2nd South Carolina
    3rd South Carolina
    7th South Carolina
    8th South Carolina
    15th South Carolina
    3rd South Carolina Battalion
Barksdale's Brigade
    Brig. Gen. William Barksdale

    13th Mississippi
    17th Mississippi
    18th Mississippi
    21st Mississippi
Cobb's Brigade
    Brig. Gen. T. R. R. Cobb
    Col. Robert McMillan
    16th Georgia
    18th Georgia
    24th Georgia
    Cobb Legion
    Phillips's Legion

Semmes's Brigade
  Brig. Gen. Paul J. Semmes
  10th Georgia
  50th Georgia
  51st Georgia
  53rd Georgia
Artillery
  Col. H. C. Cabell
  Manly's (North Carolina) Battery
  Read's (Georgia) Battery
  Richmond Howitzers (1st)
    McCarthy's Battery
  Troup (Georgia) Artillery

ANDERSON'S DIVISION
Maj. Gen. Richard H. Anderson

Wilcox's Brigade
  Brig. Gen. Cadmus M. Wilcox
  8th Alabama
  9th Alabama
  10th Alabama
  11th Alabama
  14th Alabama
Mahone's Brigade
  Brig. Gen. William Mahone
  6th Virginia
  12th Virginia
  16th Virginia
  41st Virginia
  61st Virginia
Featherston's Brigade
  Brig. Gen. W. S. Featherston
  12th Mississippi
  16th Mississippi
  19th Mississippi
  48th Mississippi (5 companies)
Wright's Brigade
  Brig. Gen. A. R. Wright
  3rd Georgia
  22nd Georgia
  48th Georgia
  2nd Georgia Battalion
Perry's Brigade
  Brig. Gen. E. A. Perry

  2nd Florida
  5th Florida
  8th Florida
Artillery
  Donaldsonville (Louisiana)
    Artillery
  Huger's (Virginia) Battery
  Lewis's (Virginia) Battery
  Norfolk (Virginia) Light Artillery
    Blues

PICKETT'S DIVISION
Maj. Gen. George E. Pickett

Garnett's Brigade
  Brig. Gen. Richard B. Garnett
  8th Virginia
  18th Virginia
  19th Virginia
  28th Virginia
  56th Virginia
Armistead's Brigade
  Brig. Gen. Lewis A. Armistead
  9th Virginia
  14th Virginia
  38th Virginia
  53rd Virginia
  57th Virginia
Kemper's Brigade
  Brig. Gen. James L. Kemper
  1st Virginia
  3rd Virginia
  7th Virginia
  11th Virginia
  24th Virginia
Jenkins's Brigade
  Brig. Gen. M. Jenkins
  1st South Carolina (Hagood's)
  2nd South Carolina (Rifles)
  5th South Carolina
  6th South Carolina
  Hampton Legion
  Palmetto Sharpshooters
Corse's Brigade
  Brig. Gen. Montgomery D. Corse

15th Virginia
17th Virginia
30th Virginia
32nd Virginia
Artillery
Dearing's (Virginia) Battery
Fauquier (Virginia) Artillery
Richmond (Fayette) Artillery

HOOD'S DIVISION
Maj. Gen. John B. Hood

Law's Brigade
Brig. Gen. E. M. Law
4th Alabama
44th Alabama
6th North Carolina
54th North Carolina
57th North Carolina
Robertson's Brigade
Brig. Gen. J. B. Robertson
3rd Arkansas
1st Texas
4th Texas
5th Texas
Anderson's Brigade
Brig. Gen. George T. Anderson
1st Georgia (Regulars)
7th Georgia
8th Georgia
9th Georgia
11th Georgia
Toombs's Brigade
Col. H. L. Benning
2nd Georgia
15th Georgia
17th Georgia
20th Georgia
Artillery
German (South Carolina) Artillery

Palmetto (South Carolina) Light
Artillery
Rowan (North Carolina) Artillery

RANSOM'S DIVISION
Brig. Gen. Robert Ransom Jr.

Ransom's Brigade
Brig. Gen. Robert Ransom Jr.
24th North Carolina
25th North Carolina
35th North Carolina
49th North Carolina
Branch's (Virginia) Battery
Cooke's Brigade
Brig. Gen. J. R. Cooke
Col. E. D. Hall
15th North Carolina
27th North Carolina
46th North Carolina
48th North Carolina
Cooper's (Virginia) Battery
First Corps Artillery
Washington (Louisiana) Artillery
Col. J. B. Walton
1st Company
2nd Company
3rd Company
4th Company
Alexander's Battalion
Lt. Col. E. Porter Alexander
Bedford (Virginia) Artillery
Eubank's (Virginia) Battery
Madison Light Artillery
(Louisiana)
Parker's (Virginia) Battery
Rhett's (South Carolina) Battery
Woolfolk's (Virginia) Battery

Lt. Gen. Thomas J. Jackson

D. H. HILL'S DIVISION
Maj. Gen. Daniel H. Hill

First Brigade
  Brig. Gen. R. E. Rodes
  3rd Alabama
  5th Alabama
  6th Alabama
  12th Alabama
  26th Alabama
Second (Ripley's) Brigade
  Brig. Gen. George Doles
  4th Georgia
  44th Georgia
  1st North Carolina
  3rd North Carolina
Third Brigade
  Brig. Gen. A. H. Colquitt
  13th Alabama
  6th Georgia
  23rd Georgia
  27th Georgia
  28th Georgia
Fourth Brigade
  Brig. Gen. Alfred Iverson
  5th North Carolina
  12th North Carolina
  20th North Carolina
  23rd North Carolina
Fifth (Ramseur's) Brigade
  Col. Bryan Grimes
  2nd North Carolina
  4th North Carolina
  14th North Carolina
  30th North Carolina
Artillery
  Maj. H. P. Jones
  Hardaway's (Alabama) Battery
  Jeff Davis (Alabama) Artillery
  King William (Virginia) Artillery
  Morris (Virginia) Artillery
  Orange (Virginia) Artillery

A. P. HILL'S DIVISION
Maj. Gen. Ambrose P. Hill

First (Field's) Brigade
  Col. J. M. Brockenbrough
  40th Virginia
  47th Virginia
  55th Virginia
  22nd Virginia Battalion
Second Brigade
  Brig. Gen. Maxcy Gregg
  Col. D. H. Hamilton
  1st South Carolina
  1st South Carolina Rifles
  12th South Carolina
  13th South Carolina
  14th South Carolina
Third Brigade
  Brig. Gen. E. L. Thomas
  14th Georgia
  35th Georgia
  45th Georgia
  49th Georgia
Fourth Brigade
  Brig. Gen. J. H. Lane
  7th North Carolina
  18th North Carolina
  28th North Carolina
  33rd North Carolina
  37th North Carolina
Fifth Brigade
  Brig. Gen. J. J. Archer
  5th Alabama Battalion
  19th Georgia
  1st Tennessee
  7th Tennessee
  14th Tennessee
Sixth Brigade
  Brig. Gen. William D. Pender
  Col. A. M. Scales
  13th North Carolina
  16th North Carolina

22nd North Carolina
34th North Carolina
38th North Carolina
Artillery
  Lt. Col. R. L. Walker
  Branch (North Carolina) Artillery
  Crenshaw (Virginia) Battery
  Fredericksburg (Virginia) Artillery
  Johnson's (Virginia) Battery
  Letcher (Virginia) Artillery
  Pee Dee (South Carolina) Artillery
  Purcell (Virginia) Artillery

EWELL'S DIVISION
Brig. Gen. Jubal A. Early

Lawton's Brigade
  Col. E. N. Atkinson
  Col. C. A. Evans
  13th Georgia
  26th Georgia
  31st Georgia
  38th Georgia
  60th Georgia
  61st Georgia
Trimble's Brigade
  Col. R. F. Hoke
  15th Alabama
  12th Georgia
  21st Georgia
  21st North Carolina
  1st North Carolina Battalion
Early's Brigade
  Col. J. A. Walker
  13th Virginia
  25th Virginia
  31st Virginia
  44th Virginia
  49th Virginia
  52nd Virginia
  58th Virginia
Hays's (First Louisiana) Brigade
  Brig. Gen. Harry T. Hays
  5th Louisiana

6th Louisiana
7th Louisiana
8th Louisiana
9th Louisiana
Artillery
  Capt. J. W. Latimer
  Chesapeake (Maryland) Artillery
  Charlottesville (Virginia) Artillery
  Courtney (Virginia) Artillery
  First Maryland Battery
  Louisiana Guard Artillery
  Staunton (Virginia) Artillery

JACKSON'S DIVISION
Brig. Gen. William B. Taliaferro

First Brigade
  Brig. Gen. E. F. Paxton
  2nd Virginia
  4th Virginia
  5th Virginia
  27th Virginia
  33rd Virginia
Second Brigade
  Brig. Gen. J. R. Jones
  21st Virginia
  42nd Virginia
  48th Virginia
  1st Virginia Battalion
Third (Taliaferro's) Brigade
  Col. E. T. H. Warren
  47th Alabama
  48th Alabama
  10th Virginia
  23rd Virginia
  37th Virginia
Fourth (Starke's) Brigade
  Col. Edmund Pendleton
  1st Louisiana (Volunteers)
  2nd Louisiana
  10th Louisiana
  14th Louisiana
  15th Louisiana
  Coppens's (Louisiana) Battalion

Artillery
Capt. J. B. Brockenbrough
Carpenter's (Virginia) Battery
Danville (Virginia) Artillery
Hampden (Virginia) Artillery
Lee (Virginia) Artillery
Lusk's (Virginia) Battery
Reserve Artillery
Brig. Gen. W. N. Pendleton
Brown's Battalion
Col. J. Thompson Brown
Brooke's (Virginia) Battery
Dance's Battery Powhatan Artillery
Hupp's Battery, Salem Artillery
Poague's (Virginia) Battery
Rockbridge Artillery
Smith's Battery, Third Howitzers
Watson's Battery, Second
Howitzers
Cutts's (Georgia) Battalion
Lane's Battery
Patterson's Battery
Ross's Battery
Nelson's Battalion
Maj. William Nelson
Kirkpatrick's (Virginia) Battery,
Amherst Artillery
Massie's (Virginia) Battery,
Fluvanna Artillery
Milledge's (Georgia) Battery
Miscellaneous Batteries
Ells's (Georgia) Battery

Nelson's (Virginia) Battery,
Hanover Artillery
Cavalry
Maj. Gen. James E. B. Stuart
First Brigade
Brig. Gen. Wade Hampton
1st North Carolina
1st South Carolina
2nd South Carolina
Cobb (Georgia) Legion
Phillips's (Georgia) Legion
Second Brigade
Brig. Gen. Fitzhugh Lee
1st Virginia
2nd Virginia
3rd Virginia
4th Virginia
5th Virginia
Third Brigade
Brig. Gen. W. H. F. Lee
2nd North Carolina
9th Virginia
10th Virginia
13th Virginia
15th Virginia
Artillery
Maj. John Pelham
Breathed's (Virginia) Battery
Chew's (Virginia) Battery
Hart's (South Carolina) Battery
Henry's (Virginia) Battery
Moorman's (Virginia) Battery

Notes

ABBREVIATIONS

B&L	Robert Underwood Johnson and Clarence Clough Buel, eds., *Battles and Leaders of the Civil War*. 4 vols. New York: Castle Books, 1956.
CCW	*Report of the Joint Committee on the Conduct of the War*. 3 pts. Washington, D.C.: Government Printing Office, 1865.
CHS	Connecticut Historical Society, Hartford
CL	University of Michigan, William L. Clements Library, Ann Arbor
CSL	Connecticut State Library, Hartford
CU	Cornell University, Department of Manuscripts and Archives, Ithaca, New York
CWMC	Civil War Miscellaneous Collection
CWTI	*Civil War Times Illustrated Collection*
DCL	Dartmouth College Library, Special Collections, Hanover, New Hampshire
Duke	Duke University, William R. Perkins Library, Durham, North Carolina
Emory	Emory University, Special Collections, Robert W. Woodruff Library, Atlanta, Georgia
FSNMP	Fredericksburg and Spotsylvania National Military Park, Fredericksburg, Virginia
GAR	Grand Army of the Republic Museum, 110th Pennsylvania Miscellaneous Letters, Philadelphia, Pennsylvania
GDAH	Georgia Department of Archives and History, Atlanta
GLC	Pierpont Morgan Library, Gilder Lehrman Collection, New York, New York
HCWRTC	Harrisburg Civil War Round Table Collection
HL	Henry E. Huntington Library, San Marino, California
HSP	Historical Society of Pennsylvania, Philadelphia
HU	Harvard University, Houghton Library, Cambridge, Massachusetts
IHS	Indiana Historical Society, Indianapolis
ISL	Indiana State Library, Indianapolis
IU	Indiana University, Lilly Library, Bloomington
LC	Library of Congress, Manuscripts Division, Washington, D.C.
LSU	Department of Archives and Manuscripts, Louisiana State University, Baton Rouge
MC	Museum of the Confederacy, Richmond, Virginia
MDAH	Mississippi Department of Archives and History, Jackson
MHC	University of Michigan, Bentley Library, Michigan Historical Collections, Ann Arbor
MHS	Massachusetts Historical Society, Boston
MOLLUS	Military Order of the Loyal Legion of the United States, Civil War Library and Museum, Philadelphia
MSH	Joseph K. Barnes, *The Medical and Surgical History of the Civil War*. 15 vols. Wilmington, N.C.: Broadfoot, 1990.
NA	National Archives, Washington, D.C.
NCDAH	North Carolina Division of Archives and History, Raleigh
NHHS	New Hampshire Historical Society, Concord
NHSL	New Hampshire State Library, Concord

NJHS	New Jersey Historical Society, Trenton
NYHS	New-York Historical Society, New York
NYPL	New York Public Library, New York
OHS	Ohio Historical Society, Columbus
OR	*War of the Rebellion: A Compilation of the Official Records of the Union and Confederate Armies.* 128 vols. Washington, D.C.: Government Printing Office, 1880–1901. All references are to series 1, volume 21, unless otherwise noted.
ORN	*Official Records of the Union and Confederate Navies in the War of the Rebellion.* 31 vols. Washington: Government Printing Office, 1894–1922.
OR Supplement	
	Supplement to the Official Records of the Union and Confederate Armies. 95 vols. Wilmington, N.C.: Broadfoot Publishing Company, 1994– .
RG	Record Group
RIHS	Rhode Island Historical Society, Providence
SCL	University of South Carolina, South Caroliniana Library, Columbia
SHC	University of North Carolina, Southern Historical Collection, Chapel Hill
SHSW	State Historical Society of Wisconsin, Madison
TSLA	Tennessee State Library and Archives, Nashville
UA	University of Alabama, William Stanley Hoole Special Collections Library, Tuscaloosa
UGa	University of Georgia, Special Collections, Athens
UR	University of Rochester, Rhees Library, Rochester, New York
USAMHI	United States Army Military History Institute, Carlisle Barracks, Pennsylvania
UT	University of Texas, Center for American History, Austin
UVa	University of Virginia, Alderman Library, Charlottesville
VHS	Virginia Historical Society, Richmond

PROLOGUE

1. Hirst, *Boys from Rockville,* 150.

2. *OR,* ser. 1, 27(1):445; Abbott, *Fallen Leaves,* 188. A captain in the 26th North Carolina drew the same historical parallel: "It was a second Fredericksburg affair, only the wrong way" (*OR,* ser. 1, 27[2]:645).

3. William F. Fox, *Regimental Losses,* 164, 182.

4. See the especially useful critique of typical battle studies in Keegan, *Face of Battle,* 27–40, 62, 65–73, though Keegan's brilliant book focuses almost exclusively on the battlefield itself.

5. For three excellent battle studies that not only perceptively analyze strategy and tactics but also pay considerable attention to the political context, see Castel, *Decision in the West;* Hennessy, *Return to Bull Run;* Sears, *Chancellorsville.*

CHAPTER ONE

1. Lincoln, *Collected Works,* 5:460–61. For useful accounts of McClellan after Antietam, see Sears, *McClellan,* 328–41; Warren W. Hassler Jr., *McClellan,* 310–13; Sears, *Landscape Turned Red,* 336–38.

2. George Brinton McClellan, *Civil War Papers,* 511, 512, 514, 516, 517, 518; *OR,* ser. 1, 19(2):549, 550–51, 51(1):937–38; James A. Ward, *That Man Haupt,* 140–41. Although McClellan often exaggerated and made excuses, supply problems had been apparent in the Army of the Potomac since Antietam, and they would persist for the rest of the year. See *New York Times,* November 2, 1862; Meade, *Life and Letters,* 1:329–30.

3. James R. Woodworth to Phoebe Woodworth, November 4, 1862, Woodworth Papers,

Hotchkiss Collection, CL; November 5, 1862, Jackson Diary, IHS. For helpful comments on the Civil War as high adventure, see Rose, *Victorian America and the Civil War,* 134–35; Sweet, *Traces of War,* 3–4.

4. Gibbon, *Recollections of the Civil War,* 94; Willard J. Templeton to his brother, November 8, 1862, Templeton Letters, NHSL; John T. Greene, *Ewing Family Letters,* 10, 24–25; Heffelfinger, "'Dear Sister Jennie,'" 214; Donaldson, *Inside the Army of the Potomac,* 158; James R. Woodworth to Phoebe Woodworth, November 7, 1862, Woodworth Papers, Hotchkiss Collection, CL; Wightman, *From Antietam to Fort Fisher,* 71.

5. Chamberlain, *Through Blood and Fire,* 31; Daniel M. Holt, *Surgeon's Civil War,* 40.

6. *Baltimore American and Commercial Advertiser,* November 4, 1862; *Boston Post,* November 7, 1862; *New York Herald,* November 4, 5, 1862; *New York Times,* November 5, 6, 1862; "Lee, Beauregard, and McClellan," *Harper's Weekly,* November 1, 1862, 690.

7. Helman, "Young Soldier in the Army of the Potomac," 148; November 7, 1862, Bailey Diary, NHHS; Thomas H. Parker, *History of the 51st,* 252–53; Willard J. Templeton to his brother, November 8, 1862, Templeton Letters, NHSL; Daniel M. Holt, *Surgeon's Civil War,* 42–43.

8. Helman, "Young Soldier in the Army of the Potomac," 149; S. Millett Thompson, *Thirteenth New Hampshire,* 22; November 7, 1862, Willard Diary, NHSL; Elisha Hunt Rhodes, *All for the Union,* 87. For a detailed summary of troop movements, see George Brinton McClellan, *McClellan's Own Story,* 645–47.

9. November 8, 1862, Willard Diary, NHSL; R. S. Robertson to his parents, November 7, 1862, Robertson Papers, FSNMP; Robert S. Robertson, "Diary of the War," 66; Wightman, *From Antietam to Fort Fisher,* 74.

10. Billings, *Hard Tack and Coffee,* 52–53; George H. Allen, *Forty-Six Months,* 149; Bruce Sutherland, "Pittsburgh Volunteers," 245; John Ripley Adams, *Memorials and Letters,* 71.

11. James B. Post to his wife, November 8, 1862, Post Papers, CWMC, USAMHI; John Ripley Adams, *Memorials and Letters,* 70; Reichardt, *Diary of Battery A,* 71; Edwin O. Wentworth to his wife, November 8, 1862, Wentworth Papers, LC; Helman, "Young Soldier in the Army of the Potomac," 148–49; Brewster, *When This Cruel War Is Over,* 187.

12. John T. Greene, *Ewing Family Letters,* 26; Reid Mitchell, *Civil War Soldiers,* 59–60.

13. Newell, *10th Regiment Massachusetts Volunteers,* 157; McClenthen, *Narrative of the Fall and Winter Campaign,* 9; William Teall to his wife, November 7, 1862, Teall Letters, TSLA; Dawes, *Sixth Wisconsin,* 105.

14. James I. Robertson Jr., *Soldiers Blue and Gray,* 68–69; Billings, *Hard Tack and Coffee,* 113–18; Robert Goldthwaite Carter, *Four Brothers in Blue,* 158.

15. Cornelius Richmond to his wife, November 7, 1862, Richmond Papers, FSNMP; William Hamilton to his mother, November 8, 1862, Hamilton Papers, LC; Relyea Memoir, 55–56, CHS; John Ripley Adams, *Memorials and Letters,* 73; Haley, *Rebel Yell and Yankee Hurrah,* 46–47.

16. See useful introductions with an emphasis on soldier reactions in Linderman, *Embattled Courage,* 115–18; James I. Robertson Jr., *Soldiers Blue and Gray,* 147–55.

17. Wightman, *From Antietam to Fort Fisher,* 74; Craft, *History of the One Hundred Forty-First Pennsylvania,* 25; Sturtevant, *Josiah Volunteered,* 59; McAllister, *Letters of Robert McAllister,* 217.

18. November 8, 1862, Woodworth Diary, Hotchkiss Collection, CL; Abiel Hall Edwards, *"Dear Friend Anna,"* 39; *MSH,* 3:19–20, 5:91–92, 197; November 3, 1862, Rice Diary, LC; Sewall D. Tilton to his sister, November 2, December 11, 1862, Tilton Papers, NHHS.

19. Edward H. Brewer to Mary Brewer, November 14, 1862, Brewer Papers, CSL; S. Millett Thompson, *Thirteenth New Hampshire,* 22; James R. Woodworth to Phoebe Woodworth, November 15, 1862, Woodworth Papers, Hotchkiss Collection, CL; William Child, *Fifth New Hampshire,* 144.

20. Washburn, *108th Regiment,* 111; *New York Tribune,* November 5, 1862; *Flemington (N.J.) Hunterdon Gazette,* December 24, 1862.

21. Bellard, *Gone for a Soldier,* 168–69; Address of Edward C. Delvan to the Army of the United States, Albany, New York, November 4, 1862, Seward Papers, UR; *New York Tribune,* November 15, 1862; Henry J. H. Thompson to his wife, November 16, 1862, Thompson Papers, Duke.

22. Wightman, *From Antietam to Fort Fisher,* 75–76; Hitchcock, *War from the Inside,* 100–101; Relyea Memoir, 57, CHS; Bellard, *Gone for a Soldier,* 170; *Rochester (N.Y.) Daily Union and Advertiser,* November 20, 1862.

23. Darius Starr to his mother, November 10, 1862, Starr Papers, Duke; James Remington to his sister, November 13, 1862, Remington Papers, RIHS; Siegel, *For the Glory of the Union,* 96; William Henry Walling to his sister, November 6, 1862, Walling Papers, CWMC, USAMHI; November 13, 1862, Jackson Diary, IHS; George Washington Whitman, *Civil War Letters,* 73.

24. For excellent discussions of northern perceptions of the South, see Wiley, *Life of Billy Yank,* 96–108; Reid Mitchell, *Civil War Soldiers,* 32–34, 94–126; Michael Barton, *Goodmen,* 7–33; Jimerson, *Private Civil War,* 131–35.

25. Royster, *Destructive War,* 85–86; Grimsley, *Hard Hand of War,* 72–73, 85–92, 96–98, 105–7. In parts of northern Virginia the destruction of property by both sides had begun much earlier. See Noel G. Harrison, "Atop an Anvil," 133–64.

26. Edwin O. Wentworth to his wife, November 8, 1862, Wentworth Papers, LC; Hartsock, *Soldier of the Cross,* 23; George Lewis, *First Rhode Island Light Artillery,* 115; Haley, *Rebel Yell and Yankee Hurrah,* 49; Isaac Lyman Taylor, "Campaigning with the First Minnesota," 232.

27. Lord, *History of the Ninth New Hampshire,* 202; *Philadelphia Evening Bulletin,* November 13, 1862; Hopkins, *Seventh Rhode Island,* 29; William Teall to his wife, November 17, 1862, Teall Letters, TSLA.

28. *New York Times,* November 13, 1862; Saum, *Popular Mood of America,* 154–55; Civil War Reminiscences, ca. 1890, U.S. History Manuscripts, IU.

29. Helman, "Young Soldier in the Army of the Potomac," 150; Siegel, *For the Glory of the Union,* 92; William Child, *Fifth New Hampshire,* 144; Roe, *Tenth Massachusetts,* 148.

30. George Lewis, *First Rhode Island Light Artillery,* 119; Dority, "Civil War Diary," 9; Isaac Lyman Taylor, "Campaigning with the First Minnesota," 231; Haley, *Rebel Yell and Yankee Hurrah,* 47; November 4, 1862, Holford Diary, LC; Heffelfinger, "'Dear Sister Jennie,'" 214.

31. George Lewis, *First Rhode Island Light Artillery,* 114–15; November 3, 1862, Jackson Diary, IHS; Kepler, *Fourth Ohio,* 86–87; Haydon, *For Country, Cause, and Leader,* 285.

32. Hitchcock, *War from the Inside,* 103; John T. Greene, *Ewing Family Letters,* 28; William Franklin Draper to his wife, November 11, 1862, Draper Papers, LC; Weygant, *One Hundred and Twenty-Fourth Regiment,* 57–58; Haydon, *For Country, Cause, and Leader,* 288–89.

33. Sturtevant, *Josiah Volunteered,* 58; McCrea, *Dear Belle,* 165; Wightman, *From Antietam to Fort Fisher,* 73–74; Gavin, *Campaigning with the Roundheads,* 201; Hartsock, *Soldier of the Cross,* 165.

34. Henry Norton, *Eighth New York Cavalry,* 49; Pettit, *Infantryman Pettit,* 36; Todd, *Seventy-Ninth Highlanders,* 253; Siegel, *For the Glory of the Union,* 92.

35. Newell, *10th Regiment Massachusetts Volunteers,* 156; Orville Thomson, *Seventh Indiana,* 137–38; Thomas H. Parker, *History of the 51st,* 254–55; Cheek and Pointon, *Sauk County Riflemen,* 215–16.

36. Thomson and Rauch, *History of the "Bucktails,"* 225–27; Walker, *Second Corps,* 135–36; John H. Rhodes, *History of Battery B,* 132–33.

37. Walker, *Second Corps,* 134–35; Currier, "From Concord to Fredericksburg," 248–49; Zerah Coston Monks to Hannah T. Rohrer, November 1, 1862, Monks-Rohrer Letters, Emory;

Moe, *Last Full Measure*, 203–4; Edward J. Nichols, *Toward Gettysburg*, 147; Rauscher, *Music on the March*, 20–29; Haley, *Rebel Yell and Yankee Hurrah*, 52.

38. John H. Rhodes, *History of Battery B*, 130–31; Willard J. Templeton to his brother, November 8–9, 1862, Templeton Letters, NHSL; William Teall to his wife, November 10, 1862, Teall Letters, TSLA; Newell, *10th Regiment Massachusetts Volunteers*, 158. For background on both the images and reality of defiant Confederate women, see Reid Mitchell, *Vacant Chair*, 89–112; Ruble, *Civil Wars*, 154–80. A child could more easily express defiance in northern Virginia than in areas under more permanent Union occupation. See Marten, *Children's Civil War*, 139–45.

39. R. S. Robertson to his parents, November 7, 1862, Robertson Papers, FSNMP; McClenthen, *Narrative of the Fall and Winter Campaign*, 18; Chamberlain, *Through Blood and Fire*, 34; Samuel S. Partridge to "Dear Ed," Partridge Letters, FSNMP; Albert Richardson, *Secret Service*, 299–300. For the persistence of civilian defiance during the war and the diverse Federal reactions, see Ash, *When the Yankees Came*, 38–44.

40. Merrill, *First Maine and District of Columbia Cavalry*, 80; *Rochester (N.Y.) Daily Union and Advertiser*, November 19, 1862; Newell, *10th Regiment Massachusetts Volunteers*, 156–57.

41. Beidelman, *Letters of George Washington Beidelman*, 142; Trobriand, *Four Years with the Army of the Potomac*, 344–45; R. S. Robertson to his parents, November 7, 1862, Robertson Papers, FSNMP.

42. Robert Goldthwaite Carter, *Four Brothers in Blue*, 156–57; Brewster, *When This Cruel War Is Over*, 187–88.

43. Hartsock, *Soldier of the Cross*, 21; Alotta, *Stop the Evil*, 33; Helman, "Young Soldier in the Army of the Potomac," 149; Robert Goldthwaite Carter, *Four Brothers in Blue*, 152.

44. Daniel M. Holt, *Surgeon's Civil War*, 44; Brewster, *When This Cruel War Is Over*, 189; *Augusta (Maine) Kennebec Journal*, November 7, 1862; *New York Tribune*, November 5, 1862; *Hartford Daily Courant*, November 5, 1862.

45. Meade, *Life and Letters*, 1:322; John Ripley Adams, *Memorials and Letters*, 71.

46. For physical descriptions of Lee at this point in the war, see Emory M. Thomas, *Lee*, 275; J. B. Jones, *Rebel War Clerk's Diary*, 1:179.

47. Douglas Southall Freeman, *Lee*, 2:415–19; Woodworth, *Davis and Lee*, 199–206; Jennings Cropper Wise, *Long Arm of Lee*, 1:327–56; Berkeley, *Four Years in the Confederate Artillery*, 30–31.

48. In examining organizational changes, I have relied on the excellent accounts in Douglas Southall Freeman, *Lee's Lieutenants*, 2:238–83; Woodworth, *Davis and Lee*, 199–206.

49. Hoole, *Lawley Covers the Confederacy*, 32; Wert, *Longstreet*, 204–8.

50. James I. Robertson Jr., *Jackson*, 631; Von Borcke, *Memoirs of the Confederate War*, 2:35–37; Pickett, *Heart of a Soldier*, 62–63; Mary Anna Jackson, *Life and Letters of Jackson*, 377.

51. Douglas Southall Freeman, *Lee's Lieutenants*, 2:310–11; Col. G. F. R. Henderson, *Jackson*, 566–67; Douglas Southall Freeman, *Lee*, 2:427; J. B. Jones, *Rebel War Clerk's Diary*, 1:179, 187–88; Emory M. Thomas, *Bold Dragoon*, 187–90; *OR*, ser. 1, 19(2):701–2, 703; Robert E. Lee, *Wartime Papers*, 333.

52. Douglas Southall Freeman, *Lee*, 2:417; Woodworth, *Davis and Lee*, 199–200; *General Orders No. 126, Army of Northern Virginia*; S. G. Pryor, *Post of Honor*, 283. For good descriptions of particular punishments during this period, see Dooley, *John Dooley, Confederate Soldier*, 73–74.

53. W. H. Andrews, *Footprints of a Regiment*, 89; Burgwyn, *Captain's War*, 31; Henry Alexander Chambers, *Diary*, 67; Greer, "All Thoughts Are Absorbed in the War," 30.

54. Michael W. Taylor, *Cry Is War, War, War*, 127; Hodijah Lincoln Meade to Richard Hardaway Meade, November 12, 1862, Meade Family Papers, VHS; Von Borcke, *Memoirs of the Confederate War*, 2:51–52; Henry Thweat Owen to Harriet Adeline Owen, November 7, 1862, Owen Papers, VHS; Cutrer and Parrish, *Brothers in Gray*, 132; Lafayette McLaws to his wife, Novem-

ber 16, 1862, McLaws Papers, SHC; Sidney Carter, *Dear Bet,* 64–65; *OR,* ser. 1, 51(2):642; November 7, 1862, Hawes Diary, VHS.

55. Judith Brockenbrough McGuire, *Diary of a Southern Refugee,* 169; *Columbus (Ga.) Daily Enquirer,* November 8, 1862; *Richmond Daily Dispatch,* November 19, 1862; *Macon (Ga.) Daily Telegraph,* November 4, 1862; Paxton, *Memoir and Memorials,* 62, 69; *Atlanta Southern Confederacy,* November 3, 1862.

56. Wiley, *Life of Johnny Reb,* 108–22; S. G. Pryor, *Post of Honor,* 283; Driver, *58th Virginia,* 37; Walters, *Norfolk Blues,* 40; Hightower, "Letters from Harvey Judson Hightower," 179; William Calder to his mother, November 11, 1862, Calder Family Papers, SHC; Henry Garrison to Emily Aurora Bosworth, November 10, 1862, Garrison Papers, Austin State University.

57. Robert A. Moore, *Life for the Confederacy,* 116; Chapla, *48th Virginia,* 42; John Howard Lewis, *Recollections from 1860 to 1865,* 61–62; Betts, *Experience of a Confederate Chaplain,* 22; William W. Bennett, *Narrative of the Great Revival,* 231–32; November 6, 1862, Ware Diary, SHC.

58. Henry Alexander Chambers, *Diary,* 68; John Bratton to his wife, November 8, 1862, Bratton Letters, SHC.

59. *OR,* ser. 4, 2:157–60; J. B. Jones, *Rebel War Clerk's Diary,* 1:183.

60. Fitzpatrick, *Letters to Amanda,* 30; November 7, 1862, Ware Diary, SHC; L. Calhoun Cooper to his mother, November 9, 1862, Cooper Letters, Kennesaw Mountain National Battlefield Park; DeNoon, *Charlie's Letters,* 88; Hatton Memoir, 355–56, LC.

61. Robert A. Moore, *Life for the Confederacy,* 116; Walter Clark, *Papers,* 1:89; Michael W. Taylor, *Cry Is War, War, War,* 128; DeNoon, *Charlie's Letters,* 88; Chamberlayne, *Ham Chamberlayne, Virginian,* 137–38; Berkeley, *Four Years in the Confederate Artillery,* 33–34; Clement Anselm Evans, *Intrepid Warrior,* 118–19; Hatton Memoir, 355–56, LC.

62. William Alexander Smith, *Anson Guards,* 165; *Richmond Daily Whig,* November 7, 1862; Long, *Memoirs of Lee,* 230; John William Jones, *Christ in the Camp,* 287–93; Berkeley, *Four Years in the Confederate Artillery,* 32–33; Garfield, *Wild Life of the Army,* 173.

63. Walter Clark, *Papers,* 1:92–93; *Richmond Daily Dispatch,* November 11, December 3, 1862; Clement Anselm Evans, *Intrepid Warrior,* 119–20; Dooley, *John Dooley, Confederate Soldier,* 70.

64. Edmund Ruffin, *Diary,* 2:489; Susan Leigh Blackford, *Letters from Lee's Army,* 132–34; Paxton, *Civil War Letters,* 61; Amanda Virginia Edmonds, *Journals,* 125.

65. Ujanirtus Allen, *Campaigning with "Old Stonewall,"* 183.

CHAPTER TWO

1. *Albany (N.Y.) Atlas and Argus,* November 1, 1862; *Rochester (N.Y.) Daily Democrat and American,* November 7, 1862.

2. James W. Geary, *We Need Men,* 32–44; *OR,* ser. 3, 2:713–14, 743, 845.

3. *New York Herald,* November 1, 14, 1862; *Albany (N.Y.) Atlas and Argus,* December 12, 1862; *Albany (N.Y.) Evening Journal,* November 14, 1862; Miller, *Camp Curtin,* 136–37; *B&L,* 3:137; Silber and Stevens, *Yankee Correspondence,* 40–41; Edward K. Russell to his mother, December 1, 1862, Kirby-Smith-Russell Collection, FSNMP.

4. *OR,* ser. 3, 2:714–16, 735, 743–45.

5. Hesseltine, *Lincoln and the War Governors,* 278–81; Saum, *Popular Mood of America,* 186–88; *OR,* ser. 3, 2:761, 765, 786, 861, 867, 935; Larsen, "Draft Riot in Wisconsin," 421–27; Current, *History of Wisconsin,* 315–19.

6. *OR,* ser. 3, 4:1265; *Janesville (Wisc.) Daily Gazette,* November 12, 1862.

7. Nevins, *War for the Union,* 2:303–5; Van Deusen, *Seward,* 327–28; Thurlow Weed Barnes, *Memoir of Thurlow Weed,* 424–25; Henry Pearson, *Wadsworth,* 150–64, 305–10.

8. Stewart Mitchell, *Horatio Seymour,* 238–54; Nevins, *War for the Union,* 2:302–3; Lathers, *Reminiscences,* 181.

9. *Albany (N.Y.) Atlas and Argus,* November 1, 1862; *Rochester (N.Y.) Daily Union and Advertiser,* November 1, 3, 1862.

10. *New York Times,* November 1–2, 4, 1862; *Albany (N.Y.) Evening Journal,* November 1, 1862; *New York Tribune,* November 3–4, 1862.

11. *Providence (R.I.) Daily Journal,* November 6, 1862; *Baltimore American and Commercial Advertiser,* November 5, 1862; Lounger, "Brethren," and "A Blunder and a Trick," *Harper's Weekly,* November 8, 1862, 707; *Hartford Daily Courant,* November 3, 1862; Strong, *Diary of George Templeton Strong,* 3:269.

12. Strong, *Diary of George Templeton Strong,* 3:270.

13. Stewart Mitchell, *Horatio Seymour,* 255; *Boston Post,* November 6, 1862; *Albany (N.Y.) Atlas and Argus,* November 20, 1862; *New York World,* November 7, 1862.

14. Two weeks before the election McClellan had privately denounced Wadsworth as "such a vile traitorous miscreant that I do not wish to see the great state of N.Y. disgraced by having such a thing at its head" (George Brinton McClellan, *Civil War Papers,* 501).

15. Whittemore and Whittemore, "Rebellious South through New York Eyes," 348–49; W. F. Searles to his brother, November 20, 1862, Searles Letters, FSNMP; Potter, *One Surgeon's Private War,* 50; Robert Gould Shaw, *Blue-Eyed Child of Fortune,* 241; Darius N. Couch, *Four Years with the Army of the Potomac,* 356; James S. Robinson to L. T. Hunt, November 7, 1862, Robinson Papers, OHS.

16. *Albany (N.Y.) Evening Journal,* November 5, 8, 1862; *Hartford Daily Courant,* November 6, 8, 1862; Thurlow Weed Barnes, *Memoir of Thurlow Weed,* 427; Strong, *Diary of George Templeton Strong,* 3:270; *Springfield (Mass.) Daily Republican,* November 6, 1862.

17. *Poughkeepsie (N.Y.) Daily Eagle,* November 5–6, 1862; *New York Tribune,* November 7, 1862; *Chicago Daily Tribune,* November 22, 1862; Henry Pearson, *Wadsworth,* 164–65; "The Result of the Election," *Independent,* November 6, 1862, 4; John Cochrane to Abraham Lincoln, November 5, 1862, Lincoln Papers, LC; Cochrane to Salmon P. Chase, November 5, 1862, Chase Papers, LC.

18. For varying assessments of the election returns, see Paludan, *"People's Contest,"* 100–101; Nevins, *War for the Union,* 2:318–19; Silbey, *Respectable Minority,* 144–46; Kleppner, *Third Electoral System,* 77, 83–84. James McPherson has argued that historians have exaggerated both Republican losses and Democratic gains, but politicians in both parties perceived the 1862 elections as a Republican debacle and acted accordingly. In hindsight the Democrats perhaps had not done as well as might have been expected, though contemporary observers made no such point. See McPherson, *Battle Cry of Freedom,* 561–62.

19. A. A. Lovett to Anson Stager, November 4, 1862, Seward Papers, UR; Lincoln, *Collected Works,* 5:496–97. See esp. a series of telegrams from various states during the first two weeks of November in the Lincoln Papers, LC.

20. Silbey, *Respectable Minority,* 66–80; *Boston Post,* November 3, 1862; Dusinberre, *Civil War Issues in Philadelphia,* 127–50; *Philadelphia Evening Bulletin,* November 1, 1862; *Washington Daily National Intelligencer,* November 7, 1862; Thaddeus Stevens, *Selected Papers,* 1:327; Nevins, *War for the Union,* 2:309–18; Strong, *Diary of George Templeton Strong,* 3:268–69. For helpful background, see Neely, *Fate of Liberty,* 52–65; Hess, *Liberty, Virtue, and Progress,* 88–97.

21. William H. Ross to James A. Bayard, November 13, 1862, Seward Papers, UR; *Indianapolis Daily State Sentinel,* November 8, 1862; John R. Emery to his mother, November 13, 1862, Emery Papers, NJHS; Paludan, *"People's Contest,"* 100–101.

22. *Albany (N.Y.) Atlas and Argus,* November 25, 1862; *Indianapolis Daily State Sentinel,* November 7, 1862; *Springfield (Mass.) Daily Republican,* November 24, 1862; Browning, *Diary,* 1:586–87; *New York Herald,* December 11, 1862.

23. *OR,* ser. 3, 4:746–47, 2:903; *New York Times,* November 20, 24, 1862; *Boston Daily Ad-*

vertiser, November 24, 1862; "The Arbitrary Arrest Business," *Harper's Weekly,* December 6, 1862, 770; *Baltimore American and Commercial Advertiser,* November 26, 1862.

24. *Times* (London), December 9–10, 1862; *New York Herald,* November 25–26, 1862; Paludan, *"People's Contest,"* 100–101.

25. Nevins, *War for the Union,* 2:307–9; Tap, "Race, Rhetoric, and Emancipation," 101–25; *New York Herald,* November 1, 4, 1862; *Boston Post,* November 4, 1862. The racist appeals were especially strong and effective in the Midwest. See Voegeli, *Free but Not Equal,* 34–38, 54–55, 60–61. Conservative soldiers in McClellan's army also rejoiced over Democratic victories and predicted that the preliminary Emancipation Proclamation would be withdrawn. See Emerson F. Merrill to his parents, November 16, 1862, Merrill Papers, FSNMP; Augustus Van Dyke to his brother, November 11, 1862, Van Dyke Papers, IHS; James B. Post to his wife, November 11, 1862, Post Papers, CWMC, USAMHI.

26. *Albany (N.Y.) Atlas and Argus,* November 10, 1862; *New York Herald,* November 5–6, 1862; *Portland (Maine) Eastern Argus,* November 13, 1862; Lindsey, *Cox,* 69–70; John S. Crocker to his wife, November 8, 1862, Crocker Letters, CU; William Henry Walling to his sister, November 20, 1862, Walling Papers, CWMC, USAMHI.

27. Charles Sumner, *Selected Letters,* 2:130; *New York Tribune,* November 19, 1862; Lydia Maria Child, *Lydia Maria Child,* 420; Irving H. Bartlett, *Wendell and Ann Phillips,* 185.

28. Phyllis F. Field, *Politics of Race in New York,* 152–53; Voegeli, *Free but Not Equal,* 55–66.

29. *Washington Daily National Intelligencer,* November 6, 1862; Browning, *Diary,* 1:592; Paludan, *"People's Contest,"* 100; Welles, *Diary of Gideon Welles,* 1:183; Richard P. L. Baber to William H. Seward, November 24, 1862, Seward Papers, UR.

30. *Philadelphia Evening Bulletin,* November 8, 1862; *Poughkeepsie (N.Y.) Daily Eagle,* November 3, 1862; Thaddeus Stevens, *Selected Papers,* 1:325–27; *Indianapolis Daily Journal,* November 26, 1862; *Cincinnati Daily Gazette,* November 6, 1862. For examples of how the absence of men in the army may have reduced the Republican vote in two districts, see Conkling, *Roscoe Conkling,* 183–85; Hollister, *Colfax,* 196–99.

31. *Albany (N.Y.) Atlas and Argus,* January 10, 1863; Lusk, *War Letters of William Thompson Lusk,* 224–25; Saum, *Popular Mood of America,* 176–81; Charles Shields Wainwright, *Diary of Battle,* 126; James Edison Decker to his father, November 30, 1862, Decker Papers, CWMC, USAMHI; November 14, 1862, Lambert Diary, IHS. The absence of a "soldier vote" in these elections makes assessing political opinion in the army tricky at best. The available evidence, however, suggests that conservatism remained strong in the ranks even though two years later, for a variety of reasons, the troops would overwhelmingly support Lincoln.

32. Strong, *Diary of George Templeton Strong,* 3:272; S. W. Oakey to Abraham Lincoln, November 5, 1862, Lincoln Papers, LC. Ominously, a number of Republicans agreed that the president and his advisers had been punished at the polls for administrative incompetence. Reports of an impending housecleaning in Washington even appeared in staunchly Republican newspapers. See *Boston Evening Transcript,* November 6, 1862; Thurlow Weed Barnes, *Memoir of Thurlow Weed,* 427–28; David Dudley Field to Abraham Lincoln, November 8, 1862, Lincoln Papers, LC; *Janesville (Wisc.) Daily Gazette,* November 6, 1862; *Yonkers (N.Y.) Examiner,* November 20, 1862; *Rochester (N.Y.) Daily Democrat and American,* November 8, 1862. Politically astute soldiers agreed that the "weakness of the President" and his administration had hurt the Republicans. See Gray and Ropes, *War Letters,* 20–21.

33. Browning, *Diary,* 1:588–89; Sandburg, *Lincoln,* 1:605–7; *Times* (London), November 21, 1862.

34. "Washington Correspondence," *Independent,* November 13, 1862, 3; Lewis F. Allen to William H. Seward, November 5, 1862, Seward Papers, UR; Nevins, *War for the Union,* 2:321–22; William Hamilton to Salmon P. Chase, November 1, 1862, Chase Papers, LC; Willet Raynor to Zachariah Chandler, December 4, 1862, Chandler Papers, LC.

35. Thorndike, *Sherman Letters,* 167–68; Garfield, *Wild Life of the Army,* 173; Lyman Trum-

bull to Zachariah Chandler, November 9, 1862, Chandler Papers, LC. There was considerable public discussion about whether the newly elected Democrats really favored a more vigorous military policy as many claimed. See *Providence (R.I.) Daily Journal,* November 1, 8, 1862; *New York Herald,* November 4, 1862; *Boston Daily Advertiser,* November 7, 1862.

36. *Philadelphia Evening Bulletin,* October 31, 1862. For the comments of moderate editors, see *New York Times,* November 5, 9, 1862; *Poughkeepsie (N.Y.) Daily Eagle,* November 7, 1862; *Boston Daily Advertiser,* November 10, 1862. For more radical opinion, see *Chicago Daily Tribune,* November 6, 1862; *Easton (Pa.) Free Press,* November 5, 1862; *Racine (Wisc.) Weekly Journal,* November 5, 1862; *Elmira (N.Y.) Weekly Advertiser,* November 15, 1862.

37. *Pittsburgh Daily Dispatch,* November 7, 1862; *Springfield (Mass.) Daily Republican,* November 7, 1862; *Watertown (N.Y.) News and Reformer,* November 6, 1862; *Newark (N.J.) Daily Advertiser,* November 5, 1862; *Boston Daily Advertiser,* November 6, 1862; "Lessons of the Elections," *Frank Leslie's Illustrated Newspaper,* November 22, 1862, 129–30.

38. Otis, *Second Wisconsin,* 64; Fiske, *Dunn Browne's Experiences in the Army,* 94–95, Gray and Ropes, *War Letters,* 94–95.

39. J. Wesley Greene to Abraham Lincoln, November 11, 1862; William Chase Barney to ?, November 23, 1862; Fernando Wood to Lincoln, December 8, 1862 (with letters), Lincoln Papers, LC; Lincoln, *Collected Works,* 5:517, 553–54. Democrats also pushed for a convention of the states to bring the Confederates back into the Union. See *Portland (Maine) Eastern Argus,* December 5, 1862; *Albany (N.Y.) Atlas and Argus,* November 25, 1862; *Harrisburg Patriot and Union,* November 8, 1862; *Newark (N.J.) Daily Advertiser,* November 25, 1862; Fisher, *Diary of Sidney George Fisher,* 441; *Congressional Globe,* 37th Cong., 3rd sess., 1862, 3–4.

40. *Baltimore American and Commercial Advertiser,* November 8, 1862; *Newark (N.J.) Daily Advertiser,* December 11, 1862; "Compromise," *Christian Advocate and Journal,* November 6, 1862, 356–57; *New York Tribune,* November 19, 1862; *Chicago Daily Tribune,* December 4, 1862.

41. *Yonkers (N.Y.) Examiner,* November 27, 1862; *Springfield (Mass.) Daily Republican,* December 6, 1862; *Cincinnati Daily Gazette,* November 19, 1862; Beecher, *Patriotic Addresses,* 398; *Congressional Globe,* 37th Cong., 3rd sess., 1862, 112–14; Scott, *One Hundred and Fifth Regiment Pennsylvania Volunteers,* 153.

42. Susan Leigh Blackford, *Memoirs of Life In and Out of the Army,* 1:230; *Richmond Daily Enquirer,* December 2, 9, 10, 1862; *Richmond Daily Whig,* November 29, December 9, 1862.

43. Chamberlayne, *Ham Chamberlayne, Virginian,* 137–38; Lafayette McLaws to his wife, November 10, 1862, McLaws Papers, SHC; Jedediah Hotchkiss to Sara Ann Comfort Hotchkiss, November 2, 1862, Hotchkiss Papers, LC; Thomas Claybrook Elder to Anna Fitzhugh Elder, November 11, 1862, Elder Papers, VHS; *New York Tribune,* November 27, 1862.

44. *Charleston Mercury,* November 5, 10, 1862; *Richmond Daily Examiner,* November 15, 1862; *Richmond Daily Whig,* December 2, 1862; *Raleigh Weekly Register,* November 12, 1862; Edmund Ruffin, *Diary,* 2:486, 488, 494–95.

45. *Lynchburg Daily Virginian,* November 1, 1862; *Richmond Daily Whig,* November 15, December 8 (quotation), 1862; *Charleston Daily Courier,* November 11, 1862; *Richmond Daily Enquirer,* November 1, 11, 1862; *Richmond Daily Dispatch,* November 10, 21, 1862; Grayson, *Witness to Sorrow,* 244; *Columbus (Ga.) Daily Enquirer,* November 5, 1862.

46. *Wilmington (N.C.) Daily Journal,* November 10, 1862; *Richmond Daily Whig,* November 11, 1862; *Macon (Ga.) Daily Telegraph,* November 10, 1862; DuBose, *Yancey,* 675–76.

47. The best treatments of the British cabinet discussions are in Howard Jones, *Union in Peril,* 162–97; Ephraim Douglass Adams, *Great Britain and the Civil War,* 2:37–59, 105–15; Crook, *North, South, and the Powers,* 227–44.

48. For French diplomacy, see Case and Spencer, *United States and France,* 347–66, 374–81; Howard Jones, *Union in Peril,* 198–206; Crook, *North, South, and the Powers,* 245–57.

49. Howard Jones, *Union in Peril,* 210–23; Ephraim Douglass Adams, *Great Britain and the Civil War,* 2:59–74; Brauer, "British Mediation and the Civil War," 49–65.

50. For contrasting accounts of how the economic interests lined up, see Ellison, *Support for Secession,* 15–154; Philip S. Foner, *British Labor and Civil War,* 29–54.

51. William H. Seward, *Works,* 5:366, 368–71; Duberman, *Charles Francis Adams,* 297–98; Bigelow, *Retrospections,* 1:574, 578–79; Henry P. Tappan to Abraham Lincoln, November 22, 1862, Lincoln Papers, LC; Lincoln, *Collected Works,* 5:518–19.

52. Howard Jones, *Union in Peril,* 208–10.

53. Case and Spencer, *United States and France,* 366–73; Ephraim Douglass Adams, *Great Britain and the Civil War,* 2:75; Carroll, *Henri Mercier and the Civil War,* 241–43; Howard Jones, *Union in Peril,* 206–8; Moran, *Journal of Benjamin Moran,* 2:1091; Bigelow, *Retrospections,* 1: 571–72; Hernon, *Celts, Catholics, and Copperheads,* 92.

54. Marx and Engels, *Civil War in the U.S.,* 258–61.

55. *Philadelphia Public Ledger,* December 8, 1862; *Boston Evening Transcript,* November 8, 1862; *Baltimore American and Commercial Advertiser,* November 18, December 12, 1862; Crook, *North, South, and the Powers,* 257–79; *New York Times,* December 1, 9, 1862; Hugh Roden to George Roden, November 12, 1862, Roden Papers, Schoff Collection, CL.

56. Katz, *Belmont,* 120; *Albany (N.Y.) Atlas and Argus,* November 13, 1862; *Washington Daily National Intelligencer,* November 14, 1862; *New York Herald,* November 3, 17, 1862.

57. *New York Times,* November 27, 1862; "The French Proposal to Mediate," *Harper's Weekly,* December 6, 1862, 770; *Hartford Daily Courant,* November 26, 1862; Joshua R. Giddings to Charles Sumner, December 1, 1862, Sumner Papers, HU; *Springfield (Mass.) Daily Republican,* November 29, 1862.

58. *ORN,* ser. 2, 3:589, 600, 602–3, 611–13; Owsley, *King Cotton Diplomacy,* 337–59, 427; J. B. Jones, *Rebel War Clerk's Diary,* 1:199–200; Meade, *Benjamin,* 267–68.

59. For examples of optimism, see *Richmond Daily Enquirer,* December 3, 1862; *Raleigh Weekly Register,* November 5, 1862; *Charleston Mercury,* December 8, 1862. For more ambivalent assessments, see *Lynchburg Daily Virginian,* November 1, 13, 1862; *Macon (Ga.) Daily Telegraph,* November 1, 1862.

60. *Milledgeville (Ga.) Southern Recorder,* November 4, 1862; *Richmond Daily Whig,* November 5, 24, 1862; *Richmond Daily Dispatch,* November 8, December 2, 1862; *Augusta (Ga.) Daily Chronicle and Sentinel,* November 14, 1862; *Charleston Mercury,* November 19, 1862; *Charleston Daily Courier,* November 14, December 2, 1862; Boney, *Letcher,* 177.

61. Edmondston, *"Journal of a Secesh Lady,"* 296.

CHAPTER THREE

1. Mary A. Livermore, *My Story of the War,* 556.

2. Hay, *Diaries and Letters of John Hay,* 218–19; Nicolay and Hay, *Lincoln,* 6:188; Mary A. Livermore, *My Story of the War,* 241–42; Lincoln, *Collected Works,* 5:484; Benjamin P. Thomas, *Lincoln,* 347; Browning, *Diary,* 1:591; John G. Nicolay to Therena Bates, November 9, 1862, Nicolay Papers, LC.

3. The conclusions drawn here about the timing of and justification for McClellan's removal are a synthesis of the following views: Michael F. Holt, "Abraham Lincoln and the Politics of Union," in John L. Thomas, *Lincoln and the American Political Tradition,* 127; Paludan, *Presidency of Lincoln,* 159–60; Nevins, *War for the Union,* 2:323–30; Comte de Paris, *Civil War in America,* 2:558; William Teall to his wife, November 7, 1862, Teall Letters, TSLA.

4. Lincoln, *Collected Works,* 5:485; *OR Supplement,* pt. 1, 3:450; Ambrose, *Halleck,* 93; Sears, *Landscape Turned Red,* 339–40. Lincoln was also acquiring greater confidence in his own ability to direct military operations. See Daniel E. Sutherland, *Fredericksburg and Chancellorsville,* 7.

5. See the various accounts by Buckingham in *Chicago Daily Tribune,* September 6, 1875; Comte de Paris, *Civil War in America,* 2:555–58n; Stine, *Army of the Potomac,* 241–42; Poore, *Burnside,* 178–80; Brown, *Cushing of Gettysburg,* 137–39.

6. In addition to the sources cited in the preceding notes, see Marvel, *Burnside*, 159–60; *CCW*, 1:650; Haydon, *For Country, Cause, and Leader*, 286.

7. *CCW*, 1:650; Herman Haupt to his wife, November 9, 1862, Haupt Letterbook, Haupt Papers, LC; George Brinton McClellan, *Civil War Papers*, 519–20. Contrary to the contemporary account in the letter to his wife, McClellan later claimed that for some time he had anticipated being removed from command. See George Brinton McClellan, *McClellan's Own Story*, 651.

8. George Brinton McClellan, *Civil War Papers*, 521; William Teall to his wife, November 9, 1862, Teall Letters, TSLA; Judd, *Story of the Thirty-Third*, 215.

9. Donaldson, *Inside the Army of the Potomac*, 159; Bayard, *Life of Bayard*, 260; James R. Woodworth to Phoebe Woodworth, November 10, 1862; Woodworth Papers, Hotchkiss Collection, CL; Daniel B. Foote to "My Dear Friend," November 10, 1862, Foote Letters, USAMHI; James B. Thomas, *Civil War Letters*, 11–12. In assessing the soldiers' reactions to McClellan's removal, I have relied heavily on letters and diaries. I consulted memoirs and regimental histories but will only cite them if they contained excerpts of contemporary responses or some particular insight not found in other sources.

10. McCrea, *Dear Belle*, 166–67; McAllister, *Letters of Robert McAllister* and; November 11, 1862, Bancroft Diary, MHI; Michael C. C. Adams, *Our Masters the Rebels*, 129–30; Fairchild, *27th Regiment*, 111; John Ripley Adams, *Memorials and Letters*, 73–74; Zerah Coston Monks to Hannah T. Rohrer, November 11, 1862, Monks-Rohrer Letters, Emory; John S. Crocker to his wife, November 11, 1862, Crocker Letters, CU.

11. November 1862, McClellan Papers, LC; Gibbon, *Recollections of the Civil War*, 96; Elisha Hunt Rhodes, *All for the Union*, 88; Garner, *Civil War World of Herman Melville*, 199–200; Welsh and Welsh, "Civil War Letters from Two Brothers," 152; Isaac Lyman Taylor, "Campaigning with the First Minnesota," 232; *Rochester (N.Y.) Daily Union and Advertiser*, November 24, 1862; *Elmira (N.Y.) Weekly Advertiser*, December 6, 1862; *Pittsburgh Daily Dispatch*, November 25, 1862.

12. Robert S. Robertson, "Diary of the War," 67; Jacob Blackington to his sister, November 10, 1862, Blackington Papers, USAMHI; McClenthen, *Narrative of the Fall and Winter Campaign*, 23; Tevis, *Fighting Fourteenth*, 55.

13. Moe, *Last Full Measure*, 204; Gibbon, *Recollections of the Civil War*, 97–98; McCrea, *Dear Belle*, 167; *New York Herald*, November 10, 1862; Haley, *Rebel Yell and Yankee Hurrah*, 50.

14. Brown, *Cushing of Gettysburg*, 139; Stephen Rich to "Brother William," November 14, 1862, Rich Papers, CWMC, USAMHI; William Hamilton to his mother, November 15, 1862, Hamilton Papers, LC; Perkins, "Letters Home," 129.

15. Abbott, *Fallen Leaves*, 142–43; Dawes, *Sixth Wisconsin*, 103; November 16, 1862, Thompson Memoir, LC; Moe, *Last Full Measure*, 204–5; Gaff, *On Many a Bloody Field*, 202; *New York Herald*, November 19, 1862; *New York Tribune*, November 28, 1862; *New York Irish-American*, December 6, 1862; James B. Thomas, *Civil War Letters*, 111–12.

16. Harper, *Civil War History of Chester County, Pennsylvania*, 176; *Philadelphia Evening Bulletin*, November 19, 1862; Nolan, *Iron Brigade*, 170–71.

17. Edward J. Nichols, *Toward Gettysburg*, 146; James R. Woodworth to his wife, November 15, 1862, Woodworth Papers, Hotchkiss Collection, CL; Edwin Winchester Stone, *Rhode Island in the Rebellion*, 177; *New York Times*, November 13, 15, 1862; *Rochester (N.Y.) Daily Democrat and American*, December 2, 1862; Beidelman, *Letters of George Washington Beidelman*, 145.

18. William F. Smith to his mother, November 14, 1862, William F. Smith Letters, Leigh Collection, USAMHI; *Elizabeth New Jersey Journal*, November 25, 1862; William Child, *Fifth New Hampshire*, 145; Bardeen, *Little Fifer's Diary*, 83; John Lord Parker, *Twenty-Second Massachusetts*, 212–14; Hyndman, *History of a Cavalry Company*, 76; Graham, *Ninth New York*, 362–63; Charles Augustus Fuller, *Recollections of the War of 1861*, 75; Floyd, *Fortieth Regi-*

ment, 182; Chapin, *History of the Thirty-fourth Regiment,* 75; Augustus Van Dyke to his brother, November 11, 1862, Van Dyke Papers, IHS; Guiney, *Commanding Boston's Irish Ninth,* 151.

19. Osborn, *No Middle Ground,* 87–88; Richard K. Halsey to "Friend Keck," December 10, 1862, King Papers, Schoff Collection, CL; Favill, *Diary of a Young Officer,* 201; William Watson, *Letters of a Civil War Surgeon,* 31; Judson, *Eighty-third Pennsylvania,* 98.

20. Washburn, *108th Regiment,* 111; Samuel Clark to his niece, November 13, 1862, Clark Letters, FSNMP; Heffelfinger, "'Dear Sister Jennie,'" 215–16; Robert S. Robertson, "Diary of the War," 66; Charles Bowers to "Dear Lydia," November 10, 1862, Bowers Papers, MHS; November 11, 1862, Thompson Memoir, LC; F. W. Eager to George B. McClellan, November 15, 1862, McClellan Papers, LC; November 15, 1862, Taggart Diary, USAMHI; *Richmond (Ind.) Palladium,* December 19, 1862.

21. Pettit, *Infantryman Pettit,* 36; Otis, *Second Wisconsin,* 65; November 9, 1862, Taggart Diary, USAMHI; Brewer, *Sixty-first Regiment,* 43–44; James Edison Decker to his father, November 1862, Decker Papers, CWMC, USAMHI; *History of the Fifth Massachusetts Battery,* 483.

22. William Child, *Fifth New Hampshire,* 145; John S. Crocker to his wife, November 8, 1862, Crocker Letters, CU; George W. Ballock to his wife, November 10, 1862, Ballock Papers, Duke; McKelvey, *Rochester in the Civil War,* 110–11; Robert S. Robertson, "Diary of the War," 67–68; November 10, 1862, Woodworth Diary, Hotchkiss Collection, CL.

23. James Lorenzo Bowen, *Thirty-Seventh Regiment,* 95; R. S. Robertson to his parents, November 10, 1862, Robertson Papers, FSNMP; Harper, *Civil War History of Chester County, Pennsylvania,* 176; Frederick, *Story of a Regiment,* 110; William Hamilton to his mother, November 15, 1862, Hamilton Papers, LC.

24. Charles H. Eagor to his wife, November 25, 1862, Eagor Letters, Leigh Collection, USAMHI; George W. Ballock to his wife, November 10, 1862, Ballock Papers, Duke; Haley, *Rebel Yell and Yankee Hurrah,* 50; Paludan, *"People's Contest,"* 319; *Rochester (N.Y.) Daily Union and Advertiser,* November 20, 1862; George W. Barr to "Vinnie," November 10, 1862, Barr Papers, Schoff Collection, CL; November 8, 1862, Richards Diary, SHSW.

25. Edward Henry Courtney Taylor to his sister, November 1862, Taylor Letters, MHC; Sears, *Landscape Turned Red,* 343–44; William H. Myers to his parents, November 20, 1862, Myers Letters, CWMC, USAMHI; James B. Post to his wife, November 11, 1862, Post Papers, CWMC, USAMHI; R. S. Robertson to his parents, November 12, 1862, Robertson Papers, FSNMP; A. C. Higley to his father, November 21, 1862, Higley Letters, FSNMP.

26. Edward Henry Courtney Taylor to his sister, November 1862, Taylor Letters, MHC; Oliver Willcox Norton, *Army Letters,* 128; Edward K. Russell to his mother, December 1, 1862, Kirby-Smith-Russell Collection, FSNMP; Gavin, *Campaigning with the Roundheads,* 209–10.

27. Amassa Cobb to "Frank," November 14, 1862, Cobb Letter, SHSW; Castleman, *Army of the Potomac,* 240–41; Samuel Edmund Nichols, *"Your Soldier Boy Samuel,"* 46–48; George Thornton Fleming, *Hays,* 279; John W. Ames to his mother, November 9, 1862, Ames Papers, USAMHI.

28. Extract from a letter from John A. Dix to his wife, November 17, 1862, McClellan Papers, LC; Gibbon, *Recollections of the Civil War,* 96; *OR,* ser. 1, 19(2):551; Robert Goldthwaite Carter, *Four Brothers in Blue,* 158; William Teall to his wife, November 10, 1862, Teall Letters, TSLA; John S. Crocker to his wife, November 9, 1862, Crocker Letters, CU; Meade, *Life and Letters,* 1:325–26; George Brinton McClellan, *Civil War Papers,* 521–22.

29. *OR,* ser. 1, 19(2):558; Marvel, *Burnside,* 161–62; William Child, *Fifth New Hampshire,* 145; William A. Moore to his father, November 18, 1862, Moore Papers, NHHS; Charles Shields Wainwright, *Diary of Battle,* 125; Louis Fortescue to "Friend Sam," November 13, 1862, Fortescue Letters, FSNMP; John S. Crocker to his wife, November 10, 1862, Crocker Letters, CU; *New York Times,* November 12, 1862; John L. Smith, *118th Pennsylvania,* 107–8.

30. November 10, 1862, Heffelfinger Diary, *CWTI,* USAMHI; Samuel B. Fischer to his sis-

ter, November 10, 1862, Fischer Letters, Leigh Collection, USAMHI; Welsh and Welsh, "Civil War Letters from Two Brothers," 152, November 20, 1862, Lambert Diary, IHS; *Rochester (N.Y.) Daily Union and Advertiser*, November 26, 1862; Tyler, *Recollections of the Civil War*, 56–57; November 10, 1862, Berry Diary, *CWTI*, USAMHI.

31. Crowell Reminiscences, 10–11, NJHS; *Rochester (N.Y.) Daily Union and Advertiser*, November 20, 22, 1862; *Newark (N.J.) Daily Advertiser*, November 17, 1862; Weymouth, *Memorial Sketch of Lieut. Edgar M. Newcomb*, 93–94; *Wellsboro (Pa.) Agitator*, December 3, 1862; Donaldson, *Inside the Army of the Potomac*, 162–63; Edward Henry Courtney Taylor to his sister, November 1862, Taylor Letters, MHC; Galwey, *Valiant Hours*, 52–53.

32. Gates, *Civil War Diaries*, 49; George Thomas Stevens, *Three Years in the Sixth Corps*, 164–65; Hartsock, *Soldier of the Cross*, 25; Francis Jewett Parker, *Thirty-Second Massachusetts*, 115–16; Alonzo D. Bump to his wife, November 10, 1862, Bump Letters, Leigh Collection, USAMHI. There was considerable debate in the New York press about whether the officers had orchestrated support for McClellan and about the enlisted men's response to the general's farewell. See *New York Tribune*, November 18, 1862; *New York Times*, November 14, 1862; *New York Herald*, November 12, 1862.

33. Edwin O. Wentworth to his father, November 10, 1862, Wentworth Papers, LC; Robert Guyton to his father, November 10, 1862, Guyton and Heasler Papers, Duke; Uriah N. Parmelee to his mother, November 10, 1862, Parmelee Papers, Duke.

34. William A. Moore to his father, November 18, 1862, Moore Papers, NHHS; Swinfen, *Ruggles' Regiment*, 13; George W. Ballock to his wife, November 10, 1862, Ballock Papers, Duke; Beidelman, *Letters of George Washington Beidelman*, 144; Barber, *Civil War Letters*, 103; John S. Crocker to his wife, November 10, 1862, Crocker Letters, CU; Louis Fortescue to "Friend Sam," November 13, 1862, Fortescue Letters, FSNMP; Robert S. Robertson, "Diary of the War," 67; George Brinton McClellan, *Civil War Papers*, 522.

35. *New York Herald*, November 11, 14, 1862; George Brinton McClellan, *Civil War Papers*, 525–28; *New York Times*, November 11, 13, 1862; John G. Nicolay to Therena Bates, November 13, 1862, Nicolay Papers, LC; Sears, *McClellan*, 345–48; *Yonkers (N.Y.) Examiner*, November 20, 1862; Matias Romero, *Mexican View of America in the 1860s*, 135.

36. *New York Herald*, November 10, 11, 13, 1862; *New York World*, November 11, 1862; *Boston Post*, November 10, 1862; *Rochester (Ind.) Weekly Sentinel*, November 22, 1862; *Harrisburg Patriot and Union*, November 11–18, 1862; *Cannelton (Ind.) Reporter*, November 14, 1862; *Portland (Maine) Eastern Argus*, November 10–11, 1862; "Our War Correspondence," *Vanity Fair*, November 22, 1862, 245; *Albany (N.Y.) Atlas and Argus*, November 11–13, 1862; *Congressional Globe*, 37th Cong., 3rd sess., 1862, 97.

37. Lydia Maria Child, *Lydia Maria Child*, 420; Charles Sumner, *Selected Letters*, 2:131–32; Charles Sumner to Lot M. Morrill, November 18, 1862, Morrill Papers, Maine Historical Society; McPherson, *Struggle for Equality*, 119; "The Pro-Slavery Reaction," *National Anti-Slavery Standard*, November 15, 1862, 2; "General McClellan," *Liberator*, November 21, 1862, 186; Edwin Wright to Salmon P. Chase, November 13, 1862, Chase Papers, LC.

38. *New York Times*, November 10–11, 1862; *Janesville (Wisc.) Daily Gazette*, November 10, 1862; Simon Cameron to William H. Seward, November 14, 1862, Seward Papers, UR; *Eau Claire (Wisc.) Free Press*, November 20, 1862; *Pittsburgh Daily Dispatch*, November 14, 1862; *Racine (Wisc.) Weekly Journal*, November 12, 1862; *Kokomo (Ind.) Howard Tribune*, November 13, 1862; *Elmira (N.Y.) Weekly Advertiser*, November 15, 1862; *Indianapolis Daily Journal*, November 11, 1862; *Chicago Daily Tribune*, November 8, 10, 1862; *Augusta (Maine) Kennebec Journal*, November 14, 1862; Gray and Ropes, *War Letters*, 19; *Boston Evening Transcript*, November 11–12, 1862.

39. *Rochester (N.Y.) Daily Democrat and American*, November 11, 1862; *Muncie (Ind.) Delaware County Free Press*, November 20, 1862; *Providence (R.I.) Daily Journal*, November 11, 1862; *Indianapolis Daily Journal*, November 12, 1862; *Springfield (Mass.) Daily Republican*,

November 11, 1862; *New York Tribune,* November 10, 15, 1862; Martin Ryerson to William H. Seward, December 13, 1862; George Washington Patterson to Seward, November 21, 1862; Elihu G. Cook to Seward, November 10, 1862; William Morris to Seward, November 10, 1862, Seward Papers, UR; Garfield, *Wild Life of the Army,* 176; Zachariah Chandler to his wife, December 4, 1862, Chandler Papers, LC; Bigelow, *Retrospections,* 1:576–77; E. M. Chester to Salmon P. Chase, November 10, 1862, Chase Papers, LC; *Watertown (N.Y.) Daily News and Reformer,* November 13, 1862; Ferris, "Civil War Diaries," 241; *Easton (Pa.) Free Press,* November 20, 1862; *Poughkeepsie (N.Y.) Daily Eagle,* November 11, 1862; *Haverhill (Mass.) Gazette,* November 14, 1862.

40. *Newark (N.J.) Daily Advertiser,* November 10, 1862; *Boston Daily Advertiser,* November 13, 1862; *Hartford Daily Courant,* November 10, 1862; *Albany (N.Y.) Evening Journal,* November 10, 14, 1862; O. Follett to Salmon P. Chase, November 12, 1862, Chase Papers, LC; *Philadelphia Evening Bulletin,* November 10, 1862; *Philadelphia Inquirer,* November 10, 1862; Elizabeth Blair Lee, *Civil War Letters,* 203–4.

41. For varying assessments of Lincoln's decision, see Col. G. F. R. Henderson, *Stonewall Jackson,* 569; Hattaway and Jones, *How the North Won,* 283; Kenneth P. Williams, *Lincoln Finds a General,* 2:479; Nevins, *War for the Union,* 2:232.

42. Hebert, *Fighting Joe Hooker,* 146–51; Chase, *Salmon P. Chase Papers,* 1:404, 411; Gurowski, *Diary,* 1:313; Gaillard Hunt, *Israel, Elihu, and Cadwallader Washburn,* 109; Henry Greenleaf Pearson, *Life of John A. Andrew,* 2:59; *OR Supplement,* pt. 1, 3:449, 453; Marx and Engels, *Civil War in the U.S.,* 210–14.

43. For two versions of this anecdote, see Fitzhugh Lee, *Lee,* 221; Edward Porter Alexander, *Fighting for the Confederacy,* 166.

44. Most of the material on Burnside's background has been drawn from William Marvel's fine biography, *Burnside,* 1–159. For useful insights on the McClellan-Burnside relationship, see also Jacob Dolson Cox, *Military Reminiscences of the Civil War,* 1:376–89.

45. Swinton, *Campaigns of the Army of the Potomac,* 231; Nicolay and Hay, *Lincoln,* 6:197–98; Kenneth P. Williams, *Lincoln Finds a General,* 2:480–82; T. Harry Williams, *Lincoln and His Generals,* 178–79; Chase, *Salmon P. Chase Papers,* 3:319; Welles, *Diary of Gideon Welles,* 1:182–83.

46. Jacob Dolson Cox, *Military Reminiscences of the Civil War,* 1:356–57; Allen Thorndike Rice, *Reminiscences of Abraham Lincoln,* 278; Clausewitz, *On War,* 146.

47. Jacob Dolson Cox, *Military Reminiscences of the Civil War,* 1:309; Dana, *Recollections of the Civil War,* 132–33; T. Harry Williams, *Lincoln and His Generals,* 178; Edward H. Brewer to his mother, November 14, 1862, Brewer Papers, CSL; John S. Crocker to his wife, November 11, 1862, Crocker Letters, CU.

48. Orlando Willcox, *Forgotten Valor,* 383; Jacob Dolson Cox, *Military Reminiscences of the Civil War,* 1:389–90; Daniel Reed Larned to Mary Burnside, November 9, 1862, Larned Papers, LC; Howard, *Autobiography,* 1:314; Woodbury, *Burnside and the Ninth Army Corps,* 174–75; Haupt, *Reminiscences of Herman Haupt,* 160; *B&L,* 3:106; *OR,* ser. 1, 19(2):557; Jacob Lyman Greene, *Franklin and the Left Wing at Fredericksburg,* 31–32n. Again Clausewitz has acute observations on the need for self-confidence in a commander and the danger of a general rising beyond his capabilities. See Clausewitz, *On War,* 108, 146.

49. Meade, *Life and Letters,* 1:325; Schurz, *Reminiscences,* 2:397–98; Alpheus Starkey Williams, *From the Cannon's Mouth,* 151.

50. Charles E. Perkins to his brother, November 11, 1862, Charles E. Perkins Papers, *CWTI,* USAMHI; December 5, 1862, Lambert Diary, IHS; Franklin William Draper to his wife, November 8, 1862, Draper Papers, LC; Wightman, *From Antietam to Fort Fisher,* 75; November 24, 1862, Taggart Diary, USAMHI.

51. Jeffries, "Diary of Lemuel Jeffries," 269–70; John S. Crocker to his wife, November 9,

1862, Crocker Letters, CU; Samuel Morrow to his brother, November 26, 1862, Morrow Papers, HCWRTC, USAMHI; Albert, *Forty-fifth Pennsylvania,* 253; Galwey, *Valiant Hours,* 53; William Houghton to his father, December 3, 1862, Houghton Papers, IHS; Cavins, *Civil War Letters of Cavins,* 106. See also the useful analysis in Marvel, "Making of a Myth," 2–3.

52. Castleman, *Army of the Potomac,* 242; Henry C. Marsh to John Marsh, November 25, 1862, Marsh Papers, ISL; Robert E. Jameson to his mother, November 16, 1862, Jameson Papers, LC; James B. Post to his wife, November 11, 1862, Post Papers, CWMC, USAMHI; William H. Armstrong, *Red-Tape and Pigeon-Hole Generals,* 225–26; *Story of the Twenty-first Connecticut,* 53.

53. George Hopper to his brother, December 3, 1862, Hopper Papers, USAMIII; Enoch T. Baker to Sarah Baker, November 12, 1862, Baker Papers, GAR; *Rochester (N.Y.) Daily Democrat and American,* November 21, 1862; *Kokomo (Ind.) Howard Tribune,* November 27, 1862; Edwin Winchester Stone, *Rhode Island in the Rebellion,* 179; Pardington, *Dear Sarah,* 39, 42; John White Geary, *Politician Goes to War,* 69; Beidelman, *Letters of George Washington Beidelman,* 144; James Remington to his father, November 17, 1862, Remington Papers, RIHS.

54. "General Ambrose E. Burnside," *American Phrenological Journal* 35 (March 1862): 49.

55. *Rochester (N.Y.) Daily Union and Advertiser,* November 10–11, 1862; *Daily（ Ohio, ）?* ber 18, 1862; *Indianapolis Daily State Sentinel,* November 11, 1862; *New York Herald,* November 11, 13, 1862.

56. *Providence (R.I.) Daily Journal,* November 10, 1862; *Eau Claire (Wisc.) Free Press,* December 4, 1862; *Albany (N.Y.) Evening Journal,* November 10, 15, 17, 1862; "The Removal of McClellan," *Harper's Weekly,* November 22, 1862, 738; *Philadelphia Inquirer,* November 17, 1862; Schuyler Colfax to Abraham Lincoln, November 10, 1862, Lincoln Papers, LC; *New York Times,* November 10, 1862.

57. Charles Sumner, *Selected Letters,* 2:132; T. Harry Williams, *Lincoln and the Radicals,* 197–98; *New York Tribune,* November 17, 1862; Gurowski, *Diary,* 2:14–15; Villard, *Memoirs,* 1:337–38; *Chicago Daily Tribune,* November 11, 1862; Charles Francis Adams, *Cycle of Adams Letters,* 1:193–96.

58. *Augusta (Ga.) Daily Chronicle and Sentinel,* November 22, 1862; James Longstreet, "The Battle of Fredericksburg," in *B&L,* 3:70; *Richmond Daily Examiner,* November 14, 1862; *Richmond Daily Dispatch,* November 20, 1862; *Richmond Daily Whig,* November 28, 1862.

59. Fleet and Fuller, *Green Mount,* 182; Thomas Claybrook Elder to Anna Fitzhugh Elder, November 16, 1862, Elder Papers, VHS; Robert A. Moore, *Life for the Confederacy,* 116; Edmund Ruffin, *Diary,* 2:489; *Richmond Daily Enquirer,* November 15, 1862. McClellan supporters in the North always claimed that Rebels greatly feared their hero. See McCrea, *Dear Belle,* 166; *Brookville (Ind.) Franklin Democrat,* November 14, 1862.

60. *Charleston Mercury,* November 14, 1862; *Macon (Ga.) Daily Telegraph,* November 18, 1862; *Richmond Daily Examiner,* November 22, 1862; *Milledgeville (Ga.) Confederate Union,* November 25, 1862; *Columbus (Ga.) Daily Enquirer,* November 17, 1862; Judith Brockenbrough McGuire, *Diary of a Southern Refugee,* 170; Susan Leigh Blackford, *Memoirs of Life In and Out of the Army,* 1:230.

61. *OR,* ser. 2, 4:949–50; Jedediah Hotchkiss to Sara Ann Comfort Hotchkiss, November 16, 1862, Hotchkiss Papers, LC; Graves, *Confederate Marine,* 94; *Richmond Daily Dispatch,* November 20, 1862; *Richmond Daily Whig,* November 14, 17, 1862; Emma Holmes, *Diary,* 210.

62. *Raleigh Weekly Standard,* November 19, 1862; Hatton Memoir, 369, LC; *Richmond Daily Whig,* November 15, 1862; Edmondston, *"Journal of a Secesh Lady,"* 301; November 27, 1862, Grimball Diary, SHC; *Wilmington (N.C.) Daily Journal,* November 18, 21, 1862; *Charleston Mercury,* November 21, 1862; *Richmond Daily Dispatch,* November 17, 1862; *Richmond Daily Examiner,* November 15, 1862.

63. November 11, 1862, Thompson Memoir, LC; Welsh and Welsh, "Civil War Letters from

Two Brothers," 152–53; Daniel Reed Larned to Mary Burnside, November 9, 1862, Larned Papers, LC; Castleman, *Army of the Potomac,* 242; November 15, 1862, Elmer Diary, CWMC, USAMHI; *New York Times,* November 12, 1862; Sprenger, *122d Regiment,* 102–3.

64. Hartsock, *Soldier of the Cross,* 27; *Rochester (N.Y.) Daily Union and Advertiser,* November 19, 1862; William Teall to his wife, November 10, 1862, Teall Letters, TSLA; George B. Felch to his father, November 11, 1862, Felch Letters, FSNMP; Cheek and Pointon, *Sauk County Riflemen,* 54–55.

65. Zerah Coston Monks to Hannah T. Rohrer, November 11, 1862, Monks-Rohrer Letters, Emory; Gavin, *Campaigning with the Roundheads,* 203; *Story of the Twenty-first Connecticut,* 53; November 9, 1862, Holford Diary, LC; James R. Woodworth to Phoebe Woodworth, November 10, 1862, Woodworth Papers, Hotchkiss Collection, CL; Haley, *Rebel Yell and Yankee Hurrah,* 52.

66. William Franklin Draper to his wife, November 11, 1862, Draper Papers, LC; Albert, *Forty-fifth Pennsylvania,* 253; *Newark (N.J.) Daily Advertiser,* November 17, 1862; November 13–14, 1862, Bailey Diary, NHHS; James Remington to his sister, November 13, 1862, Remington Papers, RIHS; Willard J. Templeton to his parents, November 12, 1862, Templeton Letters, NHSL; Beidelman, *Letters of George Washington Beidelman,* 174.

67. McCarter, *My Life in the Irish Brigade,* 68–69; Henry F. Young to "Dear Delia," November 15, 1862, Young Papers, SHSW; William Watson, *Letters of a Civil War Surgeon,* 31–32; Stephen Rich to "Brother William," November 14, 1862, Rich Papers, CWMC, USAMHI; Pardington, *Dear Sarah,* 35.

68. Small, *Road to Richmond,* 57; McAllister, *Letters of Robert McAllister,* 219; James R. Woodworth to Phoebe Woodworth, November 10, 1862, Woodworth Papers, Hotchkiss Collection, CL; S. Millett Thompson, *Thirteenth New Hampshire,* 23–24; Hartsock, *Soldier of the Cross,* 26–27; *Augusta (Maine) Kennebec Journal,* December 12, 1862; Elizabeth D. Leonard, *Yankee Women,* 120–21; November 14, 1862, Eaton Diary, SHC.

69. For a concise and cogent analysis of how Burnside planned to advance on Richmond, see Marvel, *Burnside,* 163–64. Marvel speculates that McClellan himself might have suggested the Fredericksburg route shortly before he relinquished command to Burnside.

70. *OR,* ser. 1, 19(2):546, 552–54.

71. For an excellent analysis and defense of Burnside's plan by a Confederate ordnance officer, see William Allan, "Fredericksburg," 125–26. Longstreet claimed that the Confederates' biggest worry was that Burnside would advance and defeat the divided corps of the Army of Northern Virginia in detail. Artillerist Porter Alexander later offered two contradictory assessments of Burnside's new route. See James Longstreet, "The Battle of Fredericksburg," in *B&L,* 3:85; Edward Porter Alexander, *Fighting for the Confederacy,* 166; Edward Porter Alexander, *Military Memoirs of a Confederate,* 284. For more critical comments, see Gough, *Fredericksburg and Chancellorsville,* 47–49; Whan, *Fiasco at Fredericksburg,* 19–23.

72. *OR,* ser. 1, 19(2):570; Herman Haupt to his wife, November 15, 1862, Haupt Letterbook, Haupt Papers, LC; Ambrose, *Halleck,* 9–10; Brooks, *Washington in Lincoln's Time,* 42; Doster, *Lincoln and Episodes of the Civil War,* 178–79.

73. Haupt, *Reminiscences of Herman Haupt,* 160; Herman Haupt to his wife, November 15, 1862, Haupt Letterbook, Haupt Papers, LC; *CCW,* 1:683–84; *OR,* 83–84. Halleck later claimed that he convinced Burnside to modify his original plan and have the Army of the Potomac cross upstream from the junction of the Rappahannock and Rapidan rivers. Burnside always insisted that he intended to proceed by way of Falmouth. Halleck, Burnside, Meigs, and Haupt may have briefly discussed crossing the army elsewhere, and there is also the possibility that Halleck and Burnside completely misunderstood each other; but the contemporary evidence, including Halleck's own remarks about pontoons, and the weight of historical opinion supports Burnside's version of the meeting. See *CCW,* 1:675; *OR,* 46–47; T. Harry Williams, *Lin-*

coln and His Generals, 192–93; Kenneth P. Williams, Lincoln Finds a General, 2:484–87; Whan, Fiasco at Fredericksburg, 20–21.

74. Nicolay and Hay, Lincoln, 6:198; OR, ser. 1, 19(2):574, 579, 21:84; Clausewitz, On War, 617.

75. On December 9 Maj. Gen. Henry W. Slocum's Twelfth Corps became part of the Reserve Grand Division.

76. OR, ser. 1, 19(2):583–84; Meade, Life and Letters, 1:326; CCW, 1:666; New York Tribune, November 14, 1862.

77. Trobriand, Four Years with the Army of the Potomac, 353; Clausewitz, On War, 294–95; Hagerman, Civil War and Origins of Modern Warfare, 79–80; Redway, Fredericksburg, 34–35; Whan, Fiasco at Fredericksburg, 124–25; Gough, Fredericksburg and Chancellorsville, 50–51; Castleman, Army of the Potomac, 241–42; Daniel R. Larned to Mary Burnside, November 9, 1862, and Larned to his sister, November 9, 1862, Larned Papers, LC.

78. McAllister, Letters of Robert McAllister, 220; John S. Crocker to his wife, November 13, 1862, Crocker Letters, CU; Hess, Liberty, Virtue, and Progress, 5–17.

79. McAllister, Letters of Robert McAllister, 219; James B. Post to his wife, November 15, 1862, Post Papers, CWMC, USAMHI; James Remington to his sister, November 10, 1862, Remington Papers, RIHS; Robert Gould Shaw, Blue-Eyed Child of Fortune, 255; George Henry Chandler to his mother, November 9, 1862, Chandler Papers, NHHS.

80. Roland R. Bowen, From Ball's Bluff to Gettysburg, 141; Pardington, Dear Sarah, 37; James B. Post to his wife, November 15, 1862, Post Papers, CWMC, USAMHI; William Franklin Draper to his wife, November 8, 1862, Draper Papers, LC.

81. Roland R. Bowen, From Ball's Bluff to Gettysburg, 141; Haydon, For Country, Cause, and Leader, 288; Darius Starr to his mother, November 10, 1862, Starr Papers, Duke; Uriah N. Parmelee to his mother, November 10, 1862, Parmelee Papers, Duke.

82. Albany (N.Y.) Atlas and Argus, November 11, 1862; McKelvey, Rochester in the Civil War, 110; Alexander Morrison Stewart, Camp, March, and Battlefield, 251; Alpheus Starkey Williams, From the Cannon's Mouth, 150–51; OR Supplement, pt. 1, 3:666–67; Baltimore American and Commercial Advertiser, November 13, 1862.

83. Strong, Diary of George Templeton Strong, 3:274–75; Hartford Daily Courant, November 14, 1862; Philadelphia Inquirer, November 12, 13, 1862; New York Times, November 23, 1862; New York Tribune, November 18, 1862; Chicago Daily Tribune, November 19, 1862.

CHAPTER FOUR

1. OR, ser. 1, 19(2):564–66, 571–72, and ser. 3, 2:951–52; Rusling, Men and Things I Saw in Civil War Days, 282; Haupt, Reminiscences of Herman Haupt, 159–60, 163–65, 170, 173.

2. OR, ser. 1, 19(2):559–60, 571–72, 21:147, 764, 781, 798; CCW, 1:682–83, 685–87; Comte de Paris, Civil War in America, 2:569; Duncan, Medical Department of the United States Army, 175; Haupt, Reminiscences of Herman Haupt, 165–68.

3. Gray and Ropes, War Letters, 33–34; December 6, 1862, Abernathy Diary, USAMHI; John Smart to Ann Smart, November 26, 1862, Smart Letters, FSNMP.

4. Hagerman, Civil War and Origins of Modern Warfare, 45; Samuel W. Eaton to Catherine Eaton, November 24, 1862, Eaton Papers, SHSW; Samuel W. North to "Dear Brother," November 20, 1862, North Letters, USAMHI; Welsh and Welsh, "Civil War Letters from Two Brothers," 153; James B. Post to his wife, November 11, 1862, Post Papers, CWMC, USAMHI.

5. John H. Rhodes, History of Battery B, 132; McCrea, Dear Belle, 164–65; Charles Shields Wainwright, Diary of Battle, 124, 126; History of the Fifth Massachusetts Battery, 492; Edwin Winchester Stone, Rhode Island in the Rebellion, 181–82.

6. Tobie, First Maine Cavalry, 102–3; Denison, First Rhode Island Cavalry, 178; November 17, 1862, Lloyd Diary, SHC; OR, ser. 1, 19(2):566.

7. *OR,* ser. 1, 19(2):572, 21:765–66, 774–75, 815; Locke, *Story of the Regiment,* 154–55; Von Borcke, *Memoirs of the Confederate War,* 2:57–61; *History of the Sixth New York Cavalry,* 80–82; November 10, 1862, Flack Diary, FSNMP; John S. Crocker to his wife, November 11, 1862, Crocker Letters, CU; Denison, *First Rhode Island Cavalry,* 172–73; Hopkins, *Seventh Rhode Island,* 31–32; O'Reilly, *Jackson at Fredericksburg,* 6–7.

8. For the general outlines of the march and the various departure times, see *OR,* 84; Whitney, *Hawkins Zouaves,* 164; Bosbyshell, *48th in the War,* 92; Washburn, *108th Regiment,* 111; Isaac Lyman Taylor, "Campaigning with the First Minnesota," 233.

9. Wiley, *Life of Billy Yank,* 64; James I. Robertson Jr., *Soldiers Blue and Gray,* 61–63; Bartol, *Nation's Hour,* 44–45; Howard, *Autobiography,* 1:316; Clausewitz, *On War,* 319.

10. Kenneth P. Williams, *Lincoln Finds a General,* 2:504. By November 19 all of Sumner's brigades had reached the environs of Falmouth.

11. *Story of the Twenty-first Connecticut,* 56; R. S. Robertson to his parents, November 21, 1862, Robertson Papers, FSNMP; Relyea Memoir, 62–63, CHS; Peter Welsh, *Irish Green and Union Blue,* 32.

12. Wightman, *From Antietam to Fort Fisher,* 80–81; Page, *Fourteenth Connecticut,* 70–71; John S. Crocker to his wife, November 19, 1862, Crocker Letters, CU; Beidelman, *Letters of George Washington Beidelman,* 147–48. In a new regiment three or so stragglers per day was defined as "very little straggling." See *OR Supplement,* pt. 2, 40:572. For a good description of both the physical and psychological effects of marches, see Linderman, *Embattled Courage,* 113–15.

13. J. E. Hodgkins, *Civil War Diary,* 13; Waitt, *Nineteenth Massachusetts,* 159; Aldrich, *History of Battery A,* 155; Mayo, *Civil War Letters,* 219; A. B. Martin to "Dear Ann," December 19, 1862, Martin Letter, FSNMP; Tyler, *Recollections of the Civil War,* 58–59; McCarter, *My Life in the Irish Brigade,* 76.

14. James Remington to his father, November 17, 1862, Remington Papers, RIHS; Wightman, *From Antietam to Fort Fisher,* 83; November 16, 1862, Willand Diary, NHSL; *History of the Thirty-Fifth Massachusetts Volunteers,* 71–72; *Story of the Twenty-first Connecticut,* 55; Walcott, *Twenty-First Regiment,* 228–29; McCarter, *My Life in the Irish Brigade,* 77–80.

15. Jeffries, "Diary of Lemuel Jeffries," 270; Kepler, *Fourth Ohio,* 89; Paige Memoir, 17, USAMHI; Marvel, *Ninth New Hampshire,* 86; *Story of the Twenty-first Connecticut,* 89, 91–92.

16. John S. Crocker to his wife, November 15, 1862, Crocker Letters, CU; November 19, 1862, Pope Diary, *CWTI,* USAMHI; Aldrich, *History of Battery A,* 155; Lord, *History of the Ninth New Hampshire,* 208.

17. George W. Barr to Vinnie Barr, November 19, 1862, Barr Papers, Schoff Collection, CL; John S. Crocker to his wife, November 15, 1862, Crocker Letters, CU; Wightman, *From Antietam to Fort Fisher,* 81–82; Haydon, *For Country, Cause, and Leader,* 291; Bartol, *Nation's Hour,* 46; November 16, 1862, Lloyd Diary, SHC; Rusling, *Men and Things I Saw in Civil War Days,* 282–83; Wren, *Captain James Wren's Civil War Diary,* 89; George H. Mellish to his mother, November 19, 1862, Mellish Papers, HL.

18. Edward Henry Courtney Taylor to his mother, November 20, 1862, Taylor Letters, MHC; Isaac Lyman Taylor, "Campaigning with the First Minnesota," 233; McAllister, *Letters of Robert McAllister,* 224; Richard Packard to his parents, November 24, 1862, Packard Letter, CWMC, USAMHI; Charles Shields Wainwright, *Diary of Battle,* 127; Gavin, *Campaigning with the Roundheads,* 207; Oliver Wendell Holmes, *Touched with Fire,* 72–73.

19. Siegel, *For the Glory of the Union,* 97–99; Castleman, *Army of the Potomac,* 213; *OR,* 84, 760–61; Jaques, *Three Years' Campaign,* 125–26; Cook, *Twelfth Massachusetts,* 78–79; Todd, *Ninth Regiment, N.Y.S.M.,* 219; Daniel M. Holt, *Surgeon's Civil War,* 48; Baquet, *History of the 1st New Jersey,* 58–59; November 17, 18, 20, 1862, Holford Diary, LC.

20. John Harrison Mills, *Chronicles of the Twenty-First New York,* 270–71; Maxson, *Camp Fires of the Twenty-Third,* 112; McClenthen, *Narrative of the Fall and Winter Campaign,* 27–28;

Henry C. Marsh to John Marsh, November 20, 1862, Marsh Papers, ISL; Henry Ogden Ryerson to his sister, November 21, 1862, Anderson Family Papers, NJHS; Dawes, *Sixth Wisconsin*, 106; Warren Hapgood Freeman, *Letters from Two Brothers*, 56–57.

21. Orson Blair Curtis, *History of the Twenty-Fourth Michigan*, 80–81; Wyman Silas White, *Civil War Diary*, 109–10; Charles E. Davis, *Three Years in the Army*, 157–59; William Speed to Charlotte Speed, November 21, 1862, Speed Papers, Schoff Collection, CL. Several men in both the First and Sixth Corps deserted during the march and were later court-martialed. See Index Project Summary of Courts-Martial, Fredericksburg, Woodacre, California, copies in FSNMP.

22. *OR*, 354–55, 762, 772–73, 786.

23. For marching schedules, see Thomas H. Evans, "'Cries of the Wounded,'" 29–30; John Lord Parker, *Twenty-Second Massachusetts*, 215–18; John L. Smith, *118th Pennsylvania*, 109–10. For the experiences of Sykes's men, see Brian A. Bennett, *140th New York*, 94–97; Brainard, *One Hundred and Forty-sixth New York*, 21–23; Reese, *Sykes' Regular Infantry Division*, 169–70.

24. Helman, "Young Soldier in the Army of the Potomac," 151–52. For another excellent account, see Hartwell, *To My Beloved Wife and Boy at Home*, 29.

25. Weygant, *One Hundred and Twenty-Fourth Regiment*, 58 59; *Rochester (N.Y.) Daily Democrat and American*, November 29, 1862; November 22, 1862, Mancha Diary, CWMC, USAMHI; Thomas J. Halsey, *Field of Battle*, 42; Rusling, *Men and Things I Saw in Civil War Days*, 284–85; Robert Goldthwaite Carter, *Four Brothers in Blue*, 165; November 20, 1862, Woodworth Diary, Hotchkiss Collection, CL; John W. Ames to his brother, November 24, 1862, Ames Papers, USAMHI; November 20, 1862, Schaeffer Diary, West Virginia University; Hartsock, *Soldier of the Cross*, 30–31. The periods without food may have also been longer in Hooker's grand division. See November 17, 20, 22–25, 1862, Mancha Diary, CWMC, USAMHI; Asa W. Bartlett, *History of the Twelfth New Hampshire*, 35–36; D. Porter Marshall, *Co. "K," 155th Pennsylvania*, 78.

26. Ted Alexander, *126th Pennsylvania*, 127; James H. Leonard, "Letters of a Fifth Wisconsin Volunteer," 68; Beidelman, *Letters of George Washington Beidelman*, 147; Henry F. Young to his father, December 1, 1862, Young Papers, SHSW; Zerah Coston Monks to Hannah T. Rohrer, November 20, 1862, Monks-Rohrer Letters, Emory; McAllister, *Letters of Robert McAllister*, 224–25; *OR*, 776.

27. November 19, 1862, Pope Diary, CWTI, USAMHI; Aldrich, *History of Battery A*, 155; Lord, *History of the Ninth New Hampshire*, 208; Charles Shields Wainwright, *Diary of Battle*, 127–28; Charles J. Borden to "Dear Friend," November 16, 1862, Borden Papers, Duke; Tobie, *First Maine Cavalry*, 101–2; *New York Times*, November 28, 1862; Daniel M. Holt, *Surgeon's Civil War*, 53; November 23, 1862, Holford Diary, LC; November 27, 28, 1862, Ayer Diary, Duke.

28. Alonzo Pierce to "Dear Brother Charlie," December 7, 1862, Pierce Papers, NHHS; Dawes, *Sixth Wisconsin*, 106; Catton, *Glory Road*, 67; John Ripley Adams, *Memorial and Letters*, 74; Benjamin F. Appleby to his wife, December 10, 1862, Appleby Letters, CWTI, USAMHI; Gregg, *Life in the Army*, 74–75; Morton Hayward to his sister, November 22, 1862, Hayward Letters, Leigh Collection, USAMHI. Some of the foraging described took place en route, though much of it began after the troops arrived at their destinations. There is also some material included from soldiers whose outfits arrived later in November or in early December.

29. Asa W. Bartlett, *History of the Twelfth New Hampshire*, 398–99; Hartsock, *Soldier of the Cross*, 29; *Berks and Schuylkill (Pa.) Journal*, November 22, 1862; J. Frank Sterling to his sister, November 25, 1862, Sterling Papers, Rutgers University.

30. Lusk, *War Letters of William Thompson Lusk*, 232–33; Conyngham, *Irish Brigade*, 325–27.

31. Donald L. Smith, *Twenty-fourth Michigan*, 52; Barber, *Civil War Letters*, 103; Robert Goldthwaite Carter, *Four Brothers in Blue*, 176–77; Francis Jewett Parker, *Thirty-Second Mas-*

sachusetts, 113–15; Blake, *Three Years in the Army of the Potomac,* 146; Woodward, *Third Pennsylvania Reserves,* 200.

32. Small, *Sixteenth Maine,* 52–54; Fairchild, *27th Regiment,* 113; *New York Times,* December 11, 1862.

33. Curtis C. Pollock to his mother, November 25, 1862, Pollock Papers, CWMC, USAMHI; Castleman, *Army of the Potomac,* 213–14; November 18, 1862, Mancha Diary, CWMC, USAMHI; Judd, *Story of the Thirty-Third,* 220–22; Blake, *Three Years in the Army of the Potomac,* 145–46; Letter of John Boyts, November 23, 1862, Boyts Diary, HSP.

34. Allan L. Bevan to his sister, November 24, 1862, Bevan Correspondence, CWMC, USAMHI; Robert W. Hemphill to his father, November 20, 1862, Hemphill Letter, Henry Family Papers, USAMHI; Meade, *Life and Letters,* 1:330; McAllister, *Letters of Robert McAllister,* 236; November 21, 1862, Holford Diary, LC.

35. *Philadelphia Evening Bulletin,* November 18, 1862; *New York Times,* November 18–19, 1862; Leech, *Reveille in Washington,* 220; *Albany (N.Y.) Atlas and Argus,* November 19–20, 1862; French, *Witness to the Young Republic,* 414; *Poughkeepsie (N.Y.) Daily Eagle,* November 19, 1862; *Providence (R.I.) Daily Journal,* November 19, 1862; *Hartford Daily Courant,* November 19, 21, 1862; *Springfield (Mass.) Daily Republican,* November 19, 1862; *Philadelphia Inquirer,* November 19–20, 1862; *Yonkers (N.Y.) Examiner,* November 20, 1862; *New York Tribune,* November 21, 1862.

36. *Journal of the Called Session of the Senate of Alabama,* 85; *OR,* ser. 4, 2:180; Lafayette McLaws to his wife, November 16, 1862, McLaws Papers, SHC; McPherson, *What They Fought For,* 9–25; Michael Barton, *Goodmen,* 35–44.

37. Reid Mitchell, *Civil War Soldiers,* 34–36; Wiley, *Life of Johnny Reb,* 308–15; Jimerson, *Private Civil War,* 126–29; *Richmond Daily Whig,* November 25, December 2, 11, 1862.

38. Shattuck, *Shield and Hiding Place,* 35–43; *Richmond Daily Dispatch,* November 5, 1862; *Richmond Daily Whig,* November 7, 1862; *Journal of the Senate of South Carolina,* 26–27; Drew Gilpin Faust, *Creation of Confederate Nationalism,* 22–40.

39. Vance, *Papers of Zebulon Baird Vance,* 1:304–5; *Athens (Ga.) Southern Banner,* January 21, 1863; Mrs. Dr. Welborn to Joseph E. Brown, November 16, 1862, Brown (Governors') Papers, GDAH.

40. *Journal of the Senate of South Carolina,* 26–27; *Raleigh Weekly Standard,* November 12, 1862; *Richmond Daily Enquirer,* November 14, 1862; December 1, 1862, Hamilton Diary, FSNMP; Kate Burruss to Edward M. Burruss, December 3, 1862, Burruss Papers, LSU; December 28, 1862, Simons Diary, UT.

41. *Richmond Daily Dispatch,* November 5, 1862; *Richmond Daily Enquirer,* November 4, 8, 1862; *Journal of the Called Session of the Senate of Alabama,* 14–15; November 28, 1862, Grimball Diary, SHC; *Richmond Daily Examiner,* November 7, 1862.

42. *OR,* ser. 4, 2:181–82; *Richmond Daily Enquirer,* December 10, 13, 1862; *Richmond Daily Whig,* November 21, 1862, January 7, 1863; *Charleston Daily Courier,* November 7, 1862; *Augusta (Ga.) Daily Chronicle and Sentinel,* November 15, 1862; *Wilmington (N.C.) Daily Journal,* December 3, 1862; *Richmond Daily Enquirer,* November 7, 1862; Rowland, *Davis,* 5:425–26.

43. J. B. Jones, *Rebel War Clerk's Diary,* 1:181, 184; *Richmond Daily Examiner,* November 3, 6, 14, 1862; *Richmond Daily Whig,* December 2, 1862; Daniel E. Sutherland, *Fredericksburg and Chancellorsville,* 19.

44. *OR,* ser. 4, 2:214–15; DuBose, *Yancey,* 672–74; *Richmond Daily Whig,* November 12, December 12, 1862; *Richmond Daily Enquirer,* November 20, 1862.

45. *Charleston Daily Courier,* October 31, November 6, 1862; *OR,* ser. 4, 2:154, 180–81, 186–88, 225–26; *Richmond Daily Dispatch,* November 14, 27, 1862; *Richmond Daily Whig,* November 5, 1862; *Richmond Daily Enquirer,* November 14, 1862; George K. Harlow to his father, November 15, 1862, Harlow Family Papers, VHS.

46. *Richmond Daily Examiner,* November 4, 1862; Edmondston, *"Journal of a Secesh Lady,"* 296. A concise and helpful summary of Lee's thinking and the positions of his troops is in William Allan, *Army of Northern Virginia,* 460–62.

47. Emory M. Thomas, *Bold Dragoon,* 182–86; Cook, *Wearing of the Gray,* 19; Susan Leigh Blackford, *Letters from Lee's Army,* 136.

48. Col. G. F. R. Henderson, *Civil War,* 17–18; *OR,* ser. 1, 19(2):709, 712, 716–17.

49. George William Beale, *Lieutenant of Cavalry in Lee's Army,* 56–58; *OR,* ser. 1, 19(2):710–11, 714–15, 717–18, 720; Fishel, *Secret War for the Union,* 256–57; Julian Calx Ruffin to Edmund Ruffin, November 14, 1862, Ruffin Papers, VHS. As noted earlier in this chapter, Haupt's men rebuilt this section of railroad.

50. *Richmond Daily Enquirer,* November 15, 1862; *OR,* ser. 1, 19(2):723, 21:1013–15; Edmund Ruffin, *Diary,* 2:490, 497; Julian Calx Ruffin to Edmund Ruffin, November 24, 1862, Ruffin Papers, VHS; "The New Base of Operations," *Index* (London), December 4, 1862, 88; McDaniel, *With Unabated Trust,* 112.

51. *OR,* 550–51, 1017–22; Robert E. Lee, *Wartime Papers,* 341; *Richmond Daily Whig,* November 20, 1862; J. B. Jones, *Rebel War Clerk's Diary,* 1:192. See the concise and cogent analysis of Lee's thinking in Daniel E. Sutherland, *Fredericksburg and Chancellorsville,* 111–111.

52. Dickert, *Kershaw's Brigade,* 167–69; Thomas R. Reeder to his sister, November 28, 1862, Reeder Letters, SCL; Robert A. Moore, *Life for the Confederacy,* 117; Edward M. Burruss to Kate Burruss, November 23, 1862, Burruss Papers, LSU; Henry P. Garrison to Emily Aurora Bosworth, November 25, 1862, Garrison Papers, Austin State University; Sorrel, *Recollections of a Confederate Staff Officer,* 225; Hubbert, "Diary of Mike M. Hubbert," 311.

53. Sloan, *Guilford Grays,* 53–54; November 21, 1862, Samuel Hoey Walkup Journal, Walkup Papers, SHC; Walter Clark, *Regiments and Battalions from North Carolina,* 3:69; Day, *History of Company I,* 30–31; Constantine Hege to his father, November 24, 1862, Hege Letters, Leigh Collection, USAMHI; Henry Alexander Chambers, *Diary,* 70; Burgwyn, *Captain's War,* 35.

54. *OR Supplement,* pt. 1, 3:710–11; *OR,* ser. 1, 51(2):650; Napier Bartlett, *Military Record of Louisiana,* 158; Krick, *Parker's Virginia Battery,* 88; William M. Owen, *In Camp and Battle with the Washington Artillery,* 173–74.

55. *OR,* 1025–26; O'Reilly, *Jackson at Fredericksburg,* 9; Ott, "Civil War Diary of James J. Kirkpatrick," 83–84; DeNoon, *Charlie's Letters,* 95–96; Halsey Wigfall to Louis T. Wigfall, November 23, 1862, Wigfall Papers, UT; November 21, 1862, Pickett Diary, CWTI, USAMHI; November 19–21, 1862, Ware Diary, SHC; Goodson, "Letters of Joab Goodson," 130–31; November 20, 1862, Hume Diary, LC; James C. Zimmerman to his wife, November 24, 1862, Zimmerman Papers, Duke.

56. *OR,* 1026–27; William H. Jones to his wife, November 19, 1862, William H. Jones Papers, Duke; November 19, 1862, Malloy Diary, CWMC, USAMHI; William Ross Stillwell to "My Dear Mollie," November 23, 1862, Stillwell Letters, GDAII; J. W. Armsworthy to his wife, November 23, 1862, Armsworthy Letters, FSNMP.

57. November 20, 1862, Malloy Diary, CWMC, USAMHI; William Ross Stillwell to "My Dear Mollie," November 23, 1862, Stillwell Letters, GDAH; Cauthen, *Family Letters of Three Wade Hamptons,* 88; T. R. R. Cobb to his wife, November 22, 1862, Cobb Letters, UG.

58. Edmund Ruffin, *Diary,* 2:497; J. B. Jones, *Rebel War Clerk's Diary,* 1:194; *Richmond Daily Enquirer,* November 20, 1862; *Richmond Daily Examiner,* November 21, 22, 1862; *Richmond Daily Dispatch,* November 19, 1862.

CHAPTER FIVE

1. *History of the Thirty-Fifth Massachusetts Volunteers,* 68–71; Graham, *Ninth New York,* 364.

2. Favill, *Diary of a Young Officer,* 202–3; Mulholland, "At Fredericksburg," 3; Aldrich, *His-*

tory of Battery A, 155–56; Walker, *Second Corps,* 140–41; *New York Times,* November 21, 1862; Jane Howison Beale, *Journal,* 65; *OR,* 1017–18.

3. *OR,* 787–88; November 20, 1862, Pope Diary, *CWTI,* USAMHI; Teall, "Ringside Seat at Fredericksburg," 24; Wren, *Captain James Wren's Civil War Diary,* 89; Edmondston, *"Journal of a Secesh Lady,"* 308; T. R. R. Cobb to his wife, November 22, 1862, Cobb Letters, UG; Judith Brockenbrough McGuire, *Diary of a Southern Refugee,* 171; *Richmond Daily Enquirer,* November 22, 24, 1862.

4. *CCW,* 1:652, 657–58; Villard, *Memoirs,* 1:343–44; Howard, *Autobiography,* 1:316–18; *OR,* 85–86, 777; Witherspoon, "Chapter in the History of the Defense of Fredericksburg," 14–24, VHS.

5. William Child, *Fifth New Hampshire,* 147; Augustus Van Dyke to his father, November 19, 20, 1862, Van Dyke Papers, IHS; Robert S. Robertson, "Diary of the War," 70–71; Orlando Willcox, *Forgotten Valor,* 398; *History of the Thirty-Fifth Massachusetts Volunteers,* 75; Amos Hadley, *Life of Walter Harriman,* 123. For solid defenses of Burnside's caution at this point, see Kenneth P. Williams, *Lincoln Finds a General,* 2:505; Marvel, *Burnside,* 167. For cogent criticisms of Burnside, see Edward Porter Alexander, *Fighting for the Confederacy,* 167; Palfrey, *Antietam and Fredericksburg,* 139; J. H. Moore, "Fredericksburg," 180; William Allan, "Fredericksburg," 128–29; Whan, *Fiasco at Fredericksburg,* 128; Catton, *Glory Road,* 22–23.

6. *New York Times,* November 22, 1862; *New York Herald,* November 19, 22, 1862; *New York World,* November 21, 1862.

7. *Philadelphia Inquirer,* November 21, 22, 1862; *New York Tribune,* November 22, 1862; *New York Times,* November 21, 1862; *New York Herald,* November 20, 1862.

8. *CCW,* 1:675; John Godfrey to Horace Godfrey, November 5, 16, December 1, 1862, Godfrey Papers, NHHS; Charles Francis Adams Jr., *Autobiography,* 161; Gibbon, *Recollections of the Civil War,* 107–9; McAllister, *Letters of Robert McAllister,* 238; *New York Times,* November 7, 18, 1862; J. Cutler Andrews, *North Reports the Civil War,* 320–21; Villard, *Memoirs,* 1: 347–48.

9. *OR,* 85, 104–5, 355, 773–74; *CCW,* 1:654.

10. *Manufactures of the United States in 1860,* 631; Kennedy, *Agriculture of the United States in 1860,* 162–65; *Statistics of the United States in 1860,* 485–86; *New York Tribune,* November 24, 1862; *History of the Sixth New York Cavalry,* 84–85; Tobie, *First Maine Cavalry,* 104; Willard J. Templeton to parents and sister, November 27, 1862, Templeton Letters, NHSL; *New York Herald,* November 28, 1862; McAllister, *Letters of Robert McAllister,* 229–30.

11. John S. Crocker to his wife, November 19, 1862, Crocker Letters, CU; Daggett, "Those Whom You Left behind You," 347; McCarter, *My Life in the Irish Brigade,* 82–83; Charles Shields Wainwright, *Diary of Battle,* 131; Hopkins, *Seventh Rhode Island,* 33–34; Moe, *Last Full Measure,* 207; Favill, *Diary of a Young Officer,* 20–23; *New York Herald,* December 5, 1862. For information on Falmouth before and during the war, see Noel G. Harrison, *Fredericksburg Civil War Sites,* 1:64–76. Noel Harrison's two volumes contain wonderfully detailed descriptions of numerous sites in and around Fredericksburg. His work is indispensable for any student of the Civil War in that area of Virginia.

12. *OR,* 783–84; Teall, "Ringside Seat at Fredericksburg," 24.

13. Teall, "Ringside Seat at Fredericksburg," 24; Marsena Rudolph Patrick, *Inside Lincoln's Army,* 179–80; *OR,* 784–85.

14. *OR,* 1026; Lafayette McLaws to his wife, November 22, 1862, McLaws Papers, SHC; *Richmond Daily Whig,* November 25, 1862.

15. Walcott, *Twenty-First Regiment,* 232; James R. Woodworth to Phoebe Woodworth, November 22–25, Woodworth Papers, Hotchkiss Collection, CL; John S. Crocker to his wife, November 22, 1862, Crocker Letters, CU; Barber, *Civil War Letters,* 102.

16. Noel G. Harrison, *Fredericksburg Civil War Sites,* 1:1–17; Blair, "Barbarians at Fredericksburg's Gate," 144–52; Kennedy, *Population of the United States,* 518.

17. Jane Howison Beale, *Journal,* 65–66; Kate Corbin to Sallie Munford, November 19, 1862, Munford-Ellis Papers, Duke; November 19, 1862, Alsop Diary, VHS; Lafayette McLaws to his wife, November 22, 1862, McLaws Papers, SHC; Wollard Diary, 41–42, FSNMP; Walters, *Norfolk Blues,* 43; Haggard, "Cavalry Fight at Fredericksburg," 295; James LeGrand Wilson, *Confederate Soldier,* 98–101.

18. J. B. Jones, *Rebel War Clerk's Diary,* 1:192; Edward Porter Alexander, "Battle of Fredericksburg," 382–83; Scales, "Battle of Fredericksburg," 205–6; Robert E. Lee, *Wartime Papers,* 393–94; James Drayton Nance to "My Dear Laura," November 30, 1862, Nance Papers, SCL; Susan Pendleton Lee, *Memoirs of William Nelson Pendleton,* 237; William Teall to his wife, November 29, 1862, Teall Letters, TSLA; Judith Brockenbrough McGuire, *Diary of a Southern Refugee,* 171; Jane Howison Beale, *Journal,* 66–67.

19. William M. Owen, *In Camp and Battle with the Washington Artillery,* 174; Halsey Wigfall to Louis T. Wigfall, November 23, 1862, Wigfall Papers, UT; William Ross Stillwell to "My Dear Mollie," November 23, 1862, Stillwell Letters, GDAH; Mrs. B. M. Carter, "Story of Gen. Lee and Three Children"; T. R. R. Cobb to his wife, November 22, 27, 1862, Cobb Letters, UG; Roberson, *Weep Not for Me,* 93; William Henry Tatum to his sister, November 23, 1862, Tatum Papers, VHS; Jesse S. McGee to "My dear Mollie," November 14, 1862, McGee Church & Family Papers, SCL.

20. James Power Smith, "With Stonewall Jackson," 24–25; Edward Porter Alexander, "Battle of Fredericksburg," 382–83; *Philadelphia Inquirer,* December 8, 1862; Parramore et al., *Before the Rebel Flag Fell,* 47–48; Davidson, *Diary and Letters,* 60–61; Edmondson, *My Dear Emma,* 114; Collier, *Third Arkansas Infantry,* 105; Pender, *General to His Lady,* 191; Thomas Claybrook Elder to Anna Fitzhugh Elder, November 23, 1862, Elder Papers, VHS; William Willis Blackford, *War Years with Stuart,* 187; Alexander McNeil to his wife, November 27, 1862, McNeil Letter, FSNMP.

21. *Richmond Daily Examiner,* December 3, 1862; Judith Brockenbrough McGuire, *Diary of a Southern Refugee,* 173; December 1, 1862, Hamilton Diary, FSNMP; J. E. B. Stuart to Flora Cooke Stuart, December 3, 1862, Stuart Papers, VHS.

22. J. B. Jones, *Rebel War Clerk's Diary,* 1:195; *Richmond Daily Examiner,* November 24, 1862; J. Cutler Andrews, *South Reports the Civil War,* 222; Judith Brockenbrough McGuire, *Diary of a Southern Refugee,* 172; Corsan, *Two Months in the Confederate States,* 137.

23. Judith Brockenbrough McGuire, *Diary of a Southern Refugee,* 172–74; [Putnam,] *Richmond during the War,* 201; *Richmond Daily Dispatch,* December 3, 1862; *Richmond Daily Enquirer,* December 4, 12, 1862.

24. November 25, December 6, 1862, Malloy Diary, CWMC, USAMHI; [Heinichen,] "Fredericksburg," Maryland Historical Society; November 25, 28–30, 1862, Hamilton Diary, FSNMP; Susan Leigh Blackford, *Letters from Lee's Army,* 137–38; Jane Howison Beale, *Journal,* 67–68; Napier Bartlett, *Military Record of Louisiana,* 159; Thomas R. Reeder to his sister, November 28, 1862, Reeder Letters, SCL.

25. *Richmond Daily Dispatch,* November 24, 1862; *Richmond Daily Enquirer,* November 28, 1862; John Howard Lewis, *Recollections from 1860 to 1865,* 63; Goodson, "Letters of Joab Goodson," 131; Longstreet, *From Manassas to Appomattox,* 296; McPherson, *For Cause and Comrades,* 148–53.

26. *CCW,* 1:654–55, 673–75, 677–78, 681–82; Herman Haupt to his wife, November 15, 1862, Haupt Letterbook, Haupt Papers, LC; *OR,* 47. Grand division commanders Hooker and Franklin—no friends of Burnside—later testified that the delay in the pontoons had prevented the army from quickly striking a blow at Lee. Hooker pointedly blamed Halleck and Meigs. See *CCW,* 1:662–63, 671. Even writers critical of Burnside have refused to absolve Halleck, who as usual abjured any responsibility. See Comte de Paris, *Civil War in America,* 2:564–65; Swinton, *Campaigns of the Army of the Potomac,* 236; Nevins, *War for the Union,* 2:344–45.

27. *OR*, ser. 1, 19(2):572, 581, 21:148–49, 793–94; [Woodbury,] *Halleck and Burnside*, 8–9; *CCW*, 1:663, 673.

28. *OR*, ser. 1, 19(2):580, 21:85–86, 765, 794; *CCW*, 1:663–64; *OR Supplement*, pt. 2, 44: 90–91.

29. *OR*, 47–48, 149, 794, and ser. 1, 51(1):946; *CCW*, 1:651–52, 665, 674–75, 679, 681–82; Woodbury, *Burnside and the Ninth Army Corps*, 190–96; [Woodbury,] *Halleck and Burnside*, 9–11; Whan, *Fiasco at Fredericksburg*, 24; Bruce, "Battle of Fredericksburg," 501; Clausewitz, *On War*, 139.

30. *OR*, 87, 103–4, 150, 792, 799; *CCW*, 1:664, 674; *Rochester (N.Y.) Daily Union and Advertiser*, December 12, 1862. An aggravated Burnside blamed Woodbury for the delay and on November 25 ordered the engineer's arrest. After hearing Woodbury's explanations, however, Burnside released him two days later. It seems likely that Woodbury offered some damning information about Halleck. See *OR*, 798, 802.

31. *OR*, 798–99, 802; Fishel, *Secret War for the Union*, 263–64. Even if the Federals had crossed on November 25 or November 26, as some commentators have suggested, Lee would simply have withdrawn his forces to the North Anna River. For criticism of Burnside's refusal to send troops across the Rappahannock at this time, see Stine, *Army of the Potomac*, 252; Whan, *Fiasco at Fredericksburg*, 128.

32. John S. Crocker to his wife, November 20, 1862, Crocker Letters, CU; Anthony G. Graves to his parents, November 21, 1862, Graves Letters, FSNMP; Robert Goldthwaite Carter, *Four Brothers in Blue*, 190–91.

33. Charles Frederick Taylor, "Colonel of the Bucktails," 338; George Henry Chandler to "Dear William," November 24, 1862, Chandler Papers, NHHS; Hartsock, *Soldier of the Cross*, 32; Samuel Edmund Nichols, *"Your Soldier Boy Samuel,"* 50; Lusk, *War Letters of William Thompson Lusk*, 230–31; George W. Barr to Vinnie Barr, November 23, 1862, Barr Papers, Schoff Collection, CL.

34. Relyea Memoir, 65–66, CHS; Charles Shields Wainwright, *Diary of Battle*, 128; Sprenger, *122d Regiment*, 113–14; John Henry Burnham to Sarah B. Burnham, November 25, 1862, Burnham Papers, CSL; November 25, 1862, Taggart Diary, USAMHI; Paul H. Hilliard to Lucretia Thompson, November 25, 1862, Hilliard Papers, Duke; Walcott, *Twenty-First Regiment*, 233; John S. Crocker to his wife, November 21, 24, 1862, Crocker Letters, CU; Gilbert Thompson, *Engineer Battalion*, 25.

35. Nolan, *Iron Brigade*, 176; William Henry Walling to his sister, November 24, 1862, Walling Papers, CWMC, USAMHI; Cavins, *Civil War Letters of Cavins*, 111; Hirst, *Boys from Rockville*, 42; Haley, *Rebel Yell and Yankee Hurrah*, 53; John S. Crocker to his wife, November 25, 1862, Crocker Letters, CU.

36. James I. Robertson Jr., *Jackson*, 642; Kenneth P. Williams, *Lincoln Finds a General*, 2: 501–2; *OR*, 1028–29, 1035; Jennings Cropper Wise, *Long Army of Lee*, 1:364–65. For an argument that Lee was in fact unsure of himself in late November and early December, see Woodworth, *Davis and Lee*, 209.

37. *OR*, 1018–19, 1027–29, 1031–33; Chamberlayne, *Ham Chamberlayne, Virginian*, 140–41.

38. Henry Kyd Douglas, *I Rode with Stonewall*, 203; Brogan, *American Civil War*, 92–93; Early, *Narrative of the War*, 165–66; James Power Smith, "With Stonewall Jackson," 23–24. For details of Jackson's march, see James I. Robertson Jr., *Jackson*, 642–47; Douglas Southall Freeman, *Lee's Lieutenants*, 2:317–24.

39. Davidson, *Diary and Letters*, 60; Draughton Stith Haynes, *Field Diary of a Confederate Soldier*, 23–25; Bradwell, "Georgia Brigade at Fredericksburg," 18; *Macon (Ga.) Daily Telegraph*, December 16, 1862; Cutrer and Parrish, *Brothers in Gray*, 132; John S. Brooks to Sarah A. Knox, December 2, 1862, Brooks Letters, SHC; Corsan, *Two Months in the Confederate States*, 102.

40. Gregory C. White, *31st Georgia*, 59–60; Fulton, *War Reminiscences*, 53–54; McCrady,

"Address before Virginia Division," 206–7; Worsham, *One of Jackson's Foot Cavalry*, 150–51; Caldwell, *History of a Brigade of South Carolinians*, 55–56.

41. Hatton Memoir, 359, LC; November 26–29, 1862, Jones Diary, Schoff Collection, CL; Shoemaker, *Shoemaker's Battery*, 24; Willis Lee, "Record," FSNMP; Welch, *Confederate Surgeon's Letters*, 36–37.

42. Gregory C. White, *31st Georgia*, 58; Chapla, *42nd Virginia*, 29; McDonald, *Woman's Civil War*, 92; Richard Lewis, *Camp Life of a Confederate Boy*, 35; Bone Reminiscences, NCDAH; Walter Clark, *Regiments and Battalions from North Carolina*, 1:664; *OR Supplement*, pt. 2, 48:343; J. A. Gillespie to "Dear Sallie," November 27, 1862, Gillespie Family Papers, GDAH; Sgt. John Dykes Taylor, *48th Alabama*, 13; Fitzpatrick, *Letters to Amanda*, 33, 35.

43. *OR*, 563, 1034, 1037–39, and ser. 1, 51(2):651–52; William Nelson Pendleton to Anzolette E. Pendleton, November 26, 1862, Pendleton Papers, SHC.

44. Thomas Claybrook Elder to Anna Fitzhugh Elder, November 23, 1862, Elder Papers, VHS; Edward M. Burruss to Kate Burruss, November 23, 1862, Burruss Papers, LSU; James C. Zimmerman to his wife, November 24, 1862, Zimmerman Papers, Duke; Marcus H. Hefner to his wife, November 23, 1862, Hefner Collection, NCDAH; T. R. R. Cobb to his wife, November 24, 1862, Cobb Letters, UG; Lineberger, *Letters of a Gaston Ranger*, 27; Trout, *With Jeb and Saber*, 114.

45. *Richmond Daily Examiner*, November 24, 27, 1862; *Richmond Daily Enquirer*, November 24, 26, 1862; J. B. Jones, *Rebel War Clerk's Diary*, 1:195; Edmund Ruffin, *Diary*, 2:497–98; *Raleigh Weekly Register*, November 26, 1862; *Richmond Daily Dispatch*, November 26, 1862; *Charleston Mercury*, November 27, 1862.

46. Robert E. Lee, *Wartime Papers*, 343; Milo Grow to his wife, November 25, 1862, Grow Letters, FSNMP; Berkeley, *Four Years in the Confederate Artillery*, 35; William Nelson Pendleton to Nancy Pendleton, November 27, 1862, Pendleton Papers, SHC.

47. Fishel, *Secret War for the Union*, 257; Angus James Johnston II, *Virginia Railroads in the Civil War*, 15–16. Reports about Confederate supply problems appeared in the northern press and likely intensified pressure on Burnside to advance. See, for example, *Newark (N.J.) Daily Advertiser*, November 22, 1862.

48. *OR*, ser. 1, 19(2):718, 721, 21:1012–13, 1016, 1041, 1045; Thomas Smith Ruffin to Edmund Ruffin, November 27, 1862, Ruffin Papers, VHS; Goff, *Confederate Supply*, 71–72; Terry L. Jones, *Lee's Tigers*, 139; Henry Alexander Chambers, *Diary*, 70–71. A suspicious Georgian charged that some soldiers claimed to be without shoes to avoid camp duties. See W. H. Andrews, *Footprints of a Regiment*, 95–96.

49. *OR*, ser. 1, 51(2):642; Sorrel, *Recollections of a Confederate Staff Officer*, 125–26; November 28, 1862, Wright's Georgia Brigade Order Book, CWTI, USAMHI; Walter Clark, *Papers*, 1:99; W. H. Andrews, *Footprints of a Regiment*, 93; Gregory, *38th Virginia*, 29; Gunn, *24th Virginia*, 37.

50. Worsham, *One of Jackson's Foot Cavalry*, 151; Parramore et al., *Before the Rebel Flag Fell*, 46–47; "Brunswick Guard," 8–9; Walter Clark, *Regiments and Battalions from North Carolina*, 1:168–69; December 6, 1862, Pickett Diary, CWTI, USAMHI; J. F. Coghill to his parents, December 7, 1862, Coghill Papers, Duke; William C. McClellan to his father, December 10, 1862, Buchanan and McClellan Family Papers, SHC.

51. *Richmond Daily Examiner*, November 8, 1862; *Richmond Daily Whig*, November 8, 10, 19, 26, 1862; *Raleigh Weekly Standard*, November 19, 1862; J. B. Jones, *Rebel War Clerk's Diary*, 1:186, 191.

52. *Richmond Daily Enquirer*, November 10, 13, 18, 20, 1862; *Charleston Mercury*, November 15, 1862; *Milledgeville (Ga.) Southern Recorder*, November 25, 1862; Winkler, *Confederate Capital*, 123–24; Burroughs, "Reminiscences of Fredericksburg," 636; M. A. Holden to the Secretary of War, January 11, 1863, Letters Received, microcopy 437, roll 94, NA.

53. William Ross Stillwell to "My Dear Mollie," November 30, 1862, Stillwell Letters,

GDAH; John French White to Martha Coles White, December 1, 1862, White Papers, VHS; *Lynchburg Daily Virginian,* November 24, 1862.

54. Clausewitz, *On War,* 331, 339; *OR,* ser. 1, 19(2):700–701, 716–17, 21:1016, 1018, and ser. 4, 2:192–93; Goff, *Confederate Supply,* 78–79; Hagerman, *Civil War and Origins of Modern Warfare,* 120–21.

55. *MSH,* 5:31, 104, 207; Dinkins, "Griffith-Barksdale-Humphreys Mississippi Brigade," 265; Welch, *Confederate Surgeon's Letters,* 35; *Atlanta Southern Confederacy,* November 18, 1862; November 18, 1862, Ware Diary, SHC; J. B. Jones, *Rebel War Clerk's Diary,* 1:208; Thomas J. Morrison to his mother, November 30, 1862, Morrison Letters, FSNMP; James C. Zimmerman to his wife, December 2, 1862, Zimmerman Papers, Duke.

56. Von Borcke, *Memoirs of the Confederate War,* 2:65–66, 77–80; David Holt, *Mississippi Rebel,* 131; W. G. Bean, *Sandie Pendleton,* 84–85; William M. Owen, *In Camp and Battle with the Washington Artillery,* 171; Baker, *Reminiscent Story of the Civil War,* 33–34; Trout, *With Pen and Saber,* 114; November 12, 1862, Ware Diary, SHC; Dickert, *Kershaw's Brigade,* 202–3.

57. David Holt, *Mississippi Rebel,* 131–32, 134–40; W. H. Andrews, *Footprints of a Regiment,* 96–97. Such larks became much more serious when men committed depredations on civilian property or ended up AWOL. See *OR,* 1037–38, and ser. 1, 51(2):651; Squires, "'Boy Officer' of the Washington Artillery," 20; *Milledgeville (Ga.) Southern Recorder,* December 2, 1862. One Virginian claimed that soldiers seemed to be running off every night and that a guardhouse was full of such men awaiting courts-martial. See William G. Cason to Mary Cason, December 11, 1862, Cason Letter, Gettysburg National Military Park.

58. See the useful summary of various sins in Wiley, *Life of Johnny Reb,* 36–58. See also an order prohibiting furloughs for hospital patients suffering from syphilis or gonorrhea, *Circular, Confederate States of America.*

59. November 20, 1862, Malloy Diary, CWMC, USAMHI; Shand Memoir, SCL; Johnson, *This They Remembered,* 94–95; December 8, 1862, Ware Diary, SHC; Dooley, *John Dooley, Confederate Soldier,* 78–79; Archer, "James J. Archer Letters," 138–39.

60. Sheeran, *Confederate Chaplain,* 34–35; *OR,* ser. 1, 19(2):722; W. H. Andrews, *Footprints of a Regiment,* 95; David Holt, *Mississippi Rebel,* 131; Wiley, *Life of Johnny Reb,* 37; *Atlanta Southern Confederacy,* December 18, 1862.

61. McPherson, *For Cause and Comrades,* 12; Wiley, *Life of Johnny Reb,* 192–216.

62. *OR,* 1035–36, 1069; *Richmond Daily Whig,* November 25, 27, 28, 1862; *Wilmington (N.C.) Daily Journal,* December 29, 1862; *Richmond Daily Enquirer,* December 11, 1862.

63. John Bratton to his wife, November 8, 1862, Bratton Letters, SHC; John French White to Martha Coles White, November 30, 1862, White Papers, VHS; Susan Leigh Blackford, *Letters from Lee's Army,* 140; William Ross Stillwell to "My Dear Mollie," December 11, 1862, Stillwell Letters, GDAH. Unfortunately more than a few soldiers destroyed their wives' letters for fear such intimate correspondence might fall into enemy hands. See Alfred E. Doby to his wife, January 12, 1863, Doby Letters, MC.

64. McPherson, *For Cause and Comrades,* 131–34; Robert Taylor Scott to his wife, December 10, 1862, Keith Family Papers, VHS; Patterson, *Yankee Rebel,* 83–84; Louise Haskell Daly, *Alexander Cheeves Haskell,* 87.

65. Simpson and Simpson, *Far, Far from Home,* 160; John French White to Martha Coles White, November 30, December 3, 1862, White Papers, VHS. A little over a year and a half later, White would be listed on the muster rolls as a deserter. See Jensen, *32nd Virginia,* 206.

66. S. G. Pryor, *Post of Honor,* 285, 295.

67. McDaniel, *With Unabated Trust,* 115.

68. McPherson, *For Cause and Comrades,* 134–40; James Drayton Nance to "My Dear Laura," November 30, 1862, Nance Papers, SCL; Robert Taylor Scott to his wife, November 20, 1862, Keith Family Papers, VHS; Fitzpatrick, *Letters to Amanda,* 31; J. E. B. Stuart to Flora

Cooke Stuart, November 25, 1862, Stuart Papers, VHS; J. E. B. Stuart to "Dear Lily," November 16, 1862, Stuart Papers, Duke. For a useful discussion of fathers and children, see Marten, *Children's Civil War,* 71–73.

69. Pender, *General to His Lady,* 193; Spencer, *Civil War Marriage in Virginia,* 150–52; John Bratton to his wife, November 8, December 10, 1862, Bratton Letters, SHC; Speairs and Pettit, *Civil War Letters,* 1:65–66, 68–69.

70. DeNoon, *Charlie's Letters,* 95; S. G. Pryor, *Post of Honor,* 290; James C. Zimmerman to his wife, December 2, 1862, Zimmerman Papers, Duke; Cutrer and Parrish, *Brothers in Gray,* 132; Fitzpatrick, *Letters to Amanda,* 33; Ujanirtus Allen, *Campaigning with "Old Stonewall,"* 192; Mills Lane, *"Dear Mother: Don't Grieve about Me,"* 195.

71. *Macon (Ga.) Daily Telegraph,* December 16, 1862; *OR,* ser. 4, 2:247; Jedediah Hotchkiss to Sara Ann Comfort Hotchkiss, December 7, 1862, Hotchkiss Papers, LC; James C. Zimmerman to his wife, December 4, 1862, Zimmerman Papers, Duke; T. R. R. Cobb to his wife, December 6, 1862, Cobb Letters, UG; Ella Harper to George Washington Finley Harper, November 5, 1862, Harper Papers, SHC.

72. John William Jones, *Life and Letters of Lee,* 200; Hotchkiss, *Make Me a Map of the Valley,* 96; Draughton Stith Haymon, *Field Diary of a Confederate Soldier,* 21. For useful comments on how religion offered consolation for loss but also compensation for the absence of families and a substitute for the worldly pleasures of camp life, see Samuel J. Watson, "Religion and Combat Motivation in Confederate Armies," 34–37.

73. November 20, 1862, Hopkins Diary, VHS; Hotchkiss, *Make Me a Map of the Valley,* 95; James I. Robertson Jr., *Jackson,* 650. For differing interpretations on the significance of vice and irreligion in camp, see Wiley, *Life of Johnny Reb,* 174–91; Samuel J. Watson, "Religion and Combat Motivation in Confederate Armies," 37–40; Drew Gilpin Faust, "Christian Soldiers," 79–80.

74. Drew Gilpin Faust, "Christian Soldiers," 81–88; Betts, *Experience of a Confederate Chaplain,* 22–23; Susan Pendleton Lee, *Memoirs of William Nelson Pendleton,* 238; Sidney J. Romero, "Confederate Chaplain," 127–39; Shattuck, *Shield and Hiding Place,* 63–72; Richard Irby to his wife, December 1, 1862, Irby Letters, FSNMP.

75. Ott, "Civil War Diary of James J. Kirkpatrick," 83; John William Jones, *Christ in the Camp,* 289–06; Drew Gilpin Faust, "Christian Soldiers," 63–79; Shattuck, *Shield and Hiding Place,* 43–50; James I. Robertson Jr., *Jackson,* 635.

76. William Nelson Pendleton to Nancy Pendleton, November 27, 1862, Pendleton Papers, SHC; Samuel J. Watson, "Religion and Combat Motivation in Confederate Armies," 48–55; S. G. Pryor, *Post of Honor,* 290; Oscar J. E. Stuart to his father, November 27, 1862, Dimitry Papers, Duke.

CHAPTER SIX

1. Croffut and Morris, *Connecticut during the War,* 290.

2. Daniel M. Holt, *Surgeon's Civil War,* 47; Gilbert Thompson, *Engineer Battalion,* 25; John Southard to his sister, November 30, 1862, Southard Family Papers, NYHS; S. Millett Thompson, *Thirteenth New Hampshire,* 25.

3. November 21, 1862, Lloyd Diary, SHC; Elisha Hunt Rhodes, *All for the Union,* 88; Denison, *First Rhode Island Cavalry,* 180–81; *New York Times,* November 25, 1862; November 21, 1862, Pope Diary, CWTI, USAMHI; *Berks and Schuylkill (Pa.) Journal,* November 29, 1862; November 21, 1862, Webb Diary, Schoff Collection, CL.

4. James L. Bowen, "In Front of Fredericksburg"; Charles Francis Adams, *Cycle of Adams Letters,* 1:202; *Story of the Twenty-first Connecticut,* 56–58; Spangler, *My Little War Experiences,* 58.

5. Robert Goldthwaite Carter, *Four Brothers in Blue,* 168–69; Wightman, *From Antietam to Fort Fisher,* 83; McCrea, *Dear Belle,* 169; James Remington to his father, November 21, 1862,

Remington Papers, RIHS; Edward Henry Courtney Taylor to his brother, November 29, 1862, Taylor Letters, MHC; Bartol, *Nation's Hour,* 44.

6. Robert S. Robertson, "Diary of the War," 72; John W. Ames to Fisher Ames, November 24, 1862, and Ames to his mother, November 29, 1862, Ames Papers, USAMHI; James Madison Stone, *Personal Recollections of the Civil War,* 106–7; William Watson, *Letters of a Civil War Surgeon,* 35; Haley, *Rebel Yell and Yankee Hurrah,* 53; Brewster, *When This Cruel War Is Over,* 190; Orwig, *131st Pennsylvania,* 85–86.

7. Anthony G. Graves to "Friend Jack," December 2, 1862, Graves Letters, FSNMP; Beidelman, *Letters of George Washington Beidelman,* 151; Weymouth, *Memorial Sketch of Lieut. Edgar M. Newcomb,* 97; December 1, 1862, Holford Diary, LC; *New York Herald,* December 1, 1862.

8. Wightman, *From Antietam to Fort Fisher,* 83; James R. Woodworth to Phoebe Woodworth, November 30, 1862, Woodworth Papers, Hotchkiss Collection, CL; Asa W. Bartlett, *History of the Twelfth New Hampshire,* 401–2; Nelson Ames, *History of Battery G,* 46; James B. Thomas, *Civil War Letters,* 123; *Fifty-Seventh Regiment, Pennsylvania Veteran Volunteer Infantry,* 62–63; Tyler, *Recollections of the Civil War,* 60; Daniel M. Holt, *Surgeon's Civil War,* 52–53; Alexander Morrison Stewart, *Camp, March, and Battlefield,* 265–68. The careful laying out of streets in several camps was another sign that some regiments did not expect to move until spring. See Hopkins, *Seventh Rhode Island,* 35–36; *New York Herald,* December 5, 1862.

9. David Beem to his wife, November 27, 1862, Beem Papers, IHS; Mulholland, "At Fredericksburg," 3; November 27, 1862, Pope Diary, CWTI, USAMHI; Helman, "Young Soldier in the Army of the Potomac," 153; Andrew J. Bennett, *Story of the First Massachusetts Light Battery,* 90–91; Galwey, *Valiant Hours,* 54–55; Stearns, *Three Years with Company K,* 140–41.

10. John Lord Parker, *Twenty-Second Massachusetts,* 218; November 27, 1862, Holford Diary, LC; Lord, *History of the Ninth New Hampshire,* 217; Smithe, *Glimpses of Places, and People, and Things,* 29–30; Aschmann, *Memoirs of a Swiss Officer,* 97–98; Stearns, *Three Years with Company K,* 143; Borton, *On the Parallels,* 43–44; John Day Smith, *Nineteenth Maine,* 25; Brewster, *When This Cruel War Is Over,* 190.

11. Bisbee, "Three Years a Volunteer Soldier," 116; *OR,* 370–71; *Hartford Daily Courant,* November 19, 1862; James Pratt to his wife, November 27, 1862, Pratt Collection, USAMHI; Charles R. Johnson to "Dear Nellie," November 29, 1862, Johnson Letters, Gregory A. Coco Collection, USAMHI; Hopkins, *Seventh Rhode Island,* 37; Thomas H. Parker, *History of the 51st,* 264.

12. Whitman and True, *Maine in the War for the Union,* 432–33; Helman, "Young Soldier in the Army of the Potomac," 154; Charles E. Davis, *Three Years in the Army,* 160; November 19, 1862, Willand Diary, NHSL.

13. Shannon, *Organization and Administration of the Union Army,* 1:53–103; *Albany (N.Y.) Atlas and Argus,* December 8, 1862; *New York Herald,* December 11, 1862; November 18, 1862, Pope Diary, CWTI, USAMHI; William Hamilton to his mother, November 22, 1862, Hamilton Papers, LC; John Smart to Ann Smart, November 26, 1862, Smart Letters, FSNMP; A. C. Higley to his father, December 1, 1862, Higley Letters, FSNMP; Ted Alexander, *126th Pennsylvania,* 120; James B. Thomas, *Civil War Letters,* 119.

14. Charles E. Davis, *Three Years in the Army,* 161; Billings, *Hard Tack and Coffee,* 85–86; Samuel Morrow to his brother, November 26, 1862, Morrow Papers, HCWRTC, USAMHI; Samuel W. Eaton to Catherine Eaton, December 1, 1862, Eaton Papers, SHSW; Bellard, *Gone for a Soldier,* 119; Beidelman, *Letters of George Washington Beidelman,* 148.

15. Brainard, *One Hundred and Forty-sixth New York,* 23; Len Smith to ?, December 4, 1862, Len Smith Letter, FSNMP; Rohloff C. Hacker to his parents, November 23, 1862, Hacker Brothers Papers, Schoff Collection, CL; Musgrove, *Autobiography of Captain Richard Musgrove,* 46; Zerah Coston Monks to Hannah T. Rohrer, November 25, 1862, Monks-Rohrer Letters, Emory.

16. Catton, *Glory Road*, 17; McKelvey, *Rochester in the Civil War*, 157; *Philadelphia Inquirer*, December 3, 1862; Sprenger, *122d Regiment*, 118–19; McCarter, *My Life in the Irish Brigade*, 90–91.

17. Brewster, *When This Cruel War Is Over*, 190; Helman, "Young Soldier in the Army of the Potomac," 152–53; Bellard, *Gone for a Soldier*, 120; *Springfield (Mass.) Daily Republican*, November 27, 1862; Orson Blair Curtis, *History of the Twenty Fourth Michigan*, 79; Hartsock, *Soldier of the Cross*, 32; Haley, *Rebel Yell and Yankee Hurrah*, 54; Blakeslee, *Sixteenth Connecticut*, 25.

18. Wiley, *Life of Billy Yank*, 224–26; Gerrish, *Reminiscences of the War*, 66–67; Fairchild, *27th Regiment*, 114; William Hamilton to his mother, November 22, 1862, Hamilton Papers, LC.

19. Gerrish, *Reminiscences of the War*, 64–65; Orson Blair Curtis, *History of the Twenty-Fourth Michigan*, 79; S. Millett Thompson, *Thirteenth New Hampshire*, 24.

20. Isaac Lyman Taylor, "Campaigning with the First Minnesota," 233; Ford, *Fifteenth Regiment Massachusetts Volunteer Infantry*, 221; John Ripley Adams, *Memorials and Letters*, 75; Martin A. Haynes, *Minor War History*, 78–79; *Elizabeth New Jersey Journal*, November 25, 1862; S. Millett Thompson, *Thirteenth New Hampshire*, 24; November 23, 1862, Holford Diary, LC.

21. Isaac Lyman Taylor, "Campaigning with the First Minnesota," 234; James Coburn to his parents, November 24, 1862, James P. Coburn Papers, USAMHI; William F. Smith to his mother, November 21, 1862, William F. Smith Letters, Leigh Collection, USAMHI; Albert, *Forty-fifth Pennsylvania*, 196.

22. Isaac Lyman Taylor, "Campaigning with the First Minnesota," 233–34, Weymouth, *Memorial Sketch of Lieut. Edgar M. Newcomb*, 94–96; Mayo, *Civil War Letters*, 221–22; Wren, *Captain James Wren's Civil War Diary*, 91; Haydon, *For Country, Cause, and Leader*, 293; John Henry Burnham to Sarah B. Burnham, November 25, 1862, Burnham Papers, CSL.

23. Charles Jewett Morris to his brother and sister, November 28, 1862, Morris Papers, Duke; Helman, "Young Soldier in the Army of the Potomac," 153; *New York Herald*, December 8, 1862; November 21, 1862, Pope Diary, CWTI, USAMHI. An enterprising second lieutenant decided to follow the sutlers' example and sold a $3.50 watch for $15. See Brewster, *When This Cruel War Is Over*, 196.

24. George H. Sargent to his mother, November 17, 1862, Sargent Papers, NHHS; Thomas H. Parker, *History of the 51st*, 261; *New York Times*, November 19, 1862.

25. *Rochester (N.Y.) Daily Union and Advertiser*, December 1, 1862; Fairchild, *27th Regiment*, 116–17; Currier, "From Concord to Fredericksburg," 251; Page, *Fourteenth Connecticut*, 70.

26. Billings, *Hard Tack and Coffee*, 227; Sprenger, *122d Regiment*, 104; Currier, "From Concord to Fredericksburg," 250–51.

27. Benjamin Apthorp Gould, *Military and Anthropological Statistics of American Soldiers*, 595; *MSH*, 1:174–79, 2:60–61.

28. Haydon, *For Country, Cause, and Leader*, 292; Albert W. Luther to his parents, November 27, 1862, Luther Papers, ISL; *Augusta (Maine) Kennebec Journal*, November 28, 1862.

29. Gordon Willis Jones, "Medical History of the Fredericksburg Campaign," 247; O. Leland Barlow to his sister, November 30, 1862, Barlow Papers, CSL; Robert Guyton to his father, November 23, 1862, Guyton and Heaslet Papers, Duke; Henry J. H. Thompson to Lucretia Thompson, November 22, 1862, Thompson Papers, Duke; J. Theodore Calhoun, "Rough Notes of an Army Surgeon's Experience in the Great Rebellion," *Medical and Surgical Reporter*, November 8, 1862, 150; Cutcheon, *Story of the Twentieth Michigan Infantry*, 37.

30. *MSII*, 1.1/4–79, 5:20–21, 6:650–51, 828–29; Asa W. Bartlett, *History of the Twelfth New Hampshire*, 37; Fairchild, *27th Regiment*, 115; Albert W. Luther to J. H. Luther, December 8, 1862, Luther Papers, ISL; Washburn, *108th Regiment*, 112; William Henry Walling to his sister, December 1, 1862, Walling Papers, CWMC, USAMHI; *Fifth Annual Report of the Bureau of Military Statistics*, 569–70; Francis Jewett Parker, *Thirty-Second Massachusetts*, 120–21.

31. *MSH,* 1:174–75, 2:61, 3:163–64.

32. *MSH,* 1:174–75, 3:19–20, 44–45, 117–21; Uriah N. Parmelee to his mother, November 20, 1862, Parmelee Papers, Duke; *Newark (N.J.) Daily Advertiser,* November 28, 1862; *New York Tribune,* December 2, 1862; November 29, 1862, Rice Diary, LC.

33. James R. Woodworth to Phoebe Woodworth, November 30, December 3, 4, 7, 8, 1862, Woodworth Papers, Hotchkiss Collection, CL; Nash, *Forty-fourth New York,* 449.

34. Oliver Edwards to his mother, December 10, 1862, Edwards Papers, GLC; *MSH,* 2:100; *Baltimore American and Commercial Advertiser,* December 5, 1862; William Watson, *Letters of a Civil War Surgeon,* 37–38; Hartsock, *Soldier of the Cross,* 31; Henry Ogden Ryerson to his sister, December 7, 1862, Anderson Family Papers, NJHS; James R. Woodworth to Phoebe Woodworth, December 8, 1862, Woodworth Papers, Hotchkiss Collection, CL.

35. December 8, 9, 1862, Eaton Diary, SHC; Brewster, *When This Cruel War Is Over,* 195–96; Cutcheon Autobiography, MHC; *Fifth Annual Report of the Bureau of Military Statistics,* 569; Samuel Edmund Nichols, "*Your Soldier Boy Samuel,*" 51–52; McAllister, *Letters of Robert McAllister,* 234; John W. Ames to his father, December 9, 1862, Ames Papers, USAMHI.

36. *Rochester (N.Y.) Daily Union and Advertiser,* December 10, 1862; Pardington, *Dear Sarah,* 45. Carefully kept diaries sometimes became little more than chronicles of death. See Stuckenberg, *Surrounded by Methodists,* 33–36.

37. Small, *Road to Richmond,* 58; November 23, 1862, S. W. Gordon Diary, FSNMP; Brian A. Bennett, *140th New York,* 97; December 2, 1862, Schaeffer Diary, West Virginia University; *Providence (R.I.) Daily Journal,* December 6, 1862; *Johnstown (Pa.) Cambria Tribune,* December 19, 1862; Edmund Halsey, *Brother against Brother,* 86; Hopkins, *Seventh Rhode Island,* 37; James Remington to his father, November 30, 1862, Remington Papers, RIHS.

38. Aaron K. Blake to his sister, November 16, 1862, Blake Letters, CWMC, USAMHI; Gearhart, *Reminiscences of the Civil War,* 23; Musgrove, *Autobiography of Captain Richard Musgrove,* 46; Dwight Vick to his sister, November 30, 1862, Vick Letter, CWMC, USAMHI.

39. Hartsock, *Soldier of the Cross,* 36; Henry J. H. Thompson to Lucretia Thompson, November 22, 1862, Thompson Papers, Duke; James B. Thomas, *Civil War Letters,* 123; Sprenger, *122d Regiment,* 126–27.

40. Robert Goldthwaite Carter, *Four Brothers in Blue,* 162–63; James I. Robertson Jr., *Soldiers Blue and Gray,* 81–93; McPherson, *For Cause and Comrades,* 82–90. In late November a tobacco shortage hardly improved the mood of the Federals. Some men thought the vile weed kept them healthy and, when it could not be obtained, tried smoking everything from moss to chestnut bark to coffee. See George H. Mellish to his mother, December 10, 1862, Mellish Papers, HL; Roe, *Tenth Massachusetts,* 151; George H. Allen, *Forty-Six Months,* 158; Newell, *10th Regiment Massachusetts Volunteers,* 159.

41. Waugh, "Reminiscences," FSNMP; Aldrich, *History of Battery A,* 157; Siegel, *For the Glory of the Union,* 95–96, 105–6; November 28, 1862, Pope Diary, CWTI, USAMHI.

42. McPherson, *What They Fought For,* 4–7; Kaser, *Books and Libraries in Camp and Battle,* 13–38, 46–47, 52–58; Frank and Reaves, "*Seeing the Elephant,*" 54–61; John W. Ames to Fisher Ames, November 24, 1862, Ames Papers, USAMHI; Reuben H. Humphreyville to his brother and sister, November 25, 1862, Humphreyville Papers, Chicago Historical Society; William Hamilton to his mother, November 28, 1862, Hamilton Papers, LC; *Wellsboro (Pa.) Agitator,* December 3, 1862.

43. Brooks, *Mr. Lincoln's Washington,* 38–40; *Baltimore American and Commercial Advertiser,* November 20, 1862; *OR,* 806, 810–11; Cory, "Private's Recollections of Fredericksburg," 122–24; Reid Mitchell, *Civil War Soldiers,* 69–75. For general treatment of various vices, see Billings, *Hard Tack and Coffee,* 144–54; Wiley, *Life of Billy Yank,* 247–62, 197–223; Linderman, *Embattled Courage,* 83–97, 118–24.

44. *Rochester (N.Y.) Daily Democrat and American,* December 12, 1862; Haydon, *For Coun-*

try, *Cause, and Leader,* 293–94; *New York Herald,* December 5, 1862; Walcott, *Twenty-First Regiment,* 233–34; Bellard, *Gone for a Soldier,* 170–71; Drewster, *When This Cruel War Is Over,* 190–91; Samuel Partridge to "Dear Ed," December 6, 1862, Partridge Letters, FSNMP; Charges against D. J. W. Keyes, December 4, 1862, Humphreys Papers, HSP; *MSH,* 6:890–91. The following offhand remark suggests the extent of the problem: "A good many of the men drunk yesterday and early this morning" (December 4, 1862, Woodward Diary, HL.)

45. Meyers, *Ten Years in the Ranks,* 279–80; *MSH,* 6:890–91; William Teall to his wife, November 29, 1861, Teall Letters, TSLA; William Watson, *Letters of a Civil War Surgeon,* 33; Pyne, *Ride to War,* 103–4.

46. J. E. Hodgkins, *Civil War Diary,* 14; McClenthen, *Narrative of the Fall and Winter Campaign,* 29–30; George Lewis, *First Rhode Island Light Artillery,* 121–22. The general comments in the preceding two paragraphs constitute a synthesis of ideas from several fine recent works on the common soldier: McPherson, *For Cause and Comrades,* 53–58; Reid Mitchell, *Civil War Soldiers,* 58–59; Reid Mitchell, *Vacant Chair,* 3–7, 40–54; James I. Robertson Jr., *Soldiers Blue and Gray,* 122–32; Hess, *Liberty, Virtue, and Progress,* 56–67; Jimerson, *Private Civil War,* 198–210; Frank and Reaves, *"Seeing the Elephant,"* 49–54; Linderman, *Embattled Courage,* 34–41, 47–56, 169–79.

47. Samuel S. Partridge to "Dear Ed," November 23, 1862, Partridge Letters, FSNMP; *New York Herald,* December 8, 1862; *Rochester (N.Y.) Daily Democrat and American,* December 15, 1862; November 28, 1862, Mancha Diary, CWMC, USAMHI; S. Millett Thompson, *Thirteenth New Hampshire,* 25; Dawes, *Sixth Wisconsin,* 106.

48. Reid Mitchell, *Civil War Soldiers,* 56–58; Reid Mitchell, *Vacant Chair,* 19–25; James Remington to his father, December 6, 1862, Remington Papers, RIHS; Haydon, *For Country, Cause, and Leader,* 292; Relyea Memoir, 66–67, CHS.

49. McPherson, *For Cause and Comrades,* 12–13, 131–34; U.S. Bureau of the Census, *Historical Statistics of the United States,* 2:805; Jimerson, *Private Civil War,* 4–5. The sheer volume of mail marked something of a revolution in communications because as late as 1837, the average American received about two letters a year, and even that figure is misleading because much of the correspondence involved business matters. See Pred, *Urban Growth and the Circulation of Information,* 79–81.

50. John W. Ames to Fisher Ames, November 24, 1862, Ames Papers, USAMHI; Henry Ogden Ryerson to his sister, November 21, 1862, Anderson Family Papers, NJHS; Pardington, *Dear Sarah,* 40; Welsh and Welsh, "Civil War Letters from Two Brothers," 152; McAllister, *Letters of Robert McAllister,* 235.

51. Gallman, *Mastering Wartime,* 66–68; Rohloff C. Hacker to William and Barbara Woll Hacker, November 23, 1862, Hacker Brothers Papers, Schoff Collection, CL; William Franklin Draper to his mother, November 30, 1862, Draper Papers, LC; Peter Welsh, *Irish Green and Union Blue,* 33; John R. Coye to his wife, December 5, 1862, Coye Letters, FSNMP; J. Frank Sterling to his father, November 7, 1862, Sterling Papers, Rutgers University; Samuel Morrow to his brother, November 26, 1862, Morrow Papers, HCWRTC, USAMHI; Molyneux, *Quill of the Wild Goose,* 53; Brewster, *When This Cruel War Is Over,* 192.

52. *Flemington (N.J.) Hunterdon Republican,* December 19, 1862; Pardington, *Dear Sarah,* 38; Daniel M. Holt, *Surgeon's Civil War,* 52; John S. Crocker to his wife, December 12, 1862, Crocker Letters, CU.

53. McPherson, *For Cause and Comrades,* 134–40; Reid Mitchell, *Vacant Chair,* 11–16; Castleman, *Army of the Potomac,* 216; Reid Mitchell, "Northern Soldier and His Community," 78–80; Reid Mitchell, *Civil War Soldiers,* 64–69; Chamberlain, *Through Blood and Fire,* 34–35.

54. Cavins, *Civil War Letters of Cavins,* 106; Edward H. Brewer to Mary E. Brewer, November 10, 1862, Brewer Papers, CSL; Pardington, *Dear Sarah,* 36–37.

55. Pardington, *Dear Sarah,* 45; George W. Ballock to his wife, November 10, 18, Decem-

ber 3, 1862, Ballock Papers, Duke; Ransom F. Sargent to his wife, December 2, 1862, Sargent Papers, DCL; George E. Upton to his wife, December 2, 1862, Upton Papers, NHHS. Absence from home seemed to quicken the confessional impulses in some men. A Michigan recruit so lonesome for his wife that he often kissed her picture promised to forgo whiskey and "Profane swearing." A New Yorker more candidly admitted that his "habits" were "no worse than heretofore and that, I suppose, is bad enough." How his wife interpreted a rather ambiguous pledge to "return to you as good as I left you" is not known. See Pardington, *Dear Sarah,* 40; John S. Crocker to his wife, December 11, 1862, Crocker Letters, CU.

56. George W. Ballock to his sister, November 14, 1862, and to his wife, November 25, 1862, Ballock Papers, Duke; James B. Post to his wife, November 27, 1862, Post Papers, CWMC, USAMHI; John Smart to Ann Smart, November 26, 1862, Smart Letters, FSNMP; Barber, *Civil War Letters,* 102.

57. Catherine Eaton to Samuel W. Eaton, November 12, 22, December 3, 8, 15, 1862, and James Eaton to Samuel W. Eaton, November 26, 1862, Eaton Papers, SHSW; James R. Woodworth to Phoebe Woodworth, November 12, 13, 16, 30, December 8, 1862, Woodworth Papers, Hotchkiss Collection, CL.

58. Saum, *Popular Mood of America,* 155–56; Gallman, *Mastering Wartime,* 70–83; George E. Upton to his wife, December 2, 1862, Upton Papers, NHHS; Samuel V. Dean to his wife, December 10, 1862, Dean Letters, FSNMP; Cavins, *Civil War Letters of Cavins,* 108–9; Abiel Hall Edwards, *"Dear Friend Anna,"* 41; Edwin O. Wentworth to Carrie A. Wentworth, December 1–3, 1862, and Carrie A. Wentworth to Edwin O. Wentworth, November 6, 1862, Wentworth Papers, LC. For a perceptive and sophisticated general analysis of soldiers' relations to their families, focusing on a host of fears and anxieties, see Marten, *Children's Civil War,* 68–100.

59. Abiel Hall Edwards, *"Dear Friend Anna,"* 38; Zerah Coston Monks to Hannah T. Rohrer, December 4, 1862, Monks-Rohrer Letters, Emory; Warren Hapgood Freeman, *Letters from Two Brothers,* 57; U.S. Bureau of the Census, *Historical Statistics of the United States,* 2:1057.

60. Wren, *Captain James Wren's Civil War Diary,* 91–92; George E. Upton to his wife, December 7, 1862, Upton Papers, NHHS; Hosea Towne to "Dear Friends," December 5, 1862, Towne Papers, NHHS; Keegan, *Face of Battle,* 193; Griffith, *Battle Tactics of the Civil War,* 91–115; James B. Thomas, *Civil War Letters,* 123; James Coburn to his parents, November 24, 1862, James P. Coburn Papers, USAMHI; Best, *History of the 121st New York,* 33–34.

61. McCarter, *My Life in the Irish Brigade,* 95–100.

62. *History of the Thirty-Fifth Massachusetts Volunteers,* 74; William Speed to Charlotte Speed, November 29, 1862, Speed Papers, Schoff Collection, CL; November 29, 1862, Abernathy Diary, USAMHI.

63. Barber, *Civil War Letters,* 102; S. Millett Thompson, *Thirteenth New Hampshire,* 25; William Franklin Draper to his wife, November 23, 1862, Draper Papers, LC; Anthony G. Graves to "Jack," December 2, 1862, Graves Letters, FSNMP; Hopkins, *Seventh Rhode Island,* 37. A few hardy souls seemed to enjoy picket duty—so long as there was good shelter and plenty to eat—and preferred it to camp routine. See Robert Guyton to his father, December 5, 1862, Guyton and Heaslet Papers, Duke; James Coburn to his parents, December 7, 1862, James P. Coburn Papers, USAMHI; Edwin O. Wentworth to his wife, December 1–3, 1862, Wentworth Papers, LC.

64. *OR,* 371, 1117–21; John Day Smith, *Nineteenth Maine,* 25; William Hamilton to his mother, November 22, 1862, Hamilton Papers, LC.

65. December 2, 1862, Metcalf Diary, FSNMP; Washburn, *108th Regiment,* 112; *Story of the Twenty-first Connecticut,* 63–64; Bellard, *Gone for a Soldier,* 179.

66. Rose, *Victorian America and the Civil War,* 97–103; Anthony G. Graves to his parents, November 21, December 19, 1862, Graves Letters, FSNMP; Hiram Berdan to Abraham Lincoln, November 27, 1862, Lincoln Papers, LC; Orlando Willcox to Zachariah Chandler, December 1,

1862, Chandler Papers, LC; Meade, *Life and Letters*, 1:327, 329; Cavins, *Civil War Letters of Cavins*, 112.

CHAPTER SEVEN

1. Lincoln, *Collected Works*, 5:510–11. At this same time Halleck poured out his own frustrations to Stanton about the slow movement of Federal armies, the large numbers of stragglers and deserters, and the generals' seeming inability to following up victories. See *OR*, ser. 3, 2:877–78.

2. Lincoln, *Collected Works*, 5:514–15; Daniel Reed Larned to his sister, November 27, 1862, Larned Papers, LC; Marsena Rudolph Patrick, *Inside Lincoln's Army*, 182–83; Michael C. C. Adams, *Our Masters the Rebels*, 132–34; Whan, *Fiasco at Fredericksburg*, 31.

3. *New York Times*, November 28, 30, 1862; Louis M. Starr, *Reporting the Civil War*, 127; Browning, *Diary*, 1:590; Stephen B. Oates, *Woman of Valor*, 101.

4. Zerah Coston Monks to Hannah T. Rohrer, November 20, 1862, Monks-Rohrer Letters, Emory; John D. Wilkins to his wife, November 26, 1862, Wilkins Papers, Schoff Collection, CL; Edward Henry Courtney Taylor to his sister, November 27, 1862, Taylor Letters, MHC.

5. Daniel Reed Larned to his sister, November 27, 1862, Larned Papers, LC; Trudeau, "Those Whom You Left behind You," 349; Henry Snow to his sister, December 5, 1862, Snow Letters, CHS; Cavins, *Civil War Letters of Cavins*, 111; Willard J. Templeton to his parents and sister, November 27, 1862, Templeton Letters, NHSL.

6. Jacob Pyewell to his mother, November 26, 1862, Pyewell Papers, CWMC, USAMHI; Partridge, *Letters from the Iron Brigade*, 65; John Pellett to his family, November 30, 1862, Pellett Papers, USAMHI; Franklin Sawyer to Samuel Sexton, November 26, 1862, Sexton Papers, OHS.

7. John S. Crocker to his wife, November 27, 1862, Crocker Letters, CU; Edmund Halsey, *Brother against Brother*, 87; Siegel, *For the Glory of the Union*, 101–2; Trask, *Fire Within*, 154; William Watson, *Letters of a Civil War Surgeon*, 34–35; Edwin O. Wentworth to his wife, November 26, 1862, Wentworth Papers, LC.

8. Frank Longstreet to his sister, November 26, 1862, Longstreet Papers, CWMC, USAMHI; Edward W. Steffan to his brother, November 28, 1862, Steffan Letters, FSNMP; Josiah C. Fuller to his wife, November 26, 1862, Fuller Papers, CWMC, USAMHI; Daniel M. Holt, *Surgeon's Civil War*, 51; Robert Goldthwaite Carter, *Four Brothers in Blue*, 169–70.

9. Thomas Claybrook Elder to Anna Fitzhugh Elder, November 27, 1862, Elder Papers, VHS; Corsan, *Two Months in the Confederate States*, 105; Thomas Smith Ruffin to Edmund Ruffin, November 27, 1862, Ruffin Papers, VHS; S. G. Pryor, *Post of Honor*, 288; Robert H. Simpson to "Dear Mary," November 28, 1862, Settle Papers, Duke.

10. J. B. Jones, *Rebel War Clerk's Diary*, 1:197; Samuel Schooler to Mary E. Schooler, December 1862, Schooler Papers, Duke; Judith Brockenbrough McGuire, *Diary of a Southern Refugee*, 173–74; *Richmond Daily Examiner*, November 29, 1862; *Richmond Daily Dispatch*, November 28, 1862; *Richmond Daily Whig*, November 29, 1862; *Richmond Daily Enquirer*, November 29, 1862.

11. Wren, *Captain James Wren's Civil War Diary*, 91; Albert W. Luther to his parents, November 27, 1862, Luther Papers, ISL; William Watson, *Letters of a Civil War Surgeon*, 34; Teall, "Ringside Seat at Fredericksburg," 25. Even though the Confederates were not building extensive earthworks, to nervous Federals across the river their preparations seemed formidable.

12. *Chicago Daily Tribune*, November 24, 25, 1862; *Philadelphia Inquirer*, November 25, 1862; *Easton (Pa.) Northampton County Journal*, November 26, 1862; *New York Times*, November 26, 1862; "On to Richmond Once More!," *Harper's Weekly*, November 29, 1862, 754.

13. *Hartford Daily Courant*, November 29, 1862; *New York Herald*, November 29, 1862; *Baltimore American and Commercial Advertiser*, November 29, 1862; *New York Times*, Decem-

ber 1–2, 1862; Gurowski, *Diary,* 2:25; Brooks, *Mr. Lincoln's Washington,* 28. Some editors claimed that Burnside was waiting for another Federal army to strike a diversionary blow along the James River. See *Boston Evening Transcript,* November 22, 1862; *Janesville (Wisc.) Daily Gazette,* November 25, 1862.

14. *Albany (N.Y.) Evening Journal,* November 26, 1862; *Philadelphia Inquirer,* November 26–27, 1862; *Watertown (N.Y.) Daily News and Reformer,* November 25, 1862.

15. Charles E. Davis, *Three Years in the Army,* 160; *Times* (London), December 12, 1862; *New York Herald,* November 28, 1862; *Rochester (N.Y.) Daily Union and Advertiser,* November 25, 1862.

16. J. Cutler Andrews, *North Reports the Civil War,* 322; *New York Times,* November 26–28, December 1, 1862; *New York Herald,* November 27, 1862; *Chicago Daily Tribune,* November 29, 1862; *Indianapolis Daily Journal,* December 3, 1862; *New York Tribune,* November 27, 1862.

17. Marvel, *Burnside,* 169; November 27, 1862, Latta Diary, LC; November 27, 1862, Heffelfinger Diary, *CWTI,* USAMHI; Walcott, *Twenty-First Regiment,* 233.

18. George Thomas Stevens, *Three Years in the Sixth Corps,* 164; Dwight Vick to his sister, November 30, 1862, Vick Letter, CWMC, USAMHI; Fairchild, *27th Regiment,* 115; Willard J. Templeton to his parents, November 27, 1862, Templeton Letters, NHSL; Frank Longstreet to his sister, November 29, 1862, Longstreet Papers, CWMC, USAMHI; John Day Smith, *Nineteenth Maine,* 25–26; November 27, 1862, Asa W. Bartlett, "Diary of Military Action," NHHS; Musgrove, *Autobiography of Captain Richard Musgrove,* 46.

19. November 27, 1862, Pope Diary, *CWTI,* USAMHI; November 27, 1862, Jackson Diary, IHS; November 27, 1862, Bailey Diary, NHHS; *Newark (N.J.) Daily Advertiser,* December 8, 1862; James Lorenzo Bowen, *Thirty-Seventh Regiment,* 99–100; Newell, *10th Regiment Massachusetts Volunteers,* 160.

20. *New York Herald,* December 3, 1862; Marsena Rudolph Patrick, *Inside Lincoln's Army,* 182; Joseph Bloomfield Osborn to Martha Osborn, November 27, 1862, Osborn Papers, LC; Samuel W. Eaton to Catherine Eaton, December 1, 1862, Eaton Papers, SHSW; William Franklin Draper to his mother, November 30, 1862, Draper Papers, LC.

21. Graham, *Ninth New York,* 368; Mayo, *Civil War Letters,* 222; November 27, 1862, Bancroft Diary, MHC; John H. Rhodes, *History of Battery B,* 135; *Rochester (N.Y.) Daily Democrat and American,* December 10, 1862; Newell, *10th Regiment Massachusetts Volunteers,* 159. Complaints about meager food on Thanksgiving were pervasive in the Army of the Potomac; I have found more than fifty references to the problem.

22. Denison, *First Rhode Island Cavalry,* 181; Haley, *Rebel Yell and Yankee Hurrah,* 54; Brewster, *When This Cruel War Is Over,* 192.

23. Edmund Halsey, *Brother against Brother,* 86–87; Helman, "Young Soldier in the Army of the Potomac," 153; November 27, 1862, Metcalf Diary, FSNMP.

24. James B. Post to his wife, November 27, 1862, Post Papers, CWMC, USAMHI; Wightman, *From Antietam to Fort Fisher,* 84–85; Samuel W. Eaton to Catherine Eaton, December 1, 1862, Eaton Papers, SHSW; William Hamilton to his mother, November 28, 1862, Hamilton Papers, LC; Sturtevant, *Josiah Volunteered,* 60–61; Samuel V. Dean to his wife, November 28, 1862, Dean Letters, FSNMP; William Speed to Charlotte Speed, November 29, 1862, Speed Papers, Schoff Collection, CL; Robert Goldthwaite Carter, *Four Brothers in Blue,* 178.

25. Elisha Hunt Rhodes, *All for the Union,* 88; George E. Upton to his wife, December 2, 1862, Upton Papers, NHHS.

26. Aaron K. Blake to his sister, November 30, 1862, Blake Letters, CWMC, USAMHI; James B. Post to his wife, November 27, 1862, Post Papers, CWMC, USAMHI; Robert Goldthwaite Carter, *Four Brothers in Blue,* 175; O. Leland Barlow to his sister, November 30, 1862, Barlow Papers, CSL; Ford, *Fifteenth Regiment Massachusetts Volunteer Infantry,* 220; Wightman, *From Antietam to Fort Fisher,* 82; Lusk, *War Letters of William Thompson Lusk,* 233–34; *Narragansett (R.I.) Weekly,* December 11, 1862; James R. Woodworth to Phoebe Woodworth,

November 27–28, 1862, Woodworth Papers, Hotchkiss Collection, CL. Newspaper editors offered equally sentimental descriptions of empty chairs around the Thanksgiving table. See *Hartford Daily Courant,* November 27, 1862.

27. McKelvey, *Rochester in the Civil War,* 111–12; Jeremiah Taylor, *Hamilton Brewer,* 108–9; Samuel S. Partridge to "Dear Ed," November 25, 1862, Partridge Letters, FSNMP; Miles Peabody to his parents, December 1, 1862, Peabody Letters, CWMC, USAMHI.

28. *Yonkers (N.Y.) Examiner,* November 27, 1862; "Thanksgiving Day," *Christian Inquirer,* December 6, 1862; *Boston Daily Advertiser,* November 27, 1862; *Philadelphia Public Ledger,* November 27, 1862; *Indianapolis Daily State Sentinel,* November 27, 1862; *Boston Post,* November 27, 1862.

29. *Philadelphia Inquirer,* November 27, 1862; *New York Times,* November 28, 1862; *Albany (N.Y.) Atlas and Argus,* November 27, 1862; *Albany (N.Y.) Evening Journal,* November 26, 1862.

30. *New York Times,* November 28, 1862; "Confederate Republic of Israel," *Christian Advocate and Journal,* December 11, 1862, 394; *Augusta (Maine) Kennebec Journal,* November 28, 1862; *Philadelphia Inquirer,* November 28, 1862; "Thanksgiving in Time of War," *Evangelist,* November 27, 1862, 1; *Philadelphia Evening Bulletin,* November 26, 1862; *New York Tribune,* November 28, 1862.

31. Thibaut, *Guide of Providence,* 88, George W. Ballock to his wife, November 25, 1862, Ballock Papers, Duke; Catherine Eaton to Samuel W. Eaton, November 28, 1862, Eaton Papers, SHSW; *Baltimore American and Commercial Advertiser,* November 27, 1862; *New York Tribune,* November 28, 1862; *Newark (N.J.) Daily Advertiser,* November 26, 1862; *Philadelphia Inquirer,* November 28, 1862.

32. For the ambivalence of soldiers toward religion, see Wiley, *Life of Billy Yank,* 262–74; James I. Robertson Jr., *Soldiers Blue and Gray,* 170–89. On secularization, religious language, and the search for meaning, I have especially relied on the analysis in Rose, *Victorian America and the Civil War,* 17–38, 59–67; Paludan, *"People's Contest,"* 363–65.

33. November 13, 1862, Jackson Diary, IHS; James R. Woodworth to Phoebe Woodworth, November 22–25, December 1, 1862, Woodworth Papers, Hotchkiss Collection, CL; Henry A. Allen, *Sergeant Allen and Private Renick,* 166; United States Christian Commission, *First Annual Report,* 64–65; Daniel Reed Larned to ?, December 8, 1862, Larned Papers, LC; Pardington, *Dear Sarah,* 38; Albert, *Forty-fifth Pennsylvania,* 207–8; Washburn, *108th Regiment,* 111.

34. Lord, *History of the Ninth New Hampshire,* 200–201, 207; Haydon, *For Country, Cause, and Leader,* 295; Meade, *Life and Letters,* 1:328; Sturtevant, *Josiah Volunteered,* 58–59; December 7, 1862, Webb Diary, Schoff Collection, CL.

35. Lincoln, *Collected Works,* 5:497–98; *New York Times,* November 23, 1862; Burrage, *Thirty-Sixth Massachusetts,* 25; Henry A. Allen, *Sergeant Allen and Private Renick,* 169; Alexander Morrison Stewart, *Camp, March, and Battlefield,* 262–63; Hartsock, *Soldier of the Cross,* 32; Siegel, *For the Glory of the Union,* 94; *Newark (N.J.) Daily Advertiser,* November 17, 1862.

36. *Newark (N.J.) Daily Advertiser,* December 5, 1862; Shattuck, *Shield and Hiding Place,* 51–63. Many chaplains were Methodists, though Baptists, Presbyterians, Unitarians, and Catholics also joined the ranks. Protestant officers sometimes prevented Catholics from becoming chaplains. Three priests served in the Irish brigade, however, and wartime experience likely eroded sectarian prejudice. See Paludan, *"People's Contest,"* 349; Peter Welsh, *Irish Green and Union Blue,* 35; Eastman, "Army Chaplain of 1863," 347. For a fuller account of Union chaplains generally, see Warren B. Armstrong, *For Courageous Fighting and Confident Dying,* 1–94.

37. Lord, *History of the Ninth New Hampshire,* 214, 218; McAllister, *Letters of Robert McAllister,* 226; Hartsock, *Soldier of the Cross,* 33, 35; *Newark (N.J.) Daily Advertiser,* November 28, 1862; Walcott, *Twenty-First Regiment,* 235; Beidelman, *Letters of George Washington Beidelman,* 143.

38. *New York Herald,* December 5, 1862; *Indianapolis Daily Journal,* December 11, 1862;

Cook, *Twelfth Massachusetts,* 81; John L. Smith, *118th Pennsylvania,* 106; McAllister, *Letters of Robert McAllister,* 223–24; Beidelman, *Letters of George Washington Beidelman,* 149–50.

39. Alexander Morrison Stewart, *Camp, March, and Battlefield,* 255–58; Samuel W. Eaton to Warner Eaton, December 1, 1862, Eaton Papers, SHSW.

40. Uriah N. Parmelee to his mother, December 5, 1862, Parmelee Papers, Duke; Hartsock, *Soldier of the Cross,* 26–28, 166.

41. Lincoln, *Collected Works,* 5:425.

42. *Boston Post,* November 20, 1862; "The President's Emancipation Proclamation," *Knickerbocker,* November 1862, 436–41; *Albany (N.Y.) Atlas and Argus,* November 18, 1862; *Congressional Globe,* 37th Cong., 3rd sess., 1862, 76–82, 94–100, 146–50; *New York Herald,* November 18, 1862; *Smithport (Pa.) M'Kean County Democrat,* November 29, 1862; *Indianapolis Daily State Sentinel,* November 3, 1862.

43. Lounger, "Stick to the Text," *Harper's Weekly,* December 13, 1862, 786; *Chicago Daily Tribune,* November 3, 13, 1862; *New York Times,* November 12, 1862; Henry J. Raymond to Abraham Lincoln, November 25, 1862, Lincoln Papers, LC.

44. *Providence (R.I.) Daily Journal,* November 15, 1862; "The War Policy and the Future of the South," *Christian Examiner,* November 1862, 435–54; Douglass, *Writings of Douglass,* 3:290–96; George B. Cheever to Abraham Lincoln, November 22, 1862; Horace Greeley to Lincoln, November 24, 1862; and Andrew Parker to Lincoln, November 9, 1862, Lincoln Papers, LC.

45. William F. Smith to his mother, November 7, 1862, William F. Smith Letters, Leigh Collection, USAMHI; Daniel M. Holt, *Surgeon's Civil War,* 41; Hess, *Liberty, Virtue, and Progress,* 18–22; Cavins, *Civil War Letters of Cavins,* 113–14.

46. Wiley, *Life of Billy Yank,* 109–19; Jimerson, *Private Civil War,* 27–49; McPherson, *What They Fought For,* 27–46; Milans, "Eyewitness to Fredericksburg," 22; Edwin O. Wentworth to his father, November 10, 1862, Wentworth Papers, LC.

47. McPherson, *What They Fought For,* 56–58; McPherson, *For Cause and Comrades,* 117–21.

48. Zerah Coston Monks to Hannah T. Rohrer, November 11, 1862, Monks-Rohrer Letters, Emory; John W. Ames to Fisher Ames, November 24, 1862, Ames Papers, USAMHI; Sturtevant, *Josiah Volunteered,* 60; Alexander Morrison Stewart, *Camp, March, and Battlefield,* 261–62; Hartsock, *Soldier of the Cross,* 29; Cavins, *Civil War Letters of Cavins,* 113.

49. Andrew J. Bennett, *Story of the First Massachusetts Light Battery,* 92; Abram P. Smith, *Seventy-Sixth New York,* 193–94; Haydon, *For Country, Cause, and Leader,* 291; S. Millett Thompson, *Thirteenth New Hampshire,* 30–31; Hopkins, *Seventh Rhode Island,* 30; McCarter, *My Life in the Irish Brigade,* 111–19.

50. Daniel Reed Larned to his sister, November 27, 1862, Larned Papers, LC; Silber and Stevens, *Yankee Correspondence,* 95; Jonathan Hutchinson to his home folks, December 5, 1862, Hutchinson Letters, USAMHI; Wightman, *From Antietam to Fort Fisher,* 71; December 2, 1862, Pope Diary, *CWTI,* USAMHI.

51. Edward Hall Armstrong to his father, December 18, 1862, Armstrong Letter, Duke; *OR,* ser. 1, 51(2):650–51; *Richmond Daily Enquirer,* November 20, December 3, 1862; *Richmond Daily Dispatch,* November 5, 14, December 12, 1862.

52. *Charleston Mercury,* November 29, 1862; J. B. Jones, *Rebel War Clerk's Diary,* 1:202; Sarah Morgan Dawson, *Civil War Diary,* 350; *Richmond Daily Enquirer,* December 22, 1862; *Pastoral Letter from the Bishops of the Protestant Episcopal Church,* 10–11; McPherson, *What They Fought For,* 47–56.

53. *Charleston Daily Courier,* November 17, December 5, 1862; *Richmond Daily Whig,* November 22, 1862; *Richmond Daily Enquirer,* November 12, 1862.

54. *OR,* ser. 4, 2:211; *Richmond Daily Whig,* November 20, 1862; *Journal of the Senate of South Carolina,* 13–14; Speairs and Pettit, *Civil War Letters,* 1:68, 72.

55. Fisher, *Diary of Sidney George Fisher*, 443; Dicey, *Spectator of America*, 91–92; Willard L. King, *Lincoln's Manager*, 200; Brooks, *Mr. Lincoln's Washington*, 28–29.

56. *Congressional Globe*, 37th Cong., 3rd sess., 1862, 1; Lincoln, *Collected Works*, 5:518.

57. Lincoln, *Collected Works*, 5:520, 527–37. Some historians have argued that Lincoln's message was tailored for conservative voters and marked a return to the political center (Paludan, *Presidency of Lincoln*, 160–66; Donald, *Lincoln*, 396–98; Voegeli, *Free but Not Equal*, 66), while other scholars have tried to explain away Lincoln's support for compensated emancipation by emphasizing the message's powerful rhetorical conclusion (Trefousse, *Radical Republicans*, 233–35; LaWanda Cox, *Lincoln and Black Freedom*, 10–11; McPherson, *Battle Cry of Freedom*, 562–63). These competing interpretations suggest Lincoln's own uncertainty. Exhausted and frustrated, he was hardly in top form at the end of 1862.

58. McPherson, *Struggle for Equality*, 119–20; "The President's Message," *Liberator*, December 5, 1862, 194; "Cleaning Up," *Independent*, November 20, 1862, 4; "The President's Message," *Independent*, December 4, 1862, 4; Blight, *Frederick Douglass' Civil War*, 122–47; "The Proclamation and the Message," *National Anti-Slavery Standard*, December 13, 1862, 2; "The President's Annual Message," *Evangelist*, December 4, 1862, 1. For Beecher's authorship of attacks on Lincoln published in the important religious weekly *Independent*, see Henry C. Bowen to William H. Seward, December 9, 1862, Seward Papers, UR.

59. Elizabeth Blair Lee, *Civil War Letters*, 211; *Watertown (N.Y.) Daily News and Reformer*, December 10, 1862; *Augusta (Maine) Kennebec Journal*, December 19, 1862; *New York Tribune*, December 2, 1862; *Chicago Daily Tribune*, December 3, 1862; *Boston Evening Transcript*, December 5, 1862.

60. Garfield, *Wild Life of the Army*, 185–86; *Haverhill (Mass.) Gazette*, December 5, 1862; *Newark (N.J.) Daily Advertiser*, December 2, 1862; *Springfield (Mass.) Daily Republican*, December 3, 1862; *Chicago Daily Tribune*, December 4, 1862; "Emancipation," *Christian Advocate and Journal*, December 11, 1862, 396; Browning, *Diary*, 1:591; *New York Times*, December 2, 3, 1862.

61. *Washington Daily National Intelligencer*, December 2, 1862; *New York Herald*, December 2–3, 1862; *Boston Daily Advertiser*, December 2, 1862; *Times* (London), December 17, 1862.

62. *Rochester (N.Y.) Daily Union and Advertiser*, December 2, 1862; Appendix to the *Congressional Globe*, 37th Cong., 3rd sess., 1862, 39–41; *Indianapolis Daily State Sentinel*, December 5, 1862; "The President's Message and the War," *Knickerbocker*, January 1863, 58–64; *Portland (Maine) Eastern Argus*, December 3, 1862; *Goshen (Ind.) Democrat*, December 10, 1862.

63. J. B. Jones, *Rebel War Clerk's Diary*, 1:204; "Compensated Emancipation," *Index* (London), December 18, 1862, 121; Speairs and Pettit, *Civil War Letters*, 1:74; William Nelson Pendleton to Anzolette E. Pendleton, December 7, 1862, Pendleton Papers, SHC; Edmund Ruffin, *Diary*, 2:505; Pender, *General to His Lady*, 193.

64. *Lynchburg Daily Virginian*, December 9, 1862; *Charleston Mercury*, December 11, 1862; *Richmond Daily Examiner*, December 6, 1862; Myers, *Children of Pride*, 997; December 6, 1862, Hamilton Diary, FSNMP; *Richmond Daily Dispatch*, December 6, 1862; *Richmond Daily Whig*, December 9, 1862.

65. Richard K. Halsey to "Friend Keck," December 10, 1862, King Papers, Schoff Collection, CL; December 6, 1862, Thompson Memoir, LC; Isaac Lyman Taylor, "Campaigning with the First Minnesota," 235; Oliver Willcox Norton, *Army Letters*, 128; Lusk, *War Letters of William Thompson Lusk*, 239.

66. William Houghton to his father, December 3, 1862, Houghton Papers, IHS; *Rochester (N.Y.) Daily Union and Advertiser*, December 8, 1862; Emerson F. Merrill to his parents, December 7, 1862, Merrill Papers, FSNMP.

CHAPTER EIGHT

1. Daniel Reed Larned to "My Dear Henry," November 22, 1862, Larned Papers, LC; Fishel, *Secret War for the Union,* 265–66; *OR,* ser. 3, 3:293; Joseph C. Kennedy to Ambrose E. Burnside, December 1, 1862, Burnside Papers, entry 159, box 4, NA.

2. *OR,* 812–13, 819, and ser. 1, 51(1):952; E. V. Sumner to Ambrose E. Burnside, November 23, 1862, Burnside Papers, entry 159, box 3, NA; John S. Crocker to his wife, November 29, 1862, Crocker Letters, CU; William Teall to his son-in-law and wife, December 1, 1862, Teall Letters, TSLA.

3. *OR,* 61, 87, 355–56, 780, 787; Brainerd, *Bridge Building in Wartime,* 98–106; William F. Smith, *Autobiography,* 59–60; William F. Smith, "Franklin's 'Left Grand Division,'" in *B&L,* 3:128–29; *CCW,* 1:652, 661, 666; Marvel, *Burnside,* 169–70; Whan, *Fiasco at Fredericksburg,* 29–30.

4. *ORN,* ser. 1, 5:182–89; *OR,* 642–43; *OR Supplement,* pt. 2, 10:180; O'Reilly, *Jackson at Fredericksburg,* 11–12; Jennings Cropper Wise, *Long Arm of Lee,* 1:365–66.

5. Anson Stager to Abraham Lincoln, December 1, 1862, Lincoln Papers, LC; William F. Smith, *Autobiography,* 60; Meade, *Life and Letters,* 1:335; Joseph E. Hooker to Edwin M. Stanton, December 4, 1862, Stanton Papers, LC; John Godfrey to Horace Godfrey, December 6, 1862, Godfrey Papers, NHHS; December 6, 1862, Thompson Memoir, LC.

6. December 3, 1862, Jackson Diary, IHS; Edward Henry Courtney Taylor to his sister, November 29, 1862, Taylor Letters, MHC; Samuel S. Partridge to "Dear Ed," November 30, 1862, Partridge Letters, FSNMP; Augustus Van Dyke to his father, December 1, 1862, Van Dyke Papers, IHS.

7. Reardon, "Forlorn Hope," 85–86; *History of the Fifth Massachusetts Battery,* 491–92; James H. Leonard, "Letters of a Fifth Wisconsin Volunteer," 68; Trobriand, *Our Noble Blood,* 81; Zerah Coston Monks to Hannah T. Rohrer, December 5, 1862, Monks-Rohrer Letters, Emory.

8. Bright and Bright, *"Respects to All,"* 33; Flauvius Bellamy to E. F. Bellamy, December 1, 1862, Bellamy Papers, ISL; Robert Goldthwaite Carter, *Four Brothers in Blue,* 180.

9. Bright and Bright, *"Respects to All,"* 34; Henry C. Marsh to John Marsh, December 5, 1862, Marsh Papers, ISL; Oliver Willcox Norton, *Army Letters,* 127–28; George W. Ballock to his wife, December 3, 1862, Ballock Papers, Duke. On the difficulty of getting an army moving again after a delay in camp, see Keegan, *Face of Battle,* 292–93. Even at this late date, rumors persisted that the Army of the Potomac might be moved elsewhere or that a thirty-day armistice was in the offing. See William Speed to Charlotte Speed, November 29, 1862, Speed Papers, Schoff Collection, CL; Miles Peabody to his parents, December 1, 1862, Peabody Letters, CWMC, USAMHI; December 2, 1862, Jackson Diary, IHS.

10. Robert E. Lee, *Recollections and Letters,* 85; Douglas Southall Freeman, *Lee,* 2:438–41; Robert E. Lee, *Wartime Papers,* 343; *OR,* 551–52, 1042–43, 1049–50, 1052; Fitzhugh Lee, *Lee,* 234–35; *Richmond Daily Enquirer,* December 3, 1862.

11. Klein, *Edward Porter Alexander,* 50–51; Longstreet, *From Manassas to Appomattox,* 300; *OR Supplement,* pt. 1, 3:711–13; William M. Owen, *In Camp and Battle with the Washington Artillery,* 174–76; *OR,* ser. 1, 51(2):564; Edward Porter Alexander, *Fighting for the Confederacy,* 167–68; Susan Pendleton Lee, *Memoirs of William Nelson Pendleton,* 235. At this stage of the war, extensive earthworks were not yet being built to protect infantry, and Lee may also have been trying to induce Burnside to attack by not having the defenses appear too formidable. See Hagerman, *Civil War and Origins of Modern Warfare,* 122–25; Sorrel, *Recollections of a Confederate Staff Officer,* 125; Douglas Southall Freeman, *Lee,* 2:441–42.

12. *OR,* 1043–44, 1046–47; *OR Supplement,* pt. 1, 3:712–13; Walters, *Norfolk Blues,* 45.

13. *OR,* 1035, 1040; James Power Smith, "With Stonewall Jackson," 27; Edmondson, *My Dear Emma,* 122; W. G. Bean, *Sandie Pendleton,* 85; Ujanirtus Allen, *Campaigning with "Old Stonewall,"* 192; James C. Zimmerman to his wife, December 4, 1862, Zimmerman Papers,

Duke. Reports of powerful Confederate earthworks began appearing in the northern press; one staff officer was sure that Lee's forces numbered at least 180,000 men. See *New York Times,* December 9, 1862; *Indianapolis Daily Journal,* December 8, 1862; John S. Crocker to his wife, December 3, 1862, Crocker Letters, CU.

14. Henry F. Young to his father, December 1, 1862, Young Papers, SHSW; John Godfrey to Horace Godfrey, December 1, 1862, Godfrey Papers, NHHS; Bartol, *Nation's Hour,* 46–47; Lewis Nettleton to "My own dear love," November 30, 1862, Nettleton-Baldwin Family Papers, Duke; Anthony G. Graves to his friend Jack, December 2, 1862, Graves Letters, FSNMP; William Hamilton to his mother, November 30, 1862, Hamilton Papers, LC.

15. Craig L. Dunn, *Iron Men, Iron Will,* 144; Reuben Schell to his father, December 4, 1862, Schell Letters, FSNMP; *Rochester (N.Y.) Daily Union and Advertiser,* December 10, 1862; Washburn, *108th Regiment,* 112; James T. Odem to Eleanor Odem, December 3, 1862, Odem Papers, UVa; Pardington, *Dear Sarah,* 45–46. Some social psychologists have defined rumors as word-of-mouth information passed along "without secure standards of evidence being present," but sociologists have preferred to assume that rumors can be either true or false—a proposition that is much more useful for historians. Cf. Allport and Postman, *Psychology of Rumor,* ix; Shibutani, *Improvised News,* 17; Kapferer, *Rumors,* 2–16. Camp rumors tended to multiply and contradict one another, thus making analysis of particular rumors difficult at best.

16. McAllister, *Letters of Robert McAllister,* 233; Hemmenway, "Reminiscence," *CWTI,* USAMHI; Paludan, *"People's Contest,"* 319.

17. Brian A. Bennett, *140th New York,* 99; Charles Francis Adams, *Cycle of Adams Letters,* 1: 203; Virgil W. Mattoon to his father, December 5, 1862, Mattoon Papers, CHS; Philip Hacker to William Hacker and Barbara Woll Hacker, November 29, 1862, Hacker Brothers Papers, Schoff Collection, CL; Hosea Towne to "Dear Friends," December 5, 1862, Towne Papers, NHHS; Milans, "Eyewitness to Fredericksburg," 21–22.

18. Dawes, *Sixth Wisconsin,* 107; John S. Crocker to his wife, December 5, 1862, Crocker Letters, CU; McCrea, *Dear Belle,* 170; Edward Henry Courtney Taylor to his brother, November 29, 1862, Taylor Letters, MHC. For general insights on the exchange of rumors as a group activity, see Shibutani, *Improvised News,* 9–16. Of some comfort to the historian is the argument that the exact source of a rumor is not that important. By the same token, however, to refer to rumors as simply "spontaneous" begs a number of historical questions. See Kapferer, *Rumors,* 19–20.

19. W. H. Andrews, *Footprints of a Regiment,* 96; December 5, 1862, Jones Diary, Schoff Collection, CL; William Calder to his mother, December 8, 1862, Calder Family Papers, SHC; Hotchkiss, *Make Me a Map of the Valley,* 97.

20. *Savannah Republican,* December 15, 1862; December 7, 1862, Ware Diary, SHC; T. R. R. Cobb to his wife, December 6, 1862, Cobb Letters, UG.

21. William Rhadamanthus Montgomery, *Georgia Sharpshooter,* 74; Edmund Ruffin, *Diary,* 2:505; Burgwyn, *Captain's War,* 39.

22. John S. Brooks to Sarah A. Knox, December 5, 1862, Brooks Letters, SHC; Krick, *30th Virginia,* 33; Paxton, *Memoir and Memorials,* 74–75; Calhoun Green Clay to ?, December 11, 1862, Clay Family Papers, VHS; Hatton Memoir, 370, LC; Jeremiah M. Tate to his sister, December 11–13, 1862, Tate Papers, GLC; James A. Wilson to his wife, December 6, 1862, James Albert Wilson Letter, FSNMP; Irby, *Historical Sketch of the Nottoway Grays,* 23; Thomas Ruffin, *Papers,* 3:281; Edmondson, *My Dear Emma,* 114; *Contributions to a History of the Richmond Howitzer Battalion,* 143; Thomas J. Morrison to his father, December 8, 1862, Morrison Letters, FSNMP.

23. Simpson and Simpson, *Far, Far from Home,* 164–65; Roberson, *Weep Not for Me,* 152; Henry P. Garrison to Emily Aurora Bosworth, December 9, 1862, Garrison Papers, Austin State University; William Henry Tatum to his brother, December 10, 1862, Tatum Papers, VHS; Torrence, "Diary and Letters of Leonidas Torrence," 499–500; Constantine Hege to his father,

December 8, 1862, Hege Letters, Leigh Collection, USAMHI. Reports that Confederates were still wearing summer clothing appeared in the northern press and likely contributed to expectations that Burnside would whip the ragtag Rebels. See *New York Herald,* December 5, 1862; Edward Bates, *Diary,* 268; Herman Haupt to his wife, December 9, 1862, Haupt Letterbook, Haupt Papers, LC.

24. *OR,* ser. 4, 2:229–31; *Richmond Daily Whig,* December 4, 1862; Robert A. Moore, *Life for the Confederacy,* 102; *Columbus (Ga.) Daily Enquirer,* December 15, 1862; *Richmond Daily Examiner,* December 5, 1862.

25. Louise Haskell Daly, *Alexander Cheeves Haskell,* 87; Iobst and Manarin, *Bloody Sixth,* 102–3; William Calder to his mother, December 8, 1862, Calder Family Papers, SHC; *Atlanta Southern Confederacy,* December 18, 1862.

26. Chapla, "Quartermaster Operations in the Forty-second Virginia," 13–14; Constantine A. Hege to his parents, December 18, 1862, Hege Letters, Leigh Collection, USAMHI; John S. Brooks to Sarah A. Knox, December 2, 1862, Brooks Letters, SHC; Welch, *Confederate Surgeon's Letters,* 37; *Richmond Daily Enquirer,* December 13, 1862; *Richmond Daily Dispatch,* December 10, 1862; *Richmond Daily Whig,* December 10, 1862. Reports of barefoot Rebel deserters on short rations appeared in the northern press on the very eve of the battle of Fredericksburg. See *New York Herald,* December 12, 1862.

27. James C. Zimmerman to his wife, December 2, 1862, Zimmerman Papers, Duke; December 4–5, 1862, Ware Diary, SHC; *Savannah Republican,* December 15, 1862.

28. Francis Warrington Dawson, *Reminiscences of Confederate Service,* 83–84; Susan Leigh Blackford, *Letters from Lee's Army,* 140; J. W. Armsworthy to his wife, December 4, 1862, Armsworthy Letters, FSNMP; Susan Pendleton Lee, *Memoirs of William Nelson Pendleton,* 236–38; Cutrer and Parrish, *Brothers in Gray,* 135; *Macon (Ga.) Daily Telegraph,* December 16, 1862; Edgar Allan Jackson, *Three Rebels Write Home,* 63.

29. Von Borcke, *Memoirs of the Confederate War,* 2:82–84; William M. Owen, *In Camp and Battle with the Washington Artillery,* 177.

30. Foster, *New Jersey and the Rebellion,* 529; Croffut and Morris, *Connecticut during the War,* 288–89; Thorpe, *Fifteenth Connecticut Volunteers,* 29–30; John Russell Bartlett, *Memoirs of Rhode Island Officers,* 238; S. Millett Thompson, *Thirteenth New Hampshire,* 27–28, 31–32; December 1–6, 1862, Abernathy Diary, USAMHI; Ephraim Jackson to "Dear Brother and Sister," December 20, 1862, Jackson Letters, FSNMP; John Leonard to his father, December 7, 1862, Leonard Letters, CWMC, Yale; Alonzo Pierce to "Dear Brother Charlie," December 7, 1862, Pierce Papers, NHHS.

31. *Flemington (N.J.) Hunterdon Republican,* December 24, 1862; Newton Martin Curtis, *From Bull Run to Chancellorsville,* 219–20; Best, *History of the 121st New York,* 34–38; Henry Ogden Ryerson to his sister, December 7, 1862, Anderson Family Papers, NJHS; Michie, *Life and Letters of Emory Upton,* 70–71.

32. Judd, *Story of the Thirty-Third,* 233–35; December 5, 7, 1862, Taylor Diary, FSNMP; *Newark (N.J.) Daily Advertiser,* December 12, 13, 1862; Fairchild, *27th Regiment,* 115–16; Benedict, *Vermont in the Civil War,* 1:337–38; Castleman, *Army of the Potomac,* 253.

33. Brewster, *When This Cruel War Is Over,* 194–95.

34. December 1, 1862, Jackson Diary, IHS; *New York Times,* December 10, 1862; December 5–6, Furst Diary, HCWRTC, USAMHI; *History of the Fifth Massachusetts Battery,* 494; Davenport, *Fifth New York Volunteer Infantry,* 335; George H. Allen, *Forty-Six Months,* 159–60; Seigel, *For the Glory of the Union,* 103–4; December 6, 1862, Berry Diary, *CWTI,* USAMHI; December 6, 1862, Heffelfinger Diary, *CWTI,* USAMHI.

35. December 7, 1862, Pope Diary, *CWTI,* USAMHI; Haydon, *For Country, Cause, and Leader,* 295; J. E. Hodgkins, *Civil War Diary,* 15; Bruce Sutherland, "Pittsburgh Volunteers," 248.

36. Richard K. Halsey to "Friend Keck," December 10, 1862, King Papers, Schoff Collection, CL; Lord, *History of the Ninth New Hampshire*, 221.

37. Trobriand, *Four Years with the Army of the Potomac*, 361; Davenport, *Fifth New York Volunteer Infantry*, 336; Pettit, *Infantryman Pettit*, 40; Wren, *Captain James Wren's Civil War Diary*, 93; Franklin Boyts to his brother, December 9, 1862, Boyts Diary, HSP.

38. Samuel S. Partridge to "Dear Ed," December 6, 1862, Partridge Letters, FSNMP; Thomas H. Evans, "'Cries of the Wounded,'" 30; Martin A. Haynes, *Minor War History*, 80–81; Gay, "Gay Letters," 388; Lord, *History of the Ninth New Hampshire*, 220–21; December 7, 1862, Shepard Diary, FSNMP; John Lord Parker, *Twenty-Second Massachusetts*, 221; December 6, 1862, Keiser Diary, HCWRTC, USAMHI; John T. Greene, *Ewing Family Letters*, 30. On the other hand, a particularly hearty Hoosier lying on the ground under three blankets in a muslin tent claimed that he "never slept better or more comfortable in my life" (December 6, 1862, Jackson Diary, IHS).

39. John Lord Parker, *Twenty-Second Massachusetts*, 221; Bardeen, *Little Fifer's Diary*, 98; McNamara, *History of the Ninth Massachusetts*, 241.

40. J. E. Hodgkins, *Civil War Diary*, 15; Kearney, "Letters from the Field," 185; December 8, 1862, Furst Diary, HCWRTC, USAMHI; McAllister, *Letters of Robert McAllister*, 230; *Religion, for Country, Cause, and Leader*, 294; Emerson F. Merrill to his parents, December 7, 1862, Merrill Papers, FSNMP.

41. James Remington to his father, December 8, 1862, Remington Papers, RIHS; December 1, 6, 1862, Thompson Memoir, LC; Charles E. Davis, *Three Years in the Army*, 160; Asa W. Bartlett, *History of the Twelfth New Hampshire*, 37; Lord, *History of the Ninth New Hampshire*, 222; Loren H. Goodrich to "Dear Friends," December 9, 1862, Goodrich Papers, CHS; Willard J. Templeton to his brother, December 7, 1862, Templeton Letters, NHSL; James Coburn to his parents, December 7, 1862, James P. Coburn Papers, USAMHI; *Fifth Annual Report of the Bureau of Military Statistics*, 572–73; Samuel S. Partridge to "Dear Ed," December 9, 1862, Partridge Letters, FSNMP.

42. S. Millett Thompson, *Thirteenth New Hampshire*, 32–33; John Lord Parker, *Twenty-Second Massachusetts*, 221; Gearhart, *Reminiscences of the Civil War*, 23; Sprenger, *122d Regiment*, 128–30; Cook, *Twelfth Massachusetts*, 79; Powell, *Fifth Corps*, 366; *New York Times*, December 9, 1862; *Johnstown (Pa.) Cambria Tribune*, December 19, 1862; *Albany (N.Y.) Atlas and Argus*, December 10, 1862; *New York Herald*, December 10, 1862; *MSH*, 5:473; December 7, 1862, Stoner Diary, FSNMP; December 6, 1862, S. W. Gordon Diary, FSNMP; Reese, *Sykes' Regular Infantry Division*, 173; Orson Blair Curtis, *History of the Twenty-Fourth Michigan*, 83–84; Pardington, *Dear Sarah*, 47; Asa W. Bartlett, *History of the Twelfth New Hampshire*, 37.

43. Walcott, *Twenty-First Regiment*, 235–36; A. C. Higley to his father, December 6, 1862, Higley Letters, FSNMP; *Wellsboro (Pa.) Agitator*, December 17, 1862; George E. Upton to his wife, December 7, 1862, Upton Papers, NHHS; *OR*, 377; December 3, 1862, Jackson Diary, IHS; Brian A. Bennett, *140th New York*, 101; James Remington to his father, December 6, 1862, Remington Papers, RIHS. Although shoe shortages in the Army of the Potomac were not nearly so politically controversial as those in the Army of Northern Virginia, one letter from an Indiana regiment (published in an ardently Republican newspaper) claimed there were hardly any barefoot men in the camps. See *Indianapolis Daily Journal*, December 5, 1862.

44. Daniel M. Holt, *Surgeon's Civil War*, 56; Lusk, *War Letters of William Thompson Lusk*, 240–41; Washburn, *108th Regiment*, 112; John W. Ames to his father, December 9, 1862, Ames Papers, USAMHI; Wren, *Captain James Wren's Civil War Diary*, 94.

45. John T. Greene, *Ewing Family Letters*, 29; Glover, *Bucktailed Wildcats*, 167; William Speed to Charlotte Speed, November 29, 1862, Speed Papers, Schoff Collection, CL; *Pittsburgh Daily Dispatch*, December 9, 1862; Lord, *History of the Ninth New Hampshire*, 221; December 6, 1862, Seage Diary, MHC; Brewster, *When This Cruel War Is Over*, 193; Edward K. Russell to

his mother, December 1, 1862, Kirby-Smith-Russell Collection, FSNMP; Uriah N. Parmelee to his mother, December 5, 1862, Parmelee Papers, Duke; William Hamilton to his mother, November 28, 1862, Hamilton Papers, LC; December 8, 1862, Abernathy Diary, USAMHI.

46. December 3, 1862, Pope Diary, CWTI, USAMHI; Washburn, 108th Regiment, 112; William Teall to his wife, December 7, 1862, Teall Letters, TSLA; Lucius B. Shattuck to "Dear Ellen," December 11–14, 1862, Shattuck Letters, MHC.

47. Rochester (N.Y.) Daily Union and Advertiser, December 12, 1862; James Remington to his father, November 30, December 8, 1862, Remington Papers, RIHS; Bellard, Gone for a Soldier, 179; December 2, 1862, Jackson Diary, IHS; Weymouth, Memorial Sketch of Lieut. Edgar M. Newcomb, 99. The men also began sending home lists of favorite foods for their families to provide in Christmas boxes. See George H. P. Rowell to his parents, December 3, 1862, Rowell Papers, NHHS; Beidelman, Letters of George Washington Beidelman, 151–52; Samuel V. Dean to his wife, December 5, 1862, Dean Letters, FSNMP.

48. These estimates on pay come from scores of comments in soldier diaries and letters.

49. James Lorenzo Bowen, Thirty-Seventh Regiment, 100; Smithe, Glimpses of Places, and People, and Things, 30; Henry L. Campbell to his mother, December 7, 1862, Campbell Papers, Duke; Newell, 10th Regiment Massachusetts Volunteers, 160; Albany (N.Y.) Atlas and Argus, December 5, 1862.

50. New York Times, December 9, 1862; Bright and Bright, "Respects to All," 33; Anthony G. Graves to his friend Jack, December 2, 1862, Graves Letters, FSNMP; December 5, 1862, Lambert Diary, IHS; Oliver Willcox Norton, Army Letters, 129. A War Department report was unclear about the number of men on the army payroll but naturally blamed the Treasury Department for delays in paying the troops. See "Number of Soldiers on the Pay-Roll of the Army," House Executive Document, no. 40, 37th Cong., 3rd sess., 1862, 2–4.

51. James T. Odem to Eleanor Odem, December 2, 1862, Odem Papers, UVa; Johnstown (Pa.) Cambria Tribune, December 12, 1862; James B. Thomas, Civil War Letters, 121; Naum Hass Apgar to his brother, December 8, 1862, GAR; Brookville (Ind.) Franklin Democrat, December 26, 1862.

52. Cornelius Richmond to his wife, December 9, 1862, Richmond Papers, FSNMP; James B. Post to his wife, December 10, 1862, Post Papers, CWMC, USAMHI.

CHAPTER NINE

1. George E. Upton to his wife, December 7, 1862, Upton Papers, NHHS; Curtis C. Pollock to his wife, December 9, 1862, Pollock Papers, CWMC, USAMHI; William Henry Walling to his sister, December 9, 1862, Walling Papers, CWMC, USAMHI.

2. Joseph Bloomfield Osborn to his brother, December 7, 1862, Osborn Papers, LC; George E. Upton to his wife, December 7, 1862, Upton Papers, NHHS; John T. Greene, Ewing Family Letters, 31; Lord, History of the Ninth New Hampshire, 221; Edwin O. Wentworth to his wife, December 9, 1862, Wentworth Papers, LC.

3. J. T. Kenyon to his father, December 8, 1862, Kenyon Letters, FSNMP; Peter Welsh, Irish Green and Union Blue, 37; Donaldson, Inside the Army of the Potomac, 170; George Washington Whitman, Civil War Letters, 74; Haydon, For Country, Cause, and Leader, 295; Edwin O. Wentworth to his wife, December 9, 1862, Wentworth Papers, LC; December 9, 1862, Boyts Diary, HSP.

4. John S. Crocker to his wife, December 7, 8, 1862, Crocker Letters, CU; Naum Hass Apgar to his brother, December 8, 1862, GAR; Cornelius Richmond to his wife, December 9, 1862, Richmond Papers, FSNMP; James B. Thomas, Civil War Letters, 123.

5. Marvel, "Making of a Myth," 4–5; OR, 105; Kenneth P. Williams, Lincoln Finds a General, 2:520–21; Thomas L. Livermore, Numbers and Losses, 96; Welcher, Union Army, 1:701. Thaddeus S. C. Lowe's reconnaissance balloons had helped Burnside discover the position of Jackson's troops at Skinker's Neck. That may have led him to exaggerate Rebel numbers,

but it also suggested the possibility of attacking before Lee could reassemble his scattered forces. See Thaddeus S. C. Lowe, "My Balloons in War and Peace," American Institute of Aeronautics and Acronautics Papers, LC; Fishel, *Secret War for the Union*, 267–68; Edward Porter Alexander, *Military Memoirs of a Confederate*, 288.

6. *New York Herald*, December 8, 1862; *Philadelphia Inquirer*, December 1–2, 1862; *Baltimore American and Commercial Advertiser*, December 4, 1862; *Chicago Daily Tribune*, December 10, 1862; *New York Times*, November 29, December 5, 1862; Zachariah Chandler to his wife, December 3, 1862, Chandler Papers, LC; Charles Sumner, *Selected Letters*, 2:133. This apparent confidence in Burnside, however, did not run deeply. In Washington and in the army, rumors that Hooker would soon take over the command persisted. See *New York Times*, December 4, 1862; December 4, 1862, Webb Diary, Schoff Collection, CL.

7. *Albany (N.Y.) Atlas and Argus*, December 1, 5, 1862; *Boston Post*, December 1, 3, 1862; *Rochester (N.Y.) Daily Union and Advertiser*, November 28, 1862; "War Correspondence," *Vanity Fair*, December 20, 1862, 297; *New York Herald*, December 5, 1862. Thurlow Weed's newspaper organ, a notable voice of Republican conservatism, agreed that the same people who had been impatient with McClellan were now criticizing Burnside. See *Albany (N.Y.) Evening Journal*, November 19, 1862.

8. *Boston Post*, December 4, 1862; *Baltimore American and Commercial Advertiser*, December 1, 1862; *New York Tribune*, December 1, 1862; *Philadelphia Inquirer*, November 29, December 1, 1862.

9. *Chicago Daily Tribune*, November 30, 1862; *Indianapolis Daily Journal*, December 11, 1862; *New York Tribune*, December 9, 1862; *New York Times*, November 29, 1862.

10. *OR Supplement*, pt. 1, 3:669; *New York Times*, December 2, 6, 1862; *New York Tribune*, December 8, 1862; *Baltimore American and Commercial Advertiser*, December 2, 1862; *New York Herald*, December 13, 1862; Horace Greeley, "The Collapse at Hand," *Independent*, December 4, 1862, 1.

11. *Indianapolis Daily Journal*, December 1, 1862; *Poughkeepsie (N.Y.) Daily Eagle*, December 5, 1862; *Rochester (N.Y.) Daily Democrat and American*, December 2, 1862; *Boston Evening Transcript*, December 1, 1862; Gray and Ropes, *War Letters*, 44; *New York Herald*, December 8, 12, 1862; *Albany (N.Y.) Evening Journal*, November 28, December 11, 12, 1862; Lounger, "Expectations," *Harper's Weekly*, December 13, 1862, 787.

12. *Poughkeepsie (N.Y.) Daily Eagle*, December 10, 1862; *Flemington (N.J.) Hunterdon Republican*, December 19, 1862; Zachariah Chandler to his wife, December 10, 1862, Chandler Papers, LC.

13. Welton, *Caldwell Letters*, 159; Lucy B. Meade to Alexander Brown, December 11, 1862, Brown Papers, Duke; December 7, 1862, Hamilton Diary, FSNMP; J. H. Wallace to William Ware, December 5, 1862, National Bank of Fredericksburg Correspondence, FSNMP; *Richmond Daily Enquirer*, December 2, 1862; *Richmond Daily Examiner*, December 1, 1862.

14. *Richmond Daily Dispatch*, December 3, 1862; *Charleston Mercury*, December 5, 13, 1862; *Richmond Daily Enquirer*, December 2, 5, 1862; *Macon (Ga.) Daily Telegraph*, December 5, 1862; *Richmond Daily Whig*, December 10, 13, 1862; *Richmond Daily Examiner*, December 10, 1862; *Charleston Daily Courier*, December 4, 12, 1862. Rumors that Burnside had been replaced by Hooker also circulated in the Confederacy. See J. B. Jones, *Rebel War Clerk's Diary*, 1:203; Edmondston, "Journal of a Secesh Lady," 312; *Raleigh Weekly Register*, December 10, 1862.

15. *Richmond Daily Examiner*, December 3, 4, 1862; *Wilmington (N.C.) Daily Journal*, December 4, 1862; *Augusta (Ga.) Daily Chronicle and Sentinel*, December 8, 1862; Boney, *Letcher*, 177; Benjamin Hill Jr., *Hill*, 272; Edmund Ruffin, *Diary*, 2:501–2; *Charleston Mercury*, December 2, 12, 1862.

16. *OR*, 13–16; Clement Anselm Evans, *Confederate Military History*, 6:179–80; Rea, *Sketches from Hampton's Cavalry*, 61–62. A captain in the 3rd Pennsylvania Cavalry, careless in guarding key roads around Hartwood Church, was immediately cashiered.

17. *OR,* 27–28; George William Beale, *Lieutenant of Cavalry in Lee's Army,* 58–62; R. Channing Price to his sister, December 4, 1862, Price Papers, SHC.

18. *OR,* 28–30; *Philadelphia Inquirer,* December 10, 1862. Had Burnside used his cavalry more effectively during the weeks leading up to the battle of Fredericksburg not only could he have acquired more accurate knowledge of Confederate numbers and positions, but he would have further strained his opponents' already depleted resources. Stuart had driven his men and horses to the limits of their endurance. Hampton in particular complained that hard service had badly reduced his forces. See J. E. B. Stuart to Flora Cooke Stuart, December 2, 1862, Stuart Papers, VHS; Cauthen, *Family Letters of Three Wade Hamptons,* 87–89; *OR,* 1040–41, 1045, 1047–48; Balfour, *13th Virginia Cavalry,* 11; William Willis Blackford, *War Years with Stuart,* 187–88.

19. Thomas R. Reeder to his sister, November 28, 1862, Reeder Letters, SCL; William Nelson Pendleton to Nancy Pendleton, November 27, 1862, Pendleton Papers, SHC; T. R. R. Cobb to his wife, November 27, 1862, Cobb Letters, UG; George Hopper to his brother, December 3, 1862, Hopper Papers, USAMHI; Daggett, "Those Whom You Left behind You," 347; Ott, "Civil War Diary of James J. Kirkpatrick," 84; Coles, *From Huntsville to Appomattox,* 76; H. S. Hall, "Fredericksburg and Chancellorsville," 187–88.

20. Abernathy, *Our Mess,* 17; Driver, *1st Virginia,* 51; Favill, *Diary of a Young Officer,* 207; Ansell W. White to his mother, December 10, 1862, White Letters, Leigh Collection, USAMHI; James Drayton Nance to "My Dear Laura," November 30, 1862, Nance Papers, SCL; Coles, *From Huntsville to Appomattox,* 77; Cory, "Private's Recollections of Fredericksburg," 124–27; Albert, *Forty-fifth Pennsylvania,* 196.

21. Pettit, *Infantryman Pettit,* 38; Walker, *Second Corps,* 142; McCrea, *Dear Belle,* 169; Lafayette McLaws to his wife, December 3, 1862, McLaws Papers, SHC; Gavin, *Campaigning with the Roundheads,* 208.

22. *New York Times,* November 26, 1862; Judd, *Story of the Thirty-Third,* 229; Charles R. Johnson to "Nellie," December 1862, Johnson Letters, Gregory A. Coco Collection, USAMHI; Blake, *Three Years in the Army of the Potomac,* 146–47; *New York Tribune,* November 22, 1862; B. F. Taylor, "Fredericksburg Campaign with the Army of the Potomac," 46–47.

23. Lafayette McLaws to his wife, December 3, 1862, McLaws Papers, SHC; Alexander Cheeves Haskell to his mother, December 10, 1862, Haskell Papers, SHC; Susan Leigh Blackford, *Letters from Lee's Army,* 139–40; Cutrer and Parrish, *Brothers in Gray,* 135; Richard Irby to his wife, December 1, 1862, Irby Letters, FSNMP; William Calder to mother, December 1, 1862, Calder Family Papers, SHC. I have found twenty-five statements from Lee's soldiers that they did not expect to fight any time soon and only ten from soldiers who thought otherwise.

24. William S. White, "Diary of the War," 142; Archie K. Davis, *Boy Colonel of the Confederacy,* 216; *Macon (Ga.) Daily Telegraph,* December 16, 1862; J. E. B. Stuart to "Dear Lily," December 5, 1862, Stuart Papers, Duke.

25. Pender, *General to His Lady,* 190–91; Robert E. Lee, *Wartime Papers,* 351; DeNoon, *Charlie's Letters,* 99; December 11, 1862, Malloy Diary, CWMC, USAMHI; *OR,* 1052–54; Jefferson Davis, *Papers,* 8:533–35; Woodworth, *Davis and Lee,* 208.

26. *OR,* 1057; William Allan, *Army of Northern Virginia,* 468–69; *Baltimore American and Commercial Advertiser,* December 15, 1862; J. B. Jones, *Rebel War Clerk's Diary,* 1:204; Col. G. F. R. Henderson, *Civil War,* 49–52, 105–6. Thomas Livermore estimated Lee's "effectives" at slightly over 73,000; see Thomas L. Livermore, *Numbers and Losses,* 96. It is worth noting that Lee's defensive preparations consisted largely of taking advantage of the natural terrain in the deployment of his forces rather than in constructing field fortifications.

27. Jennings Cropper Wise, *Long Arm of Lee,* 1:371–73; Edward Porter Alexander, *Fighting for the Confederacy,* 168; Long, "McClellan and Burnside," 1; Col. G. F. R. Henderson, *Jackson,* 572–73; Dabney, *Jackson,* 595.

28. *B&L*, 3:107–8, 129–30; Herman Haupt to his wife, December 9, 1862, Haupt Letter-book, Haupt Papers, LC; *OR Supplement*, pt. 1, 3:684; Stephen B. Oates, *Woman of Valor*, 103; J. Cutler Andrews, *North Reports the Civil War*, 323.

29. Noel G. Harrison, *Fredericksburg Civil War Sites*, 1:102–6; Marsena Rudolph Patrick, *Inside Lincoln's Army*, 186; *B&L*, 3:108, 126; Howard, *Autobiography*, 1:321–22. I have greatly benefited from William Marvel's sympathetic, perceptive, and generally persuasive analy-sis of Burnside's thinking and difficulties during this period, in Marvel, *Burnside*, 171–72. To keep the Confederates from concentrating their forces, Burnside had Federal pickets at Port Royal convey false information to their Rebel counterparts and even had a corduroy road constructed opposite Skinker's Neck. Union gunboats also steamed up the Rappahannock, exchanged fire with Confederate artillery, and remained in position even after the Army of the Potomac began crossing at Fredericksburg. See O'Reilly, *Jackson at Fredericksburg*, 12–14; *ORN*, ser. 1, 5:190–98.

30. Bruce, "Battle of Fredericksburg," 505; December 9–10, 1862, Rice Diary, FSNMP; McAllister, *Letters of Robert McAllister*, 238–39; William Teall to his wife, December 10, 1862, Teall Letters, TSLA; Wren, *Captain James Wren's Civil War Diary*, 94; S. Millett Thompson, *Thirteenth New Hampshire*, 35; *History of the 121st Regiment Pennsylvania Volunteers*, 28

31. December 10, 1862, Taylor Diary, FSNMP; John R. Coye to his wife, December 10, 1862, Coye Letters, FSNMP; John W. Ames to his father, December 9, 1862, Ames Papers, USAMHI; *New York Irish-American*, January 3, 1863; Dexter, *Seymour Dexter*, 114–15; McCarter, *My Life in the Irish Brigade*, 140–42.

32. *B&L*, 3:86; Giles, *Rags and Hope*, 147–48; Cogswell, *Eleventh New Hampshire*, 64.

33. Stephen B. Oates, *Woman of Valor*, 105; Orwig, *131st Pennsylvania*, 96; Howard, *Auto-biography*, 1:327; Small, *Road to Richmond*, 59. For a general treatment of prebattle appre-hension and preparation, see Keegan, *Face of Battle*, 237–38.

34. William Gilson to his wife, December 10, 1862, Gilson Letter, FSNMP; George H. Mellish to his mother, December 10, 1862, Mellish Papers, HL; Virgil W. Mattoon to his mother, December 10, 1862, Mattoon Papers, CHS; Ansell W. White to his mother, December 10, 1862, White Letters, Leigh Collection, USAMHI; James R. Woodworth to Phoebe Woodworth, December 10, 1862, Woodworth Papers, Hotchkiss Collection, CL.

35. James B. Post to his wife, December 10, 1862, Post Papers, CWMC, USAMHI; *Lan-caster (Pa.) Daily Evening Express*, December 23, 1862; John Russell Bartlett, *Memoirs of Rhode Island Officers*, 239; Lusk, *War Letters of William Thompson Lusk*, 242–43; Robert Goldthwaite Carter, *Four Brothers in Blue*, 185; George L. Prescott to ?, December 10, 1862, Prescott Papers, MHS. For a useful discussion of the relationship between tension, plausibility, and the will to believe favorable rumors, see Kapferer, *Rumors*, 65–83.

36. Castleman, *Army of the Potomac*, 256–57; Dawes, *Sixth Wisconsin*, 108; Samuel K. Zook to E. J. Wade, December 10, 1862, Zook Papers, CWMC, USAMHI. Psychologists have analyzed the persistence of wishful thinking, but they have also noted, without necessarily worrying about the apparent contradiction, the prevalence of dark rumors. In part, bad news simply spreads more rapidly and readily. See Kapferer, *Rumors*, 132–35.

37. *Flemington (N.J.) Hunterdon Republican*, December 19, 1862; Asa W. Bartlett, *History of the Twelfth New Hampshire*, 492; Daniel M. Holt, *Surgeon's Civil War*, 57–58; December 11, 1862, Elmer Diary, CWMC, USAMHI; William Watson, *Letters of a Civil War Surgeon*, 40; Brewster, *When This Cruel War Is Over*, 198–99.

38. McPherson, *For Cause and Comrades*, 77–82; Small, *Sixteenth Maine*, 57–58; Craft, *His-tory of the One Hundred Forty-First Pennsylvania*, 30; Waitt, *Nineteenth Massachusetts*, 164; Henry, "Fredericksburg," 99–100; Joseph Bloomfield Osborn to Mary Osborn, December 10, 1862, Osborn Papers, LC. For Federals and Confederates alike, patriotism and nationalism were abstract but nevertheless real ideas that motivated many soldiers. Commanding officers

could thus straightforwardly instruct men to do their duty, noting that the folks back home expected no less. See McPherson, *For Cause and Comrades,* 90–103; Sprenger, *122d Regiment,* 133–34; John H. Rhodes, *History of Battery B,* 136.

39. McAllister, *Letters of Robert McAllister,* 239; *Newark (N.J.) Daily Advertiser,* December 18, 1862; December 10, 1862, Jackson Diary, IHS; December 11, 1862, Lewis Nettleton Diary, Nettleton-Baldwin Family Papers, Duke; Sturtevant, *Josiah Volunteered,* 67. For an analysis of the relationship between religious faith and battle performance, see Samuel J. Watson, "Religion and Combat Motivation in Confederate Armies," 29–34.

40. Gregg, *Life in the Army,* 75–76; Gaff, *On Many a Bloody Field,* 208.

41. McPherson, *For Cause and Comrades,* 67–71; December 6, 9, 1862, Abernathy Diary, USAMHI; Virgil W. Mattoon to his mother, December 10, 1862, Mattoon Papers, CHS; Lusk, *War Letters of William Thompson Lusk,* 243; Orlando Willcox, *Forgotten Valor,* 403; December 11, 1862, Woodworth Diary, Hotchkiss Collection, CL; Henry Brantingham to his wife, December 8, 9, 1862, Brantingham Letters, USAMHI.

42. McPherson, *For Cause and Comrades,* 36–38, 52–53; William Teall to his wife, December 10, 1862, Teall Letters, TSLA; Edward J. Nichols, *Toward Gettysburg,* 149; *History of the 121st Regiment Pennsylvania Volunteers,* 28; Pullen, *Twentieth Maine,* 46; Frank Moore, *Rebellion Record,* 6:96; John R. Coye to his wife, December 10, 1862, Coye Letters, FSNMP.

43. Hartsock, *Soldier of the Cross,* 36–37.

44. J. E. Brown to Mollie Matthews, December 10, 1862, Matthews Papers, MC; Edward Porter Alexander, "Battle of Fredericksburg," 385; M[oxley] Sorrel to Edward Porter Alexander, December 10, 1862, Alexander Papers, SHC; Longstreet, *From Manassas to Appomattox,* 301.

45. Shotwell, *Papers of Randolph Abbott Shotwell,* 1:395–96; Susan Leigh Blackford, *Letters from Lee's Army,* 143–45; Pender, *General to His Lady,* 194; W. H. Andrews, *Footprints of a Regiment,* 98–99.

46. *CCW,* 1:652–53, 667; *OR,* 63–64, and ser. 1, 51(2):955. Burnside was still apparently relying on balloon reconnaissance to determine Lee's positions. The heretofore idle cavalry received vague orders to follow the infantry divisions as they crossed the river. See William Allan, *Army of Northern Virginia,* 470; Col. G. F. R. Henderson, *Civil War,* 37–41; Col. G. F. R. Henderson, *Jackson,* 574; *CCW,* 1:747–48.

47. Walker, "Couch at Fredericksburg"; Walker, *Second Corps,* 145; Jacob Lyman Greene, *Franklin and the Left Wing at Fredericksburg,* 10; Palfrey, *Antietam and Fredericksburg,* 141, 143; Whan, *Fiasco at Fredericksburg,* 128–29.

48. Col. G. F. R. Henderson, *Civil War,* 42; Clausewitz, *On War,* 433, 533.

49. *OR,* 87–88, 840–41, 954–56, and ser. 1, 51(2):856; Woodbury, *Burnside and the Ninth Army Corps,* 211–12. Evidently appalled at the prospect of crossing directly into Fredericksburg, the engineers returned to their camps on the night of December 9 singing a line from an old British soldier's song: "O why should we be melancholy boys, Whose business tis to die" (Brainerd, *Bridge Building in Wartime,* 107–8).

50. *OR,* 842, 845; John W. Ames to his father, December 9, 1862, Ames Papers, USAMHI; McClenthen, *Narrative of the Fall and Winter Campaign,* 32.

CHAPTER TEN

1. Weather Data, Georgetown Weather Station, December 11–15, 1862, FSNMP (unless otherwise specified, all other references to temperatures during the battle of Fredericksburg and the Mud March come from this source); Billings, *Hard Tack and Coffee,* 384–88; Forbes, *Thirty Years After,* 13; *OR,* ser. 1, 29(2):465–66. Clausewitz commented that weather is seldom a decisive factor in battle but that fog could be an exception to this rule; see Clausewitz, *On War,* 143.

2. *OR,* 169, 173–74, 201, 203, 214–16, 452–53, 514, 621; Gilbert Thompson, *Engineer Battal-*

ion, 25–26; *New York Times,* December 14, 1862; O'Reilly, *Jackson at Fredericksburg,* 15–16. A third bridge was constructed the following day; see *OR,* 107–8. After the war a brief, pointless controversy erupted in the columns of the *National Tribune* about the relative contribution of the Regulars and the New Yorkers to the laying of these pontoons. See Beardsley, "Crossing at Fredericksburg," 3; Willey, "Who Laid the Pontoons at Fredericksburg?," 3; U. D. Wood, "Who Laid the Pontoons?," 3; Gilbert Thompson, "U.S. Engineer Battalion," 3; Vogl, "Who Laid the Pontoons?," 3; P. M. Evans, "Who Laid the Pontoons?," 3; Gilbert Thompson, "Who Laid the Pontoons?," 3.

3. *OR,* 106–7, 448–49, 844; Marvel, *Burnside,* 175–76; *Atlas to Accompany the Official Records,* plate XXX, maps 3 and 4. Some historians have suggested that Burnside should have hurried Franklin's men across the bridges and marched them toward Fredericksburg to flank the Confederates out of the town. See Whan, *Fiasco at Fredericksburg,* 130–31; Kenneth P. Williams, *Lincoln Finds a General,* 2:524–25; Daniel E. Sutherland, *Fredericksburg and Chancellorsville,* 37–38.

4. *OR,* 523, 534–36; *Pittsfield (Mass.) Sun,* January 1, 1863; *B&L,* 3:131; James Lorenzo Bowen, *Thirty-Seventh Regiment,* 108–9; Woodbury, *Second Rhode Island,* 127–28; William P. Carmany to his brother and sister, December 10, 1862, Carmany Papers, William L Collection, CT; Alonzo Hunt Rhodes, *All for the Union,* 89–90, 92; Nelson V. Hutchinson, *Seventh Massachusetts Volunteer Infantry,* 110–11; Frank C. Park to "Friends at Home," December 17, 1862, Park Letter, FSNMP; *Springfield (Mass.) Daily Republican,* December 19, 1862. Franklin later informed McClellan that because it was getting dark, he had asked Burnside to delay crossing the bulk of Left Grand Division until the following day. See Franklin to McClellan, December 23, 1862, McClellan Papers, LC.

5. Seigel, *For the Glory of the Union,* 107–8; Locke, *Story of the Regiment,* 157–58; Orson Blair Curtis, *History of the Twenty-Fourth Michigan,* 88; Lucius B. Shattuck to Ellen Shattuck, December 11–14, 1862, Shattuck Letters, MHC; December 11, 1862, S. W. Gordon Diary, FSNMP; Werkheiser Memoir, 3, FSNMP.

6. Alexander Morrison Stewart, *Camp, March, and Battlefield,* 278; Tyler, *Recollections of the Civil War,* 64–65; December 11, 1862, Halsey Diary, USAMHI; Kearney, "Letters from the Field," 187; *OR Supplement,* pt. 2, 46:581.

7. Bates Alexander, "Seventh Regiment," October 25, 1895; John Harrison Mills, *Chronicles of the Twenty-First New York,* 273–74; Haley, *Rebel Yell and Yankee Hurrah,* 55–56; Bicknell, *History of the Fifth Maine,* 167. Fear often spawned strange mishaps. When a sergeant in the 19th Indiana carelessly shot off a finger, his comrades might easily have wondered just how accidental it was. See December 11, 1862, Jackson Diary, IHS.

8. Brainerd, *Bridge Building in Wartime,* 110.

9. Ibid., 108–15; *OR,* 168, 170, 175–76, 179–80; *Cahors (N.Y.) Cataract,* December 20, 1862; *OR Supplement,* pt. 2, 44:91, 108–9, 123, 178.

10. Bruce, "Battle of Fredericksburg," 510; *OR,* 170, 226, 258–59, 349–50; Favill, *Diary of a Young Officer,* 208–9.

11. *OR,* 578.

12. *OR,* 546–47; Douglas Southall Freeman, *Lee,* 2:444; Edward Porter Alexander, "Battle of Fredericksburg," 384–85; Robert E. Lee to William M. McDonald, April 15, 1868, Lee Letterbook, VHS.

13. *OR,* 568–69; William Allan, *Army of Northern Virginia,* 472; Wert, *Longstreet,* 209–12.

14. *OR,* 578; Jennings Cropper Wise, *Long Arm of Lee,* 1:369–71; Edward Porter Alexander, "Battle of Fredericksburg," 382–83; William M. Owen, *In Camp and Battle with the Washington Artillery,* 181–82.

15. *OR,* 545, 573–76, 1058, and ser. 1, 51(2):661; December 11, 1862, Latrobe Diary, VHS; Musselman, *Caroline Light, Parker, and Stafford Light Virginia Artillery,* 53.

16. *OR,* 600, 605; *B&L,* 3:86; Clement Anselm Evans, *Confederate Military History,* 4:365;

Dinkins, "Barksdale's Mississippi Brigade," 257. In examining the role of Barksdale's men in the fighting on December 11, I have heavily relied on the thorough and perceptive tactical analysis in Hawley, "Barksdale's Mississippi Brigade."

17. *B&L,* 3:86–87; Dinkins, "Barksdale's Mississippi Brigade," 257; Cummings, "Bombardment of Fredericksburg," 253; Hawley, "Barksdale's Mississippi Brigade," 12–13; Longstreet, *From Manassas to Appomattox,* 300–301; *OR,* 578, 601, 604–5; Oscar J. E. Stuart to Anne E. Stuart, December 17, 1862, Dimitry Papers, Duke; *Richmond Daily Examiner,* December 12, 1862. Some soldiers still saw such sharpshooting as cowardly and unsporting, but such qualms would rapidly disappear. See Linderman, *Embattled Courage,* 147–55. Three dozen Federal guns had been hauled down to the riverbank to support the bridge builders. Aside from the obvious fog problem, the guns themselves proved less than reliable—five stock-trails were shattered by the force of firing. In his official report General Hunt pulled no punches: "They [several twelve-pounders] were defective, and is almost needless to say, contract work, the contractors being Wood Brothers, of New York" (*OR,* 182).

18. Marsena Rudolph Patrick, *Inside Lincoln's Army,* 187; Woodbury, *Burnside and the Ninth Army Corps,* 213; Charles Carelton Coffin, *Four Years of Fighting,* 142–44; Judd, *Story of the Thirty-Third,* 238; *New York Times,* December 13, 1862; Teall, "Ringside Seat at Fredericksburg," 23–24.

19. *OR,* 180–82, 196, 827–28; Naisawald, *Grape and Canister,* 236–41; William Teall to his wife, December 11, 1862, Teall Letters, TSLA; Tom Josiah to his wife, December 11, 1862, Josiah Letter, FSNMP; Robert S. Robertson, "Diary of the War," 73; Longacre, *Man behind the Guns,* 129–34.

20. *OR,* 191, 194–95, 199, 204–5, 267, 335; Whan, *Fiasco at Fredericksburg,* 40. According to one estimate the Federals fired some 9,000 rounds. See George N. Barnard to his father, December 16, 1862, Barnard Papers, MHS.

21. Thomas H. Parker, *History of the 51st,* 268–69; Henry J. H. Thompson to his wife, December 11, 1862, Thompson Papers, Duke; Bicknell, *History of the Fifth Maine,* 168–69.

22. Galwey, *Valiant Hours,* 56; Brainard, *One Hundred and Forty-sixth New York,* 29; John S. Crocker to his wife, December 11, 1862, Crocker Letters, CU; Wightman, *From Antietam to Fort Fisher,* 86; d'Entremont, *Southern Emancipator,* 175–76.

23. December 11, 1862, Willand Diary, NHHS; George H. Allen, *Forty-Six Months,* 173–74; David Beem to his wife, December 18, 1862, Beem Papers, IHS; Elias H. W. Peck to his wife, December 12, 1862, Richardson Collection, ISL.

24. Henry Lewis to "Cousin Charlie," January 3, 1863, Lewis Letters, GLC; Bruce, *Twentieth Massachusetts,* 208–9; John H. Rhodes, *History of Battery B,* 138–39; Walter A. Eames to his wife, December 20, 1862, Eames Letters, USAMHI; *Rochester (N.Y.) Daily Democrat and American,* December 22, 1862; Chapin, *History of the Thirty-fourth Regiment,* 80; Bryan Grimes to his brother William, December 25, 1862, Grimes Family Papers, SHC; Amory Allen to his parents, December 17, 1862, Allen Letter, FSNMP.

25. Sanford, *Fighting Rebels and Redskins,* 191; John H. Rhodes, *History of Battery B,* 137–38; William Chambers Bartlett, "Incident of Fredericksburg," 468–69; Judith Brockenbrough McGuire, *Diary of a Southern Refugee,* 180; Thomas Rice, "All the Imps of Hell Let Loose," 13; Croffut and Morris, *Connecticut during the War,* 291; Brogan, *American Civil War,* 100.

26. *New York Irish-American,* January 3, 1863; *New York Tribune,* December 12, 1862; *Richmond Daily Examiner,* December 18, 1862; Susan Leigh Blackford, *Letters from Lee's Army,* 149; Henry Willis to his father, December 15, 1862, Henry Willis Letter, FSNMP; J. H. Wallace to William Ware, December 13, 1862, National Bank of Fredericksburg Correspondence, FSNMP; Samuel S. Partridge to "Dear Ed," December 17, 1862, Partridge Letters, FSNMP. After the Federals occupied the town, some of the volunteer firemen among them tried to douse the flames, but during the night "falling timbers from the burning houses would crash among the embers and send up showers of sparks" ("Personal Recollections of the First Battle

of Fredericksburg," 4, UT). See also Joseph Ripley Chandler Ward, *One Hundred and Sixth Pennsylvania,* 114. Despite what seemed to many observers a devastating bombardment, defective guns and ammunition hampered Federal gunners all day. According to Hunt the 20-pounder Parrotts sometimes posed as much threat to Union soldiers as to Confederates. Besides their doubtful accuracy, these guns tended to burst. Some shells exploded prematurely, making artillerists reluctant to fire them over friendly forces. The most common problem was poorly made fuses that either failed to ignite or did so too quickly. See *OR,* 189–90, 192, 200–202, 207, 211, 225; *New York Times,* January 11, 1863.

27. *Philadelphia Inquirer,* December 13, 1862; Lucius B. Shattuck to "Dear Ellen," December 11, 1862, Shattuck Letters, MHC; Willard J. Templeton to his sister, December 11, 1862, Templeton Letters, NHSL; Beidelman, *Letters of George Washington Beidelman,* 166.

28. Griner, "Civil War of a Pennsylvania Trooper," 50–51; December 11, 1862, Butler Diary, Schoff Collection, CL; December 11, 1862, Gilpin Diary, LC; *History of the 127th Regiment Pennsylvania Volunteers,* 118; Chamberlain, *Through Blood and Fire,* 38.

29. Charles Thomas Bowen to his wife, December 18, 1862, Bowen Letter, FSNMP; Locke, *Story of the Regiment,* 159; Virgil W. Mattoon to his mother, December 10–15, 1862, Mattoon Papers, CHS.

30. Douglas Southall Freeman, *Lee,* 2:446; Robert E. Lee, *Wartime Papers,* 357–58; Polley, *Soldier's Letters to Charming Nellie,* 88; *Richmond Daily Dispatch,* December 22, 1862.

31. Abernathy, *Our Mess,* 18–19; December 11, 1862, Henley Diary, FSNMP; J. C. Lloyd, "Battles of Fredericksburg," 500; Robert A. Moore, *Life for the Confederacy,* 122; Hawley, "Barksdale's Mississippi Brigade," 15–16.

32. *OR,* 579, 603, 606–7, 618–19; Lang, "Letters of Lang," 344–45; Oscar J. E. Stuart to Annie E. Stuart, December 17, 1862, Dimitry Papers, Duke.

33. *OR,* 601; Douglas Southall Freeman, *Lee,* 2:447; Hotchkiss, *Make Me a Map of the Valley,* 99; William M. Owen, *In Camp and Battle with the Washington Artillery,* 180.

34. Boggs, *Alexander Letters,* 243–44; Edward Porter Alexander, *Fighting for the Confederacy,* 170–71; William Ross Stillwell to "My Dear Mollie," December 14, 1862, Stillwell Letters, GDAH; Patterson, *Yankee Rebel,* 87–88.

35. *Times* (London), January 1, 1863; *Baltimore American and Commercial Advertiser,* December 15, 1862; Robert Franklin Fleming Jr., "Recollections," FSNMP; Susan Leigh Blackford, *Letters from Lee's Army,* 150; Noel G. Harrison, *Fredericksburg Civil War Sites,* 2.8–9; Jane Howison Beale, *Journal,* 127–29; Alvey, *History of the Presbyterian Church of Fredericksburg,* 41; Asa W. Bartlett, *History of the Twelfth New Hampshire,* 405; *Raleigh Weekly Register,* January 7, 1863. One account of civilians under fire composed years afterward included a stereotypical tale of slaves hiding in a cellar with their white family. Loyal "Uncle Charles" loudly prayed for "old missus and de chillens" but also bravely went upstairs for food in the midst of the shelling. A white woman asked "Aunt Sally" to go back up to the kitchen, but the slave refused, saying that she doubted "Gin'l Lee hisself cud stan' up making coffee under that tornady" (Mrs. Frances Bernard Goolrick, "Shelling of Fredericksburg," 573–74, and "Frightful Experiences at Fredericksburg," 513). Even after the Federals occupied the town, a seventy-year-old woman who had braved the bombardment in her house continued to spout "secesh" talk to the officers using it as a headquarters. See Charles Howard to his mother, December 13, 1862, Brooks Collection, LC.

36. Blair, "Barbarians at Fredericksburg's Gate," 154; Frank Moore, *Rebellion Record,* 6:97; [Heinichen,] "Fredericksburg," Maryland Historical Society; *Raleigh Weekly Register,* January 7, 1863; "Battle of Fredericksburg," 262; Hotchkiss, *Make Me a Map of the Valley,* 99; December 12, 1862, Butler Diary, Schoff Collection, CL; William Henry Tatum to his brother, December 17, 1862, Tatum Papers, VHS; David Holt, *Mississippi Rebel,* 141–45.

37. Lacy, "Lee at Fredericksburg," 604; J. E. B. Stuart to Flora Cooke Stuart, December 9–10, 1862, Stuart Papers, VHS; J. E. Brown to Mollie Matthews, December 10, 1862, Matthews

Papers, MC; William M. Owen, *In Camp and Battle with the Washington Artillery*, 181; Jane Howison Beale, *Journal*, 131–33; Cadmus Wilcox to his sister, December 17, 1862, Wilcox Papers, LC; Von Borcke, *Memoirs of the Confederate War*, 2:94–100; Mrs. Frances Bernard Goolrick, "Shelling of Fredericksburg," 574.

38. December 11, 1862, Malloy Diary, CWMC, USAMHI; *Richmond Daily Enquirer*, December 13, 15, 1862; Oscar J. E. Stuart to Annie E. Stuart, December 17, 1862, Dimitry Papers, Duke; George Clark, *Glance Backward*, 27; Stiles, *Four Years under Marse Robert*, 128; *Richmond Daily Examiner*, December 15, 1862; Jane Howison Beale, *Journal*, 133; McCrea, *Dear Belle*, 173; *New York Times*, December 14, 1862.

39. Berkeley, *Four Years in the Confederate Artillery*, 35–36; Conn, "Conn-Brantley Letter," 439; Shotwell, *Papers of Randolph Abbott Shotwell*, 1:407; Susan Pendleton Lee, *Memoirs of William Nelson Pendleton*, 240–41; Lacy, "Lee at Fredericksburg," 606; *Athens (Ga.) Southern Banner*, January 7, 1863; Pender, *General to His Lady*, 193–94; December 12, 1862, Hume Diary, LC; McDonald, *Woman's Civil War*, 98–99; *Richmond Daily Dispatch*, December 13, 16, 1862; *Lynchburg Daily Virginian*, December 16, 1862; William Wallace White to "Dear Mitt," December 24, 1862, White Letters, GDAH.

40. *CCW*, 1:656; *OR*, 88–89, 170, 175–76, 179–80; Howard, *Autobiography*, 1:323; Marsena Rudolph Patrick, *Inside Lincoln's Army*, 187–88. Porter Alexander believed that some of Burnside's troops should have crossed in boats before the fog lifted and could have easily done so. See Edward Porter Alexander, *Military Memoirs of a Confederate*, 291.

41. *OR*, 221–22, 282–83; *OR Supplement*, pt. 2, 30:671, 680; Brainerd, *Bridge Building in Wartime*, 116–17; Herring, "Crossing of the Rappahannock by the 7th Mich.," 3; Oesterle Memoir, 6, *CWTI*, USAMHI; Frank Moore, *Rebellion Record*, 6:101–2; Whan, *Fiasco at Fredericksburg*, 41; Stephen B. Oates, *Woman of Valor*, 107. A thirteen-year-old drummer, Robert Henry Hendershot, supposedly exemplified the bravery of the Michigan troops. Young Hendershot helped push the boats into the water and, against orders, insisted on crossing with the other soldiers. Apparently something of a hellion, Hendershot did not quite live up to his newly minted boy hero image when he later enthusiastically helped plunder Fredericksburg. Nevertheless, exaggerated newspaper stories of his dash made him an overnight celebrity. He later met Lincoln in Washington and appeared at P. T. Barnum's museum in New York. Separating truth from romance in any account of the Hendershot episode remains difficult. See *Baltimore American and Commercial Advertiser*, December 31, 1862; Charles Carelton Coffin, *Four Years of Fighting*, 149; Gerry, *Robert Henry Hendershot*, 2–45.

42. *OR*, 283–84, 600–601; Howard, *Autobiography*, 1:324–25; Sidney B. Vrooman to Zachariah Chandler, December 25, 1862, Chandler Papers, LC; Hawley, "Barksdale's Mississippi Brigade," 18–19.

43. Weymouth, *Memorial Sketch of Lieut. Edgar M. Newcomb*, 106–8; Captain John G. B. Adams, "Sunshine and Shadows of Army Life," 452; Waitt, *Nineteenth Massachusetts*, 165–72; Moncena Dunn, "Fredericksburg," 6; *B&L*, 3:121; John Gregory Bishop Adams, *Reminiscences of the Nineteenth Massachusetts Regiment*, 50–53; J. E. Hodgkins, *Civil War Diary*, 16; Frinfrock, *Across the Rappahannock*, 28; Hawley, "Barksdale's Mississippi Brigade," 18–19; December 19, 1862, E. P. Miller Diary, FSNMP; Henry Ropes to John Codman Ropes, December 18, 1862, Ropes Letters, Boston Public Library. A surgeon in the Second Corps later claimed that Sumner had ordered his men to kill any man, woman, or child found in a house from which shots were fired at the Union soldiers, but there is no corroborating evidence for this story. See Grant Memoir, 2, NYHS.

44. *OR*, 283–84; Waitt, *Nineteenth Massachusetts*, 171; Bruce, *Twentieth Massachusetts*, 198–205; Miller and Mooney, "20th Massachusetts and the Street Fight for Fredericksburg," 113–21; Whan, *Fiasco at Fredericksburg*, 41–42; Henry Ropes to John Codman Ropes, December 18, 1862, Ropes Letters, Boston Public Library; George N. Macy to "Dear Colonel," December 20, 1862, Hancock Papers, USAMHI; Stephen Longfellow, "Fredericksburg," 3; Miller and

Mooney, *Civil War,* 83–90; Abbott, *Fallen Leaves,* 15; Dinkins, "Barksdale's Mississippi Brigade," 257–58.

45. Miller and Mooney, "20th Massachusetts and the Street Fight for Fredericksburg," 122; Henry Ropes to John Codman Ropes, December 18, 1862, Ropes Letters, Boston Public Library; Miller and Mooney, *Civil War,* 142–93 passim; George N. Macy to "Dear Colonel," December 20, 1862, Hancock Papers, USAMHI; Oliver Wendell Holmes, *Touched with Fire,* 90–91.

46. *OR,* 583; List of casualties from Barksdale's Brigade, December 18, 1862, McLaws Papers, SHC; J. E. Hodgkins, *Civil War Diary,* 16; *MSH,* 10:531; 11:234, 255, 264, 271, 12:505, 507, 632, 885–86; December 18, 1862, E. P. Miller Diary, FSNMP.

47. *OR,* 174, 310, 331, 345–46, 579, 603, 605; B. Dailey to Julia Dailey, December 14, 1862, Dailey Papers, FSNMP; December 11, 1862, Henderson Diary, FSNMP; "The Eighty-Ninth Infantry at Fredericksburg," in *Third Annual Report of the State Historian of New York,* 49–55; *OR Supplement,* pt. 2, 45:370.

48. *OR,* 569, 601, 606; Lafayette McLaws, "The Battle of Fredericksburg," in *Addresses Delivered before the Confederate Veterans Association of Savannah,* 76–77; *B&L,* 3:88–89; Whan, *Fiasco at Fredericksburg,* 42–43; Hawley, "Barksdale's Mississippi Brigade," 19 ; Otiles, Four Years under Morse Robert, 130–31; Douglas Southall Freeman, *Lee's Lieutenants,* 2:337–38.

49. Bliss Memoir, 4:20, USAMHI; Daniel Reed Larned to "Dear Henry," December 11, 1862, Larned Papers, LC; *OR,* 64, 846.

50. *OR,* 65, 218–19, 262–63, 285; Henry Ropes to John Codman Ropes, December 18, 1862, Ropes Letters, Boston Public Library; Gregg, *Life in the Army,* 79; *History of the 127th Regiment Pennsylvania Volunteers,* 119–21.

51. *OR,* 277–78; McDermott, *69th Pennsylvania,* 23; *Philadelphia Inquirer,* January 2, 1863; Joseph Ripley Chandler Ward, *One Hundred and Sixth Pennsylvania,* 112–13; John Day Smith, *Nineteenth Maine,* 30; Banes, *Philadelphia Brigade,* 135–37; Walter A. Eames to his wife, December 20, 1862, Eames Letters, USAMHI; Dority, "Civil War Diary," 10.

52. *OR,* 331–32; Wightman, *From Antietam to Fort Fisher,* 86–87; Bruce, "Battle of Fredericksburg," 518–20; R. P. Staniels to "My Darling Selina," December 16, 1862, Staniels Letter, FSNMP; S. Millett Thompson, *Thirteenth New Hampshire,* 37–40.

53. Von Borcke, *Memoirs of the Confederate War,* 2:101–2; *OR,* 578–80, 588, 608–9, 625, and ser. 1, 51(2):659–61; Burroughs, "Reminiscences of Fredericksburg," 636; Coles, *From Huntsville to Appomattox,* 78. Yet on the night of December 11, Lee still remained somewhat uncertain of Burnside's intentions, and he left half of Jackson's men guarding possible crossing points downstream.

54. Goodson, "Letters of Joab Goodson," 134; W. H. Burgess to David McKnight, December 20, 1862, McKnight Family Papers, UT; Stearns, *Three Years with Company K,* 146; December 11, 1862, Ware Diary, SHC; Thomas Rowland to "Dear Aunt Emily," December 21, 1862, Rowland Papers, MC; Shand Memoir, 162, SCL; December 11, 1862, Shipp Diary, VHS.

55. McKinney, *Life in Tent and Field,* 81–82; Tillinghast, *Twelfth Rhode Island,* 26–27, 242–44; Jacob Henry Cole, *Under Five Commanders,* 105; McCarter, *My Life in the Irish Brigade,* 147–52; Sawyer, *Military History of the 8th Ohio,* 91; Relyea Memoir, 70, CHS.

56. Tillinghast, *Twelfth Rhode Island,* 217–18; McCarter, *My Life in the Irish Brigade,* 146–47; Robert Goldthwaite Carter, *Four Brothers in Blue,* 192–93; Goss, *Recollections of a Private,* 123–24; December 11, 1862, Charles S. Granger Diary, CWMC, USAMHI.

57. Frank Moore, *Rebellion Record,* 6:92; *Fifth Annual Report of the Bureau of Military Statistics,* 722; Hartsock, *Soldier of the Cross,* 37; Samuel Penniman Bates, *History of the Pennsylvania Volunteers,* 4:148; *History of the 127th Regiment Pennsylvania Volunteers,* 121–22; Ayling, *Yankee at Arms,* 81–82; McKelvcy, *Rochester in the Civil War,* 158–59; *Albany (N.Y.) Atlas and Argus,* January 1, 1863; Brian A. Bennett, *140th New York,* 104; J. E. Hodgkins, *Civil War Diary,* 16.

58. *Albany (N.Y.) Atlas and Argus,* December 15, 1862; Lapham, "Recollections of the Twelfth R.I. Volunteers," 19; Brainerd, *Bridge Building in Wartime,* 114–16; Bruce, *Twentieth Massachusetts,* 206; Osborn, *No Middle Ground,* 92; *New York Irish-American,* January 3, 1863.

CHAPTER ELEVEN

1. Even sympathetic historians have criticized Burnside for not attacking on December 12 before Lee could reunite his scattered forces. See Marvel, *Burnside,* 178; Marvel, "Making of a Myth," 22–23; Whan, *Fiasco at Fredericksburg,* 130; Nevins, *War for the Union,* 2:347–48. For a pointed, concise, and perceptive critique of Burnside's early tactical mistakes, see Daniel E. Sutherland, *Fredericksburg and Chancellorsville,* 38–39.

2. Marvel, *Burnside,* 178–79; Marsena Rudolph Patrick, *Inside Lincoln's Army,* 188; William Teall to his wife, December 12, 1862, Teall Letters, TSLA; Tillinghast, *Twelfth Rhode Island,* 31.

3. OR, 269, 276, 289–90, 304; Kepler, *Fourth Ohio,* 92–93; Borton, *On the Parallels,* 57–58; Cory, "Private's Recollections of Fredericksburg," 135–36; Baxter, *Gallant Fourteenth,* 116–17; *MSH,* 10:626; J. E. Hodgkins, *Civil War Diary,* 16–17; Charles H. Eagor to his wife, December 12, 1862, Eagor Letters, Leigh Collection, USAMHI.

4. OR, 226, 240, 254, 260–61; McCarter, *My Life in the Irish Brigade,* 154–59; Mulholland, *116th Pennsylvania,* 53–54; Favill, *Diary of a Young Officer,* 210; Sheldon, *"Twenty-Seventh,"* 24–25; *MSH,* 10:711, 1000; December 12, 1862, Willand Diary, NHSL; *New York Irish-American,* January 3, 1863.

5. OR, 315–16; Thorpe, *Fifteenth Connecticut Volunteers,* 33; December 12, 1862, Pope Diary, *CWTI,* USAMHI; Hopkins, *Seventh Rhode Island,* 39–40; *Boston Journal,* n.d., FSNMP.

6. Walcott, *Twenty-First Regiment,* 240; Haydon, *For Country, Cause, and Leader,* 296–97; December 12, 1862, Cutcheon Autobiography, MHC; A. A. Batchelder to his parents, December 16, 1862, Batchelder Letter, FSNMP; Burrage, *Thirty-Sixth Massachusetts,* 26; Henry A. Allen, *Sergeant Allen and Private Renick,* 169; R. P. Staniels to "My Darling Selina," December 16, 1862, Staniels Letter, FSNMP; December 12, 1862, Charles S. Granger Diary, CWMC, USAMHI; Henry Lewis to "Dear Cousin Charlie," January 3, 1863, Lewis Letters, GLC; Bliss Memoir, 4:21–22, USAMHI; Bartol, *Nation's Hour,* 48–49. Around 2:00 P.M. Brig. Gen. Amiel Whipple's small Third Corps division began crossing the river to the strains of a band from the 12th New Hampshire playing "Bully for You." A well-aimed Rebel shell ended the concert, shattering the bass drum and scattering the musicians, much to the amusement of onlookers. Crowded Fredericksburg could accommodate no more troops. After crouching along the riverbank dodging Confederate artillery rounds, this division had to retreat back across the bridge. Even this minor fiasco had produced a scattering of casualties among troops under fire for the first time. See OR, 110, 358; Walcott, *Twenty-First Regiment,* 240; Sprenger, *122d Regiment,* 139–41; Isaac Morrow to his brother, December 21, 1862, Morrow Papers, HCWRTC, USAMHI; Paige Memoir, 20–21, USAMHI; December 12, 1862, Mancha Diary, CWMC, USAMHI; Nathan Chesley to "Friend Sawyer," December 19, 1862, Chesley Letter, FSNMP; Asa W. Bartlett, *History of the Twelfth New Hampshire,* 40–41; *OR Supplement,* pt. 2, 39:459.

7. OR, 108–9, 523, 527; Edmund Halsey, *Brother against Brother,* 92; *Flemington (N.J.) Hunterdon Republican,* December 26, 1862; December 12, 1862, S. W. Gordon Diary, FSNMP; *Pittsfield (Mass.) Sun,* January 1, 1863; Joseph Bloomfield Osborn to Joseph M. Osborn, December 18, 1862, Osborn Papers, LC; *OR Supplement,* pt. 1, 3:782, pt. 2, 40:540; Foster, *New Jersey and the Rebellion,* 505; December 12, 1862, Halsey Diary, USAMHI; Haines, *15th New Jersey,* 30; John Ripley Adams, *Memorials and Letters,* 81; Henry Ryerson to his sister, December 23, 1862, Anderson Family Papers, NJHS. After the Sixth Corps had crossed, Brig. Gen. George D. Bayard's cavalry brigade moved slowly over the bridges and skirmished with Confederate pickets beyond the railroad. Whether these forays provided any useful intelligence information is doubtful, though ironically they largely marked the extent to which Burn-

side used his cavalry during the battle. See O'Reilly, *Jackson at Fredericksburg*, 23–24; *OR*, 199; Tobie, *First Maine Cavalry*, 105–6; William Penn Lloyd, *First Reg't Pennsylvania Reserve Cavalry*, 38; December 12, 1862, Lloyd Diary, SHC; Pyne, *Ride to War*, 104–6.

8. *OR*, 109, 453; Charles Shields Wainwright, *Diary of Battle*, 137–38; Charles E. Davis, *Three Years in the Army*, 162; Gearhart, *Reminiscences of the Civil War*, 24–25.

9. *OR*, 485–86, 510; James B. Thomas, *Civil War Letters*, 126–27; *OR Supplement*, pt. 1, 3: 686–87; Lucius B. Shattuck to Ellen Shattuck, December 11–14, 1862, Shattuck Letters, MHC; Dawes, *Sixth Wisconsin*, 109–10; Otis, *Second Wisconsin*, 66; Maxson, *Camp Fires of the Twenty-Third*, 117–18; Orson Blair Curtis, *History of the Twenty-Fourth Michigan*, 89–90; Darius Starr to his mother, December 25, 1862, Starr Papers, Duke.

10. Best, *History of the 121st New York*, 41; *B&L*, 3:142; Woodward, *Our Campaigns*, 232.

11. Noel G. Harrison, *Fredericksburg Civil War Sites*, 2:14–15; Galwey, *Valiant Hours*, 58; John Worthington Ames, "Under Fire," 440; Abraham Welch to his sister, December 27, 1862, Welch Letter, SHC; S. Millett Thompson, *Thirteenth New Hampshire*, 76; Augustus Van Dyke to his brother, December 23, 1862, Van Dyke Papers, IHS; *Philadelphia Inquirer*, December 15, 1862; Thomas Rice, "All the Imps of Hell Let Loose," 13; Page, *Fourteenth Connecticut*, 60; Roberts, *House Undivided*, 140.

12. Winn, *Musico at Fredericksburg*, 44; *History of the 127th Regiment Pennsylvania Volunteers*, 122–23; Frank Moore, *Rebellion Record*, 5:98. Although Mark Grimsley is right that much of the looting was aimed at wealthy secessionists, he exaggerates the restraining influence of high-ranking officers and ignores the fact that many soldiers proved less than discriminating in their choice of targets. A Lutheran chaplain believed that several Union generals actually wanted the looting to take place. See Grimsley, *Hard Hand of War*, 108–9; Stuckenberg, *Surrounded by Methodists*, 38.

13. Cory, "Private's Recollections of Fredericksburg," 134–35; Kepler, *Fourth Ohio*, 92; R. S. Robertson to his parents, December 12, 1862, Robertson Papers, FSNMP; J. E. Hodgkins, *Civil War Diary*, 17; E. A. Walker to "Friend Knight," January 24, 1863, Walker Letters, Leigh Collection, USAMHI.

14. McKelvey, *Rochester in the Civil War*, 160–61; Croffut and Morris, *Connecticut during the War*, 291–92; Walker, *Second Corps*, 154; Thomas Rice, "All the Imps of Hell Let Loose," 12; Joseph Ripley Chandler Ward, *One Hundred and Sixth Pennsylvania*, 114–15; Todd Reminiscences, 78, SHC.

15. David Beem to his wife, December 18, 1862, Beem Papers, IHS; Milo Grow to his wife, December 18, 1862, Grow Letters, FSNMP; Waitt, *Nineteenth Massachusetts*, 176.

16. O. Leland Barlow to his sister, December 16, 1862, Barlow Papers, CSL; Charles J. Borden to "Dear Friend," December 18, 1862, Borden Papers, Duke; G. O. Bartlett to Ira Andrews, December 18, 1862, Bartlett Papers, GLC; *Lancaster (Pa.) Daily Evening Express*, December 23, 1862; Lord, *History of the Ninth New Hampshire*, 224–25, 249; Baxter, *Gallant Fourteenth*, 115; Robert S. Robertson, "Diary of the War," 74; John L. Smith, *118th Pennsylvania*, 122; Oliver Willcox Norton, *Army Letters*, 129; *Philadelphia Inquirer*, January 2, 1863; S. Millett Thompson, *Thirteenth New Hampshire*, 45.

17. Bruce, "Battle of Fredericksburg," 521, 527–28; Reichardt, *Diary of Battery A*, 74; McCarter, *My Life in the Irish Brigade*, 156–57; Asaph R. Tyler to his wife, December 15, 1862, Tyler Letters, FSNMP; Moe, *Last Full Measure*, 210–11; Amory Allen to his parents, December 17, 1862, Allen Letter, FSNMP; Hopkins, *Seventh Rhode Island*, 42; Wren, *Captain James Wren's Civil War Diary*, 97; Ford, *Fifteenth Regiment Massachusetts Volunteer Infantry*, 223.

18. John S. Weiser to his parents, January 1, 1863, Weiser Papers, CWMC, USAMHI; Isaac Lyman Taylor, "Campaigning with the First Minnesota," 236; Henry H. Holt to Luther Eaton, December 17, 1862, Holt Letters, Leigh Collection, USAMHI; Dority, "Civil War Diary," 10; Thomas D. Grover Smith to "Dear Mother," December 18, 1862, Thomas D. Grover Smith Letter, Turner Collection, USAMHI; Beidelman, *Letters of George Washington Beidelman*, 166–67;

Joseph Ripley Chandler Ward, *One Hundred and Sixth Pennsylvania*, 115; Charles Augustus Fuller, *Recollections of the War of 1861*, 78.

19. Mulholland, *116th Pennsylvania*, 54–55; McCarter, *My Life in the Irish Brigade*, 161; Robert Goldthwaite Carter, *Four Brothers in Blue*, 193–94; J. L. Smith to his mother, December 26, 1862, John L. Smith Letters, FSNMP.

20. Spangler, *My Little War Experiences*, 62; Joseph Ripley Chandler Ward, *One Hundred and Sixth Pennsylvania*, 115; S. Millett Thompson, *Thirteenth New Hampshire*, 42; Howard, *Autobiography*, 1:325; Hough, "Battle of Fredericksburg," 13, FSNMP; Waitt, *Nineteenth Massachusetts*, 174–75.

21. Walker, *Second Corps*, 153–54; December 12, 1862, Butler Diary, Schoff Collection, CL; *History of the Thirty-Fifth Massachusetts Volunteers*, 81–82; Waitt, *Nineteenth Massachusetts*, 175–76; Reese, *Sykes' Regular Infantry Division*, 186.

22. Cory, "Private's Recollections of Fredericksburg," 136; *Minnesota in the Civil and Indian Wars*, 1:29; Imholte, *First Minnesota*, 108; Aldrich, *History of Battery A*, 160; Powell, *Fifth Corps*, 398; Currier, "From Concord to Fredericksburg," 252–53; Bruce, "Battle of Fredericksburg," 528.

23. Abbott, *Fallen Leaves*, 155–56; G. O. Bartlett to Ira Andrews, December 18, 1862, Bartlett Papers, GLC; Cavins, *Civil War Letters of Cavins*, 122; Marvel, *Ninth New Hampshire*, 995–96; Henry Grimes Marshall to "Dear Folks at Home," Marshall Papers, Schoff Collection, CL.

24. George W. Ballock to his wife, December 18, 1862, Ballock Papers, Duke; P. H. Hilliard to his wife, December 21, 1862, Hilliard Papers, Duke; George W. Barr to Vinnie Barr, December 18, 1862, Barr Papers, Schoff Collection, CL; Henry Willis to his father, December 15, 1862, Henry Willis Letter, FSNMP; Charles Dwight Chase to his father, January 11, 1862, Chase Papers, NHHS; Willard J. Templeton to his sister, December 11, 1862, Templeton Letters, NHSL; Charles F. Stinson to his mother, December 17, 1862, Stinson Letters, USAMHI; A. B. Martin to "Dear Ann," December 19, 1862, Martin Letter, FSNMP; Thomas Rice, "All the Imps of Hell Let Loose," 13.

25. Gambone, *Zook*, 106; December 12, 1862, Henderson Diary, FSNMP; McCrea, *Dear Belle*, 175; December 12, 1862, Pope Diary, *CWTI*, USAMHI; Robert Goldthwaite Carter, *Four Brothers in Blue*, 209; *Indianapolis Daily Journal*, December 24, 1862.

26. Joseph N. Haynes to his father, December 21, 1862, Haynes Papers, Duke; A. A. Batchelder to his parents, December 16, 1862, Batchelder Letter, FSNMP; Aaron K. Blake to his sister, December 18, 1862, Blake Letters, CWMC, USAMHI; Ephraim Jackson to "Dear Brother and Sister," December 20, 1862, Jackson Letters, FSNMP; December 14, 1862, Rice Diary, FSNMP; Beidelman, *Letters of George Washington Beidelman*, 162–63.

27. *New York Tribune*, December 15, 1862; John S. Crocker to his wife, December 12, 1862, Crocker Letters, CU; Thomas Rice, "All the Imps of Hell Let Loose," 14; December 19, 1862, Webb Diary, Schoff Collection, CL.

28. Roland R. Bowen, *From Ball's Bluff to Gettysburg*, 141; Royster, *Destructive War*, 253–54; Everard H. Smith, "Chambersburg"; Reid Mitchell, *Vacant Chair*, 7–11; Ellis M. Stevens to Daniel Stevens, December 12, 1862, Stevens Papers, CSL.

29. *OR*, 222; Chamberlain, *Through Blood and Fire*, 44–45; *New York Herald*, December 14, 1862; Cory, "Private's Recollections of Fredericksburg," 134; S. Millett Thompson, *Thirteenth New Hampshire*, 41, 99; Simonton, "Recollections of Fredericksburg," 257–58; *Under the Maltese Cross*, 105. Couch did not repeat his claim in a later article for the *Century Magazine* series but instead admitted that there had been "considerable looting" (*B&L*, 3:108).

30. *Minnesota in the Civil and Indian Wars*, 1:29; *OR*, 344; December 12, 1862, Butler Diary, Schoff Collection, CL; Cowtan, *Services of the Tenth New York Volunteers*, 161–62; Howard Owen Edmonds, *Owen-Edmonds*, 41–42; Borton, *Awhile with the Blue*, 37; *B&L*, 3: 108–9; Hopkins, *Seventh Rhode Island*, 42–43; Marsena Rudolph Patrick, *Inside Lincoln's Army*, 188–89.

31. George L. Prescott to ?, December 11–12, 1862, Prescott Papers, MHS; Tillinghast, *Twelfth Rhode Island*, 175; *Rochester (N.Y.) Daily Democrat and American*, December 27, 1862; Herbert C. Mason to his father, December 17, 1862, Mason Letter, FSNMP; John Godfrey to Horace Godfrey, December 14, 1862, Godfrey Papers, NHHS; ? (an unidentified member of the 24th New York) to "Dear Jeemes," December 18, 1862, Lyons Family Papers, U.S. Military Academy; Darrohn, "Recollections," 8–9, FSNMP; R. P. Staniels to "My Darling Selina," December 16, 1862, Staniels Letter, FSNMP.

32. John Wilkins to his wife, December 18, 1862, Wilkins Papers, Schoff Collection, CL; Baxter, *Gallant Fourteenth*, 115; Abraham Welch to his sister, December 27, 1862, Welch Letter, SHC; Osborne, *Twenty-Ninth Massachusetts*, 205.

33. Civil War Damage Inventories, Drawer 491, Clerk of the Circuit Court of Fredericksburg; December 29, 1862, Alsop Diary, VHS; Jane Howison Beale, *Journal*, 74–75.

34. *Richmond Daily Enquirer*, December 22, 1862; *Charleston Daily Courier*, January 8, 1863; Figg, *"Where Men Only Dare to Go!,"* 94; Blake, *Three Years in the Army of the Potomac*, 157; Goss, *Recollections of a Private*, 134; Thomas Rice, "All the Imps of Hell Let Loose," 14.

35. December 12, 1862, Latrobe Diary, VHS; Oscar J. E. Stuart to Annie E. Stuart, December 17, 1862, Dimitry Papers, Duke; Francis Marion Coker to his wife, December 18, 1862, Coker Letters, UG; John F. Sale to ? December 23, 1862, Sale Letter, FSNMP; Isaac Howard to his father, December 25, 1862, Howard Family Papers, SHC; Thomas Rice, "All the Imps of Hell Let Loose," 14.

36. *Augusta (Ga.) Daily Constitutionalist*, January 4, 1863; *Richmond Daily Dispatch*, December 18, 1862; *Richmond Daily Enquirer*, December 18, 22, 1862; Blair, "Barbarians at Fredericksburg's Gate," 156–58; *Richmond Daily Dispatch*, December 15, 1862; *Charleston Daily Courier*, January 8, 1863; *Atlanta Southern Confederacy*, January 7, 1863. Editor Edward Pollard included poignant details of refugee suffering, the bombardment of Fredericksburg, and the sack of the town in his yearly compilation of contemporary war history. See Pollard, *Southern History of the War*, 1:540–41, 547–49.

37. *Richmond Daily Dispatch*, December 23, 1862; *Richmond Daily Enquirer*, December 20, 1862; Edmondston, *"Journal of a Secesh Lady,"* 322. Although northern newspapers barely reported, let alone criticized, the soldiers' behavior, a *New York Times* editorial later conceded that plundering by Federal armies would most likely spur the Rebels to redouble their efforts to win independence. See *New York Times*, January 4, 1863.

38. Professor Lowe had his balloon ready to go, and signal stations had been established; but Burnside learned little about the strength or deployment of Lee's forces. Fog and smoke along with sometimes sloppy staff work hampered communication. For intelligence problems, see William Allan, "Fredericksburg," 133; *OR*, ser. 3, 3:294; *OR Supplement*, pt. 1, 10: 446; Hagerman, *Civil War and Origins of Modern Warfare*, 80–81.

39. *OR*, 89–91, 109, and ser. 1, 51(1):1021; *B&L*, 3:109, 133–34; *CCW*, 1:707; Jacob Lyman Greene, *Franklin and the Left Wing at Fredericksburg*, 12–13; William B. Franklin to St. Clair Mulholland, January 13, 1881, Mulholland Collection, MOLLUS; Marvel, *Burnside*, 180. With regard to the advice of his generals, Burnside either refused to commit himself or left the impression that he would follow their counsel (much of the evidence is sketchy, contradictory, or of questionable authority).

40. "Personal Recollections of the First Battle of Fredericksburg," 8, UT; *OR*, 545, 1060.

41. *OR*, 569–70; *B&L*, 3:89–91; Walters, *Norfolk Blues*, 47; Patterson, *Yankee Rebel*, 85. This officer in his own way simply echoed the classic definition of a strong defensive position. See Clausewitz, *On War*, 409.

42. Hotchkiss, *Make Me a Map of the Valley*, 99–100; Lenoir Chambers, *Jackson*, 2:277–80; *OR*, 641, 1060; O'Sullivan, *55th Virginia*, 42; James Power Smith, "With Stonewall Jackson," 28; W. G. Bean, *Sandie Pendleton*, 87.

43. Conn, "Conn-Brantley Letter," 439; W. H. Andrews, *Footprints of a Regiment*, 97;

Samuel D. Buck, *With the Old Confeds,* 71; Walter Clark, *Regiments and Battalions from North Carolina,* 2:476.

44. Early, *Narrative of the War,* 170; Handerson, *Yankee in Gray,* 52; Edward Waterman to his sisters, December 19, 1862, Waterman-Bacon-Sanders Family Papers, Houston Regional Library; December 12, 1862, Hodnett Diary, UDC Bound Typescripts, GDAH.

45. *OR,* 643; W. R. M. Slaughter to his sister, January 4, 1863, Slaughter Letters, VHS; Hubbell, *Confederate Stamps, Old Letters, and History,* appendix, 8; Edward Hall Armstrong to his father, December 18, 1862, Armstrong Letter, Duke; John S. Brooks to Sarah A. Knox, December 20, 1862, Brooks Letters, SHC; Laboda, *From Selma to Appomattox,* 68; William S. White, "Diary of the War," 144–45.

46. "Personal Recollections of the First Battle of Fredericksburg," 1, UT; *OR,* 588; Dickert, *Kershaw's Brigade,* 182; Coles, *From Huntsville to Appomattox,* 80; Mary Anna Jackson, *Life and Letters of Jackson,* 397.

47. O'Reilly, *Jackson at Fredericksburg,* 23; *B&L,* 3:136; Judd, *Story of the Thirty-Third,* 252–53; Coles, *From Huntsville to Appomattox,* 77; Noel G. Harrison, *Fredericksburg Civil War Sites,* 2:76–82; Charles Shields Wainwright, *Diary of Battle,* 138–39.

48. Villard, *Memoirs,* 1:360–61; December 12, 1862, Charles S. Granger Diary, CWMC, USAMHI; John Smart to Ann Smart, December 17, 1862, Smart Letters, FSNMP; Mulholland, *116th Pennsylvania,* 55; Loyd Harris, "Army Music," 291–92.

49. Charles E. Davis, *Three Years in the Army,* 162–63; Cook, *Twelfth Massachusetts,* 80; George H. Allen, *Forty-Six Months,* 164–67; *Elizabeth New Jersey Journal,* January 6, 1863; Blakeslee, *Sixteenth Connecticut,* 28; Cogswell, *Eleventh New Hampshire,* 66.

50. Ford, *Fifteenth Regiment Massachusetts Volunteer Infantry,* 224–25; December 12, 1862, Shepard Diary, FSNMP; William Child, *Fifth New Hampshire,* 155; December 12, 1862, Pope Diary, *CWTI,* USAMHI; Corby, *Memoirs of Chaplain Life,* 131; Joseph E. Grant, *Flying Regiment,* 47; Bosbyshell, *48th in the War,* 96; Virgil W. Mattoon to his mother, December 10–15, 1862, Mattoon Papers, CHS; Peter Welsh, *Irish Green and Union Blue,* 43; December 12, 1862, Furst Diary, HCWRTC, USAMHI.

51. Hess, *Union Soldier in Battle,* 1–9; Blake, *Three Years in the Army of the Potomac,* 149.

52. James R. Woodworth to Phoebe Woodworth, December 12, 1862, Woodworth Papers, Hotchkiss Collection, CL; Melcher, *With a Flash of His Sword,* 11; Favill, *Diary of a Young Officer,* 210; Baxter, *Gallant Fourteenth,* 117; J. Cutler Andrews, *North Reports the Civil War,* 325; *Philadelphia Inquirer,* December 15, 1862; Charles F. Powell to his parents, December 12, 1862, Powell Papers, CWMC, USAMHI.

53. Hess, *Union Soldier in Battle,* 29–32; December 12, 1862, Charles S. Granger Diary, CWMC, USAMHI; William Child, *Fifth New Hampshire,* 152; Cavins, *Civil War Letters of Cavins,* 120; O'Reilly, "Pennsylvania Reserves at Fredericksburg," 8; Trobriand, *Four Years with the Army of the Potomac,* 363–64.

54. Hess, *Union Soldier in Battle,* 122–26; McAllister, *Letters of Robert McAllister,* 240; Charles H. Eagor to his wife, December 12, 1862, Eagor Letters, Leigh Collection, USAMHI; Hackett, *Christian Memorials,* 79–81.

CHAPTER TWELVE

1. Douglas Southall Freeman, *Lee,* 2:451; Clausewitz, *On War,* 103–4, 186, 249. For evidence of Burnside's physical and mental exhaustion, see Marvel, *Burnside,* 174–206 passim.

2. Undated statement of James Allen Hardie, ca. December 1862, and Extract of Letter from Hardie to Ambrose E. Burnside, March 12, 1863?, Hardie Papers, LC; *OR,* 90–91, and ser. 1, 51(1):1021; *CCW,* 1:707; Marvel, *Burnside,* 203–4. Reynolds had also stayed up—until 3:00 A.M.—before going to bed in disgust. See *B&L,* 3:133. Franklin later testified that "the staff officer who brought the order" strengthened his restrictive interpretation of Burnside's order. See *CCW,* 1:709–10.

3. *OR*, 457.

4. Historians have usually made cases either for or against Burnside, but what John Keegan has labeled the "accusatorial" approach to battle history tends to oversimplify greatly the many factors affecting the outcome of a battle, including communications and staff work. See Keegan, *Face of Battle*, 75–77.

5. *OR*, 90, 110, 114.

6. Haley, *Rebel Yell and Yankee Hurrah*, 57; Castleman, *Army of the Potomac*, 260; *OR*, ser. 1, 51(1):1021; *B&L*, 3:133–34; *CCW*, 1:708, 710; William B. Franklin to George B. McClellan, December 23, 1862, McClellan Papers, LC. Franklin also claimed to have discussed the order with Reynolds and Smith. In an appearance before the Joint Committee on the Conduct of the War only a few days after the battle, Burnside attributed the failure of Franklin's attack to the strength of the Confederate positions. But during additional testimony in early February 1863, he sharply criticized Franklin for "a lack of alacrity and strict adherence to the spirit of the plan" that prevented a successful assault on the high ground near Hamilton's Crossing. Privately he claimed to have trusted Franklin's discretion. Surely, Burnside said, Franklin realized that "I did not cross more than 100,000 [men] over the river to make a reconnaissance." See *CCW*, 1:655–56, 723–24; Ambrose E. Burnside to Mr. Sturgis? June 4, 1913, Burnside Papers, entry 159, box 3, NA.

7. See, for example, Jennings Cropper Wise, *Long Arm of Lee*, 1:380–81. Later critics of Burnside's tactics have thoroughly dissected and criticized the orders issued on December 13. See, for example, Jacob Lyman Greene, *Franklin and the Left Wing at Fredericksburg*, 16–19; Palfrey, *Antietam and Fredericksburg*, 162–65. Some students of the battle have maintained that the attack orders were vague because Burnside had thoroughly discussed his plans with Franklin and the other generals on December 12. See, for example, Woodbury, *Burnside and the Ninth Army Corps*, 228–29; Marvel, *Burnside*, 175–76; A. Wilson Greene, "Opportunity to the South," 312–13. Artillery officers testified that Franklin hardly needed the entire Sixth Corps to guard the bridges and suggested that he should have launched a much stronger attack. Hooker agreed with this assessment in his congressional testimony. Even commentators most critical of Burnside have pointed to Franklin's timidity and what the artillery chief of the First Corps deemed his "natural laziness." Given his engineering background, Franklin may also have been inclined toward a strict interpretation of Burnside's orders. See [De Peyster,] "Fredericksburg," 201–7; *CCW*, 1:670, 670, 687–90; Charles Shields Wainwright, *Diary of Battle*, 147–48. Part of the difficulty with the battle plan may also have stemmed from the anomalous position of both the grand division and corps commanders in the recently reorganized Army of the Potomac. To be sure, Franklin's defenders have also been quick to adopt his interpretation of Burnside's orders. See Swinton, *Campaigns of the Army of the Potomac*, 248; Col. G. F. R. Henderson, *Civil War*, 66–67; Whan, *Fiasco at Fredericksburg*, 132; Jacob Lyman Greene, *Franklin and the Left Wing at Fredericksburg*, 19, 31, 35–38. The soundest conclusion is that both Burnside and Franklin bore considerable responsibility for the ineffectual assault on the Rebel right. Confederate defensive positions as well as the tactical performance of commanders and troops on both sides also greatly influenced the results of the fighting on this part of the field.

8. Charles, "Events in Battle of Fredericksburg," 66.

9. Whan, *Fiasco at Fredericksburg*, 47–49; Col. G. F. R. Henderson, *Civil War*, 36, 47; *OR*, 378.

10. Clausewitz, *On War*, 348.

11. A. Wilson Greene, "Opportunity to the South," 296–97; O'Reilly, *Jackson at Fredericksburg*, 38; Susan Leigh Blackford, *Letters from Lee's Army*, 145–46; Early, *Narrative of the War*, 167–68; *OR*, 449, 453. Shortly after the battle, Franklin greatly exaggerated the steepness of Prospect Hill, falsely reporting it "well abattied." The enemy's lines, he said, were "impregnable." See William B. Franklin to George B. McClellan, December 23, 1862, McClellan

Papers, LC. Federal cavalry had not reconnoitered the ground; Yankee horsemen did little during the battle itself but watch. "Cold, idle, and anxious," Charles Francis Adams Jr. described them. See *OR,* 220–21; *Indianapolis Daily Journal,* December 20, 1862; Denison, *First Rhode Island Cavalry,* 182–83; William Penn Lloyd, *First Reg't Pennsylvania Reserve Cavalry,* 38; Charles Francis Adams, *Cycle of Adams Letters,* 1:211.

12. *OR,* 630–31; Col. G. F. R. Henderson, *Civil War,* 62; Whan, *Fiasco at Fredericksburg,* 61; O'Reilly, *Jackson at Fredericksburg,* 27–29. During the morning D. H. Hill's Division moved into a position in reserve behind Early and Taliaferro.

13. *OR,* 636–37; A. Wilson Greene, "Opportunity to the South," 300–301; Jennings Cropper Wise, *Long Arm of Lee,* 1:377–82. I have relied heavily on the meticulous analysis of artillery placement in O'Reilly, *Jackson at Fredericksburg,* 29–32. For tactical details and analysis of the fighting on the Confederate right, O'Reilly's book is superb.

14. Two regiments from Col. John M. Brockenbrough's rightmost Virginia brigade later moved to support Archer, while the rest backed up Walker's batteries. Pender's brigade was stationed to the left and rear of Lane's brigade and behind Davidson's artillery. Brig. Gen. Edward L. Thomas's Georgia brigade held a position to the rear of the gap between Pender and Lane.

15. *OR,* 630–32, 653–64; O'Reilly, *Jackson at Fredericksburg,* 27–28.

16. *OR,* 645; Pender, *General to His Lady,* 191; James I. Robertson Jr., *Hill,* 157–61, 167–68.

17. Von Borcke, *Memoirs of the Confederate War,* 2:114; Sorrel, *Recollections of a Confederate Staff Officer,* 131; Lenoir Chambers, *Jackson,* 2:383; John William Jones, *Christ in the Camp,* 88; John W. Stevens, *Reminiscences of the Civil War,* 89–90; Col. G. F. R. Henderson, *Jackson,* 578–79; Douglas Southall Freeman, *Lee's Lieutenants,* 2:346–47; Worsham, *One of Jackson's Foot Cavalry,* 152–53. Some sources claimed that Jackson noticed the gap and even predicted the Federals would attack there, but several authorities have raised objections to this version of events and have argued that Jackson deserves some criticism for the faulty brigade alignment. See Dabney, *Jackson,* 610; Douglas Southall Freeman, *Lee's Lieutenants,* 2:341–42; Nolan, "Confederate Leadership at Fredericksburg," 39–40; James I. Robertson Jr., *Jackson,* 651–53.

18. *CCW,* 1:710; *OR,* 91, 449–50, 453–54; Hitchcock, *War from the Inside,* 101; Meade, *Life and Letters,* 1:334, 342–43; O'Reilly, *Jackson at Fredericksburg,* 196–97; William B. Franklin to John C. Ropes, May 15, 1895, Ropes Papers, Boston University.

19. *CCW,* 1:702; Meade, *Life and Letters,* 1:332, 339, 341–42. Meade's division was reportedly the smallest in the First Corps, though Reynolds later testified it was the largest. Frank O'Reilly notes that some of Meade's troops had been detached for other duties, but the numbers remain uncertain. See O'Reilly, *Jackson at Fredericksburg,* 202.

20. Charles Shields Wainwright, *Diary of Battle,* 143; George Meade (the general's son) to his mother, December 21, 1862, Meade Papers, HSP; O'Reilly, *Jackson at Fredericksburg,* 35–36; *OR,* 91. Franklin and Burnside likely were still confused about the road system, and Burnside apparently wanted the troops moved farther down the Richmond Stage Road to flank the Confederate right. For a detailed analysis of this question, see Marvel, *Burnside,* 185–86.

21. *OR,* 510–11; *Philadelphia Inquirer,* December 25, 1862; *History of the 121st Regiment Pennsylvania Volunteers,* 30; Charles Shields Wainwright, *Diary of Battle,* 139.

22. *B&L,* 3:77; Von Borcke, *Memoirs of the Confederate War,* 2:116–17; [De Peyster,] "Fredericksburg," 199; Charles, "Events in Battle of Fredericksburg," 66; Walter H. Taylor, *Four Years with General Lee,* 80; L. Minor Blackford, *Mine Eyes Have Seen the Glory,* 207–8; Davidson, *Diary and Letters,* 63; December 13, 1862, Jones Diary, Schoff Collection, CL; Mockbee, "Historical Sketch of the 14th Tennessee," 33, MC.

23. *OR,* 533; Sorrel, *Recollections of a Confederate Staff Officer,* 131; Von Borcke, *Memoirs of the Confederate War,* 2:117; Jedediah Hotchkiss to Sara Ann Comfort Hotchkiss, December 13,

1862, Hotchkiss Papers, LC. For various versions of the first quotation, see the *Times* (London), January 13, 1863; James Power Smith, "With Stonewall Jackson," 30; Dabney, *Jackson*, 611.

24. Charles Minor Blackford to Mary Blackford, January 12, 1863, Blackford Family Papers, SHC; William Willis Blackford, *War Years with Stuart*, 192–93; Edward Porter Alexander, *Fighting for the Confederacy*, 173–74; William Woods Hassler, *Pelham*, 138; Von Borcke, *Memoirs of the Confederate War*, 2:112–13.

25. William Woods Hassler, *Pelham*, 145; O'Reilly, *Jackson at Fredericksburg*, 40–41; Shreve, "Reminiscences," 5–6, Jefferson County Museum; R. Channing Price to his mother, December 17, 1862, Price Papers, SHC.

26. Bates Alexander, "Seventh Regiment," October 25, 1895; O'Reilly, *Jackson at Fredericksburg*, 42–43; *OR*, 185–86, 199–200, 458, 510–11; Harper, *Civil War History of Chester County, Pennsylvania*, 181–82; Shreve, "Reminiscences," 5–6, Jefferson County Museum; Whan, *Fiasco at Fredericksburg*, 132–33; Samuel Penniman Bates, *History of the Pennsylvania Volunteers*, 4:30–31; *History of the 121st Regiment Pennsylvania Volunteers*, 30–31.

27. Jennings Cropper Wise, *Long Arm of Lee*, 1:382–83; William Woods Hassler, *Pelham*, 145–46; O'Reilly, *Jackson at Fredericksburg*, 43–46; *OR*, 91, 458, 510–11, 514, 15; Cooke, "Right at Fredericksburg," 1; Naisawald, *Grape and Canister*, 249–50.

28. *OR Supplement*, pt. 1, 1, 110–111; *OR*, 91, 458, 511, 514–15.

29. Mertz, "Jackson's Artillerists," 77–78; Cooke, *Wearing of the Gray*, 122–23; *OR*, 547, 631; George William Beale, *Lieutenant of Cavalry in Lee's Army*, 63–64.

30. *CCW* 1:708; *OR* 215, 461–62, 466, 468; *OR Supplement*, pt. 1, 3:688; Irvin Cross Wills to James W. Wills, January 1, 1863, Wills Family Papers, VHS.

31. *OR*, 461–62, 476–77; *OR Supplement*, pt. 1, 3:688, 779–80; Lucius B. Shattuck to Ellen Shattuck, December 11–14, 1862, Shattuck Letters, MHC; Orson Blair Curtis, *History of the Twenty-Fourth Michigan*, 91–92.

32. Charles Shields Wainwright, *Diary of Battle*, 141; *OR*, 454, 458; Milans, "Eyewitness to Fredericksburg," 23; Naisawald, *Grape and Canister*, 250–51; Gearhart, *Reminiscences of the Civil War*, 25; O'Reilly, *Jackson at Fredericksburg*, 48. The sources are inconsistent on times and duration of the various artillery attacks. I have largely followed O'Reilly's lead on these matters. Part of the problem stems from the fact that during artillery duels, and indeed combat in general, men do not accurately note the time. See Dean, *Shook over Hell*, 64–65.

33. *OR*, 649, 679; Robert H. Moore, *Danville, Eight Star, New Market, and Dixie Artillery*, 25–27; Bohannon, *Giles, Allegheny, and Jackson Artillery*, 28; Carmichael, *Purcell, Crenshaw, and Letcher Artillery*, 102–3; December 13, 1862, Jones Diary, Schoff Collection, CL; December 13, 1862, O'Farrell Diary, MC.

34. McIntosh Manuscript, 7–10, SHC; Hatton Memoir, 373–79, LC; *OR*, 636; Mertz, "Jackson's Artillerists," 82–85; Kimble, "Company A," MC; Dabney, *Jackson*, 613–14; Walter Clark, *Regiments and Battalions from North Carolina*, 2:556, 4:236; Nisbet, *Four Years on the Firing Line*, 123. For a discussion of the psychological impact of coming under intense artillery fire, see Dean, *Shook over Hell*, 65–66.

35. *OR*, 454; O'Reilly, *Jackson at Fredericksburg*, 49–51.

36. Pennypacker, *Meade*, 100; McIntosh Manuscript, 9–10, SHC; McCreery Recollections, section 10, 1862–63, VHS; Cooke, "Right at Fredericksburg," 1; *OR*, 480, 637–38, 645–46, 649; O'Reilly, *Jackson at Fredericksburg*, 51–53; Jennings Cropper Wise, *Long Arm of Lee*, 1:383–84.

37. *OR*, 631; McIntosh Manuscript, 10, SHC; December 13, 1862, Furst Diary, HCWRTC, USAMHI; Isaac Hall, *History of the Ninety-Seventh New York*, 110; Catton, *Glory Road*, 44; Small, *Sixteenth Maine*, 72.

38. McClenthen, *Narrative of the Fall and Winter Campaign*, 37; Bates Alexander, "Seventh Regiment," November 3, 1895; *OR*, 486, 482–83, 514; Samuel Penniman Bates, *History of the Pennsylvania Volunteers*, 4:30–31; *MSH*, 2:131, 7:201; *OR Supplement*, pt. 2, 58:88.

39. L. Minor Blackford, *Mine Eyes Have Seen the Glory*, 208–9; *Charleston Daily Courier*,

December 13, 1862; William Meade Dame to his mother, December 15, 1862, Dame Letters, FSNMP; Carmichael, *Purcell, Crenshaw, and Letcher Artillery,* 149.

40. *OR,* 186, 450, 483, 515–17, 637; Samuel Penniman Bates, *History of the Pennsylvania Volunteers,* 2:969; Charles E. Davis, *Three Years in the Army,* 164–65; Small, *Road to Richmond,* 65.

41. *OR,* 637–39, 677, 679; Robert H. Moore, *Danville, Eight Star, New Market, and Dixie Artillery,* 25–27; Fonerden, *Carpenter's Battery,* 41–42; Jennings Cropper Wise, *Long Arm of Lee,* 1:384–85.

42. *OR,* 650, 662; Walter Clark, *Regiments and Battalions from North Carolina,* 1:664–65.

43. *OR,* 649; Cooke, "Right at Fredericksburg," 1; December 13, 1862, Jones Diary, Schoff Collection, CL; McIntosh Manuscript, 9–10, SHC; Brunson, *Pee Dee Light Artillery,* 23–24; *Charleston Daily Courier,* 13, 1862; Carmichael, *Lee's Young Artillerist,* 75; *MSH,* 10:743; Carmichael, *Purcell, Crenshaw, and Letcher Artillery,* 105.

44. Driver, *1st and 2nd Rockbridge Artillery,* 34–36; *OR,* 638–39; O'Reilly, *Jackson at Fredericksburg,* 58; Jennings Cropper Wise, *Long Arm of Lee,* 1:385; Steve Dandridge to his mother, December 19, 1862, Bedinger-Dandridge Family Papers, Duke; *Richmond Daily Whig,* January 9, 1863.

45. Charles Shields Wainwright, *Diary of Battle,* 141; *OR,* 458–59; Naisawald, *Grape and Canister,* 254–55.

46. William S. White, "Diary of the War," 146–47; Edward A. Moore, *Cannoneer under Jackson,* 161–63; Poague, *Gunner with Stonewall,* 54–55; Driver, *1st and 2nd Rockbridge Artillery,* 34–36; William B. Bailey to C. C. Bailey, December 17, 1862, Bailey Letters, HCWRTC, USAMHI; *OR,* 186; Lee Memoir, 4–6, FSNMP.

47. O'Reilly, *Jackson at Fredericksburg,* 64–65; *CCW,* 1:705. For a thorough and perceptive assessment of the performance of Jackson's artillery, see Mertz, "Jackson's Artillerists," 94–95.

48. Scales, "Battle of Fredericksburg," 212–13; Edward Waterman to his sisters, December 19, 1862, Waterman-Bacon-Sanders Family Papers, Houston Regional Library.

CHAPTER THIRTEEN

1. Mulholland, "At Fredericksburg," 3. For a pointed critique of the conventional "battle piece," see Keegan, *Face of Battle,* 69–73. For common physical and psychological reactions of soldiers heading into combat, see Wiley, *Life of Billy Yank,* 69–70; McPherson, *For Cause and Comrades,* 36–45; Hess, *Union Soldier in Battle,* 15–19.

2. Cleaves, *Meade,* 91; Bates Alexander, "Seventh Regiment," November 3, 1895.

3. *OR,* 518–19; O'Reilly, *Jackson at Fredericksburg,* 36; Thomson and Rauch, *History of the "Bucktails,"* 233; Samuel Penniman Bates, *History of the Pennsylvania Volunteers,* 1:585; *History of the 121st Regiment Pennsylvania Volunteers,* 32–33; December 13, 1862, Taggart Diary, USAMHI.

4. Silas W. Crocker, "Charge of the Pennsylvania Reserves," 3; Hess, *Union Soldier in Battle,* 45–54; Keegan, *Face of Battle,* 36–40.

5. Samuel Penniman Bates, *History of the Pennsylvania Volunteers,* 1:31; *Philadelphia Inquirer,* December 25, 1862; *OR,* 511, 513, 518–19; O'Reilly, "Pennsylvania Reserves at Fredericksburg," 16–17.

6. Sypher, *History of the Pennsylvania Reserve Corps,* 414–15; *OR,* 511, 518–19; Samuel Penniman Bates, *History of the Pennsylvania Volunteers,* 1:551, 2:699–700; Silas W. Crocker, "Charge of the Pennsylvania Reserves," 3; Krick, "Maxcy Gregg," 293–310; *OR,* 646–47, 651–52; Caldwell, *History of a Brigade of South Carolinians,* 57–61; O'Reilly, *Jackson at Fredericksburg,* 85–88; Outz, "Maxcy Gregg at Fredericksburg," 15–23; Norton Reunion Speech, 1886, SCL; Benson, *Berry Benson's Civil War Book,* 31–33; Clement Anselm Evans, *Confederate Military History,* 6:171–72.

7. Caldwell, *History of a Brigade of South Carolinians,* 61–62; Clement Anselm Evans, *Confederate Military History,* 6:172; *MSH,* 11:268, 12:555; *OR,* 519–20, 560; O'Reilly, *Jackson at Fredericksburg,* 88, Samuel Penniman Bates, *History of the Pennsylvania Volunteers,* 4:30–31; *History of the 121st Regiment Pennsylvania Volunteers,* 32–33; *Philadelphia Inquirer,* December 25, 1862.

8. O'Reilly, *Jackson at Fredericksburg,* 63; Archer, "James J. Archer Letters," 139; *Atlanta Southern Confederacy,* December 30, 1862; Keeley, "Civil War Diary Relates Records of Famous Company"; *OR,* 657–58, 660–61; Dyer and Moore, *Tennessee Civil War Veterans Questionnaires,* 2:637.

9. Whether the Georgians had actually dug rifle pits or held a shallow depression is unclear in the contemporary accounts.

10. Woodward, *Our Campaigns,* 235–36; December 13, 1862, Woodward Diary, HL; Samuel Penniman Bates, *History of the Pennsylvania Volunteers,* 1:585–86, 2:727–28, 851–52; *Carlisle (Pa.) Herald,* December 26, 1862; *Cumberland Valley (Pa.) Journal,* December 18, 1862; *OR,* 560, 658–59, 660; *Atlanta Southern Confederacy,* December 30, 1862; Keeley, "Civil War Diary Relates Records of Famous Company"; Folsom, *Heroes and Martyrs of Georgia,* 35; O'Reilly, *Jackson at Fredericksburg,* 88–92. After-action reports sometimes refer to the "collapse" of a regiment; in this case, "collapse" meant a withdrawal and at least 100 men taken prisoner. Yet the numbers hardly recapture the horror. Take, for instance, the case of an unidentified private who was struck in the front of the head, suffered a severe skull fracture, was captured, was transported to a Washington hospital, was operated on for the removal of several bone fragments, but finally succumbed to pneumonia. See *MSH,* 7:258.

11. Benneville Schell to his father, December 28, 1862, Schell Letters, FSNMP; *OR,* 661; Lindsley, *Military Annals of Tennessee,* 326; Mockbee, "Historical Sketch of the 14th Tennessee," 34, MC.

12. J. H. Moore, "Fredericksburg," 182–83; *OR,* 646, 657, 659–60; F. S. Harris, "Gen. Jas. J. Archer," 19; Fite Memoir, 80–81, TSLA; Lindsley, *Military Annals of Tennessee,* 238; Archer, "James J. Archer Letters," 138.

13. O'Reilly, *Jackson at Fredericksburg,* 36; Warner, *Generals in Blue,* 246; November 8, 1862, Eaton Diary, SHC.

14. O'Reilly, *Jackson at Fredericksburg,* 77; *Atlanta Southern Confederacy,* December 30, 1862; *OR,* 657, 661; Lindsley, *Military Annals of Tennessee,* 326; Thomson and Rauch, *History of the "Bucktails,"* 233–35; Mockbee, "Historical Sketch of the 14th Tennessee," 34, MC.

15. *OR,* 521–22; Samuel Penniman Bates, *History of the Pennsylvania Volunteers,* 2:670, 791, 821, 851–52, 884–85; *Pittsburgh Daily Dispatch,* December 22, 1862; Bright and Bright, "Respects to All," 33–34; *Beaver (Pa.) Weekly Argus,* December 24, 1862; *OR Supplement,* pt. 2, 58: 683; *CCW,* 1:692; *OR,* 139–40, 512; *Pittsburgh Post,* December 24, 1862; December 13, 1862, Taggart Diary, USAMHI.

16. *OR,* 520; O'Reilly, *Jackson at Fredericksburg,* 36, 83; Bates Alexander, "Seventh Regiment," November 10, December 6, 1895; December 13, 1862, Heffelfinger Diary, CWTI, USAMHI; *Cumberland Valley (Pa.) Journal,* December 18, 1862.

17. Samuel Penniman Bates, *History of the Pennsylvania Volunteers,* 1:614–15, 639; Woodward, *Third Pennsylvania Reserves,* 208–9; Milans, "Eyewitness to Fredericksburg," 23.

18. *OR,* 520; Samuel Penniman Bates, *History of the Pennsylvania Volunteers,* 2:762, 4:464–65; Gearhart, *Reminiscences of the Civil War,* 26–27; December 13, 1862, Boyts Diary, HSP. The figures include some casualties sustained during the later Confederate counterattack. Given the number of serious leg wounds in both regiments, Lane's North Carolinians must have paid some heed to the officers' standard admonitions to fire low. See *MSH,* 11:232, 240, 275, 276, 286, 294, 299, 330, 12:443–44, 475, 482, 504, 519, 524, 526, 535, 543, 605, 793, 794, 800.

19. *OR,* 654; Walter Clark, *Regiments and Battalions from North Carolina,* 1:657; William G. Morris to his wife, December 18, 1862, Morris Letter, SHC.

20. *OR,* 654; J. H. Lane, "Twenty-Eighth North Carolina Infantry," 332; Walter Clark, *Regiments and Battalions from North Carolina,* 2:475; William G. Morris to his wife, December 18, 1862, Morris Letter, SHC.

21. Gibbon, *Recollections of the Civil War,* 100–101; Isaac Hall, *History of the Ninety-Seventh New York,* 109.

22. Small, *Road to Richmond,* 62–65; *CCW,* 1:691, 700, 715; *OR,* 480; Charles Shields Wainwright, *Diary of Battle,* 139.

23. Warner, *Generals in Blue,* 495–96; Jack D. Welsh, *Medical Histories of Union Generals,* 332; *OR,* 484, 503; Samuel Penniman Bates, *History of the Pennsylvania Volunteers,* 10:867. For conflicting accounts of and rationalizations for the behavior of the 88th Pennsylvania, see *OR,* 508–9; Samuel Penniman Bates, *History of the Pennsylvania Volunteers,* 5:70–71; Vautier, *88th Pennsylvania,* 90–91.

24. *OR,* 503, 505–8, 654; Locke, *Story of the Regiment,* 163–65; John D. Withrow to Sarah Withrow, December 28, 1862, Withrow Letters, FSNMP; Todd, *Ninth Regiment, N.Y.S.M.,* 224–25; Jaques, *Three Years' Campaign,* 128–29; December 13, 1862, Robert S. Coburn Diary, *CWTI,* USAMHI; *OR Supplement,* pt. 2, 45:214–29; *MSH,* 11:262, 296, 12:471, 484, 495, 534, 550, 580; *Philadelphia Press,* December 27, 1862; Isaac Hall, *History of the Ninety-Seventh New York,* 111–12; Howard Thomas, *Boys in Blue from the Adirondack Foothills,* 114.

25. *OR,* 496–97, 499–501, 503, 654; Charles Shields Wainwright, *Diary of Battle,* 143–44; Walter Clark, *Regiments and Battalions from North Carolina,* 2:475, 556–57; Frinfrock, *Across the Rappahannock,* 87; Scales, "Battle of Fredericksburg," 209–10; Wetmore, "Story of a New York Boy at Fredericksburg," 3; Howard Thomas, *Boys in Blue from the Adirondack Foothills,* 111–12; McClenthen, *Narrative of the Fall and Winter Campaign,* 44.

26. *OR,* 480, 486–87, and ser. 1, 51(1):172; *CCW,* 1:715; McClenthen, *Narrative of the Fall and Winter Campaign,* 38. The regiments joining Root were the 12th Massachusetts, the 88th Pennsylvania, and the 136th Pennsylvania.

27. William F. Fox, *Regimental Losses,* 132; *OR,* 488–90, 646, 654–55; *Augusta (Maine) Kennebec Journal,* January 2, 1863; *OR Supplement,* pt. 2, 25:592–93; Small, *Road to Richmond,* 66–67; Bisbee, "Three Years a Volunteer Soldier," 116; Small, *Sixteenth Maine,* 65–67, 72–81; William G. Morris to his wife, December 18, 1862, Morris Letter, SHC; Irving Smith to Lusey Smith, December 22, 1862, Smith Papers, Duke; Walter Clark, *Regiments and Battalions from North Carolina,* 1:374–75, 2:35–36.

28. *OR,* 493, 498; Cook, *Twelfth Massachusetts,* 80, 83; Isaac Tichenor to Michael Leonard, March 17, 1893, Tichenor Letter, FSNMP.

29. *OR,* 491–92; *OR Supplement,* pt. 2, 45:557; Kress, *Memoirs,* 3–4; Barber, *Civil War Letters,* 109.

30. *OR,* 494–95, 502; McCoy, "107th Penna. Vet. Volunteers"; Samuel Penniman Bates, *History of the Pennsylvania Volunteers,* 3:858, 5:71; James B. Thomas, *Civil War Letters,* 124–25, 127–28, 130; Vautier, *88th Pennsylvania,* 91.

31. Palfrey, *Antietam and Fredericksburg,* 158–59; *OR,* 454, 519; Samuel Penniman Bates, *History of the Pennsylvania Volunteers,* 2:851–52; Charles Shields Wainwright, *Diary of Battle,* 143–44.

32. *OR,* 646, 651; Dunaway, *Reminiscences,* 56–57; O'Sullivan, *55th Virginia,* 42.

33. Early, *Narrative of the War,* 170–73; Greer, "All Thoughts Are Absorbed in the War," 30; *OR,* 663–64.

34. *OR,* 647, 664–65, 669–70; Early, *Narrative of the War,* 172–73; *Macon (Ga.) Daily Telegraph,* January 6, 1863; Bradwell, "Georgia Brigade at Fredericksburg," 19; Mills Lane, *"Dear Mother: Don't Grieve about Me,"* 202; Stiles, *Four Years under Marse Robert,* 135; *Sandersville Central Georgian,* January 14, 1863; *Savannah Republican,* January 6, 1863.

35. *OR,* 520–21, 664, 673–74; Ashcraft, *31st Virginia,* 43; Early, *Narrative of the War,* 173–74; Harper, *Civil War History of Chester County, Pennsylvania,* 181; Gearhart, *Reminiscences of the*

Civil War, 26–29; *Winchester (Va.) Times,* February 11, 1891; Wingfield, "Diary of Capt. H. W. Wingfield," 20 21. Walker's men had passed through Brig. Gen. Elisha F. Paxton's "Stonewall Brigade" from Jackson's old division. The division was now commanded by Brig. Gen. William B. Taliaferro.

36. *OR,* 664, 672; Nisbet, *Four Years on the Firing Line,* 124; Early, *Narrative of the War,* 174; William Calvin Oates, *War between Union and Confederacy,* 166; Edward Waterman to his sisters, December 19, 1862, Waterman-Bacon-Sanders Family Papers, Houston Regional Library; McClendon, *Recollections of War Times,* 159–60; S. G. Pryor, *Post of Honor,* 299–300.

37. Meade, *Life and Letters,* 1:338; *B&L,* 3:136; *OR,* 72, 90, 113–14, 355, 358–59, 361–62, 364; *CCW,* 1:704–5, 708; *OR Supplement,* pt. 1, 3:767–71.

38. *CCW,* 1:691–92, 705–6; *OR,* 512. Birney later testified that he received only one request for assistance from Meade. See *CCW,* 1:706. Both Birney's division and, later, Sickles's division had been detached from Hooker's control, and Franklin does not appear to have been coordinating the various commands.

39. Pennypacker, *Meade,* 102; Hitchcock, *War from the Inside,* 134–35; Thomson and Rauch, *History of the "Bucktails,"* 236.

40. Cleaves, *Meade,* 92–93; George G. Meade to his wife, December 30, 1862, and William B. Franklin to Meade, March 25, 1863, Meade Papers, HSP; Meade, *Life and Letters,* 1:337–40. Meade's censure of Reynolds in the December 30, 1862, letter to his wife was excised from the published version of the general's correspondence. In his official report, congressional testimony, and private correspondence Franklin passed the proverbial buck to Reynolds, claiming the impracticality of using Smith's Sixth Corps to support the attack. His excuses for the timid use of his sizable forces shifted and multiplied as time went on. See *OR,* 449–50; *CCW,* 1: 661–62; William B. Franklin to St. Clair A. Mulholland, January 13, 1881, Mulholland Collection, MOLLUS; William B. Franklin to George B. McClellan, December 23, 1862, McClellan Papers, LC. Reynolds took a similar tack. He told the Joint Committee on the Conduct of the War that the troops supporting Meade had not moved quickly enough, but he dithered about who might have been responsible for the delay. In his official report Reynolds claimed the Confederates' strong position had foiled the "brilliant attack," though privately and before the committee he also faulted the performance of Meade's and Gibbon's divisions. See *CCW,* 1:699–700; *OR,* 455; Edward J. Nichols, *Toward Gettysburg,* 155.

41. *OR,* 522; *Berks and Schuylkill (Pa.) Journal,* January 10, 1863; Bates Alexander, "Seventh Regiment," December 20, 1895; Kerbey, *On the War-Path,* 133–34; George H. Allen, *Forty-Six Months,* 163–64.

42. Reuben Schell to his father, December 17, 1862, Schell Letters, FSNMP; *OR,* 139–40, 512–13; Nathan Pennypacker to ?, December 15, 1862, Pennypacker Letters, Chester County Historical Society; *CCW,* 1:702; Frinfrock, *Across the Rappahannock,* 99; Charles Frederick Taylor, "Colonel of the Bucktails," 356; James H. McIlwaine to Emma McIlwaine, December 14, 1862, McIlwaine Letters, Leigh Collection, USAMHI; Franklin Boyts to his parents, December 21, 1862, Boyts Diary, HSP.

43. Franklin Boyts to his parents, December 21, 1862, Boyts Diary, HSP; Richard K. Halsey to "Friend Keck," December 15, 1862, King Papers, Schoff Collection, CL; William Hamilton to his mother, December 18, 1862, Hamilton Papers, LC; Bates Alexander, "Seventh Regiment," December 20, 1895.

CHAPTER FOURTEEN

1. *OR,* 91–92; Robert S. Robertson, "Diary of the War," 75; *New York Herald,* December 17, 1862; Herman Haupt to his wife, December 13, 1862, Haupt Letterbook, Haupt Papers, LC; Clausewitz, *On War,* 140; Jacob Lyman Greene, *Franklin and the Left Wing at Fredericksburg,* 25–26n. Shortly before the attacks began on the Federal right, one of Lowe's balloons ascended; it went up again two hours later, and yet again around 4:00 P.M. The fog and smoke

likely prevented the men from seeing much, and there is no evidence that Burnside gained any useful intelligence in this way. See *OR*, ser. 3, 3:294; William Teall to his wife, December 13, 1862, Teall Letters, TSLA; *Philadelphia Inquirer*, December 16, 1862. For an analysis arguing that Burnside was in essence reversing his battle plan and hoping that an attack by his right might bolster the assault by his left, see Daniel E. Sutherland, *Fredericksburg and Chancellorsville*, 51–52.

2. Welcher, *Union Army*, 1:708–9; Noel G. Harrison, *Fredericksburg Civil War Sites*, 2:120–21, 134–38, 160–61; *OR*, 617–18, and ser. 1, 51(2):954; Longstreet, *From Manassas to Appomattox*, 298; William Teall to his wife, December 9, 1862, Teall Letters, TSLA; Marsena Rudolph Patrick, *Inside Lincoln's Army*, 188; [De Peyster,] "Fredericksburg," 200–201; Marvel, *Burnside*, 188–89.

3. Longstreet, *From Manassas to Appomattox*, 298; *B&L*, 3:88; William Allan, *Army of Northern Virginia*, 468; Squires, "'Boy Officer' of the Washington Artillery," 20; Boggs, *Alexander Letters*, 244; Col. G. F. R. Henderson, *Civil War*, 44–46.

4. Hagerman, *Civil War and Origins of Modern Warfare*, 88, 122–23; Griffith, *Battle Tactics of the Civil War*, 117–35; Col. G. F. R. Henderson, *Civil War*, 48, 63; *OR*, 565–66, 587; Edward Porter Alexander, *Military Memoirs of a Confederate*, 279; Edward Porter Alexander, *Fighting for the Confederacy*, 175. In a much-cited passage Longstreet quoted Porter Alexander as saying, "General, we cover that ground now so well that we will comb it as with a fine-tooth comb. A chicken could not live on that field when we open on it." Alexander later wrote that he did not remember making such a remark. See *B&L*, 3:79; Edward Porter Alexander, *Fighting for the Confederacy*, 169.

5. Col. G. F. R. Henderson, *Civil War*, 63; *OR*, 552–53, 569–70.

6. *OR*, 570; *B&L*, 3:75–76; Speairs and Pettit, *Civil War Letters*, 1:75; Edward Porter Alexander, *Fighting for the Confederacy*, 172; Longstreet, *From Manassas to Appomattox*, 308.

7. *OR*, 90.

8. *OR*, 94; Marvel, *Burnside*, 204–5; Marvel, "Making of a Myth," 17–21; Clausewitz, *On War*, 95, 209, 360; William F. Smith to John C. Ropes, March 9, 1895, Ropes Papers, Boston University. Burnside apparently knew little about the terrain (especially the millrace, the Sunken Road, and the stone wall), and by remaining at the Phillips House, he could not see the strength of the Confederate positions. At 9:30 A.M. on December 13 Federal signal officers sent Sumner information about rifle pits and other entrenchments in the Confederate line, but nothing about the Sunken Road or the stone wall. See William Allan, *Army of Northern Virginia*, 481; Col. G. F. R. Henderson, *Civil War*, 52–53; Hagerman, *Civil War and Origins of Modern Warfare*, 79, 81; *OR*, 119, 151–56; *OR Supplement*, pt. 1, 10:444–48; Cushing, "Acting Signal Corps," 102.

9. William Teall to his wife, December 13, 1862, Teall Letters, TSLA; *CCW*, 1:660; *B&L*, 109–10; *OR*, 222, 286. Although Couch could communicate with the Lacy House by telegraph, first the fog and, later, dense smoke blocked Sumner's view of the fighting. See *OR*, 165–66; *OR Supplement*, pt. 1, 10:448–49; Robert S. Robertson, "Diary of the War," 75.

10. Warner, *Generals in Blue*, 161–62; Patricia L. Faust, *Encyclopedia of the Civil War*, 292; Howard, *Autobiography*, 1:338; Cavins, *Civil War Letters of Cavins*, 112; Elizabeth Blair Lee, *Civil War Letters*, 229.

11. *OR*, 570, and ser. 1, 51(2):661–62; Galwey, *Valiant Hours*, 59–60; Longstreet, *From Manassas to Appomattox*, 308; Edward Porter Alexander, *Fighting for the Confederacy*, 176–77; Baker, *Reminiscent Story of the Civil War*, 44–45; December 13, 1862, Latrobe Diary, VHS; *B&L*, 3:97.

12. The 1st Delaware had been detached from French's Third Brigade.

13. As a tactical response to growing firepower, West Point instructors began to emphasize the deployment of more skirmishers than had been used in the past, and this became standard procedure during the war. Another development—seen on several occasions during

the battle of Fredericksburg—was for troops to advance at the double-quick. See McWhiney and Jamieson, *Attack and Die*, 99–100; Hagerman, *Civil War and Origins of Modern Warfare*, 10, 20.

14. Charles Careleton Coffin, *Four Years of Fighting*, 158; *OR*, 286–87, 291–92, 570; Lamb, "Battle of Fredericksburg," 236; *Battle-Fields of the South*, 508–9; *Charleston Daily Courier*, January 8, 1863; Edward Porter Alexander, "Battle of Fredericksburg," 449–50; December 13, 1862, Latrobe Diary, VHS; *B&L*, 3:79; Jennings Cropper Wise, *Long Arm of Lee*, 1:387. The Federal artillery fire from Stafford Heights directed against Longstreet's gunners was not especially effective in part because of the distances involved but also because of defective shells that either exploded prematurely or did not explode at all. See *OR*, 184, 192, 195; Thomas H. Parker, *History of the 51st*, 280–81.

15. *B&L*, 3:79; *OR*, 291–92, 298, 570; Sawyer, *Military History of 8th Ohio*, 93–95; Franklin Sawyer, newspaper clipping in Samuel Sexton Civil War Memoirs, Sexton Papers, OHS; Baker, *Reminiscent Story of the Civil War*, 47–48; *Battle-Fields of the South*, 508; Noel G. Harrison, *Fredericksburg Civil War Sites*, 2:172–73; *OR Supplement*, pt. 2, 51:46.

16. *OR*, 292, 306; Kepler, *Fourth Ohio*, 93–96; Jeffries, "Diary of Lemuel Jeffries," 270; Seville, *First Delaware*, 56–57; Harper, *Civil War History of Chester County, Pennsylvania*, 179. At least three members of the First Delaware did not survive amputations, a lieutenant died at home a month later from a head wound, and one private who had been hit in the lower third of his right thigh had to suffer through three amputations between December 14, 1862, and May 7, 1864. See *MSH*, 7:120, 10:752, 11:252, 257, 12:632.

17. Borton, *Awhile with the Blue*, 38–39; *OR*, 74, 287, 292; unsigned report (courier or staff officer?), December 15, 1862, Kimball Collection, IU; Jennings Cropper Wise, *Long Arm of Lee*, 1:388–89. Kimball's seemingly cool indifference led some soldiers to conclude that he would readily sacrifice their lives for a promotion, but even the general's critics conceded his bravery. See Charles Gibson to his sister, January 6, 1863, Gibson Letters, FSNMP.

18. Landon, "Letters to the Vincennes Western Sun," 338–39; Cavins, *Civil War Letters of Cavins*, 118, 120; December 13, 1862, Lambert Diary, IHS; Augustus Van Dyke to his father, December 14, 1862, Van Dyke Papers, IHS. For a fine discussion of how Union soldiers found it difficult to describe their combat experiences, see Hess, *Union Soldier in Battle*, 45–54.

19. Baxter, *Gallant Fourteenth*, 118–19; Charles Gibson to his sister, January 6, 1863, Gibson Letters, FSNMP; Cavins, *Civil War Letters of Cavins*, 120; Sawyer, *Military History of the 8th Ohio*, 100. Some initially reticent soldiers became much more voluble in memoirs as time and distance made more graphic descriptions easier to write. Compare, for example, David Beem to his wife, December 14, 1862, Beem Papers, IHS, and Beem Memoir, FSNMP.

20. Civil War soldiers in similar hot spots, fearing either to advance or to retreat, would often stop and occasionally exchange shots at close range, rarely with good result. Nor was the tactic effective at Fredericksburg. See Griffith, *Battle Tactics of the Civil War*, 137–63.

21. Foster, *New Jersey and the Rebellion*, 519–21; Borton, *Awhile with the Blue*, 40–52; Borton, *On the Parallels*, 62–70; *OR*, 74; Isaac Hillyer to his wife, December 18, 20, 1862, Hillyer Letters, FSNMP.

22. *OR*, 290, 292–93, 295, 299; Foster, *New Jersey and the Rebellion*, 570–71; Edward Hutchinson to "Dear Emma," December 18, 1862, Hutchinson Letters, FSNMP; December 13, 1862, Rice Diary, FSNMP; Sawyer, *Military History of the 8th Ohio*, 95.

23. William M. Owen, *In Camp and Battle with the Washington Artillery*, 184; McCash, *Cobb*; Rufus Kilpatrick Porter, "Sketch of General T. R. R. Cobb," 184–93; W. H. Kirkpatrick to J. C. Newton, January 25, 1863, UDC Bound Typescripts, GDAH.

24. *OR*, 608, 625; Rufus Kilpatrick Porter, "Sketch of General T. R. R. Cobb," 194–96; "General Thomas R. R. Cobb"; *Athens (Ga.) Southern Banner*, December 24, 1862; Sutton, *Civil War Stories*, 19–24; Charles, "Events in Battle of Fredericksburg," 66; *Atlanta Southern Confederacy*, December 31, 1862. The more common reference to the "slaughter pen" at

Fredericksburg refers to the area between the railroad and the Richmond Stage Road on the Union left.

25. *OR,* 287, 303, 308; Cowtan, *Services of the 10th New York Volunteers,* 162–63; George F. Hopper to his brother, December 21, 1862, Hopper Papers, USAMHI; Cory, "Private's Recollections of Fredericksburg," 137.

26. Hitchcock, *War from the Inside,* 115–28, 141–45; Cory, "Private's Recollections of Fredericksburg," 136–38; *OR,* 309; Samuel Penniman Bates, *History of the Pennsylvania Volunteers,* 4:244. An officer in the 8th Ohio thought that few of Andrews's troops actually reached Kimball's position. See Sawyer, *Military History of the 8th Ohio,* 95–96.

27. *OR,* 300–302; Samuel Penniman Bates, *History of the Pennsylvania Volunteers,* 4:206; Hirst, *Boys from Rockville,* 73–74; Darrohn, "Recollections," 9, FSNMP; Spangler, *My Little War Experiences,* 64–67; Page, *Fourteenth Connecticut,* 81–92; *Rochester (N.Y.) Daily Democrat and American,* December 23, 1862; Amory Allen to his parents, December 17, 1862, Allen Letter, FSNMP; Croffut and Morris, *Connecticut during the War,* 292–93; McKelvey, *Rochester in the Civil War,* 161–62; Washburn, *108th Regiment,* 26–27, 113, 238. The types of wounds for these regiments are carefully documented in *MSH,* 7:122, 250–51, 266, 9:243, 10:632, 707, 773, 774, 964, 987, 11:269, 270, 329, 12:468, 481, 532, 733–34. A few pieces of artillery behind French's men supported the attack, but their position and the terrain undermined their effectiveness. See *OR,* 289; Nelson Ames, *History of Battery G,* 51–53; John Pellett to his family, December 21, 1862, Pellett Papers, USAMHI.

28. Edward H. Brewer to Mary Brewer, December 27, 1862, Brewer Papers, CSL; McKelvey, *Rochester in the Civil War,* 162; *OR,* 131; George F. Hopper to his brother, December 21, 1862, Hopper Papers, USAMHI; Walker, *Second Corps,* 192–93; John S. Weiser to his parents, December 17, 1862, Weiser Papers, CWMC, USAMHI; Nevins, *War for the Union,* 2:348.

29. *OR,* 580, 588–89, 607–8, 629–30; Rufus Kilpatrick Porter, "Sketch of General T. R. R. Cobb," 194–96; Preston, "Death of Cobb," 28–41; Joseph Henry Lumpkin to his daughter, December 30, 1862, Lumpkin Papers, UG; Jack D. Welsh, *Medical Histories of Confederate Generals,* 43.

30. *OR,* 222; David M. Jordan, *Hancock,* 57; McCarter, *My Life in the Irish Brigade,* 86–88.

31. *OR,* 227, 258–61; *Third Annual Report of the State Historian of New York,* 39; Sheldon, *"Twenty-Seventh,"* 21; Samuel K. Zook to E. J. Wade, December 16, 1862, Zook Papers, CWMC, USAMHI; George C. Case to his parents, December 17, 1862, Case Letters, FSNMP; *Fourth Annual Report of the Bureau of Military Statistics,* 557; Frederick, *Story of a Regiment,* 134; Walker, *Second Corps,* 168–70; Favill, *Diary of a Young Officer,* 211–12, 216. A member of the 57th New York was shocked to see a "motley crowd of men" still cavorting about in women's clothes while others continued to loot the city. One especially brazen fellow was lugging about a stuffed alligator. See Favill, *Diary of a Young Officer,* 210–11.

32. Gambone, *Zook,* 116; *OR,* 130; *Philadelphia Inquirer,* December 16, 1862; *MSH,* 10:703, 705, 708, 714, 749, 760, 764, 801, 940, 952, 968, 977, 982, 11:141, 172, 238, 259, 265, 269, 299, 300, 388, 400, 403, 12:452, 456, 468, 471, 509, 511, 524, 532, 606, 794–5, 821, 884.

33. Longstreet, *From Manassas to Appomattox,* 308; *OR,* 570, 608, 625–26, 629–30; Jennings Cropper Wise, *Long Arm of Lee,* 1:389–90; *Charleston Daily Courier,* December 30, 1862; Walter Clark, *Regiments and Battalions from North Carolina,* 2:297, 439, 3:69–70; *OR Supplement,* pt. 1, 3:808–9; Alexander Routh to ?, December 22, 1862, Routh Letter, East Carolina University; December 13, 1862, Samuel Hoey Walkup Journal, Walkup Papers, SHC; Sloan, *Guilford Grays,* 55–56.

34. Conyngham, *Irish Brigade,* 330–37; Maria Lydig Daly, *Diary of a Union Lady,* 201–2; Cavanagh, *Memoirs of Gen. Thomas Francis Meagher,* 466–67.

35. Thomas Rice, "Desperate Courage," 60; Burton, *Melting Pot Soldiers,* 119–21.

36. Thomas Rice, "Desperate Courage," 62; *OR,* 240; McCarter, *My Life in the Irish Brigade,* 15–16, 70.

37. *OR*, 241; Bosbyshell, *48th in the War*, 96–97; Cavanagh, *Memoirs of Gen. Thomas Francis Meagher*, 466–67; McCarter, *My Life in the Irish Brigade*, 164–67, 71; Harper, *Civil War History of Chester County, Pennsylvania*, 177; *Third Annual Report of the State Historian of New York*, 40; *New York Irish-American*, January 3, 10, 1863; Conyngham, *Irish Brigade*, 341–42, 348; Mulholland, *116th Pennsylvania*, 43.

38. Mulholland, "At Fredericksburg," 3; Mulholland, "Battle of Fredericksburg," 1; Mulholland, *116th Pennsylvania*, 60–62; McCarter, *My Life in the Irish Brigade*, 171–75; *OR*, 249.

39. Conyngham, *Irish Brigade*, 342–43; Mulholland, *116th Pennsylvania*, 62–63; *Philadelphia Grand Army Scout and Soldiers' Mail*, October 6, 1883; *OR*, 246, 248–50; *New York Irish-American*, January 3, 1863; Thomas Rice, "Desperate Courage," 64; McCarter, *My Life in the Irish Brigade*, 175–76.

40. Mulholland, *116th Pennsylvania*, 64–67; *OR*, 248; *Philadelphia Grand Army Scout and Soldiers' Mail*, October 6, 1883; *OR*, 246, 250–51; Thomas Rice, "Desperate Courage," 68; Power Memoir, FSNMP; Peter Welsh, *Irish Green and Union Blue*, 43, 46; *Third Annual Report of the State Historian of New York*, 40–43; McCarter, *My Life in the Irish Brigade*, 176–81; *New York Irish-American*, December 27, 1862, January 3, 10, 1863. The shouting, the close physical contact on the battlefield, the presence of friends, and the tight-knit character of the companies all created horror and buttressed courage. Adrenaline rushes, moments of remarkable calmness, and the maddening sight of dead and wounded comrades all sustained even hopeless assaults such as the attack of the Irish Brigade at Fredericksburg. See Hess, *Union Soldier in Battle*, 110–22; McPherson, *For Cause and Comrades*, 36–45.

41. Thomas Rice, "Desperate Courage," 64, 66; "Sacrifice of Federals at Fredericksburg," 370; *Richmond Daily Whig*, December 24, 1862; Col. G. F. R. Henderson, *Civil War*, 74–75; Woods Reminiscences, UDC Bound Typescripts, 147–48, GDAH; William M. Owen, *In Camp and Battle with the Washington Artillery*, 187; Pickett, *Heart of a Soldier*, 65–66; Jane Howison Beale, *Journal*, 76; Patterson, *Yankee Rebel*, 90–91. Cobb's well-sheltered brigade had fewer casualties than many single regiments in the various Federal brigades, and many of the injuries were minor. See *OR*, 558; *Athens (Ga.) Southern Banner*, December 24, 1862; *Augusta (Ga.) Daily Constitutionalist*, December 27, 1862.

42. *OR*, 244; Conyngham, *Irish Brigade*, 344–35; *Third Annual Report of the State Historian of New York*, 44; *OR Supplement*, pt. 2, 44:471; *New York Irish-American*, December 27, 1862; Samuel Penniman Bates, *History of the Pennsylvania Volunteers*, 3:1129–30; Peter Welsh, *Irish Green and Union Blue*, 40. Descriptions of a brigade reduced to a shadow of its former self quickly reached the northern press. See *Philadelphia Inquirer*, December 16, 1862; *Albany (N.Y.) Evening Journal*, December 20, 1862.

43. Uriah N. Parmelee to his mother, November 20, 1862, Parmelee Papers, Duke; Warner, *Generals in Blue*, 63–64; *OR*, 233–34; Stuckenberg, *Surrounded by Methodists*, 41; William Child, *Fifth New Hampshire*, 152; December 13, 1862, Willand Diary, NHSL; Rodney H. Ramsey to his father, December 27, 1862, Ramsey Letter, NHHS; *Third Annual Report of the State Historian of New York*, 39.

44. *OR*, 230, 233–35, 238; December 13, 1862, Willand Diary, NHSL; William Child, *Fifth New Hampshire*, 150, 154–61, 164–65; Waite, *New Hampshire in the Great Rebellion*, 283–84. Cross was hit by a sizable shell fragment in the breast and another small piece that knocked out two teeth. Spitting out blood and sand, he could not move and so lay there in a deadly crossfire between the Rebels in front and friendly troops in the rear. "I awaited death," he later scribbled in his journal. See William Child, *Fifth New Hampshire*, 152–53.

45. Henry, "Fredericksburg," 100. *OR*, 230, 233, 236, 238–39; December 13, 1862, Kerr Diary, FSNMP; Samuel V. Dean to his wife, December 17, 19, 1862, Dean Letters, FSNMP; Samuel Penniman Bates, *History of the Pennsylvania Volunteers*, 4:519 20. Colonel Cross later claimed both publicly and privately that several new—albeit unnamed—regiments had faltered during the fight, that officers without a scratch feigned being wounded to leave the

field, and that consequently his New Hampshire boys had suffered much higher casualties. See *OR*, 235; William Child, *Fifth New Hampshire*, 154. For a sobering account of the wounded in the 145th Pennsylvania, see Stuckenberg, *Surrounded by Methodists*, 43–44.

46. Charles Augustus Fuller, *Recollections of the War of 1861*, 78–80; *OR*, 236–38; Civil War Reminiscences, ca. 1890, 36–38, U.S. History Manuscripts, IU; *Elmira (N.Y.) Weekly Advertiser*, December 27, 1862.

47. George W. Ballock to Jenny Ballock, December 18, 1862, Ballock Papers, Duke; Uriah N. Parmelee to his mother, December 18, 1862, Parmelee Papers, Duke; William F. Fox, *Regimental Losses*, 139, 281, 301; Walker, *Second Corps*, 192; *OR*, 129, 228, 231; Mulholland, *116th Pennsylvania*, 54–55; Hancock, *Reminiscences of Winfield Scott Hancock*, 92–93; Charles Amory Clark, "Campaigning with the Sixth Maine," 416; George W. Barr to Vinnie Barr, December 21, 1862, Barr Papers, Schoff Collection, CL. In letters written home the men often detailed the exact losses in their own companies. See Levi L. Carr to his sister, December 26, 1862, Carr Letter, CWMC, USAMHI.

48. John R. Brooke to St. Clair Augustin Mulholland, January 8, 1881, Mulholland Collection, MOLLUS; Edward Porter Alexander, "Battle of Fredericksburg," 450–52; Samuel K. Zook to E. J. Wade, December 16, 1862, Zook Papers, CWMC, USAMHI; *Philadelphia Inquirer*, December 25, 1862; David M. Jordan, *Hancock*, 63; Walker, *Second Corps*, 172–74; Mulholland, "Battle of Fredericksburg," 1; William M. Owen, *In Camp and Battle with the Washington Artillery*, 195–96; *New York Times*, June 16, 1889; Alotta, *Stop the Evil*, 59; December 13, 1862, Willand Diary, NHSL; *CCW*, 1:658.

49. Favill, *Diary of a Young Officer*, 212; George C. Case to his parents, December 17, 1862, Case Letters, FSNMP; William Child, *Fifth New Hampshire*, 153; Harper, *Civil War History of Chester County, Pennsylvania*, 183–84; Borton, *On the Parallels*, 70–71, 73–74.

50. McCarter, *My Life in the Irish Brigade*, 183–86; Rodney H. Ramsey to his father, December 27, 1862, Ramsey Letter, NHHS; *OR*, 257; Gambone, *Zook*, 125. For a discussion of how people surrounded by the dead expect to be killed themselves, see Lifton, *History and Human Survival*, 159–64. Although Lifton primarily studied survivors of Hiroshima, his insights on psychological responses to death are consistent with and shed additional light on soldier experiences at Fredericksburg.

51. *New York Irish-American*, January 3, 1863; Sheldon, *"Twenty-Seventh,"* 28–30; *Philadelphia Grand Army Scout and Soldiers' Mail*, October 6, 1883; *OR*, 242–44, 250; Corby, *Memoirs of Chaplain Life*, 133; Borton, *On the Parallels*, 79; Cowtan, *Services of the Tenth New York Volunteers*, 168; Thomas Rice, "Desperate Courage," 70. Meagher's performance at Fredericksburg—hobbled by a badly bruised knee, he went back into town for a horse and missed the attack—raised some questions. How serious was the knee injury? Had he been reluctant to stand with his men? No direct evidence from Irish Brigade troops supports any imputations of cowardice. Hancock's report explicitly defended Meagher, but the sudden withdrawal of the two New York regiments is not that easy to explain. Was Meagher's report on Fredericksburg so long—over six pages in the *Official Records*—because he sought to cover up his own derelictions in a flood of verbiage? Perhaps, but the sketchy record also justifies giving the always controversial Meagher the benefit of considerable doubt. See *OR*, 228, 240–46; Burton, *Melting Pot Soldiers*, 124–25; Athearn, *Meagher*, 120; Villard, *Memoirs*, 1:371.

52. Hagerman, *Civil War and Origins of Modern Warfare*, 3–27; Griffith, *Battle Tactics of the Civil War*, 29–60, 73–90; Frank and Reaves, "Seeing the Elephant," 101–3; *OR*, ser. 3, 2: 736–37. Because the Federals also had to advance uphill (however slightly), the Confederates had geometrical and psychological advantages. See Clausewitz, *On War*, 352.

CHAPTER FIFTEEN

1. Stegeman, *These Men She Gave*, 72; Hodijah Lincoln Meade to Jane Eliza Meade, December 17, 1862, Meade Family Papers, VHS; McCreery Recollections, section 10, 1862–63, VHS;

Pendleton, "On Marye's Hill," 1; William M. Owen, *In Camp and Battle with the Washington Artillery*, 186–87.

2. *OR*, 586–87; William Henry Tatum to his brother, December 17, 1862, Tatum Papers, VHS; December 13, 1862, Duffey Diary, VHS; Edward Porter Alexander, *Fighting for the Confederacy*, 172–73, 175–76; Jennings Cropper Wise, *Long Arm of Lee*, 1:388–89; Speairs and Pettit, *Civil War Letters*, 1:78–79; Charles Minor Blackford to Mary Blackford, December 14, 1862, Blackford Family Papers, SHC. One of the guns exploded on the thirty-ninth round; the other, on the fifty-fourth round. Although Lee and Longstreet were standing nearby when one of the pieces burst, they were unharmed.

3. Sorrel, *Recollections of a Confederate Staff Officer*, 127; *OR*, 580, 592–99, 625; *B&L*, 3:81, 92; *OR Supplement*, pt. 2, 64:424–25; Wyckoff, *Second South Carolina*, 53–58; Shand Memoir, SCL; Dickert, *Kershaw's Brigade*, 183–88; *Newberry (S.C.) Herald and News*, January 3, 1902; Wyckoff, *Third South Carolina*, 86–95; Simpson and Simpson, *Far, Far from Home*, 165–67; E. R. Willis to his father, December 18, 1862, E. R. and McKibben Willis Letters, FSNMP.

4. Robert Franklin Fleming Jr., "Recollections," FSNMP; Dickert, *Kershaw's Brigade*, 203; Shand Memoir, SCL; Wyckoff, *Second South Carolina*, 56.

5. *B&L*, 3:113; *OR*, 223. Before sending Howard in, Couch reportedly transmitted a dispatch through the signal corps saying, "It is only murder now." On its face this does not sound like a message normally sent through such a channel, and the source is distinctly unfriendly to Burnside. The truth of the statement, however, is undeniable. See Walker, *Second Corps*, 175.

6. John Ripley Adams, *Memorials and Letters*, 91; Ford, *Fifteenth Regiment Massachusetts Volunteer Infantry*, 218; John A. Carpenter, *Sword and Olive Branch*, 39–40; Charles H. Howard to his mother, December 13, 1862, Brooks Collection, LC.

7. *OR*, 263, 278, 281; Banes, *Philadelphia Brigade*, 140–42; *Philadelphia Inquirer*, December 31, 1862, January 2, 1863; McDermott, *69th Pennsylvania*, 24; Samuel Penniman Bates, *History of the Pennsylvania Volunteers*, 4:148; *History of the 127th Pennsylvania*, 125–31; Gregg, *Life in the Army*, 80. The 127th Pennsylvania was also sent forward with Owen's brigade because the 71st Pennsylvania had been detached for picket duty. Howard later described meeting the wounded Col. Nelson Miles of the 61st New York who—though seated on a stretcher and holding the "lips" of his neck wound together with his fingers—offered suggestions on where to reinforce Hancock. See Howard, *Autobiography*, 1:342.

8. *OR*, 263, 284–86; Waitt, *Nineteenth Massachusetts*, 178–83; J. E. Hodgkins, *Civil War Diary*, 17–18; John Gregory Bishop Adams, *Reminiscences of the Nineteenth Massachusetts Regiment*, 53–54; Bruce, *Twentieth Massachusetts*, 215–16, 221–22; George N. Macy to "Dear Colonel," December 20, 1862, Hancock Papers, USAMHI; Gray and Ropes, *War Letters*, 55; Abbott, *Fallen Leaves*, 148–52; Miller and Mooney, *Civil War*, 92. A second lieutenant in the 19th Massachusetts was later awarded the Medal of Honor for grabbing both the regimental and national colors as a cannonball tore through the U.S. flag. See U.S. Army Department, *Medal of Honor*, 119. Given the heavy losses on December 11 in Hall's brigade, it is difficult to separate the totals for December 13, and the estimate of 500 casualties is conservative. See also the long list of officers killed or wounded in Walker, *Second Corps*, 193–95.

9. *OR*, 130, 263, 269, 274–75; *Minnesota in the Civil and Indian Wars*, 1:29–30; Imholte, *First Minnesota*, 110; Moe, *Last Full Measure*, 212–13; Chapin, *History of the Thirty-fourth Regiment*, 81–84; Ford, *Fifteenth Regiment Massachusetts Volunteer Infantry*, 229; Charles H. Eagor to his wife, December 14, 1862, Eagor Letters, Leigh Collection, USAMHI; Roland R. Bowen, *From Ball's Bluff to Gettysburg*, 141.

10. *OR*, 311, 316, 318–19, 325, 330; George Washington Whitman, *Civil War Letters*, 75–76; McCrea, *Dear Belle*, 176. Sturgis had earlier attempted to wrest command of the Ninth Corps from Willcox based on seniority. In light of this dispute it is certainly noteworthy that Sturgis's was the first division in the Ninth Corps to be sent into the bloodbath. See Orlando Willcox, *Forgotten Valor*, 396.

11. Wren, *Captain James Wren's Civil War Diary,* 108; C. L. Rundlett to his parents, January 30, 1863, Rundlett Letter, FSNMP. The accusation was also made later that Ferrero had melodramatically promised to lead the charge but then was not seen again until the guns fell silent. See Cogswell, *Eleventh New Hampshire,* 46.

12. *OR,* 326, 329; Willard J. Templeton to his sister, December 11–14, 1862, Templeton Letters, NHSL; Cogswell, *Eleventh New Hampshire,* 23–24, 45–48, 51–57, 481–82, 553–54; Paige, *Experiences in the Civil War,* 31–36; Currier, "From Concord to Fredericksburg," 254–55. Ferrero's men reportedly fired between 60 and 200 rounds each.

13. *OR,* 327; James Madison Stone, *Personal Recollections of the Civil War,* 110–12; Walcott, *Twenty-First Regiment,* 240–43, 251; *New York Times,* March 11, 1885; Stephen B. Oates, *Woman of Valor,* 113–14.

14. *History of the Thirty-Fifth Massachusetts Volunteers,* 84–90; *OR,* 328–30; Thomas H. Parker, *History of the 51st,* 268–73; Frank Moore, *Rebellion Record,* 6:102–3; December 13, 1862, Pope Diary, *CWTI,* USAMHI; James Pratt to his wife, December 16, 1862, Pratt Collection, USAMHI. On the many arm wounds and amputations, see *MSH,* 10:537, 576, 592, 705, 706, 710, 724, 752, 757, 763, 771, 976, 977, 983.

15. George Washington Whitman, *Civil War Letters,* 78–79; Edward Porter Alexander, *Military Memoirs of a Confederate,* 304–5; William M. Owen, *In Camp and Battle with the Washington Artillery,* 187–88; *OR,* 555; Berkeley, *Four Years in the Confederate Artillery,* 36–37; *Macon (Ga.) Daily Telegraph,* December 29, 1862; Lucius S. J. Owen to his mother, January 5, 1863, Owen Letters, *CWTI,* USAMHI; Jennings Cropper Wise, *Long Arm of Lee,* 1:387.

16. *OR,* 316, 319–21, 323–24; Lord, *History of the Ninth New Hampshire,* 196–97, 226–27, 243–44; Marvel, *Ninth New Hampshire,* 99–103; Tillinghast, *Twelfth Rhode Island,* 37–41, 176–78, 204–5; Bosbyshell, *48th in the War,* 97–98; Joseph Gould, *Story of the Forty-eighth,* 97–103; Joseph E. Grant, *Flying Regiment,* 48–53; Lapham, "Recollections of the Twelfth R.I. Volunteers," 27–35; December 13, 1862, Beddall Diary, CWMC, USAMHI; George Henry Chandler to "Dear William," December 18, 1862, Chandler Papers, NHHS; Jackman, *Sixth New Hampshire,* 122, 127–28; A. A. Batchelder to his parents, December 16, 1862, Batchelder Letter, FSNMP.

17. *OR,* 323; Hopkins, *Seventh Rhode Island,* 43–48, 325–26; Bliss Memoir, 4:25–30, 39, USAMHI; U.S. Army Department, *Medal of Honor,* 119; *Narragansett (R.I.) Weekly,* December 25, 1862.

18. Henry C. Heisler to his sister, December 18, 1862, Heisler Papers, LC; *OR,* 117, 129–32.

19. *OR,* 647, 662; Davidson, *Diary and Letters,* 63–65; Walter Clark, *Regiments and Battalions from North Carolina,* 1:375, 665–66, 2:170, 586.

20. *OR,* 646, 652–53, 655; Folsom, *Heroes and Martyrs of Georgia,* 149; *Augusta (Ga.) Daily Constitutionalist,* December 23, 1862, January 14, 1863; Walter Clark, *Regiments and Battalions from North Carolina,* 2:36; *Macon (Ga.) Daily Telegraph,* December 30, 31, 1862; *Atlanta Southern Confederacy,* January 13, 1862; Fitzpatrick, *Letters to Amanda,* 37. It is also important to remember that even though A. P. Hill's line had been penetrated, Brig. Gen. William B. Taliaferro's entire division was only lightly engaged. Posted behind Gregg's and Thomas's brigades, this mixture of Virginia, Louisiana, and Alabama regiments sustained a few casualties from the shelling. Bull Paxton's brigade eventually moved forward along the military road to aid Gregg's shattered command. Some of Gregg's South Carolinians appeared so demoralized that they hardly wished to be rallied, but by the time Paxton had reached them (rather tardily, according to Frank O'Reilly, the closest student of the fighting), the Yankees were more or less in full retreat. In describing their experience most soldiers stressed their continuous and terrifying exposure to Union shelling. See *OR,* 675–78, 680–87; O'Reilly, *Jackson at Fredericksburg,* 122–24; Edwin G. Lee to F. W. M. Holliday, December 22, 1862, Holliday Papers, Duke; G. R. Bedinger to his mother, December 23, 1862, Bedinger-Dandridge Family Papers, Duke; "Last Roll," 419; Samuel J. C. Moore to Ellen Moore, December 15, 1862, Samuel

.J. C. Moore Papers, SHC; Joseph W. Griggs to his father, December 19, 1862, Griggs Family Papers, VHS; December 13, 1862, Firebaugh Diary, SHC.

21. *OR*, 450, 520; Woodward, *Third Pennsylvania Reserves*, 209–10; Bates Alexander, "Seventh Regiment," December 6, 20, 1895; *Philadelphia Inquirer*, December 25, 1862; Samuel Penniman Bates, *History of the Pennsylvania Volunteers*, 85, 791; *Beaver (Pa.) Weekly Argus*, December 24, 1862; December 13, 1862, Taggart Diary, USAMHI.

22. Woodward, *Our Campaigns*, 186; Nathan Pennypacker to ?, December 19, 1862, Pennypacker Letters, Chester County Historical Society; A. J. Alexander, "Fredericksburg"; *OR*, 359. Stoneman's description also included Gibbon's forces.

23. *OR*, 664–65; William Calvin Oates, *War between Union and Confederacy*, 166–67; Early, *Narrative of the War*, 175; Henry W. Thomas, *Doles Cook Brigade*, 225; Nisbet, *Four Years on the Firing Line*, 124–25; Ujanirtus Allen, *Campaigning with "Old Stonewall,"* 194–95.

24. *OR*, 664–65; Mills Lane, *"Dear Mother: Don't Grieve about Me,"* 202. For a perceptive critique of these impetuous and piecemeal counterattacks, see Col. G. F. R. Henderson, *Civil War*, 107–8. Perhaps to palliate the behavior of his own men, Col. Clement A. Evans—who took command of the brigade after Atkinson was wounded—reported that a treacherous Yankee had pretended to surrender and had then attempted to fire at his captors before a "bayonet thrust" from a brave captain in the 33rd Georgia "prevented the intended barbarism" (*OR*, 670).

25. *CCW*, 1:705–6; *OR*, 362, 368, 373; Trobriand, *Four Years with the Army of the Potomac*, 370.

26. I have followed Gary Gallagher's lead in rendering this quotation. See Gallagher, *Fredericksburg Campaign*, vii, xii.

27. Mills Lane, *"Dear Mother: Don't Grieve about Me,"* 202; *OR*, 670–71; *Augusta (Ga.) Daily Chronicle and Sentinel*, January 15, 1863; *Savannah Republican*, January 6, 1863.

28. *OR*, 484, 671; Naisawald, *Grape and Canister*, 256–57.

29. Samuel Penniman Bates, *History of the Pennsylvania Volunteers*, 3:249–50; Ellis C. Strouss to his mother, December 19, 1862, Strouss Papers, *CWTI*, USAMHI.

30. *OR*, 362, 373–75; Edward Kalloch Gould, *Major-General Hiram Berry*, 218–19; Houghton, *Seventeenth Maine*, 28–33; *Portland (Maine) Eastern Argus*, December 27, 1862; Haley, *Rebel Yell and Yankee Hurrah*, 58–59; Petty, "History of 37th New York," 117. Other than the 5th Michigan, which actually charged toward Atkinson's men, Berry's brigade suffered only "light casualties." This phrase appears in much Civil War battle history, but in this case it still meant that more than seventy men were hit. See O'Reilly, *Jackson at Fredericksburg*, 149; *OR*, 134.

31. Crotty, *Four Years in the Army of the Potomac*, 73; *OR*, 364, 671; *OR Supplement*, pt. 1, 3:767–71; George Lewis, *First Rhode Island Light Artillery*, 129–32; Edwin Winchester Stone, *Rhode Island in the Rebellion*, 188; *Savannah Republican*, December 22, 1862; Bradwell, "Georgia Brigade at Fredericksburg," 19; *Macon (Ga.) Daily Telegraph*, January 6, 1863; *Augusta (Ga.) Daily Chronicle and Sentinel*, January 15, 1863; Gregory C. White, *31st Georgia*, 62–64; Mills Lane, *"Dear Mother: Don't Grieve about Me,"* 202.

32. *OR*, 365–67; Babcock, "114th Regiment Pennsylvania Volunteers," 1; Hagerty, *Collis' Zouaves*, 125–38; Hays, *Sixty-Third Regiment Pennsylvania Volunteers*, 165–66; Grew, *Fredericksburg*; *Philadelphia Inquirer*, December 19, 1862. Collis was later awarded the Medal of Honor for leading this timely charge. See U.S. Army Department, *Medal of Honor*, 119. Robinson's other four regiments remained behind lying in the mud supporting batteries. Although Birney later praised his division for standing firm and the new regiments for fighting well, other accounts suggested considerable straggling, including men cowering along the riverbank. See Samuel Penniman Bates, *History of the Pennsylvania Reserves*, 4:674; Scott, *One Hundred and Fifth Regiment Pennsylvania Volunteers*, 66–67; Craft, *History of the One Hundred Forty-First Pennsylvania*, 31–33, 37; *OR*, 363; James Coburn to his parents, December 17,

1862, James P. Coburn Papers, USAMHI; Bloodgood, *Personal Reminiscences of the War,* 50–52; *Kokomo (Ind.) Howard Tribune,* December 25, 1862; McCabe Memoir, 9, FSNMP; Charles Shields Wainwright, *Diary of Battle,* 144; Martin A. Haynes, *Second New Hampshire,* 145–46.

33. Gregory C. White, *31st Georgia,* 65–66; *OR,* 366, 671; *Carlisle (Pa.) Herald,* December 26, 1862; Samuel Penniman Bates, *History of the Pennsylvania Volunteers,* 2:728; Grew, *Fredericksburg.*

34. O'Reilly, *Jackson at Fredericksburg,* 167; Bradwell, "Georgia Brigade at Fredericksburg," 19–20; *Savannah Republican,* January 6, 1863; George W. Nichols, *Soldier's Story of His Regiment,* 60–61.

35. *CCW,* 1:715–16; Gibbon, *Recollections of the Civil War,* 104; *OR,* 459, 480, 482, 484, 487–88, 492, 499, 501, and ser. 1, 51(1):172; Charles Shields Wainwright, *Diary of Battle,* 143; Samuel Penniman Bates, *History of the Pennsylvania Volunteers,* 5:153–54; McClenthen, *Narrative of the Fall and Winter Campaign,* 39–41; McCreery Recollections, section 10, 1862–63, VHS; Kress, *Memoirs,* 4; James B. Thomas, *Civil War Letters,* 127–30; Isaac Tichenor to Michael Leonard, March 17, 1893, Tichenor Letters, FSNMP; Vautier, *88th Pennsylvania,* 91. For a careful analysis of the complex tactics, again see O'Reilly, *Jackson at Fredericksburg,* 159–65.

36. Small, *Road to Richmond,* 67; December 13, 1862, Brown Diary, CWMC, USAMHI; *OR,* 138; Small, *Sixteenth Maine,* 66–67; Samuel C. Starrett to his father, December 24, 1862, Starrett Letter, FSNMP.

37. McClendon, *Recollections of War Times,* 62; William Alexander Smith, *Anson Guards,* 168; W. R. M. Slaughter to his sister, January 4, 1863, Slaughter Letters, VHS; Trobriand, *Four Years with the Army of the Potomac,* 370–71.

38. *OR,* 92–94.

39. *OR,* 93–94, 111, 118–19, 128, 450, and ser. 1, 51(1):1020–21. *CCW,* 1:709–11; William B. Franklin to George G. Meade, April 1, 1863, Meade Papers, HSP; Woodbury, *Burnside and the Ninth Army Corps,* 221–22. Birney believed there was still more than enough time for Franklin to have launched another assault on the Confederate left. See *CCW,* 1:707. Even Burnside's critics have questioned Franklin's performance. See Palfrey, *Antietam and Fredericksburg,* 174–82; Kenneth P. Williams, *Lincoln Finds a General,* 2:531–32. It is difficult to defend Franklin's actions on December 13, but a case can certainly be made against an attack by his rather widely scattered forces. See Whan, *Fiasco at Fredericksburg,* 71–72, 133; Warren W. Hassler, *Commanders of the Army of the Potomac,* 166; William Allan, *Army of Northern Virginia,* 508–9. For the closest analysis of the orders, see Marvel, *Burnside,* 191–92. Why Burnside dispatched staff officers with orders rather than using the telegraph wire from the Phillips House to Franklin's headquarters is a mystery. There was apparently confusion at the time when the wire was strung, and the contemporary evidence is uncertain and contradictory. See *OR Supplement,* pt. 1, 10:446–47; Plum, *Military Telegraph,* 1:335–36; *OR,* 153–54, 157–59; Cushing, "Acting Signal Corps," 103.

40. *OR,* 462, 476; Marvel, *First New Hampshire Battery,* 26–28; McKelvey, *Rochester in the Civil War,* 114–15; December 13, 1862, Holford Diary, LC; Lucius B. Shattuck to "Dear Ellen," December 11–13, 1862, Shattuck Letters, MHC; William Speed to Charlotte Speed, December 29, 1862, Speed Papers, Schoff Collection, CL; Vaclav Dusek to his parents, December 1862, Dusek Reminiscence, FSNMP; Gaff, *On Many a Bloody Field,* 210; Partridge, *Letters from the Iron Brigade,* 68.

41. Smithe, *Glimpses of Places, and People, and Things,* 32–33; *Watertown (N.Y.) Daily News and Reformer,* December 26, 1862; Virgil W. Mattoon to his mother, December 10–15, 1862, Mattoon Papers, CHS; Gates, *"Ulster Guard,"* 524–25; Dexter, *Seymour Dexter,* 117; John Lucas Harding to his father, December 16, 1862, Harding Manuscripts, IU; Abram P. Smith, *Seventy-Sixth New York,* 188–92; Orville Thomson, *Seventh Indiana,* 143.

42. *CCW,* 1:709; *OR,* 523–24, 647; Walter Clark, *Regiments and Battalions from North Carolina,* 4:169–70; O'Reilly, *Jackson at Fredericksburg,* 168–69; Samuel B. Fisher to his sister,

December 18, 1862, Fisher Letters, Leigh Collection, USAMHI; *OR Supplement,* pt. 2, 40:47. After crossing the railroad and running into Confederate reinforcements, Hatch was hit in the right thigh. He died after an amputation; his last recorded words were "Tell my friends I charged upon that Railroad and took it." See *MSH,* 11:237; *Newark (N.J.) Daily Advertiser,* December 26, 1862.

43. *OR,* 622–24; Confederate Soldier Reminiscence, "My War Story," NCDAH; Hatton, "Gen. Archibald Campbell Goodwin," 134; William H. Clairville to Mary Clairville, December 17, 1862, Clairville Papers, Rutgers University; Walter Clark, *Regiments and Battalions from North Carolina,* 3:268–69, 406–9; J. W. Armsworthy to his wife, December 18, 1862, January 12, 1863, Armsworthy Letters, FSNMP.

44. Baquet, *History of the 1st New Jersey,* 225–28; *OR,* 140–41, 528, 558; Foster, *New Jersey and the Rebellion,* 95–96, 505–6; Henry Odgen Ryerson to his sister, December 23, 1862, Anderson Family Papers, NJHS; Haines, *15th New Jersey,* 31–33; Polley, *Hood's Texas Brigade,* 139; Walter Clark, *Regiments and Battalions from North Carolina,* 1:309; Kenneth W. Jones, "Fourth Alabama Infantry," 200–201; Wagner, *Letters of William F. Wagner,* 26–27. The Sixth Corps' medical director reported 457 casualties of 22,000 effectives. See *MSH,* 2:134.

45. Hugh Roden to his family, November 19, 1862, Roden's Papers, William L. Goodman, UL, CCW, 1:766–7; *OR,* 360, 378–79, 383; O'Reilly, *Jackson at Fredericksburg,* 172–73; *OR Supplement,* pt. 1, 3:718–19; *Elizabeth New Jersey Journal,* January 6, 1863; December 13, 1862, Charles P. Perkins Diary, CWTI, USAMHI.

46. Samuel Penniman Bates, *History of the Pennsylvania Volunteers,* 5:386; Dexter E. Buell, *Company B, 27th New York,* 16; George H. Mellish to his mother, January 2, 1863, Mellish Papers, HL; Woodbury, *Second Rhode Island,* 132; John S. Bumps to his mother, December 19, 1862, Hunter Family Papers, CWMC, USAMHI.

47. Bicknell, *History of the Fifth Maine,* 173; *Newark (N.J.) Daily Advertiser,* December 30, 1862; *OR,* 531–32; Samuel Penniman Bates, *History of the Pennsylvania Volunteers,* 7:1; *Philadelphia Inquirer,* December 27, 1862; Sanford McCall to his niece, December 17, 1862, McCall Letters, Western Michigan University.

48. George Chandler to his father, December 25, 1862, Chandler Letters, FSNMP; Siegel, *For the Glory of the Union,* 109–11; Evan Rowland Jones, *Four Years in the Army of the Potomac,* 100–101; John Southard to his sister, December 22, 1862, Southard Family Papers, NYHS; *Pittsfield (Mass.) Sun,* January 1, 1863; Morton Hayward to his sister, December 19, 1862, Hayward Letters, Leigh Collection, USAMHI; *Fourth Annual Report of the Bureau of Military Statistics,* 580; William P. Carmany to his brother and sister, December 19, 1862, Carmany Papers, Schoff Collection, CL; Tyler, *Recollections of the Civil War,* 65; Sanford Truesdale to his sister, December 17, 1862, Truesdale Papers, University of Chicago; Joseph Bloomfield Osborn to Joseph M. Osborn, December 18, 1862, Osborn Papers, LC. When some black servants joined the 20th New York behind an embankment, white officers and men drove them away with bayonets. "Let the damned nigger[s] be killed—how dare they come here among white men," one fellow shouted. See George E. Stephens, *Voice of Thunder,* 215.

49. Mundy, *No Rich Men's Sons,* 100; *Albany (N.Y.) Atlas and Argus,* December 23, 1862; *Albany (N.Y.) Evening Journal,* December 23, 1862; *MSH,* 12:735; Best, *History of the 121st New York,* 42–43; James Lorenzo Bowen, *Thirty-Seventh Regiment,* 112–13; December 13, 1862, Taylor Diary, FSNMP; Howard Thomas, *Boys in Blue from the Adirondack Foothills,* 113; *Fifth Annual Report of the Bureau of Military Statistics,* 723–25. Burns's division, which had relieved the Sixth Corps guarding the bridges, also came under fire but, even worse, had to watch the terrible slaughter throughout the day. Before crossing Deep Run, the men had witnessed the first charges on the stone wall and now feared joining the fight themselves. "The anxiety and mental suffering I experienced during the day and night was the worst I ever passed through," wrote one assistant surgeon. Some men kept springing to their feet in expectation of heading into action. Despite several close calls, the entire division had suffered only twenty-seven

casualties. See *OR,* 132; Cutcheon Autobiography, MHC; Joseph P. Vickers to his parents, December 16, 1862, Vickers Letter, FSNMP; Haydon, *For Country, Cause, and Leader,* 297–98; George B. Felch to his father, December 15, 1862, Felch Letters, FSNMP.

50. Hagerman, *Civil War and Origins of Modern Warfare,* 6–13; Royster, *Destructive War,* 34–47, 68–78; Clausewitz, *On War,* 206, 370; Cooke, *Jackson,* 232; Dabney, *Jackson,* 619–21. Jackson would have undoubtedly agreed with Clausewitz that tactical success leads to strategic victory. See Clausewitz, *On War,* 228.

51. Daniel E. Sutherland, *Fredericksburg and Chancellorsville,* 59; *OR,* 638–40; Poague, *Gunner with Stonewall,* 55–59; Driver, *1st and 2nd Rockbridge Artillery,* 34–36; Jennings Cropper Wise, *Long Arm of Lee,* 1:391–92; O'Reilly, *Jackson at Fredericksburg,* 175–76.

52. Orson Blair Curtis, *History of the Twenty-Fourth Michigan,* 93–94; William Speed to Charlotte Speed, December 15, 1862, Speed Papers, Schoff Collection, CL; John Wesley St. Clair to his family, December 17, 1862, St. Clair Letters, SHSW; Dawes, *Sixth Wisconsin,* 110–11; John Harrison Mills, *Chronicles of the Twenty-First New York,* 276–79; Henry F. Young to his father, December 17, 1862, Young Papers, SHSW; *OR Supplement,* pt. 1, 3:690–94; *OR,* 474–75.

53. Clausewitz, *On War,* 526; Caldwell, *History of a Brigade of South Carolinians,* 61; James I. Robertson Jr., *Jackson,* 660–61; Hotchkiss, *Make Me a Map of the Valley,* 100; *OR,* 647, 652, 666, 687; Early, *Narrative of the War,* 176–78; O'Reilly, *Jackson at Fredericksburg,* 176–77. A ferocious fighter, Hood later claimed he was ready to advance when Jackson's orders were countermanded. In his official report Longstreet praised the late afternoon charge of Law's brigade, but controversy later erupted about Hood's apparent passivity. Pickett supposedly suggested a flank attack against Franklin's right. Longstreet claimed that such a move would have been consistent with the day's orders and would have brought destruction of Burnside's army. But in light of the Confederate victory, Longstreet did not press the matter of Hood's negligence. The evidence does suggest that Hood was behaving with what was for him unusual caution on December 13, but how much his men might have accomplished is doubtful, given the strength of Franklin's reserves. See Hood, *Advance and Retreat,* 49–50; *OR,* 570; Walter Harrison, *Pickett's Men,* 71–72; Longstreet, *From Manassas to Appomattox,* 317; B&L, 3: 84; *OR Supplement,* pt. 1, 3:804–5.

54. Von Borcke, *Memoirs of the Confederate War,* 2:128–30; Cooke, "Right at Fredericksburg," 1; Vivian Minor Fleming Reminiscence, 22–23, FSNMP; L. Minor Blackford, *Mine Eyes Have Seen the Glory,* 209–10; Charles Minor Blackford to Mary Blackford, January 12, 1863, Blackford Family Papers, SHC.

55. O'Reilly, *Jackson at Fredericksburg,* 178–80; *OR,* 360, 463, 634; *OR Supplement,* pt. 1, 3:693; W. R. M. Slaughter to his sister, January 4, 1863, Slaughter Letters, VHS; Edward Hall Armstrong to his father, December 18, 1862, Armstrong Letter, Duke; Norman, *Portion of My Life,* 156–57; Hubbell, *Confederate Stamps, Old Letters, and History,* appendix, 8; December 13, 1862, Pickens Diary, UA.

56. *OR,* 558–62.

57. Spencer, *Civil War Marriage in Virginia,* 150.

CHAPTER SIXTEEN

1. Herman Haupt to his wife, December 13, 1862, Haupt Letterbook, Haupt Papers, LC; Clausewitz, *On War,* 102, 106, 190, 211, 240; Keegan, *Face of Battle,* 106; Marvel, *Burnside,* 192–93.

2. *CCW,* 1:667; Daniel Reed Larned, Pencil Notes on the Battle of Fredericksburg, December 11–15, 1862, Larned Papers, LC; *OR,* 95, 356–57. Only old Sumner remained steadfast. In fact, Burnside and several staff officers worried that he might impetuously cross the river to personally join one of the assaulting columns. See Whittier, "Comments on the Peninsular Campaign," 288–89; Sanford, *Fighting Rebels and Redskins,* 192–93.

3. *OR*, 95, 356; *CCW*, 1:667, 669–70, 723–25; *B&L*, 3:114; Stine, *Army of the Potomac*, 289–90; Sanford, *Fighting Rebels and Redskins*, 193.

4. *OR*, 399, 404–5; Robert Goldthwaite Carter, *Four Brothers in Blue*, 213; George M. Barnard to his father, December 16, 1862, Barnard Papers, MHS. It is worth noting that Butterfield had written about the shock value of assault tactics in battle. See Hagerman, *Civil War and Origins of Modern Warfare*, 19–20. After the meeting with Burnside, Hooker brought several batteries across the river. But the artillery already in town had been firing for several hours with little effect, and the battery commanders appeared more interested in protecting their guns from Rebel shells than in attacking the Confederate positions. Only seven of nineteen batteries attached to Sumner's grand division went into action. See *CCW*, 1:667; Naisawald, *Grape and Canister*, 246; *OR*, 183, 193; *OR Supplement*, pt. 2, 3:742–43, 745–46.

5. *OR*, 72, 116, 162, 404–5. Ironically, some Pennsylvania soldiers in Griffin's division had played euchre that morning while waiting to cross the river. See John L. Smith, *118th Pennsylvania*, 120–21.

6. *OR*, 408–9; Powell, *Fifth Corps*, 388–89n; John Lord Parker, *Twenty-Second Massachusetts*, 225–26; Everson, "Forward Against Marye's Heights," 1; William W. Hemmenway "Reminiscence," CWII, USAMHI; George M. Barnard to his father, December 16, 1862, Barnard Papers, MHS.

7. Despite using some cavalry and four infantry companies, General Patrick could not clear the town of looters. See Marsena Rudolph Patrick, *Inside Lincoln's Army*, 189.

8. John L. Smith, *118th Pennsylvania*, 122–25; Samuel Penniman Bates, *History of the Pennsylvania Volunteers*, 6:1311; J. L. Smith to "Dear Mother," December 26, 1862, John L. Smith Letters, FSNMP; Donaldson, *Inside the Army of the Potomac*, 179–89.

9. John Lord Parker, *Twenty-Second Massachusetts*, 224–28; Edwin C. Bennett, *Musket and Sword*, 114–17; Robert Goldthwaite Carter, *Four Brothers in Blue*, 194–97, 206–9; *Rochester (N.Y.) Daily Union and Advertiser*, December 20, 26, 1862; *Rochester (N.Y.) Daily Democrat and American*, December 22, 1862; Mundy, *2d Maine*, 216–18. The brigade suffered some 500 casualties. See *OR*, 135.

10. *OR*, 570–71, and ser. 1, 51(1):174–75.

11. William M. Owen, *In Camp and Battle with the Washington Artillery*, 188–94; Boggs, *Alexander Letters*, 244–45; *B&L*, 3:93; *OR*, 576; Krick, *Parker's Virginia Battery*, 99–100; Edward Porter Alexander, "Battle of Fredericksburg," 545–55; Dickert, *Kershaw's Brigade*, 188–89.

12. *OR*, 407–8; *History of the Fifth Massachusetts Battery*, 496–510; Waugh, "Reminiscences," FSNMP.

13. *OR*, 185, 267–68, 580–81; *OR Supplement*, pt. 1, 3:764–65, Walker, *Second Corps*, 177–79; John H. Rhodes, *History of Battery B*, 139–40; Chester F. Hunt to his mother, December 19, 1862, Hunt Letter, USAMHI; *Providence (R.I.) Daily Journal*, December 24, 1862; Henry Ropes to "Dear John," December 20, 1862, Ropes Letters, Boston Public Library.

14. *OR*, 311, 393, 397; Samuel Penniman Bates, *History of the Pennsylvania Volunteers*, 4:1310; Joseph H. Leighty to his sister, December 26, 1862, Leighty Papers, CWMC, USAMHI; James Crowther to his sister, December 28, 1862, GAR.

15. *OR*, 405, 410; Zerah Coston Monks to Hannah T. Rohrer, December 17, 1862, Monks-Rohrer Letters, Emory; Guiney, *Command Boston's Irish Ninth*, 154–55; McNamara, *History of the Ninth Massachusetts*, 254–59; Samuel Penniman Bates, *History of the Pennsylvania Volunteers*, 3:455–56; George H. Nichols to his mother, December 14, 1862, Nichols Letters, Schoff Collection, CL; Francis Jewett Parker, *Thirty-Second Massachusetts*, 129–32; *Albany (N.Y.) Evening Journal*, December 20, 1862; Haerrer, *With Drum and Gun in '61*, 87; December 13, 1862, Bancroft Diary, MHC.

16. See the older but cogent critique of these assault tactics in Col. G. F. R. Henderson, *Civil War*, 91–93.

17. *OR*, 411–13; Melcher, *With a Flash of His Sword,* 11–13; Chamberlain, *Through Blood and Fire,* 38–40; Chamberlain, "My Story of Fredericksburg," 152–53; Gerrish, *Reminiscences of the War,* 76–78; December 13, 1862, Berry Diary, *CWTI,* USAMHI; Samuel Penniman Bates, *History of the Pennsylvania Volunteers,* 4:1253; Simonton, "Recollections of Fredericksburg," 252–54; *Brunswick (Maine) Telegraph,* January 2, 1863; Judson, *Eighty-third Pennsylvania,* 101–5.

18. Anthony G. Graves to his father, December 19, 1862, Graves Letters, FSNMP; Nash, *Forty-fourth New York,* 115; *MSH,* 10:710, 711, 730, 920, 11:268, 285, 303, 12:472, 482, 798.

19. Orwig, *131st Pennsylvania,* 113–14; *Under the Maltese Cross,* 95; *OR,* 72, 116, 223–24; *New York Times,* December 17, 1862; *B&L,* 3:114–15. In examining the performance of Humphreys's division, I have relied heavily on Reardon, "Forlorn Hope," 80–112.

20. *OR,* 223–24, 399, 430–31; Carswell McClellan, *General Humphreys at Malvern Hill and Fredericksburg,* 10–15; *Under the Maltese Cross,* 537; Nathaniel W. Brown to Albert M. Given, December 23, 1862, Brown Letter, FSNMP; Beidelman, *Letters of George Washington Beidelman,* 167.

21. Humphreys, *Andrew Atkinson Humphreys,* 178–80; "The Battle of Fredericksburg," *Harper's Weekly,* January 10, 1863, 17; *Under the Maltese Cross,* 96–98; Hartsock, *Soldier of the Cross,* 38. Nearly a quarter-century later, of course, he considered the whole attack "a very great mistake." See Humphreys, *Humphreys at Fredericksburg,* 27.

22. *OR,* 431; Kerbey, *On the War-Path,* 145–46. A member of the 131st Pennsylvania later described Mexican War veteran Allabach as having "an eye like an eagle . . . the finest looking officer I ever saw. He was a brave man, a great soul" (Hutchison, "Fredericksburg," 271).

23. *OR,* 443–48; Samuel Penniman Bates, *History of the Pennsylvania Volunteers,* 4:225–26; December 13, 1862, Cavada Diary, HSP; Hartsock, *Soldier of the Cross,* 39; Nathaniel W. Brown to Albert M. Given, December 23, 1862, Brown Letter, FSNMP; Orwig, *131st Pennsylvania,* 115–18.

24. Helman, "Young Soldier in the Army of the Potomac," 154; *OR,* 74, 132; Humphreys, *Humphreys at Fredericksburg,* 12–13. Partisans of the Second Corps hotly denied that their men posed any serious obstacle or tried to discourage Humphreys's men, and heated postwar controversy eventually erupted. See Walker, *Second Corps,* 181–87; Carswell McClellan, *General Humphreys at Malvern Hill and Fredericksburg,* 23–24.

25. Jennings Cropper Wise, *Long Arm of Lee,* 1:396–97; Edward Porter Alexander, *Fighting for the Confederacy,* 177–79; [Heinichen,] "Fredericksburg," Maryland Historical Society; Longstreet, *From Manassas to Appomattox,* 312–13; *OR,* 590; Shand Memoir, SCL. Porter Alexander later described Humphreys's late afternoon charge as "utterly hopeless" but representing a "high type of disciplined valor" (Edward Porter Alexander, *Military Memoirs of a Confederate,* 307). As the double-shotted canister devastated Humphreys's regiments, one survivor from an earlier assault reportedly commented, "Great gods, if only one of those shells would take Burnside on the head" (Kepler, *Fourth Ohio,* 98).

26. Nathaniel W. Brown to Albert M. Given, December 23, 1862, Brown Letter, FSNMP; *OR,* 431; W. C. Ward, "Unable to Help," 3; John C. Anderson to his family, January 10, 1863, Anderson Letter, FSNMP. At the same time, Humphreys shifted Tyler's brigade to the left of Hanover Street in preparation for these troops to join the assault. See *OR,* 431. Less than a month before the battle, a pious lady had written to Humphreys warning that the general's reputation as a "profane swearer" placed not only his own soul at risk but the army's fate as well. Humphreys replied after Fredericksburg that he never swore at the Almighty, only at his fellow man. See J. D. Mather to Humphreys, November 19, 1862, and Humphreys to Mather, January 1, 1863, Humphreys Papers, HSP.

27. *OR,* 432, 444–48; Orwig, *131st Pennsylvania,* 118–19; *Under the Maltese Cross,* 101, 539–40; December 13, 1862, Cavada Diary, HSP; Nathaniel W. Brown to Albert M. Given, December 23, 1862, Brown Letter, FSNMP.

28. Carswell McClellan, *General Humphreys at Malvern Hill and Fredericksburg,* 20–23; *Philadelphia Inquirer,* December 18, 1862; *OR,* 74, 275, 437, 439–40; Werkheiser Memoir, 9–10, FSNMP; Rowe, *Sketch of the 126th Pennsylvania,* 15–18.

29. Welsh and Welsh, "Civil War Letters from Two Brothers," 156–59; *OR,* 437, 440; Samuel Penniman Bates, *History of the Pennsylvania Volunteers,* 4:128–29; December 13, 1862, Cavada Diary, HSP; William O. Campbell Memoir, 8–9, FSNMP; John Phillips to his family, December 18, 1862, Phillips Letters, FSNMP; Rowe, *Sketch of the 126th Pennsylvania,* 18–19; Werkheiser Memoir, 12–13, FSNMP.

30. Humphreys, *Andrew Atkinson Humphreys,* 180; Hutchison, "Fredericksburg," 268–69; *OR,* 137, 440–41; Samuel Penniman Bates, *History of the Pennsylvania Volunteers,* 4:185, 225–26, 283, 8:802; *Philadelphia Inquirer,* December 18, 1862; Hartsock, *Soldier of the Cross,* 39–42; List of killed and wounded in Humphreys's division, December 16, 1862, Humphreys Papers, HSP. At least nineteen of the seriously wounded men in the division later died after amputations. See *MSH,* 11:47, 239, 262, 266, 270, 271, 303, 380–81, 12:490, 504, 511, 518, 526, 747, 793, 798.

31. *OR,* 312, 332, 338–39; Marvel, *Burnside,* 195; Wightman, *From Antietam to Fort Fisher* 89–90; John England to Ellen Hargeddon, December 17, 1862, England Papers, NYPL

32. *OR,* 332–33, 344; [?] December 13, 1862, Harvey Henderson Diary, FSNMP; *OR Supplement,* pt. 2, 42:773.

33. *OR,* 332, 335–37, 343–47; Kimball, *Company I, 103 N.Y.S.V.,* 117; Joseph H. Haynes to his father, December 21, 1862, Haynes Papers, Duke. For a good description of how Confederate artillery responded to Getty's assault, see Edward Porter Alexander, *Fighting for the Confederacy,* 179.

34. R. P. Staniels to "My Darling Selina," December 16, 1862, Staniels Letter, FSNMP; *OR,* 338, 340–41; Henry H. Holt to Luther Eaton, December 17, 1862, Holt Letters, Leigh Collection, USAMHI; S. Millett Thompson, *Thirteenth New Hampshire,* 45–62, 65–69, 94; Aaron F. Stevens to "Dear kindred and friends," January 5, 1863, Aaron F. Stevens Papers, NHHS; Charles F. Stinson to his mother, December 17, 1862, Stinson Letters, USAMHI; Ephraim Jackson to "Dear Brother and Sister," December 13, 1862, Jackson Letters, FSNMP; *Portsmouth (N.H.) Daily Morning Chronicle,* December 29, 1862; Aaron K. Blake to his sister, December 18, 1862, Blake Letters, CWMC, USAMHI.

35. *OR,* 332–33, 348, 352–54; Gallup, "Connecticut Yankee at Fredericksburg," 203; Henry Lewis to "Dear Cousin Charlie," January 3, 1863, Lewis Letters, GLC; *Providence (R.I.) Daily Journal,* December 27, 1862; Lewis Nettleton to "My own dear love," January 18, 1863, Nettleton-Baldwin Family Papers, Duke; Henry Grimes Marshall to Hattie Marshall, December 14, 1862, Marshall Papers, Schoff Collection, CL; Henry J. H. Thompson to Lucretia Thompson, December 11–15, 19, 1862, Thompson Papers, Duke; Asaph R. Tyler to his wife, December 15, 1862, Tyler Letters, FSNMP.

36. *OR,* 116–17, 336, 357, 415, 418–22, 424–25; *CCW,* 1:668–69; Powell, *Fifth Corps,* 387–88; John D. Wilkins to his wife, December 15, 18, 1862, Wilkins Papers, Schoff Collection, CL; Charles Thomas Bowen to his wife, December 18, 1862, Bowen Letter, FSNMP; Anderson, "Civil War Recollections of the Twelfth Infantry," 391; Thomas H. Evans, "'Cries of the Wounded,'" 30–31. Howard's men complained that Humphreys's retreating troops were little more than a "mob." Like most of the withdrawals that day, this one was disorderly. Isolated regiments remained in position only to discover that the rest of the brigade had slipped back into town. "We returned tired, forsaken, and dispirited," one member of the 155th Pennsylvania wrote. "Our bands mournfully filling the air with requiems for the dead." See Beidelman, *Letters of George Washington Beidelman,* 168; *OR,* 74, 278–79, 432; Welsh and Welsh, "Civil War Letters from Two Brothers," 156–57; *Under the Maltese Cross,* 102–3; Reardon, "Forlorn Hope," 80, 98. In Sykes's division Brig. Gen. Gouverneur Kemble Warren's brigade of New Yorkers remained in reserve behind Buchanan and Andrews. Even these men suffered from

Rebel shells. See *Rochester (N.Y.) Daily Union and Advertiser,* December 27, 1862; *Rochester (N.Y.) Daily Democrat and American,* December 27, 1862; McKelvey, *Rochester in the Civil War,* 203–4.

37. Daniel Reed Larned to "My Dear Henry," December 16, 1862, Larned Papers, LC; John Smart to Ann Smart, December 13, 1862, Smart Letters, FSNMP; Bicknell, *History of the Fifth Maine,* 177; Hitchcock, *War from the Inside,* 127; Walcott, *Twenty-First Regiment,* 244–45; Werkheiser Memoir, 13–15, FSNMP; *History of the Thirty-Fifth Massachusetts Volunteers,* 90; *Annals of the War,* 261.

38. Reuben Kelley to his sister, January 8, 1863, Kelley Letters, FSNMP; Thomas H. Evans, "'Cries of the Wounded,'" 32; David V. Lovell to his sister, December 19, 1862, Lovell Letter, Gregory A. Coco Collection, USAMHI; Brogan, *American Civil War,* 97; Scott, *One Hundred and Fifth Regiment Pennsylvania Volunteers,* 67; Isaac Morrow to his brother, December 21, 1862, Morrow Papers, HCWRTC, USAMHI; Houghton, *Seventeenth Maine,* 33; *Annals of the War,* 264; McKelvey, *Rochester in the Civil War,* 204. To some men on both sides, the sounds of the wounded horses seemed almost worse than the soldiers' cries, a phenomenon also observed in the Napoleonic wars. See *History of 127th Regiment Pennsylvania Volunteers,* 133; Brett Memoir, 14, FSNMP; Keegan, *Face of Battle,* 201–2.

39. Grimes, *Extracts of Letters,* 25; Riggs, *13th Virginia,* 28; *Fredericksburg Free Lance,* December 24, 1910; Sanford W. Branch to his mother, December 17, 1862, Sexton Collection, UG; Dickert, *Kershaw's Brigade,* 196–97; Benson, *Berry Benson's Civil War Book,* 33; Ujanirtus Allen, *Campaigning with "Old Stonewall,"* 197; Hunter, *Johnny Reb and Billy Yank,* 316; *New York Herald,* December 17, 1862. On the limits of humans' ability to close the mind to such horrors, see Lifton, *History and Human Survival,* 153–54.

40. Mundy, *2nd Maine,* 219; S. Millett Thompson, *Thirteenth New Hampshire,* 69; Jackman, *Sixth New Hampshire,* 125–26; *Annals of the War,* 261; Hartsock, *Soldier of the Cross,* 42; December 13, 1862, Taylor Diary, FSNMP.

41. Robert Goldthwaite Carter, *Four Brothers in Blue,* 198; Amos Hadley, *Life of Walter Harriman,* 132; *New York Tribune,* December 27, 1862; Peter Welsh, *Irish Green and Union Blue,* 46; *New York Irish-American,* December 27, 1862; Kepler, *Fourth Ohio,* 97–98; Robert S. Roberston, "Diary of the War," 75; *MSH,* 2:102. One badly wounded soldier, who apparently feared being taken prisoner, mistook approaching Federals for Confederates and committed suicide. See Thomas H. Evans, "'Cries of the Wounded,'" 33.

42. McCarter, *My Life in the Irish Brigade,* 189–95.

43. *Annals of the War,* 262; *MSH,* 2:102, 131; Mulholland, *116th Pennsylvania,* 52–53; Haines, *15th New Jersey,* 35; Gordon Willis Jones, "Medical History of the Fredericksburg Campaign," 251–52; *OR,* 163; Letterman, *Medical Recollections of the Army of the Potomac,* 73; William Child, *Fifth New Hampshire,* 163. One surgeon complained that some amputations were so poorly performed that a second operation was then required, though given the numbers of wounded and the conditions in the buildings, that is hardly surprising. See Castleman, *Army of the Potomac,* 262.

44. Bardeen, *Little Fifer's Diary,* 122–23; Duncan, *Medical Department of the United States Army,* 191; Mulholland, *116th Pennsylvania,* 52–53; Castleman, *Army of the Potomac,* 262; Abraham Welch to his sister, December 27, 1862, Welch Letter, SHC. Although the cramped quarters and time of year made Fredericksburg distinctive from most other Civil War engagements, the experiences of the wounded on the field and their first hours in the hospitals fell into a familiar pattern. See Hess, *Union Soldier in Battle,* 32–37.

45. Keegan, *Face of Battle,* 195–97; Melcher, *With a Flash of His Sword,* 13–14; George M. Barnard to his father, December 16, 1862, Barnard Papers, MHS; John W. Ames to his mother, December 15, 1862, Ames Papers, USAMHI; Kerbey, *On the War-Path,* 155; *Baltimore American and Commercial Advertiser,* January 2, 1863.

46. Simonton, "Recollections of Fredericksburg," 254; Brainard, *One Hundred and Forty-*

sixth New York, 36; Henry Lewis to "Dear Cousin Charlie," January 3, 1863, Lewis Letters, GLC; Joseph Bloomfield Osborn to Joseph M. Osborn, December 18, 1862, Osborn Papers, LC; Thomas H. Evans, "'Cries of the Wounded,'" 32; *Albany (N.Y.) Atlas and Argus,* January 1, 1863; Davenport, *Fifth New York Volunteer Infantry,* 345.

47. *OR,* 65, 73, and ser. 1, 51(1):1025; *CCW,* 1:653, 709; William Teall to his wife, December 13, 1862, Teall Letters, TSLA; *B&L,* 3:117, 127, 137. Franklin later vaguely informed McClellan that he had supported Burnside's plan even though Sumner and Hooker appeared "demoralized." See Franklin to McClellan, December 23, 1862, McClellan Papers, LC.

48. Longstreet, *From Manassas to Appomattox,* 316; *OR,* 546, 555, and ser. 1, 51(2):662; Clausewitz, *On War,* 258, 263. Stuart and Hood may have argued that the Federals were whipped and would not attack, but the evidence on this is doubtful. See Henry Kyd Douglas, *I Rode with Stonewall,* 205–6; Hood, *Advance and Retreat,* 50; Cooke, "Right at Fredericksburg," 1. Jackson's most careful biographer has raised doubts about the oft-told tale of Jackson dozing off during the meeting, suddenly awakening, and declaring the Confederates should drive the Yankees into the river. See James I. Robertson Jr., *Jackson,* 662.

49. *OR,* 566, and ser. 1, 51(2):662, Longstreet, *From Manassas to Appomattox,* 316; Hagerman, *Civil War and Origins of Modern Warfare,* 123; Wyckoff, *Second South Carolina,* 81–82, Caldwell, *History of a Brigade of South Carolinians,* 65; McNamara, *History of the Ninth Massachusetts,* 261; Jennings Cropper Wise, *Long Arm of Lee,* 1:397–98; G. M. Sorrel to Edward Porter Alexander, December 13, 1862 (two dispatches), Alexander Papers, SHC.

50. S. G. Pryor, *Post of Honor,* 299; Charles Minor Blackford to Mary Blackford, December 14, 1862, Blackford Family Papers, SHC; Handerson, *Yankee in Gray,* 53–54; Charles, "Events in Battle of Fredericksburg," 67; December 13, 1862, Wise Diary, Duke.

51. *Johnstown (Pa.) Cambria Tribune,* December 26, 1862; Samuel K. Zook to E. J. Wade, December 16, 1862, Zook Papers, CWMC, USAMHI.

CHAPTER SEVENTEEN

1. John Worthington Ames, "Under Fire," 432; A. A. Batchelder to his parents, December 16, 1862, Batchelder Letter, FSNMP; Sprenger, *122d Regiment,* 144–45; Musgrove, *Autobiography of Captain Richard Musgrove,* 50; Samuel Edmund Nichols, *"Your Soldier Boy Samuel,"* 58; Thomas Bowen to his wife, December 18, 1862, Bowen Letter, FSNMP.

2. *History of the Fifth Massachusetts Battery,* 508; Ted Alexander, *126th Pennsylvania,* 130; W. C. Ward, "Unable to Help," 3; *Lancaster (Pa.) Daily Evening Express,* December 23, 1862; Brian A. Bennett, *140th New York,* 108–9.

3. Thomas Bowen to his wife, December 18, 1862, Bowen Letter, FSNMP; Weygant, *One Hundred and Twenty-Fourth Regiment,* 71–72; Sim Siggins to Hannah T. Rohrer, December 22, 1862, Monks-Rohrer Letters, Emory; *Under the Maltese Cross,* 108–10; Aaron K. Blake to his sister, December 15, 1862, Blake Letters, CWMC, USAMHI.

4. *Story of the Twenty-first Connecticut,* 73–74; Thorpe, *Fifteenth Connecticut Volunteers,* 36–37; Aaron F. Stevens to his family, January 5, 1863, Aaron F. Stevens Papers, NHHS; John Godfrey to Horace Godfrey, December 14, 1862, Godfrey Papers, NHHS; Castleman, *Army of the Potomac,* 263–64; *History of the Thirty-Fifth Massachusetts Volunteers,* 90–91.

5. December 14, 1862, Charles S. Granger Diary, CWMC, USAMHI; December 14, 1862, Pope Diary, CWTI, USAMHI; Washburn, *108th Regiment,* 113; Lusk, *War Letters of William Thompson Lusk,* 247; December 14–15, 1862, Woodworth Diary, Hotchkiss Collection, CL; Joseph Bloomfield Osborn to Martha Osborn, December 15, 1862, Osborn Papers, LC; *Albany (N.Y.) Atlas and Argus,* January 1, 1863. At Burnside's headquarters a soldier heard that Lincoln had sent instructions that no fighting should take place on the Sabbath. See Oliver S. Collidge to ?, December 14, 1862, Coolidge Papers, Duke.

6. Hooker opposed abandoning Fredericksburg but did not support another frontal assault.

7. William Teall to his wife, December 14, 1862, Teall Letters, TSLA; *OR*, 65, 120–21, 312; Todd, *Seventy-Ninth Highlanders*, 264–65; *CCW*, 1:653; Burrage, *Thirty-Sixth Massachusetts*, 27–28; John Godfrey to Horace Godfrey, December 14, 1862, Godfrey Papers, NHHS; G. M. Cutts to Ambrose E. Burnside, December 14, 1862, Franklin Papers, LC; *B&L*, 3:117–18; Orlando Willcox, *Forgotten Valor*, 391, 404–6; Charles Shields Wainwright, *Diary of Battle*, 145; Daniel Reed Larned, Pencil Notes on the Battle of Fredericksburg, December 11–15, 1862, Larned Papers, LC. For an excellent analysis of Burnside's thinking, see Marvel, *Burnside*, 197–200.

8. William Allan, *Army of Northern Virginia*, 517–18; William Allan, "Fredericksburg," 144–45; *B&L*, 3:82; Brogan, *American Civil War*, 96; Hood, *Advance and Retreat*, 50–51.

9. December 14, 1862, Latrobe Diary, VHS; December 14, 1862, O'Farrell Diary, MC; Thomas Rowland to his mother, December 14, 1862, Rowland Papers, MC; Berkeley, *Four Years in the Confederate Artillery*, 37; Henry Thweatt Owen to Harriet Adeline Owen, December 14, 1862, Owen Papers, VHS; Scharf, *Personal Memoirs of Jonathan Thomas Scharf*, 55; *Athens (Ga.) Southern Banner*, January 7, 1863.

10. Kershaw, "Richard Kirkland," 186–88; "Fellow Feeling in the Army"; Trantham, "Richard R. Kirkland," 105.

11. Robert Franklin Fleming Jr., "Recollections," 4, FSNMP; Parramore et al., *Before the Rebel Flag Fell*, 49; David Emmons Johnston, *Story of a Confederate Boy in the Civil War*, 172; Milo Grow to his wife, December 15, 1862, Grow Letters, FSNMP.

12. *OR*, 571, 590; Ott, "Civil War Diary of James J. Kirkpatrick," 89; Edward E. Sill to his sister, December 20, 1862, Sill Letters, Duke.

13. *OR*, 418–19; Reese, *Sykes' Regular Infantry Division*, 182–85.

14. *OR*, 420, 425–27; *MSH*, 2:134; Reese, *Sykes' Regular Infantry Division*, 175–82; John D. Wilkins to his wife, December 18, 1862, Wilkins Papers, Schoff Collection, CL; John W. Ames to his mother, December 15, 1862, Ames Papers, USAMHI; John Worthington Ames, "Under Fire," 433–39; December 14, 1862, Bacon Diary, FSNMP; Charles Thomas Bowen to his wife, December 18, 1862, Bowen Letter, FSNMP; *Rochester (N.Y.) Daily Democrat and American*, December 27, 1862; Thomas H. Evans, "'Cries of the Wounded,'" 33. Andrews's brigade suffered 140 casualties. Given the men's position for much of the day, it is not surprising that most of the wounds were in the upper extremities, the back muscles, or the posterior. See *OR*, 426; *MSH*, 2:133, 135. A member of the 14th U.S. Infantry who slipped away into town under fire felt guilty about tempting God by "exposing myself so" (December 14, 1862, Bacon Diary, FSNMP).

15. Simonton, "Recollections of the Fredericksburg," 254–56; Thomas Gouldsberry to his brother, December 25, 1862, Gouldsberry Letter, FSNMP; Apted Memoir, CWMC, USAMHI; Charles Bowers to "Dear Lydia," December 19, 1862, Bowers Papers, MHS; Nash, *Forty-fourth New York*, 116; George M. Barnard to his father, December 16, 1862, Barnard Papers, MHS; December 14, 1862, Bancroft Diary, MHC; G. M. Sorrel to Edward Porter Alexander, December 14, 1862 (three dispatches), Alexander Papers, SHC; Edward Porter Alexander, *Fighting for the Confederacy*, 180; *OR*, 546; December 14, 1862, Seage Diary, MHC.

16. *OR*, 411; Melcher, *With a Flash of His Sword*, 14–15; Zerah Coston Monks to Hannah T. Rohrer, December 17, 1862, Monks-Rohrer Letters, Emory; John L. Smith, *118th Pennsylvania*, 132; Gerrish, *Reminiscences of the War*, 78–79; Donaldson, *Inside the Army of the Potomac*, 189–90.

17. J. L. Smith to "Dear Mother," December 26, 1862, John L. Smith Letters, FSNMP; Robert Goldthwaite Carter, *Four Brothers in Blue*, 200–201, 208–9; John Lord Parker, *Twenty-Second Massachusetts*, 230–32; December 14, 1862, Lockey Diary, MHC; James R. Woodworth to Phoebe Woodworth, December 15, 1862, Woodworth Papers, Hotchkiss Collection, CL; *OR Supplement*, pt. 2, 28:437, 446; Captain Charles A. Stevens, *Berdan's Sharpshooters*, 222–23. Even in Hancock's division, which had already sustained so many casualties, several more

men suffered serious wounds that required amputations. See *MSH*, 10:723, 11:148, 286, 12:797.

18. Moe, *Last Full Measure*, 215; *OR*, 2:73–74; December 14, 1862, Cavada Diary, HSP; Orwig, *131st Pennsylvania*, 126–27; Nathaniel W. Brown to Albert M. Given, December 23, 1862, Brown Letter, FSNMP; Isaac Lyman Taylor, "Campaigning with the First Minnesota," 237.

19. *OR*, 634–35, 643, 666; James I. Robertson Jr., *Jackson*, 663; Von Borcke, *Memoirs of the Confederate War*, 2:135–36; Hotchkiss, *Make Me a Map of the Valley*, 100–101; Walter Clark, *Regiments and Battalions from North Carolina*, 1:143.

20. *OR*, 685, 687; Coles, *From Huntsville to Appomattox*, 83; Von Borcke, *Memoirs of the Confederate War*, 2:136–37; Walter Clark, *Regiments and Battalions from North Carolina*, 1:143; *OR Supplement*, pt. 2, 1:180, 6:410, 48:250; Samuel J. C. Moore to Ellen Moore, December 15, 1862, Samuel J. C. Moore Papers, SHC; December 14, 1862, Ware Diary, SHC; Joseph W. Griggs to his father, December 19, 1862, Griggs Family Papers, VHS; Ujanirtus Allen, *Campaigning with "Old Stonewall,"* 195.

21. *Winchester (Va.) Times*, February 11, 1891; December 14, 1862, Hawes Diary, VHS; Edward Waterman to his sisters, December 19, 1862, Waterman-Bacon-Sanders Family Papers, Houston Regional Library.

22. George E. Stephens, *Voice of Thunder*, 213; *OR*, 488; December 14, 1862, Latta Diary, LC; Blake, *Three Years in the Army of the Potomac*, 152–53; Samuel Penniman Bates, *History of the Pennsylvania Volunteers*, 6:1185; Woodward, *Third Pennsylvania Reserves*, 218–19; Hanifen, *History of Battery B, First New Jersey Artillery*, 37–38; *OR Supplement*, pt. 1, 3:755–56, 759. Federal batteries occasionally lobbed shells into the woods, but official reports indicate that relatively few rounds were fired. See *OR*, 365; *OR Supplement*, pt. 1, 3:695, 748, 760–61, 768; George Lewis, *First Rhode Island Light Artillery*, 133–34.

23. Martin A. Haynes, *Second New Hampshire*, 147–48; *OR*, 383; Martin A. Haynes, *Minor War History*, 82; McAllister, *Letters of Robert McAllister*, 245–46; Bellard, *Gone for a Soldier*, 183.

24. *OR*, 120, 363; *OR Supplement*, pt. 1, 3:800, and pt. 2, 40:601; Virgil W. Mattoon to his mother, December 10–15, 1862, Mattoon Papers, CHS; Darius Starr to his mother, December 25, 1862, Starr Papers, Duke; Wyman Silas White, *Civil War Diary*, 113–14; Thomas J. Halsey, *Field of Battle*, 46; Best, *History of the 121st New York*, 44; Lucius B. Shattuck to Ellen Shattuck, December 11–14, 1862, Shattuck Letters, MHC; Haines, *15th New Jersey*, 34; Houghton, *Seventeenth Maine*, 34; Storey, *History of Cambria County*, 250; Elisha Hunt Rhodes, *All for the Union*, 90–91; Milans, "Eyewitness to Fredericksburg," 22–23.

25. George H. Allen, *Forty-Six Months*, 170–71; *New York Irish American*, December 27, 1862; Small, *Road to Richmond*, 69; Borton, *Awhile with the Blue*, 54; Edward Kalloch Gould, *Major-General Hiram Berry*, 227; S. Millett Thompson, *Thirteenth New Hampshire*, 74–75.

26. John R. Young to Maria Van Wagonen, December 29, 1862, Van Wagonen Papers, University of Oregon; Anecdotes of Rev. Dr. J. P. Smith, ca. 1897, Hotchkiss Papers, LC; A. J. Alexander, "Fredericksburg"; Haley, *Rebel Yell and Yankee Hurrah*, 60–61.

27. Blake, *Three Years in the Army of the Potomac*, 154; W. R. M. Slaughter to his sister, January 4, 1863, Slaughter Letters, VHS; Houghton, *Seventeenth Maine*, 33; *OR Supplement*, pt. 1, 3:789–90.

28. Anecdotes of Rev. Dr. J. P. Smith, ca. 1897, Hotchkiss Papers, LC; Charles R. Johnson to "Dear Nellie," December 1862, Johnson Letters, HCWRTC, USAMHI; Goss, *Recollections of a Private*, 133–34; Bosbyshell, *48th in the War*, 100.

29. *Augusta (Ga.) Daily Chronicle and Sentinel*, December 27, 1862; Scott, *One Hundred and Fifth Regiment Pennsylvania Volunteers*, 67; Perkins Memoir, 7, NHHS; Charles R. Johnson to "Dear Nellie," December 15, 1862, Johnson Letters, HCWRTC, USAMHI; James T. Odem to Eleanor Odem, December 19, 1862, Odem Papers, UVa.

30. Tapert, *Brothers' War,* 121; Hartsock, *Soldier of the Cross,* 44; "Personal Recollections of the First Battle of Fredericksburg," 18–19, UT; Cook, *Twelfth Massachusetts,* 80–81; L. Minor Blackford, *Mine Eyes Have Seen the Glory,* 210–12. Temperatures rose high enough during the day for bodies to putrefy.

31. *History of the Fifth Massachusetts Battery,* 510–11; Herman Haupt to his wife, December 15, 1862, Haupt Letterbook, Haupt Papers, LC; *Philadelphia Inquirer,* December 23, 1862; Asaph R. Tyler to his wife, January 17, 1863, Tyler Letters, FSNMP; Siegel, *For the Glory of the Union,* 115; Oliver Wendell Holmes, *Touched with Fire,* 78. For perceptive analyses of the soldiers' responses to battlefield deaths, see Hess, *Union Soldier in Battle,* 37–44; Linderman, *Embattled Courage,* 124–28; Frank and Reaves, *"Seeing the Elephant,"* 105–8. For a general discussion of burial details, see Dean, *Shook over Hell,* 68.

32. For insights based on a much more overwhelming experience of death, the bombing of Hiroshima, see Lifton, *History and Human Survival,* 127–28, 153–54. For a description of how the Civil War hardened soldiers to scenes of death and helped them suppress sentiment and sensibility, see Laderman, *Sacred Remains,* 137–40.

33. Catton, *Never Call Retreat,* 24; Richard Lewis, *Camp Life of a Confederate Boy,* 37; Coles, *From Huntsville to Appomattox,* 84; December 16, 1862, Conway Diary, GDAH; Shand Memoir, SCL; Burgwyn, *Captain's War,* 42; John L. G. Wood to his father, December 18, 1862, John L. G. Wood Letters, UDC Bound Typescripts, GDAH; December 15, 1862, Pickens Diary, UA; William Calvin Oates, *War Between Union and Confederacy,* 168; Braddock Memoir, 25–26, MC. An artillery private tried to grab a pair of boots but desisted when he tugged on one boot and much of the man's leg came with it (the dead man had received a mortal wound right above the knee). See Walters, *Norfolk Blues,* 49. One unlucky Rebel donned a Yankee overcoat and was mistakenly shot dead by a Confederate sharpshooter. For enterprising lads, it was worth taking a chance because even a bloody and soiled coat might fetch $40 in camp. See W. R. M. Slaughter to his sister, January 4, 1863, Slaughter Letters, VHS; L. Calhoun Cooper to his mother, December 18, 1862, Cooper Letters, Kennesaw Mountain National Battlefield Park.

34. *Richmond Daily Examiner,* December 19, 1862; December 17, 1862, Duffey Diary, VHS; William Henry Tatum to John Tatum, December 17, 1862, Tatum Papers, VHS; Thomas Claybrook Elder to Anna Fitzhugh Elder, December 21, 1862, Elder Papers, VHS.

35. Rankin, *23rd Virginia,* 54; Loehr, *First Virginia Regiment,* 32; Fletcher, *Rebel Private,* 51; Ujanirtus Allen, *Campaigning with "Old Stonewall,"* 206; William S. Campbell to his cousin, December 17, 1862, William S. Campbell Letter, FSNMP; Trowbridge, *The South,* 107; *Charleston Daily Courier,* January 8, 1863; Berkeley, *Four Years in the Confederate Artillery,* 39. Some men had a superstitious aversion to touching dead Yankees, and when one scavenger discovered a Bible on a body, he suddenly realized that these fellows, too, believed they were fighting for the right. See Young, "Civil War Letters of Abram Hayne Young," 59; Abernathy, *Our Mess,* 20.

36. Small, *Road to Richmond,* 69–70; Henry Grimes Marshall to "Dear Folks at Home," December 20, 1862, Marshall Papers, Schoff Collection, CL; William Teall to his wife, December 16, 1862, Teall Letters, TSLA; *OR,* 261–62; December 17, 1862, Pope Diary, *CWTI,* USAMHI; Roland R. Bowen, *From Ball's Bluff to Gettysburg,* 141. Federals foraging for food also took shoes, coats, and blankets from dead comrades. When the enemy stripped the dead, of course that became an outrage, but both attitudes and practices showed how inured some men had grown to corpses on battlefields. See Robert Goldthwaite Carter, *Four Brothers in Blue,* 197–98; *Annals of the War,* 265; Lord, *History of the Ninth New Hampshire,* 230.

37. Cavins, *Civil War Letters of Cavins,* 118; Heffelfinger, "'Dear Sister Jennie,'" 217; S. Millett Thompson, *Thirteenth New Hampshire,* 86; Allen Landis to his parents, January 1, 1863, Landis Papers, LC; Haley, *Rebel Yell and Yankee Hurrah,* 60; John Dragoo to Daniel and Abigail Dragoo, December 18, 1862, Dragoo Papers, ISL. Northern newspaper coverage of Rebel "out-

rages" was surprisingly restrained. See *New York Herald,* December 19, 1862; *New York Tribune,* December 18, 1862; *Baltimore American and Commercial Advertiser,* December 23, 1862.

38. Mills Lane, *"Dear Mother: Don't Grieve about Me,"* 208; December 16, 1862, Ware Diary, SHC; Shotwell, *Papers of Randolph Abbott Shotwell,* 1:432. A Richmond editor duly noted how careless the Federals had been with their dead but gently suggested that if Confederates really needed to strip the bodies, they should at least leave the underwear. See *Richmond Daily Enquirer,* December 22, 1862.

39. Laderman, *Sacred Remains,* 130–31; Francis Marion Coker to his wife, December 18, 1862, Coker Letters, UG; Bryan Grimes to his brother, December 25, 1862, Grimes Family Papers, SHC; *Richmond Daily Dispatch,* December 20, 1862; *Lynchburg Daily Virginian,* December 20, 1862.

40. *OR,* 212–22; Robert Goldthwaite Carter, *Four Brothers in Blue,* 198; John Lord Parker, *Twenty-Second Massachusetts,* 232; Nathaniel W. Brown to Albert M. Given, December 23, 1862, Brown Letter, FSNMP; Haley, *Rebel Yell and Yankee Hurrah,* 61; Walker, *Second Corps,* 188; *History of the 127th Regiment Pennsylvania Volunteers,* 136–40; Jennings Cropper Wise, *Long Arm of Lee,* 1:400.

41. December 14, 1862, Hodnett Diary, UDC Bound Typescript, GDAH; James Harvey Wood, *The War m. Dauhl Muit, Mississippi Rebel,* 145; Gunn, *24th Virginia,* 38, Robert A. Moore, *Life for the Confederacy,* 124; December 15, 1862, Copenhaver Diary, CWMC, USAMHI; Hotchkiss, *Make Me a Map of the Valley,* 101.

42. McCreery Recollections, section 10, 1862–63, VHS; Stiles, *Four Years under Marse Robert,* 137; *Richmond Daily Dispatch,* December 22, 1862; Conn, "Conn-Brantley Letter," 439.

43. *Augusta (Maine) Kennebec Journal,* January 2, 1863; Oliver S. Coolidge to ?, December 14–15, 1862, Coolidge Papers, Duke; Chamberlain, *Through Blood and Fire,* 43; Tyler, *Recollections of the Civil War,* 66; Edward K. Russell to his mother, December 14, 1862, Kirby-Smith-Russell Collection, FSNMP.

44. James Longstreet to R. H. Anderson, December 15, 1862, Alexander Papers, SHC; *Richmond Daily Dispatch,* December 22, 1862; *OR,* 566–67, 576–77; W. H. Burgess to David McKnight, December 20, 1862, McKnight Family Papers, UT; Boggs, *Alexander Letters,* 245–46; Ott, "Civil War Diary of James J. Kirkpatrick," 89; Burgwyn, *Captain's War,* 40; Henry Alexander Chambers, *Diary,* 76. An excitable Virginian in Anderson's division claimed there was cannonading along the lines all day. See December 15, 1862, Shipp Diary, VHS.

45. *New York Irish-American,* December 27, 1862, January 10, 1863; Conyngham, *Irish Brigade,* 354; McNamara, *History of the Ninth Massachusetts,* 267; Cavanagh, *Memoirs of Gen. Thomas Francis Meagher,* 471–72; Edward Field, "Irish Brigade," 585–86; Mulholland, *116th Pennsylvania,* 60–61. The original plans had been to hold the banquet in a festively decorated log house in the brigade's camp across the river.

46. Wingfield, "Diary of Capt. H. W. Wingfield," 21; December 15, 1862, Hawes Diary, VHS; James I. Robertson Jr., *Jackson,* 664.

47. *OR Supplement,* pt. 1, 3:756; *OR,* 122; William H. Clairville, "Battle of Fredericksburg," 83, Clairville Papers, Rutgers University; Houghton, *Seventeenth Maine,* 34–35; Babcock, "114th Regiment Pennsylvania Volunteers," 1; Haley, *Rebel Yell and Yankee Hurrah,* 61; John F. Hartwell to his wife, December 17, 1862, Hartwell Papers, FSNMP; December 15, 1862, Furst Diary, HCWRTC, USAMHI; Elisha Hunt Rhodes, *All for the Union,* 91.

48. Vail, *Reminiscences of a Boy in the Civil War,* 99–100; *MSH,* 11:226; December 15, 1862, Jackson Diary, IHS; Craig L. Dunn, *Iron Men, Iron Will,* 149.

49. D. R. E. Winn to his wife, December 18, 1862, Winn Letters, Emory; Francis Marion Coker to his wife, December 16, 1862, Coker Letters, UG; Hotchkiss, *Make Me a Map of the Valley,* 101; December 15, 1862, Hodnett Diary, UDC Bound Typescripts, GDAH; Milo Grow to his wife, December 15, 1862, Grow Letters, FSNMP; Samuel J. C. Moore to Ellen Moore, December 15, 1862, Samuel J. C. Moore Papers, SHC.

50. William Watson, *Letters of a Civil War Surgeon,* 41; A. B. Williams to his father, December 15, 1862, Williams Letters, University of Rochester; John S. Crocker to his wife, December 15, 1862, Crocker Letters, CU; Henry Willis to his father, December 15, 1862, Henry Willis Letter, FSNMP; Edward K. Russell to his mother, December 14, 1862, Kirby-Smith-Russell Collection, FSNMP.

51. Sturtevant, *Josiah Volunteered,* 75; Robert Goldthwaite Carter, *Four Brothers in Blue,* 199; Daniel E. Underhill to Samuel E. Underhill, December 15, 1862, Underhill Letter, FSNMP; John Harrison Mills, *Chronicles of the Twenty-First New York,* 279; Cornelius Richmond to his wife, December 15, 1862, Richmond Papers, FSNMP; Hartsock, *Soldier of the Cross,* 45; Amos Hadley, *Life of Walter Harriman,* 139; Robert S. Robertson, "Diary of the War," 76.

52. *OR,* 75, 121, 124–25; *B&L,* 3:118; William Teall to his wife, December 15, 1862, Teall Letters, TSLA; *CCW,* 1:659; Edwin V. Sumner to Ambrose E. Burnside, December 14, 1862, Stuart Collection, LC; Daniel Reed Larned, Pencil Notes on the Battle of Fredericksburg, December 11–15, 1862, Larned Papers, LC.

53. *OR,* 122, and ser. 1, 51(1):958; Marvel, *Burnside,* 199–200.

54. Daniel Reed Larned to "My Dear Henry," December 16, 1862, Larned Papers, LC; *OR,* 124, 451; Robert Goldthwaite Carter, *Four Brothers in Blue,* 205; John L. Smith, *118th Pennsylvania,* 137; J. L. Smith to his mother, December 26, 1862, John L. Smith Letters, FSNMP; Teall, "Ringside Seat at Fredericksburg," 30. At 5:30 P.M. Hooker remained unsure whether the retreat was to take place. See *OR,* 124.

55. P. A. O'Connell to A. W. Dougherty, December 13, 1862, entry 544, Field Hospital Records, Adjutant General's Records, NA; *MSH,* 2:102–3; Hirst, *Boys from Rockville,* 76; McCarter, *My Life in the Irish Brigade,* 202–4. Many of the wounded had been removed during the preceding two days as well.

56. O'Reilly, *Jackson at Fredericksburg,* 187–88; James B. Thomas, *Civil War Letters,* 127–28; Bates Alexander, "Seventh Regiment," December 20, 1895; December 15, 1862, Latta Diary, LC; John Ripley Adams, *Memorials and Letters,* 78; Lucius B. Shattuck to "Dear Gill and Mary," December 16, 1862, Shattuck Letters, MHC; December 15, 1862, Furst Diary, HCWRTC, USAMHI; Hartwell, *To My Beloved Wife and Boy at Home,* 35.

57. Joseph Bloomfield Osborn to Joseph M. Osborn, Osborn Papers, LC; Edmund Halsey, *Brother against Brother,* 95; December 15, 1862, Holford Diary, LC; *OR,* 451.

58. *OR,* 124; Henry Grimes Marshall to "Dear Folks at Home," December 20, 1862, Marshall Papers, Schoff Collection, CL; Lapham, "Recollections of the Twelfth R.I. Volunteers," 36–37; Pullen, *Twentieth Maine,* 56–58; Tillinghast, *Twelfth Rhode Island,* 62–63.

59. Favill, *Diary of a Young Officer,* 213–14; Musgrove, *Autobiography of Captain Richard Musgrove,* 51–52; Galwey, *Valiant Hours,* 66; S. Millett Thompson, *Thirteenth New Hampshire,* 78; December 15, 1862, Charles S. Granger Diary, CWMC, USAMHI; Aldrich, *History of Battery A,* 165–66; Currier, "From Concord to Fredericksburg," 256; Todd, *Seventy-Ninth Highlanders,* 60; *OR,* 401.

60. *OR,* 76, 125–26, 401; *Brunswick (Maine) Telegraph,* January 2, 1863; Nash, *Forty-fourth New York,* 116–17; Judson, *Eighty-third Pennsylvania,* 107–9; J. L. Smith to his mother, December 15, 1862, John L. Smith Letters, FSNMP; Donaldson, *Inside the Army of the Potomac,* 192; James R. Woodworth to Phoebe Woodworth, December 17, 1862, Woodworth Papers, Hotchkiss Collection, CL; Graves Memoir, 6, FSNMP; December 15, 1862, Stoner Diary, FSNMP; Nathaniel W. Brown to Albert M. Given, December 23, 1862, Brown Letter, FSNMP; December 15, 1862, Pope Diary, *CWTI,* USAMHI; *Fourth Annual Report of the Bureau of Military Statistics,* 155. A regimental historian later recalled the "intense agony" of men suffering from diarrhea who had not been able to move for more than a day. See Thomas H. Parker, *History of the 51st,* 274–75.

61. McKelvey, *Rochester in the Civil War,* 205–6; Donaldson, *Inside the Army of the Potomac,* 192–93; Welsh and Welsh, "Civil War Letters from Two Brothers," 156–57; Davenport, *Fifth*

New York Volunteer Infantry, 352–57; *OR Supplement,* pt. 2, 42:636; Brainard, *One Hundred and Forty-sixth New York,* 42–44; Tilney, *My Life in the Army,* 34–38; *OR,* 401, 415–16.

62. *OR,* 403; Rowe, *Sketch of the 126th Pennsylvania,* 22–24; "An Adventure at Fredericksburg."

63. John Smart to Ann Smart, December 17, 1862, Smart Letters, FSNMP; *OR,* 172–73, 175, 178; Charles Shields Wainwright, *Diary of Battle,* 146; Gilbert Thompson, *Engineer Battalion,* 27.

64. December 15, 1862, Furst Diary, HCWRTC, USAMHI; Bellard, *Gone for a Soldier,* 186; Sanford Truesdale to his sister, December 17, 1862, Truesdale Papers, University of Chicago; Vail, *Reminiscences of a Boy in the Civil War,* 100–101; December 16, 1862, Taylor Diary, FSNMP; Houghton, *Seventeenth Maine,* 35–36; Dority, "Civil War Diary," 11–12; December 16, 1862, Berry Diary, *CWTI,* USAMHI; Hanifen, *History of Battery B, First New Jersey Artillery,* 40; Robert Goldthwaite Carter, *Four Brothers in Blue,* 209–10.

65. Tillinghast, *Twelfth Rhode Island,* 64–65; Hopkins, *Seventh Rhode Island,* 50; Edward Hutchinson to "Dear Emma," December 22, 1862, Hutchinson Letters, FSNMP; Haley, *Rebel Yell and Yankee Hurrah,* 62; Henry Grimes Marshall to "Dear Folks at Home," December 20, 1862, Marshall Papers, Schoff Collection, CL; Galwey, *Valiant Hours,* 66–67; Hagerty, *Collis' Zouaves,* 129–30; Frank O. Park to "Friends at Home," December 17, 1862, Park Letter, FSNMP; William B. Jordan Jr., *Red Diamond Regiment,* 30; Wyman Silas White, *Civil War Diary,* 117.

66. Abraham Welch to his sister, December 27, 1862, Welch Letter, SHC; Nathaniel W. Brown to Albert M. Given, December 23, 1862, Brown Letter, FSNMP; Alexander Way to his wife, December 17, 1862, Way Letters, FSNMP; McKelvey, *Rochester in the Civil War,* 163; McAllister, *Letters of Robert McAllister,* 242; December 16, 1862, Pope Diary, *CWTI,* USAMHI; Ayling, *Yankee at Arms,* 85; December 18, 1862, Latta Diary, LC.

67. Reardon, "Forlorn Hope," 102; Weygant, *One Hundred and Twenty-Fourth Regiment,* 73; Thomas H. Evans, "'Cries of the Wounded,'" 38; William H. Clairville to Mary Clairville, December 17, 1862, Clairville Papers, Rutgers University; Gallup, "Connecticut Yankee at Fredericksburg," 204.

68. Edward Porter Alexander, "Battle of Fredericksburg," 463–64; *OR,* 333; Speairs and Pettit, *Civil War Letters,* 1:75; John F. Hartwell to his wife, December 17, 1862, Hartwell Papers, FSNMP; Dawes, *Sixth Wisconsin,* 114; Von Borcke, *Memoirs of the Confederate War,* 2:147; Bidwell, *Forty-ninth New York Volunteers,* 139–40; Milo Grow to his wife, December 16, 1862, Grow Letters, FSNMP.

69. Sorrel, *Recollections of a Confederate Staff Officer,* 136–37; Samuel V. Dean to his wife, December 19, 1862, Dean Letters, FSNMP; William Teall to his wife, December 17, 1862, Teall Letters, TSLA; Currier, "From Concord to Fredericksburg," 257; Hopkins, *Seventh Rhode Island,* 51; William M. Owen, *In Camp and Battle with the Washington Artillery,* 195–97; Frederick, *Story of a Regiment,* 126; *Fitchburg (Mass.) Sentinel,* January 2, 1863. Bodies were dumped in these trenches despite War Department orders about specifying the place of burial and marking the graves with headboards. See Laderman, *Sacred Remains,* 118–19.

70. Landon, "Letters to the Vincennes Western Sun," 340; Lord, *History of the Ninth New Hampshire,* 250; Hough, "Battle of Fredericksburg," 14, FSNMP; Darrohn, "Recollections," FSNMP; George E. Stephens, *Voice of Thunder,* 214.

71. Rauscher, *Music on the March,* 34; *OR,* 555, 641, 673, and ser. 2, 2:115–17; Marsena Rudolph Patrick, *Inside Lincoln's Army,* 199; William Teall to his wife, December 17, 1862, Teall Letters, TSLA; Bloodgood, *Personal Reminiscences of the War,* 57; L. Minor Blackford, *Mine Eyes Have Seen the Glory,* 212–13; Samuel Penniman Bates, *History of the Pennsylvania Volunteers,* 6:1185n; December 14, 1862, Hamilton Diary, FSNMP; Ujanirtus Allen, *Campaigning with "Old Stonewall,"* 201. In Richmond prisoners from Fredericksburg languished in filthy conditions, witnessed several amputations, and occasionally died. See December 18, 1862–

January 10, 1863, Heffelfinger Diary, *CWTI,* USAMHI; George W. Grant to his sister, January 19, 28, 1863, Grant Papers, Duke; *Richmond Daily Dispatch,* January 1, 1863.

72. John Smart to his wife, December 13, 1862, Smart Letters, FSNMP; *Augusta (Maine) Kennebec Journal,* January 2, 1863; Judd, *Story of the Thirty-Third,* 251–52; *New York Herald,* December 17, 1862; "Sacrifice of Federals at Fredericksburg," 370.

73. Philip H. Powers to his wife, December 17, 1862, Powers Letters, Leigh Collection, USAMHI; D. R. E. Winn to his wife, December 18, 1862, Winn Letters, Emory; *Richmond Daily Enquirer,* December 18, 1862; *Augusta (Ga.) Daily Constitutionalist,* December 28, 1862, January 4, 1863; Jesse H. H. Person to his mother, December 25, 1862, Presley Carter Person Papers, Duke; Davenport, *Fifth New York Volunteer Infantry,* 357; Von Borcke, *Memoirs of the Confederate War,* 2:148–49. Shortly after the war a young man showed a northern reporter to the icehouse burial ground. See Trowbridge, *The South,* 112.

74. Craig L. Dunn, *Iron Men, Iron Will,* 151; James Coburn to his parents, December 17, 1862, James P. Coburn Papers, USAMHI; Stephen S. Rogers to his mother, December 16, 1862, Rogers Papers, Illinois State Historical Library; December 16, 1862, Jackson Diary, IHS; Otis, *Second Wisconsin,* 67; Castleman, *Army of the Potomac,* 267; McAllister, *Letters of Robert McAllister,* 243; Albert, *Forty-fifth Pennsylvania,* 253–54; Henry F. Young to his father, December 17, 1862, Young Papers, SHSW; Robert S. Robertson, "Diary of the War," 76–77; Pardington, *Dear Sarah,* 48; Edward K. Russell to his mother, December 17, 1862, Kirby-Smith-Russell Collection, FSNMP; R. S. Robertson to his parents, December 24, 1862, Robertson Papers, FSNMP; William Hamilton to his mother, December 18, 1862, Hamilton Papers, LC; Joseph P. Vickers to his parents, December 16, 1862, Vickers Letter, FSNMP.

75. *OR,* 548–49; James I. Robertson Jr., *Jackson,* 664; Scharf, *Personal Memoirs of Jonathan Thomas Scharf,* 57; *B&L,* 3:82–83; Clausewitz, *On War,* 84; Early, *Narrative of the War,* 180–82; Redway, *Fredericksburg,* 201, 218–19; Cooke, *Lee,* 192; Jedediah Hotchkiss to Sara Ann Comfort Hotchkiss, January 23, 1863, Hotchkiss Papers, LC. Only a few Confederates claimed that they had expected the Yankees to withdraw. See Von Borcke, *Memoirs of the Confederate War,* 2:142; Walter Clark, *Regiments and Battalions from North Carolina,* 2:226; Grimes, *Extracts of Letters,* 26–27. For perceptive and contrasting analyses of whether Lee should have been more aggressive, see Jennings Cropper Wise, *Long Arm of Lee,* 1:400–404; Col. G. F. R. Henderson, *Civil War,* 95–100.

76. Gannon, *Irish Rebels,* 147; David L. Bozeman to his wife, December 17, 1862, Bozeman Letters, FSNMP; Bryan Grimes to William Grimes, December 18, 1862, Grimes Family Papers, SHC; *Battle-Fields of the South,* 515; Joseph N. Haynes to his father, January 7, 1863, Haynes Papers, Duke; Malone, *Whipt 'em Everytime,* 66–67; December 16, 1862, Jones Diary, Schoff Collection, CL; Ott, "Civil War Diary of James J. Kirkpatrick," 89–90. Because of the Union withdrawal, the Confederates captured substantial amounts of arms, ammunition, accouterments, and food. See *OR,* 571, 588; *Richmond Daily Enquirer,* December 18, 1862.

77. For incisive comments on defining and assessing defeat, see Clausewitz, *On War,* 142, 227, 230, 233–34, 254.

CHAPTER EIGHTEEN

1. Thomas L. Livermore, *Numbers and Losses,* 96; *OR,* 129–42, 558–62.

2. For estimates that were remarkably close to the reported numbers, see G. O. Bartlett to Ira Andrews, December 18, 1862, Bartlett Papers, GLC; Henry J. H. Thompson to Lucretia Thompson, December 19, 1862, Thompson Papers, Duke; Electus W. Jones to his parents, December 17, 1862, Electus W. Jones Papers, Duke.

3. Haydon, *For Country, Cause, and Leader,* 299; John F. Hartwell to his wife, December 17, 1862, Hartwell Papers, FSNMP; Jonathan Hutchinson to his family, December 20, 1862, Hutchinson Letters, USAMHI.

4. Donaldson, *Inside the Army of the Potomac*, 189; Gallup, "Connecticut Yankee at Fredericksburg," 203; George M. Barnard to his father, December 16, 1862, Barnard Papers, MHS; Emerson F. Merrill to his parents, December 17, 1862, Merrill Papers, FSNMP; J. McDonald to his sister, December 19, 1862, Lt. J. McDonald Letters, FSNMP; George A. Spencer to his mother, December 25, 1862, Spencer Papers, GLC; Joseph N. Haynes to his father, December 21, 1862, Haynes Papers, Duke; P. Borary to Johnny Borary, December 18, 1862, Borary Papers, GLC; William Speed to Charlotte Speed, December 29, 1862, Speed Papers, Schoff Collection, CL; William M. Sheppard to his wife, December 17, 1862, Sheppard Letter, FSNMP; Pardington, *Dear Sarah*, 49.

5. Thomas Claybrook Elder to Anna Fitzhugh Elder, December 21, 1862, Elder Papers, VHS; Cadmus Marcellus Wilcox to his sister, December 17, 1862, Wilcox Papers, LC; W. H. Burgess to David McKnight, December 20, 1862, McKnight Family Papers, UT; William Rhadamanthus Montgomery, *Georgia Sharpshooter*, 77; Borden, *Legacy of Fanny and Joseph*, 130; William Henry Tatum to his brother, December 17, 1862, Tatum Papers, VHS; Cutrer and Parrish, *Brothers in Blue*, 139; Hodijah Lincoln Meade to Jane Eliza Meade, December 17, 1862, Meade Family Papers, VHS; Isaac Howard to his father, December 25, 1862, Howard Family Papers, SHC; Unknown Soldier to "Dear Cousin," December 19, 1862, Unknown Soldier Letter, FSNMP; William Henry Cocke to John Cocke, December 25, 1862, Cocke Family Papers, VHS; John R. Damron to his father, December 17, 1862, Damron Letter, University of Tennessee; J. S. Wilson to his father, December 19, 1862, Wilson Papers, MDAH; E. R. Willis to his father, December 18, 1862, E. R. and McKibben Willis Letters, FSNMP; James T. McElvaney to his mother, December 19, 1862, McElvaney Letter, FSNMP; Mills Lane, *"Dear Mother: Don't Grieve about Me,"* 217–18; Austin, *Georgia Boys with "Stonewall" Jackson*, 58.

6. Jesse S. McGee to "My Dear Mollie," December 20, 1862, McGee-Charles Family Papers, SCL; *Augusta (Ga.) Daily Chronicle and Sentinel*, December 27, 1862; *Augusta (Ga.) Daily Constitutionalist*, December 27, 1862; *Charleston Daily Courier*, December 19, 1862; J. B. Jones, *Rebel War Clerk's Diary*, 1:216–17; Edmondston, *"Journal of a Secesh Lady,"* 320.

7. *New York Tribune*, December 18, 23, 1862; *Chicago Daily Tribune*, December 18, 1862; Brooks, *Mr. Lincoln's Washington*, 51; Emerson F. Merrill to his parents, December 21, 1862, Merrill Papers, FSNMP; *Harrisburg Patriot and Union*, December 20, 1862; *Albany (N.Y.) Atlas and Argus*, January 9, 1863.

8. Todd Reminiscences, 75–76, SHC; John Bratton to his wife, December 16, 1862, Bratton Letters, SHC; Shand Memoir, SCL; William C. McClellan to his father, December 25, 1862, Buchanan and McClellan Family Papers, SHC; William Rhadamanthus Montgomery, *Georgia Sharpshooter*, 78; *Charleston Daily Courier*, December 31, 1862; L. Minor Blackford, *Mine Eyes Have Seen the Glory*, 213; *Atlanta Southern Confederacy*, December 27, 1862.

9. J. E. B. Stuart to George Washington Custis Lee, December 18, 1862, Stuart Papers, Duke; William Willis Blackford, *War Years with Stuart*, 196; Charles, "Events in Battle of Fredericksburg," 68; Susan Leigh Blackford, *Letters from Lee's Army*, 149; December 14, 1862, J. M. Mitchell Diary, FSNMP; Isaac Howard to his father, December 25, 1862, Howard Family Papers, SHC; E. R. Willis to his father, December 18, 1862, E. R. and McKibben Willis Letters, FSNMP; Edward E. Sill to his sister, December 20, 1862, Sill Letters, Duke.

10. Trout, *With Pen and Saber*, 126; Jedediah Hotchkiss to Sara Ann Comfort Hotchkiss, December 17, 1862, Hotchkiss Papers, LC; W. R. M. Slaughter to his sister, January 4, 1863, Slaughter Letters, VHS; *Augusta (Ga.) Daily Constitutionalist*, December 23, 1862; *OR*, 628.

11. Robert H. Simpson to "Dear Mary," December 16, 1862, Settle Papers, Duke; *Athens (Ga.) Southern Banner*, January 7, 1863; J. G. Montgomery to his brother and sister, January 9, 1863, Montgomery Letter, FSNMP; *Charleston Daily Courier*, January 17, 1863; Henry Calvin Conner to "Dear Ellen," December 18, 1862, Conner Papers, SCL; Brogan, *American Civil War*, 98–99; William Henry Stewart, *Pair of Blankets*, 75; "Battle of Fredericksburg," 263.

12. Walters, *Norfolk Blues,* 49; W. H. Andrews, *Footprints of a Regiment,* 98; Hightower, "Letters from Harvey Judson Hightower," 180; *Charleston Daily Courier,* January 9, 1863.

13. December 16, 1862, Latrobe Diary, VHS; S. G. Pryor, *Post of Honor,* 296; McPherson, *For Cause and Comrades,* 148–53; Rev. Nicholas A. Davis, *Campaigns from Texas to Maryland,* 104; *Athens (Ga.) Southern Banner,* January 14, 1863; *Richmond Daily Dispatch,* December 23, 1862; Charles Kerrison to "Uncle Edwin," December 18, 1862, Kerrison Family Papers, SCL; Thomas Claybrook Elder to Anna Fitzhugh Elder, December 21, 1862, Elder Papers, VHS; Benjamin Lewis Blackford to William Blackford, December 23, 1862, Blackford Family Papers, SHC; Brogan, *American Civil War,* 96. On how fighting can stir up "national" hatred where none existed before a war, see Clausewitz, *On War,* 138. For long-term effects of seeing so many dead on a battlefield, see Dean, *Shook over Hell,* 67–68.

14. Spencer, *Civil War Marriage in Virginia,* 152; McDaniel, *With Unabated Trust,* 122; Milo Grow to his wife, December 16, 1862, Grow Letters, FSNMP.

15. *Richmond Daily Enquirer,* December 15, 16, 24, 25, 1862; *Milledgeville (Ga.) Southern Recorder,* January 6, 1863; *Richmond Daily Examiner,* December 16, 1862; *Charleston Mercury,* December 17, 23, 1862; *Augusta (Ga.) Daily Chronicle and Sentinel,* January 1, 1863; *Wilmington (N.C.) Daily Journal,* January 9, 1863; *Raleigh Weekly Register,* December 31, 1862; *Raleigh Weekly Standard,* December 31, 1862, January 7, 1863; *Richmond Daily Dispatch,* December 15, 1862.

16. J. Cutler Andrews, *North Reports the Civil War,* 74; *New York Tribune,* December 15, 16, 20, 1862; *New York Times,* December 15, 16, 18, 1862; *Philadelphia Inquirer,* December 15, 17, 1862; *Baltimore American and Commercial Advertiser,* December 23, 1862; Royster, *Destructive War,* 240; *Boston Evening Transcript,* December 15, 1862; *New York Herald,* December 16, 1862; *Hartford Daily Courant,* December 19, 23, 1862; *Flemington (N.J.) Hunterdon Gazette,* December 24, 1862; *Rochester (N.Y.) Daily Democrat and American,* December 23, 1862; *Carlisle (Pa.) Herald,* December 26, 1862.

17. McDonald, *Woman's Civil War,* 100; Emma Holmes, *Diary,* 218; Lusk, *War Letters of William Thompson Lusk,* 252–53; Catherine Eaton to Samuel W. Eaton, December 15, 1862, Eaton Papers, SHSW; Anzolette E. Pendleton to William Nelson Pendleton, December 18, 1862, Pendleton Papers, SHC; L. Minor Blackford, *Mine Eyes Have Seen the Glory,* 207.

18. Orson Blair Curtis, *History of the Twenty-Fourth Michigan,* 107; Brainerd, *Bridge Building in Wartime,* 309; Susan Leigh Blackford, *Letters from Lee's Army,* 149–50; Samuel V. Dean to his wife, December 22, 1862, Dean Letters, FSNMP; Henry Wadsworth Longfellow, *Letters,* 4:304; Robert Wentworth to his daughter, December 25, 1862, Wentworth Papers, LC; Gearhart, *Reminiscences of the Civil War,* 32; Haley, *Rebel Yell and Yankee Hurrah,* 60.

19. Lifton, *History and Human Survival,* 169, 172–73; Becker, *Denial of Death,* 2.

20. Abbott, *Fallen Leaves,* 160; Welsh and Welsh, "Civil War Letters from Two Brothers," 161; Orson Blair Curtis, *History of the Twenty-Fourth Michigan,* 82; Guiney, *Commanding Boston's Irish Ninth,* 155; Kate Stone, *Journal,* 164–65.

21. Welsh and Welsh, "Civil War Letters from Two Brothers," 155; Walter A. Eames to his wife, December 14, 16, 18, 1862, Eames Letters, USAMHI; Rohloff C. Hacker to his parents, December 18, 1862, Philip Hacker to his parents, December 31, 1862, January 14, 1863, Philip Hacker to his father, January 5, 1863, Philip Hacker to his mother, January 18, February 1, 1863, Hacker Brothers Papers, Schoff Collection, CL.

22. *Rochester (N.Y.) Daily Union and Advertiser,* January 3, 1863; William Teall to his wife, December 17, 1862, Teall Letters, TSLA; *Rochester (N.Y.) Daily Democrat and American,* January 23, 1863; January 9, 1863, Shand Memoir, SCL; Walt Whitman, *Walt Whitman's Civil War,* 30–31; George Washington Whitman, *Civil War Letters,* 77–78; Laderman, *Sacred Remains,* 108–9; Gallman, *Mastering Wartime,* 57–60, 77; Gallman, *North Fights the Civil War,* 74–77. A correspondent at Falmouth later reported that a dead Rebel officer's body had been returned

to his family through the lines. He hoped that such an act of charity would "do much towards mitigating the horrors of this unnatural contest" (*New York Herald,* January 11, 1863). In the nineteenth century, middle- and upper-class people especially felt a strong need to grieve tangibly and publicly. See Pike and Armstrong, *Time to Mourn,* 11.

23. Abbott, *Fallen Leaves,* 150; J. C. Allen to "Cousin Sallie," December 18, 1862, Milner Collection, GDAH; John H. Mitchell to Rebecca Mitchell, December 17, 1862, John Mitchell Letters, FSNMP; Hartsock, *Soldier of the Cross,* 169; G. A. Evans, undated statement, Brown Papers, Virginia Polytechnic; Laderman, *Sacred Remains,* 132–33; Hagerty, *Collis' Zouaves,* 133–34; Cary, *George William Curtis,* 60; Paludan, *"People's Contest,"* 319; J. T. Carpenter to Katie Froneberger, January 13, 1863, Carpenter Letter, FSNMP; Thomas Bell to "Dear Sir," January 4, 1863, GAR; Norman W. Camp to Amanda Wolcott, December 20, 1862, Wolcott Letters, FSNMP. Whether Brown actually spoke the words quoted is not that important because they shed light on several common themes in the deaths of soldiers. Evangelicals increasingly emphasized reunion of families in the afterlife, rejecting traditional notions of the corpse representing sinful humanity. See Laderman, *Sacred Remains,* 51–58; Ann Douglas, "Heaven Our Home," 65–68.

24. Raymond, "Extracts from the Journal of Henry J. Raymond," 410–20; Brainerd, *Bridge Building in Wartime,* 219; Whitman (?), *Prisoners,* March 11, 1097; William Withington to his wife, December 18, 1862, Withington Papers, MHC; Grant Memoir, 4, NYHS; *German Reformed Messenger,* January 7, 1863, 2; Miller and Mooney, *Civil War,* 24. For an argument that the Civil War generation experienced a "morbid" fixation on the dead body, see Laderman, *Sacred Remains,* 73–85.

25. Paludan, *"People's Contest,"* 365–66; Miller and Mooney, *Civil War,* 24, 137; Ruggles, "Soldier and a Letter," 89; McDonald, *Woman's Civil War,* 100; Gallman, *Mastering Wartime,* 54–56.

26. Conyngham, *Irish Brigade,* 356–59; *New York Times,* January 17, 1863; "Mass for the Dead Soldiers of the Irish Brigade," *Frank Leslie's Illustrated Newspaper,* February 7, 1863, 304–5; *New York Irish-American,* January 24, 1863; *New York Tablet,* January 24, 1863; Cavanagh, *Memoirs of Gen. Thomas Francis Meagher,* 477. This first St. Patrick's Cathedral, still standing at the corner of Mulberry and Prince streets, should not be confused with the present St. Patrick's Cathedral.

27. Borden, *Legacy of Fanny and Joseph,* 130–31, 134–36, 139, 143. The pious believed that heaven released one from life's trials, and reassurances about their passing to a better world provided considerable comfort. For a general discussion of this point, see Lifton, *History and Human Survival,* 174–75. The death of so many away from home, bereft of their women relatives and their own clergymen, caused further social strain by depriving families of the increasingly elaborate and prolonged rituals of grief. Unfortunately, students of death have largely ignored the Civil War's massive carnage in assessing social attitudes and practices. See Ann Douglas, "Heaven Our Home," 49–68.

28. Royster, *Destructive War,* 250–51; *Richmond Daily Dispatch,* December 16, 25, 1862; *Providence (R.I.) Daily Journal,* December 13, 1862; "Remarks at the Funeral of Lt. Col. J. B. Curtis, December 17, 1862," *Christian Inquirer,* December 27, 1862, n.p.; *Wellsboro (Pa.) Agitator,* January 4, 1863. It seemed especially touching when a sickly youth defied his parents' wishes, endured the hardships of camp life, and then fell in battle. See *Richmond Daily Whig,* December 24, 1862.

29. *Christian Reformed Messenger,* January 7, 1863, 2; *Raleigh Weekly Standard,* January 7, 1863; Molyneux, *Quill of the Wild Goose,* 61; Bacon, *Memorial of William Kirkland Bacon,* 20–41, 51–62, 78–81; Means, *Waiting for Daybreak,* 6–9; Goolsby, "Crenshaw Battery," 349. On both the importance and the limits of religion as consolation, see Drew Gilpin Faust, *Riddle of Death,* 22–23.

30. United States Christian Commission, *First Annual Report,* 39–40; David Beem to his wife, January 22, 1863, Beem Papers, IHS; William W. Bennett, *Narrative of the Great Revival,* 243–44; Means, *Waiting for Daybreak,* 12–13; Weymouth, *Memorial Sketch of Lieut. Edgar M. Newcomb,* 111–21.

31. Sweet, *Traces of War,* 15–34; Haines, *15th New Jersey,* 34; Samuel J. Watson, "Religion and Combat Motivation in Confederate Armies," 41–48; Edward P. Smith, *Incidents of the Christian Commission,* 49–50; Mulholland, *116th Pennsylvania,* 53; United States Christian Commission, *First Annual Report,* 39; Laderman, *Sacred Remains,* 98–99; *German Reformed Messenger,* January 7, 1863, 2. For a fine general discussion of northern soldiers coming to terms with death, see Reid Mitchell, *Vacant Chair,* 138–50.

32. Holland, *Pierce M. B. Young,* 70; Edward Porter Alexander, *Fighting for the Confederacy,* 177; William Rhadamanthus Montgomery, *Georgia Sharpshooter,* 77; *OR,* 582; *Athens (Ga.) Southern Banner,* December 17, 24, 1862; Stegeman, *These Men She Gave,* 78; Joseph Henry Lumpkin to his daughter, December 30, 1862, Lumpkin Papers, UG; *OR,* 1067–68; *B&L,* 3: 93–94; Confederate Soldier to "Dear Molly," December 16–17, 1862, UDC Bound Transcripts, GDAH.

33. Slaughter, *Life of Randolph Fairfax,* 5–16, 34–47; Randolph Barton, *Recollections,* 37; James Power Smith, "With Stonewall Jackson," 31; Minor Memoir, 136, UVa; Judith Brockenbrough McGuire, *Diary of a Southern Refugee,* 179; John William Jones, *Christ in the Camp,* 69–70. For similar themes, see Burrows, *Memoirs of Lewis Minor Coleman,* 3–44; Renfroe, *Model Confederate Soldier,* 4–16.

34. Bartol, *Nation's Hour,* 3–25, 46, 53, 55, 58; John W. Ames to his mother, December 22, 1862, Ames Papers, USAMHI; *Boston Daily Advertiser,* December 20, 1862.

35. Richard Frederick Fuller, *Chaplain Fuller,* 292–93, 302–4, 310–21; Richard F. Fuller to Charles Sumner, December 15, 1862, January 19, 1863, Sumner Papers, HU; Charles Carelton Coffin, *Four Years of Fighting,* 150–52; *Boston Evening Transcript,* December 15, 1862. Funeral sermons for men with abolitionist antecedents commonly employed the antithesis between words and actions that Lincoln used so effectively in the Gettysburg Address. See Wills, *Lincoln at Gettysburg,* 55–62.

36. Jack D. Welsh, *Medical Histories of Union Generals,* 23; Bayard, *Life of Bayard,* 261, 274–77, 320–23; A. J. Alexander, "Fredericksburg"; Potter, *One Surgeon's Private War,* 53; December 13, 1862, Lloyd Diary, SHC; *Evangelist,* February 5, 1863, 2; Strong, *Diary of George Templeton Strong,* 3:279–80; McCrea, *Dear Belle,* 176–77; Elizabeth Blair Lee, *Civil War Letters,* 216; *New York Tribune,* December 15, 1862; Gurowski, *Diary,* 2:34–35; *New York Herald,* December 17, 1862.

37. *OR,* 646, 1067; Boteler, "At Fredericksburg with Stonewall," 82; James Power Smith, "With Stonewall Jackson," 34; McIntosh Manuscript, 11–12, SHC; Krick, "Maxcy Gregg," 293; J. Monroe Anderson to "Dear Misses Gregg," January 9, 1863, Gregg Papers, SCL; December 15, 1862, Hamilton Diary, FSNMP; Palmer, *Address Delivered at the Funeral of General Maxcy Gregg,* 3–11; *Journal of the House of Representatives of South Carolina,* 192–93; *Charleston Daily Courier,* December 15, 1862; *Charleston Mercury,* December 15, 1862; Francis Pickens to "Dear Miss Gregg," December 28, 1862, Alexander Cheeves Haskell Papers, SHC. On stoic death in the Civil War era, see Saum, *Popular Mood of America,* 110–13; Linderman, *Embattled Courage,* 64–65. On the sometimes contradictory components of southern honor, see Wyatt-Brown, *Southern Honor.*

38. William Calder to his mother, December 15, 1862, Calder Family Papers, SHC; D. R. E. Winn to his wife, December 18, 1862, Winn Letters, Emory; William H. Clairville to his sister, December 17, 1862, Clairville Papers, Rutgers University; Jedediah Hotchkiss to Sara Ann Comfort Hotchkiss, December 17, 1862, Hotchkiss Papers, LC; Speairs and Pettit, *Civil War Letters,* 1:82; Hartsock, *Soldier of the Cross,* 44; E. R. Willis to his father, December 18, 1862, E. R.

and McKibben Willis Letters, FSNMP; Myers, *Children of Pride*, 1001; DeNoon, *Charlie's Letters*, 115; George M. Barnard to his father, December 16, 1862, Barnard Papers, MHS; Beidelman, *Letters of George Washington Beidelman*, 162.

39. William M. Sheppard to his wife, December 17, 1862, Sheppard Letter, FSNMP; A. A. Batchelder to his parents, December 16, 1862, Batchelder Letter, FSNMP; William Fermoil to his family, December 24, 1862, Fermoil Letter, FSNMP; Sypher, *History of the Pennsylvania Reserve Corps*, 418–19. Gerald Linderman points to a declining faith in divine protection during the course of the war, but what is perhaps more remarkable is how many soldiers and civilians held fast to this notion with sometimes only slight modifications. See Linderman, *Embattled Courage*, 158–59.

40. McCarthy, *Detailed Minutiae of Soldier Life*, 94; Palfrey, *Antietam and Fredericksburg*, 166. For useful general discussions of how little soldiers usually saw, see Keegan, *Face of Battle*, 46–54, 101, 128–31; Hess, *Union Soldier in Battle*, 9–15.

41. Hess, *Union Soldier in Battle*, 19–21; McPherson, *For Cause and Comrades*, 12; Frank and Reaves, "Seeing the Elephant," 92–93; W. H. Burgess to David McKnight, December 20, 1862, McKnight Family Papers, UT; P. E. Fouts to his parents, February 1, 1863, Fouts Collection, NCDAH.

42. R. J. Robertson to his parents, December 13, 1862, Robertson Papers, FSNMP; Abraham Welch to his sister, December 27, 1862, Welch Letter, SHC; Holsinger, "How Does One Feel under Fire?," 294–96; Clausewitz, *On War*, 85, 89, 167; William Hamilton to his mother, December 24, 1862, Hamilton Papers, LC; W. H. Andrews, *Footprints of a Regiment*, 97–98; Saum, *Popular Mood of America*, 153–54; McPherson, *For Cause and Comrades*, 62–67. Hatred could help fearful men still thinking of their families at home become killers. See Reid Mitchell, *Civil War Soldiers*, 75–82.

43. Frederick, *Story of a Regiment*, 116–17; Jacob Henry Cole, *Under Five Commanders*, 105; Waitt, *Nineteenth Massachusetts*, 183; Hopkins, *Seventh Rhode Island*, 47; J. H. Lane, "Twenty-Eighth North Carolina Infantry," 332–33. For the only Bible anecdote from Fredericksburg that I have found, see Kaser, *Books and Libraries in Camp and Battle*, 50.

44. Hartwell, *To My Beloved Wife and Boy at Home*, 36; Asa W. Bartlett, *History of the Twelfth New Hampshire*, 738; Reuben Schell to his father, December 17, 1862, and Benneville Schell to his father, December 28, 1862, Schell Letters, FSNMP; Treichler, "Sketch of Battle of Fredericksburg," USAMHI; Edmund Halsey, *Brother against Brother*, 95; Waitt, *Nineteenth Massachusetts*, 173.

45. John Toffey to his brother, December 23, 1862, Toffey Papers, Rutgers University; Wiley, *Life of Billy Yank*, 68; Edwin O. Wentworth to his wife, December 26, 1862, Wentworth Papers, LC; John C. Anderson to his family, January 10, 1863, Anderson Letter, FSNMP; Small, *Road to Richmond*, 68, 71; OR, 255, 300, 412; Frank and Reaves, "Seeing the Elephant," 110–19; Dean, *Shook over Hell*, 54–55, 72–75; Linderman, *Embattled Courage*, 17–35; Hess, *Union Soldier in Battle*, 73–82, 95–102; Clausewitz, *On War*, 101. The fear might continue after the battle ended. In late December, only days after Fredericksburg, a member of the 9th New Hampshire tried to fight the Rebels in his sleep and ended up putting a bullet through his foot. See Lord, *History of the Ninth New Hampshire*, 248. For a useful, though excessively psychoanalytical, discussion of how courage involves overcoming the fear of death, see Becker, *Denial of Death*, 11–13.

46. John Gregory Bishop Adams, *Reminiscences of the Nineteenth Massachusetts Regiment*, 52; Charles E. Davis, *Three Years in the Army*, 165–66; Linderman, *Embattled Courage*, 11–15, 32–33; *New York Tribune*, December 17, 1862; Reid Mitchell, *Vacant Chair*, 25–30; Waugh, "Reminiscences," 12, FSNMP. In 1888 recently elected Pennsylvania senator Matthew S. Quay received a Medal of Honor for leading a regiment in Humphreys's division during their late afternoon charge toward the stone wall. Quay's bravery was rather vaguely described, and

one suspects possible political influence; but a brigade commander recalled Quay saying right before the battle, "I would rather die, and be called a fool, than live, and be called a coward." See Mulholland, *Congress Medal of Honor Legion,* 171–73; Quay File, FSNMP.

47. *Baltimore American and Commercial Advertiser,* January 2, 1863; Linderman, *Embattled Courage,* 62–64, 160–61; *OR,* 224; Hess, *Union Soldier in Battle,* 82–93.

48. *Athens (Ga.) Southern Banner,* January 7, 1863; *Richmond Daily Whig,* December 18, 1862; *OR,* 594, 597, 671, and ser. 1, 51(2):663.

49. Clausewitz, *On War,* 113; Linderman, *Embattled Courage,* 15–16, 98–102, 26–27; Frank and Reaves, *"Seeing the Elephant,"* 37–41; Royster, *Destructive War,* 256–57, 264–65; Edwin Wentworth to his wife, January 12, 1863, Wentworth Papers, LC. Even the association of courage with manliness occasionally received a sharp blow. When a Hoosier major heard that a Pennsylvania corporal promoted to sergeant for "gallant conduct" at Fredericksburg had just had a baby, he could only wonder, "What use have we for women if soldiers in the army can give birth to children?" (Cavins, *Civil War Letters of Cavins,* 132).

50. Reid Mitchell, "Northern Soldier and His Community," 84–88; Keegan, *Face of Battle,* 73–74, 187–92; Linderman, *Embattled Courage,* 43–47; *OR,* 251, 269–70, 288.

51. *Easton (Pa.) Free Press,* December 18, 1862; *OR,* 187, 309, 319, 624; Robert Franklin Fleming Jr., "Recollections," FSNMP; Edwin Wentworth to his wife, December 26, 1862, Wentworth Papers, LC; *New York Herald,* December 18, 1862.

52. Clausewitz, *On War,* 138, 187; Alcott, *Hospital Sketches,* 34–35; William Hamilton to his mother, December 28, 1862, Hamilton Papers, LC; George C. Case to his parents, December 17, 1862, Case Letters, FSNMP; Edwin Wentworth to his wife, January 5, 1863, Wentworth Papers, LC; Keegan, *Face of Battle,* 35; Linderman, *Embattled Courage,* 73–79; James Crowther to his sister, December 28, 1862, GAR. For excellent analyses of battle as an act of will and the impulse toward self-sacrifice, see Keegan, *Face of Battle,* 296; Hess, *Liberty, Virtue, and Progress,* 42–55.

53. Index Project Summary of Courts-Martial, Fredericksburg, Woodacre, California, copies in FSNMP; Wightman, *From Antietam to Fort Fisher,* 91; Ujanirtus Allen, *Campaigning with "Old Stonewall,"* 198–99. These statements about the fighting at Fredericksburg are consistent with James McPherson's estimate that about half the men in any given regiment did most of the fighting. See McPherson, *For Cause and Comrades,* 6–7. The Lowry project on court-martial records promises to be of enormous value to students of the Civil War.

54. John L. Smith, *118th Pennsylvania,* 112–14; Goodson, "Letters of Joab Goodson," 136; Zerah Coston Monks to Hannah T. Rohrer, January 1863, Monks-Rohrer Letters, Emory; Paige Memoir, 24–25, USAMHI; Small, *Road to Richmond,* 70–71; W. C. Ward, "Unable to Help," 3; Waitt, *Nineteenth Massachusetts,* 184; Brinton, *Memoirs,* 219.

55. Goss, *Recollections of a Private,* 132–33; McClenthen, *Narrative of the Fall and Winter Campaign,* 46; Blake, *Three Years in the Army of the Potomac,* 151–52; Pile Memoir, 7, TSLA; Sarah Emma Evelyn Edmonds, *Nurse and Spy in the Union Army,* 304–5; Bloodgood, *Personal Reminiscences of the War,* 52–53; Gaff, *On Many a Bloody Field,* 210.

56. Dickert, *Kershaw's Brigade,* 197–98; Orwig, *131st Pennsylvania,* 114–15; Wyckoff, *Third South Carolina,* 93; James Harvey Wood, *The War,* 109; Robert Franklin Fleming Jr., "Recollections," FSNMP.

57. McPherson, *For Cause and Comrades,* 8–9, 59–61; William Hamilton to his mother, December 28, 1862, Hamilton Papers, LC; Robert Franklin Fleming Jr., "Recollections," 2, FSNMP; December 20, 1862, Dodge Diary, LC; J. McDonald to his sister, December 19, 1862, Lt. J. McDonald Letters, FSNMP; *Rochester (N.Y.) Daily Democrat and American,* January 13, 27, 1863; Hirst, *Boys from Rockville,* 78–79; *Philadelphia Inquirer,* January 21, 1863.

58. Index Project Summary of Courts-Martial, Fredericksburg, Woodacre, California, copies in FSNMP; William B. Jordan Jr., *Red Diamond Regiment,* 32; Ujanirtus Allen, *Campaigning with "Old Stonewall,"* 204; O. Leland Barlow to his sister, December 29, 1862, Barlow

Papers, CSL; Thorpe, *Fifteenth Connecticut Volunteers*, 40; David Emmons Johnston, *Story of a Confederate Boy in the Civil War*, 174–75; January 18, 1863, Hadley Diary, NHHS; Henry A. Allen, *Sergeant Allen and Private Renick*, 177; January 2, 1863, Cowin Diary, UA; Robert Goldthwaite Carter, *Four Brothers in Blue*, 210.

59. Keegan, *Face of Battle*, 297–98; Clausewitz, *On War*, 260; December 21, 1862, Malloy Diary, CWMC, USAMHI; Means, *Waiting for Daybreak*, 3–7. For a helpful discussion of the sometimes contradictory efforts to interpret massive numbers of dead as part of a larger cause while also giving meaning to individual sacrifices, see Laderman, *Sacred Remains*, 130.

CHAPTER NINETEEN

1. Heller and Heller, *Confederacy Is on Her Way up the Spout*, 81; December 14, 1862, Malloy Diary, CWMC, USAMHI; *OR*, 557–58, 648; *Atlanta Southern Confederacy*, December 27, 1862; *Richmond Daily Examiner*, December 16, 1862. The reader will soon notice that much more attention is given to the treatment of the Federal wounded. This is because the Yankees faced a much larger task and also because the Union sources are much richer.

2. *Richmond Daily Dispatch*, December 16, 1862; Bacot, *Confederate Nurse*, 169; Mary Janes Lucas to "Dear Nannie," December 20, 1862, Lucas-Ashley Family Papers, Duke; Judith Brockenbrough McGuire, *Diary of a Southern Refugee*, 176–77; Katharine M. Jones, *Ladies of Richmond*, 146.

3. *MSH*, 2:100, 102, 130; Gordon Willis Jones, "Medical History of the Fredericksburg Campaign," 241–48; Hough, "Battle of Fredericksburg," 8, FSNMP; A. O'Connell to Dr. A. W. Dougherty, December 13, 1862, entry 544, Field Hospital Records, Adjutant General's Records, NA; Letterman, *Medical Recollections of the Army of the Potomac*, 51–57, 65–66.

4. Letterman, *Medical Recollections of the Army of the Potomac*, 24–30; *New York Tribune*, December 2, 1862; Heffelfinger, "'Dear Sister Jennie,'" 217; Small, *Sixteenth Maine*, 81; Hopkins, *Seventh Rhode Island*, 45; Sypher, *History of the Pennsylvania Reserve Corps*, 420–21; U.S. Army Department, *Medal of Honor*, 120.

5. *MSH*, 12:923–24, 937–38; A. O'Connell to Dr. A. W. Dougherty, December 13, 1862, entry 544, Field Hospital Records, Adjutant General's Records, NA; Samuel J. C. Moore to Ellen Moore, December 15, 1862, Samuel J. C. Moore Papers, SHC; Duncan, *Medical Department of the United States Army*, 185–86; Herbert C. Mason to his father, December 17, 1862, Mason Letter, FSNMP; Grant Memoir, NYHS; Hurd Memoir, USAMHI; *OR*, 406.

6. Douglas and Brink, *Reports of the Sanitary Commission after Fredericksburg*, 11–12; *MSH*, 2:103, 134; Hough, "Battle of Fredericksburg," 7, FSNMP; *OR*, 313, 419; Curtis C. Pollock to his mother, December 18, 1862, Pollock Papers, CWMC, USAMHI; Duncan, *Medical Department of the United States Army*, 180, 187, 190.

7. James I. Robertson Jr., *Soldiers Blue and Gray*, 160; William H. Clairville, "Battle of Fredericksburg," 83, Clairville Papers, Rutgers University; Castleman, *Army of the Potomac*, 267–68; *Philadelphia Public Ledger*, January 3, 1863; *New York Irish-American*, December 27, 1862.

8. Lord, *History of the Ninth New Hampshire*, 240–42; Walt Whitman, *Walt Whitman's Civil War*, 236–37; Tillinghast, *Twelfth Rhode Island*, 223–24; George H. Allen, *Forty-Six Months*, 173.

9. A. O'Connell to Dr. A. W. Dougherty, December 13, 1862, entry 544, Field Hospital Records, Adjutant General's Records, NA; Grant Memoir, 2–3, NYHS; Duncan, *Medical Department of the United States Army*, 192, 196–99; *MSH*, 2:101–2, 131; *OR*, 377; Letterman, *Medical Recollections of the Army of the Potomac*, 69–71; Gordon Willis Jones, "Medical History of the Fredericksburg Campaign," 248–49. See the map of the division hospitals in Duncan, *Medical Department of the United States Army*, 193.

10. Duncan, *Medical Department of the United States Army*, 180, 196–97; Locke, *Story of the Regiment*, 166–67; December 12, 1862, Bailey Diary, NHHS; Hough, "Battle of Fredericksburg," 8, FSNMP; Hopkins, *Seventh Rhode Island*, 49; Colston, "Personal Experiences," FSNMP; William H. Stiles to his mother, December 15, 1862, Mackay and Stiles Family Papers,

SHC; Fitzpatrick, *Letters to Amanda,* 38. Sanitary Commission officials, War Department inspectors, congressmen, and newspaper correspondents generally praised the operations of the division hospitals near Fredericksburg. See Douglas and Brink, *Reports of the Sanitary Commission after Fredericksburg,* 12–13, 27–28; Duncan, *Medical Department of the United States Army,* 178–79; Letterman, *Medical Recollections of the Army of the Potomac,* 90; *Philadelphia Inquirer,* December 22, 1862; *Albany (N.Y.) Evening Journal,* December 27, 1862.

11. *MSH,* 2:130; William Child, *Fifth New Hampshire,* 163; Bisbee, "Three Years a Volunteer Soldier," 117; Abraham Welch to his sister, December 27, 1862, Welch Letter, SHC; *Albany (N.Y.) Atlas and Argus,* December 27, 1862; *OR,* 958; Howard Thomas, *Boys in Blue from the Adirondack Foothills,* 114–15; William Watson, *Letters of a Civil War Surgeon,* 42; Stuckenberg, *Surrounded by Methodists,* 46; Duncan, *Medical Department of the United States Army,* 180–81. For the deficiencies of individual hospitals, see Douglas and Brink, *Reports of the Sanitary Commission after Fredericksburg,* 17–26.

12. Letterman, *Medical Recollections of the Army of the Potomac,* 57–63; *New York Irish-American,* December 27, 1862; *Albany (N.Y.) Atlas and Argus,* December 15, 1862; Hough, "Battle of Fredericksburg," 8, FSNMP. For reports of Confederate shells striking hospitals in Fredericksburg, including one account of an already badly mangled Pennsylvanian who was killed by a shell just as the surgeons were preparing to amputate one of his legs, see Brinton, *Memoirs,* 214–15; McCarter, *My Life in the Irish Brigade,* 201–2; Thomson and Rauch, *History of the "Bucktails,"* 240.

13. Letterman, *Medical Recollections of the Army of the Potomac,* 60–61; "Volunteer Surgeons," *Medical and Surgical Reporter,* November 8, 1862, 158–59; "The Care of the Wounded on the Battle-Field," *Medical and Surgical Reporter,* January 24, 1863, 341–42; Bardeen, *Little Fifer's Diary,* 115; *New York Herald,* November 28, 1862; *Richmond Daily Whig,* November 27, 1862; *OR,* 342; William Watson, *Letters of a Civil War Surgeon,* 41, 45; *MSH,* 2:104.

14. Hough, "Battle of Fredericksburg," 15, FSNMP; Lord, *History of the Ninth New Hampshire,* 231; Trobriand, *Four Years with the Army of the Potomac,* 378–79; December 15, 1862, Charles S. Granger Diary, CWMC, USAMHI; Walter Clark, *Regiments and Battalions from North Carolina,* 2:475–76; *Kokomo (Ind.) Howard Tribune,* January 8, 1863.

15. Mary Edwards Walker, "Incidents Connected with the Army," Walker Papers, Syracuse University; Frank Moore, *Rebellion Record,* 6:93; Abraham Welch to his sister, December 27, 1862, Welch Letter, SHC; Gordon Willis Jones, "Medical History of the Fredericksburg Campaign," 251; Letterman, *Medical Recollections of the Army of the Potomac,* 76–86.

16. Rollins, "'Give My Love to All,'" 28; *MSH,* 8:451, 12:440; Arthur T. Chapin to his sister, December 20, 1862, Chapin Letter, USAMHI; McCarter, *My Life in the Irish Brigade,* 198–201.

17. *MSH,* 2:130, 133; Letterman, *Medical Recollections of the Army of the Potomac,* 79–86; Gilbreath Reminiscences, 52–53, ISL; Castleman, *Army of the Potomac,* 265; Frank Moore, *Rebellion Record,* 6:93. More than a month before the battle, advertisements for artificial limbs appeared in various periodicals, and a Federal commission had met in New York to determine what kinds of prostheses the government would provide. See *Harper's Weekly,* November 1, 1862, 703; *New York Tribune,* November 13, 1862.

18. Burroughs, "Reminiscences of Fredericksburg," 637; S. Millett Thompson, *Thirteenth New Hampshire,* 86; [Heinichen,] "Fredericksburg," Maryland Historical Society; Small, *Road to Richmond,* 68; Susan Leigh Blackford, *Letters from Lee's Army,* 150; Todd Reminiscences, 78, SHC.

19. Paludan, *"People's Contest,"* 325; Edwin C. Bennett, *Musket and Sword,* 118–19; Holsinger, "How Does One Feel under Fire?," 296; December 13, 1862, Bailey Diary, NHHS; George H. Allen, *Forty-Six Months,* 172–73.

20. Henry Lewis to "Dear Cousin Charlie," January 3, 1863, Lewis Letters, GLC; McCarter, *My Life in the Irish Brigade,* 207; Mulholland, "Battle of Fredericksburg," 1; Siegel, *For the*

Glory of the Union, 114–16; Castleman, *Army of the Potomac,* 272; Hopkins, *Seventh Rhode Island,* 49.

21. December 14, 1862, Bescancon Diary, Duke; Hartsock, *Soldier of the Cross,* 45; *New York Herald,* December 15, 1862; Frank Moore, *Women of the War,* 536–40; Paludan, *"People's Contest,"* 355; Stephen B. Oates, *Woman of Valor,* 117. Sometimes female volunteers could be less than sensitive themselves. As a surgeon was operating on a man who had been shot in the groin, a nurse flippantly remarked to the poor soldier, "How hard [it is] to lose so many privates on the field and then come here and lose your own" (George H. Patch to his mother, December 23, 1862, Patch Papers, Leigh Collection, USAMHI). Dr. Mary Walker, who had arrived in November, was still resented by male surgeons. See Elizabeth D. Leonard, *Yankee Women,* 122–23.

22. Stephen B. Oates, *Woman of Valor,* 101–3, 109–12, 119–20; Clara Barton to Mary Norton, January 19, 1863, Norton Papers, Duke.

23. Elizabeth D. Leonard, *Yankee Women,* 122–23; December 13, 15, 1862, Eaton Diary, SHC; Frank Moore, *Women of the War,* 119–21. For a general discussion of how hospital conditions affected doctors, nurses, and visitors, see Dean, *Shook over Hell,* 77–80.

24. Douglas and Brink, *Reports of the Sanitary Commission after Fredericksburg,* 1–3; Brinton, *Personal Memoirs,* 59–60; Corby, *Memoirs of Chaplain Life,* 134–35; *New York Herald,* December 22, 1862; United States Christian Commission, *First Annual Report,* 34, 39, 57–58, 64–65; United States Christian Commission, *Second Annual Report,* 33–34; James Grant, "Flag and the Cross," 53–54, LC. Also maintaining ties between communities, churches, and soldiers, local aid societies sent supplies and agents to the camps. See *Haverhill (Mass.) Gazette,* December 17, 1862; Washburn, *108th Regiment,* 37–38; Foster, *New Jersey and the Rebellion,* 523n.

25. Linderman, *Embattled Courage,* 130–33; Edward Louis Edes to his father, December 19, 1862, Edes Papers, MHS; *Kokomo (Ind.) Howard Tribune,* December 25, 1862; Donaldson, *Inside the Army of the Potomac,* 189; *Evangelist,* February 5, 1863, 2; Gregory C. White, *31st Georgia,* 66; Julian, *Political Recollections,* 225–26. For the first few days after the battle, company rolls sometimes listed nearly as many absent as present; a New York regimental clerk reported that several men were in some hospital ("don't know where"). See December 15–16, 1862, Robinson Diary, DCL; Borton, *Awhile with the Blue,* 53–54; *OR Supplement,* pt. 2, 47: 490–92.

26. Cogswell, *Eleventh New Hampshire,* 554–55; Stephen B. Oates, *Woman of Valor,* 115; Walt Whitman, *Walt Whitman's Civil War,* 39; December 16, 1862, Eaton Diary, SHC; *Indianapolis Daily Journal,* December 29, 1862; George W. Barr to Vinnie Barr, December 18, 1862, Barr Papers, Schoff Collection, CL; George H. Patch to his mother, December 23, 1862, Patch Papers, Leigh Collection, USAMHI; John England to Ellen Hargeddon, December 17, 1862, England Papers, NYPL. In closing a letter to a friend, a New York lieutenant unintentionally revealed why there were relatively few detailed descriptions of field hospitals right after a battle: "If I ever see you again I'll tell you things [that] will make your blood run cold and freeze the very marrow in your bones, but such things only make a letter disgusting— and to me, seeing them is terrible enough without deliberately recounting them" (Samuel S. Partridge to "Dear Ed," December 17, 1862, Partridge Letters, FSNMP).

27. Miller and Mooney, *Civil War,* 90–92, 116; December 14, 15, 17, 1862, Kerr Diary, FSNMP; J. E. Hodgkins, *Civil War Diary,* 18–19.

28. United States Christian Commission, *First Annual Report,* 35; Linderman, *Embattled Courage,* 27–32; John R. Coye to his wife, December 24, 1862, Coye Letters, FSNMP; *Baltimore American and Commercial Advertiser,* December 15, 1862; Cowtan, *Services of the Tenth New York Volunteers,* 170; *Kokomo (Ind.) Howard Tribune,* January 8, 1863; Hartsock, *Soldier of the Cross,* 43–44; Haines, *15th New Jersey,* 34.

29. A. B. Martin to "Dear Ann," December 19, 1862, Martin Letter, FSNMP; Douglas and Brink, *Reports of the Sanitary Commission after Fredericksburg*, 17–26; "Army and Navy News," *Medical and Surgical Reporter*, December 27, 1862, 299–300; Walt Whitman, *Walt Whitman's Civil War*, 39; Cavins, *Civil War Letters of Cavins*, 120.

30. Lord, *History of the Ninth New Hampshire*, 631–32; Marvel, *Ninth New Hampshire*, 111–12.

31. McCarter, *My Life in the Irish Brigade*, 195–98; Stephen B. Oates, *Woman of Valor*, 118; William Child, *Fifth New Hampshire*, 163–64; December 14, 1862, Eaton Diary, SHC; Borton, *On the Parallels*, 56; Lord, *History of the Ninth New Hampshire*, 240; Walt Whitman, *Walt Whitman's Civil War*, 29; D. Porter Marshall, *Co. "K," 155th Pennsylvania*, 80. As John Keegan pointed out about Waterloo, it is often forgotten in battle accounts that the dying continued for several days after a battle; see Keegan, *Face of Battle*, 202. For Civil War battles of course—mostly because of improved medical treatment that kept the mortally wounded alive longer—deaths might continue for weeks and even months after a battle.

32. Letterman, *Medical Recollections of the Army of the Potomac*, 87; Potter, *One Surgeon's Private War*, 54; December 18–21, 1862, Kerr Diary, FSNMP.

33. Letterman, *Medical Recollections of the Army of the Potomac*, 87–88; December 17, 1862, Taggart Diary, USAMHI; Samuel W. Eaton to Eddie Eaton, December 15, 1862, Eaton Papers, SHSW; United States Christian Commission, *First Annual Report*, 33–34; Edward P. Smith, *Incidents of the Christian Commission*, 49; McCarter, *My Life in the Irish Brigade*, 204–6; *History of 127th Regiment Pennsylvania Volunteers*, 253; "Sacrifice of Federals at Fredericksburg," 370; *MSH*, 2:103–4, 132.

34. McCarter, *My Life in the Irish Brigade*, 205, 208; Douglas and Brink, *Reports of the Sanitary Commission after Fredericksburg*, 7; Duncan, *Medical Department of the United States Army*, 205; Stephen B. Oates, *Woman of Valor*, 119; *MSH*, 2:104, 133, 12:957–71.

35. McCarter, *My Life in the Irish Brigade*, 209–11; Duncan, *Medical Department of the United States Army*, 207; Stillé, *History of the United States Sanitary Commission*, 371–72; Locke, *Story of the Regiment*, 168–69; Stuckenberg, *Surrounded by Methodists*, 47; Ropes, *Civil War Nurse*, 111; *MSH*, 2:133; Walt Whitman, *Walt Whitman's Civil War*, 40; Bliss Memoir, 4: 36–37, USAMHI. The steamship ride took eight hours.

36. Duncan, *Medical Department of the United States Army*, 205; McCarter, *My Life in the Irish Brigade*, 211; United States Christian Commission, *First Annual Report*, 34–35; Brooks, *Mr. Lincoln's Washington*, 45–46; Von Olnhausen, *Adventures of an Army Nurse*, 56. Some of the wounded would eventually be transferred to Philadelphia. Families now had to scan the hospital lists in the newspapers for word of their loved ones. See Ropes, *Civil War Nurse*, 113; Miller, *Camp Curtin*, 148–49; *Philadelphia Inquirer*, December 22, 1862, January 7, 12, 1863; *New York Tribune*, December 27, 1862. Confederates also had to rely on hospital lists and other incomplete sources for news of the wounded. Few accounts of treatment in the Richmond hospitals have survived. Two soldiers with painful but not especially serious wounds offered generally favorable assessments of hospital conditions in the Confederate capital. See Fitzpatrick, *Letters to Amanda*, 40–43; December 20–30, 1862, Malloy Diary, CWMC, USAMHI; *Lynchburg Daily Virginian*, December 17, 1862.

37. Ropes, *Civil War Nurse*, 112; Wheelock, *Boys in White*, 67; *MSH*, 6:897–99, 910, 913–15, 917–20, 936–42, 12:837–39; Duncan, *Medical Department of the United States Army*, 181; "The Discharge of the Wounded and Sick Soldiers from the Service," *Medical and Surgical Reporter*, December 13, 20, 1862, 273; Walt Whitman, *Walt Whitman's Civil War*, 47–50; Stuckenberg, *Surrounded by Methodists*, 48. Brooks carefully distinguished between the recently constructed, whitewashed structures that appeared to be model facilities, the well-organized hospitals supervised by the Sanitary Commission, and the notoriously overcrowded and unsanitary buildings that had been used since the beginning of the war; see Brooks, *Mr. Lincoln's Washington*, 47–50.

38. Alcott, *Hospital Sketches*, 25–29; Ropes, *Civil War Nurse*, 115–16; Walt Whitman, *Walt Whitman's Civil War*, 85–91.

39. William Houghton to his father, December 22, 1862, Houghton Papers, IHS; Alcott, *Hospital Sketches*, 30–31; Joseph H. Leighty to his sister, January 1, 1863, Leighty Papers, CWMC, USAMHI; J. E. Hodgkins, *Civil War Diary*, 20. Of course it is significant that such favorable reports usually came from men with relatively minor injuries.

40. J. F. Hodgkins, *Civil War Diary*, 21; Heffelfinger, "'Dear Sister Jennie,'" 217; Edwin C. Bennett, *Musket and Sword*, 120–23. Clara Barton and Senator Henry Wilson of Massachusetts arranged for Sgt. Thomas Plunkett, who had been so badly wounded during Ferrero's attack toward the stone wall and had endured the amputation of both arms, to return to Massachusetts. After seeing Plunkett in Washington, even the hard-bitten Wilson was shaken. "My God! What a Price!" he exclaimed. "And where is the end?" See *MSH*, 10:974; Stephen B. Oates, *Woman of Valor*, 119. See the account of Plunkett's wounding in Chapter 15 above.

41. Mary Edwards Walker, "Incidents Connected with the Army," no 1, Walker Papers, Syracuse University; H. O. Thomas to William Oland Bourne, September 27, 1862, Bourne Papers, LC; Alcott, *Hospital Sketches*, 36–37, 91–92.

42. *MSH*, 7:205, 239, 263–65, 8:299–300, 361–62. The standard Confederate surgical manual recommended a more conservative approach to serious head wounds and opposed trephining altogether. See Chisolm, *Manual of Military Surgery*, 294–96.

43. *MSH*, 8:431–32, 554, 9:260; Alcott, *Hospital Sketches*, 35–36.

44. *MSH*, 9:455, 11:83, 85–86, 170, 366. In 1869 a private in Sykes's division finally had a bullet extracted from his right shoulder. A sergeant in Humphreys's division was not nearly so fortunate; with a ball still lodged in his hip joint, in 1874 he died from the wound. See *MSH*, 10:484, 11:25–26.

45. Ropes, *Civil War Nurse*, 120; *MSH*, 10:870, 12:625, 892.

46. *MSH*, 10, 717–18, 11:301; Mary Edwards Walker, "Incidents Connected with the Army," no. 3, Walker Papers, Syracuse University; John Lord Parker, *Twenty-Second Massachusetts*, 236–37.

47. *MSH*, 10:748, 11:22, 357, 366, 381, 12:633, 828, 839–40, 443–44. "Sloughing" refers to dead tissue separating itself from healthy tissue. Hospital reports do not always make clear distinctions between gangrene and other types of infections, including the commonly reported pyemia.

48. Wheelock, *Boys in White*, 79–80; George Thornton Fleming, *Hays*, 286; Alcott, *Hospital Sketches*, 84–86; Gilbreath Reminiscences, 53–55, ISL; Kepler, *Fourth Ohio*, 196–97.

49. Von Olnhausen, *Adventures of an Army Nurse*, 57–58; Alcott, *Hospital Sketches*, 29–30, 33, 37–38, 40–41, 43; Alcott, *Journals of Louisa May Alcott*, 113 15; Hackett, *Christian Memorials*, 104, Wheelock, *Boys in White*, 60–61, 71–72; Stephen B. Oates, *Woman of Valor*, 121.

50. Alcott, *Journals of Louisa May Alcott*, 110–11, 113; *Philadelphia Evening Bulletin*, January 6, 1863; Wheelock, *Boys in White*, 72–73; Laderman, *Sacred Remains*, 131–32. For helpful treatments of the soldiers longing for feminine touches and attempts to describe wartime suffering in conventionally sentimental language, see Reid Mitchell, *Vacant Chair*, 71–87; Frederickson, *Inner Civil War*, 87–88. Back home, ladies' aid societies sponsored relief fairs or gathered special food for shipment to the hospitals. See *Albany (N.Y.) Atlas and Argus*, December 18, 27, 1862; Gallman, *Mastering Wartime*, 130; *New York Times*, December 16, 1862.

51. Alcott, *Hospital Sketches*, 31, 80–84; United States Christian Commission, *First Annual Report*, 34, 36; Ropes, *Civil War Nurse*, 95–99.

52. *Fourth Annual Report of the Bureau of Military Statistics*, 558; Alcott, *Hospital Sketches*, 30, 49–59; Ropes, *Civil War Nurse*, 117–18; Lusk, *Letters of William Thompson Lusk*, 253.

53. Jeffrey D. Marshall, *War of the People*, 130–31; Alcott, *Hospital Sketches*, 45–46. For a careful analysis of psychological problems suffered by Civil War soldiers, see Dean, *Shook over Hell*.

54. *Rochester (N.Y.) Daily Democrat and American,* January 14, 1863; ? to Mrs. Sarah Shure, December 25, 1862, Shure Letters, USAMHI. Private Shure died on December 29. See Samuel Penniman Bates, *History of the Pennsylvania Volunteers,* 7:272.

CHAPTER TWENTY

1. David Horner Bates, *Lincoln in the Telegraph Office,* 113; Miers, *Lincoln Day by Day,* 3: 155; Sid Denning to Anson Stager, December 11, 12, 1862; J. G. Garland to Stager, December 11, 1862 (three dispatches); A. H. Caldwell to Stager, December 12, 1862; O. H. Dorrance to Stager, December 12, 1862; E. V. Sumner to Mrs. Sumner, December 11, 1862, Lincoln Papers, LC. The presence of these telegrams in the Lincoln papers strongly suggests that the president either read them at the War Department or they were later sent to the Executive Mansion. The Associated Press had a close relationship with the administration and became a quasi-official source of war news. See Richard A. Schwarzlose, *Newsbrokers,* 1:242–54; Blondheim, *News over the Wires,* 129–40.

2. A. H. Caldwell to Anson Stager, December 13, 1862 (three dispatches); Sid Denning to Stager, December 13, 1862; J. G. Garland to Stager, December 13, 1862 (two dispatches); Stager to Edwin M. Stanton, December 13, 1862 (two dispatches), Lincoln Papers, LC; *New York Times,* December 13, 1862. The reference to the "first redoubt" being taken likely referred to the false reports during the late afternoon that some of Couch's troops had gained a foothold on Marye's Heights. It is doubtful that the *Times* quoted Lincoln accurately, but the report surely raised false and unreasonable hopes in the North.

3. *OR,* 65; Welles, *Diary of Gideon Welles,* 1:192; *OR Supplement,* pt. 1, 3:671; George Thornton Fleming, *Hays,* 283; Gaillard Hunt, *Israel, Elihu, and Cadwallader Washburn,* 206; Willard L. King, *Lincoln's Manager,* 206. The "first ridge" in Burnside's dispatch likely referred to the swale where so many Federals had taken shelter. One of Lincoln's secretaries, John G. Nicolay, had left Washington to visit Burnside. He did not arrive at Falmouth until noon on December 14, and what information he conveyed to the president is unknown. See John G. Nicolay to Therena Nicolay, December 11, 17, 1862, Nicolay Papers, LC; Lincoln, *Collected Works,* 5:552, 6:2.

4. Haupt, *Reminiscences of Herman Haupt,* 177; Villard, *Memoirs,* 1:384–91. Haupt's account is believable though he may have exaggerated Lincoln's reaction. Clearly perplexed, the president had decided not to accompany his wife to church that morning and summoned former secretary of war and Pennsylvania Republican wire-puller Simon Cameron to Washington. See Browning, *Diary,* 1:495; Lincoln, *Collected Works,* 6:2.

5. Willard L. King, *Lincoln's Manager,* 207; Sandburg, *Lincoln,* 1:630–31; Gurowski, *Diary,* 2:29; Browne, *Every-day Life of Abraham Lincoln,* 573–74.

6. Herman Haupt to his wife, December 18, 1862, Haupt Letterbook, Haupt Papers, LC; Browning, *Diary,* 1:596; Gibbon, *Recollections of the Civil War,* 106; Francis Becknell Carpenter, *Inner Life of Abraham Lincoln,* 177; Stephen B. Oates, *Lincoln,* 327; Nevins, *War for the Union,* 2:352; Mary A. Livermore, *My Story of the War,* 561. Sight of the Fredericksburg wounded may have further depressed the president. Both Lincoln and his wife visited hospitals shortly after the battle. See McCarter, *My Life in the Irish Brigade,* 217; Gilbreath Reminiscences, 55, ISL.

7. Leech, *Reveille in Washington,* 222; George Thornton Fleming, *Hays,* 284; *OR Supplement,* pt. 1, 3:672–73; Ethan Allan Hitchcock to "Dear Mrs. Mann," December 15, 1862, Hitchcock Papers, LC; Browning, *Diary,* 1:596; Welles, *Diary of Gideon Welles,* 1:193; Logsdon, *White,* 92; Matias Romero, *Mexican View of America in the 1860s,* 138. Brigadier general and recently elected Ohio congressman James A. Garfield took a much longer view of the Fredericksburg debacle. A proponent of aggressive strategy, he welcomed Burnside's "bloody work" and maintained that the only way to preserve the republic was to "pulverize the great rebel armies." See Garfield, *Wild Life of the Army,* 198–99.

8. J. Cutler Andrews, *North Reports the Civil War*, 333–34; Gobright, *Recollection of Men and Things at Washington*, 318; Robert Luther Thompson, *Wiring a Continent*, 373; Pratt, *Stanton*, 262–63; *Rochester (N.Y.) Daily Democrat and American*, December 18, 1862.

9. *Chicago Daily Tribune*, December 12, 1862; *New York Times*, December 12, 1862; *New York Tribune*, December 12, 1862; *Albany (N.Y.) Atlas and Argus*, December 12, 1862; *Philadelphia Inquirer*, December 12, 1862; *Providence (R.I.) Daily Journal*, December 12, 1862.

10. *Chicago Daily Tribune*, December 13, 1862; *Philadelphia Public Ledger*, December 13, 1862; *Albany (N.Y.) Atlas and Argus*, December 13, 1862.

11. J. Cutler Andrews, *North Reports the Civil War*, 330; *New York Herald*, December 14, 1862; *New York Times*, December 14, 1862; Leech, *Reveille in Washington*, 221.

12. *Newark (N.J.) Daily Advertiser*, December 15, 1862; *Philadelphia Public Ledger*, December 15, 1862; *New York Times*, December 15, 1862; *Boston Evening Transcript*, December 15, 1862; O'Connor, *Civil War Boston*, 121; *Springfield (Mass.) Daily Republican*, December 15, 1862; *Philadelphia Inquirer*, December 15, 1862; *New York Tribune*, December 15, 1862; *Boston Daily Advertiser*, December 15, 1862.

13. *Baltimore American and Commercial Advertiser*, December 16, 1862; *Albany (N.Y.) Evening Journal*, December 16, 1862; *Philadelphia Public Ledger*, December 16, 1862; *Providence (R.I.) Daily Journal*, December 16, 1862; *New York Times*, December 16, 1862; *Newark (N.J.) Daily Advertiser*, December 16, 1862; *Philadelphia Inquirer*, December 16, 17, 1862; *Washington Daily National Intelligencer*, December 16, 1862; *Hartford Daily Courant*, December 16, 17, 1862; J. Cutler Andrews, *North Reports the Civil War*, 335. Banks was in fact sailing for New Orleans to assume command in the Department of the Gulf.

14. Lincoln remarked to one of his secretaries, William O. Stoddard, that even if the Army of the Potomac kept suffering the same proportion of casualties, the Confederates would soon be "wiped out to the last man." Whether or not Stoddard was quoting the president directly, his account contained one especially telling passage: "No general yet found can face the arithmetic, but the end of the war will be at hand when he shall be discovered" (Stoddard, *Inside the White House*, 101).

15. *Rochester (N.Y.) Daily Democrat and American*, December 17, 19, 20, 1862; *Philadelphia Inquirer*, December 17–20, 22, 1862; "The Repulse at Fredericksburg," *Independent*, December 18, 1862, 4; *Easton (Pa.) Free Press*, December 18, 1862; *New York Times*, December 18–19, 1862, January 7, 1863; *Kokomo (Ind.) Howard Tribune*, December 18, 1862; *Albany (N.Y.) Evening Journal*, December 17, 1862; *Boston Evening Transcript*, December 17, 22, 1862. Even a Rochester Democratic editor hedged his bets, claimed to be still hopeful, but for good measure wished that Burnside would not have to face, à la McClellan, political interference from Washington. See *Rochester (N.Y.) Daily Union and Advertiser*, December 15, 1862.

16. *New York Tribune*, December 16, 1862; *Poughkeepsie (N.Y.) Daily Eagle*, December 20, 1862; *Springfield (Mass.) Daily Republican*, December 17, 18, 1862.

17. *New York Times*, December 17, 18, 1862; *Indianapolis Daily Journal*, December 15, 1862; *Albany (N.Y.) Atlas and Argus*, December 15–16, 1862; J. Cutler Andrews, *North Reports the Civil War*, 335; *Richmond Daily Dispatch*, December 22, 1862; Bosse, *Civil War Newspaper Maps*, 113; *New York Herald*, December 17, 21, 1862. Swinton's December 13 dispatch did not appear in print until December 17.

18. *New York Times*, December 17, 1862; *New York Herald*, December 17, 1862; *Albany (N.Y.) Evening Journal*, December 18, 1862; *Rochester (N.Y.) Daily Union and Advertiser*, December 17, 1862; *Boston Post*, December 17, 1862. A leading Catholic weekly carried somber headlines: "Great Disaster in the Army of the Potomac"; "Terrible Slaughter of the Best Blood of the Country" (*Boston Pilot*, December 27, 1862).

19. Strong, *Diary of George Templeton Strong*, 3:276–78; Elizabeth Blair Lee, *Civil War Letters*, 214–15. A disaster such as Fredericksburg of course created a great demand for news, but many citizens had already grown skeptical of press accounts. In such an atmosphere, rumors

helped people make some sense of a seemingly dangerous, chaotic situation. See Shibutani, *Improvised News,* 31–46, 57–59, 163–64.

20. Ferris, "Civil War Diaries," 242; Maria Bryant to John Emory Bryant, December 14, 1862, Bryant Papers, Duke; Strong, *Diary of George Templeton Strong,* 3:279; Benjamin F. Butler, *Correspondence,* 2:539; Fisher, *Diary of Sidney George Fisher,* 444; Royster, *Destructive War,* 237–39, 246–47; Maria Lydig Daly, *Diary of a Union Lady,* 208–9. During a period of what one sociologist has termed "sustained collective tension," civilians (and soldiers) exchanged rumors in an effort to comprehend a chaotic situation. Rumors can flourish in the absence of "news" but also when there is a surfeit of news, especially unreliable news. See Shibutani, *Improvised News,* 46–49, 64–65; Allport and Postman, *Psychology of Rumor,* 1.

21. Royster, *Destructive War,* 241; Gallman, *North Fights the Civil War,* 77–80; Gay, "Gay Letters," 389–90; McKelvey, *Rochester in the Civil War,* 113–14; *Indiana (Pa.) Weekly Democrat,* December 25, 1862.

22. William C. Davis, *Davis,* 482–84; *OR,* 1062–63; Jefferson Davis, *Papers,* 8:549, 552–53.

23. J. B. Jones, *Rebel War Clerk's Diary,* 1:210–13; Edmund Ruffin, *Diary,* 2:509; Kean, *Inside the Confederate Government,* 33; Katharine M. Jones, *Ladies of Richmond,* 146.

24. J. Cutler Andrews, *South Reports the Civil War,* 223–31; Corsan, *Two Months in the Confederate States,* 82–83; *Augusta (Ga.) Daily Chronicle and Sentinel,* December 13, 1862; *Richmond Daily Dispatch,* December 15, 1862; *Richmond Daily Whig,* December 15, 1862; *Richmond Daily Enquirer,* December 15–17, 1862; *Columbus (Ga.) Daily Enquirer,* December 16, 1862.

25. Judith Brockenbrough McGuire, *Diary of a Southern Refugee,* 174–75; Welton, *Caldwell Letters,* 162–63; December 14, 1862, Hume Diary, LC; McDonald, *Woman's Civil War,* 99; Frobel, *Civil War Diary of Anne S. Frobel,* 142, 144–45; Lucy Rebecca Buck, *Shadows of My Heart,* 164; Eppes, *Through Some Eventful Years,* 190; Robert Patrick, *Reluctant Rebel,* 67–68; Edmondston, *"Journal of a Secesh Lady,"* 315–22. For a discussion of Confederate politics in the aftermath of Fredericksburg, see Chapter 23 below.

26. Klement, *Copperheads in the Middle West,* 39; Bogue, "Cutler's Congressional Diary," 319–20; Nevins, *War for the Union,* 2:351–52; John Jay to Charles Sumner, December 18, 1862; George F. Williams to Sumner, December 19, 1862; and several other letters, December 1862, Sumner Papers, HU; Moses H. Grinnell to William H. Seward, December 17, 1862; C. Becker Jr. to Seward, December 23, 1862; Jonathan Longfellow to Seward, December 25, 1862, Seward Papers, UR.

27. Van Deusen, *Seward,* 335–41; Paludan, *Presidency of Lincoln,* 168–71, 174–75; Niven, *Chase,* 308–10; Blue, *Chase,* 191–92; Nevins, *War for the Union,* 2:335, 353n; "The Cabinet and the Country," *National Anti-Slavery Standard,* November 29, 1862, 2; Fessenden, *Fessenden,* 1:264.

28. Van Deusen, *Seward,* 341–44; Gurowski, *Diary,* 2:23–24, 34; "Secretary Seward and Emancipation," *National Anti-Slavery Standard,* December 20, 1862, 2; Dicey, *Spectator of America,* 97–98; Charles Francis Adams, *Cycle of Adams Letters,* 1:199; Logsdon, *White,* 92; Tap, *Over Lincoln's Shoulder,* 144.

29. Fessenden, *Fessenden,* 1:231–36; Browning, *Diary,* 1:596–98; Lafayette S. Foster to Hamilton Fish, December 16, 1862, Fish Papers, LC. Lincoln's refusal to approve the executions of more than 300 Sioux after an uprising in Minnesota the preceding summer also stoked Wilkinson's anger. As if he already did not have enough to disturb his sleep, the president had to decide which Indians would die. Thirty-eight were eventually executed at Mankato, Minnesota, on December 26. See *Congressional Globe,* 37th Cong., 3rd sess., 1862, 13; *New York Times,* December 8, 1862; Alexander Ramsey to Abraham Lincoln, November 28, 1862, Lincoln Papers, LC; Welles, *Diary of Gideon Welles,* 1:186; Lincoln, *Collected Works,* 5:493, 525–26, 537–38, 542–53, 550–51, 6:6; *OR,* ser. 2, 2:84, 125.

30. Donald, *Lincoln,* 401; William H. Seward to Abraham Lincoln, December 16, 1862, Lincoln Papers, LC; Fessenden, *Fessenden,* 1:236–38; Browning, *Diary,* 1:598–99.

31. Jacob F. Collamer to Abraham Lincoln, December 18, 1862, Lincoln Papers, LC; Lincoln, *Collected Works*, 6:9; Fessenden, *Fessenden*, 238–43; Browning, *Diary*, 1:600–601; Zachariah Chandler to his wife, December 18, 1862, Chandler Papers, LC.

32. Edward Bates, *Diary*, 268–70; Welles, *Diary of Gideon Welles*, 1:194–99; Fessenden, *Fessenden*, 1:243–48.

33. Welles, *Diary of Gideon Welles*, 1:199–204; Edward Bates, *Diary*, 270–71.

34. Charles Sumner, *Selected Letters*, 2:133; Randall, *Lincoln the President*, 2:243; French, *Witness to the Young Republic*, 415; Bogue, "Cutler's Congressional Diary," 320; *Newark (N.J.) Daily Advertiser*, December 22, 1862; *Watertown (N.Y.) Daily News and Reformer*, December 22, 1862.

35. Moran, *Journal of Benjamin Moran*, 2.1098, 1100–1101; Charles Francis Adams, *Cycle of Adams Letters*, 1:221–22; December 27–29, 1862, Adams Diary, MHS. Minister Adams no doubt was also worried about his son Charles Francis Jr. serving in the cavalry.

36. *Times* (London), December 26, 29, 30, 1862, January 2, 3, 5, 9, 13, 14, 1863; Marx and Engels, *Civil War in the U.S.*, 263–64; *London Illustrated News*, January 10, 1863, 38–39. Whether Lee could follow up his victory was debated in London, though some British commentators even concluded that Fredericksburg marked a genuine turning point in the war and that the United States might even break up into three separate nations. See "The Battle of Fredericksburg," *Saturday Review* (London), January 3, 1863, 2–3; "Fort Sumter to Fredericksburg," *Quarterly Review* (London), April 1863, 352–53.

37. Henry Shelton Sanford to William H. Seward, December 30, 1862, and Richard M. Blatchford to Seward, January 2, 1863, Seward Papers, UR; Bayard Taylor to Simon Cameron, January 3, 1863, Cameron Papers, LC. Conversely, news of the European reaction to Fredericksburg added to the despair in the American press. See *New York Herald*, January 15, 1863.

38. *ORN*, ser. 2, 3:629–33, 653–54, 662–63; Vance, *Papers of Zebulon Baird Vance*, 2:18.

39. "The Battle of Fredericksburg," *Index* (London), January 1, 1863, 155; "The Only Road to Peace," *Index*, January 8, 1863, 168; *ORN*, ser. 2, 3:619–25, 649, 651–53; *Charleston Mercury*, January 21, 1863.

40. *ORN*, ser. 2, 3:634–35; Case and Spencer, *United States and France*, 382–97; Owsley, *King Cotton Diplomacy*, 438–40; Crook, *North, South, and the Powers*, 279–82; Howard Jones, *Lincoln and a New Birth of Freedom*, 147–48, 157. There was some fear in Washington that the Fredericksburg defeat would rekindle European mediation efforts. See Du Pont, *Civil War Letters*, 2:323; Gurowski, *Diary*, 2:56–57.

41. J. E. B. Stuart to Flora Cooke Stuart, December 9–10, 1862, Stuart Papers, VHS; *Richmond Daily Whig*, December 11, 1862; *Richmond Daily Examiner*, December 17, 1862; Edmund Ruffin, *Diary*, 2:517, 528, 534.

42. William Johnson Pegram to Virginia Johnson McIntosh, January 8, 1863, Pegram-Johnson-McIntosh Family Papers, VHS; January 8, 1863, Cowin Diary, UA; *Charleston Daily Courier*, January 10, 1863; *Richmond Daily Examiner*, January 12, 1863; *ORN*, ser. 2, 3:658–59. Confederates also sounded increasingly contemptuous of what one Richmond editor called "those two old painted mummies, Russell and Palmerston" (*Richmond Daily Whig*, December 29, 1862).

43. December 22, 1862, Taggart Diary, USAMHI; McAllister, *Letters of Robert McAllister*, 244; John White Geary, *Politician Goes to War*, 72–73; Weld, *War Diary and Letters*, 154–56.

44. Edmondston, "*Journal of a Secesh Lady*," 321–22; McDonald, *Woman's Civil War*, 108–9; *Charleston Mercury*, December 31, 1862; *Richmond Daily Enquirer*, December 27, 1862; Kean, *Inside the Confederate Government*, 35; Richard Henry Watkins to Mary Watkins, December 28–29, 1862, Watkins Papers, VHS; Lucy Rebecca Buck, *Shadows of My Heart*, 168; Edmund Ruffin, *Diary*, 2:518–19; *Charleston Daily Courier*, December 24, 1862; *Richmond Daily Dispatch*, December 24, 1862; Thomas Claybrook Elder to Anna Fitzhugh Elder, December 27,

1862, Elder Papers, VHS; S. G. Pryor, *Post of Honor,* 302–3; W. T. Kinzer to his mother and sister, December 25, 1862, Kinzer Letter, West Virginia University.

45. *New York Times,* December 13, 16, 1862; *New York Herald,* December 16–18, 1862; *New York Tribune,* December 16, 1862; "The Price of Gold," *Banker's Magazine and Statistical Register,* January 1863, 560; "Notes on the Money Market," *Banker's Magazine and Statistical Register,* January 1863, 573; "The Price of Gold," *Banker's Magazine and Statistical Register,* January 1863, 647; Wesley C. Mitchell, *History of the Greenbacks,* 196, 211, 423–24; *Baltimore American and Commercial Advertiser,* January 21, 1863; Roll, "Interest Rates and Price Expectations," 478–79. Military news often arrived at the so-called Gold Room in New York from War Department dispatches before it reached the newspapers, and the major gold traders had other sources of confidential information. Gold prices also fluctuated during this period in response to the fate of congressional legislation making greenbacks legal tender. It is difficult to measure the effects of Fredericksburg as compared with other war news—mostly bad—on the New York financial markets. For differing interpretations of how price fluctuations related to war news, see Wesley C. Mitchell, "Value of the 'Greenbacks' during the Civil War," 144–45, 155; Wesley C. Mitchell, *History of the Greenbacks,* 216; Guinnane, Rosen, and Willard, "Greenback Prices," 313–28; McCandless, "Money, Expectations, and the Civil War," 661–71. The January rise in gold prices likely also reflected the passage of a bill in Congress increasing the volume of greenbacks. See Willard, Guinnane, and Rosen, "Turning Points in the Civil War," 1013. Gold prices were calculated according to the number of paper dollars it would take to buy 100 gold dollars. So if the price was 130, it would take 130 paper dollars to purchase 100 gold dollars. The higher the price of gold, the weaker both the dollar and public confidence.

46. Longstreet, *From Manassas to Appomattox,* 317; *Charleston Daily Courier,* December 27, 1862; J. B. Jones, *Rebel War Clerk's Diary,* 1:223; U.S. Bureau of the Census, *Historical Statistics of the United States,* 1:165, 201, 212, 214, 2:1104, 1118; Wesley C. Mitchell, *History of the Greenbacks,* 101–5, 248; Andreano, *Economic Impact of the Civil War,* 178–79, 181. Whether wages lagged significantly behind price increases has been the subject of considerable debate. For useful summaries and data, see Paludan, *"People's Contest,"* 113, 182–83; Gallman, *Mastering Wartime,* 225–26, 271–72.

47. U.S. Bureau of the Census, *Historical Statistics of the United States,* 2:993; *Rochester (N.Y.) Daily Union and Advertiser,* November 18, 1862; *New York Herald,* November 10, 15, 1862, January 5, 1863; *Portland (Maine) Eastern Argus,* November 19, 1862; *Albany (N.Y.) Atlas and Argus,* December 9, 1862.

48. "The Money Question," *Harper's Weekly,* November 15, 1862, 722; Oberholtzer, *Jay Cooke,* 1:223–26; Chase, *Salmon P. Chase Papers,* 3:327–28, 335, 375–76; *Philadelphia Inquirer,* November 1, 1862; Hammond, *Sovereignty and an Empty Purse,* 285–317.

49. Clausewitz, *On War,* 592.

50. Melville, *Collected Poems of Herman Melville,* 404; Garner, *Civil War World of Herman Melville,* 207–8, 215–16. Literary scholar Stanton Garner has argued that Melville's "Inscription for the Slain at Fredericksburg" was the only one of his war poems actually written during the war.

CHAPTER TWENTY-ONE

1. Caleb H. Beal to his parents, December 13, 1862, Beal Papers, MHS; Willard J. Templeton to his brother, December 15–16, 1862, Templeton Letters, NHSL; Adam Muenzenberger to his wife, December 17, 1862, Muenzenberger Letters, FSNMP; Marvel, *Ninth New Hampshire,* 116; James R. Woodworth to Phoebe Woodworth, December 28, 1862, Woodworth Papers, Hotchkiss Collection, CL. On the need of frustrated people to analyze the question of responsibility, see Allport and Postman, *Psychology of Rumor,* 37–38.

2. David Beem to his wife, December 18, 1862, Beem Papers, IHS; Nash, *Forty-fourth New York,* 120–21.

3. R. S. Robertson to his parents, December 15, 1862, Robertson Papers, FSNMP; George W. Ballock to his wife, December 18, 1862, Ballock Papers, Duke; December 21, 1862, Webb Diary, Schoff Collection, CL; Landon, "Letters to the Vincennes Western Sun," 340.

4. *Newark (N.J.) Daily Advertiser,* December 24, 1862; A. Wilson Greene, "Opportunity to the South," 295; Augustus Van Dyke to his brother, December 23, 1862, Van Dyke Papers, IHS; Edmund Halsey, *Brother against Brother,* 96; Molyneux, *Quill of the Wild Goose,* 54–55; Henry Snow to his sister, December 29, 1862, Snow Letters, CHS; Cavins, *Civil War Letters of Cavins,* 120; Reichardt, *Diary of Battery A,* 77; Sturtevant, *Josiah Volunteered,* 78–80. The sources cited for general comments on demoralization in the Army of the Potomac represent a cross section of various corps and ranks from private to major.

5. Pettit, *Infantryman Pettit,* 50; *Pittsfield (Mass.) Sun,* January 1, 1863; Henry J. H. Thompson to Lucretia Thompson, December 21, 1862, Thompson Papers, Duke; December 15, 1862, Bacon Diary, FSNMP; R. S. Robertson to his parents, December 24, 1862, Robertson Papers, FSNMP; McAllister, *Letters of Robert McAllister,* 242; December 18, 1862, Dodge Diary, LC; Lusk, *War Letters of William Thompson Lusk,* 245–48; Clarence Whedon to his sister, January 4, 1863, Whedon Papers, Schoff Collection, CL.

6. J. L. Smith to his mother, December 15, 1862, John L. Smith Letters, FSNMP; Frinfrock, *Across the Rappahannock,* 146; Wiley, "Soldier's Life," 71–72; Henry Ogden Ryerson to his sister, December 23, 1862, Anderson Family Papers, NJHS; George M. Barnard to his father, December 16, 1862, Barnard Papers, MHS; Winfield Scott Hancock to Zachariah Chandler, December 19, 1862, Chandler Papers, LC.

7. John D. Wilkins to his wife, December 18, 1862, Wilkins Papers, Schoff Collection, CL; Abbott, *Fallen Leaves,* 152; Anthony G. Graves to his father, December 19, 1862, Graves Letters, FSNMP; William Speed to his sister, December 29, 1862, Speed Papers, Schoff Collection, CL; Jacob W. Haas to Frederick Haas, December 18, 1862, Haas Papers, HCWRTC, USAMHI.

8. Elisha Hunt Rhodes, *All for the Union,* 91–92; Joseph H. Haynes to his father, January 7, 1863, Haynes Papers, Duke; Robert Gould Shaw, *Blue-Eyed Child of Fortune,* 267; R. P. Staniels to "My Darling Selina," December 16, 1862, Staniels Letter, FSNMP; E. H. Wade to "Dear Nell," December 16, 1862, Wade Letters, CL; December 14, 1862, Taggart Diary, USAMHI; Pardington, *Dear Sarah,* 49; December 13, 1862, Willand Diary, NHSL; Robert Goldthwaite Carter, *Four Brothers in Blue,* 198. On the problem of death without purpose, see Lifton, *History and Human Survival,* 153, 176–77; Drew Gilpin Faust, *Riddle of Death,* 25–26.

9. Augustus C. Buell, "*Cannoneer,*" 44; Rodney H. Ramsey to his father, December 27, 1862, Ramsey Letter, NHHS; George H. Bradley to "Dear Friends at Home," December 20, 1862, Bradley Papers, Yale University; *Washington Daily National Intelligencer,* December 29, 1862; *Ebensburg (Pa.) Democrat and Sentinel,* January 7, 1863; Frinfrock, *Across the Rappahannock,* 125; Hess, *Liberty, Virtue, and Progress,* 32–41; Frank and Reaves, "*Seeing the Elephant,*" 199–25; Clausewitz, *On War,* 231; Laderman, *Sacred Remains,* 101.

10. *Brunswick (Maine) Telegraph,* January 16, 1863; Emerson F. Merrill to his parents, December 24, 1862, Merrill Papers, FSNMP; *Philadelphia Press,* December 27, 1862; James Madison Stone, *Personal Recollections of the Civil War,* 117–18; Craft, *History of the One Hundred Forty-First Pennsylvania,* 46; Walt Whitman, *Walt Whitman's Civil War,* 36; William Child, *Fifth New Hampshire,* 150.

11. Foote, *Civil War,* 2:116, 118–19; Haines, *15th New Jersey,* 37; John England to Ellen Hargeddon, December 17, 1862, England Papers, NYPL; *History of the Thirty-Fifth Massachusetts Volunteers,* 94–95; James Pratt to his wife, December 19, 1862, Pratt Collection, USAMHI; Osborn, *No Middle Ground,* 96; William Watson, *Letters of a Civil War Surgeon,* 42–43; Nathan

Chesley to "Friend Sawyer," December 19, 1862, Chesley Letter, FSNMP; Charles H. Eagor to his wife, December 20, 1862, Eagor Letters, Leigh Collection, USAMHI; George W. Ballock to his sister, December 25, 1862, Ballock Papers, Duke.

12. John Southard to his sister, December 22, 1862, Southard Family Papers, NYHS; McPherson, *For Cause and Comrades,* 32–33; A. B. Martin to "Dear Ann," December 19, 1862, Martin Letter, FSNMP; David V. Lovell to his sister, December 19, 1862, Lovell Letter, Gregory A. Coco Collection, USAMHI; James Coburn to his parents, December 17, 1862, James P. Coburn Papers, USAMHI; Joseph Bloomfield Osborn to his brother, December 26, 1862, Osborn Papers, LC; Cornelius Richmond to his wife, December 25, 1862, Richmond Papers, FSNMP; Gaff, *On Many a Bloody Field,* 213; Alexander Morrison Stewart, *Camp, March, and Battlefield,* 280; William Child, *Fifth New Hampshire,* 166; Molyneux, *Quill of the Wild Goose,* 55; O. Leland Barlow to his sister, December 29, 1862, Barlow Papers, CSL; Samuel C. Starrett to David Starrett, December 24, 1862, Starrett Letter, FSNMP. When a despairing young Hoosier cut off his right thumb with an ax, his comrades doubted it was an accident. See Gaff, *On Many a Bloody Field,* 213.

13. For examples of this sentiment from various ranks and corps, see Gallup, "Connecticut Yankee at Fredericksburg," 204; Charles F. Stinson to his mother, December 21, 1862, Stinson Letters, USAMHI; Pettit, *Infantryman Pettit,* 41; Isaac Morrow to his brother, December 21, 1862, Morrow Papers, HCWRTC, USAMHI; Matrau, *Letters Home,* 39; Aaron K. Blake to his sister, December 26, 1862, Blake Letters, CWMC, USAMHI; Edwin O. Wentworth to his wife, December 22, 1862, Wentworth Papers, LC.

14. Hartwell, *To My Beloved Wife and Boy at Home,* 40; Siegel, *For the Glory of the Union,* 116; McPherson, *For Cause and Comrades,* 156; Uriah N. Parmelee to his mother, December 26, 1862, Parmelee Papers, Duke; Bardeen, *Little Fifer's Diary,* 123–24; John R. Coye to his wife, December 17, 1862, Coye Letters, FSNMP; John R. McClure, *Hoosier Farmboy in Lincoln's Army,* 32.

15. Curtis C. Pollock to his mother, December 18, 1862, Pollock Papers, CWMC, USAMHI; Hartwell, *To My Beloved Wife and Boy at Home,* 37–38; Dwight P. Peck to "Dear Friends at Home," January 1, 1863, Dwight P. Peck Letter, FSNMP; Edwin O. Wentworth to his wife, December 22, 1862, Wentworth Papers, LC; John T. Greene, *Ewing Family Letters,* 33; Ephraim Jackson to "Dear Brother and Sister," December 20, 1862, Jackson Letters, FSNMP; Samuel Edmund Nichols, *"Your Soldier Boy Samuel,"* 58–59; Jimerson, *Private Civil War,* 229; George E. Upton to his wife, December 23, 1862, Upton Papers, NHHS; James Pratt to his wife, December 30, 1862, Pratt Collection, USAMHI.

16. David Jones to John Jordan Jr., December 16, 1862, David Jones Letters, FSNMP.

17. John Harrison Mills, *Chronicles of the Twenty-First New York,* 280–81; Douglas and Brink, *Reports of the Sanitary Commission after Fredericksburg,* 13; Haydon, *For Country, Cause, and Leader,* 299; McAllister, *Letters of Robert McAllister,* 249; William Watson, *Letters of a Civil War Surgeon,* 44; Wren, *James Wren's Civil War Diary,* 126; *New York Times,* December 21, 1862; *New York Herald,* December 21, 1862; *Philadelphia Inquirer,* December 18, 1862; *Providence (R.I.) Daily Journal,* December 31, 1862; Joseph E. Grant, *Flying Regiment,* 66–68; December 17–31, 1862, Furst Diary, HCWRTC, USAMHI. For a helpful analysis arguing that the army—even right after Fredericksburg—was not as demoralized as historians have often assumed, see A. Wilson Greene, "Morale, Maneuver, and Mud," 177–79. For discussions about distinctions between complaining and defeatism along with attention to the remarkable resilience of Civil War soldiers, see McPherson, *For Cause and Comrades,* 9–10; Frank and Reaves, *"Seeing the Elephant,"* 126–27.

18. Rose, *Victorian America and the Civil War,* 224–28; Reid Mitchell, *Vacant Chair,* 154–60; Frank and Reaves, *"Seeing the Elephant,"* 129–40; McAllister, *Letters of Robert McAllister,* 241; Charles Eagor to his wife, January 19, 1863, Eagor Letters, Leigh Collection, USAMHI; Hess, *Union Soldier in Battle,* 127–57; Robert Goldthwaite Carter, *Four Brothers in Blue,* 212; McPher-

son, *For Cause and Comrades*, 34–35; McKelvey, *Rochester in the Civil War*, 117; George W. Barr to Vinnie Barr, December 29, 1862, Barr Papers, Schoff Collection, CL.

19. Sullivan D. Green to "Friend Kittie," December 25, 1862, Green Papers, MHC; Brewster, *When This Cruel War Is Over*, 205; Reardon, "Forlorn Hope," 101; O'Reilly, *Jackson at Fredericksburg*, 194; John W. Ames to his mother, December 22, 1862, Ames Papers, USAMHI; Robert Goldthwaite Carter, *Four Brothers in Blue*, 215; John S. Crocker to his wife, December 16, 1862, Crocker Letters, CU; John Smart to Ann Smart, December 17, 1862, Smart Letters, FSNMP; McPherson, *For Cause and Comrades*, 153–55; George W. Barr to Vinnie Barr, December 25, 1862, Barr Papers, Schoff Collection, CL. For a discussion of how armies sustain their fighting spirit after a defeat, see Clausewitz, *On War*, 187.

20. December 21, 1862, Halsey Diary, USAMHI; James Laird to his wife, December 16, 1862, Laird Letter, FSNMP; George W. Ballock to his wife, December 14, 1862, Ballock Papers, Duke; John Claude Buchanan to Sophie Buchanan, December 15, 1862, Buchanan Family Papers, MHC; *History of the Thirty-Fifth Massachusetts Volunteers*, 97; John Ripley Adams, *Memorials and Letters*, 79; Alexander Morrison Stewart, *Camp, March, and Battlefield*, 282–83.

21. Garfield, *Wild Life of the Army*, 200; John Claude Buchanan to Sophie Buchanan, January 8, 1863, Buchanan Family Papers, MHC; *Newark (N.J.) Daily Advertiser*, January 19, 1863; William Adams, "Politics and the Pulpit," *American Presbyterian and Theological Review*, January 1863, 122–45; Reid Mitchell, *Vacant Chair*, 115–16; Fairchild, *27th Regiment*, 131; John Ripley Adams, *Memorials and Letters*, 84–85.

22. Anson B. Shuey to Sarah Shuey, December 16, 1862, Shuey Letter, FSNMP; John Ripley Adams, *Memorials and Letters*, 93; Castleman, *Army of the Potomac*, 265–66.

23. Nolan, "Confederate Leadership at Fredericksburg," 44; Gallagher, "Yanks Have Had a Terrible Whipping," 129–35; *OR*, 549; Robert E. Lee, *Wartime Papers*, 365, 380–81; Heth, "Letter from Henry Heth," 153–54. Gallagher's essay presents the best analysis of Confederate response to the battle, though he admits that Lee's apparent disappointment with the outcome cannot be entirely explained.

24. *Charleston Mercury*, December 15, 1862; James Edmond Hall, *Diary of a Confederate Soldier*, 66–67; December 16, 1862, Hamilton Diary, FSNMP; William B. Bailey to C. C. Bailey, December 17, 1862, Bailey Letters, HCWRTC, USAMHI; December 28, 1862, Dulany Diary, VHS.

25. *OR Supplement*, pt. 2, 71:46; Hodijah Lincoln Meade to Jane Eliza Meade, December 17, 1862, Meade Family Papers, VHS; Thomas Rowland to "Dear Aunt Emily," December 21, 1862, Rowland Papers, MC; *OR*, ser. 4, 2:293; *Richmond Daily Examiner*, December 17, 1862; Isaac Howard to his father, December 23, 1862, Howard Family Papers, SHC; W. H. Burgess to David McKnight, December 20, 1862, McKnight Family Papers, UT; Jedediah Hotchkiss to Sara Ann Comfort Hotchkiss, December 13–14, 1862, Hotchkiss Papers, LC; R. Channing Price to his mother, December 23, 1862, Price Papers, SHC; John Andrew Ramsay to "Cousin Julius," December 17, 1862, Ramsay Papers, SHC.

26. LePore, *Name of War*, xiv, 240; *Richmond Daily Examiner*, December 17, 1862; *Richmond Daily Enquirer*, December 18, 22, 1862; *Richmond Daily Dispatch*, December 20, 1862; Charles Kerrison to his uncle, December 18, 1862, Kerrison Family Papers, SCL; C. H. Jones to his mother, December 16, 1862, Robert Hairston Papers, SHC; *Times* (London), January 7, 1863; *Richmond Daily Whig*, December 16, 1862; *Augusta (Ga.) Daily Constitutionalist*, December 23, 1862; Unknown Soldier to "Dear Cousin," December 19, 1862, Unknown Soldier Letter, FSNMP; Philip H. Powers to his wife, December 17, 1862, Powers Letters, Leigh Collection, USAMHI; Thomas Claybrook Elder to Anna Fitzhugh Elder, December 21, 1862, Elder Papers, VHS; Richard Irby to his wife, December 19, 1862, Irby Letters, FSNMP. Porter Alexander even claimed that if the Yankees had fought as well as the Confederates, they "would have carried the position at the Marye's house at the *first* assault" (Boggs, *Alexander Letters*, 246).

27. William Henry Cocke to John Cocke, December 25, 1862, Cocke Family Papers, VHS;

Richmond Daily Examiner, January 3, 1863; Mortimer Johnson to his wife, December 18[?], 1862, Johnson Family Papers, Virginia Military Institute Archives; *Richmond Daily Whig,* December 16, 24, 29, 1862; *Lynchburg Daily Virginian,* December 22, 1862; *Richmond Daily Dispatch,* December 16–17, 1862; *Richmond Daily Examiner,* December 16, 1862; *Richmond Daily Enquirer,* December 20, 1862; Speairs and Pettit, *Civil War Letters,* 1:80; *Wilmington (N.C.) Daily Journal,* December 29, 1862.

28. James I. Robertson Jr., *Hill,* 170; *OR Supplement,* pt. 2, 72:278; Emma Holmes, *Diary,* 222; Isaac Howard to his father, December 25, 1862, Howard Family Papers, SHC; *Richmond Daily Dispatch,* December 18–19, 1862; *Richmond Daily Examiner,* December 15, 1862; *Columbus (Ga.) Daily Enquirer,* December 19, 1862; *Macon (Ga.) Daily Telegraph,* December 18–19, 1862, January 6, 1863; *Atlanta Southern Confederacy,* December 24, 31, 1862; *Augusta (Ga.) Daily Constitutionalist,* December 23, 1862; Fitzpatrick, *Letters to Amanda,* 39; William C. McClellan to his father, December 25, 28, 1862, Buchanan and McClellan Family Papers, SHC; *Charleston Mercury,* December 22, 1862; *Charleston Daily Courier,* December 19, 1862; J. B. Jones, *Rebel War Clerk's Diary,* 1:221.

29. Philip H. Powers to his wife, December 25, 1862, Powers Letters, Leigh Collection, USAMHI; Augusta J. Evans to Jabez Lamar Monroe Curry, December 20, 1862, Curry Papers, LC; *Richmond Daily Dispatch,* December 20, 23–24, 1862; Milo Grow to his wife, December 15, 17, 1862, Grow Letters, FSNMP; *Macon (Ga.) Daily Telegraph,* December 25, 1862; *Richmond Daily Whig,* December 30, 1862; W. R. M. Slaughter to his sister, January 4, 1863, Slaughter Letters, VHS; *Raleigh Weekly Standard,* January 7, 1863.

30. *Richmond Daily Enquirer,* December 20, 1862; Robert Brooke Jones to "Dearest Bettie," December 17, 1862, Jones Family Papers, VHS; Jefferson Davis, *Papers,* 9:11–12; *Raleigh Weekly Register,* December 24, 1862; *Lynchburg Daily Virginian,* December 18, 1862; *Charleston Daily Courier,* December 31, 1862; Richard Lewis, *Camp Life of a Confederate Boy,* 36.

31. *Richmond Daily Enquirer,* December 18, 1862; Charles Minor Blackford to Mary Blackford, January 12, 1863, Blackford Family Papers, SHC; Welch, *Confederate Surgeon's Letters,* 39; Paxton, *Memoir and Memorials,* 85–86; *Athens (Ga.) Southern Banner,* January 7, 1863; L. Calhoun Cooper to his mother, December 18, 1862, Cooper Letters, Kennesaw Mountain National Battlefield Park; William B. Bailey to C. C. Bailey, December 17, 1862, Bailey Letters, HCWRTC, USAMHI; *Atlanta Southern Confederacy,* December 25, 1862.

32. *Richmond Daily Dispatch,* January 1, 1863; *Richmond Daily Whig,* January 6, 1863; *Lynchburg Daily Virginian,* December 16, 1862; *Richmond Daily Examiner,* December 24, 1862; *Charleston Daily Courier,* December 17, 1862; Richard L. Dabney to George W. Payne, January 2, 1863, Dabney Family Papers, VHS; *OR,* 549–50, 1085–86. About this same time misleading reports of a Confederate "victory" at Murfreesboro, Tennessee, sent Confederate hopes soaring even higher. See *Richmond Daily Whig,* January 3, 1863; *Richmond Daily Dispatch,* January 5, 1863; Borden, *Legacy of Fanny and Joseph,* 141.

33. Mary Anna Jackson, *Life and Letters of Jackson,* 386; Hotchkiss, *Make Me a Map of the Valley,* 102–3; December 28, 1862, Maury Diary, LC; Jedediah Hotchkiss to Sara Ann Comfort Hotchkiss, December 21, 1862, Hotchkiss Papers, LC; *OR,* 644; Cadmus Marcellus Wilcox to his sister, December 17, 1862, Wilcox Papers, LC; Myers, *Children of Pride,* 1001; Oscar J. E. Stuart to Adelaide L. Stuart, January 6, 1863, Dimitry Papers, Duke; *Charleston Daily Courier,* December 31, 1862; Robert Taylor Scott to his wife, December 31, 1862, Keith Family Papers, VHS.

34. *Charleston Daily Courier,* January 3, 1863; Roberson, *Weep Not for Me,* 95; James T. McElvaney to his mother, December 19, 1862, McElvaney Letter, FSNMP; Mary Anna Jackson, *Life and Letters of Jackson,* 387–88; Burrows, *New Richmond Theater,* 3–16.

35. Emerson F. Merrill to his parents, December 17, 21, 1862, Merrill Papers, FSNMP; Uriah N. Parmelee to his mother, December 26, 1862, Parmelee Papers, Duke; Henry F. Young to "Dear Delia," December 31, 1862, Young Papers, SHSW; A. J. Wilson to his parents, Decem-

ber 24, 1862, A. J. Wilson Letter, FSNMP; William L. Orr to Margaret Small Orr, December 21, 1862, Orr Family Papers, IU; David Dunkle to Uriah Thompson, January 3, 1863, Dunkle Letters, CWMC, USAMHI; J. L. Willy to his wife, December 17, 1862, Willy Letters, HCWRTC, USAMHI; Augustus Van Dyke to his brother, December 28, 1862, Van Dyke Papers, IHS; Wiley, *Life of Billy Yank,* 280; Tucker, *Hancock,* 113; Jimerson, *Private Civil War,* 200.

36. Charles Thomas Bowen to his wife, December 18, 1862, Bowen Letter, FSNMP; Edward Louis Edes to his father, December 26, 1862, Edes Papers, MHS; Wightman, *From Antietam to Fort Fisher,* 94; *Boston Daily Advertiser,* December 18, 1862; Henry F. Young to his father, December 17, 1862, Young Papers, SHSW; Abbott, *Fallen Leaves,* 155; Nancy Polk Lasselle to Mary Niles, January 7, 1863, U.S. History Manuscripts, IU; Loren H. Goodrich to "Dear Friends," December 1862, Goodrich Papers, CHS; Thomas H. Parker, *History of the 51st,* 280–81.

37. *OR Supplement,* pt. 1, 3:673; Clark S. Edwards to his wife, January 14, 1863, Edwards Papers, USAMHI; Frinfrock, *Across the Rappahannock,* 145; William Watson, *Letters of a Civil War Surgeon,* 43; George H. Legate to his sister, December 27, 1862, Legate Letter, Gregory A. Coco Collection, HCWRTC, USAMHI.

38. O. Leland Barlow to his father, December 14, 1862, Barlow Papers, CSL; *Washington Daily National Intelligencer,* December 18, 1863; *Harrisburg Patriot and Union,* December 19, 1862; *New York World,* December 19, 1862; *New York Tribune,* December 27, 1862.

39. Samuel W. Eaton to Eddie Eaton, December 15, 1862, Eaton Papers, SHSW; December 19, 1862, Dodge Diary, LC; *Albany (N.Y.) Atlas and Argus,* December 24, 1862; *New York World,* December 19, 1862; George M. Barnard to his father, December 20, 1862, Barnard Papers, MHS; Meade, *Life and Letters,* 1:341; Charles Shields Wainwright, *Diary of Battle,* 156.

40. *New York Herald,* December 17, 22, 1862; Strong, *Diary of George Templeton Strong,* 3:281; John Hancock Douglas to his brother, December 25, 1862, Douglas Papers, LC; Brooks, *Washington in Lincoln's Time,* 36–37, 62; Welles, *Diary of Gideon Welles,* 1:206; *OR,* ser. 3, 2:953–54; Gurowski, *Diary,* 2:21; Fessenden, *Fessenden,* 1:248.

41. Bliss Memoir, 4:44, USAMHI; James Edison Decker to his father, December 17, 1862, Decker Papers, CWMC, USAMHI; *New York Irish-American,* January 10, 1863; Caleb H. Beal to his parents, December 23, 1862, Beal Papers, MHS; John Ripley Adams, *Memorials and Letters,* 88–89.

42. *Fifth Annual Report of the Bureau of Military Statistics,* 725–26; Edmund Halsey, *Brother against Brother,* 97–98; Joseph Bloomfield Osborn to his father, December 18, 1862, Osborn Papers, LC; Henry H. Young to his mother, December 29, 1862, Young Papers, CWMC, USAMHI; Samuel V. Dean to his wife, December 22, 1862, Dean Letters, FSNMP; William Hamilton to his mother, December 24, 1862, Hamilton Papers, LC.

43. December 15, 1862, Lambert Diary, IHS; George Barnard to his father, December 18, 1862, Barnard Papers, MHS; A. J. Wilson to his parents, December 24, 1862, A. J. Wilson Letter, FSNMP; Isaac Lyman Taylor, "Campaigning with the First Minnesota," 238; Gifford Taylor, *Gouverneur Kemble Warren,* 97.

44. Abbott, *Fallen Leaves,* 149; Anson B. Shuey to Sarah Shuey, December 16, 1862, Shuey Letter, FSNMP; McKelvey, *Rochester in the Civil War,* 164; R. S. Robertson to his parents, December 24, 1862, Robertson Papers, FSNMP; Robert Goldthwaite Carter, *Four Brothers in Blue,* 210–11; *New York Irish-American,* December 27, 1862; L. B. Havern to Simeon Whiteley, December 16, 1862, Whiteley Papers, Illinois State Historical Library. Some soldiers claimed that McClellan had been seen in camp. Although most rumors, especially those right after a battle, tend to be dark, reports of McClellan's imminent return proved the exception to the rule. In this case perhaps, the false reports initially did more to boost than to depress morale. See James Jenkins Gillette to his mother, December 17, 1862, Gillette Papers, LC; Zerah Coston Monks to Hannah T. Rohrer, December 21, 1862, Monks-Rohrer Letters, Emory; Kapferer, *Rumors,* 132–35; Shibutani, *Improvised News,* 146–47.

45. *Richmond Daily Examiner,* December 18, 1862; Garfield, *Wild Life of the Army,* 201–2; *New York Herald,* December 19, 1862, January 10, 1863; *Boston Post,* December 22, 1862; *Harrisburg Patriot and Union,* January 12, 1863; Francis Preston Blair Sr. to Abraham Lincoln, December 18, 1862, Lincoln Papers, LC; Edward Bates, *Diary,* 270; Gurowski, *Diary,* 2:42, 105; *Pittsburgh Daily Dispatch,* January 22, 1863.

46. Reuben H. Humphreyville to his sister, January 2, 1863, Humphreyville Papers, Chicago Historical Society; Oliver Willcox Norton, *Army Letters,* 129; George H. Patch to his mother, December 21, 1862, Patch Papers, Leigh Collection, USAMHI; John Southard to his sister, December 22, 1862, Southard Family Papers, NYHS. In assessing soldier reaction to Burnside after Fredericksburg, I have relied almost exclusively on diaries and letters. After the fact, many remembered considering Burnside a fool from the start, so memoirs and regimental histories should be used sparingly.

47. R. S. Robertson to his parents, December 15, 1862, Robertson Papers, FSNMP; Uriah N. Parmelee to his mother, December 26, 1862, Parmelee Papers, Duke; Trobriand, *Four Years with the Army of the Potomac,* 400–401; William P. Carmany to his sister, December 19, 1862, Carmany Papers, Schoff Collection, CL; George H. Bradley to his home folks, December 20, 1862, Bradley Papers, Yale University; Charles H. Eagor to his wife, December 16, 1862, Eagor Letters, Leigh Collection, USAMHI.

48. Abbott, *Fallen Leaves,* 152; Donaldson, *Inside the Army of the Potomac,* 192; Teall, "Ringside Seat at Fredericksburg," 31; Walker, *Second Corps,* 198; Uriah N. Parmelee to his mother, December 26, 1862, Parmelee Papers, Duke.

49. Elmer Bragg to his father, December 23, 1862, Bragg Letters, DCL; George Thornton Fleming, *Hays,* 288; Elisha Hunt Rhodes, *All for the Union,* 92; Edwin Winchester Stone, *Rhode Island in the Rebellion,* 191–92; *Indianapolis Daily Journal,* December 25, 1862; Woolsey, *Hospital Days,* 58; John S. Crocker to his wife, December 17, 19, 1862, Crocker Letters, CU; Edward Burns to ?, December 1862, Van Wagonen Papers, University of Oregon; Herbert C. Mason to his father, December 17, 1862, Mason Letter, FSNMP; Castleman, *Army of the Potomac,* 272–73.

50. George W. Coon to his mother, December 23, 1862, Coon Papers, FSNMP; William Teall to his wife, December 16, 1862, Teall Letters, TSLA; Herman Haupt to his wife, December 18, 1862, Haupt Letterbook, Haupt Papers, LC; Marsena Rudolph Patrick, *Inside Lincoln's Army,* 194; Daniel Reed Larned to "Dear Henry," December 16, 1862, Larned Papers, LC; *OR,* 66–67. In his report on the campaign Burnside noted that because he was a relatively new face in the Army of the Potomac, many officers had lacked confidence in him. Also, a campaign begun so late in the year had been risky. Moreover, soldiers unpaid for several months added to the "gloom and despondency" that seemed to dog the army. See *OR,* 96.

51. Marsena Rudolph Patrick, *Inside Lincoln's Army,* 194; *New York Tribune,* December 17, 1862; Gurowski, *Diary,* 2:31; Zachariah Chandler to his wife, December 18, 21, 1862, Chandler Papers, LC. For differing interpretations of how the committee investigated Fredericksburg, see T. Harry Williams, *Lincoln and the Radicals,* 201–5; Tap, *Over Lincoln's Shoulder,* 144–47; Marvel, *Burnside,* 206–7.

52. *CCW,* 1:654–56.

53. William Teall to his wife, December 17–20, 1862, Teall Letters, TSLA; Julian, *Political Recollections,* 224–25; *CCW,* 1:656–63.

54. William B. Franklin to George B. McClellan, December 23, 1862, McClellan Papers, LC; *OR,* 868–70; Lincoln, *Collected Works,* 6:15, 15–16n; Samuel E. Lyon to Salmon P. Chase, January 6, 1863, Chase Papers, LC.

55. *CCW,* 1:665–73; John Godfrey to Horace Godfrey, December 16, 1862, Godfrey Papers, NHHS; *New York Herald,* December 22, 1862; Charles Shields Wainwright, *Diary of Battle,* 149, 153; *OR,* ser. 1, 32(2):468.

56. *Boston Daily Advertiser,* December 18, 1862; *Washington Daily National Intelligencer,*

December 22, 1862; Richard Dodge to Simon Cameron, December 25, 1862, Cameron Papers, LC.

57. William Harris to George Hopper, December 26, 1862, Hopper Papers, USAMHI; *Cannelton (Ind.) Reporter,* December 26, 1862; *Albany (N.Y.) Atlas and Argus,* December 19, 1862.

58. *Baltimore American and Commercial Advertiser,* December 17, 1862; *Albany (N.Y.) Atlas and Argus,* December 17, 18, 1862; "The Reverse at Fredericksburg," *Harper's Weekly,* December 27, 1862, 818.

59. *Portland (Maine) Eastern Argus,* December 16–18, 1862; *Albany (N.Y.) Atlas and Argus,* December 15, 17, 1862; *Harrisburg Patriot and Union,* December 18, 1862; *Indianapolis Daily State Sentinel,* December 17, 1862; *New York Herald,* December 16, 1862; *Philadelphia Public Ledger,* December 17, 1862; *Boston Post,* December 18, 1862; *Rochester (N.Y.) Daily Union and Advertiser,* December 18, 1862; *Springfield (Mass.) Daily Republican,* December 20, 1862; "The Civil War: A Week of Grave Events," *Albion,* December 20, 1862, 606–7.

60. Raymond, "Extracts from the Journal of Henry J. Raymond," 424; *New York Times,* January 27, 1863; Ambrose E. Burnside to Lincoln, December 19, 20, 1862, Lincoln Papers, LC; Lincoln, *Collected Works,* 6:10; Daniel Reed Larned to his sister, December 19, 1862, Larned Papers, LC; W. Thiel Appleton to Ambrose E. Burnside, December 23, 1862, Burnside Papers, entry 159, box 3, NA. For the most part Republican editors stuck by Burnside. Vice-President Hannibal Hamlin saw no reason to dump a general for "one mistake." See *Chicago Daily Tribune,* December 19, 1862; *Cahors (N.Y.) Cataract,* December 20, 1862; *Watertown (N.Y.) Daily News and Reformer,* December 17, 1862; *Providence (R.I.) Daily Journal,* December 17, 18, 1862; H. Draper Hunt, *Hamlin,* 166.

61. *OR,* 66–67. Drafts of Burnside's letter dated December 19 are in both the Lincoln and Stanton papers with the notation that it was to be sent to the Associated Press. See Burnside to Halleck, December 19, 1862, Lincoln Papers, LC; Burnside to Halleck, December 19, 1862, Stanton Papers, LC.

62. John Claude Buchanan to Sophie Buchanan, December 24, 1862, Buchanan Family Papers, MHC; Charles Gibson to his sister, January 6, 1863, Gibson Letters, FSNMP; Castleman, *Army of the Potomac,* 274; Dexter, *Seymour Dexter,* 124, 130; December 23, 1862, Dodge Diary, LC; Abbott, *Fallen Leaves,* 156–57; Donaldson, *Inside the Army of the Potomac,* 196. Meade and Franklin were not impressed by the letter but pitied Burnside. See Meade, *Life and Letters,* 1:341; William B. Franklin to George B. McClellan, December 23, 1862, McClellan Papers, LC. Rebels dismissed the general's confession of failure as a weak effort to cover up administration blunders. "To sacrifice an army to please a cabinet and to curry favor with a mob is a crime that cannot be excused," the Confederacy's London propaganda organ huffed. Several verses of broadside doggerel ridiculed a general who "basely bows at Lincoln's toes." See *Richmond Daily Examiner,* December 30, 1862; *Atlanta Southern Confederacy,* January 7, 1863; "General Burnside's Report and Sworn Statement," *Index* (London), January 8, 1863, 170; Shelton, *Downfall of Burnside.*

63. *Boston Evening Transcript,* December 23, 1862; *Rochester (N.Y.) Daily Democrat and American,* December 23, 1862; *Philadelphia Inquirer,* December 23, 1862; *Providence (R.I.) Daily Journal,* December 23, 1862; Hay, *Lincoln's Journalist,* 324–27; *Cincinnati Daily Gazette,* December 23, 1862; *Springfield (Mass.) Daily Republican,* December 23, 1862; *New York Times,* December 23–24, 30, 1862; *Albany (N.Y.) Evening Journal,* December 23, 1862; *New York Tribune,* December 23, 1862; Whittemore and Whittemore, "Rebellious South through New York Eyes," 349; Strong, *Diary of George Templeton Strong,* 3:282; Chase, *Salmon P. Chase Papers,* 3:345; D. Robinson to William H. Seward, December 23, 1862, Seward Papers, UR; J. Van Buren to Ambrose E. Burnside, December 23, 1862, Burnside Papers, entry 159, box 3, NA.

64. *Rochester (N.Y.) Daily Union and Advertiser,* December 23, 1862; *Philadelphia Public*

Ledger, December 25, 1862; *Harrisburg Patriot and Union,* December 23, 1862; *Yonkers (N.Y.) Examiner,* December 25, 1862; *New York Herald,* December 23, 26, 1862.

65. Lincoln, *Collected Works,* 6:13. Lincoln scholars, including notables such as James G. Randall, David Donald, Stephen Oates, and Phillip Paludan, do not even mention the document. The president's private secretaries, Nicolay and Hay, along with Carl Sandburg and Benjamin Thomas quoted from it but left off the statement about the casualties. See Nicolay and Hay, *Lincoln,* 6:211; Sandburg, *Lincoln,* 1:632; Benjamin P. Thomas, *Lincoln,* 350.

66. *OR,* 68; Charles Shields Wainwright, *Diary of Battle,* 149–50. For defenses of Lincoln's reasoning, see Walt Whitman, *Walt Whitman's Civil War,* 38–39; "The Cabinet Imbroglio," *Harper's Weekly,* January 3, 1863, 2.

67. *Harrisburg Patriot and Union,* December 27, 1862; *Albany (N.Y.) Atlas and Argus,* December 25, 1862; *Boston Post,* January 1, 1863. Confederates also ridiculed Lincoln's effort to turn a defeat into a victory. See *Lynchburg Daily Virginian,* January 4, 1863.

68. Tap, *Over Lincoln's Shoulder,* 147; Catton, *Never Call Retreat,* 58–59; Daniel Reed Larned to "Dear Henry," December 26, 1862, Larned Papers, LC; *New York Times,* December 26, 1862; *Pittsburgh Daily Dispatch,* December 27, 1862; *Springfield (Mass.) Daily Republican,* December 25, 1862; *Rochester (N.Y.) Daily Union and Advertiser,* December 27, 1862; James H. Leonard, "Letters of a Fifth Wisconsin Volunteer," 70; Charles Shields Wainwright, *Diary of Battle,* 155; Eliza Wilkes to John Wilkes, January 4, 1863, Wilkes Family Papers, Duke; *Portland (Maine) Eastern Argus,* December 27, 1862. In April 1863 Franklin issued a pamphlet attempting to vindicate his reputation. This scathing, self-serving, and ultimately unpersuasive review of the controversy neither helped him nor hurt Burnside. Franklin's attempt to portray himself as a naive innocent without political friends was laughable. See *OR,* ser. 1, 51(1):1019–33; Ambrose E. Burnside to James Allen Hardie, May 14, 1863, Hardie Papers, LC; Tap, *Over Lincoln's Shoulder,* 161.

69. *New York Tribune,* December 15–17, 19, 24–25, 1862; *New York Herald,* December 25, 1862.

CHAPTER TWENTY-TWO

1. *Providence (R.I.) Daily Journal,* December 20, 1862; *Waukesha (Wisc.) Freeman,* December 23, 1862; *New York Times,* December 25, 1862; *Chicago Daily Tribune,* December 25, 1862; *Hartford Daily Courant,* December 24, 1862; *New York Tribune,* December 24, 1862; *Baltimore American and Commercial Advertiser,* December 27, 1862; *New York Herald,* December 24, 1862.

2. John F. Hartranft to Sallie Hartranft, December 16, 1862, Hartranft Letter, FSNMP; December 16, 1862, Mancha Diary, CWMC, USAMHI; Rusling, *Men and Things I Saw in Civil War Days,* 292; Wightman, *Antietam to Fort Fisher,* 93; Charles A. Legg to his parents, December 17, 1862, Legg Papers, Duke; Sanford Truesdale to his sister, December 17, 1862, Truesdale Papers, University of Chicago; Lucius B. Shattuck to "Dear Ellen," December 17–21, 1862, Shattuck Letters, MHC; *Lancaster (Pa.) Daily Evening Express,* December 23, 1862; Charles F. Stinson to his mother, December 21, 1862, Stinson Letters, USAMHI; Edwin O. Wentworth to his wife, December 22, 1862, Wentworth Papers, LC; Pettit, *Infantryman Pettit,* 41; December 21, 1862, Boyts Diary, HSP; Emory Upton to his sister, December 23, 1862, Upton Letter, HCWRTC; Augustus Van Dyke to his brother, December 28, 1862, Van Dyke Papers, IHS; George Henry Chandler to his mother, December 25, 1862, Chandler Papers, NHHS. For an insightful general discussion of how rumors are constructed and discussed in the absence of reliable information and how their discussion also helps people cope with monotony and routine, see Shibutani, *Improvised News,* 55–56, 70–73.

3. Cook, *Twelfth Massachusetts,* 85; Wyman Silas White, *Civil War Diary,* 117–18; Craft, *History of the One Hundred Forty-First Pennsylvania,* 39; January 5, 7, 1863, Hadley Diary, NHHS; *Haverhill (Mass.) Gazette,* January 23, 1863; Robert S. Robertson, "Diary of the War," 77; George A. Seaman to Olivia Seaman, December 24, 1862, Seaman Letters, FSNMP; Virgil W.

Mattoon to "Dear Brother John," December 28, 1862, Mattoon Papers, CHS; McAllister, *Letters of Robert McAllister,* 254.

4. Houghton, *Seventeenth Maine,* 37; Hitchcock, *War from the Inside,* 145–46; Bloodgood, *Personal Reminiscences of the War,* 58–59.

5. Information on the huts came from twenty detailed descriptions in diaries, letters, newspapers, regimental histories, and memoirs. On various dimensions, see *Narragansett (R.I.) Weekly,* January 8, 1863; Storey, *History of Cambria County,* 251; George Chandler to his father, December 25, 1862, Chandler Letters, FSNMP; *Wellsboro (Pa.) Agitator,* January 4, 1863; Galwey, *Valiant Hours,* 71; Fairchild, *27th Regiment,* 128.

6. McCrea, *Dear Belle,* 179; Albert Foster to his daughter, January 4, 1862, Foster Letters, FSNMP; Stearns, *Three Years with Company K,* 151–52; Nathaniel W. Brown to Albert M. Given, December 23, 1862, Brown Letter, FSNMP; Frederick, *Story of a Regiment,* 137.

7. Pettit, *Infantryman Pettit,* 42; McKelvey, *Rochester in the Civil War,* 116; John Harrison Foye to his father, January 14, 1863, Foye Papers, NHHS; David Beem to his wife, December 25, 1862, Beem Papers, IHS; *History of the Fifth Massachusetts Battery,* 521.

8. Cavins, *Civil War Letters of Cavins,* 120; *History of the Thirty-Fifth Massachusetts Volunteers,* 93; John Day Smith, *Nineteenth Maine,* 34; Hitchcock, *War from the Inside,* 147; Peter Welsh, *Irish Green and Union Blue,* 51–52, 55; Jacob Henry Cole, *Under Five Commanders,* 123; Matrau, *Letters Home,* 40; Billings, *Hard Tack and Coffee,* 74–78; John Ripley Adams, *Memorials and Letters,* 94–95; Daniel M. Holt, *Surgeon's Civil War,* 65; Samuel S. Partridge to "Dear Ed," January 6, 1863, Partridge Letters, FSNMP.

9. David Beem to his wife, December 18, 1862, Beem Papers, IHS; January 15, 1863, Marshall Diary, LC; Charles H. Eagor to his wife, December 20, 1862, Eagor Letters, Leigh Collection, USAMHI; Samuel S. Partridge to "Dear Ed," January 17, 1863, Partridge Letters, FSNMP; Aaron Blake to his sister, January 11, 1863, Blake Letters, CWMC, USAMHI; Isaac Lyman Taylor, "Campaigning with the First Minnesota," 238; Haydon, *For Country, Cause, and Leader,* 299–301.

10. George M. Barnard to his father, December 21, 1862, Barnard Papers, MHS; Lewis Nettleton to "My own dear love," December 20, 1862, Nettleton-Baldwin Family Papers, Duke; David W. Benjamin to his sister, December 27, 1862, Benjamin Letter, Leigh Collection, USAMHI; Hopkins, *Seventh Rhode Island,* 52–53; O. Leland Barlow to his sister, January 20, 1863, Barlow Papers, CSL; Rusling, *Men and Things I Saw in Civil War Days,* 291.

11. Sprenger, *122d Regiment,* 181; S. Millett Thompson, *Thirteenth New Hampshire,* 98; Pullen, *Twentieth Maine,* 63–65; Solomon Dodge to "Dear Brother Charles," December 30, 1862, Dodge Papers, NHHS; Marbaker, *Eleventh New Jersey,* 29–30.

12. Walt Whitman, *Walt Whitman's Civil War,* 36; Glazier, *Three Years in the Federal Cavalry,* 114–15; Samuel Penniman Bates, *History of the Pennsylvania Volunteers,* 4:186; Reeves, *Twenty-Fourth New Jersey,* 24; Hopkins, *Seventh Rhode Island,* 54; Foster, *New Jersey and the Rebellion,* 571; Gavin, *Campaigning with the Roundheads,* 227; Hitchcock, *War from the Inside,* 147.

13. Henry J. H. Thompson to Lucretia Thompson, December 19, 1862, Thompson Papers, Duke; Thomas J. Halsey, *Field of Battle,* 52; Wren, *Captain James Wren's Civil War Diary,* 126–27; Hartwell, *To My Beloved Wife and Boy at Home,* 37; Wyman Silas White, *Civil War Diary,* 119; Brian A. Bennett, *140th New York,* 123; John March Cate to his wife, December 24, 1862, Cate Letters, FSNMP; S. Millett Thompson, *Thirteenth New Hampshire,* 87; Henry Ogden Ryerson to his sister, January 13, 1863, Anderson Family Papers, NJHS; Orson Blair Curtis, *History of the Twenty-Fourth Michigan,* 107; Niven, *Connecticut for the Union,* 94–95; *Ebensburg (Pa.) Democrat and Sentinel,* January 14, 1863; *Albany (N.Y.) Atlas and Argus,* December 24, 1862. The comment about British workers referred to relief efforts to help the unemployed in the north of England suffering from the so-called cotton famine, a point of great sensitivity in Anglo-American relations at this time.

14. O. Leland Barlow to his sister, December 29, 1862, Barlow Papers, CSL; Peter Welsh, *Irish Green and Union Blue,* 45; McKelvey, *Rochester in the Civil War,* 45.

15. O. Leland Barlow to his father, January 13, 1863, Barlow Papers, CSL; Pettit, *Infantry-man Pettit,* 52; Darius Starr to his mother, January 15, 1863, Starr Papers, Duke; Solomon Dodge to "Dear Brother Charles," December 30, 1862, Dodge Papers, NHHS; Oliver S. Coolidge to ?, December 27, 1862, Coolidge Papers, Duke.

16. Hopkins, *Seventh Rhode Island,* 51; Gallup, "Connecticut Yankee at Fredericksburg," 204; December 20, 1862, Brown Diary, CWMC, USAMHI; John Southard to his sister, December 22, 1862, Southard Family Papers, NYHS; John W. Ames to his mother, December 29, 1862, Ames Papers, USAMHI; Zerah Coston Monks to Hannah T. Rohrer, December 28, 1862, Monks-Rohrer Letters, Emory; Orson Blair Curtis, *History of the Twenty-Fourth Michigan,* 109.

17. David Beem to his wife, December 21, 1862, Beem Papers, IHS; Best, *History of the 121st New York,* 53–54; Houghton, *Seventeenth Maine,* 42; James Lorenzo Bowen, *Thirty-Seventh Regiment,* 115–16; Benjamin Apthorp Gould, *Military and Anthropological Statistics of American Soldiers,* 10, 594–95; S. Millett Thompson, *Thirteenth New Hampshire,* 93; Hopkins, *Seventh Rhode Island,* 51; Lucius B. Shattuck to "Dear Ellen," December 21–24, 1862, Shattuck Letters, MHC.

18. S. Millett Thompson, *Thirteenth New Hampshire,* 93; Foster, *New Jersey and the Rebellion,* 522; Craft, *History of the One Hundred Forty-First Pennsylvania,* 41–44; Blakeslee, *Sixteenth Connecticut,* 29; David Lane, *Soldier's Diary,* 25.

19. James R. Woodworth to Phoebe Woodworth, December 19, 1862, Woodworth Papers, Hotchkiss Collection, CL; *MSH,* 3:77; Robert W. Hemphill to his father, December 18, 1862, Hemphill Letter, Henry Family Papers, USAMHI; Asa W. Bartlett, *History of the Twelfth New Hampshire,* 516; Crowinshield, *First Regiment Massachusetts Cavalry,* 105; *Rochester (N.Y.) Daily Union and Advertiser,* January 7, 1863; Haines, *15th New Jersey,* 37; Foster, *New Jersey and the Rebellion,* 387; Haley, *Rebel Yell and Yankee Hurrah,* 62–63.

20. Orson Blair Curtis, *History of the Twenty-Fourth Michigan,* 102–3; Lord, *History of the Ninth New Hampshire,* 628–31; December 24, 1862, Eaton Diary, SHC; Pardington, *Dear Sarah,* 53. It is understandable that many of the boys preferred home remedies, from cayenne pepper to various tonics and elixirs to a daily dousing of the head in cold water. One Pennsylvanian astutely warned that sickly soldiers could easily "become victims of quackery." See Edwin O. Wentworth to his wife, December 22, 1862, Wentworth Papers, LC; January 11, 1863, Eaton Diary, SHC; Peter Welsh, *Irish Green and Union Blue,* 52; January 7, 1863, Halsey Diary, USAMHI; *Albany (N.Y.) Atlas and Argus,* January 5, 1863; *Ebensburg (Pa.) Democrat and Sentinel,* January 14, 1863.

21. Asa W. Bartlett, *History of the Twelfth New Hampshire,* 704; Sturtevant, *Josiah Volunteered,* 80; "Army Correspondence," *German Reformed Messenger,* January 14, 1863, 1; December 21, 1862, Eaton Diary, SHC; December 20, 1862, Halsey Diary, USAMHI. For a good sense of how one regiment that had barely been engaged at Fredericksburg suffered serious losses from disease in December 1862 and January 1863, see the individual cases noted in Brainard, *One Hundred and Forty-sixth New York,* 312–415 passim.

22. December 26, 1862, Mancha Diary, CWMC, USAMHI; Washburn, *108th Regiment,* 114; Cutcheon, *Story of the Twentieth Michigan Infantry,* 46; Sprenger, *122d Regiment,* 168–69; Weygant, *One Hundred and Twenty-Fourth Regiment,* 76–77; Daniel M. Holt, *Surgeon's Civil War,* 57; Walt Whitman, *Walt Whitman's Civil War,* 35–36; December 25, 862, Eaton Diary, SHC.

23. Wightman, *From Antietam to Fort Fisher,* 93; Henry C. Heisler to his sister, December 22, 1862, Heisler Papers, LC.

24. For typical schedules, see Vautier, *88th Pennsylvania,* 93; Wightman, *From Antietam to Fort Fisher,* 95; Peter Welsh, *Irish Green and Union Blue,* 51; *History of the Fifth Massachusetts Battery,* 529–30.

25. Small, *Sixteenth Maine,* 84–87; Henry F. Young to his father, January 9, 1862, Young

Papers, SHSW; Brainard, *One Hundred and Forty-sixth New York*, 47–50; Cudworth, *First Regiment (Massachusetts Infantry)*, 332; Elisha Hunt Rhodes, *All for the Union*, 95–96; James B. Thomas, *Civil War Letters*, 131–33; Jacob Henry Cole, *Under Five Commanders*, 121; Frederick, *Story of a Regiment*, 135–36.

26. Craig L. Dunn, *Iron Men, Iron Will*, 153; December 21, 1862, Gilpin Diary, LC; Richard Henry Watkins to Mary Watkins, December 20, 1862, Watkins Papers, VHS; John R. Coye to his wife, January 7, 1863, Coye Letters, FSNMP; Lucius B. Shattuck to "Dear Gill and Mary," December 16–18, 1862, Shattuck Letters, MHC; Reid Mitchell, *Civil War Soldiers*, 37–38; Haydon, *For Country, Cause, and Leader*, 300; *Fourth Annual Report of the Bureau of Military Statistics*, 580; Philip Hacker to William Hacker and Barbara Woll Hacker, January 6, 1863, Hacker Brothers Papers, Schoff Collection, CL; Loren H. Goodrich to "Dear Friends," January 5, 1863, Goodrich Papers, CHS.

27. Pettit, *Infantryman Pettit*, 47; David Beem to his wife, January 4, 1863, Beem Papers, IHS; George W. Ballock to Jenny Ballock, December 18, 1862, Ballock Papers, Duke; Pettit, *Infantryman Pettit*, 45; Haydon, *For Country, Cause, and Leader*, 300; January 5, 1863, Taber Diary, CWTI, USAMHI; Charles H. Brewster to ?, January 14, 1863, Brewster Collection, Northampton Historical Society.

28. Samuel R. Partridge to "Dear Lu," January 9, 1863, Partridge Letters, FSNMP; Jacob F. Smith to "Dear Callie," February 5, 1863, Jacob F. Smith Letter, CWMC, USAMHI; Craig L. Dunn, *Iron Men, Iron Will*, 153; George E. Upton to his wife, January 15, 1863, Upton Papers, NHHS; December 23, 1862, Dodge Diary, LC; Haley, *Rebel Yell and Yankee Hurrah*, 64; David Beem to his wife, December 18, 1862, Beem Papers, IHS; December 27, 1862, Taggart Diary, USAMHI.

29. William Speed to his sister, December 29, 1862, Speed Papers, Schoff Collection, CL; Matrau, *Letters Home*, 40; United States Christian Commission, *First Annual Report*, 36–37, 58–59, 63–64; Charles Carelton Coffin, *Four Years of Fighting*, 174–75; Solomon Dodge to "Dear Brother Charles," December 30, 1862, Dodge Papers, NHHS; *History of the Fifth Massachusetts Battery*, 523; Peter Welsh, *Irish Green and Union Blue*, 55; S. Millett Thompson, *Thirteenth New Hampshire*, 96, 98; Melcher, *With a Flash of His Sword*, 20; Forbes, *Thirty Years After*, 133; Reeves, *Twenty-Fourth New Jersey*, 26; Robert Goldthwaite Carter, *Four Brothers in Blue*, 213.

30. *Rochester (N.Y.) Daily Democrat and American*, January 8, 17, 1863; Brian A. Bennett, *140th New York*, 120; Washburn, *108th Regiment*, 115; John Gregory Bishop Adams, *Reminiscences of the Nineteenth Massachusetts*, 60–61.

31. Hartsock, *Soldier of the Cross*, 46; December 21, 1862, Taggart Diary, USAMHI; Reeves, *Twenty-Fourth New Jersey*, 25; Henry Grimes Marshall to "Dear Hattie," January 25, 1863, Marshall Papers, Schoff Collection, CL; January 4, 1863, Henry C. Marsh Diary, Marsh Papers, ISL; Henry Snow to his mother, December 25, 1862, Snow Letters, CHS; Hartsock, *Soldier of the Cross*, 48–49; S. Millett Thompson, *Thirteenth New Hampshire*, 98; *Newark (N.J.) Daily Advertiser*, January 6, 1863. In the Irish Brigade, Chaplain William Corby held daily mass for some time after the battle of Fredericksburg. See Corby, *Memoirs of Chaplain Life*, 135–36; Peter Welsh, *Irish Green and Union Blue*, 41.

32. United States Christian Commission, *First Annual Report*, 57; Charles H. Eagor to his wife, January 4, 1863, Eagor Letters, Leigh Collection, USAMHI; Washburn, *108th Regiment*, 114; January 18, 1863, Jackson Diary, IHS; Hartsock, *Soldier of the Cross*, 52; John Harrison Foye to his sister, January 30, 1863, Foye Papers, NHHS; Sim Siggins to Hannah T. Rohrer, January 25, 1863, Monks-Rohrer Letters, Emory.

33. James R. Woodworth to his wife, December 28, 1862, January 7, 1863, Woodworth Papers, Hotchkiss Collection, CL; Josiah W. Perry to Phoebe Perry, January 15, 1863, Perry Papers, Illinois State Historical Library; January 25, 1863, Stevens Diary, USAMHI; George E. French to his mother, January 1, 1863, French Papers, Leigh Collection, USAMHI; Charles Augustus Fuller, *Recollections of the War of 1861*, 76; Andrew J. Bennett, *Story of the First Mas-*

sachusetts Light Battery, 99–100; Haines, *15th New Jersey,* 37; Alexander Morrison Stewart, *Camp, March, and Battlefield,* 290–93; United States Christian Commission, *First Annual Report,* 59–60; Virgil W. Mattoon to "Dear Brother John," December 28, 1862, Mattoon Papers, CHS.

34. Sturtevant, *Josiah Volunteered,* 81; Melcher, *With a Flash of His Sword,* 18; *Carlisle (Pa.) Herald,* December 26, 1862; *Hartford Daily Courant,* January 14, 1863; Robert Guyton to his father, December 28, 1862, Guyton and Heaslet Papers, Duke; January 15–16, 1863, Stevens Diary, USAMHI; Clark S. Edwards to his wife, January 5, 1863, Edwards Papers, USAMHI.

35. Kibler, "Letters from a Confederate Soldier," 125; December 17, 1862, Firebaugh Diary, SHC; James T. McElvaney to his mother, December 19, 1862, McElvaney Letter, FSNMP; *OR Supplement,* pt. 2, 6:294; Alexander Routh to ?, December 22, 1862, Routh Letter, East Carolina University; W. H. Andrews, *Footprints of a Regiment,* 100; J. F. Shaffner to "My Dearest Friend," December 21, 1862, Shaffner Papers, NCDAH.

36. William Alexander Smith, *Anson Guards,* 173; Welch, *Confederate Surgeon's Letters,* 41; Thomas Claybrook Elder to Anna Fitzhugh Elder, December 21, 1862, Elder Papers, VHS; Robert Taylor Scott to his wife, December 31, 1862, Keith Family Papers, VHS; Richard Lewis, *Camp Life of a Confederate Boy,* 37; S. G. Pryor, *Post of Honor,* 267.

37. Dobbins, *Grandfather's Journal,* 120–21; McCreery Recollections, section 10, 1862–63, VHS; January 17, 1863, Cowin Diary, UA; Napier Bartlett, *Military Record of Louisiana,* 164; Manarin, *15th Virginia,* 36; Lee A. Wallace Jr., *17th Virginia,* 42.

38. David L. Bozeman to his wife, January 18, 1863, Bozeman Letters, FSNMP; DeNoon, *Charlie's Letters,* 124–25; Jonathan Fuller Coghill to "Dear Pappy, Ma, and Mit," January 25, 1863, Coghill Letters, Auburn University Archives; Krick, *30th Virginia,* 34; McMurry, *Hood,* 67; "Letters from the Front," 157.

39. Ujanirtus Allen, *Campaigning with "Old Stonewall,"* 200; Reidenbaugh, *33rd Virginia,* 56; Robert A. Moore, *Life for the Confederacy,* 125; Jensen, *32nd Virginia,* 106–7; Walter Clark, *Regiments and Battalions from North Carolina,* 2:297; Austin, *Georgia Boys with "Stonewall" Jackson,* 58.

40. Jennings Cropper Wise, *Long Arm of Lee,* 1:425–26; Bone Reminiscences, NCDAH; Driver, *52nd Virginia,* 31–32; J. G. Montgomery to his family, January 9, 1863, Montgomery Letter, FSNMP; William Ross Stillwell to "My Dear Mollie," December 14, 1862, Stillwell Letters, GDAH; Pipes Memoir, 15, VHS; *OR,* 1097.

41. Chapla, "Quartermaster Operations in the Forty-second Virginia," 19–20; James H. Simpson to his mother, December 25, 1862, Allen and Simpson Family Papers, SHC; Cutrer and Parrish, *Brothers in Gray,* 138; Emory M. Thomas, *Confederate Nation,* 190–91; Bell, *11th Virginia,* 36; Walter Clark, *Regiments and Battalions from North Carolina,* 2:586; *OR,* 1097–99; Michael W. Taylor, *Cry Is War, War, War,* 129; James T. McElvaney to his mother, December 19, 1862, McElvaney Letter, FSNMP.

42. *OR,* 1088–90, 1100–1101, 1109–11, and ser. 1, 51(2):667. One problem was that Northrop waited until after the battle of Fredericksburg to order additional supplies from the lower South. See Goff, *Confederate Supply,* 80–81.

43. Caldwell, *History of a Brigade of South Carolinians,* 70; Terry L. Jones, *Lee's Tigers,* 140; Musselman, *Caroline Light, Parker, and Stafford Light Virginia Artillery,* 55; December 18, 22, 1862, Ware Diary, SHC; Thomas Claybrook Elder to Anna Fitzhugh Elder, December 27, 1862, Elder Papers, VHS.

44. William Meade Dame to "Dear Nell," January 1863, Dame Letters, FSNMP; Carmichael, *Purcell, Crenshaw, and Letcher Artillery,* 106; Hartley, *Stuart's Tarheels,* 183; Krick, *30th Virginia,* 34–35.

45. Thomas J. Morrison to his mother, December 20, 1862, Morrison Letters, FSNMP; Dobbins, *Grandfather's Journal,* 117; Chapla, *42nd Virginia,* 30–32; Hagood, "Memoirs," 92, SCL; James W. Espy to Alexander H. Stephens, December 30, 1862, Stephens Papers, LC;

Edwin G. Lee to Frederick W. M. Holliday, December 22, 1862, Holliday Papers, Duke; Clement Anselm Evans, *Confederate Military History*, 8:860. Officers' slaves, too, got sick and had to be sent home. See John Bratton to his wife, January 1, 1863, Bratton Letters, SHC.

46. J. F. Shaffner to "My dearest friend," December 21, 1862, Shaffner Papers, NCDAH; *OR*, 1084–85; Henry Kyd Douglas to Helen Macomb Boteler, December 22, 1862, Douglas Papers, Duke; January 23, 1863, Ware Diary, SHC; Constantine Hege to his parents, December 21, 1862, Hege Letters, Leigh Collection, USAMHI; Edward E. Sill to his sister, December 20, 1862, Sill Letters, Duke; Jensen, *32nd Virginia*, 107; December 27, 1862, January 1, 1863, Pickens Diary, UA. Though not as severe as in warmer weather, diarrhea still plagued many soldiers. "When one's bowels get wrong here, it is difficult to correct them with the diet we have," an Alabama lieutenant observed. See Burgwyn, *Captain's War*, 44; James M. Simpson to his mother, December 25, 1862, and Simpson to his wife, January 6, 1863, Allen and Simpson Family Papers, SHC; Cutrer and Parish, *Brothers in Gray*, 139–40; Ujanirtus Allen, *Campaigning with "Old Stonewall,"* 211; January 17, 1863, Ware Diary, SHC; Spears and Pettit, *Civil War Letters,* 1:89.

47. Robert E. Lee, *Wartime Papers*, 379–81.

48. Henry Clay Krebs to Lizzie Beard, December 25, 1862, Krebs Papers, Duke; William D. Henderson, *10th Virginia* 43, December 25, 1862, Shipp Diary, VHS; J. F. Shaffner to "My dearest friend," December 26, 1862, Shaffner Papers, NCDAH; Malone, *Whipt 'em Everytime*, 67; Iobst and Manarin, *Bloody Sixth*, 108; Henry Alexander Chambers, *Diary*, 78; Alexander E. Pendleton to his sister, December 28, 1862, Pendleton Papers, SHC; Ujanirtus Allen, *Campaigning with "Old Stonewall,"* 199–200. For a useful though at times overblown analysis of changing Christmas customs and their significance, see Nissenbaum, *Battle for Christmas*.

49. Bell, *11th Virginia*, 36; Driver, *52nd Virginia*, 30; Isaac Howard to his father, December 25, 1862, Howard Family Papers, SHC; Manarin, *15th Virginia*, 36; Trout, *With Pen and Saber*, 129; Jensen, *32nd Virginia*, 107; David Holt, *Mississippi Rebel*, 155–58.

50. William Henry Cocke to John Cocke, December 26, 1862, Cocke Family Papers, VHS; Chamberlayne, *Ham Chamberlayne, Virginian*, 151; Riggs, *13th Virginia*, 28; William C. McClellan to his father, December 28, 1862, Buchanan and McClellan Family Papers, SHC; David L. Bozeman to his wife, December 27, 1862, Bozeman Letters, FSNMP; Joslyn, *Charlotte's Boys*, 141.

51. Edgar Allan Jackson, *Three Rebels Write Home*, 81; Burgwyn, *Captain's War*, 45; Irvin Cross Wills to James W. Wills, January 1, 1863, Wills Family Papers, VHS; Pierrepont, *Reuben Vaughan Kidd*, 319; Mills Lane, *"Dear Mother: Don't Grieve about Me,"* 208; Jeremiah M. Tate to his sister, February 14, 1863, Tate Papers, GLC; Balfour, *13th Virginia Cavalry*, 11; Krick, *Parker's Virginia Battery*, 106.

52. George Wise, *Seventeenth Virginia*, 132; Patterson, *Yankee Rebel*, 91; Bryan Grimes to William Grimes, December 26, 1862, Grimes Family Papers, SHC; December 24, 1862, Ware Diary, SHC; December 25, 1862, E. P. Miller Diary, FSNMP; December 24, 1862, Hodnett Diary, UDC Bound Typescripts, GDAH; Richard Lewis, *Camp Life of a Confederate Boy*, 38.

53. Accounts of Christmas Day in the Army of Northern Virginia confirm Reid Mitchell's argument that long-held notions about Confederates as devout Christian soldiers need revising. See Reid Mitchell, "Christian Soldiers?," 297–309.

54. Thomas Claybrook Elder to Anna Fitzhugh Elder, December 27, 1862, Elder Papers, VHS; Francis P. Fleming, "Fleming in the War for Southern Independence," 48–49; December 25, 1862, Jones Diary, Schoff Collection, CL; W. H. Andrews, *Footprints of a Regiment*, 100 101; Henry P. Garrison to Emily Aurora Bosworth, January 4, 1863, Garrison Papers, Austin State University; Halsey Wigfall to Charlotte Wigfall, December 26, 1862, Wigfall Papers, UT.

55. Philip H. Powers to his wife, December 25, 1862, Powers Letters, Leigh Collection, USAMHI; Miles H. Hill to his sister, December 24, 1862, Morgan-Hill Family Papers, Troup County Archives; H. Waters Berryman to his mother, December 27, 1862, Berryman Let-

ter, USAMHI; Hightower, "Letters from Harvey Judson Hightower," 180; Dobbins, *Grandfather's Journal,* 116; Samuel J. C. Moore to his wife, December 25, 1862, Samuel J. C. Moore Papers, SHC; Young and Young, *56th Virginia,* 69–70; James I. Robertson Jr., *4th Virginia,* 23; William G. Bean, "House Divided," 407; D. R. E. Winn to "Dear Fannie," December 23, 1862, Winn Letters, Emory.

56. *Charleston Daily Courier,* December 24, 1862; *Richmond Daily Dispatch,* December 24, 25, 29, 1862; J. B. Jones, *Rebel War Clerk's Diary,* 1:224; Katharine M. Jones, *Ladies of Richmond,* 147; Welton, *Caldwell Letters,* 166–67; Lee A. Wallace Jr., *1st Virginia,* 38; December 25, 1862, Hamilton Diary, FSNMP; December 25, 1862, Penrose Diary, LSU; Greer, "All Thoughts Are Absorbed in the War," 35.

57. *Milledgeville (Ga.) Confederate Union,* December 30, 1862; *Charleston Mercury,* December 25, 1862; December 25, 1862, Ware Diary, SHC; J. F. Shaffner to "My dearest friend," December 26, 1862, Shaffner Papers, NCDAH; *Richmond Daily Examiner,* December 25, 1862.

58. *Richmond Daily Whig,* December 24, 1862; *Richmond Daily Dispatch,* December 25, 1862; *Richmond Daily Enquirer,* December 25, 1862; *Charleston Daily Courier,* December 25, 1862; Simpson and Simpson, *Far, Far from Home,* 168.

59. John R. McClure, *Hoosier Farmboy in Lincoln's Army,* 35; Cornelius Richmond to his wife, December 25, 1862, Richmond Papers, FSNMP; James H. Leonard, "Letters of a Fifth Wisconsin Volunteer," 69; Aldrich, *History of Battery A,* 167; Bright and Bright, *"Respects to All,"* 36; George H. Patch to his mother, December 27, 1862, Patch Papers, Leigh Collection, USAMHI; Haydon, *For Country, Cause, and Leader,* 301; *Wellsboro (Pa.) Agitator,* January 4, 1863; John D. Withrow to Sarah Withrow, December 28, 1862, Withrow Letters, FSNMP; Molyneux, *Quill of the Wild Goose,* 55.

60. Edward Henry Courtney Taylor to his brother, January 7, 1863, Taylor Letters, MHC; J. L. Smith to his mother, December 26, 1862, John L. Smith Letters, FSNMP; *History of the Sixth New York Cavalry,* 88; Edmund Halsey, *Brother against Brother,* 97; Curtis C. Pollock to his mother, December 27, 1862, Pollock Papers, CWMC, USAMHI; Joseph H. Leighty to his sister, December 25, 1862, GAR.

61. Pettit, *Infantryman Pettit,* 44; Harper, *Civil War History of Chester County, Pennsylvania,* 187; Henry Grimes Marshall to "Dear Folks at Home," December 25, 1862, Marshall Papers, Schoff Collection, CL; Jacob Henry Cole, *Under Five Commanders,* 121; Allan L. Bevan to his sister, January 1, 1863, Bevan Correspondence, CWMC, USAMHI; Edward W. Steffan to his brother, December 27, 1862, Steffan Letters, FSNMP; Dawes, *Sixth Wisconsin,* 115.

62. J. L. Smith to his mother, December 26, 1862, John L. Smith Letters, FSNMP; Haley, *Rebel Yell and Yankee Hurrah,* 63–64; William Hamilton to his mother, December 28, 1862, Hamilton Papers, LC; Weygant, *One Hundred and Twenty-Fourth Regiment,* 78–79; Cudworth, *First Regiment (Massachusetts Infantry),* 333; John W. Ames to his mother, January 4, 1863, Ames Papers, USAMHI; Solomon Dodge to his brother, December 30, 1862, Dodge Papers, NHHS; Henry Butler to his wife, December 30, 1862, Butler Papers, Castine Public Library.

63. Henry C. Heisler to his sister, January 5, 1863, Heisler Papers, LC; Hitchcock, *War from the Inside,* 148–49; *Rochester (N.Y.) Daily Union and Advertiser,* January 5, 1863; Cavins, *Civil War Letters of Cavins,* 130; Reeves, *Twenty-Fourth New Jersey,* 23–24; *New York Times,* December 30, 1862; Donaldson, *Inside the Army of the Potomac,* 196.

64. John Godfrey to Horace Godfrey, December 28, 1862, Godfrey Papers, NHHS; Louis Fortescue to "Friend Sam," January 9, 1863, Fortescue Letters, FSNMP; David Beem to his wife, December 25, 1862, Beem Papers, IHS; Conyngham, *Irish Brigade,* 360–61; December 25, 1862, Holford Diary, LC; Molyneux, *Quill of the Wild Goose,* 58; Gaff, *On Many a Bloody Field,* 213; George E. Stephens, *Voice of Thunder,* 219; Hitchcock, *War from the Inside,* 153–57; George W. Barr to Vinnie Barr, December 25, 1862, Barr Papers, Schoff Collection, CL. Some men decorated their camps with holly or even Christmas trees; others organized races and games. As with the Confederates, there were apparently few religious observances. See Trask,

Fire Within, 163–64; William Hamilton to his mother, January 6, 1863, Hamilton Papers, LC; Mulholland, *116th Pennsylvania,* 72; Hitchcock, *War from the Inside,* 149–51; Trobriand, *Our Noble Blood,* 88–89; David Beem to his wife, December 25, 1862, Beem Papers, IHS.

65. December 25, 1862, Taggart Diary, USAMHI; George W. Ballock to Jenny Ballock, December 23, 25, 1862, Ballock Papers, Duke; Lewis Nettleton to "My own dear love," December 25, 1862, Nettleton-Baldwin Family Papers, Duke; George W. Barr to Vinnie Barr, December 25, 1862, Barr Papers, Schoff Collection, CL; Cavins, *Civil War Letters of Cavins,* 126; John Claude Buchanan to Sophie Buchanan, December 31, 1862, Buchanan Family Papers, MHC; Hartsock, *Soldier of the Cross,* 47; Washburn, *108th Regiment,* 114; John R. McClure, *Hoosier Farmboy in Lincoln's Army,* 32; David Beem to his wife, December 25, 1862, Beem Papers, IHS; George H. Legate to his sister, December 27, 1862, Legate Letter, Gregory A. Coco Collection, HCWRTC, USAMHI.

66. December 25, 1862, Bacon Diary, FSNMP; James R. Woodworth to Phoebe Woodworth, December 25, 1862, Woodworth Papers, Hotchkiss Collection, CL; Molyneux, *Quill of the Wild Goose,* 56; John Claude Buchanan to Sophie Buchanan, December 24, 1862, Buchanan Family Papers, MHC; Edward Hutchinson to "Dear Emma," December 22, 1862, Hutchinson Letters, FSNMP; John Harrison Foye to his sister, January 18, 1863, Foye Papers, NHHS; Lois Hill, *Poems and Songs of the Civil War,* 118. For the *Christmas Eve* drawing, see *Harper's Weekly,* January 3, 1863, 8.

67. For representative Christmas advertising, see *New York Herald,* December 23, 1862; *New York Tribune,* December 23, 1862; *Baltimore American and Commercial Advertiser,* December 10, 15, 23, 1862; *Albany (N.Y.) Atlas and Argus,* December 17, 25, 27, 1862; *Springfield (Mass.) Daily Republican,* December 24, 1862; O'Connor, *Civil War Boston,* 122.

68. Ferris, "Civil War Diaries," 242; *Springfield (Mass.) Daily Republican,* December 27, 1862, January 5, 1863; Brooks, *Mr. Lincoln's Washington,* 52; *Philadelphia Inquirer,* December 27, 1862.

69. *New York Herald,* December 25, 1862; *Philadelphia Inquirer,* December 25, 1862; Strong, *Diary of George Templeton Strong,* 3:282; Thomas Gouldsberry to his brother, December 25, 1862, Gouldsberry Letter, FSNMP.

70. *New York Irish-American,* December 27, 1862; Dexter, *Seymour Dexter,* 130. The unnamed Irishman might have been even more depressed had he known that on Christmas Day several aldermen visited a cemetery near St. Patrick's Cathedral, which had been set aside for the burial of Catholic soldiers. See *New York Herald,* December 25, 1862.

71. *Boston Evening Transcript,* December 24, 1862; *Hartford Daily Courant,* December 25, 1862; Lounger, "Holy-Time," *Harper's Weekly,* January 10, 1863, 18; "Christmas Greeting," *Independent,* December 25, 1862, 4; Isaac Lyman Taylor, "Campaigning with the First Minnesota," 239.

CHAPTER TWENTY-THREE

1. Robert Taylor Scott to his wife, January 5, 1863, Keith Family Papers, VHS; William Rhadamanthus Montgomery, *Georgia Sharpshooter,* 13.

2. January 1, 1863, Ware Diary, SHC; Clement Anselm Evans, *Intrepid Warrior,* 125–26; Wingfield, "Diary of Capt. H. W. Wingfield," 21–22; Patterson, *Yankee Rebel,* 91–92; Edmund Ruffin, *Diary,* 2:524; Edmondston, *"Journal of a Secesh Lady,"* 326–29; Cumming, *Journal,* 82.

3. Clement Anselm Evans, *Intrepid Warrior,* 131; J. B. Jones, *Rebel War Clerk's Diary,* 1: 228; Jefferson Davis, *Papers,* 9:8; Henry Alexander Chambers, *Diary,* 80; Susan Leigh Blackford, *Letters from Lee's Army,* 152–53; Lucy Rebecca Buck, *Shadows of My Heart,* 171; *Macon (Ga.) Daily Telegraph,* January 2, 1863; *Charleston Mercury,* January 1, 1863; Sarah Morgan Dawson, *Civil War Diary,* 380–81.

4. Sprenger, *122d Regiment,* 172; Philip Piper to his cousin, January 7, 1863, GAR.

5. John L. Smith, *118th Pennsylvania,* 158; January 1, 1863, S. W. Gordon Diary, FSNMP;

William B. Jordan Jr., *Red Diamond Regiment,* 34; Trobriand, *Four Years with the Army of the Potomac,* 397–98; Ayling, *Yankee at Arms,* 89; Todd, *Seventy-Ninth Highlanders,* 267; McAllister, *Letters of Robert McAllister,* 251; Siegel, *For the Glory of the Union,* 118. For connections between drinking and liberty, see Rorabaugh, *Alcoholic Republic,* esp. 35.

6. December 31, 1862, Webb Diary, Schoff Collection, CL; Isaac Lyman Taylor, "Campaigning with the First Minnesota," 240; Robert S. Robertson, "Diary of the War," 78; *Albany (N.Y.) Atlas and Argus,* January 1, 1863.

7. The points about morality and providence are brilliantly discussed in Diggins, *Lost Soul of American Politics,* 312–33, 346.

8. It is easy when discussing "freedom" in the Civil War era to assume that emancipation was all but inevitable and give short shrift to competing visions of freedom. Eric Foner's recent survey of the subject, while acknowledging that "both sides fought the Civil War in the name of freedom," adopts a tone suggesting that the triumph of progressive notions about freedom was not seriously in doubt. See Eric Foner, *Story of American Freedom,* 95–100.

9. Harriet Beecher Stowe to Charles Sumner, December 13, 1862; John Murray Forbes to Sumner, December 18, 1862; John D. Baldwin to Sumner, December 30, 1862, Sumner Papers, HU; B. Birdsoll to Zachariah Chandler, December 22, 1862, Chandler Papers, LC; Sylvanus Cobb to Abraham Lincoln, December 27, 1862, Lincoln Papers, LC; Strong, *Diary of George Templeton Strong,* 3:284; Charles Sumner, *Selected Letters,* 2:135–36.

10. Beecher, *Patriotic Addresses,* 403–21; *Chicago Daily Tribune,* December 19, 1862; George E. Stephens, *Voice of Thunder,* 216–19; Irving H. Bartlett, *Wendell and Ann Phillips,* 166.

11. Ropes, *Civil War Nurse,* 114–15; Browning, *Diary,* 1:602; Joseph H. Geiger to Salmon P. Chase, December 27, 1862, Chase Papers, LC.

12. *New York Tribune,* December 26–27, 1862; "Fredericksburg and Washington," *National Anti-Slavery Standard,* December 27, 1862, 2; "God's Ways Not Our Ways," *Evangelist,* January 1, 1863, 1; Resolution of Conference of Baptist Ministers to Abraham Lincoln, December 24, 1862, Seward Papers, UR. In arguing that emancipation would bring military victory, abolitionists and their Republican allies echoed Clausewitz's contention that an ambitious "policy" objective would infuse energy into an army. See Clausewitz, *On War,* 606–7, 610, 642.

13. *Indianapolis Daily State Sentinel,* December 18, 1862; *New York Herald,* December 18, 1862.

14. Miers, *Lincoln Day by Day,* 3:159; Welles, *Diary of Gideon Welles,* 1:209–11; Chase, *Salmon P. Chase Papers,* 3:350–51; Browning, *Diary,* 1:606–7; Sandburg, *Lincoln,* 2:14; Poore, *Perley's Reminiscences of Sixty Years in the National Metropolis,* 2:136.

15. Brooks, *Washington in Lincoln's Time,* 48–49; Brooks, *Mr. Lincoln's Washington,* 58–60; Welles, *Diary of Gideon Welles,* 1:212; Poore, *Perley's Reminiscences of Sixty Years in the National Metropolis,* 2:137; Frederick W. Seward, *Reminiscences of a War-Time Statesman and Diplomat,* 227; Francis Becknell Carpenter, *Inner Life of Lincoln,* 87.

16. Lincoln, *Collected Works,* 6:28–30. For a brief, analytical, and carefully balanced appraisal of the Emancipation Proclamation, see Paludan, *Presidency of Lincoln,* 187–89.

17. Stephen B. Oates, *Woman of Valor,* 118–19; Cary, *George William Curtis,* 161; John Murray Forbes to Zachariah Chandler, January 26, 1862, Chandler Papers, LC; "Why a Prolonged War?," *Liberator,* January 29, 1863, 18; Thaddeus Stevens, *Selected Papers,* 1:357; *New York Tribune,* January 13, 1863; Paludan, *Presidency of Lincoln,* 190–91.

18. Douglass, *Writings of Douglass,* 3:305–10; Douglass, *Life and Times,* 427–30; Quarles, *Negro in the Civil War,* 170–74. For accounts of similar celebrations elsewhere, see McPherson, *Negro's Civil War,* 50, 81; Quarles, *Negro in the Civil War,* 174–75; Dusinberre, *Civil War Issues in Philadelphia,* 151–53.

19. "The New Year," *Independent,* January 1, 1863, 4; "The Edict of Freedom," *Independent,* January 8, 1863, 8; "The Happy New Year," *National Anti-Slavery Standard,* January 10, 1863, 2; *Poughkeepsie (N.Y.) Daily Eagle,* January 3, 1863; *Cincinnati Daily Gazette,* January 3, 1863;

Chicago Daily Tribune, January 2, 1863; Strong, *Diary of George Templeton Strong,* 3:286; *Boston Daily Advertiser,* January 1, 1863; *Springfield (Mass.) Daily Republican,* January 2, 1863; *Boston Evening Transcript,* January 2, 1863.

20. *New York World,* January 6, 1863; "Mr. Lincoln Proclaims Emancipation," *Albion,* January 3, 1863, 6–7; *Indianapolis Daily State Sentinel,* January 1, 1863; Klement, *Copperheads in the Middle West,* 43–45; *New York Herald,* January 1, 1863; *Harrisburg Patriot and Union,* December 3, 1862, January 3, 1863; *Albany (N.Y.) Atlas and Argus,* January 3, 6, 1863. Historian John Hope Franklin noted how Democratic editors responded in remarkably mild language. This is partly true, and even the Republican press did not comment extensively on the final Emancipation Proclamation. But it is also important to keep in mind that the Democrats had many other issues with which to browbeat the administration. The failures of the Army of the Potomac, the new calls for peace, the coming inauguration of Horatio Seymour as governor of New York, and the prospects for foreign intervention in the war all consumed increasing amounts of editorial space. See Franklin, *Emancipation Proclamation,* 118–24.

21. Welles, *Diary of Gideon Welles,* 1:212–13; Browning, *Diary,* 1:609, 612–13, 618–19; *Rochester (N.Y.) Daily Union and Advertiser,* January 5, 1863; Thomas Ewing Sr. to William H. Seward, January 13, 1863, and William Crafts to Seward, January 24, 1863, Seward Papers, UR; *Albany (N.Y.) Evening Journal,* January 7, 14, 30, 1863; *New York Times,* January 3, 9, 1863.

22. Edward W. Peck to his mother, January 3, 1863, Peck Letters, CWMC, USAMHI; Gaff, *On Many a Bloody Field,* 215–16; Abbott, *Fallen Leaves,* 161; *Rochester (N.Y.) Daily Union and Advertiser,* January 20, 1863; Charles Shields Wainwright, *Diary of Battle,* 156; McKelvey, *Rochester in the Civil War,* 119–20.

23. John C. Ellis to his nephew, January 1863, Ellis-Marshall Papers, HCWRTC, USAMHI; Gay, "Gay Letters," 390; Joseph Bloomfield Osborn to Mary Osborn, Osborn Papers, LC.

24. Kearney, "Letters from the Field," 189–90; Jonathan Hutchinson to his home folks, January 7, 1863, Hutchinson Letters, USAMHI; G. O. Bartlett to Ira Andrews, January 11, 1863, Bartlett Papers, GLC; Daniel Faust to his mother, January 5, 1863, Faust Papers, HCWRTC, USAMHI; January 2, 1863, Dodge Diary, LC; "Alarming Evidence of Demoralization in the Army," *Old Guard,* February 1863, 36; *Rochester (N.Y.) Daily Union and Advertiser,* January 22, 1863; Gaff, *On Many a Bloody Field,* 215–16. Some officers attempted to resign in protest over the Emancipation Proclamation, but Burnside and Sumner quickly put a halt to that ploy. See Ambrose E. Burnside to William B. Franklin, January 18, 1863, Burnside Letterbook, Dispatches, December 26, 1862–January 20, 1863, RIHS; *New York Tribune,* January 21, 1863; *Baltimore American and Commercial Advertiser,* January 22, 1863; Raymond, "Extracts from the Journal of Henry J. Raymond," 421.

25. John R. McClure, *Hoosier Farmboy in Lincoln's Army,* 35–36; Landon, "Letters to the Vincennes Western Sun," 341; "Alarming Evidence of Demoralization in the Army," *Old Guard,* February 1863, 36; Daniel M. Holt, *Surgeon's Civil War,* 61; December 15, 1862, Boyts Diary, HSP; George E. Stephens, *Voice of Thunder,* 214; Morton Hayward to his sister, December 23, 1862, Hayward Letters, Leigh Collection, USAMHI. Ironically, racial prejudice helped build support for the enrollment of black troops. "The true question," Hannah Ropes believed, "was whether we would have sons sacrificed, or the blacks, for whose freedom this war is waged." Such reasoning helped convince white soldiers that black regiments might redound to their advantage. See *Philadelphia Evening Bulletin,* November 12, 1862; Ropes, *Civil War Nurse,* 114–15; McPherson, *For Cause and Comrades,* 126–28.

26. Jacob W. Haas to Frederick Haas, January 3, 1863, Haas Papers, HCWRTC, USAMHI; Gaff, *On Many a Bloody Field,* 215.

27. Edward Henry Courtney Taylor to his sister, January 15, 1863, Taylor Letters, MHC; Joseph Ripley Chandler Ward, *One Hundred and Sixth Pennsylvania,* 128; Banes, *Philadelphia Brigade,* 148–49; Anson B. Shuey to his wife, January 11, 1863, Shuey Papers, CWMC, USAMHI; Thomas H. Parker, *History of the 51st,* 282. James McPherson's careful analysis

rightly notes that Lincoln's decision did not cause a morale crisis in the army. Yet despite the complexity of soldier opinion, there is little doubt that the Emancipation Proclamation at least contributed to morale problems among Burnside's men. See McPherson, *For Cause and Comrades,* 121–26.

28. *Brunswick (Maine) Telegraph,* January 16, 1863; January 14, 1863, Stevens Diary, USAMHI; Stearns, *Three Years with Company K,* 152; Isaac Lyman Taylor, "Campaigning with the First Minnesota," 242; John Ripley Adams, *Memorials and Letters,* 92–93; Gates, *Civil War Diaries,* 60; David Beem to his wife, January 8, 1863, Beem Papers, IHS; *History of the Fifth Massachusetts Battery,* 526; Gaff, *On Many a Bloody Field,* 216; William Franklin Draper to his father, January 9, 1863, Draper Papers, LC. James McPherson has argued that the majority of Federal soldiers favored emancipation and, along with Reid Mitchell, has pointed out the strength of pragmatic arguments in the evolution of military attitudes. Yet McPherson acknowledged that opinion seemed to be running the other way during the winter of 1862–63, certainly the case in the Army of the Potomac. See McPherson, *What They Fought For,* 60–64; Reid Mitchell, *Civil War Soldiers,* 126–31. For a good narrative account of soldier reactions that emphasizes diversity, change over time, and finally steadfast patriotism, see William C. Davis, *Lincoln's Men,* 99–108.

29. *Richmond Daily Examiner,* January 7, 1863; January 1, 1863, Harriet Ellen Moore Diary, SHC; *Augusta (Ga.) Daily Chronicle and Sentinel,* January 9, 1863; Hotchkiss, *Make Me a Map of the Valley,* 107; *Macon (Ga.) Daily Telegraph,* January 8, 1863; *Richmond Daily Dispatch,* January 6, 1863. At this point the southern press was still reporting the battle of Stones River as a Rebel victory.

30. John G. Nicolay to Therena Nicolay, January 11, 1863, Nicolay Papers, LC; P. C. Smith to Salmon P. Chase, January 1, 1863, Chase Papers, LC; Nevins, *War for the Union,* 2:351; T. Harry Williams, *Lincoln and the Radicals,* 242–43; Catton, *Never Call Retreat,* 58; Edward L. Pierce, *Memoir and Letters of Sumner,* 4:114; Kapferer, *Rumors,* 132–35. For a concise discussion of speculation about a so-called Northwest Confederacy, see McPherson, *Battle Cry of Freedom,* 593.

31. Nicholas B. Wainwright, "Loyal Opposition in Philadelphia," 298–99; Roseboom, *History of Ohio,* 404; *Congressional Globe,* 37th Cong., 3rd sess., 1862, 2, 26–37, 86–90, 227; *Albany (N.Y.) Atlas and Argus,* December 6, 1862; *Newark (N.J.) Daily Advertiser,* January 20, 1863. Prisoners whom Democrats considered martyrs to liberty, Republicans dismissed as either cheating contractors or traitors. See *Augusta (Maine) Kennebec Journal,* December 19, 1862; *Philadelphia Inquirer,* December 24, 1862; *New York Tribune,* December 9, 1862.

32. Stewart Mitchell, *Horatio Seymour,* 260–67; George Brinton McClellan, *Civil War Papers,* 537; George B. McClellan Democratic Club, Morrisania, N.Y., to George B. McClellan, January 16, 1863, McClellan Papers, LC; Thurlow Weed to William H. Seward, November 20, 1862, January 1, 1863, Seward Papers, UR.

33. Stewart Mitchell, *Horatio Seymour,* 267–71; *New York World,* January 9, 1863; *Albany (N.Y.) Atlas and Argus,* January 9, 1863; *Philadelphia Public Ledger,* January 7, 1863; *New York Herald,* January 8, 1863; *New York Irish-American,* January 17, 1863; *Boston Pilot,* January 24, 1863. Mark Neely has pointed out that the question of civil liberties became a more attractive issue for northern Democrats after the fall elections. See Neely, *Fate of Liberty,* 192–95. Weed's newspaper organ praised Seymour's message overall but declared him wrong on the issue of arbitrary arrests. See *Albany (N.Y.) Evening Journal,* January 7, 1863.

34. *New York Tribune,* January 8, 1863; *Yonkers (N.Y.) Examiner,* January 15, 1863; *Philadelphia Evening Bulletin,* January 6, 1863; *Poughkeepsie (N.Y.) Daily Eagle,* January 8, 1863; *New York Times,* January 8, 9, 1863.

35. Chase, *Salmon P. Chase Papers,* 3:329; Welles, *Diary of Gideon Welles,* 1:219; John A. Dix to Edwin M. Stanton, January 1, 1863, Lincoln Papers, LC; Douglass, *Writings of Douglass,* 3:314–17. In light of the later draft riots in the city, Dix proved something of a prophet.

36. Nevins, *War for the Union*, 2:341–42; Fernando Wood to Abraham Lincoln, December 8, 17, 1862, and Horace Greeley to Lincoln, December 12, 1862, Lincoln Papers, LC; Lincoln, *Collected Works*, 5:553–54; Raymond, "Extracts from the Journal of Henry J. Raymond," 705; Van Deusen, *Greeley*, 288–97; Carroll, *Henri Mercier and the Civil War*, 254–59; N. P. Tallmadge to William H. Seward, January 7, 1863, Seward Papers, UR. One of the informal diplomats was recently elected New York congressman Fernando Wood, a notorious Tammany Hall Democrat. For the international context of these peace rumors, see Howard Jones, *Lincoln and a New Birth of Freedom*, 159–61.

37. *Albany (N.Y.) Atlas and Argus*, January 5, 1863; Shankman, *Pennsylvania Antiwar Movement*, 108–9; "What Is the War Coming To?," *Knickerbocker*, January 1863, 44; Fisher, *Diary of Sidney George Fisher*, 445; Dusinberre, *Civil War Issues in Philadelphia*, 153–56.

38. *Congressional Globe*, 37th Cong., 3rd sess., 1862, 15; *New York Times*, December 13, 1862; Klement, *Limits of Dissent*, 122–28; *Appendix to Congressional Globe*, 37th Cong. 3rd sess., 1862, 52–60; Klement, *Copperheads in the Middle West*, 42; *New York Herald*, January 3, 1863; Silbey, *Respectable Minority*, 90–110; *Springfield (Mass.) Daily Republican*, December 24, 1862; Tap, *Over Lincoln's Shoulder*, 143–44; Bogue, "Cutler's Congressional Diary," 321.

39. W. R. Holloway to John G. Nicolay, January 1, 1863, and Henry B. Carrington to Abraham Lincoln, January 14, 1863, Lincoln Papers, LC; Hill, ser. 3, 3:4; Stampp, *Indiana Politics during the Civil War*, 169–76; *Indianapolis Daily Journal*, January 10, 1863; *Indianapolis Daily State Sentinel*, January 16, 1863; Terrill, *Indiana in the War of the Rebellion*, 301–15.

40. Klement, *Copperheads in the Middle West*, 52–67.

41. Joseph H. Geiger to Salmon P. Chase, November 7, 18, 1862, Chase Papers, LC; Chase, *Salmon P. Chase Papers*, 3:312–14, 325–26; Zachariah Chandler to his wife, January 15, 1863, Chandler Papers, LC; Trefousse, *Wade*, 192; Blue, *Chase*, 194–95.

42. Zachariah Chandler to his wife, January 8, 17, 1863, Chandler Papers, LC; George, *Zachariah Chandler*, 97–99; *Watertown (N.Y.) Daily News and Reformer*, January 15, 1863.

43. Simon Cameron to Edwin M. Stanton, November 24, 1862, Stanton Papers, LC; Cameron to Abraham Lincoln, January 13, 1863, Lincoln Papers, LC; Bradley, *Cameron*, 226–32; *Philadelphia Evening Bulletin*, January 12, 1863; *New York Tribune*, January 13, 1863; *Philadelphia Inquirer*, January 14, 1863; Fisher, *Diary of Sidney George Fisher*, 446; *Harrisburg Patriot and Union*, January 22, 1863; Welles, *Diary of Gideon Welles*, 1:223.

44. *Pittsburgh Daily Dispatch*, January 16, 1863; Gurowski, *Diary*, 2:59–60; *New York Tribune*, January 22, 1863; Brooks, *Mr. Lincoln's Washington*, 81–83; Edward Warren to Charles Sumner, January 17, 1863, Sumner Papers, HU.

45. *Newark (N.J.) Daily Advertiser*, December 26, 1862; *Augusta (Maine) Kennebec Journal*, January 9, 1863; *New York Tribune*, January 27, 1863; "No Surrender," *Harper's Weekly*, January 31, 1863, 66; Freidel, *Union Pamphlets on the Civil War*, 1:503–11.

46. *Newark (N.J.) Daily Advertiser*, December 31, 1862, January 10, 1863; *Hartford Daily Courant*, January 23, 1863; *Poughkeepsie (N.Y.) Daily Eagle*, January 17, 1863.

47. Motley, *Correspondence*, 2:103; *Boston Evening Transcript*, January 17, 1863; *Chicago Daily Tribune*, January 21, 1863; "Secession at Home," *Independent*, January 22, 1863, 4; *Congressional Globe*, 37th Cong., 3rd sess., 1862, 314–18; *Albany (N.Y.) Evening Journal*, January 15, 1863.

48. Charles Gibson to his sister, January 6, 1863, Gibson Letters, FSNMP; Reuben Kelley to his sister, January 15, 1863, Kelley Letters, FSNMP; Richard J. Gist to his aunt, January 7, 1863, Gist Family Papers, LC; James T. Odem to Eleanor Odem, January 1, 1863, Odem Papers, UVa; A. Caldwell to his brother, January 1, 1863, Caldwell Family Papers, CWTI, USAMHI. One historian has suggested that Fredericksburg raised fundamental questions about whether a democracy was too weak and inefficient to defeat what some northerners considered to be a centralized southern despotism. See Michael C. C. Adams, *Our Masters the Rebels*, 136–37.

49. James Bloomfield Osborn to Joseph M. Osborn, December 18, 1862, Osborn Papers,

LC; Edwin Wentworth to his wife, December 26, 1862, Wentworth Papers, LC; December 22, 1862, Lewis Nettleton Diary, Nettleton-Baldwin Family Papers, Duke; James T. Odem to Eleanor Odem, January 13, 1863, Odem Papers, UVa; McPherson, *For Cause and Comrades,* 99; Naum Hass Apgar to John A. Apgar, January 1, 1863, GAR.

50. Charles Jewett Morris to his brother and sister, January 8, 1863, Morris Papers, Duke; *Brookville (Ind.) Franklin Democrat,* January 23, 1863; Marsena Rudolph Patrick, *Inside Lincoln's Army,* 197–98, 201; Brewster, *When This Cruel War Is Over,* 205; Edwin Wentworth to his wife, January 2, 1863, Wentworth Papers, LC; McKelvey, *Rochester in the Civil War,* 114; Augustus Van Dyke to his brother, December 23, 1862, Van Dyke Papers, IHS; George H. Patch to his mother, December 27, 1862, Patch Papers, Leigh Collection, USAMHI. Exaggerated reports of northern unrest—including supposed riots in New York and Boston—also proved disheartening. See Murton S. Tanner to his mother, December 27, 1862, Tanner Letter, CWMC, USAMHI.

51. David Beem to his wife, January 8, 1863, Beem Papers, IHS; January 11, 1863, Plumb Diary, CWMC, USAMHI; Sawyer, *Military History of the 8th Ohio,* 102; Oliver Edwards to his mother, January 13, 1863, Edwards Papers, GLC; Kepler, *Fourth Ohio,* 103; Flauvius Bellamy to his brother, January 16, 1863, Bellamy Papers, ISL; Cavins, *Civil War Letters of Cavins,* 126, 134; January 19, 1863, Stevens Diary, USAMHI; Moe, *Last Full Measure,* 219; Robert Goldthwaite Carter, *Four Brothers in Blue,* 233.

52. Confederate Soldier to "Dear Molly," December 14, 1862, UDC Bound Typescripts, GDAH; Fitzpatrick, *Letters to Amanda,* 39; Kibler, "Letters from a Confederate Soldier," 124; J. B. Jones, *Rebel War Clerk's Diary,* 1:215; Jedediah Hotchkiss to Sara Ann Comfort Hotchkiss, December 17, 1862, Hotchkiss Papers, LC; Irvin Cross Wills to James W. Wills, January 1, 1863, Wills Family Papers, VHS; Carson, *Life, Letters, and Speeches of James Louis Petigru,* 465; Breckinridge, *Lucy Breckinridge of Grove Hill,* 93. Assessing Confederate opinion in this period is complicated because many soldiers and civilians also realized that success might still depend on victories in the western theater. The inconclusive battle of Murfreesboro made the prospect of peace appear more problematic. See Archer, "James J. Archer Letters," 140–41; Spencer, *Civil War Marriage in Virginia,* 153–54; W. R. M. Slaughter to his sister, January 4, 1863, Slaughter Letters, VHS; *Augusta (Ga.) Daily Chronicle and Sentinel,* January 4, 1863; Henry P. Garrison to Emily Aurora Bosworth, January 4, 1863, Garrison Papers, Austin State University.

53. *Augusta (Ga.) Daily Chronicle and Sentinel,* December 21, 1862; S. G. Pryor, *Post of Honor,* 298; *Lynchburg Daily Virginian,* January 9, 1863; Graves, *Confederate Marine,* 98; Maggie Iredell to Cadwallader Jones, December 28, 1862, Jones Papers, SHC; McDonald, *Woman's Civil War,* 115; Edmund Ruffin, *Diary,* 2:521–22, 526–27, 540–42; *Wilmington (N.C.) Daily Journal,* December 23, 1862.

54. Edmund Ruffin Jr. to Edmund Ruffin, December 27, 1862, Edmund Ruffin Papers, VHS; January 4, 17, 1863, Cowin Diary, UA; *Augusta (Ga.) Daily Chronicle and Sentinel,* December 27, 1862; McDonald, *Woman's Civil War,* 116–17; *Charleston Mercury,* January 27, 1863; *Atlanta Southern Confederacy,* January 8, 1863; Speairs and Pettit, *Civil War Letters,* 1:90–91; Edmund Ruffin, *Diary,* 2:539; J. B. Jones, *Rebel War Clerk's Diary,* 1:236; *Raleigh Weekly Register,* December 31, 1862; *Macon (Ga.) Daily Telegraph,* December 20, 1862.

55. Allston, *South Carolina Rice Plantation,* 192; Robert Taylor Scott to his wife, January 5, 1863, Keith Family Papers, VHS; S. G. Pryor, *Post of Honor,* 297; William G. Bean, "House Divided," 410; Clement Anselm Evans, *Intrepid Warrior,* 131–32.

56. "Proceedings of the First Confederate Congress," 191; House Resolution by Mr. Foster, January 20, 1863; House Bill No. 25, January 13, 1863; *Richmond Daily Examiner,* January 21, 1863; Edmund Ruffin, *Diary,* 2:550–52; J. B. Jones, *Rebel War Clerk's Diary,* 1:230; *Charleston Mercury,* January 26, 1863; *Richmond Daily Dispatch,* January 26, 1863. Realistic Confederates also recognized that the Yankees could throw still more troops into the fray and that south-

ern armies had best prepare for spring offensives. See Lang, "Letters of Lang," 345; *Richmond Daily Dispatch,* January 6, 1863.

57. John Bratton to his wife, January 1, 1863, Bratton Letters, SHC; *Milledgeville (Ga.) Confederate Union,* January 20, 1863; *Augusta (Ga.) Daily Chronicle and Sentinel,* January 6, 1863; *Charleston Mercury,* January 13, 1863; James I. Robertson Jr., *Stonewall Brigade,* 178; *Richmond Daily Whig,* January 5, 1863.

58. *Charleston Daily Courier,* January 21, 1863; *Raleigh Weekly Register,* December 31, 1862; *Raleigh Weekly Standard,* December 31, 1862; *Richmond Daily Enquirer,* December 17, 1862; Alfred E. Doby to his wife, January 18, 1863, Doby Letters, MC. For an extended discussion on how the Confederates developed rival political cultures of national unity and libertarianism, see Rable, *Confederate Republic.*

59. Jefferson Davis, *Papers,* 8:566–67, 9:11–15.

60. James D. Richardson, *Messages and Papers,* 1:276–77, 290–93; Alfred E. Doby to his wife, January 15, 1863, Doby Letters, MC; Judith Brockenbrough McGuire, *Diary of a Southern Refugee,* 183–84; *Richmond Daily Whig,* January 16, 1863; *Charleston Mercury,* January 23, 1863.

61. Lerner, "Money, Prices, and Wages," 15; *Report of the Secretary of the Treasury*, 1, 11, 11, 11, 11, 11, 11, 11, 1, 589–89; "Proceedings of the First Confederate Congress," 122; Lucy A. Caldwell et al. to John Letcher, Letcher Papers, Library of Virginia; "A Lady" to John Gill Shorter, January 19, 1863, Shorter Papers, Alabama Department of Archives and History; *Richmond Daily Dispatch,* December 29, 1862; Bessie Martin, *Desertion of Alabama Troops,* 126–38; *Laws of the State of Mississippi,* 68–72, 79–81; *House Bill No. 20 . . . January 28, 1863.* Freedom remained so precious in part because southern women had made so many sacrifices. Despite a falling off in ladies' aid society activity, soldiers duly noted the connection between female charity and the defense of southern liberty. See *Charleston Daily Courier,* January 24, 1863; Speairs and Pettit, *Civil War Letters,* 1:84; Lang, "Letters of Lang," 346.

62. *Richmond Daily Enquirer,* November 20, 1862; "Proceedings of the First Confederate Congress," 126–28, 149–50.

63. *Richmond Daily Enquirer,* December 22, 1862; *OR,* ser. 4, 2:262–63, 294–95; "Proceedings of the First Confederate Congress," 128–29, 171–75, 180–84; J. B. Jones, *Rebel War Clerk's Diary,* 1:242.

64. Mollie Harris to Jefferson Davis, January 30, 1863, Letters Received, microcopy 437, roll 94, NA; Adelia Ethridge to Davis, December 22, 1862, Letters Received, microcopy 437, roll 126, NA; Mrs. L. W. Nicholson to John J. Pettus, December 17, 1862, Pettus Papers, MDAH. For numerous petitions in December 1862 and January 1863 from women trying to get their men out of the army for various reasons, see Confederate Secretary of War papers cited above. For examples of draft resistance and disaffection in some areas, see *OR,* ser. 4, 2:258; Tatum, *Disloyalty in the Confederacy,* 46–49, 58–59, 99.

65. *Richmond Daily Whig,* December 19, 1862, January 3, 1863; *Richmond Daily Enquirer,* December 18, 1862; *Charleston Mercury,* January 5, 1863; *Richmond Daily Dispatch,* December 15, 1862.

CHAPTER TWENTY-FOUR

1. *OR,* 886; Marvel, *Burnside,* 208; *CCW,* 1:716–17, 726, 747–50.

2. *CCW,* 1:716; *OR,* 95, 899–901; Abiel Hall Edwards, *"Dear Friend Anna,"* 42; Bellard, *Gone for a Soldier,* 190–92; Virgil W. Mattoon to his brother, December 28, 1862, Mattoon Papers, CHS; Fairchild, *27th Regiment,* 131; Felix Brannigan to his sister, December 27, 1862, Brannigan Papers, LC; John W. Ames to his mother, December 29, 1862, Ames Papers, USAMHI; *History of the Fifth Massachusetts Battery,* 521–22; Charles Francis Adams, *Cycle of Adams Letters,* 1:225–32; McNamara, *History of the Ninth Massachusetts,* 270–71; Robert Goldthwaite Carter, *Four Brothers in Blue,* 217–20; John L. Smith, *118th Pennsylvania,* 152–56;

Captain Charles A. Stevens, *Berdan's Sharpshooters*, 226–28; *Kokomo (Ind.) Howard Tribune*, January 15, 1863; Brewster, *When This Cruel War Is Over*, 205.

3. John Godfrey to Horace Godfrey, December 28, 1862, Godfrey Papers, NHHS; Rusling, *Men and Things I Saw in Civil War Days*, 292–93; Felix Brannigan to his sister, December 29, 1862, Brannigan Papers, LC; Charles Shields Wainwright, *Diary of Battle*, 153; George E. Stephens, *Voice of Thunder*, 219–20.

4. William W. Burns to S. S. Cox, January 12, 1863, Dearborn Collection, HU; Trobriand, *Our Noble Blood*, 90; Winslow, *Sedgwick*, 52–53.

5. John Newton to George W. Cullum, December 3, 1862, Cullum Papers, Allegheny College; John Cochrane to Salmon P. Chase, December 19, 1862, Chase Papers, LC; Warner, *Generals in Blue*, 86–87, 334–45. Cochrane's dour assessment of army morale may have been influenced by his chronic bronchitis and an increasingly painful double hernia. See Jack D. Welsh, *Medical Histories of Union Generals*, 71.

6. *CCW*, 1:730–31, 735, 741, 745–46; *OR*, 1009–10. Franklin's testimony on his conversations with subordinates was confusing if not mendacious. He admitted knowing that Newton planned to "see influential people" about morale problems and Burnside's plans but denied knowing of any effort "to see the President, or anybody else who had any power in the matter" (*CCW*, 1:711–12). For extremely helpful but somewhat differing accounts of Burnside in Washington, see Marvel, *Burnside*, 209–10; Sears, *Chancellorsville*, 4–8.

7. *CCW*, 1:731–33, 737–38, 740–44. For an excellent account of the Newton-Cochrane affair, see Sears, *Chancellorsville*, 1–4.

8. *OR*, 900–902. Lincoln called off the operation without apparently consulting Halleck or Stanton. See *CCW*, 1:722–23.

9. *CCW*, 1:722, 750–52; Walter Phelps to his wife, December 31, 1862, Phelps Letters, FSNMP; Weld, *War Diary and Letters*, 157; James S. Graham to his grandfather, January 2, 1863, Graham Letters, FSNMP; Hopkins, *Seventh Rhode Island*, 53; Marsena Rudolph Patrick, *Inside Lincoln's Army*, 197–98. As if to confirm the claims made by Newton and Cochrane, a soldier in Sturgis's division heard several men say they would not cross the river again. See James Pratt to his wife, January 1, 1863, Pratt Collection, USAMHI.

10. Welles, *Diary of Gideon Welles*, 1:211; *CCW*, 1:717–18; Daniel R. Larned to his uncle, January 1, 1863, Larned Papers, LC; Meade, *Life and Letters*, 1:343–44; Marvel, *Burnside*, 209–10. In a later conversation with Franklin, Burnside learned that it had been Newton and Cochrane who had visited Lincoln. See *CCW*, 1:722–23.

11. Daniel Reed Larned to his uncle, January 1, 1863, Larned Papers, LC; *OR*, 941–42, 945; Meade, *Life and Letters*, 1:344; Burnside memorandum, May 24, 1863, Burnside Papers, entry 159, box 3, NA; Raymond, "Extracts from the Journal of Henry J. Raymond," 422; *OR*, 1006–12.

12. Welles, *Diary of Gideon Welles*, 1:209; *OR*, 940–41; Nicolay and Hay, *Lincoln*, 6:215.

13. Mrs. Austin Blair to William Withington, December 30, 1862, and Benjamin Baker to Withington, December 30, 1862, Withington Papers, MHC; David Green to Sullivan Green, December 30, 1862, Sullivan Green Papers, MHC; Hollister, *Colfax*, 203; "The Battle of Fredericksburg," *Scientific American*, December 27, 1862, 402.

14. *OR*, 1008, 1010–11; *CCW*, 1:718; Marvel, *Burnside*, 210–11; Meade, *Life and Letters*, 1:344.

15. Marsena Rudolph Patrick, *Inside Lincoln's Army*, 200; Meade, *Life and Letters*, 1:346; John Godfrey to his brother, January 4, 9, 1863, Godfrey Papers, NHHS; Hebert, *Fighting Joe Hooker*, 164–65; T. Harry Williams, *Lincoln and the Radicals*, 265; Gates, *Civil War Diaries*, 60.

16. Uriah N. Parmelee to his mother, January 14, 1863, Parmelee Papers, Duke; *New York Irish-American*, January 3, 1863; R. S. Robertson to his parents, January 9, 1863, Robertson Papers, FSNMP; Zerah Coston Monks to Hannah T. Rohrer, January 1863, Monks-Rohrer Letters, Emory; Trobriand, *Our Noble Blood*, 92; Henry F. Young to his father, January 9, 1863, Young Papers, SHSW.

17. Uriah N. Parmelee to his mother, January 1, 1863, Parmelee Papers, Duke; Cavins, *Civil War Letters of Cavins*, 130; Allan L. Bevan to his sister, January 1, 1863, Bevan Correspondence, CWMC, USAMHI; Guiney, *Commanding Boston's Irish Ninth*, 161; George Washington Whitman, *Civil War Letters*, 79.

18. *Philadelphia Inquirer*, January 5, 7, 1863; *New York Herald*, January 6, 1863; *Haverhill (Mass.) Gazette*, January 2, 1863; William R. Williams to his wife, January 4, 1863, Williams Papers, CWMC, USAMHI; Edmund Halsey, *Brother against Brother*, 103; William Franklin Draper to his father, January 9, 1863, Draper Papers, LC. For additional evidence of rebounding morale, see A. Wilson Greene, "Morale, Maneuver, and Mud," 190–91.

19. John D. Withrow to Sarah Withrow, December 28, 1862, Withrow Letters, FSNMP; Samuel Parmelee to his mother, December 26, 1862, Parmelee Papers, Duke; John T. Greene, *Ewing Family Letters*, 35; Aaron K. Blake to his sister, January 11, 1863, Blake Letters, CWMC, USAMHI; Edward W. Peck to his mother, January 3, 1863, Peck Letters, CWMC, USAMHI; Henry Lewis to his cousin, January 3, 1863, Lewis Letters, GLC.

20. Edwin Wentworth to his wife, January 5, 1863, Wentworth Papers, LC; Weston, *Picket Pins and Sabers*, 36; McKelvey, *Rochester in the Civil War*, 164; Sears, *Chancellorsville*, 15; William Hamilton to his brother, January 3, 1863, and Hamilton to his mother, January 6, 1863, Hamilton Papers, LC; *Williamsburg (Pa.) Democrat and Sentinel*, January 14, 1863.

21. S. B. Tarleton to "Dear Amy," January 12, 1863, Tarleton Letter, CWMC, USAMHI; Matrau, *Letters Home*, 40.

22. Philip Hacker to William and Barbara Woll Hacker, January 6, 1863, Hacker Brothers Papers, Schoff Collection, CL; S. Millett Thompson, *Thirteenth New Hampshire*, 101–2; John Ripley Adams, *Memorials and Letters*, 93. Soldiers and their families reportedly complained of too much "hard biscuit and stinking meat" while Lincoln "lives on Roast Beef and every delicacy he wants" (C. Ainslie to William H. Seward, January 8, 1863, Seward Papers, UR).

23. George H. Mellish to his mother, January 2, 1863, Mellish Papers, HL; Sprenger, *122d Regiment*, 179; Letterman, *Medical Recollections of the Army of the Potomac*, 94–95; Benedict, *Vermont in the Civil War*, 1:347. The health of some regiments had become unusually good. See Charles Piper to cousin, January 7, 1863, GAR; Cavins, *Civil War Letters of Cavins*, 129.

24. Reeves, *Twenty-Fourth New Jersey*, 24; Rufus P. Stanick to "My Darling Selina," January 5–6, 1863, Stanick Letter, Virginia Polytechnic; *OR*, 958; Charles Dwight Chase to his father, January 11, 1863, Chase Papers, NHHS; Craft, *History of the One Hundred Forty-First Pennsylvania*, 45–46; John T. Greene, *Ewing Family Letters*, 35–36.

25. *MSH*, 2:130, 134; Peter Welsh, *Irish Green and Union Blue*, 51; *OR*, 957–58.

26. Edmund Halsey, *Brother against Brother*, 102; Musgrove, *Autobiography of Captain Richard Musgrove*, 55–56; Catton, *Glory Road*, 93; January 13, 1862, Asa W. Bartlett, "Diary of Military Action," NHHS; Sprenger, *122d Regiment*, 173–74, 176, 179, 184, 188–89.

27. January 11, 1863, Mancha Diary, CWMC, USAMHI; Daniel M. Holt, *Surgeon's Civil War*, 62–63; Washburn, *108th Regiment*, 115; Cornelius Richmond to his wife, January 3, 1863, Richmond Papers, FSNMP.

28. January 10, 21, 1863, Eaton Diary, SHC; Jonathan Hutchinson to his home folks, January 7, 1863, Hutchinson Letters, USAMHI; *Philadelphia Inquirer*, January 7, 1863; William Franklin Draper to his wife, January 18, 1863, Draper Papers, LC; Reeves, *Twenty-Fourth New Jersey*, 27–28; Orson Blair Curtis, *History of the Twenty-Fourth Michigan*, 108; S. Millett Thompson, *Thirteenth New Hampshire*, 99–100; United States Christian Commission, *First Annual Report*, 62; Locke, *Story of the Regiment*, 177.

29. David Lane, *Soldier's Diary*, 25; A. B. Martin to "Dear Ann," December 19, 1862, Martin Letter, FSNMP; Loren H. Goodrich to "Dear Friends," January 5, 1863, Goodrich Papers, CHS; John W. Ames to his mother, January 12, 1863, Ames Papers, USAMHI.

30. Alexander Way to his wife, December 18, 1862, Way Letters, FSNMP; Hartwell, *To My Beloved Wife and Boy at Home*, 36–38; George E. Upton to his wife, January 18, 1863, Upton

Papers, NHHS; Cavins, *Civil War Letters of Cavins,* 130; John Vestal Hadley, "Indiana Soldier in Love and War," 222.

31. Henry Grimes Marshall to "Dear Hattie," December 28, 1862, Marshall Papers, Schoff Collection, CL; Henry F. Young to "Dear Delia," January 25, 1863, Young Papers, SHSW; William Franklin Draper to his wife, January 18, 1863, Draper Papers, LC; Pardington, *Dear Sarah,* 51–52; John R. Coye to his wife, December 19, 1862, Coye Letters, FSNMP; Jacob Bechtel to "Miss Cannie," January 15, 1863, Bechtel Letters, Gettysburg National Military Park; Hagerty, *Collis' Zouaves,* 131–32. Loneliness, sentimental attachments to home, and the desire to maintain family ties led soldiers to exchange pictures with their loved ones and kept photographers in camp busy. See Hopkins, *Seventh Rhode Island,* 51; January 3, 1863, Pope Diary, *CWTI,* USAMHI; Perkins, "Letters Home," 130.

32. James P. Coburn to his father, January 28, 1863, James P. Coburn Papers, USAMHI; Peter Welsh, *Irish Green and Union Blue,* 60; Ford, *Fifteenth Regiment Massachusetts Volunteer Infantry,* 233–34; John Vestal Hadley, "Indiana Soldier in Love and War," 224.

33. *Rochester (N.Y.) Daily Union and Advertiser,* January 3, 1863; James B. Thomas, *Civil War Letters,* 141; January 13, 1863, Thompson Memoir, LC; Peter Welsh, *Irish Green and Union Blue,* 59; Osborne, *Twenty-Ninth Massachusetts,* 214; Glazier, *Three Years in the Federal Cavalry,* 122; James T. Odem to Eleanor Odem, January 15, 1863, Odem Papers, UVa; James L. Converse to his wife, January 16, 1863, Converse Letters, Chicago Historical Society; George H. Allen, *Forty-Six Months,* 184–85.

34. Josiah W. Perry to his brother, December 23, 1862, Perry Papers, Illinois State Historical Library; John S. Weiser to his parents, January 1, 1863, Weiser Papers, CWMC, USAMHI; Oliver Willcox Norton, *Army Letters,* 129–30; Walker, *Second Corps,* 198–99; Barber, *Civil War Letters,* 111; Molyneux, *Quill of the Wild Goose,* 59–60; McAllister, *Letters of Robert McAllister,* 243; James B. Thomas, *Civil War Letters,* 133; Donaldson, *Inside the Army of the Potomac,* 198; William Watson, *Letters of a Civil War Surgeon,* 72.

35. Cushing, "Acting Signal Corps," 103–4; *Ebensburg (Pa.) Democrat and Sentinel,* January 7, 1863; Henry Grimes Marshall to his home folks, December 25, 1862, Marshall Papers, Schoff Collection, CL; John R. Coye to his wife, January 7, 1863, Coye Letters, FSNMP; Charles B. Sloan to Lt. Col. Dickinson, January 5, 1863, Lincoln Papers, LC; Best, *History of the 121st New York,* 52–53; Barber, *Civil War Letters,* 114; McAllister, *Letters of Robert McAllister,* 253; Newell, *10th Regiment Massachusetts Volunteers,* 181; James B. Thomas, *Civil War Letters,* 139; Charles Frederick Taylor, "Colonel of the Bucktails," 357. Capt. Charles B. Sloan of the 114th Pennsylvania, the officer whose plea reached the president, was discharged with a surgeon's certificate in March. See Samuel Penniman Bates, *History of the Pennsylvania Volunteers,* 6:1202.

36. Chase, *Salmon P. Chase Papers,* 3:357–59; *Congressional Globe,* 37th Cong., 3rd sess., 1862, 199–200; Wesley C. Mitchell, "Greenbacks and the Cost of the Civil War," 154–55; Lincoln, *Collected Works,* 6:60–61; Wesley C. Mitchell, *History of the Greenbacks,* 105.

37. *Philadelphia Inquirer,* December 30, 1862, January 12, 1863; *Springfield (Mass.) Republican,* January 22, 1863; William Claflin to Charles Sumner, January 17, 1863, Sumner Papers, HU; *New York Herald,* December 27, 1862; *Baltimore American and Commercial Advertiser,* January 15, 1863; *Portland (Maine) Eastern Argus,* December 30, 1862; John March Cate to his wife, December 24, 1862, Cate Letters, FSNMP; A. J. Wilson to his parents, December 24, 1862, A. J. Wilson Letter, FSNMP; Moe, *Last Full Measure,* 220.

38. Peter Welsh, *Irish Green and Union Blue,* 52; Marsena Rudolph Patrick, *Inside Lincoln's Army,* 201; General Order No. 3, 16th Connecticut, January 17, 1863, Burnham Papers, CSL; Gaff, *On Many a Bloody Field,* 216–17. Complaints about a shortage of good officers— no doubt exacerbated by heavy Fredericksburg casualties—contributed to the uneven discipline. Harsh punishments only further alienated enlisted men. "It was such officers," a young private recalled, "who received a stray ball occasionally on the field of battle" (Bellard, *Gone*

for a Soldier, 187–88). See also Osborn, *No Middle Ground*, 99; Favill, *Diary of a Young Officer*, 216, 218.

39. Banes, *Philadelphia Brigade*, 148; Brian A. Bennett, *140th New York*, 116; George Lewis, *First Rhode Island Light Artillery*, 142–43; Gavin, *Campaigning with the Roundheads*, 232; Daniel M. Holt, *Surgeon's Civil War*, 69. In analyzing the extent of desertion, I have followed the treatment in Sears, *Chancellorsville*, 18. For interesting attempts to play down the number of deserters, see Kenneth P. Williams, *Lincoln Finds a General*, 2:553; A. Wilson Greene, "Morale, Maneuver, and Mud," 179.

40. Reid Mitchell, *Vacant Chair*, 30–31; Alotta, *Stop the Evil*, 66–67, 76–79; James Lorenzo Bowen, *Thirty-Seventh Regiment*, 116; Jimerson, *Private Civil War*, 232; Zerah Coston Monks to Hannah T. Rohrer, January 17, 1863, Monks-Rohrer Letters, Emory; Marsena Rudolph Patrick, *Inside Lincoln's Army*, 201–2; Henry J. H. Thompson to Lucretia Thompson, January 7, 1863, Thompson Papers, Duke.

41. Marvel, *Ninth New Hampshire*, 116–17; Small, *Sixteenth Maine*, 89; *OR*, 985, and ser. 1, 25(2):73.

42. James S. Graham to his grandfather, January 1, 1863, Graham Letters, FSNMP; Houghton, *Seventeenth Maine*, 41–42; Harper, *Civil War History of Chester County, Pennsylvania*, 287; 861 January 18, 1863, Stevens Diary, USAMHI; Craft, *History of the One Hundred Forty-First Pennsylvania*, 46; January 18, 1863, Madill Diary, Gregory A. Coco Collection, HCWRTC, USAMHI; Bloodgood, *Personal Reminiscences of the War*, 59; Haley, *Rebel Yell and Yankee Hurrah*, 66–67; William Watson, *Letters of a Civil War Surgeon*, 49–50.

43. Haley, *Rebel Yell and Yankee Hurrah*, 66; *Rochester (N.Y.) Daily Union and Advertiser*, January 12, 1863; Asa W. Bartlett, *History of the Twelfth New Hampshire*, 56–58; Reuben Schell to his father, January 1863, Schell Letters, FSNMP; Locke, *Story of the Regiment*, 180–81; *Albany (N.Y.) Atlas and Argus*, January 12, 19, 1863; Fessenden, *Fessenden*, 1:265.

44. *Augusta (Maine) Kennebec Journal*, January 2, 1863; *Philadelphia Inquirer*, January 5, 1863; *Wellsboro (Pa.) Agitator*, January 4, 1863; McPherson, *For Cause and Comrades*, 99; Barber, *Civil War Letters*, 111–12; Stephen M. Pingree to his cousin, January 6, 1863, Pingree Papers, Vermont Historical Society; David Beem to his wife, January 4, 8, 11, 1863, Beem Papers, IHS; Bicknell, *History of the Fifth Maine*, 188–89.

45. Jacob H. Haas to Frederick Haas, January 3, 1863, Haas Papers, HCWRTC, USAMHI; Clausewitz, *On War*, 189; January 1, 1863, Webb Diary, Schoff Collection, CL.

46. January 5, 1863, Jackson Diary, IHS; January 7, 1863, Pope Diary, *CWTI*, USAMHI; Henry Butler to his wife, January 18, 1863, Butler Papers, Castine Public Library; Pettit, *Infantryman Pettit*, 51–52.

47. Marsena Rudolph Patrick, *Inside Lincoln's Army*, 199; *OR*, 944–45, 953–54; Lincoln, *Collected Works*, 6:46–48.

48. Meade, *Life and Letters*, 1:346; *Albany (N.Y.) Atlas and Argus*, January 6, 1863; *OR*, ser. 3, 3:294; Wightman, *From Antietam to Fort Fisher*, 93; Henry Lewis to his cousin, January 3, 1863, Lewis Letters, GLC; Hopkins, *Seventh Rhode Island*, 54; January 8, 1863, Madill Diary, Gregory A. Coco Collection, MCWRTC, USAMHI; *OR*, 749–51; D. P. Woodbury to Orrin E. Hine, January 2, 1863, Hine Papers, LC; Robert S. Robertson, "Diary of the War," 80; John S. Weiser to his parents, January 12, 1863, Weiser Papers, CWMC, USAMHI; *New York Times*, January 8, 1863; *Rochester (N.Y.) Daily Union and Advertiser*, January 12, 1863; *OR Supplement*, pt. 1, 3:679; Brooks, *Mr. Lincoln's Washington*, 65–67; Daniel Reed Larned to "My Dear Henry," January 9, 1863, and Larned to his sister, January 11, 1863, Larned Papers, LC.

49. Sears, *Chancellorsville*, 15; Cudworth, *First Regiment (Massachusetts Infantry)*, 334–35; S. Millett Thompson, *Thirteenth New Hampshire*, 96–97; Rufus P. Stanick to "My Darling Selina," January 5–6, 1863, Stanick Letter, Virginia Polytechnic; Brian A. Bennett, *140th New York*, 123; January 6, 1863, Pope Diary, *CWTI*, USAMHI; Teall, "Ringside Seat at Fredericksburg," 33; Joseph N. Haynes to his father, January 7, 1863, Haynes Papers, Duke.

50. William Franklin Draper to his mother, January 5, 1863, Draper Papers, LC; Franklin Sawyer to Samuel Sexton, January 5, 1863, Sexton Papers, OHS; Partridge, *Letters from the Iron Brigade,* 72; *New York Herald,* January 11, 1863.

51. *Richmond Daily Whig,* December 20, 1862; *Richmond Daily Enquirer,* December 17, 22, 1862; Lineberger, *Letters of a Gaston Ranger,* 31; Isaac Howard to his father, December 25, 1862, Howard Family Papers, SHC; Joslyn, *Charlotte's Boys,* 143–44; December 23, 1862, Jones Diary, Schoff Collection, CL; S. G. Pryor, *Post of Honor,* 300; James C. Zimmerman to his brother, December 30, 1862, Zimmerman Papers, Duke.

52. *Augusta (Ga.) Daily Chronicle and Sentinel,* December 18, 1862; *Charleston Mercury,* December 20, 1862; S. G. Pryor, *Post of Honor,* 296; Mills Lane, *"Dear Mother: Don't Grieve about Me,"* 208; Cadmus Marcellus Wilcox to his sister, December 17, 1862, Wilcox Papers, LC; Charles Kerrison to his uncle, December 18, 1862, Kerrison Family Papers, SCL; Micah Jenkins to his wife, December 21, 1862, Jenkins Papers, Duke.

53. A. Wilson Greene, "Morale, Maneuver, and Mud," 198–99; Susan Pendleton Lee, *Memoirs of William Nelson Pendleton,* 250–51; Hotchkiss, *Make Me a Map of the Valley,* 103; *OR,* 689–97, 870; J. E. B. Stuart to Flora Cooke Stuart, December 22, 1862, Stuart Papers, VHS; Plum, *Military Telegraph,* 1:356–58; Cauthen, *Family Letters of Three Wade Hamptons,* 89–90; *Richmond Daily Whig,* December 24, 1862; *Augusta (Ga.) Daily Constitutionalist,* January 3, 1863; Thomas Ruffin, *Papers,* 3:282.

54. *OR,* 731–35, 1075–76; Richard Henry Watkins to Mary Watkins, December 28–29, 1862, Watkins Papers, VHS; R. Channing Price to his sister, January 2, 1863, Price Papers, SHC; Robert Brooke Jones to "Dearest Bettie," January 5, 1863, Jones Family Papers, VHS. Federal reports greatly exaggerated Confederate numbers but failed to conceal Yankee ineptitude. "Fruitless" was the word one New Yorker chose to describe efforts to cut off Stuart's retreat. The mere mention of the Rebel cavalry chieftain struck terror among sutlers and in the North made Stuart appear nearly as invincible as Jackson. See *OR,* 968, 887, 893; Alpheus Starkey Williams, *From the Cannon's Mouth,* 156–57; Alfred Pleasonton to "Dear General," January 8, 1863, Pleasonton Papers, LC; James R. Woodworth to Phoebe Woodworth, January 5, 1863, Woodworth Papers, Hotchkiss Collection, CL; Landon, "Letters to Vincennes Western Sun," 342; Gray and Ropes, *War Letters,* 57; Frank Longstreet to his sister, December 31, 1862, Longstreet Papers, CWMC, USAMHI; *OR Supplement,* pt. 1, 3:674–75; *Albany (N.Y.) Atlas and Argus,* January 5, 1863.

55. Robert E. Lee, *Wartime Papers,* 384, 386, 388–90; Welch, *Confederate Surgeon's Letters,* 41–42; Woodworth, *Davis and Lee,* 213–15.

56. Walter Clark, *Regiments and Battalions from North Carolina,* 2:558–59; James I. Robertson Jr., *Jackson,* 438–39; Cooke, *Jackson,* 240.

57. J. F. Shaffner to "My dearest friend," December 21, 1862, Shaffner Papers, NCDAH; William B. Pettit to his wife, December 16, 1862, Pettit Papers, SHC; Jedediah Hotchkiss to Sara Ann Comfort Hotchkiss, January 11, 1863, Hotchkiss Papers, LC.

58. Thomas Claybrook Elder to Anna Fitzhugh Elder, December 27, 1862, Elder Papers, VHS; Ujanirtus Allen, *Campaigning with "Old Stonewall,"* 205; Stikeleather Reminiscences, 35, NCDAH; Edward Porter Alexander, *Fighting for the Confederacy,* 187; Hubbert, "Diary of Mike M. Hubbert," 313; Hodijah Lincoln Meade to his mother, February 10, 1863, Meade Family Papers, VHS; Dickert, *Kershaw's Brigade,* 205; O'Sullivan, *55th Virginia,* 43; *Charleston Daily Courier,* February 5, 1863; Dobbins, *Grandfather's Journal,* 119; Ott, "Civil War Diary of James J. Kilpatrick," 94.

59. Polley, *Hood's Texas Brigade,* 139–40; Richard Lewis, *Camp Life of a Confederate Boy,* 37–38; Napier Bartlett, *Military Record of Louisiana,* 164–66; Coward, *South Carolinians,* 74; Redwood, "Johnny Reb at Play," 35–36.

60. December 28, 1862, Ware Diary, SHC; Carmichael, *Purcell, Crenshaw, and Letcher Artillery,* 151; Alfred E. Doby to his wife, January 15, 1863, Doby Letters, MC.

61. William W. Bennett, *Narrative of the Great Revival*, 252–53.

62. David Holt, *Mississippi Rebel*, 139; Lineberger, *Letters of a Gaston Ranger*, 31; Richard Henry Watkins to Mary Watkins, January 4, 1863, Watkins Papers, VHS; Welch, *Confederate Surgeon's Letters*, 40–41.

63. William G. Bean, "House Divided," 408–9; William Alexander Smith, *Anson Guards*, 174; John William Jones, *Christ in the Camp*, 242–45, 295–311; William W. Bennett, *Narrative of the Great Revival*, 251–57; Stiles, *Four Years under Marse Robert*, 139–43; Abernathy, *Our Mess*, 21–22; Shattuck, *Shield and Hiding Place*, 97–98.

64. January 18, 1863, Firebaugh Diary, SHC; Fitzpatrick, *Letters to Amanda*, 39; Paxton, *Memoir and Memorials*, 86. Paxton would be killed at Chancellorsville.

65. Simpson and Simpson, *Far, Far from Home*, 167; Francis Marion Coker to his wife, December 18, 1862, Coker Letters, UG; Alfred E. Doby to his wife, January 20, 25, 1863, Doby Letters, MC; Jedediah Hotchkiss to Sara Ann Comfort Hotchkiss, January 23, 1863, Hotchkiss Papers, LC.

66. Ujanirtus Allen, *Campaigning with "Old Stonewall,"* 203; Jedediah Hotchkiss to Sara Ann Comfort Hotchkiss, January 11, 1863, Hotchkiss Papers, LC; Spears and Pettit, *Civil War Letters*, 1:85–86; McDaniel, *With Unabated Trust*, 124; James M. Simpson to Addie Simpson, January 6, 1863, Allen and Simpson Family Papers, SHC.

67. Thomas Claybrook Elder to Anna Fitzhugh Elder, January 3, 1863, Elder Papers, VHS; S. G. Pryor, *Post of Honor*, 304; Pender, *General to His Lady*, 195–96; Richard Irby to his wife, December 19, 1862, Irby Letters, FSNMP; Borden, *Legacy of Fanny and Joseph*, 127–29; William Ross Stillwell to "My Dear Mollie," December 1862, Stillwell Letters, GDAH; Hester Reeve to Edward Payson Reeve, December 22, 1862, Reeve Papers, SHC; Fitzpatrick, *Letters to Amanda*, 39; Elizabeth Preston Allan, *Margaret Junkin Preston*, 159–60. For an excellent discussion of the war's impact on children's play, see Marten, *Children's Civil War*, 158–66.

68. William Ross Stillwell to "My dear Mollie," January 15, 1863, Stillwell Letters, GDAH; Samuel H. Walkup to his wife, January 1, 1863, Walkup Papers, SHC; Constantine Hege to his parents, December 21, 1862, Hege Letters, Leigh Collection, USAMHI; Lineberger, *Letters of a Gaston Ranger*, 32; Clement Anselm Evans, *Intrepid Warrior*, 133–34; S. G. Pryor, *Post of Honor*, 301–2; Jonathan Fuller Coghill to his home folks, January 25, 1863, Coghill Letters, Auburn University Archives; J. G. Montgomery to "Dear Bro Arthur and Sister Bettie," January 9, 1863, Montgomery Letter, FSNMP; Lang, "Letters of Lang," 345; Jedediah Hotchkiss to Sara Ann Comfort Hotchkiss, December 17, 1862, Hotchkiss Papers, LC.

69. John Lee Holt, *I Wrote You Word*, 122; Young and Young, *56th Virginia*, 69; Ruffner, *44th Virginia*, 34; S. Millett Thompson, *Thirteenth New Hampshire*, 98; Henry A. Allen, *Sergeant Allen and Private Renick*, 175; James I. Robertson Jr., *Jackson*, 676; Mary Anna Jackson, *Life and Letters of Jackson*, 388; James I. Robertson Jr., *Hill*, 170; Lee A. Wallace Jr., *1st Virginia*, 104; DeNoon, *Charlie's Letters*, 118.

70. Caldwell, *History of a Brigade of South Carolinians*, 71; Dickert, *Kershaw's Brigade*, 205; January 25, 1863, E. P. Miller Diary, FSNMP; W. H. Andrews, *Footprints of a Regiment*, 99; December 21, 1862, Jones Diary, Schoff Collection, CL; Edward Stuart to his sister, December 27, 1862, Dimitry Papers, Duke.

71. Goolsby, "Crenshaw Battery," 350; Worsham, *One of Jackson's Foot Cavalry*, 155–56; December 19, 1862, Hatton Memoir, 383, LC; January 20, 1863, Ware Diary, SHC; Edward M. Burruss to Kate Burruss, January 19, 1863, Burruss Papers, LSU; Jere Malcolm Harris to his sister, December 26, 1862, Jere Malcolm Harris Letter, FSNMP.

CHAPTER TWENTY-FIVE

1. *New York Times*, January 13, 1863; McAllister, *Letters of Robert McAllister*, 256–57.

2. Horace Greeley, "A Great War in Winter," *Independent*, January 15, 1863, 1; *New York Times*, January 16, 1863; Brooks, *Mr. Lincoln's Washington*, 70–71; *Chicago Daily Tribune*, Janu-

ary 17, 1863; *New York Herald,* January 10, 18, 1863; *Washington Daily National Intelligencer,* January 12, 1863; *Rochester (N.Y.) Daily Union and Advertiser,* January 16, 1863.

3. *CCW,* 1:719; *Philadelphia Inquirer,* January 16, 1863; Marvel, *Burnside,* 212; *OR,* 961, 965, 969; January 13, 1863, Henry Taylor Diary, FSNMP; Henry Ogden Ryerson to his sister, January 13, 1863, Anderson Family Papers, NJHS.

4. Daniel Reed Larned to "My Dear Henry," January 16, 1863, Larned Papers, LC; Marsena Rudolph Patrick, *Inside Lincoln's Army,* 202–3; *CCW,* 1:728–29; A. Wilson Greene, "Morale, Maneuver, and Mud," 195; *ORN,* ser. 1, 5:213–14; Clausewitz, *On War,* 271.

5. Robert S. Robertson, "Diary of the War," 81; O. Leland Barlow to his brother, January 14, 1863, Barlow Papers, CSL; Abiel Hall Edwards, *"Dear Friend Anna,"* 45. "Our Potomac army . . . can do nothing but dissolve, decompose, and die," Senator Sumner feared. "There must be a speedy extrication, or its present encampment will be a Golgotha" (Charles Sumner, *Selected Letters,* 2:138).

6. Flauvius Bellamy to his sister, January 16, 1863, Bellamy Papers, ISL; Melcher, *With a Flash of His Sword,* 18; Fiske, *Dunn Browne's Experiences in the Army,* 110–11; Raymond, "Extracts from the Journal of Henry J. Raymond," 420; Josiah W. Perry to Phoebe Perry, January 11, 1863, Perry Papers, Illinois State Historical Library.

7. Edwin Winchester Stone, *Rhode Island in the Rebellion,* 198; William Franklin Draper to his wife, January 18, 1863, Draper Papers, LC; Zerah Coston Monks to Hannah T. Rohrer, January 13, 1863, Monks-Rohrer Letters, Emory; James R. Woodworth to Phoebe Woodworth, January 17, 1863, Woodworth Papers, Hotchkiss Collection, CL.

8. Fessenden, *Fessenden,* 1:266; Bogue, "Cutler's Congressional Diary," 323–24; Zachariah Chandler to his wife, January 22, 1863, Chandler Papers, LC.

9. *Rochester (N.Y.) Daily Union and Advertiser,* January 23, 1863; *New York Tribune,* January 21, 23, 1863.

10. Douglas Southall Freeman, *Lee's Lieutenants,* 2:428–29; Edgar Allan Jackson, *Three Rebels Write Home,* 29–30; *OR,* 1088, 1091–92, 1096–97, 1103–4, 1108; J. B. Jones, *Rebel War Clerk's Diary,* 1:239.

11. January 16, 1863, Madill Diary, Gregory A. Coco Collection, HCWRTC, USAMHI; *OR,* 76–77, and ser. 1, 51(1):973; January 16, 1863, Mancha Diary, CWMC, USAMHI; S. Millett Thompson, *Thirteenth New Hampshire,* 100; George W. Barr to Vinnie Barr, January 16, 1863, Barr Papers, Schoff Collection, CL; James B. Thomas, *Civil War Letters,* 139–40; Haydon, *For Country, Cause, and Leader,* 305; James P. Coburn to his home folks, January 16, 1863, James P. Coburn Papers, USAMHI.

12. January 17, 1863, Madill Diary, Gregory A. Coco Collection, HCWRTC, USAMHI; James Bloomfield Osborn to Mary Osborn, January 17, 1863, Osborn Papers, LC; Stephen M. Pingree to "Cousin Augustus," January 17, 1863, Pingree Papers, Vermont Historical Society; Kepler, *Fourth Ohio,* 102; Samuel R. Beardsley to his wife, January 17, 1863, Beardsley Papers, USAMHI; January 17, 1863, Bacon Diary, FSNMP; *OR,* 975; January 17, 1863, Asa W. Bartlett, "Diary of Military Action," NHHS; George H. Mellish to his mother, January 17, 1863, Mellish Papers, HL. One befuddled volunteer had heard various rumors that the army might be going to Fredericksburg, Washington, or New Orleans. See Charles Littlefield to his wife, January 17, 1863, Littlefield Letters, CWMC, USAMHI.

13. James R. Woodworth to Phoebe Woodworth, January 18, 1863, Woodworth Papers, Hotchkiss Collection, CL; S. Millett Thompson, *Thirteenth New Hampshire,* 100; James Lorenzo Bowen, *Thirty-Seventh Regiment,* 118; Pardington, *Dear Sarah,* 62; McKelvey, *Rochester in the Civil War,* 118–19; Raymond, "Extracts from the Journal of Henry J. Raymond," 420; *OR,* 977; Meade, *Life and Letters,* 1:347; McAllister, *Letters of Robert McAllister,* 258; Charles Shields Wainwright, *Diary of Battle,* 157; William Franklin Draper to his wife, January 18, 1863, Draper Papers, LC.

14. Henry Van Aernum to his daughter, January 19, 1863, Van Aernum Papers, FSNMP;

Raymond, "Extracts from the Journal of Henry J. Raymond," 420–21; Charles Shields Wainwright, *Diary of Battle*, 157–58; McAllister, *Letters of Robert McAllister*, 259; January 19, 1863, Eaton Diary, SHC. Troops from Maj. Gen. Franz Sigel's Reserve Grand Division (the Eleventh and Twelfth Corps) were in position near Stafford Court House and Fairfax to support any movement by the other three grand divisions.

15. Daniel M. Holt, *Surgeon's Civil War*, 68; Charles H. Eagor to his wife, January 19, 1863, Eagor Letters, Leigh Collection, USAMHI; Reuben H. Humphreyville to his sister, January 19, 1863, Humphreyville Papers, Chicago Historical Society; January 19, 1863, Madill Diary, Gregory A. Coco Collection, HCWRTC, USAMHI; James A. Carman to his uncle, January 19, 1863, Carman Family Collection, USAMHI; John Pellett to his family, January 19, 1863, Pellett Papers, USAMHI; Abbott, *Fallen Leaves*, 162–63.

16. *OR*, 127.

17. James A. Graham to Ellen Lee, January 20, 1863, Graham Letters, FSNMP; Catton, *Glory Road*, 85; Burrage, *Thirty-Sixth Massachusetts*, 30; Page, *Fourteenth Connecticut*, 107–8; Welsh and Welsh, "Civil War Letters from Two Brothers," 160; Locke, *Story of the Regiment*, 180; Abbott, *Fallen Leaves*, 163–64; Henry Ropes to "Dear John," January 21, 1863, Ropes Letters, Boston Public Library.

18. Sanford Truesdale to his sister, January 20, 1863, Truesdale Papers, University of Chicago; Osborn, *No Middle Ground*, 104; James Edison Decker to his father, January 20, 1863, Decker Papers, CWMC, USAMHI; McCrea, *Dear Belle*, 181–82; Isaac Lyman Taylor, "Campaigning with the First Minnesota," 243; McClenthen, *Narrative of the Fall and Winter Campaign*, 48–49; Lusk, *War Letters of William Thompson Lusk*, 271–72; Mayo, *Civil War Letters*, 224–25. The prospect of battle also awakened a strange lust. "The idea of another fight makes me wild almost," Larned admitted. "I long to hear the guns again. It is one of the most exciting things I ever experienced, and if it could be rid of the awful horrors & agony, it could be beautiful" (Daniel Reed Larned to his sister, January 20, 1863, Larned Papers, LC).

19. *OR*, 79–80, 986. Hooker had earlier refused to attend a council of war to discuss the plan. See John Godfrey to Horace Godfrey, January 13, 1863, Godfrey Papers, NHHS.

20. Hays, *Sixty-Third Regiment Pennsylvania Volunteers*, 168–69; Donaldson, *Inside the Army of the Potomac*, 205; Samuel S. Partridge to "Dear Ed," January 25, 1863, Partridge Letters, FSNMP; *OR Supplement*, pt. 2, 16:478, 507; January 20, 1863, Madill Diary, Gregory A. Coco Collection, HCWRTC, USAMHI; Craft, *History of the One Hundred Forty-First Pennsylvania*, 47–48; January 20, 1863, Stevens Diary, USAMHI; McAllister, *Letters of Robert McAllister*, 260–61; Bellard, *Gone for a Soldier*, 196–97; Cudworth, *First Regiment (Massachusetts Infantry)*, 339.

21. Blake, *Three Years in the Army of the Potomac*, 159–60; Asa W. Bartlett, *History of the Twelfth New Hampshire*, 54–55. Humor did not mask more serious demoralization. A lieutenant in Griffin's division reported, "No one cared, no one had confidence, and it made not the slightest difference whether they stayed in camp or inaugurated a campaign" (Donaldson, *Inside the Army of the Potomac*, 205).

22. *OR*, 78–79; *OR Supplement*, pt. 2, 45:580; John Vestal Hadley, "Indiana Soldier in Love and War," 226; Edmund Halsey, *Brother against Brother*, 105–6.

23. Charles Shields Wainwright, *Diary of Battle*, 158; Bicknell, *History of the Fifth Maine*, 190–93; H. S. Hall, "Fredericksburg and Chancellorsville," 191; Charles E. Davis, *Three Years in the Army*, 187–88; Siegel, *For the Glory of the Union*, 121.

24. Dority, "Civil War Diary," 12; Waugh, "Reminiscences," FSNMP; *History of the Fifth Massachusetts Battery*, 534–35; Samuel S. Partridge to "Dear Ed," January 25, 1863, Partridge Letters, FSNMP; *OR Supplement*, pt. 2, 16:507; John W. Ames to his mother, January 25, 1863, Ames Papers, USAMHI; Trobriand, *Four Years with the Army of the Potomac*, 407; January 20, 1863, Bacon Diary, FSNMP; Haley, *Rebel Yell and Yankee Hurrah*, 67; January 20, 1863, James P. Coburn Diary, James P. Coburn Papers, USAMHI.

25. James B. Thomas, *Civil War Letters,* 142; Dawes, *Sixth Wisconsin,* 116; Sanford Truesdale to his sister, January 26, 1863, Truesdale Papers, University of Chicago; Gaff, *On Many a Bloody Field,* 217; McClenthen, *Narrative of the Fall and Winter Campaign,* 50–51; January 20, 1863, Bailey Diary, DCL; Bright and Bright, *"Respects to All,"* 37; Craig L. Dunn, *Iron Men, Iron Will,* 155; Fairchild, *27th Regiment,* 134–35. They might have envied their comrades in Sumner's Right Grand Division, badly bloodied at Fredericksburg but not in the vanguard this time. Burnside instructed his most faithful subordinate to hold his command in readiness to support Hooker and Franklin. See *OR,* 78.

26. Davenport, *Fifth New York Volunteer Infantry,* 366; Donaldson, *Inside the Army of the Potomac,* 206; January 21, 1863, Bacon Diary, FSNMP; John D. Cooper to his daughter, January 25, 1863, Cooper Papers, DCL; Bardeen, *Little Fifer's Diary,* 149; January 21, 1863, Hadley Diary, NHHS; Van Santvoord, *One Hundred and Twentieth New York,* 39–40; January 21, 1863, Cavada Diary, HSP.

27. Kearney, "Letters from the Field," 189–90; Weygant, *One Hundred and Twenty-Fourth Regiment,* 81–82; Sprenger, *122d Regiment,* 192–93; Pullen, *Twentieth Maine,* 68–69; James R. Woodworth to Phoebe Woodworth, January 21, 1863, Woodworth Papers, Hotchkiss Collection, CL; Brian A. Bennett, *140th New York,* 125–26; Powell, *Fifth Corps,* 408–9; Robert Goldthwaite Carter, *Four Brothers in Blue,* 225–26.

28. James B. Thomas, *Civil War Letters,* 142; *OR Supplement,* pt. 2, 45:580; Elisha Hunt Rhodes, *All for the Union,* 97; Haines, *15th New Jersey,* 38–39; Abiel Hall Edwards, *"Dear Friend Anna,"* 47; Dawes, *Sixth Wisconsin,* 116–17; George H. Mellish to his mother, January 24, 1863, Mellish Papers, HL; Twitchell, *Carpetbagger from Vermont,* 50; *Berkshire County (Mass.) Eagle,* January 29, 1863.

29. January 21, 1863, Holford Diary, LC; January 21, 1863, Bailey Diary, DCL; January 21, 1863, Charles P. Perkins Diary, *CWTI,* USAMHI; Best, *History of the 121st New York,* 51–52; Sanford Truesdale to his sister, January 26, 1863, Truesdale Papers, University of Chicago.

30. Daniel M. Holt, *Surgeon's Civil War,* 66; Pullen, *Twentieth Maine,* 61; Foote, *Civil War,* 2:129; Charles Littlefield to his wife, January 24, 1863, Littlefield Letters, CWMC, USAMHI; Hitchcock, *War from the Inside,* 164; Billings, *Hard Tack and Coffee,* 72; Robert S. Robertson, "Diary of the War," 82. For a useful analysis of both the soil and the storm system, see Winters, *Battling the Elements,* 33–39.

31. *OR,* 989–90, 1000–1001; Locke, *Story of the Regiment,* 182; Gilbert Thompson, *Engineer Battalion,* 28; *Kokomo (Ind.) Howard Tribune,* February 5, 1863; Roe, *Tenth Massachusetts,* 168; *OR Supplement,* pt. 2, 16:508; Craft, *History of the One Hundred Forty-First Pennsylvania,* 48; Hagerty, *Collis' Zouaves,* 167.

32. Relyea Memoir, 88, CHS; H. S. Hall, "Fredericksburg and Chancellorsville," 191–92; Bidwell, *Forty-ninth New York Volunteers,* 28; *History of the Fifth Massachusetts Battery,* 535–36; Sprenger, *122d Regiment,* 195; Louis Fortescue to "Friend Sam," January 1863, Fortescue Letters, FSNMP; Blake, *Three Years in the Army of the Potomac,* 160–61; William H. Peacock to "Sarah," January 28, 1863, Peacock Papers, CWMC, USAMHI; Bellard, *Gone for a Soldier,* 196–97; John W. Ames to his mother, January 25, 1863, Ames Papers, USAMHI; Swinfen, *Ruggles' Regiment,* 17.

33. John Godfrey to Horace Godfrey, January 13, 1863, Godfrey Papers, NHHS; William Boston to "Aunt Rosa," January 30, 1863, Boston Papers, MHC; *History of the 127th Regiment Pennsylvania Volunteers,* 273; Forbes, *Thirty Years After,* 209; Glover, *Bucktailed Wildcats,* 183; James R. Woodworth to Phoebe Woodworth, January 25, 1863, Woodworth Papers, Hotchkiss Collection, CL; Perkins Memoir, 8, NHHS; Cudworth, *First Regiment (Massachusetts Infantry),* 339; Dayton E. Flint to his father, January 27, 1863, Flint Letters, CWMC, USAMHI; Hitchcock, *War from the Inside,* 165–66. Perhaps some 100 to 150 horses and mules were lost; one officer estimated their value at $50,000. See Orville Thomson, *Seventh Indiana,* 148; Stephen Z. Starr, *Union Cavalry,* 1:336–37; James B. Thomas, *Civil War Letters,* 143. Not

surprisingly, the Mud March gave birth to tall tales about mules sinking so deep that only their ears could still be seen, or an entire wagon train being swallowed. One raconteur told about a pair of mules that disappeared into the earth and were next seen plowing a field in China. See Catton, *Glory Road,* 88; Craig L. Dunn, *Iron Men, Iron Will,* 155–56; Cook, *Twelfth Massachusetts,* 87; Orville Thomson, *Seventh Indiana,* 147.

34. Daniel Reed Larned to "My Dear Henry," January 21, 1863, Larned Papers, LC; Raymond, "Extracts from the Journal of Henry J. Raymond," 421; Cogswell, *Eleventh New Hampshire,* 66; George H. P. Rowell to his parents, January 24, 1863, Rowell Papers, NHHS; Howard Coffin, *Full Duty,* 142; George Thomas Stevens, *Three Years in the Sixth Corps,* 176; Robert S. Robertson, "Diary of the War," 82; *OR,* 752, 990–91.

35. Raymond, "Extracts from the Journal of Henry J. Raymond," 421–22; *OR,* 81–82, 994.

36. John D. Cooper to his daughter, January 25, 1863, Cooper Papers, DCL; Bardeen, *Little Fifer's Diary,* 150; Dority, "Civil War Diary," 13; James R. Woodworth to Phoebe Woodworth, January 25, 1863, Woodworth Papers, Hotchkiss Collection, CL; Elisha Hunt Rhodes, *All for the Union,* 97; *OR Supplement,* pt. 2, 40:540; Hartwell, *To My Beloved Wife and Boy at Home,* 44; Daniel M. Holt, *Surgeon's Civil War,* 71; *OR,* 1003.

37. Bloodgood, *Personal Reminiscences of the War,* 70; Charles E. Davis, *Three Years in the Army,* 191; Robert G. Robertson, "Diary of the War," 80; Sprenger, 122d Regiment, 196–97; Hartwell, *To My Beloved Wife and Boy at Home,* 44; Joseph Bloomfield Osborn to Mary Osborn, January 25, 1863, Osborn Papers, LC; Edwin Wentworth to his wife, January 25, 1863, Wentworth Papers, LC; Dayton E. Flint to his father, January 27, 1863, Flint Letters, CWMC, USAMHI; Abram P. Smith, *Seventy-Sixth New York,* 202; Walker, *Second Corps,* 200. Some enlisted men received fines for straggling—better than marching in the mud, one private decided. A few soldiers remained defiantly in the woods and dared anyone to arrest them, but most apparently received lenient treatment. See Gilbert Crocker, "Gilbert Crocker's Civil War," 66; *Albany (N.Y.) Atlas and Argus,* January 30, 1863; Marbaker, *Eleventh New Jersey,* 32–34.

38. Haley, *Rebel Yell and Yankee Hurrah,* 70; *History of the 121st Regiment Pennsylvania Volunteers,* 41; Craig L. Dunn, *Iron Men, Iron Will,* 156; Edward Cotter to his brother, January 23, 1863, Cotter Letter, CWMC, USAMHI; John Henry Burnham to Sarah B. Burnham, January 26, 1863, Burnham Papers, CSL; Howard Thomas, *Boys in Blue from the Adirondack Foothills,* 125; James Madison Stone, *Personal Recollections of the Civil War,* 124; Reeves, *Twenty-Fourth New Jersey,* 28; S. Millett Thompson, *Thirteenth New Hampshire,* 103.

39. January 23, 1863, Horace Currier Diary, SHSW; Marvel, *First New Hampshire Battery,* 32–33; Dawes, *Sixth Wisconsin,* 117–18; January 24, 1863, Jackson Diary, IHS; January 23, 1863, Diary of Private Elisha Dean, SHSW; Partridge, *Letters from the Iron Brigade,* 76.

40. Terry A. Johnston, "*Him on the One Side and Me on the Other,*" 123; Gay, "Gay Letters," 394; William B. Jordan Jr., *Red Diamond Regiment,* 38; Craig L. Dunn, *Iron Men, Iron Will,* 155; *OR Supplement,* pt. 2, 61:81; Zerah Coston Monks to Hannah T. Rohrer, January 25, 1863, Monks-Rohrer Letters, Emory; Bellard, *Gone for a Soldier,* 198; *OR,* ser. 1, 25(2):77–78; Index Project Summary of Courts-Martial, Fredericksburg, Woodacre, California, copies in FSNMP; *Rochester (N.Y.) Daily Union and Advertiser,* January 29, 1863; Sanford Truesdale to his sister, January 26, 1863, Truesdale Papers, University of Chicago.

41. Fairchild, *27th Regiment,* 135; January 23, 1863, Henry Starke Seage Diary, MHC; Gavin, *Campaigning with the Roundheads,* 235; January 23, 1863, Bescancon Diary, Duke; *OR Supplement,* pt. 2, 45:580; James Pratt to his wife, January 23, 1863, Pratt Collection, USAMHI; William Boston to "Aunt Rosa," January 30, 1863, Boston Papers, MHC; Daniel M. Holt, *Surgeon's Civil War,* 71.

42. January 22–23, 1863, S. W. Gordon Diary, FSNMP; January 22–24, 1863, Stevens Diary, USAMHI; Hartsock, *Soldier of the Cross,* 51; Perkins Memoir, 8, NHHS; Reminisco, *Life in the Union Army,* 20; January 25, 1863, Halsey Diary, USAMHI; Bliss Memoir, 4:46, USAMHI;

Haines, *15th New Jersey,* 40; January 24, 1863, Fribley Diary, CWMC, USAMHI; John Lord Parker, *Twenty-Second Massachusetts,* 244–45; Robert Goldthwaite Carter, *Four Brothers in Blue,* 226–27; John L. Smith, *118th Pennsylvania,* 162–63.

43. Nolan, *Iron Brigade,* 192; Sprenger, *122d Regiment,* 197; S. Millett Thompson, *Thirteenth New Hampshire,* 102–31; January 16–20, 1863, Stoner Diary, FSNMP; Duncan, *Medical Department of United States Army,* 208–9; January 24, 1863, Eaton Diary, SHC; Roe, *Tenth Massachusetts,* 168; Aldrich, *History of Battery A,* 168; Baquet, *History of the 1st New Jersey,* 205; Edwin O. Wentworth to his wife, January 25, 1863, Wentworth Papers, LC.

44. Charles Jewett Morris to his brother and sister, January 27, 1863, Morris Papers, Duke; Levander Sawtelle to "Respected friend and brother," January 25, 1863, Sawtelle Letters, CWMC, USAMHI; Thorpe, *Fifteenth Connecticut Volunteers,* 42; James R. Woodworth to Phoebe Woodworth, January 25, 1863, Woodworth Papers, Hotchkiss Collection, CL; John Ripley Adams, *Memorials and Letters,* 96–97; Wightman, *From Antietam to Fort Fisher,* 104.

45. *Berkshire County (Mass.) Eagle,* January 29, 1863; *New York Times,* January 26, 1863; Humphreys, *Andrew Atkinson Humphreys,* 182; Meade, *Life and Letters,* 1:349; William Watson, *Letters of a Civil War Surgeon,* 50–51; Henry Grimes Marshall to "Dear Hattie," January 25, 1863, Marshall Papers, Schoff Collection, CL; Flauvius Bellamy to his parents, January 25, 1863, Bellamy Papers, ISL; Jacob F. Smith to "Dear Callie," February 5, 1863, Jacob F. Smith Letter, CWMC, USAMHI; January 22, 1863, Bailey Diary, DCL; John Vestal Hadley, "Indiana Soldier in Love and War," 227.

46. Ayling, *Yankee at Arms,* 94; Charles Bowers to "Dear Lydia," January 23, 1863, Bowers Papers, MHS; Isaac Lyman Taylor, "Campaigning with the First Minnesota," 244; J. L. Smith to "Dear Mother," January 25, 1863, John L. Smith Letters, FSNMP; Samuel S. Partridge to "Dear Ed," Partridge Letters, FSNMP; Howard Coffin, *Full Duty,* 143; Edward Henry Courtney Taylor to "Bill," January 25, 1863, Taylor Letters, MHC; Sears, *Chancellorsville,* 20; George W. Barr to Vinnie Barr, January 21, 1863, Barr Papers, Schoff Collection, CL; Robert Goldthwaite Carter, *Four Brothers in Blue,* 228–29; Marsena Rudolph Patrick, *Inside Lincoln's Army,* 206–7; Hagerty, *Collis' Zouaves,* 168; Haydon, *For Country, Cause, and Leader,* 307; Donaldson, *Inside the Army of the Potomac,* 205; Sprenger, *122d Regiment,* 196; Sim Siggins to Hannah T. Rohrer, January 25, 1863, Monks-Rohrer Letters, Emory.

47. Lewis Nettleton to "My own dear love," January 25, 1863, Nettleton-Baldwin Family Papers, Duke; William L. Orr to Margaret Small Orr, January 28, 1863, Orr Family Papers, IU; Marsena Rudolph Patrick, *Inside Lincoln's Army,* 205–6; *Johnstown (Pa.) Cambria Tribune,* January 30, 1863.

48. Edwin Wentworth to his wife, January 25, 1863, Wentworth Papers, LC; Edward Henry Courtney Taylor to "Bill," January 25, 1863, Taylor Letters, MHC; James P. Coburn to his father, January 28, 1863, James P. Coburn Papers, USAMHI.

49. Alpheus Starkey Williams, *From the Cannon's Mouth,* 159–60; Hartsock, *Soldier of the Cross,* 52; Dayton E. Flint to his father, January 27, 1863, Flint Letters, CWMC, USAMHI; William Franklin Draper to his wife, January 23, 1863, Draper Papers, LC.

50. J. C. Lee to Ellen Lee, January 24, 1863, Graham Letters, FSNMP; John D. Cooper to his daughter, January 25, 1863, Cooper Papers, DCL; Nolan, *Iron Brigade,* 193; Smithe, *Glimpses of Places, and People, and Things,* 40–43; Brewer, *Sixty-first Regiment,* 47; Edward J. Nichols, *Toward Gettysburg,* 158–59.

51. Robert Taylor Scott to his wife, January 30, 1863, Keith Family Papers, VHS; Edmund Ruffin, *Diary,* 2:557–58; *Charleston Daily Courier,* January 31, 1863; Edmondston, *"Journal of a Secesh Lady,"* 352. After Fredericksburg and the Mud March, rumors of Federal demoralization made it easy for Confederates to indulge in wishful thinking. Recent "news" had been so positive, making even ambiguous information grounds for Pollyannaish assessments. See Allport and Postman, *Psychology of Rumor,* 43–45.

52. Molyneux, *Quill of the Wild Goose,* 66; Galwey, *Valiant Hours,* 74; Sears, *Chancellors-*

ville, 20; William Howard Mills, "From Burnside to Hooker," 50; Jeffries, "Diary of Lemuel Jeffries," 271–72.

53. Douglas Southall Freeman, *Calendar of Confederate Papers,* 382; "Letters from the Front," 157–58; *Charleston Daily Courier,* January 29, February 5, 1863; Jonathan Fuller Coghill to "Dear Pappy, Ma, and Mit," January 25, 1863, Coghill Letters, Auburn University Archives; J. F. Shaffner to "My dearest friend," January 22, 1863, Shaffner Papers, NCDAH; Perry, "Whip the Devil and His Hosts," 42; William Ross Stillwell to his wife, February 1, 1863, Stillwell Letters, GDAH.

54. *New York Tribune,* January 24, 26–27, 1863; *New York Herald,* January 24, 1863; *Boston Post,* January 26, 1863; Strong, *Diary of George Templeton Strong,* 3:289–90; H. Draper Hunt, *Hamlin,* 166; *CCW,* 1.716; *New York Times,* January 24, 27, 1863.

55. Raymond, "Extracts from the Journal of Henry J. Raymond," 423; *OR,* 998–99; Ambrose E. Burnside to ?, May 24, 1863, Burnside Papers, entry 159, box 3, NA. Burnside had earlier ordered the arrest of Brooks on grounds of insubordination Brooks stoutly denied that he had used "language tending to demoralize his command" but expressed some confidence in Hooker. See William T. H. Brooks to his father, February 17, 1863, Brooks Papers, USAMHI.

56. Raymond, "Extracts from the Journal of Henry J. Raymond," 703–4; Daniel Read Larned to Mrs. Ambrose E. Burnside, January 28, 1863, Larned Papers, LC; *CCW,* 1:719–20; Ambrose E. Burnside to Abraham Lincoln, January 23, 1863, Lincoln Papers, LC; Lincoln, *Collected Works,* 6:74.

57. Raymond, "Extracts from the Journal of Henry J. Raymond," 704; Daniel Read Larned to Mrs. Ambrose E. Burnside, January 28, 1863, Larned Papers, LC; *CCW,* 1:720.

58. Welles, *Diary of Gideon Welles,* 1:229–30; Niven, *Chase,* 314; Raymond, "Extracts from the Journal of Henry J. Raymond," 705; *OR,* 1004, 1007, 1009; *CCW,* 720–21.

59. *OR,* 1004–5; Raymond, "Extracts from the Journal of Henry J. Raymond," 706, 708.

60. Bliss Memoir, 4:48–49, USAMHI; Marsena Rudolph Patrick, *Inside Lincoln's Army,* 208; Daniel Read Larned to Mrs. Ambrose E. Burnside, January 28, 1863, Larned Papers, LC; Louis Fortescue to "Friend Sam," January 1863, Fortescue Letters, FSNMP; *OR,* 1005. Although the account of Burnside's final days with the Army of the Potomac presented here differs slightly in detail and more in tone and emphasis, I have greatly benefited from two excellent accounts: Marvel, *Burnside,* 213–17; A. Wilson Greene, "Morale, Maneuver, and Mud," 205–15.

61. Meade, *Life and Letters,* 1:351; Pettit, *Infantryman Pettit,* 53–54; January 28, 1863, Nathan B. Webb Diary, Schoff Collection, CL; A. S. West to his father, 1863, West Letters, FSNMP; Haydon, *For Country, Cause, and Leader,* 308; William Watson, *Letters of a Civil War Surgeon,* 51; Wyman Silas White, *Civil War Diary,* 125–26; Robert S. Robertson, "Diary of the War," 84; Moe, *Last Full Measure,* 221; E. A. Walker to "Friend Knight," January 24, 1863, Walker Letters, Leigh Collection, USAMHI.

62. Isaac Lyman Taylor, "Campaigning with the First Minnesota," 245; Joseph Harrison Law to Mary E. Law, January 26, 1863, Law Family Papers, CWMC, USAMHI; William Franklin Draper to his father, January 26, 1863, Draper Papers, LC; Bright and Bright, *"Respects to All,"* 38.

63. Joseph Hooker to "Dr. Wilkes," January 29, 1863, Annmary Brown Military Collection, Brown University; George Henry Hood to "Dear Etta," January 26, 1863, Hood Papers, Duke; Charles Jewett Morris to his brother and sister, January 27, 1863, Morris Papers, Duke; Hugh Roden to George Roden, February 1, 1863, Roden Papers, Schoff Collection, CL; Jacob F. Smith to "Dear Callie," February 5, 1863, Jacob F. Smith Letter, CWMC, USAMHI; William A. Guest to his father, January 30, 1863, Guest Papers, CWMC, USAMHI; Washburn, *108th Regiment,* 115; Louis Langer to Mr. and Mrs. John W. Scales, January 31, 1863, Scales Family Papers, CWMC, USAMHI; William Boston to "Aunt Rosa," January 30, 1863, Boston Papers, MHC.

Hooker eventually learned of General Orders No. 8 and wrote a long letter to Stanton, essentially a diatribe accusing Burnside of everything from cowardice at First Bull Run to blundering at Antietam to "madness" at Fredericksburg to being a two-faced liar. See *OR*, ser. 1, 25(2):855–56.

64. Lusk, *War Letters of William Thompson Lusk,* 274–75; Sears, *Chancellorsville,* 16; Wightman, *From Antietam to Fort Fisher,* 106; George H. Mellish to his mother, January 29, 1863, Mellish Papers, HL; O. Leland Barlow to his sisters, January 26, 1863, Barlow Papers, CSL; Uriah N. Parmelee to his brother, January 26, 1863, Parmelee Papers, Duke.

65. McPherson, *For Cause and Comrades,* 156; Gray, *Hidden Civil War,* 133; Jimerson, *Private Civil War,* 232; Edward W. Steffan to Gus Steffan, January 31, February 2, 1863, Steffan Letters, FSNMP.

66. Franklin Sawyer to Samuel Sexton, February 2, 1863, Sexton Papers, OHS; John Ripley Adams, *Memorial and Letters,* 98–99; George Henry Chandler to his mother, January 27, 1863, Chandler Papers, NHHS; Thomas Bell to "Dear Friend," January 1863, GAR; Charles Bowers to "Dear Lydia," January 23, 1863, Bowers Papers, MHS.

67. Peter Welsh, *Irish Green and Union Blue,* 65–67. Welsh continued to serve his adopted country until he was mortally wounded at the battle of Spotsylvania.

68. *Washington Daily National Intelligencer,* January 28, 1863; Brooks, *Mr. Lincoln's Washington,* 83–84; Thorndike, *Sherman Letters,* 187; Chase, *Salmon P. Chase Papers,* 3:375, 377–78; T. Harry Williams, *Lincoln and the Radicals,* 242.

69. *Philadelphia Evening Bulletin,* January 27, 1863; Mrs. Austin Blair to William Withington, January 29, 1863, Withington Papers, MHC.

EPILOGUE

1. December 28, 1862, Maury Diary, LC; Charles Minor Blackford to Mary Blackford, January 12, 1863, Blackford Family Papers, SHC; Simpson and Simpson, *Far, Far from Home,* 169; L. Minor Blackford, *Mine Eyes Have Seen the Glory,* 213; William Murdock Parsley to his mother, January 4, 1863, Parsley Papers, SHC; *Charleston Daily Courier,* January 17, 31, 1863. Mary Tom found the Baptist church in much better shape than she had expected, even though shells had damaged the spire, smashed windows, and struck the organ. See Mary Tom to Mary Anna McGuire Claiborne, December 29, 1862, Claiborne Family Papers, VHS.

2. Shand Memoir, SCL; J. H. Wallace to William Ware, December 28, 1862, National Bank of Fredericksburg Correspondence, FSNMP; W. L. Masten to his brother, March 16, 1863, Masten Letter, FSNMP; Douglas H. Gordon to Ann Eliza Gordon, January 27, 31, 1863, Douglas H. Gordon Letters, FSNMP; S. G. Pryor, *Post of Honor,* 299.

3. December 13–14, 1862, Hamilton Diary, FSNMP; Jane Howison Beale, *Journal,* 75–78; Dobbins, *Grandfather's Journal,* 116; Mrs. Frances Bernard Goolrick, "Shelling of Fredericksburg," 574; George J. Nicholson to Charles W. Wellford, December 22, 1862, Schooler Papers, Duke; December 29, 1862, January 1, 1863, Alsop Diary, VHS.

4. *Atlanta Southern Confederacy,* December 27, 1862; Delia Smith Taylor to Anna McGuire Claiborne, March 5, 1863, Claiborne Family Papers, VHS; Jedediah Hotchkiss to Sara Ann Comfort Hotchkiss, January 21, 1863, Hotchkiss Papers, LC; January 20, 1863, Maury Diary, LC. Several cold and hungry refugees (including one woman in her nineties) drifted into the Federal camps. At least one Fredericksburg child ended up in an orphan asylum near Washington, D.C. See Pencil Notes on the Battle of Fredericksburg, December 11–15, 1862, Larned Papers, LC; Castleman, *Army of the Potomac,* 270–72; Elizabeth Blair Lee, *Civil War Letters,* 278.

5. Robert E. Lee, *Wartime Papers,* 382; December 29, 1862, Alsop Diary, VHS; Jedediah Hotchkiss to Sara Ann Comfort Hotchkiss, December 21, 1862, Hotchkiss Papers, LC; William H. Jones to his wife, December 23, 1862, William H. Jones Papers, Duke. Anger over the destruction of the town and suffering of the refugees made some Confederates rejoice

at seeing so many dead Yankees scattered about the streets and yards. Jedediah Hotchkiss hoped he would never see another town so ruined unless it was that "sink of iniquity" Washington, D.C. See Shotwell, *Papers of Randolph Abbott Shotwell*, 1:435–36; R. Channing Price to his mother, December 23, 1862, Price Papers, SHC; Jedediah Hotchkiss to Sara Ann Comfort Hotchkiss, January 21, 1863, Hotchkiss Papers, LC. Even a Pennsylvania corporal noted how pitiful it was to see "young women here who were once comfortable dressed in clothing made of old grain sacks and blankets" (Pettit, *Infantryman Pettit*, 43–44).

6. Allbritton, "Third Arkansas," 161; January 1863 passim, Slaughter Papers, HL; *Charleston Daily Courier*, December 31, 1862; Ruffner, *44th Virginia*, 35; *OR*, ser. 1, 51(2):665–66; Conn and Conn, "Letters of Two Confederate Officers," 187; List of Richmond Howitzers' Contributions, n.d., MC; Burgwyn, *Captain's War*, 44; Douglas Southall Freeman, *Calendar of Confederate Papers*, 254; Susan Leigh Blackford, *Letters from Lee's Army*, 149; January 2, 1863, Pickens Diary, UA; Hotchkiss, *Make Me a Map of the Valley*, 106–7; December 21, 1862, Pickett Diary, *CWTI*, USAMHI; Riggs, *7th Virginia*, 18; J. C. C. Sanders to "Dear Fannie," January 3, 1862[3], Sanders Letters, FSNMP; Perry, "Whip the Devil and His Hosts," 42; James Power Smith, "With Stonewall Jackson," 60.

7. Dobbins, *Grandfather's Journal*, 116; *Richmond Daily Dispatch*, January 1, 1863; *Richmond Daily Enquirer*, December 29, 1862.

8. *Athens (Ga.) Southern Banner*, January 14, 1863; *Lynchburg Daily Virginian*, December 16, 1862; *Richmond Daily Enquirer*, December 23, 1862; *Augusta (Ga.) Daily Constitutionalist*, January 8, 1863; *Charleston Mercury*, January 24, 1863; William M. Blackford to Montgomery Slaughter, March 30, 1863, Slaughter Papers, HL; Lucy Rebecca Buck, *Shadows of My Heart*, 166, 174–76.

9. Blair, "Barbarians at Fredericksburg's Gate," 158–59; *Charleston Daily Courier*, January 3, 1863; *Augusta (Ga.) Daily Constitutionalist*, January 21, 1863; January 1863 passim and unidentified clipping, Lynchburg, Virginia, February 17, 1863, Slaughter Papers, HL; Massey, *Refugee Life in the Confederacy*, 252–55; Dobbins, *Grandfather's Journal*, 116–17; *Richmond Daily Dispatch*, December 24, 1862, January 5, 1863.

10. Charlotte E. Lomax to Montgomery Slaughter, January 31, 1863; E. M. Hunter to Slaughter, February 6, 1863; Harriet Barbour to Slaughter, February 26, 1863; Mrs. Joseph B. Anderson to Slaughter, February 24, 1863; William J. Jones to ?, April 10, 1863; Matelda Barnett to Slaughter, February 1863, all in Civil War Damage Inventories, Clerk of the Circuit Court of Fredericksburg; unidentified clipping with letter from Montgomery Slaughter, March 13, 1863, Slaughter Papers, HL.

11. Blair, "Barbarians at Fredericksburg's Gate," 160–62; Trowbridge, *The South*, 106–7, 109, 113; Conwell, *Magnolia Journey*, 8, 10; *Philadelphia Weekly Times*, August 6, 1881; Edward King, *Great South*, 796.

12. *MSH*, 12:840–41. Serving in Caldwell's brigade of Hancock's division, Zuelch had been in the thick of the fight on December 13. For other examples of long recovery periods, see *MSH*, 12:487, 545. Although the vast majority of cases in the *Medical and Surgery History* (the best source for information on the long-term fate of the seriously wounded) are of Federal soldiers, many Confederates experienced similar torments.

13. *MSH*, 8:289, 10:648, 11:14–15, 248; Bengtson and Kuz, *Photographic Atlas of Civil War Injuries*, 111.

14. Marvel, *Ninth New Hampshire*, 113; *MSH*, 9:12, 287, 309. Men who managed to survive serious abdominal wounds usually did not live into the 1870s.

15. *MSH*, 11:148, 12:429, 553, 635. Historians know surprisingly little about the long-term psychological effects of Civil War combat on the soldiers. For a penetrating analysis and case studies, especially for Indiana (largely western theater) volunteers who suffered some kind of posttraumatic stress disorder, see Dean, *Shook over Hell*, 91.

16. For examples of the stirring, often sentimental, and ephemeral poetry inspired by the

battle of Fredericksburg, see McCarter, *My Life in the Irish Brigade,* 230–33; Charles Carelton Coffin, *Fours Years of Fighting,* 145, 147; Owen, *Christmas Reminiscence of Fredericksburg.*

17. The exchange of news and rumors—a persistent activity in both camp and home— allowed the venting of frustrations but also shaped social life. People reacted to the latest reports and to one another's understanding of both the recent past and the immediate future. What the psychological and sociological literature on rumor reveals is the central importance of exploring the perceptions of the men in uniform and their families. Conversations in camp and at home became prime indicators of morale. See Kapferer, *Rumors,* 41–50; Shibutani, *Improvised News,* 163–64, 175–77.

18. The military situation in the western theater had, of course, been much more fluid and largely favored the Federals. At the same time, after Fredericksburg, people could hardly foresee the ferocity of the more than two more years of deadly fighting in the eastern theater that still lay ahead.

19. "Many Prominent Persons Present," 174–78; Reardon, "Forlorn Hope," 106; Kerbey, *On the War-Path,* 160–66; Werkheiser Memoir, 19, FSNMP.

20. [De Peyster,] "Fredericksburg," 201; Hutchison, "Fredericksburg," 267; Cavanagh, *Memoirs of Gen. Thomas Francis Meagher,* 470–71; Pepper, *Under Three Flags,* 333.

21. *OR,* ser. 1, 27(2):645; *Richmond Daily Whig,* July 12, 1863; J. S. Wood Reminiscences, 11, Personal Papers, GDAH; Dickert, *Kershaw's Brigade,* 190–91; Longstreet, *From Manassas to Appomattox,* 314–15; Bruce, "Strategy of the Civil War," 461–62.

Bibliography

MANUSCRIPTS
Alabama Department of Archives and History, Montgomery
    John Gill Shorter (Governors') Papers
Allegheny College, Lawrence Lee Pelletien Library, Meadville, Pennsylvania
    George W. Cullum Papers
Auburn University, Archives and Manuscripts Department, Auburn, Alabama
    Jonathan Fuller Coghill Letters
Stephen F. Austin State University, Special Collections, Nacodoches, Texas
    Henry Parks Garrison Papers, Quillian Garrison Research Collection
Boston Public Library, Boston, Massachusetts
    Henry Ropes Letters
Boston University, Department of Special Collections, Boston, Massachusetts
    John C. Ropes Papers, Massachusetts Military Historical Society Collection
Brown University, John Hay Library, Special Collections, Providence, Rhode Island
    Annmary Brown Military Collection
Castine Public Library, Castine, Maine
    Henry Butler Papers
Chester County Historical Society, West Chester, Pennsylvania
    Nathan Pennypacker Letters
Chicago Historical Society, Chicago, Illinois
    James L. Converse Papers
    Reuben H. Humphreyville Papers
Clerk of the Circuit Court of Fredericksburg, Virginia
    Civil War Damage Inventories
Connecticut Historical Society, Hartford
    Loren H. Goodrich Papers
    Littlefield Family Papers
    Virgil W. Mattoon Papers
    William H. Relyea Memoir
    Henry Snow Letters
Connecticut State Library, Hartford
    O. Leland Barlow Papers
    Edward H. Brewer Papers
    John Henry Burnham Papers
    Daniel Stevens Papers
Cornell University, Department of Manuscripts and Archives, Ithaca, New York
    John S. Crocker Letters, Frank S. Brockett Collection
Dartmouth College Library, Special Collections, Hanover, New Hampshire
    Smith G. Bailey Diary
    Elmer Bragg Letters and Diary
    John D. Cooper Papers
    Oscar D. Robinson Diary
    Ransom F. Sargent Papers
Duke University, William R. Perkins Library, Durham, North Carolina

Edward Hall Armstrong Letter, Confederate States of America Archives, Officers and
     Soldiers Letters, Army Miscellany
H. G. Ayer Diary
George Williamson Ballock Papers
Nathan T. Bartley Papers, Confederate Veteran, 1861–1931, box 1
Bedinger-Dandridge Family Papers
Henry Bescancon Diary
Charles J. Borden Papers
Harriette Branham Diary
Alexander Brown Papers
John Emory Bryant Papers
Anna B. Campbell Papers
Lunsford Cherry Papers
James O. Coghill Papers
Oliver S. Coolidge Papers
Mary A. Councill Papers
John B. S. Dimitry Papers
Henry Kyd Douglas Papers
John B. Evans Papers
George W. Grant Papers
Robert Guyton and James B. Heaslet Papers
Edward Harden Papers
Joseph N. Haynes Papers
Paul Herman Hilliard Papers
Frederick W. M. Holliday Papers
George Henry Hood Papers
Micah Jenkins Papers
Electus W. Jones Papers
William H. Jones Papers
Henry Clay Krebs Papers
Emma A. Legg Papers
Lucas-Ashley Family Papers
Charles Jewett Morris Papers
Munford-Ellis Papers
Nettleton-Baldwin Family Papers
Mary Norton Papers
Samuel and Uriah N. Parmelee Papers
Presley Carter Person Papers
Charles S. Powell Reminiscences
Mary E. Schooler Papers
Thomas Lee Settle Papers
Edward E. Sill Letter
Evin Smith Papers
John M. Snider Papers
Darius Starr Papers
James Ewell Brown Stuart Papers
Henry J. H. Thompson Papers
U.S. Army Archives, Miscellaneous Papers
Wilkes Family Papers
George Newton Wise Diary
James C. Zimmerman Papers

East Carolina University, Special Collections, Greenville, North Carolina
    Alexander Routh Letter, Hugh Harrison Mills Collection
Emory University, Special Collections, Robert W. Woodruff Library, Atlanta, Georgia
    William Macon Crumley, Personal Reminiscences of the Civil War
    John A. Everett Letter
    Monks-Rohrer Letters
    David Read Evans Winn Letters
Fredericksburg and Spotsylvania National Military Park, Fredericksburg, Virginia (largely
    copies from miscellaneous collections and descendants of soldiers)
    Amory Allen Letter
    John C. Anderson Letter
    J. W. Armsworthy Letters
    Cyrus Bacon Diary
    Charles Barber Letters
    A. A. Batchelder Letter
    David Beem Memoir and Letters
    Charles Thomas Bowen Letter
    David L. Bozeman Letters
    Martin W. Brett Memoir
    Nathaniel W. Brown Letter
    William O. Campbell Memoir
    William S. Campbell Letter
    J. T. Carpenter Letter
    George C. Case Letters
    John March Cate Letters
    George Chandler Letters
    Nathan Chesley Letter
    Samuel Clark Letters
    W. B. Colston, "Personal Experiences of Captain W. B. Colston"
    George W. Coon Papers
    Samuel Coplan, "Account of Sam Coplan's Role in the Battle of Fredericksburg during
        the Civil War"
    John R. Coye Letters
    B. Dailey Papers
    William Meade Dame Letters
    Morris R. Darrohn, "Recollections of My Army Life"
    Samuel V. Dean Letters
    Vaclav Dusek Reminiscence
    George B. Felch Letters
    William Fermoil Letter
    George W. Flack Diary
    Erasmus Fleming Letter
    Robert Franklin Fleming Jr., "Recollections of the Battle of Fredericksburg"
    Vivian Minor Fleming Reminiscence
    Louis Fortescue Letters
    Albert Foster Letters
    John Z. Gayle Letter
    Charles Gibson Letters
    Charles H. Gilley Letters
    William Gilson Letter
    Douglas H. Gordon Letters

S. W. Gordon Diary
Silas Gore Letters
Thomas Gouldsbery Letter
James S. Graham Letters
Anthony G. Graves Memoir and Letters
Milo Grow Letters
Henry W. Grubbs Letter
Maria Hamilton Diary, "An Eyewitness Account of the Battle of Fredericksburg"
Jere Malcolm Harris Letter
John H. Harris Diary
John Hartranft Letter
John F. Hartwell Papers
John W. Haverstick Letter
Harvey Henderson Diary
Albert Wymer Henley Diary
A. C. Higley Letters
Isaac Hillyer Letters
Franklin B. Hough, "Battle of Fredericksburg"
Thomas Jefferson Howarth Memoir
Edward B. Hutchinson Letters
Richard Irby Letters
Ephraim Jackson Letters
Arch F. Jones Letter
David Jones Letters
Tom Josiah Letter
Reuben Kelley Letters
J. T. Kenyon Letters
Robert A. Kerr Diary
Kirby-Smith-Russell Collection
James Laird Letter
Willis Lee, "Record of Willis Lee's Service in the Confederate Army, Richmond
    Howitzers"
Richard McCabe Memoir
Lt. J. McDonald Letters
John McDonald Letter
Guilford D. Mace Letter
James T. McElvaney Letter
Alexander McNeil Letter
A. B. Martin Letter
Herbert C. Mason Letter
W. L. Masten Letter
Emerson F. Merrill Papers
Martin Van Buren Metcalf Diary
E. P. Miller Diary
William A. Miller Letter
J. M. Mitchell Diary
John Mitchell Letters
J. G. Montgomery Letter
Thomas J. Morrison Letters
William Goodrich Morton Letters
Adam Muenzenberger Letters

National Bank of Fredericksburg Correspondence
Thomas J. Owen, "Back in War Times"
Frank C. Park Letter
Samuel Selden Partridge Letters
Abel G. Peck Letter
Dwight P. Peck Letter
Lucy Chandler Pendleton Reminiscences
John W. Phillips Letters
C. Powell Letter
Kenneth H. Power Memoir
Matthew Quay File
H. M. Reed Letters
Joshua Rice Diary
Cornelius Richmond Papers
R. S. Robertson Papers
C. L. Rundlett Letter
John F. Sale Letter
J. C. G. Sanders Letter
Reuben and Benneville Schell Letters
Charles A. Seaman Letters
W. F. Searles Letters
Joseph M. Shepard Diary
William M. Sheppard Letter
Anson B. Shuey Letter
John Smart Letters
John L. Smith Letters
Len Smith Letter
Ellis Spear, "My Story of Fredericksburg and Comments Thereon By One Who Was
    There," and Spear Letters
R. P. Staniels Letter
Samuel C. Starrett Letter
Edward W. Steffan Letters
Charles J. Stoner Diary
Henry Taylor Diary
Isaac S. Tichenor Letter
Augustus Tuttle Letter
Asaph R. Tyler Letters
Daniel Underhill Letter
Unknown Soldier (apparently 48th Virginia) Letter
Henry Van Aernum Papers
Joseph P. Vickers Letter
William A. Waugh, "Reminiscences of the Rebellion or What I Saw as a Private Soldier
    of the 5th Mass. Light Battery from 1861–1863"
Alexander Way Letters
Weather Data, December 11–15, 1862, January 20–22, 1863
Martin L. Werkheiser Memoir
A. S. West Letters
E. R. and McKibben Willis Letters
Henry Willis Letter
A. J. Wilson Letter
James Albert Wilson Letter

John D. Withrow Letters
Aaron C. Wolcott Letters
Leander E. Wollard Diary
Georgia Department of Archives and History, Atlanta
    Joseph E. Brown (Governors') Papers
    Confederate Soldier Letter, December 14, 1862, UDC Collection
    Charles J. McDonald Conway Diary
    Gillespie Family Papers
    James M. Goldsmith, "Record of James Manning Goldsmith being Taken Prisoner"
    Richard W. Milner Collection
    Sidney J. Richardson Letters
    William Ross Stillwell Letters
    William W. White Letters
    J. S. Wood Reminiscences, Civil War Miscellany
    UDC Bound Typescripts
        Confederate Soldier to "Dear Molly"
        William H. Hodnett Diary
        William Moore Jones Reminiscences
        William H. Kirkpatrick Letter
        John L. G. Wood Letters
        Joseph White Woods Reminiscences
Gettysburg National Military Park, Gettysburg, Pennsylvania
    Jacob Bechtel Letters
    William G. Cason Letter
Grand Army of the Republic Museum, Philadelphia, Pennsylvania
    110th Pennsylvania Miscellaneous Letters
Harvard University, Houghton Library, Cambridge, Massachusetts
    Frederick W. Dearborn Collection
        William W. Burns Letter
        Regis De Trobriand Letter
    Charles Sumner Papers
Historical Society of Pennsylvania, Philadelphia
    Franklin Boyts Diary
    Adolph Fernandez Cavada Diary
    Andrew A. Humphreys Papers
    George Gordon Meade Papers
Samuel Houston Regional Library, Liberty, Texas
    Waterman-Bacon-Sanders Family Papers
Henry E. Huntington Library, San Marino, California
    George H. Mellish Papers
    Montgomery Slaughter Papers
    Union Soldier Diary
    Evan M. Woodward Diary
Illinois State Historical Library, Springfield
    Josiah W. Perry Papers
    Stephen S. Rogers Papers
    Simeon Whiteley Papers
Index Project Summaries of Courts Martial, Dr. Thomas P. Lowry, Woodacre, California
Indiana Historical Society, Indianapolis
    David E. Beem Papers
    William Houghton Papers

William N. Jackson Diary
George Washington Lambert Diary
Augustus M. Van Dyke Papers
Indiana State Library, Indianapolis
Flauvius J. Bellamy Papers
John Dragoo Papers
Erasmus Gilbreath Reminiscences
James H. Luther Papers
Henry C. Marsh Papers
Mildred Knight Richardson Collection
Indiana University, Lilly Library, Bloomington
J. Lucas Harding Manuscripts
Nathan Kimball Collection
Orr Family Papers
U.S. History Manuscripts
Nancy Polk Lasselle Letter
Civil War Reminiscences of a Soldier in Co. C, 6th NY, 1861–1864
Jefferson County, West Virginia, Museum
George R. Shreve, "Reminiscences of the Stuart Horse Artillery," R. Preston Chew
Papers
Kennesaw Mountain National Battlefield Park, Kennesaw, Georgia
L. Calhoun Cooper Letters
Library of Congress, Manuscripts Division, Washington, D.C.
American Institute of Aeronautics and Astronautics Papers
William Bourne Papers
Felix Brannigan Papers
William E. Brooks Collection
Simon Cameron Papers
Zachariah Chandler Papers
Salmon P. Chase Papers
Jabez Lamar Monroe Curry Papers
George S. Dennison Papers
Theodore Dodge Diary
John Hancock Douglas Papers
William Franklin Draper Papers
Hamilton Fish Papers
William B. Franklin Papers
James Jenkins Gillette Papers
Samuel J. B. V. Gilpin Diary, E. N. Gilpin Papers
Gist Family Papers
James Grant, "The Flag and the Cross: A History of the United States Christian
Commission"
George Washington Hall Papers
William Hamilton Papers
James Henry Hammond Papers
James Allen Hardie Papers
John William Ford Hatton Memoir
Lewis M. Haupt Papers
Henry C. Heisler Papers
Orrin E. Hine Papers
Ethan Allan Hitchcock Papers

Lyman C. Holford Diary
Jedediah Hotchkiss Papers
Henry Hotze Papers
Fannie Page Hume Diary
Robert Edwin Jameson Papers
James Kelaher Letter
Allen Landis Papers
Daniel Read Larned Papers
James William Latta Diary
Abraham Lincoln Papers
George B. McClellan Papers
William Ogden McDonald Papers
Daniel W. Marshall Diary
Betty Herndon Maury Diary
John G. Nicolay Papers
Joseph Bloomfield Osborn Papers
Alfred Pleasonton Papers
David A. Rice Diary
M. Shuler Diary
Edwin M. Stanton Papers
Alexander H. Stephens Papers
George Hay Stuart Collection
Gilbert Thompson Memoir (diary)
Lyman Trumbull Papers
Benjamin Franklin Wade Papers
Israel Washburn Papers
Edwin O. Wentworth Papers
Cadmus Marcellus Wilcox Papers
Lawrence Wilson Diary
Library of Virginia, Richmond
John Letcher (Governors') Papers
Louisiana State University, Department of Archives and Manuscripts, Louisiana and Lower
Mississippi Valley Collection, Baton Rouge
Edward M. Burruss Papers
Ann Wilkinson Penrose Diary
Maine Historical Society, Portland
Lot M. Morrill Papers
Maryland Historical Society, Baltimore
[Edward L. Heinichen,] "Fredericksburg, Battle of, Description by Unknown Soldier,"
Civil War Collection
Massachusetts Historical Society, Boston
Charles Francis Adams Diary, Adams Family Papers
George M. Barnard Papers
Caleb H. Beal Papers
Charles Bowers Papers
Edward Louis Edes Papers
Thomas S. Howland Papers
George L. Prescott Papers
Military Order of the Loyal Legion of the United States, Civil War Library and Museum,
Philadelphia
St. Clair Augustin Mulholland Collection

Mississippi Department of Archives and History, Jackson
  John J. Pettus (Governors') Papers
  J. J. Wilson Papers
Pierpont Morgan Library, Gilder Lehrman Collection, New York, New York
  G. O. Bartlett Papers
  P. Borary Papers
  Oliver Edwards Papers
  Henry Lewis Letters
  George A. Spencer Papers
  Jeremiah M. Tate Papers
Museum of the Confederacy, Richmond, Virginia
  J. A. Braddock Memoir
  Alfred E. Doby Letters
  Junius Kimble Reminiscences
  List of Richmond Howitzers' Contributions for Subscription to Relief of Fredericksburg
    Sufferers
  Mary Matthews Papers
  R. T. Mockbee, "Historical Sketch of the 11th Tennessee Regiment of Infantry"
  John O'Farrell Diary
  Kate Mason Rowland Papers
National Archives, Washington, D.C.
  Adjutant General's Office Records, RG 94
  Ambrose E. Burnside Papers, General's Papers and Generals' Reports and Books, RG 94
  Letters Received by the Confederate Secretary of War, RG 109
New Hampshire Historical Society, Concord
  John Batchelder Bailey Diary
  Asa W. Bartlett, "Diary of Military Action of 12th New Hampshire Volunteers"
  Charles P. Chamberlain Papers
  George Henry Chandler Papers
  Charles Dwight Chase Papers
  Solomon Dodge Jr. Papers
  John Harrison Foye Papers
  John Godfrey Papers
  Frances Henry Goodall Papers
  Sylvester Erwin Hadley Diary
  William Adams Moore Papers
  N. B. Perkins Memoir
  Alonzo Pierce Papers
  Rodney H. Ramsey Letter, Miscellaneous Civil War Letters
  George H. P. Rowell Papers
  George H. Sargent Papers
  Aaron F. Stevens Papers
  John O. Stevens Papers
  Sewell D. Tilton Papers
  Hosea Towne Papers
  George E. Upton Papers
New Hampshire State Library, Concord
  Willard J. Templeton Letters
  Herbert J. Willand Diary
New Jersey Historical Society, Trenton
  Anderson Family Papers

Josiah J. Brown Reminiscence
Charles Crowell Reminiscences
John R. and Alla M. Emery Papers
John Vance Powers Papers
New-York Historical Society, New York
E. DeLoss Burton Papers
George Fischer Letter
Gabriel Grant Memoir
Southard Family Papers
New York Public Library, New York
John England Papers, U.S. Army Collection, 1862–1863
Northampton Historical Society, Northampton, Massachusetts
Charles H. Brewster Collection
North Carolina Division of Archives and History, Raleigh
J. W. Bone Reminiscences, Lowry Shufford Collection, Civil War and Confederate
    Material
Noah Collins Diary, Isaac S. Loudon Collection
Confederate Soldier Reminiscence, "My War Story," Lowry Shufford Collection
P. E. Fouts Collection
Marcus H. Hefner Collection
James H. Lane, "Incidents of Gallantry: Men of 7th, 28th, 37th NC"
R. B. Manning Diary, William H. S. Burgwyn Diary
Melinda Ray Diary, Civil War Collection
A. M. Scales Letters
J. F. Shaffner Papers
J. A. Stikeleather Reminiscences
Ohio Historical Society, Columbus
James S. Robinson Papers
Samuel Sexton Papers
Rhode Island Historical Society, Providence
Ambrose E. Burnside Letterbook
James Remington Papers
Rutgers University Special Collections, New Brunswick, New Jersey
William Howard Clairville Papers
J. Frank Sterling Papers
John J. Toffey Papers
State Historical Society of Wisconsin, Madison
Henry W. Beecham Letters
Amassa B. Cobb Letter
Horace Currier Diary
Diary of Private Elisha Dean
Edward Dwight Eaton Papers
Alonzo V. Richards Diary
John Weslie St. Clair Letters
W. K. Wright Collection
Henry F. Young Papers
Syracuse University Library, Special Collections Department, Syracuse, New York
Mary Edwards Walker Papers
Tennessee State Library and Archives, Nashville
John A. Fite Memoir
George C. Pile Memoir

William W. Teall Letters
Troup County Archives, LaGrange, Georgia
    Morgan-Hill Family Papers
University of Alabama, William Stanley Hoole Special Collections Library, Tuscaloosa
    John Cowin Diary
    Samuel Pickens Diary
University of Chicago Library, Chicago, Illinois
    Sanford Truesdale Papers
University of Georgia, Special Collections, Athens
    Carlton-Newton-Mell Collection
    T. R. R. Cobb Letters
    Francis Marion Coker Letters, Hodgson Heidler Collection
    J. H. Lumpkin Papers
    Margaret Branch Sexton Collection
University of Houston, Special Collections, Houston, Texas
    William Wilberforce Edgerton Papers
University of Michigan, Bentley Library, Michigan Historical Collections, Ann Arbor
    John Milton Bancroft Diary
    William Boston Papers
    Buchanan Family Papers
    Byron Mac Cutcheon Autobiography
    Sullivan D. Green Papers
    George Lockey Diary
    Henry Starke Seage Diary
    Lucius B. Shattuck Letters
    Edward Henry Courtney Taylor Letters
    William Herbert Withington Papers
University of Michigan, William L. Clements Library, Ann Arbor
    Lawrence Hotchkiss Collection
        James R. Woodworth Diary and Letters
    Schoff Civil War Collection
        George W. Barr Papers
        Francis Butler Diary
        Adam and William Carmany Papers
        Hacker Brothers Papers
        William Ellis Jones Diary
        Josiah Edmond King Papers
        Henry Grimes Marshall Papers
        George H. Nichols Letters
        Edgar A. Phelps Papers
        Hugh P. and George Roden Papers
        William Speed Papers
        Edward H. Wade Letters
        Nathan B. Webb Diary
        Clarence Whedon Papers
        John D. Wilkins Papers
University of North Carolina, Southern Historical Collection, Chapel Hill
    Edward Porter Alexander Papers
    Allen and Simpson Family Papers
    Blackford Family Papers
    John Bratton Letters

John Stanley Brooks Letters
Buchanan and McClellan Family Papers
Calder Family Papers
William R. Cox Papers
Harriet H. A. Eaton Diary
Samuel Angus Firebaugh Diary
Meta Morris Grimball Diary
Grimes Family Papers
Robert Hairston Papers
Eli Spinks Hamilton Papers
George Washington Finley Harper Papers
Alexander Cheeves Haskell Papers
Howard Family Papers
Cadwallader Jones Papers
William Penn Lloyd Diary
Jacob Lyons Diary
David Gregg McIntosh Manuscript
Mackay and Stiles Family Papers
Lafayette McLaws Papers
Harriet Ellen Moore Diary
Samuel J. C. Moore Papers
William G. Morris Letter
Eliza Hall Parsley Papers
William Nelson Pendleton Papers
William B. Pettit Papers
Phifer Family Papers
R. Channing Price Papers
John A. Ramsay Papers
Edward Payson Reeve Papers
William L. Saunders Papers
W. H. T. Squires Papers
Westwood Todd Reminiscences
Samuel Hoey Walkup Papers
Thomas Lewis Ware Diary
Abraham Welch Letter
Whitaker-Snipes Family Papers
Amanda Worthington Diary
University of Oregon, Knight Library, Special Collections, Eugene
    Maria Van Wagonen Papers
University of Rochester, Rhees Library, Rochester, New York
    William Henry Seward Papers
    Albert B. Williams Letters
University of South Carolina, South Caroliniana Library, Columbia
    Henry Calvin Conner Papers
    Maxcy Gregg Papers
    James R. Hagood, "Memoirs of the 1st South Carolina Regiment of Volunteer Infantry"
    Kerrison Family Papers
    McGee-Charles Family Papers
    William R. Montgomery Reminiscences and Letters
    James Drayton Nance Papers
    J. J. Norton Reunion Speech

James Reeder Letters
Robert B. Shand Memoir, Shand Family Papers
University of Tennessee, Knoxville
    John D. Damron Letter, Ann Penn Wray Collection
University of Texas, Center for American History, Austin
    McKnight Family Papers
    "Personal Recollections of the First Battle of Fredericksburg Fought on December 13,
        1862, as Seen from an Artillery Position on the Hill at Hamilton's Crossing"
    Lizzie Simons Diary
    Louis T. Wigfall Papers
University of Virginia, Alderman Library, Charlottesville
    Carter Minor Memoir
    James T. Odem Papers
U.S. Army Military History Institute, Carlisle Barracks, Pennsylvania
    William J. Abernathy Diary
    Alexander W. Acheson Papers, Pennsylvania Save the Flag Collection
    John W. Ames Papers
    Samuel R. Beardsley Papers
    H. Water, Perryman Letter
    Lyman and Jacob Blackington Papers
    Zenas R. Bliss Memoir
    Henry Brantingham Letters, Joseph Bilby Collection
    William T. H. Brooks Papers
    Carman Family Collection
    Arthur T. Chapin Letter
    Civil War Miscellaneous Collection
        Alfred M. Apted Memoir
        Samuel A. Beddall Diary
        Clarence H. Bell Letters
        Allan L. and John H. Bevan Correspondence
        Aaron K. Blake Letters
        Orrel Brown Diary
        Robert A. Browne Papers
        Lewis L. Carr Letter
        Albert H. Carter Letters
        John B. Copenhauer Diary
        Edward Cotter Letter
        James Edison Decker Papers
        David Dunkle Letters
        Robert W. Elmer Diary
        Timothy C. Emerton Letters
        Henry Fical Letters
        Dayton E. Flint Letters
        Charles W. Fribley Diary
        Josiah C. Fuller Papers
        Charles S. Granger Diary
        Luther A. Granger Papers
        William A. Guest Papers
        Hunter Family Papers
        Law Family Papers
        Joseph H. Leighty Papers

Michael Leonard Letters
Albert Little Letter
Charles H. Littlefield Letters
Frank Longstreet Papers
Charles A. Malloy Diary
Joseph Franklin Mancha Diary
William A. Moore Memoir
John Morton Letters
William H. Myers Letters
Samuel W. North Letters
William Penn Oberlin Papers
John O'Connell Memoir
Richard Packard Letter
Miles Peabody Letters
William H. Peacock Papers
Edward W. Peck Letters
Isaac Plumb Diary
Curtis C. Pollock Papers
James B. Post Papers
Charles F. Powell Papers
Jacob Pyewell Papers
Stephen Rich Papers
Levander Sawtelle Letters
Scales Family Papers
Anson B. Shuey Papers
Jacob F. Smith Letter
Murton S. Tanner Letter
S. B. Tarleton Letter
Dwight Vick Letter
William H. Walling Papers
John S. Weiser Papers
William R. Williams Papers
Henry H. Young Papers
Samuel K. Zook Papers
Civil War Times Illustrated Collection
Benjamin F. Appleby Letters
John Berry Diary
Caldwell Family Papers
Robert S. Coburn Diary
Jacob Heffelfinger Diary
William W. Hemmenway, "Reminiscence of Battle of Fredericksburg, Va., 1862"
John D. McQuaide Letters
Frederick W. Oesterle Memoir
Lucius S. J. Owen Letters
Charles E. Perkins Papers
Charles P. Perkins Diary
George S. Pickett Diary
Albert A. Pope Diary
George S. Rollins Autopsy and Letters
Henry Sprague Letter
Ellis C. Strouss Papers

Joseph S. C. Taber Diary
Wright's Georgia Brigade Order Book
James P. Coburn Papers
Gregory A. Coco Collection
    Charles R. Johnson Letters
    David V. Lovell Letter
Walter A. Eames Letters
Clark S. Edwards Papers, Wiley Sword Collection
Daniel B. Foote Letters
Edward Halsey Diary, Halsey Collection
Winfield Scott Hancock Papers
Harrisburg Civil War Round Table Collection
    William Britton Bailey Jr. Letters
    Gregory A. Coco Collection
        George H. Legate Letter
        Henry J. Madill Diary
    Hannah Delp Papers
    Isaac Newton Durboraw Papers
    Ellis-Marshall Papers
    Daniel Faust Papers
    Luther C. Furst Diary
    Jacob W. Haas Papers
    John W. Joyce Papers
    Henry Keiser Diary
    Isaac and Joseph Morrow Papers
    Emory Upton Letter
    J. L. Willy Letters
Henry Family Papers, Ronald D. Boyer Collection
George F. Hopper Papers
Chester F. Hunt Letter, Earl M. Hess Collection
Daniel Emerson Hurd Memoir, William Marvel Collection
Jonathan Hutchinson Letters, Norwich Civil War Round Table Collection
Lewis Leigh Collection
    David W. Benjamin Letter
    Alonzo D. Bump Letters
    Charles H. Eager Letters
    Samuel B. Fischer Letters
    Timothy Fonley Letter
    George E. French Papers
    Morton Hayward Letters
    Constantine A. Hege Letters
    Henry H. Holt Letter
    James H. McIlwaine Letters
    George H. Patch Papers
    Philip H. Powers Letters
    William F. Smith Letters
    E. A. Walker Letters
    Ansell W. White Letters
Charles C. Paige Memoir, Wendell W. Lang Jr. Collection
John Pellett Papers
Walter Phelps Letters

James Pratt Collection
John F. Shure Letters, Michael Winey Collection
Thomas D. Grover Smith Letter, Justin Turner Collection
Thomas White Stevens Diary
Charles F. Stinson Letters, Michael Musick Collection
Robert Taggart Diary, Jay Luvaas Collection
James M. Treichler, "Sketch of Battle of Fredericksburg," Northwest Corner Civil War
    Round Table Collection
Twentieth Massachusetts Diary, Massachusetts MOLLUS Collection
Michael J. Vreeland Papers
U.S. Military Academy, West Point, New York
    Lyons Family Papers
Vermont Historical Society, Montpelier
    Stephen M. Pingree Papers
Virginia Historical Society, Richmond
    Lizzie Maxwell Alsop Diary
    Claiborne Family Papers
    Clay Family Papers
    Cocke Family of Portsmouth Family Papers
    Dabney Family Papers
    Thomas F. Darby Papers
    Edward Samuel Duffey Diary
    Mary Eliza Dulany Diary
    Thomas Claybrook Elder Papers
    Griggs Family Papers
    Harlow Family Papers
    Samuel Horace Hawes Diary
    Abner Crump Hopkins Diary
    Jones Family Papers
    Keith Family of Fauquier Co. Papers
    Keith Family Papers
    Osmun Latrobe Diary
    Robert E. Lee Letterbook, Lee Family Papers
    John VanLew McCreery Recollections
    McGuire Family Papers
    Meade Family Papers
    William Y. Mordecai Papers
    Henry Thweatt Owen Papers
    Pegram-Johnson-McIntosh Family Papers
    James Eldred Phillips Memoir
    David Washington Pipes Memoir
    Elizabeth Gordon Reynolds Recollections
    Edmund Ruffin Papers
    John Simmons Shipp Diary
    W. R. M. Slaughter Letters
    James Ewell Brown Stuart Papers
    William Henry Tatum Papers
    Lucy Thornton Papers
    Richard Henry Watkins Papers
    John French White Papers
    Wills Family Papers

T. D. Witherspoon, "A Chapter in the History of the Defense of Fredericksburg"
Virginia Military Institute Archives, Lexington
  Johnson Family Papers
Virginia Polytechnic Institute and State University, Special Collections, Blacksburg
  Washington Brown Papers
  Rufus P. Stanick Letter
Western Michigan University, Kalamazoo
  Sanford McCall Letters
West Virginia University, Morgantown
  W. T. Kinzer Letter
  Lewis Schaeffer Diary
Yale University, New Haven, Connecticut
  George H. Bradley Papers
  Civil War Miscellaneous Collection
    James B. Dawley Letters
    John Leonard Letters

CONTEMPORARY PERIODICALS

Albion
American Phrenological Journal
American Presbyterian and Theological Review
Bankers' Magazine and Statistical Register
Brownson's Quarterly Review
Christian Advocate and Journal
Christian Examiner
Christian Inquirer
Continental Monthly
Danville Quarterly Review
Evangelist
Frank Leslie's Illustrated Newspaper
German Reformed Messenger
Harper's Weekly
Independent
Knickerbocker
Liberator
London Illustrated News
Medical and Surgical Reporter (Philadelphia)
National Anti-Slavery Standard
Old Guard
Quarterly Review (London)
Saturday Review (London)
Scientific American
Southern Illustrated News
Southern Literary Messenger
Vanity Fair

NEWSPAPERS

Albany (N.Y.) Atlas and Argus
Albany (N.Y.) Evening Journal
Athens (Ga.) Southern Banner
Athens (Bradford Co., Pa.) Gazette

Atlanta Constitution Magazine
Atlanta Southern Confederacy
Augusta (Ga.) Daily Chronicle and Sentinel
Augusta (Ga.) Daily Constitutionalist
Augusta (Maine) Kennebec Journal
Baltimore American and Commercial Advertiser
Beaver (Pa.) Weekly Argus
Berks and Schuylkill (Pa.) Journal
Berkshire County (Mass.) Eagle
Boston Daily Advertiser
Boston Evening Transcript
Boston Journal
Boston Pilot
Boston Post
Brookville (Ind.) Franklin Democrat
Brunswick (Maine) Telegraph
Cahors (N.Y.) Cataract
Cannelton (Ind.) Reporter
Carlisle (Pa.) Herald
Charleston Daily Courier
Charleston Mercury
Chicago Daily Tribune
Cincinnati Daily Gazette
Columbus (Ga.) Daily Enquirer
Cumberland Valley (Pa.) Journal
Easton (Pa.) Free Press
Easton (Pa.) Northampton County Journal
Eau Claire (Wisc.) Free Press
Ebensburg (Pa.) Democrat and Sentinel
Elizabeth New Jersey Journal
Elmira (N.Y.) Weekly Advertiser
Fitchburg (Mass.) Sentinel
Flemington (N.J.) Hunterdon Gazette
Flemington (N.J.) Hunterdon Republican
Fredericksburg Free Lance
Goshen (Ind.) Democrat
Harrisburg Patriot and Union
Hartford Daily Courant
Haverhill (Mass.) Gazette
Index (London)
Indiana (Pa.) Weekly Democrat
Indianapolis Daily Journal
Indianapolis Daily State Sentinel
Janesville (Wisc.) Daily Gazette
Johnstown (Pa.) Cambria Tribune
Kokomo (Ind.) Howard Tribune
Lancaster (Pa.) Daily Evening Express
Lynchburg Daily Virginian
Macon (Ga.) Daily Telegraph
Milledgeville (Ga.) Confederate Union
Milledgeville (Ga.) Southern Recorder

Muncie (Ind.) Delaware County Free Press
Narragansett (R.I.) Weekly
Newark (N.J.) Daily Advertiser
New York Daily Tribune
New York Herald
New York Irish-American
New York Tablet
New York Times
New York World
Philadelphia Evening Bulletin
Philadelphia Inquirer
Philadelphia Press
Philadelphia Public Ledger
Philadelphia Grand Army Scout and Soldier's Mail
Pittsburgh Daily Dispatch
Pittsfield (Mass.) Sun
Portland (Maine) Eastern Argus
Portsmouth (N.H.) Daily Morning Chronicle
Poughkeepsie (N.Y.) Daily Eagle
Providence (R.I.) Daily Journal
Racine (Wisc.) Weekly Journal
Raleigh Weekly Register
Raleigh Weekly Standard
Richmond Daily Dispatch
Richmond Daily Examiner
Richmond Daily Enquirer
Richmond Daily Whig
Richmond (Ind.) Palladium
Rochester (Ind.) Weekly Sentinel
Rochester (N.Y.) Daily Democrat and American
Rochester (N.Y.) Daily Union and Advertiser
Sandersville Central Georgian
Savannah Republican
Smithport (Pa.) M'Kean County Democrat
Springfield (Mass.) Daily Republican
Times (London)
Washington Daily National Intelligencer
Watertown (N.Y.) Daily News and Reformer
Waukesha (Wisc.) Freeman
Wellsboro (Pa.) Agitator
Wilmington (N.C.) Daily Journal
Winchester (Va.) Times
Yonkers (N.Y.) Examiner

PRINTED PRIMARY SOURCES

Books, Broadsides, Government Publications, and Pamphlets

Abbott, Henry Livermore. *Fallen Leaves: The Civil War Letters of Major Henry Livermore Abbott.* Edited by Robert Garth Scott. Kent, Ohio: Kent State University Press, 1991.

Abernathy, William Meshack. *Our Mess: Southern Gallantry, and Privations.* McKinney, Tex.: McKintex Press, 1977.

Adams, Charles Francis. *A Cycle of Adams Letters, 1861–1865*. 2 vols. Edited by Worthington Chauncey Ford. Boston: Houghton Mifflin, 1920.

Adams, Charles Francis, Jr. *Charles Francis Adams, 1835–1915: An Autobiography*. Boston: Houghton Mifflin, 1916.

Adams, John Gregory Bishop. *Reminiscences of the Nineteenth Massachusetts Regiment*. Boston: Wright and Potter, 1899.

Adams, John Ripley. *Memorial and Letters of Rev. John R. Adams, Chaplain of the Fifth Maine and the One Hundred Twenty-First New York Regiments during the War of the Rebellion*. Privately printed, 1890.

Addresses Delivered before the Confederate Veterans Association of Savannah, Georgia, 1895. Savannah, Ga.: George H. Nichols, 1895.

Adjutant and Inspector General's Office. *General Orders No. 97, December 1, 1862*. N.p., n.d.

———. *General Orders No. 104, December 13, 1862*. N.p., n.d.

Albert, Allen Diehl. *History of the Forty-fifth Regiment Pennsylvania Veteran Volunteer Infantry, 1861–1865*. Williamsport, Pa.: Grit Pub. Co., 1912.

Alcott, Louisa May. *Hospital Sketches*. Edited by Bessie Z. Jones. Cambridge, Mass.: Harvard University Press, 1960.

———. *The Journals of Louisa May Alcott*. Edited by Joel Myerson and Daniel Shealy. Boston: Little, Brown, 1989.

Aldrich, Thomas M. *The History of Battery A, First Regiment Rhode Island Light Artillery in the War to Preserve the Union, 1861–1865*. Providence, R.I.: Snow and Farnham, 1904.

Alexander, Edward Porter. *Fighting for the Confederacy: The Personal Recollections of General Edward Porter Alexander*. Edited by Gary W. Gallagher. Chapel Hill: University of North Carolina Press, 1989.

———. *Military Memoirs of a Confederate: A Critical Narrative*. New York: Da Capo Press, 1993.

Alexander, Ted, ed. *The 126th Pennsylvania*. Shippensburg, Pa.: Beidel Printing House, 1984.

Allan, William. *The Army of Northern Virginia in 1862*. Boston: Houghton Mifflin, 1892.

Allen, George H. *Forty-Six Months with the Fourth R.I. Volunteers in the War of 1861 to 1865*. Providence, R.I.: J. A. and R. A. Reid, 1887.

Allen, Henry A. *Sergeant Allen and Private Renick*. Edited by Martin Litvin. Galesburg, Ill.: Mother Bickerdyke Historical Collection, 1971.

Allen, Ujanirtus. *Campaigning with "Old Stonewall": Confederate Captain Ujanirtus Allen's Letters to His Wife*. Edited by Randall Allen and Keith S. Bohannon. Baton Rouge: Louisiana State University Press, 1998.

Allston, Robert F. W. *The South Carolina Rice Plantation as Revealed in the Papers of Robert F. W. Allston*. Edited by J. H. Easterby. Chicago: University of Chicago Press, 1945.

American Annual Cyclopedia and Register of Important Events, 1862, 1863. New York: Appleton, 1863–64.

Ames, Nelson. *History of Battery G, First Regiment, New York Light Artillery*. Marshalltown, Iowa: Marshall Printing, 1900.

Andrews, W. H. *Footprints of a Regiment: A Recollection of the 1st Georgia Regulars*. Edited by Richard M. McMurry. Atlanta: Longstreet Press, 1992.

Annals of the War. Philadelphia: Times Publishing, 1879.

Armstrong, William H. *Red-Tape and Pigeon-Hole Generals, As Seen from the Ranks during a Campaign of the Army of the Potomac*. New York: Carleton, 1864.

Aschmann, Rudolf. *Memoirs of a Swiss Officer in the American Civil War*. Edited by Heinz K. Meier. Translated by Hedwig D. Rappolt. Bern: Herbert Lang, 1972.

Atlas to Accompany the Official Records of the Union and Confederate Armies. Washington, D.C.: Government Printing Office, 1891–95.

Aubery, Cullen Bullard. *Recollections of a Newsboy in the Army of the Potomac, 1861-1865*. Milwaukee: n.p., 1904.

Auchmuty, Richard Tylden. *Letters of Richard Tylden Auchmuty, Fifth Corps, Army of the Potomac*. Privately printed, 189-.

Ayling, Augustus D. *A Yankee at Arms: The Diary of Lieutenant Augustus D. Ayling, 29th Massachusetts Volunteers*. Edited by Charles F. Herberger. Knoxville: University of Tennessee Press, 1999.

Bacon, William Johnson. *Memorial of William Kirkland Bacon, Late Adjutant of the Twenty-Sixth Regiment of New York State Volunteers*. Utica, N.Y.: Roberts, Printer, 1863.

Bacot, Ada W. *A Confederate Nurse: The Diary of Ada W. Bacot, 1860-1863*. Edited by Jean V. Berlin. Columbia: University of South Carolina Press, 1994.

Baker, Henry H. *A Reminiscent Story of the Great Civil War, Second Paper, a Personal Experience*. New Orleans: Ruskin Press, 1911.

Banes, Charles. *History of the Philadelphia Brigade*. Philadelphia: Lippincott, 1876.

Baquet, Camille. *History of the 1st Brigade, New Jersey Volunteers from 1861 to 1865*. Trenton, N.J.: MacCrellish, State Printers, 1910.

Barber, Charles. *The Civil War Letters of Charles Barber, Private, 104th New York Volunteer Infantry*. Edited by Raymond C. Barber and Mary H. Swanson. Torrance, Calif.: Gary E. Swanson, 1991.

Bardeen, Charles W. *A Little Fifer's Diary*. Syracuse, N.Y.: Printed by the author, 1910.

Barnes, Joseph K. *The Medical and Surgical History of the Civil War*. 15 vols. Wilmington, N.C.: Broadfoot, 1990.

Barnes, Thurlow Weed. *Memoir of Thurlow Weed*. Boston: Houghton Mifflin, 1884.

Bartlett, Asa W. *History of the Twelfth Regiment New Hampshire Volunteers in the War of the Rebellion*. Concord, N.H.: Ira C. Evans, 1897.

Bartlett, John Russell. *Memoirs of Rhode Island Officers Who Were Engaged in the Service of Their Country during the Great Rebellion of the South*. Providence, R.I.: Sidney S. Rider and Brother, 1867.

Bartlett, Napier. *Military Record of Louisiana, Including Biographical and Historical Papers Relating to the Military Organizations of the State*. Baton Rouge: Louisiana State University Press, 1964.

Bartol, Cyrus Augustus. *The Nation's Hour: A Tribute to Major Sidney Willard, Delivered in the West Church, December 21*. Boston: Walker, Wise, 1862.

Barton, Randolph. *Recollections, 1861-1865*. Baltimore: Thomas A. Evans, 1913.

Bassett, H. M. *From Bull Run to Bristow Station*. St. Paul, Minn.: North Central Pub. Co., 1962.

Bates, David Homer. *Lincoln in the Telegraph Office: Recollections of the United States Military Telegraph Corps during the Civil War*. New York: Century Co., 1907.

Bates, Edward. *The Diary of Edward Bates, 1859-1866*. Washington, D.C.: American Historical Association, 1933.

Bates, Samuel Penniman. *A Brief History of the One Hundredth Regiment*. New Castle, Pa.: W. B. Thomas, 1884.

———. *History of the Pennsylvania Volunteers, 1861-1865*. 10 vols. Wilmington, N.C.: Broadfoot, 1993.

Battle-Fields of the South, From Bull Run to Fredericksburgh . . . By an English Combatant. New York: John Bradburn, 1864.

Bayard, Samuel John. *The Life of George Dashell Bayard*. New York: G. P. Putnam's Sons, 1874.

Beale, George William. *A Lieutenant of Cavalry in Lee's Army*. Boston: Gorham Press, 1918.

Beale, Jane Howison. *The Journal of Jane Howison Beale of Fredericksburg, Virginia, 1850-1862*. Fredericksburg, Va.: Historic Fredericksburg Foundation, 1995.

Beecher, Henry Ward. *Patriotic Addresses in America and England from 1850 to 1885.* Edited by John R. Howard. New York: Fords, Howard, and Hulbert, 1891.

Beidelman, George Washington. *The Civil War Letters of George Washington Beidelman.* Edited by Catherine H. Vanderslice. New York: Vantage Press, 1978.

Bellard, Alfred. *Gone for a Soldier: The Civil War Memoirs of Private Alfred Bellard.* Edited by David Herbert Donald. Boston: Little, Brown, 1975.

Benedict, G. G. *Vermont in the Civil War: A History of the Part Taken by the Vermont Soldiers and Sailors in the War for the Union.* 2 vols. Burlington, Vt.: Free Press Association, 1886.

Bengtson, Bradley P., and Julian E. Kuz. *Photographic Atlas of Civil War Injuries.* Grand Rapids, Mich.: Medical Staff Press, 1996.

Bennett, Andrew J. *The Story of the First Massachusetts Light Battery, Attached to the Sixth Army Corps.* Boston: Deland and Barta, 1886.

Bennett, Edwin C. *Musket and Sword, or The Camp, March, and Firing Line in the Army of the Potomac.* Boston: Coburn Pub. Co., 1900.

Bennett, William W. *A Narrative of the Great Revival Which Prevailed in the Southern Armies.* Harrisonburg, Va.: Sprinkle Publications, 1989.

Benson, Berry. *Berry Benson's Civil War Book: Memoirs of a Confederate Scout and Sharpshooter.* Edited by Susan W. Benson. Athens: University of Georgia Press, 1992.

Berkeley, Henry Robinson. *Four Years in the Confederate Artillery: The Diary of Private Henry Robinson Berkeley.* Edited by William H. Runge. Chapel Hill: University of North Carolina Press, 1961.

Betts, Alexander Davis. *Experience of a Confederate Chaplain, 1861–1864.* Edited by W. A. Betts. N.p., n.d.

Bicknell, George W. *History of the Fifth Regiment Maine Volunteers, Comprising Brief Descriptions of its Marches, Engagements, and General Services from the Date of Its Muster in, June 24, 1861 to the Time of its Must Out, July 27, 1864.* Portland, Maine: Hall L. Davis, 1871.

Bigelow, John. *Retrospections of an Active Life.* 5 vols. New York: Baker and Taylor, 1909.

Billings, John D. *Hard Tack and Coffee, or The Unwritten Story of Army Life.* Boston: George M. Smith, 1887.

Bird, Edgeworth, and Sallie Bird. *The Granite Farm Letters: Civil War Correspondence of Edgeworth and Sallie Bird.* Athens: University of Georgia Press, 1988.

Black, Harvey. *A Surgeon with Stonewall Jackson: The Civil War Letters of Dr. Harvey Black.* Edited by Glenn L. McMullen. Baltimore: Butternut and Blue, 1995.

Blackford, L. Minor. *Mine Eyes Have Seen the Glory: The Story of a Virginia Lady, Mary Berkeley Minor Blackford, 1802–1896.* Cambridge, Mass.: Harvard University Press, 1954.

Blackford, Susan Leigh. *Memoirs of Life In and Out of the Army in Virginia During the War Between the States.* 2 vols. Lynchburg, Va.: J. P. Bell, 1894–96.

———, ed. *Letters from Lee's Army; or, Memoirs of Life in and out of the Army in Virginia during the War between the States.* New York: Charles Scribner's Sons, 1947.

Blackford, William Willis. *War Years with Jeb Stuart.* New York: Charles Scribner's Sons, 1945.

Blake, Henry Nicholls. *Three Years in the Army of the Potomac.* Boston: Lee and Shepard, 1865.

Blakeslee, Bernard F. *History of the Sixteenth Connecticut Volunteers.* Hartford, Conn.: Case, Lockwood, and Brainard, 1875.

Bloodgood, John D. *Personal Reminiscences of the War.* New York: Hunt and Eaton, 1893.

Boggs, Marion Alexander, ed. *The Alexander Letters, 1787–1900.* Athens: University of Georgia Press, 1980.

Borden, Winifred, ed. *The Legacy of Fannie and Joseph.* N.p., 1992.

Borton, Benjamin. *Awhile with the Blue; or, Memories of War Days, the True Story of a Private.* Passaic, N.J.: William Taylor, 1898.

———. *On the Parallels; or, Chapters of Inner History, A Story of the Rappahannock.* Woodstown, N.J.: Monitor-Register, 1903.

Bosbyshell, Oliver Christian. *The 48th in the War, Being a Narrative of the 48th Regiment, Infantry, Pennsylvania Veteran Volunteers, during the War of the Rebellion.* Philadelphia: Avil Printing Co., 1895.

Bosse, David. *Civil War Newspaper Maps: A Historical Atlas.* Baltimore: Johns Hopkins University Press, 1993.

Bowen, James Lorenzo. *History of the Thirty-Seventh Regiment Mass. Volunteers, in the Civil War of 1861–1865.* Holyoke, Mass.: Clark W. Bryan, 1884.

Bowen, Roland R. *From Ball's Bluff to Gettysburg . . . and Beyond: The Civil War Letters of Private Roland E. Bowen, 15th Massachusetts Infantry, 1861–1864.* Edited by Gregory A. Coco. Gettysburg, Pa.: Thomas Publications, 1994.

Brainerd, Wesley. *Bridge Building in Wartime: Colonel Wesley Brainerd's Memoir of the 50th New York Volunteer Engineers.* Edited by Ed Malles. Knoxville: University of Tennessee Press, 1997.

Breckinridge, Lucy. *Lucy Breckinridge of Grove Hill: The Journal of a Virginia Girl, 1862–1864.* Edited by Mary D. Robertson. Kent, Ohio: Kent State University Press, 1981.

Brewster, Charles Harvey. *When This Cruel War Is Over: The Civil War Letters of Charles Harvey Brewster.* Edited by David W. Blight. Amherst: University of Massachusetts Press, 1992.

Bright, Adams S., and Michael S. Bright. *"Respects to All": Letters of Two Pennsylvania Boys in the War of the Rebellion.* Edited by Aida Craig Truxall. Pittsburgh: University of Pittsburgh Press, 1962.

Bright, John. *Speeches of John Bright, M.P., on the American Question.* Boston: Little, Brown, 1865.

Brinton, John Hill. *Personal Memoirs of John H. Brinton, Major and Surgeon U.S.V., 1861–1865.* New York: Neale, 1914.

Brogan, Hugh, ed. *The American Civil War: Extracts from the Times, 1860–1865.* London: Times Newspapers, 1975.

Brooks, Noah. *Mr. Lincoln's Washington: Selections from the Writings of Noah Brooks, Civil War Correspondent.* Edited by P. J. Staudenraus. South Brunswick, N.J.: Yoseloff, 1967.

———. *Washington, D.C., in Lincoln's Time.* Edited by Herbert Mitang. Chicago: Quadrangle Books, 1971.

Browning, Orville Hickman. *The Diary of Orville Hickman Browning.* 2 vols. Edited by Theodore Calvin Pease and James G. Randall. Springfield: Illinois State Historical Library, 1925–32.

Buck, Lucy Rebecca. *Shadows of My Heart: The Civil War Diary of Lucy Rebecca Buck.* Edited by Elizabeth R. Baer. Athens: University of Georgia Press, 1997.

Buck, Samuel D. *With the Old Confeds: Actual Experiences of a Captain in the Line.* Baltimore: H. E. Houck, 1925.

Buell, Augustus C. *"The Cannoneer": Recollections of Service in the Army of the Potomac.* Washington, D.C.: National Tribune, 1890.

Buell, Dexter E. *A Brief History of Company B., 27th Regiment N.Y. Volunteers.* Lyons, N.Y.: Office of the Republican, 1874.

Burgwyn, William H. S. *A Captain's War: The Letters and Diaries of William H. S. Burgwyn, 1861–1865.* Edited by Herbert M. Schiller. Shippensburg, Pa.: White Mane, 1994.

Burrage, Henry Sweetser. *History of the Thirty-Sixth Regiment Massachusetts Volunteers, 1862–1865.* Boston: Rockwell and Churchill, 1884.

Burrows, John Lansing. *The Christian Scholar and Soldier: Memoirs of Lewis Minor*

Coleman . . . Lieut. Col. of First Regiment Virginia Artillery. Richmond: Smith, Bailey, 1864.

———. *The New Richmond Theater: A Discourse Delivered on Sunday, February 8, 1863, in the First Baptist Church, Richmond, VA.* Richmond: Smith, Bailey, 1863.

Butler, Benjamin F. *Private and Official Correspondence of Gen. Benjamin F. Butler during the Period of the Civil War.* 5 vols. Edited by Jessie Ames Marshall. Privately printed, 1917.

Caldwell, J. F. J. *The History of a Brigade of South Carolinians Known First as "Gregg's" and Subsequently as "McCowan's Brigade."* Philadelphia: King and Baird, 1866.

Canfield, William A. *A History of William A. Canfield's Experience in the Army.* Manchester, N.H.: Charles F. Livingston, 1869.

Cantrell, Oscar Alexander. *Sketches of the First Regiment Georgia Volunteers together with the History of the 56th Regiment Georgia Volunteers, to January 1, 1864.* Atlanta: Intelligencer Presses, 1864.

Carpenter, Francis Becknell. *The Inner Life of Abraham Lincoln: Six Months at the White House.* New York: Hurd and Houghton, 1870.

Carson, James Petigru. *Life, Letters, and Speeches of James Louis Petigru.* Washington, D.C.: W. H. Lowdermilk, 1920.

Carter, Robert Goldthwaite. *Four Brothers in Blue, or Sunshine and Shadows of the War of the Rebellion: A Story of the Great Civil War from Bull Run to Appomattox.* Austin: University of Texas Press, 1978.

Carter, Sidney. *Dear Bet: The Carter Letters, 1861–1863: The Letters of Lieutenant Sidney Carter, Company A, 14th Regiment, South Carolina Volunteers, Gregg's-McCowan's Brigade, CSA, to Ellen Timmons Carter.* Edited by Bessie Mell Lane. Clemson, S.C.: B. M. Lane, 1978.

Carter, William Giles Harding. *From Yorktown to Santiago with the Sixth U.S. Cavalry.* Baltimore: Lord Baltimore Press, 1900.

Castleman, Alfred Lewis. *The Army of the Potomac, Behind the Scenes: A Diary of Unwritten History, from Organization of the Army by General George McClellan, to the Close of the Campaign in Virginia, during the First Day of January, 1863.* Milwaukee: Strickland and Co., 1863.

Cauthen, Charles Edward, ed. *Family Letters of Three Wade Hamptons, 1782–1901.* Columbia: University of South Carolina Press, 1953.

Cavanagh, Michael. *Memoirs of Gen. Thomas Francis Meagher.* Worcester, Mass.: Messenger Press, 1892.

Cavins, Elijah Henry Clay. *The Civil War Letters of Col. Elijah H. C. Cavins, 14th Indiana.* Compiled by Barbara A. Smith. Owensboro, Ky.: Cook-McDowell, 1981.

Chamberlain, Joshua Lawrence. *Through Blood and Fire: Selected Civil War Papers of Major General Joshua Lawrence Chamberlain.* Mechanicsburg, Pa.: Stackpole, 1996.

Chamberlaine, William W. *Memoirs of the Civil War between Northern and Southern Sections of the United States of America, 1861–1865.* Washington, D.C.: Byron S. Adams, 1912.

Chamberlayne, John Hampden. *Ham Chamberlayne, Virginian: Letters and Papers of an Artillery Officer in the War for Southern Independence.* Richmond: Dietz, 1932.

Chambers, Henry Alexander. *Diary of Captain Henry A. Chambers.* Edited by T. H. Pearce. Wendell, N.C.: Broadfoot's Bookmark, 1983.

Chase, Salmon P. *The Salmon P. Chase Papers.* 4 vols. Kent, Ohio: Kent State University Press, 1993–.

Child, Lydia Maria. *Lydia Maria Child: Selected Letters, 1817–1880.* Edited by Milton Meltzer and Patricia G. Holland. Amherst: University of Massachusetts Press, 1982.

Child, William. *A History of the Fifth New Hampshire Regiment New Hampshire Volunteers, in the American Civil War, 1861–1865.* Bristol, N.H.: R. W. Musgrove, 1893.

Chisolm, J. Julian. *A Manual of Military Surgery for the Use of Surgeons in the Confederate States Army*. 3rd ed. Columbia, S.C.: Evans and Cogswell, 1864.

Circular, Confederate States of America, Surgeon General's Office, November 29, 1862. N.p., n.d.

Clark, George. *A Glance Backward; or, Some Events in the Past History of My Life*. Houston: Rein and Sons, 1914.

Clark, Walter. *Histories of the Several Regiments and Battalions from North Carolina in the Great War, 1861-'65*. 5 vols. Raleigh, N.C.: Nash Brothers, 1901.

———. *The Papers of Walter Clark*. 2 vols. Edited by Aubrey Lee Brooks and Hugh Talmage Lefler. Chapel Hill: University of North Carolina Press, 1948.

Clay-Clopton, Virginia. *A Belle of the Fifties: Memoirs of Mrs. Clay of Alabama, Covering Social and Political Life in Washington and the South, 1863-66*. Edited by Ada Sterling. New York: Doubleday, Page, 1905.

Cochrane, John. *The War for the Union: Memoir of Gen. John Cochrane*. New York: n.p., 1875.

Coffin, Charles Carelton. *The Boys of '61, or Four Years of Fighting with the Army and Navy*. Boston: Dana Estes, 1899.

———. *Four Years of Fighting: A Volume of Personal Observations with the Army and Navy*. Boston: Ticknor and Fields, 1866.

Cogswell, Leander Winslow. *A History of the Eleventh New Hampshire Regiment, Volunteer Infantry, in the Rebellion War, 1861-1865*. Concord, N.H.: Republican Press Association, 1891.

Cole, Jacob Henry. *Under Five Commanders; or, a Boy's Experience with the Army of the Potomac*. Paterson, N.J.: New Print Co., 1906.

Coles, R. T. *From Huntsville to Appomattox: R. T. Coles's History of 4th Regiment, Alabama Volunteer Infantry, C.S.A., Army of Northern Virginia*. Edited by Jeffrey D. Stocker. Knoxville: University of Tennessee Press, 1996.

Conkling, Alfred R. *The Life and Letters of Roscoe Conkling*. New York: Charles L. Webster, 1889.

Contributions to a History of the Richmond Howitzer Battalion, Pamphlets Nos. 2 and 3. Richmond: Carlton and McCarthy, 1883-86.

Conwell, Russell. *Magnolia Journey: A Union Veteran Revisits the Former Confederate States*. Edited by Joseph C. Carter. University: University of Alabama Press, 1974.

Conyngham, Captain D. P. *The Irish Brigade and Its Campaigns*. New York: William McSorley, 1867.

Cook, Benjamin F. *History of the Twelfth Massachusetts Volunteers*. Boston: Twelfth Regiment Association, 1882.

Cooke, John Esten. *A Life of Gen. Robert E. Lee*. New York: Appleton, 1871.

———. *The Life of Stonewall Jackson*. Richmond: Ayres and Wade, 1863.

———. *Wearing of the Gray: Being Personal Portraits, Scenes, and Adventures of the War*. Edited by Philip Van Doren Stern. Bloomington: Indiana University Press, 1959.

Corby, William. *Memoirs of Chaplain Life: Three Years with the Irish Brigade in the Army of the Potomac*. Edited by Lawrence Frederick Kohl. New York: Fordham University Press, 1992.

Corsan, W. C. *Two Months in the Confederate States: An Englishman's Travels through the South*. Baton Rouge: Louisiana State University Press, 1996.

Coward, Asbury. *The South Carolinians: Colonel Asbury Coward's Memoirs*. Edited by Natalie Jenkins Bond and Osmun Latrobe Coward. New York: Vantage Press, 1968.

Cowtan, Charles W. *Services of the Tenth New York Volunteers (National Zouaves) in the War of the Rebellion*. New York: Charles H. Ludwig, 1882.

Cox, Jacob Dolson. *Military Reminiscences of the Civil War.* 2 vols. New York: Charles Scribner's Sons, 1900.

Craft, David. *History of the One Hundred Forty-First Regiment, Pennsylvania Volunteers, 1862–1865.* Towanda, Pa.: Reporter-Journal, 1885.

Croffut, W. A., and John M. Morris. *The Military and Civil History of Connecticut during the War of 1861–65.* New York: Ledyard Bill, 1868.

Crotty, Daniel G. *Four Years Campaigning in the Army of the Potomac.* Grand Rapids, Mich.: Dygert Brothers, 1874.

Crowinshield, Benjamin William. *A History of the First Regiment of Massachusetts Cavalry Volunteers.* Boston: Houghton Mifflin, 1891.

Cudworth, Warren Handel. *History of the First Regiment (Massachusetts Infantry) from the 25th of May, 1861 to the 25th of May, 1864.* Boston: Walker, Fuller, 1866.

Cumming, Kate. *Kate: The Journal of a Confederate Nurse.* Edited by Richard Barksdale Harwell. Baton Rouge: Louisiana State University Press, 1959.

Curtis, Newton Martin. *From Bull Run to Chancellorsville: The Story of the Sixteenth New York Infantry.* New York: G. P. Putnam's Sons, 1906.

Curtis, Orson Blair. *History of the Twenty-Fourth Michigan of the Iron Brigade, Known as the Detroit and Wayne County Regiment.* Detroit: Winn and Hammond, 1891.

Cutcheon, Byron Mac. *The Story of the Twentieth Michigan Infantry, July 15th, 1862, to May 30th, 1865.* Lansing, Mich.: Robert Smith Printing Co., 1904.

Cutler, Julia P. *Life and Times of Ephraim Cutler.* Cincinnati: Robert Clarke and Co., 1890.

Cutrer, Thomas W., and T. Michael Parrish, eds. *Brothers in Gray: The Civil War Letters of the Pierson Family.* Baton Rouge: Louisiana State University Press, 1997.

Dabney, Robert Lewis. *Life and Campaigns of Lieut.-Gen. Thomas J. Jackson.* Harrisonburg, Va.: Sprinkle Publications, 1983.

Daly, Maria Lydig. *Diary of a Union Lady, 1861–1865.* Edited by Harold Earl Hammond. New York: Funk and Wagnalls, 1962.

Dana, Charles A. *Recollections of the Civil War.* New York: Appleton, 1898.

Daniel, Frederick S. *Richmond Howitzers in the War: Four Years Campaigning with the Army of Northern Virginia.* Richmond: n.p., 1891.

Davenport, Alfred A. *Camp and Field Life of the Fifth New York Volunteer Infantry (Duryee Zouaves).* New York: Dick and Fitzgerald, 1879.

Davidson, Greenlee. *Captain Greenlee Davidson, C.S.A.: Diary and Letters, 1851–1863.* Verona, Va.: McClure Press, 1975.

Davis, Charles E. *Three Years in the Army: The Story of Thirteenth Massachusetts Volunteers, from July 16, 1861, to August 1, 1864.* Boston: Estes and Lauriat, 1894.

Davis, Jefferson. *The Papers of Jefferson Davis.* 10 vols. Edited by Lynda Lasswell Crist and Mary Seaton Dix. Baton Rouge: Louisiana State University Press, 1995.

[Davis, Oliver Wilson]. *Life of David Bell Birney, Major-General, United States Volunteers.* Philadelphia: King and Baird, 1867.

Davis, Rev. Nicholas A. *The Campaigns from Texas to Maryland.* Richmond: Office of the Presbyterian Committee of Publication of the Confederate States, 1863.

Dawes, Rufus Robinson. *Service with the Sixth Wisconsin Volunteers.* Marietta, Ohio: E. R. Alderman and Sons, 1890.

Dawson, Francis Warrington. *Reminiscences of Confederate Service, 1861–1865.* Edited by Bell I. Wiley. Baton Rouge: Louisiana State University Press, 1980.

Dawson, Sarah Morgan. *Sarah Morgan Dawson: The Civil War Diary.* Edited by Charles East. Athens: University of Georgia Press, 1991.

Day, William A. *A True History of Company I, 49th Regiment, North Carolina Troops, in the Great Civil War between the North and the South.* Newton, N.C.: Enterprise Job Office, 1893.

DeLeon, T. C. *Four Years in Rebel Capitals*. Mobile, Ala.: Gossip Printing Co., 1890.

Denison, Frederic. *Sabres and Spurs: The First Regiment Rhode Island Cavalry in the Civil War, 1861–1865*. Baltimore: Butternut and Blue, 1994.

DeNoon, Charles E. *Charlie's Letters: The Correspondence of Charles E. DeNoon*. Edited by Richard T. Couture. Farmville, Va.: R. Couture, 1982.

Dexter, Seymour. *Seymour Dexter, Union Army: Journal and Letters of Civil War Service in Company K, 23rd New York Volunteer Regiment of Elmira, with Illustrations*. Edited by Carl A. Morrell. Jefferson, N.C.: McFarland and Co., 1996.

Dicey, Edward. *Spectator of America*. Edited by Herbert Mitang. Chicago: Quadrangle Books, 1971.

Dickert, D. Augustus. *History of Kershaw's Brigade, with Complete Roll of Companies, Biographical Sketches, Incidents, Anecdotes, Etc*. Newberry, S.C.: Elbert H. Aull, 1899.

Diman, George Waters. *Autobiography and Sketches of My Travels by Sea and Land*. Bristol, R.I.: Semi-Weekly Bristol Phoenix, 1896.

Dinkins, James. *1861 65, by an Old Johnnie: Personal Recollections and Experiences in the Confederate Army*. Dayton, Ohio: Morningside, 1975.

Dobbins, Austin C. *Grandfather's Journal: Company B, Sixteenth Mississippi Infantry Volunteers Harris' Brigade, Anderson's Division, A.N.V.* Dayton, Ohio: Morningside, 1988.

Donaldson, Francis Adams. *Inside the Army of the Potomac: The Civil War Experience of Captain Francis Adams Donaldson*. Edited by J. Gregory Acken. Mechanicsburg, Pa.: Stackpole, 1998.

Dooley, John Edward. *John Dooley, Confederate Soldier: His War Journal*. Edited by Joseph T. Durkin. Notre Dame, Ind.: University of Notre Dame Press, 1983.

Doster, William Emile. *Lincoln and Episodes of the Civil War*. New York: G. P. Putnam's Sons, 1915.

Douglas, Henry Kyd. *I Rode with Stonewall, being Chiefly the War Experiences of the Youngest Member of Jackson's Staff from the John Brown Raid to the Hanging of Mrs. Surratt*. Chapel Hill: University of North Carolina Press, 1940.

Douglas, J. H., and C. M. Brink. *Reports of the Operations of the Inspectors and Relief Agents of the Sanitary Commission after the Battle of Fredericksburg*. New York: William C. Byant, 1863.

Douglass, Frederick. *Life and Times of Frederick Douglass*. Cleveland: George M. Rewell, 1883.

———. *The Life and Writings of Frederick Douglass*. 5 vols. Edited by Philip S. Foner. New York: International Publishers, 1952.

Dunaway, Wayland Fuller. *Reminiscences of a Rebel*. New York: Neale, 1913.

Duncan, Louis C. *The Medical Department of the United States Army in the Civil War*. Gaithersburg, Md.: Olde Soldier Books, 1987.

Du Pont, Samuel Francis. *Samuel Francis Du Pont: A Selection from His Civil War Letters*. 3 vols. Edited by John D. Hayes. Ithaca, N.Y.: Cornell University Press, 1969.

Dyer, Gustavus W., and John Trotwood Moore. *The Tennessee Civil War Veterans Questionnaires*. 5 vols. Easley, S.C.: Southern Historical Press, 1985.

Early, Jubal Anderson. *Narrative of the War between the States*. New York: Da Capo Press, 1989.

Edmonds, Amanda Virginia. *Journals of Amanda Virginia Edmonds: Lass of the Mosby Confederacy, 1859–1867*. Edited by Nancy Chapplear Baird. Stephens City, Va.: Commercial Press, 1984.

Edmonds, Howard Owen. *Owen-Edmonds, Incidents of the American Civil War, 1861–1865*. Chicago: Lakeside Press, 1928.

Edmonds, Sarah Emma Evelyn. *Nurse and Spy in the Union Army*. Hartford, Mich.: W. S. Williams, 1865.

Edmondson, James K. *My Dear Emma: War Letters of Col. James K. Edmondson, 1861–1865*. Edited by Charles Turner. Verona, Va.: McClure Press, 1978.

Edmondston, Catherine Ann Devereux. *"Journal of a Secesh Lady": The Diary of Catherine Ann Devereux Edmondston*. Edited by Beth G. Crabtree and James W. Patton. Raleigh, N.C.: Division of Archives, 1979.

Edwards, Abiel Hall. *"Dear Friend Anna": The Civil War Letters of a Common Soldier from Maine*. Edited by Beverly Hayes Kallgren and James L. Crouthamel. Orono: University of Maine Press, 1992.

Edwards, John Frank. *Army Life of Frank Edwards, Confederate Veteran, Army of Northern Virginia*. LaGrange, Ga.: n.p., 1911.

Ely, Ralph. *With the Wandering Regiment: The Diary of Captain Ralph Ely of the Eighth Michigan Infantry*. Edited by George M. Blackburn. Mount Pleasant: Central Michigan University Press, 1965.

Eppes, Susan Bradford. *Through Some Eventful Years*. Gainesville: University of Florida Press, 1968.

Evans, Clement Anselm. *Intrepid Warrior: Clement Anselm Evans, Confederate General from Georgia: Life, Letters, and Diaries of the War Years*. Edited by Robert Grier Stephens Jr. Dayton, Ohio: Morningside, 1994.

———, ed. *Confederate Military History*. Extended ed. 17 vols. Wilmington, N.C.: Broadfoot, 1987.

Fairchild, Charles Bryant. *History of the 27th Regiment N.Y. Vols., Being a Record of its More than Two Years of Service in the War for the Union*. Binghamton, N.Y.: Carl and Matthews, 1888.

Favill, Josiah Marshall. *The Diary of a Young Officer Serving with the Armies of the United States during the War of the Rebellion*. Chicago: R. R. Donnelley, 1909.

Fessenden, Francis. *Life and Public Services of William Pitt Fessenden*. 2 vols. Boston: Houghton Mifflin, 1907.

Fifth Annual Report of the Chief of the Bureau of Military Statistics. Albany, N.Y.: C. Van Benthuysen, 1868.

Figg, Royal W. *"Where Men Only Dare to Go!" or, the Story of a Boy Company (C.S.A.)*. Richmond: Whittet and Shepperson, 1885.

Fisher, Sidney George. *A Philadelphia Perspective: The Diary of Sidney George Fisher Covering the Years 1834–1871*. Edited by Nicholas B. Wainwright. Philadelphia: Historical Society of Pennsylvania, 1967.

Fiske, Samuel Wheelock. *Mr. Dunn Browne's Experiences in the Army*. Boston: Nichols and Noyes, 1866.

Fitzpatrick, Marion Hill. *Letters to Amanda: The Civil War Letters of Marion Hill Fitzpatrick, Army of Northern Virginia*. Edited by Jeffrey C. Lowe and Sam Hodges. Macon, Ga.: Mercer University Press, 1998.

Fleet, Betsey, and John D. P. Fuller, eds. *Green Mount: A Virginia Plantation Family during the Civil War*. Lexington: University Press of Kentucky, 1962.

Fleming, Francis Philip. *Memoir of Capt. C. Seton Fleming of the Second Florida Infantry, C.S.A.* Jacksonville, Fla.: Times-Union Publishing House, 1884.

Fleming, George Thornton, ed. *Life and Letters of Alexander Hays*. Pittsburgh: Gilbert Adams Hays, 1919.

Fletcher, William A. *Rebel Private: Front and Rear*. Edited by Bell I. Wiley. Austin: University of Texas Press, 1954.

Floyd, Frederick Clark. *History of the Fortieth (Mozart) Regiment, New York Volunteers*. Boston: F. H. Gibson, 1909.

Folsom, James Madison. *Heroes and Martyrs of Georgia: Georgia's Record in the Revolution of 1861*. Macon, Ga.: Burke, Boykin, 1864.

Fonerden, Clarence Albert. *A Brief History of the Military Career of Carpenter's Battery.* New Market, Va.: Henkel and Co., 1911.

Forbes, Edwin. *Thirty Years After: An Artist's Memoir of the Civil War.* Edited by William J. Cooper Jr. Baton Rouge: Louisiana State University Press, 1993.

Ford, Andrew Elmer. *The Story of the Fifteenth Regiment Massachusetts Volunteer Infantry in the Civil War, 1861–1864.* Clinton, Mass.: W. J. Coulter, 1898.

Fort, John Porter. *John Porter Fort, a Memorial and Personal Reminiscences.* New York: Knickerbocker Press, 1918.

Foster, John G. *New Jersey and the Rebellion: History of the Services of the Troops and People of New Jersey in Aid of the Union Cause.* Newark, N.J.: Martin R. Dennis, 1868.

Fourth Annual Report of the Bureau of Military Statistics. Albany, N.Y.: C. Van Benthuysen, 1867.

Fox, Gustavus Vasa. *Confidential Correspondence of Gustavus Vasa Fox, Assistant Secretary of the Navy, 1861–1865.* 2 vols. Edited by Robert Means Thompson and Richard Wainwright. Freeport, N.Y.: Books for Libraries Press, 1972.

Frederick, Gilbert. *The Story of a Regiment, Being a Record of the Military Services of the Fifty-Seventh New York State Volunteer Infantry in the War of the Rebellion, 1861–1865.* Chicago: C. H. Morgan, 1895.

Freeman, Warren Hapgood. *Letters from Two Brothers Serving in the War for the Union.* Cambridge, Mass.: H. O. Houghton, 1871.

Freidel, Frank, ed. *Union Pamphlets of the Civil War.* 2 vols. Cambridge, Mass.: Harvard University Press, 1967.

French, Benjamin Brown. *Witness to the Young Republic: A Yankee's Journal, 1828–1870.* Edited by Donald B. Cole and John J. McDonough. Hanover, N.H.: University Press of New England, 1989.

Frobel, Anne S. *The Civil War Diary of Anne S. Frobel of Wilton Hill, Virginia.* Edited by Mary H. Lancaster and Dallas M. Lancaster. Florence, Ala.: Birmingham Printing and Publishing, 1986.

Fuller, Charles Augustus. *Personal Recollections of the War of 1861, as Private, Sergeant and Lieutenant in the Sixty-first Regiment, New York Volunteer Infantry.* Sherburne, N.Y.: News Job Printing House, 1906.

Fuller, Edward H. *Battles of the Seventy-seventh New York State Foot Volunteers, Third Brigade, Sixth Corps, Second Division.* Gloversville: n.p., 1901.

Fuller, Richard Frederick. *Chaplain Fuller, Being a Life Sketch of a New England Clergyman and Army Chaplain.* Boston: Walker, Wise, 1863.

Fulton, William F. *The War Reminiscences of William F. Fulton, Fifth Alabama Battalion, Archer's Brigade, A P Hill's Light Division.* Gaithersburg, Md.: Butternut Press, 1986.

Galwey, Thomas Francis. *The Valiant Hours: Narrative of "Captain Brevet," an Irish-American in the Army of the Potomac.* Edited by W. S. Nye. Harrisburg, Pa.: Stackpole, 1961.

Garfield, James A. *The Wild Life of the Army: Civil War Letters of James A. Garfield.* Edited by Frederick D. Williams. East Lansing: Michigan State University Press, 1964.

Gates, Theodore Burr. *The Civil War Diaries of Col. Theodore B. Gates, 20th New York State Militia.* Hightstown, N.J.: Longstreet House, 1991.

———. *The "Ulster Guard" [20th N.Y. State Militia] and the War of the Rebellion.* New York: Benjamin H. Tyrrel, 1879.

Gearhart, Edwin R. *Reminiscences of the Civil War.* Stroudsburg, Pa.: Daily Record Press, 1901.

Geary, John White. *A Politician Goes to War: The Civil War Letters of John White Geary.* Edited by William Alan Blair. University Park: Pennsylvania State University Press, 1995.

General Orders Nos. 126, 127, 138, Army of Northern Virginia, November 12, 14, December 31, 1862. N.p., n.d.

Gerrish, Theodore. *Army Life: A Private's Reminiscences of the Civil War.* Portland, Maine: Hoyt, Fogg, and Donham, 1882.

Gibbon, John. *Personal Recollections of the Civil War.* New York: G. P. Putnam's Sons, 1928.

Giles, Valerius Cincinnatus. *Rags and Hope: The Recollections of Val C. Giles, Four Years with Hood's Brigade, Fourth Texas Infantry, 1861–1865.* Edited by Mary Lasswell. New York: Coward-McCann, 1961.

Glazier, Willard. *Three Years in the Federal Cavalry.* New York: R. H. Ferguson and Co., 1870.

Glenn, William Wilkins. *Between North and South: A Maryland Journalist Views the Civil War.* Rutherford, N.J.: Fairleigh Dickinson University Press, 1976.

Gobright, L. A. *Recollection of Men and Things at Washington.* Philadelphia: Claxton, Remsen, and Haffelfinger, 1869.

Goddard, Samuel A. *Letters on the American Rebellion.* 1870. Reprint, New York: Books for Libraries Press, 1971.

Goss, Warren Lee. *Recollections of a Private.* New York: Thomas Y. Crowell, 1890.

Gould, Benjamin Apthorp. *Investigations in the Military and Anthropological Statistics of American Soldiers.* New York: Hurd and Houghton, 1869.

Gould, Joseph. *The Story of the Forty-eighth: A Record of the Campaigns of the Forty-eighth Regiment Pennsylvania Veteran Volunteer Infantry.* Philadelphia: Alfred M. Slocum, 1908.

Gracey, Samuel L. *Annals of the Sixth Pennsylvania Cavalry.* Philadelphia: E. H. Butler, 1868.

Graham, Matthew John. *The Ninth Regiment, New York Volunteers (Hawkins' Zouaves), Being a History of the Regiment and Veteran Association, from 1860 to 1900.* New York: E. P. Corby, 1900.

Grant, Joseph E. *The Flying Regiment: Journal of the Campaign of the 12th Regt. Rhode Island Volunteers.* Providence, R.I.: Sidney S. Rider and Brothers, 1865.

Graves, Henry Lea. *A Confederate Marine: A Sketch of Henry Lea Graves with Excerpts from the Graves Family Correspondence, 1861–1865.* Tuscaloosa, Ala.: Confederate Pub. Co., 1963.

Gray, John Chipman, and John Codman Ropes. *War Letters, 1862–1865.* Edited by Worthington C. Ford. Boston: Houghton Mifflin, 1927.

Grayson, William J. *Witness to Sorrow: The Antebellum Autobiography of William J. Grayson.* Edited by Richard J. Calhoun. Columbia: University of South Carolina Press, 1990.

Greeley, Horace. *The American Conflict: A History of the Great Rebellion in the United States of America, 1860–65.* 2 vols. Hartford, Conn.: O. D. Case, 1866.

Greene, John T., ed. *The Ewing Family Civil War Letters.* East Lansing: Michigan State University Press, 1994.

Gregg, J. Chandler. *Life in the Army, in the Departments of Virginia, and the Gulf.* 2nd ed. Philadelphia: Perkinpine and Higgins, 1868.

Grew, William. *Fredericksburg, December 13, 1862.* Broadside signed by William Grew, private, Co. I, 114th P.V., Regimental Historian. Copy in Henry E. Huntington Library, San Marino, Calif.

Grimes, Bryan. *Extracts of Letters of Major-General Bryan Grimes to His Wife, Written While in Active Service in the Army of Northern Virginia. Together with Some Personal Recollections of the War, Written by Him after Its Close, etc.* Edited by Gary W. Gallagher. Wilmington, N.C.: Broadfoot, 1986.

Grow, Milo. *Milo Grow's Letters from the Civil War.* Lake Seminde, Ga.: Privately printed for the Grow Family Reunion, 1986.

Guiney, Patrick R. *Commanding Boston's Irish Ninth: The Civil War Letters of Colonel*

Patrick R. Guiney, Ninth Massachusetts Volunteer Infantry. Edited by Christian G. Samito.
New York: Fordham University Press, 1998.

Hackett, Horatio Balch. *Christian Memorials of the War; or, Scenes and Incidents Illustrative of Religious Faith and Principle, Patriotism, Bravery of our Army.* Boston: Guild and Lincoln, 1864.

Hadley, Amos. *Life of Walter Harriman, with Selections from His Speeches and Writings.* Boston: Houghton Mifflin, 1888.

Haerrer, William. *With Drum and Gun in '61: A Narrative of the Adventures of William Haerrer of the Fourteenth New York State Volunteers.* Greenville, Pa.: Beaver Print Co., 1908.

Haines, Alanson A. *History of the 15th New Jersey Volunteer Infantry.* New York: Jenkins and Thomas, 1883.

Haley, John. *The Rebel Yell and the Yankee Hurrah: The Civil War Journal of a Maine Volunteer.* Edited by Ruth L. Silliker. Camden, Maine: Down East Books, 1985.

Hall, Isaac. *History of the Ninety-Seventh Regiment, New York Volunteers in the War for the Union.* Utica, N.Y.: L. C. Childs and Son, 1890.

Hall, James Edmond. *The Diary of a Confederate Soldier: James E. Hall.* Edited by Ruth Woods Dayton. Lewisburg, W.Va.: n.p., 1961.

Halsey, Edmund. *Brother against Brother. The Lost Civil War Diary of Lt. Edmund Halsey.* Edited by Bruce Chadwick. Secaucus, N.J.: Birch Lane Press, 1997.

Halsey, Thomas J. *Field of Battle: The Civil War Letters of Thomas J. Halsey.* Washington, D.C.: National Geographic Society, 1996.

Hamlin, Charles Eugene. *The Life and Times of Hannibal Hamlin.* 2 vols. Port Washington, N.Y.: Kennikat Press, 1971.

Hancock, Almira R. *Reminiscences of Winfield Scott Hancock.* New York: Charles L. Webster, 1887.

Handerson, Henry Ebenezer. *Yankee in Gray: The Civil War Memoirs of Henry E. Handerson, with a Selection of His Wartime Letters.* Cleveland: Press of Western Reserve University, 1962.

Hanifen, Michael. *History of Battery B, 1st New Jersey Artillery.* Hightstown, N.J.: Longstreet House, 1991.

Harper, Douglas R. *"If Thee Must Fight": A Civil War History of Chester County, Pennsylvania.* West Chester, Pa.: Chester County Historical Society, 1990.

Harrison, Walter. *Pickett's Men: A Fragment of War History.* New York: Van Nostrand, 1870.

Hartsock, Andrew Jackson. *Soldier of the Cross: The Civil War Diary and Correspondence of Rev. Andrew Jackson Hartsock.* Edited by James C. Duram and Eleanor A. Duram. Manhattan, Kans.: Military Affairs/Aerospace Historian, 1979.

Hartwell, John F. L. *To My Beloved Wife and Boy at Home: The Letters and Diaries of Orderly Sergeant John F. L. Hartwell.* Edited by Ann Hartwell Britton and Thomas J. Reed. Madison, N.J.: Fairleigh Dickinson University Press, 1998.

Haskell, John Cheeves. *The Haskell Memoirs.* Edited by Gilbert E. Govan and James W. Livingood. New York: Putnam, 1960.

Haskin, William L. *The History of the First Regiment of Artillery.* Portland, Maine: B. Thurston and Co., 1879.

Haupt, Herman. *Reminiscences of General Herman Haupt.* Milwaukee: Wrights and Joys, 1901.

Hay, John. *Lincoln and the Civil War in the Diaries and Letters of John Hay.* Edited by Tyler Dennett. New York: Dodd, Meade, 1939.

———. *Lincoln's Journalist: John Hay's Anonymous Writings for the Press, 1860–1864.* Edited by Michael Burlingame. Carbondale: Southern Illinois University Press, 1998.

Haydon, Charles B. *For Country, Cause, and Leader: The Civil War Journal of Charles B. Haydon*. Edited by Stephen W. Sears. New York: Ticknor and Fields, 1993.

Haynes, Draughton Stith. *The Field Diary of a Confederate Soldier*. Darien, Ga.: Ashantilly Press, 1963.

Haynes, Martin A. *A History of the Second Regiment, New Hampshire Volunteer Infantry in the War of the Rebellion*. Lakeport, N.H.: privately printed, 1896.

———. *A Minor War History, Compiled from a Soldier Boy's Letters to "The Girl I Left Behind Me," 1861–1864*. Lakeport, N.H.: Private print of Martin A. Haynes, 1916.

Hays, Gilbert Adams. *Under the Red Patch: Story of the Sixty-Third Regiment Pennsylvania Volunteers, 1861–1864*. Pittsburgh: Market Review Pub. Co., 1908.

Headley, P. C. *Massachusetts in the Rebellion*. Boston: Walker, Fuller, 1866.

Heller, J. Roderick, III, and Carolynn Ayres Heller, eds. *The Confederacy Is on Her Way up the Spout: Letters to South Carolina, 1861–1864*. Athens: University of Georgia Press, 1992.

Hill, Benjamin, Jr. *Senator Benjamin H. Hill of Georgia, His Life, Speeches and Writings*. Atlanta: H. C. Hudgins, 1891.

Hill, Lois, ed. *Poems and Songs of the Civil War*. New York: Fairfax Press, 1990.

Hirst, Benjamin. *The Boys from Rockville: Civil War Narratives of Sgt. Benjamin G. Hirst, Company D, 14th Connecticut Volunteers*. Edited by Robert L. Bee. Knoxville: University of Tennessee Press, 1998.

A Historical Sketch of the Quitman Guards, Company E, Sixteenth Mississippi Regiment, Harris' Brigade. New Orleans: Isaac T. Hinton, 1866.

History of the 121st Regiment Pennsylvania Volunteers. Rev. ed. Philadelphia: Catholic Standard and Times, 1906.

History of the 127th Regiment Pennsylvania Volunteers, Familiarly Known as the "Dauphin County Regiment." Lebanon, Pa.: Report Pub. Co., 1902.

History of the Fifth Massachusetts Battery. Boston: Luther E. Cowles, 1902.

History of the Fifty-Seventh Regiment, Pennsylvania Veteran Volunteer Infantry, First Brigade, First Division, Third Corps, and Second Brigade, Third Division, Second Corps, Army of the Potomac. Meadville, Pa.: McCoy and Calvin, 1904.

History of the First Regiment Minnesota Volunteer Infantry, 1861–1864. Stillwater, Minn.: Easton and Masterman, 1916.

History of the Sixth New York Cavalry (Second Ira Harris Guard), Second Brigade, First Division, Cavalry Corps, Army of the Potomac, 1861–1865. Worcester, Mass.: Blanchard Press, 1908.

History of the Third Pennsylvania Cavalry, Sixtieth Regiment Pennsylvania Volunteers in the American Civil War. Philadelphia: Franklin Printing, 1905.

History of the Thirty-Fifth Regiment Massachusetts Volunteers, 1862–1865. Boston: Mills, Knight, 1884.

Hitchcock, Frederick Lyman. *War from the Inside: The Story of the 132nd. Regiment Pennsylvania Volunteer Infantry in the War for the Suppression of the Rebellion, 1862–1863*. Philadelphia: Lippincott, 1904.

Hodgkins, J. E. *The Civil War Diary of Lieut. J. E. Hodgkins: 19th Massachusetts Volunteers from August 11, 1862 to June 3, 1865*. Camden, Maine: Picton Press, 1994.

Hollister, O. J. *Life of Schuyler Colfax*. New York: Funk and Wagnalls, 1886.

Holmes, Emma. *The Diary of Miss Emma Holmes*. Edited by John F. Marszalek. Baton Rouge: Louisiana State University Press, 1979.

Holmes, Oliver Wendell. *Touched with Fire: Civil War Letters and Diary of Oliver Wendell Holmes, Jr., 1861–1864*. Edited by Mark de Wolfe Howe. Cambridge, Mass.: Harvard University Press, 1946.

Holt, Daniel M. *A Surgeon's Civil War: The Letters and Diary of Daniel M. Holt*. Edited by

James M. Greiner, Janet L. Coryell, and James R. Smither. Kent, Ohio: Kent State University Press, 1994.

Holt, David. *A Mississippi Rebel in the Army of Northern Virginia: The Civil War Memoirs of Private Daniel Holt.* Edited by Thomas D. Cockrell and Michael B. Ballard. Baton Rouge: Louisiana State University Press, 1996.

Holt, John Lee. *I Wrote You Word: The Poignant Letters of Private Holt.* Edited by James A. Mumper. Lynchburg, Va.: H. E. Howard, 1991.

Hood, John Bell. *Advance and Retreat: Personal Experiences in the United States and Confederate States Armies.* Edited by Richard N. Current. Bloomington: Indiana University Press, 1959.

Hopkins, William P. *The Seventh Regiment Rhode Island Volunteers in the Civil War, 1861–1865.* Providence, R.I.: Providence Press, 1903.

Hotchkiss, Jedediah. *Make Me a Map of the Valley: The Civil War Journal of Stonewall Jackson's Topographer.* Edited by Archie P. McDonald. Dallas: Southern Methodist University Press, 1973.

Houghton, Edwin B. *The Campaigns of the Seventeenth Maine.* Portland, Maine; Short and Loring, 1866.

House Bill No. 20. January 13, 1863. Richmond: n.p., 1863.

House Bill No. 25, January 13, 1863. Richmond: n.p., 1863.

Howard, Oliver Otis. *Autobiography of Oliver Otis Howard.* 2 vols. New York: Baker and Taylor, 1907.

Hubbell, Raynor. *Confederate Stamps, Old Letters, and History.* Griffin, Ga.: n.p., 1959.

Humphreys, Henry Hollingsworth. *Major General Andrew Atkinson Humphreys at Fredericksburg, Va., December 13th, 1862, and Farmville, Va., April 7, 1865.* Chicago: R. R. McCabe and Co., 1896.

Hunt, Gaillard. *Israel, Elihu, and Cadwallader Washburn: A Chapter in American Biography.* New York: Macmillan, 1925.

Hunter, Alexander. *Johnny Reb and Billy Yank.* New York: Neale, 1905.

Hutchinson, Gustavus B. *A Narrative of the Formation and Services of the Eleventh Massachusetts Volunteers.* Boston: Alfred Mudge and Sons, 1893.

Hutchinson, Nelson V. *History of the Seventh Massachusetts Volunteer Infantry in the War of the Rebellion.* Taunton, Mass.: Ezra Davol, 1890.

Hyde, Thomas Worcester. *Following the Greek Cross; or, Memories of the Sixth Army Corps.* Boston: Houghton Mifflin, 1894.

Hyndman, William. *History of a Cavalry Company: A Complete Record of Company "A," 4th Penn'a Cavalry.* Philadelphia: James B. Rodgers, 1870.

Irby, Richard. *The Captain Remembers: The Papers of Captain Richard Irby.* Edited by Virginia Fitzgerald Jordan. Blackstone, Va.: Nottoway County Historical Association, 1975.

———. *Historical Sketch of the Nottoway Grays, Afterwards Company G, Eighteenth Virginia Regiment, Army of Northern Virginia.* Richmond: J. W. Fergusson and Son, 1878.

Jackman, Lyman. *History of the Sixth New Hampshire Regiment in the War for the Union.* Concord, N.H.: Republican Press Association, 1891.

Jackson, Edgar Allan. *Three Rebels Write Home.* Franklin, Va.: News Pub. Co., 1955.

Jackson, Mary Anna. *Life and Letters of General Thomas J. Jackson.* New York: Harper and Brothers, 1892.

Jaques, John Wesley. *Three Years' Campaign of the Ninth N.Y.S.M. during the Southern Rebellion.* New York: Hilton and Co., 1865.

Johnson, Robert Underwood, and Clarence Clough Buel, eds. *Battles Leaders of the Civil War.* 4 vols. New York: Castle Books, 1956.

Johnston, David Emmons. *The Story of a Confederate Boy in the Civil War.* Portland, Ore.: Glass and Prudhomme, 1914.

Johnston, Terry A., ed. *"Him on the One Side and Me on the Other": The Civil War Letters of Alexander Campbell, 79th New York Infantry Regiment, and James Campbell, 1st South Carolina Battalion.* Columbia: University of South Carolina Press, 1999.

Jones, Evan Rowland. *Four Years in the Army of the Potomac: A Soldier's Recollections.* London: Tyne Pub. Co., 1881.

Jones, J. B. *A Rebel War Clerk's Diary at the Confederate States Capital.* 2 vols. Philadelphia: Lippincott, 1866.

Jones, John William. *Christ in the Camp, or Religion in Lee's Army.* Richmond: B. F. Johnson, 1887.

———. *Life and Letters of Robert Edward Lee: Soldier and Man.* New York: Neale, 1906.

———. *Personal Reminiscences of General Robert E. Lee.* Richmond: United States Historical Society Press, 1989.

Jones, Katharine M., ed. *Ladies of Richmond.* Indianapolis: Bobbs-Merrill, 1962.

Jones, Terry L., ed. *The Civil War Memoirs of Captain William J. Seymour: Reminiscences of a Louisiana Tiger.* Baton Rouge: Louisiana State University Press, 1991.

Joslyn, Mauriel Phillips, ed. *Charlotte's Boys: Civil War Letters of the Branch Family of Savannah.* Berryville, Va.: Rockbridge Publishing, 1996.

Journal of the Called Session, 1862, and the Second Regular Annual Session of the Senate of the State of Alabama. Montgomery, Ala.: Montgomery Advertiser Book and Job Office, 1863.

Journal of the House of Representatives of the State of Mississippi, December Session of 1862, and November Session of 1863. Jackson, Miss.: Cooper and Kimball, 1864.

Journal of the House of Representatives of the State of South Carolina, Being the Session of 1862. Columbia, S.C.: Charles P. Pelham, 1862.

Journal of the Senate of South Carolina, Being the Session of 1862. Columbia, S.C.: Charles P. Pelham, 1862.

Journal of the Senate of the State of Georgia, at the Annual Session of the General Assembly . . . 1862. Milledgeville, Ga.: Houghton, Nisbet, and Barnes, 1862.

Judd, David Wright. *The Story of the Thirty-Third N.Y.S. Vol.; or, Two Years Campaigning in Virginia and Maryland.* Rochester, N.Y.: Benton and Andrews, 1864.

Judson, Amos M. *History of the Eighty-third Regiment Pennsylvania Volunteers.* Dayton, Ohio: Morningside, 1986.

Julian, George W. *Political Recollections, 1840 to 1872.* Westport, Conn.: Negro Universities Press, 1970.

Kean, Robert Garlick Hill. *Inside the Confederate Government: The Diary of Robert Garlick Hill Kean.* Edited by Edward Younger. New York: Oxford University Press, 1957.

Kennedy, Joseph C. G. *Agriculture of the United States in 1860; Compiled from the Original Returns of the Eighth Census.* Washington, D.C.: Government Printing Office, 1864.

———. *Population of the United States in 1860; Compiled from the Original Returns of the Eighth Census.* Washington, D.C.: Government Printing Office, 1864.

Kepler, William. *History of the Three Months' and Three Years' Service, from April 16, 1861, to June 22d, 1864, of the Fourth Regiment Ohio Volunteer Infantry in the War for the Union.* Cleveland: Leader Printing, 1886.

Kerbey, Major J. O. *On the War-Path: A Journey over the Historic Grounds of the Late Civil War.* Chicago: Donohue, Henneberry, 1890.

Kimball, Orville Samuel. *History and Personal Sketches of Company I, 103 N.Y.S.V., 1862–1864.* Elmira, N.Y.: Facts Print, 1900.

King, Edward. *The Great South.* Edited by W. Magruder Drake and Robert R. Jones. Baton Rouge: Louisiana State University Press, 1972.

Kress, John Alexander. *Memoirs of Brigadier General John Alexander Kress.* N.p., 1925.

Lane, David. *A Soldier's Diary, the Story of a Volunteer.* Jackson, Mich.: n.p., 1905.

Lane, Mills, ed. *"Dear Mother: Don't Grieve about Me. If I Get Killed, I'll Only Be Dead."
Letters from Georgia Soldiers in the Civil War.* Savannah, Ga.: Beehive Press, 1977.

Lathers, Richard. *Reminiscences of Richard Lathers: Sixty Years of a Busy Life in South
Carolina, Massachusetts, and New York.* New York: Grafton Press, 1907.

*Laws of the State of Mississippi Passed at a Called and Regular Session of the Mississippi
Legislature, Held in Jackson and Columbus, Dec. 1862 and Nov. 1863.* Selma, Ala.: Cooper
and Kimball, 1864.

Lee, Elizabeth Blair. *Wartime Washington: The Civil War Letters of Elizabeth Blair Lee.* Edited
by Virginia Jeans Laas. Urbana: University of Illinois Press, 1991.

Lee, Fitzhugh. *General Lee.* New York: Appleton, 1894.

Lee, Robert E. *Recollections and Letters of Robert E. Lee.* Garden City, N.Y.: Doubleday,
Page, 1924.

———. *The Wartime Papers of R. E. Lee.* Edited by Clifford Dowdey and Louis H. Manarin.
New York: Bramhill House, 1961.

Lee, Susan Pendleton. *Memoirs of William Nelson Pendleton.* Philadelphia: Lippincott, 1893.

Letterman, Jonathan. *Medical Recollections of the Army of the Potomac.* New York:
Appleton, 1866.

Lewis, George. *The History of Battery E, First Regiment Rhode Island Light Artillery, in the
War of 1861 and 1865 to Preserve the Union.* Providence, R.I.: Snow and Farnham, 1892.

Lewis, John Howard. *Recollections from 1860 to 1865.* Washington, D.C.: Peake and
Co., 1895.

Lewis, Richard. *Camp Life of a Confederate Boy.* Charleston, S.C.: News and Courier Book
Presses, 1883.

Lincoln, Abraham. *The Collected Works of Abraham Lincoln.* 9 vols. Edited by Roy P. Basler.
New Brunswick, N.J.: Rutgers University Press, 1954.

Lindsley, John Berrien, ed. *Military Annals of Tennessee, Confederate.* Nashville: J. J.
Lindsley, 1886.

Lineberger, James W. *Letters of a Gaston Ranger.* Edited by Hugh Douglas Pitts. Richmond:
privately printed, 1991.

Lines, Amelia Akehurst. *To Raise Myself a Little: The Diaries and Letters of Jennie, a Georgia
Teacher, 1861–1886.* Edited by Thomas Dyer. Athens: University of Georgia Press, 1982.

Livermore, Mary A. *My Story of the War: A Woman's Narrative of Four Years Personal
Experience.* Hartford, Conn.: A. D. Worthington and Co., 1890.

Lloyd, William Penn. *History of the First Reg't Pennsylvania Reserve Cavalry, From its
Organization, August, 1861, to September, 1864.* Philadelphia: King and Baird, 1864.

Locke, William Henry. *The Story of the Regiment.* Philadelphia: Lippincott, 1868.

Long, A. L. *Memoirs of Robert E. Lee.* Secaucus, N.J.: Blue and Grey Press, 1983.

Longfellow, Henry Wadsworth. *The Letters of Henry Wadsworth Longfellow.* 4 vols. Edited
by Andrew Hillen. Cambridge, Mass.: Harvard University Press, 1967–82.

Longstreet, James. *From Manassas to Appomattox: Memoirs of the Civil War in America.*
Edited by James I. Robertson Jr. Bloomington: Indiana University Press, 1960.

Lord, Edward Oliver. *History of the Ninth Regiment, New Hampshire Volunteers in the War of
the Rebellion.* Concord, N.H.: Republican Press Association, 1895.

Lusk, William Thompson. *War Letters of William Thompson Lusk.* New York: privately
printed, 1911.

McAllister, Robert. *The Civil War Letters of General Robert McAllister.* Edited by James I.
Robertson Jr. New Brunswick, N.J.: Rutgers University Press, 1965.

McCarter, William. *My Life in the Irish Brigade: The Civil War Memoirs of Private William*

McCarter, 116th Pennsylvania Infantry. Edited by Kevin E. O'Brien. Campbell, Calif.: Savas Publishing, 1996.

McCarthy, Carlton. *Detailed Minutiae of Soldier Life in the Army of Northern Virginia, 1861–1865.* Richmond: William L. Sheppard, 1884.

McClellan, Carswell. *General Andrew A. Humphreys at Malvern Hill, July 1, 1862, and Fredericksburg, Va., December 13, 1862, A Memoir.* St. Paul, Minn.: privately printed, 1888.

McClellan, George Brinton. *The Civil War Papers of George B. McClellan: Selected Correspondence, 1860–1865.* Edited by Steven W. Sears. New York: Ticknor and Fields, 1989.

———. *McClellan's Own Story.* New York: Charles L. Webster, 1887.

McClellan, Henry Brainerd. *I Rode with Jeb Stuart: The Life and Campaigns of Major General J. E. B. Stuart.* Bloomington: Indiana University Press, 1958.

McClendon, William Augustus. *Recollections of War Times, by an Old Veteran While under Stonewall Jackson and Lieutenant General James Longstreet.* Montgomery, Ala.: Paragon Press, 1909.

McClenthen, Charles S. *Narrative of the Fall and Winter Campaign, by a Private Soldier of the 2nd Div., 1st Army Corps, Containing a Detailed Description of the "Battle of Fredericksburg."* Syracuse, N.Y.: Masters and Lee, 1863.

McClure, Alexander. *Recollections of Half a Century.* Salem, Mass.: Salem Press, 1904.

McClure, John R. *Hoosier Farmboy in Lincoln's Army: The Civil War Letters of Pvt. John R. McClure.* Edited by Nancy Niblack Baxter. Indianapolis: Guild Press, 1992.

McCrea, Tully. *Dear Belle: Letters from a Cadet and Officer to His Sweetheart, 1858–1865.* Edited by Catherine S. Crary. Middletown, Conn.: Wesleyan University Press, 1965.

McDaniel, Henry Dickerson. *With Unabated Trust: Major Henry McDaniel's Love Letters from Confederate Battlefields as Treasured in Hester McDonald's Bonnet Box.* Edited by Anita B. Sims. Monroe, Ga.: Historical Society of Walton County, 1977.

McDermott, Anthony Wayne. *A Brief History of the 69th Regiment Pennsylvania Veteran Volunteers.* Philadelphia: D. J. Gallagher and Co., 1889.

McDonald, Cornelia Peake. *A Woman's Civil War: A Diary, with Reminiscences of the War, from March 1862.* Edited by Minrose C. Gwin. Madison: University of Wisconsin Press, 1992.

McGuire, Judith Brockenbrough. *Diary of a Southern Refugee During the War.* New York: E. J. Hale, 1867.

McKelvey, Blake, ed. *Rochester in the Civil War.* Rochester, N.Y.: Rochester Historical Society, 1944.

McKinney, Edward Pascal. *Life in Tent and Field, 1861–1865.* Boston: Richard G. Badger, 1922.

McNamara, Daniel George. *The History of the Ninth Regiment Massachusetts Volunteer Infantry, Second Brigade, First Division, Fifth Army Corps, Army of the Potomac, June 1861–June 1864.* Boston: E. B. Stillings, 1899.

Macon, Emma Cassandra Riely, and Reuben Conway Macon. *Reminiscences of the Civil War.* Privately printed, 1911.

McPherson, James M. *The Negro's Civil War: How American Negroes Felt and Acted during the War for the Union.* New York: Vintage, 1965.

Malone, Barlett Yancey. *Whipt 'em Everytime: The Diary of Bartlett Yancey Malone, Co. H., Sixth N.C. Regiment.* Edited by William Whatley Pierson. Jackson, Tenn.: McCowat-Mercer Press, 1960.

Manufactures of the United States in 1860; Compiled from the Original Returns of the Eighth Census. Washington, D.C.: Government Printing Office, 1865.

Marbaker, Thomas D. *History of the Eleventh New Jersey Volunteers from its Organization to Appomattox*. Trenton, N.J.: MacCrellish and Quigley, 1898.

Mark, Penrose G. *Red: White: and Blue Badge, Pennsylvania Veteran Volunteers, a History of the 93rd Regiment*. Harrisburg, Pa.: Aughinbaugh Press, 1911.

Marshall, D. Porter. *Company "K," 155th Pennsylvania Volunteer Zouaves, a Detailed History of its Organization and Service to the Country during the Civil War*. N.p., 1888.

Marshall, Jeffrey D., ed. *A War of the People: Vermont Civil War Letters*. Hanover, N.H.: University Press of New England, 1999.

Marx, Karl, and Frederick Engels. *The Civil War in the U.S.* 3rd ed. New York: International Publishers, 1961.

Matrau, Henry. *Letters Home: Henry Matrau of the Iron Brigade*. Edited by Marcia M. Reid-Green. Lincoln: University of Nebraska Press, 1993.

Maxson, William P. *Camp Fires of the Twenty-Third, Sketches of Camp Life, Marches, and Battles of the Twenty-Third Regiment, N.Y.V.* New York: Davies and Kent, 1863.

Mayo, Perry. *The Civil War Letters of Perry Mayo*. Edited by Robert W. Hodge. East Lansing: Publications of the Museum, Michigan State University, 1967.

Meade, George. *The Life and Letters of George Gordon Meade*. 2 vols. New York: Charles Scribner's Sons, 1913.

Means, John Oliver. *Waiting for Daybreak: A Discourse at the Funeral of Lieut. Edgar M. Newcomb, of the Mass. 19th reg't who died December 20, 1862, of Wounds Received at Fredericksburg, Preached in Park Street Church, December 27*. Boston: Alfred A. Mudge and Sons, 1863.

Melcher, Holman S. *With a Flash of His Sword: The Writings of Major Holman S. Melcher*. Edited by William B. Styple. Kearny, N.J.: Belle Grove Pub. Co., 1994.

Melville, Herman. *Collected Poems of Herman Melville*. Edited by Howard P. Vincent. Chicago: Packard and Co., 1947.

Merrill, Samuel H. *The Campaigns of the First Maine and District of Columbia Cavalry*. Portland, Maine: Bailey and Noyes, 1866.

Meyer, Henry Codington. *Civil War Experiences under Bayard, Gregg, Kilpatrick, Custer, Raulston, and Newberry, 1862, 1863, 1864*. New York: Knickerbocker Press, 1911.

Meyers, Augustus. *Ten Years in the Ranks, U.S. Army*. New York: Stirling Press, 1914.

Mills, John Harrison. *Chronicles of the Twenty-First Regiment, New York State Volunteers*. Buffalo: John M. Layton, 1867.

Minnesota in the Civil and Indian Wars. 2 vols. St. Paul: Pioneer Press, 1890–93.

Molyneux, Joel. *Quill of the Wild Goose: Civil War Letters and Diaries of Private Joel Molyneux, 141st Pennsylvania Volunteers*. Edited by Kermit Molyneux Bird. Shippensburg, Pa.: Burd Street Press, 1996.

Montgomery, Walter Alexander. *The Days of Old and the Years That Are Past*. N.p., n.d.

Montgomery, William Rhadamanthus. *Georgia Sharpshooter: The Civil War Diary and Letters of William Rhadamanthus Montgomery*. Edited by George Montgomery Jr. Macon, Ga.: Mercer University Press, 1997.

Moore, Edward A. *The Story of a Cannoneer under Stonewall Jackson*. New York: Neale, 1907.

Moore, Frank. *Women of the War; Their Heroism and Self-Sacrifice*. Hartford, Conn.: S. S. Scranton, 1866.

———, ed. *The Rebellion Record: A Diary of American Events*. 11 vols. New York: Putnam and Van Nostrand, 1861–68.

Moore, Robert A. *A Life for the Confederacy as Recorded in the Pocket Diaries of Pvt. Robert A. Moore, Co. G, 17th Mississippi Regiment, Confederate Guards*. Edited by James W. Silver. Jackson, Tenn.: McCowat-Mercer Press, 1959.

Moran, Benjamin. *The Journal of Benjamin Moran, 1857–1865.* Edited by Sarah Agnes Wallace and Frances Elma Gillespie. 2 vols. Chicago: University of Chicago Press, 1949.

Morgan, William Henry. *Personal Reminiscences of the War of 1861–5.* Lynchburg, Va.: J. P. Bell, 1911.

Motley, John Lothrop. *The Correspondence of John Lothrop Motley.* 2 vols. Edited by George William Curtis. New York: Harper and Brothers, 1889.

Mulholland, St. Clair Augustine. *The Story of the 116th Regiment, Pennsylvania Infantry, War of Secession, 1862–1865.* Philadelphia: F. McManus Jr. and Co., 1903.

Musgrove, Richard Watson. *Autobiography of Captain Richard W. Musgrove.* Bristol, N.H.: n.p., 1921.

Myers, Robert Manson, ed. *The Children of Pride: A True Story of Georgia and the Civil War.* New Haven, Conn.: Yale University Press, 1972.

Nagle, Theodore M. *Reminiscences of the Civil War.* Erie, Pa.: Dispatch Printing, 1923.

Nash, Eugene Arus. *A History of the Forty-fourth Regiment New York Volunteer Infantry in the Civil War, 1861–1865.* Chicago: R. R. Donnelley and Sons, 1911.

National Tribune Scrap Book, Number 1. Washington, D.C.: National Tribune, n.d.

Newell, Joseph Keith. *"Ours": Annals of the 10th Regiment Massachusetts Volunteers, in the Rebellion.* Springfield, Mass.: C. A. Nichols and Co., 1875.

Nichols, George W. *A Soldier's Story of His Regiment (61st Georgia) and Incidentally of the Lawton-Gordon-Evans Brigade, Army of Northern Virginia.* Kennesaw, Ga.: Continental Book Co., 1961.

Nichols, Samuel Edmund. *"Your Soldier Boy Samuel": Civil War Letters of Lieut. Samuel Edmund Nichols of the 37th Regiment Massachusetts Volunteers.* Buffalo, N.Y.: privately printed, 1929.

Nichols, Wesley. *Autobiography and Civil War Recollections.* Leesville, S.C.: Twin-County News, 1915.

Nicolay, John G., and John Hay. *Abraham Lincoln: A History.* 10 vols. New York: Century Co., 1890.

Nisbet, James Cooper. *Four Years on the Firing Line.* Edited by Bell Irvin Wiley. Jackson, Tenn.: McCowat-Mercer Press, 1963.

Norman, William M. *A Portion of My Life; Being a Short and Imperfect History Written While a Prisoner of War on Johnson's Island, 1864.* Winston-Salem, N.C.: J. F. Blair, 1959.

Norton, Henry. *Deeds of Daring; or, History of the Eighth New York Volunteer Cavalry.* Norwich, N.Y.: Chenango Telegraph, 1889.

Norton, Oliver Willcox. *Army Letters, 1861–1865.* Chicago: O. L. Denning, 1903.

Noyes, George Freeman. *The Bivouac and the Battlefield; or, Campaign Sketches in Virginia and Maryland.* New York: Harper and Brothers, 1863.

Oates, William Calvin. *The War between the Union and the Confederacy and Its Lost Opportunities, with a History of the 15th Alabama Regiment.* New York: Neale, 1905.

Official Records of the Union and Confederate Navies in the War of the Rebellion. 31 vols. Washington, D.C.: Government Printing Office, 1894–1922.

Orwig, Joseph Ray. *History of the 131st Pennsylvania Volunteers, War of 1861–5.* Williamsport, Pa.: Sun Book and Job Printing, 1902.

Osborn, Thomas Ward. *No Middle Ground: Thomas Ward Osborn's Letters.* Hamilton, N.Y.: Edmonston, 1993.

Osborne, William H. *The History of the Twenty-Ninth Regiment of Massachusetts Volunteer Infantry, in the Late War of the Rebellion.* Boston: Albert J. Wright, 1877.

Otis, George H. *The Second Wisconsin Infantry.* Edited by Alan D. Gaff. Dayton, Ohio: Morningside, 1984.

Owen, Frederick Wooster. *A Christmas Reminiscence of Fredericksburg.* Morristown, N.J.: n.p., 1895.

Owen, Thomas James. *"Dear Friends at Home . . .": The Letters and Diary of Thomas James Owen, Fiftieth New York Volunteer Engineer Regiment, during the Civil War.* Edited by Dale F. Floyd. Washington, D.C.: U.S. Government Printing Office, 1985.

Owen, William M. *In Camp and Battle with the Washington Artillery of New Orleans.* Boston: Ticknor and Co., 1885.

Page, Charles Davis. *History of the Fourteenth Regiment Connecticut Volunteer Infantry.* Meriden, Conn.: Horton Printing, 1906.

Paige, Charles C. *Story of the Experiences of Lieut. Charles C. Paige in the Civil War of 1861–5.* Franklin, N.H.: Journal-Transcript Press, 1911.

Palmer, Benjamin Morgan. *Address Delivered at the Funeral of General Maxcy Gregg in the Presbyterian Church, Columbia, SC, December 20, 1862.* Columbia, S.C.: Southern Guardian Steam-Power Press, 1863.

Pardington, John H. *Dear Sarah: Letters Home from a Soldier in the Iron Brigade.* Edited by Coralou Peel Lassen. Bloomington: Indiana University Press, 1999.

Parker, Francis Jewett. *The Story of the Thirty Second Regiment Massachusetts Infantry.* Boston: C. W. Calkins, 1880.

Parker, John Lord. *History of the Twenty-Second Massachusetts Infantry, the Second Company Sharpshooters, and Third Light Battery in the War of the Rebellion.* Boston: Rand Avery, 1887.

Parker, Thomas H. *History of the 51st Regiment of P.V., and V.V.* Philadelphia: King and Baird, 1869.

Parramore, Thomas C., Annie B. Darden, Frank Roy Johnson, and E. Frank Stevenson, eds. *Before the Rebel Flag Fell: Five Viewpoints on the Civil War.* Murfreesboro, N.C.: Johnson Publishing, 1965.

Partridge, George W. *Letters from the Iron Brigade: George Washington Partridge, Jr., 1839–1863: Civil War Letters to His Sisters.* Edited by Hugh L. Whitehouse. Indianapolis: Guild Press, 1994.

Pastoral Letter from the Bishops of the Protestant Episcopal Church to the Clergy and Laity of the Church in the Confederate States of America. Delivered before the General Council, in St. Paul's Church, Augusta, November 22, 1862. Augusta, Ga.: Steam Power Press Chronicle and Sentinel, 1862.

Pate, Henry Clay. *Proceedings of the General Court Martial, in The Case of Lieut Col. H. Clay Pate, 5th Va. Cavalry.* Richmond: n.p., 1863.

Patrick, Marsena Rudolph. *Inside Lincoln's Army: The Diary of Marsena Rudolph Patrick, Provost Marshal General, Army of the Potomac.* Edited by David S. Sparks. New York: Yoseloff, 1964.

Patrick, Robert. *Reluctant Rebel: The Secret Diary of Robert Patrick, 1861–1865.* Edited by F. Jay Taylor. Baton Rouge: Louisiana State University Press, 1959.

Patterson, Edmund DeWitt. *Yankee Rebel: The Civil War Journal of Edmund DeWitt Patterson.* Edited by John G. Barrett. Chapel Hill: University of North Carolina Press, 1966.

Paxton, Elisha Franklin. *The Civil War Letters of General Frank "Bull" Paxton, CSA, a Lieutenant of Lee and Jackson.* Edited by John G. Paxton. Hillsboro, Tex.: Hill Junior College Press, 1978.

———. *Memoir and Memorials: Elisha Franklin Paxton.* New York: De Vinne, 1905.

Pender, William Dorsey. *The General to His Lady: The Civil War Letters of William Dorsey Pender to Fanny Pender.* Edited by William W. Hassler. Chapel Hill: University of North Carolina Press, 1965.

Pepper, George W. *Under Three Flags; or, The Story of My Life as Preacher, Captain in the Army, Chaplain and Consul.* Cincinnati: Curts and Jennings, 1899.

Pettit, Frederick. *Infantryman Pettit: The Civil War Letters of Corporal Frederick Pettit.* Edited by William Gilfillan Gavin. Shippensburg, Pa.: White Mane, 1990.

Phillips, Ulrich B., ed. *The Correspondence of Robert Toombs, Alexander H. Stephens, and Howell Cobb.* Washington, D.C.: American Historical Association, 1913.

Pickett, George Edward. *The Heart of a Soldier as Revealed in the Intimate Letters of Genl. George E. Pickett.* New York: Seth Moyle, 1913.

Pierce, Edward L. *Memoir and Letters of Charles Sumner.* 4 vols. Boston: Roberts Brothers, 1894.

Poague, William Thomas. *Gunner with Stonewall: Reminiscences of William Thomas Poague, a Memoir, Written for His Children in 1903.* Edited by Monroe F. Cockrell. Jackson, Tenn.: McCowat-Mercer Press, 1957.

Poe, Clarence, ed. *True Tales of the South at War: How Soldiers Fought and Families Lived, 1861–1865.* Chapel Hill: University of North Carolina Press, 1961.

Polk, J. M. *The Confederate Soldier and Ten Years in South America.* Austin, Tex.: Van Boeckmann-Jones, 1910.

Pollard, Edward A. *Life of Jefferson Davis with a Secret History of the Southern Confederacy.* Freeport, N.Y.: Books for Libraries Press, 1969.

———. *Southern History of the War.* 2 vols. New York: Fairfax Press, 1977.

Polley, Joseph Benjamin. *Hood's Texas Brigade: Its Marches, Its Battles, Its Achievements.* Dayton, Ohio: Morningside, 1976.

———. *A Soldier's Letters to Charming Nellie.* New York: Neale, 1908.

Poore, Benjamin Perley. *Perley's Reminiscences of Sixty Years in the National Metropolis.* 2 vols. Tecumseh, Mich.: A. W. Mills, 1886.

Post, Marie Caroline. *The Life and Memoirs of Comte Regis de Trobriand.* New York: E. P. Dutton, 1910.

Potter, William W. *One Surgeon's Private War: Doctor William W. Potter of the 57th New York.* Shippensburg, Pa.: White Mane, 1996.

Powe, James Harrington. *Reminiscences and Sketches of Confederate Times.* Columbia, S.C.: R. L. Bryan, 1909.

Pryor, Mrs. Roger A. *Reminiscences of Peace and War.* New York: Macmillan, 1924.

Pryor, S. G. *A Post of Honor: The Pryor Letters, 1861–1863.* Fort Valley, Ga.: Garret Publications, 1989.

Public Laws of the State of North Carolina (1862–63). Raleigh, N.C.: W. W. Holden, 1863.

[Putnam, Sallie Brock]. *Richmond during the War; Four Years of Personal Observation.* New York: Carleton, 1867.

Pyne, Henry Rogers. *Ride to War: The History of the First New Jersey Cavalry.* Edited by Earl Schenck Miers. New Brunswick, N.J.: Rutgers University Press, 1961.

Ray, Frederic E. *"Our Special Artist": Alfred R. Waud's Civil War.* Mechanicsburg, Pa.: Stackpole, 1994.

Rea, D. B. *Sketches from Hampton's Cavalry, Embracing the Principal Exploits of the Cavalry in the Campaigns of 1862 and 1863.* Columbia, S.C.: South Carolinian Steam Press, 1864.

Reeves, James Johnson. *History of the Twenty-Fourth Regiment, New Jersey Volunteers.* Camden, N.J.: S. Chew, 1889.

Reichardt, Theodore. *Diary of Battery A, First Regiment, Rhode Island Light Artillery.* Providence, R.I.: N. Bangs Williams, 1865.

Reid, Whitelaw. *A Radical View: The "Agate" Dispatches of Whitelaw Reid, 1861–1865.* 2 vols. Memphis: Memphis State University Press, 1976.

Reminisco, Don Pedro Quarendo. *Life in the Union Army; or, Notings and Reminiscences of a Two Years' Volunteer.* New York: H. Dexter, 1863.

Renfroe, Rev. J. J. D. *A Model Confederate Soldier, Being a Brief Sketch of the Rev. Nathaniel D. Renfroe, Lieutenant of A Company in the Fifth Alabama Battalion, of General*

A. P. Hill's Division, Who Fell in the Battle of Fredericksburg, December 13th, 1862. N.p., 1863.

Report of the Joint Committee on the Conduct of the War. 3 pts. Washington, D.C.: Government Printing Office, 1865.

Report of the Secretary of the Treasury . . . January 10, 1863. Richmond: n.p., 1863.

Rhodes, Elisha Hunt. *All for the Union: The Civil War Diaries and Letters of Elisha Hunt Rhodes.* Edited by Robert Hunt Rhodes. New York: Orion Books, 1991.

Rhodes, John H. *The History of Battery B, First Regiment Rhode Island Light Artillery in the War to Preserve the Union, 1861–1865.* Providence, R.I.: Snow and Farnham, 1894.

Rice, Allen Thorndike, ed. *Reminiscences of Abraham Lincoln by Distinguished Men of His Time.* New York: North American Review, 1889.

Richardson, Albert. *The Secret Service, the Field, the Dungeon, and the Escape.* Hartford, Conn.: American Publishing, 1865.

Richardson, James D., ed. *The Messages and Papers of Jefferson Davis and the Confederacy.* 2 vols. New York: Chelsea House, 1966.

Ripley, William Y. W. *Vermont Riflemen in the War for the Union.* Rutland: Tuttle and Co., 1883.

Roberson, Elizabeth Whitley. *Weep Not for Me Dear Mother.* Washington, D.C.: Venture Press, 1991.

Roe, Alfred Seelye. *The Tenth Regiment Massachusetts Volunteer Infantry, 1861–1864, a Western Massachusetts Regiment.* Springfield, Mass.: F. A. Bassette, 1909.

Romero, Matias. *A Mexican View of America in the 1860s: A Foreign Diplomat Describes the Civil War and Reconstruction.* Edited by Thomas Schoonover. Rutherford, N.J.: Fairleigh Dickinson University Press, 1991.

Ropes, Hannah. *Civil War Nurse: The Diary and Letters of Hannah Ropes.* Edited by John R. Brumgardt. Knoxville: University of Tennessee Press, 1980.

Rorabaugh, W. J. *The Alcoholic Republic: An American Tradition.* New York: Oxford University Press, 1979.

Rowe, David Watson. *A Sketch of the 126th Regiment Pennsylvania Volunteers.* Chambersburg, Pa.: Printed at the Office of the "Franklin Repository," Cook and Hays Publishers, 1869.

Rowland, Dunbar, ed. *Jefferson Davis, Constitutionalist: His Letters, Papers, and Speeches.* 10 vols. Jackson: Mississippi Department of Archives and History, 1923.

Ruffin, Edmund. *The Diary of Edmund Ruffin.* 3 vols. Edited by William K. Scarborough. Baton Rouge: Louisiana State University Press, 1972–89.

Ruffin, Thomas. *The Papers of Thomas Ruffin.* 4 vols. Edited by James G. de Roulhac Hamilton. Raleigh, N.C.: Edwards and Broughton, 1918–20.

Rusling, James Fowler. *Men and Things I Saw in Civil War Days.* New York: Eaton and Mains, 1899.

Sanford, George B. *Fighting Rebels and Redskins: Experiences in Army Life of Colonel George B. Sanford, 1861–1892.* Edited by E. R. Hagemann. Norman: University of Oklahoma Press, 1969.

Sawyer, Franklin. *A Military History of the 8th Regiment Ohio Volunteer Infantry.* Edited by George A. Groot. Cleveland: Fairbanks and Co., 1881.

Schalk, Emil. *Campaigns of 1862 and 1863.* Philadelphia: Lippincott, 1863.

Scharf, Jonathan Thomas. *The Personal Memoirs of Jonathan Thomas Scharf of the First Maryland Artillery.* Baltimore: Butternut and Blue, 1992.

Scheibert, Captain Justus. *Seven Months in the Rebel States during the North American War, 1863.* Translated by Joseph C. Hayes. Edited by W. Stanley Hoole. Tuscaloosa, Ala.: Confederate Pub. Co., 1958.

Schurz, Carl. *Intimate Letters of Carl Schurz.* Edited by Joseph Schafer. Madison: State Historical Society of Wisconsin, 1928.

———. *Reminiscences of Carl Schurz.* 3 vols. New York: McClure, 1907–8.

Seville, William P. *History of the First Regiment, Delaware Volunteers.* Wilmington: Historical Society of Delaware, 1884.

Seward, Frederick W. *Reminiscences of a War-Time Statesman and Diplomat, 1830–1915.* New York: G. P. Putnam's Sons, 1916.

Seward, William H. *The Works of William H. Seward.* 5 vols. Edited by George E. Baker. Boston: Houghton Mifflin, 1853–84.

Shaw, Robert Gould. *Blue-Eyed Child of Fortune: The Civil War Letters of Colonel Robert Gould Shaw.* Edited by Russell Duncan. Athens: University of Georgia Press, 1992.

Sheeran, James B. *Confederate Chaplain: A War Journal.* Edited by Joseph T. Durkin. Milwaukee: Bruce Pub. Co., 1960.

Sheldon, Winthrop Dudley. *The "Twenty-Seventh": A Regimental History.* New Haven, Conn.: Morris and Benham, 1866.

Shelton, William J. *The Downfall of Burnside.* Lynchburg, Va.: Johnson and Schaffter, 1863[?].

Shoemaker, John J. *Shoemaker's Battery: Stuart's Horse Artillery, Pelham's Battalion.* Memphis: S. C. Toof, 1908.

Shotwell, Randolph Abbott. *The Papers of Randolph Abbott Shotwell.* 3 vols. Edited by J. G. de Roulhac Hamilton. Raleigh: North Carolina Historical Commission, 1929–36.

Silber, Nina, and Mary Beth Stevens, eds. *Yankee Correspondence: Civil War Letters between New England Soldiers and the Home Front.* Charlottesville: University Press of Virginia, 1996.

Simpson, Dick, and Tally Simpson. *Far, Far from Home: The Wartime Letters of Dick and Tally Simpson, 3rd South Carolina Volunteers.* Edited by Guy R. Everson and Edward H. Simpson. New York: Oxford University Press, 1994.

Slaughter, Rev. Philip. *A Sketch of the Life of Randolph Fairfax, A Private in the Ranks of the Rockbridge Artillery, Attached to the "Stonewall Brigade."* Richmond: Tyler, Allegre, and McDaniel, Enquirer Job Office, 1864.

Sloan, John Alexander. *Reminiscences of the Guilford Grays, Co. B, 27th N.C. Regiment.* Washington, D.C.: R. O. Polkinhorn, 1883.

Small, Abner Ralph. *The Road to Richmond: The Civil War Memoirs of Major Abner R. Small of the Sixteenth Maine Volunteers, Together with the Diary Which He Kept When He Was a Prisoner of War.* Edited by Harry Adams Small. Berkeley: University of California Press, 1939.

———. *The Sixteenth Maine Regiment in the War of the Rebellion, 1861–1865.* Portland, Maine: B. Thurston and Co., 1886.

Smith, Abram P. *History of the Seventy-Sixth Regiment, New York Volunteers.* Syracuse, N.Y.: Truair, Smith and Miles, 1867.

Smith, Edward P. *Incidents of the United States Christian Commission.* Philadelphia: Lippincott, 1869.

Smith, James E. *A Famous Battery and its Campaigns, 1861–'64.* Washington, D.C.: W. H. Lowdermilk, 1892.

Smith, John Day. *The History of the Nineteenth Regiment of Maine Volunteer Infantry, 1862–1865.* Minneapolis: Great Western, 1909.

Smith, John L. *History of the 118th Pennsylvania Volunteers, Corn Exchange Regiment.* Philadelphia: J. L. Smith, 1905.

Smith, William Alexander. *The Anson Guards, Company C, Fourteenth Regiment North Carolina Volunteers, 1861–1865.* Charlotte, N.C.: Stone Pub. Co., 1914.

Smith, William F. *The Autobiography of Major General William F. Smith, 1861–1864.* Edited by Herbert M. Schiller. Dayton, Ohio: Morningside, 1990.

Smithe, George C. *Glimpses of Places, and People, and Things. Extracts from Published Correspondence and Other Writings, 1861–1886.* Ypsilanti, Mich.: Ypsilantian Press, 1887.

Sorrel, Gilbert Moxley. *Recollections of a Confederate Staff Officer.* Edited by Bell Irvin Wiley. Jackson, Tenn.: McCowat-Mercer Press, 1958.

Spangler, Edward Webster. *My Little War Experiences with Historical Sketches and Memorabilia.* New York: Daily Pub. Co., 1904.

Speairs, Arabella, and William Beverly Pettit. *Civil War Letters of Arabella Speairs and William Beverly Pettit of Fluvanna County, Virginia, March 1862–March 1865.* 2 vols. Edited by Charles W. Turner. Roanoke, Va.: Virginia Lithography and Graphics Company, n.d.

Speer, William Henry Asbury. *Voices from Cemetery Hill: The Civil War Diary, Reports, and Letters of Colonel William Henry Asbury Speer.* Edited by Allen Paul Speer. Johnson City, Tenn.: Overmountain Press, 1997.

Spencer, Carrie Esther, ed. *A Civil War Marriage in Virginia: Reminiscences and Letters.* Boyce, Va.: Carr Pub. Co., 1956.

Sprenger, George ? *? History of the Camp and Field Life of the 122d Regiment, Penn'a Volunteers.* Lancaster, Pa.: New Era, 1885.

Statistics of the United States in 1860; Compiled from the Original Returns and Being the Final Exhibit of the Eighth Census. Washington, D.C.: Government Printing Office, 1866.

Stearns, Austin C. *Three Years with Company K.* Edited by Arthur A. Kent. Rutherford, N.J.: Fairleigh Dickinson University Press, 1976.

Stephens, George E. *A Voice of Thunder: The Civil War Letters of George E. Stephens.* Edited by Donald A. Yacovone. Urbana: University of Illinois Press, 1997.

Stephens, Robert, ed. *Intrepid Warrior: Clement Anselm Evans, Confederate General from Georgia: Life, Letters, and Diaries of the War Years.* Dayton, Ohio: Morningside, 1992.

Stevens, Captain Charles A. *Berdan's United States Sharpshooters in the Army of the Potomac, 1861–1865.* Dayton, Ohio: Morningside, 1972.

Stevens, George Thomas. *Three Years in the Sixth Corps: A Concise Narrative of Events in the Army of the Potomac, from 1861 to the Close of the Rebellion, April 1865.* Albany: S. R. Gray, 1866.

Stevens, John W. *Reminiscences of the Civil War.* Hillsboro, Tex.: Mirror Printing, 1902.

Stevens, Thaddeus. *The Selected Papers of Thaddeus Stevens.* 2 vols. Edited by Beverly Wilson Palmer and Holly Byers Ochoa. Pittsburgh: University of Pittsburgh Press, 1997.

Stewart, Alexander Morrison. *Camp, March, and Battlefield.* Philadelphia: James B. Rodgers, 1865.

Stewart, William Henry. *A Pair of Blankets: War-Time History in Letters to the Young People of the South.* New York: Broadway Pub. Co., 1911.

Stiles, Robert. *Four Years under Marse Robert.* New York: Neale, 1903.

Stillé, Charles J. *History of the United States Sanitary Commission.* Philadelphia: Lippincott, 1866.

Stine, James Henry. *History of the Army of the Potomac.* Philadelphia: J. B. Rodgers, 1892.

Stoddard, William O. *Inside the White House: Memoirs and Reports of Lincoln's Secretary.* Edited by Michael Burlingame. Lincoln: University of Nebraska Press, 2000.

Stone, Edwin Winchester. *Rhode Island in the Rebellion.* Providence, R.I.: George H. Whitney, 1864.

Stone, James Madison. *Personal Recollections of the Civil War.* Boston: published by the author, 1918.

Stone, Kate. *Brokenburn: The Journal of Kate of Stone, 1861–1868.* Edited by John Q. Anderson. Baton Rouge: Louisiana State University Press, 1955.

The Story of the Twenty-first Regiment, Connecticut Volunteer Infantry, during the Civil War, *1861–1865, by Members of the Regiment.* Middletown, Conn.: Stewart Printing Co., 1900.

Strong, George Templeton. *The Diary of George Templeton Strong.* 4 vols. Edited by Allan Nevins and Milton Halsey Thomas. New York: Macmillan, 1952.

Stuart, James E. B. *The Letters of General J. E. B. Stuart.* Edited by Adele H. Mitchell. N.p.: Stuart-Mosby Historical Society, 1990.

Stuckenberg, John H. W. *I'm Surrounded by Methodists: Diary of John H. W. Stuckenberg, Chaplain of the 145th Pennsylvania Volunteer Infantry.* Edited by David T. Hedrick and Gordon Barry Davis Jr. Gettysburg, Pa.: Thomas Publications, 1995.

Sturtevant, Arnold H., ed. *Josiah Volunteered: A Collection of Diaries, Letters, and Photographs of Josiah H. Sturtevant, His Wife, Helen, and His Four Children.* Farmington, Maine: Knowlton and McLeary, 1977.

Sumner, Charles. *The Selected Letters of Charles Sumner.* 2 vols. Edited by Beverly Wilson Palmer. Boston: Northeastern University Press, 1990.

Sumner, George C. *Battery D, First Rhode Island Light Artillery in the Civil War, 1861–1865.* Providence, R.I.: Rhode Island Printing Co., 1897.

Supplement to the Official Records of the Union and Confederate Armies. 95 vols. Wilmington, N.C.: Broadfoot, 1994– .

Sutton, E. H. *Civil War Stories, Written by E. H. Sutton.* Demorest, Ga.: Banner Printing Co., 1910.

Swinton, William. *Campaigns of the Army of the Potomac.* New York: Charles B. Richardson, 1866.

Sypher, Josiah Rinehart. *History of the Pennsylvania Reserve Corps.* Lancaster, Pa.: Elias Barr and Co., 1865.

Tapert, Annette, ed. *The Brothers' War: Civil War Letters to Their Loved Ones from the Blue and Gray.* New York: Random House, 1988.

Taylor, Jeremiah. *The Sacrifice Consumed: Life of Edward Hamilton Brewer, Lately a Soldier in the Army of the Potomac.* Boston: Henry Hoyt, 1863.

Taylor, Michael W., ed. *The Cry Is War, War, War: The Civil War Correspondence of Lts. Burwell Thomas Cotton and George Job Huntley, 34th Regiment North Carolina Troops.* Dayton, Ohio: Morningside, 1994.

Taylor, Sgt. John Dykes. *History of the 48th Alabama Volunteer Infantry Regiment.* Edited by William Stanley Hoole. Dayton, Ohio: Morningside, 1982.

Taylor, Walter H. *Four Years with General Lee.* Edited by James I. Robertson Jr. Bloomington: Indiana University Press, 1962.

———. *General Lee: His Campaigns in Virginia, 1861–1865.* Dayton, Ohio: Morningside, 1975.

Terrill, W. H. H. *Indiana in the War of the Rebellion: Report of the Adjutant General.* Indianapolis: Indiana Historical Society, 1960.

Tevis, C. *The History of the Fighting Fourteenth.* New York: Brooklyn Eagle Press, 1911.

Third Annual Report of the State Historian of the State of New York, 1897. New York: Wynkoop Hallenbeck Crawford, 1898.

Thomas, Henry W. *The History of the Doles-Cook Brigade, Army of Northern Virginia.* Dayton, Ohio: Morningside, 1988.

Thomas, James B. *"I Never Want to Witness Such Sights": The Civil War Letters of First Lieutenant James B. Thomas, Adjutant, 107th Pennsylvania Volunteers.* Edited by Mary Warner Thomas and Richard A. Sauers. Baltimore: Butternut and Blue, 1995.

Thompson, S. Millett. *Thirteenth Regiment of New Hampshire Volunteer Infantry in the War of the Rebellion, 1861–1865.* Boston: Houghton Mifflin, 1888.

Thomson, Orville. *From Philippi to Appomattox: Narrative of the Service of the Seventh Indiana Infantry in the War for the Union.* N.p., 190-.

Thomson, Osmund Rhodes Howard, and William H. Rauch. *History of the "Bucktails," Kane Rifle Regiment of the Pennsylvania Reserve Corps (13th Pennsylvania Reserves, 42nd of the Line)*. Philadelphia: Electric Printing, 1906.

Thorndike, Rachel Sherman, ed. *The Sherman Letters: Correspondence between General Sherman and Senator Sherman from 1837 to 1891*. New York: Da Capo Press, 1969.

Thorpe, Sheldon Brainerd. *The History of the Fifteenth Connecticut Volunteers in the War for the Defense of the Union, 1861–1865*. New Haven, Conn.: Price, Lee and Adkins, 1893.

Tillinghast, Pardon Elisha. *History of the Twelfth Regiment Rhode Island Volunteers in the Civil War, 1862–1863*. Providence, R.I.: Snow and Farnham, 1904.

Tilney, Robert. *My Life in the Army: Three Years and a Half with the Fifth Army Corps, Army of the Potomac, 1862–1865*. Philadelphia: Ferris and Leach, 1912.

Tobie, Edward Parsons. *History of the First Maine Cavalry, 1861–1865*. Boston: Emery and Hughes, 1887.

Todd, William. *History of the Ninth Regiment, N.Y.S.M., N.G.S. N.Y., 1845–1888*. New York: J. S. Ogilvie, 1889.

———. *The Seventy-Ninth Highlanders, New York Volunteers in the War of the Rebellion, 1861–1865*. Albany: Brandow, Barton, 1886.

Trask, Kerry A. *Fire Within: A Civil War Narrative from Wisconsin*. Kent, Ohio: Kent State University Press, 1995.

Trobriand, Régis de. *Four Years with the Army of the Potomac*. Translated by George K. Dauchy. Boston: Ticknor and Co., 1889.

———. *Our Noble Blood: The Civil War Letters of Regis de Trobriand*. Edited by William B. Styple. Kearny, N.J.: Belle Grove, 1997.

Trout, Robert J., ed. *With Pen and Saber: The Letters and Diaries of J. E. B. Stuart's Staff Officers*. Mechanicsburg, Pa.: Stackpole, 1995.

Trowbridge, J. T. *The South: A Tour of its Battle-Fields and Ruined Cities*. Hartford, Conn.: L. Stebbins, 1866.

Turner, Justin G., and Linda Levitt Turner. *Mary Todd Lincoln: Her Life and Letters*. New York: Knopf, 1972.

Twitchell, Marshall Harvey. *Carpetbagger from Vermont: The Autobiography of Marshall Harvey Twitchell*. Edited by Ted Tunnell. Baton Rouge: Louisiana State University Press, 1989.

Tyler, Mason Whiting. *Recollections of the Civil War with Many Original Diary Entries and Letters*. New York: G. P. Putnam's Sons, 1912.

Under the Maltese Cross, Antietam to Appomattox, the Loyal Uprising in Western Pennsylvania, Campaigns 155th Pennsylvania Regiment Narrated by Rank and File. Akron, Ohio: Werner, 1910.

United States Christian Commission. *First Annual Report*. Philadelphia: n.p., 1863.

———. *Second Annual Report*. Philadelphia: n.p., 1864.

U.S. Bureau of the Census, *Historical Statistics of the United States*. 2 vols. Washington, D.C.: Government Printing Office, 1975.

Vail, Enos Ballard. *Reminiscences of a Boy in the Civil War*. Brooklyn: printed by the author, 1915.

Vance, Zebulon Baird. *The Papers of Zebulon Baird Vance*. 2 vols. Edited by Frontis W. Johnston and Joe A. Mobley. Raleigh, N.C.: Division of Archives and History, 1963– .

Van Santvoord, Cornelius. *The One Hundred and Twentieth Regiment, New York State Volunteers, a Narrative of its Services in the War for the Union*. Rondout, N.Y.: Kingston Freeman, 1894.

Vanscoten, M. *The Conception, Organization and Campaigns of "Company H," 4th Penn. Reserve, Volunteer Corps, 33rd Regiment in Line, 1861–5*. Tunkhannock, N.J.: Baldwin and Chapman, 1885.

Vautier, John D. *History of the 88th Pennsylvania Volunteers in the War for the Union, 1861–1865.* Philadelphia: Lippincott, 1894.

Veil, Charles Henry. *The Memoirs of Charles Henry Veil: A Soldier's Recollections of the Civil War and Arizona Territory.* Edited by Herman J. Viola. New York: Orion Books, 1993.

Villard, Henry. *Memoirs of Henry Villard, Journalist and Financier, 1835–1900.* 2 vols. Boston: Houghton Mifflin, 1904.

Von Borcke, Heros. *Memoirs of the Confederate War for Independence.* 2 vols. New York: Peter Smith, 1938.

Von Olnhausen, Mary. *Adventures of an Army Nurse in Two Wars, Edited from the Diary and Correspondence of Mary Phinney, Baroness Von Olnhausen.* Edited by James Phinney Munroe. Boston: Little, Brown, 1903.

Wagner, William F. *Letters of William F. Wagner, Confederate Soldier.* Edited by John M. Hatley and Linda B. Huffman. Wendell, N.C.: Broadfoot, 1983.

Wainwright, Charles Shields. *A Diary of Battle: The Personal Journals of Colonel Charles S. Wainwright, 1861–1865.* Edited by Allan Nevins. New York: Harcourt, Brace and World, 1962.

Waite, Otis F. R. *New Hampshire in the Great Rebellion.* Claremont, N.H.: Tracy, Chase, 1870.

Waitt, Ernest Linden. *History of the Nineteenth Regiment Massachusetts Volunteer Infantry, 1861–1865.* Salem, Mass.: Salem Press, 1906.

Walcott, Charles Folsom. *History of the Twenty-First Regiment in the War for the Preservation of the Union, 1861–1865.* Boston: Houghton Mifflin, 1882.

Walker, Francis. *General Hancock.* New York: Appleton, 1898.

———. *History of the Second Army Corps in the Army of the Potomac.* New York: Charles Scribner's Sons, 1886.

Walters, John. *Norfolk Blues: The Civil War Diary of the Norfolk Light Artillery Blues.* Edited by Kenneth Wiley. Shippensburg, Pa.: Burd Street Press, 1997.

Ward, Joseph Ripley Chandler. *History of the One Hundred and Sixth Regiment Pennsylvania Volunteers, 2d Brigade, 2d Division, 2d Corps, 1861–1865.* Philadelphia: Grant, Faires and Rodgers, 1883.

War of the Rebellion: A Compilation of the Official Records of the Union and Confederate Armies. 128 vols. Washington, D.C.: Government Printing Office, 1880–1901.

Washburn, George H. *A Complete History and Record of the 108th Regiment N.Y. Vols. from 1862 to 1894.* Rochester, N.Y.: E. R. Andrews, 1894.

Watson, William. *Letters of a Civil War Surgeon.* Edited by Paul Fatout. West Lafayette, Ind.: Purdue University Press, 1961.

Welch, Spencer Glasgow. *A Confederate Surgeon's Letters to His Wife.* New York: Neale, 1911.

Weld, Stephen Minot. *War Diary and Letters of Stephen Minot Weld, 1861–1876.* Cambridge, Mass.: Riverside Press, 1911.

Welles, Gideon. *The Diary of Gideon Welles, Secretary of the Navy under Lincoln and Johnson.* 3 vols. Edited by Howard K. Beale. New York: Norton, 1960.

Welsh, Peter. *Irish Green and Union Blue: The Civil War Letters of Peter Welsh, Color Sergeant, 28th Regiment Massachusetts Volunteers.* Edited by Lawrence Frederick Kohl and Margaret Cosse Richard. New York: Fordham University Press, 1986.

Welton, J. Michael, ed. *"My Heart Is So Rebellious": The Caldwell Letters, 1861–1865.* Warrenton, Va.: Fauquier National Bank, n.d.

Westbrook, Robert S. *History of the 49th Pennsylvania Volunteers.* Altoona, Pa.: Altoona Times, 1898.

Weston, John Burden. *Picket Pins and Sabers: The Civil War Letters of John Burden Weston.* Edited by Robert W. and Nancy D. Frost. Ashland, Ky.: Economy Printers, 1977.

Weygant, Charles H. *History of the One Hundred and Twenty-Fourth Regiment, N.Y.S.V.*
Newburgh, N.Y.: Journal Print House, 1877.

Weymouth, Albert Blodgett. *A Memorial Sketch of Lieut. Edgar M. Newcomb of the
Nineteenth Mass. Vols.* Malden, Mass.: Alvin G. Brown, 1883.

Wheelock, Julia S. *The Boys in White; the Experience of a Hospital Agent in and Around
Washington.* New York: Lange and Hillman, 1870.

White, Wyman Silas. *The Civil War Diary of Wyman S. White, First Sergeant of Company "F"
of the 2nd United States Sharpshooter Regiment (New Hampshire Men) in the Army of the
Potomac, 1861–1865.* Edited by Russell C. White. Baltimore: Butternut and Blue, 1993.

Whitman, George Washington. *Civil War Letters of George Washington Whitman.* Edited by
Jerome M. Loving. Durham, N.C.: Duke University Press, 1975.

Whitman, Walt. *Walt Whitman's Civil War.* Edited by Walter Lowenfels. New York:
Knopf, 1961.

Whitman, William E. S., and Charles H. True. *Maine in the War for the Union: A History of
the Part Borne by Maine Troops.* Lewiston, Maine: Nelson, Dingley Jr. and Co., 1865.

Whitney, John H. *The Hawkins Zouaves (Ninth N.Y.V.), Their Battles and Marches.* New York:
published by the author, 1866.

Wightman, Edward King. *From Antietam to Fort Fisher: The Civil War Letters of Edward King
Wightman, 1862–1865.* Edited by Edward G. Longacre. Rutherford, N.J.: Fairleigh
Dickinson University Press, 1985.

Willcox, Orlando. *Forgotten Valor: The Memoirs, Journals, and Civil War Letters of
Orlando B. Willcox.* Edited by Robert Garth Scott. Kent, Ohio: Kent State University
Press, 1999.

Williams, Alpheus Starkey. *From the Cannon's Mouth: The Civil War Letters of General
Alpheus S. Williams.* Edited by Milo M. Quaife. Detroit: Wayne State University
Press, 1959.

Wilson, James LeGrand. *The Confederate Soldier.* Edited by James W. Silver. Memphis:
Memphis State University Press, 1972.

Winkler, Angelina Virginia. *The Confederate Capital and Hood's Texas Brigade.* Austin, Tex.:
Eugene Von Boeckmann, 1894.

Wise, George. *History of the Seventeenth Virginia Infantry, C.S.A.* Baltimore: Kelly,
Piet, 1870.

Wood, James Harvey. *The War: "Stonewall" Jackson, His Campaigns and Battles, the
Regiment as I Saw Them.* Cumberland, Md.: Eddy Press, 1910.

[Woodbury, Augustus]. *General Halleck and General Burnside.* Boston: John Wilson and
Son, 1884.

Woodbury, Augustus. *Major General Ambrose E. Burnside and the Ninth Army Corps.*
Providence, R.I.: S. S. Rider and Brother, 1867.

———. *The Second Rhode Island Regiment, a Narrative of Military Operations.* Providence,
R.I.: Valpey, Angell, 1875.

Woodward, Evan Morrison. *History of the Third Pennsylvania Reserves.* Trenton, N.J.:
MacCrellish and Quigley, 1883.

———. *Our Campaigns; or, the Marches, Bivouacs, Battles, Incidents of Camp Life and
History of Our Regiment during its Three Years Term of Service.* Philadelphia: John E.
Potter, 1865.

Woolsey, Jane S. *Hospital Days.* New York: Van Nostrand, 1870.

Worsham, John H. *One of Jackson's Foot Cavalry: His Experience and What He Saw during
the War, 1861–1865.* New York: Neale, 1912.

Wray, William James. *History of the Twenty-third Pennsylvania Volunteer Infantry, Birney's
Zouaves.* Philadelphia: n.p., 1904.

Wren, James. *Captain James Wren's Civil War Diary: From New Bern to Fredericksburg.*
Edited by John Michael Priest. Shippensburg, Pa.: White Mane, 1990.

Articles

Adams, Captain John G. B. "Sunshine and Shadows of Army Life." In *Civil War Papers Read before the Commandery of the State of Massachusetts Military Order of the Loyal Legion of the United States,* 2:447–63. Wilmington, N.C.: Broadfoot, 1993.

Alexander, A. J. "Fredericksburg: Recollections of the Battle." *Philadelphia Weekly Press,* February 23, 1887.

Alexander, Bates. "Seventh Regiment." *Hummelstown (Pa.) Sun,* October 25, November 3, 10, December 6, 20, 1895, January 10, 1896.

Alexander, Edward Porter. "The Battle of Fredericksburg." *Southern Historical Society Papers* 10 (August and September, October and November 1882): 382–92, 445–64.

———. "Confederate Artillery Service." *Southern Historical Society Papers* 11 (February–March 1883): 98–113.

Allan, William. "Fredericksburg." *Papers of the Military Historical Society of Massachusetts* 3 (1899): 122–49.

Ames, John Worthington. "Under Fire." *Overland Monthly* 3 (1869): 432–41.

"An Adventure at Fredericksburg." *Brooklyn Advance* 12 (1885): 120–21.

Anderson, Thomas McArthur. "Civil War Recollections of the Twelfth Infantry." *Journal of the Military Service Institution of the United States* 41 (1907): 379–93.

Archer, James Jay. "The James J. Archer Letters: A Marylander in the Civil War." Edited by C. A. Porter Hopkins. *Maryland Historical Magazine* 56 (June 1961): 125–49.

Babcock, William A. "The 114th Regiment Pennsylvania Volunteers in the Late War." *Philadelphia Weekly Times,* April 24, 1886.

Barrow, Henry W. "Civil War Letters of Henry W. Barrow to John W. Fries." *North Carolina Historical Review* 34 (January 1957): 68–85.

Bartlett, William Chambers. "An Incident of Fredericksburg." *United Service* (Philadelphia), n.s., 2 (November 1889): 467–71.

"Battle of Fredericksburg: Recollections of It, and Bombardment of the City." *Southern Historical Society Papers* 19 (January 1876): 262–63.

Bean, William G. "A House Divided: The Civil War Letters of a Virginia Family." *Virginia Magazine of History and Biography* 59 (October 1951): 397–422.

Beardsley, H. H. "The Crossing at Fredericksburg." *National Tribune,* June 28, 1888.

Bisbee, George D. "Three Years a Volunteer Soldier in the Civil War, Antietam to Appomattox." In *War Papers Read before the Commandery of the State of Maine, Military Order of the Loyal Legion of the United States,* 4:114–49. Wilmington, N.C.: Broadfoot, 1992.

Bogue, Allan G. "William Parker Cutler's Congressional Diary of 1862–63." *Civil War History* 33 (December 1987): 315–30.

Boteler, Alexander Robinson. "At Fredericksburg with Stonewall." *Civil War Times Illustrated* 36 (December 1997): 20–22, 78–83.

Bowen, James L. "In Front of Fredericksburg." *Philadelphia Weekly Times,* December 2, 1882.

Bradwell, I. G. "The Georgia Brigade at Fredericksburg." *Confederate Veteran* 30 (January 1922): 18–20.

"Brunswick Guard." *Southern Historical Society Papers* 28 (January–December 1900): 8–14.

Burroughs, Sam R. "Reminiscences of Fredericksburg." *Confederate Veteran* 16 (December 1908): 636–37.

Butler, H. A. "Fredericksburg—Personal Reminiscences." *Confederate Veteran* 14 (April 1906): 181.

Carter, Mrs. B. M. "Story of Gen. Lee and Three Children." *Confederate Veteran* 5 (January 1897): 18–19.

Chamberlain, Joshua Lawrence. "My Story of Fredericksburg." *Cosmopolitan* 54 (December 1912): 148–59.

Charles, R. K. "Events in Battle of Fredericksburg." *Confederate Veteran* 14 (February 1906): 65–68.

Clark, Charles Amory. "Campaigning with the Sixth Maine." In *War Sketches and Incidents as Related by Companions of the Iowa Commandery Military Order of the Loyal Legion of the United States*, 2:389–439. Wilmington, N.C.: Broadfoot, 1994.

Cobb, Howell. "Howell Cobb Papers." Edited by R. P. Brooks. *Georgia Historical Quarterly* 6 (December 1922): 355–94.

Cody, Barnett H. "Letters of Barnett Hardeman Cody and Others, 1861–1864," pt. 2. *Georgia Historical Quarterly* 23 (December 1939): 362–80.

Commodore. "The Funny Side of Army Life." *National Tribune*, April 25, 1889.

"A Confederate Veteran." *Southern Historical Society Papers* 19 (January 1891): 257–61.

Conn, Charles Augustus. "Conn-Brantley Letter, 1862." Edited by T. Conn Bryan. *Georgia Historical Quarterly* 55 (Fall 1971): 437–41.

Conn, William Thomas, and Charles Augustus Conn. "Letters of Two Confederate Officers: William Thomas Conn and Charles Augustus Conn." Edited by T. Conn Bryan. *Georgia Historical Quarterly* 46 (June 1962): 174–95.

Cooke, John Esten. "The Right at Fredericksburg." *Philadelphia Weekly Times*, April 26, 1879.

Cory, Eugene A. "A Private's Recollections of Fredericksburg." In *Personal Narratives of Events in the Rebellion, Being Papers Read before the Rhode Island Soldiers and Sailors Historical Society*, 4:117–42. Wilmington, N.C.: Broadfoot, 1993.

Crocker, Gilbert. "Gilbert Crocker's Civil War, 24th Regt., N.Y.V." Edited by Rodney E. Johnson. *Oswego County Historical Society Publications* 24 (1961): 48–75.

Crocker, Silas W. Company I, 6th PA Reserves. "The Charge of the Pennsylvania Reserves." *National Tribune*, January 10, 1889.

Cummings, C. C. "Battle of Fredericksburg, December 13, 1862." *Confederate Veteran* 23 (August 1915): 358.

———. "The Bombardment of Fredericksburg." *Confederate Veteran* 23 (June 1915): 253–54.

Currier, John Charles. "From Concord to Fredericksburg." In *Civil War Papers of the California Commandery and the Oregon Commandery of the Military Order of the Loyal Legion of the United States*, 244–59. Wilmington, N.C.: Broadfoot, 1995.

Cushing, Samuel T. "The Acting Signal Corps." In *War Talks in Kansas: A Series of Papers Read before the Kansas Commandery of the Military Order of the Loyal Legion of the United States*, 92–108. Wilmington, N.C.: Broadfoot, 1992.

Daggett, George Henry. "Those Whom You Left behind You." In *Glimpses of the Nation's Struggle: Papers Read before the Minnesota Commander of the Military Order of the Loyal Legion of the United States*, 5:332–64. Wilmington, N.C.: Broadfoot, 1992.

Daves, Graham. "Twenty-Second North Carolina Infantry." *Southern Historical Society Papers* 24 (January–December 1896): 256–67.

Dent, Stephen. "With Cobb's Brigade at Fredericksburg." *Confederate Veteran* 22 (November 1914): 500–501.

[De Peyster, John Watts]. "Fredericksburg: Who was Responsible for the Repulse?" *Onward* 2 (September 1869): 199–208.

Dinkins, Captain James. "Barksdale's Mississippi Brigade at Fredericksburg." *Confederate Veteran* 34 (July 1926): 256–59.

———. "Griffith-Barksdale-Humphreys Mississippi Brigade and Its Campaigns." *Southern Historical Society Papers* 32 (January–December 1904): 250–74.

Dority, Orin G. "The Civil War Diary of Orin G. Dority," pts. 1 and 2. *Northwest Ohio Quarterly* 37 (Winter 1964–65, Summer 1965): 7–26, 104–14.

Dunn, Moncena. Lt. Col. 19th Mass. "Fredericksburg, How the 19th Mass. Charged Across the River." *National Tribune,* August 19, 1886.

Dyer, Alexander Byrdie. "Fourth Regiment of Artillery." *Journal of Military Service Institution of the United States* 11 (1890): 843–67.

Early, Jubal Anderson. "Stonewall Jackson at Fredericksburg, a Letter from Jubal A. Early." *Historical Magazine* (Morrisania), ser. 2, vol. 8 (July 1870): 32–35.

Eastman, William R. "The Army Chaplain of 1863." In *Personal Recollections of the War of the Rebellion: Addresses Delivered before the New York Commandery of the Loyal Legion of the United States,* 4 vols., edited by A. Noel Blakeman, 4:338–50. Wilmington, N.C. Broadfoot, 1992.

Evans, P. M. "Who Laid the Pontoons?" *National Tribune,* October 18, 1888.

Evans, Thomas H. "'The Cries of the Wounded Were Piercing and Horrible.'" *Civil War Times Illustrated* 7 (July 1968): 28–38.

Everson, Erastus W. "Forward Against Marye's Heights." *Philadelphia Weekly Times,* March 4, 1882.

"Fellow Feeling in the Army." *Confederate Veteran* 2 (November 1894): 339.

Ferris, Anna M. "The Civil War Diaries of Anna M. Ferris." Edited by Harold B. Hancock. *Delaware History* 9 (April 1961): 221–64.

Field, Edward. "The Irish Brigade." *United Service* (Philadelphia), n.s., 1 (June 1889): 575–92.

Fleming, Francis P. "Francis P. Fleming in the War for Southern Independence: Soldiering with the 2nd Florida Regiment." Edited by Edward C. Williamson. *Florida Historical Quarterly* 28 (July 1949): 38–52.

Gallup, Frances E. "A Connecticut Yankee at Fredericksburg." Edited by Richard Lowitt. *Military Affairs* 19 (Winter 1955): 203–4.

Gay, Samuel Frederick. "The Gay Letters: A Civil War Correspondence." Edited by Max L. Heyman Jr. *Journal of the West* 9 (July 1970): 377–412.

"Gen. R. E. Lee to Gen. T. J. Jackson." *Southern Historical Society Papers* 39 (April 1914): 1.

Gibson, Drury P. "Letters from a North Louisiana Tiger." Edited by Debra Nance Laurence. *North Louisiana Historical Association Journal* 10, no. 4 (1979): 130–47.

Goodson, Joab. "Letters of Captain Joab Goodson, 1862–1864," pts. 1 and 2. Edited by W. Stanley Hoole. *Alabama Review* 10 (April, July 1957): 126–53, 215–31.

Goody, Thomas. "The 89th New York." *National Tribune,* April 26, 1888.

Goolrick, Mrs. Frances Bernard. "Frightful Experiences at Fredericksburg." *Confederate Veteran* 18 (November 1910): 513.

———. "The Shelling of Fredericksburg." *Confederate Veteran* 25 (December 1917): 573–74.

Goolrick, Mrs. John T. "Ladies' Memorial Association of Fredericksburg, Va." *Confederate Veteran* 24 (October 1916): 472.

Goolsby, J. C. "Crenshaw Battery, Pegram's Battalion, Confederate States Artillery." *Southern Historical Society Papers* 28 (January–December 1900): 336–76.

Greer, George H. T. "All Thoughts Are Absorbed in the War." *Civil War Times Illustrated* 17 (December 1978): 30–35.

Griner, Joseph Addison. "The Civil War of a Pennsylvania Trooper." Edited by Daniel H. Woodward. *Pennsylvania Magazine of History and Biography* 87 (January 1963): 39–62.

Hadley, John Vestal. "An Indiana Soldier in Love and War: The Civil War Letters of John V. Hadley." Edited by James I. Robertson Jr. *Indiana Magazine of History* 59 (September 1963): 189–288.

Haggard, Horatio C. "Cavalry Fight at Fredericksburg." *Confederate Veteran* 21 (June 1913): 295.

Hall, H. S. "Fredericksburg and Chancellorsville." In *War Talks in Kansas: A Series of Papers Read before the Kansas Commandery of the Military Order of the Loyal Legion of the United States*, 185–205. Wilmington, N.C.: Broadfoot, 1992.

Harris, Loyd G. "Army Music." In *War Papers and Personal Reminiscences, 1861–1865. Read before the Commandery of the State of Missouri, Military Order of the Loyal Legion of the United States*, 287–94. Wilmington, N.C.: Broadfoot, 1992.

Heffelfinger, Jacob. "'Dear Sister Jennie—Dear Brother Jacob': The Correspondence between a Northern Soldier and His Sister in Mechanicsburg, Pennsylvania, 1861–1864," pt. 2. Edited by Florence C. McLaughlin. *Western Pennsylvania Historical Magazine* 60 (July 1977): 203–24.

Helman, Howard. "A Young Soldier in the Army of the Potomac: Diary of Howard Helman, 1862." Edited by Arthur W. Thurner. *Pennsylvania Magazine of History and Biography* 87 (April 1963): 139–55.

Henry, William W. "Fredericksburg, My First Battle." *Blue and Gray* 5 (February 1895): 99–101.

Herring, Sergeant H. "Crossing of the Rappahannock by the 7th Mich." *National Tribune*, April 29, 1897.

Heth, Henry. "Letter from Major General Henry Heth, of A. P. Hill's Corps, A.N.V." *Southern Historical Society Papers* 4 (October 1077). 151–60.

Hightower, Harvey Judson. "Letters from Harvey Judson Hightower, a Confederate Soldier, 1862–1864." Edited by Dewey W. Grantham Jr. *Georgia Historical Quarterly* 40 (June 1956): 174–89.

Hodgkins, N. M. "The 'Macon Light Artillery' at Fredericksburg." *Southern Historical Society Papers* 11 (February–March 1883): 138–39.

Holmes, John Rush. "The Civil War Letters of John Rush Holmes." Edited by Ida Bright Adams. *Western Pennsylvania Historical Magazine* 44 (June 1961): 15–27.

Holsinger, Frank. "How Does One Feel under Fire?" In *War Talks in Kansas: A Series of Papers Read before the Kansas Commandery of the Military Order of the Loyal Legion of the United States*, 290–304. Wilmington, N.C.: Broadfoot, 1992.

Hosford, John W. "A Florida Soldier in the Army of Northern Virginia: The Hosford Letters." Edited by Knox Mellon Jr. *Florida Historical Quarterly* 46 (January 1968): 243–71.

Hubbert, Mike M. "The Travels of the 13th Mississippi Regiment: Excerpts from the Diary of Mike M. Hubbert of Attala County (1861–1862)." Edited by John F. Fisher. *Journal of Mississippi History* 45 (November 1983): 288–313.

Humphreys, Andrew Atkinson. "The Army of the Potomac, General Humphreys at Fredericksburg." *Historical Magazine* (Morrisania), ser. 2, vol. 5 (June 1869): 353–56.

Hunt, Henry J. "Artillery." *Papers of the Military Historical Society of Massachusetts* 13 (1888): 91–125.

Hutchison, Joseph G. "Fredericksburg." In *War Sketches and Incidents as Related by Companions of the Iowa Commandery Military Order of the Loyal Legion of the United States*, 2:255–73. Wilmington, N.C.: Broadfoot, 1994.

"Incidents at Fredericksburg." *Confederate Veteran* 4 (September 1896): 305–7.

Jeffries, Lemuel. "'The Excitement Had Begun!': The Civil War Diary of Lemuel Jeffries, 1862–1863." Edited by Jason H. Silverman. *Manuscripts* 30 (Fall 1978): 265–78.

Jones, J. William. "Gen. A. P. Hill: Partial Sketch of His Thrilling Career." *Confederate Veteran* 1 (August 1893): 233–36.

———. "Stonewall Jackson." *Southern Historical Society Papers* 19 (January 1891): 145–64.

"Jubal Early to One of His Chaplains." *Confederate Veteran* 13 (October 1905): 459.

Kearney, Philip J. "Letters from the Field, Written to his Relatives by Major Philip J.

Kearney, Eleventh New Jersey." *Historical Magazine* (Morrisania), ser. 2, vol. 7 (March 1870): 184–95.

Keeley, John. "Civil War Diary Relates Records of Famous Company." *Atlanta Constitution Magazine,* March 15, 1931.

Kershaw, General J. B. "Richard Kirkland, the Humane Hero of Fredericksburg." *Southern Historical Society Papers* 8 (April 1880): 186–88.

Kibler, James Allen. "Letters from a Confederate Soldier." *Tyler's Quarterly* 31 (1949–50): 120–27.

Kinsolving, Roberta Cary Corbin. "Stonewall Jackson in Winter Quarters." *Confederate Veteran* 20 (January 1912): 24–26.

Kitchen, D. C. "Burnside's Mud March." *Philadelphia Weekly Times,* March 4, 1882.

Lacy, J. Horace. "Lee at Fredericksburg." *Century Magazine* 32 (August 1886): 605–8.

Lamb, John. "The Battle of Fredericksburg." *Southern Historical Society Papers* 27 (January–December 1899): 231–40.

Landon, William D. "Fourteenth Indiana Regiment, Letters to the Vincennes Western Sun." *Indiana Magazine of History* 33 (September 1937): 325–48.

Landry, R. Prosper. "The Donaldsonville Artillery at the Battle of Fredericksburg." *Southern Historical Society Papers* 23 (January–December 1895): 198–202.

Lane, J. H. "Twenty-Eighth North Carolina Infantry." *Southern Historical Society Papers* 24 (January–December 1896): 324–39.

Lang, David. "Civil War Letters of Colonel David Lang." Edited by Bertram H. Groene. *Florida Historical Quarterly* 54 (January 1976): 340–66.

Lapham, Oscar. "Recollections of Service in the Twelfth Regiment R.I. Volunteers." In *Personal Narratives of Events in the Rebellion, Being Papers Read before the Rhode Island Soldiers and Sailors Historical Society,* 5:1–37. Wilmington, N.C.: Broadfoot, 1993.

"The Last Roll." *Confederate Veteran* 14 (September 1906): 414–21.

Leonard, James H. "Letters of a Fifth Wisconsin Volunteer." Edited by R. G. Plumb. *Wisconsin Magazine of History* 3 (1919): 52–83.

"Letters from the Front." *Confederate Veteran* 26 (April 1918): 157–58.

Lloyd, J. C. "The Battles of Fredericksburg." *Confederate Veteran* 23 (November 1915): 500–502.

Long, A. L. "McClellan and Burnside." *Philadelphia Weekly Times,* January 16, 1886.

Longfellow, Stephen. "Fredericksburg." *National Tribune,* February 23, 1888.

Lowe, D. R. "Perilous Service at Fredericksburg." *Confederate Veteran* 17 (May 1909): 236–37.

Lyle, John N. "Stonewall Jackson and Maxcy Gregg." *Confederate Veteran* 8 (December 1900): 538.

McCarter, William. "Fredericksburg, As Seen by One of Meagher's Irish Brigade." *National Tribune,* July 29, 1886.

McClellan, Major H. B. "'The Gallant Pelham' and His Gun at Fredericksburg." *Southern Historical Society Papers* 12 (October–November–December 1884): 466–70.

McCoy, T. F. "The 107th Penna. Vet. Volunteers at South Mountain, Antietam and Fredericksburg." *Philadelphia Press,* January 4, 1888.

McCrady, Edward. "Address before the Virginia Division of Army of Northern Virginia, at their Reunion on the Evening of October 21, 1886." *Southern Historical Society Papers* 14 (January–December 1886): 181–222.

McGuire, Hunter Holmes. "General Thomas J. Jackson." *Southern Historical Society Papers* 19 (January 1891): 298–318.

Mehen, J. R. "An Incident of Fredericksburg." *Confederate Veteran* 23 (September 1915): 407–8.

Milans, Henry G. "Eyewitness to Fredericksburg." *North-South Trader's Civil War* 19 (Christmas 1992): 20–24.

Mills, William Howard. "From Burnside to Hooker: Transfer of the Army of the Potomac, 1863." *Magazine of American History* 15 (January 1885): 44–56.

"Monument to the Confederate Dead at Fredericksburg, Virginia, Unveiled June 10, 1891." *Southern Historical Society Papers* 18 (January–December 1890): 397–406.

Moore, J. H. "Fredericksburg." *Southern Bivouac*, n.s., 2 (August 1886): 179–84.

Mulholland, St. Clair A. "At Fredericksburg." *National Tribune*, October 8, 1881.

———. "The Battle of Fredericksburg." *Philadelphia Weekly Times*, April 23, 1881.

"On Historic Spots." *Southern Historical Society Papers* 36 (January–December 1908): 197–209.

"Pelham at Fredericksburg." *Confederate Veteran* 3 (April 1895): 111.

Pendleton, D. D. "On Marye's Hill." *Philadelphia Weekly Times*, March 26, 1887.

Perkins, Charles E. "Letters Home: Sergeant Charles E. Perkins in Virginia, 1862." Edited by Ray Henshaw and Glenn W. LaFantasie. *Rhode Island History* 39 (November 1980): 107–31.

Perry, Eugene O. "Whip the Devil and His Hosts: The Civil War Letters of Private Eugene O. Perry of Hood's Brigade." Edited by Harold B. Simpson. *Chronicles of Smith County, Texas* 6 (Fall 1967): 10–15, 33–49.

Pierce, Francis E. "I have with the reg't been through a terrible battle." *Civil War Times Illustrated* 1 (December 1962): 6–9, 28–32.

Porter, Rufus Kilpatrick. "Sketch of General T. R. R. Cobb." *Land We Love* 3 (July 1867): 183–97.

"Proceedings of the First Confederate Congress." *Southern Historical Society Papers* 47 (December 1930): 1–229.

Purifoy, John. "Was This a Coincidence?" *Confederate Veteran* 9 (April 1901): 167.

Raymond, Henry W., ed. "Extracts from the Journal of Henry J. Raymond." *Scribner's Monthly*, January, March 1880, 419–24, 703–10.

Redwood, Allen C. "Johnny Reb at Play." *Scribner's Monthly*, November 1878 79, 33–37.

"Reports of the First, Seventh, and Seventeenth Virginia Regiments in 1862." *Southern Historical Society Papers* 38 (January–December 1910): 262–67.

Robertson, Robert S. "Diary of the War by Robert S. Robertson." Edited by Charles N. Walker and Rosemary Walker. *Old Fort News* 28 (April–June 1965): 59–118.

Rollins, George S. "'Give My Love to All': Civil War Letters of George S. Rollins." Edited by Gerald S. Henig. *Civil War Times Illustrated* 11 (November 1972): 16–28.

Ruggles, Emmeline. "A Soldier and a Letter." *Confederate Veteran* 38 (March 1930): 89–90.

"Sacrifice of Federals at Fredericksburg." *Confederate Veteran* 1 (December 1893): 370–71.

Scales, Alfred M. "Battle of Fredericksburg." *Southern Historical Society Papers* 40 (September 1915): 195–223.

Shumate, B. Y. H. "Some Recollections of Fredericksburg." *Confederate Veteran* 21 (July 1913): 342–43.

Simonton, Edward. "Recollections of the Battle of Fredericksburg." In *Glimpses of the Nation's Struggle: Papers Read before the Minnesota Commander of the Military Order of the Loyal Legion of the United States*, 2:245–66. Wilmington, N.C.: Broadfoot, 1992.

"Sixteenth Georgia at Fredericksburg." *Confederate Veteran* 7 (December 1899): 546.

Smith, James Power. "With Stonewall Jackson in the Army of Northern Virginia." *Southern Historical Society Papers* 43 (August 1920): 1–110.

Squires, Charles W. "The 'Boy Officer' of the Washington Artillery." *Civil War Times Illustrated* 14 (May 1975): 10–17, 19–23.

Stiles, Robert. "Monument to the Confederate Dead at the University of Virginia." *Southern Historical Society Papers* 21 (January–December 1893): 15–37.

"Strange Freak in the Army." *Confederate Veteran* 2 (November 1894): 335.

Suddath, James Butler. "From Sumter to the Wilderness: Letters of Sergeant James Butler Suddath, Co. E, 7th Regiment S.C.V." Edited by Frank B. Williams Jr. *South Carolina Historical Magazine* 58 (January, July 1962): 1–12, 93–104.

Taylor, B. F. "Fredericksburg Campaign with the Army of the Potomac." In *War of the Sixties,* edited by Edward R. Hutchins, 37. New York: Neale, 1900.

Taylor, Charles Frederick. "Colonel of the Bucktails: Civil War Letters of Charles Frederick Taylor." Edited by Charles F. Hobson and Arnold Shankman. *Pennsylvania Magazine of History and Biography* 97 (July 1973): 333–61.

Taylor, Isaac Lyman. "Campaigning with the First Minnesota: A Civil War Diary." Edited by Hazel C. Wolf. *Minnesota History* 25 (March, June, September, December 1944): 11–39, 117–52, 224–57, 342–61.

Teall, William W. "Ringside Seat at Fredericksburg." *Civil War Times Illustrated* 4 (May 1965): 17–34.

"Tennesseans at Fredericksburg." *Confederate Veteran* 9 (February 1901): 66–67.

Thompson, Gilbert. "U.S. Engineer Battalion, Their Services at Fredericksburg." *National Tribune,* August 16, 1888.

————. "Who Laid the Pontoons?" *National Tribune,* November 8, 1888.

Thompson, William Y. "The U.S. Sanitary Commission." *Civil War History* 2 (June 1956): 41–63.

Tillinghast, Pardon Elisha. "Reminiscences of Service with the Twelfth Rhode Island Volunteers and a Memorial of Col. George H. Browne." In *Personal Narratives of Events in the Rebellion, Being Papers Read before the Rhode Island Soldiers and Sailors Historical Society,* 5:171–221. Wilmington, N.C.: Broadfoot, 1993.

Tolley, William P. "Campaigns by Army of Northern Virginia." *Confederate Veteran* 8 (March 1900): 109–10.

Torrence, Leonidas. "The Road to Gettysburg: The Diary and Letters of Leonidas Torrence of the Gaston Guards." Edited by Haskell Monroe. *North Carolina Historical Review* 36 (October 1959): 476–517.

Trantham, William D. "Wonderful Story of Richard R. Kirkland." *Confederate Veteran* 16 (March 1908): 105.

Vogl, F. "Who Laid the Pontoons?" *National Tribune,* October 11, 1888.

Walker, Francis A. "Couch at Fredericksburg." *National Tribune,* October 21, 1886.

Ward, W. C. "Unable to Help." *National Tribune,* March 1, 1894.

Welsh, George Wilson, and Philip Rudsil Welsh. "Civil War Letters from Two Brothers." *Yale Review* 18 (September 1928): 148–61.

Wetmore, Ezra F. "Story of a New York Boy at Fredericksburg." *National Tribune,* May 9, 1895.

White, Herman Lorenzo. "The White Papers: Letters (1861–1865) of Pvt. Herman Lorenzo White, 22nd Regiment Massachusetts Volunteers." Edited by Kathleen Kroll and Charles Moran. *Massachusetts Review* 18 (Summer 1977): 248–70.

White, William S. "A Diary of the War." In *Contributions to a History of the Richmond Howitzer Battalion, Pamphlet No. 2,* 89–286. Richmond: Carlton and McCarthy, 1883.

Whittemore, Charles, and Ruth Whittemore. "'Despotism of Traitors': The Rebellious South through New York Eyes." Edited by Walter Rundell Jr. *New York History* 45 (October 1964): 331–67.

Whittier, Charles A. "Comments on the Peninsular Campaign of General McClellan." *Papers of the Military Historical Society of Massachusetts* 1 (1878): 279–300.

Willey, T. L. "Who Laid the Pontoons at Fredericksburg?" *National Tribune,* July 26, 1888.

Wilson, James Harrison. "Major-General Andrew Atkinson Humphreys." *Papers of the Military Historical Society of Massachusetts* 10 (1893): 71–96.

Wingfield, Henry Wyatt. "Diary of Capt. H. W. Wingfield, 58th Virginia Regiment." *Bulletin of the Virginia State Library* 16 (July 1927): 7–47

Wood, U. D. "Who Laid the Pontoons?" *National Tribune,* November 22, 1888.

Young, Abram Hayne. "Civil War Letters of Abram Hayne Young." *South Carolina Historical Magazine* 78 (January 1977): 56–70.

SECONDARY SOURCES

Books

Adams, Ephraim Douglass. *Great Britain and the American Civil War.* 2 vols. New York: Longmans, Green, 1925.

Adams, Michael C. C. *Our Masters the Rebels: A Speculation on Union Military Failure in the East, 1861–1865.* Cambridge, Mass.: Harvard University Press, 1978.

Allan, Elizabeth Preston. *The Life and Letters of Margaret Junkin Preston.* Boston: Houghton Mifflin, 1903.

Allport, Gordon W., and Leo Postman. *The Psychology of Rumor.* New York: Henry Holt, 1947.

Alotta, Robert I. *Stop the Evil: A Civil War History of Desertion and Murder.* San Rafael, Calif.: Presidio, 1978.

Alvey, Edward, Jr. *History of the Presbyterian Church of Fredericksburg, Virginia.* Fredericksburg, Va.: Session of the Presbyterian Church of Fredericksburg, 1976.

Ambrose, Stephen E. *Halleck: Lincoln's Chief of Staff.* Baton Rouge: Louisiana State University Press, 1962.

Andreano, Ralph, ed. *The Economic Impact of the American Civil War.* Cambridge, Mass.: Schenkman, 1962.

Andrews, J. Cutler. *The North Reports the Civil War.* Pittsburgh: University of Pittsburgh Press, 1955.

———. *The South Reports the Civil War.* Princeton, N.J.: Princeton University Press, 1970.

Armstrong, Warren B. *For Courageous Fighting and Confident Dying: Union Chaplains in the Civil War.* Lawrence: University Press of Kansas, 1998.

Ash, Stephen V. *When the Yankees Came: Conflict and Chaos in the Occupied South, 1861–1865.* Chapel Hill: University of North Carolina Press, 1995.

Ashcraft, John M. *31st Virginia Infantry.* Lynchburg, Va.: H. E. Howard, 1988.

Athearn, Robert Greenleaf. *Thomas Francis Meagher: An Irish Revolutionary in America.* Boulder: University of Colorado Press, 1949.

Austin, Aurelia. *Georgia Boys with "Stonewall" Jackson: James Thomas Thompson and the Walton Infantry.* Athens: University of Georgia Press, 1967.

Bache, Richard Meade. *Life of General George Gordon Meade, Commander of the Army of the Potomac.* Philadelphia: Henry T. Coates, 1897.

Balfour, Daniel T. *13th Virginia Cavalry.* Lynchburg, Va.: H. E. Howard, 1986.

Bartlett, Irving H. *Wendell and Ann Phillips: The Community of Reform, 1840–1880.* New York: Norton, 1979.

Barton, Michael. *Goodmen: The Character of Civil War Soldiers.* University Park: Pennsylvania State University Press, 1981.

Baxter, Nancy Niblack. *Gallant Fourteenth: The Story of an Indiana Civil War Regiment.* Traverse City, Mich.: Pioneer Study Center Press, 1980.

Bean, W. G. *Stonewall's Man: Sandie Pendleton.* Chapel Hill: University of North Carolina Press, 1959.

Becker, Ernest. *The Denial of Death.* New York: Free Press, 1973.

Bell, Robert T. *11th Virginia Infantry.* Lynchburg, Va.: H. E. Howard, 1985.

Bennett, Brian A. *Sons of Old Monroe: A Regimental History of Patrick O'Rorke's 140th New York Volunteer Infantry.* Dayton, Ohio: Morningside, 1992.

Best, Isaac O. *History of the 121st New York State Infantry.* Chicago: James H. Smith, 1921.

Bidwell, Frederick David. *History of the Forty-ninth New York Volunteers.* Albany, N.Y.: J. B. Lyon, 1916.

Bigelow, John. *The Campaign of Chancellorsville.* New Haven, Conn.: Yale University Press, 1910.

Blight, David W. *Frederick Douglass' Civil War: Keeping Faith in Jubilee.* Baton Rouge: Louisiana State University Press, 1989.

Blondheim, Menahem. *News over the Wires: The Telegraph and the Flow of Public Information in America, 1844–1897.* Cambridge, Mass.: Harvard University Press, 1994.

Blue, Frederick J. *Salmon P. Chase: A Life in Politics.* Kent, Ohio: Kent State University Press, 1987.

Bohannon, Keith S. *The Giles, Allegheny, and Jackson Artillery.* Lynchburg, Va.: H. E. Howard, 1990.

Boney, F. N. *John Letcher of Virginia: The Story of Virginia's Civil War Governor.* Tuscaloosa: University of Alabama Press, 1966.

Bradley, Erwin Stanley. *Simon Cameron: Lincoln's Secretary of War.* Philadelphia: University of Pennsylvania Press, 1966.

Brainard, Mary Genevie Green. *Campaigns of the One Hundred and Forty-sixth Regiment New York Volunteers.* New York: G. P. Putnam's Sons, 1915.

Bremner, Robert H. *The Public Good: Philanthropy and Welfare in the Civil War Era.* New York: Knopf, 1980.

Brewer, Abraham Titus. *History of the Sixty-first Regiment Pennsylvania Volunteers, 1861–1865.* Pittsburgh: Art Engraving and Printing, 1911.

Bridges, Hal. *Lee's Maverick General: Daniel Harvey Hill.* New York: McGraw-Hill, 1961.

Brown, Kent Masterson. *Cushing of Gettysburg: The Story of a Union Artillery Commander.* Lexington: University Press of Kentucky, 1993.

Browne, Francis Fisher. *The Every-day Life of Abraham Lincoln.* Minneapolis: Northwestern Pub. Co., 1887.

Bruce, George Anson. *The Twentieth Regiment of Massachusetts Volunteer Infantry, 1861–1865.* Boston: Houghton Mifflin, 1906.

Brunson, Joseph W. *Historical Sketch of the Pee Dee Light Artillery, Army of Northern Virginia.* Winston-Salem, N.C.: Stewart Printing House, 1927.

Bryan, T. Conn. *Confederate Georgia.* Athens: University of Georgia Press, 1953.

Burton, William L. *Melting Pot Soldiers: The Union's Ethnic Regiments.* Ames: Iowa State University Press, 1988.

Bushong, Millard Kessler. *Old Jube: A Biography of General Jubal A. Early.* Boyce, Va.: Carr Pub. Co., 1955.

Carman, Harry J., and Reinhard H. Luthin. *Lincoln and the Patronage.* New York: Columbia University Press, 1943.

Carmichael, Peter S. *Lee's Young Artillerist: William R. J. Pegram.* Charlottesville: University Press of Virginia, 1995.

———. *The Purcell, Crenshaw, and Letcher Artillery.* Lynchburg, Va.: H. E. Howard, 1990.

Carpenter, John A. *Sword and Olive Branch: Oliver Otis Howard.* Pittsburgh: University of Pittsburgh Press, 1964.

Carroll, Daniel B. *Henri Mercier and the American Civil War.* Princeton, N.J.: Princeton University Press, 1971.

Cary, Edward. *George William Curtis.* Boston: Houghton Mifflin, 1894.

Case, Lynn M., and Warren F. Spencer. *The United States and France: Civil War Diplomacy.* Philadelphia: University of Pennsylvania Press, 1970.

Castel, Albert. *Decision in the West: The Atlanta Campaign of 1864.* Lawrence: University Press of Kansas, 1992.

Catton, Bruce. *Glory Road: The Bloody Route from Fredericksburg to Gettysburg.* Garden City, N.Y.: Doubleday, 1952.

———. *Never Call Retreat.* Garden City, N.Y.: Doubleday, 1965.

Chambers, Lenoir. *Stonewall Jackson.* 2 vols. New York: William Morrow, 1959.

Chapin, Louis N. *A Brief History of the Thirty-fourth Regiment N.Y.S.V.* New York: n.p., 1903.

Chapla, John David. *42nd Virginia Infantry.* Lynchburg, Va.: H. E. Howard, 1983.

———. *48th Virginia Infantry.* Lynchburg, Va.: H. E. Howard, 1989.

Cheek, Philip, and Mair Pointon. *History of the Sauk County Riflemen, Known as Company "A," Sixth Wisconsin Veteran Volunteer Infantry, 1861–1865.* Madison, Wisc.: Democrat Printing Co., 1909.

Clausewitz, Carl von. *On War.* Edited and translated by Michael Howard and Peter Paret. Princeton, N.J.: Princeton University Press, 1984.

Cleaves, Freeman. *Meade of Gettysburg.* Norman: University of Oklahoma Press, 1960.

Coffin, Howard. *Full Duty: Vermonters in the Civil War.* Woodstock, Vt.: Countryman Press, 1993.

Cole, Arthur Charles. *The Sesquicentennial History of Illinois: The Era of the Civil War, 1848–1870.* Urbana: University of Illinois Press, 1987.

Collins, Calvin L. *"I Will Die In My Pit!": The Story of the Third Regiment, Arkansas Infantry, C.S.A.* Little Rock: Pioneer Press, 1959.

Comte de Paris. *History of the Civil War in America.* 4 vols. Translated by Louis F. Tasistro. Philadelphia: Joseph H. Coates, 1875.

Cox, LaWanda. *Lincoln and Black Freedom: A Study in Presidential Leadership.* Columbia: University of South Carolina Press, 1981.

Crook, D. P. *The North, the South, and the Powers, 1861–1865.* New York: John Wiley and Sons, 1974.

Current, Richard N. *The History of Wisconsin: The Civil War Era, 1848–1873.* Madison: State Historical Society of Wisconsin, 1976.

Curry, Leonard P. *Blueprint for Modern America: Nonmilitary Legislation of the First Civil War Congress.* Nashville: Vanderbilt University Press, 1968.

Daly, Louise Haskell. *Alexander Cheeves Haskell: The Portrait of a Man.* Wilmington, N.C.: Broadfoot, 1988.

Darter, Oscar H. *The History of the Fredericksburg Baptist Church, Fredericksburg, Virginia.* Richmond: Garrett and Massie, 1960.

Davis, Archie K. *Boy Colonel of the Confederacy: The Life and Times of Henry King Burgwyn, Jr.* Chapel Hill: University of North Carolina Press, 1985.

Davis, William C. *Jefferson Davis: The Man and His Hour.* New York: Harper Collins, 1991.

———. *Lincoln's Men: How President Lincoln Became Father to an Army and a Nation.* New York: Free Press, 1999.

Dean, Eric T., Jr. *Shook over Hell: Post-Traumatic Stress, Vietnam, and the Civil War.* Cambridge, Mass.: Harvard University Press, 1997.

Dell, Christopher. *Lincoln and the War Democrats: The Grand Erosion of Conservative Tradition.* Rutherford, N.J.: Fairleigh Dickinson University Press, 1975.

d'Entremont, John. *Southern Emancipator: Moncure Conway, the American Years, 1832–1865.* New York: Oxford University Press, 1987.

Diggins, John Patrick. *The Lost Soul of American Politics: Virtue, Self-Interest, and the Foundations of Liberalism.* New York: Basic Books, 1984.

Divine, John E. *8th Virginia Infantry.* Lynchburg, Va.: H. E. Howard, 1983.

Donald, David Herbert. *Charles Sumner and the Rights of Man.* New York: Knopf, 1970.

———. *Lincoln.* New York: Simon and Schuster, 1995.

———. *Lincoln Reconsidered: Essays on the Civil War Era.* 2nd ed. New York: Vintage, 1961.

Driver, Robert J., Jr. *The 1st and 2nd Rockbridge Artillery*. Lynchburg, Va.: H. E. Howard, 1987.

———. *1st Virginia Cavalry*. Lynchburg, Va.: H. E. Howard, 1991.

———. *52nd Virginia Infantry*. Lynchburg, Va.: H. E. Howard, 1986.

———. *58th Virginia Infantry*. Lynchburg, Va.: H. E. Howard, 1990.

Duberman, Martin. *Charles Francis Adams, 1807-1886*. Stanford, Calif.: Stanford University Press, 1960.

DuBose, John Witherspoon. *The Life and Times of William Lowndes Yancey*. 1892. Reprint, New York: Peter Smith, 1942.

Dunn, Craig L. *Iron Men, Iron Will: The Nineteenth Indiana Regiment of the Iron Brigade*. Indianapolis: Guild Press, 1995.

Dusinberre, William. *Civil War Issues in Philadelphia, 1856-1865*. Philadelphia: University of Pennsylvania Press, 1965.

Dyer, Frederick H. *A Compendium of the War of the Rebellion*. Dayton, Ohio: Morningside, 1978.

Ellison, Mary. *Support for Secession: Lancashire and the American Civil War*. Chicago: University of Chicago Press, 1972.

Faust, Drew Gilpin. *The Creation of Confederate Nationalism: Ideology and Identity in the Civil War South*. Baton Rouge: Louisiana State University Press, 1988.

———. *"A Riddle of Death": Mortality and Meaning in the American Civil War*. Gettysburg, Pa.: Gettysburg College, 1995.

Faust, Patricia L., ed. *Historical Times Illustrated Encyclopedia of the Civil War*. New York: Harper and Row, 1986.

Field, Phyllis F. *The Politics of Race in New York: The Struggle for Black Suffrage in the Civil War Era*. Ithaca, N.Y.: Cornell University Press, 1982.

Fishel, Edwin C. *The Secret War for the Union: The Untold Story of Military Intelligence in the Civil War*. Boston: Houghton Mifflin, 1996.

Fleming, Vivian Minor. *Battles of Fredericksburg and Chancellorsville*. Richmond: W. C. Hall, 1921.

Flower, Frank Abial. *Edwin McMasters Stanton: The Autocrat of Rebellion, Emancipation, and Reconstruction*. Akron, Ohio: Saalfield, 1905.

Foner, Eric. *The Story of American Freedom*. New York: Norton, 1998.

Foner, Philip S. *British Labor and the American Civil War*. New York: Holmes and Meier, 1981.

Foote, Shelby. *The Civil War: A Narrative*. 3 vols. New York: Random House, 1958–74.

Fox, William F. *Regimental Losses in the American Civil War, 1861-1865*. Dayton, Ohio: Morningside, 1985.

Frank, Joseph Allan, and George A. Reaves. *"Seeing the Elephant": Raw Recruits at the Battle of Shiloh*. New York: Greenwood Press, 1989.

Franklin, John Hope. *The Emancipation Proclamation*. Garden City, N.Y.: Doubleday, 1963.

Frederickson, George M. *The Inner Civil War: Northern Intellectuals and the Crisis of the Union*. New York: Harper and Row, 1965.

Freeman, Douglas Southall. *A Calendar of Confederate Papers*. Richmond: Confederate Museum, 1908.

———. *Lee's Lieutenants*. 3 vols. New York: Charles Scribner's Sons, 1942–44.

———. *R. E. Lee: A Biography*. 4 vols. New York: Charles Scribner's Sons, 1934–35.

Frinfrock, Bradley. *Across the Rappahannock: From Fredericksburg to the Mud March*. Bowie, Md.: Heritage Books, 1994.

Furgurson, Ernest B. *Chancellorsville, 1863: The Souls of the Brave*. New York: Knopf, 1992.

Gaff, Alan D. *On Many a Bloody Field: Four Years in the Iron Brigade*. Bloomington: Indiana University Press, 1996.

Gallagher, Gary W., ed. *The Fredericksburg Campaign: Decision on the Rappahannock.* Chapel Hill: University of North Carolina Press, 1995.

Gallman, J. Matthew. *Mustering Wartime: A Social History of Philadelphia during the Civil War.* Cambridge: Cambridge University Press, 1990.

———. *The North Fights the Civil War: The Home Front.* Chicago: Ivan R. Dee, 1994.

Gambone, A. M. *"If Tomorrow Night Finds Me Dead": The Life of General Samuel K. Zook.* Baltimore: Butternut and Blue, 1996.

———. *Major-General John Frederick Hartranft: Citizen Soldier and Pennsylvania Statesman.* Baltimore: Butternut and Blue, 1995.

Gannon, James P. *Irish Rebels, Confederate Tigers: The 6th Louisiana Volunteers, 1861–1865.* Campbell, Calif.: Savas Publishing, 1998.

Garner, Stanton. *The Civil War World of Herman Melville.* Lawrence: University Press of Kansas, 1993.

Gavin, William G. *Campaigning with the Roundheads: The History of the Hundredth Pennsylvania Veteran Volunteer Infantry Regiment in the American Civil War, 1861–1865.* Dayton, Ohio: Morningside, 1989.

Geary, James W. *We Need Men: The Union Draft in the Civil War.* DeKalb: Northern Illinois University Press, 1991.

George, Mary Karl. *Zachariah Chandler: A Political Biography.* East Lansing: Michigan State University Press, 1969.

Gerry, H. E. *Camp Fire Entertainment and True History of Robert Henry Hendershot, the Drummer Boy of the Rappahannock.* Chicago: Hack and Anderson, 1898.

Glover, Edwin A. *Bucktailed Wildcats, a Regiment of Civil War Volunteers.* New York: Yuseloff, 1960.

Goff, Richard D. *Confederate Supply.* Durham, N.C.: Duke University Press, 1969.

Gough, John Edmond. *Fredericksburg and Chancellorsville: A Study of the Federal Operations.* London: Hugh Rees, 1913.

Gould, Edward Kalloch. *Major-General Hiram G. Berry, His Career as a Contractor, Bank President, Politician, and Major-General of Volunteers in the Civil War.* Rockland, Maine: Courier-Gazette, 1899.

Gray, Wood. *The Hidden Civil War: The Story of the Copperheads.* New York: Viking Press, 1942.

Greene, Jacob Lyman. *Gen. William B. Franklin and the Operations of the Left Wing at the Battle of Fredericksburg, December 13, 1862.* Hartford, Conn.: Belknap and Warfield, 1900.

Gregory, G. Howard. *38th Virginia Infantry.* Lynchburg, Va.: H. E. Howard, 1988.

Griffith, Paddy. *Battle Tactics of the Civil War.* New Haven, Conn.: Yale University Press, 1989.

Grimsley, Mark. *The Hard Hand of War: Union Military Policy toward Southern Civilians, 1861–1865.* Cambridge: Cambridge University Press, 1995.

Gunn, Ralph White. *24th Virginia Infantry.* Lynchburg, Va.: H. E. Howard, 1987.

Gurowski, Adam. *Diary.* 3 vols. New York: Burt Franklin, 1968.

Hagerman, Edward. *The American Civil War and the Origins of Modern Warfare.* Bloomington: Indiana University Press, 1988.

Hagerty, Edward J. *Collis' Zouaves: The 114th Pennsylvania Volunteers in the Civil War.* Baton Rouge: Louisiana State University Press, 1997.

Hammond, Bray. *Sovereignty and an Empty Purse: Banks and Politics in the Civil War.* Princeton, N.J.: Princeton University Press, 1970.

Harrison, John M. *The Man Who Made Nasby, David Ross Locke.* Chapel Hill: University of North Carolina Press, 1969.

Harrison, Noel G. *Fredericksburg Civil War Sites*. 2 vols. Lynchburg, Va.: H. E. Howard, 1995.

Hartley, Chris J. *Stuart's Tarheels: James B. Gordon and His North Carolina Cavalry*. Baltimore: Butternut and Blue, 1996.

Hassler, Warren W. *Commanders of the Army of the Potomac*. Baton Rouge: Louisiana State University Press, 1962.

———. *General George B. McClellan: Shield of the Union*. Baton Rouge: Louisiana State University Press, 1957.

Hassler, William Woods. *A. P. Hill: Lee's Forgotten General*. Richmond: Garrett and Massie, 1957.

———. *Colonel John Pelham: Lee's Boy Artillerist*. Richmond: Garrett and Massie, 1960.

Hattaway, Herman, and Archer Jones. *How the North Won: A Military History of the Civil War*. Urbana: University of Illinois Press, 1983.

Hebert, Walter H. *Fighting Joe Hooker*. Indianapolis: Bobbs-Merrill, 1944.

Henderson, Col. G. F. R. *The Civil War: A Soldier's View*. Edited by Jay Luvaas. Chicago: University of Chicago Press, 1958.

———. *Stonewall Jackson and the American Civil War*. New York: Grosset and Dunlap, 1898.

Henderson, William D. *12th Virginia Infantry*. Lynchburg, Va.: H. E. Howard, 1984.

Hennessy, John J. *Return to Bull Run: The Campaign and Battle of Second Manassas*. New York: Simon and Schuster, 1993.

Hernon, James. *Celts, Catholics, and Copperheads: Ireland Views the American Civil War*. Columbus: Ohio State University Press, 1968.

Hess, Earl J. *Liberty, Virtue, and Progress: Northerners and Their War for the Union*. New York: New York University Press, 1988.

———. *The Union Soldier in Battle: Enduring the Ordeal of Combat*. Lawrence: University Press of Kansas, 1997.

Hesseltine, William B. *Lincoln and the War Governors*. New York: Knopf, 1955.

Holland, Lynwood M. *Pierce M. B. Young: The Warwick of the South*. Athens: University of Georgia Press, 1964.

Hoole, William Stanley. *Lawley Covers the Confederacy*. Tuscaloosa, Ala.: Confederate Pub. Co., 1964.

Humphreys, Henry H. *Andrew Atkinson Humphreys: A Biography*. Philadelphia: John C. Winston, 1924.

Hunt, H. Draper. *Hannibal Hamlin of Maine, Lincoln's First Vice President*. Syracuse, N.Y.: Syracuse University Press, 1969.

Imholte, John Quinn. *The First Volunteers: History of the First Minnesota Volunteer Regiment, 1861–1865*. Minneapolis: Ross and Haines, 1963.

Iobst, Richard W., and Louis H. Manarin. *The Bloody Sixth: The Sixth North Carolina Regiment, Confederate States of America*. Raleigh: North Carolina Confederate Centennial Commission, 1965.

Jensen, Les. *32nd Virginia Infantry*. Lynchburg, Va.: H. E. Howard, 1990.

Jimerson, Randall C. *The Private Civil War: Popular Thought during the Sectional Conflict*. Baton Rouge: Louisiana State University Press, 1988.

Johnson, Mary N. *This They Remembered*. Washington, Ga.: Washington Pub. Co., 1986.

Johnston, Angus James, II. *Virginia Railroads in the Civil War*. Chapel Hill: University of North Carolina Press, 1961.

Jones, Howard. *Abraham Lincoln and a New Birth of Freedom: The Union and Slavery in the Diplomacy of the Civil War*. Lincoln: University of Nebraska Press, 1999.

———. *Union in Peril: The Crisis over British Intervention in the Civil War*. Chapel Hill: University of North Carolina Press, 1992.

Jones, Terry L. *Lee's Tigers: The Louisiana Infantry in the Army of Northern Virginia*. Baton Rouge: Louisiana State University Press, 1987.

Jordan, David M. *Winfield Scott Hancock: A Soldier's Life*. Bloomington: Indiana University Press, 1988.

Jordan, William B., Jr. *Red Diamond Regiment: The 17th Maine Infantry, 1862–1865*. Shippensburg, Pa.: White Mane, 1996.

Kapferer, Jean-Noël. *Rumors: Uses, Interpretations, and Images*. New Brunswick, N.J.: Transaction Publishers, 1990.

Kaser, David. *Books and Libraries in Camp and Battle: The Civil War Experience*. Westport, Conn.: Greenwood Press, 1984.

Katz, Irving. *August Belmont: A Political Biography*. New York: Columbia University Press, 1968.

Keegan, John. *The Face of Battle*. New York: Viking, 1976.

King, Willard L. *Lincoln's Manager: David Davis*. Cambridge, Mass.: Harvard University Press, 1960.

Klein, Maury. *Edward Porter Alexander*. Athens: University of Georgia Press, 1971.

Klement, Frank L. *The Copperheads in the Middle West*. Chicago: University of Chicago Press, 1960.

———. *Dark Lanterns, Secret Political Societies, Conspiracies, and Treason Trials in the Civil War*. Baton Rouge: Louisiana State University Press, 1984.

———. *The Limits of Dissent: Clement L. Vallandigham and the Civil War*. Lexington: University Press of Kentucky, 1970.

Kleppner, Paul. *The Third Electoral System, 1853–1892: Parties, Voters, and Political Cultures*. Chapel Hill: University of North Carolina Press, 1979.

Krick, Robert K. *30th Virginia Infantry*. Lynchburg, Va.: H. E. Howard, 1985.

———. *Fredericksburg Artillery*. Lynchburg, Va.: H. E. Howard, 1987.

———. *Lee's Colonels: A Biographical Register of the Field Officers of the Army of Northern Virginia*. 3rd ed. Dayton, Ohio: Morningside, 1991.

———. *Parker's Virginia Battery*. 2nd ed. Wilmington, N.C.: Broadfoot, 1988.

Laboda, Lawrence R. *From Selma to Appomattox: The History of the Jeff Davis Artillery*. Shippensburg, Pa.: White Mane, 1994.

Laderman, Gary. *Sacred Remains: American Attitudes toward Death, 1799–1883*. New Haven, Conn.: Yale University Press, 1996.

Leech, Margaret. *Reveille in Washington, 1860–1865*. New York: Harper and Brothers, 1941.

Leonard, Elizabeth D. *Yankee Women: Gender Battles in the Civil War*. New York: Norton, 1994.

Leonard, Thomas C. *News for All: America's Coming-of-Age with the Press*. New York: Oxford University Press, 1995.

———. *The Power of the Press: The Birth of American Political Reporting*. New York: Oxford University Press, 1986.

Lepore, Jill. *The Name of War: King Phillip's War and the Origins of American Identity*. New York: Knopf, 1998.

Lifton, Robert Jay. *History and Human Survival: Essays on the Young and Old, Survivors and the Dead, Peace and War, and on Contemporary Psychohistory*. New York: Random House, 1970.

Linderman, Gerald F. *Embattled Courage: The Experience of Combat in the American Civil War*. New York: Free Press, 1987.

Lindsey, David. *"Sunset" Cox: Irrepressible Democrat*. Detroit: Wayne State University Press, 1959.

Livermore, Thomas L. *Numbers and Losses in the Civil War in America, 1861–1865*. Bloomington: Indiana University Press, 1957.

Loehr, Charles T. *War History of the Old First Virginia Infantry Regiment.* Dayton, Ohio: Morningside, 1970.

Logsdon, Joseph. *Horace White, Nineteenth Century Liberal.* Westport, Conn.: Greenwood Press, 1971.

Longacre, Edward G. *The Man behind the Guns: A Biography of General Henry J. Hunt, Commander of Artillery, Army of the Potomac.* South Brunswick, N.J.: A. S. Barnes, 1977.

Luvaas, Jay. *The Military Legacy of the Civil War: The European Inheritance.* Chicago: University of Chicago Press, 1959.

McCash, William B. *Thomas R. R. Cobb: The Making of a Southern Nationalist.* Macon, Ga.: Mercer University Press, 1983.

McMurry, Richard M. *John Bell Hood and the War for Southern Independence.* Lexington: University Press of Kentucky, 1982.

McPherson, James M. *Battle Cry of Freedom: The Civil War Era.* New York: Oxford University Press, 1988.

———. *For Cause and Comrades: Why Men Fought in the Civil War.* New York: Oxford University Press, 1997.

———. *The Struggle for Equality: Abolitionists and the Negro in the Civil War and Reconstruction.* Princeton, N.J.: Princeton University Press, 1964.

———. *What They Fought For, 1861–1865.* Baton Rouge: Louisiana State University Press, 1994.

McWhiney, Grady, and Perry D. Jamieson. *Attack and Die: Civil War Military Tactics and the Southern Heritage.* University: University of Alabama Press, 1982.

Manarin, Louis H. *15th Virginia Infantry.* Lynchburg, Va.: H. E. Howard, 1990.

Marten, James. *The Children's Civil War.* Chapel Hill: University of North Carolina Press, 1998.

Martin, Bessie. *Desertion of Alabama Troops from the Confederate Army.* New York: AMS Press, 1966.

Martin, David G. *The Fluvanna Artillery.* Lynchburg, Va.: H. E. Howard, 1992.

Marvel, William. *Burnside.* Chapel Hill: University of North Carolina Press, 1991.

———. *The First New Hampshire Battery, 1861–1865.* South Conway, N.H.: Lost Cemetery Press, 1985.

———. *Race of the Soil: A History of the Ninth New Hampshire.* Wilmington, N.C.: Broadfoot, 1988.

Massey, Mary Elizabeth. *Refugee Life in the Confederacy.* Baton Rouge: Louisiana State University Press, 1964.

Mattern, Carolyn J. *Soldiers When They Go: The Story of Camp Randall, 1861–1865.* Madison: State Historical Society of Wisconsin, 1981.

Maxwell, William Quentin. *Lincoln's Fifth Wheel: The Political History of the U.S. Sanitary Commission.* New York: Longmans, Green, 1956.

Meade, Robert Douthat. *Judah P. Benjamin: Confederate Statesman.* New York: Oxford University Press, 1943.

Michie, Peter Smith. *The Life and Letters of Emory Upton, Colonel of the Fourth Regiment of Artillery.* New York: Appleton, 1885.

Miers, Earl Schenck. *Lincoln Day by Day: A Chronology, 1809–1865.* 3 vols. Dayton, Ohio: Morningside, 1991.

Miller, Francis Trevelyan. *Photographic History of the Civil War.* 10 vols. New York: Review of Reviews, 1912.

Miller, Randall M., Harry S. Stout, and Charles Reagan Wilson, eds. *Religion and the American Civil War.* New York: Oxford University Press, 1998.

Miller, Richard F., and Robert F. Mooney. *The Civil War: The Nantucket Experience.* Nantucket, Mass.: Wesco Publishing, 1994.

Miller, William J. *The Training of an Army: Camp Curtin and the North's Civil War.* Shippensburg, Pa.: White Mane, 1990.

Mills, George H. *History of the 16th North Carolina Regiment.* Hamilton, N.Y.: Edmonston, 1992.

Mitchell, Reid. *Civil War Soldiers: Their Expectations and Experiences.* New York: Simon and Schuster, 1988.

———. *The Vacant Chair: The Northern Soldier Leaves Home.* New York: Oxford University Press, 1993.

Mitchell, Stewart. *Horatio Seymour of New York.* Cambridge, Mass.: Harvard University Press, 1938.

Mitchell, Wesley C. *A History of the Greenbacks.* Chicago: University of Chicago Press, 1903.

Moe, Richard. *The Last Full Measure: The Life and Death of the First Minnesota Volunteers.* New York: Henry Holt, 1993.

Moore, Robert H. *The Danville, Eight Star, New Market, and Dixie Artillery.* Lynchburg, Va.: H. E. Howard, 1989.

Mulholland, St. Clair Augustine. *Military Order Congress Medal of Honor Legion of the United States.* Philadelphia: Town Printing, 1905.

Mundy, James H. *No Rich Men's Sons: The First Maine Volunteer Infantry.* Cape Elizabeth, Maine: Harp Publications, 1994.

———. *Second to None: The Story of the 2d Maine Volunteer Infantry Regiment.* Scarborough, Maine: Harp Publications, 1992.

Musselman, Homer D. *The Caroline Light, Parker, and Stafford Light Virginia Artillery.* Lynchburg, Va.: H. E. Howard, 1992.

Naisawald, L. Van Loan. *Grape and Canister: The Story of the Field Artillery in the Army of the Potomac, 1861–1865.* New York: Oxford University Press, 1960.

Neely, Mark E., Jr. *The Fate of Liberty: Abraham Lincoln and Civil Liberties.* New York: Oxford University Press, 1991.

Nevins, Allan. *The War for the Union.* 4 vols. New York: Charles Scribner's Sons, 1959–71.

Nichols, Edward J. *Toward Gettysburg: A Biography of John F. Reynolds.* University Park: Pennsylvania State University Press, 1958.

Nissenbaum, Stephen. *The Battle for Christmas.* New York: Knopf, 1996.

Niven, John. *Connecticut for the Union: The Role of the State in the Civil War.* New Haven, Conn.: Yale University Press, 1965.

———. *Salmon P. Chase: A Biography.* New York: Oxford University Press, 1995.

Nolan, Alan. *The Iron Brigade.* 3rd ed. Berrien Springs, Mich.: Hardscrabble Books, 1983.

Oates, Stephen B. *With Malice toward None: The Life of Abraham Lincoln.* New York: Harper and Row, 1977.

———. *A Woman of Valor: Clara Barton and the Civil War.* New York: Free Press, 1994.

Oberholtzer, Ellis Paxson. *Jay Cooke: Financier of the Civil War.* 2 vols. Philadelphia: George W. Jacobs, 1907.

O'Connor, Thomas H. *Civil War Boston: Home Front and Battlefield.* Boston: Northeastern University Press, 1997.

O'Reilly, Frank. *The Fredericksburg Campaign: "Stonewall" Jackson at Fredericksburg, the Battle of Prospect Hill, December 13, 1862.* Lynchburg, Va.: H. E. Howard, 1993.

O'Sullivan, Richard. *55th Virginia Infantry.* Lynchburg, Va.: H. E. Howard, 1989.

Owsley, Frank Lawrence. *King Cotton Diplomacy: Foreign Relations of the Confederate States of America.* Rev. ed. Chicago: University of Chicago Press, 1959.

Palfrey, Francis Winthrop. *The Antietam and Fredericksburg.* New York: Charles Scribner's Sons, 1882.

Paludan, Phillip Shaw. *"A People's Contest": The Union and the Civil War, 1861–1865.* New York: Harper and Brothers, 1988.

————. *The Presidency of Abraham Lincoln.* Lawrence: University Press of Kansas, 1994.

Pearson, Henry. *James S. Wadsworth of Geneseo.* New York: Charles Scribner's Sons, 1913.

Pearson, Henry Greenleaf. *The Life of John A. Andrew: Governor of Massachusetts, 1861–1865.* 2 vols. Boston: Houghton Mifflin, 1904.

Pennypacker, Isaac Rusling. *General Meade.* New York: Appleton, 1901.

Pierrepont, Alice V. D. *Reuben Vaughan Kidd, Soldier of the Confederacy.* Petersburg: n.p., 1947.

Pike, Martha V., and Janice Gray Armstrong. *A Time to Mourn: Expressions of Grief in Nineteenth Century America.* Stony Brook, N.Y.: Museums at Stony Brook, 1980.

Plum, William Rattle. *The Military Telegraph during the Civil War in the United States.* 2 vols. New York: Arno Press, 1974.

Poore, Benjamin Perley. *The Life and Public Services of Ambrose E. Burnside, Soldier, Citizen, Statesman.* Providence, R.I.: J. A. and R. A. Reid, 1882.

Porter, George H. *Ohio Politics during the Civil War Period.* New York: Columbia University Press, 1911.

Powell, William Henry. *The Fifth Army Corps.* New York: G. P. Putnam's Sons, 1896.

Pratt, Fletcher. *Stanton: Lincoln's Secretary of War.* New York: Norton, 1953.

Pred, Allan R. *Urban Growth and the Circulation of Information: The United States System of Cities, 1790–1840.* Cambridge, Mass.: Harvard University Press, 1973.

Pullen, John J. *The Twentieth Maine, a Volunteer Regiment in the Civil War.* Philadelphia: Lippincott, 1957.

Quarles, Benjamin. *The Negro in the Civil War.* Boston: Little, Brown, 1963.

Rable, George C. *Civil Wars: Women and the Crisis of Southern Nationalism.* Urbana: University of Illinois Press, 1989.

————. *The Confederate Republic: A Revolution against Politics.* Chapel Hill: University of North Carolina Press, 1994.

Randall, James G. *Lincoln the President.* 4 vols. New York: Dodd, Mead, 1945–55.

Rankin, Thomas M. *23rd Virginia Infantry.* Lynchburg, Va.: H. E. Howard, 1985.

Rauscher, Frank. *Music on the March, 1862–'65, with the Army of the Potomac, 114th Regiment, P. V., Collis' Zouaves.* Philadelphia: William F. Fell, 1892.

Redway, George William. *Fredericksburg, a Study in War.* New York: Macmillan, 1906.

Reese, Timothy J. *Sykes' Regular Infantry Division: A History of Regular United States Infantry Operations in the Civil War's Eastern Theater.* Jefferson, N.C.: McFarland, 1990.

Reidenbaugh, Lowell. *33rd Virginia Infantry.* Lynchburg, Va.: H. E. Howard, 1982.

Rhodes, James Ford. *History of the United States from the Compromise of 1850 to the Final Restoration of Home Rule at the South in 1877.* 7 vols. New York: Macmillan, 1892–1906.

Riggs, David F. *7th Virginia Infantry.* Lynchburg, Va.: H. E. Howard, 1982.

————. *13th Virginia Infantry.* Lynchburg, Va.: H. E. Howard, 1989.

Roberts, Allen E. *House Undivided: The Story of Freemasonry and the Civil War.* New York: Macoy Publishing, 1961.

Robertson, James I., Jr. *4th Virginia Infantry.* Lynchburg, Va.: H. E. Howard, 1982.

————. *General A. P. Hill: The Story of a Confederate Warrior.* New York: Random House, 1987.

————. *Soldiers Blue and Gray.* Columbia: University of South Carolina Press, 1988.

————. *The Stonewall Brigade.* Baton Rouge: Louisiana State University Press, 1963.

————. *Stonewall Jackson: The Man, the Soldier, the Legend.* New York: Macmillan, 1997.

Rodenbough, Theodore F., ed. *Uncle Sam's Medal of Honor.* New York: G. P. Putnam's Sons, 1886.

Rose, Anne C. *Victorian America and the Civil War.* Cambridge: Cambridge University Press, 1992.

Roseboom, Eugene H. *History of the State of Ohio: The Civil War Era, 1850–1873.* Columbus: Ohio State Archaeological and Historical Society, 1944.

Royster, Charles. *The Destructive War: William Tecumseh Sherman, Stonewall Jackson, and the Americans.* New York: Knopf, 1991.

Ruffner, Kevin C. *44th Virginia Infantry.* Lynchburg, Va.: H. E. Howard, 1987.

Sandburg, Carl. *Abraham Lincoln: The War Years.* 4 vols. New York: Harcourt, Brace, 1939.

Saum, Lewis O. *The Popular Mood of America, 1860–1890.* Lincoln: University of Nebraska Press, 1990.

Schwarzlose, Richard A. *The Newsbrokers.* 2 vols. Evanston, Ill.: Northwestern University Press, 1989.

Scott, Kate M. *History of the One Hundred and Fifth Regiment of Pennsylvania Volunteers.* Philadelphia: New-World Pub. Co., 1877.

Sears, Stephen W. *Chancellorsville.* Boston: Houghton Mifflin, 1996.

———. *Controversies and Commanders: Dispatches from the Army of the Potomac.* Boston: Houghton Mifflin, 1999.

———. *George B. McClellan, the Young Napoleon.* New York: Ticknor and Fields, 1988.

——— *Landscape Turned Red: The Battle of Antietam.* New York: Ticknor and Fields, 1983.

Shackelford, George G. *George Wythe Randolph and the Confederate Elite.* Athens: University of Georgia Press, 1988.

Shankman, Arnold M. *The Pennsylvania Antiwar Movement, 1861–1865.* Rutherford, N.J.: Fairleigh Dickinson University Press, 1980.

Shannon, Fred. *The Organization and Administration of the Union Army.* 2 vols. Cleveland: Arthur H. Clarke, 1928.

Shattuck, Gardiner H., Jr. *A Shield and Hiding Place: The Religious Life of the Civil War Armies.* Macon, Ga.: Mercer University Press, 1987.

Shaw, Maurice F. *Stonewall Jackson's Surgeon: Hunter Holmes McGuire, a Biography.* Lynchburg, Va.: H. E. Howard, 1993.

Shibutani, Tamotsu. *Improvised News: A Sociological Study of Rumor.* Indianapolis: Bobbs-Merrill, 1966.

Siegel, Alan A. *For the Glory of the Union: Myth, Reality, and the Media in Civil War New Jersey.* Rutherford, N.J.: Fairleigh Dickinson University Press, 1984.

Silbey, Joel H. *A Respectable Minority: The Democratic Party in the Civil War Era, 1860–1868.* New York: Norton, 1997.

Simpson, Harold Brown. *Gaines Mill to Appomattox: Waco and McLennan County in Hood's Texas Brigade.* Waco, Tex.: Texian Press, 1963.

Smith, Donald L. *The Twenty-fourth Michigan of the Iron Brigade.* Harrisburg, Pa.: Stackpole, 1963.

Smith, William Ernest. *The Francis Preston Blair Family in Politics.* 2 vols. New York: Macmillan, 1933.

Stackpole, Edward J. *Drama on the Rappahannock: The Fredericksburg Campaign.* Harrisburg, Pa.: Stackpole, 1957.

Stampp, Kenneth M. *Indiana Politics during the Civil War.* Indianapolis: Indiana Historical Bureau, 1949.

Stannard, David E., ed. *Death in America.* Philadelphia: University of Pennsylvania Press, 1975.

Starr, Louis M. *Reporting the Civil War: The Bohemian Brigade in Action, 1861–1865.* New York: Collier, 1962.

Starr, Stephen Z. *The Union Cavalry in the Civil War.* 3 vols. Baton Rouge: Louisiana State University Press, 1979–85.

Steele, Mathew Forney. *American Campaigns.* Harrisburg, Pa.: Telegraph Press, 1909.

Stegeman, John F. *These Men She Gave: The Civil War Diary of Athens, Georgia.* Athens: University of Georgia Press, 1964.

Stewart, James Brewer. *Wendell Phillips: Liberty's Hero.* Baton Rouge: Louisiana State University Press, 1986.

Storey, Henry Wilson. *History of Cambria County [Pa.].* 2 vols. New York: Lewis Pub. Co., 1907.

Sutherland, Daniel E. *Fredericksburg and Chancellorsville: The Dare Mark Campaign.* Lincoln: University of Nebraska Press, 1998.

———. *Seasons of War: The Ordeal of a Confederate Community.* New York: Free Press, 1995.

Sweet, Timothy. *Traces of War: Poetry, Photography, and the Crisis of the Union.* Baltimore: Johns Hopkins University Press, 1990.

Swinfen, David B. *Ruggles' Regiment: The 122nd New York Volunteers in the American Civil War.* Hanover, N.H.: University Press of New England, 1982.

Tap, Bruce. *Over Lincoln's Shoulder: The Committee on the Conduct of the War.* Lawrence: University Press of Kansas, 1998.

Tatum, Georgia Lee. *Disloyalty in the Confederacy.* Chapel Hill: University of North Carolina Press, 1934.

Taylor, Gifford. *Gouverneur Kemble Warren: Life and Letters of an American Soldier.* Boston: Houghton Mifflin, 1932.

Thomas, Benjamin P. *Abraham Lincoln: A Biography.* New York: Knopf, 1952.

Thomas, Benjamin P., and Harold M. Hyman. *Stanton: The Life and Times of Lincoln's Secretary of War.* New York: Knopf, 1962.

Thomas, Emory M. *Bold Dragoon: The Life of J. E. B. Stuart.* New York: Harper and Row, 1986.

———. *The Confederate Nation, 1861–1865.* New York: Harper and Row, 1979.

———. *Robert E. Lee: A Biography.* New York: Norton, 1995.

Thomas, Howard. *Boys in Blue from the Adirondack Foothills.* Prospect, N.Y.: Prospect Books, 1960.

Thomas, John L., ed. *Abraham Lincoln and the American Political Tradition.* Amherst: University of Massachusetts Press, 1986.

Thompson, Gilbert. *The Engineer Battalion in the Civil War.* Washington, D.C.: Press of the Engineer School, 1910.

Thompson, Robert Luther. *Wiring a Continent: The History of the Telegraph Industry in the United States, 1832–1866.* Princeton, N.J.: Princeton University Press, 1947.

Trefousse, Hans L. *Benjamin Franklin Wade: Radical Republican from Ohio.* New York: Twayne, 1963.

———. *The Radical Republicans: Lincoln's Vanguard for Racial Justice.* New York: Knopf, 1968.

Trulock, Alice Rains. *In the Hands of Providence: Joshua L. Chamberlain and the American Civil War.* Chapel Hill: University of North Carolina Press, 1992.

Tucker, Glenn. *Hancock the Superb.* Indianapolis: Bobbs-Merrill, 1960.

U.S. Army Department. Public Information Division. *The Medal of Honor of the United States Army.* Washington, D.C.: Government Printing Office, 1948.

Van Deusen, Glyndon G. *Horace Greeley: Nineteenth-Century Crusader.* Philadelphia: University of Pennsylvania Press, 1953.

———. *William Henry Seward.* New York: Oxford University Press, 1967.

Vinovskis, Maris A., ed. *Toward a Social History of the American Civil War: Exploratory Essays.* Cambridge: Cambridge University Press, 1990.

Voegeli, V. Jacque. *Free but Not Equal: The Midwest and the Negro during the Civil War.* Chicago: University of Chicago Press, 1967.

Wallace, Lee A., Jr. *1st Virginia Infantry.* Lynchburg, Va.: H. E. Howard, 1984.
————. *5th Virginia Infantry.* Lynchburg, Va.: H. E. Howard, 1988.
———— *17th Virginia Infantry.* Lynchburg, Va.: H. E. Howard, 1990.
————. *A Guide to Virginia Military Organizations, 1861–1865.* Rev. 2nd ed. Lynchburg, Va.:
    H. E. Howard, 1986.
Wallace, Willard M. *The Soul of the Lion: A Biography of General Joshua L. Chamberlain.*
    New York: Thomas Nelson and Sons, 1960.
Ward, James A. *That Man Haupt: A Biography of Herman Haupt.* Baton Rouge: Louisiana
    State University Press, 1973.
Warner, Ezra J. *Generals in Blue: Lives of the Union Commanders.* Baton Rouge: Louisiana
    State University Press, 1964.
————. *Generals in Gray: Lives of the Confederate Commanders.* Baton Rouge: Louisiana
    State University Press, 1959.
Weber, Thomas. *The Northern Railroads in the Civil War, 1861–1865.* New York: King's
    Crown Press, 1952.
Welcher, Frank J. *The Union Army, 1861–1865: Organizations and Operations, the Eastern
    Theater.* Bloomington: Indiana University Press, 1989.
Welsh, Jack D. *Medical Histories of Confederate Generals.* Kent, Ohio: Kent State University
    Press, 1995.
————. *Medical Histories of Union Generals.* Kent, Ohio: Kent State University Press, 1996.
Wert, Jeffrey D. *General James Longstreet, the Confederacy's Most Controversial Soldier: A
    Biography.* New York: Simon and Schuster, 1993.
Whan, Vorin E. *Fiasco at Fredericksburg.* State College: Pennsylvania State University
    Press, 1961.
White, Gregory C. *A History of the 31st Georgia Volunteer Infantry.* Baltimore: Butternut and
    Blue, 1997.
Wiley, Bell Irvin. *The Life of Billy Yank: The Common Soldier of the Union.* Indianapolis:
    Bobbs-Merrill, 1952.
————. *The Life of Johnny Reb: The Common Soldier of the Confederacy.* Indianapolis:
    Bobbs-Merrill, 1943.
Williams, Kenneth P. *Lincoln Finds a General: A Military Study of the Civil War.* 5 vols. New
    York: Macmillan, 1949–59.
Williams, T. Harry. *Lincoln and His Generals.* New York: Knopf, 1952.
————. *Lincoln and the Radicals.* Madison: University of Wisconsin Press, 1941.
Wills, Gary. *Lincoln at Gettysburg: The Words That Remade America.* New York: Simon and
    Schuster, 1992.
Winslow, Robert Elliott, III. *General John Sedgwick: The Story of a Union Corps Commander.*
    Novato, Calif.: Presidio, 1982.
Winters, Harold A. *Battling the Elements: Weather and Terrain in the Conduct of War.*
    Baltimore: Johns Hopkins University Press, 1998.
Wise, Jennings Cropper. *The Long Arm of Lee; or, The History of the Artillery of the Army of
    Northern Virginia.* 2 vols. Lynchburg, Va.: J. P. Bell, 1915.
Wood, Forrest G. *Black Scare: The Racist Response to Emancipation and Reconstruction.*
    Berkeley: University of California Press, 1968.
Woodworth, Steven E. *Davis and Lee at War.* Lawrence: University Press of Kansas, 1995.
Wyatt-Brown, Bertram. *Southern Honor: Ethics and Behavior in the Old South.* New York:
    Oxford University Press, 1982.
Wyckoff, Mac. *A History of the Second South Carolina Infantry, 1861–1865.* Fredericksburg,
    Va.: Sergeant Kirkland's Museum, 1994.
————. *A History of the Third South Carolina Infantry, 1861–1865.* Fredericksburg, Va.:
    Sergeant Kirkland's Museum, 1995.

Young, William A., Jr., and Patricia C. Young. *56th Virginia Infantry.* Lynchburg, Va.: H. E. Howard, 1990.

Articles

Allbritton, Orval E. "The Third Arkansas Regiment from Formation to Fredericksburg." *Arkansas Historical Quarterly* 16 (Summer 1957): 150–62.

Blair, William A. "Barbarians at Fredericksburg's Gate: The Impact of the Union Army on Civilians." In *The Fredericksburg Campaign: Decision on the Rappahannock,* edited by Gary W. Gallagher, 142–70. Chapel Hill: University of North Carolina Press, 1995.

Brauer, Kinley J. "British Mediation and the American Civil War: A Reconsideration." *Journal of Southern History* 38 (February 1972): 49–64.

Bruce, George Anson. "The Battle of Fredericksburg, December 13, 1862." In *Papers of the Military Historical Society of Massachusetts,* 15 vols., 9:497–537. Wilmington, N.C.: Broadfoot, 1989–90.

———. "The Strategy of the Civil War." In *Papers of the Military Historical Society of Massachusetts,* 15 vols., 13:393–483. Wilmington, N.C.: Broadfoot, 1989–90.

Chapla, John D. "Quartermaster Operations in the Forty-second Virginia Infantry Regiment." *Civil War History* 30 (March 1984): 5–30.

Douglas, Ann. "Heaven Our Home: Consolation Literature in the Northern United States, 1830–1880." In *Death in America,* edited by David E. Stannard, 49–68. Philadelphia: University of Pennsylvania Press, 1975.

Faust, Drew Gilpin. "Christian Soldiers: The Meaning of Revivalism in the Confederate Army." *Journal of Southern History* 53 (February 1987): 63–90.

Gallagher, Gary W. "The Yanks Have Had a Terrible Whipping: Confederates Evaluate the Battle of Fredericksburg." In *The Fredericksburg Campaign: Decision on the Rappahannock,* edited by Gary W. Gallagher, 113–141. Chapel Hill: University of North Carolina Press, 1995.

"General Thomas R. R. Cobb." *Confederate Veteran* 7 (July 1899): 309.

"George Ely Pingree." In *Military Essays and Recollections: Papers Read before the Commandery of the State of Illinois, Military of the Loyal Legion of the United States and Memorials of the Deceased Companions,* 8 vols., 8:611–13. Wilmington, N.C., 1992–93.

Greene, A. Wilson. "Morale, Maneuver, and Mud: The Army of the Potomac, December 16, 1862–January 26, 1863." In *The Fredericksburg Campaign: Decision on the Rappahannock,* edited by Gary W. Gallagher, 171–227. Chapel Hill: University of North Carolina Press, 1995.

———. "Opportunity to the South: Meade versus Jackson at Fredericksburg." *Civil War History* 33 (December 1987): 295–314.

Guinnane, Timothy W., Harvey S. Rosen, and Kristen L. Willard. "Messages from 'The Den of Wild Beasts': Greenback Prices Commentary on the Union's Prospects." *Civil War History* 41 (December 1995): 313–28.

Harris, F. S. "Gen. Jas. J. Archer." *Confederate Veteran* 3 (January 1895): 18–19.

Harrison, Noel G. "Atop an Anvil: The Civilians' War in Fairfax and Alexandria Counties, April 1861–April 1862." *Virginia Magazine of History and Biography* 106 (Spring 1998): 133–64.

Hatton, Clarence R. "Gen. Archibald Campbell Goodwin." *Confederate Veteran* 28 (April 1920): 133–36.

Hawley, Steve C. "Barksdale's Mississippi Brigade at Fredericksburg." *Civil War History* 40 (March 1994): 5–24.

"History of the 48th Virginia Infantry." *Historical Society of Washington County, Virginia, Publications,* ser. 2, no. 7 (Winter–Spring 1968–69): 5–38.

Jones, Gordon Willis. "The Medical History of the Fredericksburg Campaign: Course and Significance." *Journal of the History of Medicine and Allied Sciences* 10 (July 1963). 241–56.

Jones, Kenneth W. "The Fourth Alabama Infantry: A Fighting Legion." *Alabama Historical Quarterly* 38 (Fall 1976): 171–203.

Krick, Robert K. "Maxcy Gregg: Political Extremist and Confederate General." *Civil War History* 19 (December 1973): 293–313.

Larsen, Lawrence H. "Draft Riot in Wisconsin, 1862." *Civil War History* 7 (December 1961): 421–27.

Lerner, Eugene M. "Money, Prices, and Wages in the Confederacy." In *The Economic Impact of the American Civil War,* edited by Ralph Andreano, 11–40. Cambridge, Mass.: Schenkman, 1962.

McCandless, George T., Jr. "Money, Expectations, and the U.S. Civil War." *American Economic Review* 86 (June 1996): 661–71.

"Many Prominent Persons Present." *Southern Historical Society Papers* 36 (January–December 1908): 174 79.

Marvel, William. "The Making of a Myth: Ambrose E. Burnside and the Union High Command at Fredericksburg." In *The Fredericksburg Campaign: Decision on the Rappahannock,* edited by Gary W. Gallagher, 1–25. Chapel Hill: University of North Carolina Press, 1995.

Mertz, Gregory A. "'A Severe Day on All the Artillery': Stonewall Jackson's Artillerists and the Defense of the Confederate Right." *Civil War Regiments* 4, no. 4 (1995): 70–99.

Miller, Richard F., and Robert F. Mooney. "Across the River and into the Streets: The 20th Massachusetts Infantry and the Street Fight for Fredericksburg." *Civil War Regiments* 4, no. 4 (1995): 101–26.

Mitchell, Reid. "Christian Soldiers? Perfecting the Confederacy." In *Religion and the American Civil War,* edited by Randall M. Miller, Harry S. Stout, and Charles Reagan Wilson, 297–309. New York: Oxford University Press, 1998.

———. "The Northern Soldier and His Community." In *Toward a Social History of the American Civil War: Exploratory Essays,* edited by Maris A. Vinovskis, 78–92. Cambridge: Cambridge University Press, 1990.

Mitchell, Wesley C. "Greenbacks and the Cost of the Civil War." *Journal of Political Economy* 5 (March 1897): 117–56.

———. "The Value of the 'Greenbacks' during the Civil War." *Journal of Political Economy* 6 (March 1898): 139–67.

Nolan, Alan T. "Confederate Leadership at Fredericksburg." In *The Fredericksburg Campaign: Decision on the Rappahannock,* edited by Gary W. Gallagher, 26–47. Chapel Hill: University of North Carolina Press, 1995.

O'Reilly, Frank A. "'Busted Up and Gone to Hell': The Assault of the Pennsylvania Reserves at Fredericksburg." *Civil War Regiments* 4, no. 4 (1995): 1–27.

Outz, Clay. "Maxcy Gregg and His Brigade of South Carolinians at the Battle of Fredericksburg." *South Carolina Historical Magazine* 95 (January 1994): 6–26.

Owen, Allison. "Record of an Old Artillery Organization." *Field Artillery Journal* 4 (January–March 1914): 5–18.

Petty, A. Milburn. "History of 37th Regiment, New York Volunteers." *Journal of the Irish American Historical Society* 31 (1937): 101–37.

Preston, David L. "'The Glorious Light Went Out Forever': The Death of Brig. Gen. Thomas R. R. Cobb." *Civil War Regiments* 4, no. 4 (1995): 28–46.

Reardon, Carol. "The Forlorn Hope: Brig. Gen. Andrew A. Humphreys's Pennsylvania Division at Fredericksburg." In *The Fredericksburg Campaign: Decision on the*

Rappahannock, edited by Gary W. Gallagher, 80–112. Chapel Hill: University of North Carolina Press, 1995.

Rice, Thomas. "All the Imps of Hell Let Loose." *Civil War Times Illustrated* 22 (June 1983): 8–15.

———. "Desperate Courage." *Civil War Times Illustrated* 29 (November–December 1990): 58–70.

Roll, Richard. "Interest Rates and Price Expectations during the Civil War." *Journal of Economic History* 32 (June 1972): 476–98.

Romero, Sidney J. "The Confederate Chaplain." *Civil War History* 1 (June 1955): 127–40.

Rorabaugh, W. J. "Who Fought for the North in the Civil War? Concord, Massachusetts, Enlistments." *Journal of American History* 73 (December 1986): 695–701.

Smith, Everard H. "Chambersburg: Anatomy of a Confederate Reprisal." *American Historical Review* 96 (April 1991): 432–55.

Sutherland, Bruce. "Pittsburgh Volunteers with Sickles' Excelsior Brigade." Pt. 3, "Fredericksburg and Chancellorsville." *Western Pennsylvania Historical Magazine* 45 (September 1962): 241–62.

Tap, Bruce. "Race, Rhetoric, and Emancipation: The Election of 1862 in Illinois." *Civil War History* 39 (June 1993): 101–25.

Wainwright, Nicholas B. "The Loyal Opposition in Civil War Philadelphia." *Pennsylvania Magazine of History and Biography* 88 (July 1964): 294–315.

Watson, Samuel J. "Religion and Combat Motivation in the Confederate Armies." *Journal of Military History* 58 (January 1994): 29–55.

Wiley, Bell Irvin. "The Soldier's Life, North and South: Letters Home Tell Adventures of Two Foes." *Life,* February 3, 1961, 64–77.

Willard, Kristen L., Timothy W. Guinnane, and Harvey S. Rosen. "Turning Points in the Civil War: Views from the Greenback Market." *American Economic Review* 96 (September 1996): 1001–18.

Thesis

Ott, Eugene Matthew. "The Civil War Diary of James J. Kirkpatrick, Sixteenth Mississippi Infantry, C.S.A." Master's thesis, Texas A&M University, 1984.

Index

Abbott, Henry L., 1–2, 171
Adams, Charles Francis, Sr., 39, 333
Adams, Henry, 333
Alabama troops
—Infantry
5th Battalion, 214
Albany Atlas and Argus, 28
Albany Daily Democrat and American, 28
Albany Evening Journal, 145, 327
Alcohol, 14–15, 24, 94, 108, 175, 179, 364–65, 367, 372, 419, 481 (n. 44)
Alcott, Louisa May, 3, 317–18, 320–21
Alexander, Edward Porter, 135, 160, 165, 221, 270, 500 (n. 40), 514 (n. 4), 526 (n. 25)
Allabach, Peter H., 261–63, 526 (n. 22)
Allen, Ujanirtus, 26, 362
Alley, Leander F., 241, 294
Ambulances, 281–82, 308–9
American Journal of Medical Science, 312
Amputations, 312–13, 319, 528 (n. 43), 544 (n. 17). *See also* Surgery
Amsden, Frank, 20
Anderson, George T., 404
Anderson, Richard H., 78, 160, 220, 273
Anderson, Robert, 216
Andrew, John A., 29
Andrews, George L., 266
Andrews, Johnson W., 226–27
Antietam, Battle of, 8, 21, 51
Aquia Creek, Va., 64, 77, 316–17, 419
Archer, James J., 13, 94, 193, 207–8, 214, 246
Army of Northern Virginia: corps created in, 21–22; troop strength of, 148
Army of the Potomac: creation of grand divisions in, 59–60; drilling in, 113; troop strength of, 144; letter from Lincoln to, 352–53; Hooker appointed to command, 422–23
Arnold, Isaac, 325
Artillery: Confederate, 80–81, 135, 148–49, 160, 193, 199–203, 221, 230, 279–80, 519 (n. 2), 526 (n. 25); Federal, 162–64, 197, 198–203, 253, 258–59, 498 (nn. 17, 20), 499 (n. 26), 509 (n. 32), 515 (n. 14), 516

(n. 17), 525 (n. 4), 531 (n. 22). *See also* names of specific units
Atkinson, Edward N., 214–15, 246, 248, 252
Aurora borealis, 279
Averell, William Woods, 389–90

Ballock, George W., 111
Balloons, 132, 492–93 (n. 5), 505 (n. 38), 513 (n. 1)
Bank of Virginia, 177
Banks, Nathaniel P., 325
Banks Ford, 408, 412–13
Barbour, William, 210
Barksdale, William E., 136, 160–61, 165–66, 168–71
Barnes, Joseph A., 256–57
Barrett, James, 169
Bartol, Cyrus Augustus, 297
Barton, Clara, 149, 151, 168, 313, 320
Baseball, 360
Baxter, Henry, 168
Baya, William, 165
Bayard, George D., 298, 502 (n. 7)
Beale, Jane Howison, 80, 84, 166
Beecher, Henry Ward, 37, 129, 373
Belle Plain, Va., 88
Bendix, John E., 226
Benjamin, Judah P., 334
Bennett, James Gordon, 374
Berlin, Md., 87
Bernard, Alfred, 157
Bernard, Arthur, 187, 193
Bernard House, 427
Berry, Hiram G., 247
Bingham, John A., 383
Birney, David B. 203, 215–16, 246–48, 521 (n. 32), 522 (n. 39)
Bliss, Zenas R., 243, 423
Boisol, David, 319
Borden, Fannie, 295
Boston Post, 11, 353
Bowen, Roland E., 62, 181–82, 241
Boyd, Andrew, 14
Brackett, John M., 107
Brainerd, Wesley, 158–59

Brandon, Lane, 171
Brantingham, Henry, 153
Brewster, Charles Harvey, 138, 152
Bright, John, 39
Brockenbrough, John B., 193, 199, 200, 201
Brockenbrough, John M., 214, 246, 508
  (n. 14)
Brooks, Noah, 317, 546 (n. 37)
Brooks, William T. H., 138, 250–51, 421–22,
  585 (n. 55)
Brown, Washington, 293, 539 (n. 23)
Browning, Orville Hickman, 35, 332
Bryant, William Cullen, 337
Buchanan, Robert C., 266
Buckingham, Catharnius P., 43–44
Buell, Don Carlos, 43
Burials, 276–79, 284–85, 294–95, 535
  (n. 69), 567 (n. 70)
Burns, William W., 175–76, 249, 523 (n. 49)
Burnside, Ambrose E., 2; and removal of
  McClellan, 43–44; background and early
  Civil War career of, 50–52; physical description of, 52; phrenological profile of,
  53–54; appointment of, to command,
  53–56; campaign plans of, 56–59, 66–
  73, 144, 466 (nn. 69, 73), 494 (n. 18);
  arrives at Fredericksburg, 80; and campaign delay, 81–83, 132–33; and demand
  for surrender of Fredericksburg, 83–
  84; and delay of pontoons, 87–88, 474
  (n. 30); soldiers' assessment of, 88–
  89, 117; meets with Lincoln, 116–17; and
  Thanksgiving, 119; public assessment
  of, 144; Confederate assessment of, 147,
  344–45, 466 (n. 71), 559 (n. 62); and
  battle plans, 149–50, 154–55, 174, 184–
  85, 190–91, 484 (n. 13), 495 (n. 29), 502
  (n. 1), 505 (n. 39), 507 (nn. 6, 7), 508
  (n. 20), 514 (n. 1); and crossing into
  Fredericksburg, 161–62, 171, 497 (nn. 3,
  4) 500 (n. 40); and failure of artillery
  bombardment, 168; and decision to
  attack Confederate right, 218, 221, 514
  (n. 8); gives attack orders to Franklin,
  249–50, 522 (n. 39); and continued Federal attacks toward stone wall, 255–56,
  261; and night after battle, 269–70; and
  decision to stop attacks, 272; and debate
  about renewing attacks, 281; and treatment of wounded, 316; wires Lincoln
  about battle, 324; assessment of, after

Fredericksburg, 348–49, 558 (n. 50);
  and testimony before Joint Committee
  on the Conduct of the War, 349–50;
  and letter written after Fredericksburg, 351–52; and campaign plans after
  Fredericksburg, 389–94, 401–2, 408–
  10, 574 (n. 10); soldiers criticize, after
  Fredericksburg, 394; and Mud March,
  410–19; after Mud March, 411–12, 415,
  418–19, 421–22, 582 (n. 25); soldiers'
  attitudes toward, after Mud March, 420;
  removed from command, 422–23
Butterfield, Daniel, 256, 269, 525 (n. 4)

Cabinet Crisis, 330–32
Caldwell, Emilie, 183
Caldwell, John C., 233–35
Cameron, Simon, 382, 548 (n. 4)
Caroline Street, 160, 163, 168, 180
Carr, Joseph B., 252, 275
Carroll, Samuel S., 259
Carter, Robert, 12
Carter, Walter, 342
Castleman, Alfred, 343
Casualties: Federal, 158–59, 165, 168–70,
  175–76, 200–201, 205, 209–10, 212, 214,
  222–35, 238–44, 247–50, 252–53, 257–68,
  272, 274, 276, 283, 284, 288–322, 431–32,
  511 (nn. 10, 18), 515 (n. 16), 517 (n. 44),
  518 (n. 47), 519 (n. 8), 520 (n. 15), 521
  (n. 30), 523 (n. 49), 527 (n. 30), 528
  (n. 41), 530 (nn. 14, 17), 544 (n. 12), 545
  (n. 25); Confederate, 165, 166, 170, 173,
  197, 199, 202, 205–8, 230, 238, 244, 246–
  47, 251, 253–54, 258, 284, 288, 295–300,
  517 (n. 41). See also Death
Cavalry, 65–66, 76–77, 146, 389–90, 402–3,
  410, 493 (n. 16), 494 (n. 18), 496 (n. 46),
  502 (n. 7), 578 (n. 54)
Cavanagh, James, 232
Cavins, Elijah H. C., 115, 126, 225
Chamberlain, Joshua Lawrence, 9, 111
Chamberlayne, Ham, 364
Chandler, Zachariah, 144–45, 349, 381–82,
  410
Chaplains, 98, 119, 124, 153, 320–21, 485
  (n. 36)
Charleston Mercury, 56, 91, 92, 344–45, 386
Chase, Nellie, 313
Chase, Salmon P., 35–36, 52, 330, 332, 336,
  374, 381, 398

Chatham (Lacy House), 150, 272, 430
Chicago Tribune, 36–37, 118, 125, 325, 376
Christian Commission, 296, 314, 316–17, 360
Christian soldiers, 295–300
Christmas, 328, 363–66, 366–69, 566 (n. 64)
Civilians, 15–19, 183–84, 455 (nn. 39, 40), 499 (n. 35). *See also* Refugees
Clark, James, 283
Clark, James Freeman, 298
Clausevitz, Karl von, 66–67, 87–88, 154, 192, 221, 301, 303, 305, 337, 409, 432, 464 (n. 48), 496, (n. 1), 538 (n. 13), 568 (n. 12)
Clothing, 12, 24–25, 90–93, 102–3, 136, 140, 356–57, 362, 490 (n. 23)
Cobb, Thomas R. R., 70, 87, 220, 221, 226, 228, 296–97
Cochrane, John, 32, 390–91, 421, 574 (n. 5)
Cole, Andrew, 431
Collis, Charles H. T., 248
Comstock, Cyrus B., 87, 155
Connecticut troops
—Artillery
1st Heavy, 162
—Infantry
8th, 159
14th, 1–2, 227
15th, 14
16th, 272
21st, 68, 107
27th, 229
Conscription, 28–30, 75–76, 387–88
Cooke, Jay, 336
Cooke, John Esten, 197
Cooke, John Roger, 220, 226, 230, 238
Corbin, Kate, 84
Corby, William, 236
Corps: created in Army of Northern Virginia, 21–22
Couch, Darius N., 150, 182, 221–22, 238–39, 244, 256, 258, 280, 504 (n. 29), 519 (n. 5)
Courage, 152, 274, 301–3, 341, 434–35, 519 (n. 8), 542 (n. 49)
Cowardice, 303–5
Cox, Samuel S., 33–34
Crenshaw Battery, 202
Cross, Robert E., 233, 517 (n. 44), 517 (n. 45)
Crutchfield, Stapleton, 193

Culpeper, Va., 23, 27
Curtin, Andrew, 29
Cutler, William Parker, 330

Darlington, Henry A., 224
Davidson, Greenlee, 193, 200–202, 253
Davis, Jefferson, 75–76, 328–29, 371, 386–87, 410
Death, 14, 105, 113, 140, 277–78, 288–300, 315–16, 320–21, 358, 395–96, 480 (n. 36), 518 (n. 50), 538 (n. 22), 539 (nn. 27, 28), 541 (n. 45), 546 (n. 31)
Deep Run, 156, 176, 192, 193, 250, 251, 523 (n. 49)
Defensive position: Confederate, 488 (n. 11), 489 (n. 13), 494 (n. 26)
Dehon, Arthur, 216
Delaware troops
—Infantry
1st, 225, 515 (n. 16)
Demming, Sid, 323
Desertion, 398–400, 406, 419, 469 (n. 21). *See also* Discipline
Devens, Charles, Jr., 157
Dickinson, George, 241
Diplomacy, International: in context of Fredericksburg campaign, 38–41, 332–35
Discipline: military, 18, 23–24, 108–10, 177–84, 186, 399–400, 406, 476 (n. 57), 576 (n. 38), 583 (n. 37). *See also* Desertion
Disease, 13, 93, 105–7, 140, 152, 357, 363, 534 (n. 60). *See also* Illness
Dix, John A., 30, 380
Doubleday, Abner, 194, 198, 250
Douglass, Frederick, 125, 375–76, 380
Draper, William Franklin, 394
Drilling: in Army of the Potomac, 113
Drouyn de Lhuys, Edouard, 38
Dumfries, Va., 146, 402–3

Early, Jubal A., 25, 185–86, 193, 214–15, 248, 253, 275
Eaton, Catherine, 112, 122, 291
Eaton, Harriet, 313, 316
Eaton, Samuel, 112
Edmonds, Amanda, 64
Edmondston, Catherine, 40, 329
Elections (1862–63), 30–38, 381–82, 457 (nn. 14, 18), 458 (nn. 25, 31, 32), 459 (n. 35)
Ellett, James, 199

Emancipation Proclamation, 33–34, 373–
78, 569 (nn. 20, 24, 28)
Engels, Frederick, 39
Eulogies, 294–300
Evans, Clement A., 246, 521 (n. 24)

Fairfax, Randolph, 297
Falmouth, Va., 83
Fear, 541 (n. 45)
Featherston, Winfield Scott, 164–65
Ferrero, Edward, 241–42, 422, 520 (n. 11)
Fessenden, William Pitt, 330, 400, 410
Financial markets, 335–36, 552 (n. 45)
Fires: camp, 102, 136
Fiser, John 161
Florida troops
—Infantry
   8th, 161, 170
Floyd, Lawrence, 229
Foltz, Samuel, 114
Foner, Eric, 568 (n. 8)
Food, 12, 15, 25, 56–57, 68, 92–93, 103–4,
   120–21, 136, 140–41, 187, 271, 357, 362–
   63, 364, 366–67, 394–95, 469 (n. 25),
   484 (n. 21), 492 (n. 47), 575 (n. 22)
Foraging, 15–18, 71–72, 178–79, 454 (n. 25),
   469 (n. 28)
Forney, John W., 326
Franklin, John Hope, 569 (n. 20)
Franklin, William B.: background of,
   and appointment to grand division
   command, 60; and march toward Fredericksburg, 69; and campaign strategy,
   133; and crossing of troops, 157–58;
   and battle plans, 184–85, 473 (n. 26),
   529 (n. 47); on eve of battle, 187; and
   battle orders, 190–92, 195, 506 (n. 2),
   507 (n. 6), 508 (n. 20); and failure of
   Meade's attack, 216, 507 (n. 11), 513
   (n. 40); and retreat, 245; and Burnside's
   late afternoon orders to attack, 249–
   50, 522 (n. 39); and Joint Committee
   on the Conduct of the War, 350, 560
   (n. 68), 574 (n. 6); and campaign plans
   after Fredericksburg, 390–91; and Mud
   March, 411, 418; Burnside's attempt to
   dismiss, 422; and departure from Army
   of the Potomac, 423
Fraternization, 146–47, 276, 359
Fredericksburg, Va.: Federals demand
   surrender of, 83–84; description of,
84; departure of refugees from, 84–86;
bombardment of, 162–64, 166–67, 498
(n. 26), 499 (n. 35), 586 (n. 1); sack of,
177–84, 271, 503 (n. 12), 505 (n. 37), 516
(n. 31), 525 (n. 7), 586 (n. 5); battlefield
in, described, 192–94; Federal withdrawal from, 282–87; impact of battle
on, 427–35
Freeman, Elizabeth, 291
Fremont, John C., 117
French, William H., 174–75, 221–28, 256,
266
Fuller, Arthur B., 298
Fuller, Margaret, 298

Gambling, 94, 108, 176, 398
Gangrene, 319. *See also* Illness
Garfield, James A., 25–26, 130, 348, 548
(n. 7)
Garland, J. G., 323
Garrison, William Lloyd, 129
George, Samuel W., 358
Georgia troops
—Infantry
   1st, 365
   11th, 362
   12th, 96
   13th, 215, 521 (n. 24)
   18th, 24
   19th, 207
   21st, 26, 362
   24th, 230
   35th, 244
   45th, 244
   49th, 244
   51st, 291
Getty, George W., 138, 264–66
Gettysburg, Battle of, 1–2, 434–35
Gibbon, John, 1, 44, 132–33, 176, 194, 200,
   210–14, 244, 248–49
Gove, George S., 14
Grand Divisions: creation of, in Army of
   the Potomac, 59–60
Granger, Charles 272
Gray, Ruffin "Bud", 295
Greeley, Horace, 30–31, 34, 82, 129, 145,
   354, 379, 380, 408, 425
Greenbacks, 335–36
Greensboro, Ala., 295
Gregg, Maxcy, 13, 193–94, 205–6, 215,
   298–99

Griffin, Charles, 256–58
Grimsley, Mark, 503 (n. 12)
Grow, Milo, 291

Hacker, Philip, 293
Haley, John, 13, 16
Hall, James, 201
Hall, Norman J., 168, 239–40
Halleck, Henry W.: and Burnside's plans
  for McClellan, 7; and removal of McClel-
  lan, 43; and Burnside's campaign plans,
  58–59, 116, 466 (n. 73), 483 (n. 1); and
  pontoons, 87–88, 473 (n. 26); and Burn-
  side's battle plans, 154; and crossing into
  Fredericksburg, 171; and debate about
  renewing attacks, 281; and blame for
  Fredericksburg, 347–48; and Burnside's
  letter, 351; and campaign plans after
  Fredericksburg, 388–89, 391–401, 408
Hall's Battery, 247–48
Halstead, Murat, 149–50
Hamilton, David H., 206
Hamilton, Maria, 86
Hamilton's Crossing, Va., 91, 157, 185, 186,
  193, 214
Hampton, Wade, 146, 402–3, 494 (n. 18)
Hancock, Winfield Scott, 1, 18, 72, 150, 175,
  228–36, 256, 339
Hanover Street, 219, 222, 239
Hardie, James A., 190–91, 218, 249
Harland, Edward, 265–66
Harper's Weekly, 118, 261, 368
Harrison, Noel, 472 (n. 11)
Hartsock, Andrew Jackson, 124
Hartwood Church, Va., 70, 82, 146
Hatch, William B., 250, 523 (n. 42)
Haupt, Herman, 9, 58–59, 63, 324
Hawkins, Rush C., 171, 264–65, 269–70
Hay, John, 352
Haydon, Charles, 17, 69, 356
Hazard, John G., 258–59
Hazel Run, 192, 220, 283
Heffelfinger, Jacob, 16
Heisler, Henry C., 243–44, 358
Heisler, Joseph, 358
Helman, Howard, 70–71
Hendershott, Robert Henry, 500 (n. 51)
Hightower, Harvey, 18
Hill, Ambrose P., 22, 185, 193–94, 253–54,
  275, 329
Hill, Benjamin H., 146

Hill, Daniel Harvey, 133, 185–86, 197,
  253–54, 275, 346
Hirst, Benjamin, 1–2
Hodgkins, Joseph E., 68
Hoke, Robert F., 215, 246
Holden, William W., 345
Holmes, Emma, 291
Holmes, Oliver Wendell, Jr., 69, 170
Home, 95–97, 110–13, 122, 151–52, 364–66,
  368–69, 396–97, 405–6, 482 (n. 55), 576
  (n. 31)
Homer, Peter W., 105
Hood, John B., 78, 157, 160, 220, 250–51,
  275, 524 (n. 53), 529 (n. 48)
Hooker, Joseph E.: as possible McClellan replacement, 43, 50; rumored appointment of, to command, 53, 493
  (n. 6); appointment of, to grand division command, 60; and march toward
  Fredericksburg, 70; description of, 82;
  proposes to cross Rappahannock, 82–83;
  and campaign strategy, 133, 473 (n. 26);
  and battle orders, 191, 507 (n. 7); and
  objections to continued Federal assaults
  toward stone wall, 255–56; and fear of
  Confederate counterattack, 266; during night after battle, 269; and debate
  about renewing attacks, 281; gives testimony before Joint Committee on the
  Conduct of the War, 350; and campaign
  plans after Fredericksburg, 390; and
  Mud March, 418; Burnside's attempt to
  dismiss, 421–22; appointed to command
  Army of the Potomac, 422–23; soldiers'
  attitudes toward, 424; and artillery, 525
  (n. 4)
Horses, 64–65, 77, 528 (n. 38), 582 (n. 33)
Hospitals, 14, 106, 268–69, 307–22, 358,
  544 (nn. 10, 12), 545 (n. 26), 546 (nn. 36,
  37)
Hotchkiss, Jedediah, 196, 403–4
Hotze, Henry, 333
Howard, Oliver Otis, 67, 150, 151, 171, 179,
  239–41
Howison's Hill, 237
Hughes, John (archbishop), 230
Humphreys, Andrew Atkinson, 45, 260–64,
  420, 526 (nn. 21, 24, 25, 26), 527 (nn. 30,
  36)
Hunt, Henry J., 162
Hurkamp, John, 273

Huts, 140, 355–56, 362, 419. *See also* Shelter; Tents

Illness, 57, 395, 562 (nn. 20, 21), 565 (n. 46), 575 (nn. 23, 35). *See also* Disease
Indiana troops
—Infantry
14th, 115, 126, 225, 377
19th, 123
Inflation, 25, 104, 387, 479 (n. 23)
Irish Brigade, 67, 164, 173, 175, 188, 230–33, 236, 268, 276, 278, 280, 294–95, 309, 311, 349, 356, 369, 397, 424, 518 (n. 51), 533 (n. 45)
Iron Brigade, 15, 198, 250, 347, 395

Jackson, Conrad Feger, 195, 200, 205, 207–9, 245
Jackson, Miss., 386
Jackson, Thomas J.: appointment of, to corps command, 21–22; description of, 21–22, 90; and Federal march toward Fredericksburg, 77; and march from Shenandoah Valley, 89–91; religious views of, 98; and Confederate artillery, 135; and preparations for Federal attack, 185–87; and A. P. Hill, 194; observes Federal advance, 196; during early morning artillery duel, 199; proposes counterattack, 252–54; waits for Federals to renew attacks, 275; (n. 48); and Maxcy Gregg, 298; and religion in aftermath of Fredericksburg, 346; and military plans after Fredericksburg, 403; and gap in lines, 508 (n. 17); and meeting on night of December 13, 529 (n. 48)
James, William, 151
Jastram, Pardon S., 248
Jeffords, Susan Emeline, 145
Johnston, Joseph E., 20
Joint Committee on the Conduct of the War, 349–50, 353, 421, 560 (n. 68), 574 (n. 6)
Jones, David, 341
Julian, George W., 350

Kargé, Joseph, 146
Keegan, John, 452 (n. 4), 507 (n. 4), 546 (n. 31)
Kershaw, James B., 172, 237–38

Kimball, Nathan, 222–25, 515 (n. 17)
King, Preston, 331
Kirkland, Richard 273
Krebs, Henry, 363–64

Lacy, J. Horace, 150
Lane, James H., 186, 210, 215, 244, 248
Lang, David, 165
Larned, Daniel Reed, 132, 422
Lattimer, Joseph W., 250
Law, Evander M., 250
Leavens, Lewis, 243
Lee, Robert E.: confidence of, 2; description of, 19–20; reacts to McClellan's advance, 22–23; and religion, 25, 97–98; and Federal march toward Fredericksburg, 76–78; and arrival of Federal troops at Fredericksburg, 89–91, 474 (n. 31); and supply problems, 92–93; and gambling, 94; and Fredericksburg defenses, 134–35, 171; and Federal crossing of Rappahannock, 159–60; and Federal bombardment of Fredericksburg, 164; and preparations for Federal attack, 185–87; and Jackson's tactical suggestions, 194; on Pelham, 198; watches Federal attacks, 237; and Confederate artillery fire, 243; on repulse of Federal assaults, 246; and night after battle, 270; waits for renewed Federal attacks, 272–73; and response to Federal withdrawal from Fredericksburg, 286; and Maxcy Gregg, 298; and reaction to Fredericksburg victory, 343–44; and Christmas, 363; Jefferson Davis praises, 386; and military preparations after Fredericksburg, 402–3; and Burnside's campaign plans after Fredericksburg, 410; and Fredericksburg refugees, 428–29; and Burnside's battle plans, 501 (n. 53)
Lentz, John, 283
Letcher, John, 37, 40, 146
Letterman, Jonathan, 308, 310, 314, 316
Letters, 94–96, 110–12, 396, 476 (n. 63), 481 (n. 49)
Lice, 12
Lincoln, Abraham, 3; McClellan questions judgement of, 7–8; and 1862 elections, 35–36; and possible foreign mediation

offer, 39; and military strategy, 42, 460 (n. 4); and removal of McClellan, 42–43; and appointment of Burnside, 51–53; and Burnside's campaign plans, 116–17; and Sabbath observance in army, 123; and slavery, 125–31, 487 (n. 57); and Annual Message to Congress, 128–29; and news from Fredericksburg, 323–25, 548 (nn. 1, 4, 14); and cabinet crisis, 330–32; and Burnside's letter, 351–52; and letter to Army of the Potomac, 352–53; and Joint Committee on the Conduct of the War, 353; and Emancipation Proclamation, 373–76; and Burnside's campaign plans after Fredericksburg, 391–92, 401; and soldiers' pay, 398; and removal of Burnside from command, 422; and rumored orders against fighting on the Sabbath, 409 (n. 5), visits Washington hospitals, 548 (n. 6); and Sioux Indians, 550 (n. 29)

Lincoln, Mary, 369
Linderman, Gerald, 541 (n. 39)
Lockert, James W., 208
Longfellow, Henry Wadsworth, 291
Longstreet, James, 238, 273; appointment of, to corps command, 21; description of, 21; and shoe shortage, 92; and battle preparations, 153; position of, on December 11, 160; and bombardment of Fredericksburg, 165; observes Federal advance, 196; and defensive preparations, 220–22; and artillery, 222, 230; late afternoon orders of, 258; and orders to Hood, 524 (n. 53)
Lowe, Thaddeus Sobieski Constantine, 132, 505 (n. 38), 513 (n. 1)
Luse, William H., 161
Lyle, Peter, 212

Macy, George N., 169
Madison Parish, La., 292
Magilton, Albert, 195, 204–5, 209–10, 245
Maine troops
—Artillery
2nd Battery, 201
—Infantry
2nd, 419
6th, 252
16th, 151, 213, 249, 319, 414

17th, 13, 16, 247, 359, 418
19th, 303
20th, 9, 19, 111, 260, 274
Mannsfield, 187
Marble, Manton, 82
Marching, 10–11, 66–73, 89–91, 138, 410–19, 468 (n. 12), 469 (n. 21)
Marshall, John W., 226
Marvel, William, 466 (n. 69)
Marx, Karl, 3, 39, 333
Marye's Heights, 160, 166, 191, 192, 219–20, 222, 224, 226, 229, 230, 238, 239, 258, 272
Mason, James M., 40, 334
Mason, John S., 224–25
Massachusetts troops
—Artillery, Light
5th Battery (E), 258
—Infantry
1st, 252
10th, 16, 19, 138, 152
15th, 62, 179, 241, 412
18th, 257
19th, 68, 168–69, 180, 239–40, 295, 301, 314, 519 (n. 8)
20th, 1–2, 169–71, 180, 240–41, 291
21st, 108, 242
22nd, 88, 257, 342, 419
24th, 357–58
28th, 230–31, 233
32nd, 259–60
35th, 127, 242
36th, 394
37th, 15, 89, 113, 157
Mattoon, Virgil, 361
McAllister, Robert, 60–61, 71, 110, 408
McCabe, William Gordon, 368
McCandless, William, 204
McCarter, William, 114, 151, 232, 268, 311–12
McClellan, George B., 394; influence of, on army, 2; and approach to war, 7–8; and Lincoln administration, 7–8; and campaign after Antietam, 7–20; soldiers' affection for, 9, 44–47, 69, 150, 463 (n. 32); and conscription, 29; and Democrats, 31; and political influence in Army of the Potomac, 35; and 1862 elections, 36, 457 (n. 14); strategy of, 42–43; removal of, 42–50, 461 (n. 7); soldiers' criticism of, 47; and relationship with

Burnside, 50–51; and Federal soldiers, 117; on Burnside, 132; and George B. Bayard, 298; calls for return to command of, 348; Confederate reaction to, 465 (n. 59)

McClure, Alexander K., 434

McCreary, David B., 234

McIntosh, David, 199

McLaws, Lafayette, 74, 77–78, 84, 147, 159, 160–61, 170, 185, 220, 228, 238, 273

McMillan, Robert, 230, 233

McPherson, James M., 457 (n. 18), 542 (n. 53), 569–70 (nn. 27, 28)

Meade, George G.: and foraging, 18, and morale, 20; and appointment of Burnside, 53; and Burnside's campaign plans, 73; and promotions, 115; and Hooker, 133; and crossing Rappahannock, 176; description of, 195; and orders to begin attack, 195–96; and stalled attack, 199; and attack on Confederate right, 204; and Gibbon's assault on Confederate right, 212; and Confederate counterattack, 215–16; and retreat, 244–45; and Mud March, 420; and removal of Burnside, 423; size of division of, 508 (n. 19); and lack of support for attack, 513 (n. 40)

Meade, Lucy, 145

Meagher, Thomas Francis, 45, 230–33, 276, 295, 518 (n. 51)

Means, J. O., 306

Medill, Joseph, 125

Meigs, Montgomery, 9, 58, 65, 87, 89, 118

Melish, George, 411

Melville, Herman, 3, 337

Memminger, Christopher G., 387

Mercier, Henri, 380

Michigan troops
—Infantry
2nd, 105, 356
5th, 247, 293, 521 (n. 30)
7th, 168, 169, 431
24th, 16, 198, 250, 358

Milans, Henry G., 275

Miles, Nelson, 234, 519 (n. 7)

Millrace, 219, 224, 229, 239, 265

Minnesota troops
—Infantry
1st, 370

Mississippi troops
—Infantry
13th, 160, 165
16th, 404
17th, 160–61, 165, 170
18th, 98, 160–61, 170
21st, 160, 165, 170–71

Mitchell, Reid, 570 (n. 28)

Morale, 19–20, 26, 69, 73–77, 79, 91, 117–19, 134–36, 141–48, 151–54 172, 187–88, 271–72, 275–76, 280–81, 335, 338–48, 354–63, 366, 369–70, 372, 380–88, 393–407, 409–26, 433–34, 495 (n. 38), 497 (n. 7), 554 (nn. 12, 17), 572 (n. 56), 574 (n. 9), 580 (nn. 5, 18, 21)

Morgan, Edwin D., 122, 230

Morgan, Sarah, 372

Morrow, Henry A., 198

Morton, Oliver P., 381

Mozart Requiem, 294

Mud March, 410–19

Murphey, Josiah, 169, 314–15

Music, 151, 294

Myers, Abraham C., 92

Nagle, James, 243–44

Nantucket Island, Mass., 294

Napoleon III, 38–39, 334

Neely, Mark, 570 (n. 33)

Newcomb, Edgar M., 295–96, 306

New Hampshire troops
—Infantry
5th, 14, 233–35, 340
6th, 243
11th, 11, 241–42
12th, 502 (n. 6)
13th, 57, 138, 265, 357

New Jersey troops
—Cavalry
1st, 105, 146
—Infantry
4th, 250–51
11th, 408
15th, 250
23rd, 251
24th, 225, 357
25th, 264–65
26th, 418
28th, 153, 225–26

Newton, John, 138, 390–91, 421

New Year's Day, 371–72
New York: gubernatorial election in, 30–32; financial markets in, 335–36
New York Anglo-African, 373
New York Herald, 49, 104, 145, 327, 352, 353, 360
New York Times, 82, 117, 119, 123–24, 125, 145, 318, 325, 327, 376, 380, 408, 418, 421
New York Tribune, 14, 289, 291, 324, 353
New York troops
—Engineers
15th, 156
50th, 31, 87, 158–59, 318
—Infantry
4th, 227
5th, 234
7th, 234–35, 431
9th, 15, 264
10th, 249
13th, 109, 120
14th, 260
20th, 523 (n. 48)
24th, 361
26th, 212
34th, 241
37th, 247
38th, 246
42nd, 412
44th, 106, 112, 114, 260, 338
51st, 108, 242
55th, 188, 249
57th, 229–30, 235, 516 (n. 31)
61st, 234, 519 (n. 7)
63rd, 231, 235
64th, 234
69th, 231–33, 294
79th, 72, 89
83rd, 212
88th, 231
89th, 170, 265
94th, 213
97th, 212
104th, 213
105th, 213, 248
108th, 14, 228
121st, 355
124th, 358
140th, 399
New York World, 31, 82
Nicolay, John G., 42–43, 548 (n. 3)

North Anna River, 77–78, 343
North Carolina troops
—Infantry
7th, 210, 213
16th, 250
18th, 210, 213
24th, 229
26th, 452 (n. 2)
27th, 228
28th, 210, 212, 213
33rd, 210, 212, 213
37th, 210, 212, 213
46th, 228
48th, 230
54th, 250 51
57th, 250–51
Northrop, Lucius B., 25, 363
Nugent, Robert, 233
Nunnally, Matthew Talbot, 362
Nurses, 313, 317, 320, 545 (n. 21)

O'Brien, William Smith, 39
Occoquan, Va., 402–3
Ohio troops
—Infantry
4th, 224
8th, 222–23, 225, 516 (n. 26)
Orange Plank Road, 219–20, 222, 224, 273, 412
O'Reilly, Frank A., 509 (n. 32), 520 (n. 20)
Osborn, Joseph Bloomfield, 418
Ouellet, Thomas, 294
Owen, Joshua T., 239

Palmer, Benjamin Morgan, 299–300
Palmer, Oliver H., 227–28
Palmerston, John Henry Temple, Lord, 38
Parke, John G., 412
Parker, Albert E., 170
Patrick, Marsena Rudolph, 83, 399, 409, 423, 525 (n. 7)
Patterson, Edward, 165–66
Paxton, Elisha Franklin, 24, 26, 405, 520 (n. 20)
Pay: soldiers', 141–42, 397–98, 492 (n. 50)
Peace: rumors of, 36–38, 379–81, 383–87, 459 (n. 39)
Peagram, William R. J., 202
Pee Dee Artillery, 202
Pelham, John, 196–98, 200, 202

Pender, William Dorsey, 130, 147, 154, 244, 248, 406, 508 (n. 14)
Pendleton, William Nelson, 91
Pennsylvania troops
—Artillery, Light
Battery A, 200
—Infantry
11th, 212
26th, 252
48th, 178–79, 243–44, 358
53rd, 229, 236
57th, 247
63rd, 247–48
71st, 519 (n. 7)
81st, 234–5
88th, 212, 213, 248–49, 512 (n. 23)
90th, 212, 248
107th, 213
110th, 259, 372
114th, 247–48, 285, 575 (n. 35)
116th, 114, 231–32
118th, 257, 419
121st, 72, 207
122nd, 358, 395
123rd, 319
126th, 263
127th, 173, 239, 519 (n. 7)
129th, 263–64, 266, 434
131st, 16, 262–63
132nd, 227
133rd, 56, 71, 89
134th, 263
136th, 213–14
142nd, 210, 215, 217
145th, 234, 431
155th, 527 (n. 36)
—Infantry Reserves, 195
1st, 197, 205
2nd, 207
3rd, 209–10, 275
4th, 209–10
5th, 209, 300
6th, 205
7th, 207, 209, 217, 245
8th, 210
9th, 209, 216
10th, 209, 328
11th, 207, 209, 217
12th, 209
13th, 18, 205, 207, 208–9, 217
Perkins, Augustus, 158

Pettit, Arabella Speairs, 97
Pettit, William B., 97
Pettus, John J., 388
Philadelphia Inquirer, 73, 82, 144, 326
Phillips, Wendell, 374
Phillips House, 161, 191, 218, 219, 256, 269, 272
Pickens, Francis, 75, 298
Pickets, 113–14, 482 (n. 63)
Pickett, George E., 1, 160, 221, 258, 275, 434–35
Piper, Philip, 372
Plundering: of the dead, 277–78, 532 (nn. 33, 35, 36), 533 (n. 38)
Plunkett, Thomas, 242, 547 (n. 40)
Poague, William T., 253
Pollock's Mill, 162
Pontoons, 87–88, 118, 155–59, 283, 473 (n. 26), 497 (n. 2)
Port Conway, Va., 133
Port Royal, Va., 116, 133
Post, James, 12
Pratt, George C. 170
Pratt, Joseph, 197
Preston, Margaret Junkin, 406
Princess Anne Street, 164, 170
Prisoners, 285, 311, 535 (n. 71)
Prospect Hill, 191, 193, 198, 199, 202, 207, 246, 250
Prostitutes, 14–15
Pryor, Shepherd Green, 96

Quay, Matthew S., 541 (n. 46)

Racism: among soldiers, 377–78. *See also* Emancipation Proclamation; Slavery
Raff, George W., 29
Railroads, 63–64, 66, 91
Raleigh North Carolina Standard, 345, 386
Ransom, Robert, Jr., 77–78, 160, 220, 226, 228, 230, 238
Rappahannock River, 23
Raymond, Henry J., 125, 421, 422
Reagan, John H., 95
Recreation: in armies, 93–94, 107–8, 137–38, 360–61, 365, 403–4
Rectortown, Va., 43
Refugees, 84–86, 166–67, 427–30, 586 (n. 4)
Religion, 25–26, 74, 97–99, 119, 121–25, 152–54, 172, 272, 295–300, 304, 342–43,

346–47, 360–61, 365, 404–5, 406, 477
(n. 72), 541 (n. 39)
Remington, James, 141
Reynolds, John F., 176, 187, 194–95, 198,
200, 216, 506 (n. 2), 513 (n. 40)
Rhode Island troops
—Infantry
7th, 141, 243, 423
12th, 172, 257, 284
Rhodes, Elisha Hunt, 11
Richmond Daily Dispatch, 76, 79, 168, 184,
378
Richmond Daily Enquirer, 75, 77, 81, 92, 118,
184, 291, 344–45, 387
Richmond Daily Examiner, 75, 79, 167, 344,
378
Richmond Daily Whig, 37, 56, 74, 92, 130
Richmond Howitzers, 201, 344
Richmond Stage Road, 157, 176, 191, 195,
196, 203, 215, 248, 250, 251
Robinson, John C., 247–48
Rockbridge Artillery, 202, 253, 297
Rodes, Robert E., 276
Root, Adrian R., 213–14, 248
Ropes, Henry, 169
Rowland, Kate Mason, 329
Ruffin, Edmund, 26, 37, 79, 334, 371
Ruggles, Francis Dunbar, 294
Rumors, 88, 135–36, 143–46, 292–93,
354–55, 488 (n. 9), 489 (n. 15, 18), 495
(n. 35), 529 (n. 5), 549 (n. 19), 550
(n. 20), 557 (n. 44), 560 (n. 2), 572
(n. 50), 580 (n. 12), 584 (n. 51), 588
(n. 17): of peace, 36–38, 379–81, 383–87,
459 (n. 39)
Russell, Lord John, 38

Sadley, A. D., 170
Saint George's Episcopal Church, 164, 427
Saint Patrick's Cathedral (New York, N.Y.),
294–95
Salem Church, 85
Salem, Va., 43
Sanitary Commission, 313–14, 316–17
Sawyer, Franklin, 222, 224, 225
Scientific American, 393
Seddon, James A., 75–76
Seward, Frederick, 375
Seward, William H., 30, 39, 330–32
Seymour, Horatio, 30–32, 41, 379–80
Shanties. *See* Huts

Shelter: in armies, 11–12, 24. *See also* Huts;
Tents
Sherman, John, 331, 425
Shoes, 24–25, 90–93, 136, 140, 362, 491
(n. 43)
Shorter, John Gill, 74
Shure, John, 322
Sickles, Daniel E., 63, 251–52
Sigel, Franz, 59
Simpson, John, 200
Sinclair, William, 195, 199, 204–5, 207, 245
Skinker's Neck, Va., 133, 185
Skirmishers, 514 (n. 13)
Slaughter, Montgomery, 83, 290, 429
Slaughter, Philip, 297
Slaughter pen, 247
Slavery, 125–31, 523 (n. 48). *See also* Eman-
cipation Proclamation
Slidell, John, 334
Sloan, Charles B., 575 (n. 35)
Small, Abner, 106, 249
Smith, Elizabeth Walton, 368–69
Smith, Gerritt, 374
Smith, James Power, 199
Smith, William F. (Baldy), 133, 138, 191,
221, 249–52, 350, 390–91, 411, 422
Southard, Lucy, 183
South Carolina troops
—Infantry
1st, 206
2nd, 238, 262, 273
3rd, 238
6th, 25
7th, 184
Orr's Rifles, 205–6
Spaulding, Ira, 87
Springfield Daily Republican, 326
Stafford Heights, 158, 159, 162, 164, 166,
192, 197, 221, 273
Stager, Anson, 133, 323–24
Stansbury's Hill, 224
Stanton, Edwin M., 7, 63, 82–83, 332, 348,
351, 393–94, 423
Stephens, Alexander H., 127
Stephens, George, 373–74
Sterling, Frank, 72
Stevens, Aaron F., 265
Stewart, Alexander M., 124
Stiles, W. H., 215
Stockton, Thomas B. W., 260
Stoddard, William O., 548 (n. 14)

Stone, Kate, 292–93
Stones River, Battle of (Murfreesboro), 572 (n. 52)
Stone wall, 219–20, 235, 263, 289–90
Stowe, Harriet Beecher, 373
Stratton House, 263
Stretchers, 274
Strong, George Templeton, 31, 62, 327, 369, 421
Stuart, J. E. B., 22, 76–77, 80, 96, 193, 196, 253, 329, 334, 402–3, 529 (n. 48)
Sturgis, Samuel D., 175, 241–44, 266, 280, 422, 519 (n. 10)
Sully, Alfred, 182, 241, 302–3
Sully, Thomas, 182
Sumner, Charles, 34, 49, 144, 331
Sumner, Edwin V.: background of, and appointment to command grand division, 59–60; description of, 81; proposes to cross Rappahannock, 81–82; and demand for surrender of Fredericksburg, 83–84; and campaign strategy, 133; and Burnside battle plans, 150; orders given to, 157, 174–75, 191; and attack toward stone wall, 221; and night after battle, 269; and news from Fredericksburg, 323–24; arrives at Falmouth, 468 (n. 10); and orders on treatment of Confederates, 500 (n. 43); and support for Burnside's attacks, 524 (n. 2)
Sunderland, Byron, 128
Sunken Road, 219, 239, 243
Surgeons, 310–11, 318–19
Surgery, 547 (n. 44). See also Amputations
Sutlers, 15, 104–5
Swain, Jacob G., 169
Sweitzer, Jacob, 259–60
Swinton, William, 82, 327, 408–9
Sykes, George, 266, 273–74

Taliaferro, William B., 193, 253–54, 275, 520 (n. 20)
Tannery, 273
Taylor, Edward, 117
Taylor, Isaac, 370
Taylor, Nelson, 200, 211–12, 248
Taylor's Hill, 192
Telegraph (Lee's) Hill, 160, 196, 224, 227, 237, 243, 246
Telegraph Road, 219–20, 222, 224, 256
Templeton, Willard, 11

Tennessee troops
—Infantry
7th, 208
14th, 207–8
Tents, 11–12, 24, 101, 136, 139, 362. See also Huts; Shelter
Thanksgiving, 119–22, 484 (n. 21), 485 (n. 26)
Thomas, Edward L., 244, 248, 508 (n. 14)
Thompson, Henry, 14
Tilton, Sewall, 13
Times (London), 333
Tobacco, 480 (n. 40)
Torbert, Alfred T. A., 176, 250–51
Tredegar Iron Works, 127
Trephining, 318–19, 547 (n. 42)
Trobriand, Regis de, 249
Trumbull, Lyman, 36, 330
Tyler, Erastus B., 263–64

United States Ford, 409
United States Regular Army troops
—Artillery
5th, 162
—Infantry
2nd Sharpshooters, 176
3rd, 273
4th, 273
14th, 530 (n. 14)

Vallandingham, Clement L., 381
Vance, Zebulon, 74, 333
Vermont troops
—Infantry
6th, 411
Vick, Dwight, 107
Villard, Henry, 324
Vinton, Francis L., 138
Virginia troops
—Cavalry
9th, 146
—Infantry
22nd Battalion, 214
32nd, 96
40th, 214
47th, 214
48th, 25
55th, 214

Wade, Benjamin F., 330, 381
Wadsworth, James S., 30, 284

Wainwright, Charles, 187, 198–99, 201, 202, 413

Walker, James A., 215, 244–45

Walker, Mary, 57, 545 (n. 21)

Walker, Reuben Lindsay, 193, 199, 200

Walton, James B., 224

Ward, J. Hobart, 246–47

Warren, Gouverneur K., 348

Warrenton, Va., 9, 26, 48, 56

Washington Artillery, 78, 93, 136–37, 166, 220, 222, 224, 243, 258

Water Street, 161, 175

Weather, 57, 66–73, 91, 100–101, 136–42, 172, 190, 192, 283–84, 354–55, 409–19

Weed, Thurlow, 30, 32, 379, 493 (n. 7)

Welles, Gideon, 324, 376, 380

Welsh, Peter, 356, 424–25

Wentworth, Carrie, 110

Wentworth, Edwin O., 15, 113, 143, 302

Whipple, Amiel, 259, 502 (n. 6)

White, John French, 96

White Oak Church, 413

White Sulphur Springs, Va., 66

Whitman, George Washington, 143, 242–43, 293

Whitman, Walt, 3, 293, 318, 340, 358

Whittemore, Ruth, 31

Wightman, Edward King, 17

Wilkinson, Morton S., 330

Willard, Sidney, 297–98

Willcox, Orlando, 52, 241, 256, 280, 519 (n. 10)

William Street, 219

Willis's Hill, 226

Wilson, Henry, 375

Wisconsin troops

—Infantry

  5th, 343

  6th, 18, 45

  7th, 198

Women, 18–19, 75, 84–86, 108–9, 112–13, 359–60, 404, 547 (n. 50), 573 (nn. 61, 64)

Wood, Fernando, 36–38, 571 (n. 36)

Woodbury, Daniel, 87–88, 159, 418, 474 (n. 30)

Woodward, Evan M., 207

Woodworth, James R., 106, 112

Wounded, 267–68, 528 (n. 44), 546 (n. 36). See also Casualties

Wright, Ernest, 18

Yancey, William Lowndes, 38

Zook, Samuel K., 229, 270

Zuelch, George, 431